Dictionary of Business Biography

Dictionary of Business Biography

A Biographical Dictionary of Business Leaders Active in Britain in the Period 1860–1980

edited by

David J Jeremy

Research Fellow, Business History Unit
London School of Economics and Political Science

Foreword by HRH The Duke of Edinburgh

Volume I
A-C

London
Butterworths
1984

England	Butterworth & Co (Publishers) Ltd, 88 Kingsway, LONDON WC2B 6AB
Australia	Butterworth Pty Ltd, SYDNEY, MELBOURNE, BRISBANE, ADELAIDE, and PERTH
Canada	Butterworth & Co (Canada) Ltd, TORONTO
	Butterworth & Co (Western Canada) Ltd, VANCOUVER
New Zealand	Butterworths of New Zealand Ltd, WELLINGTON
Singapore	Butterworth & Co (Asia) Pte Ltd, SINGAPORE
South Africa	Butterworth Publishers (Pty) Ltd, DURBAN
USA	Mason Publishing Co, ST PAUL, Minnesota
	Butterworths Legal Publishers, SEATTLE, Washington; BOSTON, Massachusetts; and AUSTIN, Texas
	D & S Publishers, CLEARWATER, Florida

© London School of Economics and Political Science 1984

ISBN *for the complete set of volumes:*   0 406 27340 5
      for this volume: 0 406 27341 3

Typeset by Whitefriars Composertype Ltd, Chichester
Printed by The Whitefriars Press Ltd, Tonbridge

Foreword

   BUCKINGHAM PALACE.

While it seems to be generally acknowledged that wealth has to be created before it can be spent, there is a curious reluctance to acknowledge or to record the achievements of the great wealth creators of modern times. Details of the lives of famous artists, authors, playwrights, scientists, statesmen and inventors are readily available, but there is little or nothing about the entrepreneurs who made Britain, for a time, one of the wealthiest countries in all history.

The Dictionary of Business Biography is the first attempt to fill this gap in the national record and in doing so it provides a fascinating glimpse behind the scenes of the business world. Every one of the subjects in this dictionary is unique in one way or another and the string of the businesses they founded and managed are equally remarkable.

The Dictionary of Business Biography is a most valuable and interesting addition to the many distinguished works of reference available to scholars and researchers and I believe that those involved in this pioneer project deserve to be congratulated.

1983

v

Introduction

Leslie Hannah and David J Jeremy

This *Dictionary* presents more than 1,000 individual biographies in five volumes. As a collective biography of entrepreneurs it covers those active in this country during the critical period of Britain's possession and then loss of international industrial leadership between 1860 and the present. Current wisdom among economic and business historians alleges that beginning in the 1870s there was a failure of entrepreneurial skill and drive, to which must be attached a large share of the blame for Britain's 'declining rate of growth of industrial production, the relative deterioration in her international position and the sluggish rise in productivity'.[1] Most recently Martin Wiener has colourfully projected this view of Britain's performance over the last century in a much-quoted work of historical synthesis:

> As a rule, leaders of commerce and industry in England over the past century have accommodated themselves to an élite culture blended of preindustrial aristocratic and religious values that inhibited their quest for expansion, productivity and profit.[2]

'Explaining the "British disease" (of relative industrial decline)', noted Ralf Dahrendorf in the book based on his television series, 'has become a popular sport among scholars and journalists alike'.[3]

The *Dictionary of Business Biography* represents the first comprehensive and systematic attempt to place generalisations about British entrepreneurs on a sure foundation of biographical data. It has been undertaken by the Business History Unit which was set up at the London School of Economics and Imperial College with industrial support in 1978-79. Similar studies had been discussed earlier and, although these schemes did not come to fruition, they helped to prepare a climate of opinion sympathetic towards a major study of entrepreneurship in Britain. Happily, this materialised in 1979 when the Social Science Research Council funded the newly-formed Business History Unit to conduct a five-year study, to produce this dictionary, and a computerised data bank incorporating standardised biographical information from which a collective biography, analysing the group's characteristics, might be constructed.[4] In this way it is hoped to present both qualitative and quantitative perspectives on Britain's entrepreneurial leadership over the past century and thereby to provide the 'hard' evidence about the origins, career patterns, wealth and creative role of the nation's entrepreneurs which historians (and policy-makers) may use with confidence.

In selecting subjects for entry we aimed for coverage of the whole

1 Peter L Payne, *British Entrepreneurship in the Nineteenth Century* (Macmillan, 1974), 45.
2 Martin Wiener, *English Culture and the Decline of the Industrial Spirit, 1850-1980* (Cambridge University Press, 1981), 127.
3 Ralf Dahrendorf, *On Britain* (BBC Publications, 1982), 21-22.
4 The data bank will be made available to scholars on the completion of the study.

spectrum of business, ranging from mining and manufacturing through public utilities, construction and services to distribution. We excluded academics, civil servants, trade unionists and agriculturists where their involvement in the business world was incidental to their central career. We also excluded those who were still active on a full time basis in their major business role. Entrepreneurs in the whole of the United Kingdom are included, except that Scottish businessmen and women who were not active south of the border (but would otherwise have qualified for entry) are to be the subject of a separate study being conducted at the University of Glasgow by Professor Slaven and his colleagues. While we sought a balance between the various industries, we were not able to obtain a coverage as wide as we would have wished in some sectors — notably in the wholesaling and retailing trades — because of the paucity of information. By contrast, in those industries which are much studied by historians — notably railways or textiles — we had a plethora of potential subjects and we have exercised a stern selection procedure to remove all except the pivotal personalities in order that such sectors should not have an excessive weight.

The criteria for selection were catholic: rogues like Horatio Bottomley appear as well as Smilesian heroes like Thomas Beecham, or Billy Butlin. There are men who have built up large businesses, as well as those whose significance derives from having inherited a business only to run it down. The chief executives of large banks or leading manufacturing corporations or the nationalised industry giants are here, but also pioneers of modern advertising like Samuel H Benson, whose firms were quite small. Decorative chairmen, with strings of associated company directorships, have been admitted rarely. Those who have had real impact, good or bad, whatever their position or title, are the ones who have qualified for entry. Above all it is *business* achievement — rather than activity in charitable, political or community work — which the editor has taken as his guide. The process of selection was assisted by the advice of the many specialist colleagues who are listed in the acknowledgements. The result is neither a random nor a stratified sample, but it does, we suggest, provide a balanced and comprehensive coverage of those who have made a significant contribution to business leadership in Britain over the last 120 years.

Acknowledgements

The Editorial Advisory Board and the *DBB* editor are first and foremost grateful to the Social Science Research Council for its imaginative and large-scale support of this project. Without the SSRC's decisive act of faith the plan to prepare a definitive data bank on modern British entrepreneurs would still be under discussion. The grant was awarded on the recommendation of the SSRC's Economic and Social History Committee, under the chairmanship of Professor John Saville.

Secondly the projectors and editor of the *DBB* are deeply indebted to the many individuals who have served on the advisory committees (one for each major industry) which guided our initial choice of entries and then to those (now numbering nearly 500) who have enthusiastically responded to the invitation to contribute biographies. As may be seen from the list of the contributors to Volume I they have come from various backgrounds but chiefly from academic history and economic history departments, from company archives and boardrooms and from museums; some are now retired; others are embarking on their careers as historians.

The editor of the *DBB* has also relied heavily on the generous refereeing services of a large number of specialist historians. To them the project is heavily indebted for anonymous but extremely valuable comments which have improved the accuracy and the elegance of many entries. The following list records those on whose advice the editor has gratefully drawn:

Margaret Ackrill, Alison Adburgham, Angela Airey, Bernard Alford, Roger Alford, Jake Almond, Donald Anderson, Charles Andrews, John Armstrong, William Ashworth, Peter Atkins, Jill Austin, David Avery, Colin Baber, Philip Bagwell, Theo Barker, Neville Bartlett, Victor Belcher, Joyce Bellamy, Maurice W Beresford, Janet Blackman, Gerry Bloomfield, Michael Bonavia, John Booker, Jonathan Boswell, Sue Bowden, Brian Bowers, Gordon Boyce, Trevor Boynes, R Bracegirdle, Lord Briggs of Lewes, John Briggs, Frank Brittain, Keith Brooker, Peter Brooks, the late Elizabeth Brunner, Kathleen Burk, Gillian Burke, Roger Burt, Gordon Bussey, Michael Bywater, David Cannadine, Forrest Capie, Donald Cardwell, Josef Cassis, Harold Catling, Francis Celoria, Philippe Chalmin, Bill Chaloner, Geoffrey Channon, Stanley Chapman, Olive Checkland, Roy Church, Joe Clarke, Leslie Clarkson, Esmond Cleary, Roy Coad, R W M Clouston, Hugh Cockerell, Donald Coleman, Ed Cooney, Tony Corley, Tom Corran, Philip Cottrell, Robin Craig, L M Cullen, Richard Davenport-Hines, Alun Davies, Peter Davies, Martin Daunton, Roberta Dayer, Marguerite Dupree, Pat Dutton, J B F Earle, David Edgerton, J R Edwards, Cyril Ehrlich, Dennis Ellam, Charlotte Erickson, Malcolm Falkus, Douglas Farnie, Peter Fearon, Ronald Ferrier, David Fieldhouse, Robert Fitton, Claude Fivel-Demoret, G A Fletcher, Roderick C Floud, James Foreman-Peck, Martin Gaskell, Harriet Geddes, Keith Geddes, Brian Gee, R Gibson-Jarvie, John Goodchild, Jordan Goodman, Howard Gospel, Terry Gourvish, Margaret Gowing, Derek Green, Edwin Green, Robert Greenhill, Colin Griffin, Clifford Gulvin, Bill Gunston, L F Haber, Rosalind Hadden, Leslie Hannah, John Harris, Negley Harte, Charles Harvey, Mike Hatchett, Kevin Hawkins, Roy Hay, John Hibbs, Robin Higham, Jim Holderness, Graeme Holmes, Tony Howe, Kenneth Hudson, Pat Hudson, Leslie Hunt, David Iredale, John Iredale, Robert Irving, Gordon Jackson, Russell Jackson, David Jenkins, David Johnson, W Johnson, Jim Johnston, Charlie Jones, Edgar Jones,

George A Jones, Geoffrey Jones, Simon Katzenellenbogen, Shirley Keeble, Marian Kent, John Killick, John King, Maurice W Kirby, Robert Kirk, Sir Arthur Knight, David Kynaston, Joan Lane, Rodney Law, Rachael Lawrence, Stephen Lawrence, Joseph Leckey, the late Alan Lee, Wayne Lewchuk, Colin Lewis, Jonathan Liebenau, Jean Lindsay, Stafford Linsley, Craig Littler, Ian Stewart Lloyd, Roger Lloyd-Jones, Rachel Low, Campbell McMurray, John Malin, Roger Manvell, Sheila Marriner, Peter Marsh, J D Marshall, Sir Peter Masefield, John Mason, Bill Mathew, Peter Mathias, Helen Meller, Joe Melling, Keith Middlemas, Bill Milligan, Leonard Minkes, Brian Mitchell, Donald Moggridge, Peter Morris, Michael Moss, Charles Munn, Christopher Murphy, Robert Murphy, Basil Murray, Ted Musson, Norman Mutton, John Myerscough, Terry Nevett, Chris Niblett, Ian Nicholson, Ian Norrie, Paul Nunn, Derek Oddy, George Odey, John Orbell, Richard Overy, Robert Parker, Linda Parry, Peter Payne, Alan Pearsall, Maurice Pearton, Ronald Peddie, Denys Pegg, David Phillips, Bill Philpott, D C M Platt, the late Ken Ponting, Michael Port, Dilwyn Porter, Leslie Pressnell, Trevor Raybould, Gordon Read, Bill Reader, Basil Reckitt, M C Reed, Richard H Reed, Hew Reid, D G Rhys, David Richardson, Gordon Rimmer, Robert Ring, Michael Robbins, Richard Roberts, Mary Rose, David Rowe, Bill Rubinstein, Peter Russell, Leonard Sainer, Andrew Saint, Michael Sanderson, Christopher Schmitz, Henry Schollick, Christine Shaw, Eric Sigsworth, Aubrey Silberston, Colin Simmons, Douglas Simmons, Jack Simmons, Tony Slaven, Judy Slinn, Eynon Smart, Barbara Smith, Richard Storey, Frank Strahan, Sir John Summerson, Barry Supple, Barry Sutton, Philip Sykes, Jennifer Tann, Arthur Taylor, W A Thomas, Michael Thompson, Bill Thurlow, Steve Tolliday, Alistair Tough, Rick Trainor, Clive Trebilcock, Lloyd Trott, Gordon Tucker, Gerard Turnbull, John Turner, Alison Turton, Geoffrey Tweedale, Jean-Jacques Van Helten, Kathleen Wain, David Wainwright, Peter Wardley, Ron Weir, Fred Wellings, Oliver Westall, Tim Whitney, Mira Wilkins, John Williams, Trevor Williams, Charles Wilson, Richard Wilson, Chris Wrigley, Robert Wyatt, Stephanie Zarach, Jonathan Zeitlin.

We are in addition much obliged and grateful to all those in public libraries, learned institutions, government agencies and company headquarters who have so willingly supplied the *DBB* editorial staff with a variety of materials with which to augment biographical entries.

Certain individuals have been especially helpful to the project and must be particularly thanked: Professor T C Barker, whose brainchild the *DBB* was, for his constant interest and enthusiasm; Professor John Saville and Dr Joyce Bellamy of the *Dictionary of Labour Biography,* for their advice when the project began in January 1980; Professors Sydney Checkland and Tony Slaven, Dr Charles Munn, Mrs Sheila Hamilton and Mr Nick Morgan of the *Dictionary of Scottish Business Biography,* for their exchange of biographical information on subjects with Scottish origins and connections; Professor Charlotte Erickson (then of the LSE, now of Cambridge), Professor Harold Perkin of Lancaster University, and Professor Colin Harbury of the City University, for the loan of their biographical work cards; Mrs Thea Elliott, for the loan of her late husband's research notes on British MPs; Peter Wakeford, Richard Kacznyski, Robert Clark and Bob Jackson of the LSE's Computer Services, for their unending patience in helping the *DBB* team with the new microcomputer technology; David Ellsworth of the LSE's Geography Department, for providing photographic copies of our illustrative materials; and lastly Patrick D C Davis, the LSE's Publications Officer, for his wise and professional advice in our negotiations with publishers.

To Professor Leslie Hannah, Director of the Business History Unit since its foundation, must be paid a special tribute. With Professor T C Barker, he was the original architect of the *DBB* project. Then, as a joint editor, he was heavily involved for the project's first three years, critically reading and commenting on every entry submitted and counselling on a range of policies, from author recruitment to publishing contracts. Latterly his other duties have prevented him from continuing this commitment and from participating in the final editing, but he has remained finally responsible for the project.

The *DBB* office was well served by a series of secretarial and research staff: Mrs Shirley Keeble, Miss Jill Gosling, Mrs Greta Edwards and Mrs Dawn Waldron, began the development of our filing system. Miss Helen Jeffries, gave final shape to the *DBB*'s office organisation and, with Miss Alex Kidner, began the arduous work of entering the A-C biographies on the word processor. In 1982-83 this work was continued and completed for Volume I by Miss Kidner and Miss Margaret Kiely.

At the editorial level Dr Christine Shaw, who joined the staff in July 1980, has been a steady and efficient, part time, deputy editor. She has helped to identify subjects for inclusion in the paper, publishing and distribution industries and has strengthened the substance of a number of entries. All the current members of the *DBB* staff have shared in the demanding tasks of proof-reading.

Illustrations, collated and organised by Miss Kidner, have come from a variety of sources, including art galleries, company archives, local public libraries and private owners. We are grateful to all those who have helped us locate them; for any unwitting infringements of copyright, we proffer our apologies. The assembly of illustrations and various other editorial burdens have been lightened by the efficient support of the design and production staff at Butterworths.

In conclusion I would like to emphasise that this biographical dictionary, intended as a major reference tool for the historical profession, is essentially the product of the collective efforts of the present generation of (mostly economic and business) historians. Without the cooperation of advisors, contributors and referees outside the *DBB* office and the sustained efforts of all the staff within that office, it would not have been possible to meet the time limits set by the SSRC grant or the publisher's deadlines. To all I wish to express my deep and sincere thanks. This does not, of course, implicate them in any way in any faults or omissions that remain.

David J Jeremy

List of Contributors to Volume I

R B Adams   Chief Executive and Managing Director, P&O Group, London.

Angela Airey   Newcastle upon Tyne.

Sir Peter Allen   formerly Chairman, ICI, PLC, London.

J K Almond   Senior Lecturer, Department of Metallurgy and Materials, Teesside Polytechnic.

Donald Anderson   Director, Quaker House Colliery Co Ltd, Ashton-in-Makerfield, Lancashire.

Peter J Atkins   Administrative Assistant, Department of Geography, University of Durham.

Colin Baber   Lecturer, Department of Economics, University College Cardiff.

Philip S Bagwell   Professor, formerly of the Polytechnic of Central London.

H R Balston   Turriff, Aberdeenshire.

K A Barlow   Keeper of Technology, North Western Museum of Science and Industry, Manchester.

Sir Basil Bartlett, Bt   Holland Park, London.

J Neville Bartlett   Lecturer, Department of Economic History, University of Aberdeen.

Joyce M Bellamy   Editor, *Dictionary of Labour Biography,* Department of Economic and Social History, University of Hull.

C Leslie Bibby   formerly Director of J Bibby & Sons Ltd, Liverpool.

J Benjamin Bibby   Director, J Bibby & Sons Ltd, Liverpool.

R M Black   BICC Research, London.

Janet M Blackman   Lecturer, Department of Economic and Social History, University of Hull.

Katherine V Bligh   Record Office, House of Lords, London.

G T Bloomfield   Professor and Chairman of the Department of Geography, University of Guelph, Ontario.

Sue Bowden   Research Student, Business History Unit, London School of Economics and Political Science.

Brian Bowers	Deputy Keeper, Department of Electrical Engineering, Communications and the Earth, Space and Mathematical Sciences, Science Museum, London.
Faith Bowers	Research Student, Theology Department, King's College, London.
Emily Boyle	School of Marketing and Business Policy, Ulster Polytechnic.
Trevor Boyns	Lecturer, Department of Economics, University College, Cardiff.
Robert Bracegirdle	Keeper, Museum of Technology, Leicester.
P Stanley Briggs	formerly of Department of Food and Leather, Leeds University.
Frank Brittain	Southgate, London.
Keith Brooker	East Yorkshire College of Further Education.
R H Bulmer	Hereford.
Z Burianova	Research Student, King's College, Cambridge.
Kathleen Burk	Lecturer, Department of Humanities, Imperial College of Science and Technology, London.
Gill Burke	Senior Lecturer in Social Administration, School of Social Science and Business Studies, Polytechnic of Central London.
David Burrage	Group Public Relations Manager, Richard Costain Ltd, London.
Gordon Bussey	Historical Advisor, Philips Electronics.
Michael H Caine	Chairman, Booker McConnell PLC, London.
Forrest Capie	Senior Lecturer in Economics, Centre for Banking and International Finance, The City University Business School, London.
David G Carpenter	John Mowlem & Co Ltd, Brentford, Middlesex.
Stanley D Chapman	Reader (Business History), Department of Economic and Social History, University of Nottingham.
Roy Church	Professor of Economic History, School of Economic and Social Studies, University of East Anglia.
Joe F Clarke	Principal Lecturer, Department of Humanities, Newcastle upon Tyne Polytechnic.
Esmond J Cleary	Senior Lecturer, Department of Economics, University College of Swansea.
J B M Coates	formerly Group Chairman, Coates Brothers & Co Ltd, London.

Hugh Cockerell	Professor, Gresham College, City University, London.
D C Coleman	Professor of Economic History, Pembroke College, Cambridge.
Robert Copeland	Historical Consultant, Spode Ltd, Stoke on Trent.
T A B Corley	Senior Lecturer, Department of Economics, University of Reading.
Tom Corran	Fielding Newson-Smith, London.
P L Cottrell	Lecturer, Department of Economic and Social History, University of Leicester.
Elizabeth Crittall	Institute of Historical Research, University of London.
R F Currie	Editor, *Classic Motor Cycle*, Surrey.
Jenny Davenport	London.
R P T Davenport-Hines	Research Officer, Business History Unit, London School of Economics and Political Science.
Roberta A Dayer	State University of New York at Buffalo, USA.
Susan I Dench	Carlisle.
Madge Dresser	Senior Lecturer, Department of Humanities, Bristol Polytechnic.
Marguerite W Dupree	Fellow, Wolfson College, Cambridge.
David Edgerton	Research Student, Department of Social and Economic Studies, Imperial College of Science and Technology, London.
J R Edwards	Lecturer, Department of Accountancy and Financial Control, University College, Cardiff.
Cyril Ehrlich	Professor, Department of Economic and Social History, The Queen's University of Belfast.
Dennis Ellam	formerly Secretary of the National Federation of Wholesale Grocers.
D A Farnie	Reader in Economic History, Department of History, University of Manchester.
*C A Farquharson-Roberts	Cobham Archivist, Flight Refuelling Ltd, Dorset.
Sue Farrant	Senior Lecturer, Department of Humanities, Brighton Polytechnic.
R W Ferrier	Company Historian, BP, Britannic House, London.
Claude Fivel-Demoret	Université de Paris-Sorbonne and Business Archives Council.

Katherine A Fricker   St Albans School, Bedford.

Honor Godfrey   Company Archivist, Reckitt & Colman, Norwich.

John Goodchild   Principal Local Studies Officer and Archivist, Wakefield M D Libraries.

T R Gourvish   Senior Lecturer, School of Economic and Social Studies, University of East Anglia.

Robert G Greenhill   Senior Lecturer, School of Business Studies, City of London Polytechnic.

A A Hall   Researcher with the Coal Board History Project.

Leslie Hannah   Professor of Business History and Director, Business History Unit, London School of Economics and Political Science.

⋆A E Harrison   Department of Economics and Related Studies, University of York.

Kevin Hawkins   formerly with the Management Centre, University of Bradford.

Roy Hay   Professor, School of Social Sciences, Deakin University, Victoria, Australia.

Robin Higham   Professor, Department of History, Kansas State University, USA.

Sir Maurice Hodgson   formerly Chairman, ICI, PLC.

Len Holden   Research Student, School of Economic and Social Studies, University of East Anglia.

Jim Holderness   School of Economic and Social Studies, University of East Anglia.

Graeme M Holmes   Senior Lecturer, Department of Economics and Banking, University of Wales Institute of Science and Technology.

L B Hunt   formerly with Johnson, Matthey & Co, Ltd, London.

John A Iredale   Lecturer, Project Planning Centre for Developing Countries, University of Bradford.

R J Irving   Courage Brewing Ltd.

Helen Jeffries   formerly secretary, *Dictionary of Business Biography,* Business History Unit, London School of Economics and Political Science.

D T Jenkins   Lecturer, Department of Economic and Related Studies, University of York.

David J Jeremy   Research Fellow, Business History Unit, London School of Economics and Political Science.

D S Johnson	Lecturer, Department of Economic and Social History, The Queen's University of Belfast.
Walford Johnson	Lecturer, Department of Economics, The New University of Ulster, Coleraine.
Edgar Jones	GKN Group Historian, London.
H Kay Jones	formerly Director, Butterworths, London.
L J Jones	Department of Economic and Social History, University of Birmingham.
S E Katzenellenbogen	Senior Lecturer, Department of History, University of Manchester.
Shirley Keeble	Research Student, Business History Unit, London School of Economics and Political Science.
H B Kerr	Chairman, James Carmichael (Contractors), London.
Cyril A Kidd	formerly Company Secretary, Selection Trust Ltd, London.
Alexandra Kidner	Researcher, Business History Unit, London School of Economics and Political Science.
Robert Kirk	Research Student, Department of Economics, University of Salford.
Robert Knight	formerly Executive Vice-Chairman, Bowater Corporation PLC.
David Kynaston	formerly Research Student, Department of Economic History, London School of Economics and Political Science.
Joseph Leckey	Archivist, Irish Railway Records Society, Ballygowan, Co Down.
S M Linsley	Editor, *Industrial Archaeology Review,* Department of Adult Education, University of Newcastle upon Tyne.
Peter T Marsh	Professor and Director, Department of History, Syracuse University, New York, USA.
J D Marshall	Centre for North-West Regional Studies, University of Lancaster.
Sir Peter Masefield	formerly Chairman of British European Airways and the London Transport Executive.
John J Mason	Lecturer, Department of Economics and Economic History, Manchester Polytechnic.
C E Meakin	Lecturer, Department of History, Nene College, Northampton.
A L Minkes	Professor (Business Organisation), Department of Industrial Economics and Business Studies, University of Birmingham.

Basil Murray	Archivist, Cadbury-Schweppes Ltd, Birmingham.
Norman Mutton	Head of School of Economics, Department of Government and Economics, City of Birmingham Polytechnic.
T R Nevett	Principal Lecturer, Department of Business Studies, Polytechnic of the South Bank, London.
Paul Nunn	Department of History, City of Sheffield Polytechnic.
E A Olive	formerly Public Relations Officer, Aveling-Barford Ltd, Grantham, Lincs.
M J Orbell	Archivist, Baring Bros Ltd, London.
Henry W Parris	University of Reading.
J F Parsons	formerly Director of Education, County Borough of Bournemouth.
A W H Pearsall	Historian, National Maritime Museum, London.
Charles R Perry	Professor, Department of History, University of the South, Sewanee, Tennessee, USA.
David C Phillips	Archivist, Institute of Agricultural History and Museum of English Rural Life, University of Reading.
Andrew N Porter	Lecturer, Department of History, King's College, London.
H J Potterton	formerly Joint Managing Director of Currys Ltd.
Stephen Rabson	Group Librarian, P&O Information & Public Relations, London.
John Rackham	Editor, *Information Transfer.*
J Gordon Read	Keeper of Archives, Merseyside County Museums, Liverpool.
W J Reader	Texaco Visiting Fellow, Business History Unit, London School of Economics and Political Science.
Peter N Reed	Assistant Director, Merseyside County Museums, Liverpool.
R H Reed	Archivist, National Westminster Bank Ltd, London.
Hew F Reid	Director of Studies, Department of Furniture Technology, Buckinghamshire College of Higher Education.
R W Rennison	New Works Engineering, Newcastle & Gateshead Water Co.
Jeffrey Richards	Senior Lecturer, Department of History, Lancaster University.

W G Rimmer	Professor, Department of Economic History, University of New South Wales, Australia.
R H G Ring	formerly Managing Director of Dents.
David E Roberts	Senior Lecturer, Department of Economics and Public Administration, Trent Polytechnic.
Catherine M Ross	Research Student, Department of Economics, University of Newcastle upon Tyne.
D J Rowe	Lecturer, Department of Economics, University of Newcastle upon Tyne.
Peter E Russell	Research Student, Department of History of Science and Technology, University of Manchester Institute of Science and Technology.
Leonard Sainer	Chairman, Sears Holdings Ltd, London.
Michael Sanderson	Senior Lecturer, School of Economics and Social Studies, University of East Anglia.
Alan J Scarth	Assistant Keeper (Collections Management), Merseyside Maritime Museum.
Christopher Schmitz	Lecturer, Department of Modern History, University of St Andrews.
J W Scott	Partner, Clifford-Turner, London.
Christine Shaw	Research Officer, Business History Unit, London School of Economics and Political Science.
Eric Sigsworth	School of Humanities, Humberside College of Higher Education.
Jack Simmons	Professor, formerly Department of History, University of Leicester.
P Eynon Smart	formerly with The Institute of Bankers, London.
Barbara M D Smith	Lecturer, Centre for Urban and Regional Studies, University of Birmingham.
Michael Stammers	Keeper of Maritime History, County Museum, Liverpool.
Richard A Storey	Archivist, Modern Records Centre, University of Warwick Library.
G Barry Sutton	Executive Director, IDV (UK), Harlow, Essex.
Pat M Thane	Lecturer, Goldsmith's College, London.
F M L Thompson	Director, Institute of Historical Research, London.

Alistair G Tough	Assistant Archivist, Modern Records Centre, University of Warwick Library.
R H Trainor	Lecturer, Department of Economic History, University of Glasgow.
G L Turnbull	Senior Lecturer, Department of Economic History, University of Leeds.
John Turner	Lecturer, Department of History, Bedford College, London.
Alison Turton	Company Archivist, House of Fraser PLC, Glasgow.
Geoffrey Tweedale	Research Student, Economic History Department, London School of Economics and Political Science.
A C Twort	Consultant, Binnie & Partners, London.
Jean J Van Helten	Department of History, La Trobe University, Victoria, Australia.
Sean Vertigan	Postgraduate Student, University of Nottingham.
David E Wainwright	London.
Oliver M Westall	Lecturer, Department of Economics, University of Lancaster.
Raymond R Wile	Associate Professor, Department of History, Queen's College, The City University of New York, USA.
L John Williams	Senior Lecturer, Department of Economics, The University College of Wales, Aberystwyth.
Charles Wilson	Professor, Jesus College, Cambridge.
Kevin Wilson	Assistant Press Officer, Royal Doulton Tableware Ltd, Stoke-on-Trent.
Humphrey Wynn	Air Historical Branch, Ministry of Defence, London.

* Now (July 1983) deceased

Notes to Readers

1 Biographies are in the alphabetical sequence of subjects' family names. In the case of *hyphenated* surnames the first name in the compound family name determines the sequence.

2 In entry headings the title 'Lord' has been confined to barons, holders of the lowest degree in the British peerage; holders of degrees above baron have been given their exact peerage title, 'Viscount', 'Duke' etc. Peers are all listed in the alphabetical sequence of *family* names, not titles.

3 Place-names are normally used according to the contemporary usage pertaining to the particular entry.

4 County boundaries are usually those prevailing before the reorganisation of local government in 1975.

5 For a note on British currency usage, see abbreviations (below), under £.

6 Foreign words have not been italicised.

7 The place of publication in bibliographical references is London, unless otherwise stated.

8 In the case of books running to several editions, bibliographical information is provided for the first or major edition.

9 Cross references to entries in the *Dictionary of National Biography*, *Who's Who of British Members of Parliament* and *Who Was Who* are regularly provided in the lists of sources but in many cases contributors have relied on ampler or more recently discovered sources.

Abbreviations

AA	Automobile Association *or* anti-aircraft
AC	Alternating current
& Co	and Company
ADC	aide-de-camp
AEG	Allgemeine Elektrizitäts Gesellschaft
AEI	Associated Electrical Industries
AFC	Air Force Cross
AG	Aktien-gesellschaft (joint-stock company)
AGM	Annual General Meeting
am	ante meridien (before noon)
APCM	Associated Portland Cement Manufacturers
APOC	Anglo Persian Oil Co
ARP	air-raid precautions
Aslef	Associated Society of Locomotive Engineers and Firemen
ATV	Associated Television
b	born
BA	Bachelor of Arts
BAT	British American Tobacco Co
Bateman	John Bateman, *Great Landowners of Great Britain* (Harrison, 1879).
BBFT	British Bank for Foreign Trade
BC & CC	British Cocoa & Chocolate Co
BCe	Birth certificate from General Register Office, St Catherines House, London WC2B 6JP
BCe (Scots)	Scottish birth certificate from The Registrar General, New Register House, Edinburgh EH1 3YT

BDC	British Dyestuffs Corporation
BEA	British European Airways
BEF	British Expeditionary Force
bhp	brake horsepower
BICC	British Insulated Callender's Cables
BISF	British Iron and Steel Federation
BL	British Library, Great Russell Street, London WC1B 3DG
BLPES	British Library of Political and Economic Science, London School of Economics and Political Science, Portugal Street, London WC2A 2HD
BOAC	British Overseas Airways Corporation
Boase	Frederic Boase, *Modern English Biography, Containing Memoirs of Persons Who Have Died since 1850* (6 vols, Truro: Netherton & Worth, 1892-1921).
BP	British Petroleum
BPC	British Printing Corporation
BPCM	British Portland Cement Manufacturers
BS	Bachelor of Surgery (Britain) *or* Bachelor of Science (USA) *or* Bristol-Siddeley
BSc	Bachelor of Science (Britain)
BSA	Birmingham Small Arms
BSC	British Steel Corporation
Bt	Baronet
Burke's Landed Gentry	*Burke's Landed Gentry* (Burke's Peerage Ltd. Various editions since 1836; edition identified by date).
Burke's Peerage and Baronetage	*Burke's Peerage and Baronetage* (Burke's Peerage [Genealogical Books] Ltd. Various editions since 1826; edition identified by date).
BVC	British Vacuum Cleaner
ca	circa
CB	Companion of the Bath

CBE	Commander (of the Order) of the British Empire
CBI	Confederation of British Industry
CEGB	Central Electricity Generating Board
ch	chapter
CIE	Companion of the Order of the Indian Empire
C-in-C	Commander-in-Chief
CMG	Companion of the Order of St Michael and St George
CND	Campaign for Nuclear Disarmament
Co	Company
Col	Colonel
comp	compiled, compiler
Complete Peerage	George Edward Cokayne, *The Complete Peerage of England, Scotland, Ireland, Great Britain and the United Kingdom, Extant Extinct or Dormant* (13 vols, St Catherine Press, 1910-59).
C Reg	Companies Registration Office file(s); microfiche versions of the files have been obtained from Companies Registration Office, 55 City Road, London EC1 Y1BB
C Reg(w)	Notes made from company files subsequently despatched to the PRO and there subjected to a random destruction rate of 80–90 per cent.
CRO	County Record Office
cwt	hundredweight (112 pounds, avoirdupois)
d	died
d (following a monetary figure)	pence [See note under £ at the end of this list]
DAB	*Dictionary of American Biography* edited by Allen Johnson and Dumas Malone (22 vols, New York: Charles Scribner's Sons, 1928-1944).
DBB	*Dictionary of Business Biography*
DCe	Death certificate from General Register Office, St Catherines House, London WC2B 6JP
DCL	Doctor of Civil Law *or* Distillers Co Ltd

DCM	Distinguished Conduct Medal
DD	*Directory of Directors* (annual, East Grinstead: Thomas Skinner Directories, 1880-1983).
DH	De Havilland
DL	Deputy-Lieutenant
DLB	*Dictionary of Labour Biography* edited by Joyce M Bellamy and John Saville (6 vols, Macmillan, 1972-82, in progress).
DLitt	Doctor of Letters
DNB	*Dictionary of National Biography* edited by Leslie Stephen and Sidney Lee (63 vols, Oxford University Press, 1885-1933).
DSc	Doctor of Science
DSIR	Department of Scientific and Industrial Research
DWB	*Dictionary of Welsh Biography down to 1940* edited by Sir John Edward Lloyd and R T Jenkins (The Honourable Society of Cymmrodorion, 1959).
ECSC	European Coal and Steel Community
Edwards seminar paper.	Almost 450 papers, chiefly by businessmen and women presented in Professor Ronald S Edwards' Seminar at the LSE, 1946-1973, on 'Problems in Industrial Administration' (in BLPES Manuscripts). A number of these papers were published in *Business Enterprise* (Macmillan, 1959), *Studies in Business Organisation* (Macmillan, 1961) and *Business Growth* (Macmillan, 1966) edited by R S Edwards and H Townsend.
EEC	European Economic Community
EFTA	European Free Trade Association
Elliott research notes.	The biographical research notes on British MPs (mostly of the twentieth century) compiled by the late Anthony Elliott and kindly loaned to the *DBB* project by his widow Mrs Thea Elliott.
EMGAS	East Midlands Gas
EMI	Electric & Musical Industries
Erickson workcards.	Biographical workcards prepared by Professor Charlotte Erickson on steel and hosiery leaders, for her book *British Industrialists. Steel and Hosiery, 1850-1950* (Cambridge: Cambridge University Press for the National Institute of Economic and Social Research, 1959) and kindly loaned by her to the *DBB* project.

ETU	Electrical Trades Union
F	Fahrenheit (temperature)
FBI	Federation of British Industries
FCS	Fellow of the Chemical Society (now FRCS)
fl	floreat (flourished)
Foster, *Alumni Oxonienses.*	Joseph Foster, *Alumni Oxonienses, The Members of the University of Oxford 1715-1886* (4 vols, Oxford: James Parker & Co, 1891).
FRS	Fellow of the Royal Society
GEC	General Electric Co
GER	Great Eastern Railway
GBE	Knight *or* Dame Grand Cross of the British Empire
GCVO	Knight *or* Dame Grand Cross of the Royal Victorian Order
GDP	Gross Domestic Product
GHQ	General Headquarters
GLC	Greater London Council
GKN	Guest, Keen & Nettlefolds
GmbH	Gesellschaft mit beschrankter Haftung (private limited liability company)
GNP	Gross National Product
GRA	Greyhound Racing Association Ltd
GWR	Great Western Railway
HC	House of Commons
HM	His/Her Majesty/Majesty's
HMV	His Master's Voice
Hon	Honourable
hp	horsepower
HP	Handley Page

HT	High Tension
IAL	Imperial Airways Ltd
IBA	Independent Broadcasting Authority
ibid	ibidem (the same source as the one previously quoted)
ICE	Institution of Civil Engineers
ICI	Imperial Chemical Industries
IEE	Institution of Electrical Engineers
IG	Interessengemeinschaft (combine)
IME	Institution of Mechanical Engineers
Inc	Incorporated
JISI	*Journal of the Iron and Steel Institute*
JP	Justice of the Peace
Jr	Junior
KBE	Knight Commander of the Order of the British Empire
KCB	Knight Commander of the Order of the Bath
KCMG	Knight Commander of the Order of St Michael and St George
KCVO	Knight Commander of the Royal Victorian Order
KG	Knight of the Order of the Garter
kV	kilovolt
kW	kilowatt
£	£: see end of list
lb	pound(s), weight
LCC	London County Council
Lieut Col	Lieutenant Colonel
LLB	Bachelor of Laws
LLD	Doctor of Laws

LMS	London, Midland & Scottish Railway *or* London Missionary Society
LNER	London & North Eastern Railway
LNWR	London & North Western Railway
LSE	London School of Economics and Political Science, Houghton Street, London WC2A 2AE
Ltd	Limited
MA	Master of Arts
MC	Military Cross
MCe	Marriage certificate from General Register Office, St Catherine's House, London WC2B 6JP
MCe (Irish)	Irish marriage certificate from The Registrar General, Oxford House, 49/55 Chichester Street, Belfast BT1 4HL (Northern Ireland), or The Registrar General, Custom House, Dublin 1 (Southern Ireland)
MCe (Scots)	Scottish marriage certificate from The Registrar General, New Register House, Edinburgh EH1 3YT
MM	Military Medal
MMS	Methodist Missionary Society
MVO	Member of the Royal Victorian Order
MW	megawatt(s)
NAAFI	Navy, Army, and Air Force Institutes
NCB	National Coal Board
NCO	non-commissioned officer
nd	no date
NEDC	National Economic Development Council
NHS	National Health Service
NLR	North London Railway
np	no place
NPA	Newspaper Proprietors' Association

NRA	National Register of Archives, Quality House, Quality Court, London WC2A 1HP
NV	naamloze vennootschap (limited company)
OB St John	British Order of the Hospital of St John of Jerusalem
ODI	Overseas Development Institute
OPEC	Organisation of Petroleum Exporting Countries
OTC	Officers' Training Corps
P&O	Peninsular & Oriental Steamship Co
PA	Press Association
passim	here and there
PC	Privy Councillor
PD	*Parliamentary Debates* (Hansard)
PEP	Political and Economic Planning, now the Policy Studies Institute, London
pH	measure of hydrogen in concentration (indicating level of acidity)
PhD	Doctor of Philosophy
PLC (*or* plc)	public limited company
pm	post meridien (afternoon)
PP	*Parliamentary Papers*
pp	privately printed or published
PrC	Probate Calendar in Principal Registry of the Family Division, Somerset House, Strand, London WC2R 1LP
PRO	Public Record Office, Chancery Lane, London WC2A 1LR, or Ruskin Avenue, Kew, Richmond, Surrey TW9 4DU
psi	pounds per square inch
Pty	Proprietary (limited company in Australia, New Zealand, South Africa)
PVC	polyvinyl chloride
qv	quod vide (which see; cross reference to another entry)

qqv	{same, but see several entries}
RA	Royal Artillery *or* Royal Academician
RAC	Royal Automobile Club
R&D	research and development
RAF	Royal Air Force
RAFVR	Royal Air Force Volunteer Reserve
RAOC	Royal Army Ordnance Corps
RASC	Royal Army Service Corps
RC	Royal Commission
RCA	Radio Corporation of America
RE	Royal Engineers
REA	Royal Exchange Assurance
rep	reprinted
RFC	Royal Flying Corps
RIBA	Royal Institute of British Architects
Rly	Railway
RM	Royal Marines
RN	Royal Navy
RNAS	Royal Naval Air Service
RNR	Royal Naval Reserve
RNVR	Royal Naval Volunteer Reserve
RO	Record Office
RPM	resale price maintenance
RSA	Royal Society of Arts
RUSI	Royal United Services Institute
s (following a monetary figure)	shillings [see note under £ at the end of this list]

SA	Société Anonyme (limited liability company)
SC	Select Committee
Scots DBB	*Dictionary of Scottish Business Biography,* Department of Economic History, Glasgow University
SHAEF	Supreme Headquarters, Allied Expeditionary Forces
Singer, *History of Technology.*	Charles Singer, E J Holmyard, A R Hall and Trevor Williams (eds), *A History of Technology* (7 vols, Oxford: Clarendon Press, 1954-78).
SOAS	School of Oriental and African Studies, London University
SR	Southern Railway
Sr	Senior
SSRC Elites data.	Biographical workcards from SSRC project on 'The Economic Worth of Elites in British Society since 1880' conducted by Professor H J Perkin of Lancaster University, and kindly loaned by him to the *DBB* project.
STOL	Short take-off and landing
sv	sub verbo (under the heading cited)
TA	Territorial Army
TD	Territorial Decoration
Times *Prospectuses.*	*Prospectuses of Public Companies Including the Number of Bonds Drawn and Cancelled. Reprinted from the Advertisement Columns of the Times* (biannual, Times Publishing Co Ltd, 1891-1964).
TV	television
TUC	Trades Union Congress
UDC	Urban District Council
UK	United Kingdom
USA	United States of America
USAF	United States Air Force
V	volt(s)
VCH	*Victoria History of the Counties of England*

Venn, *Alumni Cantabrigienses.*	John Venn and J A Venn, *Alumni Cantabrigienses. A Biographical List of All Known Students, Graduates and Holders of Office at the University of Cambridge, from the Earliest Times to 1900* Part II *1752 to 1900* (6 vols, Cambridge: Cambridge University Press, 1946-54)
V/STOL	vertical or short take-off and landing
VTOL	vertical take-off and landing
Will	Will of subject (unless otherwise stated) in Principal Registry of the Family Division, Somerset House, London WC2R 1LP
WPM	Wallpaper Manufacturers
WW	*Who's Who* (annual, Adam & Charles Black, 1849-1983).
WWMP	Michael Stenton and Stephen Lees (eds), *Who's Who of British Members of Parliament. A Biographical Dictionary of the House of Commons* (4 vols, Hassocks, Sussex: Harvester Press, 1976-81).
WWW	*Who Was Who, 1897-1980* (8 vols, Adam & Charles Black, 1920-81).
WWW Theatre	*Who Was Who in the Theatre, 1912-1976* (Detroit: Gale Research Co, 1978)
YMCA	Young Men's Christian Association
£	Pound (monetary). In all entries, for dates before 15 February 1971 (when Britain switched to a decimal currency) the pound quoted is the old one, ie divided into 20 shillings each of 12 pence. Monetary sums under this old system are expressed as follows: £2 12s 6d. The decimal system abandoned shillings and divided the pound into 100 pence. The conversion rate for shillings is therefore one (old) shilling of 12 pence to five decimal pence.

ABERCONWAY, 1st Lord

see MACLAREN, Charles Benjamin Bright

ADAM, William

(1828-1898)

Carpet manufacturer

William Adam (from the supplement to the Kidderminster Shuttle *17 Dec 1898).*

William Adam was born at Paisley on 10 June 1828, the son of Peter Adam, a handloom woollen weaver, and his wife Elisa.

He began his career as a handloom cotton weaver in Paisley, subsequently working as a warehouseman. After moving to Glasgow, he became a foreman in James Templeton's carpet manufacturing business, where he became familiar with the Chenille Axminster handloom weaving process patented by his employer in 1839. In the late 1850s he moved to Kidderminster to introduce the process to Brinton & Lewis, a leading Brussels carpet manufacturer. But within a year he and George Race, a cashier of the firm, had founded their own Chenille Axminster rug manufacturing firm. The partnership was dissolved in 1862 and Adam then became manager of the rug making firm of H R Willis of Kidderminster where he remained for nearly seven years.

Adam at last found real scope for his ability in 1869 when he went into partnership with Michael Tomkinson (qv) in Kidderminster, founding the carpet manufacturing firm of Tomkinson & Adam. Tomkinson supplied the commercial drive and acumen. Adam confined himself to technical and production matters, solving the practical problems involved as the firm converted to powerloom production and greatly enlarged its scale of operations.

Spool Axminster powerlooms were in full production soon after Tomkinson purchased the British rights from their American inventor in 1878. But Adam's outstanding achievement was the invention of a successful setting powerloom (more complicated than the weft powerloom) for weaving Chenille Axminster carpeting, patented in 1882. James Templeton & Co, which had developed a less efficient loom, paid £5,000 for a licence to use the invention and licences were granted to two other firms, whilst Tomkinson & Adam speedily installed 80 looms of their own.

Adam was a deacon of the Kidderminster Congregational Church for

I

over twenty years, until his death, and its treasurer for nearly as many. He was a life member of the executive of the Worcestershire Union of Congregational Churches. He strongly supported the temperance movement and was a vice-president of the Midland Temperance League. He made numerous charitable donations to individuals and to Congregational churches in Worcestershire, usually shunning publicity; his largest recorded gift was £1,250 towards the cost of Baxter Congregational Church, Kidderminster, erected in 1884.

He married twice: firstly, in 1854, to Agnes Thomson of Paisley (d 1878) by whom he had six children; secondly, in 1879 to Emma Grigg of Kidderminster who bore him two sons. His eldest sons, Peter and William, became his partners in the firm and survived their father. William Adam died on 13 December 1898. He left a 2,000 acre estate in Gloucestershire, purchased for nearly £50,000 in 1897, and a personal estate valued at £211,291 gross.

JAMES NEVILLE BARTLETT

Sources:

Unpublished

Hereford and Worcester County Museum, Hartlebury, Tomkinson & Adam Price List, Oct 1869.

PRO: RG9 2079, 2080.

BCe (Scots).

MCe (Scots).

PrC.

Published

James Neville Bartlett, *Carpeting the Millions: the Growth of Britain's Carpet Industry* (Edinburgh: John Donald 1978).

Kidderminster Shuttle 25 Sept 1897, 17 Dec 1898, 10 Nov 1900.

Frederick H Young, *A Century of Carpet Making 1839-1939* (Glasgow: James Templeton & Co, 1943).

ADAMS, William

(1823-1904)

Locomotive and marine engineer

William Adams was born at Limehouse, East London, on 15 October 1823, the son of John Samuel Adams, the resident engineer of the East & West India Dock Co. After a private education at Moorgate, he went at an early age into the engineering department of the East & West India Docks. He was then apprenticed to Miller & Ravenhill, marine engineers of Blackwall. In the 1840s he worked in the yards at Marseilles and Genoa of P Taylor & Co, marine engineers, supervising the erection of engines and overseeing their trials. During the Year of Revolutions, 1848, Adams joined the Sardinian Navy, spending four years afloat as a marine engineer. He returned to England after his marriage in 1852 to Isabella Park in Genoa, where her father, Charles P Park, was a marine engineer.

During the late 1850s Adams shifted from marine to locomotive engineering after working with H Martin between 1852 and 1855. In the mid-1850s he surveyed a railway route on the Isle of Wight, acted as superintendent of Cardiff Docks and designed and laid out the Bow workshops of the North London Railway. This last commission paved the way for Adams's appointment in 1855 as first locomotive superintendent of the North London Railway. Initially Adams developed the existing types of locomotive employed by the NLR, not designing his own until 1863. Two years later his 51 class appeared: this was not only a larger locomotive, with a boiler pressure of 160 psi, but also incorporated his own type of bogie which allowed lateral movement about the pivot, an important advance. Another particular feature of the locomotives that he produced for the NLR and, subsequently, the Great Eastern Railway, was a sandbox mounted on top of the boiler. His expertise by now not only encompassed design and production engineering, but also traffic management, marked by his introduction of block train sets which were to run on the NLR until the 1930s. The high point of his work for the NLR was his no 1 class of 1868, outside-cylinder 4-4-OT engines, which became the company's standard passenger engine with 74 built. Proving exceptionally dependable, they lasted up to fifty years.

Adams's style of management developed at the Bow works; he was quiet, unassuming, even easy-going but his physique made him a daunting presence at a first meeting. Likened to a general in a southern European army, this Victorian pater familias (he had ten children) was a jovial man, his house being renowned for lavish dinner parties and musical evenings which frequently centred upon the host, who was a singer and entertainer of some repute. He gave generous support to social and philanthropic schemes, especially those for railway employees, like the Bow and Bromley Institute. Adams's position as a professional engineer at the end of the 1860s was marked publicly by his presidency of the Society of Engineers in 1870.

ADAMS William

In 1873 Adams succeeded S W Johnson as the locomotive superintendent of the Great Eastern Railway. He reconstructed the Great Eastern's Stratford works and, as with the NLR, developed its rolling stock. He designed four classes of locomotives for the GER and, in catering for the line's growing London suburban traffic, continued his predecessor's 0-4-4T types. The refurbishment of the company's works took some time so Adams's Class 61 tanks were built by contract, as were the 4-4-0s of 1876 and 1877. The latter proved to be too heavy for their stipulated task and so were quickly switched from passenger to freight work. His introduction of the 2-6-0 to British tracks in 1879/80 was a disaster for, despite their exceptional power, these 'Moguls' proved to be uneconomic and consequently were scrapped after a very short working life of eight years. There is some doubt as to whether these engines were not to be 0-6-0s, their leading pony truck being a modification introduced by Massey Bromley, Adams's successor at the GER.

Adams was also responsible for the motive power of the London Tilbury & Southend Railway, which was closely associated with the GER and which became responsible for the provision of locomotives, following the expiry of the contractors' lease over its lines. The LT&SR general manager, A L Stride, chose a tank engine (a locomotive carrying its own coal and water, as opposed to a tender engine) in order to overcome the problems of reversing at Tilbury, an intermediate yet terminal station. Stride consulted with Adams over the layout of the LT&SR's works at Plaistow and Adams was responsible for the detailed design and specification of the 4-4-2 tank engines which worked the line from the late 1870s, and continued to be built, in modified form, until 1930.

In 1878 Adams moved from the Great Eastern to the London & South Western Railway, and now received a salary of £1,500 per annum. The L&SWR was in great difficulties in the late 1870s because William George Beattie, its mechanical engineer, proved relatively incompetent after succeeding his father in the post. The size of the task confronting Adams was daunting, one measure being the inability of the Nine Elms Works, due to the pressure of repairs and its constricted site, to erect new locomotives until the late 1880s.

Adams solved the London & South Western's motive power problems firstly by modernising, through rebuilding, existing Joseph Beattie engines; secondly, by altering the layout of the workshops at Nine Elms; and thirdly by introducing new classes which had initially to be built under contract. One major problem, as with the Great Eastern, was London suburban traffic. Adams took the approach that he had used with the North London - a 4-4-0 design. While the first three classes of engine had his boilers and bogies, there are indications, as with later designs, that a substantial part in their conception was played by Hermann Lange of Beyer Peacock, the Manchester firm of locomotive engineers.

Adams's locomotives were splendidly proportioned and were generally 'gadget-free', unlike the Beattie engines that they replaced. Their success came from robust construction, large bearing services and free steaming. Adams laid great stress upon economical running and tests with an express design in the 1890s yielded results in terms of coal consumption per indicated hp hour equal to those achieved by the *Caldicot Castle* thirty-five years later. Adams experimented briefly with compounding but the only unusual point of his locomotives from the mid-1880s was the vortex blast pipe for which he held the patent (in conjunction with his nephew Henry) which produced a more uniform flow through the firebox.

Adams's most notable contribution to British locomotive development came at the end of his career in the 1890s when he sucessfully met the challenge of producing express engines capable of pulling heavier trains at higher speeds. These were a series of 60 4-4-0 designs divided into four classes of which both the T3 and T6 were capable of sustaining 80 mph in favourable circumstances, a notable achievement for the 1890s. In the mid-1890s Adams's mind gave way and it is highly probable that his works manager, W F Pettigrew, undertook a not insignificant part of the design of these classes. Their joint work was marked by the award of both a Telford Premium and a George Stephenson medal by the Institution of Civil Engineers in 1895 for their paper 'Trials of an Express Locomotive'.

The problems of continuing loss of memory became so grave for William Adams that he was forced to retire in 1895, but he handed over to Dugald Drummond (qv) a locomotive department second to none in the British Isles. He spent his last years gardening at his family home, Carlton House, at the top of Putney Hill, and died on 7 August 1904, leaving £63,672 gross.

P L COTTRELL

Writings:

(with W F Pettigrew) 'Trials of an Express Locomotive' *Minutes of the Institution of Civil Engineers* 125 (1896).

Sources:

Unpublished

PrC.

Information from Michael Robbins.

Published

E L Ahrons, *The British Steam Railway Locomotive* (Locomotive Publishing Co, 1927).

Colin Langley Aldrich, *Great Eastern Locomotives Past and Present, 1862-1948* (Brightlingsea: E V Aldrich, 5th ed, 1949).

Cecil J Allen, *The Great Eastern Railway* (Shepperton: Ian Allan, 1955).

Donald L Bradley, *Locomotives of the London & South Western Railway* (2 vols, Railway Correspondence and Travel Society, 1965, 1967).

Henry C Casserley, *London & South Western Locomotives* (Shepperton: Ian Allan, 1971).

Cuthbert Hamilton Ellis, *The South Western Railway* (George Allen & Unwin, 1956).

ADAMS William

—, *Twenty Locomotive Men* (Ian Allan, 1958).

Tony Fairclough and Alan Wills (eds), *Southern Steam Locomotive Survey. The Adams Classes* (Truro: D Bradford Barton, 1978).

Sam Fay, *A Royal Road* (Kingston-on-Thames: W Drewett, 1882).

Kenneth H Leech, 'Tilbury Tanks' in B Reed (ed), *Locomotives in Profile* (4 vols, Windsor: Profile Publications, 1971-74) 3.

Locomotive Magazine 49 (1943), 50 (1944).

Chapman F D Marshall, *History of the Southern Railway* (Southern Railway Co, 1936).

John Marshall, *A Biographical Dictionary of Railway Engineers* (Newton Abbot: David & Charles, 1978).

Minutes of the Proceedings of the Institution of Civil Engineers 157 (1904).

National Railway Museum, *North London Railway* (HMSO, 1979).

Oswald S Nock, *The London & South Western Railway* (Shepperton: Ian Allan, 1967).

Michael Robbins, *The North London Railway* (Godalming: Oakwood Press, 1937).

Daniel Adamson (courtesy of the Manchester Ship Canal Co).

ADAMSON, Daniel

(1820-1890)

Engineer and promoter of the Manchester Ship Canal

Daniel Adamson was born at Shildon, County Durham, on 30 April 1820, the thirteenth of the fifteen children of Daniel Adamson, landlord of the *Grey Horse* (now the *Surtees Arms*) at Shildon, and his wife Ann née Gibson. From the public house, his father operated a horse-drawn passenger coach, the *Perseverance*, on the Stockton & Darlington Railway.

His father sent Daniel to the Quaker School, Old Shildon, where he received thorough instruction in mathematics. On his thirteenth birthday he left school to become an apprentice of Timothy Hackworth, engineer to the Stockton & Darlington Railway.

On completing his apprenticeship in 1841, Adamson qualified as both an engineer and draughtsman. He claimed the rare distinction of having created a complete locomotive at the age of nineteen. After Hackworth set up on his own in 1840, Adamson continued to work under his successor,

William Bouch, as managing draughtsman, then as superintendent of stationary engines, finally, in 1847, becoming general manager of the Stockton & Darlington engine works.

In 1850 Adamson resigned of his own free will to become manager of Heaton Foundry in Stockport and, among other activities, planned and constructed a cotton mill. From there he moved to establish his own ironworks at Newton Moor and Hyde Junction, near Dukinfield, six miles from Manchester, works which became world famous and which still (1983) exist as part of the Acrow group. From this works the 'Manchester' boilers, pioneered by Hackworth, were sent all over the world. The range of products of Daniel Adamson & Co are evident from the firm's illustrated catalogue, no 4 (ca 1870), in which they announce themselves as manufacturers of stationary, expansive, condensing, high pressure and compound engines, stationary blowing engines and pumping engines, locomotive steam engines, steam cranes and hoists, iron and steel bridges, iron roofs, beams and pillars, complete gas works, hydraulic lifts for warehouses, rivetting and rivet-making machines, testing machines to test up to 200 tons, Adamson's patent hydraulic lifting jacks, castings of every description, gun metal, valves, and so forth. The works expanded rapidly and, covering four acres, were rebuilt to his designs in 1872-73. By the time Adamson died in 1890, he employed 600 men and paid out £40,000 per annum in wages. A considerable export trade was conducted, with not only European but world-wide connections.

Resuming his earlier interest in the cotton industry from Stockport days, he established the Newton Moor Spinning Co in 1861, with a capital of £30,000 of which £1,000 came from Adamson himself. A second mill was built in 1874, and by 1883 the total capacity of both mills, in which £220,000 had been invested, was 107,000 spindles.

Adamson entered the field of primary production in 1863, erecting the Yorkshire Steel & Iron Works at Penistone. These were the first works in the country to depend wholly upon the large scale manufacture of Bessemer steel. As the engineer of the works, he supplied the engines, boilers and Bessemer steel plant from his establishment at Newton Moor, the whole enterprise becoming operational in thirteen months. He soon afterwards sold the Yorkshire Steel & Iron Works at a considerable profit to Charles Cammell & Co, of Sheffield. Ever an opportunist, his chance meeting with a farmer who showed him some lumps of iron ore found on his land in Lincolnshire led to a new departure in the founding of the North Lincolnshire Iron Co at Frodingham, for the production of pig iron in 1864-65. Adamson overcame the difficulty of the lime content of the ore by adding local siliceous ore. This was a major contribution to the development of the Lincolnshire iron field. Adamson remained chairman of the company for over twenty years.

Although the Newton Moor boiler works were not the largest in the country, they had an unrivalled reputation for quality. Following in the steps of Hackworth, Adamson constantly experimented and improved, hence the numerous patents taken out by him between 1852 and 1887, mostly for improving the design and manufacture of boilers. His major achievement in this area was to develop economical high-pressure boilers using the anti-collapsive flange seam as a ring joint (1852). Ten years later he patented the technique of drilling, instead of punching, rivet holes in boiler plates.

Being as interested in metallurgy as in engineering, he was a pioneer in the use of steel for boilers, from 1857. He succeeded in persuading John Platt (qv) of Oldham, the well-known machinery manufacturer, to buy six Bessemer steel boilers in 1860. Over the period 1860-1890 he produced some 3,000 high pressure boilers according to methods which were widely followed. He mastered the technique of welding mild steel and was adept at the testing and chemical analysis of ferrous metals.

His work was professionally recognised. For his Wheelock (USA patent) engine he was awarded a gold medal at the Inventions Exhibition in London in 1885. At the Edinburgh International Exhibition of 1886 his horizontal engine supplied power for electric lighting and for this he received another gold medal. Probably his crowning award was the Bessemer gold medal, which he received from Sir Henry Bessemer (qv) himself, in 1889, for his role in the development of uses for Bessemer steel.

As a measure of his European reputation, shortly before his death he visited Elba at the request of the Italian Government, to report upon the potential of its iron mines. Thus as both an engineer and a metallurgist, Adamson made a most significant contribution to the advance of technology throughout the nineteenth century.

Adamson's outstanding contribution to nineteenth century business, however, came with his crucial involvement in the Manchester Ship Canal scheme. As chairman of the Provisional Committee of the Manchester Ship Canal he was chiefly responsible for promoting the idea of the Manchester Ship Canal. To his experience in engineering and transportation he added a relentless drive and enthusiasm which despised opposition, and a homespun North-country bluntness and tenacity which endeared him to the common man. Like Gladstone, he trusted the 'masses' rather than the 'classes' and became something of a celebrity as a speaker on the Canal issue. Opposition was strong: from the railway companies and from the Mersey Docks & Harbour Board, which was largely dominated by Liverpool shipowners and merchants, who had a vested interest in blighting the Canal scheme and were able to marshall an impressive array of alleged facts and figures in support of their case. There was also early opposition from C P Scott, editor of the *Manchester Guardian* (who later claimed that he had advised those originally interested in the ship canal idea to go to Adamson for leadership!).

Adamson never claimed that the Canal was his idea. Newspaper correspondence; interest on the part of the Manchester Chamber of Commerce; plans for a tidal navigation to Manchester drafted by Hamilton Fulton, civil engineer; and the example of the Clyde, as improved by the Glasgow merchants; all focused attention on the issue, from 1876 onwards. The earliest correspondent, a Manchester Scot, George Hicks, then approached Adamson. He in turn consulted his old friend, James Abernethy, civil engineer, and got an encouraging opinion. A spell of illness, however, hindered Adamson from taking up the matter until he arranged the crucial public meeting at his house, The Towers, Didsbury, Manchester, on 27 June 1882. There the mayors of Manchester and the surrounding towns, along with leaders of trade and industry, co-

operative and labour movements, heard Fulton and Edward Leader
Williams, then engineer of the Bridgewater Canal, speak. Leader
Williams was to become the engineer of the Ship Canal. Adamson took
the chair, Fulton sketched the main engineering features and estimated
the cost at £4.5 million. Hicks outlined the commercial case. He believed
the Canal would earn £750,000 a year. A provisional committee was
appointed to take the matter further and form a company to be called the
Manchester Tidal Navigation Co. At this meeting, Adamson met
Marshall Stevens (qv), a Liverpool shipping agent, who became his
indefatigable first lieutenant.

Later that year, Leader Williams's scheme for a Ship Canal with locks
was chosen in the light of further investigation. Adamson accepted this
amendment. Manchester Chamber of Commerce and Manchester and
Salford Corporations pledged support and a mass meeting of working
men gave unanimous approval. On 15 December 1882 the first bill was
deposited. It was rejected by a Committee of the Lords; in 1884 a second
bill was rejected by the Commons. Then despite bitter opposition,
municipal rate support was pledged. In 1885 the third bill passed both
Houses, receiving the Royal Assent on 6 August 1885. It included a clause
to purchase the Bridgewater Canal, a profitable 'feeder' undertaking.
This was Adamson's finest hour. He was met at Stockport by a brass
band, triumphal arches and addresses of welcome from his workmen and
other representatives of labour. He prophesied that in five years the Canal
shares would be doubled in value and trebled in ten years and that the
Canal would save £1 million a year to the trade of the district.

Adamson had immense confidence in local financial backing from all
classes. Working men, he felt, knew their livelihoods depended on it. His
own men contributed £444. One pet idea of his was the Co-operative
Share Distribution Co, which enabled shares to be acquired by weekly
instalments of 1s each. Sadly, however, the provisional prospectus of 1885
failed to raise more than £750,000, so the assistance of Rothschilds was
sought. They agreed to help on the stiff condition that interest would be
paid on the capital during construction. Adamson believed that
subscriptions would come in without this proviso. An act was obtained
permitting this, and Rothschilds sought to raise £6 million on the Stock
Market while the promotors raised £2 million locally. Vested interests
again brought about failure.

A drastic reappraisal was needed. At this point, unfortunately,
Adamson's rugged individuality, outspokenness and propensity for
excitement ceased to be an advantage. He had stirred up widespread
enthusiasm and momentum. Now shrewder financial brains and more
diplomatic tongues needed to take over. A consultative committee with
power to report on the whole scheme was appointed. It included landed
proprietors; also those newly won to the scheme. Adamson did not
welcome it. When it recommended that the board should be
reconstructed, his natural dominance became intolerance; he refused to
move the adoption of the report. He held that he had done all possible to
strengthen the board and blamed inadequate canvassing. Sir Joseph Lee
(qv), chairman of Tootals, the deputy chairman of the board, then moved
the adoption of the report. Adamson thereupon offered to resign if the
report were passed. Even the chairman of the Co-operative Wholesale

Society, a staunch friend of Adamson's, supported the report and expressed the hope that Adamson and Sir Joseph Lee would be reconciled. On 10 February 1887, Lord Egerton of Tatton was elected chairman, Sir Joseph Lee being re-elected as deputy. Adamson thereupon resigned, though he continued to support the Ship Canal scheme publicly. Without his rugged determination and demagogic approach, the scheme would never have been launched.

Adamson's wilder predictions for the Canal were indeed chimerical, but its most important effect was in breaking the monopoly of the Mersey Docks & Harbour Board and of the railway companies, and thus lowering the rates of carriage of goods whether or not the Canal was used. This was Adamson's main objective. The Port of Manchester's trade as a percentage of that of the whole UK never reached double figures. The Canal company paid its first dividend in 1915.

Adamson had led a very full life. He was a member of the Institution of Mechanical Engineers from 1859, a member of council from 1876, and a vice-president from 1885; a member of the Iron and Steel Institute from its foundation in 1869, member of council from 1873, vice-president in 1885 and president, 1887-88; member of the Institution of Civil Engineers from 1877; a member of the Geological Society from 1875, also of the British Iron Trades Association, the Railway and Canal Traders' Association and the Society of Arts. He was president of the North Staffordshire Institute of Mechanical and Mining Engineers, a member of the Institute of Mining and Mechanical Engineers of Newcastle upon Tyne, the Cleveland Institution of Engineers, the Manchester Geographical Society, the Manchester Literary and Philosophical Society, and others. He was a director of the Manchester Chamber of Commerce and a JP for Cheshire from 1876 and later also for the City of Manchester. In 1873 he became a member of Dukinfield Local Board, becoming chairman in 1875, retaining that position till his resignation from the board in 1879. As chairman of the Waterworks Committee in 1874, he secured the transference of the waterworks to the Ashton Joint Waterworks Committee. He was active in promoting the joint local authority ownership of the gas works, the development of sewage works and the increase of postal, telegraphic and banking facilities.

His interest in education was evident in his membership of the Dukinfield Library and of the Astley Institute, of which he was president, from 1883 to 1886. He contributed to prizes and scholarships and was particularly concerned to promote the teaching of science. He left £260 to the Dukinfield Village Library. He was president of the North Cheshire Agricultural Society in 1876. Politically he was a Liberal, but he was not set on political advancement. In 1888 he contested Heaton Norris for Lancashire County Council against Sir Henry Houldsworth, losing by only 306 votes. There were proposals to bring him forward as a parliamentary candidate, but he declined on health grounds. At heart he had little patience with the formalities of party political organisation. Similarly, his religion was a practical, broad and non-dogmatic Anglicanism.

As a self-made man, he was not embarrassed by his hard-earned riches. His palatial house called The Towers (now the Shirley Institute), bought in 1874 at the bargain price of £11,000, where he had liveried servants, was in Didsbury, one of the more salubrious districts of Manchester. He also had a hunting lodge in Flintshire.

He was a firm disciplinarian, but generally popular with his workmen. He welcomed trade unions, providing they played a subsidiary but supportive role to management. He could be intolerant and scathing with competitors and opponents; on the other hand, he was totally devoid of humbug. Adamson remained a thoroughly practical engineer and, at a meeting of the Manchester Association of Engineers in 1881, he expressed his scorn for college-educated Whitworth Scholars. In appearance, he had a commanding presence. A well-built figure with a fine beard, he was, at least on formal occasions, immaculate in his dress.

Adamson died on 13 February 1890. He was survived by a widow, Mary, and two daughters: Alice Ann, the wife of Joseph Leigh, one-time mayor of, and MP for, Stockport, later knighted for his work as a director of the Canal; and Lavinia, the wife of William J Parkyn, his partner and manager of the Dukinfield works. Daniel Adamson left an estate valued at £71,065 gross.

J GORDON READ

Writings:

'On High Pressure Steam Generally and its Application to Quadruple Engines' *JISI* 1875.

'On the Mechanical & Other Properties of Iron & Mild Steel' *ibid* 1878.

'Properties of Puddled Iron, Ingot Iron & Steel for Constructive Purposes' *Proceedings of North Staffordshire Institute of Mechanical Mining Engineers* 4, part 2 (1879).

'On a Horizontal Compound-Lever Testing Machine of 15,000 powers, with a further Recording Lever of 150,000 powers' *JISI* 1888.

Minutes of Evidence given by Proponents and Opponents of the Manchester Ship Canal Bill (6 vols, pp by Waterlow & Sons, 1883-85) copy in Greater Manchester CRO, Manchester Ship Canal Co archives.

British Patents:

1852 (14,259)	1863 (3,233)	1871 (344)	1881 (544)
1853 (2,793)	1865 (1,291)	1873 (900)	1887 (534)
1858 (1,674)	1866 (166)	1875 (3,099)	1887 (535)
1861 (52)	1867 (1,517)	1878 (401)	1888 (10,061)
1862 (1,820)	1869 (1,377)	1878 (5,080)	

Sources:

Unpublished

Greater Manchester Archives, County Hall, Manchester, Daniel Adamson, personal and business records.

Lancashire RO, Bow Lane, Preston, DDX/101; DDBe.

ADAMSON Daniel

Manchester Central Library, St Peter's Square, Manchester, pamphlets, cuttings, etc (Local History Library).

Merseyside County Archives, 64 Islington, Liverpool, MDHB, Legal, N series (Manchester Ship Canal) Parliamentary Papers.

PrC.

Personal information from Mrs P Parkyn, widow of R W Parkyn, great-grandson of Daniel Adamson.

Published

T Ashbury, *Jubilee of Manchester Association of Engineers* (Manchester, 1905).

Ashton-under-Lyne Reporter 18 Jan 1890.

Auckland Chronicle 24 Apr 1876.

Boase.

The Engineer 17 Jan 1890.

Engineering 14 Apr 1876.

Douglas A Farnie, *Manchester Ship Canal and the Rise of the Port of Manchester* (Manchester: Manchester University Press, 1980).

JISI 3 (1890).

Bosdin T Leech, *History of the Manchester Ship Canal* (2 vols, Sherratt & Hughes, 1907).

Manchester City News 18 Jan 1890.

Manchester Examiner 14 Jan 1890.

Manchester Faces and Places 1 (1890).

Manchester Guardian 14 Jan 1890.

Manchester Ship Canal Company Past and Present (Manchester: Public Relations Department, Port of Manchester, 1978).

A Memorial to Daniel Adamson (Dukinfield: pp, 1935).

Proceedings of the Geological Society 46 (1890).

Proceedings of the Institution of Civil Engineers 100 (1890).

Proceedings of the Institution of Mechanical Engineers (1870).

Proceedings of the Manchester Literary and Philosophical Society (1890).

Spennymoor Times 5 May 1876.

The Towers, Didsbury (Manchester: Shirley Institute, 1976).

Robert Young, *Timothy Hackworth and the Locomotive* (Co Durham: Shildon, 2nd ed, 1975).

ADDIS, Sir Charles Stewart

(1861-1945)

Banker and government financial adviser

Sir Charles S Addis (from The First Fifty Years of the Institute of Bankers 1879–1929, *Blades, East & Blades, 1929).*

Charles Stewart Addis was born in Edinburgh on 23 November 1861, the eleventh child of Rev Thomas Addis, a Free Church of Scotland minister, and his wife, Robina née Thorburn. Although he was a gifted student, Charles rebelled against the rigorous academic demands which his father made of him and quit the Edinburgh Academy at the age of sixteen, determined to make his own way as a merchant. He became an apprentice for Peter Dawie & Co, General Importers, in Leith. Following his apprenticeship, Addis set off for London in 1880 where he obtained a position with the Hongkong & Shanghai Banking Corporation, and began to study Chinese in evening classes at King's College in the Strand.

An important turning point in the young Scotsman's career came in 1883 when he was transferred to Singapore and then to the head office in Hong Kong. Over the next twenty years, Addis held a variety of positions with the HSBC in China, Burma and India, becoming acquainted with a large number of European and Asian leaders and gaining unique experience in the field of international finance and diplomacy.

In 1905 Addis was appointed to the London office of the Hongkong & Shanghai Bank, where he became senior manager in 1911. His new duties included membership of the board of directors of the British & Chinese Corporation and the Chinese Central Railways, both of which were partially owned by the Bank. In addition, Addis was appointed British Censor to the State Bank of Morocco and became a director of the Eastern Telegraph Co Ltd. His achievement in organising the first international banking consortium for China was rewarded with a knighthood in 1913. Sir Charles's success in gaining government backing for the Hongkong & Shanghai Bank in the Reorganisation Loan of 1913 to China gave the bank great advantages over its other British competitors.

While Sir Charles continued to be deeply involved in China affairs throughout his career, the move to London had enlarged the scope of his interests and broadened his expertise. In 1914 he became a member of the Council of the Royal Economic Society, which put him in close contact with academic theorists such as John Maynard Keynes (qv). Later membership in such groups as the Tuesday Club, the Royal Institute of International Affairs and the Reform and Athenaeum Clubs enabled Sir Charles to exchange views with leading statesmen and men of affairs.

During the First World War, Addis's knowledge of international markets and credit conditions became especially valuable to the Government as Britain strove to meet the financial burdens caused by war. In 1918 Sir Charles was appointed to the Cunliffe Committee which, having currency and foreign exchanges under consideration, recommended a return to gold after the war was over. The next year he was appointed a director of the Bank of England, shortly thereafter becoming a member of the important Committee of Treasury. Following the war Addis served on the Committee on Indian Currency in 1920 and as a financial expert to the Genoa Conference in 1922. He was elected president of the Institute of Bankers in 1921.

Despite these new responsibilities, Sir Charles continued to influence Far Eastern affairs, being regularly consulted by the Foreign Office and the Cabinet throughout the 1920s. His position as manager of the British Group of the China Consortium (which he had helped to reorganise in 1920) involved regular consultations with his American counterparts in the house of Morgan. Through such contacts, Addis was able to preserve the dominant influence of the Hongkong & Shanghai Bank over China's financial affairs, and was rewarded with the KCMG in 1921.

As close friend and advisor to Montagu Norman (qv), Governor of the Bank of England, Addis supported Britain's return to the Gold Standard in 1925 and consistently fought for the principles of free trade. In 1924 Sir Charles became involved in the reparations question when he became British director of the Reichsbank, which was reorganised as part of the Dawes Plan. In order to carry out his Reichsbank responsibilities, Addis began to study German at the age of sixty-three. Five years later he helped to draft the Young Plan for German reparations, which included plans for a Bank of International Settlements. Addis became a director and vice-president of the Bank of International Settlements. Following his retirement from the Bank of England and the Bank of International Settlements, Addis spent two months in Canada in 1933 as a member of the Royal Commission on Banking for Canada.

While Sir Charles's great achievements partially can be explained by intellectual ability and physical vitality, of greater significance were his indomitable will, personal integrity and spiritual strength. Addis's philosophy best can be summarised by the scriptural verse which he often quoted: 'to whom much is given of him shall much be required.' Although not dogmatic, Addis remained a confirmed believer, not only in God but in the perfectibility of man. He viewed his own efforts as a contribution to world peace.

While home on his second leave in 1894, Addis met and married Elizabeth Jane McIsaac; their long and happy marriage produced six sons and seven daughters. With his wife and children, to whom he was intensely devoted, he shared his love of music, literature and nature. Sir Charles's last years were spent at Woodside, a lovely estate forty miles south of London in Sussex. He became a church warden in the little church at Frant, where he is buried. He died on 14 December 1945, leaving £114,299 gross.

ROBERTA A DAYER

Writings:

In the late 1880s and 1890s, Addis contributed articles to *The Chinese Times* (Tientsin) and the *North China Daily News* (Shanghai). Since the articles were unsigned, information concerning their authorship must come from other sources, such as letters and diaries. Addis also wrote a column called 'Notes by Quidnunc', for the *News*, and helped with 'Peking Notes' in the *Times*. The titles below are a selection from a larger but still incomplete list of writings and speeches deposited in the *DBB* files.

'The Wedding Rice' *The Chinese Times* 4 June 1887.

'Exchange' *ibid* 9 Nov 1889.

'New Railroads in China' *ibid* 16 Nov 1889.

'Notes by Quidnunc' *North China Daily News* Mar-Dec 1890.

'How to Spend Money' An address to the Young Men's Christian Association, Shanghai, *North China Herald* 6 Mar 1896.

'Corea under the Russians, The Issacher of the East' *The United Services Magazine* 15 (June 1897).

'The Daily Exchange Quotations' Literary & Debating Society, Shanghai, 4 Feb 1903. Printed as a pamphlet by the *North China Herald*.

'Chinese Railways' *Journal of the Royal Society of Arts* 57 (21 May 1909).

'A British Trade Bank' *The Economic Journal* 26 (Dec 1916).

'Bank Reserves and Depreciation' *ibid* 27 (Sept 1917).

'Problems of British Banking' *Edinburgh Review* 228 (July 1918).

'The Economics of a War Indemnity', an address to the Institute of Bankers *The Nation* 108 (12 April 1919).

'European Policy and Finance in China' *Living Age* 350 (28 June 1919).

'The Victory Loan' *Review of Reviews* 60 (July 1919).

'Finance of China' *Edinburgh Review* 230 (Oct 1919).

'The China Consortium' *Times* 14 Oct 1920.

'Changes in China in the Past Twenty Years' *The Bankers Magazine* 104 (May 1922).

'Back to the Gold Standard' *The Accountants' Magazine* 28 (Jan 1924).

'Discussion on Monetary Reform' *Economic Journal* 34 (June 1924).

'Chinese Tariff Revision' *Times* 26 Nov 1925.

'Comments on Hu Shih speech' *Journal of the Royal Institute of International Affairs* 5 (9 Nov 1926).

'The Bank of International Settlements' *Journal of Institute of Bankers* 51 (May 1930).

'Outlook for International Cooperation in Finance' *Proceedings of the Academy of Political Science* 14 (Jan 1931).

'The New Monetary Technique' *Quarterly Review* 269 (July 1937).

'Liberal Economy' *Spectator* 160 (4 Feb 1938).

Sources:

Unpublished

Federal Reserve Bank of New York: Benjamin Strong papers.

PRO: British Foreign Office, Cabinet Office and Treasury Records.

ADDIS Sir Charles Stewart

School of Oriental and African Studies, London: Sir Francis Aglen papers.

United States National Archives, Washington DC, Department of State records.

University of Toronto Library: J O P Bland papers.

Woodside, Frant, Sussex: Addis Papers.

PrC.

BCe (Scots).

MCe (Scots).

Interviews with the late Sir William Addis KBE, CMG, MA and the late Sir John Addis KCMG (sons of Sir Charles); the late Lady Bernard, Lady Lawrence, Miss Addis OBE, Mrs Edmund Booth, the Hon Mrs M K Geddes, Mrs J E Pownall (daughters of Sir Charles); Mrs Michael Warr (daughter-in-law of Sir Charles); Lt Commander Charles Addis (grandson of Sir Charles); and Lady Montagu Norman, widow of Lord Norman and friend of Miss Addis.

David McLean, 'British Banking and Government in China: The Foreign Office and the Hongkong and Shanghai Bank 1895-1913' (Cambridge PhD, 1972).

Published

Maurice Collis, *Wayfoong: The Hongkong and Shanghai Banking Corporation* (Faber & Faber, 1965).

Roberta A Dayer, *Bankers and Diplomats in China 1917-1925: The Anglo-American Relationship* (Frank Cass & Co, 1981).

Economic Journal 56 (Sept 1946).

E J S, 'Gold and Sir Charles Addis' *The Spectator* 19 Jan 1924.

'Men of Mark: Sir Charles Addis' *The Financial News* 17 Dec 1930.

Donald E Moggridge, *British Monetary Policy 1924-1931: The Norman Conquest of $4.86* (Cambridge: Cambridge University Press, 1972).

Richard S Sayers, *The Bank of England 1891-1944* (3 vols, Cambridge: Cambridge University Press, 1976).

Times 15 Dec 1945.

WWW.

Sir John Aird. Watercolour by Sir Leslie Ward, signed Spy (courtesy of the National Portrait Gallery, London).

AIRD, Sir John

(1833-1911)

Civil engineering contractor

John Aird was born on 3 December 1833, the only child of John Aird (1800-76) and his wife Agnes née Bennett, daughter of Charles Bennett of Lambeth, Surrey. John Aird Sr had originated from Ross-shire, and, for twenty years, worked as superintendent at the Phoenix Gas Co's works in Greenwich, before setting up his own contracting business, John Aird & Sons, in 1848. This became a substantial contracting business, laying gas and water mains both in England and abroad. John Aird Jr left school at the age of eighteen, having received a private education at Greenwich and Southgate, and joined his father's firm. Before long he was involved in the important task of removing the Crystal Palace buildings, erected by his father, from Hyde Park to Sydenham. By the age of twenty-one, he had been given almost complete charge of the Berlin Water Co, formed in 1852 by Sir Charles Fox and Thomas Crompton in partnership with John Aird Sr.

While his father still controlled the main operation of the firm, Aird undertook several contracting projects abroad for waterworks, gasworks and drainage systems. In 1860 the firm went into partnership with the contractors Lucas Bros, to form Lucas & Aird. After the amalgamation was completed in 1870, Aird finally took over his father's position by becoming the chief and, although younger than Charles Lucas, very much the dominant partner. He was, however, responsible for the firm's largest works of the 1860s, the first of which was the Beckton gasworks, finished in 1870.

At Beckton, Lucas & Aird constructed a gasworks capable of carrying one million cubic feet of gas a day to the City of London and Westminster (and soon serving nearly all London north of the Thames) in order to satisfy the rising demand for gas. The plant, which significantly reduced the unit cost of gas production, made the Gas Light & Coke Co the leading metropolitan gas company and induced many small gas companies to amalgamate with it.

Lucas & Aird's other major work of the 1860s was the construction of the Millwall Docks, commissioned in 1864 by the Millwall Freehold Land & Dock Co. Begun in June 1865, in collaboration with the engineer John Fowler (qv), it was finished in only three years, and covered 36 acres.

For twenty years, Lucas & Aird held a virtual monopoly of London dock work. The 1870 amalgamation, which set up an interlocking financial structure and so increased capital resources, combined with John Aird's shrewd financial sense (he had links with the Barings and the Rothschilds) placed the firm in a strong financial position. They were, therefore, able to respond to the ever-increasing need for docks, generated by the near-doubling of traffic entering the port of London in the decade 1860-70. They built quickly and well, thereby encouraging new trade and keeping costs and repairs low. Using a previously unseen degree of mechanisation, Lucas & Aird, following Alexander Randall's design, over fifteen years substantially extended the Victoria Dock, which became the Royal Albert Dock and robbed the inefficient South-West India Dock of its steam traffic. They also took over, and finished in two years, work on the Tilbury Dock for the East & West India Dock Co, which inefficient contractors had been unable to complete.

Although their contracts centred on the Thames, Lucas & Aird also planned 60 miles of industrial railway network in Hull, and, in 1885, having ensured much publicity, Aird built the West Highland railway for the North British Railway Co, at a tender price of £2.25 million. He relished the tricky task of building across marshland, where he developed the method of constructing embankments out of brushwood and logs covered with ash and earth. His plans to continue and link the railway with Inverness, however, were rejected, and by the time the Crofters' Commission had persuaded the Government to provide help for the Highlands, Aird was working abroad on the Nile and no longer available.

John Aird's interest in small English works began to decline after the failure of Lucas & Aird to secure a contract for the Manchester Ship Canal as a result of financial squabbles between Rothschilds and the promoters of the project. Charles Lucas died in 1895, and, aware of growing competition from new men, such as John Jackson (qv) and Weetman Pearson (qv), Aird turned to Egypt, where John Aird & Co (as the firm became after Lucas's death) were responsible for the building of the Aswan Dam, the greatest single work carried out by British contractors before that time, and the Assyut Barrage. Approached by Ernest Cassel (qv), Aird undertook to complete the two projects in five years at a cost of £1.5 million. Aird won the contract, signed on 22 February 1898, in preference to Pearsons. The immense size of the projected Aswan Dam and the problems caused by excavation difficulties and annual flooding meant that the work proved to be far more expensive that Aird had originally estimated. With 20,000 men (90 per cent natives) working on day and night shifts at one point, in a race against time and floods, Aird finished the Aswan Dam in June 1902, a year ahead of schedule, but at an extra cost of £500,000.

Aird was again forced to take risks in the construction of the Assyut Barrage, where a low flood left him with the choice of failing crops or the possibility of the loss of three years' work. He chanced the latter by letting the river into the canal, and, again, his gamble paid off, although not without a long battle filling in new holes in the dam with stones dropped from barges.

At the age of seventy and with a high reputation in Egypt, Aird contracted for a complex reservoir plan on the Aswan itself, where contraction and expansion caused by wide climatic variations proved to be the greatest problem. It was completed after his death. His last work on the Nile took the form of a barrage at Esneh, between Aswan and Assyut, finished eighteen months ahead of schedule, under the control of Murdock Macdonald, once on Aird's staff, and then Director General of Reservoirs in Egypt.

Back in England and fighting against Pearsons' increasing competition in dock-building, Aird won a contract in 1902 to build the Royal Edward

Docks at Avonmouth. Again, the site was a treacherous one, but the 30-acre dock was completed in 1908 and opened in July of that year by the King.

This was almost Aird's last public function, as, some months previously, a stroke (probably the result of overwork in the Egyptian heat) left him partially paralysed. Having virtually retired, he left the firm in the hands of his sons, Malcolm and Charles, and a son-in-law. They embarked on a difficult contract for improvements for the Singapore Tanjong Pagar Dock Co which proved so troublesome that the STP Dock Co brought in another firm of contractors in 1911. Airds sued for misrepresentation and seizure of property which led to a long court case. John Aird & Co eventually settled out of court and lost over £1 million, as a result of which the firm was liquidated by the brothers.

Although Aird's sons were much to blame for this disastrous failure (they relied entirely on the Singapore engineers without visiting the site themselves), John Aird had never helped them gain any insight into the firm and its methods, rather despising them for being on a lower intellectual level than himself. Described as 'a tall, florid giant with prominent features, blue eyes and a deep commanding voice, and a beard which he wore longer and more splendid as he grew older' {Middlemas (1963) 131}, John Aird was often stubborn and short-tempered. Sure of his own judgement, foresight and ideas, he treated his workers fairly but with total autocracy, which did not endear him to them.

Outside work, he was a great patron of contemporary arts, sitting on the Council of Art Union of London from 1891 until his death. He was also an enthusiastic mason (Senior Grand Deacon). A staunch Conservative and Unionist, Aird was MP for North Paddington, 1887-1906, and in 1900-2 was first mayor of Paddington, where he was a respected and popular personality. His other posts and honours included those of: major and honorary lieutenant colonel of the Engineer and Railway Volunteer Staff Corps; associate of the Institution of Civil Engineers (1859); member of the Iron and Steel Institute (1887); member of the Royal Commission on the Depression of Trade (1886); and the title of Grand Cordon of Medjideh (for services on the Nile) (1902). He was created a baronet in 1901.

John Aird married in 1855, Sarah née Smith (d 1909), by whom he had two sons and seven daughters; she was the daughter of Benjamin Smith, a wealthy wharfinger of Deptford Green, but despite her father's influence, Sarah had had remarkably little influence on her husband's business life. Sir John Aird died on 6 January 1911 at Wilton Park, Beaconsfield, Bucks, his place of retirement. He left an estate valued at £1,101,489 gross.

HELEN E JEFFRIES

Sources:

Unpublished

MCe.

PrC.

Published

Builder 13 Jan 1911.

DNB.

Robert K Middlemas, *The Master Builders* (Hutchinson, 1963).

Times Jan 7, 12, Mar 23 1911.

WWMP.

WWW.

AIREDALE, 1st Lord
see **KITSON, James**

AIREY, Sir Edwin
(1878-1955)

Builder and contractor

Edwin Airey was born in Leeds on 7 February 1878. His parents, William Airey and his wife Elizabeth née Robinson, came from a village in Wensleydale and brought their children up strictly as Wesleyan Methodists. Edwin, the younger son, attended the new Central Higher Grade School in Leeds and later the Yorkshire College. At fourteen he became an apprentice joiner in Wood & Airey, a firm of builders in which his father was a partner. In 1895, William Airey set up on his own and eight years later took his son into partnership. Like the mass of small local builders, William Airey & Son speculated in the construction of dwelling houses and undertook alterations and repairs. Their permanent staff numbered three: a clerk, a joiner and a mason. The proprietors did their own estimating and as skilled tradesmen carried out all brickwork and woodwork. Other tasks were put out to sub-contractors.

William Airey died in 1905 and Edwin assumed control of the business. As his father had remarried in 1899 and produced two more children, Edwin had to buy out his step-mother. This strained his resources at a time when housing demand fell somewhat and he had to support a growing family. Airey therefore turned his administrative and financial skills to the growth area of general contracting. In 1909 he secured a contract to construct a clothing factory for the Hunslet Co-operative Wholesale Society. Other major projects followed, including a new Teachers' Training College at Bingley. By 1914, the success of the firm was assured. Airey now had sufficient resources to tender for more complex constructions though he still assumed direct responsibility for work that involved the traditional building crafts, employing upwards of 100 men on his sites.

During the First World War, Airey built ordnance factories, gun testing and firing ranges. In 1915 he became a consultant in the Ministry of Munitions and produced his first invention, a portable aircraft hangar. After the war, when the Government subsidised local authority housing, Airey designed a Duo-slab system of construction using pre-fabricated concrete slabs and secured valuable public housing contracts on sites as far afield as Edinburgh, Bristol and northern France, as well as Leeds where he built 800 houses by this method in the Meanwood Valley.

In the later 1920s, major public and private building projects were launched in inner city areas and Airey's more notable building achievements in Leeds included the Headrow Store for Lewis's Ltd (1932), the Brotherton Library at Leeds University (1933), the two-way grandstand at Headingley Sports Ground (1933), and the Queen's Hotel for the LMS railway (1936). The concentration of his resources on fewer sites provided Airey with opportunities to introduce innovations which economised on materials, transport and the utilisation of hired plant. The Headrow department store, for instance, was completed in seventy weeks, twenty weeks ahead of schedule, a fine example of pre-planning. The facing stone for this building, which covered the largest area of any department store in the provinces, was hoisted to a higher floor and lowered into position by 40 travelling blocks. The steelwork in the same building was redesigned to incorporate another Airey invention, the reinforced floor 'Aerodome' which was displayed at the Building Trades Exhibition in London in 1931. The saving in steel costs alone more than outweighed the expense of the 'Aerodome' floors in the building. In the construction of the Brotherton Library, which cost £120,000, the concrete to support the dome surmounting the vast circular reading room was poured into a spider's web of angle-iron and shuttering; this was subsequently dismantled, completing a procedure which halved the cost of the traditional method.

By the early 1930s, William Airey & Son ranked amongst the top 1 per cent of builders in the UK and employed over 800 men, almost a tenth of the workforce in the local building industry. In addition, Airey was the principal owner of the Pioneer Brick & Tile Co which had plants throughout the West Riding.

At the end of the Second World War, when subsidised public housing was once more assigned a high priority, large contractors developed the off-site production of standardised components. The two-storey Airey House, designed in 1946 for the Ministry of Health to supplement traditional construction in rural areas, was based on pre-cast concrete piers and panels that could be erected quickly without bricklayers and plasterers. Under government guarantee the company built 20,000 houses on this system between 1945 and 1950.

Airey's services both during and immediately after the First World War were recognised by the conferment of a knighthood in 1922. Sir Edwin Airey was fellow of the Institute of Builders and a member of the Institute of Structural Engineers. He served as president both of the National and Yorkshire Federation of Building Trades Employers, and as chairman of the Commercial Travellers Association. In 1944 he was High Sheriff of Yorkshire, and was invested in 1949 as a Commander of the Order of Orange-Nassau. The ruling Conservative Party in the Leeds City Council nominated him as Lord Mayor in 1923 although he had never participated in local politics. Airey held office in many voluntary organisations in Leeds: treasurer in his Methodist chapel; provincial rank in the freemasons (1908); and as chairman of the Board of the Leeds Public Dispensary (1922-29), of the Leeds Choral Union in 1933, of the Rugby League Council, and, for thirty-one years, of the board of the Leeds Cricket, Football & Athletic Co Ltd. Sir Edwin Airey died on 14 March 1955 leaving £52,166 gross. He was survived by his wife, Edith (née Greaves) whom he married in 1904, a son and three daughters.

W GORDON RIMMER

Sources:

Unpublished

BCe.

MCe.

PrC.

Interview with Lady Airey and George Airey, 26 July 1961.

Published

The Architect and Building News 3 May 1946.

Marian Bowley, *Innovations in Building Materials* (Duckworths, 1958).

—, *The British Building Industry. Four Studies in Response and Resistance to Change* (Cambridge: Cambridge University Press, 1966).

Asa Briggs, *Friends of the People* (Batsford, 1958).

E E Dodd, *History of Bingley* (Bingley: Harrison, 1958).

Christopher G Powell, *An Economic History of the British Building Industry, 1815-1979* (Methuen, 1980).

A Thompson, *Library Buildings of Britain and Europe* (Butterworth, 1963).

Times 15 March 1955.

WWW.

Yorkshire Evening Post 14 March 1955.

William M Aitken, Lord Beaverbrook. Oil painting by Walter Sickert, dated 1935 (courtesy of the National Portrait Gallery, London).

AITKEN, William Maxwell

1st Lord Beaverbrook

(1879-1964)

Newspaper proprietor

William Maxwell Aitken, the fifth of nine surviving children, was born at Maple, Ontario, on 25 May 1879, and brought up at Newcastle, New Brunswick. His father, William Cuthbert Aitken, was a Presbyterian minister who had emigrated to Canada from Scotland in 1864. His mother, Jane née Noble, was the daughter of a prosperous storekeeper and farmer of Scottish Presbyterian stock.

As a boy Maxwell was clever, restless and mischievous, idle in school and difficult at home. His principal interest was in making money by various schemes, including, when he was thirteen, the launch of a weekly newspaper, called *The Leader*, which appeared just three times.

Failing in Latin in the entrance exams to Dalhousie University, at sixteen Aitken began work in a drug store for $1 a week, and then as a clerk in a lawyer's office, but he could never settle to anything for very long. He sold insurance, then sold bonds (which proved far more profitable) and then began buying and selling companies. He raised money from a variety of sources, from individuals approached in door to door selling (a not unusual method of selling bonds in Canada), to banks. He supplied the local press with favourable information about the companies he wanted to sell, seeing newspapers as an instrument of propaganda long before he owned any. With the aid of John Stairs, a leading financier in Halifax, in 1903 he also started his own finance company, Royal Securities Corporation, the first bond-selling company in Eastern Canada.

In 1906 Aitken moved Royal Securities to Montreal, where he became the leading promoter of a wave of company mergers which affected every industry in Canada. Aitken had a hand in many of these mergers, in iron and steel, railways, hydro-electric power, paper, flour and cement. He was also concerned with the promotion of companies in the West Indies. These deals made him a sterling millionaire by the age of thirty, but left most of the companies with which he was concerned weakened by over-capitalisation. The most notorious instance was that of the Canada Cement Co, which brought together 11 of the 23 Canadian Cement producers. The total assets of all 23 was $15 million: the new merger was capitalised at $38 million of which $32.5 million was eventually issued. Contemporary reports probably exaggerated his profits from this and other deals, but Aitken's life-long reluctance to provide convincing evidence to refute the accusations of malpractice which persisted in Canada and had recurrent echoes in Britain, made it impossible to determine how much profit he did make, and how exactly he came by it.

On 17 July 1910 Aitken set sail for England with his wife and infant son Max. He came to England on business, being contracted to sell $5 million

23

worth of shares in Price Brothers, a large pulp and paper concern. Whilst he was staying in London, his private solicitor, C H Cahan (later a Canadian Cabinet minister) began to blackmail him over questionable dealings in the cement mergers. Aitken paid up to keep him quiet but decided to remain in England. He kept up his Canadian business interests until his death, and they provided the bulk of his income, but a major storm over Canada Cement in which Aitken was blamed for the doubling of the price of cement as well as for making excessive profits, effectively prevented him from playing a part in Canadian public life.

On settling in England he continued to buy and sell companies. His first venture was the purchase that summer of the major share-holding in Rolls Royce which had come onto the market after the death of Charles Rolls (qv). Aitken put a business associate, Edward Goulding, MP for Worcester (later Lord Wargrave), on the board as his representative. Goulding remained on the board when Aitken sold out in 1913 at a considerable profit. Another early venture was the purchase in 1911 of the Colonial Bank, which had a large business in the West Indies. He joined the board in 1914, becoming chairman a year later. Concentrating on extending the bank's operation in West Africa he had soon doubled its assets from £3.46 million to £6.75 million. After the war he sold out to Barclays.

Soon after Aitken settled in England, he became involved in British politics, prompted by Edward Goulding and Andrew Bonar Law, another business acquaintance and then a leading Unionist MP. At Law's suggestion he was offered the Unionist candidacy for Ashton-under-Lyne, and he successfully contested the seat in the general election of December 1910. At that time political parties subsidised various newspapers, usually in the guise of an investment in shares by some individual of substance, who frequently added his own investment. Early in January 1911 Aitken had already been approached by Canadian-born Ralph Blumenfeld, the editor of the *Daily Express*, and he gave him a loan of £25,000. In 1912 Aitken became one of three nominal holders of £10,000 subscribed by the Unionist party for ordinary shares in the *Express*, and on his own account lent a further £40,000 as a first mortgage, with the condition that the *Daily Express* should publish paragraphs on his activities for propaganda use in his constituency.

In addition to the *Express* Aitken lent his support to the *Globe*, a moribund evening paper which he bought for £40,000, £25,000 of which was provided by Unionist sources. He showed no interest in running the paper, which continued to lose money and in 1914 Aitken paid Dudley Docker (qv) £5,000 to take it off his hands.

In November 1916 Aitken bought the controlling shareholding in the *Daily Express* for £17,500 to prevent the closure of the paper and the consequent loss of the sums he had lent as a mortgage. Before taking this step he sought the advice of Lord Rothermere (qv), who urged him to buy the paper whilst refusing to join the deal himself as it would lead him into direct rivalry with his brother, Lord Northcliffe (qv).

At first Aitken paid little attention to his new acquisition. Politics absorbed his chief energies. At the time he was involved in the political manoeuvring which led to the resignation of Asquith and the appointment of Lloyd George as prime minister in 1916. He was rewarded by a peerage in 1916, and in 1918 by appointments as Chancellor of the Duchy of Lancaster, and Minister of Information.

After the war Aitken, now Lord Beaverbrook, concentrated his energies on the *Daily Express*. He took active and vigorous control and added to his shareholding until he owned, directly or indirectly, 100 per cent of the shares. In November 1918 he launched the *Sunday Express*, designed to fill the gap between the serious and the sensational Sunday papers, and to prevent his printing presses lying idle one day a week. Far more expensive than he had bargained for, *The Sunday Express* cost him £500,000 in the first two years, and needed nearly £2 million before it was finally established as a sound business concern. But at length he succeeded in his aim of providing a popular, unsophisticated, respectable Sunday paper. Beaverbrook himself was its chief columnist and showed some style and flair as a popular journalist.

In 1923 Beaverbrook bought the newspapers of the dying Sir Edward Hulton (qv) for £6 million, selling them again to Rothermere within a week for the same price, but keeping one Hulton paper for himself. This was the *Evening Standard*, whose office in St Bride's Street, next to the offices of the *Daily Express*, had long been coveted by Beaverbrook. The *Standard* had a limited 'quality' readership, half that of its rival the *Evening News*, and Beaverbrook, while aiming to increase its circulation, did not change the character of the paper to suit a more popular audience.

Beaverbrook showed no interest in acquiring provincial newspapers in competition with Rothermere or the Berry brothers (qqv) and Iliffe (qv). But he did establish local *Express* offices and presses in Manchester, Birmingham and Glasgow to aid growth in circulation. In 1928 he went a step further by giving the Glasgow office complete independence, calling the paper the *Scottish Daily Express*, and added the *Evening Citizen* which he had purchased from George Outram. Bids to acquire more national newspapers, the *Sunday Times* and the *Daily Chronicle*, were unsuccessful.

The *Daily Express* had begun to show a good profit, and the *Sunday Express* to cease to make a loss, by 1922. During the 1920s and 1930s, the circulation and profits of Beaverbrook's papers grew rapidly. His Canadian investments provided his income, while he put most of his newspaper profits back into the papers. Paradoxically, Beaverbrook's newspaper profits included the income from a substantial holding in the Daily Mail Trust, a holding company set up after Northcliffe's death in 1922. The Trust bought 49 per cent of Beaverbrook's holdings in London Express Newspapers for £200,000 and 80,000 Daily Mail Trust shares. When Beaverbrook acquired the *Evening Standard*, the Daily Mail Trust took 49 per cent, paying Beaverbrook with a further 40,000 shares in the Trust. These arrangements not only diversified Beaverbrook's financial interests in the UK but also allowed him to call on Rothermere's considerable experience in newspaper finance. The financial interlocking between the two most popular daily papers did not prevent their editors from engaging in a whole-hearted battle for circulation with each other and with other rival papers, particularly the *Daily Herald*. Free gifts, insurance schemes and competitions probably had little permanent effect on the circulation of the papers concerned, and though Beaverbrook occasionally complained about the expense of this war, he enjoyed the fight too much to leave the field to his rivals.

Beaverbrook's and Rothermere's companies were also for a while joint owners of a newsprint mill on the Mersey with a third company, Bowaters. The mainstay of the new Bowater's Mersey Paper Mills Ltd was to be a twenty-year contract with London Express Newspapers Ltd, starting from 1931. (Alarm when other of Beaverbrook's newspaper rivals, the Berry brothers took over Lloyds, the biggest newsprint manufacturers in Britain in 1927, had prompted Beaverbrook to cancel the *Daily Express*'s long standing contract with that mill, and make alternative arrangements for the supply of newsprint to his papers.) Beaverbrook's papers took half of the £400,000 ordinary share capital, Rothermere £100,000 and Bowaters £100,000. Relations between the directors he appointed to the BMPM board and Eric Bowater (qv) were suspicious and difficult, and Bowater seized the opportunity of buying Rothermere's shares for his company in 1932. Beaverbrook was outraged at what he regarded as Rothermere's desertion, and offered to buy Rothermere's holdings in the mill and in Bowaters himself, but was outmanoeuvred by Eric Bowater and forced to sell the *Express* holding in the mill.

The acrimony generated by the episode, and the intensification of the circulation war in the early 1930s made the financial links between the Daily Mail Trust and Express Newspapers seem increasingly anomalous. In 1932-33 Beaverbrook bought out the 80,000 shares which the Trust held in the Express for just over £550,000 and then sold his Trust shares for a considerably larger sum. In May 1933 the remaining link with the Trust was broken when Beaverbrook bought its shares in the *Evening Standard* for £275,000.

Circulation of the *Daily Express* grew from under 250,000 in 1922 to over 2 million in 1933 and 4 million in 1950, and for many years the paper proudly claimed the 'World's Largest Daily Net Sale', being ahead of both the *Daily Mirror* and the *Daily Herald*. The circulation of the *Sunday Express* rose to over 2.5 million in 1948, 3.25 million in 1954 and 4.4 million in September 1963.

Much of the credit for this success was due to Beaverbrook himself. The telephone lines hummed day and night whether he was in London, or Cherkley his country home, or in one of his other houses in Jamaica, the Bahamas or southern France. His editors had to go to see him, wherever he was, promptly and at short notice. His telephone and 'soundscriber' were always by his side. As soon as he had an idea or a message for someone he dictated it into his 'soundscriber'. He scrutinised his own and all the national papers every day. He often wrote leading articles, and some of the other columns as well, without putting his name to them. He created the feeling that his papers were something special to work for and although his staff were not highly paid, he encouraged the myth that they were by suddenly increasing, sometimes doubling, the salaries of his editors and top journalists. He had the ability to spot and encourage young talent.

Although Beaverbrook learned a lot about journalism from his first editor, Blumenfeld, he never mastered the technical aspects of running a newspaper. Probably his most important discovery was the young Canadian E J Robertson, who managed his newspapers for thirty years. Robertson was tough, bold and unerringly accurate in his financial intuitions. Beaverbrook knew he could rely on him entirely. Perhaps his second most important find was Arthur Christiansen, who was editor of the *Daily Express* for twenty-four years. Appointed at the age of twenty-nine in 1933 he headed a bright young team of journalists and writers which became known as Beaverbrook's 'eager eaglets'. Many talented cartoonists, journalists and writers were attracted to Beaverbrook's newspapers — including Osbert Lancaster, Cummings, Low and Vicky, Tom Driberg, Arnold Bennett, Harold Nicolson, Bruce Lockhart, J M Keynes (qv), Peter Howard, Michael Foot who edited the *Standard* during the Second World War, Frank Owen and Percy Cudlipp.

In his evidence to the Royal Commission on the Press Beaverbrook told them, 'I ran the paper purely for the purpose of making propaganda and with no other object' {RC on the Press (1947-8) Cmd 7416, 4}. He waged many political campaigns through his papers and failed in most of them. His most determined effort was the promotion of his Empire Crusade for free trade with the Empire and protective tariffs against other imports, which began in 1929. For a while, he made a thorough nuisance of himself to the Conservative party in particular, nagging away on the subject through his newspapers, public speeches and personal contacts, and running Crusade candidates at by-elections. But he failed to win the support of any major politician, and the Crusade ground to a halt in 1933, though some Empire Crusade Clubs survived for several years after that. Another, more controversial campaign was his insistence that his newpapers should proclaim, right up to the middle of 1939, that there would be no war: gloom he felt, would be bad for the circulation figures and advertisement revenue. He also waged more personal battles and vendettas through his papers. Certain individuals must not be mentioned, others must be mentioned favourably, or unfavourably. His goading of Stanley Baldwin throughout the 1920s stung Baldwin in March 1931 into his famous remark that Beaverbrook (and Rothermere) sought 'power without responsibility — the prerogative of the harlot throughout the ages.' Beaverbrook's glee in the pursuit of his vendettas made some see him as a lovable naughty boy who had never grown up, while others thought of him as malicious, even evil. Without achieving lasting political power or influence, Beaverbrook did at least succeed in having fun. The reactions to his propaganda were negative rather than positive. But his papers reflected his readers' feelings and attitudes as well as Beaverbrook's preoccupations, and it was this which accounts for their success.

Although in his later years Beaverbrook's attention to the daily minutiae of his papers became somewhat less close he never lost interest in them, nor did he relinquish control before his death. In 1954, he transferred all his voting shares, worth about £1.5 million, in Beaverbrook Newspapers (as London Express Newspapers was now to be called) to the Beaverbrook Foundation and subsequently gave some of his non-voting shares to the Foundation as well, passing the rest to his family. The income of the Foundation was devoted to various charitable purposes in the UK and in New Brunswick, including assistance to the Presbyterian Church, building hospitals, and purchasing manuscripts and works of art for galleries and libraries. Beaverbrook was to be chairman of the Foundation for life and was to be succeeded by his son Max. Though technically the Foundation, and not Beaverbrook personally, controlled the newspapers, in fact Beaverbrook ran the papers just as he had before. In 1960 he set up a Canadian Beaverbrook Foundation, endowing it with $1.3 million of his American investments. The rest of the Canadian fortune, $4.5 million American investments and $10 million of investments in Canada, was bequeathed to the Foundation on his death. These Foundations took over the charitable payments Beaverbrook was already making; and he sometimes supplemented their income from his own as well. He could be very generous to friends, and employees, in need — though this great generosity contrasted with a curious parsimony in some minor matters.

Politically, Beaverbrook was an eccentric radical who was increasingly ignored by the Conservative Party. Such political influence as he had derived from his personal friendships, rather than his political ideas or his propaganda campaigns. In 1916 he had played a part in the appointment of Lloyd George as prime minister, and in 1922, by persuading Bonar Law to put himself forward as an alternative candidate for the premiership, he had a hand in Lloyd George's downfall. His friendship with Churchill brought him into the Government during the Second World War as Minister of Aircraft Production in 1940-41, Minister of Supply from 1941 to 1942, and Lord Privy Seal from 1943 to 1945: his chief task in these appointments was to listen to, encourage and amuse Churchill. He loved being at the centre of things, whether socially or politically.

He married in January 1906 Gladys, daughter of General Charles Drury of Halifax, and had two sons and a daughter. His first wife died in 1927 and in 1963 he married Marcia Anastasia, 'Cristofer', the widow of his old friend and fellow Canadian speculator Sir James Dunn (qv). He died at Cherkley on 9 June 1964, just after he had celebrated in great style his eighty-fifth birthday. His estate in England was proved at £379,530.

Beaverbrook's elder son, Sir Maxwell Aitken, took control of the papers, until illness forced him to sell out to the Trafalgar House Group in 1977.

KATHERINE V BLIGH *and* CHRISTINE SHAW

Writings:

Canada in Flanders (2 vols, Hodder & Stoughton, 1915 and 1917).

Success (Stanley Paul & Co, 1921 and numerous later editions).

Politicians and the Press (Hutchinson, 1926).

Politicians and the War (vol 1, Thornton Butterworth, 1928, vol 2, Lane Publications, 1932).

Empire Free Trade ... The New Policy For Prosperity (Daily Express, 1929).

My Case for Empire Free Trade (The Empire Crusade, 1930).

High Wages: a Manifesto to Trade Unionists (Daily Express, ca.1930).

The Resources of the British Empire (Lane Publications, 1934).

(with the Very Rev W R Inge, G D Cole and others) *The Causes of War* (New York: The Telegraph Press, 1935).

'We Hired the Money - They Hired the Soldiers', reprinted from the *Daily Express* (1939).

PP, RC on the Press (1947-8) Cmd 7416.

My Televised and Broadcast Speeches on the History of **The Times** (Daily Express Office, 1952).

Men and Power (Hutchinson, 1956).

Friends - Sixty Years of Intimate Personal Relations with Richard Bedford Bennett (Heinemann, 1959).

Courage - The Story of Sir James Dunn (Collins, 1961).

The Divine Propagandist (Heinemann, 1962).

The Decline and Fall of Lloyd George (Collins, 1963).

My Early Life (Canada: Atlantic Advocate, 1964).

The Abdication of King Edward VIII, ed A J P Taylor (Hamish Hamilton, 1966).

Sources:

Unpublished

House of Lords RO, Beaverbrook Papers.

PrC.

Published

Viscount Camrose, *British Newspapers and their Controllers* (Cassells, 1949).

Arthur Christiansen, *Headlines All My Life* (Heinemann, 1961).

DNB.

Peter Howard, *Beaverbrook. A Study of Max the Unknown* (Hutchinson, 1964).

C J Humbro, *Newspaper Lords in British Politics* (Macdonald, 1958).

R T Naylor, *The History of Canadian Business 1867-1914* (2 vols, Toronto: James Lorimer, 1975)

William J Reader, *Bowater. A History* (Cambridge University Press, 1981).

A J P Taylor, *Beaverbrook* (Hamish Hamilton, 1972).

Times 10 June 1964.

Francis Williams, *Dangerous Estate* (Longmans, Green & Co, 1957).

Alan Wood, *The True History of Lord Beaverbrook* (Heinemann, 1965).

WWMP.

WWW.

ALDENHAM, 1st Lord Aldenham
see GIBBS, Henry Hucks

Mr George Ale

Sir George Alexander, 1909.
Watercolour by Sir Bernard
Partridge (courtesy of the National
Portrait Gallery, London).

ALEXANDER, Sir George

(1858-1918)

Actor-manager

George Alexander Gibb Samson (known by his stage-name George Alexander) was born at Reading, on 19 June 1858, the only son of William Murray Samson, and his wife Mary Ann née Longman. His father had an extensive agency in the dry goods trade in the West of England. George received most of his education at Stirling High School, which he left at fifteen to start in business with Leaf & Co, drapers' warehouseman, of Old Change. While so engaged in commerce he became very active in amateur dramatics in London and this experience aroused his desire to act professionally. Accordingly he left Leafs and joined a repertory company in Nottingham to embark on a professional career in 1879. He toured in various companies before making his London début at the Court in 1881. It was then his good fortune to join Irving's Lyceum company where he stayed for the rest of the decade, save for a period with John Hare at the St James Theatre in 1883. Then, after a short trial management at the Avenue in 1889, he took the lease of the St James Theatre in November 1890, beginning with typical flair by installing electric lighting and re-upholstering the seats. So began Alexander's actor-managership of the St James which lasted until his death in 1918, one of the most outstanding examples of successful business entrepreneurship in the theatre of the time.

Alexander's tenure of the St James Theatre from 1890 to 1918 was marked by three characteristics, artistic, social and financial. Artistically he provided a stage for much of the important new British drama of the time. This included notably the work of Wilde (*Lady Windermere's Fan, The Importance of Being Earnest, An Ideal Husband*), Pinero (*The Second Mrs Tanqueray*), Anthony Hope (*The Prisoner of Zenda*) and much other work by R C Carton, Sutro and others.

Alexander's forte was the production and playing of polished Society drama and indeed he created the roles of 'John Worthing' and 'Aubrey Tanqueray'. He made the St James one of the most fashionable social centres of London life. The emphasis on the highest standards of order, taste and elegance drew the cultivated and wealthy to his audiences.

Thirdly, this was good business. Of the plays produced between 1891 and 1914, 27 ended in loss and 26 in profit. But the 26 successful plays made six times as much again as the losses on the 27. Only in one year, 1894-95, did Alexander have to work for less than nothing. The profits could be vast: his most lucrative was *His House in Order* which earned £35,000 clear profit; *Earnest* and *Tanqueray* both earned between £21,000 and £22,000. His net earnings from his 26 profitable plays were £269,400. Alexander was the direct lessee of the St James and he employed his own business manager. He was very careful over his control of his business affairs, having been cheated by an absconding manager during his preparatory tenure of the Avenue. His prudence and entrepreneurial flair were rewarded and on his death he left the third largest fortune among contemporary actor-managers.

Alexander's high business abilities carried over into many spheres beside his own theatre. He was especially keen on the institutions for the financial safeguard of the actor's life, being a director of the Royal General Theatrical Fund (the actors' pension scheme), a trustee of the Actors' Benevolent Fund and president of the King George V Pension Fund. He was also a vice-president of the Actors' Association and of the Theatrical Managers' Association. Beyond the theatre he had public interests. He was a JP and in 1907 he was elected to the London County Council on which he served for six years until 1913, representing South St Pancras. A E W Mason notes that he 'brought to his new duties the studious care which he had given to his theatre' {Mason (1935) 185}, as a conscientious researcher on social questions and a polished speaker. He was invited to stand as a Conservative MP, but his own deteriorating health and a likely defeat (by John Burns at Battersea) forced him to decline. For his theatrical and public services he was knighted in 1911. The honorary degree of LLD was also conferred upon him by the University of Bristol in 1912.

Alexander was a man of great charm and, being graced with a most handsome presence both in young and middle age, was one of the first of the matinée idols. More important, he was one of the new breed of gentlemanly, socially acceptable actors of late Victorian and Edwardian times, and had a wide circle of titled friends. Sartorially punctilious, he was a pioneer of fashion, notably in the modern turnover soft collar. Sir George lived in some style in Pont Street and at Little Court, a country house at Chorley Wood. Untreatable diabetes led to his premature death from consumption on 16 March 1918. He was survived by his wife Florence, daughter of Edward Theleur, whom he married in August 1882; her taste had contributed much to the dignity and style for which Alexander had made the St James famous. He left £97,919 gross.

MICHAEL SANDERSON

Writings:

Practical Hints on Adopting the Stage as a Profession. An address delivered at the Athenaeum hall (Leeds, nd).

Sources:

Unpublished

British Theatre Museum, papers of Sir George Alexander.

BCe.

MCe.

PrC.

Published

DNB.

Raymond Mander and Joe Mitchenson, *Lost Theatres of London* (New English Library, 1976).

Alfred E W Mason, *Sir George Alexander and the St James Theatre* (Macmillan & Co, 1935).

Owen Nares, *Myself and Some Others* (Duckworth, 1925).

PP, HC, 1909 (303) VIII Report of the Joint Select Committee on Stage Plays (Censorship).

Times 16 Mar 1918.

WWW.

John D Allcroft, ca 1878–80. Portrait by Sir Francis Grant PRA (courtesy of Sir Philip and Lady Magnus-Allcroft).

ALLCROFT, John Derby

(1822-1893)

Glove manufacturer and merchant

John Derby Allcroft was born in Worcester on 19 July 1822, the only son of Jeremiah Macklin Allcroft and Hannah, daughter of Thomas Derby of Birmingham. His father was in partnership with the bachelor brothers John and William Dent, leading glove and leather manufacturers and merchants, who traded from warehouses in Worcester and London as J & W Dent & Co.

From teenage years Allcroft was intimately associated with the company, receiving practical training under his father. He displayed ability, diligence and integrity and when the partners retired they sold the business on 1 January 1846 to him and three other employees. Allcroft was then only twenty-three. The company's name was later changed to Dent, Allcroft & Co but continued to sell under the Dent label.

At this time Worcester was the centre of the glove industry, organised on a domestic system and using techniques unchanged for centuries. The number of master glovers fell from 120 to 40 between 1826 and 1848 because their trade in ladies' gloves, in home and overseas markets, had been lost to cheaper French Kids. Domestic population growth and a rising standard of living, together with the expansion of world trade increased demand for gloves, which Allcroft, once in charge of the soundly-based Dent business, was not slow to meet.

One of his first steps was to replace the London premises in Wood Street with a commanding headquarters (which survived with its early organisation intact until 1940). He next turned to the manufacturing side of the business which had three glove and leather production sites in different parts of Worcester. These Allcroft centralized in a specially adapted factory at Palace Yard (near the Cathedral) in 1853. At this date the indoor employees numbered less than 200; twenty-five years later there were 1,000. Allcroft knew that major cost savings could be achieved by the skilful handling of leather and that technical perfection was of the highest importance in an era when fit and elegance counted for so much in the fashion of gloves. In a labour-intensive industry no compromise could be allowed, meticulous work was demanded. It was his insistence on quality workmanship that was a major factor in the company's continued success. To this end Allcroft was a strong disciplinarian. His foremen and examiners asserted their power with conspicuous strictness, imbuing the employees with the desire for high achievement.

> As everyone knows, this house gained their important reputation by reason of their general standard of excellence and thoroughly reliable quality and whatever they undertake is done with care and thoroughly. {*Drapers Record* 27 Sept 1919}

Allcroft's workpeople also knew him as a generous and kindly employer who rewarded talent. As a result the morale of the company was high, bringing with it increased energy.

Allcroft, like his predecessors, controlled his own selling. After the advent of free trade in 1826 admitted cheaper continental gloves to Britain, the company accepted the competitive challenge and moved more strongly into European and American markets. Allcroft organised the existing functions of manufacturer and merchant on an international scale and the company's buyers had access to nearly every European manufacturer. In the twenty-five years to 1884 turnover advanced fourfold to 1.02 million dozen pairs. At this date the company's factories, leather yards, buying agencies and selling branches outside the UK were located in New York, Paris, Grenoble, Fontaine, Brussels, Ceroux Mousty, Halberstadt, Leipzig, Prague, and Naples. Dents had became the pre-eminent company in the world and its name a household word.

By 1873 Allcroft, now aged fifty-one and the sole partner, wished to retire in order to devote more time to his other interests. He suggested a partnership to a friend of his own age, Captain James Cundy, invalided some years earlier from the Indian Army, and with whom Allcroft had worked closely on religious and philanthropic activities. At this date Allcroft's capital holding was £500,000 and the goodwill valued at £120,000.

The new partnership between Allcroft and Cundy and Timothy Bevington required a degree of profit-sharing, especially with the firm's buyers who in 1873 held 6 per cent of the capital. By 1886 this amounted to 14 per cent (£97,650) of the firm's capital of £694,250. Allcroft himself maintained a connection with the firm and the partners benefited from his counsel for two decades.

John Derby Allcroft was Lord of the Manors of Stokesay and Onibury in Shropshire, an 8,500 acre estate which he purchased in 1869. He restored Stokesay Castle, a thirteenth-century fortified manor house and in 1889-90 he built a mansion with 100 rooms on the estate. Allcroft was DL for London, JP for Shropshire and its High Sheriff in 1893. He was Conservative MP for Worcester 1878-80.

Allcroft was a staunch Evangelical Anglican, being president of the Church Pastoral Aid Society and a generous donor to the Corporation of the Sons of Clergy, the British and Foreign Bible Society and the YMCA (giving £5,000 to secure Exeter Hall as the YMCA's headquarters in 1881). He endowed five churches, three in London and two on his estate. He gave generously to the building of numerous other churches. He was elected governor of Christ's Hospital in 1849 and was its treasurer between 1873 and 1891.

Among the charities he liberally supported were a number associated with glove and leather trade institutions and several hospitals like the Royal Hospital for Incurables, and St Mary's Hospital. A strong freemason, Allcroft was a Grand Treasurer in the Grand Lodge with the distinction of having a lodge named after him. Allcroft was also a fellow of the Royal Geographical Society and of the Royal Astronomical Society.

Allcroft was twice married: firstly in 1854 to Mary Annette, daughter of Rev Thomas Martin. After her death in 1857 he married in 1864 Mary Anne Jewell, eldest daughter of John Blundell of Timsbury Manor, Hampshire. They had four sons and two daughters, but Allcroft considered none of his sons potential businessmen so did not encourage them to succeed him. One did join the firm, but without distinguishing himself.

John Derby Allcroft died on 29 July 1893 at his home in Lancaster Gate, London, leaving effects of £492,063 gross.

ROBERT H G RING

Sources:

Unpublished

Worcester RO, St Peter's parish register.

E D Macphee, 'Notes on Dent Allcroft & Co Ltd' and other MSS in possession of author.

MCe.

PrC.

Information from the Clerk, Christ's Hospital.

Interview with Sir Philip Magnus-Allcroft.

Published

The Christian 3 Aug, 7 Sept 1893.

The City Press 2, 5 Aug 1893.

The Drapers Record 27 Sept 1919.

The Shrewsbury Chronicle 11 Aug 1893.

John Summerson, *Victorian Architecture* (New York: Columbia University Press, 1970).

Times 1 Aug 1893.

The Warehouseman & Draper 5 Aug 1893.

The Worcester Advertiser 30 Mar 1878.

The Worcester Chronicle 10 July 1867.

WWMP.

ALLEN, Samuel

(1848-1911)

Metal manufacturer

Samuel Allen was born in Wharf Street, Birmingham on 19 August 1848, the son of James Allen, a merchant's clerk, and his wife Sarah Ann née Wilson. His father later became a partner in Barker & Allen, the successor to the firm of Webb & Barker, which had developed the production of nickel and 'German silver' (an alloy of nickel, copper and zinc) for the electro-plating industry of Birmingham and elsewhere. German silver could be cast or wrought before plating, thus giving it an advantage over copper. It was also capable of being made into fancy patterned wire for decorative purposes.

After attending the city's King Edward VI School, Samuel Allen began his commercial career with J H Hopkins & Sons in Granville Street, Birmingham, and then joined his father in Barker & Allen. The two bought the firm in 1883 and in 1897 transferred to a new site at Springhill on which rolling mills and casting shops were erected. After his father's death, Allen continued as sole proprietor, but in 1898 the firm became a private limited company, with Allen as managing director and his two sons as members of the board. The firm traded largely in Europe, but had a substantial share of the Indian market and outlets in the USA and Canada.

Allen's main strengths seem to have been his ability to organise on a substantial scale and make judicious commercial moves at the opportune moment. His father, along with Stephen Barker, had pioneered some of the technical processes involved in nickel production from the 1840s onwards. The son saw to it that machinery was kept up-to-date, full electrification for light and power was installed in 1908 and premises were expanded in Birmingham and Sheffield. Close attention was paid to foreign markets and Allen travelled extensively on the Continent. Nevertheless, the impression is that Allen closely followed the market rather than led, and this may be the secret of his success.

He was not greatly involved in affairs outside the firm, but was a member of the Marston Green Relief Committee and the Infirmary Management Committee. He was active in the Chamber of Commerce, following its reconstruction around 1900, being elected to its Council and serving on its General Purposes Committee. He was treasurer from 1907 until his death in 1911. In June of that year he was elected to the Birmingham Board of Guardians for Rotton Park Ward.

Early in November 1911 he suffered a stroke at a meeting of the board, and died on 4 November, predeceased by two days by his wife. He was survived by two sons, John H Allen and Thomas Allen, both of whom became directors of the company. He left £33,489 gross.

J ROY HAY

Sources:

Unpublished

BCe.

PrC.

Published

Steven Barker, 'Nickel German Silver Manufacture' in Samuel Timmins (ed), *The Resources, Products and Industrial History of Birmingham and the Midland Hardware District* (Robert Hardwick, 1866).

Birmingham Mail 8 Nov 1948.

Birmingham Weekly Post 9 Nov 1911.

Industrial World Aug 1935.

'Midland Captains of Industry' 47, 'Samuel Allen' *Birmingham Gazette and Express* 22 Jan 1908.

George H Wright, *Chronicles of the Birmingham Chamber of Commerce* (Birmingham: Birmingham Chamber of Commerce, 1913).

ALLEN, William Edward

(1860-1919)

Poster printer and theatre owner

William Edward Allen was born in Belfast on 2 March 1860, the third son of a printer, David Allen, and his wife Agnes, née Jamieson. Allen's parents were Presbyterian, and they gave their five children a strict Sabbatarian upbringing, although this discipline relaxed somewhat as the family became more affluent. William was educated at the Belfast Academical Institute, the first of his sons that David could afford to send there. On leaving school in 1876, William joined his eldest brother David's firm, Cullen, Allen & Co, a produce-exporting and shipping business, as a clerk at a salary of £6 a year. His brother, who had been away at the time, did not in fact approve of this appointment.

About 1882, William moved to his father's business at a salary of £120 a year. The firm was reorganised in 1884, becoming David Allen & Sons. The 'Sons' were William, allotted £1,000 of the £18,000 nominal capital, and his elder brother Robert, allotted £2,000. In addition the brothers were each debited with £5,000, which they were to pay out of their earnings, with 5 per cent interest due on the outstanding balance. William considered the value put on the firm's assets quite unrealistic: he thought £10,000 a more accurate evaluation of a plant he later recalled as 'farcical' and of the 'most modest' business his father was doing. {Allen (1957) 104}

But William's flair and energy, supported by Robert's patience and experience, soon made an impact. From the mid-1880s the Belfast plant was increasingly devoted to lithographic printing for commercial and theatrical customers. William urged upon his father the desirability of the firm having an office in London to exploit the market there, particularly the theatrical touring companies. In 1888 William and Robert opened an office just off Leicester Square, in the heart of theatrical London. Robert disliked the city and soon left. David ordered William to return to Belfast too, but William, who thoroughly enjoyed the pace and excitement of working for capricious and disorganised theatrical customers, disobeyed his father. He persuaded Fred Mouillot, a leading manager of touring companies, to sign a long-term contract which did much to establish the firm's reputation as printers of theatrical posters. When David came to London in 1890, he was convinced that William was making a success of this business, and agreed to the installation of letterpress machinery in Leicester Street.

While David's health precluded his active involvement in the business for some years prior to his death in 1903, the firm, under William's energetic management, and in response to the expansion of theatrical touring companies, continued to grow rapidly. A Manchester office was opened in 1893 to keep up with provincial orders, and agencies in New York and Australia looked after touring companies overseas. In 1895 a new lithographic works was built on a 12 acre site at Harrow. Paying great attention to the artistic and technical quality of their work, and operating one of the largest lithographic plants in the country, David Allens was now the leading printer of theatrical posters, and had a worldwide reputation in this field. It became a public company in 1897; the share capital of £150,000 was divided between the partners, who were joined in 1895 by William's younger brother, Sam. The £85,000 of 4.5 per cent debenture stock was over-subscribed by four times (mostly at Belfast), within two hours of its issue. William and Robert became joint managing directors of the company. No deliberate effort was made to diversify into other sorts of printing business in the years before the war, when many other larger London printing firms who had formerly specialised in, say, lithography or letterpress, began to expand their interests into other areas of the trade, so that they could compete for all kinds of printing contracts. But David Allens did diversify into fields associated with their theatrical printing: the management of theatres and billposting.

William became involved in the management of theatres in the 1890s, initially through Fred Mouillot. No records survive of the early years of the David Allen Theatres Co, but it evidently flourished. By 1915 the company owned the freeholds of five theatres (four in the provinces, one at Deptford) together worth £89,000, and also had substantial holdings in several provincial theatre companies. Much of the responsibility for the management of these ventures was borne by William's wife, Sarah Collett, whom he had married in 1898. She was the daughter of a spendthrift barrister who had died when she was only three. Her mother, and later Sarah herself, had earned their living on the stage, and Sarah had achieved some success under the stage name Cissy Grahame (she was known within the family as Cissy).

William was also a director of David Allen & Sons Billposting Co, registered in 1905 with a capital of £30,000. This business had been steadily built up since 1887, first in Ireland, then in Liverpool and southwest Scotland; by 1908 the company claimed to be the largest billposting firm in the world. William had little to do with its routine management, which was largely undertaken by his brother-in-law, J O Rogers, until his death in 1909. This company had initially at least been thought of as a provision for Roger's wife Sarah, William's sister. However, the billposting business came into its own after William's death, when a combination of the declining popularity and prosperity of the theatre, and government action, dealt a severe blow to the interests he had built up.

This government action was the wartime requisitioning and compulsory purchase of the firm's Harrow printing works in 1918. No satisfactory replacement was ever found, and the printing business suffered badly after the war. But the £315,000 compensation did at least help to solve some festering family quarrels, allowing the liquidation of a large debt the younger brother Sam had owed to Robert before his death in 1912, and which William had felt obliged to ensure that Sam repaid to Robert's widow and child. In 1916 William, chairman of David Allens since 1913, had wanted to buy the extravagant and inattentive Sam out of the firm, and bring in Cissy, who had done much valuable work for the business, as a director, but the rest of the family would not hear of it. Now William acquired the holding of Robert's estate in David Allen & Sons, which gave him 57 per cent of the ordinary share capital. Most of the shares in the billposting company were held by David Allen & Sons, while the rest were divided amongst the family, including William. When William died on 12 April 1919 (leaving an estate proved at £88,267 gross), the family was no longer in a position to oppose Cissy's taking a prominent position in the direction of the firm as joint managing director with Sam; William's and Cissy's three sons were trained under her.

William's considerable energies seem to have been largely taken up by business, but then this did entail a great deal of very pleasurable social life in the cause of maintaining his vital theatrical contacts. Before his marriage he had enjoyed yachting, but had given it up to please Cissy. Afterwards, that part of his taste for romanticism and adventure that was not sufficiently satisfied by his involvement with the theatre, found an outlet in the month he spent every spring in Monte Carlo gambling, in a modest way, at the Casino.

CHRISTINE SHAW

Sources:

Unpublished

PrC.

B W E Alford, 'The London Letterpress Printing Industry, 1850-1941' (London PhD, 1962).

Published

William E D Allen, *David Allens, the History of a Family Firm 1857-1957* (John Murray, 1957).

William Beable, *Romance of Great Businesses* (2 vols, Heath Cranton, 1926).

ALLHUSEN, Christian Augustus Henry

(1806-1890)

Chemical manufacturer

Christian Augustus Henry Allhusen was born in Kiel on 2 December 1806, the son of Carl Christian Allhusen, a merchant, and Anna

ALLHUSEN Christian Augustus Henry

Christian A H Allhusen (courtesy of the Newcastle & Gateshead Water Co).

Margaretha, née Schroder. Of their five sons and two daughters, Christian was the fourth son. Following the French occupation of Schleswig-Holstein and the seizure of the family residence, the family broke up, two of the older brothers emigrating to England where they engaged in the grain trade. Christian Allhusen arrived in England at the age of nineteen, having already worked in the grain trade at Rostock. In Newcastle upon Tyne he joined his two brothers and was taken into partnership by them, an arrangement which lasted until his brothers left Tyneside, one emigrating to North America and the other moving to London.

Allhusen was then joined by Henry Bolckow (qv), with whom he had worked in Rostock, and the two men formed a partnership, first as grain merchants but later as ship and insurance brokers, operating under the name Christian Allhusen & Co. The partnership between the two men was dissolved in 1840 when Bolckow joined with John Vaughan (qv) and set up Teesside's first ironworks and Allhusen, although not himself a chemist, entered the growing Tyneside chemical industry by purchasing the soap works, then in a moribund state, of Charles Attwood & Co, established in Gateshead in the 1820s.

Allhusen's venture was successful and after trading under a variety of names the firm was registered in 1871 as the Newcastle Chemical Works Co with a capital of £510,000. As a manufacturer of alkali using the Leblanc process the company began to decline in the latter part of the nineteenth century and Allhusen, although an astute businessman, was unable to distribute dividends to the holders of ordinary shares during the 1880s. The decline in trade, general throughout the chemical industry on Tyneside, led in 1883 to a reduction in the company's capital to £300,000. As a manufacturer, Allhusen was not an innovator but nevertheless was constantly seeking and adopting improvements in manufacturing methods, never risking failure by limiting expenditure on the construction of plant.

To house his workpeople, or perhaps as a speculation, Allhusen in 1868 purchased some 40 acres of land near his works in east Gateshead, while in the western part of the town he was one of the promoters, and later a director, of the Redheugh Bridge Co, established in 1866 to provide a road-crossing of the River Tyne. He was a member of the Gateshead Town Council from 1849 until 1853 and in that year put forward a plan for the improvement of the river quay there. The proposal did not succeed, largely due to a lack of co-operation by the North Eastern Railway, the involvement of which was vital, but it had the virtue of bringing about the demolition of some of the town's worst housing. As a representative of the town he was elected a member of the Tyne Improvement Commission in 1852, a position from which he resigned three years later.

Allhusen was not a scientist in his own right. His skill lay in adopting the latest innovations in manufacture and using his commercial abilities to promote his products. It is ironic that it was due to his initiative, at least in part, that the chemical industry came to decline on the Tyne only to flourish on the Tees. Following a lead given by Bolckow in 1862, Allhusen, with others, instigated the drilling for salt, one of the basic raw materials in the manufacture of alkali, on Teesside, at first with the intention of conveying it to the Tyne works for processing. However, principally because the Solvay process superseded the earlier Leblanc process of alkali manufacture, the chemical industry shifted entirely to Teesside leaving its Tyneside parent to decline rapidly.

Allhusen's interests outside the chemical industry were many. He was a director of the Marine Insurance Co, the Northfleet Coal & Ballast Co, the Brazil Great Southern Railway, the British Land & Mortgage Co of America, the International Bank of London, the New Oriental Bank Corporation, the Metropole Hotel Co and the Newcastle & Gateshead Water Co. In this last concern Allhusen had a financial interest virtually from its formation in 1845 and in 1857 he became a director; active in the company's management, he remained on the board of directors for forty-two years in spite of having moved from Tyneside in 1872.

In addition to his directorships Allhusen was a large shareholder in the Northumberland & Durham District Bank. When it failed in 1857 it was he who proposed that a body of its shareholders should be responsible for the continued operation of the Derwent Ironworks Co, indebted to the bank to a total of £1 million and so liable to closure following the bank's collapse. By his efforts the ironworks continued in production, Allhusen becoming chairman of the committee managing its affairs. As the Consett Iron Co, the business was registered in 1864 with a capital of £400,000.

In religion, Allhusen was an Anglican and in politics, a Liberal. He was an advocate of free trade and supported Cobden's scheme for negotiating a treaty of commerce with France, representing the chemical manufacturers of the North-East at the Paris conferences. He was also instrumental in inviting Gladstone, Chancellor of the Exchequer, to Newcastle in 1862, a move initiated in recognition of the latter's efforts in securing the treaty between Britain and France.

Allhusen was undoubtedly a man of great power and influence in the area, politically active, as were other chemical manufacturers. While he created employment for many, and amassed a huge personal fortune for himself, he was not of a benevolent nature, a fact regretted by the contemporary press.

Allhusen married Anne, the daughter of John Shield of Broomhaugh, in 1835 and over the next decade produced a family of four sons. From 1842 the family lived in Elswick Hall, Newcastle, but later moved to Stoke Court, Buckinghamshire. The move caused some local controversy because it was hoped that Allhusen would bestow his property upon the town as a park. Such munificence was not part of Allhusen's character and the grounds were purchased by a group of businessmen who subsequently sold them, at a loss, to the Corporation.

Narrowly predeceased by his wife, Allhusen died on 13 January 1890 at Stoke Poges, leaving his chemical interests under the control of his son, Wilton, and a nephew, Alfred; another son continued to operate Allhusen's shipping concern in Newcastle. His estate amounted to £1,126,852 gross. His works did not long continue unchanged. Immediately after his death they, and all others in Tyneside, became part of the United Alkali Co; the rationalisation which ensued brought about the closure of all but the factories of Allhusen and Tennant.

R W RENNISON

ALLHUSEN Christian Augustus Henry

Writings:

Report of the Commissioners Appointed to Inquire into the Present State of the River Tyne (HMSO, 1855).

Sources:

Unpublished

Gateshead Central Library, Borough of Gateshead Minute Books (1849-53).

Newcastle & Gateshead Water Co, Newcastle upon Tyne, Minute Books (1845-90).

PrC; Will.

Information from Lt Col R C Allhusen (1981).

Published

John Fenwick Allen, 'Industrial Celebrities: Christian Allhusen' *Chemical Trade Journal* 5 Apr 1890.

William A Campbell, *The Old Tyneside Chemical Trade* (Newcastle upon Tyne: University of Newcastle upon Tyne, 1964).

William Fordyce, *A History of Coal, Coke, Coalfields and Iron Manufacture in Northern England* (Sampson Low Son & Co, 1860).

Newcastle Daily Chronicle 14 Jan 1890.

Northern Tribune 1 (1854).

ALLPORT, Sir James Joseph

(1811-1892)

Railway manager

James Joseph Allport was born in Birmingham on 27 February 1811, the third son of William Allport, a gun maker of 8 Whittall Street (and for a time prime warden of the Birmingham Proof House Co), and Phoebe, the daughter of Joseph Dickinson of Woodgreen, Staffordshire. Little is known about his early life, but a private education in Belgium was cut short on the death of his father in 1823, and he returned to Birmingham to help his mother manage the family business.

Allport's long career in railways began in 1839, when he joined the newly-opened Birmingham & Derby Junction Railway Co as chief clerk, based at Hampton Junction (Hampton-in-Arden). In the 'Mania' atmosphere of company promotion and merger he rose rapidly in the company: goods superintendent in 1840; traffic superintendent in 1843; and then, through George Hudson's influence, traffic superintendent, at a salary of £250 a year, of the Newcastle & Darlington Junction Railway Co in 1844. Under Hudson's influence the Newcastle & Darlington developed into a large company, taking Allport with it. In 1845 he was appointed manager and superintendent of the Great North of England Railway, a few months before its acquisition by the Newcastle & Darlington, later known as the York, Newcastle & Berwick Railway Co. By 1849 Allport was calling himself 'manager' of this important company, which enjoyed access to both the flourishing freight business of the North East and the lucrative passenger traffic of the east coast route from England to Scotland.

Allport thus acquired considerable experience of traffic management and a reputation for skill in handling inter-company negotiations. Above all, however, he had a flair for public relations. His later claim to have originated the idea of a Railway Clearing House for the exchange of traffic between companies has been disputed and dispelled, but he was prominent in its deliberations. He also became well known for his special expresses, including the train he organised in August 1845 to take the news of Hudson's election as MP for Sunderland to London in a record eight hours. Finally, he is thought to have been responsible for the first application of hydraulic power on the railways, in the goods crane at Newcastle.

Shortly after Hudson's empire collapsed in 1849 Allport became manager of the Manchester, Sheffield & Lincolnshire Railway. Earning £1,200 a year, Allport's stay in Manchester was relatively brief, though he placed both passenger and freight traffic on a secure footing. Possibly he felt constrained by the need to work closely with a directorial committee of consultation. At any rate, when in 1853 he was offered the post of general manager of the Midland, with a salary of £1,500 a year, he accepted with alacrity.

Undoubtedly, Allport's major contribution to railway management was made with the Midland, which he served for four decades as general manager (1853-57, 1860-80) and director (1857-60, 1880-92). When he joined the company in October 1853, it was a rag-bag of assorted lines, dominated by Mark Huish and the London & North Western, and still suffering financially from Hudson's mismanagement. Almost immediately, Allport revived the Midland's traffic position, and by 1857 he was able to leave Derby to join Palmer's, the Jarrow shipbuilders, as managing director.

Allport's railway career might well have ended with his move into shipbuiding, but he had retained a close contact with his former employers by joining the board of directors. In April 1860 he was persuaded to return as general manager (he resigned as a director) in order to protect the Midland's independent existence, which was threatened by both the London & North Western and the Great Northern. Not only did Allport succeed in maintaining the company's independence, but he was also responsible for its transformation into a coherent network with its own access to London. The company's St Pancras station and hotel (opened in 1868) were as much a monument to Allport and the Liberal business interests of the East Midlands as to their designer, Sir George Gilbert Scott (qv).

Allport served as general manager until 1880. Under his management the Midland grew steadily, with new routes to London, Manchester and Carlisle, and access to Bristol and Swansea in the West and to Norwich and Yarmouth in the East. Expansion was costly, but it did not dim the company's profitability. Ordinary dividends averaged 6 per cent from 1853 to 1880, more than double the return in the years 1849-52, before Allport's arrival. Profits were in part a result of the lucrative freight traffic in coal, bricks and Burton beer. However, passenger traffic was an important element also, and here Allport's skills as a marketing manager became renowned. The Midland was one of the last main lines to be built into London and it had to win traffic by improving services and cutting fares. Allport's initiative in the 1870s transformed the approach of the major railway companies to long-distance business. In 1872 the Midland began to carry third-class passengers on all its trains, and three years later first-class fares were reduced to the level of second-class, and the latter was abolished. Further evidence of aggressive marketing came with the introduction in 1874 of Pullman Cars. Allport thus proved himself to be a leading figure in encouraging the improvement in quality of service and lower fares which initiated the inter-railway competition of the late nineteenth century. He retired, at the age of sixty-nine, receiving a 'golden handshake' of £10,000 and a seat on the board, which he retained until his death. His success was publicly marked with a knighthood in 1884.

Allport also found time for membership of the boards of non-railway companies. He was chairman of Brown Marshalls, the General Hydraulic Power Co, and United Asbestos, and a director of several other companies, including the Lion Fire Insurance Co (with James Staats Forbes (qv)) and Samuel Fox & Co. He was also a Derbyshire JP and while not active in politics certainly shared the Liberal sympathies of several of the Midland's directors. Above all, however, he will be remembered as the outstanding railway manager of the middle decades of the nineteenth century. He was confident and enterprising, and he combined the skills of the negotiator, marketing manager, and administrator. He was the general manager par excellence and, indeed, one of the early advocates of such an official. 'I have always been of the opinion', he wrote to the directors of the York, Newcastle & Berwick on 26 December 1849, 'that unity of management consolidated in the hands of one paid officer acting under instructions from the Board will prove most advantageous to the interests of the Company and induce the most prompt and efficient working of its affairs' {PRO RAIL 772/4}.

He married in 1832 Ann (d 1886), daughter of John Gold of Birmingham; they had two sons and three daughters. Sir James Allport died on 25 April 1892 leaving £194,032 gross.

T R GOURVISH

Sources:

Unpublished

PRO, RAIL 36/2, 3, board minutes of Birmingham & Derby Junction Rly; RAIL 232/2-4, board minutes of Great North of England Rly; RAIL 772/4-9, board minutes of York Newcastle & Berwick Rly; RAIL 491/13-26, board minutes of Midland Rly; RAIL 772/3, board minutes of Newcastle & Darlington Junction Rly.

PrC.

Published

Geoffrey Channon, 'A Nineteenth-Century Investment Decision: the Midland's London Extension' *Economic History Review* 2nd ser, 25 (1972).

DNB.

George Dow, *Great Central* I (Locomotive Publishing Co, 1959).

Engineering 29 Apr 1892.

Railway News 30 Apr 1892.

Railway Official Gazette 14 May 1892.

W W Tomlinson, *The North Eastern Railway: Its Rise and Development* (Newcastle upon Tyne: Andrew Reid, 1915).

AMBLER, Geoffrey Hill

(1904-1978)

Worsted spinner and inventor

Geoffrey H Ambler. Drawing by Sherlock Evans (from Journal of the Bradford Textile Society *1950–51).*

Geoffrey Hill Ambler was born at Baildon near Bradford on 23 June 1904, the son of Fred Ambler, a worsted spinner of Dumb Mills, Bradford, and his wife Annie née Hill, and grandson of Sir James Hill, 1st Bt, (1849-1936), the founder of the family firm of Sir James Hill & Sons Ltd in 1891. He attended Shrewsbury School and Clare College, Cambridge, where he took a degree in engineering and economics, and also obtained a rowing blue. In 1925 he became president of the University Rowing Club and was in the winning boat against Oxford in 1924, 1925 and 1926. He entered the wool industry in 1926 as trainee manager in the family firm. In that year also, he took up flying with the Yorkshire Aviation Club; flying was to become his main interest for the next twenty years. In 1931 he was commissioned into the Royal Auxiliary Air Force; at the beginning of the war he was commanding 609 Fighter Squadron at Yeadon, now the Leeds/Bradford airport. In 1942 he was made Commandant of the Royal Observer Corps; by 1945 he was Senior Air Staff Officer at Fighter Command, and he retired with the rank of Air Vice Marshal. During his service he received the following honours and decorations: AFC, 1940; OBE, 1941; ADC to the King, 1943; CBE, 1944; CB, 1946.

After the war he rejoined the family firm and became chairman in 1949. His interest in the combined areas of engineering and textiles led him, after considerable fundamental work, in 1946 to the invention of the Ambler Superdraft Unit (ASD). This was a device which could be added to existing worsted spinning machinery which enabled much higher drafts to be used than previously, 100-150 as against 10-12. This made possible the elimination of the two previous operations with a consequent saving in machinery, labour, floor space, power and waste.

The ASD was introduced at about the same time as the Autoleveller of George Raper (qv) and together their innovations revolutionised the post-war worsted spinning industry. The theoretical work was continued by Miss Margaret Hannah at Leeds University in 1948 and the production of the units was undertaken through Rose Bros of Gainsborough. Ambler's only publication was in the *Journal of the Bradford Textile Society* (1950-51), the report of an occasion when he addressed that Society. In his talk he is reported to have said that it was his intention to 'give the home trade first go ... but that he had safeguarded his overseas patent rights'. Later in a press statement he said orders were being taken from overseas.

In 1960 he was awarded an honorary fellowship of the Textile Institute and in 1966 the honorary degree of Doctor of Law was conferred upon him by Leeds University.

His textile peers considered Geoffrey Ambler a capable technologist, a good inventor and a popular associate; he had a retiring nature and was perhaps a planner rather than an entrepreneur. Business activities were not his outstanding forte although for many years he was a member of the Worsted Spinners' Federation board, the Wool Textile Delegation, the Wool (and Allied) Textile Employers' Council and was also a local director of Martins Bank. He was appointed a DL for West Yorkshire in 1949.

In February 1974 the family business was sold for £150,000 to Hield Bros, Bradford; at the time it was indicated that the pre-tax profit up to 1973 was running at an annual rate of not less than £30,000. The firm had a workforce of approximately 200.

Geoffrey Ambler married Phoebe née Gaunt in 1940, and they had three daughters. Ambler died on 26 August 1978. He was said to be working on a new invention connected with worsted spinning at the time of his death. He left £114,351 gross.

JOHN A IREDALE

Writings:

'The Ambler Superdraft' *Journal of the Bradford Textile Society* (1950-51).

Sources:

Unpublished

BCe.

MCe.

PrC.

Published

File of newspaper cuttings, mostly from the *Telegraph & Argus*, Bradford, in the Bradford Public Library.

Textile Institute and Industry Oct 1978.

WWW.

ANDERSON, Sir Alan Garrett

(1877-1952)

Shipping line owner and executive

Alan Garrett Anderson was born in London on 9 March 1877, only son and second child of James George Skelton Anderson and his wife Elizabeth née Garrett (1836-1917). His father was nephew of James Anderson (qv), senior partner of Anderson, Anderson & Co and was himself a partner. His mother was the first woman to qualify as a doctor. Alan was sent first to Elstree School, whence he won a King's Scholarship to Eton, and then proceeded to Trinity College Oxford, where in addition to a good academic career, he also distinguished himself in rowing.

In 1897 he joined the family firm, of which his father was now senior partner. By then, the business was principally the joint management, with F Green & Co, of the Orient Steam Navigation Co owning six passenger ships providing, in conjunction with the Pacific Steam Navigation Co, a fortnightly contract mail service between London and Australia via Suez. The P&O Co provided a service in the intervening weeks, though as an entirely separate organisation. In 1900 Alan Anderson became a partner. Although he was thus born into the business, his ability and his enduring interest in ships soon made it clear that he would be a potential successor to his father and great-uncle, in the careful and devoted control of a business which always aimed at the highest standards. The Orient Co was reorganised financially in 1901, and its prosperity was still delicate for the first few years of Alan's career.

A major challenge came in 1906, when the Pacific Co was acquired by Owen Philipps (qv) whose Royal Mail Steam Packet Co took over the Pacific Steam Navigation share in the Orient-Pacific service. It seems clear that Philipps wished to establish himself in the Australian service, for difficulties soon sprang up (and the Royal Mail put one of its most modern ships on the service). Eventually in July 1907 the RMSP gave notice of its withdrawal from the joint service, no doubt anticipating that the Andersons and the Greens would not have the resources to replace their ships. Alan Anderson's father had died earlier in 1907, leaving James Anderson's son, Kenneth Skelton Anderson, as senior partner with Alan and Irvine Geddes, cousins, as colleagues: all relatively young men, but very determined. Anderson and the Green partners, particularly Sir Frederick Green and Sir Thomas Devitt, wanted to preserve the service all of them had seen grow from the beginning. By great exertions, and thanks to the high standing of both families, the seemingly impossible was achieved, and five new and larger ships were built in time to take over as the Royal Mail vessels were withdrawn. Moreover, the venture succeeded financially, and a sixth ship was soon added. By 1912 the Orient Line was owner of one of the finest passenger fleets afloat and financially healthy. It is difficult to distinguish the contributions of individuals, but it is worthy of note that when in 1911 the Midland Railway took over the London Tilbury & Southend Railway, Alan Anderson, as representing one of the principal users of Tilbury Docks, was invited to join the Midland board. He remained on the Midland board and that of its successor, the London Midland & Scottish Railway, until nationalisation.

Alan Anderson's abilities had also been noticed elsewhere, and soon after the outbreak of war, he was asked by Lord Runciman to assist the Board of Trade in connection with the blockade of the Central Powers. Later, he was appointed to the Royal Commission on Wheat Supplies, and subsequently became chairman of the Wheat Executive controlling the distribution of wheat to the western allies; he visited Washington with Balfour's mission in 1917 in this connection. Soon afterwards, Sir Eric Geddes (qv), son of his aunt, invited Alan Anderson to become Controller of the Navy in order to improve the production of ships. In all these tasks, his ability, tempered with humour and generosity, allowed him to achieve good results. He became KBE in 1917, and was asked to join the board of the Bank of England in 1918.

Anderson had now to return to the affairs of the Orient Line. The Green family wished to retire, and the P&O Co, with whom the Australia service had long been shared, acquired much of their interest in the Orient. The two firms were merged into Anderson, Green & Co which continued to manage the Orient Co. Four of its fine ships had been lost in the First World War. One new ship was completed, but three ex-German vessels had to be employed as stopgaps. However the P&O backing rendered replacement much easier than in the 1907 crisis, five new and even larger vessels being built through the 1920s. The P&O link also provided Alan Anderson with an entry into wider spheres of shipping, as he became one of the most valued colleagues of Lord Inchcape (qv) and a director of the P&O and British India companies. He was president of the

Chamber of Shipping in 1924-25, and Deputy-Governor of the Bank of England in 1925-26. In 1927, on the retirement of Sir Kenneth Anderson, he became senior partner of Anderson, Green.

The Orient Line survived the storm of 1929 well, although one or two of the ships built in 1909 were retired perhaps slightly early. By 1933 design of a new ship was in active preparation, and Sir Alan's son Colin took a leading part in her interior layout, for which the *Orion* and her later sister *Orcades* set new standards. In 1935 Sir Alan became Conservative MP for the City, although he did not find Parliament congenial and retired in 1940 to make way for Sir Andrew Duncan (qv) and to return to his previous wheat role. In August 1941 he was appointed chairman of the Railway Executive Committee and Controller of Railways in the Ministry of War Transport, posts he held until the end of the war, using again his broad outlook, energy and ability to delegate to sound effect in a post where tact was often called for.

After the war he retired from the Orient, although he still took great interest in the new ships. His railway connections ended with nationalisation.

Sir Alan was tall and impressive. He took a deep interest in detail, but retained a broad outlook and could encompass the widest problems. Not content with owning ships, his main interest was yachting, beginning at Aldeburgh in his early days; he successively owned several yachts and was a member of a number of yacht clubs, including the Royal Yacht Squadron. He also followed his mother's great work by supporting various hospitals and associated organisations, particularly the Elizabeth Garrett Anderson Hospital, the London School of Medicine for Women and the Royal Free Hospital. In his later years he took much interest in international commercial co-operation and was vice-president and then president of the International Chamber of Commerce. He was president of the Institution of Marine Engineers in 1928, of the Association of Chambers of Commerce in 1933-34, DL of the County of London, and High Sheriff in 1922, director of the Suez Canal Co, governor of Eton College and an honorary fellow of his old college at Oxford. He was a Trustee of the Seamen's Pension Fund, and a member of the Royal Commission on the National Debt, and he helped to found the British Provident Association for Hospital and Additional Services.

His honours included the Order of the Crown of Italy, the Légion d'Honneur and the Order of the White Rose of Finland; he was an honorary captain RNR.

He married in 1903 Muriel Ivy, daughter of G W Duncan of Richmond. They had four children; the two sons, Colin Skelton and Donald Forsyth (qv) went into the Orient and P&O companies respectively. The daughters are Diana Elizabeth and Hermione Charteris.

Sir Alan Anderson died on 4 May 1952 leaving £169,017 gross.

ALAN W H PEARSALL

Sources:

Unpublished

National Maritime Museum, P&O Archives, OSN/31/7-10, Historical Notes on Orient S N Co.

PrC.

PRO, RAIL 1007/422, RAIL 1057/3367-68, Records of London Midland & Scottish Railway Co.

Published

Louisa G Anderson, *Elizabeth Garrett Anderson* (Faber & Faber, 1939).

DNB.

John M Maber, *North Star to Southern Cross* (Prescot: T Stephenson & Sons, 1967).

Joan G Manton, *Elizabeth Garrett Anderson* (Methuen & Co, 1965).

Charles F Morris, *Origins, Orient and Oriana* (Brighton: Teredo Books Ltd, 1980).

Syren & Shipping 6 July 1938.

Times 5 May 1952.

WWW.

Sir Donald F Anderson (courtesy of P&OSN Co).

ANDERSON, Sir Donald Forsyth

(1906-1973)

Shipping industry leader

Donald Forsyth Anderson was born in Paddington, London on 3 September 1906, the second son of Sir Alan Garrett Anderson (qv), a shipbroker, and his wife Muriel Ivy Anderson née Duncan. His grandmother was Dr Elizabeth Garrett Anderson, the first woman to qualify as a doctor in England.

Educated at Eton and Trinity College, Oxford, Anderson joined the family business of Anderson, Green & Co Ltd, shipbrokers and managers of the Orient Line, in 1928. Orient Line operated only passenger liners on the Australian run, but it played a part in industry affairs quite disproportionate to its size and it produced seven presidents of the Chamber of Shipping: Sir Donald was one, as were his father, his brother, his grandfather and three cousins.

In 1933-34, Anderson accompanied the chairman of Peninsular & Oriental Steam Navigation Co, the Hon Alexander Shaw (later Lord Craigmyle) and his wife on a visit to India and Australia, and joined P&O in the latter year.

In September 1939 Anderson joined the Ministry of Shipping, later the Ministry of War Transport. In 1941, he was appointed to the British Merchant Shipping Mission to the United States in Washington and he remained there until recalled to join the P&O board in June 1943 by Sir William Currie, who had by then replaced Lord Craigmyle as P&O chairman. He became a managing director in 1946, deputy chairman in 1950, and he succeeded Sir William Currie as chairman on 1 April 1960.

By 1950, the date of Anderson's appointment as deputy chairman of P&O, the necessary steps had been taken by P&O and its subsidiary companies to replace ships lost during the war. However, no one saw more clearly than Anderson the need for P&O to broaden the base of its shipping operations. The accelerated development of air transport due to the technological advances made during the war posed a major threat for a group which operated passenger and cargo liner services to Australia, New Zealand, the Far East and the Indian sub-continent while the aspirations of the newly independent India, Pakistan, Burma and Ceylon to develop their own fleets were also bound to make inroads into traditional P&O business. In 1955 Anderson presented a paper to the P&O board recommending a programme of tanker building; this was accepted and led to the first substantial entry into tanker operation by an independent British shipowner. Anderson had also been advocating the building of bulk carriers but no progress was made at the time due to the degree of independence still vested in the subsidiary companies. The first rather tentative steps to reshape the loose association of subsidiary companies which comprised the P&O Group into an organisation more capable of facing the problems of the post-war era were taken in 1955; the capital structure was reorganised and the chairmen of some major subsidiary companies were invited to join the P&O board.

As chairman, Anderson moved towards the rationalisation of the group's shipping activities and a management structure based on a functional rather than a geographical basis. One of his first acts on becoming chairman was to preside over the absorption of his family firm, the Orient Line, into P&O so that the passenger liners of P&O and Orient in the UK and Australia trade came under a single management. Trident Tankers was formed in 1962 as a specialist management company for all the group tankers, which were owned by various subsidiary companies, and with responsibility for further developments in tankers, gas carriers and oil, bulk, or ore carriers. Two companies predominantly involved in running shelter deck tramp ships were merged as Hain-Nourse in 1965 and this company had the responsibility for the bulk carriers which progressively came into service from that year. Anderson meanwhile instigated with Erling Naess the formation of a joint company, Associated Bulk Carriers, for the operation of these vessels, a type of ship of which P&O had no experience at the time. Although the final stage of the restructuring was not taken until Anderson's successor (his cousin F I Geddes) was in the chair, the P&O board were clear as to the steps which were necessary and the decision to call in McKinsey & Co to act as a

ANDERSON Sir Donald Forsyth

Moreton Bay, *one of the first class of ships built for OCL, Sir Donald Anderson's Chief legacy to P&O (courtesy of Overseas Containers Ltd).*

catalyst was taken a few months before his retirement on 2 September 1971.

Anderson's greatest service to P&O was, without doubt, the initiative he took in conjunction with Sir John Nicholson, chairman of Ocean Steam Ship Co Ltd, for P&O and Ocean to containerise their liner trades jointly. They recognised that the investment required to containerise a major liner trade was likely to be beyond the capability of any British shipping company on its own, involving as it would the complete re-tonnaging of the trade in a very short space of time quite apart from the enormous ancillary investment in containers, terminals, computer systems for container control and inland depots. He realised also the complications which would arise in each trade over historic conference rights. If they could find other like-minded shipowners prepared to integrate their liner business with P&O and Ocean it would facilitate the introduction of containerisation, and invitations were consequently extended to Sir Nicholas Cayzer of British and Commonwealth Shipping Co Ltd and to Sir Errington Keville of Furness, Withy & Co Ltd: together they formed the consortium of Overseas Containers Ltd in 1965. The philosophy adopted was of complete integration of all the deep sea liner trades of all four groups and under Anderson's leadership the new consortium got away to a successful start and set the pattern for the future.

Shipping was going through a period of recession when Anderson took over the chairmanship and the performance of the new chairman was bound to come under close scrutiny by the shareholders' committee which had been established in 1955 to seek improved performance and higher dividends. In defending the performance of P&O from criticism he referred at the annual dinner of the Liverpool Shipping Staffs Association in 1955 to his shareholder critics as 'business parasites' who were trying to 'suck the lifeblood' of the shipping industry by demanding higher dividends; the furore which this caused necessitated a handsome apology by Anderson at the AGM in 1956. It was, therefore, an act of considerable courage that he was prepared to propose to stockholders in 1962, at a time when shipping was still in the doldrums, the redevelopment of the Group's Leadenhall Street properties. The opportunity had to be taken at once due to the acquisition of the adjoining site by Commercial Union; they proposed a joint develoment but if P&O did not agree they intended to go ahead with developing their own site and the opportunity for P&O with its extensive but shallow frontage on Leadenhall Street and St Mary Axe would have been lost forever. The proposal could all too easily have been misrepresented as the P&O board and employees seeking to improve their own working conditions when shareholders were being inadequately rewarded, but it was nevertheless approved by stockholders thanks to Anderson's advocacy and it has proved an excellent investment for P&O.

Various proposals were made during Anderson's chairmanship for P&O to diversify into areas away from shipping, but while giving careful consideration to such proposals he felt there were sufficient opportunites for diversification in shipping and he turned his back on the alternatives. After his retirement he emerged as a strong opponent of the proposed merger between P&O and Bovis and it is widely held that his eventual intervention was decisive in persuading stockholders to reject the deal.

Anderson was a brilliant man, positive and strong in his approach to any problem. He listened carefully to all points of view, although impatient of anything or anybody who was second rate, but once he had heard all viewpoints he was incisive in his decision taking. He was rather reserved and consequently appeared somewhat aloof in manner, but he was excellent company with those he knew and a good after-dinner-speaker with a keen wit. He was a good horseman and loved the country.

He was chairman of the British Shipping Federation from 1950 to 1962 and as such president of the International Shipping Federation and joint chairman of the National Maritime Board; in November 1963 he was elected president of the British Shipping Federation. He was president of the Chamber of Shipping in 1953-54. He was also president of the Institute of Shipping and Forwarding Agents, 1953; president of the Institute of Marine Engineers, 1956-57; chairman of the British Liner Committee, 1956-58; and president of the Institute of Export, 1961-63. He was a member of the Minister of Transport's Shipping Advisory Panel, 1962-64.

Anderson was an Honorary Captain RNR (awarded in recognition of outstanding support given by the P&O Group to the Royal Naval Reserve in the postwar years), an honorary member of the Honourable Company of Master Mariners (1964), an Elder Brother of the Corporation of Trinity House (1965) and an Honorary Brother of Hull Trinity House. He was honorary treasurer (1948-60) and then president (1961-73) of the Seafarers' Education Service, and vice-president of the British Ship Adoption Society from 1963 to 1973. Outside shipping, his directorships included those of the Bank of Australasia, 1936-51, and its successor Australia & New Zealand Banking Group, 1951-73; and Times Newspapers, 1967-73 (he was one of the 'national directors' appointed when the company was formed). He was for twenty years treasurer and for nine years (1964-73) chairman of the Council of the Royal Free Hospital School of Medicine, the third generation of his family to serve the school. He was also a member of the governing body of the London Graduate School of Business Studies.

He was made an Officer of the Order of Orange-Nassau in 1946 for services to the Netherlands. Following his term as president of the British Chamber of Shipping, he was knighted in 1954. In March 1959, he received the decoration of Commendatore dell'Ordine al Merito della

Repubblica Italiana. He was appointed a DL for the County of Gloucester in 1969.

During the voyage to India in 1934 he met his future wife, Elaine Llewellyn, eldest daughter of Sir David Llewellyn and sister of Colonel Harry Llewellyn of showjumping fame; they married in 1935 and there were four daughters of the marriage. Sir Donald died on 20 March 1973 leaving £693,067 gross.

STEPHEN RABSON *and* R B ADAMS

Sources:

Unpublished

National Maritime Museum, P&O papers.

P&O headquarters, unpublished papers.

PrC.

Personal knowledge.

Published

Times 22 Mar 1973.

Wavelength (P&O house magazine) special issue 1973.

WWW.

ANDERSON, James

(1811-1897)

Shipowner

James Anderson was born at Peterhead on 17 May 1811, son of John Ford Anderson (1784-1812), a surgeon, and his wife Margaret, daughter of James Skelton, merchant and shipowner of that port. The boy was educated privately under the care of Rev Francis Nicol, DD, principal of University College, St Andrew's, a great-uncle of his mother, upon whom the upbringing of the children had fallen after the early death of their father. James was intended for the law but the family circumstances, and it may be inferred, James's own interests derived from the Skelton ships,

James Anderson (from The Journal of Commerce & Shipping Telegraph *1934).*

led to him joining, in 1828, James Thomson & Co of 8 Billiter Square, London, a firm of merchants, shipbrokers and shipowners, specialising in the Jamaica trade and the Skeltons' agents in London.

James showed considerable aptitude for business and an absorbing interest in ships, and in 1842 he became a partner. The firm began to take advantage of the widening opportunities for trade, beginning to load ships for other West Indian ports, for the west coast of both Americas, and from 1851, for Australia. Anderson soon became the dominant partner. He appeared on the Committee of Lloyds Register of Shipping, on the London Marine Board, and in 1860 he became chairman of the General Shipowners Society. Anderson turned the firm on a new course by asking the firm of Thomas Bilbe & Co of Rotherhithe, with whom Thomsons were associated, to build a fine clipper, the *Orient*. He loaded her for Adelaide and built up a good business there. More clippers were added and these well-maintained and hard-sailed ships brought the 'Orient Line' renown for speed and reliability. The firm's ships also sailed to other Australian ports, and eventually the firm loaded about 20 vessels a year.

In 1854 his nephew, James George Skelton Anderson (1838-1907), son of his elder brother, Rev Alexander Anderson, entered the firm and became a partner in 1863, when the title was changed to Anderson, Thomson & Co. In 1869 the last Thomson retired, two more brothers of J G S Anderson joined (A G and W R Anderson) and the firm was now Anderson, Anderson & Co.

The same year saw the opening of the Suez Canal, which, together with the steady improvement in the efficiency of the steam engine, compelled ship owners in the Australian trade to consider the use of steam. James and his nephews, cautious though they were, wished to remain in the lead. After some experimental voyages, they had the opportunity in 1877 to charter four ships from the Pacific Steam Navigation Co (PSN Co). While the results of these voyages were successful, the capital needed to place the undertaking on a permanent basis was so large that other partners were necessary. Another influential firm in the trade, F Green & Co, were also turning to steam and agreed to form the Orient Steam Navigation Co, registered on 12 February 1878, the two firms acting as joint managers.

The venture was bold, as they did not have a mail contract, but the company was initially successful and soon had to increase the frequency of its sailings from monthly to fortnightly, with the aid of further PSN Co ships and its own remarkable new ship *Orient*. In the next ten years, which financially were not very rewarding, the Orient Co built two more fine vessels, and by maintaining the high standards set by its predecessors in sail, established itself in the front rank. In 1888 it obtained a share of the main Australian mail contract. The older interests of the firm were still maintained too, although the course of trade, no less than the preoccupation with the Orient line, led to gradual contraction.

James Anderson was described as a cautious Scot, Presbyterian by faith, Liberal in politics, but never concerning himself greatly outside his own business. To that he was deeply committed, as he had a love of ships in themselves as well as a grasp of business. His standards were high: his ships had to be well built and cared for, for they were driven hard to make fast passages. James was also chairman of the Scottish Provincial

Orient (courtesy of the National Maritime Museum, London).

Insurance Co, a director of the Bank of British Columbia, where his firm had interests, and a fellow of the Royal Geographical Society.

He married in 1849, Elizabeth, daughter of John Murray, Surgeon-General. They had two sons and six daughters. The younger son, the future Sir Kenneth Skelton Anderson (1866-1942), entered the family firm in 1888 and rose to be its senior partner. Similarly, the descendants of J G S Anderson also entered the firm: Alan (later Sir Alan) G Anderson (qv), and his sons, Colin and Donald (qv) (who were both knighted in their turn). James Anderson's elder son, Hugh (1865-1928), turned to the medical world in which the family was also extremely distinguished, and became yet another Anderson knight. James Anderson retired in 1889, and died at his home, Frognal Park, Hampstead, on 1 September 1897. He left an estate valued at £133,855 gross.

ALAN W H PEARSALL

Sources:

Unpublished

National Maritime Museum, P&O Archives, OSN/31/7-10, Historical notes on Orient S.N.Co.

PrC.

Published

Illustrated London News 30 Oct 1897.

Sir Clement W Jones, *Pioneer Shipowners* (Liverpool: C Birchall & Sons, 1935).

Lloyd's Register of Shipping.

A Basil Lubbock, *The Colonial Clippers* (Glasgow: J Brown & Son, 1921).

John M Maber, *North Star to Southern Cross* (Prescot: T Stephenson & Sons, 1967).

Mercantile Navy List.

Charles F Morris, *Origins, Orient and Oriana* (Brighton: Teredo Books Ltd, 1980).

David Pollock, *Modern Shipbuilding and the Men Engaged in It* (E & F N Spon, 1884).

Hew Scott, *Fasti Ecclesiae Scoticanae* 6 (Edinburgh: Oliver & Boyd, 1926).

Syren & Shipping 6 July 1938.

Times 3 Sept 1897.

ANDERSON, Sir John

(1814-1886)

Government arsenal manager

John Anderson was born at Woodside near Aberdeen on 9 December 1814, three months after the death of his father, a merchant in the village. He was brought up by his mother and stepfather, Irvine Kempt, who was manager of the machine shop in Gordon Barran & Co's cotton mills at Woodside.

Through his stepfather's influence, John Anderson secured a clerical job in the cotton mills when he left parish school. At the age of eighteen he entered a seven years' apprenticeship in the mills' workshops and in his spare time studied in the Aberdeen Mechanics' Institute. On completing his apprenticeship in 1839 he went south to the major engineering centres in England, spending short periods at the engineering works of William Fairbairn & Co, and Sharpe, Roberts & Co, both at Manchester, and then the works of Penn at Greenwich and of David Napier in London.

On Napier's recommendation he moved to Woolwich Arsenal in 1842 to take charge of bronze gun manufacture, starting as foreman. Anderson found the Arsenal labouring under obsolete methods and equipment. With the support of his military superior, Colonel William B Dundas, Inspector of Artillery and of the Royal Brass Foundry, Anderson reformed his department, converting the Brass Foundry into an engineering workshop which made machinery for other departments as well as itself. Throughout the 1840s Anderson acquired ideas and machines from Europe and America and invented many of his own machines, frequently in his spare time. His ingenuity marked him out. By 1853 he was engineer in the Royal Brass Foundry and the following year he was appointed engineer to the Inspector of Artillery's Department, with a salary of £400 per annum rising by annual increments of £50 to £700 per annum.

Anderson was most influential in introducing into Britain the American system of manufacture, characterised by standardised parts and interchangeability. In the early 1850s the Government's adoption of the Minié rifle musket exposed the weaknesses of the English small arms manufacture: a cumbersome contract system exploited by gun makers' price rings and handicraft techniques, which were compounded by labour disputes in the early 1850s and an inelastic labour supply during the Crimean War. Contrasting American methods were advertised at the Crystal Palace Exhibition of 1851 and the New York Exhibition of 1853, the latter reported by Joseph Whitworth (qv) and George Wallis. Anderson, who visited Samuel Colt's London pistol factory to see the techniques of partial interchangeability, was convinced that a government factory could be tooled to make small arms entirely by machinery. With this in view, and faced by strong opposition from the private arms makers, the Ordnance Board sent a small delegation (the Small Arms Committee), including Anderson, to the USA in 1854. On Anderson's evidence the Board decided to build an American-style armoury at Enfield. With the assistance of an American engineer (James H Burton) and several American workmen, Anderson supervised its construction (1855-56), the installation of American machinery and the production of an elaborate system of gauges, essential for the manufacture of precision-made standardised parts and interchangeability of rifle components. By 1861 the Enfield Armoury was making nearly 100,000 rifles a year and in 1862 had a net profit of £14,000.

Next to the Enfield Armoury, Anderson's other major achievement was the renovation of the government gunpowder mills at Waltham Abbey. High gunpowder stocks in 1815 had induced a long neglect: by 1840 the largely-wooden mills were almost worn out. Anderson designed or invented a new line of equipment, made of iron; the most important single piece was his machine for granulating gunpowder, which replaced the older, very dangerous method of hand-corning. At the same time he relocated the machinery to minimise the risk of explosions.

Apart from numerous technological contributions, Anderson was responsible for a thorough reorganisation of government munitions factories. He rearranged the sequence of the work process, introduced a system of wage differentials, and brought in incentive payment schemes. In 1859 Anderson was appointed assistant superintendent of machinery under Sir William Armstrong (qv) and then superintendent of machinery in 1866 with a salary of £1,000 per annum. He retired in 1872.

Anderson served on the juries of the international exhibitions of his day: London, 1862; Paris, 1867; Vienna, 1873; and Philadelphia, 1876. He received the honorary degree of LLD from St Andrews in 1871 and was knighted and made a member of the Légion d'Honneur in 1878. In 1881 he presented a free library of 50,000 volumes, costing £6,000, to his native village.

Anderson married in 1840 Eliza, daughter of William Norrie, a merchant of London. He died at St Leonard's-on-Sea on 28 July 1886, leaving £49,888 gross.

DAVID J JEREMY

Writings:

A General Statement of the Past and Present Condition of the Several Manufacturing Branches of the War Department (HMSO, 1857).

'On the Application of Machinery in the War Department' *Journal of the Society of Arts* 5 (1857).

'On Some Applications of the Copying or Transfer Principle in the Production of Wooden Articles' *Proceedings of the Institution of Mechanical Engineers* 1858.

'On the Applications of the Copying Principle in the Manufacture and Rifling of Guns' *ibid* 1862.

'Iron and Steel as Materials for Rifled Cannon' *Journal of the Royal United Service Institution* 6 (1863).
'On the Materials and Structures of Rifled Cannon' *ibid* 9 (1865).

PP, 1867-68 (4) XXX, Report on Machine Tools.

PP, Report on the Paris Universal Exhibition 1867 (1867-68) C3968.

'On Applied Mechanics' *Journal of the Society of Arts* 17 (1869).

The Strength of Materials and Structures (Longmans & Co, 1872).

Statement of Services Performed by John Anderson, Superintendent of Machinery to the War Department from the Year 1842 to the Present Time (pp, C A MacIntosh, 1873).

PP, Reports on the Philadelphia International Exhibition of 1876 (1877) C 1774, 'Machines and Tools for Working Metals, Wood, and Stone'.

Sources:

Unpublished

MCe.

PrC.

Published

Oliver E G Hogg, *The Royal Arsenal. Its Background, Origin and Subsequent History* (2 vols, Oxford University Press, 1963).

Proceedings of the Institution of Civil Engineers 86 (1886).

Proceedings of the Institution of Mechanical Engineers Aug 1886.

Nathan Rosenberg (ed), *The American System of Manufactures. The Report of the Committee on the Machinery of the United States, 1855; and the Special Reports of George Wallis and Joseph Whitworth, 1854* (Edinburgh: Edinburgh University Press, 1969).

Times 29 July 1886.

ANDERSON, Sir William

(1835-1898)

Director general of the Royal Ordnance Factories

William Anderson was born at St Petersburg, Russia on 5 January 1835, fourth son of John Anderson, partner in Messrs Matthews Anderson, St Petersburg bankers and merchants, and his wife Frances, daughter of Dr Robert Simpson. He was educated at the High Commercial School in St Petersburg, where he became proficient in Russian, German and French, and was captain of the school and silver medallist in 1849. His unusual foreign education resembled that of another innovator of British munitions production, H S B Brindley (qv). Anderson studied in 1849-51 in the Applied Sciences Department of King's College, London, of which he remained an associate during his engineering pupillage in Manchester during 1851-54 with Sir William Fairbairn (1789-1874).

Between 1855 and 1864 Anderson was manager and then partner in the Dublin engineering firm of Courtney Stephens, specialising in the construction of bridges, cranes, signals and railway fittings. In Ireland Anderson developed the then rudimentary theory of diagonally braced girders, and was the first engineer to use the braced web in cranes. In 1863 he was president of the Institution of Civil Engineers in Ireland, but returned to England in 1864 as partner in the Southwark engineering firm of Easton & Amos (afterwards Easton & Anderson). He superintended the erection of their new Erith Ironworks, where pumping machinery, cranes, boilers and paper and sugar machinery were manufactured. During the following decade he worked at the design of centrifugal pumps, and both designed and built three sugar-mills for the Khedive of Egypt, for which he was awarded a Watt medal and a Telford premium. He also received a Telford medal and premium for his construction of Antwerp waterworks, with its revolving iron purifier. He was a member of the Institution of Civil Engineers from 1869, joining its council in 1886 and becoming vice-president in 1896.

Anderson designed several naval gun mountings for Russia and Britain, as well as a high-angle fire mortar mounting for the USA. Around 1888 Anderson was asked by the War Office to design the machinery for making the revolutionary new smokeless explosive, cordite: following his appointment in August 1889 as Director General of the Royal Ordnance Factories (ROF), this work was transferred to his eldest son. The circumstances in which Easton & Anderson subsequently secured the contract to provide the equipment to make cordite were widely censured.

As Director General of the ROF, Anderson was responsible for Waltham Abbey gunpowder works, the small-arms factories at Enfield and Sparkbrook, and Woolwich Arsenal. It was the latter that he was appointed to reform. In the 1880s Woolwich comprised three manufacturing departments: the Royal Laboratory (formed in 1696), the Royal Gun Factory (1716) and the Royal Carriage Department (1803).

> Each, within its self-appointed shell of independence, jealousy and *amour propre*, had pursued its course and developed its character to its own liking ... Each had its own foundries, forges, carpenters' shops, railway engines and rolling-stock; each was completely equipped to produce its special output {Hogg (1963) 840, 875}.

Woolwich was not only poorly prepared and equipped to expand in a national emergency, but its different departments blocked one another with jealous resentment, used their own officials to inspect their products and those of private manufacturers, and lacked expert engineering advice. Thus in 1887 there was no metallurgist at Woolwich and no chemist at Waltham. The Earl of Morley's committee (1886-87) on the Manufacturing Departments of the Army reported that the War Office's Director of Artillery, as nominal head of the ROF, was too busy to exercise proper control, and that most inefficiencies and abuses were due to this cause. As an initial reform the first Director General of Ordnance Factories, a military officer called Eardley Maitland (1833-1911), was selected in 1888. He made little mark, and Anderson was appointed to succeed him in 1889 in the hope that his civilian business expertise would be valuable. Whereas Maitland had an annual salary of £1,800, Anderson from private industry commanded £2,500 per annum. In contrast his successor, another soldier, Colonel Sir Edmond Bainbridge (1841-1911), was paid only £1,800 per annum in 1899-1903.

It fell to Anderson to implement the post-Morley reforms, but it was his misfortune to take office just as the Naval Defence Act of 1889 started an upsurge in armament orders and distracted attention from reform. Anderson created an inspectorate branch; a centralised administrative headquarters was established; the stores branches of the factories were united; coal was henceforth bought in bulk; factory accounting was modernised and centralised in 1890; and against the weight of prejudice and tradition, he tried to reduce duplication, and induce co-operation, between the different manufacturing departments. Anderson had a measure of success, but suffered from delays in obtaining authority for some changes, and met resistance to his attempted centralisation. Indeed the squabbling and obstruction between the different departments was implacable. He failed to obtain the full factory integration envisaged by Morley, and died before it was possible to transform Woolwich's layout as he desired. Radical layout changes were indispensable to make Woolwich efficient: but as late as 1919 it remained 'a manufacturing maze and muddle' with 'its labyrinth of narrow twisting streets and alleys, threading their ways among dark and old shops in many of which it is difficult to get folk to work' {*PP* (1919) Cmd 229, 177}.

Anderson chaired a departmental committee on Ordnance Factory Accounting in 1891 which led to annual savings of £18,000, but the obstacles to the spirit of his recommendations were insurmountable. According to the official who re-designed the Woolwich accounts in the early 1890s, the Arsenal was then

> largely in the hands of military officers who, in matters of pure industrial administration, were themselves also very much in the hands of managers and assistant managers ... who ... were not generally men with engineering degrees ... but men who had grown up from the bench. The general disposition was to regard accounts as an unfortunate necessity about which

the less said, the better ... when offered to take any information out of the accounts which the superintendents and managers might find useful ... they asked for nothing; and when put that information before them which thought they ought to be in a position to refuse, they made no use of it {PRO Munitions 4/6375, evidence of Sir Charles Harris to costs sub-committee of committee on ROF, 27 Jan 1919}.

It was not until twenty years after Anderson's death that Sir Mark Webster Jenkinson (qv) obliged the audit at Woolwich to include the cash, which sometimes was as much as £250,000.

About £14,000 set aside for machinery depreciation under the new accounts was misappropriated for building extensions, and the ROF's output in the 1890s was produced on deteriorating machinery, working overtime, without addition to the total capital stock employed. By the end of the century the ROF's equipment was decaying; this misuse of resources negated Anderson's attempts at higher efficiency through centralisation. The productive inefficiency of the machinery, and the nullity of factory managers, necessitated in a time of expanding orders an increase in the manufacturing workforce from 9,890 in 1886 to 12,160 in 1895 and 15,434 in 1898, making Woolwich one of the largest manufacturing establishments in Britain and creating considerable labour problems. Paradoxically the ROF's design departments remained grossly under-staffed, especially in draughtsmen.

Anderson tried to compensate for the business incompetence of the ROF by aggressive competition with private armourers, but only increased his difficulties by over-stretching facilities. Although the Morley committee had adjured to the contrary, the ROF's proportion of British naval and military orders rose from 50 per cent in 1890-91 to 60 per cent in 1895-96, with Anderson making particular efforts to win orders for big guns. This policy almost broke companies like Hotchkiss, and forced steel manufacturers like Albert Vickers (qv) to form 'rings' as a defence against Anderson's competition. It also meant that the ROF had little reserve manufacturing power to expand in a crisis like the Boer War. Anderson was as unpopular with the private manufacturers as with the Woolwich Superintendents. Thus in 1895 Nobel Explosives sued him for infractions of their cordite patents, but the House of Lords found in Anderson's favour. The Court of Appeal gave judgement for him in a similar case brought by Sir Hiram Maxim in 1897. It is nevertheless likely that Anderson was implicated in pirating the invention of cordite, and 'allegations that the War Office were a den of thieves for inventors were not wholly unfounded' {Trebilcock (1966) 376}.

Anderson was President of Section G of the British Association meeting at Newcastle in 1889, for which Durham University awarded him the honorary degree of DCL. Elected FRS in 1891, he was president of the Institution of Mechanical Engineers in 1892-93, vice-president of the Society of Arts, consulting engineer to the Royal Agricultural Society, visitor of the Royal Institution, and a member of the Iron and Steel Institute. He wrote most of the Russian material in the Foreign Abstracts of the *Proceedings* of the Institution of Civil Engineers, and translated the works of Chernoff on steel and Kalakoutsky on internal stresses in cast-iron and steel. Some of his multitude of technical papers are listed below. He was lieutenant-colonel of the Engineer and Railway Volunteer Staff

Corps, receiving the CB in 1895 and a knighthood in 1897. He was also first chairman of the Erith Local Board of Health, a member of the Erith School Board 1870-98, a licensed lay reader and for twenty-five years superintendent of Sunday Schools at Christ Church, Erith. In his death-throes he was heard to mutter his customary address to his Sunday School pupils.

In November 1856 Anderson married, at Knighton, Radnorshire, Emma Eliza, daughter of Rev J R Brown of Knighton, by whom he had several children. He died of dropsy and heart disease on 11 December 1898 at Woolwich Arsenal, leaving £10,770. Significantly his successor Bainbridge was appointed not Director General of the ROF but Chief Superintendent, a change that denoted the defeat of Anderson's attempts to tame and centralise the other departmental superintendents; and in 1899 the ROF's top management was reorganised so that more power resided with soldiers than civilians. The business understanding of the arsenals remained primitive, and Anderson's best efforts were frustrated.

R P T DAVENPORT-HINES

Writings:

'On Beams and Girder Bridges' *Transactions of the Institution of Civil Engineers of Ireland* 5 (1860).

'On a New Method of Shoring Adopted in Moving the Two Lower Floors of the Royal Bank, Dublin' *ibid* 5 (1860).

'Description of a Joint Chair for Bridge Rails Designed by Marcus Harty, Engineer to the Dublin and Drogheda Railway' *ibid* 6 (1863).

'Description of a Six-Ton Crane with Curved, Diagonally Braced Jib' *ibid* 6 (1863).

'On Railway Bridges of Small Span, and Cross Beams of Railway Bridges' *ibid* 8 (1868).

Presidential address of 11 Dec 1867 *ibid* 8 (1868).

'The Aba-el-Wakf Sugar Factory' *ibid* 35 (1872).

'Notes of a Visit Paid to Some Peatworks in the Neighbourhood of St Petersburg in May 1875' *Minutes of Proceedings of the Institution of Civil Engineers* 41 (1875).

'Experiments and Observations on the Emission of Heat by Hot-water Pipes' *ibid* 48 (1877).

'The Antwerp Waterworks' *ibid* 72 (1883).

'Notes of a journey through the N E Portion of the Delta of the Nile in April 1884' *ibid* 76 (1884).

'Conversion of Heat into Useful Work' *Journal of Society of Arts* 33 (1884-85).

'On the Generation of Steam, and the Thermo-dynamic Problems Involved' *Heat in Its Mechanical Applications* (Institution of Civil Engineers, 1885).

'On New Applications of the Mechanical Properties of Cork to the Arts' *Proceedings of the Royal Institution* 11 (1886).

ANDERSON Sir William

On the Conversion of Heat into Work. A Practical Handbook on Heat-Engines (Whittaker & Co, 1887).

'The Development of Graphic Methods in Mechanical Science' *Report of British Association* (1889).

'The Molecular Structure of Matter' *ibid* (1889).

'Action of Waves and Currents in Estuaries' *ibid* (1890).

'Revolving Purifier for the Treatment of Water by Metallic Iron' *ibid* (1891).

Presidential address *Proceedings of the Institution of Mechanical Engineers* 1892.

'The Interdependence of Abstract Science and Engineering' (James Forrest lecture) *Minutes of Proceedings of the Institution of Civil Engineers* 114 (1893).

Sources:

Unpublished

Ministry of Defence, Whitehall, reports of the Directors of Army Contracts (1889-1899), Old War Office Library.

PRO, papers of the McKinnon Wood committee on Royal Ordnance Factories (1918-1919), Munitions 4/5329, Munitions 4/6368, Munitions 4/6375.

—, War Office papers.

PrC.

Information from Clive Trebilcock.

Published

Arms and Explosives 1888-99.

DNB.

Oliver F G Hogg, *The Royal Arsenal* (2 vols, Oxford University Press, 1963).

Men of the Time (1895).

Minutes of Proceedings of the Institution of Civil Engineers 135 (1899).

PP Lord Marchamley, supplementary report to McKinnon Wood committee's report to Minister of Munitions on Royal Ordnance Factories, Woolwich (1919) Cmd 229.

Times 12 Dec 1898.

Clive Trebilcock, 'A Special Relationship - Government, Rearmament and the Cordite Firms' *Economic History Review* 2nd series 19 (1966).

WWW.

Edmund G Angus (courtesy of the Central Library, Newcastle upon Tyne).

ANGUS, Edmund Graham

(1889-1983)

Oil seal manufacturer and North East industrialist

Edmund Graham Angus was born at Westgate, Newcastle upon Tyne, on 9 June 1889, the son of Col William Mathwin Angus, a leather merchant, and his wife Sarah née Graham. He was educated at Felsted School. In 1906 he joined the family firm, served in the Boston office 1910-11 and became a director in 1920. He became a managing director in 1932 (a position he held until 1958) and chairman in 1933 (a position he held until 1964, when on his retirement he was made the first president of the company).

In 1936 the firm extended its interests with the establishment of an oil seal division with a factory at Walker, on the Tyne east of Newcastle, to manufacture seals for the lubrication systems of high-speed machinery. The division experienced considerable expansion culminating in the opening of a new factory at Wallsend in 1956, then the largest oil seal factory in Europe. By the 1960s it was claimed that the firm was the world's largest manufacturer of fire hoses. An industrial rubber plant at Cramlington New Town in Northumberland was opened and the Newcastle city centre works, which had become inconvenient, was closed. From a level of about 500 in the early 1930s the group's UK employment exceeded 3,000 in the mid-1950s and reached 3,700 in 1963. A large number of UK subsidiaries were established while many subsidiaries were established abroad, with, for instance, a Canadian factory set up in 1951. George Angus & Co Ltd was merged with Dunlop Ltd as Dunlop Angus Industrial Group in 1968.

Angus was also active in business affairs outside his own industry, holding the following positions: director of Newcastle & Gateshead Water Co, Moor Line, Tyne Tees Television Ltd; chairman of the local board of Royal Insurance Co Ltd; member of the local board of Lloyds Bank Ltd and of the North Eastern Electricity Board; and president of Newcastle Permanent Building Society. In addition he was chairman of the Northern Regional Council of the FBI and president of Newcastle and Gateshead Chamber of Commerce.

Apart from directing the fortunes of the family firm for a considerable period E G Angus had a very active public life. He was commissioned in 1906 and posted to the Hebburn Battery of the 1st Newcastle Royal Garrison Artillery Volunteers, a regiment commanded by his father. He served in France and Flanders with the 50th (Northumbrian) Division Artillery 1914-19, winning the MC in 1915. He was awarded the TD in 1922 and commanded the 74th Northumberland Field Regiment from 1925 until 1932 (with the rank of colonel from 1929). During the Second World War he commanded the 8th Heavy AA Regiment, RA, Home Guard; was awarded the CBE in 1944; and in 1950 was appointed Honorary Colonel of the 274th Field Regiment, RA (TA), (a new title for the old 74th he had previously commanded). This position he retained until 1956 when he retired after the highly unusual feat of having been on the active list for fifty years.

E G Angus was appointed a DL of the County of Durham in 1945 and a JP for Northumberland in 1948. In 1966 he was made a Knight of the Order of St John of Jerusalem and in 1974 a fellow of the Royal Society of Arts. He was a member of the Carlton, Northern Counties and Union (Newcastle upon Tyne) Clubs and his chief leisure activity was horticulture.

In 1922 he married Bridget Ellen Isabella Spencer (of the Newburn steelworks family) who was responsible for building up the famous Ravenstone herd of goats. They had three sons and a daughter. Col Angus died on 19 March 1983.

D J ROWE

Sources:

Unpublished

BCe.

Published

Industrial Tyneside Feb 1955.

Newcastle Journal 26 Feb 1955.

Newcastle Life Oct 1961.

Voice of North East Industry Dec 1963.

WW 1982.

ANGUS, George

(1821-1890)

Leather belt manufacturer

George Angus was born in Gateshead in 1821, the son of William Angus. In 1836 he was apprenticed to the leather business which his grandfather had begun in 1788. It had commenced with the sale of leather from premises in the Close, Newcastle upon Tyne, and currying was added in 1810.

At the end of George's apprenticeship in 1843 the manufacture of india rubber was added and the basis on which future expansion would take place was in existence. Expansion led to the taking of premises in Grey Street for the rubber business but these were destroyed by fire in 1867, and in the following year the whole business was established in new and larger works which were opened off Grainger Street, Newcastle, in the centre of town and near the Central Station. Here the firm built up a large trade in the manufacture of driving belts, hose pipe and leather and rubber goods for industrial customers throughout the world with a branch established in Johannesburg before the First World War. In 1888 the firm was converted into a limited company with George Angus, previously senior partner, as chairman. By this time there were warehouses and branches in Liverpool, Cardiff, Manchester, Leeds, Birmingham, Glasgow and London and the firm employed thirty-two travellers. A subsidiary leather business was developed in Liverpool from 1874 under one of George's sons, John Henry Angus, and branches were established in Northampton, Leicester, Kettering and London with a New York office in 1880 and shortly afterwards one in Boston.

George Angus played little active part in public life, although he was elected a member of Newcastle Town Council in 1857. He was a Baptist and much involved in the work of the Newcastle Baptist Church and was a supporter of many charities, especially those concerned with Christian, childrens' and young persons' work. He had thirteen children (four sons and nine daughters) and lived at Low Gosforth Hall to the north of Newcastle. He left an estate valued at £171,619 when he died on 18 November, 1890.

After his death the business was run largely by two of his sons who were joint managing directors, John Henry Angus (d 1930, leaving £160,074 gross) who was also chairman, and Colonel William Mathwin Angus (d 1934 leaving nearly £29,000 gross). They were responsible for taking the firm in two new directions in the period just before the First World War. In recognition of the changes taking place in power transmission they commenced the manufacture of gears, while they also moved into the production of canvas, which was more durable than leather for hose and belting, with the takeover of a textile firm at Bentham, Yorkshire. Here in 1910 they erected a new mill, which was further extended in 1922. The really major expansion of the firm was, however, to come with the fourth generation of the family, especially under Edmund Graham Angus (qv).

D J ROWE

Sources:

Unpublished

PrC.

Published

Industrial Tyneside Feb 1955.

Newcastle Journal 26 Feb 1955.

Newcastle Life Oct 1961.

Voice of North East Industry Dec 1963.

WW 1982.

ARMSTRONG, William George

1st Lord Armstrong of Cragside

(1810-1900)

Engineering equipment and armaments manufacturer and shipbuilder

William G Armstrong (from Mrs Stuart Menzies, Modern Men of Mark, *Herbert Jenkins Ltd, 1921).*

William George Armstrong was born in Newcastle upon Tyne on 26 November 1810, the only son of William Armstrong (1778-1857), a corn merchant of Newcastle, who in his adult life developed a passion for mathematics and became a significant political figure on Tyneside, shifting as he grew older from a somewhat reactionary position to that of a Whig reformer. His mother, Ann née Potter, was the daughter of William née Potter of Walbottle House.

A delicate child, W G Armstrong was fascinated by mechanics, an interest undimmed by his school career in private schools and at the Bishop Auckland Grammar School. From school, however, he went as an articled clerk to a firm of solicitors. After further legal studies in London with his brother-in-law William Henry Wilson, a special pleader at Lincoln's Inn, he became in 1833 a partner in the firm of Newcastle solicitor Armorer Donkin, then styled 'Messrs Donkin, Stable & Armstrong'. The connections which this practice developed with important North-Eastern companies, families and estates were soon to become extremely valuable to Armstrong.

In the mid-1830s, while still practising as a solicitor, Armstrong renewed his interest in mechanical contrivances, especially in devices which could utilise water to generate motive power; by the mid-1840s he was also experimenting with hydro-electricity and was elected a Fellow of the Royal Society in 1846 in recognition of his experimental work. But, more importantly, his appointment in 1845 as secretary to the Whittle Dene Water Co, newly formed to improve Newcastle's water supply, established his position within Tyneside's tight circle of industrialists. Armstrong's uncle, A L Potter, a noted coalowner, was chairman of the company. Its joint managing directors were G W Cruddas, shipowner and railway director, and R Lambert, lawyer and wine merchant. Later, from 1855 to 1867, Armstrong was the company's chairman. Before he resigned as secretary in 1847, Armstrong turned to his colleagues when he began to put his experiments to practical use.

In 1846, with Potter, Cruddas, Lambert and Donkin, and with assurance of markets from James Meadows Rendel FRS, a dock engineer, Armstrong formed the Newcastle Cranage Co, to supply hydraulic cranes. The following year the same men formed Armstrong & Co with a capital of £20,000 and commenced business on a five-and-a-half acre site to the west of Newcastle at Elswick, lying between the tidal Tyne and the Newcastle & Carlisle Railway. Initially they employed 20-30 men.

The works were established to design, manufacture, assemble and supply hydraulic machinery of a novel kind; Armstrong's influence here probably justifies the claims that he was the father of hydraulic engineering. Amongst the earliest orders were quayside cranes (for Jesse Hartley at Liverpool), mine winding engines and a printing press engine. Armstrong's invention of the hydraulic accumulator in 1850-51, enabling higher hydraulic pressures to be achieved and replacing the former need for reservoirs, made hydraulic power systems more compact, flexible and widely applicable. Demand for hydraulic machinery came from canal and railway companies, shipyards, dockyards, ports and harbours; with the development of the works assured, expansion was financed by ploughing back profits. By March 1852 some 352 workers were employed and about 60 cranes were being built yearly.

During the Crimean War, and again encouraged by Rendel, Armstrong turned his inventive talents to the improvement of military equipment, especially to the development of a superior field gun. The concept was not new but Armstrong succeeded in solving the metallurgical and mechanical problems that had defeated other engineers. Within twelve months he completed his first field gun, a 3-pounder, coil breech-loader with an inner tube of steel rifled on Armstrong's polygroove plan; by 1857 his 18-pounder, tested on the Shoebury ranges, was more accurate over two miles than a smooth bore equivalent over one mile. An official committee, set up in 1858, had the unenviable task of deciding which method of rifling, that of Armstrong or that of his rival Joseph Whitworth (qv), should be adopted. Since Whitworth had not yet built a field gun, but only designed one, and since Armstrong's gun was 57 times more accurate than common artillery, Armstrong's gun was selected by the War Office. In 1859 its maker was appointed the Government's Engineer for Rifled Ordnance and superintendent of the Royal Gun Factory, Woolwich, and, at the same time, was knighted. Armstrong added eleven patents for ordnance and projectiles to three already obtained for hydraulic machinery, but believing that the only justification for patents was to ensure the option of manufacturing one's own inventions, he donated his patents to the nation. The Elswick Ordnance Co, with a capital of £50,000 guaranteed by the Government, was formed with premises adjacent to the Elswick Works in order to make guns of Armstrong's design for the British Government. Armstrong had no financial involvement with the new company although its principal partners were also partners in the engineering works. He saw it as a complement to Woolwich in making Armstrong guns. George Rendel, son of James Rendel and long-time advisor to Armstrong, was appointed manager, and Andrew Noble (qv), who had been secretary to the Special Committee on Rifled Cannons and a member of the Ordnance Select Committee, was soon persuaded to join the company as joint manager.

Armstrong's success was blighted firstly by Whitworth's followers who in press and in Parliament, until Whitworth's death, advocated the use of homogeneous metal, a polygonal bore and a choked (tapered) barrel in contrast to Sir William's coiled tubing of forged steels. Secondly it was diminished by the conservatism of Service officers who preferred obsolete muzzle loading guns and cannon balls. Government orders were drastically reduced from a total value of £1,063,000 between 1859 and 1863 to about £60,000 between 1864 and 1878.

In 1863 Armstrong resigned his government position and restructured his business. The Ordnance Works were merged with the engineering works and the combined works concentrated on securing overseas arms contracts. Armstrong, now supported by G W Cruddas and the three sons of his old friend James Rendel, built up a new trade, based on foreign rather than domestic markets in armaments, supplying Russia, Austria, Italy, Spain, Egypt, Denmark, Holland, Chile and Peru with heavy guns in the late 1860s. From 1870 Armstrongs made under licence an early machine-gun, the American Gatling gun.

In 1868 the Elswick firm began to co-operate with Charles Mitchell & Co in building warships at their Walker-on-Tyne yard, some five miles downstream from Elswick. About 20 warships were built under this arrangement by 1882. However, the replacement, in 1876, of Newcastle's low stone bridge by the present hydraulic swing bridge (designed and built by the Elswick Works), enabled up-river dredging and a new shipyard to be developed at Elswick.

In 1882, Armstrong and Mitchell amalgamated their respective concerns under the title Sir W G Armstrong Mitchell & Co Ltd, the new company immediately offering shares to the public to raise the £2 million capital needed to finance the operation, a new open-hearth steel works and a shipyard at Elswick. Blast furnaces had been installed in the mid-1860s and the clear intention was to be able to produce, at Elswick, warships from raw materials. Dividends of 9 per cent were paid at the end of the first year. The steel works and shipyard were in operation by 1884, the former being managed by Col H C S Dyer (qv), brought into the company for that purpose, while in charge of the Elswick naval yard was Sir William White, formerly Chief Constructor to the Royal Navy. The subsequent interchangeability of key personnel from within the Admiralty to management positions at Elswick, and vice versa, became and remained a feature of the Elswick Works. These close contacts and those also cultivated between Elswick and the naval establishments of many other countries, helped to keep a full order book over the following three decades. In addition Armstrong's armaments salesmen were quick to capitalise on international friction wherever it surfaced. Warships destined for navies throughout the world streamed from Elswick's slipways while the Walker yard concentrated on merchant ships. Net profits generally increased as the century proceeded, dividends never falling below 7.75 per cent. Between 1868, when co-operation between Armstrong and Mitchell began, and the outbreak of the First World War, some 127 warships had been built or were under construction.

In 1885, a factory was opened near Naples to make guns for the Italian Government, and in 1897, ten years after the death of its founder, Joseph Whitworth's Openshaw works were purchased outright by Armstrong, Mitchell & Co who had raised their capital to £3 million in 1895; the new company was styled Sir W G Armstrong, Whitworth & Co Ltd. International demand for armaments of all forms was growing rapidly; the British navy's estimates for new naval constructions for 1896-97 was £7 million and the merger offered additional capacity and expertise for the Tyneside firm. The merger also provided competition for the fast growing and, by the late nineteenth century, more innovative armaments firm developed by the Vickers brothers (qv) in Sheffield. In 1897 Vickers had purchased the Naval Construction & Armaments Co Ltd at Barrow, thus enabling the combined works to provide a vertically integrated production system for ships of war and their equipment. Moreover the directors of Vickers, each an expert in his own field, were able to weld together a flexible and dynamic organisation, in contrast to the situation at Elswick where, from the 1870s, Armstrong gradually relinquished his personal control, and perhaps lost interest in the business. Andrew Noble, brought into the Elswick Ordnance Company at the age of twenty-nine, assumed autocratic and conservative control of the Elswick works during the last quarter of the nineteenth century, and the degree of ossification which accompanied his rise to power was in fact largely his responsibility.

As the Elswick works grew from 1846 onwards, its workforce enjoyed a status unusual in engineering concerns: apprenticeships were much coveted but not easily won and an Armstrong training, in any facet of the firm's organisation, was seen as giving a secure future or a passport to higher things. The Elswick Mechanics Institute, founded ca 1852, and the school established in 1866 for the technical training of the children of his workforce reflected Armstrong's view that 'habits of industry' should be inculcated at an early age and maintained through life. Armstrong welcomed the educational movement that produced schools, mechanics' institutes and free libraries, and was pleased to have played his own small part in it, but in 1883 he argued that there might be some danger in 'men being over-educated for the humbler positions which must be filled by great numbers of the population ... school education for the mass of the people should not be prolonged beyond the limit prescribed by tenderness of age, and consequent unfitness of labour.' {'Social Matters' *Northern Union of Mechanics' Institutes* 1883}

It seems clear that the course and outcome of the 1871 engineers' strike in support of the nine-hour day added to Armstrong's sense of disillusionment, first felt in the 1860s when the British establishment declined to support the Elswick Ordnance Co. As the major industrialist on Tyneside, Armstrong was an essential target for the leaders of the nine-hour movement, still more so as Armstrong and his partners took the lead in forming an employers' association to promote employer cooperation in combating workers' militancy. In May 1871 about 2,700 men struck at Elswick and about 5,000 men at other Tyneside factories handed in their strike notices. It was not until October that the strike ended when the employers conceded the workers' demands. Throughout the strike the employers' association, strongly led by Armstrong, remained stubborn and inflexible, reflecting the pattern of non-co-operation which seems to have developed at the Elswick Works itself. It was Armstrong's faulty leadership of the employers that prolonged the strike and lost them whatever public support they might have had. Armstrong's consequent loss of public esteem strengthened his resolve to leave the general management of his works to the Nobles and, to a lesser extent, the Rendels. By 1900, Armstrong, Whitworth & Co employed some 25,000 workers on 300 acres of sites. Although the company had been well served by its workforce the Elswick Works lost their vigour during the twentieth century. New products were introduced, but rarely with success; only during war preparations did the Elswick Works flourish. Now (1982) it has been completely abandoned.

Throughout his life, Armstrong displayed a wide range of interests. From 1863 he transformed a barren and rocky moor above Rothbury into a sylvan park centred on his mansion 'Cragside', designed by Norman Shaw and incorporating glass designed by William Morris (qv) in the library's bay windows. Moreover, in his laboratory at Cragside Armstrong continued to experiment, but mainly with electricity, perhaps his real love. During early 1872 Armstrong made his first journey outside Europe, travelling overland through Europe to Egypt. He studied people and archaeology as he journeyed, and lectured about his travels on his return. In 1894 he purchased Bamburgh Castle (Northumberland) and its estate for £60,000, restoring the castle, according to one critic, with the 'acme of expenditure' but the 'nadir of intelligent achievement' {Pevsner (1957) 80}. At his death he owned over 10,000 acres in Northumberland.

Armstrong was a considerable benefactor to Newcastle upon Tyne, in particular in the foundation of its present university. He acquired much of Jesmond Dene, transformed it into a 93-acre park and presented it to the city together with the high level bridge that still crosses it. Never heavily involved in politics, he nevertheless stood for parliament as a Liberal Unionist candidate in 1886, but without success. He was raised to the peerage as Baron Armstrong of Cragside in 1887 and served on Northumberland County Council, 1889-92. He received numerous academic and scientific distinctions, being president of the Institution of Mechanical Engineers in 1861, 1862 and 1869, of the Institution of Civil Engineers in 1882, of the North of England Institution of Mining and Mechanical Engineers, 1872-75 and of the Literary and Philosophical Society of Newcastle, 1860-1900.

He married Margaret Ramshaw, daughter of a Newcastle engineer, in 1834. She was a forceful woman who supported her husband's endeavours. They had no children. Lord Armstrong died on 27 December 1900, leaving £1,400,682 gross.

STAFFORD M LINSLEY

Writings:

'On the Application of a Column of Water as a Motive Power for Driving Machinery' *Mechanics Magazine* 1840.

'On the Electricity of Effluent Steam' *Philosophical Magazine* 1841-43.

'On the Application of Water Pressure as a Motive Power' *Proceedings of the Institution of Civil Engineers* 9 (1850).

'On Concussion of Pump Valves' *ibid* 12 (1853).

On the Use of Steam Coals of the Hartley District in Marine Boilers (Newcastle upon Tyne: A Reid, 1858).

'Water-pressure Machinery' *Proceedings of the Institution of Mechanical Engineers* (1858).

letter on 'The Armstrong Guns' *Times* 25 Nov 1861.

'Inaugural address' *The Industrial Resources of the District of the Three Northern Rivers: the Tyne, Wear and Tees Including the Reports on the Local Manufacturers Read before the British Association in 1863* ed Sir G Armstrong, I Lowthian Bell, John Taylor and Dr Richardson (Newcastle upon Tyne: A Reid, 1864).

'A Three-powered Hydraulic Engine' (*ibid*).

'The Construction of Wrought-Iron Rifled Field Guns Adopted for Elongated Projectiles' (*ibid*).

'Artillery' *Proceedings of the Institution of Mechanical Engineers* (1869).

'The Coal Supply' (Newcastle upon Tyne: North of England Institute of Mining and Mechanical Engineers, 1873).

A Visit to Egypt in 1872 (Newcastle upon Tyne: J M Carr, 1874).

'History of Modern Developments of Water-pressure Machinery' *Proceedings of the Institution of Civil Engineers* 1 (1877).

Proposals for a System of Technical Education (Livery Companies Committee, 1878).

'National Defences' *Proceedings of the Institution of Civil Engineers* 1 (1882).

Utilisation of National Forces (York: British Association, 1883).

'Social Matters' *Northern Union of Mechanics' Institutes* (Newcastle upon Tyne: 1883).

'The Vague Cry for Technical Education' *Nineteenth Century* 24 (July 1888).

'The Cry for Useless Knowledge' *ibid* 24 (Nov 1888).

'The New Naval Programme' *ibid* 25 (1889).

'An Induction Machine' *Proceedings of the Royal Society* (1892).

'Recent Discussions on the Abolition of Patents' 1893. (in *DNB* but untraced).

'Novel Effects of Electric Discharge' *Proceedings of the Royal Society* (1893).

Electric Movement in Air and Water (Smith & Elder, 1897).

A Supplement to Lord Armstrong's Work on Electric Movement in Air and Water (Smith & Elder, 1899).

ARMSTRONG William George

Sources:

Unpublished

Papers privately held by S M Linsley, compiled by A R Fairbairn.

Tyne and Wear CRO, Armstrong papers.

PrC.

Published

Edward Allen et al, *The North-East Engineers' Strike of 1871* (Newcastle upon Tyne: Frank Graham, 1971).

C D P Benwell, *The Making of a Ruling Class* (Newcastle upon Tyne: C D P Benwell, 1978).

A Cochrane, *The Early History of Elswick* (Newcastle upon Tyne: Mawson Swan & Morgan Ltd, 1909).

DNB.

David Dougan, *The Great Gunmaker* (Newcastle upon Tyne: Frank Graham, 1971).

Norman McCord, *North East England* (Batsford, 1979).

Sir Nicholas B L Pevsner, *Buildings of England: Northumberland* (Harmondsworth: Penguin Books, 1957).

A Saunders and N J Smith, 'Hydraulic Cranes from Armstrong's Elswick Works 1846-1936, a Product Life Cycle in Capital Goods' *IMRA Journal* May 1970.

John D Scott, *Vickers: A History* (Weidenfeld & Nicholson, 1962).

Singer, *History of Technology* 4, 5.

Clive Trebilcock, *The Vickers Brothers* (Europa Publications, 1977).

WWW.

ASHFIELD, Lord Ashfield of Southwell
see STANLEY, Albert Henry

ASHTON, Lord Ashton
see WILLIAMSON, James

ASPINALL, John Audley Frederick

(1851-1937)

Railway engineer and manager

John A F Aspinall (courtesy of the National Railway Museum, York).

John Audley Frederick Aspinall was born in Liverpool on 25 August 1851. His father was John Bridge Aspinall QC. His great-grandfather and his uncle had both been mayors of Liverpool and his father was later Recorder there. Aspinall was educated at Beaumont College, Berkshire (1863-68), where his interest in engineering showed itself in the school workshops. In 1868, he entered the London & North Western Railway works at Crewe as a pupil of John Ramsbottom and later of F W Webb, who appointed him assistant manager of the steelworks. In 1875 he became manager of the Great Southern & Western Railway works near Dublin, and later the company's Locomotive Superintendent. In 1886, he returned to England as Chief Mechanical Engineer of the Lancashire & Yorkshire Railway, in succession to Barton Wright. The company was moving its works to a new site at Horwich. Aspinall successfully completed this project which eventually employed 11,000 men. He found 55 types of locomotive in use, but carried standardization practically to its limits by building large numbers of engines to a few simple designs, notably his 0-8-0 freight and his 2-4-2 tank engines. Starting in 1889, 667 locomotives were built at Horwich in ten years: enough to replace two-thirds of the stock he inherited. Aspinall was a pioneer of large locomotives on British railways. His 4-4-2, introduced in 1899, could haul 1,000 tons and greatly increased receipts per train mile.

In 1899, Aspinall succeeded J H Stafford as the Lancashire & Yorkshire's general manager, an exceptional promotion for a mechanical engineer. His regime was marked by growth and innovation. Before he took over, the L & Y was notorious for poor quality of service and a conservative attitude to passenger pricing. Aspinall reversed these trends. To compete with electric trams, he began electrifying suburban lines. The Liverpool-Southport line became, in 1904, one of the earliest such schemes in this country. He improved the company's docks at Goole and expanded shipping services to the continent and Ireland through the ports of Goole, Fleetwood and Liverpool. In 1914, the company owned more ships than any other British railway. Against fierce competition, Aspinall captured a large share of the expanding coal traffic, notably by gaining control of the Dearne Valley Railway of which he became managing director. On retiring from the post of general manager in 1919, Aspinall joined the board but resigned in October of that year on his appointment as Consulting Mechanical Engineer to the newly-established Ministry of Transport. He retained that post until 1927. The L & Y had a continuing presence in the LMS after grouping in 1923, largely because of its revival under Aspinall.

Aspinall served as chairman of the General Managers' Conference of the Railway Clearing House. He was a member of the Vice-regal

Commission on Irish Railways, 1906-1910, and during the First World War, sat on the Railway Executive Committee. He became Honorary Associate Professor of Railway Engineering in the University of Liverpool in 1902, and was chairman of the Faculty of Engineering, 1908-1915. In that capacity, he raised funds for the erection of an engineering laboratory. Outstanding among many professional honours were his presidencies of the Institutions of Mechanical Engineers, 1909-10, and Civil Engineers, 1919. He was knighted in 1917.

Aspinall was a Roman Catholic. In 1874, he married Gertrude Helen, daughter of F B Schrader, a leather factor of Liverpool. They had one son and two daughters. Lady Aspinall died in 1921. Sir John died on 19 January 1937, leaving an estate valued at £121,784 gross.

HENRY W PARRIS

Writings:

'Experiments on the Tractive Resistance of Loaded Railway-Wagons' *Proceedings of the Institution of Civil Engineers* 1904.

Express locomotives ... Report by Mr Aspinall (Brussels: P Weissenbruch, 1895) Reprinted from *Bulletin of the International Railway Congress* (1895).

'Train-Resistance' *Proceedings of the Institution of Civil Engineers* 1902.

Sources:

Unpublished

Lancashire RO, MS DDX 87.

PrC; Will.

Published

H O Aspinall, *The Aspinwall & Aspinall Families of Lancashire AD 1189-1923* (Exeter: W Pollard & Co, 1923).

Bradford Observer 22 Sept 1892.

Cassier's Magazine 15 (1898-9).

Cuthbert H Ellis, *20 Locomotive Men* (Ian Allan, 1958).

Engineer 22 Jan 1937.

Gore's Liverpool Directory 1853.

John Marshall, *The Lancashire & Yorkshire Railway* (3 vols, Newton Abbot: David & Charles, 1969-72).

—, *A Biographical Dictionary of Railway Engineers* (Newton Abbot: David & Charles, 1978).

Eric Mason, *Lancashire & Yorkshire Railway in the 20th Century* (2nd ed, Allan, 1975).

Modern Transport 23 Jan 1937.

Proceedings of the Institution of Mechanical Engineers 15 (1937).

Railway Gazette 22 Jan 1937.

Times 20, 23, 26 Jan 1937.

WWW.

ATHERTON, Giles

(1852-1931)

Hat manufacturer

Giles Atherton was born in Stockport on 31 January 1852, the son of James A Atherton, a bobbin turner and his wife Elizabeth née McKinsey, of Longshut Lane. The Athertons had for centuries lived in Bowden and were a well-established artisan family in Stockport by the nineteenth century. Atherton served an apprenticeship to the hatting trade with two leading firms: S R Carrington & Sons and Christy & Co. After completing his apprenticeship, he started out on his own account as a hat-body maker in the Carrs, Waterloo, Stockport. Business prospered, and in 1879 Atherton moved to larger premises at Virginia Mills, Higher Hillgate, Stockport. He continued as a hat-body maker, but he soon diversified his activities to include electrical engineering and the manufacture of machinery for hat-making. In 1900 Atherton moved his hat manufacturing business onto an international scale by amalgamating with John Turner of Denton, who had two branches in the United States at Newark, New Jersey and Danbury, Connecticut. The Turner family managed the Denton and American branches, while Atherton and his sons, W H and G Dilke Atherton, managed the Stockport business. During the First World War Turner, Atherton & Co was controlled by the Ministry of Munitions and produced 5,000 15 pounder shells per week. After 1918, the firm soon returned to peacetime production levels. Atherton acquired a wide reputation in the hatting trade: probably 85-90 per cent of the machine-made hats produced in the 1930s were manufactured on machines built by his firm, and many of these machines were invented by Atherton himself.

Atherton also became closely involved with the other major industrial occupation in Stockport at the end of the nineteenth century: cotton spinning. He was the founder and chairman of the Stockport Ring Spinning Co in 1893. This company employed 500 people by 1896. He was widely respected as a member of the Manchester Royal Exchange. In the 1920s he strove hard to counteract the effects of industrial depression: he wanted to see the production and selling price of yarns strictly controlled. Just before his death, he was delighted to hear that his Number Three Mill was on full-time again.

As a respected business man, Atherton became chairman or a director of several other companies. He was chairman of the Egyptian Cotton Mills at Boulac, Cairo, and of Showell's Stockport Brewery. He was director of Dean & Co (Stockport) Ltd, the Stockport Borough Carriage Co and the Hazel Grove Rubber Co.

Atherton became closely involved in municipal politics: a Liberal, he was a Stockport councillor, 1887-94, alderman, 1895-1904 and served as mayor of Stockport, 1896-98 and 1903-4. As mayor, he campaigned hard for the building of a new town hall, and in October 1904, he laid its foundation stone. In his earlier mayoralty, in 1898, he had laid the foundation stone for the new north wing of Stockport Infirmary, to commemorate Queen Victoria's Diamond Jubilee. Whilst on the Council, he spoke forcibly in favour of modernisation: for the electric lighting of the town (achieved in 1900); the electrification of the tramways (achieved in 1901: he was the first chairman of the Electricity committee); the purchase of the waterworks from a private company (1899); the demolition of insanitary dwellings; the creation of parks and open spaces; and the installation of a fire alarm system in Stockport.

Atherton had many other interests, besides business and politics. He was a staunch Unitarian, a borough JP from 1900, a life governor of Stockport Infirmary, a president of Stockport Cricket Club and a vice-president of Stockport Amateur Operatic Society. He travelled widely in Europe, America and India, and in 1889, after his first wife's death, he made a tour of the world, visiting Australia, New Zealand, San Francisco and New York. He died on 9 October 1931, leaving £198,012 gross. He was survived by his sons, and his second wife, Mary, the daughter of John Marshall (a former alderman of Stockport), whom he had married in 1890. W H Atherton succeeded his father as chairman of his companies.

KATHERINE A FRICKER

Writings:

Two Voyages. Constantinople and the East. Round the World (Stockport: Cheshire County News Co, 1890)

Sources:

Unpublished

Stockport Borough Library, Stockport, Hurst MSS 2.

BCe.

PrC.

Published

William Astle, *History of Stockport* (Stockport: Swain & Co Ltd, 1922).

Cheshire Year Book 1897.

Kelly's Directory 1902.

Stockport Advertiser 16 Oct 1931.

Stockport Advertiser Supplement 1932.

Stockport Express Annual 1923.

AUSTIN, Herbert

Lord Austin of Longbridge
(1866-1941)

Motor car manufacturer

Herbert Austin (courtesy of the British Motor Industry Heritage Trust (BL Heritage Ltd)).

Herbert Austin was born at Little Missenden in Buckinghamshire on 8 November 1866, the second son of Giles Stevens Austin, a farm bailiff who before long moved to Yorkshire to become bailiff on Earl Fitzwilliam's Wentworth estate, and his wife Clara Jane née Simpson, daughter of a Rotherhithe Customs officer. Here Austin attended the village school before proceeding to Rotherham Grammar School, followed by two years at Brampton Commercial College in preparation for a career as an architect. After a shortlived apprenticeship with his paternal uncle (architect to Earl Fitzwilliam), in 1883 Austin turned his back on architecture in preference for engineering. A visiting Australian uncle persuaded Austin to travel back with him to Melbourne, where he was manager of Richard Parks & Co, an engineering firm. Under that uncle's tutelage, the young man's engineering apprenticeship began. Two years later he trained as a mechanic at Longlands' Foundry, at the same time attending evening classes at the Hotham Arts School in Melbourne, where at the age of twenty-one he became a prize-winning student. His design and estimates for a swing bridge over the Yarra River received special commendation though they failed to win the award.

In 1887 he took up his first appointment as manager of a small engineering firm which among its activities included the supply of parts for machinery. This brought him into contact with Frederick York Wolseley, a Dublin emigrant turned sheep farmer, and before long Austin had patented improvements to the sheep shearing machinery which was Wolseley's main item of production. In 1893 Wolseley purchased Austin's patents in return for shares in his company, and in the same year Austin agreed to manage the Wolseley Sheep Shearing Machine Co which had in the meantime removed its operations to England. In 1895, on Austin's initiative, the company purchased the Sydney Works in Alma Street in Aston, Birmingham, for the purpose of manufacturing rather than assembling the sheep shearing machinery on which the company's reputation - by then in decline - was based. Austin widened the range of products to include machine tools and bicycle parts, undertaking various other classes of engineering work, too. In search of new engineering developments during the 1890s, his interests turned to the internal combustion engine and its application to wheeled vehicles.

His first motorized vehicle, a two horsepower machine, was probably built in 1895, and resembled the small wheeled Bollée which he saw in Paris in 1894. His second vehicle, which was completed in 1896, was built with the support of the Wolseley directors who agreed to invest in this venture under Austin's personal supervision. Two years later the Wolseley Autocar number 1 incorporated several Austin patents taken out in conjunction with the WSSM Co, while the third Wolseley car, Austin's first four-wheeled voiturette of entirely British construction, won the *Daily Mail*'s first prize in the Auto Clubs' 1,000 Mile Trial held in 1900. Austin's reputation as a leading innovator was thus established.

Nonetheless, he received no further financial support from Wolseley for developing the commercial production of motor cars. Following disagreement with WSSM Co, Austin secured backing from Sir Hiram Maxim of Vickers, who bought the relevant car and machine tool patents from the WSSM Co (on whose board Austin remained for thirty-two years). In 1901 they formed the Wolseley Tool & Motor Co Ltd, with a capital of £40,000 and Austin became the managing director. However, the Vickers' connection was shortlived, for disagreement over engine design and manufacturing losses led to Austin's departure to form his own company in 1905. Based at Longbridge in a disused printing works, the Austin Motor Co produced its first motor car within one year, and in 1914, when annual production reached 1,500, the firm became a public company, with Austin as the major shareholder. The private Austin Co was sold to the new Austin Motor Co (1914) Ltd, which had a nominal capital of £650,000, for £399,993.

Austin continued to live up to his reputation as a distinguished inventor, and it was inventive genius rather than managerial competence which enabled the company to survive the acute post-war financial crisis that forced the company into the hands of the Official Receiver in 1921. In the reconstruction which followed, the key managerial functions of finance, production and organisation were transferred to men specially recruited for the task on the insistence of the company's creditors. Austin remained chairman of the company but the death of his son in 1915 seems to have destroyed his interest in the future of the institution he had created, invention and design absorbing most of his energies after reconstruction. The autocratic style of management exercised before the company was reorganised in 1921-22 was impossible thereafter due to the strength of the debenture holders, and in particular the Midland Bank.

The 1922 Austin Seven (courtesy of the British Motor Industry Heritage Trust (BL Heritage Ltd)).

This was so even though Austin continued to own at least one-fifth of all voting shares in the company. On those occasions when he pronounced upon labour relations his hostility towards trade unions was barely concealed, which, consistent with the company's policy, earned for the Longbridge management a reputation among trade unions and the Engineering Employers' Federation as unhelpful and uncooperative. Austin's post-war commercial achievements depended upon his design of the Austin Twelve, Seven and Ten, models which underpinned the company's revival in the 1920s and 1930s and enabled the firm to become one of the Big Three motor manufacturers in Britain. From £425,000 in 1913 the company's turnover grew to £1.6 million in 1922 and then £10.9 million in 1939. Net trading profits in the 1920s and 1930s varied between 8 and 15 per cent. The firm employed 8,000 in 1922 and 20,000 by 1939; its output rose from 46,562 vehicles of all types in 1929 to 76,482 (excluding commercial vehicles) in 1939.

Austin's professional standing was acknowledged by his election as president of the Institute of British Carriage and Automobile Manufacturers, of the Institution of Automobile Engineers (1930), and of the Institution of Production Engineers. He was also elected to honorary life membership of the Institution of Mechanical Engineers and of the Institute of British Foundrymen; and became president of the Society of Motor Manufacturers and Traders (1934) and of the Shadow Aero Engine Committee.

In politics he was a Conservative, serving as MP for the King's Norton division of Birmingham between 1918 and 1924 when he was an almost silent advocate of the need for 'businessmen's government'. Religion, defined in broadest terms, seems to have played little part in his life until after his son's death, when he embraced the philosophy of Pelmanism. His charitable donations included £250,000 to the Cavendish Laboratory in Cambridge in 1932. The knighthood conferred upon him in 1917 became a baronetcy in 1934 and a peerage in 1936.

He married in 1887 Helen Dron, daughter of an Australian merchant, James Dron; they had two daughters and a son. At his death on 23 May 1941 at the age of seventy-four Lord Austin of Longbridge, engaged still in designing Austin motor cars, left £509,712 gross. His great rival Lord Nuffield (qv), whose wealth much exceeded that, regarded him as one of the best motor engineers in the world.

ROY CHURCH

Writings:

'The Future Trend of Automobile Design' *Institution of Automobile Engineers*, Presidential address, 1930.

Sources:

Unpublished

BCe.

PrC.

Published

Roy A Church, *Herbert Austin: the British Motor Car Industry to 1941* (Europa Publications, 1979).

DNB.

WWMP.

WWW.

AVEBURY, 1st Lord Avebury
see LUBBOCK, John

Thomas L Aveling (courtesy of the Institute of Agricultural History, Reading).

AVELING, Thomas Lake

(1856-1931)

Steam roller and agricultural machinery manufacturer

Thomas Lake Aveling was born at Ruckinge, near Ashford, Kent on 25 August, 1856, the son of Thomas Aveling and his wife Sarah née Lake. His father went into business in Ruckinge in 1850 as a farmer and agricultural contractor; his interests eventually turned toward machinery production and in 1856 he purchased a small millwrighting shop and foundry in Rochester. Aveling Sr soon developed a fascination for self-moving steam engines, especially traction engines of which he was a pioneer designer and builder. He went into partnership with Richard Thomas Porter in 1862, the concern trading as Aveling & Porter, and in 1865 the firm produced the first ever steam roller.

Young Thomas Aveling grew up in this atmosphere of technical innovation and after leaving school, he was duly educated in all the departments of the firm, developing a particular interest in road roller manufacture. In 1881 T L Aveling was given control of the firm by his father, who died the following year. When the concern became a private limited company in 1895, styled Aveling & Porter Ltd, Aveling became managing director and chairman.

Aveling's particular contribution to the firm was to develop and maintain their specialisation in steam roller production. Such was his success that Aveling & Porter became the premier UK steam roller makers, in much the same way that the business of Robert Fowler (qv) dominated UK ploughing engine production. Aveling & Porter accounted for about 70 per cent of the total UK steam roller market during 1880-1922. A thriving export market was also cultivated and new improvements introduced, such as compounding in the 1880s and tandem rollers in 1902. Aveling was also aware of the value of sub-contracting the production of items of equipment involving different manufacturing processes from engine building. Aveling thrashing machines were produced complete with Aveling nameplates by Nalder & Nalder Ltd at Challow, Berkshire. During the First World War Aveling reorganised the Rochester works to make use of jigs for the manufacture of standardised components. The firm's principal weakness lay in Aveling's persisting commitment to steam engineering. This meant that the major development of the motor roller was carried out by one of the firm's competitors, Barford & Perkins Ltd of Peterborough, later headed by Edward Barford (qv).

Aveling was the architect of Agricultural & General Engineers Ltd (AGE), a merger in the agricultural machinery industry in which members of the Aveling and Garrett families were prominent. AGE was registered on 4 June, 1919, with an authorised capital of £8 million, as a holding company that eventually comprised 14 different concerns. Its object was to form an alliance against American competition, by rationalising production and centralising purchasing and sales. The reality was quite different. The firms in AGE were an extraordinary mixture, many suffering from a decline of the family inspiration that had originally created them and many also still fatally geared towards steam engineering. More progressively minded concerns, such as Ransomes and Rustons wisely kept clear. Individual company interests soon became apparent and plans for centralised buying and sales were abandoned. The larger concerns, such as Aveling & Porter, also tended to benefit to the detriment of the weaker members, which may well have been T L Aveling's intention.

It is uncertain if Aveling foresaw all these problems in 1919. The first head of the combine was Archibald W Machonochie, a neighbour of Aveling in Kent who began in business as a jam and pickle manufacturer and a director of the Great Eastern Railway. He resigned in 1921 when the market for AGE shares was still favourable. His replacement was the enigmatic figure of Gwilym E Rowland, who maintained his position by a policy of divide and rule among the constituent firms. By 1928, both AGE and Aveling & Porter Ltd were in a very unhealthy state. Much of the 20 acre Rochester site was idle with the remainder on short time working. In the same year Aveling & Porter Ltd formed a joint roller marketing company with their erstwhile competitors and fellow AGE members, Barford & Perkins Ltd. Talks eventually followed on rationalising and centralising their joint production, the very objectives AGE had been set up to achieve back in 1919. T L Aveling retired from the Rochester firm in 1928. He was spared the sight of the collapse of AGE in 1932 which his family firm only survived by a merger with Barford & Perkins, ironically financed by three firms, Ransomes, Rustons and Listers, all of whom had kept clear of the ill-fated combine.

Aveling maintained a dutiful public life. He was a council member and president of the Smithfield Club, a president of the Agricultural Engineers Association and a council member and finance steward of the Royal Agricultural Society of England. Like many such firms, Aveling & Porter Ltd dominated the livelihood of the town where they were located, employing 1,500 men at their peak. Aveling, as a result, found himself involved in local affairs, such as the Medway Conservancy Board, though he did refuse an offer of the mayoralty of Rochester. His principal efforts were directed towards the firm and reports describe him as hard working and energetic, though some of his competitors thought him a sharp practitioner.

Aveling married Rosita Marion Porter in 1890, a niece of Richard Thomas Porter. She committed suicide in 1904 though she did bear him two sons, Thomas and Arthur. Aveling himself died on 5 October 1931 while addressing a meeting of a local nursing association. He left an estate of £65,677 gross.

DAVID C PHILLIPS

Sources:

Unpublished

BCe.

PrC.

Published

Chatham News 9 Oct 1931.

The Engineer 152 (1931).

The Implement and Machinery Review 57 (1931-32).

Robert A Whitehead, *A Century of Steam Rollers* (Allan, 1975).

—, *Garrett 200* (1978).

AVERY, Thomas

(1813-1894)

Scale manufacturer

Thomas Avery was born in Birmingham in 1813, the second son of William Avery, scale-maker, and his wife Lucy. Privately educated, he entered the family business of W & T Avery, at 12 Digbeth, in 1828 as a traveller. In 1843, on the death of their father, Thomas and his brother William became sole partners and joint managers of the business.

Clearly Thomas Avery played a crucial part in expanding the firm which by 1865 had become one of the largest scale-making enterprises in England, employing nearly 400 men, a threefold increase over 1843. While William supervised manufacturing, Thomas as commercial manager promoted sales and travelled widely. Particular lines, such as counter machines, beam scales and platform weighers, were promoted vigorously through participation in trade exhibitions, and likely patents were quickly purchased. To the existing premises in Digbeth and Moat Lane, Averys added the firm of Thomas Bourne, purchased in 1848, and, in the 1850s, land and buildings in Mill Lane.

In return the firm provided a good income. Thomas's total earnings in the fourteen years before 1864 were over £57,000 and he withdrew his accumulating capital at quite a fast rate, at one point up to £14,000 in a year. Some at least of this was for land purchase. This deviation from an entrepreneurial pattern of profits ploughed back is perhaps to be explained by domestic circumstances. He remained childless and thus had little incentive to check present consumption for future security.

A Conservative in politics, but of a liberal type, Avery entered Birmingham Town Council in 1862, finding an outlet for what was called 'his unconscious and uncontrollable verbosity' {*Town Crier* May 1886}. He gained a reputation opposing the ruling 'economist' group, and campaigned for improved public health facilities, a cause which triumphed in 1875 with his appointment as chairman of the water committee during the mayoralty of Joseph Chamberlain (qv). Mayor of Birmingham in 1866-68 and again in 1881-82, he finally resigned from the council only in 1892.

Avery's evident intention, confirmed in 1864 when he dissolved the partnership and withdrew his remaining capital, was to pursue politics exclusively, but William Avery's death in 1874 recalled him as executor and effective manager until 1881. These were years of increasing competition and shrinking profits and it was Avery, the sole executor with direct experience, who held the business together. Informal agreements with Pooleys, the major domestic rivals, limited competition in the 1870s, so Avery vigorously pursued sales by establishing branches (the first being London, in 1876), and winning Empire markets by a mixture of direct selling and local agents. Australia, India and South Africa were the chief of these, but Thomas seems to have planned the later continental and South American agencies. By the time of his second retirement the firm probably provided work for well over 700.

Avery was prominent in Birmingham public life as a magistrate and indefatigable committee member until his death on 17 February 1894; he left £230,723 gross.

L J JONES

Writings:

An Examination of the Scheme of Mr Alderman Osborne for the Removal of the Cattle Market from Smithfield (Birmingham: M Billing, Son & Co, 1865).

On the Municipal Expenditure of the Borough of Birmingham (Birmingham, 1865).

The Corporation of Birmingham and the Water Supply of the Town. A Statement Addressed to the Members of the Town Council (Birmingham: 'Journal' Printing Offices, 1869).

Birmingham Water Undertaking (Birmingham, 1882).

(with William Avery) *Suggestions for the Amendment of the Law Relating to Weights and Measures* (Birmingham: W & T Avery, 1888).

Sources:

Unpublished

Avery's Ltd, Smethwick, company archives.

PrC.

Barbara M D Smith, 'History of W & T Avery, 1736-1939' (copy in Birmingham Reference Library, Local Studies Department).

G H Osborne, 'Collection of Newspaper Cuttings' 2 (1881-95) (Copy in Birmingham Reference Library).

Published

W & T Avery, *Weighing throughout the Ages: A History of Scales from 2000 BC to the Present Time* (Birmingham: W & T Avery, 1928).

E T Leigh Bennett, *Weighing the World* (Birmingham: W & T Avery, 1930).

Birmingham Daily Post 24 Feb 1894.

Birmingham Faces and Places 1888.

L H Broadbent, *The Avery Business 1730-1918* (Birmingham: W & T Avery, 1949).

Edgbastonia 3 (1883).

Morning News 15 Nov 1875.

A Short History of the Progress of Averys (Birmingham: W & T Avery, 1907).

Town Crier May 1886.

B

BADER, Ernest

(1890-1982)

Plastics manufacturer and pioneer of industrial democracy

Ernest Bader was born at Regensdorf near Zurich on 24 November 1890, the youngest of the 13 children of a Protestant (Reformed) Swiss farmer, Gottlieb Bader and his wife, Barbara née Meier. He formed indelible impressions during his teenage years from his father who separated from the family for two years and then, burdened by bank debts, sought occasional relief in drinking.

BADER Ernest

Ernest Bader (courtesy of Scott Bader Co Ltd).

Ernest left school at the age of twelve and, after several low-paid clerical jobs, became stock clerk in a silk factory. Following compulsory military service, he emigrated in 1912 to England where two of his elder sisters, already in north London, found him lodgings with a widow in Ferme Park. Within two months he secured a clerical job with a silk merchant at 18s a week. Through a deepening friendship with his landlady's daughter, Annie Eliza Dora Scott (1884-1979), he was drawn into a local Baptist church (though he never became a member) and, seeking with his fiancée new truth, developed an interest in the health and breath culture of Mazdaznan.

The outbreak of war in 1914 took him back to Switzerland, but starting to think on his own he became a pacifist, returned to England and with Dora joined the newly-formed Fellowship of Reconciliation. He and Dora were married in 1915 and Ernest took a job with the Belgian Bank in London. They moved in 1917 to Stanford-le-Hope, Essex, to be in the vicinity of the community formed for conscientious objectors by Reginald Sorensen (1891-1971), the Unitarian and Christian Socialist. Here the Baders stayed until 1940.

In 1920 Ernest rented an office in Finsbury Square, London, and set himself up as an import agent, relying on his linguistic skills, his Swiss connections and his very persuasive personality. A partnership with a fellow Swiss, Otto Marti, provided further capital and they secured the agencies for celluloid sheet (later made into penny windmills), rod and tube and for low-viscosity nitrocellulose, a quick-drying lacquer giving a better gloss to linseed oil in car paint. In 1923 they formed a company, Scott Bader & Co Ltd, and recruited one or two staff including Sarah Gaetsky, a hard-working young saleswoman.

Marti parted from Bader in 1930 but reappeared on the board in 1932 when Ernest started to manufacture pigment pastes in factory premises at Stratford, East London. The manufacturing side grew more rapidly after Bader recruited a professional chemist, Courtney Bryson, in 1938, and by the outbreak of war the firm had a staff of over 40. By 1939 its turnover was £215,000, with an after tax profit of £3,651, compared to its turnover of £4,250 and an after tax profit of £394 in 1923.

The bombing of London prompted Bader to move his factory and office into the country, to Wollaston Hall, near Wellingborough, in 1940. During the war the company expanded from 40 to 70 employees and Ernest, still a pacifist, found himself reluctantly and indirectly supporting the war effort with his paint resins. Foundations for future growth were laid by John Hand, an industrial chemist, whom Ernest recruited from a rival firm, headed by John Coates (qv). Hand visited New York in 1945 and returned with licences for Scott Bader to manufacture four products which gave the company an assured corner of the paint and plastics markets: polyester resins (from Marco), paint driers (from Nuodex), polymer emulsions (from Polyco) and alkyd resins (from Syntex).

A new factory was constructed in what had been the home park at Wollaston Hall. Rapid expansion in 1948 brought personnel problems and before the factory's completion a small group of career chemists, apprised of the American formulations, absconded to South Africa to set up a rival operation. Overstretched by investment in new plant, which took months to get into production, Bader was at his most 'autocratic, dictatorial and paternalistic' {Hoe (1978) 102}; to reduce his overheads he peremptorily sacked half a dozen employees and precipitated a strike in November 1948 which brought in the Chemical Workers' Union. Eventually the dispute was settled, and because it paid relatively high wages, and more importantly developed on a common ownership basis, the company was free of labour disputes thereafter. But Ernest Bader, now a Quaker, was strengthened in his belief that there had to be an alternative to confrontation between management and workers.

Inspired by Ernst Abbé (founder of Zeiss), George Goyder, Wilfred Wellock and Harold Farmer, all exponents of worker participation in firm ownership, Bader instructed his legal advisers to draft a scheme for his ideas. Their efforts produced the Scott Bader Commonwealth Ltd (SBC), a company limited by guarantee, having no share capital and registered in 1951. The share capital of Scott Bader Ltd, the operating company, was increased (by capitalising reserves) from £10,000 to £50,000, of which 90 per cent was in the name of the SBC which, as a registered charity, could decide both the size and charitable directions of profit distribution. After 1953 up to a maximum of 40 per cent of Scott Bader Ltd's profits could be equally divided between staff bonus (including production bonus) and charity (largely for the Third World), with the remaining 60 per cent of profits kept for taxation and reserves. In practice, the ploughback was normally 80 per cent. Originally, two-thirds of an individual's bonus was based on his wage or salary and one-third on merit (as rated by superiors). This only lasted two to three years, members deciding merit judgement was impossible: it was agreed that everyone should have an equal bonus, to reflect the egalitarian philosophy of the Commonwealth.

The SBC had 145 members (about three employees were not accepted by their fellow members) and in theory it was run by a board of 14 individuals: nine elected by the SBC members, the treasurer and the secretary of the operating company, one outsider and Ernest Bader. In practice Ernest dominated the scheme by sheer force of personality and retention of the majority of founders' shares by which alone the articles of association might be changed or the board restructured or dismissed. He saw himself as guide, teacher, disciplinarian and ideas man and with persuasive passion imposed his views on issues like alcohol, gambling, war (all of which he fiercely opposed) in quarrelsome board meetings. Not until his son Godric (who joined the company as a chemist in 1948) became managing director in 1957 and then chairman in 1966 did the paternalist atmosphere change.

Ernest, though not unhappy about giving up his shares, flatly rejected at this time the prospect of employees electing directors. He finally relinquished his founders' shares in 1963, following an action research study of the company conducted by an American Quaker and sociology professor, Fred Blum, assisted by Roger Hadley. This was followed by a small-group re-education programme for managers and workers. In the revisions of 1963 power passed from Ernest Bader to the members of the Commonwealth, but trustees were appointed by members as guardians of the movement towards a self-governing community of work. The seven trustees, including three outsiders (Bob Edwards, secretary of the Chemical Workers' Union and later MP; Dr, later Baroness, Mary Stocks; and Dr Fritz Schumacher) played an important role in restraining Ernest and preserving commitment to an ideal. The nature of the latter was made explicit in the revised articles of association in 1963:

> The Commonwealth is an expression of the age-old ideal taught by all great religions of a brotherhood of all men ... It is seeking through, and beyond, all material ends to foster conditions for the growth of personality truly related to God and man. Power should come from within the person and the community, and be made responsible to those it affects. The ultimate criterion in the organization of work should be human dignity and service to others instead of solely economic performance. We feel mutual responsibility must permeate the whole community of work and be upheld by democratic participation and the principle of trusteeship.

Between 1951 and 1966 when Ernest Bader retired, Scott Bader Co Ltd's turnover rose from £624,000 to £8,341,000; profits from £73,000 to £170,300; and employees from 161 to 323.

In the 1960s and 1970s, Bader took up a number of other causes: world government; the peace movement (he joined CND); training programmes at Wollaston for people from developing countries; Schumacher's Intermediate Technology Development Group; and another small firm, Trylon, dedicated to developing resins for artists' materials for use in school and in small-scale industries. With Dora he went on several world trips to India and Africa, still questing for new solutions to the warring nature of mankind, and to the paradox of his own personality: a man who sought freedom in industry and society but who felt the greatest impulsions to master others. For his work in developing new models of co-operative decision making, Birmingham University awarded him an honorary Doctorate of Social Sciences in 1978.

The Baders adopted three children and had two of their own, Godric (b 1923) and Erica (1927-48). Ernest Bader died on 5 February 1982 leaving an estate valued at ca £10,000 gross.

DAVID J JEREMY

Writings:

A Call for Ownership in Industry as an Alternative to a War-Based Society and to Communism (Wellingborough: Scott Bader Ltd, 1951).

(with Godric Bader) *From Profit Sharing to Common Ownership. A Practical Example of Growth from the Old to the New* (Wellingborough: Scott Bader Commonwealth Ltd, 1956-57).

'From Profit Sharing to Common Ownership: An Experiment in Industrial Democracy' *Journal of Current Social Issues* 10 (1971-72).

Economics and the Living Spirit or, What Can We Learn from the Scott Bader Commonwealth (Rushden, Northants: Stanley C Hunt (Printers) Ltd, 1975).

Sources:

Unpublished

C Reg: Scott Bader Co Ltd (189,141). Scott Bader Commonwealth Ltd (496,082).

MCe.

Interview with Godric Bader, 19 Apr 1982 and subsequent telephone conversations.

Roger Hadley, 'Participation and Common Ownership. A Study in Employee Participation in a Common Ownership Firm' (London PhD, 1971).

Published

Fred H Blum, *Work and Community: The Scott Bader Commonwealth and the Quest for a New Social Order* (Routledge & Kegan Paul, 1968).

—, *Ethics of Industrial Man. An Empirical Study of Religious Awareness and the Experience of Society* (Routledge & Kegan Paul, 1970).

George Goyder, *The Responsible Worker* (Hutchinson, 1975).

Susanna Hoe, *The Man Who Gave His Company Away. A Biography of Ernest Bader, Founder of the Scott Bader Commonwealth* (Heinemann, 1978).

Brian Parkyn, *Democracy, Accountability and Participation in Industry* (Bradford: MCB General Management Ltd, 1979).

The Reactor Mar 1982 (memorial issue).

Ernest F Schumacher, *Small Is Beautiful* (Blond & Briggs, 1973).

Scott Bader, *A Kind of Alchemy* (Wellingborough: Scott Bader Ltd, 1973).

Times 8 Feb 1982.

Folkert Wilken, *The Liberation of Work* (Routledge & Kegal Paul, 1969).

—, *The Liberation of Capital* (George Allen & Unwin, 1982).

BAGNALL, John Nock

(1826-1884)

Ironmaster

John Nock Bagnall was born in West Bromwich on 30 May 1826, the eldest son of the ironmaster Thomas Bagnall (1799-1885) and Mary Keen Bagnall (d 1831), daughter of the local businessman John Nock. Educated in the classics by local clergymen, J N Bagnall completed his studies in Germany. After returning to the Black Country in 1844 to enter the family business, Bagnall pursued interests in astronomy and, especially, in industrial and local history. He reprinted a seventeenth-century metallurgical tract and wrote a carefully researched history of Wednesbury. A teetotaller as well as a lover of music, Bagnall combined 'great tenacity' in his opinions with a 'genial and frank bearing' {Willett (1885) 10}.

Like many other major Black Country businesses, the family firm had developed rapidly from modest origins in the late eighteenth century when John Nock Bagnall's grandfather John (d 1829), the son of a mining surveyor, founded the business. By the 1850s, the peak decade of the region's iron industry, John Bagnall & Sons was among the largest businesses in the Black Country. The family had several pits, six blast furnaces and three finished ironworks (with 85 puddling furnaces and 20 mills and forges) in the eastern half of the district. As in other local firms, this plant often did not work at capacity; yet the output of the Bagnalls' business was among the highest in the region. In addition, as one of the Black Country's influential 'marked bar' houses, Bagnall iron had a high reputation at home and abroad: 'no name has stood higher in the commercial world' {*Wolverhampton Chronicle*, 11 Mar 1863}. Consequently the firm's partners were significant, though never preeminent, figures in the local iron trade's efforts to regulate production, prices and wages. Moreover, by the early 1870s 'several colossal fortunes had been amassed, and ... nearly every branch of the family (either directly or indirectly) had been enriched' {Hackwood (1891) ch 46}. William and James Bagnall left personal estates approximately valued at £140,000 (1863, revised 1870) and £250,000 (1872) respectively. Their brother Thomas (£5,900) and nephew John Nock (£5,671) compensated for relatively small amounts with valuable real estate.

The firm's prospects worsened as near exhaustion of local raw materials, along with competition from regions enjoying lower transport costs and more advanced methods, began to afflict the Black Country iron industry. The Bagnalls, however, escaped the worst effects of this decline by disposing of the business in 1873 to a limited company, a device just becoming fashionable in the West Midlands. John Bagnall & Sons Ltd, launched by an unscrupulous promoter during a final brief boom in the district's iron trade, received an enthusiastic response from local applicants for shares. Yet the new firm soon had to write off much of its capital and contract its operations. J N Bagnall's cousin William Gordon Bagnall served as chairman of the stabilized limited company for a time, but by the early twentieth century even this final link with the family had been broken.

John Nock Bagnall became a principal partner in the firm during its mid-nineteenth century peak. Between 1845 and 1857 he managed the family's Capponfield Furnaces near Bilston. The young Bagnall applied himself enthusiastically to all aspects of the operation, and the Capponfield enterprise apparently proved at least as profitable as the business generally.

Bagnall's most distinctive contribution to the firm lay in industrial relations, an important aspect of a business which employed more than 2,000 men in its various plants and pits. Firmly convinced of the 'responsibility of capital in reference to labour', and desiring to bring together the rich and the poor {Willett (1885) 11, 51}, John Nock was the most enthusiastic advocate of paternalistic provision for employees in a firm which from the 1840s led the way in this field among Black Country businesses. Bagnall campaigned vigorously against truck, and he backed the family's early abandonment of Sunday work. In addition, he played a key role both in the firm's establishment of schools and in its provision of Anglican chapels attached to the principal works. Bagnall formed a sick and accident club, supplied model cottages for leading workmen and organised recreational facilities such as playing fields, reading rooms and brass bands. He was closely involved in these projects: Bagnall ran a magic lantern show to lure men to the night school, for example, and conversed with employees in dialect on Christian name terms.

Such benevolence proved no panacea for labour troubles. For instance, in 1858 local organisers pointed out to strikers that the firm cut wages along with other employers. Yet the Bagnalls' well-supported facilities for workers apparently assisted them in recruiting high quality workmen. Also, the family's labour practices helped to reinforce the advantages that Black Country employers enjoyed in dealing with early attempts at trade unionism. Although compulsion as well as persuasion was involved, the miners employed by the Bagnalls and other paternalistic employers were among the first to return to work in the 1864 coal strike, for example. In addition, the firm's efforts convinced middle-class opinion in the Black Country that 'Messrs Bagnall ... do not merely regard their workmen as the sellers of so much labour for so much wages' {*Wolverhampton Chronicle*, 18 June 1862}.

J N Bagnall retired from the firm in 1861, aged only thirty-five, soon after the departure of his father and brothers. Thomas and his eldest son established country seats with the handsome financial settlements which evidently accompanied their withdrawals. John Nock, who had lived since 1854 on the edge of West Bromwich and had qualified for the first edition of Walford's *County Families* six years later, took up residence in 1863 at Shenstone Moss, near Lichfield. Father and son reached Burke's *Landed Gentry* in 1882. Yet it would be wrong simply to label either the Bagnall family generally, or J N Bagnall in particular, as 'gentrified'. James never abandoned his house in West Bromwich; W G Bagnall later launched a successful engineering enterprise; and John Nock's brothers Charles and Thomas set up as Teesside ironmasters. Nor did J N Bagnall become a stereotypical country gentleman during his long retirement. He remained on friendly terms with leading Black Country ironmasters, though beyond holding railway shares he seems not to have had any residual business interests. More importantly, Bagnall devoted his leisure not to rural sports but to an intensified involvement in religious and civic affairs, thereby expanding the scope of the paternalism which had marked his managerial career. These activities, though partly diverted to his new country neighbourhood, remained centred on the Black Country, which lay only about ten miles from his adopted home. Thus Bagnall, like other local businessmen who moved to the fringes of the district, altered rather than severed his ties to the public life of the area. In a region which craved glamour, the urban leadership of top businessmen may have been enhanced rather than diminished once the trappings of gentility had supplemented the prestige flowing from industrial wealth.

Early in the century the Bagnalls had been enthusiastic Wesleyans, and his father attempted to keep the young John Nock loyal to the chapel. But the boy was influenced by the keen Anglicanism of his mother's family, and the Bagnalls themselves were turning to the Church by the 1830s. As an adult J N Bagnall, like many of the district's foremost ironmasters, became an Anglican. He strenuously opposed the campaign for disestablishment, addressing hundreds of meetings as president of the South Staffordshire branch of the English Church Union. Even more controversially, as a High Churchman he supported innovations such as daily services and surpliced choirs, and he actively defended clergymen (such as his son-in-law, the vicar of West Bromwich) who were prosecuted for Ritualism. Yet, if such activities sometimes exasperated Dissenter and Low Churchman alike, Bagnall won widespread approval for generous support of less contentious religious activities. For example, he endowed the new district church of St James, Wednesbury and served as its churchwarden for many years. As one of the first licensed lay readers Bagnall also assisted local efforts to attract more workingmen to organised religion by conducting missions in working-class districts.

In secular affairs, too, Bagnall was a prominent participant in the increasingly diverse activities undertaken by Black Country businessmen. Some of this involvement was political. Like his relatives and many other ironmasters John Nock was a Tory, and a sufficiently loyal and active partisan to be mentioned as a possible Conservative candidate for South Staffordshire in 1865. Bagnall also served briefly on elected local boards where he supported strong public health measures. Like some of his fellow industrialists, however, Bagnall made a more significant contribution in the less turbulent sphere of county affairs. Placed on the Staffordshire Bench very young in 1853, he appeared regularly at petty sessions. There, despite the family firm's conventional attitude toward workingmen's breaches of labour law, Bagnall gained a reputation for fairness and was appealed against only once. A DL from 1859, in 1875 (twelve years after his father) Bagnall became one of the first veterans of Black Country business to be named high sheriff. The Volunteer Force also attracted much of John Nock's time and energy. He launched, subsidised and captained the Bilston Corps; later he advanced to a lieutenant colonelcy and command of a battalion. In addition, initiatives aimed at 'improving' the working class attracted his attention outside the workplace as they had within it. A critic of the pub and of youthful rowdiness, Bagnall was an enthusiastic advocate of temperance, supporting organisations as diverse as the Church of England Temperance Society and the United Kingdom Alliance. More positively, he backed an Anglican workingmen's society.

In 1848 he had followed the local tradition of close ties among business families by marrying Mary Ann Ward, the daughter of a Wolverhampton ironmaster. They had three sons and five daughters. Bagnall died at Shenstone, Staffordshire on 18 October 1884.

Although less responsive to popular preferences than the emerging generation of local leaders, Bagnall had retained general esteem on the eastern side of the Black Country because of his evident sincerity and the profusion of his public-spirited activities. For some years a managing partner of importance, he became, especially after his retirement, a respected public representative of a major business family. By conspicuously discharging the religious and civic responsibilities expected of those who amassed industrial wealth, Bagnall assisted the deepening of public involvement by the district's elite that in turn helped to maintain a social atmosphere favourable to business. This contribution was more enduring than his effort to establish a landed family: by the turn of the century John Nock Bagnall's descendants had vanished both from the *Landed Gentry* and from *County Families*.

RICHARD H TRAINOR

Writings:

(ed) *Dud Dudley's Metallum Martis: or, Iron Made with Pit-Coale, Sea-Coale, &c ...* (apparently West Bromwich, 1851).

A History of Wednesbury, in the County of Stafford ... Embracing an Account of the Coal and Iron Trade (Wolverhampton: William Parke, 1854).

PP, HC 1854 (382) XVI, SC Payment of Wages Bill.

Sources:

Unpublished

Staffordshire RO, Hatherton MS (D260/M/F/5/6/2).

C Reg: John Bagnall & Sons Ltd (7,101).

PrC: Wills of William (1863), James (1872), John Nock (1884) and Thomas Bagnall (1885).

Richard H Trainor, 'Authority and Social Structure in an Industrialized Area: a Study of Three Black Country Towns, 1840-1890' (Oxford DPhil, 1981).

Published

George C Allen, *The Industrial Development of Birmingham and the Black Country 1860-1927* (George Allen & Unwin, 1929).

Bilston Weekly Herald 25 Oct 1884.

Boase.

Burke's Landed Gentry 1882, 1898.

Dudley Herald 20 Jan 1872.

John F Ede, *History of Wednesbury* (Wednesbury: Wednesbury Corporation, 1962).

Free Press (West Bromwich) 25 Oct 1884.

Walter K V Gale, *The Black Country Iron Industry: a Technical History* (Iron and Steel Institute, 1966).

Frederick W Hackwood, *History of Tipton* (Dudley: Dudley Herald, 1891).

Norman Mutton, 'The Marked Bar Association: Price Regulation in the Black Country Iron Trade' *West Midlands Studies* 9 (1976).

PP, RC Children's Employment (Mines) (1842) 381.

PP, HC 1845 (360) XI, SC Oxford, Worcester and Wolverhampton Railway.

Staffordshire Advertiser 24 Mar 1877, 25 Oct 1884.

VCH Staffordshire vols 2, 17.

Edward Walford, *The County Families of the United Kingdom* (Robert Hardwicke 1st ed, 1860; Chatto & Windus 40th ed, 1900).

Wednesbury and West Bromwich Advertiser 13, 20 Jan 1872.

Weekly News (Oldbury) 25 Oct 1884.

Mary Willett, *John Nock Bagnall: a Memoir by His Daughter* (J Masters & Co, 1885).

Wolverhampton Chronicle 18 June 1862, 11 Mar 1863, 19 Oct 1864, 22 Oct 1884.

BAILLIEU, Clive Latham

1st Lord Baillieu

(1889-1967)

Mining financier

Clive Latham Baillieu was born in Australia on 24 September 1889, the eldest son of William Lawrence Baillieu (1859-1936), Australian financier and politician, and his wife Bertha Mary (1862-1925), only daughter of Edward Latham (1839-1905), founder of Carlton's brewery in Australia (who in 1895 married W L Baillieu's sister). His father began as an auctioneer and estate agent, subsequently becoming a mining financier with worldwide interests; his political detractors attributed to him the motto, 'When on thin ice, skate fast'. Clive Baillieu was educated at Melbourne Church of England School until 1908 when he went to Trinity College, Melbourne; in 1911 he went to read law at Magdalen College, Oxford, and was a rowing blue in 1913. Called to the bar at the Inner Temple in 1915, in that year he married Ruby Florence Evelyn (died 1962), daughter of William Clark, an Australian-born sharebroker in London who was one of his father's chief associates (his father having entered the London Stock Exchange in 1902). He served in 1915-18 with the Australian Flying Corps and in 1918-19 with the RAF, being mentioned in despatches and receiving the OBE in 1918.

After the war Baillieu entered business. He worked in his father's London office in collaboration with another old family associate, W S Robinson (qv), and in August 1923 joined the board of the New Zealand Loan & Mercantile Agency Ltd, where he remained for over forty years,

J H Stainton, *The Making of Sheffield 1865-1914* (Sheffield: Weston, 1924).

The Stock Exchange Official Year-Book 1947.

WWMP.

WWW.

BAKER, Arthur

(1881-1969)

Paper industry executive

Arthur Baker was born in Kirkstall near Leeds on 14 July 1881, the eldest son among three boys and one girl of John Edward Baker, a blacksmith who later became a district supervisor for an insurance company, and Rhoda Ellen Baker née Smith. After the family moved to Lancashire he was educated at Bury Grammar School and the Manchester College of Science and Technology. Here he read chemical engineering with a view to taking an administrative post in industry, though he never took a degree. After a spell with Olive Bros, papermakers of Bury, he joined the Wallpaper Manufacturers Ltd at Darwen in 1901 as a chemist. That year he was awarded an Honours Medal in 'Paper Manufacture'. In 1908 he was appointed chief chemist at the Wallpaper Manufacturers' new paper mill at Greenhithe, Kent and in 1912 became deputy manager.

During the First World War he returned to Darwen to manage his firm's Hollins Mill which had been turned over to munitions work and at the end of the war was promoted general manager of two of his company's paper mills there, as well as of the mill at Greenhithe, Kent. In 1920 he was appointed director and general manager of Empire Paper Mills Ltd, the firm which operated the Greenhithe Mill after it was acquired by the Harmsworth Group in 1919.

During his time with Empire, Baker went to Newfoundland in 1922-23 to advise the Treasury on the affairs of the Newfoundland Power & Paper Co, Corner Brook (later to be acquired by Bowater in 1938) whose debentures were guaranteed by the British Government. On behalf of the Papermakers' Association of Great Britain and Ireland Arthur Baker organised the installation and start-up of a small model paper machine and auxiliary plant at the British Empire Exhibition at Wembley in 1924. The actual making of paper on site on this miniature scale was the subject of much interest to the many exhibition visitors, including professional paper manufacturers.

In the same year he was approached by Eric Vansittart Bowater (qv) to take over the supervision, planning and construction of the new Bowater paper mill which had been begun on a site fronting the River Thames at Northfleet, Kent and which, being built by Armstrong Whitworth's subsidiary Armstrong Construction Ltd under Glynn West (qv), had encountered many technical and financial difficulties. Arthur Baker was hired on nearly all his own stiff terms, at a salary of £4,000 a year. As general manager and director he was given, and took, authority to change the layout of the Northfleet Mill which temporarily exacerbated the acute cash problems but eventually provided Bowaters with a first class mill. Production began and in 1926 was briefly interrupted by the General Strike, during which the mill was requisitioned by the Government to produce paper for the *British Gazette*.

He was then appointed joint managing director of Bowater's Paper Mills Ltd (with Eric V Bowater) and was responsible for the extensions to the mill in 1928. Designed to produce 50,000 tons a year from two paper machines, Baker's changes and the addition of two more machines raised capacity to 120,000 tons of newsprint a year by 1930. He was also closely concerned with the selection of a site and the development of the new Bowater's Mersey paper mill on the Manchester Ship Canal at Ellesmere Port in Cheshire. This mill was built in the short space of eleven months in 1930 primarily to supply newsprint for the northern editions of national daily newspapers which by then were being printed in Manchester.

When Eric Bowater decided to combat the rise of wood pulp prices by expanding in Canada, Baker played a leading part in preparing the plans. In turn this led to the acquisition in 1938 of the large newsprint mill at Corner Brook, Newfoundland and its name changed to Bowater's Newfoundland Pulp & Paper Mills Ltd. This mill became an important supplier of pulp and paper to the United Kingdom during the Second World War when domestic production was severely curtailed. As in the First World War Baker took charge of the munitions work to which the UK mills were temporarily converted and was chairman of the Jettison Fuel Tank Group which produced lightweight disposable fuel tanks to enable aircraft to fly much longer distances.

He actively participated in the post-war planning for the Bowater organisation and was in charge of a team exploring suitable areas for expansion in North America. He himself visited 22 sites, mostly in the Tennessee Valley, and within twelve months found, in 1951, the site at Calhoun, Tennessee where the Bowaters Southern Paper Corporation mill was built. Initially producing 130,000 tons of paper a year, this became the largest newsprint mill in the southern United States. Arthur Baker sat on the board of the BSPC until 1956.

Baker's service with Bowater spanned thirty-five years until he retired in 1959. His principal appointments included joint managing director of the parent company and director of operations of all Bowater mills in the United Kingdom and overseas until 1946. He was subsequently Chief Technical Advisor to the chairman of the board, Sir Eric Bowater, up to the time of his retirement but he continued his interest in the industry until his death.

Outside the Bowater company, Baker played a prominent part in the affairs of the British Paper and Board Makers Association (BPBMA) and

The Management Team of Bowaters Paper Mills, Northfleet, at the opening of the mill in 1926. Arthur Baker at centre. The tents belong to soldiers occupying the paper mill, to protect it from strikers during the General Strike (courtesy of Robert Knight).

the Employers' Federation of Paper Makers (now amalgamated under the title British Paper and Board Industry Federation). He became a leading expert on industrial relations and served as President of the Federation from 1924 until 1959, making a major contribution to the long record of harmonious relations between employers and employed in the paper industry. He was also instrumental in introducing chemistry into the craft of pulp and paper making, which until he founded the Technical Section of the BPBMA in 1920, had largely been carried out by practical paper makers and engineers. Baker clearly saw that paper making was a joint effort by all three.

Arthur Baker, or AB as he was affectionately known, served the pulp, paper and allied industries in Great Britain and indeed the world for nearly seventy years and his success as a leader and a leading industrialist was widely recognised. He was awarded the CBE in 1955 for services to the paper industry. His principal recreation was his business and the industry he served, but late in life he took up ski-ing, mastered the art and continued to ski in Switzerland each winter until his death. He married Annie Talbot, daughter of William Talbot, a retired picture framer, in 1908; they had two sons. Arthur Baker died on 3 November 1969 at the age of eighty-eight, leaving £107,077 gross.

ROBERT KNIGHT

Writings:

The Wedge Method of Sampling Wood Pulp (British Paper & Board Makers' Association, 1955).

Sources:

Unpublished

BCe.

MCe.

PrC.

Published

William J Reader, *Bowater. A History* (Cambridge: Cambridge University Press, 1981).

BAKER, Sir Benjamin

(1840-1907)

Railway and civil engineer

Benjamin Baker was born at Keyford near Frome in Somerset on 31 March 1840, the son of Benjamin Baker Sr and his wife Sarah née Hollis. His father came from Carlow in Ireland and became principal assistant at ironworks at Tondu, Glamorgan. Young Benjamin was educated at Cheltenham Grammar School until 1856 and then was apprenticed to H H Price at the Neath Abbey Iron Works for four years. Afterwards he went to London and spent two years as assistant to W Wilson on the Grosvenor Road railway bridge and Victoria station, London. In 1861-62 he moved to the office of Mr (later Sir) John Fowler (qv). His later partnerships were with Arthur Cameron Hurtzig, at Queen Anne's Mansions, Middlesex, and, from 1904, with Frederick Shelford, at 35a Great George Street, Westminster.

He is remembered mainly for his work on London's Underground, the Forth Bridge, and the Aswan Dam. From 1861 he was engaged on the Metropolitan (Inner Circle) railway and St John's Wood extension. In 1869 he became Fowler's chief assistant on the construction of the District railway from Westminster to the City. Fowler and Baker (partners after 1875) were consulting engineers on the world's first deep-level tube railway, the City and South London line, opened in 1890. With J H Greathead (qv) they were joint engineers for the Central tube line, opened in 1900. Baker's pioneering work on the tube system included locating stations at summits to facilitate braking and acceleration, and the 30 feet diameter tube of the C&SLR's Euston extension.

With Sir John Fowler and Sir William Arrol, the contractor, Baker designed the Forth Bridge in 1880 which, completed ten years later, was built on the cantilever principle and used steel made by the new Gilchrist-Thomas process.

The Aswan Dam he planned with Sir John Aird (qv) and he redesigned the dam to double its capacity, though he did not live to see these later designs implemented. After the completion of the Forth Bridge there were few major engineering works in the world on which he and Sir John Fowler were not consulted. He was responsible for work in Australia, West Africa, South Africa, Canada, and Ireland, where his Barrow viaduct had foundations 100 feet below low water. He was associated with the Blackwall Tunnel, Tower Bridge, and, with Sir John Wolfe Barry (qv), the Avonmouth and Hull Docks.

He was elected an associate member of the Institution of Civil Engineers in 1867, a member in 1877, and was its president in 1895. He was a member of the Institution of Mechanical Engineers, and an honorary member of the American and Canadian Societies of Engineers. His KCMG on the completion of the Forth Bridge in 1890 was followed by his KCB on the completion of the Aswan Dam in 1902, and the Order of Medjidie, First Class. He became a Fellow of the Royal Society, 1890, and was awarded the Poncelet Prize of the French Academy of Sciences, and honorary degrees of the Universities of Edinburgh, Cambridge, and Dublin.

Sir Benjamin was valued as an arbitrator and expert witness, and served on the Board of Trade's Light Railway Commission, and on the Engineering Standards Committee, and was a lay member of the Ordnance Committee. He never married. Short in stature, he was reserved, personally courageous, and had a dry sense of humour. Engineering tables he dismissed as being 'as reliable as Old Moore's Almanack' {Rolt (1962) 163}, believing as he did that theory was no substitute for experience. He was concerned for the better provision of hospitals and education, and was a generous supporter of the British Association, the Institution of Civil Engineers, and the Royal Institution where he attended his last meeting just two days before his fatal heart attack on 19 May 1907. His estate was valued at £182,582 gross.

JOSEPH LECKEY

Writings:

Diagrams Giving Weights of Girders up to 200 feet Span (E & F N Spon, 1866).

Long-span Railway Bridges (E & F N Spon, 1867, and later editions).

On the Strengths of Beams, Columns and Arches (E & F N Spon, 1870).

The Actual Lateral Pressure of Earthwork (New York: D Van Nostrand, 1881).

Some Notes on the Working Stress of Iron and Steel (New York: 1886).

Pont sur la Manche. Avant-projets de MM Schneider et Cie (1889).

Report of Committee Appointed to Inquire into the Working of the London County

Council Generating Station at Greenwich in its Relation to the Royal Observatory (HMSO, 1907).

The Forth Bridge (Spottiswoode & Co, 1882).

Address to the Institution of Civil Engineers (W Clowes & Sons, 1895).

Sources:

Unpublished

BCe.

PrC.

Published

Theodore C Barker and Michael Robbins, *A History of London Transport* (2 vols, George Allen & Unwin, 1974).

DNB.

John Marshall, *A Bibliographical Dictionary of Railway Engineers* (Newton Abbot: David & Charles, 1978).

Railway Gazette 6 (24 May 1907).

Railway News 87 (18 and 25 May 1907).

Railway Times 91 (18 and 25 May 1907).

Lionel T C Rolt, *Great Engineers* (G Bell & Sons, 1962).

WWW.

Sir Michael E Balcon (courtesy of the National Film Archive/Stills Library).

BALCON, Sir Michael Elias

(1896-1977)

Film producer and executive

Michael Elias Balcon, known always to his friends and associates as 'Mick', was born in Birmingham on 19 May 1896, the fourth child and youngest son of Louis Balcon, master clothier, and his wife Laura née Greenberg. He had two brothers and two sisters. Devoted to his mother, he saw comparatively little of his father during childhood, since Louis, afflicted with wanderlust, spent much time in South Africa. Michael Balcon described his middle-class Jewish family as 'respectable but impoverished' {Balcon (1969) 2}. He and his brothers all won scholarships to George Dixon Grammar School in Birmingham. 'My school career was undistinguished' {*ibid* 5}, he recalled, and he felt himself overshadowed both academically and in sports by his brother Chandos, 'Shan'. Shan won a scholarship to Birmingham University and later, after serving in the army during the First World War, joined 'Mick' in his film company and worked with him in various capacities until his death in 1947.

The family's financial situation caused Michael Balcon to leave school at seventeen and get a job as an apprentice in the diamond-buying department of a manufacturing jeweller. When war broke out in 1914, he was rejected for military service because of a defective left eye. Instead he went to work for the Dunlop Rubber Co, rising to be personal assistant to the managing director, Sir Arthur Du Cros (qv). 'I must admit that the business grounding I received has stood me in good stead in my chosen career as a film producer and executive' {*ibid* 10}, he said of this period. But the job bored him and when, after the war, he met again an old Birmingham friend, Victor Saville, who had become a film renter, they joined forces. With backing from yet another Birmingham friend, Oscar Deutsch (qv), they formed in 1919 Victory Motion Pictures Ltd, to operate as film renters in the Midlands. But this only whetted their appetites to produce their own films and so in 1920 they moved to London and began producing short advertising films. The opportunity to move on to full-scale production arose in 1923 when an old Birmingham acquaintance, J Graham Cutts, a former cinema manager with aspirations to be a director, obtained an option on the film rights of a West End stage success, *Woman to Woman*. They obtained financial backing from the film renter C M Woolf (qv), whose niece Saville had married in 1920, and from Oscar Deutsch, eventually raising the £30,000 necessary to produce the film. It was a success but two follow-up films flopped, Woolf and Deutsch withdrew their support and the partnership collapsed. Saville went off to Gaumont to begin an eminent career as producer-director. Balcon and Cutts founded Gainsborough Pictures in 1924, obtained financial backing from Gaumont and, in a bold move, managed to purchase Islington Studios for £14,000 from Paramount Pictures who were closing down their British production operations. At Islington, they launched a programme of film production.

Gainsborough films were distributed by C M Woolf's W & F Film Distributors, which was taken over by Ostrer's Gaumont British Picture Corporation. In 1928 they floated Gainsborough as a public company, in association with Gaumont British, and in 1932, Balcon, already managing director of Gainsborough, became production chief at Gaumont British, although he had no seat on its board. He now embarked on a punishing schedule of work, producing up to 20 films a year at Gaumont's Shepherd's Bush and Gainsborough's Islington Studios. His concerns were 'overall policy, contractual arrangements with stars and directors, the buying of stories, problems of copyright and a hundred and one other things' {Balcon (1969) 114}. The policy of the company was to produce films with international appeal in order to break into the American market. To this end, Balcon produced the Jessie Matthews musicals, Alfred Hitchcock thrillers, George Arliss biographical pictures, Jack Hulbert comedies and several expensive historical epics. The result of the workload for Balcon was a nervous breakdown but he bounced back again after a period of rest. The films failed to make the hoped-for breakthrough into the American market, partly due to the restrictive practices of the Hollywood companies, and the boom in film production of the early 1930s began to collapse in 1936. Gaumont British ran into serious financial difficulties, cut back on production and eventually ceased production altogether. Balcon's contract expired in 1936 and he left to become head of production of the new British operations of the Hollywood giant Metro-Goldwyn-Mayer, hoping by genuine Anglo-American co-operation to stimulate the British film industry. But the constraints placed on his operations were so great that he quarrelled with Metro's chief, Louis B Mayer, and resigned after completing only one film (*A Yank at Oxford*). He was replaced by Victor Saville.

Balcon now set up a small production company (Balford) with director Walter Forde and at the invitation of Reginald Baker, an old friend and a director of Ealing Studios, they took their unit there to start production of some inexpensive feature films, in 1938. Balcon was soon invited to take over as head of production at Ealing from Basil Dean. He joined the board of directors and over the next twenty years and through 95 films he proceeded to turn the name Ealing Studios into one of the most celebrated in film history.

'The studio with the team spirit' was one slogan that Dean had had painted on the wall of the studio at Ealing and it was a slogan Balcon tried to live up to. There was a permanent staff at Ealing and Balcon ran the studio by committee, with regular round table meetings to discuss projects and current productions. If there was a consensus in favour of a particular production, Balcon would back it even if he had misgivings himself. He consistently promoted and backed up-and-coming young technicians and creative artists, though he remained very possessive of them. Michael Relph, a product of the 'Balcon Academy', described him as not just a film producer, more a cinema impresario. Not only did he assemble a talented team of film-makers, but he made creative contributions to their work by encouraging original screenplays rather than adaptations, importing documentarists to give a more realistic feel to films, and commissioning modern artists to design Ealing's film posters.

Balcon described the ideal producer: 'as absorbent as a sponge, as indulgent as a father, as hard as steel and as patient as Job' {Balcon (1933) 5-7}. He sought to become this ideal producer and his associates testify to his great courage and vision, his tenacity and phenomenal energy, his personal charm and persuasiveness and as the mainspring of his success, artistic flair coupled with keen business acumen. A real bond developed between Balcon and his film-makers, a bond based, as Ivor Montagu observed, on the recognition that 'he, like them, really enjoyed making films' {Montagu (1977) 9}.

In 1939, he prepared a memorandum on how films could be utilised in the national interest in wartime. But the Government showed little interest. Indeed when war broke out, it was announced that all cinemas would be closed and studios requisitioned. Balcon was instrumental in helping to whip up a press campaign to get the Government to change its mind. The change of mind came quickly, the importance of film both to entertain and to instruct was appreciated and Ealing played a major role in the dramatisation of the concept of 'The People's War'.

Finance was always tight at Ealing and although its parent company, Associated Talking Pictures Ltd, had been floated as a public company with a nominal share capital of £125,000, only a small amount of that had been subscribed and the financing of the company fell principally on the directors themselves. In order to guarantee the future, Balcon arrived in 1947 at an arrangement with the Rank Organisation, the major force in the British cinema at that time. He negotiated a contract which guaranteed distribution of Ealing's films in return for a 50 per cent stake in them. Balcon received a place on the board of the Rank companies but, more important, complete production autonomy. Backed by this, Ealing went on to produce a stream of prestigious and popular films, notably the celebrated 'Ealing comedies', one of the glories of the British cinema.

However, financial problems curbed his activities at Ealing. With the retirement from the Ealing board of Stephen Courtauld, always its chief financial backer, and with a large overdraft and rising costs, Balcon decided to finance future operations by the sale of the studios. In 1955, therefore, Ealing Studios were sold to the BBC for £350,000. Rather than be swallowed up by the Rank Organisation, Balcon moved his Ealing unit to the Borehamwood Studios of Metro-Goldwyn-Mayer. However the loss of its base meant the loss of the old Ealing spirit and it became clear that the great days of Ealing were past. After only six more films, the arrangement with MGM was ended and in 1957 Ealing's assets were sold to Associated British Picture Corporation. The last film to be produced under the Ealing trademark (*The Siege of Pinchgut*) was released by them in 1959. The Ealing unit was finally dispersed.

Balcon now founded an independent production company, Michael Balcon Productions, and produced two films, *The Long and the Short and the Tall* (1961) and *Sammy Going South* (1963). But he was becoming more and more preoccupied with the problems faced by independent producers in getting their films made and shown. In 1951, as an adviser to the National Film Finance Corporation, he had encouraged the setting up of a company which would provide finance, production facilities and opportunities for aspiring film-makers. He was chairman of this company, Group 3, from 1951 to 1954 but because of the stranglehold of the big circuits and internal differences of opinion on policy, the company failed to make a breakthrough. The same idea, however, lay behind Bryanston, founded in 1959 to act as an umbrella organisation for independent producers. Balcon became its chairman upon the demise of Ealing and under its auspices many of the now classic films of the 'British New Wave' cinema were financed and produced. But it too finally failed to make headway and its assets were sold to Associated Rediffusion Television in 1963. Balcon made his final bid to resolve the problems of the independent producer when he became chairman of the group which in 1964 bought British Lion, to provide yet another outlet for the independents. Disagreements at board level led to his resignation in 1965. From 1965 until 1967 he was chairman of Anglo-Enterprise Film Productions, a subsidiary of the Canadian Enterprise Co, which announced plans to initiate a major schedule of productions. Nothing was forthcoming and as the British film industry plunged into its latest financial crisis, from which it has yet to emerge, Balcon's active involvement in film production ceased.

BALCON Sir Michael Elias

He continued to be active, however, in the world of film culture. From 1964 to 1972 he was a governor of the British Film Institute and from 1963 to 1971 chairman of its production board. He served on the councils of the London Academy of Music and Drama, the Royal College of Art (of which he became senior fellow in 1967) and the Society of Film and Television Arts. Despite his deep involvement in films, he found time to interest himself in television. He was part of a consortium which bid unsuccessfully for the Anglia Television franchise, and from 1960 until 1971 he was a director of Border Television.

His dedication and his achievement in his chosen profession were recognised by honours both at home and abroad. He was knighted in 1948 and was made a Knight (First Class) of the Order of St Olav of Norway in 1953. In 1977 the French Government made him a Chevalier des Arts et des Lettres. He was awarded an honorary DLitt by Birmingham University in 1967 and by Sussex University in 1975. He was a fellow of the British Film Academy and an honorary fellow of the British Kinematograph Society. In 1954 he received the Selznick Gold Laurel Award 'for consistent contribution through the production of motion pictures to goodwill among the peoples of the world'. Although he gave 'walking' as his recreation in *Who's Who*, the film industry was his life.

In 1924 Balcon married South-African born Aileen Leatherman, who was in 1946 awarded the MBE for her Red Cross work during the Second World War. They had two children, Jill, born in 1925, and Jonathan, born in 1931. Sir Michael Balcon died at the age of eighty-one at his home, Upper Parrock, in Sussex, on 17 October 1977. He left an estate valued at £272,880 gross.

JEFFREY RICHARDS

Writings:

'The Function of the Producer', *Cinema Quarterly* 2 (Autumn 1933).

'Realism or Tinsel' Workers Film Association pamphlet (1943) reprinted in Monja Danischewsky (ed), *Michael Balcon's 25 Years in Films* (1947).

'The Producer' British Film Institute Summer School Lecture (1945).

Introduction to E Lindgren, F Hardy and R Manvell, *20 Years of British Films* (Falcon Press, 1947).

'The Eye Behind the Camera' in M Balcon et al, *Saraband for Dead Lovers: the Film and its Production* (1948).

'Let British Films be Ambassadors to the World' *Kine Weekly* 11 Jan 1945.

'The Road to Survival' *ibid* 14 Dec 1950.

Film Production and Management (British Institute of Management, 1950).

'Ten Years of British Films' *Sight and Sound* supplement 'Films in 1951'.

'The Challenge Ahead' *Financial Times* supplement 23 Sept 1957.

'An Author in the Studio' *Films and Filming* July 1957.

'British Film Production' *British Kinematography* 46 (1965).

'Training for Film and Television at the Royal College of Art' *Daily Cinema* 4 Mar 1966.

A Lifetime of Films (Hutchinson, 1969).

'From Korda to Bryanston' *Film and TV Technician* Oct 1971.

'50 years as a Professional Survivor' *ibid* Nov 1971.

Sources:

Unpublished

BCe.

PrC.

Published

Charles Barr, *Ealing Studios* (Newton Abbot: David & Charles, 1977).

Ernest Betts, *The Film Business: a History of British Cinema, 1896-1972* (Allen & Unwin, 1973).

Thomas E B Clarke, *This Is Where I Came In* (Joseph, 1974).

Daily Mirror 18 Oct 1977.

Daily Telegraph 18 Oct 1977.

Monja Danischewsky (ed), *Michael Balcon's 25 Years in Films* (World Film Publications, 1947).

—, *White Russian, Red Face* (Gollancz, 1966).

J Ellis, 'Made in Ealing' *Screen* 16 (Spring 1975).

Evening Standard 18 Oct 1977.

Financial Times 21 Oct 1977.

Guardian 18 Oct 1977.

Hollywood Reporter 18 Oct 1977.

Rachael Low and Geoff Brown, *Der Produzent: Michael Balcon und der englishche Film* (Berlin: Verlage Volken Speiss, 1981).

I Montagu, M Relph and A Hitchcock, 'Michael Balcon 1896-1977' *Sight and Sound* 47 (Winter 1977).

Charles Oakley, *Where We Came In* (Allen & Unwin, 1964).

PEP, *The British Film Industry* (1952).

George Perry, *Forever Ealing* (Pavilion, 1981).

C Rollins and R J Wareing, *Victor Saville* (BFI, 1972).

Screen International 22 Oct 1977.

Times 18, 22 Oct 1977.

Variety 19 Oct 1977.

Alan Wood, *Mr Rank* (Hodder & Stoughton, 1952).

WWW.

BALDWIN, Alfred

(1841-1908)

Iron and steel manufacturer

Alfred Baldwin was born at Stourport, Worcestershire, on 4 June 1841, the youngest son of George Pearce Baldwin, a small scale iron founder of Stourport, and Sarah Chalkley, the eldest daughter of Rev Jacob Stanley, a distinguished Wesleyan Methodist minister who in 1845 was president of the Methodist Conference. The Baldwin family had for centuries been Shropshire yeomen, until in the early nineteenth century Alfred's grandfather was attracted across the county boundary by Stourport's industrial activities. After attending a number of private schools, Alfred entered the family firm of iron makers, E P & W Baldwin, which had been set up in 1849 in order to acquire the Wilden iron and tin works at Stourport, where tinplate was first manufactured in 1753. Here Alfred was introduced to, and quickly succeeded in mastering, both the technical and commercial sides of the iron industry, and by his middle twenties was an indispensable member of the firm.

Alfred Baldwin's early career was spent establishing Wilden as an efficient and substantial producer of iron and tinplate. In the early 1870s the works included seven puddling furnaces, two forges and two sheet mills, and by the time he became the firm's principal partner in 1881, three additional mills had been erected and the annual production stood at 75,000 boxes of tinplates; terneplates were also manufactured. Baldwin rapidly established a reputation as a benevolent employer at the works and the patriarch of the Wilden district of Stourport. By the late 1880s he had built a school, a church and a vicarage at Wilden and also established a farm adjacent to the works. By 1890, he had introduced into the Wilden works most of the improved conditions which the more benevolent employers of the day were practising, including a works medical service, a scheme for the encouragement of the education of workers' children and the maintenance of high standards of safety and cleanliness.

Alfred's ambitions extended beyond Wilden, though the Wilden works remained his base. The Swindon Tinplate Works, near Dudley, was acquired in 1873 with its 12 puddling furnaces and two mills. Significant extensions of the firm's activities really started when it entered South Wales. In 1886 Alfred Baldwin set up a separate company, Alfred Baldwin & Co Ltd, with an authorised capital of £50,000, which began the erection of the six-mill Panteg Tinplate Works, near Pontypool, in Monmouthshire. Two years later the company acquired the Lower Mills Works at Pontypool where it commenced rolling steel sheet for galvanising. The firm's involvement in the Pontypool district was furthered in 1892 when it restarted the Pontymoile Tinplate Works in conjunction with Wright, Butler & Co. Both the Panteg and the Pontymoile works actually commenced production in 1895, the former devoting itself to high quality tinplate production while Pontymoile concentrated on the manufacture of galvanised sheets. In addition, Alfred Baldwin developed a commercial interest in the manufacture of paper, and by the end of the nineteenth century the company controlled a few paper mills in the Midlands, though little is known about this side of his business.

The extension of Baldwin's interests into Monmouthshire brought him into close association with the firm of Wright, Butler & Co, a relationship which was to lay the foundations of large scale developments in the future. Colonel John Roper Wright (qv) had assisted William Siemens (qv) in producing the first ingot of steel by the open-hearth process in 1866 at Birmingham; Isaac Butler owned the Panteg Steel Works and in 1876 supplied a steel bloom to the Bradley Tinplate Works, at Bilston, Staffordshire, which was the first sheet steel to be rolled in Britain. Wright and Butler in 1878 formed a company which subleased the Elba Steel Works at Gowerton, near Swansea; in 1882 they purchased the Panteg Steel Works; and as a result of Wright's association with Siemens were well placed to start activities at the Landore Steel Works, Swansea, when the latter relinquished his interests there in 1888, and finally purchased those works in 1900. The 1890s saw the various interests of Baldwin and his associates successively expanding, increasingly reinforcing one another, furthering Baldwin's position and influence and at the same time in themselves becoming increasingly dependent upon his individual dynamism and leadership.

Eventually Baldwin achieved the aim which had motivated his business strategy for over a decade. He brought together these various interests under unified control, thus creating an organisational unit which was able to take advantage of the scale economies which British industry was beginning to enjoy at the start of the twentieth century. On 7 April 1902, under Alfred Baldwin's chairmanship, Baldwins Ltd was registered with an authorised capital of £850,000, to acquire the assets of five interrelated firms and to embark upon rapid expansion by systematically absorbing both competing and allied activities. The incorporation of Baldwins brought together E P & W Baldwins Ltd, which operated four works at Wilden, Stourvale (near Kidderminster), Swindon (near Dudley) and Cokeley (near Brierley Hill); Wright, Butler & Co with its steel works at Landore, Gowerton, Panteg and Cwmavon (near Port Talbot) and its Primitura and Monges haematite iron ore mines in northern Spain; Alfred Baldwin & Co Ltd, which controlled amongst other interests the Panteg and the Pontymoile tinplate and galvanising works; the Bryn Navigation Colliery Co Ltd (near Port Talbot); and the Blackwall Galvanised Iron Co Ltd of London. The board of directors under Baldwin's chairmanship comprised Col J Roper Wright, Isaac Butler, Stanley Baldwin (Alfred's son), Samuel Lammas Dore, Aubrey Butler and W Charles Wright. Thus there was formed, largely under Alfred Baldwin's direction, an organisation which was to become one of the giants of the British steel industry in the twentieth century. Another major step in this direction was taken in 1906 when Baldwins reopened the Port Talbot Steel Works which, during succeeding decades, was to become one of the company's major production centres.

In addition to his central position in the growing British steel industry of the late nineteenth and early twentieth centuries, Alfred Baldwin moved into wider industrial affairs and into public life. His commercial interests were not confined to steel making, and at various times he was a director of the Golden River Quenselle Co, Archibauld Kernick & Sons, the Anglo American Tin Stamping Co, and the Bentong Straits Tin Co. In addition in 1896 he was made chairman of the board of the Metropolitan Bank (of England and Wales) which under his guidance was transformed from a local Birmingham bank to a powerful national financial institution in the space of a decade. He was also unanimously elected chairman of the GWR's board in 1905 in succession to Lord Cawdor. In 1892 he entered parliament as the Unionist MP for the Bewdley (West Worcestershire) constituency, representing it until his death in 1908. A progressive Conservative, Alfred Baldwin was an ardent supporter of Joseph Chamberlain's (qv) tariff reform policy and an opponent of Home Rule for Ireland, of the disestablishment of the Church of England, and of Local Option in abolishing public houses; but he seldom spoke in the House. By the end of the nineteenth century he was also a JP for both Staffordshire and Worcestershire, and a DL for Worcestershire. Though raised as a Wesleyan, he became a High Anglican when he was in his mid twenties.

In 1866 Alfred Baldwin married Louisa, one of the seven talented children of the Rev George Brown MacDonald, a Wesleyan minister of Wolverhampton. One of Louisa's sisters, Alice, became the mother of Rudyard Kipling and another, Georgiana, married Edward (later Sir Edward) Burne-Jones. Baldwin had only one child, Stanley, who succeeded him as MP for Bewdley and later became prime minister. Alfred Baldwin died suddenly on 13 February 1908 at the age of sixty-seven, leaving £199,376 gross.

COLIN BABER *and* TREVOR BOYNS

Sources:

Unpublished

British Steel Corporation Archives, Spencer Works, Llanwern, miscellaneous records deposited by David Bryn.

PrC.

Published

Edward Henry Brooke, *Chronology of the Tinplate Works of Great Britain* (Cardiff: William Lewis, 1944).

James C Carr and Walter Taplin, *History of the British Steel Industry* (Oxford: Basil Blackwell, 1962).

Journal of the Institution of Mechanical Engineers 1908.

Journal of the Iron and Steel Institute 1908.

Keith Middlemas and John Barnes, *Baldwin. A Biography* (Weidenfeld & Nicolson, 1969).

Walter E Minchinton, *The British Tinplate Industry. A History* (Oxford: Clarendon Press, 1957).

Times 14 Feb 1908.

Western Mail 14 Feb 1908.

WWMP.

BALFOUR, Alexander

(1824-1886)

South American merchant

Alexander Balfour was born at Levenbank, Leven, Fifeshire, on 2 September 1824, the eldest son of Henry Balfour, a foundry owner of Leven, and Agnes née Bisset. He attended Leven Parish School, Dundee Academy and, briefly, St Andrew's University. Balfour first entered business with an uncle in Dundee but established his reputation in Liverpool with Graham Kelly & Co, after experience in the Mexican trade with Manuel Blandin. In February 1851, together with Stephen Williamson and David Duncan, two other young clerks from Fifeshire, he formed a partnership with capital from Williamson's family to ship manufactures to Chile on consignment or joint account, which minimised risks and capital requirements, making it possible for the young firm to survive. In 1863, Duncan withdrew to join what became Duncan Fox, leaving Balfour and Williamson to reconstruct the firm with new, junior partners.

Balfour Williamson's letters, typical of Victorian business correspondence, despaired of commercial prospects on the Pacific coast. Erratic long-distance communication created misunderstandings and inaccurate market intelligence; working capital was scarce, since credit was expensive in Chile where buyers delayed payment while sellers in Britain demanded prompt settlement; and fluctuating local exchanges and product prices raised real difficulties which threatened the firm's stability. In the crisis of 1857, for example, falling sales, rising stocks and bad debts in Chile without financial accommodation in Liverpool would have toppled the house but for the continuing support of Williamson's family. Yet, in fact, the house quickly prospered. Debts repaid and momentum recovered, Balfour Williamson entered California, where in 1865 junior partners established Balfour Guthrie, and confidently survived the 1867 crisis. The firm not only diversified geographically but also sectorally. Limited purchasing power along the Pacific and the need for return cargoes encouraged it to develop local primary products. The house invested capital in land, a convenient alternative to loss-making remittances from the Pacific, and in high risk-high return infrastructural projects which the public avoided. The partners managed local mines, floated companies to work concessions, arranged agencies and drew commissions on shipments to and from Europe. Balfour Williamson contributed to local industrialisation, processing primary commodities and reorganising local enterprises with additional funds and fresh management to become a leading miller on the west coast. The house also entered the important business service sector of warehousing, shipping and insurance agencies. Eventually, the firm turned, in the absence of local financial facilities, to merchant banking, offering farm mortgages and loans through investment and trust agencies. By the mid 1880s Balfour Williamson's capital exceeded £750,000, earning valuable overseas income in business typical of British merchants abroad.

Alexander Balfour was central to this expansion, possessing the capacity for hard work, prudence, and realism typical of successful Scottish businessmen. His strength was everyday attention to administrative detail and sober judgement which complemented Williamson's more imaginative approach. Of great importance, too, were his solid commercial principles of integrity and trust which enhanced his firm's reputation for fair dealing. Yet, Balfour was the subject of his partners' scathing criticism. His complex character, though it mellowed in later life, included a hasty temper, intense convictions and at times headstrong impetuosity which must have exacerbated relations with Duncan who blamed Balfour for mismanagement in 1857. Balfour's caution was unsuited to Latin America where flexibility and flair were required and which he visited infrequently leaving much of the overseas business to the more daring Williamson. Increasingly, Williamson, who made the crucial choice between Balfour and Duncan, was looked upon as the head of the firm, although the two partners held equal interest.

Balfour's career outside business was less controversial. Accumulating wealth and reputation but a devout Christian, he devoted time, energy and resources to social improvement in a genuine philanthropic spirit. His major interests in Liverpool, Scotland and the Pacific coast were temperance, seamen's conditions and child welfare. His public career included representation for St Peters Ward (1873-79) on Liverpool City Council and service as a JP for Denbighshire but he consistently refused to stand for Parliament, in contrast to his partner. While neither austere nor extravagant, Balfour's success permitted him to indulge in painting, music and travel.

Although rejecting extensive landowning as an outlet for his fortune, he settled his family on an estate near Chester (close enough to Liverpool for daily contact) where he acted as an improving landlord.

He married Mary Jessie, third daughter of Rev Roxburgh by whom he had at least four children. Ill-health, the untimely death of his eldest son and something of a spiritual depression troubled his later years. He died without retiring on 16 April 1886, shortly after an unsuccessful operation to remove a cancerous growth, and left £132,148 gross in the UK.

ROBERT GREENHILL

Writings:

Licence Reform. The Reform of the Licence Law in Sweden and the Gothenburg System. A Letter Addressed to W E Gladstone (Simpkin, Marshall & Co, 1876).

Intemperance and the Licensing System (Strahan & Co Ltd, 1881).

Sources:

Unpublished

Merseyside County Archives, Bryson Collection, Balfour Williamson Correspondence D/B/1/2-8.

University College London, Balfour Williamson & Company Archives.

PrC.

Published

Lord Forres, *Balfour Williamson & Company and Allied Firms: Memoirs of a Merchant House* (pp, Butler & Tanner Ltd, 1929).

Wallis Hunt, *Heirs of Great Adventure: The History of Balfour Williamson & Co* (2 vols, Balfour, Williamson & Co, 1951-60).

R H Lundie, *Alexander Balfour: A Memoir* (Nisbet & Co, 1889).

Liverpool Daily Post 17 Apr 1886.

Times 22 Apr 1886.

BALFOUR, Arthur

1st Lord Riverdale of Sheffield

(1873-1957)

Steel manufacturer

Arthur Balfour was born, by his account, in London, on 9 January 1873, the elder of the two sons of Herbert Balfour. The birth was not registered. He was educated at a Methodist School, Ashville College, Harrogate. At the age of fourteen he became an office boy in the firm of Seebohm & Dieckstahl, a prominent Sheffield steel-making enterprise headed by Robert Schott. Having been orphaned, both Arthur and his brother

Bertram had gone to Sheffield in the care of their godmother when she became Robert Schott's wife.

The company had a world-wide export trade in crucible steel products, and in 1887 Arthur Balfour was sent to the USA and Canada to gain experience. In 1892, greatly impressed with American progress and efficiency, he returned with his brother, Bertram, and found employment in a foundry at Buffalo. Within four years he had been promoted from the shop floor to general manager of the works. In 1896 Schott persuaded him to return to Sheffield to become a director of Seebohm & Dieckstahl, with full control of the production side of the business. In 1899 the firm became a limited company with Schott and Balfour holding the controlling interest.

In 1899 Balfour married Frances Josephine Keighley, daughter of Charles Henry Bingham, a partner in the silver and electroplating firm of Walker & Hall. After his wedding he made a tour of the world with her, visited the overseas branches of Seebohm & Dieckstahl in China, Japan, America and Canada, and took the opportunity to establish new agencies. In the USA he learned of the latest American developments in high-speed steel technology and on his return to Sheffield immediately put the results into practice. The company thus became a world pioneer in the production of the improved tool steel and the product found a ready market in the USA. Broughton Engineers Tool Works and C Meadows & Co Ltd were acquired as the firm expanded.

In 1915 Robert Schott died and Balfour became the principal shareholder and virtual owner of the company, which became Arthur Balfour & Co Ltd. He was also chairman of the High Speed Steel Alloys Ltd, Widnes, which was formed to safeguard supplies of alloys during the First World War. In the formation of the Widnes company, which consisted of a federation of special steel-makers, most of whom were Sheffield firms, Balfour had a chance to display those personal qualities as an organiser and diplomat that may have been instrumental in bringing him to the Government's attention. He later used the federation as a means to further the special steel trade's interests in the USA, where, in 1921, he became the first British industrialist to speak before the US Senate.

After the outbreak of war in 1914 Balfour also became a member of the Advisory Committee on War Munitions, the Industrial Advisory Committee to the Treasury, and, later, the Advisory Council for Scientific and Industrial Research, the Engineering Industries Committee, and Lord Balfour's Committee on Commercial and Industrial Policy. In 1919 he was elected president of the Sheffield Chamber of Commerce. In the difficult post-war years the Government made frequent use of his services. Chief among these in 1924 was his chairmanship of the Government Committee on Industry and Trade. The final report, which appeared in 1929, was in nine sections, and contained a searching examination of Britain's industrial base and made recommendations concerning the country's future ability to compete in overseas markets against rising economic nationalism.

Ironically, Balfour's own company epitomised many of the problems which the Committee had so extensively documented. Like many Sheffield tool steel firms, Balfour's was a product of nineteenth century conditions: producing a variety of items besides tool steel, which were then sold by personalised selling methods, it was very much dependent upon the kind of individualism which the Report had criticised. In the inter-war years, however, when the Sheffield steel trade faced problems stemming from the introduction of new electric steel technology and the loss of old markets, such as the US, Balfour's company, in common with many of its Sheffield competitors, remained organised on family lines.

The enterprise was designed to function effectively whilst its directors and representatives were abroad, and so Balfour's heavy involvement with public affairs may not necessarily have damaged the firm. Balfour's frequent absences were filled by his brother Bertram, who had returned from the USA, and his two sons, Robert Arthur Balfour, who joined the firm at the earliest opportunity in 1918, and Francis Henry Balfour. Gerald John Balfour, the eldest son of Bertram, was also a member of the board. These were the men who were responsible for replacing the company's American trade with markets in South America and New Zealand, areas where world competition in tool steel was less severe.

The Second World War seems to have been the turning point in the firm's fortunes. Bertram died during the war and Arthur Balfour's health went into decline. Owing to the war, no managerial replacements were forthcoming, so the company was weakened precisely when intense efforts to modernise and rebuild trade were required. Though the business escaped nationalisation, financial difficulties were only resolved when it became a public company in 1950 with a capital of £500,000. Robert Balfour, and his son Mark, continued the family connection, though Arthur Balfour was still associated with the enterprise until his death.

In 1911 Balfour became Master Cutler, the second youngest in the four hundred year-old history of the Cutlers' Company of Sheffield. He was most active in the field of Government-industry relations. In 1913 he was appointed a member of the Royal Commission on Railways. He served as leading British delegate to the Consultative Committee of the Economic Conference at Geneva. In 1930 he became a member of the Economic Advisory Council of the Cabinet, of the Advisory Council of the Department of Overseas Trade, and of the Imperial Economic Committee. In 1931 he was chairman of the UK Trade Mission to Egypt, and of the Budget Committee of the International Chamber of Commerce.

Balfour was created a baronet in 1929 and in 1935 became First Lord Riverdale of Sheffield. In 1937 he became chairman of the advisory committee of the Privy Council for Scientific and Economic Research, and later of the British Air Mission to Canada. He had been appointed vice-chairman of the British Council in 1935, and was president from 1947 to 1950.

Despite his extensive record of public service, Arthur Balfour shunned publicity and it is difficult to identify the qualities that contributed to his success. Characterised as an all-rounder with abilities as a good salesman, he also had a prodigious appetite for travel (he had visited the USA 73 times by sea), an old-fashioned business routine, a love of Sheffield and a commitment to its products, and orthodox economic ideas, with a belief in retrenchment and a hatred of inflation. Politically, he was a Conservative, though his views never conflicted with his career of public service under various Governments: a career which reflected his intense patriotism and his fascination with the industrial organisation of his own country and its place in world trade.

Arthur Balfour died in Sheffield on 7 July 1957, leaving £87,226 gross.

GEOFFREY TWEEDALE

Writings:

The Imperial Conference, with Special Reference to Commerce and Trade Cust Foundation Lecture (Nottingham, 1924).

Reports of Committee on Industry and Trade, 6 vols (HMSO, 1925-28).

PP, Final Report of the Committee on Industry and Trade (1929) Cmd 3282.

PP, Report of Departmental Committee on Fire Brigade Services (1936) Cmd 5224.

Sources:

Unpublished

Sheffield City Library, Archives Division, Balfour Darwins Ltd, day books, company minutes, production records and papers relating to subsidiaries (BDR 1-143).

PrC.

Kenneth C Barraclough, 'The Development of the Early Steel-Making Processes: an Essay in the History of Technology' (Sheffield PhD, 1981).

Published

Arthur Balfour & Co Ltd, *A Centenary 1865-1965* (Nottingham: Arthur Balfour & Co, 1967).

DNB.

Times 8 July 1957.

WWW.

BALFOUR, George

(1872-1941)

Utility engineering consultant

George Balfour was born in Portsmouth on 30 November 1872, the third son and fourth child of William Balfour (1836-1926), a skilled millwright from Dundee working in the Portsmouth dockyard, and of Susan née Phippard, a Dorset woman. He was educated at Mile End Academy and Plymouth Technical Institute, but at sixteen he left for a five year apprenticeship in mechanical engineering with a small Dundee firm with which the family had connections. The apprenticeship involved arduous hours for low pay; but he pursued his education at evening classes at University College, Dundee, developing some mathematical as well as practical engineering skills. He qualified as a journeyman fitter in August 1893 and became a municipal corporation engineer in 1894, but was not elected as a member of the Institution of Mechanical Engineers until 1902. He became an associate member of the Institution of Electrical Engineers in 1898 and a full member in 1904. His later associate membership of the Institution of Civil Engineers was honorary in nature, but, as was common at the time, the earlier elections were based not only on apprenticeship qualification but on the subsequent practical experience acquired as an engineer. In the decade after qualifying he worked on a range of projects for the construction and management of tramways and electricity supply undertakings in Scotland, including Edinburgh Corporation. He became a partner in a Dundee firm of electrical engineers, Lowden Bros, in 1899.

In the autumn of 1902, Balfour moved to become chief commercial engineer of the London branch of an American engineering firm, J G White & Co, of which G M Booth (qv) later acquired control. He was responsible for obtaining orders for tramways and electric utilities in Britain, which brought him board appointments in several of the customer undertakings, such as the Scottish Central Power Co, the Fife Tramways, Light & Power Co and the Dundee & Broughty Ferry Tramways (of all of which he was managing director). These were years of considerable expansion in both these industries, as electricity was being widely applied in transport and industry, and the young Balfour decided to set up on his own account, leaving the firm in 1907. He remained on amicable terms with his former employers, taking over some of their contracts, and the following year he persuaded his former colleague, J G White's secretary, Andrew Beatty, to join him. Beatty's experience and training as an accountant were to be an invaluable asset in their new venture and the partnership remained a happy one until Beatty's death in 1934.

Balfour Beatty was registered as a private company in January 1909, its capital of £50,000 being subscribed by the eponymous partners and a few friends. An Edinburgh office was opened in 1910, though London remained their headquarters, despite a strong Scottish flavour in their management. Initially they were involved in the finance and management of electricity and tramways companies, their first major contract being for £141,450 for the construction of the Dunfermline tramway, but they were later greatly to expand the civil engineering and construction side of their activities under the leadership of Andrew McTaggart. By the outbreak of war Balfour was a director of electrical supply companies at Arbroath, Fife, Halesowen and Mansfield. In the First World War, they were involved, among other works, in the building of army camps and of a hydro-electric scheme at Kinlochleven for the British Aluminium Co.

Although Balfour came from a Nonconformist, Gladstonian Liberal background, he soon acquired a distinct dislike of the new direction of Lloyd George's redistributive Liberalism, and before the war had unsuccessfully contested two elections in the Govan division of Lanark against radical candidates. In 1918 he was elected as Unionist MP for Hampstead, a seat he retained until his death. Unlike many businessmen MPs, he was a frequent Commons speaker, principally in defence of individualism against socialism. The general tone of his speeches was reactionary, whether in opposing votes for women or in resisting state intervention to improve the uneconomic existing structure of electricity supply: the industry he knew best in Britain. He was able to defeat the Eric Geddes (qv) proposals of 1919 for electricity reorganisation, but in 1926 the Federation of British Industries decisively rejected his uncompromising pro-private enterprise stance, and supported the Conservative Government's establishment of a state-appointed Central Electricity Board under Sir Andrew Duncan (qv) to co-ordinate electricity generation. Balfour led the diehard opposition on this as on other issues, causing much pain to Conservative whips, but having little real impact. His main initiatives were largely counter-productive, even to his own objectives. Section 13 of the 1926 Act, for example, which he initiated, set up a complex pricing structure for bulk electricity, ostensibly designed to safeguard private interests. In fact it proved wasteful of skilled resources and created so many anomalies that it became a major plank in the case successfully advanced by those who advocated further reorganisation of electric utilities, or even complete nationalisation. Although he was a member of the Carlton Club, Balfour was never taken very seriously in the inner councils of the Conservative party, and he remained an individualist rebel by nature rather than a member of the Establishment, despite his clear enjoyment of an expensive lifestyle. He was chairman of the City Group of the India Defence League in 1933.

His influence on the Government's industrial policy, at a time when more subtle capitalists were recognising the need for new forms of collaboration with a newly-democratised state in the interests of social harmony and efficient responses to foreign competition, was, then, largely counter-productive. Yet his business achievements stand in stark contrast to this, for, while he maintained a negative attitude to all state initiatives in electricity (consenting only to collaborate with them to the extent that the law required), he did build up the largest private enterprise grouping in the industry, accounting for 6 per cent of all electricity sales in Britain by the 1930s. He was able to achieve this through what was essentially a reverse take-over of the private Balfour Beatty Co in 1922, which gave him improved access to finance, while retaining effective managerial control in his hands. A new company, Power Securities Ltd, was formed in October 1922, with an issued capital of £1 million, half in 7 per cent preference and half in ordinary shares. £100,000 of the ordinary and all of the preference shares were issued to the public, but the remaining, controlling £400,000 of ordinary shares went to the partners in Balfour Beatty and to three manufacturing firms with which Balfour had become associated: British Thomson-Houston (later AEI), Armstrong, Whitworth and Babcock & Wilcox. For £220,000 Power Securities acquired the ordinary share capital of Balfour Beatty (which accounted for 44 per cent of Power Securities' assets), as well as interests in various utility companies to which the old firm were usually engineers and managers. In the following ten years a further £21 million was raised on the stock market for expansion of the utilities businesses. Balfour was chairman of Power Securities and was director and/or chairman of many of the utilities in which they were interested. As chairman of the London Power Co, for example, he was able to rationalise generation in the London area and construct the new Battersea power station, but his attempts to achieve an effective private enterprise distribution system were less successful, and reorganisation on this side had to be tackled after his death by the state initiatives which Balfour so disliked. Other areas of operation of the Power Securities/Balfour group in financial or technical and managerial control of utilities included South Wales, Scotland, Lancashire and the Midlands. In Scotland, Balfour Beatty were responsible for two major hydro-electric developments: the Grampian scheme, as engineers and contractors for the Grampian Electricity Supply Co; and the Lochaber Power Scheme, as main contractors for the British Aluminium Co. The firm also expanded overseas, with widespread interests developing in the major traditional areas of British influence. In Iraq, for example, they began a four year contract to build the River Tigris control barrage in 1934, and in East Africa and elsewhere they were involved in electricity and railway contracts. Unlike many British firms of engineering consultants, Balfour Beatty could offer wider packages, including contracting, finance and continuing management where necessary, and this gave them a strong competitive advantage in some tenders. They were, then, one of the more financially successful and dynamic (and by the end of the 1930s one of the largest) firms in national and international utility contracting. Balfour's other directorates at that time included the Sphere Investment Trust, the Atlas Electric & General Trust and the Commercial Bank of Scotland.

He married in 1901 Margaret Malloch, daughter of Baillie David Mathers JP, proprietor of a temperance hotel in Dundee (who left £6,874 in 1907); she outlived him by thirty-three years. They had one daughter and four sons, two of whom entered the business after their father's death when they had qualified, one as a solicitor and one as an engineer. George Balfour died on 26 September 1941 after a short illness. The £191,591 gross which he left is little more than his personal shareholding in the firm in the early 1920s and may not represent his true accumulated wealth.

LESLIE HANNAH

BALFOUR George

Writings:

For his Commons speeches see *PD, HC* 1918-41.

'Postwar Legislation and its Effect on the Electricity Supply Industry' *Journal of the Institution of Electrical Engineers* 1922.

Report of the Committee on Cement Production (HMSO, 1941).

Sources:

Unpublished

Electricity Council, Millbank, London, archives.

North Western Electricity Board, archives.

BCe.

PrC.

Alexander T Scott, unpublished typescript biography of George Balfour in the possession of the Balfour family.

Elliott research notes.

Published

Economist 4 Nov 1922, 12 Feb 1927, 11 Feb 1939.

'The Founder: George Balfour, J.P. M.P.' *Balfour Beatty Review* 17-18 (June and Nov 1960).

Leslie Hannah, *Electricity before Nationalisation. A Study of the Development of the Electricity Supply Industry in Britain to 1948* (Macmillan, 1979).

Alexander T Scott, *Balfour Beatty: Fifty Years 1909-1959* (pp, Balfour Beatty, 1959).

WWMP.

WWW.

Jabez S Balfour. Watercolour by Sir Leslie Ward, signed Spy (courtesy of the National Portrait Gallery, London).

BALFOUR, Jabez Spencer

(1843-1916)

Building society executive and property developer

Jabez Spencer Balfour was born in Marylebone, London on 4 September 1843, the younger son of James Balfour, a marine store dealer in Chelsea who, after his marriage in 1839 moved to Maida Vale, and gave his occupation as a 'temperance lecturer' {BCe} in 1843. James Balfour became a messenger in the Ways and Means Office in the House of Commons and in 1856 figured as one of the founding directors of the Temperance Permanent Building Society on whose board he served until 1878. Balfour's mother, Clara Lucas née Lydell, a Baptist, became a distinguished temperance orator and author, and began as a protégée of Rev Jabez Burns, for whom Balfour was named and whose son, Dawson, married Balfour's sister.

Spencer Balfour, as he was known in his prosperous days, was educated in Northern France and Germany. His first employment was at Westminster with a firm of parliamentary agents. He then became managing clerk with another such firm before becoming a junior partner in a third. In 1866 he married Ellen, a daughter of James Whittle Mead of Westbourne Park, London. They had a son and a daughter.

Balfour's career as a parliamentary agent was abandoned in 1870 when the growing Liberator Building Society, formed by Balfour (as vice-chairman) and others in June 1868, took all his attention as its secretary. He fully utilised his family connections in its formation and the resulting list of officers, board members and arbitrators was such as to command immediate and widespread support in Nonconformist and temperance circles. The image was consolidated by advertising that loans were available not only for houses but also for the building of chapels. Even more important was Balfour's use of his religious and temperance connections to build up a vast agency organisation among ministers and laymen, paying commission at a rate of 1 per cent for the first year and 0.5 per cent on the amount of subscriptions thereafter to those who brought in money. Over its life the Liberator paid more than £140,000 in commission. With such agents, church and chapel halls were natural 'branch offices' helping to reinforce the images of caution and security which, with a 'remunerative rate of interest', were the keynotes of the Society's publicity.

Balfour was an innovator in his extensive use of publicity. The name chosen, the Liberator, was already well known in dissenting circles as the title of the monthly journal of the Liberation Society, as the Society for the Liberation of Religion from State Patronage and Control was known. Agents of the building society were well armed with persuasive publicity on thrift, self-help and owner-occupation (the Society's motto was 'Libera sedes liberum facit': a free house makes a man free). An illustrated almanack was widely distributed and in comparison with other building societies, press advertising was considerable. Balfour himself was a fluent and eloquent lay preacher and used his talents in the Liberator's cause in lecturing on thrift and on housing.

Having created an effective framework for business success, Balfour implemented it with skill and energy. The Liberator grew at a rate which far outstripped anything that the building society world had yet seen. Assets were nearly £70,000 after only three years and over £500,000 after seven years. The first statistics published by the Chief Registrar of Building Societies were for the year 1876 and showed that there were only eight societies with assets of over £500,000, a level usually achieved after more than twenty years of operations. By 1879 the Liberator, after only eleven years, was the largest society with assets of £1,254,000, just ahead of the twenty-four year old Leeds Permanent. Rapid growth was particularly important to Balfour himself; when he gave up his parliamentary agency partnership to become secretary of the Liberator, as he later wrote,

> I stipulated that my remuneration should be largely dependent on ultimate success and in consequence the change entailed upon me, for the first year or two, a considerable diminution in income. Both undertakings were very successful under my management and I fully shared in their prosperity {Balfour (1907) 2}.

One of the abiding frustrations of successful building society executives is that such societies are, as far as actual building construction is concerned, passive institutions. Building societies provide finance but the decision to build, and what and where to build, lies with others. Balfour met this difficulty by using the Lands Allotment Co (formed in November 1867) to buy land and develop housing estates on it. Purchasers of these houses would finance their purchases by borrowing from the Liberator. By 1872 Balfour was managing director of both enterprises but whatever his position (and he was later to change on more than one occasion to ordinary board member or vice-president) he was clearly the inspiration and the dominant force behind them.

For some years these businesses proceeded on orthodox lines: the Lands Allotment Co, joined in 1875 by the House & Land Investment Trust Ltd, developed estates and the Liberator lent on mortgage both to purchasers from these companies and to the general public. As was typical of building societies before 1914 advances were not only to owner occupiers but also to those investing in house property to let. There were also advances directly to the companies to finance their operations but such advances were not very important at first; by 1880 these formed about 20 per cent of the Liberator's assets. Thereafter the scene changed rapidly and by 1885 typical building society loans on individual houses formed only 15 per cent of the Liberator's assets. The rest was advanced to companies and mainly within the Balfour group which expanded rapidly after 1880. From 1882 it had its own bank with the formation of the London & General Bank. In 1884 the Building Securities Co was formed to acquire the building business of a Croydon friend of Balfour, J W Hobbs: J W Hobbs & Co Ltd was then launched as a public company, to give the group its own construction capability. The Building Securities Co continued in existence, after that flotation, as an investment company. The business of

George Newman, Surveyors, was acquired in 1886 and another property development company was started in 1888, the Real Estates Co. In 1891 Balfour, in partnership with a nephew, established a financial agency, thereby completing an integrated property investment and development group.

Balfour's interests were not confined to his own group of enterprises. He sat on the board of a number of other concerns such as the Edinburgh & Glasgow Assurance Co and the Debenture Corporation. He also had an interest in the Mersey Docks and (with Lord Sudeley) in the Pell Investment & Improvement Co which held land in the United States. Balfour was later to estimate his yearly income for the years around 1890 at £3,000 from his directorships and other active business interests and a further £1,000 to £2,000 of investment income.

In 1869 Balfour moved to Croydon, to Wellesley House, and played an important part in the public life of Croydon before moving onto the national stage. In 1874 he headed the poll in the School Board election, a feat he was to repeat in 1877 and again in 1880. In 1881 he was elected a governor of Whitgift Hospital. When Croydon became a borough in June 1883 Balfour was elected its first mayor and was re-elected the following November. During his mayoralty the local press reported him entertaining on a lavish scale and opening his purse to charities of all descriptions. He regularly attended Congregationalist services and presented a clock and bells to the West Croydon Congregational Chapel. Balfour was a JP for Surrey and, later, for both London and Oxfordshire. His Oxfordshire connection began when he acquired a small estate at Burcot, beside the Thames, in parcels from 1886. He was to spend more than £10,000 improving it; he built cottages, and a village institute as well as providing allotments and a recreation ground. He also bought a farm on the Isle of Wight where his mother had spent her childhood. In 1887, after his daughter's marriage, he left Croydon to live at Marlborough Gate. He was a member of the Devonshire and the City Liberal Clubs.

On the national stage Balfour was one of Tamworth's two Liberal MPs, 1880-85; after being defeated in three other parliamentary elections he was returned to the Commons in 1889, unopposed, at a by-election at Burnley and retained this seat at the 1892 general election. Balfour rarely spoke in the House. He was on the radical wing of the Liberal Party, a strong supporter of Gladstone and firm for Irish Home Rule. He was generous in his financial support of the Liberal party and keenly disappointed when he did not get office with the Liberal victory in the summer of 1892. By that time rumours of the failing fortunes of the Balfour companies could well have been abroad.

However the centre of Balfour's life was property development; here he saw himself as the creator of great suburban estates covered with well designed, built and appointed houses. In developing Whitehall Court he pioneered the fashionable flat system in London. His other London developments included the hotels Cecil and Victoria as well as further flats in the Albert and the Carlyle Mansions. In the Isle of Wight there was a vast land reclamation project at Bembridge.

The 1880s were difficult times in the property market with falling prices the norm. The Liberator directors, while publicly projecting an image of care and prudence, sought new, but often dubious, ways of maintaining their profits. A favourite enterprise was for Balfour, Hobbs or Newman to obtain an option on an estate, or even purchase it outright, then to sell the option or estate to one of the four property companies at an excessive price, the full purchase money being borrowed from the Liberator. If, having purchased a property at these inflated prices, the property did not produce sufficient income to pay both dividends to the property company shareholders and the mortgage interest to the Liberator, there was no problem. Any shortfall could always be made good with a further advance from the Liberator. No additional security was given; the valuation of the original security was merely increased to cover the new loan. Put another way, interest to Liberator shareholders was being paid out of current receipts on share and deposit accounts. So long as the Society continued to grow rapidly the precise nature of the enterprise could be concealed. At the 1888 meeting of the Society there were strong suggestions that the rate of interest paid to depositors be reduced. The directors, while promising to give the suggestion close attention, not unnaturally decided to leave the rate unchanged. When new funds were not available to meet commitments, deeds held by the Liberator as security for its advances were used to raise money elsewhere at rates of interest eventually as high as 17.5 per cent, compared with the 4 or 5 per cent at which building societies were borrowing from the public. Balfour's management style was described as 'very aggressive; it was all done at red hot speed and he talked all the time'. {*Westminster Popular* no 5} Certainly Balfour needed little sleep, usually taking no more than four hours a night. He had a rapid grasp of figures with which he persuaded his fellow directors to let him manage everything. No functions were delegated, no discussion was allowed. A resolution of the board of the Building Securities Co of 16 March 1887 reflected this spirit in conferring on Balfour unlimited powers of investment in any company he thought fit.

The crash came for the Balfour group when its banking concern, the London & General Bank, suspended payments on 2 September 1892. The Liberator and the property companies quickly followed. There were public meetings and a shareholders' committee was formed with a view to a reconstruction of the group, but a compulsory winding-up order was made on 4 October 1892. As regards the Liberator, the Official Receiver found that of its £3,423,074 mortgage assets, 93 per cent was lent to Balfour companies: J W Hobbs & Co, 61 per cent; House & Land Investment Trust, 18 per cent and the Real Estates Co, 14 per cent. He found that the Society's assets consisted almost entirely of second and third mortgages. The prior mortgagees had, in a number of cases, gone in and were in a position to sell.

The affairs of the Liberator, the Lands Allotment Co and the House & Land Investment Trust were so intertwined that eventually the United Realisation Co was formed to take over the assets of all three in May 1895. By raising £2 million to meet prior claims amounting to £690,000 and to cover £1,310,000 for completing properties under construction, it was calculated that £2,600,000 could be realised. This left £600,000 for creditors of the three companies. Liberator depositors were given shares in the United Realisation Co, 5s per £1 of deposits; depositors with the House & Land Investment Trust got 1s per £1; and those in the Lands Allotment Company 4s per £1. Shareholders received nothing.

On 11 December 1892 two of Balfour's associates J W Hobbs and H G Wright were arrested and charged with forgery and conspiracy to obtain money by false pretences from the Liberator; these charges were later extended to include conspiring with Balfour to obtain money from another company. Balfour fled the country on 18 December, later claiming and regretting that he did so much against his will and only on legal advice. He took refuge, as 'J Butler', in the Argentine. As soon as his whereabouts became known (in April 1893) his extradition was sought, a move which hastened the Argentine's ratification of its extradition treaty with the UK (negotiated in 1888). Balfour disappeared again, this time for Jujuy province, 800 miles from Buenos Aires in the far north-west of the Argentine on the Chilean and Bolivian borders. Here he rented a portion of forest and hoped to maintain himself selling timber. His whereabouts became known again and he was arrested at Salta in January 1894. Balfour fought hard against his extradition. He achieved a series of sympathetic reports in *La Nación* which he later reprinted and circulated. He was not finally handed over to British custody until 7 April 1895.

On 6 May Balfour was charged with falsifying accounts and circulating them to attract investors to take shares in the Lands Allotment Co (Balfour on 21 counts) and also with fraudulently applying funds of the Home & Land Investment Trust to purposes other than those of that Trust (26 counts). On the first indictment Balfour was sentenced to seven years' penal servitude on each of the 21 counts (to run concurrently) and similarly for the 26 counts of the second indictment, totalling fourteen years in all. Hobbs and Newman whose trials had been completed in 1893, were also treated severely, being sentenced respectively to twelve and five years' imprisonment.

Balfour served most of his sentence in Parkhurst prison where he was both librarian and organist. He was a model prisoner and was released with full remission for good conduct on 14 April 1906. Met by his son and returned to his family, he was soon employed writing a series of articles for Northcliffe Newspapers on his prison experiences; these were later collated and published as *My Prison Life*.

Subsequently Balfour lived at Clapham and had an office in Chancery Lane where he was in business as a consulting engineer, never displaying evidence of enjoying any ill-gotten gains. In his new work he made visits to West and South Africa, Australia and New Zealand and apparently thrived until the outbreak of war which forced him to give up his consultancy. In 1915, when he was seventy-two years old, he went to Burma expecting to get employment in the management of a large tin mine at Nan Ta near the Chinese border, but was refused on account of his age. He returned to Britain to spend Christmas with his son and grandchildren. On 23 February 1916 he was travelling to Swansea to take up an appointment with the Morriston Colliery when he had a heart attack and was dead when taken from the train at Newport. At the time of his death Balfour was living in a flat at Ladbroke Grove with his wife.

The Liberator débâcle led to the reform of building societies in the Act of 1894, and to a remarkable relief fund. In addition to its depositors the Liberator in 1891 had 11,825 shareholders who were owed £1,661,000. A report of the fund in 1897 showed that of those seeking relief 1,460 were widows or spinsters over sixty years old of whom 670 were more than

BALFOUR Jabez Spencer

seventy and 189 more than eighty years old. The Liberator relief fund continued for more than twenty years, raising over £156,000 and helping more than 3,000 cases before it faded into the larger distress of the First World War.

ESMOND J CLEARY

Writings:

My Prison Life (Chapman and Hall, 1907).

Sources:

Unpublished

BCe.

MCe.

Published

Balfour en Salta. Correspondencia de Fiat Lux, Enviado Especial de 'La Nación' (Buenos Aires: La Nación, 1894).

Esmond J Cleary, *The Building Society Movement* (Elek Books, 1965).

Croydon Times 26 Feb, 1 Mar 1916.

Henry O O'Hagan, *Leaves from My Life* (2 vols, John Lane, 1929).

PP, HC 1893-94 (297) IX, Building Societies (No 2) Bill.

Seymour J Price, *Building Societies* (Franey, 1958).

South Wales Argus 24, 26 Feb 1916.

Times 13-18 May, 26-31 Oct, 4-29 Nov, 10 Dec 1895, 28 Jan 1898, 24 Feb 1916.

Westminster Popular No 5, The story of the Liberator crash, 6 Mar 1893.

WWMP.

Charles J P Ball (courtesy of Mr C J Ball.)

BALL, Charles James Prior

(1893-1973)

Entrepreneur in magnesium alloys and plastics

Charles James Prior Ball was born at Cowes, Isle of Wight, on 15 February 1893, the elder son of George William Ball, a builder, civic leader and Wesleyan local preacher, and his wife Dora née Ball. After Cowes Grammar School, Charles went to Charterhouse and on to University College, London, where the First World War interrupted his studies. Already a Territorial Army officer, he joined the Royal Horse Artillery and served with B Battery, both in Gallipoli and on the Western Front, being awarded the MC during the Battle of the Somme and the DSO in 1918, and being three times mentioned in despatches. After the Armistice he was posted to Cologne and in six months there learned German. He returned to Aldershot and, after a shortened course at University College, was awarded a Diploma in Engineering in 1919, completing a formal education which did not include any advanced chemistry. On the strength of his qualifications he was appointed to the Armaments Sub-Commission of the Military Inter-Allied Commission of Control, serving as vice-president and then president of the Cologne District Committee. Here he supervised the destruction of more than 5,000 German armaments factories and stockpiles and learned a great deal about German advances in plastic materials and metallurgy, including magnesium alloys, which he first encountered during the war when fuse from an exploding German grenade hit him in the face with less damage than expected.

Major Ball retired from the army in 1923 with about £100 in the bank and joined F A Hughes & Co Ltd, a company originally founded in 1868 by F A Hughes, a director of the London, Tilbury & Lighterage Co Ltd, to undertake activities related to the marine functions of London, Tilbury Co. In 1923 it was importing chemicals and some of the early types of plastic. Among other products, Blaupunkt (Blue Spot) loudspeakers were imported by Hughes under licence from Telefunken. As managing director (and eventually as chairman), Ball took F A Hughes & Co to the forefront of the commercial exploitation of the new plastics and metal alloy technologies. In the mid and late 1920s he imported processes and equipment to make phenolic and cellulose acetate moulding powders, synthetic resins and later PVC materials under various subsidiaries of F A Hughes & Co (including Rockhard Resins Ltd and Cellomold Ltd based at Feltham, Middlesex, and Indurite Moulding Powders Ltd, at Radcliffe, Lancashire). Hughes purchased Turners Carbides at Hull in 1925-26; this secured a source of acetylene, a major chemical intermediate in the synthesis of organic chemicals and plastics. Later in the 1920s Ball set up Hughes' subsidiaries in South Africa (where it sold explosives) and Rhodesia.

Under rights acquired from Griesheim Elektron (part of IG

Farbenindustrie since 1925), F A Hughes Ltd in 1934 was importing and supplying 1,500 tons of magnesium alloys a year to the light alloy foundries licensed to work alloys for the manufacture of aircraft and armaments components, an amount representing the total supply for the British market. Using magnesium carbonate, a widely-occurring mineral, the IG process was superior to earlier German ones which used carnallite. Frequently operating at the interface between military and industrial activities, Ball viewed with increasing disquiet events in Germany in 1933, particularly because he depended on Continental sources for his alloys. He entered difficult negotiations with IG Farbenindustrie to secure patent rights and know-how. These were obtained in exchange for a 30 per cent interest in a new private limited company, British Magnesium (Elektronmetall) Co Ltd, which Ball formed in November 1934. To provide the investment capital necessary, ICI was involved as a joint owner holding 48 per cent of the company's capital while F A Hughes Ltd had the remaining 22 per cent. BME needed high tonnages of chlorine and ICI, which had almost a monopoly of the chlorine market, joined BME when Major Ball threatened to set up his own chlorine plant. Just over a year later the company's name was changed to Magnesium Elektron Ltd (MEL) and its nominal capital increased tenfold to £400,000.

As chairman and managing director of MEL, Major Ball was responsible for the erection of its first factory, the earliest large-scale electrolytic plant for magnesium production in the country, at Clifton Junction near Manchester, where production was started in 1936. Its alloys went primarily into lightweight structural work for airframes and aero engines. The national rearmament programme of that year and then the outbreak of war led to the expansion of the first factory and the construction of a second one, at Lowerhouse, near Burnley. In 1938-39 the firm's turnover exceeded £1 million and it employed over a thousand people. By 1943, the peak of wartime production, MEL's output reached 18,000 tons a year.

After Beaverbrook (qv) decided to expand Allied production of magnesium on the American continent, Ball went to the USA in 1941 to advise the American Government about the construction of a new magnesium plant, using the IG process (not then employed by Dow, the leading American magnesium manufacturer). Under Ball's direction a scaled-up version of the Clifton Junction factory was built for the Defense Plant Corporation of America (and was managed from 1942 by the Anaconda Copper Co) near Las Vegas, Nevada (at what later became the town of Henderson). With a capacity of 55,000 tons a year, it became the largest plant of its kind in the world. Within ten months it was in production, with personnel trained by Major Ball and his staff.

After 1945 ownership of MEL passed by stages to the Distillers Co Ltd (DCL) when it purchased FA Hughes in 1946, the IG Farbenindustrie shares in MEL (from the Custodian of Enemy Property) in 1949, and ICI's shares in MEL in 1951. DCL's interests in Hughes and MEL took Major Ball in September 1946 onto the DCL board where he joined the main board's management committee (from October 1948) and then became chairman of its Plastics Committee, 1948-52 and of its Biochemical Group, 1952-58.

Wartime expansion of magnesium extraction left the British Government with excessive ingot stocks and extensive piles of scrapped magnesium aircraft components. Major Ball foresaw that the latter posed a threat to MEL because, if stocks were released, backyard foundries could buy them cheaply and market inferior ingot to the detriment of the reputation of Elektron ingot. In typical fashion he persuaded DCL to finance the purchase of the bulk of the scrap and the Government to dispose of the ingot in a manner which would not upset normal trading. Within a very short time the Clifton site was piled high with aircraft magnesium scrap which for many years served as a reservoir of cheap metal, cushioning the effects of a depressed market and providing a stopgap until new alloys and products had been developed.

In 1938 Ball learned in Germany of the remarkable grain refining action of zirconium in magnesium. Unfortunately refinement could not be achieved without contamination. Ball realised the commercial potential if contamination could be avoided and, even during the war, solving the problem received high priority at Clifton. After 1945, Ball increased the pressure and as a reminder to himself and others he could always produce from his pocket a piece of zirconium-refined magnesium. Success was achieved in 1947 at a time when the aircraft industry was demanding stronger magnesium alloys. The new process enabled MEL to develop a whole family of new alloys to meet aircraft requirements. Within a few years Ball was able to licence the MEL processes and alloys to every country in the western world with an interest in aircraft manufacturing. After DCL decided to end its investment in light metals, it sold MEL to the British Aluminium Co Ltd which purchased a 60 per cent share in 1955 and the remainder in 1961. Major Ball retired as managing director of MEL in 1955 in order to accommodate BACo's nominee and in this way secured MEL's future. He remained as chairman of MEL until 1966.

Meantime, DCL developed its plastics interests partly through Hughes. In 1941 DCL added a 48 per cent shareholding in F A Hughes to its ownership of British Resin Products Ltd, a small manufacturer of paint and other thermosetting resins acquired in 1937. Under the DCL chairman, Graham Hayman (qv), these two subsidiaries were amalgamated in 1947 as British Resin Products Ltd (BRP) and on the DCL board Major Ball had special responsibility for setting up a new BRP factory at Barry in South Wales. (DCL had already in 1939 joined on a 50-50 basis with the British Xylonite Co to form a subsidiary, BX Plastics Ltd, for the development and production of thermoplastic materials.) Under the influence of Hayman and Ball, DCL expanded still further into other plastics growth areas by forming joint subsidiaries with British and American giants. The mid-1940s saw a radical change in the price structure of DCL's plastics feedstock base. In the Budget of 1945 the Chancellor removed the fiscal advantages of making ethylene from alcohol (effective January 1946) and simultaneously removed the import duty on hydrocarbon oils to be used in Britain in chemical manufacture. DCL therefore turned from molasses to petroleum. In 1947 it linked with the Anglo Iranian Oil Co (BP after 1955) to form British Petroleum Chemicals (whose name was changed in 1956 to British Hydrocarbon Chemicals Co Ltd); on this board Ball was influential in persuading the company to take up an exclusive licence to manufacture high density polyethylene which developed into a high tonnage product of BHC. A DCL-BF Goodrich (55-45 per cent) partnership in 1945 formed British Geon Co Ltd to manufacture PVC and later nitrile synthetic rubber, with DCL providing paste know-how and BF Goodrich resin know-how. A DCL-Dow Chemical Corporation (55-45 per cent) partnership in 1953 created Distrene Co Ltd to make polystyrene. DCL, having acquired full ownership of British Xylonite and its subsidiaries in 1961, joined Union Carbide in forming a joint (50-50) plastics fabrication company, Bakelite Xylonite. Eventually however DCL sold its chemical interests, and plastics interests in British Geon, to BP in 1967 and disposed of its other interests in petrochemicals.

Major Ball also presided over the renewed expansion of Murgatroyds (set up in 1947 by Dr Herbert Levinstein) after it was taken over by DCL and Fisons in 1954. Murgatroyds made salt, chlorine, caustic soda and related chemicals from the brine resources of central Cheshire; DCL and Fisons thus ensured chlorine supplies for their subsidiaries.

Ball retired as managing director of Hughes as well as MEL in 1955 but continued as chairman of Hughes and sat on the DCL board until 15 September 1961. Although he was less of an innovator with DCL than he was with MEL, Major Ball contributed his wide breadth of technical and managerial knowledge to DCL's entrepreneurial and managerial teams, backing it with his toughness and skill in negotiating.

Among his many other directorships were those of Sterling Metals Ltd (a subsidiary of the Birmid Group), J M Steel & Co Ltd, the British Tyre & Rubber Co Ltd, L Dennis & Co Ltd and British American Metals Co Ltd.

Charles Ball's contributions to industrial metallurgy were recognised with his election as president of the Institute of Metals in 1956 and the award both of that Institute's Platinum Medal and its fellowship. In 1960 he was given the Award of Merit of the American Magnesium Association, acknowledgement of his status as one of the world's leading authorities on magnesium alloys. In addition he was a fellow of the Royal Aeronautical Society, a fellow of University College, London and a master of the Worshipful Company of Glass Sellers.

In his spare time he enjoyed yachting, representing Britain in that sport in the 1936 Olympics and later serving as an active vice-commodore of the Royal Thames Yacht Club and as a member of the America's Cup Committee. He lived and farmed at Brown Candover, Hampshire, where he bred pedigree Friesians and Suffolk sheep, sat on the Basingstoke District Council, and was a staunch member of the parish church, being churchwarden for thirty years. In every area of his life, in industry, farming or recreational pursuits, Charles Ball displayed enormous drive and enthusiasm.

He married Eva, daughter of Herbert Lucas of Shepleigh Court, Devon, in 1920; they had two sons and one daughter. Charles Ball died on 15 October 1973 leaving £124,380 gross. His Candover estate, which he passed to a family trust, was sold in 1972 for £3.25 million.

DAVID J JEREMY

Writings:

Translation from the German of Hans Kannengiesser, *The Campaign in Gallipoli* (Hutchinson, 1928).

Translation from the German, with L H Tripp and others, of Adolf Beck, *The Technology of Magnesium and Its Alloys* (F A Hughes & Co, 1940).

Sources:

Unpublished

British Aluminium Co Ltd, press release, 14 Feb 1966.

C Reg: Magnesium Elektron Ltd (293,995).

BCe.

MCe.

PrC.

Information from C James Ball, Charles Evans, Dr John Fletcher, Dr Gordon J Lewis and E J Westnedge, also from J W Smart of DCL Head Office, Edinburgh.

Published

DCL Gazette Summer 1947.

Double-Bond (BP Chemicals house journal) Oct 1973.

Lutz F Haber, *The Chemical Industry 1900-1930: International Growth and Technological Change* (Oxford: Clarendon Press, 1971).

F A Hughes & Co Ltd, *F A Hughes Centenary Year* (Epsom, Surrey: F A Hughes & Co Ltd, 1969).

Sir Beauvoir de Lisle, *Reminiscences of Sport and War* (Eyre & Spottiswoode, 1939).

William J Reader, *Imperial Chemical Industries. A History* (2 vols, Oxford University Press, 1970 and 1975) 2.

The Gunner Jan 1974.

Magnesium Newsletter Oct-Nov 1973.

Modern Metals Sept 1946.

The Stock Exchange Official Year-Book 1945-1961.

WWW.

Charles H Balston (courtesy of Whatman Ltd).

BALSTON, Charles Henry

(1873-1957)

Paper manufacturer

Charles Henry Balston was born at Boxley Abbey near Maidstone, Kent, on 6 December 1873, the second son and seventh of 13 children of Richard James Balston, a paper manufacturer and his wife Emily, née Robinson. He attended Rose Hill School, Tunbridge Wells and Eton.

In his early life Balston had shown an interest in the law, but his father invited him to enter the family business of W & R Balston, manufacturers of high class drawing, ledger and writing papers. These were sold under the trade mark of J Whatman, a papermaker of renown who had founded the business in 1740 at Turkey Mill, Maidstone, to whose son Balston's great-grandfather, William Balston, had been apprenticed in 1774, succeeding him and in 1805 building a new mill at Springfield, near Maidstone.

Charles Balston recognised the need in the firm for more modern business methods and arranged to be employed in a London bank for a year where he gained some knowledge of accounting before entering the mill in 1891. After three years' work at the mill he was satisfied that he could be spared while he rounded off his education with three years at New College, Oxford, where he read political economy.

In 1897 he returned to the mill and became chairman and managing director, positions he held until his retirement over fifty years later. After some five years he was joined by his younger brother Frank who had qualified as an engineer, and later by the youngest brother Maurice.

By the turn of the century the company had built up a worldwide reputation, particularly for their drawing papers, which were used extensively by watercolour artists, architects, surveyors and engineers. These papers were all made by hand from rags and sized with gelatine. Quality of product was a matter of the greatest importance to Balston and he introduced a series of stringent tests to ensure that no substandard products left the mill.

During the First World War he served with the 10th Yeomanry, the Buffs. He was demobilised in 1919 with the rank of lieutenant colonel. Meanwhile at the mill two important events had occurred. In 1915 the London firm of H Reeve Angel & Co became the firm's sales agents, continuing as such until the two firms merged in 1974. The second development was an approach by the Government for the company to make laboratory filter papers, to replace those high quality filter papers used in many industrial laboratories and previously made in Germany. By the end of the war the mill had developed a line of chemical filter papers which became the leading brand in many countries. Both the drawing and the filter papers were all sold through Reeve Angel, who in 1914 had opened an office in New York, ideally placed for launching the new papers in the North American market.

The family business received a serious setback when the death of Balston's father in 1918 brought heavy death duties and encumbered the business with large bank loans. The resulting financial struggle lasted throughout most of the the interwar period, a struggle made worse by the economic climate of the 1930s. There were many years when the company, which had been incorporated as a private limited liability company in 1910, could pay no dividend and yielded little income to the family.

Yet the business underwent some modernisation. The mill's paper had always been hand-made and in the interests of quality the family had decided against installing a paper-making machine. The advent of filter paper, however, demanded that this policy should be reconsidered. An arrangement was made with Turkey Mill to produce the less expensive filter papers on their Fourdrinier machine, while the more sophisticated papers were still made by hand. The prospect of an increasing shortage of skilled paper-makers and the need for speedier production methods led to the installation in 1931 of a 60 inch Fourdrinier machine, similar to the one at Turkey Mill, so that the qualitative grades of filter paper could be made on site. Within the next five years, two more machines were installed, one for making acid washed filter papers, and another which could produce the complete range of drawing papers in a wide variety of sizes and substances. All the machine-made papers were watermarked 'Mould Made', but Balston's success in matching the quality and characteristics of hand-made paper may be measured by the fact that the majority of users found it difficult to differentiate between the two.

With the outbreak of war in September 1939 and the calling-up of young men into the forces, the managerial staff was reduced to Charles Balston, his brother Frank and his stepson (Maurice had retired some years before). On account of the filter papers, the business was designated as vital to the war effort in Britain and in North America. Balston, who was sixty-five in 1939, had to cope with the problems of obtaining all the necessary raw materials, nearly all imported; of acquiring suitable replacements for those who had been called up; and of shipping the finished goods across the Atlantic. However, possessing an amazingly tough constitution, he was determined to see the younger generation trained to his satisfaction before handing over the reins of office. He kept the business going both during and after the war and reached his eightieth year before a combination of old age and ill health persuaded him to retire.

Balston was most meticulous in everything he did and it was his habit to keep detailed notes of all his experiments written in a fine copperplate hand. He was a stern disciplinarian, as his military bearing and precise attention to sartorial detail suggested, but behind his stern approach were generosity and kindliness. He was respected by those who worked for him as a man of integrity and fairness, but those who crossed him did so at their peril. He would never accept second best and his workpeople knew it.

Among other interests Balston served as a JP from 1904 to 1939. A keen fisherman and horseman, he was for some years secretary to the Mid-Kent Staghounds. He was a competent shot with a rifle, competing at Bisley, and was an excellent carpenter.

In 1922 he married Mrs Pige Leschalles, a widow with two sons, one of whom came into the business and eventually succeeded him as chairman and managing director. He died in a Bournemouth nursing home on 2 March 1957, leaving an estate proved at £107,559 gross.

HUGH BALSTON

Sources:

Unpublished

Balston family papers.

BCe.

MCe.

PrC.

Published

Kent Messenger 8 Mar 1957.

BAMBERGER, Louis

(1852-1946)

Timber importer

Louis Bamberger was born in Holborn, London, on 23 October 1852, the son of David Bamberger, a leather merchant of German Jewish origin, and his wife Rose née Moellerich. His father had been in the leather trade but by 1851 was importing beech from central Europe for sale to piano manufacturers. Louis attended small private schools in London but when his father's business suffered from the repercussions of the Overend Gurney Bank failure in 1866, he was sent to New York to work for an uncle in the kid glove trade. A year later he returned to London to join Lee & Chapman, timber importers, as a clerk and later as a representative.

In 1874 Louis Bamberger set up on his own account, with the assistance of Prier Wotton, a timber merchant in the City of London, who augmented Bamberger's capital of £3. Little is known about the growth of the firm until after the First World War when the expansion of the motor trade created a new demand for oak, larch and decorative timbers.

By the First World War Bamberger was recognised as a leading member of his industry and served as president of the Timber Trades Federation (formed in 1891), 1916-19. During these years the trade, faced with wartime prohibitions on timber imports and government control of stocks and prices, found new cohesion and strength, and the TTF's membership topped 1,000 for the first time in 1918.

A Liberal, Louis represented Bishopsgate Ward on the Court of Common Council of the Corporation of London, 1905-12. He married Emily née Woodburn, in 1876; they had eight children. He died at the age on ninety-four on 26 January 1946, leaving an estate with a probate value of £119,659 gross.

Louis's two eldest sons, Arthur Prier ('the Major') and Harold Rudolf ('Jack') joined their father as full partners in 1921. After Louis's death the firm became a public company with an issued share capital of £600,000. Jack's two sons preserved family control until the firm merged with the International Timber Corporation in 1979.

HEW F REID

Writings:

Sixty Years in the Timber and Pianoforte Trade (Marston & Co Ltd, 1929).

Bow Bell Memories (Sampson Low, Marston & Co Ltd, 1931).

Sources:

Unpublished

BCe.

PrC.

Published

Bryan Latham, *History of Timber Trade Federation of the United Kingdom. The First Seventy Years* (Ernest Benn, 1965).

BANBURY, Frederick George

1st Lord Banbury of Southam

(1850-1936)

Stockbroker and railway chairman

Sir Frederick Banbury (from A G Gardiner, Pillars of Society, *James Nisbet & Co, 1913).*

Frederick George Banbury was born in Paddington, London on 2 December 1850, eldest son of Frederick Banbury (1827-90), stockbroker (and grandson of William Banbury, London banker) and Cecilia Laura née Cox. Educated at Winchester (1863-66) and abroad, Banbury entered the Stock Exchange in 1872, became head of Frederick Banbury & Sons in 1878, and remained in that position until 1906, when he ceased his membership and dissolved the firm.

According to his father's evidence to the Royal Commission of 1877-78, the firm specialised in arranging foreign loans, though it is possible that this emphasis became less marked later in the century. Banbury himself was a manager of the Stock Exchange from 1895 until his retirement as a broker. In that capacity he was prominent in the controversy over shareholders' voting rights following the entrance qualifications imposed in 1904 that new members were henceforth to be shareholders in the Stock Exchange. In 1905 he persuaded the existing shareholders that the maximum shareholding should be reduced, in order to make it possible for would-be new members to acquire shares, thereby accepting more readily than some other managers that there was a case for limiting membership. He then failed, however, in his attempt to alter the voting system so as to safeguard the power of the biggest shareholders, as Faithfull Begg (qv) with some rancour mobilised the smaller shareholders to defeat Banbury.

Increasingly Banbury was preoccupied by politics. He was Conservative MP for Peckham from 1892 to 1906 and for the City of London from 1906 to 1924.

> 'Banbury in his Commons days was rather more than a man and only a little less than an Estate of the Realm ... he took upon himself the functions of a Second Chamber; with this difference, that whereas a Second Chamber is principally concerned with the amendment of measures sent up to it ... Banbury was content with nothing less than their complete destruction ... by the simple expedient of talking them out ... the pages of Hansard ... are filled with Sir Frederick's funeral orations over the corpses of his victims' {Janitor (1928) 59-60}.

A reactionary who was a master of detail and parliamentary procedure, especially concerning finance bills, he invariably took a stance of Gladstonian retrenchment and scrutinised all Estimates with microscopic severity. Banbury was a member of the Select Committee on the Marconi scandal, involving Godfrey Isaacs (qv), and in 1913 cross-examined Percy Heybourn, the main jobber involved, with notable fierceness. He was also chairman of the Select Committee on the Estimates (1912), and of the Select Committee on National Expenditure (1919-20). He was a member of the House of Commons Finance Committee, and during the war sat on the government committee on fresh issues of capital.

Banbury was for many years a director of the London & Provincial Bank, and sat for forty years on the board of the Colonial Securities Trust, first as a director and then as chairman until 1928. Like his stockbroking contemporary Sir Alexander Henderson (qv) of the Great Central Railway, Banbury was sought by railwaymen for his financial expertise. He became a director of the Great Northern Railway in 1903, succeeding as chairman on Lord Allerton's death in 1917. In railways he remained true to his reputation as a die-hard, and strenuously opposed the principles of re-grouping embodied in the Railway Act of 1921. He regarded the Great Northern's share of seats on the newly constituted LNER board as inadequate, and refused to continue as a director after 1922. He was also chairman of the Railway Companies Association in 1922.

Banbury was created a baronet in 1903, was sworn to the Privy Council in 1916 and raised to the peerage in 1924. He married in 1873, in Kensington, Elizabeth Rosa (who died in 1930), daughter of Thomas Barbot Beale, of Brettenham Park, Suffolk; they had one son (killed in action in 1914) and one daughter. He and his wife were passionate supporters of the Royal Society for the Prevention of Cruelty to Animals (and he became its chairman) and of Our Dumb Friends League, and put much money and effort into canine charities. He was also a magistrate in Huntingdonshire, Wiltshire and London.

He died on 13 August 1936 at Warneford Place, Wiltshire, leaving £290,209 gross. His father had left £221,826 in 1890 and his wife left £83,224 in 1930.

DAVID T A KYNASTON *and* R P T DAVENPORT-HINES

Writings:

letters on London water supply *Times* 17, 24 Mar 1897.

letters on Sir Michael Hicks-Beach's war finance *ibid* 19 Dec 1900, 5 Mar 1901.

letter on London tube railways *ibid* 31 Oct 1902.

letter on Licensing Bill *ibid* 14 July 1904.

letter on Coal Mines (Eight Hours) Bill *ibid* 11 Dec 1908.

letters on Lloyd George and price of consols *ibid* 27 Apr, 3 May 1910, 16 June 1911.

PP, HC 1912-13 (277) VII, Report SC on Estimates.

letter on Non-Ferrous Metal Industries Bill *Times* 11 Dec 1917.

letter on conscription of wealth *ibid* 2 Jan 1918.

PP, HC 1919 (113, 142, 168, 238, 245) V, Reports SC on National Expenditure.

letter on repeal of Trades Disputes Act, *Times* 11 Feb 1919.

letter on railways' deficit *ibid* 1 Aug 1919.

PP, HC 1920 (100, 118, 138, 150, 172, 183, 209, 248) VII, Reports SC on National Expenditure.

letter on financial policy *Times* 8 Jan 1920.

letter on railwaymen and Russian war supplies *ibid* 4 June 1920.

letter on floating debt *ibid* 9 June 1920.

letter on national economy *ibid* 14 Dec 1920.

letter on appointment of Examiner of Estimates *ibid* 14 Jan 1922.

letter on Coalition government policy *ibid* 22 May 1922.

letters on railways *ibid* 26 Nov 1930, 24 Feb 1931, 18 June 1931, 24 Dec 1931, 5 Mar 1935.

letters on Budgets and death duties *ibid* 14 Mar 1934, 18 Apr 1935, 26 Apr, 4 May 1935.

Sources:

Unpublished

Guildhall Library, London, Minutes of Stock Exchange.

House of Lords Record Office, papers of A Bonar Law.

Modern Record Centre, University of Warwick, Coventry, share book and registration ledger of Frederick Banbury & Sons, 1905-6.

PRO, RAIL 236, papers of Great Northern Railway.

BCe.

PrC.

Published

Cecil J Allen, *The London & North Eastern Railway* (Allan, 1966).

Complete Peerage.

DNB.

Financial Times 14 Aug 1936.

Alfred G Gardiner, *Pillars of Society* (Nisbet, 1913).

'Janitor' (pseudonym of J G Lockhart & Mary F Lyttelton (Lady Craik)), *The Feet of the Young Men* (Duckworth, 1928).

PP, RC London Stock Exchange (1878) C 2157-1.

Times 14 Aug 1936.

John Wrottesley, *Great Northern Railway* (3 vols, Newton Abbot: David & Charles, 1979-81) 3.

WWMP.

WWW.

Sir Squire Bancroft, 1900. Oil on canvas by Hugh Goldwin Riviere (courtesy of the National Portrait Gallery, London).

BANCROFT, Sir Squire

(1841-1926)

Actor manager

Sydney Bancroft Butterfield was born at Rotherhithe on 14 May 1841, elder son of Secundus Bancroft White Butterfield (d 1848), oil merchant of Rotherhithe, and Julia née Wright; he took the name of Squire Bancroft in 1867. Educated privately in England and France, from childhood he had an ardent love of Dickens and the theatre. His first stage appearance was at the Theatre Royal in Birmingham in 1861, and he played 346 different roles in the provinces during 1861-65. His first London appearance was in April 1865 at the Little Prince of Wales Theatre in Tottenham Court Road in the inaugural production under the new management of Marie Wilton and Henry James Byron (1834-1884).

Marie Effie Wilton, whom Bancroft married in 1867 (succeeding Byron as joint manager in the same year), was born 12 January 1839, eldest of six daughters of Robert Pleydell Wilton, a provincial actor. She went on the stage as a child, and after a successful career in burlesque, borrowed £1,000 from her brother-in-law and at the age of twenty-six took over the management of the Prince of Wales Theatre. She and Squire Bancroft were partners in theatrical management throughout 1867-85, and made an enviably strong pair. All their achievements in drama and business were the result of their consonant aims, united efforts and mutual sympathy. Although Squire Bancroft took the more active part in their work, his wife continued to originate many of their best ideas and initiatives. Few marriages, and fewer entrepreneurial partnerships, can have been as fortunate; although other actor-managers who were helped by their marriages to women of artistic talents and business acumen included Sir George Alexander (qv), Arthur Bourchier (1863-1927) and Sir Charles Wyndham (1837-1919).

When Marie Wilton took over her theatre in 1865, it was known as the Queen's and was a place for low-class revelry. 'It was a well-conducted, clean little house, but oh, the audience', she wrote of her first visit to her new property:

> Some of the occupants of the stalls (the price of admission was, I think, a shilling) were engaged between the acts in devouring oranges (their faces being buried in them) and drinking ginger-beer. Babies were being rocked to sleep, or smacked to be quiet, which proceeding, had an opposite effect! A woman looked up to our box, and seeing us staring aghast ... shouted, 'Now, then, you three stuck-up ones, come out o' that, or I'll send this 'ere orange at your 'eds {Bancroft (1888) I, 178-9}.

Young Marie Wilton, and later the Bancrofts in partnership, transformed this little playhouse, and their outstanding commercial success led to widespread imitation of their methods, until the character of fashionable London theatre was wholly reformed. 'The old slovenliness, tempered with ostentation, was banished from the stage' by the Bancrofts. 'Plays were prettily and appropriately, and, as time went on, even sumptuously mounted; the characters, small or great, were well and appropriately dressed; while in front of the house increasing attention was paid to cleanliness, ventilation and the comfort of the audiences' {*Times* 20 Apr 1926}. The Bancrofts charged 6s for a stalls seat in 1865 and 10s by 1874, spending the resultant profits on prettier sets and on actors' pay. Their unprecedented liberality to actors was one of the distinctive features of their management, and this generous policy was soon adopted by other actor-managers such as Alexander, Sir Henry Irving (qv) and Sir Herbert Beerbohm Tree (qv). Thus one of their principal men who was paid £18 per week in 1867 received £60 per week for the same part in a revival of 1878: the Bancrofts' rates of pay made the stage, for the first time, a fit profession for an educated man. They demanded decency and order from their actors, and secured for drama a new era of social esteem.

Productions at the Prince of Wales appealed to educated and refined audiences, and were gracious yet realistic. 'The new school of acting dates from the early days of the Bancrofts, and was the result of a most praiseworthy stand against the absurd artificialities and conventionalities then in vogue', wrote the *Saturday Review* of 22 December 1888. 'Fashionable audiences were delighted with a system which replaced the grossest caricature of themselves, their manners and customs, with the closest and most faithful reproduction' {Nicoll (1959) 51}. The Bancrofts' management was exceptionally prosperous, and reacted on the world of London theatre. Not only was their innovation of matinée performances widely copied, but they also had far-reaching effects by replacing the cheap pit with expensive stalls seats. This change caused 'pit riots' at the Prince of Wales, and made it necessary for Bancroft to charge higher prices for his seats and hence to pay actors higher wages and to spend more on sets; but it was also a critical reform which improved the social composition and tone of his audiences. The success of these policies was so evident that, whereas no new London theatres were built in the twenty-three years before the Prince of Wales opened in 1865, some dozen theatres were built in the twenty years before the Bancrofts' retirement in 1885. They outgrew the Prince of Wales, and in 1879 assumed management of the Haymarket Theatre, which they re-built and opened in January 1880. After five more years, they determined to retire while still at the height of their acclaim, and gave their farewell performance on 20 July 1885. Their reputed profits, after twenty years of management, were £180,000.

Squire Bancroft succeeded Sir Henry Irving as president of the Actors' Association, and was saddened by its disintegration with the formation of the Reform Party and the Actors' Union soon afterwards. Nevertheless, his tact, patience and acute judgement were often sought to referee theatrical rows outside the Actors' Association and were especially valuable prior to the beginning of the London Theatre Council. In retirement Bancroft was chairman of the Foundling Hospital and a member of the governing body of Middlesex Hospital, and after 1893 raised some £20,000 for them by public readings of Dickens's *Christmas Carol*. During the First World War he gave many recitations for soldiers in hospital wards, and entertained them at the Eccentric Club. He was also president of the Royal Academy of Dramatic Art (RADA), to which he gave much constructive aid: he held £700 of debentures in RADA and donated £1,000 to build their theatre in Malet Street whose foundation stone he laid. RADA's annual gold medal is named after him. A member of the Lord Chancellor's advisory committee on licensing plays, he was knighted in the Jubilee honours of 1897, and St Andrews University awarded him an honorary LL D in 1922.

Marie Bancroft, who was converted to Roman Catholicism in 1885, was a kind, affectionate, merry woman with courage and stamina and much of her husband's shrewdness, moderation and good sense. She died at the Burlington, Folkestone, 22 May 1921, aged eighty-two, leaving £3,596 net. Her widower died 19 April 1926, at his flat in Albany, Piccadilly, aged eighty-four, leaving £174,535 net. Their only child George Pleydell Bancroft (1868-1956) was a barrister, playwright and first Administrator of RADA who married a daughter of Sir John Hare (1844-1921), the actor.

R P T DAVENPORT-HINES

Writings:

(jointly) *Mr and Mrs Bancroft On and Off the Stage* (2 vols, Richard Bentley, 1888).

(Mrs Bancroft) *Gleanings from On and Off the Stage* (Routledge, 1892).

(jointly) *The Bancrofts: Recollections of Sixty Years* (John Murray, 1909).

letter on British theatres in wartime *Times* 24 Sept 1914.

letter on Warrior's Day *ibid* 29 Mar 1921.

Empty Chairs (John Murray, 1925).

Lady Bancroft also published four works of fiction between 1890 and 1912.

Sources:

Published

George P Bancroft, *Stage and Bar* (Faber, 1939).

DNB.

Arthur C Fox-Davies, *Armorial Families* (2 vols, Hurst & Blackett, 1929-30).

Allardyce Nicoll, *A History of English Drama 1660-1900* (5 vols, Cambridge: Cambridge University Press, 1959).

Times 20 Apr 1926.

WW Theatre.

WWW.

BARBOUR, Sir John Milne

(1868-1951)

Linen manufacturer

John Milne Barbour was born in Dunmurry, Co Antrim, on 4 January 1868, the second son of John D Barbour, chairman of one of Ulster's biggest flax spinning concerns, William Barbour & Sons Ltd, and his wife Elizabeth Law Milne Barbour of Paterson, New Jersey. Milne was educated at Harrow, Brasenose College, Oxford, where he graduated in 1888, and the University of Darmstadt.

In the early 1890s he entered the family firm and in 1904 succeeded his father as chairman and managing director of the Linen Thread Co, holding these positions until 1947 and remaining on the board until his death. This combine, the largest producer of linen thread in the world, had been organised in 1898 with a capitalization of nearly £4 million to overcome 'excessive competition' in the trade. It comprised nine previously independent firms, five from Ulster (Barbours, Stewarts, Dunbar McMaster, Hayes & Lindsay, Thompson) and four from Scotland; through subsidiaries the combine also controlled much of the linen thread produced in the United States and the Empire. The sales and financial aspects of the business were coordinated from Glasgow and decisions relating to technical and manufacturing matters were taken at meetings in the Barbour Thread offices at Hilden in Ulster. The combine harmonised the selling policy of the various constituent companies, though it did not entirely stifle competition between them. Although not involved in the day to day running of the company, since his multifarious other activities precluded this, Barbour was in other ways an active chairman. He was involved in matters of general policy, presiding at board meetings and making numerous visits to the company's subsidiaries in the United States and the Empire. The overall effect of his long tenure of office is difficult to judge as it coincided with what was, in the main, a difficult period for the linen industry. The years from 1904 to 1920 were generally prosperous, but after 1921 the industry experienced a permanent and almost continuous decline in demand as fashions changed and new fibres were introduced. The output of linen thread in Ulster, almost all of it produced by the combine, fell from 48,800 cwts in 1912 to 29,000 cwts in 1935. Increasingly from the 1930s the company turned from linen to man-made fibres, a movement which was accelerated by the wartime shortage of flax. While Barbour's period of office was not in general a period of great prosperity for the company, at least it survived the difficult inter-war years and was able to adapt itself to the demand for man-made fibres after 1945.

It is, however, less as a businessman than as a politician that Milne Barbour is best remembered in Northern Ireland. This aspect of his career began in 1911 when he became president of the Belfast Chamber of Commerce. His period of office coincided with a great upsurge in political activity in Ireland relating to the 'Home Rule' question, and Barbour was chosen to give evidence as a representative of the province's economic interests to the Primrose Committee on Irish Finance. Thus began an active involvement with Ulster Unionism that was to last the rest of his life. He was Unionist MP for Co Antrim in the Northern Ireland Parliament between 1921 and 1929 and for South Antrim between 1929 and his death in 1951. In 1921 he became Parliamentary and Financial Secretary to the Ministry of Finance of Northern Ireland and between 1925 and 1941 combined the post with that of Minister of Commerce. He was made a Privy Councillor in 1926. Between 1941 and 1943 he was Minister of Finance. He was displaced after a period when much dissatisfaction had been expressed by the Unionist rank and file at the absence of any vigorous wartime mobilisation of the province's economy. As a consolation for the loss of office, Barbour received a baronetcy. His achievements as a minister were modest: unemployment in the province was high throughout his period of office, and the economy generally stagnant, though the Stormont Government lacked the financial resources which would have allowed him to pursue an activist industrial policy.

Not content with two careers, either one of which would have fully occupied men of lesser energy, Milne Barbour involved himself in many other pursuits. Those who knew him have suggested that this furious activity may have been a consequence of the death in 1910 of his wife, Eliza (née Barbour, whom he married in 1899), to whom he was deeply attached. He was a prominent freemason, though unusually for a Northern Irish politician was not an Orangeman. He was president of the Scottish Life Assurance Society; chairman of the Ulster Marine Assurance Co; a director of the Ocean Accident & Guarantee Corporation, the British United Shoe Machinery Co, and the Great Northern Railway; and a Belfast Harbour Commissioner. He was a member of the Church of Ireland Synod, president of the Church of Ireland Young Men's Society, and prominent in the movement to build a cathedral in Belfast. Barbour was also a keen sportsman, pioneering motor racing as president of the Ulster Tourist Trophy Committee and the Ulster Section of the RAC. He was involved in hospital work, serving on the boards of no less than six local institutions. His accumulation of these and many other offices verged on the obsessive.

He died at the family home in Dunmurry on 3 October 1951, survived by three daughters, his son having died in an air crash in 1937. In his will he left £177,485 gross.

DAVID S JOHNSON

Writings:

PP, SC Irish Finance, 'Primrose Committee' (1913) Cd 6299.

Numerous speeches in *Northern Ireland Parliamentary Debates (Commons)*.

Contributions to newspapers eg. *Manchester Guardian* Commercial Supplement 10 Dec 1937.

Sources:

Unpublished

Interview with Dr M F Gordon, director of Linen Thread Co during Milne Barbour's period of office.

William Black, 'Variations in the Linen Industry in Northern Ireland' (Queen's University, Belfast PhD 1955).

Published

Belfast Newsletter 4 Oct 1951.

Irish Times 4 Oct 1951.

Northern Whig 4 Oct 1951.

Linen Thread Co, *The Faithful Fibre* (Glasgow: The Linen Thread Co, 1956).

Who's Who in Commerce and Industry (New York: Institute for Research in Biography Inc, 1938).

WWW.

Edward J Barford (courtesy of Aveling Barford International Ltd).

BARFORD, Edward James

(1898-1979)

Construction equipment manufacturer

Edward James Barford was born at Fletton, Peterborough, on 23 April 1898, second of the three children of James Golby Barford, half owner of Barford & Perkins Ltd, and his wife Florence Burgess née Moon.

His grandfather, founder of the company, had been responsible for several technological developments, most notably the water ballast method of increasing the weight of a compaction roller; he had also played leading roles in the development of the Royal Agricultural and Smithfield Shows, and had been something of a benefactor to Peterborough.

After preparatory school at Broadstairs, Edward was educated at Rugby but left in 1915 to enlist in the Royal Artillery. In three years he rose from private to acting major, was twice wounded, twice mentioned in despatches, and awarded the MC. Rescued by chance from a dead wagon after Cambrai in March 1918, suffering from mustard gas and trench feet, he spent two years in military hospitals followed by protracted convalescence, during which he travelled widely and even lived as a Japanese in Japan.

His business career began in 1922 with Agricultural & General Engineers, a consortium of twelve companies organised in 1919 by T L Aveling (qv) which by 1922 wholly owned the family business. Within a year, his father, who had established Barford & Perkins as the world's foremost producers of internal combustion powered road rollers, died virtually penniless.

Working hard to support his mother, Barford quickly rose to take charge of the AGE group's export sales for some third of the world. By 1927 he had become personal assistant to the chairman, Gwilym E Rowland at a salary of £2,250 per annum, that increased to £3,250 during the following three years.

Becoming increasingly dissatisfied with higher management and board policy, he tried repeatedly, without success, to initiate investigation and reorganisation until a stormy meeting with the chairman resulted in his summary dismissal: a blow he could ill afford following his marriage in October 1928 to Grace Lowrey Stanley, younger daughter of A H Stanley, First Baron Ashfield (qv).

Still a shareholder, Barford called publicly for a full investigation by the group's auditor, publishing explanatory circulars at his own expense. Despite press publicity and City criticism of him as an unknown young upstart attacking the management of a large, influential group, he persisted until a ballot of shareholders enabled him to force the resignations of the chairman and all opposing directors.

Public confidence was shattered and residual ill-feeling frustrated Barford's attempts at the reorganisation of AGE Ltd, so liquidation followed inevitably, in February 1932. Six months without salary and the burden of his campaign costs left him several thousand pounds in debt. Nevertheless he set about salvaging the family concern and Aveling & Porter Ltd of Rochester, which had a jointly-owned company to manage sales of their road rollers since 1929 and had taken some avoiding action in anticipation of the crisis. The two firms, through world leadership in motor and steam road rollers respectively, were still viable. Against the odds, Barford succeeded and during 1933 he amalgamated the two into Aveling-Barford Ltd. At the end of that year the new company took over factory premises in Grantham, Lincolnshire, from Ruston & Hornsby Ltd, Barford's principal backers, whose board he joined in 1934.

By 1937 Barford converted Aveling-Barford Ltd into a public company with an issued capital of £320,000, its pre-tax profits for 1936 and 1937 being £39,237 and £38,392 respectively. Most of the firm's indebtedness was then paid off. With rearmament under way and war threatening, EJB, as he became known, heeding the appeal of the then Secretary for War for manufacturers to educate themselves in armaments, launched the company into the production of machine gun carriers. Without official approval, and so sacrificing government grants, he extended the factory and built 40 per cent of the carriers available to the BEF during the 1939-40 phoney war. To concentrate on this vital work, EJB relinquished his directorship of Ruston & Hornsby and refused opportunities to join national rearmament committees.

Intensive market research led EJB into the field of roller hire resulting in his take-over of the old established roller hire firm of Banes & Co, Potton, Bedfordshire in 1942, and establishing it as an associate company of Aveling-Barford. Four years later he amalgamated Banes with Eddison Steam Rolling Co to form Eddison Plant Ltd with headquarters at Belton, near Grantham. Manufacture and hire under a common head, however, did not prove a happy arrangement from any point of view, especially that of roller users, so the company was sold in 1949 to Harley Drayton's (qv) British Electric Traction Co, according to Barford, for £298,000 more than he paid for it.

He again clashed with the Establishment in 1945 when a promised allocation to Aveling-Barford of wartime shadow factories in Grantham was suddenly switched without explanation to the abortive £100 People's Car project. In the furore that followed that project's failure and subsequent re-allocation of the factories to an undischarged bankrupt, EJB strove to expose what he believed to be a major public scandal, but succeeded only in raising questions in the House to the embarrassment of the Government.

His First World War sufferings and the strains of repeated business conflicts now began to tell. A strenuous tour in Southern Africa proved the last straw, precipitating in 1947 a heart attack massive enough for specialists to advise putting his affairs quickly in order. During the early 1950s he was able to resume full time working, although he had managed in convalescence to continue political activities largely concerned with financing and supplying ideas for propaganda leaflets in the Conservative cause.

The decade saw him presiding over Aveling-Barford as it developed into the head of an international group manufacturing the most comprehensive range of capital construction equipment outside the United States, with exports consistently taking 70 per cent of production. He repeatedly preached the need for rationalisation in the British construction equipment industry and directed company policy to that end. By 1967 however, the company could no longer lead in this direction since ever greater resources were needed to remain competitive with the giants of America and Japan. The board negotiated successfully to join Leyland Motor Corporation at the end of 1967, whereupon he ceased to play a leading role in company affairs.

EJB would have liked a career in Fleet Street or in public relations for he was highly politically minded. Impatience with bureaucracy and many dealings with Government deterred him from entering Parliament, although at one stage he could have had the Conservative nomination for Grantham. He preferred to apply his lively, practical mind to putting forward ideas for simplifying administration, cutting out waste and easing the lot of the governed. Inventive too, he devised a low cost, motorised bicycle to lighten the fighting soldier's equipment burden, but much time and effort failed to interest Whitehall. Off duty he was, in his younger days, no mean tennis player, and later he found relaxation in shooting.

During his latter years with the company, he suffered not only from his heart but from eye troubles that, despite several operations, almost completely destroyed his sight. His book of reminiscences reveals an important facet of his character. Amused and intrigued by the sobriquet 'Captain of Industry', he felt that 'Lance Corporal' better suited his temperament, being neither too high nor too low. In appreciation of all who had enabled him to survive the First World War, after which he felt he lived on borrowed time, he devoted all profits from his book to eye research, the King Edward VII Hospital for Officers and the Not Forgotten Association.

His first marriage gave him a son and two daughters, but was dissolved in 1940. Four years later he married Mrs June Johnstone (née Looker), who gave him a son. Following a second divorce, he married again in 1964, Marion, elder sister of his first wife. His fourth marriage to Visnja Buric, daughter of a professional musician, took place in London shortly before his eightieth birthday.

Barford died on 11 July 1979 in King Edward VII hospital following an operation for a broken hip. He left an estate valued at £2,669,764 gross.

E A OLIVE

Writings:

Reminiscences of a Lance Corporal of Industry (Elm Tree Books, 1972).

Sources:

Unpublished

Aveling Barford Ltd, Grantham, company papers.

BCe.

MCe.

PrC.

Published

The Origin and Development of Aveling Barford Ltd (1950).

A Hundred Years of Road Rollers (Grantham: The Oakwood Press, 1975).

Daily Telegraph 18 July 1979.

Times 18 July 1979.

Times *Prospectuses* 93 (1937).

R A Whitehead, *A Century of Service. An Illustrated History of Eddison Plant Ltd* (Belton, Lincs: Eddison Plant Ltd, 1968).

—, *Garrett 200: A Bicentenary History of Garretts of Leiston, 1778-1978* (Transport Bookman Publications, 1978).

WWW.

Arthur S Barham (courtesy of Express Dairy Milk Ltd).

BARHAM, Arthur Saxby

(1869-1952)

Milk wholesaler and retailer

Arthur Saxby Barham was born in Bloomsbury, London on 17 July 1869, the youngest son of George Barham (qv), the founder of Express Dairies Ltd, and Margaret née Rainey. He was educated at University College School and in 1885 joined his father's subsidiary enterprise, the Dairy Supply Co, which dealt in wholesale milk supplies, dairy utensils and machinery. He was appointed to the board in 1889 and became managing director in 1893 at the age of twenty-four. From this date George Barham relinquished control of the day-to-day running of his business and Arthur was responsible for one of the largest companies of its type in the world.

Arthur Barham was reputedly severe but just in the conduct of his business affairs. Under his stewardship the Dairy Supply Co increased its annual turnover from £161,000 in 1893 to £581,000 in 1914, a considerable achievement given the strongly competitive nature of the dairy trade at this time. In July 1915 he signed an agreement which ratified the establishment of United Dairies, an amalgamation of the Dairy Supply Co, Wilts United Dairies and Great Western & Metropolitan Dairies. This new company was a giant in the dairy trade, with an initial capital of £1 million. It was created in response to war conditions: both men and horses were being sent to the war effort and there was a perceived need to reduce the inefficiency of duplicated rounds. Initially United Dairies was largely concerned with wholesaling, but soon a retailing function was added. Arthur was a prime mover of this fundamental restructuring of the London milk trade and he became a director of the amalgamated board.

One consequence of Arthur Barham's decision to take the Dairy Supply Co into United Dairies was the loss for the Express Dairies of its wholesale milk supply. This caused some tension with his brother Titus (qv) who, as managing director, steadfastly refused to take the Express into the United Dairies combine. Nevertheless the Dairy Supply Co and the Express maintained their links, at least until Arthur retired from the board of United in 1923.

Arthur Barham served with 19th Middlesex (Bloomsbury) Volunteer Rifles, 1888-1908, and commanded that battalion, 1904-8. In September 1914 he enlisted in Queen Victoria's Rifles, and in February 1915 was appointed to command the 2/12th London (The Rangers). He served in France and Flanders and was mentioned in despatches. As a result he was awarded the CMG. He was a JP, a member of Kent County Council from 1925 to his death, and an alderman, 1937-49.

Barham was also a representative of the British Dairy Farmers Association at the inauguration of the National Milk Publicity Council in 1920. He was a director of Unigate Ltd, Sir George's Trust Ltd, and de Berhams Ltd.

His first wife Annie née Edwards, whom he married in 1893, died in

1939, and his second wife Anna Marie née Schaufelberger, died in 1941 after one year of marriage. He died on 16 July 1952, and was survived by one of his two sons. He left £46,897 gross.

PETER J ATKINS

Sources:

Unpublished

Archival material in the possession of D G W Barham of Hole Park, Rolvenden, Kent.

BCe.

PrC.

Published

Arthur G Enock, *This Milk Business: a Study from 1895 to 1943* (H K Lewis & Co, 1943).

Alan Jenkins, *Drinka Pinta: the Story of Milk and the Industry that Serves It* (Heinemann, 1970).

Bryan Morgan, *Express Journey, 1864-1964* (Newman Neame, 1964).

Our Notebook: the House Magazine of United Dairies Oct 1923.

WWW.

BARHAM, Sir George

(1836-1913)

Milk wholesaler and retailer

George Barham, son of Robert Barham of the Strand in London, was born on 22 November 1836. After an education at private schools, he began his career in 1851 as a junior clerk in a barrister's office. Two years later he was apprenticed to a builder and learned the trade of carpentry. This occupation was insufficiently challenging, and in his spare time George worked as a 'balancer' in the milk trade transporting milk surplus to the requirements of one dealer to a dairy where a shortage had arisen. It

Sir George Barham (courtesy of Express Dairy Milk Ltd).

was hard manual work, but it gave George an entrée into the trade his father had practised since migrating to London from rural Sussex in 1827. In 1858 George Barham had saved enough capital to buy a retail dairy of his own, and he acquired a shop in Dean Street, off Fetter Lane on the fringe of the City of London.

Barham was an opportunist who profited from the exceptional circumstances which afflicted the dairy trade in the mid-1860s. The rapidly increasing demand for liquid milk from London's middle and artisan classes had not adequately been met by the urban cowkeeper from early in the decade. A number of dairies recognised that new sources would have to be tapped, and proceeded to import country milk from short distances by railway. This was difficult and costly because the railway companies were unwilling to make special arrangements in timetabling, freight rates and rolling stock for what was to them a very minor source of income. The amount of milk railed to London did increase steadily, however, and in 1864 George Barham decided to form his Express Country Milk Co. The following year this investment bore fruit in a spectacular fashion because a serious outbreak of rinderpest amongst the cows of London's cowsheds reduced the milk supply to a trickle. Barham was not the first dairyman to import milk to London by railway, but he was undoubtedly the most enterprising. He travelled to the dairying areas of England and persuaded farmers who were butter and cheese producers to sell their milk in liquid form, no mean feat in view of the ingrained custom that had built up over the decades or centuries. He was granted special concessionary freight rates by Sir James Allport (qv) of the Midland Railway and, using the new Lawrence capillary cooler adapted from the brewing process, he was able to arrange for substantial supplies to be transported from as far afield as Derbyshire. This large scale and long distance traffic was revolutionary and the milk trade was never quite the same again. When the cattle plague had run its course, the urban cowkeepers re-established themselves and the quantity of railway milk declined, but Barham and his imitators had proved that a re-structured trade was possible and even desirable. Gradually intra-urban production became uncompetitive and costly, and the appellation 'dairyman' came to mean a wholesale milk dealer or a retailer, rather than a cowkeeper.

The Express Country Milk Co expanded gradually after its initial outstanding success. In 1880 its first branch dairy was opened, and in 1881 Barham reformed his enterprise as the Express Dairy Co Ltd. In 1890 it became a public company and gained a royal warrant in 1895. George Barham avoided the fluctuating fortunes of many London dairy companies in the competitive atmosphere of the 1880s and 1890s by broadening his interests beyond milk retailing. In 1866 he had started the Dairy Supply Co for the dual purpose of milk wholesaling and the manufacture and sale of dairy utensils, and in 1885 acquired the British rights to the Laval cream separator, which in its modified form as the Alfa-Laval separator, was to transform the processing of milk. Later, with his son George Titus (qv) he started a chain of teashops. Both these diversifications were successful and provided capital for a growing network of Express milk shops and depots throughout London.

George Barham's contribution to the development of the dairy industry in England was outstanding. He not only pioneered a new supply system, but also acted as a catalyst in the development of a trade organization. He was a founder-member of the Metropolitan Dairyman's Association (1873), and the Dairy Trade and Can Protection Society (1880). He helped to found and was a trustee of the Metropolitan Dairymen's Benevolent Institution (1874), of which he was president in 1880, and joined the British Dairy Farmer's Association shortly after its formation in 1877, to become a trustee and a council member from 1880 until his death, vice-president in 1901, and president in 1908.

Barham was also active in the collection and dissemination of information about developments in dairying. He was chairman of the BDFA conferences which visited the Channel Islands in 1891, Denmark and Sweden in 1897, the Home Counties in 1902, and the Midland Counties in 1908, and acted as vice-president of jurors at the International Agricultural Exhibition at Amsterdam in 1884. At his own expense he equipped a model dairy at the Great Centennial Fair at St John's, New Brunswick in 1883, sent a private commission to encourage clean milk production in India in 1889, and organized educational demonstrations at the Jamaica Exhibition at Kingston in 1890. He also advocated rural education in Britain through the medium of travelling dairy schools, and acted as an examiner for the Dairy Produce and Minor Food Products Association. For some years he served on the governing body of the British Dairy Institute at Reading.

The public life of George Barham was distinguished. In 1874 he was called to give evidence to a parliamentary Select Committee on the working of the Adulteration of Food Act, 1872, and was influential in the amendment of certain clauses which were deemed oppressive to the dairy trade. He was also a bitter opponent of the importation of butter substitutes such as 'butterine'. This was sold fraudulently as if it were the genuine article and seriously affected the livelihood of farmhouse and factory butter producers. Barham drafted a parliamentary bill which forbad the word 'butter' appearing in the title of the substitute. A modified version eventually passed into law as the Margarine Act (1887).

When the railway companies unilaterally decided in 1893 to increase their freight rates, Barham spearheaded the dairy trade's opposition. His evidence before the various commissions of enquiry was largely instrumental in the dairy industry achieving a privileged status with respect to the tariffs charged for liquid milk. In 1896 rates on average were actually lower than in 1892.

Later, in 1900, George Barham again brought his progressive and individualistic ideas to bear upon a major problem confronting milk producers. He sat on the committee appointed by the Board of Agriculture to inquire into the standard desirable for milk quality, and produced a minority report of his own. The regulations subsequently framed were based upon this rather than upon the recommendations of the majority of committee members. In his conclusions Barham had the support of practically every dairy association in the country.

George Barham was knighted in 1904. He was a JP for Middlesex and East Sussex, mayor of Hampstead in 1905-6 and High Sheriff of Middlesex in 1907-8. He served for a time on the vestry of St George's Bloomsbury, and was twice elected to the East Sussex County Council. His one excursion into parliamentary politics was unsuccessful, when he contested West Islington for the Liberal Unionist Party in 1895. Among his many other interests he was chairman of the Hackney Carriage Proprietors' Benevolent Institution, chairman of the London General Hospital and treasurer of the headquarters fund of the 19th (Bloomsbury) Rifles.

Sir George's forbears made their fortune in the iron industry, but lost their land in 1721. In 1885 he took the opportunity of buying back the estates at Snape and Tappington Grange, Wadhurst, thereby re-establishing his family's links with Sussex. He also farmed in Middlesex.

Barham's remarkable energy is attested by the wide range of his activities and interests both within the dairy industry and in community service. He was a fluent speaker, with old-fashioned manners but also a strongly disciplinarian streak to his character. His resourcefulness, self-confidence and innovative instinct were key elements to a personality which was indelibly stamped upon the Express Dairy Co, upon the London milk trade, and indeed upon the English dairy industry. His was the dominant influence for change and improvement over a fifty-year career of distinction.

Sir George Barham died on 16 November 1913, seven years after his wife Margaret née Rainey, whom he married in 1859. His two surviving sons Arthur (qv) and George Titus also made careers in the dairy industry. His estate was valued at £259,222 gross.

PETER J ATKINS

Writings:

PP, HC 1874 (262) VI, SC on the Adulteration of Food Act.

'Butter Frauds' *Bell's Weekly Messenger* 12 Apr 1886.

'Guernseys in England' *Livestock Journal* 12 July 1886.

'The London Milk Trade' in J P Sheldon ed, *The Farm and the Dairy* (1st ed, G Bell & Sons, 1888).

'A Few Thoughts on the London Milk Trade' *Agricultural Gazette* 20 Oct 1890.

PP, HC 1890-91 (394) XIV, SC on the Railway Rates and Charges Provisional Order Bills.

'Railway Rates for Dairy Produce' *Journal of the British Dairy Farmers' Association* 6 (1891).

PP, HC 1893-94 (385) XIV, SC on Railway Rates and Charges.

PP, Departmental Committee Report into the Desirability of Regulations under Section 4 of the Sale of Food and Drugs Act 1890, for Milk and Cream: Minority Report by G Barham (1901) Cd 491.

Sources:

Unpublished

Archival material in the possession of Mr D G W Barham of Hole Park, Rolvenden, Kent.

Greater London Record Office: miscellaneous documents.

PrC.

P J Atkins, 'The Milk Trade of London, ca 1790-1914' (Cambridge PhD, 1977).

D Taylor, 'The Development of English Dairy Farming ca 1860-1930' (Oxford DPhil, 1971).

Published

Creamery Manager Dec 1913.

Dairy 25 (1913).

Dairyman, Cowkeeper and Dairyman's Journal 36 (1913).

Dairy World June 1894, July 1904, Nov 1913.

Arthur G Enock, *This Milk Business: A Study from 1895 to 1943* (H K Lewis & Co, 1943).

Express Dairy Co Ltd, *Express Story, 1864-1964* (1964).

Alan Jenkins, *Drinka Pinta: The Story of Milk and the Industry that Serves It* (Heinemann, 1970).

Journal of the British Dairy Farmers' Association 28 (1914).

Journal of the Royal Society of Arts 17 (1868).

Bryan Morgan, *Express Journey, 1864-1964* (Newman Neame, 1964).

Provisioner Jan 1881.

Railway and Lands Traffic Act, 1858: Hearing of Objections to Revised Classification of Merchandise Traffic and Charges Proposed by the Various Railway Companies (1890).

Times 18 Nov 1913, 6 Jan 1914.

WWW.

BARHAM, George Titus

(1860-1937)

Milk wholesaler and retailer

George Titus Barham was born on 22 March 1860 over the dairy shop in Dean Street, Fetter Lane, London where his father George Barham (qv)

BARHAM George Titus

George T Barham (courtesy of Express Dairy Milk Ltd).

had started his own business two years before. Barham Sr became a renowned, respected and very successful dairyman who dominated the London milk trade through his Express Dairy Co Ltd, and his son followed him into this trade after an education at University College School and several years as an invalid in an orthopaedic hospital. In 1878 Titus joined the Express Country Milk Co, as it was then called, and in 1881 he became a managing director and third member of the board.

For many years Titus lived in the shadow of his father's outstanding achievements. He played an important part in helping to build up the catering side of their enterprise and gained a wealth of experience that stood him in good stead when his father gradually relinquished power from 1893 onwards and finally died in 1913. During the First World War there was a dramatic restructuring of the London milk trade, with a realignment of both the wholesale and retail sectors. One group, United Dairies, which was created in 1915 and enlarged in 1917, by the end of the war controlled something approaching two-thirds of London's wholesale supply of liquid milk. Titus abhorred this nascent monopoly and resisted blandishments to join. His brother Arthur (qv) had taken his Dairy Supply Co into the combine and tried to persuade Titus to follow. In 1920, with his traditional wholesale supplies cut off and divorced from the profitable utensil business, George Titus must have been tempted to succumb, but the stubborn streak which characterised his decision-making, coupled with a personality clash with his brother, preserved the independence of the Express Dairy Co Ltd.

Titus Barham was not the strong and influential character his father had been. He did not leave such an indelible personal stamp on the company, one contributory factor being a painful physical disability. Nevertheless the 'Express' expanded during his time of office and, after the initial difficult years, increased its number of branches fourfold and the turnover of milk sixfold between 1913 and 1937. Titus also had his share of innovative ideas. In 1929, for instance, he initiated the first large-scale experiment in the sale of milk in cartons, although in the event it was a failure financially. He refused to retire, and in his declining years the Express Dairy Co lost its momentum.

Outside his immediate business interests, Titus Barham was active in trade organizations. He was honorary treasurer of the Metropolitan Dairymen's Benevolent Institution from 1913 until his death, and its president in 1895; he was president of the National Dairymen's Benevolent Institution (Incorporated) in 1934; for many years he was president of the Dairy Trade Protection Society; he served on the Council of the British Dairy Farmers' Association, and was its vice-president in 1916 and president in 1933-34. He was a founder-member of the English Guernsey Cattle Society in 1884, its treasurer until his death and its president in 1918 and 1934. He also presided at various times over the British Kerry Society and the Dexter Society.

Titus Barham lived in Wembley for fifty-six years. He was deeply involved with local activities and became the borough's charter mayor. He was also a founder-member of the Hampstead Lodge of freemasons and was president of the Boy Scouts Association.

Titus's interest in cattle breeding led to the development of a fine herd of pedigree shorthorns, which he kept on one of his farms, at Sudbury

Park in Middlesex. In 1908 their milk was among the first to be certified as tuberculin-tested. Sudbury Park was also the home of George Titus Barham's collection of antiques, curios and works of art, which he had built up during his extensive foreign travels and visits to auction sales at Sothebys and Christies. In his will he left the mansion, estate and collection to the public.

Titus Barham died on 8 July 1937. He was survived by his wife Florence, née Vosper, but there were no children. The unsettled estate was valued at £515,063 gross.

PETER J ATKINS

Sources:

Unpublished

BCe.

PrC.

Published

Arthur G Enock, *This Milk Business: A Study from 1895 to 1943* (H K Lewis & Co, 1943).

Harrow Observer and Gazette 16 July 1937.

Alan Jenkins, *Drinka Pinta: The Story of Milk and the Industry That Serves It* (Heinemann, 1970).

Journal of the British Dairy Farmers' Association 50 (1938).

Bryan Morgan, *Express Journey, 1864-1964* (Newman Neame, 1964).

Times 9 July, 21 Sept 1937.

WWW.

*John Baring, Lord Revelstoke.
Drawing by John Singer Sargent
(courtesy of Baring Bros & Co Ltd).*

BARING, John

2nd Lord Revelstoke

(1863-1929)

Merchant banker

John Baring was born at Kingston upon Thames, on 17 September 1863, the son of Edward Charles Baring, and a great-grandson of Sir Francis Baring, the founder of Baring Brothers, merchant bankers in London. His mother Louisa Emily Charlotte née Bulteel was daughter of John Crocker Bulteel of Lyneham in Devonshire and the grand-daughter of the Second Earl Grey, prime minister. In the nineteenth century the house of Baring, under the continuing control of the Baring family, became one of the leading issuing and accepting houses in London, but the Barings also achieved high rank in public life. John Baring's father was raised to the peerage, as First Lord Revelstoke, in 1885; his uncle Sir Evelyn Baring, was First Earl of Cromer, and British agent and consul general in Egypt (1883-1907); and his cousin was the Earl of Northbrook, Viceroy of India (1872-76).

Educated at Eton, Baring went up to Trinity College, Cambridge, matriculated in 1882, but came down before taking his degree. He entered Baring Brothers in about 1883 while his father was senior partner. For two years he learnt the ordinary routine of the office and then left for an eighteen month 'world tour' when he worked in the offices of Barings' correspondents in Boston and New York (Kidder Peabody & Co), and travelled in Mexico, Argentina, Australia, India and Egypt. He spoke fluent French and Spanish.

He was made a full partner of Baring Brothers & Co on 1 January 1890, shortly before the Baring Crisis of November that year when the house faced a severe crisis of liquidity and had to be saved from collapse by the intervention of the Bank of England and the establishment of a fund to guarantee its liabilities. On the resignation of the senior partners, John Baring, with his cousin the Hon Francis Henry Baring (1850-1915) who had been a partner since 1879, played a leading role in the reconstruction and subsequent recovery of the house and the formation of a limited company (Baring Brothers & Co Ltd) to realise the assets of the old firm. By the end of the decade Revelstoke (he succeeded to the title in 1897) had re-established the house's prestige as one of the leading merchant banks in London.

On F H Baring's retirement in December 1901 Revelstoke became senior director. Haunted all his life by the memory of the Baring Crisis he sought ability as well as breeding and connection in recruiting his fellow directors and he assembled a highly competent team. Not least amongst these were Gaspard Farrer (1860-1946), an expert on American securities who came from H S Lefevre & Co in 1902, and the Canadian, Edward Peacock (1871-1962), who came from Dominion Securities Corporation in 1924. Revelstoke saw Peacock as his eventual successor as senior director and within three years of Peacock's arrival was acting more in an advisory role rather than supervising day-to-day activities.

Revelstoke's style of leadership was autocratic. At Barings he dominated policy making and controlled all negotiations leading to issues. He travelled frequently to European financial centres such as Paris and Amsterdam, and when younger, made annual visits to North America. In communicating with overseas clients, corresponding banks forming international issuing syndicates, and agents on the spot, he was the first senior director of Barings to make extensive use of cable telegraphy.

Under Revelstoke's leadership Barings continued to issue loan stock in London for Governments, municipalities and railway companies in North and South America and in Russia, the areas in which Barings had specialised for much of the nineteenth century. There were exceptions, however, such as an issue in 1902 for the Japanese Government and issues of loan stock for American public companies including American Telephone & Telegraph Co. Issues for British companies remained at a low level with just two, for Mersey Docks & Harbour Board and London United Tramways. In the changed world that followed the First World War all issues for the USA, Canada and Russia ceased although South American, mostly Brazilian, issues continued. Barings now looked to Europe, making issues in the 1920s for the Governments of Czechoslovakia, Hungary and Belgium, and the cities of Hamburg and Berlin. Before Revelstoke's death in 1929 other issues had been made for the Japanese Government and the City of Tokyo, but just two for British companies, namely Denaby & Cadeby Main Collieries Ltd, and the Underground Electric Railways Co of London Ltd. Revelstoke oversaw a similar movement in Barings' commercial credit business, away from North America and towards Europe. As a general measure of growth of Barings' business, 'commission' income increased as follows: £106,051 (1901), £126,651 (1914), £171,501 (1919) and £203,450 (1927).

Revelstoke's influence throughout the City was immense. He was a close friend of such leading bankers and financiers as Montagu Norman (qv), Sir Charles Addis (qv) and especially Sir Ernest Cassel (qv) with whom he was involved in an ill-fated attempt at business imperialism, The The National Bank of Turkey, ca 1909. His advice was sought in many quarters, as in 1904-5 when he mediated in a furious dispute between the Cunard Steamship Co Ltd headed by the Second Lord Inverclyde, and International Maritime Marine over the setting of conference rates on the North Atlantic passenger routes. Much of his influence was exercised through his directorship of the Bank of England. He joined the Court in 1898 at the early age of thirty-five, was appointed to the Committee of Treasury in 1915, and held both positions until his death. He was a confidant of successive Governors, and, as a measure of his influence, in 1917 was invited to undertake the chairmanship of a committee to investigate the internal organisation of the Bank in the difficult circumstances of a 'quarrel' between the Governor Walter Cunliffe (qv) and the Court. His committee's recommendations formed a lasting constitutional framework for the Bank.

His advice was sought by successive Governments and by officials in the Treasury and Foreign Office. In 1902 he chaired a Royal Commission to examine the workings of the Port of London, which resulted in an amalgamation of companies to form the Port of London Authority, first headed by Hudson Kearley (qv). In 1904-6 Revelstoke was invited to offer the Treasury informal advice on the 'mix' of the funded and unfunded debt. From 1911 he was an adviser to the Committee on Imperial Defence and during the First World War played a major role in negotiations for the finance of munition purchases in Britain by the Imperial Russian Government. In 1915 Asquith considered offering him a cabinet post, and his name was mentioned in 1922 as a possible Ambassador to France. In January 1917 he was appointed a Minister Plenipotentiary and joined Lord Milner's mission as British financial representative at the Allied Conference in Petrograd. In 1929 his services were called upon once again when he joined Sir Josiah Stamp (qv) as joint British representative at the Committee of Experts to review the Dawes Plan for German Reparations, although it meant resigning his directorship of the Bank of England. On the Committee of Experts he did much to encourage the formation of the Bank for International Settlements. During the course of these negotiations he died.

An expert on international capital markets, he gave informal advice to many investors both at home and overseas. One of his most important offices was Receiver General of the Duchy of Cornwall. A close friend of the Prince of Wales, later George V, he was invited to join the Prince's Council in 1907 and became Receiver General a year later when he reorganised the Duchy's finances with marked success.

His charitable interests were largely confined to support of hospitals. He was treasurer of the King Edward Hospital Fund and chairman of Guy's Hospital's Finance Committee, and he made generous bequests to them of £100,000 and £50,000 respectively, as well as £25,000 to St Mary's Hospital Medical School.

He was appointed a Privy Councillor in 1903 and was honoured with a GCVO in 1911. He was appointed Lord Lieutenant of Middlesex in 1926 and received honours from the French, Japanese and Imperial Russian Governments. A sound and shrewd judge of men and situations, a reliable confidant and with a massive capacity for work, Revelstoke was especially marked out by his great articulation and social charm. He never married. Revelstoke died on 19 April 1929. The gross value of his estate was £2,558,779.

JOHN ORBELL

Writings:

PP, RC Port of London (1902) Cd 1151.

British Staying Power. Lord Revelstoke's Views. Anglo-American Sympathies. Interview given to the United Press of America (Sir J Causton & Sons Ltd, 1916).

Sources:

Unpublished

Baring Brothers, London, Archives.

BCe.

PrC.

Published

The Bankers' Magazine June 1929.

Marian Kent, 'Agent of Empire? The National Bank of Turkey and British Foreign Policy' *Historical Journal* 18 (1975).

Richard S Sayers, *The Bank of England 1891-1944* (3 vols, Cambridge University Press, 1976).

WWW.

Sir John Barker (courtesy of House of Fraser PLC).

BARKER, Sir John

(1840-1914)

Department store founder

John Barker was born at Loose in Kent on 6 April 1840, the son of Joseph Barker, carpenter and brewer, and his wife Ann née Sells. He was educated privately and in 1853 began a three year apprenticeship to a Maidstone draper. He gained further experience in drapery shops in Folkestone and Dover before moving to London in 1858 to join Spencer, Turner & Boldero, furnishers and drapers of Marylebone.

After a few years in London, Barker was offered a position at William Whiteley's (qv) new emporium in Westbourne Grove. He proved a talented salesman and was promoted to department manager at a salary of £300 per annum. Within a year he managed to double sales at the store and although his salary was also doubled his expectation of a partnership was disappointed. Whiteley, loath to relinquish sole control, instead offered Barker £1,000 per annum in compensation.

Barker left Whiteley in 1870 to open a small drapery shop in Kensington High Street. His partner, James Whitehead, was already a wealthy merchant and provided capital and credit without interfering in the running of the business. As managing partner Barker drew an annual salary of £250 and lived over the shop with his family. He had left a remunerative position for a speculative venture but, as part owner, was now able to use and adapt the modes of retailing which had proved successful at Whiteleys. By dealing directly with manufacturers and selling for cash he was able to keep prices low and achieve a rapid turnover.

From the outset Barker envisaged the creation of a vast department store, at a time when few shops carried a diverse stock. He took every opportunity to acquire premises. By 1880 he was trading in 15 shops in High Street and Ball Street, selling not only drapery goods but also groceries, furnishings and ironmongery.

Barker was an observant and inventive businessman, hard-working, tenacious and intolerant of idleness, yet generous and well-liked by his staff. On account of his success he became prominent in the trade and was regarded as one of its spokesmen by the 1880s. A member of the Early Closing Association, he was president of the first Early Closing Congress in 1888 and a pioneer of Saturday half-day closing. He also appeared before several Parliamentary committees investigating hours and conditions of work in shops to explain the mutual benefits of reform. Apart from shorter hours, those of his staff who lived-in enjoyed comfortable accommodation and such benefits as a social club, library and athletics facilities.

In 1893 Barker acquired Whitehead's share in the business using capital provided by his son-in-law's father, Sir Walter Gilbey of Bishop's Stortford. To satisfy a condition of the loan the firm was floated as a public company, John Barker & Co Ltd, with an authorised share capital of £330,000 and £150,000 4.5 per cent first mortage debenture stock in June 1894. Over the previous seven years the firm had averaged net profits of £28,351 annually. As vendor Barker received £402,016 15s 6d (£282,016 15s 6d in cash, the rest in shares and debenture stock in the new company), and was appointed chairman. At this date business comprised 60 departments and employed 1,400 people. Barker continued to expand the business and, in 1907, acquired Ponting Brothers, a fashion store in Kensington High Street, which had recently gone into liquidation. Barker was also chairman of Paquin Ltd of Mayfair. He continued to manage both companies until his death but, by the turn of the century, he had also begun to develop interests outside the retail trade.

During the 1890s Barker bought a 300 acre estate in Bishop's Stortford, Hertfordshire, which he farmed using the most modern methods. As a breeder of livestock he was famed for his polo ponies and flock of Syrian sheep. Barker was president of the Polo Pony Society and, in 1913, president of Essex Agricultural Society. He also involved himself in the local community by contributing to local, as well as national, charities and serving, from 1913, as chairman of the bench of magistrates.

Barker, a staunch Liberal, also embarked upon a political career. In 1889 he was amongst the first aldermen elected to the new London County Council. He was president of Hammersmith Liberal Association, councillor for Chelsea Liberal Association and founder president of Bishop's Stortford District Liberal Association. He contested Maidstone on three occasions (1888, 1898, 1900) and although finally elected in 1900 he was unseated on petition by the Conservatives. From 1906 to 1910 Barker sat as MP for Penrhyn and Falmouth. He was a member of the Reform and National Liberal Clubs. After the Boer War Barker was a prominent supporter of the Territorial Movement. He was awarded a baronetcy in the King's birthday honours list in 1908.

In 1864 he married Sarah Waspe of Tuddenham in Suffolk by whom he had a daughter, Anne Sarah, and a son, John. Barker died on 16 December 1914 at the Grange, Bishop's Stortford. His son having predeceased him, he left no heir. His estate was valued at £247,706 gross.

ALISON TURTON

Writings:

PP, HC 1886 (155) XII, SC Shop Hours Regulation Bill.

PP, HC 1892 (287) XVII, SC Shop Hours Regulation Bill.

Sources:

Unpublished

BCe.

PrC.

Published

Alison Adburgham, *Shopping in Style* (Thames & Hudson, 1979).

Herts and Essex Observer 19 Dec 1914.

Illustrated London and its Representatives of Commerce (1893).

Derek W Peel, *A Garden in the Sky. The Story of Barkers of Kensington, 1870-1957* (W H Allen, 1960).

Times 17 Dec 1914.

Times *Prospectuses* 7 (1894).

Vanity Fair 6 Jan 1910.

WWMP.

WWW.

BARLOW, Sir Robert

(1891-1976)

Manufacturer of packaging materials

Robert Barlow was born in Hackney, London, on 1 September 1891. His father, Edward C Barlow (1846-1937), was a tough, sometimes terrifying

Sir Robert Barlow (courtesy of Metal Box PLC).

cockney, almost illiterate (he left a penny-a-week school at the age of ten), fond of women, three times married. Robert, the son of Edward's second wife Annie Eleanor née Baverstock, had an older half-brother Ernest (1874-1966) and a sister. He left school, according to his own account, at lunch-time on 25 July 1907 and joined his father's business in the afternoon.

Edward Barlow set himself up in business in the East End of London in 1869 to make tin boxes: a trade then requiring little more than a stock of tinplate and solder, shears, a soldering iron, and the barest minimum of skill. Towards the end of the century, after many years of grubby insecurity (as late as the 1890s the firm had no bank account) Barlows' business began to prosper, probably under Ernest's influence, and by 1908, though still small (sales £28,810, net profit £4,800), it was thriving on the manufacture of tins for Carreras' cigarettes, Birds' Custard Powder, Brands' Essence and Brooke Bond Tea, besides other products. It was also by now in printing, as many tin-makers were. The story is that old Edward, infuriated by a supplier who failed to deliver, went out and bought a printing machine, a varnish machine and a transfer press. 'But', said Ernest, 'I know nothing about printing', to which he got the reply: 'Well, learn then. There can't be anything in it if that old fool can manage it.' {Reader (1976) 25}

In 1921, when times were hard, the leading tin-box makers of Great Britain, amongst whom Barlows were barely yet to be numbered, set up Metal Box & Printing Industries Ltd as a holding company for a half-hearted merger which amounted to little more than a cosy club for the directors of medium-sized family firms, very set in their ways. 'The purpose', said an accountant, 'was of security rather than of profit.' {*ibid*, 40} Nevertheless in its first eight years MB&PI more than doubled its profits, which shows what can be done in a managed market, and by 1929 its turnover was about £1.3 million.

'Gladly would I have joined the ship,' Robert Barlow wrote to the chairman of MB&PI when it was first formed, 'confident in the captain & my fellow adventurers.' {*ibid*, 39} His father, of whom he stood in awe, and his brother were unsatisfied with the offer made to them, and Robert, having failed to persuade them to accept, was not yet in a position to enforce his views. Frustrated, he was seen one evening in his father's house to come on to the staircase, dash his spectacles to pieces, and exclaim 'I'm sick of this life!' {*ibid*, 39}

In 1929 the comfortable world of the British tin-box makers was threatened by invasion from a different planet: the can-making industry of the USA. The leader of the invasion was American Can Co, perhaps ten times larger than MB&PI and expert in a totally different and far more sophisticated technology: the mass production of containers for the canning industry. Such an industry barely existed in the UK in 1929, with nearly all canned food imported, chiefly from the USA, but the opportunity to create one was there.

Robert Barlow, now virtually in charge of the family firm, which was smaller but more profitable than the larger subsidiaries of MB&PI, recognised the gravity of the American threat. His eighty-two-year-old father's response to an offer of take-over by American Can was to swing a chair at their representative, shouting 'Shut up you damned Yankee or I'll brain you' {*ibid*, 50}, but Robert was much cooler. 'That's all right father', he reported himself as saying, 'but we are a very small specialised firm. They know all about us and could soon shut us up.' {*ibid*, 51} Negotiations continued in New York, where no doubt American Can's men felt safer, but they broke down.

Robert Barlow accepted instead, in July 1929, an offer from MB&PI of 165,500 MB&PI £1 ordinary shares and 110,350 £1 seven per cent cumulative preference shares for the whole of Barlows' share capital of 70,000 £1 ordinary and 30,000 £1 preference. As soon as the deal was completed, he joined the MB&PI board and rapidly took over the leadership, although he was not the chairman.

With the resources of MB&PI at his disposal, Barlow proceeded to defeat the threat from American Can and seize the opportunity of establishing can-making by American methods in Great Britain. Having spurned American Can's advances, he turned to their slightly smaller competitor Continental Can, which was also seeking an entry into the British market. Instead of allowing Continental Can to take over MB&PI, Barlow negotiated with their chairman, Carle Conway (1878-1959), a group of agreements which gave Continental Can a minority interest in MB&PI and gave MB&PI, in exchange for £50,000 cash, exclusive rights in Great Britain for fifteen years to buy container machinery from Continental Can and to service and technical information, as well as patent licences.

These arrangements enabled MB&PI to negotiate long-term contracts with customers which blocked American Can's British subsidiary British Can (or any other firm) from establishing itself in can-making in the British Isles. At the same time MB&PI energetically set about taking over its more important competitors. American Can, routed by Barlow's speed and ruthlessness, and perhaps short of cash, gave up British Can for lost. After a despairing appeal to its parent for capital, British Can passed into MB&PI's control in August 1931, and American Can agreed to keep out of the British market for twenty-one years. The surrender was abject and Barlow's victory was total.

He used his victory to turn MB&PI, renamed and launched to the public as The Metal Box Co in 1930, from a loose, ill-disciplined association of family firms into a centralised autocracy over which his own authority, as managing director, was absolute. The members of the more important families resented Barlow's policy deeply, and fought back hard. In 1932 they tried to get rid of him but failed when their leader lost his nerve. Barlow, hard, wily, and, when it suited him, irresistibly charming, never lost his. 'It wasn't difficult to wait, or to make changes oft-times apparently unrelated', he told his chairman in 1934 {*ibid*, 62}. 'It may have meant sending people round the world or to South Africa or getting rid of them entirely.' {*ibid*, 62} By 1935 he could rely on enough voting power (his own and his allies') to force a conclusion. Two directors still opposed him, but against a threat of his own resignation one was obliged to resign and the other submitted. Treason against Barlow did not prosper.

This civil war was not costless. Throughout his later career Barlow never felt secure. He developed elaborate tactics to protect his position, notably the device of playing possible rivals off against each other by appointing them in pairs to positions in which they were obliged to share authority with each other. The resulting discord very efficiently deflected them from any joint assault on Barlow. It did not produce a happy working atmosphere within the company. Feeling between the sales director and the production director became so bitter that as late as the 1970s, when one had retired and the other was dead, and Barlow himself had retired, the venom was still working.

Against this turbulent background, Barlow propelled Metal Box along the path he wished the company to follow: that is, towards the manufacture of 'open-top' cans on modern high-speed machinery in preference to the manufacture of the 'general line' containers, for biscuits, confectionery, tobacco and so on, on which the older firms, including Barlow's own, had built their reputation. Throughout the 1930s depression in some parts of the UK was deep and unemployment was at levels not to be seen again for more than forty years. Nevertheless living standards were rising and the canning industry, in which Metal Box had a monopoly in the supply of cans, grew rapidly. Metal Box prospered from the start, and during the 1930s capital employed rose from just under £1.4 million to nearly £4.2 million: published profits from £103,480 to £316,368 after tax. By the time war broke out about half the turnover was coming from open-top can-making: the rest from other activities.

In 1938 Barlow lost his only son in a flying accident and over the next three or four years his first marriage went to pieces. At the same time he was taking on more and more responsibilities. He became chairman of Metal Box in 1941 and remained managing director. In April 1942 he was appointed chairman of an Industrial Panel set up by the Government to investigate production hold-ups: an appointment which brought him a great deal of work and, in 1944, a knighthood. In May 1943, looking towards Metal Box's supplies of tinplate, he joined the board of Baldwins, thereby embroiling himself in the convoluted and embittered politics of the tinplate industry.

In December 1941 an attempt was made to relieve Barlow of some of his load. Archibald McKinstry (qv), managing director of Babcock & Wilcox, was brought on to Metal Box's board as a non-executive director. He was fifteen years older than Barlow, no less heavily laden with executive duties and war work. What Metal Box urgently needed (and Barlow himself, if he could be brought to recognise the need) was not an extra director but a plan of organisation to match the size and the complexity of the business.

Robert Barlow, like many great business men, was unwilling either to delegate power or to recognise the uses of bureaucracy. It was not until 1941, after promptings from the accountants Peat, Marwick, that he consented to the appointment of a financial controller, and then he proceeded to quarrel with him. Barlow's powers of work were immense and his mental capacity matched them, but by the summer of 1943 he was close to breakdown. 'They are all plotting against me', he said. 'I've got evidence. Never be ambitious; only misery can come of it. Never try to hold a job like I hold. You'd better be dead.' {*ibid*, 145}

This was the climax, the grand climacteric, of Robert Barlow's career. Sole power, which he had fought so fiercely to win, undid him. Harold Whitehead, a management consultant, in spite of an obvious admiration for Barlow, told him what he had himself indicated to the board: that he should not try to be both chairman and managing director. Whitehead went further. He remarked on 'friction, resentment, confusion, and neglect' in inter-departmental relations, traced them to their source (the quarrel between the production director and the sales director) and drew attention to 'an exceedingly bad atmosphere in the ranks of the senior executives because of this unfortunate clash of personalities' {*ibid*, 147}. The board and the chairman, Whitehead concluded, 'must accept responsibility for its undermining influence' {*ibid*, 147}.

Whitehead, speaking with the voice of management science, proclaimed the beginning, but only the beginning, of the end of RB's personal rule and the start, only the start, of the transition to the kind of administration which Metal Box, by 1944, was of a size to need. Barlow, nevertheless, remained at the head of Metal Box's affairs, as chairman, until 1961 and on the board until 1964. In 1947 he tardily followed Whitehead's advice to give up the office of managing director but characteristically, between 1949 and 1952, he arranged to have it divided between two co-equal holders. Even after he retired, and in a tantrum sold his shares, directors and others would from time to time make a ritual pilgrimage to seek his blessing.

During the long boom after the end of the Second World War Metal Box extended very greatly, both territorially in Europe and further afield and in the scope of its activities, especially the new techniques of packaging made possible by the chemical industry's rapid development of polythene film and other plastic materials. On the plastics side, Barlow's touch may have been less sure than in the development of canning, but in the extension and defence of Metal Box's traditional operations he was as skilful and combative as ever, relying on tactics of pricing and contracting designed, to the displeasure of the Monopolies Commission in 1970, to tie customers exclusively to Metal Box.

Barlow's last battle was against Courtaulds, a considerably greater power than Metal Box, when they were so ill-advised as to venture into packaging and can-making. In December 1958 Courtaulds took over Reads, who were fighting to break Metal Box's monopoly in the manufacture of cans, though handicapped by the geographical position of their factory, in Liverpool, and by Metal Box's refusal to allow firms who hired can-closing machinery from them to run Reads' cans through it. When Courtaulds also took over the paint firm of Pinchin Johnson, with which Metal Box had collaborated in developing lacquers and varnishes for metal containers, Barlow seized the opportunity for a flank attack. Metal Box indicated to Courtaulds that collaboration with Pinchin Johnson would cease and, moreover, that Metal Box would only buy lacquers and varnishes from Pinchin Johnson up to the value of containers bought by Pinchin Johnson from Metal Box. Courtaulds capitulated. They agreed that Reads should limit production of cans to their ill-sited Liverpool factory. Barlow, at the end of his career, was as skilled and ruthless a competitor as at the beginning of it.

In 1942, after a divorce, Barlow married Margaret Rawlings whose marriage had broken down in 1938. By her, he had a daughter. His second wife was quite as distinguished on the stage as Barlow was in business, but their careers lay in such widely separated fields that theirs did not seem, on the face of things, the likeliest of marriages. Nevertheless it lasted, and it hints at the complexity of Barlow's character, in which there was a strong theatrical element. He played the part of the great captain of industry to the full, with uninhibited displays of emotion which might carry him as far as flinging a telephone across the room.

As a business man, Sir Robert Barlow displayed classic qualities. He seized the opportunity to develop the British canning industry in the unpromising atmosphere of the early 1930s and he accepted the risks inherent in doing so. He fought his rivals and competitors with cunning, ferocity, courage and complete success. By conventional standards his success was deserved and very great: Metal Box was his creation.

With Barlow's towering ability in business there seems to have co-existed a deep dislike for the life of a business man. 'I don't know why I go on with it', he once said. 'I get no happiness from it.' {*ibid*, 147} That came out at the time of the management crisis on which Whitehead reported, no doubt in a moment of bitterness and depression, but there is no reason to discount it entirely. His fight for power may have destroyed his happiness for the time being, but probably without power he could not be happy, and without engaging in business he could not be powerful. Like many holders of high office, he abandoned power with extreme reluctance and later than he should have done, even after he had several times expressed a wish to go. He made no attempt to train a successor within the company, and when a successor was brought in from outside, Barlow regarded him with malevolence.

At Barlow's driving motives one can only guess. His attitude towards his father, combining admiration with fear and perhaps dislike, was certainly important: so was the sense of insecurity which prompted him to 'divide and rule'. He had religious impulses of a Dissenting kind, but one of his critics described him to the present writer as 'an evil man'. Nevertheless he displayed his changing moods — subtle, passionate, angry, ruthless, generous, kind — with such charm and style that even many of those whom he injured would speak of him with affection.

Sir Robert Barlow died on 30 September 1976 leaving an estate valued at £43,693 gross.

W J READER

Sources:

Unpublished

BCe.

PrC.

Published

William J Reader, *Metal Box, A History* (Heinemann, 1976).
WWW.

BARLOW, William Henry

(1812-1902)

Civil engineer

William Henry Barlow was born on 10 May 1812, the son of Peter Barlow FRS, professor of mathematics at the Royal Military Academy, Woolwich. He left school at the age of sixteen, trained as an engineer in HM Dockyard, Woolwich, and later under H R Palmer at the London Docks. In 1832, Messrs Maudslay & Field sent him to Constantinople. There he erected works and machinery for re-casting and re-boring ordnance. He also reported to the Government on lighthouses in the Bosphorus, and was admitted to the order of Nischan-el-Iftikar for his services to Turkey.

Returning to England in 1838, he held a succession of engineering posts with the Manchester & Birmingham, Midland Counties and Midland Railway Cos. At the period of the Great Exhibition of 1851, he helped Joseph Paxton by calculating the strength of the ironwork for the Crystal Palace. In 1857, he set up in private practice in London but remained consulting engineer to the Midland Railway. Following Brunel's death in 1859, Barlow joined Sir John Hawkshaw (qv) and others in the scheme which completed the Clifton Bridge, a suspension bridge over the Avon at Bristol, as a memorial to their distinguished colleague. He carried the Midland Railway into London, and constructed the train shed at its terminus, St Pancras. When it opened in 1868, its 240 foot span of glass and iron was the widest in the world. In the same year, he became a director of the Indo-European Telegraph Co. Following the collapse of the Tay Bridge in 1879, Barlow served on the Court of Inquiry, and the North British Railway retained him to build a replacement. He was consulted about the Forth Bridge, though his design was not ultimately chosen, and on the construction of the Dufferin Bridge over the Ganges at Benares. In a completely different field, he advised on problems of subsidence at Ely and Lincoln Cathedrals where his plans for strengthening the fabric were adopted.

Barlow was a man of wide scientific interests. His publications included papers on electric currents on the earth's surface and on the theory of structures. He invented an instrument called the logograph, a fore-runner of the telephone and phonograph. In 1850, he was elected a Fellow of the Royal Society and was its vice-president in 1880.

He was also active in his profession, and became president of the Institution of Civil Engineers in 1879-80. Barlow served on a government committee, which reported in 1877, to establish standards for the use of steel in railway engineering. The issue had become urgent as steel became widely used. In 1881, he served on another committee which was concerned with wind pressure on railway structures. This had been a factor in the Tay Bridge disaster. The same year, he became one of the first two civilians appointed to the Ordnance Committee.

Barlow married Selina Crawford, daughter of W Caffin, of the Royal

Arsenal; they had four sons and two daughters. He died on 12 November 1902, leaving an estate valued at £68,014.

HENRY W PARRIS

Writings:

Remarks on the Different Methods of Fastening Railway Bars in their Chairs; and a Description of a New Hollow Wrought Iron Key ... with an Abstract of the Discussion upon the Paper, and upon Brockedon's Vulcanized India Rubber (W Clowes & Sons, 1845).

'On the Existence ... of the Line of Equal Horizontal Thrust in Arches' *Proceedings of the Institution of Civil Engineers* 5 (1846).

On the Spontaneous Electrical Currents Observed in the Wires of the Electric Telegraph (Taylor, 1849).

On the Construction of Permanent Way of Railways (W Clowes & Sons, 1850).

Description to Diagrams for Facilitating the Construction of Oblique Bridges (London, 1855?).

'Description of the Clifton Suspension Bridge' *Proceedings of the Institution of Civil Engineers* 26 (1867).

An Analytical Investigation of the Board of Trade Returns of the Capital and Revenue of Railways in the United Kingdom (Effingham Wilson, 1868).

Preliminary Experiments on the Mechanical and other Properties of Steel, made or Collected by a Committee of Civil Engineers (Adams Brothers, printers, 1868).

Address to the Mechanical Section of the British Association, Bradford, September 18, 1873 (1873).

PP, HC 1877 (136) LXXIII, Committee to Consider the Practicability of Assigning a Safe Coefficient for the Use of Steel in Railway Structures.

PP, Report of Court of Inquiry into Fall of a Portion of the Tay Bridge (1880) C 2616.

PP, Committee on Wind Pressure on Railway Structures (1881) C 3000.

Sources:

Unpublished

PrC; Will.

Published

Theodore C Barker and Michael Robbins, *A History of London Transport* (2 vols, George Allen & Unwin, 1963-74) 1.

George F Chadwick, *The Works of Sir Joseph Paxton, 1803-1865* (Architectural Press, 1961).

DNB.

Cuthbert H Ellis, *Midland Railway* (Ian Allan, 1953).

Lionel T C Rolt, *Isambard Kingdom Brunel* (Longmans, 1957).

Proceedings of the Institution of Civil Engineers 101 (1903).

WWW.

BARNBY, 2nd Lord Barnby
see WILLEY, Francis Vernon

BARON, Bernhard

(1850-1929)

Tobacco manufacturer

Bernhard Baron was born in the town of Brest-Litovsk, Russia, on 5 December 1850; he was of French descent.

At the age of seventeen, unable to speak a word of English, he emigrated to New York. He worked in a tobacco factory for a few shillings a week; with some tobacco lent to him by a foreman at the factory he started the manufacture of hand-made cigarettes. Baron moved to New Haven, Connecticut, where he found customers for his cigarettes among the students at Yale. The failure in 1874 of a New York bank in which he had placed the savings he was accumulating forced him once again to seek employment in a tobacco factory, that of Kinney Brothers of New York. However as soon as he had saved enough to launch out on his own again, he moved to Baltimore and began manufacturing cigars. According to Baron's own account, this business prospered so well that it became the largest undertaking of its kind south of Philadelphia. In 1890, a group of financiers persuaded him to join in a enterprise aimed at challenging the powerful tobacco trusts of the day, and during 1890-95 Baron was managing director of the National Cigarette Tobacco Co of New York.

At this time, a number of inventors were wrestling with the formidable technical problems posed by the mechanisation of cigarette manufacture. In 1872 Baron patented his first invention, a machine for making cigarettes with a tobacco cover, involving a new principle of manufacture. Baron subsequently took out between 50 and 60 patents for cigarette-making, cigarette box-making, cigar-making and tobacco-cutting. Though these patents have expired, the ideas they embodied are to be found today in many machines of this class. He made a lifetime study of tobacco culture in all its branches, from the planting of the seed to the manufacture of the finished article. During the years 1871-96 there was not a single year that Bernhard Baron did not see for himself the growing and cutting of the finest crops of Virginia and other American tobaccos.

In 1895 Baron visited England with the intention of selling rights to his cigarette-manufacturing machinery, but when he came Baron saw excellent opportunities to manufacture his Baron cigarette-making machines himself, for rental to cigarette manufacturers, and formed the Baron Cigarette Machine Co Ltd. At this time the market for cigarettes in the UK was dominated by WD & HO Wills who held the exclusive UK rights for the Bonsack cigarette-making machine, the most successful of such machines yet produced. Baron's machine compared well with those of his rivals and was taken up by John Player & Son, anxious to challenge Wills in the expanding market for machine-made cigarettes. He later sold the patent to the United Cigarette Machine Co for £120,000. A condition of the sale was that Bernhard Baron would stay in England for at least two years: he found the country so agreeable and achieved such rapid success with the new company that he decided to settle. At first, Baron did not intend taking up the manufacture of tobacco and cigarettes, but later he changed his mind and decided that whenever an opportunity arose he would begin manufacturing in Britain with his 'Baron' machine and other patent machines of his own invention and manufacture.

His opportunity came with the formation of Carreras Ltd. William Yapp, who had taken over the tobacco-blending and tobacco-retailing firm of Carreras just before the turn of the century, was anxious to share in the growing market for cigarettes, and was interested in Baron's machines. When Carreras was incorporated in 1903 as a public limited company with an issued capital of £160,000, Yapp brought Baron in as a director. In 1904 Baron became managing director, and in 1905 chairman as well; he held both positions until his death. Baron decided to challenge the Imperial Tobacco Co, into which Wills, Players and several other tobacco manufacturers had been incorporated in 1901. In 1904, an allied private company, Carreras & Marcianus Cigarette Co, was formed for the production of cigarettes with his machinery. The company operated from St James's Place, Aldgate, the former works of the Baron Cigarette Machine Co.

In 1904 Carreras & Marcianus launched three brands of machine-made cigarettes, including 'Black Cat' which was to prove the most successful Carreras brand for many years. The following year Carreras began to market these brands with special offer coupons and prize competitions: so successful were these marketing ploys that extra manufacturing facilities had to be found to cope with demand. Further brands of cigarettes were launched, and by 1909 the Baron automatic pipe filler and cartridge, which sold by the million, had been introduced.

The Bernhard Baron medal produced in 1928 and given to all employees (courtesy of Carreras Rothmans Ltd).

A new factory, the Arcadia Works, was built in City Road in 1910. A full-scale gift coupon scheme was launched that year to cultivate the loyalty of smokers. Carreras' associated interests were brought into the main company: in 1912 Carreras & Marcianus ceased to operate as a separate company and its interests were taken over by Carreras Ltd, and in 1919 the Baron Machinery Co was incorporated as a subsidiary to market Baron cigarette-making machinery. Expansion of the business continued steadily during and after the First World War. Carreras' 'Black Cat' and 'Craven A' brands were among the most serious competitors of the Imperial brands in the mid-1920s when Imperial had still to match Carreras' vigorous marketing schemes. In 1929, the year of Baron's death, the issued capital of Carreras was £1.7 million.

In 1928 the new Arcadia Works were opened at Mornington Crescent. This purpose-built building, which became a major London landmark, was the first factory to contain air-conditioning and dust-extraction. Full welfare services were also provided for the employees. At the time of the official opening of Carreras new factory each of the 3,000 employees was presented with a medal inscribed 'My thanks for all your help, Bernhard Baron, Chairman, Carreras Ltd'.

In 1926 Baron purchased Pennant Lodge at Brighton, fitted and furnished it and set up a trust fund for the management of the home, later renamed the Bernhard Baron Convalescent Home, for the use of people who were, or had been employed in domestic, manual or clerical labour, preference being given to staff of Carreras Ltd and its associated companies.

Bernhard Baron's interests and philanthropic ventures reached far beyond the tobacco business; he was renowned for his numerous large charitable benefactions, among them a donation of £65,000 towards the establishment of the St George's Jewish Settlement, Henriques Street, East London. During 1927 alone, he contributed more than £180,000 for various charitable purposes and during the course of his lifetime he is reputed to have donated about £5 million to various charities and schemes to help the poor.

Among his generous gifts to the Middlesex Hospital, of which he was vice-president, was a new children's ward. He also endowed a scholarship for research in the Ferens Institute for a British subject, and a Bernhard Baron lecture at the Royal College of Surgeons of England.

Baron was an enthusiastic supporter of the Labour party, making a considerable contribution to party funds. A great admirer of Rufus Isaacs, the First Marquess of Reading, Baron frequently consulted him about his charitable schemes, and in his will appointed him chairman of the trustees charged with the administration of his charitable bequests. When Bernhard Baron's son Louis, who had succeeded his father as chairman of Carreras, died in 1933, Reading was appointed to take his place.

Bernhard Baron married Rachel Schwartz of Washington, USA in 1880; she died in 1920. They had three daughters, Fanny Guggenheim, Amelia Schaul, Sarai Wakefield, and one son, Louis Bernhard Baron. Bernhard Baron died on 1 August 1929 and was buried at the cemetery of the Liberal Jewish Synagogue, Pound Lane, Willesden, London.

He left an estate proved at £4,944,820 gross. Apart from numerous bequests to his family and staff, he established a 'Charities Fund' from which charitable organisations of many religious denominations benefited, and declared that 'all my lifetime I have given away very large sums of money for charitable purposes without distinction of creed or religion as I love my Christian brethren as much as my Jewish brethren' {Will}.

CHRISTINE SHAW

Sources:

Unpublished

Information supplied by Carreras Rothmans Ltd.

PrC; Will.

Published

Bernard W E Alford, 'Penny Cigarettes, Oligopoly and Entrepreneurship in the UK Tobacco Industry in the Late Nineteenth Century' in Barry Supple (ed), *Essays in British Business History* (Clarendon Press, 1977).

Maurice Corina, *Trust in Tobacco. The Anglo-American Struggle for Power* (Michael Joseph, 1975).

DNB.

Marquess of Reading, *Rufus Isaacs, First Marquess of Reading 1914-35* (Hutchinson & Co, 1945).

PP, HC 1960-61 (218) XIX, Monopolies Commission Report on the Supply of Cigarettes and Tobacco and of Cigarette and Tobacco Machinery.

Times 3 Aug 1929.

WWW.

Sir John Barran (courtesy of D T Jenkins).

BARRAN, Sir John

(1821-1905)

Clothing manufacturer

John Barran was born at New Wandsworth in Surrey on 3 August 1821, the son of a London gun maker, John Barran, and his wife Elizabeth Fletcher. He was educated privately and at the age of twenty-one, in 1842, for unknown reasons he took a boat from London to Hull and travelled on to Leeds. As far as is known neither he, nor his family, had any previous connections with the district. Initially he obtained employment as an assistant in a small pawnbroking, jewellers and clothing shop owned by Thomas Gresham. Within a few months Barran set himself up in business as a tailor at Bridge End South in Leeds. In the same year he married Ann Hirst, the daughter of a local woollen manufacturer, Major Hirst; they had six sons.

By 1851 John Barran, now described as a tailor and clothes dealer, had established himself in more prestigious premises at No 1, Briggate, Leeds. By this date it would appear from a surviving stock book that he was making 'made to measure' garments and also carrying a stock of ready made items.

The main development, however, of John Barran's business commenced in the 1850s and for the next few decades he was almost continuously expanding both his factory and warehouse premises and his workforce. The first step in this expansion was his perceptive decision to attempt to adapt Singer's new sewing machine to clothing manufacture. He may have been the first to have done so in Britain. He set up a small factory in Alfred Street, Leeds but soon needed to move to larger premises at No 1 Boar Lane. By 1856 he had between 20 and 30 sewing machines at work manufacturing 'ready to wear' clothes. A doggerel about him published in the *Leeds Mercury* in December 1856 shows that his pioneering enterprise had already been recognised locally.

The next major step in the expansion of John Barran's clothing business was his invention of a band-knife for cutting cloth in quantity. In 1858 Barran visited a furniture exhibition in Leeds and saw a bandsaw for cutting furniture veneers being demonstrated. He persuaded a local engineer to modify the principle for cloth cutting. In 1867 Barran moved into yet larger premises in Park Row, Leeds and was joined in the business by his eldest son, John, who became a partner in 1871. At that date the firm was carrying a 'ready made' stock valued at £10,000. Two years later the stock valuation had increased to £15,000. John Barran's technical enterprise continued. Father and son patented a counterweighted iron, and a foot control for powered sewing machines. In 1872 the firm had some 2,000 sewing machines at work, all power-driven from a gas engine through shafting. Five years later a yet larger factory was opened in Park Square, Leeds. In the following decade another huge factory and warehouse were built. The firm employed over 2,000 hands in 1893 and over 3,000 by 1904. For much of the second half of the nineteenth century John Barran's business was recognised as holding a pre-eminent position in the 'ready to wear' trade for boys' clothes. He became known as 'the little boy's tailor', although he also made men's 'ready made' clothing. {*Textile Manufacturer* Jan 1877}.

John Barran's success and reputation may perhaps be explained in three ways. Firstly he appears to have been particularly perceptive and innovatory in his production methods. Besides those inventions already mentioned he was also instrumental in developing the 'divisional system' for the manufacture of clothing. Secondly he recognised the advantage of purpose-built premises over the small 'sweated workshops' which characterized the trade. Thirdly he has been recognised as a pioneer in the improvement of employment conditions for women and children in the clothing trade. As early as 1864 he was appealing for the working hours of girls to be reduced in the trade. He practised what he preached through paying attention to welfare provision for his workers. He tried to provide regular employment, regular hours, healthier working conditions and leisure facilities. At the firm's centenary in 1951 Dame Anne Loughton, the General Secretary of the National Union of Tailors and Garment Workers, paid tribute to him.

> 'John Barran was amongst the first to prove that the team spirit was the key to success, to expansion and the winning of great markets' {Ryott (1951) introduction}.

In the context of the Leeds economy, Barran's activity was part of a diversification away from dependence on wool textiles, a shift begun in the 1840s. By the eve of the First World War over 23,000 clothing trade workers were employed in and around the town, placing Leeds second only to London as a centre of clothing manufacture.

John Barran married for the second time in 1878. His new wife was Elizabeth, the widow of J Bilton of Scarborough. His son John died tragically in 1883, but other sons, Charles, Henry and Rowland, all became involved in running the business. His second son, Alfred, seems not to have entered the firm. John Barran however continued as chairman until 1903 and the impression survives that he remained firmly at the helm in spite of also undertaking a number of political and philanthropic activities.

He represented Leeds as Liberal MP from 1876 to 1885. Then, from 1886 to 1895 he was the Liberal MP for the East Division of the West Riding of Yorkshire (Otley Division). He served as Mayor of Leeds in 1870-71. He was a member of the Council of the Yorkshire College, the forerunner of Leeds University, and he served as the chairman of the College's Finance Committee. For a long period he was a JP both for the West Riding and for Leeds. John Barran was also a prominent Leeds Baptist. He acted as president of the local Young Men's Christian Association. He also served a term as president of Leeds Chamber of Commerce. He was created a baronet for public and political services in 1895. Sir John Barran died on 3 May 1905, leaving a personal fortune of £408,048 gross.

The firm was continued by his sons and grandsons. Charles was a partner from 1878 to 1888. Henry, John Barran's fourth son, became a partner in 1886 and succeeded him as chairman in 1903, immediately floating the firm as a public company. Henry remained chairman until 1918 and was succeeded by the fifth and youngest son, Rowland, who took the firm into the women's 'ready to wear' trade. The third generation of the family became represented when Sir John Nicolson Barran, eldest son of the founder's first son, served as a director from 1903 to 1921. By the 1950s the fifth generation of the family was entering the firm.

D T JENKINS

Sources:

Unpublished

Leeds City Archives Department, Sheepscar Library, Leeds, John Barran & Sons, Business Records.

MCe.

PrC.

Published

David W Bebbington, 'Baptist MPs in the Nineteenth Century' *The Baptist Quarterly* 29 (1981).

The Century's Progress: Yorkshire 1893.

Leeds Directory 1842.

David Ryott, *John Barran's of Leeds, 1851-1951* (Leeds: pp, 1951).

Joan Thomas, 'A History of the Leeds Clothing Industry' *Yorkshire Bulletin of Economic and Social Research* (Occasional Paper, 1955).

Wool Year Book (Manchester, 1913).

Yorkshire Post 4 May 1905.

Yorkshire Who's Who 1912.

WWMP.

WWW.

BARRATT, Arthur William

(1877-1939)

Shoe manufacturer and retailer

A W Barratt (courtesy of Stylo PLC).

Arthur William Barratt was born in Northampton on 8 October 1877, the fourth of the seven sons of John Russell Barratt, a shoe machine operator (and later a footwear retailer), and his wife Elizabeth née Yeomans. His father, formerly a silk weaver, had migrated to Northampton from Desborough in search of work some years previously. William, the name by which he was known, was educated at local board schools. An able scholar, he started work in his father's retail business, as a half-timer, on his tenth birthday.

At nineteen, he became manager of his father's third shop in Gold Street, Northampton. Within three years he moved to London to gain broader experience and became a sales assistant in a Manfields shoe shop at a weekly wage of 17s 6d plus commission. Returning to Northampton in early 1901, he managed his father's retail shop in the Drapery, but when his father's business failed in July 1902, he purchased it from him as a going concern. William then entered into partnership with his elder brother David, a shoe manufacturer's clerk. Facing large and spreading shoe retailing chains, like Manfields, the Barratts' solution was to depart radically from accepted British retailing practice. They launched a mail-order business. Their principal aim was to tap the sizeable but dispersed rural markets. Initially, they marketed footwear purchased from small, local wholesale manufacturers. Sound quality, keenly-priced footwear, supported by a full money-back guarantee quickly established public goodwill and confidence, as did the great care with which customers' orders and individual needs were attended to. A meticulous card index system was adopted to record individual customers' addresses and past purchases: by 1906, 40,000 customers had been thus indexed. Central to this sales strategy was the extensive use of catalogues and advertising in both national newspapers and periodic literature of all kinds.

At this early stage, the fundamental problem was that of under-capitalisation. Within a year of moving into a factory manufacturing operation in 1905 (the Sterling Shoe Works, College Street, Northampton) the partnership was declared bankrupt: liabilities were assessed at £9,610, assets at £2,761. The discharge was suspended for two years, because business prospects were good and the Barratts were deemed to have over-extended themselves in the face of competition in the shoe mail-order business: in the last year of trading, sales exceeded £27,000, with gross profits in excess of £7,000, the order book was full and William's advertising techniques were widely acclaimed; but overhead costs were high (over £12,000 had been expended on advertising, of which £4,547 remained unpaid).

A new private limited company was registered to acquire the bankrupt partnership on 25 January 1907, under the style W Barratt & Co Ltd. The

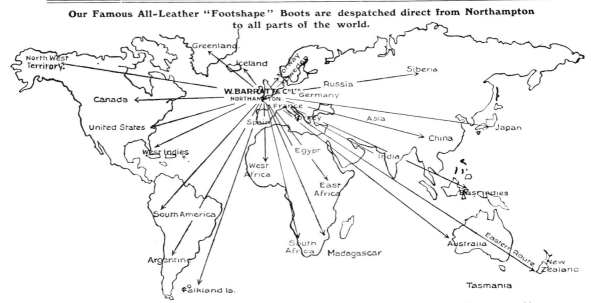

A Business on which the Sun never Sets.

Our Famous All-Leather "Footshape" Boots are despatched direct from Northampton to all parts of the world.

See book of Testimonials containing genuine letters from over sixty different countries. Post Free to any address.

An advertisement from the 1908 Barratt's Boots-by-Post Catalogue (courtesy of Stylo PLC).

purchase price of £2,287 was met by several friends: A E Catt, a prominent local businessman, John Clark, a Rushden boot manufacturer, and John H Freeborough, a Sheffield accountant. The latter became one of two directors, the other being Tom Johnson, William's father-in-law. Until the Barratts' discharge from bankruptcy in 1909, he represented their interests in the new company. Each director held half the issued preference shares, but Tom held 15 of the 20 founders' shares, giving him the controlling interest: each founders' share carried 50 votes, compared to the single vote of each preference share. Two younger brothers, Albert and Richard Barratt, received a nominal shareholding and joined the management; in 1910, John Clark joined the board. These three members provided much needed manufacturing and shoe design expertise.

The combination of Freeborough's financial judgement matched by the Barratts' enterprise clearly underpinned the success of the reformed company's first six years: by 1914 the company's assets were valued at £34,000. Profits in 1914 stood at £5,745. The rapid and consistent demand for the company's products led to the decision, in 1913, to increase substantially the organisation's scale by provision of a new factory and warehouse. This £9,000 development, known as the Footshape Boot Works, took place on a one and a quarter acre site at Kingsthorpe Road, Northampton, and was financed by two Northamptonshire Union Bank mortgages. In May 1914, the concern was converted to a public limited company. Authorised capital was increased by £46,000 to £50,000. The prospectus informs, ' ... of this sum £18,000 has already been subscribed by Founders, Directors, and their Friends, and the remaining £14,500 shares are now available for subscription, primarily by the Customers of the Company ...' {C Reg, Prospectus 2}. By December 1914 all but £884 of this latter sum had been subscribed. This pattern of share allocation and the retention of the founders' shares ensured a continued concentration of control within the company.

Following continued wartime demand, Barratts traded strongly in the inter-war period. Mail-order activity remained the sheet-anchor of the Barratt brothers' business, now under the direction of Richard, joint managing director with William, following David's retirement in 1911. A retail chain was begun in 1914, which grew to 150 shops by 1939; the long term strategy seems to have been to provide an outlet in the major towns of each English county. This development, along with their rapid emergence as a volume, wholesale producer and exporter was controlled by William, very much the architect of this growth. He also retained control of advertising, preserving a direct, personalised style. Most advertisements featured William, and carried the slogan 'Walk the Barratt Way'. This continued success was reflected by four increases in authorised capital in the period, up from £100,000 in 1919 to £1 million in 1928, undertaken to finance further additions in factory-warehouse capacity, and to finance the expanding retail chain. On each occasion the new share issue was eagerly sought. Profits of £16,566 were recorded in 1919; by 1928 they reached £95,430 and £150,171 at Barratt's death in 1939 when the authorised capital of the company still stood at £1 million.

Despite his sustained success, many in Northampton and in the trade regarded Barratt personally with only a qualified esteem. In part, this reflected stolid hostility towards his radical and very competitive marketing, particularly his egotistical advertising techniques. Possibly of greater significance, however, was his active participation in socialist politics. In 1902 he joined the vigorous Northampton branch of the Social Democratic Federation, becoming one of their most effective and uncompromising public speakers. A press election biography of 1904 suggests that Barratt's beliefs derived from his experience of shop assistants' conditions, and his study of contemporary socialist literature, principally Bellamy's *Looking Backward*. He sat as a Labour councillor at Northampton, 1929-34, being made a JP in 1930. He unsuccessfully contested the 1931 general election for Labour at Bethnal Green, London. His public life was marked by a vociferous criticism of the poor managerial quality and nepotism found in local government, and by a vehement opposition to growing militarism: his was a 'satirical and cynical spirit'. Similar criticism was apparent in trade matters. As president of the local footwear manufacturers' association in 1933 he aroused the hostility of many manufacturers by advocating a shorter working week and improved working conditions for shoe workers. He retired from active public life a year later.

His last years were marked by increased and unremitting business commitments, which hastened his death, following the early retirement of Albert in 1934, and the death of Richard in 1936. Inadequate regard seems to have been given to the question of succession: certainly William showed a marked disinclination to delegate responsibility during these later years.

An obituary offers this assessment:

'New shoes are a pleasure to me now, Mr Barratt!'

A 1939 advertisement for Barratt shoes (courtesy of Stylo PLC).

As founder of the business he blazed its trail ... but, not content with that he would continue to work hard to consolidate every new development, with the result that he wore himself out at the age of 62, and robbed himself of the life of leisure to which he was looking forward. For some time intimate friends had been trying to persuade him to relax some of his intense activities in business, but they only partially succeeded, for he was a strong believer in the personal touch. {*Northampton Independent* 15 Dec 1939}

He attempted to reconcile his socialist views with his private wealth by extensive philanthropy, and a paternalistic, autocratic concern for his work people. His model factory helped popularise air-conditioning, piped music and fluorescent lighting; he provided comprehensive social and welfare facilities, including a contribution-free pension scheme. In 1934, he provided £60,000 to endow the Barratt Maternity Hospital, Northampton, ' ... which shall be open to persons in all stations of life, and not regarded as a charity ...' {*Northampton Independent* 11 May 1934}. As a youth he had been a keen sportsman and pioneer motorcyclist, and in later life, he gave generously to local sports and was president of local rugby, football and athletic clubs.

He married Alice, daughter of Tom Johnson, a Northampton shoe finisher, in 1899. They had no issue, but there were two adopted daughters of the marriage. Barratt died at Northampton on 7 December 1939. He left £303,646 gross. Subject to numerous legacies, his estate was left in trust for his wife. On her death in 1958, a residue of over £300,000 passed to the Northampton General Hospital.

KEITH BROOKER

Sources:

Unpublished

C Reg: Stylo Barratt Shoes Ltd (91,791).

BCe.

MCe.

DCe.

PrC.

Published

Boot and Shoe Trades Journal 18 July 1902, 20 July 1906, 22 Dec 1911.

Frederick W S Craig, *British Parliamentary Election Results 1918-49* (Glasgow: Political Reference Publications, 1969).

Northampton Chronicle & Echo 8 Dec 1939.

Northampton Independent 21 Dec 1920, 3 Sept 1921, 28 Jan 1922, 8 Mar 1930, 24 Oct 1931, 31 Dec 1932, 11 May, 26 Oct 1934, 3 May 1935, 3 July 1936, 1 Jan, 4 June 1937, 1, 15 Dec 1939, 2 Feb 1940, 30 Apr 1948, 29 Aug 1952, 2 Jan 1959, 29 July 1960.

Northampton Mercury 8 Dec 1939.

'Northampton's Fine Romantic History' *Northampton Independent* 6 Mar 1936.

The Romance of Barratts (ca 1948).

Shoe and Leather News 14 Dec 1939.

'William Barratt' *Northampton Pioneer* Oct 1904.

BARRATT, Thomas James

(1841-1914)

Pioneer of mass consumer advertising

Thomas James Barratt was born at St Pancras, London, on 16 May 1841, son of Thomas Barratt, a pianoforte maker, and his wife Emma née Price. He left school at fifteen with the ambition of becoming a merchant, and by 1864 was working for Ellis & Hales, colonial brokers. According to Barratt, he left the firm after one of the partners told him 'Thomas, you know too much', and the same year obtained a job as book-keeper in the shop owned by A & F Pears, the soap makers, in Great Russell Street.

From this point his rise was meteoric, aided by his marriage in March 1865 to Mary Frances, Francis Pears's eldest daughter, whom he is reputed to have met at an academy of dancing and deportment. He soon became a traveller for the firm, and when the same year it was reorganised and its capital increased to £7,000, he was made a partner together with Francis's nineteen year-old son Andrew (qv).

Francis withdrew from the firm in 1875, leaving a loan of £4,000 to be paid off by the two remaining partners. This can have presented few problems, since by 1891 profits had reached a record level of £71,923. The following year Pears became a public company with a capital of £810,000 and Barratt as chairman and managing director. The firm paid an annual dividend of ten per cent every year until his death in 1914, in addition to which he was able to tell the ordinary general meeting in 1903 that 'After eleven years of existence they had solid property after paying off all the debts, more than sufficient in value to pay out all the debenture-holders, all the preference shareholders, and a large proportion of the ordinary shareholders'. {*Middlesex Chronicle* 7 Nov 1903}

Unlike most of his contemporaries in the soap industry, with whom he seems to have had little in common, Barratt was a firm believer in mass consumer advertising. Pears' expenditure on advertising had only totalled some £500 in eighty years, but Barratt was soon spending at the rate of £126,000 per annum and by 1903 he could tell shareholders that the firm's total promotional investment was nearing £1 million. He brought its product to the notice of the public on such a scale that Gladstone speaking in the Commons could allude to amendments 'as thick as the leaves in Vallombrosa or as plentiful as the advertisements of Pears soap' {Advertisers' Weekly *2 May 1914*}

Barratt was also notable for the promotional methods he employed. He pioneered the catch-phrase in advertising with 'Good Morning! Have you used Pears' Soap?'. He circulated French ten centime coins, at that time accepted as pennies, stamped with the word 'Pears', thus provoking the Government into buying them up to be melted down and legislating to prohibit the circulation of foreign currency. He secured endorsements from such celebrities as Lillie Langtry and Adelina Patti. He paid £2,000 for Millais' painting 'Bubbles' and proceeded to turn it into one of the most famous advertisements of all time. He commissioned advertising illustrations from leading contemporary artists, helping to some extent to bridge the gap between 'pure' and 'commercial' art. And shortly before his death he was experimenting with the use of original oil paintings on street hoardings in place of the more normal poster. He was unsuccessful, however, when Chancellor of the Exchequer Goschen rejected his offer of £100,000 for the right to advertise on the 1891 Census forms.

Pears' soap was exported successfully to markets throughout the world. Barratt himself visited the United States to supervise its introduction there, and by 1901 sales were sufficiently high for the company to spend £1,000 on an injunction against a Kansas barber named Pears whose enterprise in producing a soap under his own name was felt to be damaging its interests.

Barratt was held in great esteem by his contemporaries. Northcliffe (qv) called him 'the Father of Modern Advertising from whom I have learned so much'; Sir Thomas Dewar (qv) described him as 'a prince of commerce, a king of good fellows'; and he was commonly referred to as 'the man who washed the face of the world'. In 1889 the centenary of the founding of Pears was marked by a banquet given by the national press in Barratt's honour, some 170 representatives of newspapers from all over the world contributing to a gift of plate valued at £1,000 and an illuminated address.

He was a tall, muscular man with tremendous energy, a capacity for hard work, and an eye for detail. Almost to the end of his life he personally bought all the advertising space for his firm: something he enjoyed doing so much that he also bought on behalf of his friends.

In private life, Barratt was the owner of an impressive art collection which included engravings by George Morland, watercolours by Frank Dadd, views of Hampstead by Constable, and Landseer's 'Monarch of the Glen'. He was also a keen amateur historian, publishing a three-volume work on Hampstead which was said to have taken him thirty years to write. He was a vice-president of Hampstead Antiquarian and Historical Society, and a member of Hampstead Heath Protection Society and Hampstead Art Society. He built up a notable collection of Nelson memorabilia which included plate, a log of the *Victory* and a piano made from wood of the *Foudroyant*.

His other chief hobby was microscopy. He was a fellow of the Royal Microscopical Society, a founder of the Quekett Microscopical Society, a member of Hampstead Scientific Society and amassed a large number of slides at his Hampstead home. He was also a member of two City livery companies, a vice-president of Hampstead Wanderers Football Club and a freemason.

He died at Margate on 26 April 1914 leaving an estate valued at £405,564 gross. Chief beneficiaries under the terms of his will were two illegitimate sons by Florence Bell, a doctor's daughter, who moved into Barratt's Hampstead home and called herself 'Mrs Barratt'. His wife Mary died in greatly reduced circumstances in 1916.

TERRY NEVETT

Writings:

The Annals of Hampstead (3 vols, A & C Black, 1912).
Articles in *Advertiser's Weekly* 27 Dec 1913, 11 Apr 1914.

Sources:

Unpublished

Camden Library, Swiss Cottage, Local History Collection, papers in the Bell Moor Collection.

BCe.

PrC; Will.

Published

Advertiser's Weekly 2, 9 May 1914.

Advertising World May 1914.

C H Ward Jackson, 'The Great Persuader' *Blackwoods Magazine* Mar 1975.

Middlesex Chronicle 7 Nov 1903.

T R Nevett, *Advertising in Britain. A History* (Heinemann, 1982).

Thomas P O'Connor, appreciation in *T P's Weekly* 1 May 1914.

A and F Pears, *The History of Pears Transparent Soap* (np, nd).

Printer's Ink May 1914.

Clement K Shorter, 'The Romance of the House of Pears', reprinted from the *Sphere* with additions in *Pears Cyclopaedia* 20th ed (1916).

Times 27 Apr 1914.

Charles H Wilson, *History of Unilever* (2 vols, Cassell, 1954).

WWW.

BARROW, Harrison

(1868-1953)

Retailer, wholesaler and food manufacturer

Harrison Barrow was born in Edgbaston, Birmingham, on 12 August 1868, the son of alderman Richard Cadbury Barrow, a tea dealer (mayor of Birmingham in 1888), and Jane née Harrison, and was the great-grandson of Richard Tapper Cadbury. As such he belonged to the Barrow-Cadbury clan of Quaker businessmen which had an enormous influence on the economic, industrial and social development of Birmingham. Educated at Mason College, Birmingham and at the Lycée in Lille, he was a fluent French and German speaker and travelled widely on the Continent. He joined the family firm of Barrow's Stores at 93 Bull Street, premises which had been occupied by John Cadbury's original tea and coffee business from 1824 until taken over by Richard Cadbury Barrow in 1849. This was the time of the division of the business into a retail side (Barrow) and a manufacturing side (Cadbury).

Later, Harrison Barrow became managing director of Barrow's Stores in Corporation Street, one of the leading retail outlets in the grocery trade of the city. After his father's death the firm became a limited liability company, in 1894, with his brothers Walter, a solicitor, and Louis, an engineer with Cadburys, also on the board. The range of products sold was extended well beyond the traditional high quality beverages and spices. Barrows became a wholesale and distribution outlet as well, still trading from the single establishment. A restaurant was added in 1905, with extensions in 1909, 1921 and 1928, and the manufacture of cakes and pies was begun. In the two decades, 1898-1918, sales rose by over 33 per cent each decade. Between 1918 and 1928 the rise was only 12 per cent and the slump led to an actual decline in sales and profits, but there was a recovery so that sales rose by 22 per cent between 1928 and 1938 and by 27 per cent from 1938 to 1948. During the First World War a voluntary system of rationing for customers was introduced and this had some influence on the development of official rationing in the Birmingham area.

Barrow, like his father, was an ardent supporter of the shorter hours movement. He maintained both a Wednesday half-holiday and early closing each day, rather than the traditional practice of keeping the store open as long as customers were prepared to shop. He was chairman of the Birmingham Early Closing Association for twelve years.

Barrow's interest in politics developed early and he was elected as Liberal Councillor for Ladywood at a by-election in May 1898, becoming the youngest member of the council. At the November election he lost the seat when his name was inadvertently omitted from the voters' roll. He returned to the Birmingham Council in 1899, but was defeated in 1902 following two gestures which stemmed from his deeply-held pacifist principles. He was on the platform at the famous meeting in the Birmingham Town Hall at which Lloyd George spoke on the pro-Boer cause, and later had to be smuggled out of the hall in disguise. Barrow also opposed the granting of the freedom of the city to Lord Roberts, arguing that the honour should be confined to those who had directly served the city.

He returned to the council in 1904 for Deritend ward which he held until 1918. During these early years he campaigned for municipal ownership of the tramway system and the replacement of Birmingham's steam trams by electric trolleys. He used Glasgow as his model of a profitable municipal service, but argued that in Birmingham a unified and efficient tramway system would enable workers to live further from the centre of the city, instead of becoming overcrowded in central urban flats or tenements. Barrow became chairman of the Tramways Committee in 1907 and used the powers under the Birmingham Corporation Act of 1903 to extend the system by taking over the private operators. The system provided a net profit for the city in 1913 of £47,000.

In 1914 he turned down a unanimous invitation to become lord mayor feeling that the role required in wartime would conflict with his principles. He remained on the council and continued to make the case for those who had conscientious objections to the war. In 1918, as a member of the Friends Service Committee, he was concerned in the publication of an uncensored pamphlet entitled *The Challenge to Militarism*. For the offence he was sentenced to six months' imprisonment, of which he served five in Pentonville. He resigned his seat on Birmingham Council shortly after conviction. His return to Birmingham was celebrated by the Union of Democratic Control, who presented him with an illuminated address for his stand on civil and religious liberties.

Barrow returned to the Birmingham Council in 1922 as a Labour member, was defeated again in 1925, but regained the seat a year later. In 1930 he was elected alderman. He continued to serve on the council until 1949 in which year he received the Freedom of the City. By then he was father of the Council and had certainly fulfilled the obligation he deemed necessary for the receipt of the keys of the City. In addition to his work on transport, he was chairman of the Municipal Bank Committee and it was largely through his efforts that the Bank achieved trustee status. Barrow retained his pacifist principles, publishing a *Birmingham Peace Plan* in 1936, but he does not seem to have been as active in the movement during the Second World War.

Education was another of Barrow's major interests. He was a governor of King Edward VI's School over a long period and bailiff or chairman of the Board of Governors on two occasions. As chairman of the Estates Committee he managed the extensive properties of the foundation and was instrumental in the sale of the New Street site and the purchase of the new grounds in Edgbaston. On Birmingham Council, he chaired the Higher Education Sub-Committee and one of his last acts was to endow a foreign travel scholarship for Birmingham teachers.

He retired from the council and business in 1950 after suffering severely from arthritis for some time. He married Ethel Kenway of Neath in 1905 and she pre-deceased him in 1945. Barrow died on 15 February 1953 at the age of eighty-four. He left £34,766 gross.

ROY HAY

BARROW Harrison

Writings:

A Challenge to Militarism (Friends Service Committee, 1918).

A Birmingham Peace Plan (Leicester: The Blackfriars Press, 1936).

Sources:

Unpublished
BCe.

PrC.

Published
Barrow's Stores Ltd, *A Store Record, 1824-1949* (Birmingham, 1949).

Barrow's Stores, 1824-1924 (Birmingham, nd).

Birmingham Gazette 31 Jan 1945, 7 Apr 1948, 16 Feb 1953.

Birmingham Mail 1 July 1914, 30 July 1930, 1 Feb, 12 Apr 1949.

Birmingham Post 1 Feb 1945, 28 May 1948, 18 Jan 1949, 16 Feb 1953.

Birmingham Weekly Post 22 Feb 1919, 2 Feb 1945, 9 Apr 1948.

Norman Chamberlain, 'Municipal Government in Birmingham' *Political Quarterly* 1 (1914).

Cornish's Birmingham Year Book (1920).

Edgbastonia 18 June 1898.

Evening Dispatch 27 July 1930.

E P Hennock, *Fit and Proper Persons: Ideal and Reality in Nineteenth Century Urban Government* (Edward Arnold, 1973).

Owl 27 May 1898, 31 Oct 1908.

Sunday Mercury 6 Feb 1949.

Times 16 Feb 1953.

Town Crier 24 Oct 1902.

Iolo A Williams, *The Firm of Cadbury, 1831-1931* (Constable, 1931).

BARRY, Sir John Wolfe

(1836-1918)

Civil engineer

John Wolfe Barry, who adopted the surname of Wolfe-Barry in 1898, was born in London on 7 December 1836, youngest of the five sons of Sir Charles Barry (1795-1860) and his wife Sarah née Rowsell. His father was the architect who re-designed the Houses of Parliament after 1836, and two of his brothers, Charles Barry (born 1824) and Edward Middleton Barry (1830-80), were also architects. Another brother Alfred (1826-1910) was Bishop of Sydney and primate of Australia and Tasmania, 1876-89. John was educated at Trinity College, Glenalmond, and King's College, London, and was then apprenticed in the engineering shops of Lucas Brothers. He next became a pupil and then assistant of Sir John Hawkshaw (qv), who employed him as resident engineer in the construction of the railway stations at Charing Cross and Cannon Street, and on several Thames bridges.

In 1867 he began his own practice, becoming a member of the Institution of Civil Engineers in 1868. At this time he received a Telford medal and premium for his work on the City terminus extension of the Charing Cross Railway. For the next thirty years Barry worked indefatigably and by the turn of the century was regarded as the acknowledged head of the engineering profession in Britain. His greatest engineering work was in railways, bridges and docks. At different times he was consulting engineer to the Barry Docks & Railway Co, the Caledonian Railway, the District Railway, the Metropolitan Railway, the South Eastern Railway, the Shanghai-Nanking Railway and the Bengal-Nagpur Railway. Among lines that he constructed were the Ealing-Fulham extension of the Metropolitan-District, the Lewes and East Grinstead railway, the Mansion House-Aldgate connection on the Inner Circle line, the Ballachulish branch of the Callander-Oban railway and extensions to the Lanarkshire & Ayrshire Railway.

He was consulting engineer to most of the Thames railway bridges in London east of Westminster, such as Blackfriars. His work on Tower Bridge, completed in 1894, brought national celebrity and a CB. This contract, in which the constructors were Sir William Arrol, Lord Armstrong (qv), Herbert Bartlett (qv) and Sir John Jackson (qv), was especially complicated as the bridge had to be kept open during the work. His other railway bridges included a cantilever bridge over Loch Etive in Argyllshire.

Around 1885 Barry went into dock engineering. His first large contract was for the docks and railways at Barry in Glamorgan, but he was later responsible for the Lady Windsor Deep Lock & Graving Dock, the Alexandra Dock at Newport, Immingham Dock in Lincolnshire and the Royal Edward Dock at Avonmouth near Bristol. He was also consulting engineer for the new entrance to the Tyne docks, for the improvements to

Limehouse (London) docks, and for the extensions at Grangemouth on the Forth, at Middlesbrough and at the Surrey Commercial Docks in London. He was also consulting engineer to the Port of Bombay in India and to Durban harbour in Natal.

Barry was additionally consulting engineer to the Hong Kong Government and the estates committee of London Corporation, and was chairman of the Eastern, Eastern Extension and Western overseas cable companies. He was appointed arbitrator on many important contracts, and in 1902 was one of the three members of the Arbitration Court determining the price payable by the new Metropolitan Water Board to the eight old London water companies who claimed some £13.5 million. He also gave lucid evidence to many parliamentary committees.

In the latter stage of John Wolfe-Barry's career much of the work of his extensive practice was distributed among his four partners, G E W Cruttwell, A G Lyster and two younger members of the Barry family. His second son Kenneth Alfred Wolfe-Barry (1879-1936), after reading engineering at Trinity College, Cambridge in 1897-99, was articled to his father in 1899-1903 working on the Great Northern Railway and on London railways, and was then admitted as a partner. Like his father he was a strong supporter of Westminster Hospital, and followed him as consulting engineer to Tower Bridge. He did much dock engineering, including at Aden and Bombay. He was also consulting engineer to the Southern Punjab, Darjeeling-Himalayan, Bengal-Nagpur and Kowloon-Canton railways.

John Wolfe-Barry's nephew Arthur John Barry (1859-1944) handled the construction of many railways, docks and bridges both for his uncle's practice and on his own account. He succeeded his cousin as consulting engineer to the ports at Bombay and Aden, and although some of his public works were in Britain, he also did much in Asia. He was consulting engineer to the British & Chinese Corporation, and was involved in 1902-4 with their railway concessions in association with George Pauling and Rutherfoord Harris. He was a hard-drinking, gossipy, amorous man: 'Astonishingly interesting man Barry knows everyone and everything' one friend wrote, 'I have never seen such a mine of information' {NSWWL, Morrison diary 12 Dec 1902}. On the outbreak of the First World War he took motorised ambulance convoys to France, and was afterwards Inspector-General of the British Red Cross attached to the French Army. A lieutenant-colonel in the Engineer and Railway Staff Corps, Arthur Barry was an Officier of the Légion d'Honneur, Knight of St John of Jerusalem, held the TD and Croix de Geurre, and was created CBE in 1919. Kenneth Wolfe-Barry left £37,676 in 1936 and Arthur Barry left £16,169 in 1944.

In 1892-1906 Sir John Wolfe-Barry (he was created KCB in 1897) was a member of the International Consultative Committee of the Suez Canal, and sat on numerous government committees and commissions. These included the Royal Commission on Irish Public Works (1886-87), the West Highlands and Islands Commission (1889), the Royal Commission on Accidents to Railway Servants (1899-1900), the Royal Commission on the Port of London (1900-2), and the Royal Commission on London traffic (1903-5). He also chaired the Board of Trade's commission on Lower Thames Navigation (1894-96) and was on the inquiry committee into the vibration of London tube railways (1901-2).

He helped to found the National Physical Laboratory at Teddington, and was an associate member of the Council of the Institution of Surveyors, vice-president of the Institution of Mechanical Engineers, manager of the Royal Institution, and fellow of the Royal Society of Arts in 1898-99. He joined the Council of the Institution of Civil Engineers in 1883, and became vice-president in 1893, before serving as president in 1896 and 1897; he was made an honorary member in 1916. In 1901 the Institution at his instigation appointed a committee on standardising various kinds of iron and steel sections. This resulted in the formation of the British Engineering Standards Association, of which he became chairman.

For twenty years Barry was chairman of Westminster Hospital; he was also a member of the management committee of the Yarrow Home, and trustee of the Royal College of Surgeons' Museum from 1913. For a time he was an alderman in Westminster, was member of two City guilds, serving as Prime Warden of the Goldsmiths Company, and was a DL for London. He was at different times a member of the Senate of London University, governor of the Imperial College of Science and Technology, chairman of the Delegacy, City and Guilds Engineering College at Kensington, and a member of the Council of King's College, London.

Barry was a member of the Army Railway Council, a member of the Queen's Westminster Volunteer Battalion and Colonel of the Engineer and Railway Volunteer Staff Corps. He was a great supporter of Lord Roberts's campaign for compulsory military service in peacetime, and sat on the general council of the National Service League. 'Sir John diffused around him an atmosphere of friendly sociability comparable to that of the mess room of a good regiment' and felt a deep loyalty to the 'professional freemasonry' of civil and military engineers {*Min Proc ICE* 206 (1918) 356}. He held the Volunteer Officers' Decoration.

In 1874 he married Rosalind Grace Rowsell, daughter of a Surrey clergyman, by whom he had four sons and three daughters. Sir John Wolfe-Barry died on 22 January 1918 at his house in Chelsea leaving £278,363 gross.

R P T DAVENPORT-HINES

Writings:

Proceedings of the Institution of Civil Engineers 27 (1868).

Railway Appliances (Longmans, 1876).

Railways and Locomotives: Lectures at the School of Military Engineering, Chatham, in 1877 (Longmans, 1882).

(with Charles Welch) *History of the Tower Bridge* (Smith Elder, 1894).

(with Charles Welch) *A Short Account of the Tower Bridge* (Smith Elder, 1894).

Address on the Streets and Traffic of London (William Trounce, 1899).

Notes on the Barry Genealogy in England and Wales (Waterloo, 1906).

letter on telegraph rates *Times* 19 Nov 1908.

lecture on engineering standardisation *Times Engineering Supplement* 23 Dec 1908.

letter on F D Maurice *Times* 20 Jan 1912.

letter on coal-strike *ibid* 4 Mar 1912.

letter on sale of Westminster hospital site *ibid* 12 Jan 1914.

letter on economy of food in wartime *ibid* 5 Aug 1914.

letter on Belgian neutrality *ibid* 3 Dec 1914.

Sources:

Unpublished

New South Wales State Library, papers of G E Morrison.

PRO, Colonial Office papers.

Thomas Fisher Library, University of Toronto, papers of J O P Bland.

Published

Arthur J Barry, *Railway Expansion in China and the Influence of Foreign Powers on Its Development* (Central Asian Society, 1910).

DNB.

Arthur C Fox-Davies, *Armorial Families* (2 vols, Hurst & Blackett, 1929-30).

Keith Sinclair, 'Hobson and Lenin in Johore: Colonial Office Policy towards British Concessionaires and Investors 1878-1907' *Modern Asian Studies* 1 (1967).

Minutes of Proceedings of the Institution of Civil Engineers 206 (1917-18).

WWW.

BARTLETT, Sir Charles John

(1889-1955)

Motor car manufacturer

Charles John Bartlett was born in Bibury, Gloucestershire, on 12 December 1889, the son of George Bartlett, a miller journeyman, and Elizabeth née Stevens. He attended the village school in Bibury, and completed his formal education at Bath Technical College, training in business methods and specialising in accounting.

Sir Charles Bartlett (courtesy of Vauxhall Motors Ltd).

In 1914 he enlisted in the Devonshire and Dorsetshire Regiment in which he served throughout the First World War. He was severely wounded at the Battle of Loos, and after he recovered saw further service in France, Egypt, Mesopotamia, Palestine and Syria. Demobilized in 1919 with the rank of sergeant, the following year he joined General Motors Ltd, the London-based branch (at Hendon) of the General Motors Corporation (GM) of America, as an accounting clerk.

At Hendon Bartlett's managerial potential was recognised. His promotion was rapid and in 1926 he became managing director. While at Hendon he saw the great potential for the light truck market which was later to play a major role in the expansion of Vauxhall during the 1930s. The assembled Buicks, La Salles and Chevrolets were not selling well in the British market as passenger vehicles, so he experimented with truck bodies on the chassis and found that his vehicles sold much better in the light truck market.

In 1925 General Motors Overseas Operations (GMOO) negotiated the purchase of Vauxhall Motors Ltd at Luton, and in 1928 GM began a large capital investment programme and reorganisation of the Luton works to enable mass assembly line production. Bartlett was promoted in 1930 to the position of managing director of the enlarged Vauxhall works at Luton, by J D Mooney, the GMOO director. He was chosen because, it was said, his capabilities had been noted during the investigations and financial planning which preceded the purchase of Vauxhall. A story current at the time was that when Mooney was told by Alfred P Sloan Jr, president and chairman of GM, to pick an Englishman to run Vauxhall, he replied, 'Well I guess it had better be Charlie Bartlett; he's about as English as they come' {Platt (1980) 93}. At the time GM was acutely aware of the economic nationalism within the British motor vehicle market, promoted essentially by William Morris (qv), and were concerned to have an all-British product made by British workers. Presumably the managing director also had to be seen to be a national as well.

Vauxhall had begun car production in 1903 with an output of 43 cars. In 1905 the firm moved from Vauxhall (London) to Luton to occupy a one and a half acre site employing 180 people. By the time Charles Bartlett became managing director its production had increased to 1,278 cars on its eleven and a half acre site, employing a staff of 1,500. However, it was in the following quarter century during which Bartlett guided the fortunes of Vauxhall Motors that the company experienced one of its most important periods of growth. By the time Bartlett retired in 1954 the total output was 130,000 vehicles (cars, vans and trucks) a year, built by a labour force of 14,500 on 85 acres of site.

Under Bartlett's control the first car to roll off the assembly line was the Vauxhall Cadet, which was followed by the much more popular Light Six in 1933 and, later, by the outstandingly successful Vauxhall Ten in 1937. The greatest success, however, was in the light truck market of which 11,200 were produced in 1931 rising to a commercial vehicle output of 60,800 Bedfords by 1954. According to Sir Reginald Pearson (qv), who was later to become a member of the Vauxhall board of directors, it was Bartlett who convinced A P Sloan that a truck was the best thing for Vauxhall. Pearson describes it as a 'life saver' for Vauxhall. By the end of the 1930s Vauxhall was one of the 'Big Six' vehicle producers in Britain,

A 1930 Vauxhall Cadet (courtesy of Vauxhall Motors Ltd).

and the truck brand name, Bedford, was soon being seen in markets all over the world.

Bartlett was an industrious and able managing director and under his authority management-worker relations changed. Policy toward the workforce became more enlightened and Bartlett introduced a number of schemes to create a loyal and contented workforce. He was noted for the warmth and humanity of his approach to the job of running a large company, and many workers testify to his concern, not only about how they were coping with their jobs, but also how their wives and families were faring.

A number of policies were introduced under Bartlett's management to ensure good industrial relations and the loyalty of the workforce. The rates of pay were relatively high, resulting in wages higher than those of either Ford or Morris, and much higher than those of other Luton employers. He introduced a profit sharing scheme, to which all workers belonged, whereby they would receive a proportion of the company's profits in their pay packets each Christmas. This was introduced in 1935 and is still (1982) in being. Another of his innovations was the Management Advisory Committee (MAC) whose purpose was to enable grievances among the workforce to be dealt with quickly by a joint group made up of management, foremen and shop floor workers elected to represent the workforce. Begun by Bartlett in 1941, it was replaced increasingly by direct union negotiation in the late 1950s.

Under Bartlett's authority a group bonus system with origins in the early 1920s, was developed. Under this scheme workers were paid extra according to the output of a group of workers in each shop, excluding the skilled areas. Though it was popular with a great many workers, it was phased out in 1956 and replaced by measured day work.

He also provided a greater security of tenure so that workers were no longer automatically laid off en masse when orders were low, as they had been in the 1920s. Likewise Bartlett pursued an active policy of promoting shop floor workers to managerial positions, amongst the most notable being Sir Reginald Pearson.

Bartlett developed welfare and leisure programmes, including the provision of new canteens and the promotion of drama and sporting activities with attendant facilities. Finally, during his management the company newspaper, *The Vauxhall Mirror*, was begun to keep the workforce informed of company matters.

It is not surprising that Vauxhall was dubbed 'The turnip patch' by unionists in other car firms because of the apparently rural tranquillity in industrial relations. During Bartlett's period as managing director there were no serious industrial disputes at Vauxhall.

Despite his obvious success at managing Vauxhall, which included the huge reorganisation to mass produce Churchill tanks and Bedford army trucks during the Second World War (for which he was knighted in 1944), he did not always see eye to eye with some of the top management of the General Motors parent company. GM felt that Bartlett had been allowed to achieve too great an autonomy during the Second World War. According to M Platt 'many important war time decisions had been taken at Luton of a kind that would certainly have needed the approval of the general manager of GMOO in peacetime' {Platt (1980) 148}.

Ed Riley who replaced J D Mooney as general manager of GMOO had little empathy with Sir Charles, and their differences became open in the post-war years, particularly concerning the direction and development of Vauxhall in the late 1940s and early 1950s. Riley was determined that his ambitious plans for Vauxhall expansion should be firmly based on a product programme of his own choosing and not on an updated version of the Vauxhall Twelve which Sir Charles favoured.

On 23 April 1953 it was announced that with effect from June 1, Walter Hill would succeed Bartlett as managing director; Bartlett, who was due to

A 1931 Bedford Truck (courtesy of Vauxhall Motors Ltd).

A 1937 Vauxhall 10 (courtesy of Vauxhall Motors Ltd).

retire in 1954 upon reaching the age of sixty-five, would become chairman in the meantime, but without executive responsibility.

Beyond Vauxhall Motors, Sir Charles was active both within and outside of the motor industry. He was president of Luton Chamber of Commerce for a record of seven consecutive years between 1938 and 1945. In 1951 he was elected a fellow of the Royal Society of Arts. In July 1952 he was appointed a DL of Bedfordshire. He was vice-president of the Royal Society for the Prevention of Accidents from 1946 until 1953, in which year he succeeded Lord Llewellyn as president. In December 1954 he was appointed a member of the Eastern Electricity Board which covers the Luton area. In addition he was a council member of the British Institute of Management and also a member of the Institute of Production Engineers. He retained a lifelong love of horticulture, and was a keen cricketer and golfer and had a general interest in sport.

In 1925 he married Emily May Pincombe. They had no children. He died at 'Whitewalls', his Harpenden home in Herts, aged sixty-five, on 10 August 1955, leaving an estate declared at £42,485 gross.

LEN T HOLDEN

Writings:

Some Aspects of Management Co-ordination: Today and Tomorrow (Manchester: Manchester Municipal College of Technology, 1948).

'Management and Productivity: The Results to Be Achieved and the Penalties of Failure' *British Management Review* (1948).

Sources:

Unpublished

Modern Records Centre, University of Warwick, MSS 242:T.26 Bartlett to A P Young (qv), letters 1942-43.

BCe.

PrC.

Published

Philip W Copelin, 'Development and Organisation of Vauxhall Motors Limited' in R S Edwards and H Townsend (eds), *Studies in Business Organisation* (Macmillan, 1961).

L D Derbyshire, *The Story of Vauxhall 1857-1946* (Luton, 1946).

Len T Holden, 'Think of Me Simply as the Skipper: Industrial Relations at Vauxhall 1920-1950' *Oral History* 9 (1981).

Luton News 11 Aug 1955.

Maurice Platt, *An Addiction to Automobiles* (Warne, 1980).

Michael Sedgwick, *Vauxhall* (Beaulieu Books, 1981).

Alfred P Sloan, *My Years with General Motors* (Sidgwick & Jackson, 1965).

Times 11 Aug 1955.

Graham Turner, *The Car Makers* (Eyre & Spottiswoode, 1963).

Kenneth Ullyett, *The Vauxhall Companion* (Stanley Paul, 1971).

WWW.

BARTLETT, Sir Herbert Henry

(1842-1921)

Builder and contractor

Herbert H Bartlett (from A Record of the Works of Perry & Co Ltd*).*

Herbert Henry Bartlett was born in the small Somersetshire village of Hardington Mandeville on 30 April 1842, the son of Robert Bartlett, a carpenter, and his wife Ann née Guppy. Educated in the local schools, he intended to become an architect, and with this in mind he came to London at the age of eighteen. He took rooms in Cheapside, and was apprenticed first to an architect and then to a civil engineer. In 1865 he joined John Perry (b 1813) in a junior position.

Perry, originally a working carpenter from the East End of London, ran a successful building and construction business at the Tredegar Works at Bow, trading as Perry & Co. In 1872 he took into partnership his son William and Herbert Bartlett. John Perry then retired and a new partnership between the three Perry brothers and Herbert Bartlett was formed in 1877. It did not last long. Two of the brothers died within days of each other in 1879. The third died in 1888, leaving Herbert Bartlett the sole proprietor of Perry & Co, a position he held until his death.

Under John Perry, Bartlett assisted in the construction of St Thomas's Hospital, built in 1867-71 for a contract worth £350,000, and then one of the biggest hospitals in the world. This was followed by the Hospital for Sick Children in Great Ormond Street (1872-76), and the London Hospital which the firm extended and modernised for thirty years or more, commencing in 1870.

The firm had building maintenance contracts with the War Office (1863-82) and the Office of Works (1884-88), and also carried out work for other government departments. They built the Victoria Barracks at Portsmouth; the new wings of Burlington House, Piccadilly (1868-73); the South Kensington Museum Library; and the 570 bed Naval Hospital costing £330,000 at Chatham (1901-5).

Perhaps Bartlett's most spectacular achievement was Tower Bridge (1886-94), incorporating two steel-framed towers and a massive drawbridge which allowed vessels to move further up into the Port of London. Between 1888 and 1908 Bartlett's firm performed a large number of works — new stations, bridges, cottages, engine sheds and various improvements — for the London & South Western Railway. They also built the People's Palace at Bow (later Queen Mary College), costing £100,000 (1886), the Hotel Cecil in the Strand (1893-95), the Piccadilly Hotel (completed in eighteen months in 1908), the Guildhall School of Music (1897) and a large assortment of banks, gas works, piers, residential chambers and flats, town halls, schools and churches, including the foundations of the Roman Catholic Cathedral at Westminster (1896). Bartlett then startled London by building a large garage, completed in 1907, to house 300 electric carriages in Hertford Street, Mayfair, for the Electromobile Co.

In 1897 Herbert Bartlett signed a contract with the London & Globe Finance Corporation to perform all the civil engineering work, worth £877,000, for the construction of a deep tube under the Thames from Waterloo to Baker Street. Work began in 1898 but was temporarily stopped in 1900 when the financier behind the scheme, Whitaker Wright (qv), committed suicide. Another syndicate, the Underground Electric Railways Co of London Ltd, headed by the financier Charles Tyson Yerkes (qv), took over the line and eventually Perry & Co constructed all the tunnelling between Waterloo and Edgware Road (beyond Baker Street). The 'Bakerloo' line opened in 1906. Bartlett's firm also built twelve stations on the Bakerloo Line, including those at the Elephant & Castle, Waterloo, Trafalgar Square, Piccadilly Circus, Oxford Circus, Baker Street and Paddington. The UERL's power station for generating electricity, located at Lots Road, Chelsea, was built by Perry & Co, 1902-5.

Between 1863 and 1908 Perry & Co carried out contracts worth £6,947,507, of which hospitals represented 17 per cent, office buildings 16 per cent, hotels and restaurants 13 per cent and public buildings 11 per cent.

Tower Bridge Works 18 October 1892
(from A Record of the Works of
Perry & Co Ltd*).*

At the turn of the century, Bartlett was joined by his eldest son, Hardington Arthur Bartlett, who had been trained as an engineer by Professor Henry Robinson, Dean of King's College, London. H A Bartlett soon emerged as his father's successor within the firm. He was made consulting engineer for the Bakerloo tubes. Then he went to Spain, to build the harbour at San Sebastian, and then to Canada, where he gained further experience in railway construction. During the First World War, Sir Herbert (he was made a baronet in 1913) entrusted him with the contracts for building and maintaining a large number of military camps, mainly round Winchester. And when Perry & Co in 1919 won the contract from the Belgian Government to rebuild the entire town of Dinant, which had been badly damaged by the Germans, H A Bartlett took overall responsibility for it. However, his promise was never realised. On a fairly rough Channel crossing to Belgium in 1920 he was lost overboard. His father never recovered from the blow and died eighteen months later.

Sir Herbert Bartlett took a keen interest in all branches of the building industry, being a member of the London Master Builders' Association from its inception in 1872 and its president in 1888; an early member of the Institute of Builders, he sat on its council for over thirty years and served as its president in 1892. In 1911 he gave a sum of £30,000 to University College London, to erect buildings for the combined School of Architecture, together with the studios for the teaching of sculpture, and the rearrangement of the School of Fine Art, and the Department of Applied Statistics, including the Laboratory of Eugenics. At that time he wished to remain anonymous, but in 1919 he agreed to the publication of his name as the donor. In 1920, in recognition of his gift, the School of Architecture was renamed the Bartlett School of Architecture with his consent.

Sir Herbert was three times master of the Worshipful Company of

Baker Street and Waterloo Railway Works, 1900–5. Contractor's Locomotive in the Tunnel (from A Record of the Works of Perry & Co Ltd).

Pattenmakers and was deeply interested in, and assisted in fitting out Sir Ernest Shackleton's first expedition to the South Pole in 1907-9. For a long while Sir Herbert was Commodore of the Royal London Yacht Club and was on the council of the Yacht-Racing Association; for many years he skippered his own sailing boat, replacing it with a steam yacht when he grew too old for sailing.

His (remarkably limited) private life was very happy. He married in 1874 Ada Charlotte Barr, daughter of a City wine merchant; they had six boys and three girls. They never liked company, and never went out if they could possibly help it. Sir Herbert never owned a motor-car, and, whenever he was in London, was driven in a horse-drawn carriage between his office in Victoria Street and his large, dark house in Cornwall Gardens, which, his son Hardington once declared, was 'furnished entirely with foreclosed mortgages' {Bartlett (1978) 60}. In one respect he differed deeply from his wife. She was an ingrained Londoner, while he was a countryman at heart and would have bought a country mansion had she consented. Instead he compromised, by leasing a shoot each winter for himself and his sons. In later life Sir Herbert maintained an extraordinary patriarchal isolation. He usually dined alone, and on railway journeys always took a first-class seat, packing his wife, children and grandchildren into a third-class compartment further down the train.

To his workforce Sir Herbert was a kindly man and took immense trouble over their health and welfare. Neither he nor his wife seem to have had any feeling for religion. He built numerous churches, but entered them only for an occasional wedding or funeral. However, one of his sons, Philip, became an Anglican priest and took a living in Poplar, spending most of his life as the highly respected Rector of St Saviour's and a long-time friend of George Lansbury, the Christian Socialist. Despite his own non-observance of religious duties, Sir Herbert helped Philip in various ways and even allowed him to have all his brothers and sisters confirmed, although most of them were in advanced middle-age. Sir Herbert also bought a house near Canterbury so that all Philip's elderly parishioners could have a summer holiday.

Sir Herbert, shaken by the death of his eldest son, died at the age of seventy-nine on 28 June 1921. He left £486,680 gross but throughout his working life had been quietly buying corner sites in the City of London, and these he conveyed to a trust for his wife and children. The business passed to his second son, Robert Dudley Bartlett, whose abilities did not match his aspirations and under him the firm of Perry & Co in 1926 went bankrupt.

SIR BASIL BARTLETT, BT

Sources:

Unpublished

BCe.

MCe.

PrC.

Personal information (the author is grandson of the subject).

Published

Theodore C Barker and Michael Robbins, *A History of London Transport* (2 vols, George Allen & Unwin, 1963-74).

Sir Basil Bartlett, Bt, *Jam Tomorrow. Some Early Reminiscences* (Paul Elek, 1978).

The Builder 121 (1921).

The Builders Journal 22 Aug 1905.

Theo Crosby, *The Necessary Monument* (Studio Vista, 1970).

Daily Mail 13 Nov 1907.

The Engineer 15 Dec 1893.

Alan A Jackson, *London's Termini* (Newton Abbot: David & Charles, 1969).

Alan A Jackson and Desmond F Croome, *Rails Through the Clay. A History of London's Tube Railways* (George Allen & Unwin, 1962).

The Pictorial World 19 May 1887.

A Record of the Works of Perry & Co, Builders and Contractors (Founded AD 1837), More Particularly Dealing with Those Works Carried out under the Direction of Mr Herbert Henry Bartlett, Sole Proprietor of the Business since 1888 (pp, 1908; copy in possession of author).

Times 4 July 1921.

The Tramway and Railway World 9 Feb 1905.

University College London *Annual Reports* 1911-20.

WWW.

BARTON, Sir Harold Montague

(1882-1962)

Accountant

Sir Harold M Barton (courtesy of Ernst & Whinney).

Harold Montague Barton was born in Hull on 24 September 1882, the third son of Major Bernard Barton, JP, owner of a Hull seed-crushing mill, and Clara née Kelsey. Educated at Oundle School, he was originally articled to George Gale, a chartered accountant in Hull. He qualified in 1904 and joined Price Waterhouse in London a year later. Here he met Basil Mayhew (1884-1966) a fellow employee. Both men desired greater freedom and established their own firm in December 1907, being allowed by Price Waterhouse to retain one client each: Barton keeping Griffiths & Co, building contractors, and Mayhew, Meadow Dairy. Barton's Yorkshire origins soon proved valuable in the acquisition of the Eucryl (toothpaste manufacturers) audit as the company had their works in Hull. Mayhew, a man of distinguished appearance and gregarious character, took much responsibility for getting fresh business and entertaining clients. Barton ensured that the accounting work was efficiently undertaken, though through his membership of the Society of Yorkshiremen in London (being its chairman in 1929 and 1930) and various dining clubs he was also responsible for securing new work.

During the First World War, it was decided that Mayhew would remain in London to supervise the running of the firm, while Barton enlisted in the Artists' Rifles and attended officer training. After a short-lived attempt to standardize the Red Cross's system of accounts in India, and in response to the great and growing need for accountants to serve in public administration to regulate an increasingly complex war economy, Barton joined the Ministry of Munitions to deal with the costing of Aircraft Accounts. This experience led to his appointments in the Second World War as controller of General Aircraft Ltd (1943-45), financial director (from 1941) of the National Dock Labour Corporation (for which he was knighted in 1947), and as member of the London Price of Goods Committee (1939-42) and the Higher Appointments Committee of the Ministry of Labour and National Service (1943-44).

A Council member of the Institute of Chartered Accountants in England and Wales from 1928 to 1957, Barton was much involved in the organization of the accountancy profession. Having been elected its president in 1944-45, he then served on its Discharge Liaison Committee (like Mayhew, he had been a member of the less successful Central Demobilisation Board of 1918-20), which conducted negotiations with the Ministry of Labour to secure the speedy return of accountants from the armed forces in order to assist in the reconstruction of industry and commerce. In addition, Barton had been appointed chairman of the Institute's Taxation and Financial Relations Committee on its creation in 1942: an important body that was to conduct research into general accounting and taxation questions.

During the inter-war period Barton, Mayhew & Co grew steadily, acquiring new clients, such as the paper firm headed by Sir Eric Bowater (qv), the first agricultural marketing boards and Southern Roadways, and helped existing ones (British Mutual Bank, the Property & General Finance Corporation) to expand. As a result their staffs and number of offices had increased so that when Sir Basil Mayhew resigned from the partnership in 1936 to take up a directorship with Colmans, Harold Barton became sole senior partner, a post which he retained until his retirement in September 1954. During the period of nationalisation after 1945 Barton sat on the tribunal to determine compensation payable under the Cable and Wireless Act, and on the two Railway Conciliation Boards, becoming in 1948, with Sir Alan Rae Smith of Deloittes, the first joint auditor of the British Transport Commission.

Sir Harold Barton's career, bridging the Edwardian and post-1945 periods, covered an important transition in the accountancy profession's development. When he entered general practice, accountants, as auditors and insolvency specialists, had not earned high popular esteem; by the 1950s, the sustained service on government committees and inquiries of leading accountants like himself, supported by their professional bodies, had established the accountant's place in administration and public service.

In 1927 Barton married Joyce, second daughter of William Henry Wale, a retired manufacturer; they had one son and a daughter. Sir Harold Barton died on 20 October 1962, leaving £50,895 gross.

EDGAR JONES

Sources:

Unpublished

BCe.

MCe.

PrC.

Published

The Accountant No 4584 (27 Oct 1962).

Edgar Jones, *Accountancy and the British Economy 1840-1980, The Evolution of Ernst & Whinney* (Batsford, 1981).

WWW.

Sir Robert A Bartram (courtesy of J Clarke).

BARTRAM, Sir Robert Appleby

(1835-1925)

Shipbuilder

Robert Appleby Bartram was born at Hylton on the River Wear on 23 March 1835. His father, George Bartram (1800-1891) was a shipwright who became a junior partner of John Lister; together for sixteen years, they laid their first keel in 1838. Robert Bartram was educated in private schools, served a shipyard apprenticeship and became his father's sole partner in 1854. Output of ships from their yard remained modest, except in 1863 when four ships totalling almost 900 tons were launched. Until the retirement of George Bartram in 1871 the yard continued to build in wood.

Robert Bartram then formed a partnership with George Haswell, who had worked with the great pioneer iron shipbuilder William Pile (1823-73), and the new company built iron ships at South Dock, Sunderland, under the title Bartram, Haswell & Co. The shipyard's output was increased over the next ten years to about 12,000 tons but in the depression of the mid-1880s the yard almost disappeared. Not a single ship was launched in 1885 and only one a year in 1884 and 1886; soon after the shipyard recovered in 1889 Haswell retired. Robert Appleby's sons George and William joined their father to form the family partnership Bartram & Sons. For many years there was no expansion and output remained at about 12,000 tons. However, on the eve of the First World War it exceeded 27,000 tons per annum.

Bartram's other business interests included chairmanship of the local steelmakers Samuel Tyzack & Co and he was also a director of the Sunderland & South Shields Water Co.

Labour relations in the shipyard were normally good and Bartram was for a time chairman of the Wear Shipbuilding Conciliation Board. An active member of the employers' association, he chaired the Wear Shipbuilders' Association from 1901 to 1908 and his general interest in the trade of the port was reflected in his presidency of the Sunderland Chamber of Commerce.

Education was a lifelong interest of Bartram. He was first elected to the Hylton School Board in the 1870s and later served for twenty-three years on the Sunderland School Board, twice as chairman. He donated a thousand guineas towards the education of shipyard apprentices in memory of his son George, who died in 1910, and in 1921 he gave the borough of Sunderland 10,000 guineas to provide four scholarships and to help extend and equip the local technical college. Bartram was an elder of the local Presbyterian Church and in his will provided £4,000, the income from which was towards the minister's stipend. His many charitable and voluntary activities included the Sunderland Town and Police Court Mission, the YMCA, the Sunderland Infirmary and the Blind Institute. A JP for the borough from 1892, Bartram served on the Board of Guardians and was made a freeman of the town in November 1921; six months later he was knighted.

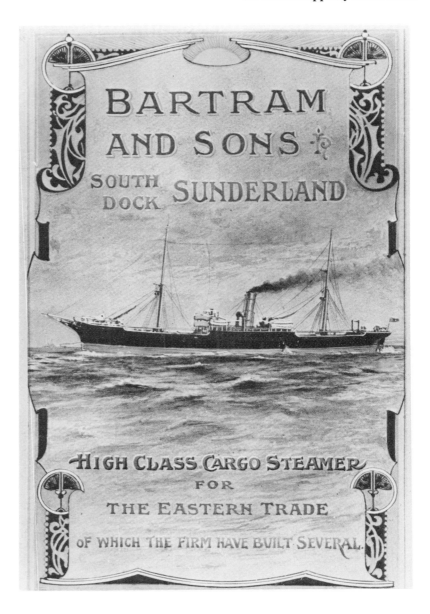

Early twentieth-century advertisement of Bartram & Sons (courtesy of Tyne & Wear Museum Service).

Bartram married twice: first Ann, daughter of the local shipbuilder William Naisby, in 1859; there were three sons and one daughter. He later married Agnes, daughter of Alexander Rhind of Newport, Fife. Sir Robert Bartram, who lived at Thornhill Park, Sunderland, died at the age of ninety on 8 August 1925 leaving £217,813 gross. The family shipyard, managed by two grandsons, was then struggling to survive.

J F CLARKE

Sources:

Unpublished

Sunderland Public Library, Corder MSS.

Tyne & Wear Archives, Papers of the Wear Shipbuilders' Association; Austin & Pickersgill Papers (includes Bartrams).

PrC.

Published

Joseph F Clarke, 'Shipbuilding on the River Wear 1780-1870' in *The Great Age of Industry in the North East* ed R W Sturgess (Durham: Durham County Local History Society, 1981).

James Jamieson (ed), *Durham at the Opening of the Twentieth Century* (Brighton: W T Pike & Co, 1906).

Shipbuilder 1922, 1925.

J W Smith and T S Holden, *Where Ships Are Born* (Sunderland: Thomas Reed & Co, 1946).

WWW.

BATEMAN, John Frederic La Trobe

(1810-1889)

Consulting hydraulic engineer

John F La Trobe Bateman in 1859 (from John F Bateman, History and Description of the Manchester Waterworks, *Manchester: T J Day, 1884).*

John Frederic La Trobe Bateman was born in the Moravian community of Lower Wyke, Halifax, on 30 May 1810, the third child of seven and eldest son of John Bateman (1772-1851) by his wife Mary Agnes, daughter of Benjamin La Trobe, a Moravian missionary at Fairfield near Ashton-under-Lyne. From the age of five, he was brought up in the Moravian community at Fairfield, Manchester, where his uncle, Frederic Foster, was pastor. A period of ten years of enlightened education shared between Moravian schools here and at Ockbrook was followed in 1825 by an apprenticeship with a Mr Dunn of Oldham, a surveyor and mining engineer.

Supported by his cousin, John Frederic Foster, a prominent magistrate, Bateman set up in 1833 as a civil engineer, land surveyor and agent. His first reservoirs were constructed at Glossop and on the River Bann, for millowners anxious to increase their production. In 1841, he became a member of the Institution of Civil Engineers. In 1844, he joined the Manchester Literary and Philosophical Society where his views on the theory of rainfall distribution were first publicised.

These views coincided with the development of the Health of Towns Movement and as a result Bateman was employed as consulting engineer to numerous works which supplied cities and towns in the UK with 'constant' water via the gravity system. He and his associate G H Hill were responsible for by far the largest number of earth embankments that form the bases of these works, many of which are functioning today (1982). Chief among them were those for Manchester and Glasgow. On completion of the latter at Loch Katrine in 1859, Bateman extended his practice by setting up a London office. Started in 1847, the Longdendale scheme for Manchester was not completed until 1876 when Bateman finally overcame the engineering difficulties that had continually beset construction. About 1865, it became obvious that the Longdendale supply would soon be insufficient. Bateman, who had given evidence to the Royal Commission on Metropolis Water Supply, was directed towards the Lake District as being an additional source for Manchester. The Thirlmere scheme was passed through Parliament in 1879 after considerable opposition and Bateman's associate, G H Hill, was eventually responsible for its construction.

Bateman was also chairman of the Shannon Inundation Inquiry. He advised on land reclamation in Spain and Majorca and was engineer for water supply to Buenos Aires. He investigated the water supply of Malta, Naples and Constantinople and was consulting engineer for Colombo Waterworks. With J W Bazalgette he worked on a scheme for the disposal of Glasgow sewage.

Bateman was elected an FRS in 1860 and president of the Institution of Civil Engineers, 1877-79. In 1883 he added the prefix surname La Trobe in recognition of his maternal grandfather. His partnership with G H Hill was dissolved in 1885, with the latter taking over all the engineering commitments.

John Bateman married in 1841 Anne, only daughter of Sir William Fairbairn; they had three sons and four daughters. Bateman died at his home, Moor Park, Farnham, on 10 June 1889, survived by his wife and six of their seven children, leaving £52,806 gross.

PETER RUSSELL

Principal Writings:

'Observations on the Relation which the Fall of Rain Bears to the Water Flowing from the Ground' *Memoirs of the Manchester Literary and Philosophical Society* 7 (1846).

'Report of the Committee for ... the Placing of Rain Gauges along the Rochdale, Ashton and Peak Forest Canals' *ibid*.

'Some Account of the Floods which Occurred at Manchester Waterworks in February 1852' *ibid* 10 (1852).

BATEMAN John Frederic La Trobe

Report on the Means of Deodorising the Sewage of Glasgow (Glasgow: G Richardson, 1858).

Reports of William Hope, J F Bateman. Iberian Irrigation Company Ltd (Printed for private circulation, 1862).

Metropolis Water Supply; on the Supply of Water to London from the Sources of the River Severn (Westminster, 1865).

Report on the Sewerage of Glasgow, Addressed to the Sanitary Committee of the Town Council ... 1 Dec 1858 (Glasgow: Robert Anderson, 1867).

On a Constant Water Supply for London (Faithfull & Head, 1867).

Report on the Drainage of Oxford (Oxford: Oxford Chronicle Co Ltd, 1867).

(with Julian J Revy) *Channel Railway. Description of a Proposed Cast-iron Tube for Carrying a Railway across the Channel between the Coasts of England and France* (Vacher & Sons, 1869).

PP, RC Water for the Metropolis and Other Large Towns, 1868-69 (1869) 4169.

Documentos Relativos a las Obras del Puerto de Buenos Aires e Informe del Injeniero J F Bateman (Buenos Aires, 1871).

Port of Buenos Ayres. Supplemental Report of John Frederic Bateman ... to Señor Don P Agote, the Minister of Finance for the Province of Buenos Ayres, on Improved Harbour Accommodation. 8th April 1871 (Kell Brothers, 1871).

Mejoras de la Ciudad de Buenos Aires; Informe sobre Drenage, Sistema de Cloacas para Desagne y sobre Provision de Agua de la Ciudad de Buenos Aires (Buenos Aires: Imprenta del Siglo, 1871).

Memoir of My Father (Sept 1873).

Address on Election as President of the Institution of Civil Engineers (W Clowes & Sons, 1878).

Report ... as to Collection and Disposal of Glasgow Sewage 7th October 1878 (Glasgow, 1878).

Meteorology: Rainfall (1881).

History and Description of the Manchester Water Works (Manchester, T J Day, 1884).

Sources:

Unpublished

PrC.

Peter E Russell, 'John Frederic La Trobe-Bateman, Water Engineer, 1810-1889' (Manchester MSc, 1980).

Published

DNB.

Proceedings of the Institution of Civil Engineers 97 (1889).

Proceedings of the Royal Society of London 46 (1889).

Peter E Russell, 'John Frederic L Trobe-Bateman (1810-1889), Water Engineer' *Newcomen Society Transactions* 52 (1980-81).

John T Batey (courtesy of the Royal Institution of Naval Architects).

BATEY, John Thomas

(1862-1951)

Naval architect and shipbuilder

John Thomas Batey was born in Newcastle upon Tyne on 28 July 1862, one of the eleven children of the tug boat operator Francis Batey (1842-1915) and Margaret née Nicholls (1842-1912). He was educated at the Royal Grammar School and in 1880, aged eighteen, he began an apprenticeship at the Hebburn shipyard of his father's friend Andrew Leslie (qv). Batey was one of the last apprentices to finish his time under the largely self-taught Scot. Through evening classes and while still an apprentice he achieved a bronze medal in naval architecture and a first-class honours degree, to become one of the few men so qualified on Tyneside at that time. While working in the Hebburn drawing office of what had become R & W Hawthorn-Leslie Ltd, Batey lectured part-time in naval architecture at Rutherford College in Newcastle.

In 1889 he became chief draughtsman at William Dobson's Low Walker shipyard and he worked there for twelve years. This smaller establishment offered limited opportunities for his talents and in 1901 he rejoined the Hebburn shipyard of Hawthorn-Leslie as chief draughtsman but in a matter of months became general manager under Herbert (later Sir Herbert) R Rowell (qv). Six years later Batey was made a director of the company. He coped successfully with a diversity of output: regular cargo vessels, naval work, many refrigeration ships, as well as almost continuous naval construction. All of this was compounded by fluctuations in orders. A profit rate of 5.1 per cent on turnover was achieved over the eight years 1907-14. Towards the end of this period pneumatic tools, a substantial investment, were introduced into the shipyard.

When Rowell became company chairman in 1916 increased managerial responsibility came Batey's way and he managed the difficult transition from war to peace-time production in the depressed inter-war years. On Rowell's death in 1921 Batey was appointed managing director. Under his careful control the Hebburn shipyard in the 1920s built some fine passenger vessels, a type of ship new to the yard. By a policy of close production control and a vigorous sales policy the shipyard was more successful than most of its rivals.

J T Batey joined the North East Coast Institution of Engineers and Shipbuilders in 1885, not long after it was founded and he played an active role in the Institution throughout his life. He served for many years on its council, frequently as chairman of key committees, was elected a fellow in 1924 and ten years later president. For more than fifty-two years Batey was a member of the Institution of Naval Architects and after years of service on their council was elected president in 1938. His continued interest in and contribution to education was recognised in an honorary DSc conferred by Durham University in 1935. A year later his status amongst the world's ship designers was reflected in his presidency of the

Hebburn Shipyard ca 1883, when John T Batey began work (from a watercolour hanging at the Hebburn Shipyard).

International Conference of Naval Architects held in New York. Batey was an early supporter of standardisation in shipbuilding and engineering and served as a member of the British Engineering Standards Association, which later became the British Standards Institution. On his retirement in 1935 the *Shipbuilder* recorded that Batey had 'always been intensely practical in his profession, combining a cautious outlook on new ideas with a readiness to accept them in full measure when once assured of their practicality.' {*Shipbuilder* (June 1936) 373}

There were few areas of shipbuilding in which Batey did not serve. His committees included the Board of Trade Advisory Committee, the Merchant Shipping Committee and the Technical Committee of Lloyd's Register. Batey played an important part in the various employers' associations and was chairman of the Tyne Shipbuilders' Association for four years and later was on the Central Board of the Shipbuilding Employers' Federation.

The helplessness of fellow workers when a serious accident occurred early in his career so troubled Batey that he determined to train volunteers to meet such emergencies. As a result he was active in the St John Ambulance Brigade until a few days before his death in 1951 and greatly treasured the honour of being a Knight Grace of the Venerable Order of the Hospital of St John of Jerusalem in England. He was president of the Hebburn Nursing Association and chairman of the Chest Hospital in the West End of Newcastle. He played tennis, bowls and billiards and enjoyed watching rugby football.

J T Batey married Adelaide Frederick Sewell (1861-1946); they had two daughters and two sons. J Leslie Batey (1896-1962) followed his father's profession of naval architect and the younger son Frank (b 1899) became managing director of the family firm Lawson-Batey Tugs Ltd, of which his father was also a director. John Thomas Batey died on 23 July 1951 leaving an estate worth £88,441 gross.

J F CLARKE

Writings:

Presidential address in *Transactions of the North East Coast Institution of Engineers and Shipbuilders* 51 (1935).

Presidential address in *ibid* 52 (1936).

Sources:

Unpublished

Tyne & Wear Archives, records of Hawthorn-Leslie, records of the North East Coast Institution of Engineers & Shipbuiders and records of the Tyne Shipbuilders Association.

PrC.

Published

Joseph F Clarke, *Power on Land and Sea. A History of Hawthorn-Leslie* (Clark Hawthorn Ltd, 1979).

Royal Institution of Naval Architects Transactions 1951.

Transactions of the North East Coast Institution of Engineers and Shipbuilders passim.

Shipbuilder June 1936.

BAXENDALE, Lloyd Henry

(1858-1937)

Road haulage industry entrepreneur

Lloyd Henry ('Harry') Baxendale was born at Totteridge near Barnet on 3 February 1858, the eldest son of Lloyd Baxendale, 'gentleman', and his wife Ellen née Turner. His grandfather Joseph Baxendale (1785-1872) had become a partner in the road haulage firm of Pickfords in 1817, had revitalised the firm and eventually in 1850 acquired ownership of it from the Pickford family. Harry's father was Joseph's second son. Educated at Eton and Christ Church College, Oxford, Harry entered Pickfords in 1879.

He was the second member of the third generation of the Baxendale family to join the firm, having been preceded by his older cousin, Joseph William Baxendale (1848-1915), the only son of Joseph Baxendale's eldest son, and was followed by his own younger brother, F H (Frank) Baxendale (1862-1918). A partnership agreement of 1894 allocated 8 shares to Joseph William the senior partner, 6 to Harry and 3 to Frank. When the firm converted to limited liability in 1901, the capital was distributed in similar proportions: Joseph William became the senior shareholder and chairman, but the active management of the business lay with Harry and Frank Baxendale.

At this stage Pickfords' principal business was as cartage and delivery agents to several railway companies. Chief amongst these was the London & North Western Railway. The decision, implemented in 1901, to break with the LNWR triggered a slump in Pickfords' fortunes and a major quarrel between the Baxendales. Joseph William resigned and withdrew; the firm's capital was heavily written down, and Harry Baxendale took over as chairman. The drain of capital, at a time when the conversion from horse to motor transport was accelerating, proved too great, however, and in 1912 the firm was forced into an alliance with its major competitor, Carter Paterson & Co. Harry Baxendale became chairman of the joint company, then the dominant combine in the road haulage industry, which from then on became the major instrument of his business interests, especially after 1920 when Pickfords passed into the ownership of the Hay's Wharf Cartage Co, a subsidiary of The Proprietors of Hay's Wharf. Throughout this time he remained a director of Pickfords but resigned from both Pickfords and Carter Paterson, when they were purchased by the four main line railway companies in 1933.

Harry Baxendale's home was Greenham Lodge, near Newbury Racecourse. Indeed he had much to do with the formation of the racecourse in 1905. He took up the suggestion of John Porter, a leading trainer, that a racecourse might appropriately be established at Newbury, the centre of an important training district, and it was laid out with grandstands on land formerly belonging to the Greenham Lodge estate. Baxendale became chairman of the Newbury Racecourse Co, which purchased the racecourse property for £30,000, and also of the Bath Racecourse Co, and whenever King George V and Queen Mary attended the Newbury races he received them. Baxendale played a full part in the sporting and social life of south Berkshire and his grounds were the scene of many big summer functions. He was active in Conservative politics, serving on the county council for six years from 1889. He was a JP for over fifty years, and chairman of the Newbury county bench 1927-35. Like his parents before him, he generously supported the parish church of St Mary the Virgin at the edge of his Greenham estate and held the office of church warden.

Harry Baxendale married Constance Louisa, daughter of Charles Raymond Pelly. They had one daughter, Christina, who married Captain the Hon Donald Erskine, the eldest son of the Sixth Lord Erskine. Harry Baxendale died on 21 May 1937 leaving an estate valued at £309,042 gross.

GERARD TURNBULL

Sources:

Unpublished

BCe.

MCe.

Prc.

Published

Richard N Hadcock, *The Story of Newbury* (Newbury: Countryside Books, 1979).

Reading Mercury 29 May 1937.

W Money, *Popular History of Newbury* (Simpkin, Marshall & Co, 1905).

Gerard Turnbull, *Traffic and Transport. An Economic History of Pickfords* (London: George Allen & Unwin, 1979).

BAYLIS, Lilian Mary

(1874-1937)

Theatre manager

Lilian Mary Baylis was born in Marylebone, London, on 9 May 1874, eldest of the ten (five surviving) children of Newton Baylis, baritone, and

Drawing of Lilian Baylis by W
Rothenstein, dated July 1922
(courtesy of John Vickers, London).

his wife Liebe Konss (anglicised to Elizabeth Cons), contralto and pianist. She was educated at home as a musician, practising five hours a day, as well as looking after the younger members of her family. She first appeared in public when only seven. In 1891-98 the family lived in South Africa, where she taught the violin, banjo, mandolin and guitar, and toured with her family in their musical troupe. Her health however gave way, and she returned to England in 1898.

Lilian Baylis' maternal aunt was

> Emma Kons (1838-1912), one of the most saintly as well as the most far-sighted of Victorian women philanthropists ... Trained under Octavia Hill as a rent collector, she revolted against the self-complacent harshness ... and became an independent manager of working-class dwellings ... Realising that what was needed, even more than sanitary but dismal homes, was the organisation of the pleasures of the poor in great cities, she in 1880 took over the management of the Victoria music hall, at that time a disreputable centre for all that was bad ... Charles Kingsley's 'licensed pit of darkness' ... and ran it as a place of popular musical entertainment, free from vice, and unsubsidised by the sale of alcoholic drink {Webb (1926) 266}.

Between 1898 and 1912 Miss Baylis was assistant manager to her aunt's celebrated coffee music-hall, just off the Waterloo Road in south London. The Victoria was run on philanthropic rather than artistic criteria, and indeed it was not until after Emma Kons's death that Lilian Baylis obtained a license for dramatic performances.

Succeeding to the management and lease on her aunt's death in July 1912, Lilian Baylis believed that God had inspired her to produce Shakespeare, opera and ballet at low prices for the working-class audience of south London. During the next six years, 'this dowdy, uneducated, eccentric, deeply religious spinster turned a dingy temperance hall in a London slum into the home of Shakespeare and opera in English with virtually no money or resources, in the middle of a world war' {Findlater (1975) 20}. Her success was such that her theatre, the Old Vic, won a national reputation, and was visited by Shakespeare-lovers from all over Britain. She herself never acted or produced, did nothing to encourage new drama, was indifferent to all theatrical productions other than her own, and resisted new ideas in stage design or lighting. Indeed a large measure of the Old Vic's wartime success must be attributed to Sir Philip Ben Greet (1857-1936), who was its producer, 1914-18.

In 1931 she re-opened Sadlers Wells Theatre in Islington, aiming that it should serve north London as the Old Vic served south London and intending that it would exchange companies with the Old Vic. After the critical meeting between the governors of the two theatres she was asked how it had gone: 'Splendidly', she replied with sincerity, 'I had the Almighty in my pocket'. In the event, there were financial difficulties after 1931, and it became necessary for the Vic to take over her drama productions while the Wells concentrated on opera and ballet, becoming the direct progenitor of the Royal Ballet. As a theatre administrator, Lilian Baylis was inefficient but peremptory. Obsessed with economy, she underpaid her actors and actresses, and was an unblushing beggar forever cadging from her patrons and friends. The Old Vic kept its audiences, and most of its performers, because it was unique in Britain as a theatre which until the late 1930s was above the commercial exigencies of the West End.

A sketch of The Old Vic by Arthur
Moreland, which appeared in the
Daily Telegraph *10 Aug 1929*
(courtesy of the Theatre Museum,
Victoria and Albert Museum).

First-rate actors were prepared to work at the Old Vic for a pittance
because it provided one of the few opportunities to play Shakespearean
roles at a time in the 1920s when Shakespeare was unfashionable in the
West End. Fine actors, such as Laurence Olivier, John Gielgud, John
Laurie, Ralph Richardson and Marie Ney, were only able to accept such
low pay because of the high fees they were earning from the British film
industry. Star salaries at the Old Vic in the 1930s were £20 per week at a
time when Olivier could command £600 a week in films, and in a real
sense, Lilian Baylis's management only survived because it was subsidised
by actors' film earnings.

Miss Baylis had an extraordinary personality. 'She was a brute, a tyrant,
ignorant, selfish, conceited ... but she was a great courageous inspired
figure also, and she was an untidy, ugly, affectionate Cockney child as
well' {Sir Hugh Walpole in Williams (1938) 5}. 'Her character combined
rare, almost bleak simplicity with canniness, an almost childlike naivety

221

with a peasant's earthy wisdom, self-defensive wariness and belligerence with vulnerable affectionate kindness' {Findlater (1975) 296}. Some of her sayings have entered theatrical legend, such as her prayer 'Dear God, please send me good actors — and cheap', or her reply to an actor who asked for a pay-rise, 'Sorry, dear, God says no'. To Queen Mary visiting the Old Vic she declared in the middle of the national anthem, 'We *always* play your husband's tune here, right through'. King George's portrait hung near one of Emma Kons (often mistaken by poorer theatre-goers as Shakespeare's mother) and she told the Queen, 'His portrait isn't as big as Emmie's, but then he hasn't done as much for the Old Vic'.

A nature lover, who was devoted to dogs, Miss Baylis had a one-room hut at Betchworth high on the South Downs. She was made an honorary MA Oxford in 1924, received an honorary LLD from Birmingham University (1934), and was made a Companion of Honour in 1929. In November 1937, just after the opening night of an Old Vic production had been postponed for the first time in her management, one of her pet dogs was run over, and her hysterical sister dropped its corpse on her while she was lying down resting. She suffered a heart attack, and died two days later on 25 November 1937 at her house in Stockwell. She never married, and left £10,037 gross.

R P T DAVENPORT-HINES

Writings:

letter on Shakespeare at the Old Vic *Times* 3 Oct 1923.

letter on St Andrew's Society for helping poor ladies *ibid* 12 July 1924.

(with Cicely Hamilton) *The Old Vic* (Cape 1926).

letter on Shoreditch Shakespeare Festival *Times* 24 June 1933.

letter on English music *ibid* 26 Feb 1937.

letter on Vic-Wells completion fund *ibid* 21 Oct 1937.

Sources:

Unpublished
PrC.

Published
John Booth, *The Old Vic 1816-1916* (Stead, 1917).

Mary Clarke, *Shakespeare at the Old Vic* (4 vols, Hamish Hamilton, 1953-58).

DNB.

Richard Findlater (KBF Bain), *Lilian Baylis, the Lady of the Old Vic* (Allen Lane, 1975).

Peter Roberts, *The Old Vic Story: a Nation's Theatre 1818-1976* (W H Allen, 1976).

Sybil and Russell Thorndike, *Lilian Baylis* (Chapman & Hall, 1938).

Ernest G Harcourt Williams, *Four Years at the Old Vic 1929-33* (Putnam, 1935).

— (ed), *Vic-Wells* (Cobden-Sanderson, 1938).

Times 26, 29, 30 Nov 1937.

WWW.

BEALE, George

(1864-1953)

Food retailer

George Beale was born at Muswell Leys, Warwickshire on 25 April 1864, the son of Thomas David Beale, a farmer, and his wife Ann née Ashby. Nothing is known of his education before he began a four-year apprenticeship to a wholesale grocer in West Bromwich. On the completion of his apprenticeship in April 1884, he joined the Maypole Dairy Co, the retail chain in the North East owned by George Watson (qv) and his brothers. Beale rose to be a chief inspector of this rapidly growing business. When he left to start on his own the Watsons, according to one of Beale's sons, gave him £1,000 as a parting gift.

He formed the Meadow Dairy Co in 1901, with a capital of just under £3,000. He put up £1,000, his wife Elizabeth (whom he had married at Newcastle upon Tyne in 1897) contributed a little money of her own, while her father William Potts, who farmed at Kenton in Northumberland, put up another £1,000. The rest of the money came from three other friends and colleagues. George Beale was to be managing director for ten years, with a salary of £25 a month, and half the net profits.

Setting out to build his own chain of food shops, on much the same lines as the Maypole stores, he opened first in Newcastle. By 1919 he had 29 branches in a number of North Eastern towns. He allowed no credit, and made no deliveries. There was very little advertising. The nearest Beale came to employing a publicity stunt was to present a silver cup for an annual football competition among local schools. Like most of his competitors in multiple food retailing, he traded in very few lines. Butter and eggs were the basis of his turnover, with some margarine, pre-packed tea, and sugar. The shops were small, and leased rather than bought: all available capital was used for trading, not for acquiring freehold sites.

In 1906, when he had 16 shops, Beale won the support of the Dutch margarine manufacturers, Van den Berghs, who were investing in several wholesale and retail companies at this period. Van den Berghs supplied £20,000 additional capital, but Beale still controlled the company for he held £21,465 of the £50,240 capital. In 1909 Van den Berghs arranged for Beale to take over the Keeloma Dairy Co, in which they also held an interest. Meadow, which became a private company, now had an authorised capital of £100,450, and, with Keeloma's 55 branches in Northumberland and Durham, controlled nearly 90 shops. In 1912 Van den Berghs increased their holding in Meadow to obtain formal control of the company.

A quiet, thoughtful man, less flamboyant than his competitors Thomas Lipton (qv) or George Watson (qv), and less in the public eye, he was more consistently successful than they, and his judgement more consistently sound. Evidently satisfied with his management of Keeloma, Van den Berghs continued to exchange their capital for George Beale's expertise, his ability to choose good staff and successfully delegate responsibility to them. In 1914 Van den Berghs reorganised the capital of Pearks' Dairies, a retail chain with over 100 stores in which they had invested heavily, to bring it under Beale's direction. Van den Berghs lent Meadow the money to take up £30,000 of Pearks' £180,000 capital. In return, Beale was to take on the management of Pearks for at least seven years for a payment of £500 a year and half the profits available for dividends. In 1916, he came south to control both companies from a new headquarters in London. From 1917 Meadow's head office was in London, although a regional headquarters was kept in Newcastle. Meadow now reverted to being a public company, with an issued capital of £276,722. Meanwhile, profits had grown from £38,424 in 1914 to £94,753 in 1918.

The end of the war brought further expansion of the Meadow Dairy Co and of Pearks, the latter mainly by opening new branches, the former by further acquisitions. Broughs was the major postwar purchase, bought for £216,000 in 1919. Broughs had been built up by Joseph Brough (qv) as a chain specialising in bulk orders delivered to women in isolated mining villages in the North East; Beale decided that new trading policies were called for to meet changing social circumstances, and ordered his managers to develop the counter trade, provide display windows, and bring in new lines. (Meadow shops were also now stocking a wider range of groceries than they had before the war, having begun to carry lines like cake and rice which Keeloma and Pearks had already sold before they came under Beale's management.)

By 1926 Beale was supervising over 800 shops, insisting on strict standards of inspection and costing to maintain efficiency; Meadow's profits that year reached £239,000. But the General Strike of 1926 caused the first real setback of Beale's career, for Meadow's branches were still concentrated in the industrial areas of the North East most heavily hit by the Strike. Meadow's profits continued to grow, but now much more slowly, a trend Van den Berghs attributed not to any failings in Beale's management, but to the shift of industrial growth and prosperity from the North East to the Midlands and the South.

Van den Berghs' continued confidence in Beale and the managers he had trained was shown when they decided to bid for control of Sir Thomas

Lipton's troubled Home & Colonial Stores. Van den Berghs assumed control of Home & Colonial after buying out Sir Thomas for £600,000 in 1927. Beale became vice-chairman, but this time there was no financial link between Home & Colonial and Meadow. Once again Beale set about introducing his men and methods to revitalise an ailing retail chain. Again he succeeded, but although the performance of Lipton's stores began to improve, that of Beale's companies was at last beginning to suffer from the drain of skilled manpower. It became apparent that for some years the Meadow Dairy Co had been benefiting by the decline of Lipton's shops. As they started to attract more customers again, it was, to some extent, at the expense of Meadow. When the formation of Unilever (of which Van den Berghs was one of the main constituents) in 1929 involved the financial integration of the Meadow Dairy Co and the Home & Colonial, Beale took the opportunity to retire from both companies and sell his holdings in Meadow.

Not that he had grown tired of business. He immediately bought a thriving southern firm with 33 small multiple stores, Green's Stores of Ilford, for £54,000, becoming the non-executive chairman. He brought his three sons into the company, selling it to them for the price he had paid for it to ensure that they owned the firm they worked for, and guided them in running and developing the business.

On retiring from the Meadow Dairy Co, George Beale also took up his father's occupation, farming, buying 1,000 acres at Pottersbury Lodge in Northamptonshire. He enjoyed all country pursuits, particularly foxhunting (he was joint master of the Grafton Foxhounds in 1934-36) and breeding hunters. He did not retire from business finally until 1947, six years before his death on 28 March 1953. His estate was proved at £276,599.

One of his sons, William (b 1908), the chairman of Green's from 1950 to 1963, became a prominent figure in the grocery trade, directing the armed forces' catering organisation, the NAAFI, in West Africa and then in Europe during the war, and serving as chairman of NAAFI from 1953 to 1961. He was knighted for his services in 1956. He served as chairman of the Multiple Grocers' Association from 1961 to 1963.

CHRISTINE SHAW

Sources:

Unpublished

BCe.

MCe.

PrC.

Information supplied by Sir William Beale, and the Multiple Retailers' Association.

Published

Economist 13 Mar 1920.

Ambrose Keevil, *The Story of Fitch Lovell* (Phillimore, 1972).

Peter Mathias, *Retailing Revolution* (Longmans, 1967).

Statist 17, 24 Sept 1927, 14 Apr 1928, 23 Feb, 6 Apr 1929.

Charles Wilson, *The History of Unilever* (2 vols, Cassell, 1954).

John E Beale (from The Richmond Magazine & Congregational Record *Vol 31 Aug 1928).*

BEALE, John Elmes

(1848-1928)

Department store retailer

John Elmes Beale was born at Weymouth on 6 December 1848, the son of John Beale, the master of a small ship, who was lost at sea when the boy was young, and his wife Fanny née Elmes. He attended Weymouth Grammar School (later Weymouth College) and then his mother arranged for him to be apprenticed to a Weymouth draper. Having completed his apprenticeship, he found employment in Sherborne. After a short period with the big Manchester wholesale warehouse of J & N Phillips, he returned to Weymouth, assisting in, and later managing a draper's shop in St Mary's Street. On 23 April 1878 he married Sarah Brickell, of Shaftesbury, and three years later, after the birth of his first son and having served eight years in the Weymouth shop, he felt it was time to branch out on his own. By this time he had saved £400 capital.

He moved to Bournemouth, which was then hardly developed but had a population of 17,000 and evidently held better prospects of commercial success than the older market towns of Dorset. The shop he rented was newly built and stood in a terrace close to Old Christchurch Road; it adjoined the Bournemouth Arcade, which, developed in the early 1870s, had shifted the commercial centre of the town from Commercial Road in the west to Old Christchurch Road, east of the Bourne Stream and the Square. His wife, a woman of great strength of character and determination, ran the shop for a couple of months until his employer released him after Christmas 1881. Their new premises had to serve as a family home, provide lodging for a first assistant, and office accommodation for a coal merchant and the YMCA, as well as his shop. Described as 'Fancy Fair', Beale's shop sold fancy goods, not to the well-to-do residents and visitors but to the new, less wealthy, holiday visitors and the lower classes in Bournemouth's suburbs, such as horsemen and gardeners, shop assistants and domestic servants. From the capital he had saved J E Beale invested in a stock of fancy goods, using the packing cases in which these were delivered to make fittings and storage fixtures.

Success was steady, especially during the summer months when large numbers of visitors from the West Country and the West Midlands came to Bournemouth's West Station (opened 1874) on day excursions by rail. These customers for spades and pails and for souvenirs to take home were greatly augmented from 1888 by the many day excursionists who came to the East (later Central) Station by the new direct rail line to Bournemouth from London and the South East.

As the fashion for seaside holidays gained momentum and more people came for longer stays in the resort and arrived with more money to spend, J E Beale, while maintaining the gift shop image of his business, began to modify the stocks he held to include more expensive items. After taking over an agency of Libertys of London, he built up a department specialising in fabrics and other manufactures from the Orient. Clearly the idea of a departmental store as it was being developed in London by Harrods and Whiteley (qv) was influencing his plans for the future. When his eldest son, John Bennett Beale, had completed training with a stationer in Southampton, he was sent to work at each of these two London firms in turn to gain the experience needed for a major expansion of the business.

By the time Bennett returned to Bournemouth in 1899 an adjoining shop had been acquired and in 1900 the shop on the other side of Fancy Fair was also added to the premises. Departments for stationery, toys, books and leather goods, as well as an expanded Gifts Department, which now included clocks, electroplated tableware, silver toilet ware and so on, were set up. As a speciality, an extended range of 'View Books' (the shop had editions of 10,000 every year or two) was put on sale. Meantime, the second son, Herbert, began training and after an apprenticeship at Hastings followed by experience under John Barker (qv) in Kensington, he also joined his father and was very soon involved in the process of planning the conversion and rebuilding of the three adjacent shops held by Fancy Fair. From among local shopowners J E Beale recruited two senior men to act as shopwalkers and managers and with their help the two eldest sons were in a position to take a major share in the running and development of the firm, permitting their father to devote more time to public affairs.

Beale, an active Wesleyan in Sherborne in the late 1860s and then in Weymouth (where he was church steward, Sunday school superintendent and local preacher in the Maiden Street Church), joined the Richmond Hill Congregational Church after he moved to Bournemouth in 1881. Here he served as a deacon, 1897-1928, and then as church treasurer, 1902-28. Among the officers and congregation were a number of local councillors associated with the faction of the town council intent upon local 'improvement' and an active role for municipal administration, sometimes ironically styled 'the Progressives'. Beale was elected to the Bournemouth Council in 1900, a few months after he was appointed a JP on the town's first Commission of the Peace. With the continuing ascendancy of the 'Progressive' faction, Beale in 1902 was elected mayor of what was now the county borough of Bournemouth; the same year he was made an alderman and sat on the Council in this capacity until 1924. During his term as mayor (he was re-elected in 1903 and 1904), important decisions were taken on the development of the sea-front, the introduction of a tramway system for Bournemouth and adjoining Poole and Christchurch; and the improvement of facilities for recreation, including municipal golf-courses, public gardens, playing fields, and the support of a municipal orchestra. All these issues were the subject of hot debate by the Council and, as mayor and chairman, J E Beale played a leading part in preserving Bournemouth's sea-front from commercial development and shaping the town as a high-class shopping centre, with a wide range of genteel entertainment and the image of a beautiful and salubrious resort. Beale and his group aimed to encourage more and more people to spend extended holidays in Bournemouth while simultaneously attracting day excursionists to a holiday resort which had avoided the brashness of many of its competitors. Beale's personal contribution to these important developments was recognised by his election as an honorary freeman of the borough. Beale was also a freemason and member of Hengist Lodge no 195.

After his three years as mayor J E Beale returned to a closer control of his business, though he remained chairman of the Public Health Committee for another twenty years. His two sons, soon to be joined by others (he had five sons and two daughters), proved their management skills and he was able to delegate to them a very large measure of responsibility as the transition of the firm to a major departmental store was carried out. This growth involved a series of expansions following the acquisition of adjacent shops, and major rebuilding schemes took place in 1905 and 1912; a third timed for 1915 was postponed. It also meant the widening of the range of goods sold and services provided. In 1920 Beales integrated with another Bournemouth retail business, that of W H Okey, drapers, of Commercial Road, in which J E Beale had held a financial interest since 1903 and in which his third son, Harold, was employed. This firm was taken over as 'Bealesons' and operated as a departmental store catering for a rather different clientele from that of the original shop. With other local businessmen, J E Beale also founded the Carlton Hotel and the family interest in this, the only independent five star hotel in Europe, remains to the present.

Beale gradually relinquished his detailed control of the business but still took part in major decisions until 1920. In the conduct of his business his great strength seems to have been a vast capacity for hard work accompanied by a willingness to trust those he employed. At the same time his strong Christian convictions shaped his attitudes to the creation of wealth and to his employees. He allowed his sons, cautiously at first, to develop the firm along the lines so successfully worked out by Gordon Selfridge (qv) in London and to back them in proposals for expansion. He was concerned for the well-being of his staff and introduced a staff superannuation scheme immediately after the First World War, and having provided for his children, he left the residue of his estate to this fund. At his death in 1928 the family business reportedly employed a staff of 700.

During the First World War he had been active in connection with many war charities, in particular the organisation of flag days and other events to assist work with the wounded, the local War Relief Committee, and for Belgian refugees who had come to Bournemouth. This war work was recognised by the award of the Belgian Médaille du Roi Albert and the Russian Cross.

John Elmes Beale died on 1 July 1928 at the age of seventy-nine, having passed over all responsibility for the firm to his sons for several years by then. He left £34,596 gross.

J F PARSONS

Sources:

Unpublished

Bournemouth Town Hall, minutes of the Bournemouth County Borough Council, 1900-28.

BCe.

MCe.

PrC.

Information from Richard Roberts.

Published

J Bennett Beale, *As I Remember It* (pp, 1967).

Bournemouth and Southampton Graphic 6 July 1928.

Bournemouth Daily Echo 2 July 1928.

Bournemouth Guardian Nov 1905, Oct 1924.

Bournemouth Times and Directory 6 July 1928.

William Henry Jacobs, *Hampshire at the Opening of the Twentieth Century* (Brighton: W T Pike & Co, 1905).

John F Parsons, *J E Beale and the Growth of Bournemouth* (3 parts, Bournemouth Local Studies Publications, 1980–82).

BEARSTED, 1st Viscount Bearsted
see SAMUEL, Marcus

Sir Alfred C Beatty in 1930 (courtesy of Selection Trust).

BEATTY, Sir Alfred Chester

(1875-1968)

Mining entrepreneur

Alfred Chester Beatty was born in New York City on 7 February 1875, the youngest of the family of three sons of John Cuming Beatty and Hetty née Bull. His father was a comfortably-off stockbroker. He attended Westminster School at Dobbs Ferry in New York and while still a boy showed a keen interest in the collection of mineral specimens. He decided to adopt mining as a career and, after a year at Princeton University, went to the Columbia School of Mines, from which he graduated at the top of his class in 1898.

After graduation, declining any further financial assistance from his father, Beatty set off for Denver in Colorado in the Rocky Mountains, which was then developing as a mining state. He tried to obtain professional work, but at first was unsuccessful and was forced to take a job as a mucker (labourer) in a small gold mine in order to make a living.

However, his ability soon showed itself and only a few months later he became manager of the mine and made a remarkable success of the job. As a result it was not long before he was able to move on and set up as a mining consultant in Denver, in which capacity he quickly gained a high reputation. Colorado in those days was still very much a part of the American 'Wild West' scene, where the carrying of guns was common. The mining fraternity was particularly inclined to lawlessness and on one occasion striking miners, whose wrath Beatty had incurred, made an attempt to kill him by letting a mine cage in which he was travelling run out of control down its shaft.

Beatty's reputation attracted the attention of the famous American mining engineer, John Hays Hammond, who in 1903 was given the job of running the Guggenheim Exploration Co, which the Guggenheim brothers had established to find mines which would assure their great smelting empire of adequate supplies of minerals. Beatty was appointed as Hammond's principal assistant and together for five years they explored the mineral potential of large areas of the American West and Mexico. They became associated in particular with the development of low-grade copper deposits on a gigantic scale which made them an economic proposition.

In addition to his work in America for the Guggenheims, Beatty carried out negotiations, on behalf of the brothers and other members of a consortium, with King Leopold II of the Belgians during 1906, which led to the establishment of the Société Internationale Forestière et Minière (Forminière) to exploit the mineral and other resources of the Kasai region of the Independent Congo State (later the Belgian Congo and now Zaire). Forminière became one of the world's largest diamond producers. In recognition of his services to the Congo, Beatty was made a Commander of the Order of Leopold II in 1932.

By 1911 Beatty was one of the top people in his profession and a wealthy man, but in that year his first wife died, leaving him with two small children to look after. He himself was in indifferent health and so shortly afterwards he decided to retire from the American mining scene and settle in London.

However, he did not remain idle for long and inspired perhaps by Herbert Hoover, another American mining engineer (later President of the USA), who had a mining consultancy practice in London, Beatty set up business in adjacent offices. As a medium for developing new mining ventures, Beatty established a small private company with a capital of £50,000 in 1914 and called it Selection Trust.

The company lay dormant during the First World War, but soon afterwards exploration activities were begun. The first successful venture was in the Gold Coast (now Ghana) where extensive deposits of alluvial diamonds were discovered. A separate public company — Consolidated African Selection Trust — was formed in 1924 to carry out the mining operations. This company proved eminently profitable right from the start and the profitability was enhanced when the operations were extended into Sierra Leone in 1934 and the exclusive right to mine diamonds throughout the whole country was obtained.

The second venture was the acquisition in 1925 of the Tetiuhe lead-zinc-silver mine near Vladivostock in far-eastern Siberia. This was a remarkable venture insofar as the USSR had nationalised all foreign interests in Russia without compensation after the Revolution in 1917. The mine was brought into production but a combination of financial and other problems prevented the operation from being a success and the property was sold to the Soviet Government in 1931.

There followed in 1926 another excursion into the field of lead-zinc-silver mining — this time in Yugoslavia, where there had been extensive mining in Roman times and the Middle Ages but where such activities had ceased some four hundred years previously with the Turkish conquest of the Balkans. Abundant traces of ancient workings still remained and Beatty was convinced that under some of these would be found major deposits too deep for the ancients to work. This proved to be the case and the Trepca mine was brought into production in 1931 and soon became the largest producer of its kind in Europe.

King Alexander of Yugoslavia took a personal interest in the Trepca development and officially opened the mine in 1930, when he awarded Chester Beatty the Grand Cordon of the Order of St Sava. This was the only occasion on which Beatty ever visited one of the mines which Selection Trust brought into existence: so confident was he in his ability to choose the right men to run operations in the field that he, the chairman of all the companies in the Selection Trust group, remained in London, from which he closely monitored the progress of his mining ventures.

By far the greatest achievement in Chester Beatty's mining career was the part he played in the development of the copperbelt of Northern Rhodesia (now Zambia). Selection Trust established one of the two major groups of companies which brought this enormous copper-bearing region into production. (The other group was set up by Sir Ernest Oppenheimer's Anglo American Corporation of South Africa.) As early as 1920 Beatty had become associated with others in exploration in Northern

Rhodesia, but later he launched his own ventures under the aegis of Selection Trust. These led firstly to the development of the Roan Antelope mine which came into production in 1931, to be followed by the Mufulira mine where production started in 1933. Around the same time the foundation work was done which enabled the Chibuluma and Chambishi mines to be brought into production in the 1950s and 1960s.

In the development of its mines Selection Trust had substantial financial assistance from the American Metal Co of New York (now Amax). With the growth of its business in the 1920s, Selection Trust had been converted into a public company and by 1933 had a capitalisation of £2.5 million. However, the vast scale of development of the Rhodesian mines necessitated outside financial help.

In spite of problems in the early 1930s caused by the world depression, the Rhodesian mines were well established by 1939 and provided a major source of supply of copper for Britain during the Second World War. It was largely for his work in Northern Rhodesia that Beatty was awarded the Gold Medal of the Institution of Mining and Metallurgy in 1935.

In all his ventures Beatty exhibited a deep sense of humanity towards his employees and he was greatly concerned about their health and welfare. For example, he engaged as a consultant Sir Malcolm Watson, one of the leading experts on tropical medicine; as a result malaria and other diseases which had previously been rife in Northern Rhodesia were largely eliminated.

In 1933 Beatty became a naturalised British subject and during the Second World War served on government committees dealing with the control of diamond dies and non-ferrous metals. He was also vice-chairman of the United Kingdom Commercial Corporation, whose chairman was Lord Swinton and whose objective was to buy up strategic supplies throughout the world and keep them out of enemy hands.

Beatty's boyhood interest in collecting continued into later life and over the years he amassed a huge and vastly valuable collection of art treasures of all kinds: paintings, ancient eastern manuscripts, rare books, antique snuff bottles and many other things. These he kept in his mansion in Kensington Palace Gardens in London.

He also became a major benefactor, his philanthropy becoming best known to the general public through his endowment of the Chester Beatty Institute for Cancer Research in London. His interest in this project extended beyond mere financial assistance for he served for several years as President of the Royal Cancer Hospital.

In 1950, at the age of seventy-five, Beatty finally retired from business. By this time the companies in the Selection Trust group together had a stock exchange value of around £40 million.

He went to live in Dublin, complaining that there were then too many restrictions in life in Britain. He took his collection of art treasures with him and built the Chester Beatty Library to house them. His public services were recognised by the British Government in 1954 when he was knighted. In 1956 he became a Freeman of Dublin and in the following year was made Eire's first honorary citizen.

Beatty was married twice; first in 1900 to Grace Madelin Rickard, by whom he had a daughter, Ninette, born in 1902 and a son Alfred Chester Jr, born in 1907. Following the death of his first wife in 1911, he married again in 1913, his second wife being Edith Dunn Stone of New York, who died in 1952.

Sir Chester died on 19 January 1968 in Monaco and was accorded a state funeral in Dublin by the Irish Government. His will revealed assets in Ireland of over £7 million, of which £6 million was represented by the Chester Beatty Library, which he left to the Irish nation.

CYRIL A KIDD *and* SIMON KATZENELLENBOGEN

Sources:

Unpublished

BP Minerals International (formerly Selection Trust), London, archives, Annual reports and chairman's statements of Selection Trust Ltd, Consolidated African Selection Trust Ltd, Tetiuhe Mining Corporation Ltd, Trepca Mines Ltd, Roan Antelope Copper Mines Ltd, Rhodesian Selection Trust Ltd and Mufulira Copper Mines Ltd - variously between 1925 and 1950.

Biographical notes on Chester Beatty, compiled by members of the Selection Trust staff (1938-66).

Speeches by Beatty at two retirement dinners in 1950.

Published

Richard J Hayes, 'Chester Beatty and his Library' *Antiquarian Bookman* 39 no 12 (20 Mar 1967).

Kenneth Bradley, *Copper Venture* (pp, Roan Antelope and Mufulira Copper Mines, 1952).

Simon Cunningham, *The Copper Industry in Zambia* (New York: Praeger, 1981).

DNB.

Sir Theodore Gregory, *Ernest Oppenheimer and the Economic Development of Southern Africa* (Cape Town: Oxford University Press, 1962).

Horizon (Zambia: Roan Selection Trust group of companies) Mar 1968.

Irish Press (Dublin) 30 Jan 1968.

Edward Jessup, *Ernest Oppenheimer — A Study in Power* (Rex Collings, 1979).

Peggy McCarthy, 'The Treasures of Shrewsbury Road' *Aramco World* (Arabian American Oil Co) Mar 1965.

'A Notable Birthday' *Mining Journal* 11 Feb 1955.

Sir Ronald L Prain, *Reflections on an Era* (Metal Bulletin Books, 1981).

Selection Trust Annual Report 1968.

Sunday Press (Dublin) 7 Feb 1965.

Times 22 Jan 1968.

Malcolm Watson, *African Highway* (John Murray, 1953).

Arthur J Wilson, *The Pick and the Pen* (Mining Journal Books, 1979).

WWW.

Zambia's Mining Industry — The First 50 Years (Ndola, Zambia: Roan Consolidated Mines, 1978).

BEAVER, Sir Hugh Eyre Campbell

(1890-1967)

Brewer and civil engineer

Sir Hugh E C Beaver (courtesy of The Brewers' Society).

Hugh Eyre Campbell Beaver was born in Johannesburg on 4 May 1890, the oldest of the three sons of Hugh Edward Campbell Beaver, who came from Montgomeryshire, and Cerise née Eyre, who was of Anglo-Irish descent. His father died in 1892, and the family returned to England. In 1904 Beaver won a scholarship to Wellington College, Berkshire, where he rose to be head boy in 1910. In the same year he failed to win a scholarship to read law at Oxford, so he sat the examination for the Indian Police instead, emerging top of the field. From 1910 to 1922 he served with the Indian police, devoting much of his time to administration and intelligence work.

On his return to England in 1922, he attracted the attention of Sir Alexander Gibb (qv), an established contractor and engineer who was his mother's neighbour and who was then launching a new type of consulting engineering practice, to serve the needs of factory production. Beaver joined the firm in the same year, and rapidly established himself. He was directly responsible for a major survey of Canadian ports in 1931, including a rebuilding of St John, New Brunswick in five months following a fire. The resulting report was published in 1932 and was subsequently implemented as the basis of the modern Canadian system of ports. Beaver was also involved in projects for Rothschilds and the Capper Pass Metallurgical Works. He became company secretary in 1931 and, a year later, a partner of Sir Alexander Gibb & Partners. In the 1930s his work concentrated on the development of Special Areas (hit most severely by the depression), in the North East and in South Wales. He was also directly responsible for the construction of the new Guinness brewery at Park Royal, London between 1932 and 1936, achieving considerable success with the company for the farsighted way in which he persuaded the directors to acquire additional land for future development and for recreational facilities. At this time he formed a close alliance with the managing director of Guinness, C J Newbold, who invited him to join the board. In the 1930s Beaver refused the invitation.

In 1940 Beaver was appointed director-general of the Ministry of Works, a crucial position, the responsibilities of which included the building and construction of the entire wartime programme of works and the supply of building materials. He was knighted for these services in 1943. Immediately after the war, he was invited, this time at the express wish of Lord Iveagh, to join Guinness as assistant managing director, under Newbold, with the particular brief of modernising the company both in methods and outlook. He took over as managing director in 1946 on the sudden death of Newbold.

Thus Beaver was launched on a career at the head of a brewing enterprise with very little experience of the supposedly mysterious art of brewery management. Over the next five years he introduced new methods of management, inspired more effective research, introduced the beginnings of a policy of diversification, saw through a notable increase in volume of exports, encouraged the development of young managers and consequently witnessed the gradual recovery of Guinness from a long period of relative stagnation.

He brought Guinness firmly into the second half of the twentieth century. His diversification policies may ultimately have proved less successful than was hoped, but seemed extremely promising and logical at the time. He was responsible for a major re-organisation of the structure of the company, dividing it into two separate trading companies, Guinness Ireland and Guinness UK, under one parent board. At the end of the 1950s he was directly responsible for the introduction of Harp Lager, initially in Ireland and subsequently in a British consortium in England, Wales and Scotland. Harp rose rapidly to become the leading brand of lager in Britain, and one of the earliest of the great successes of the lager boom of the 1960s and 1970s. His period at Guinness also saw the introduction of the *Guinness Book of Records*, which had sold over 6 million copies by his death. Again he was directly responsible for this project, the original idea for it being his own.

The results of his able management can be seen in the growth of Guinness in the 1940s and 1950s. In 1945 the pre-tax profit of the company was under £2 million; by 1947 it was £2.2 million; it subsequently rose to £4.8 million in 1948, £6.4 million in 1955, and £7.4 million in 1959, the last full year of his management. His work at Guinness showed him very much at the peak of his powers as an administrator and manager; he introduced new equipment, metal fermenting tuns, bulk delivery, and much more stringent quality control. He revised methods of budgetary control, introduced effective cost control, instituted work study, job evaluation and new works committees, and gave greater recognition to the trade union movement, supporting its growth where necessary. He left the company in very good shape on his retirement in 1960, having ensured in the 1930s that it would be well-housed, and that it would derive additional income from the leasing of land and plant in the Park Royal area.

Beaver was above all an extremely able and effective chairman of committees, as his career suggests, as well as a sharp and invigorating instigator. He had the capacity to reach the right conclusion in a very short time, often to the dismay of his colleagues, and he also had a great ability to persuade committees to reach general agreement and to accept decisions. He was amongst the earliest advocates of 'brainstorming sessions' to produce new ideas. Harp lager originated in one such session in the mid-1950s. His abilities in these directions were reflected in his work for the brewers' panels, which he handled with great skill and diplomacy. He was also a central figure in the campaign to prevent state purchase of the licensed trade following the Second World War, when his position with a company with no vested interest in tied trade helped his cause and the campaign in general. He was in line to become chairman of the Brewers' Society in 1959 when ill-health forced him to decline. He became a vice-president of the Society in 1960.

His public service after 1945 reflected his interest in the role of engineering and industry in society as a whole. From 1951 Beaver resumed his active participation in public affairs; in that year he became chairman of the British Institute of Management, and deputy chairman of the Colonial Development Corporation. In 1952 he was chairman of the Committee on Power Stations, and in 1953 he chaired the Committee on Air Pollution (known as the Beaver Committee) which resulted in the 1956 Clean Air Act. In 1954-56 he was chairman of the Advisory Council of the Department of Scientific and Industrial Research. From 1957 to 1959 he was president of the FBI and in the early 1960s he was a leading figure in the formation of the National Economic Development Council. He was awarded the KBE in 1956 in recognition of his services to the nation. He was also chairman of the Industrial Fund for the Advancement of Scientific Education in Schools, and president of both the Institute of Chemical Engineers and the Royal Statistical Society. He believed that industry should bear a part in serving Western civilisation and its way of life. Consequently he was a firm believer in support for worthy causes both socially and artistically, and influenced those around him, both individually and corporately, to support them too. Sir Hugh Beaver was forced to retire through poor health in 1960, although he continued to work unofficially on public matters thereafter.

Sir Hugh Beaver married in 1925 his second cousin, Jean Atwood Beaver, daughter of Major Robert Atwood Beaver, MD; they had two daughters before her early death in 1933. Sir Hugh Beaver died on 16 January 1967, leaving £16,500 gross.

TOM CORRAN

Writings:

Report of the Committee of Enquiry into Economy in the Construction of Power Stations (HMSO: Ministry of Fuel & Power, 1953).

PP, Report of Committee on Air Pollution (1953-54) Cmd 9322.

Sources:

Unpublished

Guinness Co, Dublin, and Park Royal, London, records.

Published

DNB.

Brewing Trade Review Feb 1967.

Guinness Time 1960.

Sir Norman Kipping, *First Beaver Memorial Lecture 1972* (Brewers' Society, 1972).

Thomas H Corran, *The Brewing Industry in Britain, 1830-1969* (forthcoming).

WWW.

BEAVERBROOK, 1st Lord Beaverbrook
see AITKEN, William Maxwell

BECKETT, Rupert Evelyn

(1870-1955)
Clearing banker

Rupert Evelyn Beckett was born at Meanwood Park, Leeds, on 2 November 1870, the third and youngest son of William Beckett Denison (1826-90), who adopted the surname Beckett in lieu of Denison in 1886 and became Conservative MP for the East Retford (1876-80) and Bassetlaw (1885-90) constituencies. Rupert Beckett's father belonged to the third generation of partners in the Leeds banking firm of Beckett & Co, originally founded by Lodge and Arthington around 1750. His mother was the Hon Helen Duncombe, daughter of the Second Lord Feversham. Beckett was brought up as a member of the Church of England and educated at Eton and Trinity College, Cambridge.

His introduction to the family banking business began at the age of nineteen when he entered the firm's principal office in Leeds to undertake junior duties. After leaving Cambridge he became a partner in the firm.

Rupert Beckett moved to Doncaster around 1895 to become the resident partner managing the Doncaster and Bradford businesses, formerly Cooke & Co, which had been absorbed by Beckett & Co in 1868. These were part of the group of branches comprising Beckett & Co, Leeds Bank, while the former businesses of Bower Hall & Co and Swann Clough & Co acquired in the 1870s were administered as a separate group under the title of Beckett & Co, York & East Riding Bank. Beckett joined the board of the Yorkshire Penny Bank, as nominee of the guaranteeing banks which took part in the reconstruction of the YPB in 1911, orchestrated by Sir Edward Holden (qv). He served for forty-four years, thirty of them as chairman.

Beckett's grandfather had been a promoter of the Great Northern Railway and instrumental in ensuring that the line from London to York did not by-pass Doncaster. Rupert Beckett became a director of the Great Northern Railway and continued on the board of its successor the London & North Eastern Railway until the nationalisation of the railways after the Second World War. He also sat on the boards of the Forth Bridge Railway, Aire & Calder Navigation, Royal Exchange Assurance, and Yorkshire Conservative Newspaper Co. His contribution to the newspaper group, which included the *Yorkshire Post*, was probably second only to his work as a banker. He was a member of the board from 1911 until his death and was chairman for thirty years earning a reputation as a champion of editorial independence.

By the First World War he had returned to Leeds and was an active member of the directing board of a munitions factory near the city and also served as a major in the Yorkshire Hussars.

In 1918 he sat on the Treasury Committee on bank amalgamations, the surge of bank mergers having been renewed with full force even before the war ended. One of the major amalgamations, that between the London County & Westminster Bank and Parr's Bank, produced the Westminster Bank, one of the 'big five'. The merger gave the new bank strong bases in London and the South East, the West Country, the East Midlands and the North West but there was a gap in representation east of the Pennines.

Rupert Beckett, then senior partner in his firm, entered into carefully guarded negotiations with the new grouping and terms were agreed for the absorption of the two Beckett banks in 1921. Thus Westminster inherited the powerful business in industrial and agricultural Yorkshire which the Becketts had been building for over a hundred and seventy years. At the time of the amalgamation the two Beckett banks had 36 offices and assets of over £12 million. The bank also gained the local knowledge and influence of the family through the appointment to the Westminster board of Rupert Beckett and his brother Gervase.

Gervase was an MP; Rupert, although a life-long supporter of the Conservative Party, resisted pressure to enter Parliament, considering that there were enough of the family at Westminster. In 1931 he had the unusual experience of being elected chairman of the bank that had taken over his own firm and he held this post for the next twenty years, leading the Westminster Bank through the economic and political troubles of the 1930s, the years of war and the period of radical social and economic change that followed. During his chairmanship the bank's assets grew from some £300 million to over £800 million and the branch network was steadily but not rashly increased in the newly-developed areas and in older centres where Westminster had not hitherto been represented.

In 1947 Beckett became chairman of the Committee of London Clearing Banks and of the British Bankers' Association. He had been made freeman of Leeds in 1931 and given an honorary LLD by the University of Leeds in 1938. He also became a JP and a DL of the West Riding.

Beckett remained active all his life, attending a board meeting at Westminster Bank's Lothbury Head Office only a few days before his death. Work for the Westminster Bank had kept him increasingly in London but he maintained his home at Shadwell, Leeds, was a regular attender at York and Doncaster race meetings, and kept in touch with the business life of the West Riding.

Rupert Beckett married in 1896 Muriel Helen Florence (d 1941) daughter of Lord Berkeley Paget; they had four daughters. He died at his apartment in the Park Lane Hotel, London, on 25 April 1955, in his eighty-fifth year, leaving £1,202,000 gross.

RICHARD REED

Sources:

Unpublished

National Westminster Bank Archives.

Published

Theodore E Gregory, *Westminster Bank through a Century* (Oxford University Press, 1936).

WWMP.

WWW.

John Bedford in 1962 (courtesy of the Drapers' Record*).*

BEDFORD, John

(1903-1980)

Head of department store chain

John Bedford was born in Birmingham on 16 January 1903, the son of John Bedford, a journeyman brass caster, and his wife, Rosalind (known as Rose) née Nicholls. John Bedford Sr started his own small brass foundry, which evidently prospered sufficiently to make it possible to plan a career in the law for his son. However, this small business later collapsed, and Bedford started work in a Birmingham department store, first as an assistant, and then as a buyer.

He joined Debenhams in 1932, when he became manager of J C Smiths, a store in Stratford upon Avon that had just been acquired by Debenhams. Three years later, he was appointed managing director of another recent acquisition of Debenhams, Arnold's of Great Yarmouth, and then in 1938, sent to Plymouth to restore the finances of the Spooners store. During the Second World War he had to tackle the problem of running Spooners in the teeth of the intensive bombing of Plymouth. Among the first buildings to be destroyed in the town centre was Spooners' premises. The morning after the destruction of these premises, Bedford, making use of his extensive Methodist and Liberal contacts in the town, arranged for the different departments to be housed in a number of small shops. He defied the bombs by erecting a one-storey building in the most devastated area of Plymouth, which survived as part of the premises for Spooners until a new store was opened in 1950. So prominent a part did he take in the city during the war, serving in the Home Guard, firewatching, publicising National Savings, active within the Chamber of Commerce, the local

Liberal Party, and the Mercantile Association, and preaching as a Methodist lay preacher on Sundays, that many people thought he had been born in Plymouth. He was involved in the planning of the new Plymouth, and in securing legislation awarding compensation to blitzed businesses.

Bedford evidently made his mark as a store manager, and he was often entrusted with the task of assessing stores offered to Debenhams. In 1948 he was elected to the main board and brought to London to tackle the lack of co-ordination in the buying for the different Debenhams stores. Initially, he still ran Spooners, and also represented the main board in the Scottish subsidiary, commuting to Scotland by sleeper. Soon, Bedford rose to be joint managing director, then in 1954 deputy chairman, and finally from 1956 chairman and managing director.

During these years Debenhams was faced by a number of problems and challenges. Some, such as war-damaged premises, and shortages and rationing of goods, were common to the whole retail trade, although these difficulties had eased by the mid-1950s. A problem Debenhams shared with other department stores was that of increasing competition from multiple and chain stores, and from mail order sales. One peculiar to Debenhams was the need to adapt to changing market conditions the organisation of by far the largest British department store group. In 1950 Debenhams owned 110 of the 140 department stores owned by groups with more than five stores each (excluding the 200 stores, many of them quite small, owned by the Co-operative Society). The Debenhams group had grown haphazardly, as stores had been acquired when and where opportunity offered. The names, the management and the individual character of each store had been maintained. The lack of centralised planning and policy, and above all the lack of centralised buying, was an increasing handicap. Multiples and chain stores, exploiting centralised buying and shop layouts and self-service techniques copied from America, offered lower prices, if on a more restricted range of goods.

Although some directors and managers defended the traditional emphasis on personal service and the preservation of the individual character of stores, Bedford realised the need for a new strategy to meet changes in consumer taste and purchasing power. He knew that the provincial stores, though lacking the prestige of Debenhams' high class London stores like Debenham & Freebody, and Marshall & Snelgrove, provided an ever-increasing share of the profits of the group. He wanted the group to continue to expand, but now with more planning and purpose, and to increase its geographical range. This expansion, and the refurbishment and re-building of old and war-damaged stores, would require more capital than the group could generate from its own resources.

Debenhams' issued capital stood at £6.2 million from 1934 to 1948, despite the acquisition of 22 retail businesses during this period. During the next few years, a total of £4.5 million of reserves were capitalised, bringing the total issued capital to £10.7 million. Bedford raised about £2 million by a rights issue in 1957 and then from 1959 to 1964 raised £7.5 million by issuing shares and £11 million by issuing debentures. This additional capital provided the finance needed for rebuilding and expansion. Three or four new retail businesses were acquired every year, and one or two small clothing manufacturers were also bought.

Bedford failed to land the biggest fish he angled for: the Harrods group of six major department stores. Discussions began between Bedford and Sir Richard Burbidge, chairman of Harrods, in June 1959 after it became known that Sir Hugh Fraser, who controlled a rapidly expanding group of department stores, was bidding for Harrods. Burbidge and his fellow directors of Harrods favoured Debenhams' offer, but they and Bedford were outmanoeuvred by Fraser who won the support of Harrods' shareholders, and with this won the battle. Bedford did not relish the fight. What had started off as a straightforward merger, he said, had been turned into a beargarden by the intervention of other people: 'I do not like takeover bids, and I do not like the people who make them' {*Times* 28 Aug 1959}. Nonetheless he was determined to win it. He took the defeat of Debenhams as a personal blow.

Bedford was only partially successful in his attempts to reorganise the Debenhams group. A conscious effort was made to increase the number of stores catering for the more popular end of the market (the bid for Harrods had run counter to this policy). It was easier to standardise the buying of goods for this end of the market, and there was some attempt to organise central buying for one or two selected lines, such as footwear and electrical goods. For many years, some goods had been offered under Debenhams' own brand names, but if central buying were to succeed, there had to be greater uniformity in Debenhams' shops. It had to be brought to the attention of customers that their local department store was in fact owned by Debenhams, so that advertising of the new bulk-bought and branded lines did not have to be encumbered with long lists of the separate Debenhams businesses. Each store began to carry notices declaring it to be 'A Debenhams Store'. But these measures were too half-hearted. Bedford failed to pursue with sufficient vigour the modernisation policies he recognised had to be applied, and allowed the discussions and debates about them to rage far too long and too vehemently. There were changes enough to upset the more traditionally-minded directors and employees, and to cause a degree of demoralisation among the staff, but not enough to make a substantial difference to Debenhams' image and performance.

Department stores were finding it increasingly difficult to hold their own in the 1960s. Mail order houses were reinforcing the challenge of the multiple shops. While businesses were still being bought and new stores opened, there began to be closures of those Debenhams' stores whose performance did not reflect the value of their assets, particularly of their sites. Selective employment tax, introduced in 1966, hit their labour-intensive department stores particularly hard: by 1970 it was costing Debenhams £2 million a year. Profits before tax fell in 1966 nearly 10 per cent on the previous year's to £7.15 million, on a turnover which had increased 4.5 per cent to £100 million. Profits continued to fall. In the year to 1 February 1969 profits before tax were £6.15 million on a turnover of £119 million. Bedford did not try to excuse results which he admitted were disappointing, although he had warned in 1966 of the inevitable problems which would be caused by the implementation of the decision to adopt, at long last, central buying in all stores, and by efforts to rationalise the group by closing the less efficient stores. Bedford retired from active management in 1970, and then from the chair in January 1971, before the full benefits of the changes he had promoted could be felt.

While these changes had troubled many of the staff of Debenhams, Bedford had tried to encourage them to identify more closely with the company by becoming shareholders in it. In 1960-61 he set aside 400,000 ordinary shares at far below the market price for offer to employees of the company. Later, he introduced a scheme enabling directors and all senior executives to acquire shares at a very favourable price. Before becoming chairman he fought for some years for the introduction of a contributory pension scheme, which was finally established in 1957. In the following year he reorganised the main board, appointing some relatively young men and making each director, except those with administrative duties at head office, chairman of a group of businesses as well as managing director of the principal store in his group. This meant that, for the first time, the main board was representative of nearly every subsidiary company in the group.

A very active managing director and chairman — as chairman he regularly visited all the Debenhams stores — Bedford had little time for outside business interests. He was a director of the Commercial Union Assurance Co from 1952 to 1973, and a member of the board of referees of the Zurich Insurance Co. For some years he served on the executive council of the Association of British Chambers of Commerce. His skill and experience in improving and rebuilding properties, and planning the layout of stores, led to his appointment in 1962 to the Banwell Committee which investigated contracts in the construction industries for the Ministry of Public Building and Works, and then to the board of the National Building Agency; he became vice-chairman of the board, and chairman of the Finance Committee. He also served as a director of London Transport. He was awarded a military MBE and the civil OBE.

His main interests outside business were religious. He was a Methodist lay preacher in Plymouth and London, sometimes preaching in the Hinde Street Methodist Church near Debenhams' headquarters. In 1961, he put forward a scheme to the Methodist Conference at Bradford for a revision of the financing of connexional activities, although, he declared, 'the mere making of money is not a virtue' {*Times* 20 Nov 1980}. He supported the retail trade charities, particularly the Cottage Homes.

Bedford was intelligent, shrewd, and hard-working; he was a good speaker, and took care to inform himself fully on matters he dealt with. His warm personality, and his reassuring presence helped him press through the reforms he knew needed to be made in Debenhams, and his physical and mental toughness helped him face the difficulties he encountered in bringing his plans to fruition.

His chief relaxation was sport and he won a number of sporting cups. When young, he played cricket and football, as well as billiards and snooker; in later years he played badminton and golf.

John Bedford married in 1927 Florence Mary, daughter of Aaron Illingworth Oddy; they had one daughter. He died on 11 November 1980, leaving an estate proved at £201,000.

CHRISTINE SHAW

Sources:

Unpublished

BCe.

MCe.

PrC.

'The Development and Organisation of Debenhams Limited' (Edwards Seminar paper 362, 1 Feb 1966).

Information provided by Miss June Bedford.

Published

Maurice Corina, *Fine Silks and Oak Counters: Debenhams 1778-1978* (Hutchinson Benham, 1978).

Greville Havenhand, *Nation of Shopkeepers* (Eyre & Spottiswoode, 1970).

Times 28 Aug 1959, 28 May 1970, 8 Jan 1971, 20 Nov 1980.

WWW.

Sir Joseph Beecham (courtesy of the Beecham Group Ltd).

BEECHAM, Sir Joseph

(1848-1916)

Patent medicine manufacturer

Joseph Beecham was born at Wigan on 8 June 1848, the eldest son of Thomas Beecham (qv), a medicine vendor, by his first wife Jane née Evans. He was educated first of all at a free school in Wigan, and after the family moved, at the Church of England Moorflat School, St Helens, which provided a good commercial education: his proficiency at arithmetic was such that he could add up long columns of four or five figures simultaneously with perfect ease. He helped his father part-time until he left school and entered the firm in about 1863. As late as 1876 father and son (the latter described in the local directory as assistant chemist) were running it with the help of only two boys: a packer and one for odd jobs. In that decade he later claimed to be working daily from 5.30 am until midnight.

His prodigious application to work was an important release for his deeply introverted nature, caused by his overbearing father and domestic tension in childhood. He found it almost impossible to meet others half-way or share his thoughts with them; the pill firm therefore remained unincorporated and under his sole ownership until he died. Yet he was quite capable of flamboyant gestures. Once in effective control of the firm, from 1881 onwards, he dramatically raised advertising expenditure from £22,000 in 1884, which was less than half that of his rival Thomas Holloway (qv) that year, to £120,000 in 1891. He broke away from wordy puffs to often illustrated fun advertisments, for instance on 'What the Wild Waves were saying' ('Try Beecham's Pills') and after the premiere of Pinero's sensational drama a spoof letter to Mr Tanqueray, suggesting the medication that might have kept his first spouse alive and thus spared the troubles with his second wife (1893). He also carried the message of his pills in free or inexpensive manuals of general knowledge and musical albums, of which millions were distributed. More adventurous, or to many, outrageous, publicity schemes included printing slogans on sails and distributing them free to boat owners, and erecting huge bill-boards near beauty spots such as Lake Windermere.

Stimulated by this very skilful, if crude, publicity, turnover between 1881 and 1890 increased by a record rate of 24 per cent a year, from £34,200 to £270,000. Joseph Beecham also opened up the overseas market, which his father had tended to neglect. Export agents were appointed for a number of countries (mainly in the British Empire) and in 1888 he introduced the pills to the American and Canadian markets, with showcards and handbills by the thousand. In about 1890 he established a manufacturing subsidiary in New York, which he supervised personally: he already had a reputation as a cosmopolitan, crossing the Atlantic some sixty times in all and claiming to have bought his tie in Cairo, his coat in Australia and his boots in San Francisco.

However, he did not maintain the firm's momentum of growth into the new century. In 1913 turnover was no more than £290,000, although net profits rose from £69,000 in 1904 (the first available date) to £111,000 in 1913, when advertising totalled about £100,000. His outside interests, already an important part of his life, now began to dominate it. As a young man he had helped to establish the St Helens cycling club in 1876 and played regularly for the cricket club there, while he had expended his sparse pocket money on the cheapest seats at classical concerts and the opera. Having become a member of St Helens Council in 1889, he caused local surprise by standing for election as mayor in 1899; he served again in 1910 and 1911. In that office he used his wealth to mount functions, whether receptions, children's parties or musical concerts, of a lavishness never before seen in the town, and to support local good causes. As chairman of the town's electricity committee from 1897 onwards, he actively promoted the expansion of local electricity undertakings and later kept the committee informed of technical advances in America and continental countries. As a result, electricity tariffs were among the lowest in the country.

In 1885 he moved to Ewanville, Huyton, near Liverpool, where he indulged in an urge for building by making various extensions, and in 1913 similarly extended his London residence, West Brow, Arkwright Road, Hampstead (now the headquarters of the railway union Aslef) adding a concert hall and a massive organ, which he played with considerable verve but little skill. He was a noteworthy philanthropist, donating £30,000 to Bedford College, London, as well as much money to a variety of musical causes. Some of his musical activities were in support of his son, (Sir) Thomas Beecham (1879-1961); he also sponsored a season of Russian grand opera and ballet at Drury Lane in 1913 and 1914, and for that service was made a knight of the Russian order of St Stanislaus. For public services and philanthropy at home, he was knighted in 1912 and two years later made a baronet.

In his Hampstead residence he had a remarkable collection of works of art, including paintings by Constable, Turner, Morland and many lesser British artists; these showed up his abiding interest in the British landscape, as did many of the water colours and drawings. He found solace in throwing off the cares of the day by, late at night, turning the spotlight on one of his paintings and spending a long time perusing every detail. He had been helped in art collecting by his friend Thomas Barratt (qv), the equally publicity-minded chairman of A & F Pears Ltd, who persuaded him to become a director of Pears in 1909. Beecham thereafter undertook Pears' as well as his own firm's business during his subsequent trips to the United States.

He made the final colourful gesture of his life in 1914. On the prompting of the financier James White (qv) he arranged to purchase from the Duke of Bedford the Covent Garden estate and market in London for £2 million, believed at that time to be the most extensive deal in landed property ever to be made in Britain. That estate included the two oldest and most prestigious London theatres, Drury Lane and the Covent Garden Opera House, where his son Thomas had already given several opera seasons.

His plan for establishing a limited company to enable the estate to be sold off in lots at a profit was frustrated by the financial crisis after the outbreak of the First World War. The consequent legal and financial problems of the uncompleted purchase visibly aged the sexagenarian Sir Joseph, and on the day when an interim settlement was to be signed, 23 October 1916, he died in his sleep of an undiagnosed heart complaint. His estate was valued at £1 million, but there were so many complexities that it had to be put into Chancery. The Duke of Bedford eventually agreed to a mortgage on the unpaid consideration, after which the estate was broken up and the mortgage finally paid off in 1922. Then in 1928, by the initiative of Philip Hill (qv), the St Helens business was separated from the estates and registered as Beechams Pills Ltd and under Hill's chairmanship started a new phase of spectacular and diversified growth.

In 1873 Joseph Beecham married in the Church of England Josephine Burnett of St Helens, daughter of a silk dealer and barber; in 1901 there was a judicial separation. Of the ten children, two sons and six daughters survived childhood. His elder son Thomas, after a brief and mutually unsatisfactory period on the publicity side of the business, went on to become a world-famous conductor, being knighted in 1916. The younger son Henry (1888-1947) took over the running of the business together with three other executors, after Joseph's death, but took no further active part after 1921.

T A B CORLEY

Sources:

Unpublished

BCe.

PrC; Will.

Published

Sir Thomas Beecham, *A Mingled Chime* (Hutchinson, 1944).

Burke's Peerage and Baronetage 1970.

Stanley D Chapman, *Jesse Boot of Boots the Chemists* (Hodder & Stoughton, 1974).

'Century of a Notable Business' *Chemist & Druggist* 10 Oct 1942.

Daily News and Leader 24 Oct 1916.

Anne Francis, *A Guinea a Box: A Biography* (Hale, 1968).

C Reginald Grundy, 'Sir Joseph Beecham's Collection at Hampstead' *The Connoisseur* 35 (1913), 38, 39 (1914).

Diana and Geoffrey Hindley, *Advertising in Victorian England, 1837-1901* (Wayland, 1972).

Alan Jefferson, *Sir Thomas Beecham: a Centenary Tribute* (Macdonald and Jane's, 1979).

Liverpool Courier 24 Oct 1916.

PP, HC 1914 (414) IX, Patent Medicines.

Francis H W Sheppard (ed), *Survey of London, vol 36: The Parish of St Paul, Covent Garden* (Athlone Press, 1970).

Times 24 Oct 1916, 26 May 1974.

Times *Prospectuses* 75 (1928).

WWW.

BEECHAM, Thomas

(1820-1907)

Patent medicine manufacturer

Thomas Beecham was born at Curbridge, Oxfordshire, on 3 December 1820, the eldest son of Joseph Beecham, an agricultural labourer, and his wife Sarah née Hunt. After a few years' free schooling locally, at the age of

Thomas Beecham (courtesy of the Beecham Group Ltd).

eight he became a shepherd's boy, and during twelve years of this kind of work he is supposed to have acquired his herbal lore and a reputation for curing animals and humans alike. From 1840 to 1847 he lived at Kidlington, rolling pills by hand for sale round about, often at neighbouring markets, and doing casual work.

In 1847 he moved to Liverpool, where he met and married Jane Evans, maid to a chemist and eight years his senior. Shortly afterwards they removed to Wigan; there he obtained a medicine licence and became a full-time vendor of his own brand of pills. His routine was to spend one day a week mixing these pills in the parlour of his terraced house, and on the other days to hawk them round the markets of the vicinity, softening up potential clients with his persuasive patter and a cautionary jar of intestinal worms.

After an unsuccessful interlude of running a herbalist's shop, at the end of 1858 or beginning of 1859, Dr Beecham (as he styled himself) took his family off to the smaller but more fume-laden town of St Helens, nine miles from Wigan. He thereafter concentrated on what were to be the two staples of the Beecham trade: a herbal or laxative pill and a cough pill. The Londoner, Thomas Holloway (qv) had already pointed the way, in 1855 spending £30,000 a year in advertising his patent medicines. Yet it was Beecham's achievement from his provincial base to outstrip all his London rivals, at a time when ordinary people were spending a growing proportion of their increased incomes on health preparations. According to the stamp duty figures, sales of such medicines more than doubled between 1852 and 1870, while real wages rose only by 18 per cent, and trebled again by 1890, real wages having risen by another 43 per cent.

Beecham first sold his pills on the St Helens market and was already declaring them 'worth a guinea a box' in the *St Helens Intelligencer* for 6 August 1859. At the same time he advertised them for sale by post from his residence at 13 Milk Street at 6d a box, 'one box sent post free for 8 stamps to any address'. In 1863, he moved to less cramped premises where he had a shed in the back garden; two years later turnover was just over £2,500, the wholesale agents being mainly in London or towns in Lancashire and Yorkshire. By 1881 turnover had increased to £34,200, a remarkable growth of nearly 18 per cent a year; nearly 50 per cent was ordered by London agents. The mail order business by then had given way almost entirely to the wholesale trade.

Following his third marriage and move to southern England in 1881, he yielded effective control of the firm to his elder son Joseph Beecham (qv), and its subsequent history is more properly narrated under the latter's name. Formally, however, Joseph did not receive a half share until 1889, being until then a salaried employee.

In appearance, Thomas Beecham never shed the aura of an unpolished rustic. With flowing hair, unkempt beard and piercing blue eyes, he was usually garbed in an antique frock coat, paper collar and hard round hat; his trousers were later described by his famous musical grandson and namesake as 'voluminous in build, of rough and thick material and variegated in hue', being 'hitched well up to the chest' {Beecham (1944) 9}. At St Helens he left the Church of England and became a Congregationalist.

Completely lacking in small-talk, temperamental and impulsive, he put off the more refined stranger, proved irresistible to the women he sought to captivate, and like many salesmen, remained a pertinacious ladies' man until well into advanced years. Yet none of his three marriages brought him lasting happiness and his first involved strife and local notoriety. Jane Beecham died in 1872 after some years of living apart. The following year he married Sarah Pemberton of Blackfriars, London, who died in 1877. In 1879 he married the twenty-eight year old Mary Sawell née Putt, a childless widow, who detested Lancashire and persuaded him to reside at Mursley Hall, Buckinghamshire, for some years. In 1884 they separated on friendly terms and he moved north again. Nine years later he built a house at Southport and in 1895 retired from the firm. He died there on 6 April 1907. By his first wife he had two sons and two daughters. Having handed over the entire business to Joseph, perhaps in exchange for an annuity, he left only £86,680 gross.

T A B CORLEY

Sources:

Unpublished

Beecham Proprietaries, St Helens, Lancs, archives.

PrC; Will.

Published

Theodore C Barker and John R Harris, *A Merseyside Town in the Industrial Revolution: St Helens 1750-1900* (Liverpool: University Press, 1954).

Sir Thomas Beecham, *A Mingled Chime* (Hutchinson, 1944).

DNB.

Anne Francis, *A Guinea a Box: A Biography* (Hale, 1968).

Terence R Nevett, *Advertising in Britain. A History* (Heinemann, 1982).

St Helens Newspaper and Advertiser 9 Apr 1907.

Times 8 Apr 1907.

BEGG, Ferdinand Faithfull

(1847-1926)

Stockbroker

Ferdinand Faithfull Begg was born in Edinburgh on 27 December 1847, the son of Rev James Begg DD, a leading Free Church minister and his wife Maria, daughter of Rev Ferdinand Faithfull, Rector of Headley, Epsom. Begg was educated privately. Between 1863 and 1872 Begg was in New Zealand, where he worked in a bank. He then returned to Scotland, took up stockbroking in 1873, and in 1885 became chairman of the Edinburgh Stock Exchange.

Two years later he moved to the London Stock Exchange and founded the stockbroking firm of Faithfull Begg & Co, from which he eventually retired in 1913. Little is known about his broking activities as such, though in 1896 he did apparently take the trouble to inspect the goldfields of West Australia, source of a boom that was shortly to supersede the more celebrated one in South African gold mines. Begg is more remembered in Stock Exchange history for his prominent reforming role both outside and inside the Committee, of which he was a member from 1904 to 1913. Two successful campaigns especially stand out, in both of which Begg represented the interests of the smaller members, even though his own firm was a relatively large one. The first was the campaign to restrict membership by insisting that new members not only be nominated by retiring members, but also be shareholders in the Stock Exchange. And when this objective was achieved in 1904, Begg was again to the fore in insisting on equitable voting rights for the smaller shareholders, a view expressed in his forceful speech at the meeting of shareholders in May 1905 and in his subsequent mobilisation of opinion. The other major campaign in which Begg was prominent eventually reached fruition in 1909, when the traditional distinction between brokers and jobbers was hardened, in order to prevent brokers from acting as dealers on the floor of the House and jobbers from 'shunting' directly with provincial exchanges. Both activities tended to be beyond the resources of the smaller members, though arguably both were beneficial to the Stock Exchange as a whole.

Begg also enjoyed a reputation outside Capel Court: following the crisis of 1893 he 'became closely identified with the resuscitation of several Australian banking institutions' {*Financial Times* 7 Dec 1926}. He unsuccessfully contested the parliamentary seat for the Kennington division of Lambeth in July 1892. Between 1895 and 1900 he was Conservative Unionist MP for the St Rollox division of Glasgow; he was later actively involved in Chamberlain's tariff campaign; and from 1912 to 1915 he was chairman of the London Chamber of Commerce, inaugurating during the First World War the Newspapers for the Fleet Fund. In general he was renowned for his loquacity and was one of life's indefatigable letter-writers to the press. According to one rather hostile verdict on Begg in 1897, 'he regards himself as a public man, and affects the exclusive, though nobody is anxious to hear his opinions a second time' {*City Punch Bowl* 13 Mar 1897}.

He married Jessie Maria, daughter of F A Cargill of Dunedin, New Zealand, in 1873. They had six children, one of whom, Francis Cargill Begg, followed him as a member of the Stock Exchange. He died on 4 December 1926, leaving £37,889.

DAVID T A KYNASTON

Writings:

Innumerable letters to the Press.

Rosebery Burns Club, Glasgow, 25 Jan 1898. Speech by F F Begg, MP, in Proposing the Toast of Caledonia and Caledonia's Bard (Edinburgh: printed for the Club, 1898).

Sources:

Unpublished

PrC.

MCe (Scots).

Guildhall Library, London, Stock Exchange Minutes.

Published

City Punch Bowl 13 Mar 1897.

Financial Times 7 Dec 1926.

Times 6 Dec 1926.

WWMP.

WWW.

BEHRENS, Sir Jacob

(1806-1889)

Woollen merchant

Sir Jacob Behrens, portrait by Ernest Sichel, 1888 (courtesy of Bradford A A Galleries & Museum).

Jacob Behrens was born at Pyrmont in Germany on 20 November 1806, the son of Nathan Behrens, a Jewish merchant who had married Clara Hahn, the daughter of a prosperous Hamburg silk merchant.

The family moved to Hamburg in 1815 and within four years Jacob was at work in his father's business, trading in woollen, worsted and cotton cloth, a great deal of which was purchased from English manufacturers and resold in the fairs and markets of northern Germany. The business was neither large nor very successful, until Jacob took over control in 1826 and began to establish new connections. He first visited England in 1832 in an attempt to persuade Thomas Clapham, a Leeds merchant who supplied him, to adopt a different finish to the goods he was supplying and to pack them in smaller bales. The attempt met with no success and a visit the following year was of little more benefit. Jacob was developing his trade in English goods profitably in northern Germany and decided to return to Leeds in 1834 to establish a small warehouse where cloth could be finished according to the requirements of his market.

The firm of Jacob Behrens was established in Leeds on 14 March 1834. Although by no means the first English branch of a German merchant firm, it soon became the first independent business when Behrens began to sell directly to Germany and not via the Hamburg business. The firm expanded rapidly. Jacob's two younger brothers, Louis and Rudolf, joined him in 1837, the former acting as an adventurous traveller in Germany for the firm.

The great majority of Behrens's business activity was with the Bradford trade and in 1838 he took the decision to move there, closer to his suppliers. He was amongst the first in the general movement of merchanting from Leeds to Bradford. Two years later Louis set up a branch of the firm in Manchester to deal in cotton goods. Their father, Nathan Behrens, died in 1842 from the shock of the disastrous Hamburg fire, but luckily the firm's stocks in Hamburg were saved.

Jacob Behrens established a reputation as a hardworking but stable and cautious businessman. His business judgements were careful and he went to great lengths to research all aspects of the trade with which he was associated. It was said that he 'lived on blue books'. He found it difficult at first to settle into Bradford society but gradually gained a respected reputation for his hard work and campaigning on behalf of the wool textile industry. He was active in the founding of the Bradford Chamber of Commerce in 1851, was its first president and remained a leading force in its activities for the rest of his life. He gave his attention to a variety of issues including the improvement of postal services and the statistics on wool textiles issued by the Board of Trade. Above all, his contribution to Bradford and the wool textile industry was through his interest in commercial treaties and other trading negotiations. He was a passionate free trader. On behalf of Bradford he paid very careful attention to commercial conditions and foreign tariffs and provided regular commercial advice to the Government. His active support to Cobden in 1860 assisted Bradford in gaining good terms in the Anglo-French treaty of commerce.

Jacob Behrens was one of the founders of the Association of Chambers of Commerce and pressure from him helped in the formation of the Commercial Department of the Foreign Office in 1872. He was knighted in 1882 for his services to commerce.

He had many local interests in Bradford, the major one of which was the well-being of the Eye and Ear Hospital, with which he was very closely involved from its foundation.

In 1844 Jacob Behrens married Doris Hoheremser, an educated member of a wealthy Jewish family from south-west Germany; they had six children. He died on 22 April 1889, five years after his wife, leaving £83,112 gross. The business was continued by his sons.

D T JENKINS

Sources:

Unpublished

MCe.

Published

Bradford Observer 23 Apr 1889.

Bradford Telegraph 23 Apr 1889.

W R Millmore, 'A Chronicle of Initiative and Progress' *Wool Record* 81 (1952).

PP, RC Depression of Industry and Trade (1886) C 4621.

A R Rollin, 'The Jewish Contribution to the British Textile Industry' *Transactions of the Jewish Historical Society of England* 17 (1948).

Eric M Sigsworth, *Black Dyke Mills: A History* (Liverpool: Liverpool University Press, 1958).

Sir Jacob Behrens, 1806-1889 (Percy Lund, Humphries & Co, ca 1925).

BEIT, Alfred

(1853-1906)

Diamond merchant and mining financier

Alfred Beit was born in Hamburg, Germany on 15 February 1853, the second of six children of Siegfried Beit (1818-81) and Laura Caroline Hahn (d 1918). His father was a silk merchant and the family, although Lutheran by religion, were descendents of Portuguese Jews who had settled in Germany in the seventeenth century.

In 1871 at the age of eighteen, Beit left for Amsterdam to learn the diamond trade after which, in 1875, he joined the Kimberley branch of the Hamburg merchant house of David Lippert & Co as a clerk. On the fields he showed a great aptitude for the diamond trade. Within three years of his arrival in Kimberley, Beit was regularly speculating in diamonds, mining claims and shares on his own account. In 1880 Beit left the employ of Lippert & Co and became the local partner of the Paris diamond merchants, Jules Porges et Cie. As a partner Beit was entitled to a third of the profits from the diamonds which were shipped to Paris and while his capital was a modest £35,000 in 1884, his understanding of market operations and some timely speculation in diamonds enabled him to increase his capital to £100,000 by 1887.

During this year Jules Porges et Cie joined Cecil Rhodes in the takeover of the Victoria Diamond Mining Co and the establishment of De Beers Consolidated Mines Ltd. Throughout the 1880s Beit was intimately involved in the complex international financial negotiations between City investors, French banks and Kimberley mine owners, which led both to the formation of De Beers in 1888 and to his own appointment as one of the company's four life governors. Meanwhile, in 1886, gold bearing ore deposits had been discovered on the Witwatersrand in the Transvaal and Beit travelled north to assess the extent and value of these new fields. With the aid of Porges's capital and access to European private banks, Beit and Porges's other partner, Julius Wernher (qv), were able to buy up claims along the Rand and float numerous, largely London-based, mining companies. In 1889 Porges retired from business, Beit returned to England where he lived until his death and Jules Porges et Cie was reconstituted as the private partnership of Wernher, Beit & Co. On the Rand the partnership owned and operated some of the richest gold mines either through inter-locking directorships, its local agents, H Eckstein & Co, or through a public holding company, Rand Mines Ltd. By the 1890s Wernher, Beit & Co and its subsidiary companies were the largest mining finance group in South Africa and in 1905, when some of the partnership's companies were reconstituted as a London-registered public company, Central Mining & Investment Corporation, it was responsible for nearly 40 per cent of South Africa's total annual output of gold. In conjunction with Julius Wernher, Beit pioneered the group system of mining on the

Rand for the purposes of financing, directing and controlling individual mining companies through a system of majority shareholding. The group system also enabled mines to pool technological, financial and managerial resources and provided a continuity of capital investment which would normally have been beyond the resources of the average, single gold mining company. Wernher, Beit & Co also had substantial interests in non-mining enterprises such as the National Bank of South Africa, the Cape Explosives Works, Fraser & Chalmers (Britain), the Pretoria Portland Cement Co and British Aluminium (Britain).

In 1889 Beit generously supported Rhodes's British South Africa Co with a personal investment of £500,000 and joined the chartered company's board. He was also chairman of the Beira Railway Co and a member of the boards of De Beers, Fraser & Chalmers and the shipping line, Woermann. The continued profitability and expansion of the Witwatersrand gold mines, however, formed the basis of Wernher, Beit & Co's expanding business empire. In 1895 Beit joined Rhodes and Leander Jameson in a conspiracy to overthrow the Boer republic and establish a regime in the Transvaal which would be more favourable to the interests of the mining industry. The Jameson Raid's failure and Beit's subsequent appearance before a Commons Select Committee on the Raid led to his resignation from the board of the BSACo and it was not until after the Boer War, in 1902, that he was reinstated and went on to become the company's vice-president in 1904. The Boer War (during which Beit spent a fortune on equipping the imperial light horse and yeomanry) led to the establishment of a British colonial administration in the Transvaal under Lord Milner which regarded the interests of the gold mines as vital to South Africa's economic development. In 1903-4 Beit persuaded the colonial administration to allow the mines to import Chinese coolies to overcome alleged shortages of African labour. During the immediate post-war period Beit also tried to restore international investor confidence in Rand gold mines and to this end he established close links with City financial institutions as well as French and German banks. Despite advocating Anglo-German financial rapprochement, he was an ardent tariff reformer. Although Beit has been described as shy and retiring, his involvement in business and politics was far from low-key. Throughout the 1890s and early 1900s he actively lobbied the British Colonial Office and successive Transvaal administrations on behalf of the gold mining industry, and established close personal contacts with politicians and bankers including Lord Milner and the Rothschilds. The extent of Beit's involvement in his partnership's affairs was, in fact, well known and led, as early as 1893, to a deterioration in his health as a result of over-work. Beit's health remained precarious and he often visited German spas for rest cures.

Beit was a collector of seventeenth century Dutch, Spanish and English paintings and in 1902 he purchased a country-house, Tewin Water in Hertfordshire, where he died on 16 July 1906. He never married and left the bulk of his private estate, valued at £8,049,885 gross, to his brother Sir Otto Beit. His public benefactions, however, amounted to £2 million, of which the bulk, some £1.2 million, was bequeathed to the Beit Trust. The Trust had originally been set up to develop transport facilities in Rhodesia and only later was its brief extended into the field of education. Generous grants have, over the years, been made to the universities at Oxford (Beit Chair) and Cape Town and Rhodes University, Grahamstown.

JEAN JACQUES VAN-HELTEN

Writings:

PP, *HC* 1897 (31) IX, Evidence before SC on Incursion into the South African Republic by an Armed Force.

Sources:

Unpublished

Rhodes House, Oxford, Beit correspondence.

Barlow Rand Ltd, Sandton, South Africa, Beit papers.

PrC.

Robert Turrell, 'Capital, Class and Monopoly: the Kimberley Diamond Fields, 1871-1899' (London PhD, 1982).

Jean Jacques Van-Helten, 'British and European Economic Investment in the Transvaal with Specific Reference to the Witwatersrand Gold Field and District, 1886-1910' (London PhD, 1981).

Published

DNB

Paul H Emden, *Jews of Britain: A Series of Biographies* (Sampson Low, Marston & Co, 1944).

G Seymore Fort, *Alfred Beit: A Study of the Man and His Work* (Ivor Nicholson & Watson, 1932).

Maryna Fraser, *All That Glittered. Selected Correspondence of Lionel Phillips, 1890-1924* (Oxford University Press, 1978).

WWW.

Sir Isaac Lowthian Bell (courtesy of the Iron & Steel Institute).

BELL, Sir Isaac Lowthian

(1816-1904)

Iron manufacturer

Isaac Lowthian Bell (most often known as Lowthian Bell) was born at Newcastle upon Tyne on 15 February 1816, the eldest of four sons (out of seven children) of Thomas Bell (1774-1845) and his wife Catherine née Lowthian. The town already breathed air heavy with fumes from local coal, iron, glass, engineering and shipbuilding works. The Bells did the same. Lowthian's father was in ironworking (the Walker works of Losh, Wilson & Bell) and connected with friends of Lord Dundonald, pioneers of the Leblanc soda process in England. He gave Lowthian his early interest in chemistry and physics and involved him in their often still mysterious relationship to industrial enterprise. The second brother, Thomas (1817-94), was also to spend his life in the iron trade. John (1818-88), the third brother, became a geologist and valuable advisor to the later Bell Brothers business.

To his father's enthusiasm and instruction, Lowthian added formal learning at Bruce's Academy, Newcastle, the kind of Dissenting Academy that leaned strongly towards the practical arts. He then spent time in Germany and Denmark before attending Edinburgh University with its still recent memories of Joseph Black. Afterwards he went to the Sorbonne, rounding off with practical work at Marseilles on alkali manufacture. Bell's continental travels left a deep influence. Though patriotic he was the least parochial of men. His knowledge of men and languages as well as his keen scientific observations of foreign science and technology were one feature that marked him off from generations of British entrepreneurs inclined to insularity. When he entered Walker's ironworks in 1835 at the age of nineteen, he was well-equipped as a chemist and metallurgist. Under the guidance of John Vaughan (qv), the firm's rolling mill superintendent, he rapidly became a leading expert on blast furnace theory and practice and new types of rolling mills. Marriage in 1842 to Margaret, daughter of Hugh Lee Pattinson, a well-known chemical manufacturer, encouraged his interest in chemistry. At Washington (Gateshead) he started in 1850 a chemical factory which, from 1860, operated the new Deville patent from France, making it the only source of aluminium in Britain. Chemical manufacture remained an important subsidiary activity to Bell. In his mid-sixties, with the help of his geologist brother, John, he developed a large salt working near their ironworks site: by 1883 it was turning out 320 tons a week. But long before that iron had become Bell's major interest.

He formed a new partnership, Bell Brothers, in 1844, to operate the Wylam Ironworks at Wylam upon Tyne. Their ironworks at Port Clarence on the north bank of the Tees, which began to produce pig iron in 1854, became one of the half-dozen largest plants in the burgeoning North-Eastern iron industry. At mid-century this region was responsible for less than a quarter of the iron manufacture in Scotland, South Wales or Staffordshire. By 1875 the Middlesbrough area alone accounted for about one-third of the whole British output of pig-iron. Bells' iron output alone rose from 13,000 tons in 1854 to just under 200,000 tons by 1878 and kept some 6,000 men in employment.

Not only did Lowthian Bell undertake to rebuild completely the works at Clarence (on Vaughan's much larger model of blast furnace) in 1865. He also leased large tracts of ironstone to supply his needs and joined with the lessor of his ironstone beds, Ralph Ward Jackson, to build the Cleveland Railway to convey his raw materials to the Clarence works. This freed him from the railway monopoly wielded by Joseph Pease, the Quaker creator of Middlesbrough and the local railway system. When Ralph Ward Jackson went bankrupt, Bell bought him out. He now controlled all his essential supplies, of coal, ironstone, and limestone, and dodged the high freight charges of the rival railways.

In 1865 the Cleveland Railway, and the West Hartlepool Harbour & Railway Co which Jackson had promoted, and of which Bell was a director, were taken over by the North Eastern Railway. Bell joined the board of the NER and remained a director until his death in 1904. From 1895 to 1904 he was deputy chairman of the company. His membership of the board exemplified the company's policy of including on its executive the leaders of local industry, commerce and agriculture. Bell ensured that the interests of the iron industry were effectively represented on the board, especially in the matter of rates; the NER developed a sliding scale of rates for the iron trade. The close links were also manifested in the railway's funding in 1877 of a series of unsuccessful experiments at Bell's ironworks, trying to rid Cleveland iron of phosphorous so that it could be used for steel rails as good as those made of haematite.

Bell's contribution to policymaking on the NER was substantial. He produced a number of major board policy papers covering areas of the business as diverse as the economics of different branches of traffic; the outcome of major investment in new technology in the company's workshops; operating costs; and the historical movement of expenditure. These papers are remarkable for the statistical concepts employed, for the lucidity of analysis and above all for their bearing on the question of costs, the most pressing business problem of the organisation at that time.

When the iron market weakened in the late 1870s and 1880s, he went rather late (in 1889) into steel making in the hope of entering the market for steel rails. But competition even here was ferocious. Bell's iron business, though labouring in the prevalent depression, kept afloat on the continuing demand by shipbuilders for iron plates and angles, and salt business also helped. But the writing was on the wall. Lowthian and his brothers were getting old. Lowthian was an entrepreneurial polymath but he had few of those acquisitive ambitions which were increasingly becoming a dominant force in the British iron and steel industry, static in the face of the increasing rivalries for both home and overseas markets. He had been the leading spokesman for the iron industry: now he was its father figure. It was too late to change his habits and talents for the different kind of enterprise displayed by, for example, his neighbour, Arthur Dorman (qv). Dorman had built his initially small Middlesbrough business up to a large diversified steel concern through shrewd human acumen. Obviously Lowthian felt his best policy was to merge his steel interests with those of Dorman, Long. In 1899 Bells became a public company. Dormans acquired a half interest. In 1902 the merger was completed by Dormans acquiring the Bells' remaining ordinary shares in exchange for 225,000 shares in Dorman, Long. Bells survived as a separate iron and steel works but much later, when the Dorman empire was itself in the straits of the inter-war depression, the Clarence works were closed. The last incident in the Bell history was the succession on the death of Sir Arthur Dorman, of Sir Hugh Bell (qv) as chairman of Dorman, Long.

Lowthian Bell was unquestionably a unique figure in a Victorian economy run largely by empiricists. An outstanding scientist, he had also a fine head for business; his business. As already noted, he was not an empire builder by conquest or purchase. He laboured on the Clarence works. But he was the unchallenged spokesman for the North-Eastern iron industry for over a quarter of a century. His scientific writings, in which the chemist, mineralogist and metallurgist were all blended, were extensive and impressive. They give him a special claim to importance in an age often regarded as a triumph of amateurism. In most large and successful firms, there will be found a balance of functions; the commercial or financial partner responsible for markets will have a technical counterpart responsible for materials, machinery, manufacture, labour, etc. (Even Ludwig Mond (qv), with whom Bell had some points of resemblance, had his Brunner (qv).) In Lowthian Bell all these managerial and technological talents were rolled into one. But excellent as his type of management was, even Bell could not escape the general nemesis of the iron trade after the arrival of cheap steel and foreign competition.

His principal works are a combination of technical research and comparative surveys of the metal industries of Britain, the USA and continental Europe. Four (which are still indispensable sources) were: *The Principles of the Manufacture of Iron and Steel* (1884); *The Iron Trade of the United Kingdom* (1886); *The Chemical Phenomena of Iron Smelting* (1872); *Notes on a Visit to Coal and Iron Mines and Ironworks in the United States* (1875). His views on the future for British industry (even in 1886) were moderately optimistic. He did not budge from his Liberal objections to protective policies. The Germans, he held, were asking for future trouble by subsidising their export trade and indulging in too much price-fixing and market-sharing. The American threat in world markets was still a long way off. But his optimism was occasionally, and wisely, tempered by reminders that 'chemists of the higher class' were more frequent in Germany than in Britain, and that British industry must deliver goods at prices competitive with those of their new rivals. Workmen must not demand excessive wages. Such reservations formed the main argument for the creation of business and professional institutes where basic problems of technology, organisation and labour relations could be thrashed out frankly. With other manufacturers, he helped to create the British Iron Trade Association (1875), the Iron and Steel Institute (1869) (of which he was president in 1873-75 and first recipient of the Bessemer gold medal in 1874), and the Institution of Mining Engineers (of which he was president in the year of his death). He was president of the BITA (1875), of the Society of the Chemical Industry (1889); he was awarded the Albert medal of the Society of Arts (1900) and the George Stephenson medal (from the Institution of Civil Engineers).

Whether he was addressing a Royal Commission or the Yorkshire Union of Mechanics or delivering any of the score of voluntary talks to enthusiasts he freely gave, his exposition was always lucid: it was also compelling, not least because his ideas (on economics, politics, social relations, and so forth) were couched in terms so reasonable and moderate as to lull his audience into agreement. In retrospect his opinions may sometimes sound complacent. In scientific argument he was invariably scientifically and rigidly faithful to his evidence and convictions. When he failed to solve the fundamental problem of eliminating phosphorus in the steel-making process, his authority was such as to persuade many a colleague that the problem was insoluble. But when Thomas and Gilchrist emerged with an apparently satisfactory process, Lowthian Bell showed characteristic generosity. When asked if rails made by the process could be introduced with safety in the construction of railways, Bell's answer was an unhesitating 'yes'.

Lowthian Bell was an affirmative man: twice mayor of Newcastle, DL and High Sheriff for the county of Durham. He stood as Liberal candidate for a North Durham seat in 1868 but was defeated; his election in 1874 was declared void; eventually he was returned for Hartlepool as an MP but, like a number of businessmen in Parliament, remained a silent one. His many academic distinctions were more to his liking than Commons business. He was FRS (1875), DCL (Durham, 1882), LLD (Edinburgh, 1893), LLD (Trinity College Dublin, 1893) and DSc Leeds (1904). He was a member of the Légion d'Honneur (1878) and, on Gladstone's nomination, a baronet (1885). When his wife died in 1886 he gave their house at Washington to be used as a home for waifs and strays. He was active in support of the Armstrong College at Newcastle. Sturdy, broad-shouldered, heavily bearded, he was an archetypal Victorian middle-class figure. Only in his passionate belief in the application of science to industry did he diverge from the norm. How effective was this dedication? It is difficult to say. One swallow did not make a summer: but it would have taken hundreds to counter the problems which brought low the British iron trade from the 1870s onwards.

Sir Isaac Lowthian Bell and his wife Margaret née Pattinson had two sons and three daughters. He died at his residence, Rounton Grange, Northallerton, on 20 December 1904, leaving £768,676 gross.

CHARLES WILSON

Selected Writings:

(ed with Sir William Armstrong et al) *The Industrial Resources of the District of the Tyne, Wear and Tees* (Longmans, 1864).

Chemical Phenomena of Iron Smelting (G Routledge & Sons, 1872).

Notes of a Visit to Coal and Iron Mines and Ironworks in the United States (Newcastle on Tyne: M & M W Lambert, 1875).

Report on the Iron Manufacture of the United States of America, and a Comparison of It with That of Great Britain (Stationery Office, 1877).

Principles of the Manufacture of Iron and Steel (G Routledge & Sons, 1884).

The Iron Trade of the United Kingdom (British Iron Trade Association, 1886).

'The Iron Trade and Allied Industries' in Thomas H Ward, *The Reign of Queen Victoria* (2 vols, Smith & Elder, 1887).

On the American Iron Trade and Its Progress During Sixteen Years (Iron & Steel Institute, 1892).

His more important articles are cited in the *DNB* entry.

Sources:

Unpublished

Messrs Dorman Long, various papers.

PrC.

Information from R J Irving.

Published

Duncan L Burn, *The Economic History of Steelmaking, 1867-1939* (Cambridge: Cambridge University Press, 1940).

Thomas H Burnham and George O Hoskins, *Iron and Steel in Britain, 1870-1930* (George Allen & Unwin, 1943).

James C Carr and Walter Taplin, *A History of the British Steel Industry* (Oxford: Basil Blackwell, 1962).

Archibald and Nan Clow, *The Chemical Revolution* (Batchworth Press, 1952).

DNB.

Robert J Irving, *The North Eastern Railway Company 1870-1914: An Economic History* (Leicester: Leicester University Press, 1976).

G Jones, 'A Description of Messrs Bell Brothers' Blast Furnaces from 1844 to 1908' *JISI* 77 (1908).

C A Hempstead (ed), *Cleveland Iron and Steel: Background and Nineteenth Century History* (British Iron & Steel Corporation, 1979).

Charles Wilson, 'Dorman Long' *Steel Review* 6 (1957).

WWMP.

WWW.

BELL, John

(1841-1911)
Railway manager

John Bell was born in 1841; very little is known of his early background. He began his business career in the head office of the Manchester, Sheffield & Lincolnshire Railway where his talents were soon recognised by that company's dynamic chairman, Edward Watkin (qv). After Watkin became chairman of the Metropolitan Railway in 1872, he recruited Bell as the company's secretary later that year.

Bell's most constructive service to the Metropolitan Railway was given in the fifteen years following his appointment as general manager in 1880. He supervised extensions to Harrow (1880), Pinner (1885), Rickmansworth (1887), Chesham (1889) and Aylesbury (1892). The policy followed was to sponsor the creation of small, nominally 'independent' companies to establish the new links and to absorb them into the main company when the pioneering work had been completed. These developments were undertaken with ambitions of making the Metropolitan a long-distance main-line railway; in this they were not successful but they paved the way for the growth of that part of suburbia known later as 'Metroland'. In this period also he showed an awareness of the possible advantages for the Metropolitan Railway of the use of electric traction. In July 1889 he authorised the testing of an electric battery locomotive and train on the company's lines between Neasden and Harrow. In the following month the directors sponsored his visit to the USA and Canada to make a study of the progress of electric traction on street tramways. Early in 1890 he travelled on one of the early electric trains of the City of London & Southwark Subway Co (which became the City & South London Railway Co later that year). In acknowledgement of his services the members of the board appointed him managing director in January 1894.

When Watkin retired from the chairmanship later in 1894 the board chose Bell to succeed him while continuing as managing director. It was not a wise decision. Thenceforward the crustier side of Bell's nature became more prominent as the burden of the combined duties of chairman and managing director became heavier. During his remaining years with the company three problems were pre-eminent: the Manchester, Sheffield & Lincolnshire (later Great Central) Railway's running powers over the Metropolitan lines to central London; the growth of omnibus competition on inner London routes; and the replacement of steam by electric traction. The Manchester, Sheffield & Lincolnshire Railway's exercise of its running powers between Quainton Road (41 miles to the north of the capital) and Baker Street were the cause of constant dispute which was aggravated by a growing animosity between its general manager, William Pollitt, and Bell. In the event Pollitt turned to the GWR which led to the building of a joint line through High Wycombe as an alternative to the Metropolitan route. Bell's mistrust and obstinacy lost his company much potential traffic. Faced with growing omnibus competition, particularly between King's Cross and Baker Street, Bell gave a lot of attention to establishing the Metropolitan Railway's own bus services when his time would have been more profitably spent in forwarding plans for railway electrification, which was the company's most urgently needed reform.

By the late 1890s, force of circumstances obliged the board of the Metropolitan Railway to give more serious attention to the electrification of its network. In 1897 the company applied to Parliament for an act to extend its powers. The report of the Board of Trade on the ventilation of its 'cut and cover' tunnels, which was the outcome of the application, concluded that 'by far the most satisfactory mode of dealing with the ventilation of the Metropolitan tunnels would be the adoption of electric traction' {GLC RO Met/19, minutes for 19 Jan 1898}. Meanwhile the construction of the Central London Railway, an electric tube line, was proceeding apace. It was James Staats Forbes (qv), chairman of the Metropolitan District Railway, who responded to these challenges in May 1898 by proposing to Bell that the two companies should conduct an experiment with electrical traction, on the DC system, between Earls Court and High Street Kensington stations, at a cost, jointly shared, of £20,000. At this stage Bell gave his full co-operation. But after the inauguration of the experimental service in January 1900 he favoured new trials with the Ganz overhead cable system while Forbes, backed by the American financier Charles Yerkes (qv), wanted to proceed as quickly as possible with the DC system. Quarrels between the two chairmen caused more delays and were only resolved when a Board of Trade arbitrator determined in favour of the Forbes plan. The failure to make speedier progress with electrification resulted in a loss of business to the company. Following the opening of the Central London Railway on 30 July 1900, the Metropolitan's figures for passengers carried dropped to 93 million compared with 96 million in 1898, though revenue rose slightly because of new goods and coal traffic coming off the Great Central Railway. Dividends on ordinary shares fell from £3 16s 3d in 1899 to £2 7s 6d in 1902.

The strains of all these conflicts and failures adversely affected Bell's health and led to his resignation from the chairmanship on 28 November 1901. For a few weeks longer he remained a member of the board without being well enough to attend its meetings. He finally relinquished his directorship on 20 February 1902. The board voted him a 'retiring allowance' of £1,500 a year, half the peak income he had received while combining the offices of chairman and managing director.

On the occasion of his retirement the *Times* and the *Railway Times* were agreed that the difficulty of combining the responsibilities of chairman and managing director and Bell's 'autocratic methods' had both contributed to the declining fortunes of the Metropolitan Railway.

Bell's principal outside interest was with the Volunteer movement in which he attained the rank of colonel. By his wife Eliza Bell he had one son and two daughters. He died on 12 February 1911, leaving £9,899 gross.

PHILIP S BAGWELL

Sources:

Unpublished

PrC; Will.

GLC Record Office, Metropolitan Railway Board Minutes Met/17-22.

Published

J Clifford Baker, *The Metropolitan Railway* (South Godstone: Oakwood Press, 1951).

Theodore C Barker and Michael Robbins, *A History of London Transport* (2 vols, Allen & Unwin, 1963-74).

John R Day, *The Story of London's Underground* (London Transport, 1969).

George Dow, *Great Central* (3 vols, Locomotive Publishing Co, 1959-65).

Alan A Jackson and Desmond F Croome, *Rails through the Clay* (Allen & Unwin, 1962).

P A Keen, 'Metropolitan Railway Road Services' *Journal of Transport History* I (1954).

Railway News 18 Feb, 29 Apr 1911.

Railway Times 6, 13, 20 July 1901.

Times 5 July 1901, 15 July 1911.

Sir Thomas H Bell (from Journal of the Iron & Steel Institute, *1907).*

BELL, Sir Thomas Hugh

(1844-1931)

Teesside industrialist

Thomas Hugh Bell was born at Walker-on-Tyne on 10 February 1844, the elder son of Sir Isaac Lowthian Bell, Bt (qv), an ironmaster, and his wife Margaret née Pattinson. Following schooling at Merchiston Castle in Edinburgh, he spent three years studying chemistry in Paris and Göttingen before entering his father's office, initially in Newcastle upon Tyne, in 1862. A year later he began to work in the ironworks belonging to his father and two uncles, at Port Clarence on the northern bank of the Tees, opposite Middlesbrough; by 1880, control of Bell Brothers' Port Clarence business was largely left in his hands. In the 1880s he and his younger brother, Charles Lowthian (1855-1906), were concerned with the first successful large-scale extraction of salt on Teesside, from beds lying 300 metres below surface. Throughout the 1890s Bell Brothers made sustained efforts to produce good open-hearth steel from Cleveland iron, and to this end technical collaboration took place with Dorman Long & Co. Bell believed that only integration and modernisation would preserve the industry's competitiveness in international markets and, indeed, he appears to have been a Teesside pioneer of rationalisation. In 1899 the Bell Brothers' partnership was converted into a public company, with members of the family holding one half of the ordinary shares, and Dorman Long, headed by Arthur J Dorman (qv), the other half. At the time, the concern had 6,000 employees, with collieries in County Durham and ironstone mines in Cleveland. The merger was taken further in 1902, when Dorman Long arranged to exchange the remaining shares held by the Bell family for ordinary stock in Dorman Long & Co Ltd. As a result, Hugh Bell became a director of Dorman Long, and for many years remained vice-chairman. At Port Clarence, a new basic open-hearth steel shop, the first in the Cleveland district to use iron made from local ores, was opened in 1901, and soon afterwards rolling mills were added. Complete amalgamation of Bell Bros with Dorman Long took place in 1923. Six years later, Bell was involved in negotiating the merger of Bolckow Vaughan with Dorman Long. Within the family firm Bell was overshadowed by his father, who remained active until his death in 1904, and then by Arthur Dorman following the merger of 1899. For only a few months between Dorman's death in February 1931 and his own in June was he chairman of Dorman Long.

Bell was a director of a number of other firms, including Channel Steel Co, Horden Collieries Ltd (chairman), Pearson & Dorman Ltd (chairman), Brunner Mond & Co Ltd, North Eastern Railway Co (vice-chairman) and its successor the London & North Eastern Railway Co, Great Eastern Train Ferries, Wilson & North Eastern Railway Shipping Co, Yorkshire Insurance Co, and Individualist Bookshop Ltd.

Bell's significant involvement in local civic affairs started in 1870, when he became a member of Middlesbrough town council, and participated in committees advocating compulsory children's schooling, a free public library, and provision of a secondary school. Later he was chairman of the Middlesbrough water undertaking, the gas and electricity committee, and the high-school management committee. For many years he promoted the cause of education, being chairman of the Middlesbrough School Board from 1888, and later procuring land for a technical and art college. Bell was twice elected mayor of Middlesbrough, in 1874 and 1883, while in 1910, although he had retired from the council in 1907, he again assumed office on the mayor's death. For more than fifty years he was one of the Tees conservancy commissioners who did much to foster the prosperity of Teesside as an industrial port, and was their chairman 1903-1931.

He was a JP for the Yorkshire North Riding, for Durham County, and for Middlesbrough. He became an alderman of the North Riding County Council, and from 1906 until his death was Lord Lieutenant of the North Riding. He was also a DL for County Durham. Before and during the First World War he sponsored the mustering of territorial troops and in 1918 was made a CB. Nationally, he served as chairman of a departmental committee charged with developing the Science Museum in South Kensington, was a member of the Board of Trade's 1916 committee to consider the international trading position of the iron and steel industry after the war, and at one time was on the board of the National Physical

Laboratory. When the Imperial College of Science and Technology was formed in 1907, he was appointed a governor; he also sat on the senate of Durham University. Honorary degrees in law were bestowed on him by Oxford, Leeds, Sheffield and Durham Universities.

Hugh Bell was a man of wide interests, personal tact and charm, with strongly-held opinions. He believed that industry could only flourish by intelligent co-operation between capital and labour. Politically, he was a staunch and outspoken Free Trader: at heart a Liberal, in 1892 he unsuccessfully contested the Middlesbrough parliamentary seat as a Unionist. In 1910 he again stood unsuccessfully, this time in the City of London as a Free Trade Liberal against the Conservative Balfour.

Bell was active within the Iron and Steel Institute. An original member at its formation in 1869, for three years, 1907-1910, he served as president, presenting the Institute with armorial bearings. When in 1921 the Institute visited Paris, Bell acted as president, and with his fluent French and German did much to placate the French steel makers who felt their country had received unjust treatment at the end of the war. In 1926 he was awarded the Iron and Steel Institute's Bessemer gold medal.

By his first marriage, to Mary Shield of Newcastle in 1867, Hugh Bell had two children, Gertrude Lowthian (1868-1926), renowned Persian scholar and diplomat, and Maurice Hugh Lowthian (1871-1944), who entered Bell Brothers' business, became a director of Dorman Long, and succeeded to the baronetcy. By his second marriage, in 1876 to Florence Olliffe (d 1930), there were three children: Hugo, Florence Elsa and Mary Katherine; these daughters became, respectively, the wives of Vice-Admiral Sir W H Richmond, president of the Imperial Defence College, and Sir Charles P Trevelyan, MP for Newcastle Central and Labour Minister of Education. Sir Hugh Bell died on 29 June 1931 leaving £260,000 gross.

J K ALMOND

Sources:

Unpublished

British Steel Corporation, Northern Regional Records Centre, Middlesbrough, Dorman Long & Co Ltd minute book, letter to shareholders of Dorman Long & Co Ltd from A J Dorman, chairman, 2 Sept 1902.

Central Reference Library, Middlesbrough, folder of news cuttings concerning Sir Hugh Bell.

PrC.

Published

JISI 124 (1931).

Harold Moore, 'The Iron and Steel Institute: Early Years' *JISI* 207 (1969).

NE Daily Gazette 29 June 1931.

WWW.

Dennis Bellamy (courtesy of Hull Daily Mail*).*

BELLAMY, Dennis

(1894-1964)

Electricity supply manager

Dennis Bellamy was born at Kettering, Northamptonshire on 18 September 1894, the fifth in a family of eight of Walter Bellamy, a shoe finisher and later foreman in the local footware industry, and his wife Mary Jane née Loasby. He attended Kettering Parish Church School until at thirteen he chose a commercial career in preference to the further academic study recommended by his headmaster.

Bellamy (or DB as he was familiarly known in later life) joined the Kettering Electricity Department as a junior clerk at a weekly wage of 3s 6d. He attended night classes for shorthand and passed a 120 word a minute examination at fifteen; he also obtained RSA book-keeping certificates. Subsequently he had mixed feelings about his youthful decision to forego higher education but admitted he 'had not much time to spare for vain regrets' {*Electra-Mag* 4 (Dec 1935) 5}.

He was fortunate, however, to have joined a progressive undertaking where the junior staff were trained in all branches of the organisation. The department operated assisted wiring schemes, hire purchase facilities, equipment hiring and a two-part tariff. This early experience proved invaluable when, after overseas service with the RAOC during the First World War (when he attained the rank of warrant officer I), Bellamy was appointed in May 1919 as senior clerk with the Kingston upon Hull Corporation Electricity Department.

The need for additional qualifications was soon apparent and, by correspondence courses, Bellamy qualified in 1926 as a member (later fellow) of the London Association of Certified and Corporate Accountants and also of the Cost and Works (later Management) Accountants. Promotion to a commercial assistant followed and, when a new engineer was appointed, Bellamy was permitted to pursue his ambition of 'going to the consumer - not waiting for the consumer to come to us' {*ibid,* 7}.

During the 1930s the citizens of Hull and adjacent areas experienced an energetic sales promotion campaign. The first electric cooker was installed in 1929, new showrooms were opened in 1933 and by 1935 some 10,000 cookers were in local use; four years later this figure had trebled. Bellamy believed in promoting electricity sales through low prices, a policy which also included rebates for early payment of accounts. He read papers at British Electrical Development Association conferences in which he stressed the need for sound sales management to be based on an accurate knowledge of supply costs for various purposes.

In the inter-war years electrical engineers were prejudiced against commercial men in managerial positions. When, in 1938, the Hull chief engineer died, only six months after Bellamy had been appointed general manager of the Hull undertaking, and was not replaced, the Incorporated Municipal Electrical Association refused to amend its articles to enable

Bellamy to represent the corporation. Thereupon the latter terminated its membership of the IMEA.

During the Second World War Bellamy was involved with many facets of public and armed forces' life in Hull. For his multifarious services to a much-bombed city he received the OBE in 1944 and became a DL of the East Riding of Yorkshire and the City and County of Kingston upon Hull in 1945.

In 1947, a few months before nationalisation of the electricity supply, he accepted an appointment as deputy chairman of the newly-created Yorkshire Electricity Board. But, about a month after the official vesting day (1 April 1948) he resigned (for personal reasons due principally to policy disagreements with the chairman) and returned to Hull as manager of the Hull sub-area of the board. Three years later, over-spending on building licences at the board's headquarters near Leeds, gave rise to a law suit, a cause célèbre known as the Scarcroft Case, which resulted in a prison sentence for the board's chairman, Colonel W M Lapper. His successor, J S Pickles resigned after nine weeks in office and Bellamy was then invited to become chairman of the board. On 25 February 1952 he took office, a position he held until his retirement ten years later.

Bellamy's initial brief was to restore public confidence in the board and among its employees where morale was low. He regarded it as a call to duty and during his chairmanship almost the whole of the board's area, from York in the north to parts of Lincolnshire, was electrified; the supply system was completely re-organised with tariffs lower than those in other areas. He was particularly concerned with attempts to improve the load factor and read papers on this subject at British Electrical Power Conventions in 1954 and 1956. Bellamy was one of the few chairmen to publicise his belief in cheap electricity: a viewpoint disputed by some economists in the early 1960s. His policies have, therefore, been subjected to critical comments in recent years.

Shortly after his retirement from the YEB, in 1962, Bellamy became chairman of the Governors of the Bradford Institute of Technology. He participated actively in the planning which preceded the Institute's transfer to university status and took an especial interest in the Emm Lane College which became a centre for management education. One of the halls of residence has been named after him.

Bellamy was associated with some 30 voluntary, sporting and professional organisations in Hull and held office as president in several of these including the Hull Rotary Club. He was one of the prime movers in the founding of a Rotary Old People's Home, was president for a time of the West Hull Men's Fellowship and of the Hull and East Riding County Centre of the St John Ambulance Association and was awarded the O B St John in 1956. Two years later he received the CBE.

Dennis Bellamy married Edith Alice, daughter of George Bailey, an insurance agent, in 1920; they had a daughter, Joyce Margaret. He died on 16 March 1964 leaving £19,971 gross.

JOYCE M BELLAMY

BELLAMY Dennis

Writings:

The Economics and Principles of Supply Costs and Tariffs (British Electrical Development Association, 1938).

The Economics of Electricity Supply (British Electrical Development Association, 1949).

Lightening the Twilight (Hull Council for Old People's Welfare, 1951).

The Development of the Domestic Load at Home and Overseas (Proceedings of British Electrical Power Convention, 1954).

The Domestic Consumer (British Electrical Power Convention, 1956).

Load Factor in the Electricity Industry (Yorkshire Electricity Board, 1958).

The Story of Rosemont House, 35 Pearson Park, Hull (Hull Rotary Club, 1962).

Sources:

Unpublished

Electricity Council, Millbank, London, papers.

BCe.

MCe.

PrC.

Published

Electra-Mag 4 (Dec 1935).

Electrical Development Association Bulletin April 1964.

Electrical Review 20 Mar 1964.

Electrical Times 19 Mar 1964.

Electricity May-June and Nov-Dec 1964.

Electronics and Power Aug 1964.

Leslie Hannah, *Electricity before Nationalisation: A Study of the Development of Electricity Supply in Britain to 1948* (Macmillan, 1979).

Times 18, 24 Mar 1964.

A Wilson, 'The Strategy of Sales Expansion in the British Electricity Supply Industry between the Wars' in Leslie Hannah (ed), *Management Strategy and Business Development: An Historical and Comparative Study* (Macmillan, 1976).

WWW.

Glyn Davies, *Building Societies and Their Branches* (Franey, 1981).

Seymour J Price, *Building Societies* (Franey, 1958).

Times 3, 10 June, 12 July 1963.

WWW.

BENHAM, James

(1820-1885)

Stove manufacturer

James Benham (courtesy of Mrs Faith Bowers).

James Benham was born in Wigmore Street, London in 1820, the son of John Lee Benham, a retail ironmonger. Benham's father began manufacturing as John Lee Benham & Sons, Ironmongers, Bathmakers, Stove, Grate and Kitchen Range Manufacturers, and Hot Water Engineers, at the corner of Welbeck Street in 1824. The showrooms were on the ground floor, with workshops below and family quarters above. Later more houses were added in Wigmore Street and behind them a factory. James, the eldest of five sons, Frederick, and eventually the youngest, John, went into the business, which grew steadily. Their father died ca 1863, and the firm flourished under James's leadership.

The first large contract came in 1841 for the kitchens of Sir Charles Barry's Reform Club of which Grissell & Peto, fellow Nonconformists, were the builders. The firm mounted a big display at the Great Exhibition, and won prize medals there and at other international exhibitions at Paris in 1855 and 1867, and London in 1862. Benhams' kitchen ranges were particularly successful, especially the combined cooking apparatus designed by the works manager, a Mr Huntley, in 1859. By 1876 this was in use in 12 military barracks, 60 workhouses, 22 hospitals, 16 schools, and 4 commercial establishments. Huntley's ship's cooking apparatus, patented in 1862, was by then installed in 84 British navy ships, 30 P&O vessels, and 12 Royal Mail steam packets; and 25 were sold abroad. In 1869 the three partners' profit was over £11,500, and in 1874 £15,000. In James's later years the firm began to decline, and once his strong leadership was removed it worsened rapidly. By 1895 there were net losses of £11,000. James's elder son Henry had left the firm to become a doctor; another son Walter remained but, like his uncles, failed to keep tight control. The firm prospered again after James's nephew Stanley reorganised the business in 1902.

James married Eliza Horsey some time before 1848, and they had at least two children. The family were vigorous Nonconformists, first in Paddington Congregational Chapel and then after 1849 in the new Bloomsbury Chapel (Baptist). They were active leaders within the church, and generous contributors to many good causes.

James Benham died on 15 June 1885, leaving £60,209 gross.

FAITH BOWERS

Sources:

Unpublished

PrC.

Published

Stanley J Benham, *Under Five Generations. The Story of Benham & Sons Ltd* (Benham & Sons, 1937).

BENN, Sir Ernest John Pickstone

(1875-1954)
Publisher and publicist

Ernest John Pickstone Benn was born in Hackney, London on 25 June 1875, the eldest son of John Williams Benn and Elizabeth née Pickstone. His father, previously a commercial traveller for a furniture company for many years, in about 1875 founded a trade journal, the *Cabinet Maker*, to advocate better design and production of furniture. Later, John Benn had a distinguished career as a long-serving Progressive member of the London County Council from its creation in 1889, and as an MP; he was made a baronet in 1914.

After spending some years at a dame's school, Ernest was educated at the City Central Foundation School. His schooling there was interrupted by an exchange visit of several months to France, with his younger brother, during which they were expelled from four schools for fighting French boys who insulted the English. Ernest returned to the City Central School, but after failing to pass the London Matriculation examinations left school, at his own request, at the age of fifteen and entered his father's office.

In later life, Benn said that he had asked to leave school as he had felt that, because of his father's preoccupation with other matters, one member of the family had to concentrate on making money. Not that he resented or rejected his father's public activities. He spent much time after office hours working as his father's electoral agent. Public service, public speaking and an independent attitude to public questions were as much part of Ernest Benn's inheritance from his father as the publishing business. Although Benn as a boy had wanted to be a missionary and had been attracted by the Salvation Army, then by Swedenborg, and then by Theism, he had come to feel the 'unwisdom of too much straining after the unknown' {Benn (1949) 29} and it was political, rather than religious, ideals which inspired his public life.

After three years as an office boy, starting at 5s a week, Benn spent six years as a traveller, selling advertisement space in the *Cabinet Maker*. He then became the manager of this journal, which was successful, and of another journal his father had started, *House*, which was not. Benn believed he learned his most valuable business lessons from the failure of *House* after a few years of publication, a failure he attributed partly to his own lack of knowledge in catering for the general reader.

Within his chosen field of technical and trade journals, he achieved great success. When John Benn was offered the *Hardware Trade Journal* by the printers Hazell, Watson & Viney in 1900, he left the management to Ernest. By launching a company, Hardware Trade Journal Ltd, with a nominal capital of £7,000, Ernest Benn bought the journal from Hazell, Watson & Viney, who agreed to accept £1,500 of shares as payment, shares which Benn repurchased over seven years. Benn took 2,500 £1 ordinary shares, as payment for his services as managing director for five years, but after the first year cancelled them, to help keep the company solvent, receiving instead an income of £300 per annum, and a quarter of any profits remaining after a 10 per cent dividend had been paid. By the third year of publication, Benn had turned a £900 loss into a £95 profit (by 1913 the profit on the journal had risen to £2,538). He bought out the shareholders other than his father, whom he had persuaded to take up £500 of shares, and in 1903 paid off Hazell, Watson & Viney (paid on credit with bills of exchange) as well, thus gaining possession once again of £2,500 of shares. He also used credit to buy a small rival paper, *Ironmongery*. By 1908 he owned practically all the shares in his company and had cleared all bills of exchange and debts.

By 1925 Benn had owned or controlled 25 papers, very largely trade journals, of which 16 had lost money, leaving the nine successful ones. He considered this an above average rate of success in publishing. When he first took over from his father, total turnover from all sources was about £5,000 per annum, with profits of about 20-25 per cent. By 1925 turnover reached £400,000 per annum, though the rate of profit on this was under 5 per cent. Benn's income by then was £10,000 per annum (by the late 1940s it was £20,000 per annum). Much of this income was ploughed back into the business: from the days when he was earning 5s a week he aimed to save half his income, and he used these savings to cover the risk of his larger transactions.

With the acquisition of *The Electrician* in 1916 and *The Gas World* a year later, Benn found himself the owner also of technical books about gas and electricity. At first he regarded these as an irritating adjunct to the main business of publishing periodicals, an unwanted distraction for his editors, and in 1920 he segregated these side-publications into a separate Book Department, with Victor Gollancz (qv) as its first manager. In 1923 (a year after he had succeeded to full control of the business and the baronetcy on his father's death) he started a book publishing company, Ernest Benn Ltd, with a nominal capital of £35,000, which took over the Book Department of Benn Brothers, and soon developed a list of more general interest. By 1929 the nominal capital had been increased to £100,000. Benn believed the risk in book publishing to be larger than in periodical publishing: while a periodical could steadily build up customers and profits each new book had to make its own way; he had always avoided publishing general interest periodicals; and he believed that businessmen should stick to the field they knew.

Sir Ernest Benn broke his own maxim more completely in 1934 when he became chairman and managing director of the United Kingdom Provident Institution, an insurance company of which he had been a director since 1931. Until his retirement from the chair in 1949, the affairs of the United Kingdom Provident took up rather more than half of the time he spent on business. His chairmanship was unremarkable except for the destruction of the head office building at 196 Strand in an air raid in 1941. This loss prompted the board to move its headquarters to a building it already owned in the City, taking it into the financial heart of London. (Similarly, Sir Ernest had favoured the removal in 1926 of the offices of Benn Brothers to a Fleet Street building costing £150,000 to build). His major contribution to United Kingdom Provident was the fostering of better staff relations by introducing a five-day week, as he had already done in his own businesses as early as 1916, and by starting a house magazine intended to give all the staff in the then rather rigidly-stratified company a sense of common identity and purpose.

This desire to increase employees' sense of participation in the concern for which they worked, which he had sought to achieve in his own business, partly by encouraging the staff to buy shares in it, was the last remnant of the socialist beliefs he had held as a young man, and which he later much regretted. His defence, in three books published in 1916-18, of trade union participation in the management of industry attracted considerable attention from politicians and the public. (At the time Benn was engaged in the highly uncharacteristic occupation of Assistant Director of Training of the Labour Supply Department of the Ministry of Munitions; he was later transferred to the Ministry of Reconstruction.) Soon, however, he became dismayed by the implications of the ideas expressed by other socialists such as the Webbs. Far from being uncomfortable in his role as a capitalist employer, Benn argued that successful and conscientious businessmen were public benefactors through the employment they provided and the wealth they created. His *Confessions of a Capitalist*, in which he expanded these ideas, was the most widely-read of all his books, going into 13 English editions, and being translated into eight foreign languages, including Japanese.

Benn's exalted view of the social utility of business brought him into conflict not only with those who advocated the expropriation of the property of businessmen but also with the advocates of the control and supervision by the state of ever larger areas of the economy and society. His excoriation of bureaucrats, as the chief agent of this continuous encroachment by the state on the liberty of the individual, probably won him wider fame and support than his celebration of the virtues of the business ethic. Together with a group of friends he founded the Individualist Bookshop in 1926, with a nominal capital of £20,000. Benn's popularity as a public speaker grew, especially with the development of the Friends of Economy movement, in which he was prominent. Started in 1931, this aimed, particularly through the organisation of large public meetings, to persuade politicians of all parties that public spending should be curbed, that people were looking to private initiatives, rather than government intervention, to overcome the country's economic difficulties. (Benn himself had been a Liberal until 1929, and always sympathised with liberal philosophy, but in that year he publicly declared his intention of voting Conservative and urged others to do so too, because he believed the Conservative position was the sounder on these issues.) The Friends of Economy movement livened up the political scene for a few years, but then faded away. The Individualist Bookshop closed in 1934, and a weekly magazine, the *Independent*, for which Benn had put up £3,000 of the capital, expired after a short and consistently unprofitable life in 1935.

The Second World War and the plethora of government controls to which it gave rise, brought renewed vigour to Benn's individualist ideas and campaigning. The Individualist Bookshop was revived in 1941, and a full-scale pamphlet campaign launched. In 1942 Benn and his collaborators, who were principally journalists and academics, with some businessmen, including the Second Lord Leverhulme and Lord Perry (qv), the chairman of Fords, published the Individualists' Manifesto and formed the Society of Individualists. Even after the war, the continuation of wartime restrictions and controls provided the Society with plenty of targets. However, Benn did not really approve of the way in which the Society of Individualists was developing, feeling that some of its supporters wanted to turn it into a subsidiary of the Conservative Party. Such disagreements contributed to a marked decline in his previously robust health.

Sir Ernest was in any case over seventy by the late 1940s, and though he still had sufficient energy to stage a one-man protest over the 1950 Census, and was prosecuted for refusing to fill in the Census form, he soon ceased to work actively for the Society. In late 1945 his second son, Glanvill, returned from the Army to chair Benn Brothers. Sir Ernest retired from the chair of the United Kingdom Provident Association in 1949 and was succeeded by his eldest son, John.

Sir Ernest was a family man. His wife, Gwendoline Dorothy Andrews, whom he married in 1903, bore him three sons and two daughters. His conviction that he was always right made him a difficult parent and employer at times, but his essential kindliness, and his ability to inspire others and bring out the best in them, more than compensated for this. His concern for others found outlet not only in his care for his employees' welfare. He annually gave about £700 to various charities and subscription lists, as well as providing help to individuals. In 1927 he sponsored the Boys' Hostel Institution, which provided residential clubs for homeless boys in London. For years, he gave £500 a year to a Boys' Hostel in Stepney named after his father, but because of increased taxation in the late 1940s, felt unable to renew the covenant, a fact he bitterly resented. He died on 16 January 1954, leaving an estate proved at £101,414 gross.

CHRISTINE SHAW

Writings:

Trade as a Science (Jarrold & Sons, 1916).

The Trade of To-morrow (Jarrolds, 1917).

Trade Parliaments and their Work (Nisbet & Co, 1918).

The Confessions of a Capitalist (Hutchinson, 1925).

The Letters of an Individualist to 'The Times' 1921-1926 (Ernest Benn, 1927).

Account Rendered: 1900-1930 (Ernest Benn, 1930).

Modern Government (Allen & Unwin, 1936).

Mind Your Own Business (Society of Individualists, 1946).

Happier Days (Ernest Benn, 1949).

A full list of his writings is in Deryck Abel, *Ernest Benn, Counsel for Liberty* (Benn, 1960).

Sources:

Unpublished

CReg: Ernest Benn Ltd (182,153).

PrC.

Information supplied by Sir John Benn, Glanvill Benn and the United Kingdom Provident Institution.

Published

Deryck Abel, *Ernest Benn, Counsel for Liberty* (Benn, 1960).

DNB.

Times 18 Jan 1954.

WWW.

BENNION, Charles

(1856-1929)

Shoe machinery manufacturer

Charles Bennion was born in Market Drayton, Shropshire on 18 October 1856, the eldest son of Thomas Platt Bennion, a well-to-do farmer, and his wife Hannah née Dale. Although expected to follow the family farming tradition he was determined to be an engineer and his father helped him gain a premium apprenticeship at the London & North Western Railway's workshops in nearby Crewe. He later worked with the marine engineers, John Penn & Sons of Greenwich, subsequently going to sea and qualifying as a second engineer.

Tiring of life at sea he took on, with his father's help, a partnership in an engineering firm in Nantwich, Cheshire, again near to the family home. Nantwich in the 1880s was a centre of boot making and here Bennion first encountered boot and shoe machinery. The partnership was unsatisfactory and he left it after a short time. In 1882 he became partner of a Mr Merry of Leicester. Merry and Bennion made a limited range of shoe machines but within a year Merry died. The valuation of the partnership property introduced Bennion to M H Pearson, son of William Pearson, already an established manufacturer of shoe machinery in Leeds. Pearson suggested joining forces with Bennion but he only took up this offer in 1886, continuing the Merry & Bennion concern for a year or so and acquiring the Leicester firm of Tomlins in this period. The resultant partnership of Pearson & Bennion became the leading concern in the UK supplying simple types of shoe machinery. Despite patent disputes which started in 1883, in particular with the English & American Shoe & General Machinery Co, Pearson & Bennion made enough progress to become a private limited company in 1890.

By the late 1880s at least four American shoe machinery companies were active in the British market, selling models (or licences to build them) of the vastly improved American machines. Pearson & Bennion built under licence for the Consolidated & Mackay Lasting Machine Co of Boston which held the patent on Matziligu's lasting machine, a sophisticated piece of technology. In a few years Pearson & Bennion outgrew their premises in Blue Boar Lane and moved to a new purpose-built factory in Belgrave Road, Leicester.

In 1899 the major American companies merged into the United Shoe Machinery Co. Bennion visited America and arranged to form the British United Shoe Machinery Co in which the USM took 79 per cent of the ordinary shares in exchange for the Goodyear Shoe Machinery Co interests in the UK. The British United Shoe Machinery Co acquired the rival English & American Co in 1901 and then built a new factory, based on American designs, on the Pearson & Bennion site in Leicester.

Bennion continued the American idea of leasing rather than selling machines, causing bitter struggles with those companies who sold machines and resolved only after Bennion's death with the acquisition of the Gimson Shoe Machinery Co. However, the British United Shoe Machinery Co progressed well under Bennion's chairmanship. He made many visits to the USA to keep in touch with latest developments and the company grew to become a major employer in Leicester as a result of his success.

Like many businessmen of the period Charles Bennion took an active part in local life. Although a life-long Conservative he did not seek prominent office. For a few years, however, he represented Newton Ward on Leicester Town Council. He was also appointed a JP for the borough from ca 1900. He was elected president of the Leicester Chamber of Commerce in 1906 and was also president of the Leicester and District Engineering Employers' Association. He was associated with freemasonry for over fifty years and for sixteen years was treasurer for the Province of Leicestershire & Rutland.

Charles Bennion was a noted philanthropist. He was a life-long supporter and life governor of the Leicester Royal Infirmary. Interested in the welfare of ex-servicemen, he helped to provide club buildings for the local branch of the British Legion. Towards the end of his life in 1928 he bought the local Bradgate Park and presented it to the people of the City and County of Leicester, one of his most generous and well remembered gifts.

Charles Bennion and his wife Marion had at least two sons and two daughters. He died on 21 March 1929, leaving £362,231 15s.

R BRACEGIRDLE

Sources:

Unpublished

BCe.

Interview with C G Bennion, grandson of Charles Bennion, 26 January 1982.

'The Origins of the British United Shoe Machinery Company Limited' (in pamphlet collection, Leicestershire RO).

Published

Leicestershire Mercury 14 July 1928, 21 Mar 1929.

Shoe and Leather News 25 Oct 1928.

Times 21 Mar 1929.

USM Today, 75th Anniversary Booklet (USM).

VCH Leicestershire I.

Wyvern 18 Mar 1898.

Henry A Benson, Lord Benson (courtesy of Lewis Photos Ltd).

BENSON, Henry Alexander

Lord Benson

(1909-)

Accountant

Henry Alexander Benson was born in Johannesburg, South Africa on 2 August 1909, the son of Alexander Stanley Benson, a solicitor and his wife Florence Mary née Cooper. He went to school in Johannesburg, first at St John's College and later at Parktown High School. Henry Benson travelled to England to enter Cooper Brothers & Co, chartered accountants, in 1926 and qualified in 1932. Encouraged by his mother, it was natural that he should choose to join this firm as he was a grandson of Francis Cooper (one of the founding brothers) and nephew of Francis D'Arcy Cooper (qv), a second-generation partner. In the practice's established tradition, he became a partner rather young, aged twenty-five in 1934.

During the Second World War, Benson served as an officer in the Grenadier Guards, attaining the rank of colonel, but when the need to re-organize the economy on a war footing became pressing and accountants were recruited into public administration, he was seconded to the Ministry of Supply to advise on the re-organization of the accounts of the Royal Ordnance Factories in 1943-44. In December 1943 he was appointed Director of Ordnance Factories. He became Controller of Building Materials at the Ministry of Works in 1945, later having the special task of advising the Minister of Health on housing production. After the war he served as a member of the Royal Ordnance Board, 1952-56.

Benson returned to Cooper Brothers from government service in 1946 and recommenced his duties as a partner. From that time John Pears and he were responsible for transforming Coopers from a family firm into a multinational accountancy practice, employing some 17,000 staff by the 1970s compared to 150 in the 1920s and about 230 in 1946. Partnerships under the style Cooper Brothers & Co had been established in Australia, on the Continent and in Africa after negotiations with local firms during the late 1940s. A major development took place in 1973 when Cooper Brothers & Co and Lybrand, Ross Brothers & Montgomery, the American accountants, adopted the common style of Coopers & Lybrand, based on an international partnership which was formed in 1957 to co-ordinate the practices existing in Britain, the United States and elsewhere abroad. His competitive and determined approach produced new clients, more offices and a broadened range of activities.

In addition, Benson sat on a considerable number of government and public committees, including the Wilson Committee (1959-60), to review work undertaken and make recommendations for further research into processes for making coal into oil, chemicals and gas, and the Fleck Advisory Committee (1953-55), to consider the organization of the

National Coal Board, of which he was deputy chairman. A member of the Crawley Development Corporation in 1947-50, he became a director and later Deputy Governor of the Hudsons Bay Company (1953-62) and Treasurer of the Open University in 1975-79. In 1963 he had been appointed a Joint Commissioner to make recommendations which led to the formation of the Confederation of British Industry. In 1967 he was appointed chairman of a committee to review the administration of the National Trust.

Following the collapse of John Bloom's Rolls Razor company in 1964 Sir Henry Benson (he was knighted in 1964 and in 1971 awarded the GBE) was appointed as joint Board of Trade inspector to investigate the affair which resulted in a report (not published) and a complex court case.

He has also been much involved in the running of the accountancy profession, being a Council member of the English Institute of Chartered Accountants from 1956 to 1975, and serving as its president in 1966. Sir Henry was largely responsible for the formation of the Accountants International Study Group in 1966 and a few years later when demands were made for more rigorous accounting standards and procedures, he played a considerable part in the formation of the International Accounting Standards Committee and was its first chairman in 1973-76. Its establishment had been preceded by difficult and protracted negotiations designed to get the world's various regulatory bodies to agree on a constitution, aims and approach so that basic accounting standards could be promulgated on an international basis. Producing a large number of accounting statements and exposure drafts, the IASC's function has been to harmonize procedures throughout the world.

In 1976-79 Sir Henry chaired the Royal Commission on Legal Services, whose mammoth report recommended amongst other things that individual solicitors or firms should be permitted a restricted right to advertise, and that the Law Society should be responsible for taking action in cases of bad professional work. Having completed this investigation into the legal profession, Sir Henry accepted an invitation in October 1979 to be the first chairman of a joint disciplinary scheme for accountants. Following his retirement from active practice in 1975 at the age of sixty-five Benson served as an Adviser to the Governor of the Bank of England, a position which he held until August 1983. In 1981 he was created a life peer.

He married Anne Virginia Macleod, daughter of Charles Macleod, a tea planter, in 1939; they had two sons and a daughter.

His career, therefore, exemplified the way in which a senior accountant can offer sustained service to public organization, the Government and the profession as a whole.

EDGAR JONES

Writings:

The Future Role of the Accountant in Practice (Institute of Chartered Accountants in England and Wales, 1958).

Report of an Inquiry into the Methods Adopted by the London Electricity Board for the Disposal of Scrap Cable (Ministry of Power, 1958).

Northern Ireland Railways: Report by H Benson (Ministry of Home Affairs, 1963).

Report on the Formation of a National Industrial Organisation by Sir H Benson, CBE and Sir Samuel Brown (Burrup, Mathieson & Co, 1964).

The Benson Report on the National Trust (National Trust, 1968).

'The Story of International Accounting Standards' *Accountancy* No 995 (July 1976).

PP, RC Legal Services (1979) Cmnd 7648.

Sources:

Unpublished

MCe.

Published

C & L Journal June 1979.

A History of Cooper Brothers & Co 1854-1954 (Cooper & Lybrand, 1954)

Geoffrey Holmes, 'Sir Henry Benson Moves on from Coopers' *Accountancy* 981 (May 1975).

Leon Hopkins, *The Hundredth Year* (Macdonald & Evans, 1980).

Christopher W Nobes and Robert H Parker, *Comparative International Accounting* (Oxford: Philip Allan, 1981).

Robert H Parker, *British Accountants: a Biographical Sourcebook* (New York: Arno Press, 1981).

WW 1982.

BENSON, Samuel Herbert

(1854-1914)

Advertising agent

Samuel Herbert Benson was born in Marylebone, London, on 14 August 1854, son of Samuel Miles Benson, a solicitor, and Philippa née Bourne. Samuel Jr was educated with a view to a legal career, but at the age of

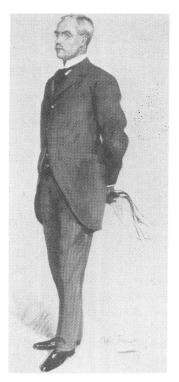

Samuel H Benson (courtesy of the History of Advertising Trust).

sixteen chanced to pick up a copy of the *Navy List* and within a month had passed an examination for entry to the Royal Navy.

For the next fifteen years he served his country with distinction, being several times mentioned in despatches. He saw service in the Ashanti War, 1874-75; commanded a cutter in an expedition against Congo pirates in 1875; took part in the Dahomey blockade, 1876-77; served at Gallipoli in the Turco-Russian War; and was in charge of the commissariat of the Naval Brigade at Suez during Lord Wolseley's expedition against Arabi Pasha in 1882 when his promising career was brought to an abrupt end by a bite on the leg from a poisonous insect. As a result he spent three years on crutches and was invalided back to London. He then became secretary to several Admiralty committees, but finding such a life incongenial, resigned from the Navy in order to pursue a career in business.

In 1886 he became manager of the Normal Co's provision factory in Aberdeen; in 1889, manager of the Bovril factory in London under John Lawson Johnston (qv); and in 1892, manager of the French factories of Betts & Co, first at Bordeaux and later at Carcassonne. Resigning after refusing to dismiss the chief clerk (an unfair action in his view) he returned to England and was unexpectedly offered the chance of handling the advertising for his former employers, Bovril, if he would become an advertising agent. Although by his own account he knew little about the subject, he accepted the challenge, and with a client of such prestige and importance his agency was in the front rank from its opening in 1893.

Benson displayed a sense of dignity and clarity of purpose which did much to raise the status of the advertising agent to that of a profession. At a time when sharp practice was commonplace and fraud by no means unknown, he became noted for his absolute integrity. A former employee wrote of him that he would discharge a man at a minute's notice for overcharging or taking advantage of a client, and while many so-called agents employed a wide range of tricks to avoid paying newspapers the agreed rate for space, Benson stated in 1913 that his agency had paid some £5,600 for space for which it had not itself been paid by advertisers. Such was the esteem in which he was held that there was a call in advertising circles for him to be awarded a knighthood.

Benson made the first attempt in Britain to set up an organisation of advertising agents which could enforce common standards and levels of service, and exclude the many charlatans and shady operators who called themselves agents but were in fact nothing of the kind. The Association of Advertising Agents failed, however, because those involved in its formation could not agree among themselves who should be eligible for membership, and they encountered considerable opposition from publishers.

He was also important as an advertising thinker. Although his writings were intended primarily to publicise his agency, they displayed a grasp of the role of advertising in the marketing process which was remarkably advanced. While most agents of the time saw advertising as a panacea, Benson emphasised the importance of studying the consumer, the trade and the competition, and of ensuring that the product was right for the market before any thought was given to promotion. At a time when most writers went little further than stressing the desirability of repetition, he argued that this was not enough and that a campaign should have objectives. And while exaggeration was commonplace, he argued that this was shortsighted since advertising was in effect trying to buy goodwill.

As a manager Benson was inclined to be somewhat remote and autocratic, suffering periods of irritability through recurrences of pain in his leg. He rewarded ability and loyalty, however, and was thought to pay the highest wages of any agent in London. He took a personal interest in the welfare of staff, helping their families in times of trouble, and drilling the boys in the agency after work out of concern for their physical well-being.

In 1885, under the patronage of Lord Randolph Churchill, he set up the Express Courier Corps, an organisation of messenger boys, which had to be abandoned under pressure from the Post Office. In 1899 he was one of the founders of the War Employment Bureau, which provided work for the wives of reservists fighting in the Boer War.

Benson married in 1882 Mary Ann Phillips, daughter of a naval paymaster-in-chief; they had three sons and two daughters. After being knocked down by a motor omnibus in Fleet Street in November 1913, he was found to be suffering from an incurable disease. Samuel Benson died on 21 July 1914 leaving an estate valued at £17,500 gross.

T R NEVETT

Writings:

Wisdom in Advertising (1901).

Force in Advertising (1904).

Benson's Facts for Advertisers (S H Benson, 1905).

letter in *Advertiser's Weekly* 6 Dec 1913.

The Advertising Equipment of S H Benson Ltd.

Sources:

Unpublished

BCe.

MCe.

PrC.

Published

Advertiser's Weekly 25 July, 1 Aug 1914.

Advertising World July, Aug 1914.

George Edgar, 'Business Builders XVI, Mr S H Benson' (magazine offprint, undated).

Peter Hadley (ed), *The History of Bovril Advertising* (Barril Ltd, 1972).

Terry R Nevett, *Advertising in Britain — A History* (Heinemann, 1982).

Stanley Piggott, *OBM 125* (pp, 1975).

Times 22 July 1914.

'Why an Association of Advertising Agents Is Impossible at Present' *Circulation Manager* Feb 1914.

Leonard H Bentall, portrait by A E Cooper (courtesy of Bentalls Ltd).

BENTALL, Leonard Hugh

(1875-1942)

Department store developer

Leonard Hugh Bentall was born at Kingston upon Thames, Surrey, on 2 September 1875, the second son and third of the four children of Frank Bentall (1843-1923), a Kingston draper, and his wife Laura née Dowman, daughter of a Southampton pharmacist.

Under Frank Bentall, a man of considerable energy and methodical habits, the family shop at 31 Clarence Street, Kingston upon Thames, was expanded from small premises, a staff of five and a first year's turnover of £200 in 1867, to half a dozen premises, rebuilt as a department store, a staff of over 100 assistants and a turnover of £60,000 when Frank retired in 1909. Enlarged markets, due to local population growth and tram and railway extensions, partly explain this, as did the firm's policy of 'a strict cash trade' {Bentall (1974) 43}. The entrepreneurial drive to seize these expanding market opportunities came chiefly from 'Mr Leonard'.

After attending a local preparatory school, Leonard Bentall was sent to New College, Eastbourne, and then Forest House, Woodford, where he became interested in practical subjects and thought of becoming an engineer.

When he left school he spent a short while in his father's shop and then, aged about nineteen, started two years as an 'improver' (one up from apprentice) at Jones & Higgins of Peckham and then a further year at Peter Jones' store in King's Road, Chelsea. He returned to his father's firm as buyer for the Manchester (goods) department (his brother George being responsible for the fancy and women's wear department), soon making his mark by his rushed visits to the City to obtain new lines, not resting until they were on display and being sold.

When his father retired in 1909 Leonard assumed the general management of the store (his elder brother George continuing as buyer for fancy goods) and recruited Herbert H Perkins from Harrods to become mail order and publicity manager. Mail order, not a success, was soon discontinued, but publicity attractions, starting with customer judging of window displays, became an integral part of Bentalls' selling techniques.

Further extensions came in 1912 after Leonard Bentall secured the freehold of three more properties in Clarence Street: now only the Clarence Arms remained, dividing the store into two sections, and this too Leonard acquired in 1919, replacing it immediately with another three storey building of Portland stone, fitted with the latest equipment like Lamson pneumatic tubes for propelling cash between counters and the central cash department, automatic 'sesame' doors and speaking tubes as in the existing premises.

The retirement of his brother George in 1917 and his plans for further expansion, already moving ahead with the purchase of more properties on Wood Street, led Leonard to convert the business into a private limited company in 1925. The directors, besides himself (as chairman) and his elder son, Gerald, were Herbert H Perkins, counting house manager, M V Harcourt, general manager, and W Astles, merchandise manager. The original nominal capital of the company was £250,000, of which £202,002 was issued. Leonard held 100,001 of the 122,000 £1 ordinary shares and 40,000 of the 80,000 £1 preference shares.

To reduce his costs, Bentall installed his own electricity generating equipment in the store's basement in 1926; by this means he undercut the Kingston electricity department's rates of 3.5d-4d a unit by 1.5d and the following year added a second generator, increasing capacity from 100 kW to 233 kW. This enabled him to indulge his fancy for numerous electrical devices: electronic calculating machines in the counting house, electric-powered equipment for opening the mail and (in the kitchens) for dishwashing, glass polishing and cutlery burnishing, as well as powered windows, ventilators and sunblinds throughout the store. To attract the custom of car owners, then the rather more wealthy members of the middle classes, he bought land on the opposite side of Wood Street and provided a covered-in car park, capable of holding 450 cars. With the Tudor restaurant (once the vicarage) in the main store block, it proved a popular attraction.

Emulating West End department stores and encouraged by continued population growth west of London, Bentall planned a major reconstruction. Designed by Sir Aston Webb & Sons, and (at Bentall's insistence) inspired by Wren's work at Hampton Court Palace nearby, the new building was commenced in 1930. Steel framed and faced with bricks and Portland stone it had three shopping floors and modern fittings (most from Gamages' new but recently-closed Oxford Street store) including escalators built specially under a licence secured by Leonard Bentall in Germany. The new shop was completed in 1935 and the following year a six storey furniture depository in Penrhyn Road was built.

In the midst of construction, the store's activities continued. The purchase of equipment from Gamages led to the recruitment of Eric Fleming as publicity director and soon Bentalls' store spectaculars were reaching new heights of sensationalism. Sir Malcolm Campbell's Bluebird racing car was displayed in 1932, followed by food and sewing exhibitions, a self-service shop of the future (of 1950) and visits by public personalities,

Architects' drawing of Bentalls (courtesy of Bentalls Ltd).

from Mantovani and Cyril Fletcher to Anita Kittner, a great attraction, who dived from a height of 63 feet near the roof of the store into a tank of water. Also in the 1930s Leonard Bentall moved into new retailing fields like motor cars, sold from 1934 onwards, and a building department whose timber framed bungalows were very popular as retirement homes on the South Coast.

There are a few measures of this growth. While the firm's authorised capital remained unchanged at £250,000 during Leonard's lifetime, profits before income tax moved between £62,000 and £103,000 a year, 1937-42. Employees numbered 500 by 1935 and 2,000 in 1946, four years after Leonard's death.

Leonard Bentall was a paternalist. He knew most of his staff, inspiring in them loyalty and, by his acerbic tongue, some fear. Certainly he kept staff on their toes by his unexpected appearances around the store. In 1925 he introduced a bonus scheme for those employees who invested 10 per cent of their wages in the Bentall business, and in 1929 started a pension fund. In the hostels in which the male and female staff were separately housed he encouraged social activities and recreations.

Outside his business Leonard Bentall was equally vigorous in his activities. For the Warehousemen, Clerks and Drapers' Schools he raised £52,000 in 1923, to build a second school at Addington; for the Kingston YMCA he raised £4,000 in 1927; and in the late 1920s he chaired the building committee responsible for a second Roberts marine mansion, at Worthing, for shop assistants needing convalescence or holidays. Like his father, Leonard Bentall was an active Congregationalist, heading the general purposes committee of Kingston Congregational church, supporting the Congregational mission at Cobham, after he moved there, and supporting an LMS missionary near Kingston, Jamaica.

He married Winifred Ivy Smith, daughter of a Kidderminster clothing manufacturer and Congregationalist, in 1902; they had two sons and four daughters. Leonard Bentall died on 24 December 1942 leaving £290,486 gross.

DAVID J JEREMY

Sources:

Unpublished

C Reg: Bentalls Ltd (203,568).

BCe.

MCe.

PrC.

Information from Rowan Bentall.

Published

Rowan Bentall, *My Store of Memories* (W H Allen, 1974).

Charles Herbert, *A Merchant Adventurer, Being the Biography of Leonard Hugh Bentall, Kingston upon Thames* (Waterlow & Sons, 1936).

Herbert H Perkins, *The Rise of Bentalls over 80 Years of Progress, 1867-1951* (Kingston upon Thames: Bentalls Ltd, 1951).

Times *Prospectuses* 99 (1946).

BERRY, Albert Eustace

(1875-1961)

Sugar refiner

Albert Eustace Berry was born in Golborn, Lancashire, on April 4 1875, seventh of the eight children of William Berry, a beer seller, and his wife Sabina née Hibbert. He grew up in Newton-le-Willows (or Newton-in-

Albert E Berry (from J L Garbutt, Manbré & Garton 1855–1955: A Hundred Years of Progress, *Manbré & Garton, 1955).*

Makerfield), where his father, a licensed victualler, was assisted by his wife and their four daughters. It is said that Albert's mother inculcated in him a certain studiousness.

At the age of seventeen he went to work in the laboratory of the United Alkali Co, in St Helen's, attending evening classes at Owens College, Manchester, where he later obtained his BSc in chemistry in 1895. He was appointed chief chemist to the company's head engineer, a post which gave him diversified experience all over the North of England. In 1897 he was offered the post of chief chemist in A Boake, Roberts & Co, of Stratford, East London, a small chemical firm; he accepted, believing that the scope for his energy would be wider in London. The company had a department producing caramel for brewers, in which Berry took great interest. He soon became the works director, and continued to further his education by taking evening classes in bacteriology at King's College, London.

Albert Berry in 1899 married Edith May Smith, daughter of a gold lace manufacturer of Hackney. They had two sons, Eustace Albert and Derbe C, who later studied chemistry and joined their father in business, in 1922 and 1928 respectively. Edith May died in 1926. Albert E Berry remarried, in 1934, to Jessie Katy Moore, daughter of a produce merchant of Wanstead, Essex.

Witnessing a change of taste among beer consumers, from the heavily malted to the lighter and sweeter beers, Berry foresaw an expansion in the market for brewing sugars. In 1906 he seized the opportunity to take over a neighbouring firm, Johnson's Saccharum Co. The assets of this firm and those of A Boake, M Roberts & Co were amalgamated to create a new firm, Sugar & Malt Products Ltd, which expanded rapidly.

During the First World War Berry participated in a rationing committee set up by the Ministry of Food to allocate sugar to brewers. Here he met other prominent members of the industry, including some directors of the Manbré Saccharine Co. This firm had been established in London in 1871 by a Frenchman, Alexandre Manbré, who had a unique patent for converting starch into sugar by a process of boiling under pressure, a method which has remained the basic principle of the industry. The firm, registered as a private limited liability company in 1874, moved to new premises in Hammersmith in 1876. In 1916 it began to experience financial difficulties and in 1919 the board invited Berry to become managing director. He refused, proposing instead to take over the ailing firm, which had large premises, and merge it with his own. His proposals were accepted and Manbré Sugar & Malt Ltd, with all its activities concentrated in Hammersmith, was formed. The capital of the new company was £700,000 (£597,000 paid-up in 1920, and wholly paid-up the year after). The first year's accounts showed assets worth £901,000; these broke the million barrier in 1921, and reached £1,396,000 in 1926. Profit also grew steadily, from £212,000 in 1920 to £350,000 in 1926.

Berry became chairman of the new concern and embarked quickly on an acquisition policy, purchasing in 1920 the Brewers' Sugar Co Ltd, Greenock; in 1921 the Liverpool Saccharine Co (founded in the 1880s by the sons of Alexandre Manbré); and in 1923 three Liverpool firms (Freeman Lloyd & Co Ltd, the Liverpool Malt Co Ltd, and Ceros Foods Ltd). In 1926 he negotiated a merger with the other major brewing sugar producer in the UK, Garton, Sons & Co Ltd which had been established in Southampton in 1855 and had moved to Battersea, London, in 1882. Berry became the first managing director of Manbré & Garton Ltd and succeeded Sir Richard Garton (qv) as chairman in 1927. The new firm's paid up capital was £1.8 million, and it showed, in 1927, assets worth £4.12 million, returning a pre-tax profit of £448,000. In 1935 the company took over the Sankey Sugar Co Ltd, of Earlstown, Lancashire, from the Dutch group Van Rossum, completing its early dramatic expansion.

In 1928 Berry invented candy sugar, which was softer and could be produced faster than sugar candy, and added it to the long range of invert sugars, glucose, colouring caramels and various gums that Manbré had already produced for the food and drink industry. Though it was hit by the depression in the sugar business in the 1930s (assets went down, from £4,239,000 in 1928 to £4,155,000 in 1932, and profits from £509,000 to £397,000 for the same dates), Manbré & Garton Ltd successfully survived, mainly due to Berry's business acumen and his interest in new developments in applied chemistry. On this subject he presented papers at the Institute of Brewers and at the Incorporated Brewers' Guild and after his retirement published two pamphlets. He was also keen on developing new technical and organisational ideas to respond to the growing demand for his products: in 1931 he initiated the use of bulk liquid sugar in the jam-making industry, and developed a fleet of liquid bulk-delivery lorries in the 1930s which vastly extended Manbré & Garton's UK market.

Berry also gradually increased the proportion of imported cane sugar used in the factory, which led to an unsuccessful attempt, in the early 1930s, to grow cane in Kenya. In 1936 however, he was asked to advise on the reorganisation and improvement of the ailing African Products Manufacturers Co Ltd, which made starch and glucose from maize at Germiston in the Transvaal. Berry's eldest son, Eustace, acted as consultant in exchange for a share in the firm's capital. Manbré & Garton acquired control of it in 1938, Berry having travelled to Germiston to assess its potential. During the Second World War, African Products Manufacturers greatly increased its share of the market and it was found necessary to create a new subsidiary, Glucose & Starch Products Ltd, with a purpose-built factory opened in 1951 in Bellville, South Africa.

Berry's advice was sought by civil servants again after the outbreak of the war in 1939. The war years, if they did not help Manbré & Garton's profit (it went down from £600,000 in 1939 to £447,000 in 1945), strengthened the firm: its assets standing at £4,922,000 in 1939, slowly accumulated to £5,249,000 in 1945. This was the result of a cautious policy of allocating only tenuous dividends. After the war, growth was steady, with assets totalling more than £6 million for the first time in 1958, a year when profit for the first time exceeded £1 million.

In the post-war years a major threat to British sugar refiners came from the Labour Government which wanted to nationalise the sugar industry in 1949-50. Resistance came primarily from Tate & Lyle, the industry's largest firm. Albert Berry played little public part in this campaign and Labour went out of office before nationalisation could be implemented.

Albert Berry retired as managing director of Manbré & Garton in 1953, leaving his two sons, Eustace and Derbe, as joint managing directors, although he remained chairman until 1959, when he was succeeded first by

Eustace, then by Derbe. When Manbré & Garton Ltd was taken over in 1976 by Tate & Lyle, it was one of the three independent sugar concerns remaining in Great Britain: Tate & Lyle dominated the domestic market; Manbré & Garton dominated the industrial users' market between the 1930s and early 1960s; and the British Sugar Corporation was, and remains, the only firm producing sugar from British beet.

During the course of his life, Albert Berry devoted most of his time to running his business, and never held any public office. He had a house and a farm at Charlwood in Surrey, as well as a shooting ground, and owned a flat in London. He regularly attended the parish church in Charlwood and his hobbies related to country-life: horse-breeding (his horses won many races in the 1920s and 1930s); hunting with the Surrey Union Foxhounds; and shooting.

Albert Eustace Berry died on 27 January 1961, and was survived by his sons and his second wife, Jessie. He left an estate of £139,741 gross.

CLAUDE FIVEL-DEMORET

Writings:

Cane Sugar versus Invert Sugar (pp, 1959).

Cane Sugar versus Invert Sugar in Brewing (Newman Neame, 1960).

Sources:

Unpublished

Office of Population Censuses and Surveys, London. Census records for 1881.

C Reg: Manbré & Garton Ltd (159,009).

BCe.

MCe.

PrC.

Information from Derbe C Berry, 1982.

Philippe Chalmin, 'L'Emergence d'une Firme Multinationale au sein de l'Economie Sucrière Mondiale: Tate & Lyle 1860-1980' (Paris-Sorbonne PhD, 1981).

Published

Philippe Chalmin, *Tate & Lyle, Géant du Sucre* (Paris: Economica, 1983).

John L Garbutt, *Manbré & Garton Ltd 1855-1955: A Hundred Years of Progress* (pp for Manbré & Garton, 1955).

International Sugar Journal May 1948.

Jeanne Stoddart, *Manbré: A Hundred Years of Sugar Refining in Hammersmith 1874-1974* (Fulham & Hammersmith Historical Society, 1974).

Times 28 Jan, 8 Mar 1961.

BERRY, Henry Seymour

1st Lord Buckland of Bwlch

(1877-1928)

Industrialist

Henry Seymour Berry was born at Merthyr Tydfil on 17 September 1877, the eldest son of John Mathias Berry, an accountant, later auctioneer and estate agent, of Merthyr Tydfil, and his wife Mary Anne née Rowe. Henry was educated privately and became a teacher. Later, abandoning teaching, he joined his father in the family estate agency. His abilities in business came to the notice of D A Thomas, later Lord Rhondda (qv) who was looking for younger men of enterprise to help in directing his colliery interests in the so-called Cambrian Combine, which was one of the larger groupings of colliery companies in South Wales. It included Consolidated Cambrian Ltd, Cambrian Collieries Ltd and Glamorgan Coal Co Ltd. The link with D A Thomas came through Henry's father, an alderman who became mayor of Merthyr Tydfil in 1911 and who had acted as parliamentary election agent for D A Thomas.

Henry Seymour Berry was associated with Thomas from 1915 onwards but the real turning-point came in 1916 when Thomas joined the Cabinet in Lloyd George's Government, leaving Berry to lead the Thomas business empire. The number of directorships held by Berry grew rapidly: by 1919 no less than 66 of them. From 1922 he relinquished many and on his death in 1928 there were just over 20. Among his more important directorships was the chairmanship of John Lysaght Ltd (integrated makers of galvanized sheets with steelworks, rolling mills and colliery interests) which came in 1919 after he purchased the firm in association with D R Llewellyn (qv) and Viscountess Rhondda, for the sum of £5 million. In turn Lysaght was acquired by Guest Keen & Nettlefolds in January 1920, but Berry remained as chairman of Lysaght and became deputy chairman of GKN and then chairman (in 1927). He did much to reorganise GKN (introducing various management committees) but was not a widely popular man. By 1921 he was also chairman and managing director of North's Navigation Collieries Ltd, Celtic Collieries Ltd and Imperial Navigation Collieries Ltd as well as chairman of Cynon Colliery Co Ltd and Britannic Coal Co Ltd. While the motivation for Berry's mergers is not entirely clear, the First World War and its aftermath did offer opportunities for take-overs in anticipation of an upturn in market demand and hence a larger share of expanding markets, an anticipation which in the 1920s was largely unfulfilled. Mergers could also provide an opportunity for achieving internal economies within firms. Overall, his importance lay in his merger activity which made him an early practitioner of the rationalisation ideas that gathered support during the 1920s. In 1924 the Berry Llewellyn-Rhondda group was described as the 'most powerful capitalist combination in the South Wales coalfield. The interests of this group extend like red threads through the mesh of capitalism in South Wales and, as in a tangled skein, it is impossible to say where they begin and where they end.' {Williams (1924) 118}

In spite of his importance in the South Wales coal industry, H S Berry does not seem to have taken a prominent part in the public pronouncements of coalowners, even if he was resolutely opposed to trade union and labour claims. He intervened once however, when with five other coalowners he called for a special meeting of the Monmouthshire and South Wales Coalowners' Association (held on 29 July 1917) to discuss the legality of arrangements made for government control of the coal mines in wartime. Otherwise, his main activity and importance were financial.

Among his non-colliery business interests were directorships of the *Western Mail*, *Merthyr Express*, *East Glamorgan Herald* and other newspapers. He was also associated with the *Sunday Times* owned by his younger brothers, J G Berry and W E Berry (qqv).

Outside business his other activities included donations to the J M Berry Technical School founded at Merthyr in memory of his father; to Merthyr General Hospital for a new wing; and to other institutions including the National Museum of Wales. He was made a Freeman of Merthyr Tydfil in 1923 and was High Sheriff of Breconshire in 1924. He served as JP both in Merthyr Tydfil and in Brecon. His association with Brecon derived from his estate at Buckland where he moved from Merthyr Tydfil in 1922. He was created a baron with the title of Buckland of Bwlch in the summer of 1926: the peerage became extinct after his death.

Berry married Gladys Mary née Sandbrook of Merthyr Tydfil in 1907 and they had five daughters. He died, after a fall from his horse, on 23 May 1928, leaving £1,116,447 gross.

GRAEME M HOLMES

Sources:

Unpublished

National Library of Wales, Monmouthshire and South Wales Coalowners' Association Minute Books, especially MG14.

PRO, Cambrian Collieries file, BT 31/31793/46172; Graigola Merthyr Co Ltd file BT 31/31020/21075.

BCe.

PrC.

Published

James C Carr and Walter Taplin, *History of the British Steel Industry* (Oxford: Blackwell, 1962).

Colliery Guardian 25 May 1928.

Charlotte Erickson, *British Industrialists. Steel and Hosiery 1850-1950* (Cambridge: Cambridge University Press, 1959).

Margaret H Mackworth (Viscountess Rhondda) and others, *D A Thomas, Viscount Rhondda* (Longmans & Co, 1921).

Who's Who in Wales (lst ed, Cardiff, 1921).

D Jeffrey Williams, *Capitalist Combination in the Coal Industry* (Labour Publishing Co, 1924)

Western Mail 24 May 1928.

WWW.

William E Berry, 1st Viscount Camrose.

James Gomer Berry, 1st Viscount Kemsley (courtesy of Lord Kemsley).

BERRY, William Ewert   and   **BERRY, James Gomer**
1st Viscount Camrose   1st Viscount Kemsley
(1879-1954)   (1883-1968)

Newspaper and periodical publishers

William Ewert and James Gomer Berry were the second and third sons of a Merthyr Tydfil estate agent, John Mathias Berry and his wife, Mary Ann, daughter of Thomas Rowe, of Pembroke Dock. William was the elder by four years: he was born on 23 June 1879, while Gomer was born on 7 May 1883. No precise details of their education have been recorded. William said of himself that he was educated privately; all that is known of Gomer's education is that it took place at Merthyr Tydfil.

At the age of fourteen, William began work as an apprentice journalist on the *Merthyr Tydfil Times*. He remained in South Wales for five years, working on various papers, before going to London in 1898. Here again he held various jobs as a reporter, before starting up on his own in 1901. With the help of a loan of £100 from his elder brother Henry Seymour (qv) he started a periodical, *Advertising World*, publishing it from a shared third-floor office in Fleet Street. After the first issue he invited Gomer, who knew nothing of journalism, to come to help him.

Thus began a partnership which was to last, in unbroken harmony, for over thirty-five years. William tended to look after the editorial aspects of their publications, while Gomer supervised the advertising, kept an eye on the circulation, and looked after the books. It would probably be unwise to assume that all the business and financial acumen was supplied by Gomer, providing a practical underpinning for his brother's journalistic flair. When approaches were made to the brothers by those with publications to sell, it was usually William they approached and he, rather than Gomer, seems to have taken the lead in subsequent negotiations. However, it is impossible to disentangle the brothers' individual contributions to their business strategy and policy, as distinct from the day-to-day running of their affairs. According to the Second Lord Burnham, who worked very closely with them, they themselves were not much concerned with the division of responsibilities. There were no rows or public disagreements to reveal differences of approach or interest. In the circumstances, it is not surprising that some of their staff succumbed to the temptation to refer to their employers by the joint epithet 'Beri-Beri'. The brothers disliked this name, but they had no objection to the other nickname, the 'Busy Bees', bestowed on them by their staff.

The *Advertising World* enjoyed sufficient success for the profit on its sale in 1905 to enable them to found a small publishing company, Ewert, Seymour & Co Ltd (the company's title suggests that Seymour was still providing some financial backing). They issued several periodicals, the most successful of which, *Boxing*, started with a print of 100,000 and reached 250,000 by about 1915.

In that year, they acquired their first newspaper, the *Sunday Times*. Founded in 1822, it had had an undistinguished career, and with a circulation of only 30,000 was losing money when they bought it. (Accounts of the price they paid vary, from £20,000 to at least £75,000; the latter figure seems more likely). They were helped to finance their acquisition by James White (qv) the financier, who provided them with a bridging loan until satisfactory arrangements had been made with their bankers.

Money was tight at the *Sunday Times* in the early days of the Berrys' regime. Gomer kept a close watch on expenses, and journalists from *Boxing* were brought in to help the meagre permanent editorial staff. William began to improve the appearance and content of the paper, paying particular attention to developing the news side, until it became a good, lively newspaper as well as a journal of opinion.

After the war, other purchases followed in rapid succession. The *Financial Times* was bought, partly for the sake of the printing works, the St Clement's Press, associated with it. In 1920, forestalled in their wish to acquire the former headquarters of W H Smith at 186 Strand by Sir Edward Iliffe (qv), the owner of Kelly's Directories and numerous trade and technical publications, they bought Kelly's Directories and the offices with it. This was the beginning of their partnership with Iliffe, which lasted until 1937. There was complete trust between the three partners; they even operated a joint bank account. Iliffe had been considering retiring from business to concentrate on politics, but changed his mind when William Berry proposed the promotion of a big public issue of shares in Associated Iliffe Press and Kelly's Directories. The issue was a great success. Other purchases made by the Berrys about this time included Cassells, the periodical and book publishers (only the periodicals were retained), and Graphic Publications, which brought them the *Daily Graphic* and two illustrated weeklies, the *Graphic* and the *Bystander*. All were bought with the intention of offering the shares to the public; all were offered before June 1921. Their progress as publishing proprietors was marked by a baronetcy for William, granted in that year (Gomer had to wait until 1928 for his).

In 1923 they nearly succeeded in buying the Hulton publishing group, but at the last minute Beaverbrook (qv) stepped in with a slightly better offer. He bought the group for £6 million cash, and almost immediately sold it to Rothermere (qv) for the same sum, keeping the *Evening Standard* for himself. Within six months the Berrys and Iliffe had persuaded Rothermere to part with the bulk of the Hulton papers for £4 million in cash and £1.5 million in debenture stock. They acquired the remaining Hulton papers from him within a few years. A new company, Allied Newspapers, was formed to own this group, with an issued capital of £8.25 million, of which the £2 million of ordinary shares were kept by the partners and their friends.

They were now among the first division of newspaper owners, and still making acquisitions. Many provincial papers were offered to them: such offers continued to be made throughout their career and they themselves never had to approach a provincial paper owner. Their importance as periodical publishers was greatly increased when in 1926 they bought the Amalgamated Press, the group founded by Northcliffe (qv), from Rothermere; the total purchase price was just over £8 million.

With the Amalgamated Press came the Imperial Paper Mills in Kent. The following year they were offered the Lloyd paper mills at Sittingbourne and Kemsley, in accordance with the wishes of Frank Lloyd (qv) who died in May 1927. Allied Newspapers paid £3.2 million for 1.6 million ordinary shares in Edward Lloyd Ltd, leaving 1.2 million £1 7 per cent preference shares with the public.

Their success was beginning to irk their major rivals. When they acquired Lloyds in 1927, Beaverbrook withdrew his newsprint contract, but there were still plenty of others to be had. Rothermere's jealousy was aroused when the partners accepted Lord Burnham's proposal in December 1927 that they should buy *The Daily Telegraph*. Rothermere read in an American paper that this meant the Berrys and Iliffe had toppled him from his position as the owner of the largest newspaper chain in the country. To challenge Allied Newspapers in its provincial strongholds, Rothermere launched Northcliffe Newspapers Ltd in 1928; by 1932 11 papers had been acquired or started. The battle was bitter and expensive, particularly in Newcastle and Bristol. Both sides were losing heavily by the competition and the costly efforts to boost advertising and circulation. An agreement was reached whereby Allied moved out of Bristol, and Rothermere closed the evening paper he had started in Newcastle. Northcliffe Newspapers was liquidated in 1932.

The early 1930s were also difficult times for the Lloyd paper mills, as for all UK paper manufacturers. The partners had interfered very little. They had kept Frank Lloyd's professional managers and followed the lines which he had mapped out before his death. Much new plant was installed, including what was claimed to be the largest and fastest paper-making machine in the world. The newsprint capacity of the mills was increased from 200,000 to 275,000 tons per annum and the total productive capacity for all kinds of paper to 320,000 tons. But while profits had reached a peak of £673,200 in 1931, by 1934 they had fallen to £388,142. Profits picked up again but it is possible that the partners may have been put off newsprint by the leaner years. Or perhaps William Berry, the chairman of Lloyds, was growing tired of the business. It was his remark to Ian Bowater at a dinner party, 'We are not newsprint manufacturers, we are journalists'

{Reader (1981) 115}, which led to the sale of Lloyds to Bowaters in July 1936. The fact that Gomer took his title, Kemsley, from one of the Lloyd mills when he was raised to the peerage in 1936 does not indicate distaste for the newsprint business on his part. (William had been given his peerage in 1929, taking the title Camrose).

If Kemsley had allowed himself to be persuaded by Camrose against his real wishes to agree to the sale of Lloyds, it could help to explain why Kemsley, Camrose and Iliffe (now Lord Iliffe) agreed to break up their partnership in January 1937. Kemsley could not have relished the prospect of always being second-in-command: Camrose was chairman and editor-in-chief of the *Daily Telegraph*, chairman of Allied Newspapers, editor-in-chief of the *Sunday Times*, and chairman of the *Financial Times* and of Kelly's Directories. To some extent Kemsley had always been in his brother's shadow, and his behaviour after the partnership ended showed he longed for a place in the limelight. But another factor was concern for the next generation. Camrose had four sons, Kemsley six, and Iliffe two, and there could be reasonable doubt whether they could work as harmoniously together as their fathers had done.

Even after the division of their empire, Camrose, Kemsley and Iliffe each had enough to make them major figures in the publishing world. Camrose took the *Daily Telegraph*, *Financial Times* and the Amalgamated Press. Kemsley took Allied Newspapers and the *Sunday Times*, and Iliffe took back Kelly's Directories under his sole control.

Amalgamated Press, with an authorised capital of £6.2 million, published 58 weekly and 21 monthly periodicals as well as children's annuals and educational works in part form. The Press also controlled four subsidiary publishing companies, and the Imperial Paper Mills; Imperial Paper owned two-thirds of the capital of the Gulf Pulp & Paper Co of Canada. Camrose had a controlling interest in the Amalgamated Press and in the *Financial Times*, which had a nominal capital of £1.5 million. He sold his interest in the *Financial Times* in 1945.

The *Daily Telegraph* was a private company in which all the ordinary capital of 40,000 £1 shares and a large proportion of the 200,000 £1 preference shares belonged to Camrose and his immediate family. The remaining preference shares were taken by Kemsley and Iliffe for a few years before Camrose and his family assumed complete ownership. Camrose said the nominal capital of the company bore no relation either to the sum that had been paid for the *Telegraph* in 1928, or the money that had been invested in a new building and plant since its purchase. The land, buildings and plant were valued at £1.3 million in 1939.

Camrose had devoted a lot of attention to the *Telegraph*, and after the partnership had broken up it continued to be his major preoccupation. Although it had never lost money in its history, its circulation was down to about 80,000. The company had been suffering from lack of investment, or perhaps from lack of intelligent investment. New printing plant had been installed in 1922 to replace the steam-driven presses used until then, yet Lord Burnham had refused to abandon the large size of paper usual in the nineteenth century but increasingly unpopular with readers in the twentieth. When the Berrys took over, Camrose decided that the plant so recently installed must be replaced; when this was done, and new offices had been built, he was ready to boost the circulation by reducing the price from 2d to 1d on 1 December 1930. The circulation, which was already recovering, doubled in a week, and continued to keep on growing, until it reached over 750,000 in 1939. Even Camrose was surprised at the market for the *Daily Telegraph*. He accomplished this striking success simply by maintaining a high standard of journalism, increasing the number of editorial pages and insisting on the widest possible coverage of home and foreign news by the *Telegraph*'s own staff. He refused to join in the battles of the circulation wars of the 1930s, when the national newspapers vied with one another in trying to attract readers by free gifts, insurance schemes and the like. There were, as Camrose put it, to be no 'cigars or nuts' from the *Telegraph* {Burnham (1955) 208} (though he was not so fastidious in the circulation war of Allied Newspapers with Northcliffe Newspapers). In 1937 he acquired the failing *Morning Post*, which he amalgamated with the *Telegraph*. During the war, in the face of severe restrictions on the supply of newsprint, Camrose sacrificed circulation rather than the quality of his newspaper, but once restrictions were relaxed after the war, the circulation passed the million mark in 1953.

Camrose was a tall, handsome, elegant man with a distinguished bearing and a quietly genial, but decisive manner. His staff respected his talents as a journalist and were not irked by his active interest in the content and appearance of the paper. Although he was perhaps readier to express blame than praise, the initial asperity of his comments would usually mellow a few hours later, and if he made a mistake himself, he was ready to acknowledge it. His main defect as a proprietor was his refusal to let any public man or movement of which he personally disapproved be mentioned favourably in his publications, even in a signed article. Named by his father (who failed to spell Ewart correctly) after the Liberal Prime Minister Gladstone, and ostensibly a Liberal for many years, he was by nature a Conservative. But he was not a 'political' proprietor, in the sense that Beaverbrook was, and Kemsley would have liked to be.

It was the general respect in which he was held in the publishing world, as well as his friendship with Churchill, that prompted his appointment soon after the outbreak of war to the post of Chief Assistant to the Minister and Controller of Press Relations in the Ministry of Information. However within a few weeks, in reconstructing the Ministry he had, as he told the House of Lords, 'organised himself out of a job' {PD Lords, 25 Oct 1939, col 1502}. He was raised to a viscountcy in the New Year Honours of 1941.

He was still taking an active part as editor-in-chief of the *Telegraph* when he died on 15 June 1954. He had already taken what he believed to be the most effective step for ensuring the preservation of the character of the newspaper he had done so much to build up, by transferring all the ordinary shares in Daily Telegraph Ltd to his sons Michael and Seymour. He had married Mary Agnes, daughter of Thomas Corns in 1905; they had four sons and four daughters. Camrose left £1,480,685 gross.

However good relations between them had been, Kemsley had had to live for over thirty years in the shadow of his elder brother. After the break-up of the Berry-Iliffe partnership in 1937 he found himself in control of Allied Newspapers, one of the two largest groups in Britain (the other being Rothermere's chain). The company owned or controlled eight morning, seven evening, six Sunday and six weekly newspapers in nine different centres. The chief provincial strongholds were Manchester, Glasgow, Cardiff, Tyneside and Sheffield. Kemsley was the largest shareholder, and by virtue of his own and his family's shareholding he had practically a controlling interest. For some years Iliffe retained a large holding in the company and was deputy chairman, but then decided to retire and sold his interests in Allied Newspapers to Kemsley, and his interests in the *Daily Telegraph* to Camrose.

Kemsley added a few more provincial papers to his group. By 1947 his papers had a combined morning circulation of 2,117,378, an evening circulation of 1,366,209 and a Sunday circulation of 5,675,919, and sold a total of 26.5 million copies a week (the comparable figures for the Rothermere group were 6,360,284 combined circulation, and 27,862,664 copies a week). The company's market value at that time was about £23 million.

Those witnesses before the Royal Commission on the Press in 1947-48 who expressed disquiet about the consequences for the freedom of the press of such concentration of ownership, usually singled out the Kemsley group for criticism. Far from taking pains to conceal from the readers of his newspapers that the papers were part of a chain owned by him, Kemsley had changed the name of Allied Newspapers to Kemsley Newspapers in 1943, and from 1945 (the year he became a viscount) each paper carried the words 'A Kemsley Newspaper' under the title block. Nor did he make any secret of his political conservatism. His editors were well acquainted with his political attitudes, and he appointed editors he felt he could work with. However, his critics before the Royal Commission failed to substantiate their claim that he issued political 'directives' to his editors. Kemsley never bought a paper for primarily political motives, whether to secure an outlet for propaganda or to silence an opponent. Nor did he ever buy a paper which he did not think he could run at a profit.

His desire to make his mark on public affairs, as Beaverbrook and Northcliffe had done, led him into some foolish situations. The most notorious was his visit to Hitler just before the outbreak of the war, a naive attempt to bring to fruition a scheme first proposed by the Nazis for an exchange of articles between British and German journals.

Kemsley's political conservatism is best seen as the exaggerated respect of an arriviste for political, social and cultural institutions. Camrose fitted easily and naturally into the world of clubs and country-houses; he was, for example, vice-commodore of the Royal Yacht Squadron from 1947 until his death. Kemsley was never quite at home, dearly though he would have liked to be so. The invariable, and rather dated, formality of his dress and manner, which made him look 'like some Edwardian grandee mixed with a suspicion of Groucho Marx' {Hobson et al (1972) xx}, the taking-up of one rich man's hobby after another, such as breeding prize cattle, giving shooting-parties, owning a yacht, without conviction or even passing interest, revealed his social unease. His exaggerated conventionality affected his newspapers, particularly his favourite *Sunday Times*, more than his political views did. Kemsley was never more pleased with his paper than when it included a signed article by some figure of social eminence and unassailable respectability (a bishop did very nicely) however dull the article might be. He once sacked an excellent art critic after an irate Royal Academician had complained to him that the man was too free in criticising the Academy's exhibitions. On such matters he would not listen to reason from his staff. On the dreadful day in September 1956, when it was learned that the great rival of the *Sunday Times*, the *Observer*, had surpassed its circulation of 625,000, Kemsley's staff replied to his rebuke with reproaches that his own prejudices were helping to make the paper less attractive than it could be. Kemsley was shaken by their criticisms, and never intervened to quite the same extent again.

Yet the journalists who worked for him respected him, for all his idiosyncracies. His passionate devotion to the *Sunday Times*, to its quality and its fortunes, infected the staff with the same enthusiasm. He was capable of flashes of journalistic intuition which would surprise them, and his judgment was often proved right. When he made a decision, he would implement it quickly. He wanted to sell his papers not by sensationalism, but by quality, by providing a thorough news service and attractive features. He attached great importance to the training of his journalists, and started the Kemsley Editorial Plan, forerunner of the National Council for the Training of Journalists. He wanted to set up a worldwide network of foreign correspondents — Ian Fleming had much to do with inspiring this idea and he ran the Foreign and Imperial News Service of Kemsley Newspapers (known as Mercury) before the success of his other creation, James Bond, diverted his attention. By then, Mercury had been much reduced in size and scope. The network had simply produced too much news for Kemsley's national papers and much had had to be placed in less suitable berths in his provincial papers. It was expensive, and not paying its way.

By the mid-1950s, other parts of Kemsley's group were beginning to give cause for concern. Too much of Kemsley's attention may have gone to the *Sunday Times*, too much money to the training schemes and the World News Service. Other papers in the Kemsley group, particularly the other national newspapers, were faltering, their sales declining, their advertising revenue disappearing. Rather than put money and effort into attempting to revive them, Kemsley sold them off. His only national daily, the *Daily Graphic*, was sold in 1952. In autumn 1955, he merged the *Sunday Chronicle* with the *Empire News*, and closed his biggest provincial paper, the *Daily Despatch*. The *Daily Mirror* took over his Manchester printing plant, and also acquired his Glasgow newspapers. In a statement issued to stockholders Kemsley said he thought the changes would 'streamline' the group and enable it to face the future 'with greater confidence and security'. But four years later, to the astonishment of Fleet Street, he sold all his holdings in Kemsley Newspapers, even his beloved *Sunday Times*, to Roy Thomson (qv).

Kemsley may have been becoming tired: he was seventy-six in 1959, and had told the Royal Commission ten years before that he was getting old and did not want any more responsibility. He could have handed over the direction of the company to his four surviving sons, who had worked with him for many years. But an unsuccessful attempt to take over Kemsley Newspapers had alarmed the family. They felt unable to sell any of their shareholding (about 40 per cent), while finding their income from the company insufficient to finance their stylish living in town and country.

The problem of death duties also loomed. The evident necessity for further closures of titles in the group, and a recent spate of labour troubles added to the attractions of disposing of the business.

Kemsley approached Roy Thomson and agreement was speedily reached. The arrangements for the sale were complicated, as Kemsley's was the larger company. Kemsley Newspapers bought Thomson's company Scottish Television, providing Thomson with a large block of shares in Kemsley Newspapers and some of the cash he needed to help him pay for Kemsley's shares. In the end, the Kemsley family realised about £5 million from the sale. Kemsley's sons stayed on to work under Thomson, but they could not adjust to the new, less patrician ways and within months all had resigned.

Kemsley came to regret having sold his papers; he retired completely from public life, and went to live in Monte Carlo where he died on 6 February 1968, leaving £310,866 gross.

He married twice. His first marriage was to Mary, the daughter of Horace G Holmes, JP, of Brondesbury Park, London; she died in 1928. They had six sons and a daughter. His second wife, whom he married in 1931, was Edith, daughter of E N Merandon du Plessis, of Mauritius; they had no children.

CHRISTINE SHAW

Writings:

Lord Camrose, *London Newspapers: Their Owners and Controllers* (Daily Telegraph & Morning Post, 1939).

PD, Lords, 5th ser 114, cols 1500-2 (25 Oct 1939).

—, *British Newspapers and Their Controllers* (Cassell, 1947).

Lord Kemsley, 'Introduction' *The Kemsley Manual of Journalism* (Cassell, 1947).

PP, RC on Press (1947-48) Cmd 7407, 7503.

Sources:

Unpublished

BCe.

Published

Linton Andrews and H A Taylor, *Lords and Laborers of the Press: Men Who Fashioned the Modern British Newspaper* (Southern Illinois University Press, 1970).

Lord Burnham, *Peterborough Court, the Story of the Daily Telegraph* (Cassell, 1955).

Colin R Coote, *Editorial: the Memoirs of Colin R Coote* (Eyre & Spottiswoode, 1965).

Hugh Cudlipp, *At Your Peril* (Weidenfeld & Nicolson, 1962).

Daily Telegraph 16 June 1954.

DNB.

Harold Hobson, Philip Knightley, and Leonard Russell, *The Pearl of Days: an Intimate Memoir of the Sunday Times 1822-1972* (Hamish Hamilton, 1972).

Memoranda of Evidence Submitted to the Royal Commission on the Press (5 vols, HMSO, 1947–8) 3.

George Murray, *The Press and the Public: the Story of the British Press Council* (Southern Illinois University Press, 1972).

PEP, *Report on the British Press* (1938).

PP, RC on Press (1961-62) Cmnd 1812.

William J Reader, *Bowater: A History* (Cambridge: Cambridge University Press, 1981).

Roy Thomson (Lord Thomson of Fleet), *After I Was Sixty* (Hamish Hamilton, 1975).

Times 16 June 1954, 7 Feb 1968.

WWW.

Sir Henry Bessemer (from J C Carr and W Taplin, History of the British Steel Industry, *Oxford: Basil Blackwell, 1962).*

BESSEMER, Sir Henry

(1813-1898)

Inventor, engineer and steel manufacturer

Henry Bessemer was born at Charlton, near Hitchin in Hertfordshire, on 19 January 1813. Descended from French Huguenot stock, his father, Anthony Bessemer, was himself a notable inventor and engineer who had been a member of the French Academy of Sciences and had attained a leading position in the Paris mint. At Charlton the elder Bessemer established a successful type-founding business in association with William Caslon.

Henry Bessemer, who is said to have inherited his father's inventing skill, after a period devoted to elementary education spent the whole of his early years developing his natural talents in his father's workshops. On 4 March 1830, at the age of seventeen, he came to London and began to put his ideas to practical effect. Though these were not always successful financially, they demonstrate the range and precociousness of his inventive gifts. There was work on the practical application of electro-plating; the embossing of metal cards and fabric; the invention of a

309

perforated die stamp; the construction of a type composing machine; the perfection of a process for making imitation Utrecht velvet; the manufacture of bronze powder and gold plate; the application of machinery to the processes of sugar refining; the production of glass plate; and the use of plumbago waste for making pencils.

In the business sphere he was less immediately successful. His invention in the 1830s of a perforated die stamp to eliminate fraud was taken up by the Government and Bessemer later claimed that it saved the country £100,000. Yet he received no reward for his work and the promise of an official appointment was not kept, though he was recognised years later by the belated bestowal of a knighthood. Bessemer apparently left government service considerably embittered.

An interest in gilt powder manufacture, however, which developed about 1840 and was carried on by Bessemer and a few trusted relatives in great secrecy for over forty years, brought rich dividends. From relatively cheap raw materials Bessemer was able to manufacture a product equal to imports costing £5 a pound, providing him with large profits which funded his later experiments in metallurgy.

The Crimean War focused Bessemer's attention indirectly on the properties of iron and steel. His previous work upon artillery had led to the development of a rotating shot. Either because there was a lack of interest from the War Office, or because his earlier differences made collaboration with the Government impossible, Bessemer took his invention to France to the Emperor Napoleon III. On trial there it soon became clear that the material available for gun construction was far too weak. Bessemer, therefore, directed his attention to the production of a stronger metal by the fusion of pig or cast iron with steel in a reverberatory or a cupola furnace. During the long series of experiments in 1855, the basic principle of the converting pneumatic process was discovered almost by accident. Noticing that some pieces of apparently unmelted pig iron, which had been exposed to an air blast, were in fact shells of decarbonised iron, Bessemer deduced that air alone was capable of producing malleable iron from pig iron without puddling. With the help of his brother-in-law, R D Allen, who supervised the practical operations at Bessemer's laboratory at Baxter House, St Pancras, a series of patents was taken out which described the mechanical details of the process and the tilting Bessemer converter. The experiments formed the basis of Bessemer's famous paper 'On the Manufacture of Iron and Steel without Fuel', which he read before the British Association meeting at Cheltenham, on 11 August 1856.

The paper caused a sensation, but the commercial exploitation of the process was delayed. Though Bessemer is said to have received £27,000 from ironmakers in different parts of the country, the early production runs were far from satisfactory and even completely unsuccessful. Bessemer was an engineer rather than a metallurgist and techniques for removing phosphorus (the significance of which was not initially appreciated) and regulating the oxygen and carbon content in the converter were still to be developed. In these circumstances Bessemer established a firm at Sheffield in 1859 to exploit the process. He was partnered by the Manchester engineering firm of William Galloway, which had supplied him with machinery for some years, by Robert

Bessemer Converter, which made the last Bessemer steel in England in 1974 at the Workington works of the British Steel Corporation, at the Kelham Island Museum, Sheffield (courtesy of G Tweedale).

Longsdon, whose source of income is not known, and by William D Allen. According to one authority the resources of the firm were as little as £12,000, of which Bessemer and Longsdon contributed about £6,000, W & J Galloway £5,000 and W D Allen £500. These were the means with which Bessemer, as managing partner, hoped to compete against the long-established Sheffield steel-making industry.

Bessemer later complained of the obstinacy of British steel-makers in refusing to try his ideas, a complaint which appears to be unjustified. Only after continuous and costly experiments had made it clear that the process depended on the use of phosphorus-free pig iron and that additions of manganese greatly improved the quality of metal produced in his converter, was Bessemer able to overcome the manufacturers' scepticism. Within two years of the foundation of Bessemer's pilot firm two of the leading Sheffield heavy steel makers, John Brown (qv) and Charles Cammell (qv), took out licences. By 1865 the Bessemer process had been adopted by all the steel-making countries of the world.

As Bessemer steel production rapidly increased world-wide, the pioneer firm remained fairly small. In 1895 the firm's paid up capital was only £96,000. But in 1873 Bessemer claimed that each of the partners in the Sheffield works had withdrawn in profit 81 times the amount of capital he originally subscribed. Not until Bessemer himself left in 1877, selling out his interest to W D Allen, did the firm become a limited company, and its shares were not marketed until 1889.

Bessemer also derived a considerable income from royalties from his patents, of which there were 43 relating to iron and steel in 1854-80 (between 1838 and 1894 Bessemer took out a total of 114 British patents). Royalties, which all went to Bessemer himself, amounted to no less than £200,000 a year during the later 1860s and by 1870 they probably totalled at least £1 million.

Once Bessemer's financial and business interest in steel manufacture ceased, he turned his attention to other matters, notably a mechanical contrivance for ships to mitigate the effects of sea-sickness. At Denmark Hill, London, he erected an observatory in his residence, and devoted a good deal of time to the construction of a telescope and the grinding of lenses. He laid out a diamond cutting and polishing plant for one of his grandsons. In the later years of his life Bessemer enjoyed a world-wide public reputation, although he made few contributions to technical literature apart from the occasional paper to bodies such as the Iron and Steel Institute, a few public addresses and letters to the *Times* and *Engineering*.

His numerous honours included the Albert gold medal of the Royal Society of Arts in 1872; the Telford gold medal and the Howard quinquennial prize of the Institution of Civil Engineers; and FRS in 1879. That year he was knighted for services to the Inland Revenue. He was honorary member of many foreign technical societies, and his reputation in the USA resulted in six manufacturing towns being named after him. In 1868 he became one of the founders of the Iron and Steel Institute, of which he was the president, 1871-73. On retiring from office he presented the Institute with an endowment for the award of a Bessemer gold medal.

Sir Henry Bessemer died at Denmark Hill on 15 March 1898, only a year after the death of his wife, Ann, daughter of Richard Allen of Amersham, whom he married in 1833. He was survived by two sons and a daughter. The gross value of his estate was £92,956, though he is said to have given a good deal of his money away in the last years of his life.

GEOFFREY TWEEDALE

Writings:

On the Resistance of the Atmosphere to Railway Trains, and a Means of Lessening the Same; together with an Account of some Improvements in Railway Carriage Axles (John Weale, 1847).

On a New System of Manufacturing Sugar from the .Cane, and its Advantages as Compared with the Method Generally Used in the West Indies, etc (W Tyler, 1852).

'On the Manufacture of Iron and Steel without Fuel' (Reprint of a paper read before the British Association, Cheltenham, 11 Aug 1856, and published in the *Times* 14 Aug).

'On the Manufacture of Malleable Iron & Steel' *Proceedings of the Institution of Civil Engineers* 18 (1858-59).

On the Manufacture of Malleable Cast Steel, its Progress and Employment as a Substitute for Wrought Iron (Pottsville, NY: B Bannan, 1865).

Presidential Address *JISI* 3 1871.

The Conveyancing of Merchandize on the Movable System, and Its Advantages as Compared with the Plateway when Forming Part of a Combined System of Road and Rail Conveyance (Bedford Press, 1883).

'On Some Early Forms of Bessemer Converters' *JISI* 1886.

'On the Manufacture of Continuous Sheets of Malleable Iron and Steel Direct from Fluid Metal' *ibid* 1891.

Sir Henry Bessemer, FRS: An Autobiography. With a Concluding Chapter by his Son, Henry Bessemer (Offices of *Engineering*, 1905).

Sources:

Unpublished

Glamorgan RO, Dowlais Iron Co Collection, Bessemer and Longsdon correspondence.

Imperial College Archives, record as a student at the Royal College of Chemistry, 1857-58, correspondence with Science & Art Department, etc, on the award of the Bessemer Medal at the Royal School of Mines, 1881. There is a complementary file at the PRO.

Kenneth C Barraclough, 'The Development of the Early Steel-Making Processes. An Essay in the History of Technology' (Sheffield PhD, 1981).

Published

F Baedeker, *Ueber das Bessemer'sche Verfahre* (Hagen, 1857).

Alan Birch, *The Economic History of the British Iron and Steel Industry 1784-1879. Essays in Industrial and Economic History with Special Reference to the Development of Technology* (Frank Cass, 1967).

John N Boucher, *William Kelly: a True History of the So-Called Bessemer Process* (Greenburg, Pa: The Author, 1924).

Duncan L Burn, *The Economic History of Steel Making, 1867-1939. A Study in Competition* (Cambridge: Cambridge University Press, 1940).

James C Carr and Walter Taplin, *A History of the British Steel Industry* (Oxford: Blackwell, 1962).

William H Chaloner, *People and Industries* (Frank Cass, 1963).

DNB.

James Dredge, 'Sir Henry Bessemer' *Transactions of the American Society of Mechanical Engineers 19* (1898).

Jan Dusánek, *Bessemerování. (A Descriptive and Statistical Account of the Inventions of Sir H Bessemer)* (Prague, 1870).

Charlotte J Erickson, *British Industrialists: Steel and Hosiery, 1850-1950* (Cambridge: Cambridge University Press, 1959).

Fortunes Made in Business (4 vols, Sampson Low & Co, 1884-87).

William T Jeans, *The Creators of the Age of Steel* (Chapman & Hall, 1884).

Ferdinand Kohn, *Iron and Steel Manufacture* (McKenzie, 1869).

Ernest F Lange, *Bessemer, Goransson and Mushet. A Contribution to Technical History* (Reprint from *Memoirs* of the Manchester Literary and Philosophical Society 57 (1913)).

Jeanne McHugh, *Alexander Holley and the Makers of Steel* (Baltimore: Johns Hopkins University Press, 1980).

Robert F Mushet, *The Bessemer-Mushet Process, or Manufacture of Cheap Steel* (Cheltenham: J J Banks, 1883).

Fred M Osborn, *The Story of the Mushets* (Thomas Nelson, 1952).

John Percy, *Metallurgy: The Art of Extracting Metals from their Ores, and Adapting them to Various Purposes of Manufacture* (John Murray, 1864).

James Riley, 'The Rise and Progress of the Scotch Steel Trade' *JISI* (1885).

Eric N Simons, 'Pioneers of the Modern Steel Industry' *Murex Review* 1 (1950).

Kenneth Warren, 'The Sheffield Rail Trade, 1861-1930: An Episode in the Locational History of the British Steel Industry', *Institute of British Geographers Transactions* 34 (1964).

WWW.

BEST, Robert Hall

(1843-1925)

Manufacturer of brass light fittings

Robert Hall Best was born at Ludgate Hill, Birmingham on 15 April 1843, the son of Robert Best, a Birmingham lamp manufacturer, and his wife Lucy, daughter of Joseph Hall, the ironmaster. He attended a school run by Dr Henry Hopkins in Summerhill Terrace and left at fifteen with a poor report in all subjects except dancing, though his practical and inventive bent was already evident. He went straight into the family business, but was left to pick up his knowledge without any serious training. In 1862 he went to Germany to learn the language and this proved to be very significant for his subsequent career. In particular, he made himself familiar with commercial German and established an understanding, perhaps somewhat romanticised over the years, of the German people and their institutions.

The following year his father died, just after the firm of Best & Hobson had moved into larger premises, the Great Bridge Works in Charlotte Street. Hobson, the manager and partner in the firm, tried to expand the business, by increasing production and by factoring bought-in items including beer engines, water closets and jewellery. In 1867 the firm failed with a deficit of over £7,000. Best was saved by the intervention of a next-door neighbour who bought up the stock and patterns of the bankrupt firm and installed his son, Harry Lloyd, as partner in the new firm of Best & Lloyd.

Best's approach to business was shaped by this early experience. He determined to preserve his independence from banks and establish the security of the business. However, once a modest level of profits had been secured his interest lay primarily in invention, design and the technical and artistic execution of the work. He also used the slack periods of the year for travel with a view to obtaining sales and commercial intelligence abroad. At one point his passport recorded over 200 crossings of the German frontier. He took over direct selling to Germany, paying off the agent who had acted for him for over a decade. Between 1863 and 1877 the firm was profitable, but in 1878, when he bought out his partner as depression began to bite, he made a loss of £1,600.

Best had a cautious, incremental approach to production and organisation. At no point did he make major changes in production processes or plant layout, preferring to make marginal adjustments to the existing site. The one experiment, taking over an adjacent red lead mill, had more to do with relationships with Best's ex-partner and Best's insatiable scientific curiosity, than with dynamic business expansion, though the new acquisition was run profitably and sold without loss in 1903. On the single occasion when major alterations were proposed for the main site by a new works manager (appointed in 1905 and widely believed to be an American), Best turned down the suggestion in favour of further piecemeal modifications of plant and processes. His dread of becoming dependent once again on outside finance seems to have been the key to this decision.

Yet the profitability of the firm hinged on a successful product innovation with the patenting of the 'Surprise' pendant gas mantle in 1893. This ingenious fitting was adjustable in both vertical and horizontal planes and was devised in response to his mother's need for an arrangement which would allow her to read in different parts of a room. But it was perfected at a time when the profits of the firm had fallen to almost zero on a turnover of £14,000. No doubt the general depression in British industry contributed to the poor performance of the firm in that year, but with the aid of the Surprise pendant there was an extraordinary recovery to a profit of £8,134 on sales of £40,325 by 1900.

Best himself acted as designer, manager and salesman for the firm until the turn of the century. Thereafter the expansion of the business led to specialist appointments and Best became more heavily involved in social, educational and welfare activities. In 1905 he led a delegation consisting of himself, W J Davis, Secretary of the Brassworkers' Union, and Charles Perks, of the Hospital Saturday charitable fund, to Berlin to study the conditions of the brass workers in that city. On their return, they published *The Brassworkers of Berlin and Birmingham: a Comparison*, which established Best's public reputation as a Germanophile social investigator. The work itself was somewhat uncritical of Berlin conditions but it contributed to the upsurge of interest in German institutions and social policies, which was the powerful background influence (both positively and negatively) on the development of social reform in Britain at the central and local level in the early years of this century. In Birmingham, Best advocated the introduction of the Elberfeld system of poor relief through the City Aid Society. Thereafter, he took up a more specific interest in post-school education through the influence of Dr Georg Kerschensteiner, the Director of Education in Munich. Through him, Best met C K Ogden, then a recent Cambridge graduate, and together they wrote *The Problem of the Continuation School and Its Successful Solution in Germany: A Consecutive Policy*, which held the trade-related schools of Munich up for emulation to the city of Birmingham, in which the skilled and craft trades still had such a dominant place. His efforts in this direction were cut short by the outbreak of the First World War, which only temporarily dampened Best's enthusiasm for things German. By then he was becoming less deeply involved in the business, though he watched over it until his death.

Best lost one son in the war, but the other survived to take over the firm and write the impressive biography on which most subsequent assessment of Robert Hall Best is based. As an employer Best was almost fanatical in his concern for standards of workmanship, but he was a humane and considerate man. Through his friendship for W J Davis he was involved in regulating conditions in the brass trades and the firm pioneered health insurance benefits beyond those provided under the National Insurance Act of 1911. As a businessman, he was an undoubted success by means which may have smacked less of the textbook than the improvisation and tactical skills of the first generation of British industrialists.

He married Maud Short, the daughter of an accountant, ca 1897; they had two sons. Best died on 1 June 1925 leaving £85,280 gross.

ROY HAY

Writings:

(with W J Davis and C Perks) *The Brassworkers of Berlin and Birmingham: A Comparison* (P S King, 1905).

The City Aid and its Future (Birmingham, 1906).

(with C K Ogden) *The Problem of the Day Continuation School and Its Successful Solution in Germany: A Consecutive Policy* (P S King, 1914).

Sources:

Unpublished

Birmingham Chamber of Commerce, Minutes (1900-14).

'A Short Life and a Gay One: A Biography of Frank Behrens Best 1893-1917' (2 vols, typescript, 1969).

BCe.

PrC.

Published

Robert Dudley Best, *Brass Chandelier* (Unwin, 1940).

Birmingham Chamber of Commerce Journal 1906-14.

Birmingham Mail 2, 4 June 1925.

Birmingham Post 2 June 1925.

Robert H Coats, *In Memoriam: Robert Hall Best* (Birmingham: Kynoch Press, 1925).

John W Hall, *The Life and Work of Joseph Hall* (Stourbridge: Mark & Moody, 1916).

Roy Hay, 'The British Business Community, Social Insurance and the German Example' in W J Mommsen (ed), *The Emergence of the Welfare State in Britain and Germany, 1850-1950* (Croom Helm, 1981).

P W Kingsford, 'R H Best, 1843-1925' *The Manager* 24 (July 1956).

Times 12, 25 Jan 1906.

BETTMANN, Siegfried

(1863-1951)

Motor cycle manufacturer

Siegfried Bettmann was born in Nuremburg, Bavaria on 18 April 1863, the only son of Meyer Bettmann, estate manager for a wealthy Bavarian landowner, and Sophie Weil. Of Jewish origin, Mayer Bettmann was himself sufficiently wealthy to be able to give young Siegfried a very good education and some assistance when he left Germany for London in November 1884. Siegfried, partly educated in Paris, spoke French and English, in addition to his native German. These skills secured him a job with Kelly's Directories, corresponding with continental manufacturers.

Finding the work dull, he left after six months, but over the next twelve months he rapidly moved from employee to owner. Kelly's work brought him a number of useful contacts. Among them was the White Sewing Machine Co of USA, whose London manager engaged Siegfried Bettmann as a commercial traveller, operating in Europe and North Africa. Having made a considerable number of commercial contacts Bettmann left the White Co and set himself up in business under the style of 'S Bettmann & Co', though at first he did not formally register his company. As an import-export agent, he mainly imported sewing machines manufactured by Biesolt & Lock, of Meissen, in Germany.

To balance this trade, Bettmann decided to export British-made bicycles, taking advantage of the prevailing cycling boom. Initially, the cycles were made for him by a Birmingham jobbing-engineering concern named William Andrews, and carried a Bettmann label, but Siegfried soon realised that sales would improve with a distinctly British trademark. The name he chose was Triumph, and in late 1885 S Bettmann & Co became the Triumph Cycle Co.

Two years later, he was joined by Maurice Schulte, a trained engineer, also from Nuremberg; from this time Triumph's fortunes improved markedly. Schulte pointed out to his partner that if the firm were to expand, it would be necessary to move from factoring into actual manufacture, and to relocate in Coventry, the centre of the British cycle trade.

Schulte took the initiative. He found suitable premises, a former ribbon factory in Much Park Street, Coventry, owned by the mayor of the city, Alderman Tomson; and the latter was persuaded to put finance into Triumph when it became a limited company.

By 1914 Bettmann had added the chairmanship of the Standard Motor Co to his duties as chairman and managing director of Triumph (in this way foreshadowing a merger that was still many years in the future) but anti-German hysteria during the First World War caused him to relinquish that position.

Relations between Bettmann and his former partner, Schulte, deteriorated so much by 1919 that the two were barely on speaking terms. Indeed, it was Bettmann who used his influence with the Triumph board to ask for Schulte's resignation (though the blow was softened by a golden handshake of £15,000).

Triumph had added motor cycles to their bicycle production in 1902 and, during the First World War, produced 30,000 motor cycles for the British and Allied forces. A further move came in 1922, when Bettmann was instrumental in adding a light car to the range. By that time the main production had moved to Priory Street, Coventry (although the original Much Park Street premises were retained for sidecar production), but these works were unsuited to car manufacture.

Bettmann had earlier talked to the Hillman concern, with a view to taking over their plant; instead, Triumph acquired the disused Dawson car factory in Clay Lane and, gradually, this became the centre of Triumph car manufacture while cycles and motor cycles continued at Priory Street.

With advancing years, Siegfried Bettmann relinquished the reins, though he was still vice-chairman in 1936 when the board decided to drop motor cycle production (the bicycle side had already been sold off) and concentrate on cars. Bettmann was not in agreement with this decision, and rather than see Triumph motor cycles disappear from the market he was instrumental in interesting John Y Sangster (qv), who already owned Ariel Motors, in taking over this side of the business.

In consequence, the Triumph car and motor cycle sides underwent complete divorce and a new firm, Triumph Engineering Ltd, was formed under Sangster's direction, to acquire Triumph motor cycle rights and continue production at Priory Street. Although he was now seventy-three, Siegfried Bettmann accepted chairmanship of Triumph Engineering, relinquishing his contact with the Triumph Motor Co. This was an astute move on the part of Sangster, for it emphasised the new firm's link with the past successful history of Triumph motor cycles, and gave confidence to dealers and customers alike that the old traditions would be maintained.

Bettmann's service with Triumph Engineering continued for only a short period, but it was of sufficient duration to see the new concern safely launched on its way to still greater glory. Ironically, the ertswhile car side of the business now ran into difficulty, and by 1939 was in the hands of the receivers, from which rescue was eventually effected. By then, though, Siegfried Bettmann had long retired from any active connection.

In the Coventry business community Bettmann took an active role as founder and president of Coventry's Chamber of Commerce. He also took a keen interest in local Coventry politics: from 1903 he was a Warwickshire JP and by 1907 he had become a Liberal member of the city council. His political activity culminated in his election as mayor of Coventry in 1913, an office he still held when the First World War broke out a year later. In the early 1920s his politics veered from Liberalism to Labour, and he later became a close friend of Ramsay MacDonald. He was a prominent freemason and founder and first-elected master of St John's Lodge, Coventry.

He married Annie Mayrick, from Shifnal, Shropshire in 1895. Bettmann died on 23 September 1951 leaving £145,204 gross.

R F CURRIE

Sources:

Unpublished

Triumph Motorcycles (Meriden) Ltd (Coventry), company archives.

PrC.

Published

Richard Langworth and Graham Robson, *Triumph Cars, The Complete 75-year History* (Motor Racing Publications Ltd, 1979).

Harry W Louis and Robert F Currie, *The Story of the Triumph Motor Cycles* (Cambridge: Patrick Stephens Ltd, 1975).

Coventry Evening Telegraph 24 Sept, 20 Dec 1951.

Coventry Standard 5 Sept 1924.

WWW.

Francis A Bevan (courtesy of Barclays Bank Ltd).

BEVAN, Francis Augustus

(1840-1919)

Clearing banker

Francis Augustus Bevan was born in Harley Street, London, on 17 January 1840, the second son of Robert Cooper Lee Bevan of Fosbury and Trent Park, and his first wife Lady Agneta Elizabeth Yorke, daughter of the Fourth Earl of Hardwicke. He was educated at Harrow, and after two years' foreign travel joined the banking partnership of Barclay, Bevan & Tritton, with which his family had been associated since 1767.

His father was the recognised leader of the London private bankers for many years, and chairman of the London Clearing Bankers from 1874 until his death in 1890; the son, who became the senior partner on his father's death, was to preside over one of the most remarkable banking developments of the period.

For many years the joint stock banks had made steady progress at the expense of the old private partnerships, which found it increasingly difficult to meet the requirements of the larger scale business that was developing throughout the century. A great many of their number were absorbed by joint stock competitors; and some of the Quaker bankers in East Anglia, who had long done business with one another and were often interconnected by marriage, discussed the possibility of frustrating piecemeal absorption by forming their own combination. There were long negotiations, which threatened to come to nothing. But in due course the Barclays in London agreed to merge with the Gurneys in Norfolk and the Backhouses in Darlington, and this alliance formed a strong nucleus around which the smaller Quaker banks were glad to group themselves. So in 1896 Barclay & Co Ltd was incorporated, combining twenty private banks with, for the most part, a common Quaker background, and combined assets of £29 million.

The directors of the new company were the partners of the combining banks, and they were also local directors, each in his old area. Bevan, as the senior Lombard Street partner, was the natural choice as chairman of this unusual gathering of largely independent-minded men. His relaxed, easy-going temperament eased what might have been a difficult position; it also meant that he was prepared to give a free hand, and consistent support and encouragement, to the new bank's first secretary, F C Goodenough (qv) who was largely to shape the new bank, and who was to succeed Bevan when the latter retired from the chairmanship in 1916.

In its first twenty years Barclays followed the example of the earlier joint stock banks, and extended its territorial cover by the acquisition of 17 other private banks. The year of Bevan's retirement, 1916, saw Barclays' first purchase of a joint stock bank, the United Counties, which began the final series of amalgamations which by the end of the decade made Barclays one of the Big Five. Barclays' total assets at the end of 1916 amounted to £117 million.

Bevan, who remained a director of the bank until his death, was a Lieutenant for the City of London, a JP and, in 1899, High Sheriff of Middlesex. His interests outside the bank were mainly associated with Evangelical and charitable enterprises. He was the treasurer of St Peter's Hospital, Covent Garden, and was active in the work of the London City Mission, the Church Patronage Trust and Christ's Hospital. The seriousness of purpose with which he undertook such work was leavened by a strong sense of humour. His recreations were music and art, cricket and horses, and he had a pioneering interest in motoring.

Bevan married firstly in 1862 Elizabeth Marianne (d 1863), daughter of Lord Charles James Fox Russell, by whom he had one son; secondly, in 1866 Constance (d 1872), daughter of Sir James Weir Hogg, Bt, by whom he had five sons, one being Gerard Lee Bevan (qv); and lastly, in 1876, Maria (d 1903), daughter of John Trotter, of Dyrham Park, Barnet, by whom he had three daughters. He died on 31 August 1919, leaving £420,921 gross.

EYNON SMART

Sources:

Unpublished

Information from T H Bevan.

MCe.

PrC.

Published

Anthony W Tuke and P W Matthews, *History of Barclays Bank Ltd* (Blades, East & Blades Ltd, 1926).

WWW.

BEVAN, Gerard Lee

(1869-1936)

Financier

Gerard Lee Bevan was born in Kensington, London on 9 November 1869, the fourth son of Francis Augustus Bevan (qv), the chairman of Barclays

Bank, and his wife Constance née Begg. He was educated at Eton (1883-88) and went up to Trinity College, Cambridge in 1889 (BA 1892), before working for two years with Barclays Bank.

In 1893 he became partner in the stockbroking firm of Ellis & Co formed in 1778. In 1912, when he owned 54 per cent of the capital of Ellis, Bevan became senior partner. Thereafter his four junior partners, the Hon Reginald Fellowes (1884-1953), Harold H Gordon, Neville F O'Brien and Frederick Tootal, had little part in the conduct of the firm. Although its turnover was at one time estimated at £12 million per annum, in the middle of the First World War Bevan lauched Ellis into heavy speculation on their own account in various industrial securities.

In 1916 Ellis & Co bought a large shareholding in the City Equitable Fire Insurance Co formed in 1908 with issued capital of £75,000 to conduct business in re-insurance. It had not been conspicuously careful, and in 1913 its declared balance on a premium income of £83,443 was only £6,853. Bevan became chairman of City Equitable in 1916, bringing on to the board with him Peter Haig-Thomas, who was then managing the Cambrian Colliery group while his uncle D A Thomas (qv) held wartime government office. From the outset Bevan dominated the board, whose other members comprised a military courtier called Sir Douglas Dawson (1854-1933), Lord Ribblesdale (1854-1925) and Lord March and Kinrara, afterwards Eighth Duke of Richmond and Gordon (1870-1935). City Equitable, like other re-insurance companies, enjoyed a war boom. Its premium income on fire account rose from £458,000 in 1917-18 to £1,190,000 in 1919-20 and £2,072,516 in 1920-21. Other business was almost equally good, and for 1919-20 and 1920-21 preference dividends were paid of 50 and 62.5 per cent and ordinary dividends amounted to 200 and 250 per cent. Ellis & Bevan's nominees held 85 per cent of the preference and 95 per cent of the ordinary shares, which at the height of the post-war boom were worth £800,000. City Equitable's profits were due to war conditions, such as the disappearance of re-insurance facilities previously offered by German and other continental companies, and the boom in marine insurance as premiums and insurance values escalated. Bevan's purchase of the company was therefore in a sense war-time profiteering which was bound to collapse in the 1920s with the restoration of traditional overseas reinsurance facilities and the collapse in marine insurance values.

However, with the pricking of the boom, and the subsequent industrial depression, the Ellis firm entered desperate straits. As early as February 1919 Bevan arranged for it to borrow £320,000 from City Equitable: by February 1921 the debt was £911,000 of which more than half was completely unsecured. From the outset in 1919 Bevan doctored City Equitable's balance-sheet. The loan of £320,000 was entered at £51,000 in the balance sheet, and the company's assets were shown as including £200,000 Treasury Bills which were not in fact their property. The accounts for 1920 and 1921 also included fictitious temporary ownership of Treasury Bills in City Equitable's published assets. Later in 1920-21 Bevan had City Equitable buy control of three small insurance offices, First National Reinsurance (formed 1919), Greater Britain (formed 1918) and the City of London (formed 1908), whose investments he then skimmed to support the accelerating deficit of both Ellis and City Equitable.

Bevan wound a skein of financial perplexities which it was impossible to unravel. In July 1921 he raised more cash by floating the City Equitable Associated Co which was to acquire the assets of the three new subsidiaries. The prospectus for the 8 per cent participating preference shares totalling £250,000 of course did not disclose the fraudulent state of the Ellis and City Equitable accounts. He was aided in this and his other deceptions by Edmund Mansell, manager of City Equitable since 1915, who by 1921 had obtained with Bevan's connivance an overdraft of £110,000 on his house from his employers, together with an annual salary of £5,000 plus 4 per cent commission on future underwriting profits.

Bevan's ruses could not save his companies from the accumulating losses of his reckless industrial investments, and in January 1922 rumours of the position led to a collapse in the price of City Equitable shares. On 3 February the company filed for bankruptcy, on 8 February Bevan disappeared and on 16 February the Ellis firm was hammered on the Stock Exchange and also went bankrupt. Apart from their debt to City Equitable of £911,000, Ellis owed £240,000 to the Lombard Street head office of Barclays Bank, and the total shortfall of the Bevan companies was finally estimated at almost £3 million. The collapse was attended by sensational publicity, not least as it coincided with the French scandal of the Banque Industrielle de Chine and with the downfall of Horatio Bottomley (qv), but had little effect on the Stock Exchange because of its rules prohibiting contango dealing.

Bevan flew to Paris, and after a hunt across Europe was arrested on 14 June in Vienna whence he was trying to reach Russia. He was disguised and using a passport in the name of Leon Vernier of Lille. After serving two months' imprisonment in Austria, he was tried at the Old Bailey in November 1922 on sixteen counts of publishing false balance sheets and fraudulent conversion, and was sentenced to seven years' penal servitude. Released from prison in 1928, he went to France and in 1929 paid Duckworths to publish a volume of his prison verse, in the manner of Swinburne, entitled *Russet and Asp*. Although to the knowledge of Antony Powell of Duckworths, only three copies were sold, London newspapers mysteriously were persuaded to put it on their published lists of bestsellers for 1929.

At the time of his downfall Bevan was part owner of a Brazilian ranch in which City Equitable invested £150,000, and was also a director of Leyland Motors, the Argentinian subsidiary of Harrods department store, Agricultural Industries Co, Chilian Stores, South American Stores and the South Brazil Electric Co. In 1918 he had arranged for Ellis's to take an option on Claridges Hotel in Paris whose capital he then reorganised and to whom City Equitable later advanced £59,000. Bevan was also involved in the South American holdings of a Mersey shipbuilder, Sir Harry Grayson (1865-1951), who became a director of City Equitable in 1917.

Bevan attributed the industrial slump which was his undoing chiefly to the high cost of coal, backed by foreign exchange difficulties and the 'nightmare of taxation'. In October 1921 he advocated that his wife's cousin, the Chancellor of the Exchequer, should cut income tax by two shillings and practise deficit budgeting until 1924 in order to revive British industry. 'It will pay us better to make some temporary addition to our indebtedness than to allow the whole fabric of industry to be crushed', he wrote in a letter in the *Times* of 12 October 1921, which makes ironic reading in retrospect. His office in Cornhill, his house off Park Lane, his apartment in the Carlton Hotel and his Wiltshire home were notably luxurious, and he had the sybaritic tastes of Whitaker Wright (qv). Like Wright, Bevan could not have sustained his frauds without the naïveté and ignorance of his aristocratic guinea-pig directors or the laxity of his accountant.

> 'The extraordinary feature of the whole affair is that nobody ... got anything out of the irregularities ... Bevan continued in the course of a year or two, by mismanagement quite incredible in its fatuity, to destroy a reinsurance company ... in fairly good repute, and to bring to bankruptcy one of the oldest firms in the Stock Exchange ... It was not for personal gain, seeing that he was himself destroyed in the general ruin, and fled the country practically penniless ... City Equitable ... failed because the assets had been muddled away' {*Economist* 9 Dec 1922}.

Bevan was an elegant, plausible man who traded on his family connections and whose hereditary privileges left him arrogant, vain and irresponsible.

Bevan married first, in 1893, Sophie (1867-1941), daughter of John Arthur Kenrick, hardware manufacturer, of Berrow Court, Edgbaston, and niece of Joseph Chamberlain (qv). By her he had two daughters. Bevan had many affairs with young women which may have contributed to the expenses which led him to fraud. His marriage was dissolved in 1928, and in April of that year he married Marie Letitia Pertuisot, a Parisian dancer who had become his mistress in 1916.

In the 1930s Bevan emigrated to Cuba and managed a distillery at Havana, where he died of sleeping sickness on 24 April 1936.

R P T DAVENPORT-HINES

Writings:

letters on trade depression *Times* 12 Oct 1921 and *Times Trade Supplement* 15 Oct 1921.

Russet and Asp (Duckworth, 1929).

Sources:

Published

Anthony D Powell, *The Strangers Are All Gone* (Heinemann, 1982).

Aylmer Vallance, *Very Private Enterprise* (Thames & Hudson, 1955).

Burke's Landed Gentry 1965.

Economist 21, 28 Jan, 18 Feb, 9 Dec 1922.

Times 1922 *passim*.

Joseph Bibby (courtesy of J Bibby & Sons PLC).

BIBBY, Joseph

(1851-1940)

Feedingstuff and food manufacturer

Joseph Bibby was born at Quernmore near Lancaster on 12 January 1851, the second of three sons of James Bibby, who owned a water-driven corn mill at Quernmore and a small farm, and of his wife Amelia née Barnett. His father was a leading member of the local Methodist community and brought up his sons as Methodists.

Joseph attended a local elementary school until the age of ten and then went to Cawthorne's Endowed School, Abbeystead, in the neighbouring valley of Wyresdale. His full-time education finished when he left school at the age of fourteen but he attended evening classes which gave him a reasonable proficiency in French and a smattering of German.

On leaving school he immediately joined his father in the family milling business and was given the task of managing a small warehouse in Lancaster which had been bought a few months previously. This gave him his first experience of commerce and although he enjoyed it he seems to have found the horizons of Lancaster too limited. In the autumn of 1872, shortly before he reached the age of twenty-two, he took a steerage passage to Canada but after spending some six months in Canada and the United States he was persuaded by his father to return home. During the next few years Joseph and his younger brother, James, increasingly took over the running of the corn milling business from their father and in 1878, when they were aged respectively twenty-seven and twenty-five, James Bibby Sr, then aged sixty-six, took them into partnership under the style of J Bibby & Sons.

Shortly before the formation of the partnership Joseph Bibby had begun to experiment with what later came to be known as 'compound feeds' for farm livestock and persuaded his father and brother to embark on their manufacture. Although he was not the originator of the idea of making compound feeds, Joseph's bold vision, enthusiasm and flair for marketing, backed up by his brother James's sound commercial and administrative skills, soon made J Bibby & Sons one of the most successful pioneers of the feed compounding industry. A mill for the production of the new feeds was opened in Lancaster in 1882. The original corn milling business was discontinued in 1885 and at about the same time a compounding mill in Liverpool was started which at first supplemented, and by 1888 had replaced, the mill in Lancaster. Following a serious fire in 1892 the Liverpool mill was rebuilt and by the turn of the century had a capacity of some 3,000 tons per week of feeds for farm animals. The firm also extended its activities by a process of vertical integration into oilseed crushing and the production of soap. These activities, and others which were added after, were located on the same site in Liverpool, a few hundred yards away from the docks through which many of the raw materials for them were imported.

Throughout the period of rapid expansion which continued up to the beginning of the First World War Joseph Bibby retained responsibility for the sale of the firm's feeds through a network of agents and merchants covering the whole of the UK. However he was often heard to remark that had it not been for an accident of birth making him a miller he would certainly have become a journalist, and he began to devote an increasing proportion of his time to writing. From 1896 until 1905 he edited *Bibby's Quarterly*. This was originally aimed at a primarily rural readership and intended at least in part as a vehicle for promoting the firm's products but it later became increasingly literary, artistic and philosophical in its content. The *Quarterly* was followed from 1906 until 1922 by *Bibby's Annual*, the work with which Joseph Bibby's name is generally associated and which achieved national fame both for its literary substance and for the quality of its full-colour reproductions of famous paintings.

Early in life Joseph Bibby had become attracted to the teachings of the Theosophical Society and in 1889 he became an active member. *Bibby's Annual* became an important platform for the promotion of Theosophical beliefs. Annie Besant, one of the founders of the Society, was a frequent contributor.

As well as numerous articles, some under his own name and some under pseudonyms, in the *Annual* and the *Quarterly*, Joseph Bibby wrote and published a number of illustrated monographs and pamphlets on such subjects as capitalism and socialism, peace and prosperity, employment and industrial relations and philosophy. Although he was interested in politics in the wider sense, party politics do not seem to have interested him greatly. However he served in 1904-11 as a Liberal member of Liverpool City Council, representing the Exchange Ward. He was elected in spite of a pledge to support any measure designed to bring about a reduction in the number of drinking saloons in the neighbourhood. He also became a JP for the City of Liverpool in 1908.

J Bibby & Sons was registered as a private limited company in 1914 with an issued capital of £500,000. James Bibby, Joseph's younger brother, became chairman and Joseph, then aged sixty-three, became vice-chairman. The rate of growth in feeds was severely checked by the war but seed-crushing flourished and the company weathered the post-war depression without too much difficulty. During the 1920s it diversified further by entering into vegetable oil refining and also carried out an ambitious rebuilding of the feed mill. James Bibby died in 1928 and Joseph succeeded him as chairman. Under Joseph's chairmanship, which continued until his death, the company introduced 'Trex', the highly successful vegetable cooking fat which made Bibbys as well known to the British housewife as it had long been to the British farmer. In the same period Bibbys also entered the paper industry. By 1940 the net assets of the company had increased to some £3 million and it employed some 5,000 people.

Joseph Bibby was not a typical capitalist of the nineteenth century. Though bold, forceful and enthusiastic in character, he would never have claimed to possess financial acumen. He was a generous man but in his personal habits thrifty and austere, abstaining always from alcohol and becoming a vegetarian on joining the Theosophical Society. His management style was paternalistic and during his lifetime the company introduced pensions for all employees, family allowances, subsidized canteen meals, joint consultation and most aspects of what was then known as welfare.

Joseph Bibby died at Bidston, Birkenhead, on 11 March 1940. He was survived by his wife, Ruth née Pye, whom he had married in 1881, and by three of his five sons, all of whom were directors of the company, and by one of his two daughters. He left £289,475 gross.

J B BIBBY *and* C L BIBBY

Writings:

Bibby's Quarterly (1896-1905).

Bibby's Annual (1902-1922, and 1936).

A Friendly Talk with Socialists and Others (Liverpool: P P Press, 1915).

The War: its Unseen Cause and Some of its Lessons (Liverpool: J Bibby & Sons, 1915).

Letters on Socialism (Liverpool: P P Press, 1915).

Social Progress. A Study in Family and Industrial Relationships (Liverpool: J Bibby & Sons, 1926).

Capitalism, Socialism and Unemployment (Liverpool: J Bibby & Sons, 1929).

Towards the Light (Liverpool: J Bibby & Sons, 1932).

On Relative Values (Liverpool: J Bibby & Sons, 1932).

Sources:

Unpublished

BCe.

Published

John B Bibby and Charles L Bibby, *A Miller's Tale. A History of J Bibby & Sons Ltd* (Liverpool: J Bibby & Sons, 1978).

John B Bibby, *The Bibbys of Conder Mill and their Descendants* (1979).

William T Stead, 'Joseph Bibby: Seed-crusher and Preacher' *Review of Reviews* June 1908.

WWW.

BICESTER, 1st Lord Bicester

see **SMITH, Vivian Hugh**

BIGELOW, Arthur Perkins

(ca 1880-1941)

Supplier of office towel services

Arthur Perkins Bigelow was born in Canada about 1880. Nothing is known of his background or parents. His first job as a soap salesman in New York brought him into contact with the new industry of office linen supply, which, although rapidly expanding in the USA, was still virtually unheard of in England. The potential demand for such an industry, however, as Bigelow realised, was vast. Over the second half of the nineteenth century the growth of banks, insurance houses and department stores in particular had resulted in a phenomenal rise in the office population, especially in the City of London. The City, far dirtier than it is today, since coal was then the main fuel used, had only one small towel supplier, the Clean Towel Supply Co, founded in 1889, which restricted its services to just a few large customers. Aware of their prospects, Bigelow and his wife sailed for England, where they arrived in April 1903.

On arrival in London, Bigelow at once purchased a supply of hand towels and obtained a laundering contract with the Kings Cross Laundry. His wife then embroidered each towel with the customer's initial (thus the company name 'Initial'), offering the customer the double advantage of a personalised service and a safeguard against infectious diseases and epidemics which might be spread through shared linen.

At first just Bigelow and his wife worked from a small rented room on the fifth floor of a Holborn office block; he acted as sales and delivery man, while she kept the books and sorted, packed and embroidered the towels, which, every evening, Bigelow took personally to the Kings Cross Laundry, at the same time collecting fresh supplies. With his modest charges (two towels changed weekly and a constant replenishment of soap for 4d a week), Bigelow soon earned himself a good reputation in the City and West End and, within two years, was employing three routemen (earning 30s a week), who collected and delivered by box tricycle. To increase his clientele, he recruited window-cleaners, office-cleaners and chimney-sweepers to canvass his service on a commission basis. In June

1905 he moved to larger premises in Great Sutton Street, Clerkenwell, which he rented for £200 a year.

The business continued to grow steadily and the new demand for linen supply encouraged other firms to set up in the same business. Generally, however, these did not prosper, since Bigelow kept a watchful eye on their growth and, once they had acquired sufficient local custom and begun to run into difficulties, bought them out and turned them into Initial branches. Among the firms that fell to Bigelow were Metropolitan Towel Service Ltd and Service Towel Supply Ltd. Bigelow attributed his success where others failed to a policy of earning comparatively small profits on a large number of transactions; operating costs were reduced in all the businesses acquired without sacrificing efficiency or quality of service.

Before very long Bigelow began to diversify his activities. His first move sprang from his annoyance that Afternoon Tea Services (who supplied tea-making apparatus on a weekly basis to Central London offices) had also moved into the area of towel supply. With two separate services to offer, Afternoon Tea had the means to attract many of Bigelow's customers and so, in 1910, Bigelow formed the Initial Tea Cabinet Co. By providing a wooden cabinet for tea storage, an electric kettle and the option of a 'tea lady', as well as the standard cups, saucers, tea and sugar, he went one better than Afternoon Tea (which he took over) and was soon serving 400 customers a day.

Bigelow's next step was to form the Initial Carrier Co. Initial previously hired horses and carts for occasional large deliveries, but Bigelow realised that, by purchasing their own, the firm could be more efficient (by meeting delivery men en route with fresh supplies), and, at the same time, make money by hiring out any of his unused capacity. A shoe-cleaning business followed in 1913 and, later, towel cabinets were introduced. These cabinets, made as components in the USA and assembled in London, cost offices 2s 2d a month (1s a week from 1914). Apart from three towels, they also contained soap, soap dish, hair brush, comb, clothes brush, nail brush and, later, a first aid kit.

The rapid growth of Bigelow's business again forced him to seek larger premises and in 1913 he moved to Goswell Road nearby, where he appointed his first sales manager at the relatively high salary of £4 10s a week.

Bigelow began to establish provincial branches in Manchester, Glasgow and other big cities. These began on a small scale, being housed in small lock-up shops, rented for 2s 6d a week and staffed by two or three men who met by box tricycle the London trains which brought and collected the fresh and used towels. The First World War curbed Initial's growth. However, Bigelow opened a Dublin branch in 1918 and, in the same year, diversified into coin-operated cigarette machines, run by the Initial subsidiary, Office Cigarette Services Ltd.

That year Initial deployed 23 tricycles and six horse vans in London and the provinces. Five years later this inventory rose to 28 tricycles, seven horse vans and ten motor vans serving London alone. The increasing volume of linen led Bigelow in 1923 to the next logical step of equipping the Goswell Road premises with its own laundering facilities. Here, a staff of 250 processed 240 tons of linen a week, and the prototype linen-folding machine was devised.

By 1928, Initial was the largest firm of its kind in Europe, with assets of £787,502 and an annual profit of £190,000. In September the public limited company, Initial Services (1928) Ltd was formed, with a nominal share capital of £625,000. Bigelow, as chairman, along with four other directors, then purchased all the servicing concerns that he had previously nominally owned, and arranged for a £5,000 extension to be built onto the Goswell Road premises. At the end of the first year, the company made a profit of £201,807, which rose to over £250,000 by 1941.

During the 1930s, Bigelow purchased a total of 14 domestic laundries and adapted them to service linen work. In 1928 a white coat and apron supply service was begun and, two years later, a towel and hairdrier rental service to hairdressers. The former service led to the setting up, in 1935, of the City Coat Manufacturing Co, in Soap Street, Manchester, as a part of the Initial subsidiary, City Laundry & Towel Services Ltd. The original staff of 20 doubled within a year and, although the company did government work during the Second World War, the growth recommenced shortly afterwards.

The last innovation under Bigelow's chairmanship was the introduction of the automatic towel cabinet in March 1937, when Initial obtained an operating licence from the US patentees, Steiner Sales Co. These cabinets, which came in 'standard' and 'midget' models, were marketed variously under the names of 'Towelflow' and 'Towelflo'. The Factories Act of 1937 benefited Initial by enforcing the provision of adequate washing facilities and protective clothing, where necessary, in offices.

Arthur Bigelow was a striking character, a 'forceful and colourful figure' {Beaver (1978) 13}, usually seen puffing on a large cigar and (even in the office) wearing a stetson, and riding in large cars. His contribution to office workers' standards of living was immense.

Bigelow himself, however, was unable to enjoy the fruits of his success since serious illness forced him to retire from active participation in the company in 1937. He returned for medical treatment to the USA, where he died in January 1941. His estate in Great Britain was proved at £364,579 gross. He was succeeded as chairman by William John Chinneck, a director on the board of Initial.

HELEN JEFFRIES

Sources:

Unpublished

PrC.

Published

Patrick Beaver, *INITIAL 1928-1978* (Stevenage: Publications for Companies, 1978).

Times *Prospectuses* 76 (1928).

BINNIE, Geoffrey Morse

(1908-)

Consulting hydraulic civil engineer

Geoffrey Morse Binnie was born in Kensington, London, on 13 November 1908, son of William James Eames Binnie, a civil engineer, and his wife Ethel née Morse. He was educated at Charterhouse, Trinity Hall, Cambridge where he read mechanical sciences, and then Zurich University. He joined the family firm of consulting engineers in 1932. The firm of Binnie & Partners was started in 1902 by his grandfather, Sir Alexander Binnie, who shortly afterwards took Geoffrey Binnie's father, W J E Binnie into partnership. From its inception the firm specialised in the utilities field of water supply, waste water treatment and disposal, irrigation, hydro-power, flood control, coastal protection, and all matters connected with hydraulic civil engineering.

Geoffrey Binnie commenced as assistant engineer on the Gorge Dam, Hong Kong, a project taking four years, 1933-37, and then became chief assistant engineer on the Eye Brook Reservoir, Northamptonshire, 1937-39. He became a partner of the firm in 1939. During the Second World War he served with the Royal Engineers in the Middle East and reached the rank of major. He returned to the family business in 1945, becoming senior partner in 1956 and holding this position until his retirement as consultant to the firm in 1973. During these post-war years he exerted a major influence on the firm's development.

Even in its early days the firm had undertaken work for both UK and overseas authorities. In the 1920s large scale projects were designed for Singapore, Rangoon, Genoa and Kano. This led in the 1930s to further major projects in Hong Kong and Burma, whilst much work continued for principal cities in the UK at Liverpool, Coventry, Oxford, Bedford, Corby, Warrington and Belfast. Geoffrey Binnie's major contribution started in 1951 when he became partner-in-charge of the design and construction supervision of the 116 metres-high concrete arch dam at Dokan in Iraq. This was the highest arch dam of wholly British design then undertaken and was remarkable for introducing new methods of structural analysis for concrete arch dams. For this work Geoffrey Binnie was awarded the George Stephenson medal of the Institution of Civil Engineers.

In 1957, with Geoffrey Binnie as senior partner, the firm was commissioned to design and supervise construction of the Mangla dam project for West Pakistan. This project, costing £130 million, personally supervised by Geoffrey Binnie, was at the time the largest ever undertaken by a private firm of consulting engineers, the dam being one of the largest in the world. The scheme was notable for its success and lack of post-completion troubles, which greatly enhanced the reputation of the firm. Much of this success can be attributed to Geoffrey Binnie's personal abilities, and the design practices set by his father and grandfather to ensure high quality output. Before the Mangla project the firm employed under 100 staff; it employed seven times that number during the peak phases of Mangla and has continued above the 1,000 mark since. The firm gained an international standing and became one of the principal agencies for exporting British civil engineering skills abroad. This expansion was achieved primarily under Geoffrey Binnie's leadership. He retired from full time work in December 1972.

Geoffrey Binnie was a vice-president of the Institution of Civil Engineers, 1970-72, and received the Institution's highest award, the Telford gold medal, in 1968. He was the first recipient of the John Smeaton gold medal awarded by the Council of Engineering Institutions. He was elected FRS in 1975 and became a founder fellow of the Fellowship of Engineering in 1976.

He married first in 1932 Yanka Paryczko (d 1964) by whom he had a son and a daughter; secondly, in 1964, he married Elspeth Maud Cicely Thompson.

A C TWORT

Writings:

Early Victorian Water Engineers (Telford, 1981).

Numerous technical papers.

Sources:

Unpublished

BCe.

Personal knowledge of the subject and firm.

Published

WW 1982.

Sir Noel Birch (courtesy of Vickers Ltd).

BIRCH, Sir James Frederick Noel

(1865-1939)

Armaments manufacturer

James Frederick Noel Birch was born at Llanrhaidr, Denbighshire, on 29 December 1865, the son of Major Richard Frederick Birch JP of Maes Elwy, St Asaph, and his wife Euphemia Mercer, daughter of James Somerville of Edinburgh. His father died in 1915 aged eighty leaving £29,583; his brother Richard Elwyn Birch was an estate agent. He was educated at Marlborough for a few months in 1879-80 and was commissioned in the Royal Artillery in 1885, subsequently attending the Royal Military Academy at Woolwich. In 1895-96 he served in South Africa. As the best four-in-hand whip in the British army, he commanded the Royal Artillery's Riding Establishment in 1905-7. In August 1914, at which date he held the rank of lieutenant-colonel, he commanded the Royal Horse Artillery in the retreat from Mons. In 1915, with the rank of brigadier general, he was on the General Staff of the Cavalry Corps, before serving as Artillery Adviser to Haig's forces in France, 1916-19. He was promoted to major general in 1917, lieutenant general in 1919, and received many British and foreign decorations, including the KCMG in 1918. After the Armistice, he held various War Office appointments, as Director of Remounts, 1920-21; Director General of the Territorial Army, 1921-23; and Master General of Ordnance (with a seat on the Army Council), 1923-27.

Although a cavalryman, Birch emerged as a progressive force in the War Office, favouring mechanisation of mobile forces. In 1924 he chaired the first meeting of the Principal Supply Officers' Committee, which signalled the start of serious attempts to rationalise the procurement of armaments in peace and war. The PSOC led to the formation of the Supply Board in 1927, and was the basis for all the administrative planning of re-armament. Birch was of great importance in these crucial early deliberations on industrial mobilization. He achieved the rank of general in 1926, and was made both KCB (1922) and GBE (1927).

In 1927 Birch retired from the army, and joined the board of Vickers, whose chairman, General Sir Herbert Lawrence (qv), had been Chief of General Staff to Haig when Birch was Artillery Adviser. Land armaments were made Birch's responsibility at Vickers, and there was much contemporary criticism, from radical pacifists, when he joined the board of an arms company straight from the War Office. Birch took the job because the munitions shortages of 1914-16 had convinced him that it was essential that Britain pay as much attention to industrial mobilization, and the strengthening of national armaments capacity, as to the armed forces themselves.

He launched his second career with gusto. The Land Armaments Department of Vickers had received very meagre orders since 1918, and had become managerially inefficient, weak in salesmanship, and hesitant in design. During 1927-29 he re-organised the department, dismissing various recherché or incompetent men, and replacing them with able young artillery officers, including the former British Deputy High Commissioner in the Rhineland, and several former military attachés. Paradoxically, in view of his military background, Birch believed that Vickers' future profits lay in industrial and commercial sales, and that any future receipts from peace-time re-armament or war-time munitions programmes should be looked upon as exceptional windfalls. Thus the military armaments turnover of Vickers-Armstrong totalled £5,857,128 in 1930-34, of which £4,199,753 came from foreign customers.

In Whitehall, Birch had the reputation of a political soldier, and he now became a political industrialist. He vigorously pressed mechanisation on the War Office, and lobbied his former colleagues on all aspects of industrial mobilization. Though he succeeded in 1929 in gaining an order to re-equip the Indian Army with Berthier machine-guns — on which weapon Vickers spent (1918-34) over £100,000 in development — he was furiously disappointed when the British Army, after years of tests, adopted a Czech-designed gun instead. Similarly the British Government's self-defeating and hollow gesture, in 1933, of a Sino-Japanese arms embargo, was actively opposed and scorned by Birch. These were only two among a multitude of reverses which he met from the political vagaries of re-armament: he felt them all keenly.

Political and diplomatic talents of a subtler kind were required by Birch abroad. In 1928 he represented Vickers at meetings in Paris when the French armourers, Schneider-Creusot, proposed a pool of world arms orders, together with Bofors; and later that year, he visited Turkey, Greece and Romania. A visit to Belgium (1930) to advise on fortifying the German frontier produced no work, and a long tour of the Baltic states in 1932 had mixed results: neither Latvia nor Lithuania agreed any contracts, but resultant business from Estonia accounted for 31 per cent of Vickers' armament exports in 1934.

When, in 1927, Vickers amalgamated their armaments and naval shipbuilding works with those of Armstrong, Whitworth, forming Vickers-Armstrong Ltd, Birch joined the new board. In 1929 the industrial-steel interests of Vickers and Cammell Laird were merged in the English Steel Corporation, of which Birch also became a director. In the period 1929-32 Birch was a dissident member of the ESC board. He disliked its chairman, George Taylor, who wanted to make the ESC autonomous, and he criticised the quality of ESC's steel for armament work. He was better satisfied with Taylor's successor, Sir Charles Craven.

Birch was tall, handsome, dapper in dress and had piercing blue eyes. He revelled in his Whitehall contacts, and in international negotiations; as a director of Vickers, he uniquely persisted in addressing the War Office as if he were still a member of the Army Council. Neither Vickers nor the War Office was spared his forthright criticism, and he was exacting, even sometimes intolerant, of his subordinates at Vickers House.

Birch married (1903) Florence Hyacinthe (1876-1938) daughter of Sir George Chetwode, sixth baronet, and grand-daughter of Michael Thomas Bass MP, the Burton-on-Trent brewer. In July 1938 ill-health obliged him to retire from all his directorships, and he died on 3 February 1939, at King's College Hospital, London, aged seventy-three. He left almost all of his estate, valued at £12,564 gross, to their son Nigel (created Lord Rhyl 1970), who promptly gave up stockbroking to enter politics.

R P T DAVENPORT-HINES

Writings:

Modern Riding, with Notes on Horse Training (Hutchinson, 1909).

Sources:

Unpublished

Imperial War Museum, Papers of Brigadier Guy Dawnay.

PRO, War Office and Supply Board Papers.

Vickers House, Vickers papers (microfilm) and J D Scott's research notes.

BCe.

MCe.

PrC.

Elliott research notes.

Richard P T Davenport-Hines, 'The British Armaments Industry 1918-36' (Cambridge PhD, 1979).

Published

Daily Telegraph 4 Feb 1939.

DNB.

Norman H Gibbs, *Rearmament Policy. History of the Second World War* Grand Strategy Series I (HMSO, 1976).

Guy Livingston, *Hot Air and Cold Blood* (Selwyn & Blount, 1933).

Stephen W Roskill, *Hankey, Man of Secrets* (3 vols, Collins, 1970-1974) 3.

John D Scott, *Vickers, A History* (Weidenfeld & Nicolson, 1962).

Times 4 Feb 1939.

Vickers News 1927-39.

WWW.

BIRD, Sir Alfred Frederick

(1849-1922)

Food manufacturer

Alfred Frederick Bird was born in Worcester Street, Birmingham on 27 July 1849, the elder son of Alfred Bird FCS, and his wife Elizabeth Lavinia née Ragg. His father, an analytical and pharmaceutical chemist, had set up a retail chemist and druggist's business in Bell Street in 1837 but had developed as a sideline the manufacture of two artificial foodstuffs, baking powder and custard powder. Alfred Jr (as he was called) attended King Edward VI's Grammar School, Birmingham, where he studied classics (allegedly as a preliminary to an intended career in law), and then at eighteen joined the family business.

Working with his father and brother in the family business, which had adopted the style of Alfred Bird & Sons, he devised another artificial foodstuff, blancmange powder. Then followed the rapid expansion of the foodstuffs manufacturing side of the business in which he took charge of both production and commercial matters. He soon had filling and wrapping machinery installed as well as an atmospheric engine. On his father's death in 1878 he became joint proprietor of the firm with his younger brother who, however, soon left the firm, leaving Alfred as the sole proprietor.

With a free hand he started to extend the Worcester Street premises, changing them from a shop with a small manufactory attached into a modern factory. At the same time that his production capacity was greatly enlarged, he gave up direct customer contact, which had hitherto been the accepted sales method for the firm, and appointed a number of agents throughout the country to direct what has been described as a potent grocery sales force, which tapped the emerging mid-Victorian mass market. Further sales expansion led to his removal to the Devonshire Works, at Moor Street, Birmingham in 1886. A fire completely destroyed those premises in 1887, but Bird was by then rich enough to construct immediately a new and purpose-built factory in Floodgate Street which the firm continued to occupy until 1964.

His major strength was undoubtedly in product development. The new products were all, in effect, 'convenience foods': resistant to rapid deterioration, compact in storage and quickly reconstituted. A few examples must suffice: an egg substitute in 1890, jelly crystals in 1895 soon followed by jelly cubes. More than 100 different lines were being produced by the time he retired in 1905. They still included some toiletry and pharmaceutical products, a relic of the firm's origins as chemists and druggists, which his successors dropped entirely so that the firm concentrated upon the specialised culinary products. Another of his strengths lay in an extensive use of modern advertising methods. He was using pictorial advertisements from 1880 and he made contractual agreements with T B Browne which set the pattern for the twentieth century system of advertising via recognised agents.

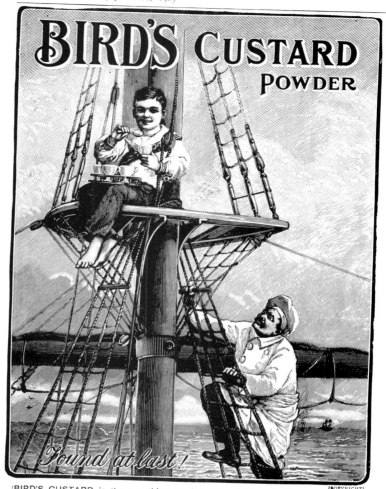

An early advertisement for Bird's Custard Powder (courtesy of Mary Evans Picture Library).

His managerial style was uncompromisingly autocratic, but he was regarded as a benevolent employer as working conditions were good and wages relatively high. In 1900, by which time he had been joined in the business by two sons, Robert Bland and Geoffrey, he sold the firm to a limited company, Alfred Bird & Sons Ltd, which had an authorised capital of £300,000. He became chairman and managing director, while the two sons and a nephew were the other directors. He retired from the business and resigned his appointments in 1905, handing over completely the direction of affairs to his son Robert.

Immediately after retiring, Alfred Bird entered national politics as a Conservative. Though unsuccessful as parliamentary candidate for the Black Country constituency of Wednesbury in 1906, he won the Wolverhampton West seat in 1910 and held it until his death. During the

First World War he served as Parliamentary Secretary to the Under Secretary of State for the Colonies.

Civic and political recognition came only after his retirement from manufacturing. He was made a JP for the county of Warwickshire in 1908, and DL of the same county in 1916. He was knighted in 1920, and was made a baronet in the New Year Honours of 1922.

An avid art collector, Bird gave some important paintings to the Houses of Parliament. Bird's other interests included world travel, mountaineering, cycling and motoring. As a young man he had been an enthusiastic cyclist, for many years holding the Land's End to John o'Groats tricycle record; as a pioneer motorist he was one of the founders of the Royal Automobile Club.

Alfred Bird married in 1875 Eleanor Frances Evans, eldest daughter of Robert Lloyd Evans, tobacconist of Handsworth. They had four sons and two daughters.

He died on 7 February 1922 in St George's Hospital, London shortly after being knocked down by a motor car in Piccadilly as he returned from a political reception. He left £653,656 gross.

NORMAN MUTTON

Sources:

Unpublished

Warwickshire RO, lists of County JP and DLs.

BCe.

MCe.

PrC.

Published

'Birmingham Chemist Who Revolutionised Food Production' *Town Cryer* (Birmingham) 4 Apr 1937.

Birmingham Evening Despatch 8 Feb 1922.

Birmingham Mail 8 Feb 1922.

Birmingham Post 13 Feb 1922.

The Food Makers (a History of General Foods Ltd) (Banbury: General Foods Ltd, 1972).

WWMP.

WWW.

Sir James Bird in 1945 (courtesy of Eric Morgan).

BIRD, Sir James

(1883-1946)

Aircraft manufacturer

James, known as Jimmy, Bird was born in London on 19 March 1883, the second son of Samuel Bird, a merchant of Calcutta, India, and East Cowes, Isle of Wight, and his wife Freda. He was educated at Marlborough and then, as a premium apprentice, joined the arms manufacturers, Armstrong Whitworth & Co, where he held a number of minor posts. In 1902, at the age of nineteen Bird set up as a consulting naval architect, a position he held until 1914; at the same time he became a director of Rennie, Forrett, a shipbuilding, engineering and dry dock company. Exactly what he did seems to be somewhat of a mystery. He began to emerge from his wealthy obscurity after 1914 when he joined the Royal Naval Air Service as an engineer officer; he received his aviator's certificate in 1915 and fairly rapidly rose to the rank of squadron commander, being appointed OBE in 1916. He became a member of the Institution of Naval Architects.

Bird himself had long been interested in aircraft (having built his first machine at Wivenhoe, Essex in 1909) and in 1916 he resigned from the RNAS with the approval of the Admiralty in order to manage the Supermarine Aviation works, then engaged on RNAS/RFC contracts. This company had been founded by Noel Pemberton-Billing and the power-boat designer Hubert Scott-Paine (qv) in 1912, but Pemberton-Billing had had to divest himself of his shares upon standing for Parliament in 1916 because of his interest in air affairs, and the company name was changed to Supermarine. Pemberton-Billing sold out to Captain A de Broughton, RFC, who in 1917 in his turn sold out to financial interests. The latter brought in Jimmy Bird as their director. Scott-Paine, managing director 1916-1923, had been given some shares by Pemberton-Billing and so for a while he and Bird were in effect joint managing directors. During this period Reginald J Mitchell (1895-1937), as chief engineer and designer began to build a reputation for himself and the firm; in 1922 Mitchell produced the Supermarine flying-boat which won the Schneider Trophy at Naples. However Scott-Paine and Bird were both strong personalities and clashes were inevitable in the strained circumstances of aviation in the 1920s. In November 1923 Bird bought out Scott-Paine at an unknown, but what Scott-Paine considered to be an impossible, price.

Bird then became the managing director (though not the sole owner) of Supermarine Aviation, until 1928, when it was sold for £400,000 to Vickers (Aviation) Ltd, part of the newly-formed Vickers-Armstrongs armaments firm which had just been created by mergers. Bird became a director of Vickers (Aviation) Ltd. At that point Supermarine were at their height, having won first and second places in the Schneider Trophy contest at Venice in 1927; shortly thereafter the RAF used four of their

Spitfire Fuselage Assembly at the Itchen works, 1939 (courtesy of Eric Morgan).

Southampton flying-boats for a 27,000-mile formation flight from England to Australia and back to Singapore. At the same time Bird became chairman of the Royal Aeronautical Society's Schneider Trophy Committee and served on the aviation committee of Lloyd's of London (the insurance exchange). Over the period 1920-45 Bird was also on the council of the Society of British Aircraft Constructors, of which he also served as deputy-chairman and honorary treasurer.

Bird, as a special director of Vickers-Armstrong, continued to manage Supermarine interests, which included the production of the successful S-5 and S-6 aircraft for the 1929 and 1931 defences of the Schneider Trophy, which then came outright to Britain. At the same time these Mitchell designs led directly to the Spitfire, which first flew in 1936 shortly before Mitchell's death. It was then taken over by his assistant, little-known Joe Smith, who developed it over the next ten years and kept it in the forefront of the battleline until it was superseded by the Gloster Meteor jet fighter. Throughout the decade from 1936, Bird supervised the expansion both of the main Supermarine plant at Woolston, Southampton, and of the shadow production of Spitfires and Seafires (the RN version of the Spitfire) in the South masterminding the subcontracting system that this necessitated, especially after enemy bombing of the main works. The only large output of Spitfires outside his control came from the Vickers-Armstrong plant at Castle Bromwich near Birmingham. He was charming and kindly, a master of detail, easy to work with. For his immense efforts, the oversight of the production of 22,759 Spitfires and Seafires, he was rewarded with a knighthood in 1945. Unfortunately the pressures of wartime management and of his other activities (he was chairman of several local Southampton companies, on the Harbour Board, and vice-commodore of the Royal Southampton Yacht Club) gave him a heart condition for which he was receiving treatment at the end of the war.

Bird appreciated other men's talents. Though not a designer, he was particularly enthusiastic at the end of the war about Joe Smith's Spiteful design, a refined Spitfire with a laminar-flow wing. As an engineer and manager Bird was a master of technical detail.

Jimmy Bird married three times. By his second wife he had a son, John Samuel, who became a test pilot. His third wife, whom he married in 1937, was Pamela, younger daughter of Arthur Ramsden. In adult life he was an avid yachtsman, golfer and shot.

On 13 August 1946 Sir James Bird was out hunting on his estate at Wickham, Hampshire when, according to the coroner's verdict, he had a heart attack which caused his gun to discharge and kill him. He left an estate of £381,024 gross.

ROBIN HIGHAM

Sources:

Unpublished

PrC.

Published

Charles F Andrews and Eric B Morgan, *Supermarine Aircraft since 1914* (1981).

DNB.

Charles G Grey, 'Jimmy Bird' *The Aeroplane* 23 Aug 1946.

Derek N James, *Schneider Trophy Aircraft 1913-1931* (Putnam, 1981).

John D Scott, *Vickers: a History* (Weidenfeld & Nicolson, 1962).

Times 15, 16, 21, 28 Aug 1946.

WWW.

BLACKBURN, Robert

(1885-1955)

Aircraft manufacturer

Robert Blackburn, portrait by Bernard Adams (courtesy of the British Aerospace Aircraft Group, Kingston Brough Division).

Robert Blackburn was born in Leeds on 26 March 1885, the son of George William Blackburn, engineer, and Kate née Naylor. He was educated at Leeds Modern School, gained an honours degree in engineering at Leeds University and was made associate member of the Institution of Civil Engineers in 1906. Then he gained practical experience with his father's company in Leeds, Thomas Green & Sons, steam roller and lawn mower manufacturers. Because of differences of view between his own academic training and contemporary engineering methods, he left Leeds for further study in Germany, Belgium and France.

In France his interest in aviation was aroused, for Paris was then a magnet for the pioneers. Working for an engineering firm in Rouen, he went to Le Mans at weekends to watch Wilbur Wright and also visited the proving-ground at Issy-les-Moulineaux near St Cloud, where Blériot, the Wright brothers, Voisin, Farman, Santos-Dumont and others tried out their machines. Fired with enthusiasm, he decided to design and build an aircraft, resigning from his company so as not to be sacked for overstaying his weekend leaves, and taking a room in Paris to work on drawings for a monoplane.

When he returned to Leeds later in 1908 he took these with him. His father, after some reluctance, gave his determined son some financial support and help in setting up a small workshop beneath a clothing factory in Benson Street, Leeds. There, with the aid of one of the factory apprentices (Harry Goodyear, who had been detailed to assist him), Robert Blackburn built his first aeroplane, a high-wing monoplane with a braced, square-shaped fuselage structure, strongly made and powered by a 35 hp Gustavus Green four-cylinder vertical engine. During April 1909 he took his monoplane up by horse-drawn furniture van to a stretch of coastal sands between Marske and Saltburn to try to get it airborne. He was unsuccessful in this, until on 24 May 1910 it flew, but crashed when he attempted a turn, leaving it severely damaged.

From the beginning Blackburn was an aeronautical designer and manufacturer: in 1910 he advertised the building of aircraft (for £700 complete) and at this date his workshop made wooden propellers. His Second Monoplane, flown from the sands at Filey, proved successful and Blackburn Aeroplanes, as his company was known, offered the type to customers for £500. The firm also built Blériot monoplanes. At this time he established a partnership with Bentfield C Hucks (famous in British aviation for the Hucks starter), who did the test flying, mostly at Filey, while Robert Blackburn concentrated on manufacturing, in Balm Road, Leeds from 1911.

His Second Monoplane made many successful flights and his third machine, *Mercury*, was exhibited at the 1911 Olympia Aero Show, where he first publicly used his company's name. The *Mercury* was the first

British aircraft to have a steel-tubed fuselage. With a government contract to produce a batch of Farnborough-designed Royal Aircraft Factory BE2Cs (two-seat biplanes ordered as standard equipment for both the Royal Flying Corps and Royal Naval Air Service), in June 1914 Blackburn formed a limited company, the Blackburn Aeroplane & Motor Co Ltd. It had an authorised capital of £20,000 in £1 shares and allowed Blackburn to find new premises, the Olympia Works at Leeds (formerly a skating rink), where it built many types of aircraft and seaplanes. Some were of original design while other types, notably BE2Cs and the Sopwith-designed Cuckoo and Baby, were built under licence. Wartime demand vastly increased the firm's size, from 20 employees in 1914 to about 2,000 in 1918. Robert Blackburn was particularly interested in developing seaplanes; and for this reason in 1916 he acquired premises at Brough, near the mouth of the Humber, in addition to his production plants at Leeds and at Sherburn-in-Elmet. Later in the war the Government commandeered the Brough site.

At Leeds the company built the first of its own aircraft to gain a production contract, the big twin-engined Kangaroo, and with this type Robert Blackburn in April 1919 started commercial air operations with the North Sea Aerial Navigation Co Ltd, though these were quickly ended in the post-war depression. During the post-war period he kept the factory going with non-aeronautical production, and in 1921 made a bold and successful bid to fulfil an Air Ministry requirement for a single-seat, carrier-borne torpedo bomber for the Fleet Air Arm, thereby commencing a long Blackburn tradition of building naval types. Between 1921 and 1928 when production ended, Blackburn built 117 of these T2 Darts. In the 1920s Blackburn built up commercial contacts abroad, especially in Greece where he helped to establish a National Aircraft Factory, for which the King of the Hellenes honoured him with the Golden Cross of the Order of the Redeemer (1927). Briefly (1927-30), with Sir Alan Cobham (qv), he operated scheduled air services in Africa but the company, Cobham-Blackburn Airlines Ltd, was forced by government policy to sell out to Imperial Airways, for a substantial sum.

With a decision crucial to his company's future, Blackburn closed down the Leeds factory after aerodrome facilities in Roundhay Park were no longer available and moved to Brough between 1928 and 1932. Prior to this move the firm had 1,000 employees at Leeds and 500 at Brough. Blackburn's situation at Brough, with ready access to the River Humber, seems to have influenced the type of aircraft the company produced, for, while its main output remained the torpedo-bombers for the Fleet Air Arm, it also designed and built (in 1927-32) a series of stately flying-boats, the Iris, Sydney and Perth, the first and last going into service with the RAF.

Landplanes, however, were not neglected, and the success of the graceful little *Bluebird IV* in the 1931 round-England King's Cup Air Race led to the transfer of the company which built the engine, Cirrus Hermes Engineering Co Ltd, from Croydon to Brough in February 1934. As Blackburn were then building large numbers of Shark torpedo aircraft under the increased Air Ministry budgets of 1933 and 1934, additional factory space had to be found by enlarging the Brough premises and also by re-opening and extending the former Olympia works at Leeds.

The prototype Universal Freighter, forerunner of the Beverley, pictured over Beverley Minster (courtesy of Humphrey Wynn).

In common with other British aircraft companies, Blackburn suffered from depressed finances in the mid-1930s, but managed to stay afloat: on 2 June 1936 the firm filed a declaration of solvency with an authorised capital of £225,000 fully paid up. It had previously (on 2 April) consolidated all its interests into one company with the formation of Blackburn Aircraft Ltd, Robert Blackburn continuing as chairman and managing director. Major F A Bumpus, who had been with the company since 1919, was chief engineer and joint managing director; Major J D Rennie was chief seaplane designer, and the other directors were Captain N W G Blackburn, H C Bevan, R R Rhodes, Squadron Leader J L N Bennett-Baggs and E Hudson.

The new company's first important act was to enter into an agreement with the Scottish shipbuilding firm William Denny & Bros Ltd, of Dumbarton, for the establishment of an aircraft factory on Clydeside. By 1937 these premises, providing more than 300,000 square feet of floor space, had been completed on land to the east of the Denny shipyard. Sir Maurice Denny joined the Blackburn Aircraft board and the company were able to move all their flying-boat activity from Brough and also to set up a Shark repair organisation separate from the main production line.

Throughout all these industrial changes and developments, and during the Second World War, Robert Blackburn, aged fifty-four at the outbreak of war, remained at the head of the company he founded. His great strength in this position lay in his personal knowledge of most of his employees, which in turn was reflected in the loyalty he inspired through his quiet, methodical and unpretentious character. He possessed the strong Yorkshire qualities of dourness and determination.

Three types of Blackburn aeroplane were in service during the war, the Skua dive-bomber and Roc fighter with the Royal Navy and the Botha torpedo-bomber with the RAF; but the company's main production work was the sub-contract manufacture of the Fairey Swordfish (1,700 of which were built) and Barracuda (635 built) and Short Sunderland flying-boat (1,700 of which were built at Dunbarton). However, the Blackburn name re-appeared with the Firebrand fleet fighter, which went into service with the Royal Navy from 1944 onwards.

After the war, Blackburn, still in control of the company he founded, secured another amalgamation (with General Aircraft Ltd in 1948), and acquired British rights for the French Turbomeca gas-turbine engines. He also saw the start of production of the Beverley heavy freighter for the RAF. During the Second World War the firm reached its highest number of employees at 17,000.

Blackburn served as vice-president of the Society of the SBAC (Society of British Aircraft Constructors, as it was then known), and was made an honorary fellow of the Royal Aeronautical Society in 1950. He received the OBE in 1918.

He married twice. By his first wife he had a son and a daughter. By his second wife Phyllis Margaret Kirton, whom he married in 1936, he had two daughters.

In 1953 he was forced by ill-health to go into semi-retirement, though still remaining chairman of Blackburn Aircraft. Robert Blackburn died suddenly on 10 September 1955, shortly after visiting the Farnborough Air Show; he left £131,785 gross.

HUMPHREY WYNN

Sources:

Unpublished

BCe.

PrC.

British Aerospace Aircraft Group, Kingston-Brough Division: unpublished outline of Blackburn's career.

Published

The Aeroplane Sept 1955.

Flight Sept 1955.

A J Jackson, *Blackburn Aircraft since 1909* (Putnam, 1968).

Harald Penrose, *British Aviation. The Pioneer Years 1908-1914* (Cassell, 1980).

—, *British Aviation. The Adventuring Years 1920-1929* (Putnam, 1973).

—, *British Aviation. Widening Horizons 1930-1934* (HMSO, 1979).

—, *British Aviation. Ominous Skies 1935-1939* (HMSO, 1980).

Journal of the Royal Aeronautical Society Sept 1955.

Shipping World 8 June 1955.

Times 12 Sept 1955.

Voice of Industry Mar 1954.

Who's Who in Commerce and Industry (New York: Institute for Research in Biography, 1938).

BLACKWELL, RICHARD

(1918-1980)

Bookseller and publisher

Richard Blackwell (courtesy of B H Blackwell Ltd).

Richard Blackwell was born in Oxford on 5 January 1918, the son of Basil Blackwell and his wife Marion, daughter of John Soans. His father already represented the third generation of the family to sell books in Oxford, and was to become one of the leading and most respected figures in the British book trade, 'in the forefront of the movement for closer co-operation and better organisation throughout the trade.' {Mumby (1949) 330} But for all his clear understanding of the business of bookselling and publishing and his concern for the welfare of the trade as a whole, Basil Blackwell remained a scholarly publisher-bookseller of a type characteristic of the nineteenth rather than the twentieth century.

Basil and his father Benjamin had created a solidly prosperous but comparatively modest bookselling and publishing firm serving the Oxford University community, including those former students who had returned to their own towns and countries but still looked to Blackwells for their supplies of learned books. It was Richard Blackwell's achievement to turn his family's firm into a major, perhaps the major, international retailer of learned and academic books and journals.

Richard Blackwell had a classical education, winning scholarships to Winchester and New College, Oxford, where he read classics. He took a first in Moderations but he did not complete his degree, leaving the University in 1939 to serve in the navy. He valued his six years of service in the navy for the broadening of his sympathies and understanding which it gave him. Yet while those who had known him as a boy appreciated the transformation of his personality brought about by his years in the navy, his reserved and often rather formal manner sometimes made it difficult for others, particularly younger members of Blackwells' staff, to appreciate the depth of his interest in and concern for their affairs.

Richard joined the family firm as a director in late 1946. His father, as chairman, continued to take a very active part in the direction of the business, but Richard took on more and more of the work and the responsibility, and his influence and enterprise were clearly apparent by the mid 1950s. Basil had a gift for giving those whose judgement he trusted their head, even while he might be slightly apprehensive about the possible results, and Richard enjoyed the benefit of his advice and consistent support.

The years after the war saw the beginning of a worldwide expansion of institutions of higher education. The reputation of Blackwells in academic circles provided Richard Blackwell with a very strong position from which to capture this rapidly growing market. University libraries throughout the English-speaking world placed standing orders with Blackwells, who not only supplied books and journals, but also helped newly-established libraries build up their collections of old and out-of-print books. Blackwells developed a complex bibliographical and book-finding service, and often libraries preferred to rely on the judgement of Blackwells' staff in compiling their orders rather than make their own selections from publishers' lists. Individual customers as well as libraries could use these facilities: Richard Blackwell said that 'Blackwell's aim, as far as is humanly possible and economically feasible, is to obtain any book from any source for any customer.' {Barker and Davies (1966) 294} There was always the danger that institutions and individuals would obtain readily available books from their nearest supplier, turning to Blackwells for the more obscure and difficult orders which were far more expensive to service. However, the steady growth and profits of the company, with turnover increasing from £250,000 in 1946 to over £30 million by the end of the 1970s, bore out Richard Blackwell's belief that what was lost on the swings of specialised book-finding services was balanced by gains on the roundabouts of bulk, and less difficult orders. Richard Blackwell's success in establishing good relations with librarians throughout the world, many of whom came to consider him a personal friend, also contributed to the consistently high proportion of turnover (over 60 per cent) represented by exports. British publishers have long looked to overseas markets for a considerable percentage of their business, but Blackwell's record as booksellers was unique. This emphasis on exports brought problems familiar to publishers (and other exporters), of vulnerability to fluctuations in the value of sterling and to disturbance of markets by political troubles, but was the main foundation of the striking post-war growth of the firm.

For many years, while Richard concentrated on bookselling, Basil continued to take particular interest in the publishing company he had set up in 1922, Basil Blackwell & Mott Ltd. (Such a combination of bookselling and publishing is rare: Heffers of Cambridge are the only other booksellers in Britain to do this.) This showed steady but unspectacular growth until Richard succeeded his father as chairman of this company in 1976 (he had been chairman of B H Blackwell Ltd, the bookselling company, since 1969). Turnover was increased from just over £1 million to over £6 million in 1979. Richard Blackwell had more to do with Blackwell Scientific Publications Ltd, a company started in 1939 with the modest nominal capital of £2,000. Its growth, particularly marked from 1960, to a turnover of more than £6 million, owed much to Per Saugman, a Dane who had joined Blackwells in 1952, becoming chairman of this company in 1973.

All the growth in assets which the expansion of these companies represented was derived from profits which the Blackwell family consistently ploughed back into their business. Many smaller businesses, such as printers, binders or other bookshops, were also acquired and run in conjunction with the major companies: 'nest eggs' as Richard Blackwell called them, which he enjoyed nurturing. He took care to master all the details of new projects, but their managers were allowed a great deal of freedom of action. Though the ultimate control of the Blackwell family was always ensured, their readiness to listen to advice helped to avoid some of the pitfalls of narrowness of outlook inherent in a tightly-knit family concern.

One of the most substantial of these nest-eggs was University Bookshops (Oxford) Ltd, which Richard Blackwell set up in 1964 in collaboration with the Oxford University Press to improve the bookselling services available to the new universities; by the end of the 1970s group turnover was over £6 million. Several companies were also acquired abroad, some of which illustrate a romantic streak in his approach to business. He was pleased to have the opportunity to buy Munksgaard of Copenhagen, for instance, because his friend Per Saugman had started his apprenticeship there in 1941. He bought a Viennese bookshop simply to keep the British flag flying in that city after a small bookshop run by the British Embassy in Vienna closed down. His major overseas purchase was the assets of the US library supply business, Richard Abel, which had become bankrupt. Its place was taken by a new company, Blackwell's North America Inc, greatly to the relief of librarians and publishers there.

His reason for acquiring the Vienna business illustrates another important aspect of his character: the value he placed on what he perceived as the traditional virtues of English society and culture. He was a solid Anglican, bore the traces of his classical education in a fondness for classical allusions and quotations, and was conservative in his social and political views. 'Imbued with an almost Victorian belief in private enterprise and the personal rewards due to individual hard work' {*Broad Sheet* March 1980}, he was determined that Blackwells should remain a family business. He was concerned at the legislation of the 1960s concerning capital gains tax and estate duties which seemed to him to threaten the survival of private and family companies. This led him, together with his old friend and financial adviser John Critchley, to help found the Smaller Businesses Association, which later became the Association of Independent Businesses, in 1968. His determination that Blackwells should maintain their leading position in bookselling did not blind him to the interests of the rest of the trade: in 1966-68 he served as president of the Booksellers' Association and he was a major witness in the successful defence of the Net Book Agreement before the Restrictive Practices Court in 1962.

In 1942 he married Marguerite Holliday, the daughter of Major Lionel Brook Holliday, governing director of a Yorkshire dyestuffs company, L B Holliday & Co Ltd; both their sons joined Blackwells. He was awarded an honorary doctorate by York University, Toronto, whose library Blackwells had done much to help create, and was elected a fellow of St Cross College, Oxford in 1978. After a long illness which he had endured with characteristic courage and reticence, he died on 26 February 1980, leaving £172,434 gross.

CHRISTINE SHAW

Writings:

'The Pricing of Books' *Journal of Industrial Economics* 2 (1954).

'The Day's Bag in a Bookshop' *Journal of Industrial Economics* 9 (1960-61).

Evidence before Restrictive Practices Court 1962 in Ronald E Barker and George R Davies (eds), *Books Are Different: An Account of the Defence of the Net Book Agreement before the Restrictive Practices Court in 1962* (Macmillan, 1966).

'The Library and the Bookseller' in *The University: The Library* (Oxford: Shakespeare Head Press, 1972).

Sources:

Unpublished

C Reg: B H Blackwell Ltd (165,100). Basil Blackwell Publisher Ltd (180,277). Blackwell Scientific Publications Ltd (349,566). University Bookshops (Oxford) Ltd (796,591).

BCe.

MCe.

PrC.

Interviews with Henry Schollick and John Critchley, and information from Miles Blackwell.

Published

Broad Sheet (Blackwells house newsletter) Mar 1980.

Frank A Mumby, *Publishing and Bookselling: A History from the Earliest Times to the Present Day* (Cape, 1949).

A L P Norrington, *Blackwell's 1879-1979. The History of a Family Firm* (Oxford: Basil Blackwell, 1983).

Times 4 Mar 1980.

WWW.

BLACKWOOD, Sir Stevenson Arthur

(1832-1893)
Manager of the Post Office

Stevenson Arthur Blackwood was born in Hampstead on 22 May 1832, the only son of Arthur Johnstone Blackwood, who served as Gentleman Usher to William IV and Victoria. Educated at Eton (1845-48) and Trinity College, Cambridge (1850-52), Blackwood entered the Treasury as a clerk on coming down from university. Even at that early point he seemed destined for the prominence and success which a man of his background, dedication and charm might expect (he was reputedly the most handsome man of his generation). From September 1854 to December 1855 he served on the Commissariat staff in the Crimea. There Blackwood underwent a religious experience which was to have a profound effect on his life. He became a committed Evangelical and devoted much time and effort to proselytizing. His speeches at the Mildmay Conferences and at Exeter Hall as well as his work in the Protestant Alliance reveal a man of sincerity and conviction (by 1878 he had also become a teetotaller). However, critics argued that Blackwood's religious views bordered on anti-Catholic bigotry, and as a result he was a figure of some controversy. In December 1858 Blackwood married Sydney, Duchess of Manchester, who shared her husband's religious views and made a happy home for him.

In 1874 Blackwood left the Treasury to become Financial Secretary to the Post Office at an annual salary of £1,500. He encountered a difficult situation at St Martin's-le-Grand. A year earlier the Post Office (and Gladstone's Government) had been shaken by the revelation that over £800,000 had been spent by a departmental administrator, Frank Ives Scudamore (qv), on the extension of the recently nationalised telegraphs without Parliamentary approval. It was hoped that Blackwood in his newly created position would impose fiscal rectitude on the wayward department or, as one wag said, the Treasury, having tried all other expedients, would test the efficacy of prayer. In fact Blackwood became imbued with the ethic that service to the public should usually come before revenue considerations.

In 1880, upon the retirement of Sir John Tilley (qv), Blackwood became Secretary to the Post Office with a salary of £1,750. In his new position Blackwood was manager of the largest business operation in Britain, commanding over 100,000 employees, receipts of £8.7 million, and a net revenue (profits) of £2.7 million. To judge his impact on this huge bureaucracy is difficult. One colleague, H Buxton Forman, felt Blackwood was not as able as some previous secretaries in mastering and directing the many aspects of the Post Office operation. Still Blackwood brought several strengths to his thirteen-year tenure of office. His skill as a negotiator contributed to the successful resolution of complicated questions at international conferences, such as the 1880 Paris Postal Congress. Moreover, he was an energetic advocate of Post Office expansion into new areas of responsibility. For example, Blackwood firmly supported the establishment of the domestic parcel post, which began to operate in 1883. He was equally convinced that the telephone would best be developed under departmental management, a judicial decision of 1880 having held that the telephone came under the Post Office's telegraphic monopoly. Still he was unable to overcome the opposition of Henry Fawcett, Postmaster General (1880-84) and Cambridge economist, who favoured local development. Blackwood's defeat on this issue contributed to the chaotic history of the telephone in Britain, until 1911 at least.

His policy on staff questions deserves some comment. Although a product of the pre-Northcote-Trevelyan era, Blackwood believed in promotion on the criterion of merit alone for the leaders of his department. This outlook led to bitter disputes with Henry Cecil Raikes, Postmaster General (1886-91), who felt seniority should also be considered. Blackwood's attitude toward the rank and file of the department was paternalistic. He encouraged the activities of clubs and societies, such as the Post Office Total Abstinence Society, which would improve the lives of his employees. However, he was completely opposed to the establishment of unions within the department. He forcefully crushed a strike among London parcel post workers in 1890, but despite his efforts the power of staff associations grew. This fact was reflected in the increasing percentage of total expenditure which wages accounted for during the last decades of the nineteenth century: while Blackwood was secretary there were two revisions of rates which added £320,000 to the Post Office wage bill in 1881-82 and £406,600 in 1890-91.

In recognition of his work in the Post Office, Blackwood was created CB in 1880 and KCB in June 1887. He was still in office when he died on 2 October 1893. As the letters of sympathy received by his family indicate, contemporaries regarded Blackwood as a model citizen, for whom service to the state and to his religion were essentially synonymous. He left £14,500 gross.

CHARLES R PERRY

Writings:

Athens and London. An Address (Morgan & Chase, 1862).

Repent and Be Converted. An Address (Morgan & Chase, 1862).

Forgiveness, Life, and Glory (J Nisbet & Co, 1864).

The Shadow and the Substance (J Nisbet & Co, 1867).

The Last Trump (Morgan & Chase, 1870).

Heavenly Places. Addresses on the Book of Joshua (J Nisbet & Co, 1872).

A Victory of Faith. A Sequel to 'Heavenly Places' (J Nisbet & Co, 1874).

Hindrances to Christian Work. An Address (J F Shaw & Co, 1876).

The Acceptable Life (Hodder & Stoughton, 1878).

Things which God Hath Joined Together. Addresses on Isaiah XLV 21-25 (J Nisbet & Co, 1878).

Heavenly Arithmetic (J Nisbet & Co, 1880).

Position and Progress. Addresses (J Nisbet & Co, 1880).

The Number 'Seven' in Scripture (Morgan & Scott, 1883).

'The Public Offices From Within' *The Nineteenth Century* 24 (1888).

Te Deum Laudamus. Being Addresses on Important Truth Therein Contained (J Nisbet & Co, 1892).

Christian Service and Responsibility. Notes of Short Addresses (Marshall Bros, 1897).

Conference Memories: Addresses given at the Mildmay Conferences between the Years 1874 and 1893 (J F Shaw & Co, 1898).

Sources:

Unpublished

Charles R Perry, 'The British Post Office, 1836-1914: A Study in Nationalisation and Administrative Expansion' (Harvard PhD, 1976).

Published

Harriet S Blackwood, *Some Records of the Life of Stevenson Arthur Blackwood* (Hodder & Stoughton, 1896).

Venn, *Alumni Cantabrigienses*.

BLAKE, Ernest Edgar

(1879-1961)

Film and photographic materials manufacturer and cinema owner

Ernest Edgar Blake was born in Bedford on 21 November 1879, one of the two sons of William Blake, a photographer and Ann Eliza née Chase. He attended Bedford Modern School and then gained experience in his father's photographic business, becoming keenly interested in the moving picture machines and celluloid ribbon film which William Friese-Greene (1855-1921) and others pioneered in the late 1880s.

Ernie (as he was known) and his brother William ('Bill') Norman Blake (1871-1934) devised a camera-cum-projector of their own and in autumn

1879 presented their first 'animatograph' show in the old schoolroom at Haynes, five miles south of Bedford. From their takings of £1 18s 4d, expenses of 4s, for hire of the schoolroom and a pony, had to be deducted. Over the next six years the Blake brothers spent many evenings taking their gas-illuminated projector and moving film round the villages of Bedfordshire and neighbouring counties, by pony and trap.

For several years after Ernie started work in London they were still showing films in and around Bedford but in 1908 the Blakes established the first regular cinema shows in Bedford itself: twice nightly presentations in the YMCA hall at the corner of Silver and Harpur Streets. The following year the Blake brothers leased the town's first cinema, the Picturedrome, built by Chethams. In 1911 they built the Empire cinema; later they built the Picturedrome and then the Playhouse in Hitchen and the Palace at Bedford. After Bill Blake died in 1934, Ernie formed a company, Granada (Bedford) Ltd, to build the Granada cinema in Bedford and to operate it as well as the Empire cinema. This gave him an important psychological, if not economic, link with his home town. Every Friday until his death he drove round Bedford in his Bentley with bills for the next week's show at the Granada.

New opportunities came in April 1903 after Ernie Blake joined Kodak Ltd, the British subsidiary (capitalised at £250,000 in 1902) of Eastman Kodak of New Jersey. He started work in the Trade Control (Dealer Sales Department) on a wage of 45s a week at the company's head office in Clerkenwell Road, London. He soon moved into the Cine Film Department and rose to become its manager in 1911.

During the First World War he served as a sergeant in motor transport in the RASC but was later commissioned in the Royal Flying Corps as a technical officer to carry out photographic duties from aircraft. After the war he returned to Kodak which was almost a monopoly supplier of film stock to the British film industry, although until the 1920s most was imported from the main Eastman Kodak plant in Rochester, New York. By the 1930s motion picture film accounted for about half of Kodak Ltd's turnover.

Ernie Blake was widely known and very popular with the men who ran the British film industry between the wars. He was known, not only as the man who sold them film stock (he described himself as a 'trader'), but as a colourful personality. He was a rugged and earthy character given to strong views and prejudices and his after-dinner speeches were famous for their 'Rabelaisian stories derived from the film business' {Corder (1974) 159}.

In 1930, the year the firm's capital was increased to £350,000, he became managing director, his appointment reflecting in part the importance of the motion picture business to Kodak. In 1946 he was appointed to the chairmanship, from which he retired in 1954.

During his period as chairman the company undertook a major programme of capital investment, building new factories in Stevenage, Kirby and Hemel Hempstead. An important innovation was the manufacture of the colour film Kodachrome, which dominated the British market. The film was first launched by Eastman Kodak in 1935 though not until 1955 did Kodak Ltd supply its own requirements.

As chairman, Blake trusted his subordinates, respecting their expertise in areas of the company's affairs he was not familiar with. He would back their judgement when he had to justify capital expenditure programmes to Eastman Kodak. Few measures of firm growth are available but by 1949 Kodak Ltd employed over 7,000 people whose wage bill totalled £2.5 million.

Blake was a keen sportsman. He played water polo for Bedford, 1897-1913, though rugby was the game with which he was most closely associated. He played for Bedford Wanderers Rugby Football Club and in 1938 became president of Bedford Rugby Football Club and of the East Midlands Rugby Union, an office he held on two occassions.

He was a founder member of the Cinema Veterans Association (1903) in 1921 and its president in 1937-38, a member of the council of the Incorporated Association of Kinematograph Manufacturers and chairman of the equipment section, chairman of the Kinematograph Manufacturers' Association, honorary fellow of the British Kinematograph Society, fellow of the Society of Motion Picture and Television Engineers (USA), member of the Cinema Consultative Committee and a member of the board of management of the Cinematograph Trade Benevolent Fund.

Blake married in 1903 Louise Batchelor, daughter of Frederick Batchelor, a pianoforte tuner of Hitchen by whom he had one son, George S W Blake, who survived him.

He resigned his directorship of Kodak Ltd in 1960 and died on 15 July 1961 leaving £97,890 gross.

D E H EDGERTON

Writings:

'The Growth and Development of Kodak' (Edwards Seminar Paper 88, 30 Jan 1951).

Sources:

Unpublished

G G Corder, 'Ernest Amor: An Appreciation' (unpublished biography, 1974).

Information from Geoffrey Bawcutt (Kodak Archivist) and Ernest Amor (manager, Kodak Ltd, 1946-66).

BCe.

MCe.

PrC.

Published

Bedfordshire Times 21 July 1961.

British Journal of Photography 4 Aug 1961.

Kinematograph Year Book 1930.

H B H Blundell ca 1890 (courtesy of Quaker House Colliery Co Ltd).

BLUNDELL, Henry Blundell-Hollinshead

(1831-1906)

Colliery owner and manager

Henry Blundell-Hollinshead Blundell was born at West Derby, Liverpool, on 24 January 1831, the son of Richard Benson Blundell-Hollinshead Blundell, a Liverpool merchant and owner of collieries at Pemberton, Wigan, Ince, Blackrod and Chorley, and his wife Jane née Leigh.

He was educated at Eton and at Christ Church, Oxford, graduating BA in 1854; he then went to Sandhurst. On leaving Sandhurst he joined the Rifle Brigade in 1855 and served in the Crimea; in 1863 he transferred to the Grenadier Guards and in 1864 passed the staff college. He subsequently served in the Sudan and Canada, and in 1876 became Adjutant General of the Home District, achieving the rank of colonel in 1882. He retired from the army in 1889 and was made a CB (Military). His brother Jonathan assisted him in running the collieries both before and after he retired from the army. However, while his brothers held shares in the colliery concern, Henry was the principal and managing partner.

Henry took over the family collieries, operated under the name of Jonathan Blundell & Son, on the death of his father in 1853. He engaged the eminent engineer William Armstrong (qv) of Newcastle, as consultant viewer. Armstrong's detailed report on the collieries resulted in the general manager and his sons (assistant managers) being dismissed. The Blackrod Colliery was already closed, but Armstrong advised Blundell to dispose of the Chorley and Wigan Collieries and concentrate his efforts on the Ince and Pemberton Collieries. The Ince Collieries had worked only the top seams but, because other collieries had been opened all round them, restricting the opportunities for expansion, it was decided not to sink the pits deeper. Instead Blundell concentrated on making Pemberton one of the largest, if not the largest, colliery in Lancashire.

Captain Henry Blundell, as he then was, immediately embarked on a programme of acquiring coal estates adjoining his own 270 acre Pemberton estate. When he purchased an estate he leased the surface but retained rights to mine the coal and acquired rights to mine under adjoining estates. In this he was assisted by his able colliery manager, William Greener, until he had amassed a mineral estate comprising upwards of 45 million tons of workable coal. In addition he leased other adjacent areas of coal comprising more than 5 million tons.

In 1868 Blundell ordered the sinking of two new deep pits, 18 feet and 16 feet in diameter and over 600 yards deep to the lowest seam of the middle coal measures. These pits were equipped with the most up-to-date plant available, and cost £100,000 to complete. The 14 workable seams had a designed output of 2,000 tons a day, or half a million tons a year. Employment was provided for 1,800 men and the coal produced was supplied to Lancashire cotton mills, gasworks, railways, ironworks, engineering works and sugar refineries, as well as domestic coal retailers.

Blundell's Pemberton Colliery, Wigan in 1932 (courtesy of Quaker House Colliery Co Ltd).

Large tonnages were exported to Ireland, South America and various other countries. James Pickering, the firm's commercial manager, introduced the system of delivering coal in bags, which limited the breakage of coal and prevented dirt, dust and annoyance. Blundells had 13 coal depots in towns on both sides of the Mersey and others at inland towns such as Wigan (where there was a very large depot) and Bury.

To house the additional miners for the new pits Colonel Blundell built Highfield colliery village. Miners' houses were provided with paved service roads behind them, privies for each house (unusual in 1870) and walled kitchen gardens, each with a pig sty at the end furthest from the house. A school, a church and houses for the schoolmaster and the curate-in-charge were added. All the teachers and the curate were paid by the Colonel who was a generous benefactor to the Pemberton district of Wigan, giving churches, schools, recreation grounds, parks and reading rooms. After an unfortunate explosion at the well-managed King Pit in October 1877, Colonel Blundell paid compensation to the victims' relatives over and above the amounts due from the Miners' Permanent Relief Fund.

Blundell converted his partnership into a limited company on 7 December 1900. The directors and sole shareholders of the new company were Colonel Henry B-H Blundell, chairman, and his brothers, Major General Richard B-H Blundell and Canon Thomas B-H Blundell, Rector of Halsall and Chaplain to Queen Victoria, the other brother, Jonathan, having died earlier. In 1900 the company had an extensive coke business with 130 beehive coke ovens in operation besides its ordinary coal trade. All of this was served by nearly 2,000 railway wagons, many of them built in the colliery workshops; six locomotives, one built by the colliery engineers; and 17 miles of sidings.

Blundell was Conservative and Unionist MP for the Ince Division of Lancashire in 1885-92 and again in 1895-1906 and took a prominent part in the debates on coal mines bills, especially the one leading to the important 1887 Coal Mines Act. He supported the Lancashire pit-brow-girls in their opposition to the clause proposed for the 1887 Act which banned them from surface work, depriving them of their jobs.

Colonel Henry Blundell married the Hon Beatrice, youngest daughter of Vice-Admiral the Hon Henry Dilkes-Byng. She had been for twelve years a Maid of Honour to Queen Victoria. Colonel Blundell built the magnificent red sandstone church of St Matthew, Highfield (the colliery village), as a memorial to her in 1894. There were no children of the marriage. Colonel Blundell died on 28 September 1906 leaving £375,939 gross.

DONALD ANDERSON

Sources:

Unpublished

In the collection of the author, Pemberton Colliery papers.

Published

Donald Anderson, 'Blundells Collieries' *Transactions of the Historical Society of Lancashire and Cheshire* 116 (1964), 117 (1965), 119 (1967).

—, *The Orrell Coalfield* (Buxton: Moorland Publishing Co, 1975).

— (with Jane Lane), *Mines and Miners of South Lancashire* (Ashton-in-Makerfield, Greater Manchester: the author, 1981).

—, *Coal. A Pictorial History of the British Coaling Industry* (Newton Abbot: David & Charles, 1982).

Wigan Observer and Wigan Examiner 1866 passim.

WWMP.

WWW.

BOLCKOW, Henry William Ferdinand

(1806-1878)

Iron and steel manufacturer

Henry William Ferdinand Bolckow was born at Sulten in the North German Grand Duchy of Mecklenberg on 8 December 1806, the son of Heinrich Bolckow, owner of a country estate, and Caroline Dussher. After being educated privately, Henry at fifteen was placed in a merchant's office in nearby Rostock. During his six years there, Bolckow met a Kiel youth, Christian Allhusen (qv) who soon departed to Newcastle upon Tyne to work with a brother; in 1827 Bolckow joined them in Newcastle as a clerk in their firm, C Allhusen & Co, engaged in the grain and shipping trades. Bolckow became a junior partner and, after twelve years in the speculative Tyneside trade, acquired a personal fortune of £40,000-£50,000.

By 1839 Bolckow met a practical ironmaker, John Vaughan (qv), and the two decided to form a partnership to exploit their combined resources of capital, financial acumen, and ironmaking skill. On the invitation of Joseph Pease, Bolckow and Vaughan turned to the small coal-shipping port of Middlesbrough, situated at the extremity of Pease's Stockton & Darlington Railway. In May 1840 they purchased six acres of land for £1,800, and a year later their jobbing ironworks opened, employing more than 100 in its forge, foundry and rolling mill. Bolckow was the business partner, leaving to Vaughan the making of products for railways, coal mines and ships. In 1846 the partners expanded into iron production by establishing blast furnaces at Witton Park in County Durham, but at this period there were occasions when financial failure was close.

However, the situation changed radically after 1850, when they began to quarry ironstone near to Middlesbrough; by late 1852 the first three blast furnaces to smelt this ore had been built nearby. Three years later, the partners possessed a dozen blast furnaces on Teesside, while other ironmakers had erected a further twenty. The population of Middlesbrough increased from 7,600 to 17,000 in five years, and by 1871 it was to increase again to 40,000. The Cleveland iron industry had emerged. In the same year, 1855, Bolckow & Vaughan supplied large quantities of cast-iron pipes for London's water mains. Throughout the 1850s, their enterprise prospered, and the partners added coal pits in Durham, limestone quarries, and fresh ironstone workings to their assets. In 1864, when the partnership was converted into a limited-liability company with a capital of £2.5 million, it was the largest then formed, and payment for the assets was fixed at close to £1 million. Manchester businessmen took a large interest in the company, of which Bolckow remained chairman until his death fourteen years later. For the seven years 1869-1875, profits available for distribution totalled £1,659,000. The nominal capital increased to £3.4 million, and over 12,000 were employed in 1875.

On Vaughan's withdrawal from active work ca 1864, Bolckow appointed a capable general manager, Edward Williams (qv), whose successor as works manager was E W Richards (qv). Bolckow supported Williams's opinion of the potential importance of the new bulk steel, and throughout the 1870s the company was involved in considerable expenditure on new plant to produce and process steel. As a result, it was able to make about 1,000 tons of steel rails a week during 1877-78, at a time when demand for iron goods had dropped to low level, and for some years after Bolckow's death it remained among the most important iron and steel companies in the world.

Bolckow desired full social acceptance in his adopted country. He became a naturalised Englishman in 1841. In the 1840s he was among the twelve improvement commissioners appointed for the new town of Middlesbrough; in 1853 he was elected its first mayor. He was one of the town's first five JPs, and a Tees conservancy commissioner; he was also DL for the North Riding of Yorkshire. In 1868, after successfully petitioning Parliament for a dispensation to enable him to qualify as an MP and a privy councillor, Bolckow was elected Liberal MP for the new Middlesbrough constituency. He held the seat until his death. A practising Anglican, Bolckow supported the temperance cause. The house he built in parkland four miles outside Middlesbrough contained a notable collection of paintings and other art objects. He seems to have been a man of sensitivity and compassion, conscious of his own good fortune compared with that of so many around him. He gave £5,000 in 1860 towards the cost of a hospital for Middlesbrough, and a few years later provided £6,600 for a primary day school as well as £30,000 for a 70 acre public park.

He had no children despite two marriages, firstly to Miriam Hay (d 1842) in 1841, and secondly to Harriet, only daughter of James Farrar of Halifax, in 1851. Despairing of producing an heir, in 1855 Bolckow invited his nephew, Carl F H Bolckow, to join him in England; after Henry's death Carl inherited the bulk of his uncle's estate and assumed the chairmanship of Bolckow Vaughan & Co Ltd.

Henry Bolckow died at Ramsgate on 18 June 1878 leaving personal effects sworn at under £800,000. He remembered five sisters, among others, in his will.

J K ALMOND

Sources:

Unpublished

British Steel Corporation, Northern Regional Records Centre, Middlesbrough. Bolckow Vaughan & Co Ltd, reports of annual meetings, 1866 to 1879.

PrC.

Published

DNB.

T Fenwick, 'H W F Bolckow' *Practical Magazine* (1873).

James S Jeans, *Pioneers of the Cleveland Iron Trade* (Middlesbrough: H G Reid, 1875).

JISI 1878.

Iron and Coal Trade Review 17 (9 Aug 1878).

Sir Hugh G Reid (ed), *Middlesbrough and Its Jubilee: A History of the Iron and Steel Industries, with Biographies of Its Pioneers* (Middlesbrough: H G Reid, 1881).

'The Jubilee of the Middlesbrough Iron Trade' *Northern Review* 17 June 1891.

Norman Moorsom, *The Birth and Growth of Modern Middlesbrough* (Middlesbrough: the author, 1967)

Ron Gott, *Henry Bolckow, Founder of Teesside* (Middlesbrough: Ron Gott, 1968).

WWMP.

BOLITHO, Thomas Bedford

(1835-1915)

Tin mine adventurer, smelter and banker

Thomas B Bolitho, by Stanhope Forbes, RA (from The First Fifty Years of the Institute of Bankers 1879–1929, *Blades, East & Blades Ltd, 1929).*

Thomas Bedford Bolitho was born in Cornwall on 5 January 1835, the third son of Edward Bolitho (1804-90), 'esquire' of Trewidden and his wife Mary, daughter of John Stephens, 'esquire' of Beerferris, Devon.

Edward Bolitho and his two brothers, Thomas Simon Bolitho (1808-81) and William (1815-95) by the 1850s had taken over the family tin smelting business (founded in the eighteenth century) of Bolitho, Sons & Co, with works at Chyandour, Calenick and Angarrack. The three brothers, apparently with little separation of responsibility between them, were key members of the Cornish 'Ring' of eight smelters which completely controlled the financing, purchasing, smelting and selling of tin. They were also major, though seldom majority, adventurers in all the noteworthy mines, such Dolcoath, Tincroft, Levant and Botallack. Furthermore, through marriage and interlocking partnerships, their bank, the Mount's Bay Bank in Penzance, was linked to other Cornish banks of consequence such as the East Cornwall Bank of Robins, Foster, Coode & Bolithos, and to Enthovens Bank of Helston. In addition they held wide interests as merchants, particularly in connection with the fishing industry.

The collapse of the price of tin from 1873 forced rapid mechanisation upon the mines. This led to heavy borrowing and the over-extension of many Cornish banks. In 1879 the West of England & South Wales Bank of Bristol failed, causing a financial panic throughout the West. A run started on the Cornish banks and Tweedy's Bank together with the Helston Union Bank crashed. The Bolithos' banking connections helped them to survive the crash of 1879; in this period too their financial interests enabled them to weather the decline of the Cornish tin industry, induced by the worldwide development of alternative sources of tin.

Thomas Bedford Bolitho was educated at Harrow and began work in the family business upon leaving school. He was admitted a full partner to Bolitho Sons & Co and to the Mount's Bay Bank in 1880. Increasingly he, together with his cousins Thomas Robins Bolitho (1840-1925) and William Edward Thomas (1862-1919) Bolitho, assumed joint responsibility for the firm's affairs, continuing the previous generation's pattern of triumvirate management with their individual responsibilities indistinguishable.

The Bolithos were deeply conservative, a weakness for their mining and smelting interests but a strength for their banking activities. They met the deepening crisis in Cornish mining defensively. As adventurers Bolitho Sons & Co do not appear to have shifted their investments on any extensive scale, although as bankers they closed many mines by refusing further loans. Those mines with which they were most closely associated remained cost book concerns and were characterised by old style management, little regard for new technology and reluctance to make fresh investment. This had tragic consequences on two occasions. At Wheal Owles Mine in 1893, eighteen men lost their lives after holing into flooded workings. The manager, by then in his eighties, had, over the years, drawn up increasingly faulty plans being unable to calculate for magnetic deviation. In 1908 the 'Man Engine' that raised and lowered miners from and to the surface, broke, but was patched up. In 1919 it collapsed again with the loss of thirty lives. Only at Basset Mines, where Thomas Bedford Bolitho was persuaded by Francis Oates (1848-1918), a mining entrepreneur, to back a capital-intensive expansion scheme on the South African model, was there a difference of approach, and this failed because of poor lodes.

The Bolithos strongly resisted challenges to the smelters' ring, such as the appearance of a new company, Penpol, formed in 1880 independently of the local ring. After the London Metal Exchange was formally instituted in 1881, thereafter determining the world price for tin, the Bolithos and their cartel apparently continued to fix Cornish tin prices for some while. Bolithos joined with Daubuz of Cavedras and Michell of Trerief to form the Cornish Consolidated Tin Smelting Co Ltd. This company continued to buy mainly Cornish ores and refused to expand production by buying much foreign ore to compensate for falling local output. Ageing equipment hampered increased productivity. A proposal by Horton Bolitho (1873-1945) that investment capital be obtained by going public, was so fiercely resisted by Thomas Bedford Bolitho and Thomas Robins Bolitho that they amended the constitution in 1908 specifically to exclude such a possibility. Other Cornish smelters, notably Williams Harvey & Co, relocated themselves at Liverpool (the main port of entry for foreign ores), re-equipping in the process, and thereby survived the depression in the home industry. In contrast, the Cornish

Consolidated Tin Smelting Co Ltd, after several loss-making years, closed in 1912. Nevertheless Thomas Bedford rescued the Cornish mines in 1914. The outbreak of war brought closure of the London Metal Exchange for three months, and the mines, unable to dispose of their tin, faced bankruptcy. Loans from Bolithos against their unsold stocks enabled the industry to survive the crisis.

As a banker, Thomas Bedford Bolitho adopted a more successful amalgamations policy. In 1889 Mount's Bay and East Cornwall Banks merged. Further amalgamations followed, notably the Redruth bank of Bain, Hitchens & Co in 1891. When Bolithos' main rival, Batten, Carne & Carne, crashed in 1896 this bank also joined the firm. Thus Bolithos as head of the newly-named Consolidated Bank of Cornwall Ltd, became the dominant financial force in the county. It was this bank, to which all the remaining mines looked for loan capital, which amalgamated with Barclays in 1905. Thomas Bedford played a leading part in negotiating the merger and remained head of the Penzance District board until 1911. Increasing ill health persuaded him to decline membership of Barclays main board, a position which was taken by his cousin Thomas Robins Bolitho. Thomas Bedford Bolitho was elected president of the Institute of Bankers in 1893.

With the ascendancy of his banking fortunes, Thomas Bedford Bolitho assumed a leading role in the political and civic life of Cornwall. In 1884 he became High Sheriff of the county. In 1885 he was elected president of the St Ives Division Liberal Association, subsequently splitting from it and joining the Unionists over the Home Rule issue. Despite these political differences however, in 1887 he was elected unopposed as MP for Penzance and St Ives, a seat he held for thirteen years, until he resigned due to ill health. Bolitho was vice-president of the Royal Cornwall Polytechnic Society, 1885-1887, and president, 1895-97. With Thomas Robins Bolitho he was joint Master of the Western Hunt until his death.

Thomas Bedford Bolitho's philanthropy towards the town of Penzance was considerable. His gifts financed the building of the Post Office, the St John's Hall, the Town Hall complex, the Penzance Seamen's Institute, the Edward Bolitho Convalescent Home (which he also endowed) and the West Cornwall Hospital. He donated £10,000 towards the building of the Newlyn Harbour Wall, thus enabling the rest to be raised from the Public Works Loans Board. His generosity was recognised in 1893 with the Freedom of Penzance.

In comparison the mining areas benefited little from his generosity. The St Just Institute is the only noticeable example of Bolitho philanthropy outside the Penzance environs. Yet at his death Thomas Bedford Bolitho was on the committees or directorates of Cooks Kitchen, Carn Brea, Levant, Tincroft, Basset Mines and Botallack mining companies. He seemed more concerned for the fishing than for the mining industry. In 1884, for example, he had been instrumental in getting the tax lifted on Cornish pilchards entering Italian ports. In 1896, he intervened in the violent dispute between Newlyn and East Coast fishermen over the Sunday fishing issue, securing the so-called 'Berington Compromise' (whereby ships could leave port on Sunday evening) paying, in addition, £700 out of his own pocket as compensation for fish thrown into the harbour during the riots.

Thomas Bedford Bolitho owned Tredwidden at Buryas Bridge, Penzance; Greenaway, near Dittisham in Devon; and Tregenna Castle, St Ives (which he sold to the Great Western Railway for a hotel). Like the rest of the family Thomas Bedford was a member of the Church of England. He married, in 1893, Frances Jane, daughter of E Carus-Wilson JP of Penmount, Truro. His only daughter, Mary, later married John Williams of Caerhays. She spent many years perfecting the gardens at Trewidden and producing new strains of camellia.

At his death on 22 May 1915 Thomas Bedford Bolitho left £550,038, a considerable increase on the £390,768 left by his father Edward, and some evidence of his acumen during a period of decline for the local economy in which he was active.

GILL BURKE

Sources:

Unpublished

Cornwall CRO, Bolitho papers, DDBL (2) 13, 38, 40; miscellaneous mining papers, DDX 104/2, 4(2), 15, 19.

MCe.

PrC.

Interviews with Major Simon Bolitho and G Salvadori (late of Barclays Bank, Penzance), both in August 1982.

Herbert Thomas, 'The Bolithos' (pp, 1914) (copy in Cornwall CRO).

Gillian M Burke, 'The Cornish Miner and the Cornish Mining Industry, 1870-1921' (London PhD, 1982).

Published

Edward Bosanketh, *Tin: A Novel* (T Fisher Unwin, 1888).

Gillian M Burke, 'The Poor Law and the Relief of Distress: West Cornwall 1870-1880' *Journal of the Royal Institution of Cornwall* 8 (1979).

Gillian M Burke and Peter Richardson, 'The Decline and Fall of the Cost Book System in the Cornish Mining Industry 1895-1914' *Business History* 23 (1981).

Anthony W Tuke and Philip W Mathews, *A History of Barclays Bank Limited* (Blades, East & Blades, 1926).

Peter A S Pool, *A History of the Town and Borough of Penzance* (Penzance: Corporation of Penzance, 1974).

PP, RC Mining Royalties (1890-91) C 6331.

PP, RC Annual Report of HM Inspectors of Mines (1894) C 7339.

PP, RC On Breaking of a Man Engine at Levant Mine, Pendeen, 1919 (1920) Cmd 557.

J A Shearne, *Cornish Banks and Bankers* (pp, 1956).

Herbert Thomas, 'Thomas Bedford Bolitho' *Journal of the Royal Cornwall Polytechnic Society* new series 5 (1923-26).

Western Morning News 24 May 1915.

WWMP.

WWW.

Sir George L F Bolton (courtesy of the Bank of England).

BOLTON, Sir George Lewis French

(1900-1982)

Banker

George Lewis French Bolton was born in Hackney, east London, on 16 October 1900, the son of William George Lewis Bolton, a shipping clerk, and his wife Beatrice Louise née French. He was educated at Leytonstone County High School and at the age of sixteen trained as a foreign exchange dealer in the London branch of the Société Générale de Paris and witnessed the wild fluctuations and heavy speculation in foreign exchanges in 1918-19. He joined the merchant banking firm of Helbert, Wagg in 1920, working in both London and Paris, and gaining experience in exchange and security arbitrage, the discount and commodity markets and international banking. He organised, and managed with conspicuous success, Helbert, Wagg's new foreign exchange department; the reputation he won there led to his recruitment in January 1933 by the Bank of England as one of their first foreign exchange specialists.

He was deputy principal of the Bank's Foreign Exchange section from September 1934 and principal from March 1936, following the death of the chief dealer, Robert Kay. As such he had charge of the market management of the floating pound sterling, with the Exchange Equalisation Account formed after the abandonment of the gold standard as his main resource. By confining the Bank's large foreign exchange dealings to a small number of approved houses, Bolton purged the London foreign exchange market of many of the innumerable and sometimes dishonest agents and small brokers who had mushroomed during the currency chaos of the 1920s. In 1937, convinced of the inevitability of war with Germany, Bolton secretly began preparations for a structure of wartime exchange control, which was smoothly implemented after the outbreak of hostilities throughout the British Empire (excepting Canada). This was the genesis of the sterling area.

Bolton was appointed adviser to the Bank of England on exchange and monetary policy in March 1941, and became increasingly crucial in high policy affecting the pound sterling and foreign exchanges. Although largely responsible for developing the sterling area and the apparatus of foreign exchange control, Bolton 'hated bureaucratic controls and interference with the business of the markets' and disliked administering regulations. 'But he was superb as a generator of ideas' and 'would produce schemes, suggestions, proposals as a machine-gun spits bullets' {Fry (1970) 22}.

In 1948 he was made an executive director of the Bank of England by the Governor, Lord Catto (qv), holding responsibility for the Bank's international dealings. During the late 1940s he had to cope with the sterling convertibility crisis, the devaluation of 1949, policy and negotiations entailed by the sterling area and the re-creation of the European monetary system, including the first European Payments Union which he helped to devise. As part of the world monetary structure created at Bretton Woods, he was British executive director of the International Monetary Fund in 1946-52 and was the IMF's alternative director (in effect Britain's financial representative) in 1952-57. He was also a director in 1949-57 of the Bank of International Settlements which had been created by European central bankers to further monetary and other co-operation. Throughout this period when Cameron Cobbold (qv) was Governor of the Bank of England, Bolton was acknowledged as the Bank's leading expert on international monetary and foreign exchange policy, but he

> was never really part of the institution. He remained a market man, a dealer at heart ... he had little patience for the routine answer and took little interest in the machinery. But he had a rare capacity for vision ... his was a strong personality; you had to be pretty determined to make your own views heard when he was about. He [was] always ... interested in human motives, in the consequences of policies for mankind. That, and his intense interest in history and world affairs, probably explained his taste for sweeping statements — a taste that ... sometimes frightened off the more pedantic officials he was trying to win over {Fry (1970) 22-23}.

In 1952 Bolton was one of the chief proponents of the ROBOT plan for a 'dash for freedom' with a floating pound, and was bitter at its rejection on obsolete political grounds. He felt impatience with Britain's subsequent slow moves towards convertibility, in which he was necessarily involved, and in 1957 left executive responsibilities at the Bank of England (although sitting as a non-executive member of the Court of Directors until 1968) to become chairman of the Bank of London & South America.

During the thirteen years before his retirement as BOLSA chairman in 1970, Bolton transformed it from a regional to an international bank and greatly expanded its business. Issued capital rose from £5.05 million in 1957 to £21.1 million in 1969; while net members' funds rose from £9.3 million to £33.6 million and gross group assets from £146 million to £790 million over the same period. He believed that the Churchill Government's decisions on sterling in 1952 had foredoomed its international role, and that BOLSA had to forge new links with the US dollar if it were to maintain business or grow. For this reason he was chiefly instrumental in developing the Eurodollar market in London. He propelled BOLSA to form jointly with the Bank of Montreal the new

Bank of London & Montreal, of which he became chairman. BOLAM rapidly expanded business in both the Caribbean and Latin America, and in 1970 became a wholly-owned subsidiary of BOLSA. Bolton also arranged, in 1965, for the Mellon Bank of Pittsburgh to acquire 15 per cent of BOLSA, thus tightening their connection with the USA. He was himself in 1961-80 a director of the Canadian Pacific Railway and its subsidiary interests in air services, oil, gas and steamships, together with Sun Life Assurance of Canada and other North American concerns.

In 1960, in order to diversify into investment and merchant banking, BOLSA bought the Balfour Williamson group, which had specialised in South American business for a century. Bolton became a director of Balfour Williamson, as well as of the Alexander Hamilton Fund SA floated by BOLSA in 1967 in association with the Royal Bank of Scotland, Banque Worms and Svenska Handelsbanken as one of the earliest offshore investment funds. He was additionally a director of the ADELA Investment Co formed in 1964 as a multi-national private investment bank for private productive enterprise in Latin America with BOLSA as a coordinator of its fifteen British shareholders.

At BOLSA Bolton was described by Sir Siegmund Warburg as 'a merchant adventurer'; half-teasingly by Sir Frank Lee of the Treasury as 'a reckless adventurer' {Fry (1970) 7, 37}; and by one journalist as an 'adventurous banker' {Sampson (1982) 332}. He introduced more progressive methods of staff recruitment and training to bring more native South Americans to positions of high responsibility, a reform which had been urged on British business in the area as early as 1928 by Sir Malcolm Robertson, the British Ambassador to Buenos Aires. Bolton also launched a major rebuilding programme of BOLSA's Latin American offices. After his retirement as chairman in 1970, he was made BOLSA's honorary president.

The range of his other activities was international. He was chairman of the Commonwealth Development Finance Co (1968-80), Premier Consolidated Oilfields (1974-76), London United Investments (from 1971), London & Bombay United Investments, and International Banking Services. Following the ructions between Sir Basil Smallpeice (qv) and 'Tiny' Rowlands, he was appointed deputy-chairman of Lonrho in 1973 and aided many of that company's 'sudden ambushes, secret penetrations and deadly raids' {Sampson (1982) 332} . He was recruited to the board of another multinational, the Rio Tinto Zinc Corporation, together with its Australian subsidiary, and the Consolidated Zinc Co. After leaving the BOLSA board he became a director of Lloyds Bank International, and also held directorships with the London International Trust, the Kuwait Investment Office, Clugston Holdings and Commonwealth Development Finance's Malaysian subsidiary.

Bolton was a member of the Kuwait Investment Advisory Committee, the Atlantic Trade Study Group, the Committee on Invisible Exports and the Group for the Formulation and Propagation of National Industry Policy. He was sheriff of London in 1952 and 1961, governor of the London School of Economics from 1961, and a member of the council of Benenden girls school in Kent. He was also chairman of the Bolton Enquiry on the future of small firms which reported in 1971, and continued to make public statements on the importance of small firms in

A BANKER'S WORLD

The Revival of the City 1957-1970

Speeches and Writings of
SIR GEORGE BOLTON

Edited by Richard Fry
with a foreword by Sir Frank Lee

HUTCHINSON OF LONDON

Title Page of G L F Bolton, A
Banker's World, *Hutchinson, 1970.*

the economy after the enquiry was concluded. He was created KCMG in 1950, and received decorations from Argentina in 1960 and Chile in 1965.

He was characterised by 'disdain for orthodoxy, enthusiasm for all that is new, searching, promising ... profound pessimism, moral fervour and vigorous pugnacity' {Bolton (1970) 183-4}. Well-read and well-informed, always lively, he was a pungent critic of British government policies from the early 1950s onwards. He alike deplored excessive government expenditure, exorbitant wage increases and monetarism, which he predicted would produce economic recession without halting inflation. Similarly he deprecated the dissolution of the sterling area, embracing Commonwealth countries, which he had helped to create, and repeatedly maintained that the economic arguments of British proponents of the Common Market were cant.

Bolton married, in March 1928, at Paddington, May, daughter of Charles Colley Howcroft, a designer, by whom he had one son and two daughters. He died on 2 September 1982, leaving £454,497 gross.

R P T DAVENPORT-HINES

Writings:

PP, Evidence (16 Dec 1957) to Tribunal of Enquiry into Allegations of Improper Disclosure of Information relating to the Raising of the Bank Rate (1958) Cmnd 350.

article on Latin American banking *Times* (Latin American supplement) 10 Aug 1959.

tribute to Sir Anthony Grafftey-Smith *ibid* 8 Nov 1960.

article on Britain and EEC *BOLSA Review* Oct 1961.

tribute to Sir Charles Hambro *Times* 2 Sept 1963.

article urging closer Anglo-USA monetary cooperation *ibid* 30 Sept 1963.

tribute to Lionel Fraser of Helbert, Wagg *ibid* 6 Jan 1965.

article on international monetary problems *Times* 25 May 1966.

article on EEC *ibid* 28 Oct 1966.

article on US banking *ibid* 8 May 1967.

article on Latin America *ibid* 5 Sept 1967.

article on sterling devaluation *ibid* 12 Sept 1967.

(jointly) *The European Capital Market* (Federal Trust for Education & Research, 1967).

article on overseas banking *Times* 21 Nov 1968.

article 'Britain's European Dilemma' *Euromoney* (London) Oct 1969.

(ed Richard Fry) *A Banker's World: The Revival of the City 1957-70. Speeches and Writings of Sir George Bolton* (Hutchinson, 1970).

letter on US dollar crisis *Times* 19 Aug 1971.

Report of Bolton Committee of Enquiry on Small Firms (1971) Cmnd 4811.

paper on stockpiling plan to spur world trade *Times* 6 April 1972.

Sources:

Unpublished
BCe.

MCe.

Published
Suzanne Cronje, *Portrait of a Multinational* (Penguin, 1976).

David Joslin, *A Century of Banking in Latin America* (Oxford University Press, 1963).

Cecil H King, *Diary 1965-70* (Cape, 1972).

Parry Committee report on Latin American studies (HMSO, 1965).

Fred Peart, letter to *Times* 15 Nov 1972.

Anthony T S Sampson, *Changing Anatomy of Britain* (Hodder & Stoughton, 1982).

Times 3 Sept 1982.

WW 1982.

BOND, Stanley Shaw

(1877-1943)
Publisher

Stanley Shaw Bond, c. 1930.

Stanley Shaw Bond was born at Wimbledon on 8 July 1877, the second son of Charles Bond, joint proprietor (with his brother Richard) of Shaw & Sons, the local government stationers, printers and publishers. They acquired this interest through their mother, Jane Shaw, the great-granddaughter of the founder of the firm. Stanley Bond was educated privately and apparently was a sickly youth.

On 8 January 1895 the proprietor of the family law publishing business of Butterworth & Co, founded in 1818, died. His executors were instructed in his will to sell the business. Charles and Richard Bond, 'trading as Shaw & Sons', made an offer of £5,500 for the goodwill, copyrights and stock, and this was accepted on 25 June 1895.

Charles Bond put in his young son Stanley (whose eighteenth birthday fell in the same month as the completion of the sale) to conduct the day-to-day business of the new acquisition. During the next twelve years the Bond brothers rationalised their business. By 1908 Shaw's publishing interests had been transferred to Butterworths; Richard had relinquished his interest in Butterworths; and Stanley was receiving a share of profits. In 1908 Charles Bond's equity in Butterworths was converted into a mortgage bearing a fixed interest, though he retained a few books as his private property, published by the firm on commission. He continued to keep a 'fatherly eye' on the business, and kept a room there, at least until 1912.

To begin with Stanley received from his father £40 a year, increased to £120 in 1899, and to £175 the next year, plus £37 10s 'share of profits'. By this time Stanley had conceived his first triumph, the 20-volume *Encyclopaedia of Forms and Precedents*. Stanley produced this at his own risk, and it was published by the firm on commission. The first volume appeared in 1902; in 1903 the project brought Stanley a profit of £1,842.

The *Encyclopaedia* was followed in 1907 by an even more ambitious publication, *Halsbury's Laws of England*. The complete re-statement of the law of England, from all sources, was the successful attempt of a young man of thirty to do something which the Government had abandoned. The 31 volumes were completed in 1917. Two other encyclopaedias rounded off Bond's plan: the *English and Empire Digest* (45 volumes, 1920-30) and *Halsbury's Statutes of England* (20 volumes, 1929-31). New editions of both the *Encyclopaedia* and *Halsbury's Laws* were published during Bond's lifetime. Other smaller encyclopaedias were developed by Bond in his later years, and two (*Court Forms* and *Words and Phrases*) were still incomplete at the time of his death.

These encyclopaedias were Bond's unique contribution to legal literature. Maurice Maxwell, a director and past chairman of the rival business, Sweet & Maxwell, attested: 'Stanley Shaw Bond introduced professionalism into law publishing, and it took the other law publishers nearly half a century to catch up with him in this respect' {Maxwell (1974) 133}. Bond was a man with a great creative talent, which he was able to bring to fruition by building up loyal and industrious teams of editors (salaried and free-lance) and salesmen. He secured lawyers of the first rank (like Lord Halsbury and Lord Atkin), as editors-in-chief.

But he had commercial flair also. He obtained subscribers by sending representatives of a high calibre to call on lawyers in their chambers and offices. He tied subscribers to him by means of annual up-dating services, which were included in the original order. He was a pioneer of 'instalment sales'.

His involvement in textbook publishing was modest, but he took a keen interest in his two weekly journals (the *Justice of the Peace*, a Shaw publication, on which he worked before the acquisition of Butterworths, and the *Law Journal*). His last triumph of personal courage and foresight was the launching of the *All England Law Reports* in 1936. This, the first weekly series of law reports, still has the largest circulation in the Commonwealth.

In 1936 Bond also took the first step towards a new ambition: to do for medicine what he had done for law. The first medical encyclopaedia was launched in that year.

Bond soon saw the potential for his publications in the Empire. He formed companies in England to trade in Australasia and India (1910), in Canada (1912) and in South Africa (1934). The London business was not incorporated until 1927, when Bond changed the name of the Canadian company to Butterworth & Co (Publishers) Ltd, increasing its authorised capital to £250,000, and transferring his London business to the company in return for shares. A company trading in Canada was incorporated in Ontario in 1931; locally incorporated companies in the other dominions did not come until after 1967. Throughout Bond's life the various businesses were personally and directly owned by him, and there was no structure of parent and subsidiary companies.

This illustrates his management style. He was an autocrat. He expected absolute loyalty to himself. He was generous in private (including generosity to staff in need), but he had the reputation of underpaying authors and employees. But it was his business, and it had to be run his way.

For many years, from 1910 to 1938, he had a trusted general manager/managing director, G C Bellew. By 1937 he had reason to doubt the quality of Bellew's management, and he was urged (particularly by his solicitor, Gilbert West) to enlarge the top management. The publishing manager, J W Whitlock, was appointed a director in April 1937, and four more were appointed in November 1937, when a new 'Working Plan' was promulgated. The curtailing of his powers did not appeal to Bellew, who left on 31 October 1938. A part-time deputy chairman and managing director was appointed, but increasingly in fact, and in name from April 1940, Bond was his own managing director. Throughout the period he was styled chairman and governing director.

Much of the profit of the business was ploughed back, and Butterworths financed its own instalment sales. But Bond tried to increase his free reserves by transactions on the stock and commodity markets. His intention thus to avoid the effect of death duties on a family business was frustrated by war conditions at the time of his death, and his trustees had to sell 39 per cent of the shares (for £231,000) to pay death duties.

Bond's private interests were shooting, stalking, golf and travel. His London home was in Cleveland Row, St James's. In 1932 he became the tenant of Braemar Castle, and in 1935 also of West Dean Park, near Chichester. At both of these he was able to pursue his interests. On the outbreak of war in 1939 many of the Butterworth staff were moved to West Dean Park. Bond acquired the smaller Dycheham Park, near Petersfield, as his private refuge, as well as continuing to use Braemar Castle, and a suite at West Dean, where he died.

He was concerned with various charitable objects. He was honorary treasurer of the Royal Association in Aid of the Deaf and Dumb, and a governor of Queen Alexandra's Hospital Home for Soldiers. In 1933 he became a member of the Central Board of Finance of the Church of England, and he was its vice-chairman at the time of his death.

In the spring of 1938 Bond (then aged sixty) announced his engagement to Miss Myrtle Fletcher, a niece of the Seventh Earl Fitzwilliam. They married in November 1938; he died four years later. Two sons were born to them, in 1940 and 1942; they and his wife survived Bond, and the company entered on a long period of being 'in trust'.

Bond died of pneumonia on 14 February 1943, aged sixty-five, when he seemed to the staff to be still a man of unbounded energy and leadership. He left £516,600 gross.

H KAY JONES

Sources:

Unpublished

Family letters and papers.

BOND Stanley Shaw

Butterworth & Co Publishers Ltd, business papers and correspondence.

Published

Aberdeen Press and Journal 17 Feb 1943.

Church of England Newspaper 19 Feb 1943.

Daily Telegraph 29 Sept 1943.

Evening Express (Aberdeen) 16, 17 Feb 1943.

Guardian 19 Feb 1943.

H K Jones, *Butterworths: History of a Publishing House* (Butterworths, 1980).

Maurice W Maxwell, 'Law Publishing: The Development of Law Publishing 1799–1974' in *Then and Now 1799–1974. Commemorating 175 Years of Law Bookselling and Publishing* (Sweet & Maxwell, 1974).

Scotsman 18 Feb 1943.

Sussex Daily News 18 Feb 1943.

Times 16 Feb 1943.

WWW.

Sir Henry C O Bonsor (courtesy of The Brewers' Society).

BONSOR, Sir Henry Cosmo Orme

(1848-1929)

Brewer

Henry Cosmo Orme Bonsor was born at Great Bookham, near Dorking, on 2 September 1848, the son of Joseph Bonsor (1807-73), 'gentleman' {BCe}, who left £300,000 at his death, and Eliza Denne née Orme. Bonsor was educated at Eton and then joined Combe & Co, brewers, in 1867. In the late 1870s he became chairman of Combe & Co, then a small London brewing firm.

During the 1880s and 1890s Combe & Co, under his chairmanship, adopted a vigorous and aggressive policy over tied trade and retailing. The company was one of the earliest of the London brewers to involve itself heavily in purchasing licensed outlets, which it often improved through judicious investment and positive marketing. There is no evidence that either Combe (or later Watney Combe Reid) had products of an outstanding quality, but their marketing made them successful.

Bonsor drove Combe & Co from a position on the periphery of the

London brewing trade in the 1870s to become, through the amalgamation of 1898, part of the largest brewing concern in London, and the nearest competitor to the giants of the industry, Bass and Guinness. His true role in bringing about the formation of Watney Combe & Reid Co Ltd in 1898 may never be fully known, but it is clear that he was the moving force as he became the company's first chairman, a position he held until 1928.

He also contributed in large measure to the growth of the National Trade Defence Association (NTDA), acting both as chairman and treasurer from its inception in 1888 until 1895. This influential position allowed him to mould the extra-parliamentary agitation of the drink trade against government interference, during a period when the temperance lobby was strong in Parliament, and also reinforced his Parliamentary authority as a spokesman for the trade.

Bonsor's experience with Watney Combe Reid was less happy. The company was floated at £15 million, an inflated valuation, and it never truly recovered its prosperity during his lifetime. The capital was subject to writing down as trade declined in the twentieth century, and Watneys lost, temporarily, its dominant position in London. Bonsor seems also to have been slow to rationalise the new company in the period before the First World War, another blow to the company's prosperity. Between 1898 and 1929 the company's assets scarcely rose, moving from £11 million to £11.5 million.

In the trade Bonsor was particularly well-respected. He was master of the Brewers' Company in 1881, was a leading figure in the creation of the Brewers' Society in 1904, and was a vice-president of the Institute of Brewing from 1904.

Outside the brewing industry Bonsor was chairman of the South Eastern Railway Co from 1898 until its amalgamation into the Southern Railway in 1923; director of the Bank of England, 1885; treasurer of Guy's Hospital; chairman of the Income Tax Commissioners for the City of London, 1886-1925; a JP and DL for Surrey and a DL and alderman of the City of London. He sat as Conservative MP for Surrey North East (Wimbledon Division) from 1885 until he retired in 1900. He was created a baronet in 1925 and was an officer of the Légion d'Honneur.

He married twice: in 1872, Emily Gertrude, daughter of James Fellowes of Kingston House, Dorset, by whom he had three sons and four daughters; after her death in 1882 he married Mabel, second daughter of James Brand, JP, of Sanderstead Court, Croydon, Surrey. His son Arthur Bonsor (1882-1966) was chairman of Watneys 1948-50 and left £166,696 gross. Sir Henry Bonsor died on 4 December 1929, leaving £717,528 gross.

TOM CORRAN

Sources:

Unpublished

BCe.

PrC.

SSRC Elites data.

Published

Brewing Trade Review 1 Jan 1980.

Henry H Janes, *The Red Barrel. A History of Watney Mann* (John Murray, 1963).

Thomas H Corran, *The Brewing Industry in Britain, 1830-1969* (forthcoming).

WWMP.

WWW.

Jesse Boot (courtesy of The Boots Co Ltd).

BOOT, Jesse

1st Lord Trent of Nottingham

(1850-1931)

Manufacturing and retail chemist

Jesse Boot was born in Nottingham on 2 June 1850, the only son of John Boot, a medical herbalist newly arrived from the country, by his second wife Mary, daughter of Benjamin Wills of Nottingham. The father was a dedicated Wesleyan preacher, but his interest in popular medicine stemmed from the Thomsonians in America rather than John Wesley's *Primitive Physic*. However, he brought an evangelistic passion from Wesleyanism into his business, using his itinerant lay ministry as a vehicle for bringing his herbal prescriptions to the poor, and passing his sense of mission on to his son, whose adult sympathies also lay with evangelical Nonconformity.

Jesse was only ten when his father died and he shortly had to leave school to help support his mother and sister, working long hours in the little herbalist shop to serve his working class clientele. The Thomsonian movement largely disappeared in America in the middle 1850s and in Britain within the next decade, but in 1870 Mrs Boot, loyally attached to the image of the business built up by her husband, still advertised herself and her son as 'medical botanists'. The working classes were now transferring their allegiance to well-advertised patent medicines, so the survival of the little shop in Goosegate demanded a recasting of policy. Boot decided to enter the proprietary medicine business in 1874 but, lacking capital to launch a remedy of his own, hit on the solution of selling a range of others' medicines at cut-prices. Backed by various local tradesmen, he launched an advertising campaign in the *Nottingham Daily*

Express in February 1877. His boldness caused a minor sensation in the town and increased his weekly takings from £20 to £100.

The success of this campaign not only launched Boot into the first rank of his branch of retail trade, but also established the cardinal points of his business policy for the rest of his long career: popular advertising, direct challenge to the 'old fashioned' retailers, high turnover and small profit margins, along with regular attempts to establish his own proprietary lines. He won the steadfast support of a circle of his friends and employees, but also provoked bitter hostility and recurrent difficulties with the vested interests. After building attractive premises in Goosegate (1883), he began to duplicate his successful formula by opening branches in Lincoln, Sheffield, and other towns within a short train journey. He had always manufactured some of his own remedies, and in 1885 began to lease space in various factories near the Midland Station. However, the most important development at this time came when Boot incorporated his rapidly growing business. A legal action that went all the way up to the House of Lords, *Pharmaceutical Society v The London & Provincial Supply Association Ltd*, produced the far-reaching decision that limited liability companies could employ qualified pharmacists. Boot grasped the opportunity to move into dispensing but, more importantly, to recruit a corps of educated managers with the capacity to maintain his proliferating retail branches. For ever enthusiastic about shop display, advertising and packaging, Boot established his own building, shopfitting and printing departments, to give the most rapid form to his endless flow of ideas. A trip to America in 1889 also enlarged his ideas on retail trade.

Boot worked so hard to build up his business that in 1886 he suffered a nervous breakdown. Packed off to Jersey for his first holiday, he fell in love with Florence Anne Rowe, who worked for her father William Rowe in a little bookshop in St Helier. After their marriage, Florence maintained her business interests by building up 'No 2 Department' (stationery, books, fancy goods, pictures and so forth) within Boot's shops. She also acted as personnel manager for all the girls employed in Boot's shops, warehouses and factories.

Meanwhile, Boot's retail expansion was threatened with containment by the vigorous growth of Taylor's Drug Stores, which spread out from Leeds, and Day's Drug Stores, which dominated the metropolitan area, and there were other growing chains in Bristol and Portsmouth. Seeking allies to conquer new territories, Boot first went into partnership with Alderman (later Sir) James Duckworth (1840-1915) of Rochdale, a Methodist tea dealer who had built up a grocery chain in Lancashire but was now increasingly involved in politics. In the 1890s Boots Cash Chemists (Lancashire) Ltd colonised much of this new territory. But Boot's greatest retail coup came in 1901 when he acquired Day's companies in London and the South of England, 65 shops and two warehouses, and formed Boots Cash Chemists (Southern) Ltd. He now began to advertise in the national press as well as the leading provincial dailies. The new acquisitions increased rather than quenched his thirst for new shops; the number of branches rose from 251 in 1901 to 560 in 1914. At the same time, he was constantly refurbishing and extending his existing shops. In 1903 one of the Nottingham shops was demolished to build a prestige departmental store in the fashionable Gothic style, and the successful experiment was soon duplicated in a sequence of other large towns. Boot's urge to build was complemented by his wife's passion for interior décor and ornamentation. In historic towns they restored or created new medieval-style shop frontages, while the approbation of good taste was also conferred by Mrs Boot's 'Booklovers' Library' and tearooms in the larger branches.

The phenomenal growth of Boots was not achieved without stiff opposition, partly from the Pharmaceutical Society, but more particularly from a militant association of small retail chemists which called itself the Proprietary Articles Trade Association. It was built up by (Sir) W S Glyn-Jones (qv) from 1896, working on the principle of using the united strength of the private chemists to force selected manufacturers to adopt resale price maintenance. Boot attacked the PATA by advertisements in the press and in his shops, and by lobbying in Parliament. He formed the Drug Companies' Association to collect support, but the overall effect was to restrain him, especially when Glyn-Jones began stirring up the Pharmaceutical Society. Six attempts were made to introduce legislation to prevent companies employing pharmacists (1903-8), all without success, but the personal toll on Jesse Boot's health was heavy.

The financing of the furious growth of Boot's business exhibited some novel features. Though he formed a sequence of companies beginning with Boot & Co Ltd in 1883, the shares were not quoted on the Stock Exchange until after the sale to Liggetts. Many of the shares were sold over the counter to Boots' customers, the managers receiving a commission on sales, while the company secretary acted as a private broker. In the early years financial support was drawn from local solicitors, tradesmen, and the Nottingham Joint-Stock Bank, but their contribution was soon dwarfed by that of hundreds of private shareholders, to whom Boot sent attractively-printed reports every quarter. Boot & Co Ltd became Boots Pure Drug Co in 1888, with subsidiary companies formed at various dates for Lancashire and for the West, South, East and North.

The First World War gave Boots the opportunity to enter the manufacture of fine chemicals, but otherwise did not change the basic structure of the business. Now gripped by chronic arthritis, Boot struggled on to the end of the war when failing health finally forced him to retire. He had no faith in his only son, John Campbell Boot, so in 1920 he sold his controlling interest to Louis K Liggett, chief of the Rexall group of chemists in America. Ownership was not repatriated until after Boot's death.

Now a bed-ridden arthritic, Boot retired to Jersey and the South of France, wondering how to dispose of the £2.275 million 'windfall' from the sale to Liggetts. He believed, not without some justification, that his wife, son and two daughters were too extravagant with his money, and he wanted to spend it on something more durable. He gave large sums to his native city to provide parks, boulevards, and hospital wards, but the main beneficiary was University College, Nottingham, which was rebuilt on a palatial scale on a greenfield site outside the town. When the building was opened by King George V in 1928, Boot, a knight since 1909 and baronet since 1916 (thanks to his gifts to the Liberal party), was created Lord Trent of Nottingham.

On Jesse Boot's death in 1931, he was succeeded by his only son J C Boot (1889-1954) who was chairman of Boots from 1926 to 1954 and first Chancellor of the University of Nottingham from 1948 to 1954. John Boot inherited his mother's good taste and 'up-market' aspirations, so that during his period of leadership the old rumbustious salesmanship steadily gave way to superior quality and service, while the efficiency of the business was improved by methods introduced from Liggetts in America.

Jesse Boot died in Jersey on 13 June 1931 leaving an estate valued at £222,317 gross in England.

S D CHAPMAN

Sources:

Unpublished

BCe.

PrC.

Published

Stanley D Chapman, *Jesse Boot of Boots the Chemists* (Hodder & Stoughton, 1974).

—, 'Jesse Boot: A Postcript' *Boots News* 7 July 1976.

DNB.

John E Greenwood, *A Cap for Boots. An Autobiography* (Hutchinson, 1977).

Times 15 June 1931.

WWW.

BOOTH, Alfred

(1834-1914)

Leather merchant and shipowner

Alfred Booth was born in Liverpool on 3 September 1834, the eldest son of Charles Booth and Emily Fletcher. Educated locally, Alfred Booth enjoyed a middle-class Liverpool background which combined business acumen with Liberal political sympathies and radical Nonconformity. His paternal grandfather, Thomas Booth, the younger son of a small landowner from near Warrington, had been apprenticed to a Liverpool corn merchant in the 1760s before becoming a successful corn factor and shipowner.

Alfred Booth did not enter the family business but from 1850 worked for the shipping agents, Lamport & Holt. His brother Charles (1840-1916), subsequently famous for his pioneering social investigations, joined him but Alfred left in 1857 for a brief appointment with Rathbones at New York, gaining valuable experience in the important Atlantic trades. Then, in 1860 Alfred Booth formed a partnership with his brother and an American, Walden, to export skins to the United States, a small, specialist enterprise, which required the detailed knowledge and contacts Booth now possessed but which did not compete with established merchant houses. Upon Walden's retirement in 1863 the partnership was reconstituted as Alfred Booth & Co of Liverpool and Booth & Co of New York with the brothers as principals.

Business, supplemented by shipping agencies and produce handling, did not immediately prosper, its diverse nature requiring funds and experience beyond the partners' resources. Alfred Booth's main interest, the leather trade, depended on a familiar pattern of commissions and sales upon consignment rather than outright ownership which tied up capital and restricted expansion. With fluctuating prices, seasonal variations, large advances to suppliers on bills of exchange, remittance problems from the United States and imperfect knowledge, success required skill and good fortune. Improving American prospects after the Civil War and investment in leather manufacturing on both sides of the Atlantic slowly brought prosperity.

Then, from 1866, a small legacy financed Booth's diversification into steamships just as the compound engine was revolutionising cargo traffic. Encouraged, perhaps, by Lamport's success in South America but, as in leather, avoiding competition with established carriers, the firm loaded for North Brazil. Again, since cargoes were small and sailing ships undercut steamers, profits eluded Booths until the 1870s, after which agreements with competitors and resistance to outsiders brought stability. Booths integrated leather and shipping into mutually supporting activities as Brazilian skins were exchanged for American produce, with the parent company acting as a holding and financing organisation. For the first twenty years success bypassed the firm, but by 1914 Booths dominated the Amazon trades, operating one of Liverpool's largest shipping fleets which had grown to over 120,000 tons, and owned the pioneering Surpass Tanning Co in America, which attained international status in kid leather.

It is tempting to ascribe this progress to the senior partner's commercial skills. Alfred Booth certainly possessed qualities crucial for business success, sound judgement, an inability to suffer fools, composure during commercial crises and an insistence upon well-defined principles for efficient day-to-day administration. His was a tactical awareness which complemented his brother's longer-term strategic sense. Yet Booth, in business from necessity not choice, clearly preferred country life on a modest income to an irksome commercial career. He retired early in 1887, before the firm's conspicuous success, although his mature judgement remained available to his successors. It is also true that Booth's early experience in product trading and shipping management, the partnership's survival in the 1860s and its financial resources, all owed much to his family's alliances with the Holts, Lamports and Rathbones, fellow Unitarians and pillars of Liverpool's commercial élite.

Luck, hard-work and adaptability, enabling him to learn quickly and profit from past mistakes were important but, as Charles Booth recognised, 'the real plan in succeeding in business is to choose such a course that the tide of affairs is with you' {John (1959) 71}. Alfred Booth's achievement was to seize opportunities in activities which proved winners. Honest, reserved and detached but inspiring loyalty and affection, Booth, therefore, represented the best tradition of Liverpool merchants.

To his business enterprise were added his considerable public and philanthropic activities as a magistrate and devout Unitarian. He married in 1867 Lydia née Butler, by whom he had six children. Alfred Booth died on 2 November 1914 leaving an estate of £43,763 gross.

ROBERT GREENHILL

Sources:

Published

Alfred Booth, 1834-1914. A Biographical Sketch (Liverpool: Henry Young & Sons Ltd, 1915).

George Chandler, *Liverpool Shipping* (Phoenix House, 1960).

Arthur H John, *A Liverpool Merchant House: Being the History of Alfred Booth and Company 1863-1958* (George Allen & Unwin, 1959).

H A Whiting, *Alfred Booth: Some Memories, Letters and Other Family Records* (1917).

Liverpool Courier 3 Nov 1914.

Liverpool Daily Post and Mercury 3 Nov 1914.

Times 3 Nov 1914.

BOOTH, George Macaulay

(1877-1971)

Entrepreneur and founder of the unit trust movement in Britain

Sketch of George M Booth by A K Lawrence RA, 1929 (from Duncan Crow, A Man of Push and Go. The Life of George Macaulay Booth, Rupert Hart-Davis, 1965).

George Macaulay Booth was born at Kensington, London, on 22 September 1877, the fourth child of Charles Booth (1840-1916) PC, FRS, of Gracedieu Manor, Loughborough, and his wife Mary Catherine (1847-1939), daughter of Charles Zachary Macaulay (1813-1886) and niece of Lord Macaulay. Charles Booth was partner in the Booth steamship line and in the Liverpool merchant house of Alfred Booth, tanners and international dealers in skins, with factories in Nottingham, Lincoln, Abingdon and Hitchin; he was also interested in Brazilian harbour development, and as the author of *Life and Labour of the People in London* (17 vols, 1891-1903), was one of the founders of British sociology. He left £150,939 in 1916.

G M Booth was educated at Harrow in 1891-95, and then travelled in France and the USA before going to Trinity College, Cambridge, in 1896. He originally wished to be a surgeon, but in 1899 entered the London office of Alfred Booth & Co, of which he took effective charge from 1908. In the new generation of Booths, G M Booth concentrated on the family's leather business while his cousin Alfred (qv) specialised in shipping. The tanning side had expanded rapidly in 1895-1905, especially in North America where the Booth's Surpass Leather Co produced about one-eighth of the 240 million square feet of kid leather annually manufactured in the USA and held a near monopoly in patent leather. Responsibility for the American business, centred on Gloversville, NY, devolved upon G M Booth who spent much time in the USA, especially before the collapse of his father's health in 1905. The Booth Steamship Line held a strong position in South American, and especially Amazon, trade, and although G M Booth had little direct responsibility for its operations, he was active in the family's investments in Argentina and Brazil. Alfred Booth & Co had a large interest in developing Manaos harbour, and G M Booth was for almost sixty years a member of the boards of Manaos Harbour Ltd and Manaos Tramways & Light Co, for much of that time as chairman.

On the outbreak of war in August 1914, Booth enabled the War Office to supplement Vickers' supply of time fuses for shells by placing orders with Burroughs, manufacturers of adding machines, and with the Zenith firm, makers of Swiss watches. He next obtained a large order of winter coats for the soldiers, and from December 1914 worked informally, but almost fulltime, getting supplies for the army. His position was regularised by his appointment to the Armaments Output Committee on 31 March 1915, and in April he became a member of the Munitions War Committee and joint head with Sir Percy Girouard (qv) of the special War Office organisation to increase munitions production. After the creation of the Ministry of Munitions, he was Director General of the Munitions Supply Department from 5 June 1915 until 20 December 1918, and chaired the Russian Supplies Committee, 1915-18. For this work he received the Russian Order of St Stanislaus and the Légion d'Honneur (1919), but, surprisingly, no British honour. There was some criticism that Booth, though 'an able shipowner' was ignorant of the 'practical basis' of armaments manufacture {PRO 30/57/73, Sir Percy Girouard of Armstrongs to Lord Kitchener, 20 March 1915}, and both Lloyd George and Addison occasionally complained that he paid more attention to the Treasury's views than to the Ministry of Munitions' policies.

Alfred Booth & Co framed an ambitious diversification programme in 1917-20, with the financial backing of Glyn's their bankers and of Robert Flemings, merchant bankers, but after the collapse of the post-war boom, the group was short of necessary capital and was financially over-extended at a time when many of its traditional markets shrivelled or disappeared. The Booth Steamship Co became the sole property of the Booth family and their associated preference shareholders in 1921, and went through difficult times before its sale to Vesteys in 1946. Alfred Booth & Co (of which G M Booth was chairman 1938-52) moved into the glue and gelatine business by buying the Lincoln firm of B Cannon, and, following its involvement in the Pavlova Leather Syndicate, began to produce leather for the glove-making industry. Increasingly they became international manufacturers and processors of the skins of kangaroos, rabbits, goats and sheep, rather than the old-style mercantile tanners, although their factories were by no means all profitable. Their American operations were hit by the taste for cheaper shoes, and consequent surplus capacity in the USA; after a long decline, Surpass's markets finally broke in 1937, leading to the closure (and in 1942 the sale) of the Gloversville works.

In September 1919 Alfred Booth & Co bought the Unit Construction Co which had been formed a few months earlier by the window manufacturer F H Crittall (qv). This company was intended to surmount the brick shortage by building homes 'fit for heroes' using standardised concrete blocks in buildings of unit dimensions. Its first major contract with Southport Borough Council was worth £221,000 (1920-23), and the first of its many Liverpool contracts was worth £613,000 (1922-24). Unit Construction's building work in 1925-39 was altogether worth about £10 million, and by 1952 it was the most profitable of Alfred Booth's subsidiaries.

In 1917, while on a munitions visit to the USA, G M Booth arranged to buy J G White & Co, public utility managers, engineering contractors and suppliers of engineering equipment. This was the English branch, formed in 1899, of an American engineering and finance house, which had been involved with Booth in the pre-war development of Manaos and Para, and the English office ran an extensive import-export business with South America. G M Booth's co-directors at Alfred Booth were less keen on this acquisition than he was, and persistently adverse post-war conditions in both South America and Britain withered White's mercantile and engineering business until it was little more than a finance house living off its earlier investments. It was re-sold in 1929 to its founder J G White, but re-purchased in 1931 by G M Booth in association with Alec Drummond and Walter Burton-Baldry (1888-1940), a London stockbroker. Reconstructed as White, Drummond & Co, with Booth as chairman, it continued to deplete its engineering operations, except as administrative managers of tramways and lighting installations at Singapore, Shanghai, Manaos and (until a rupture in 1943) Para in Brazil. From the outset Booth regarded White Drummond as more important for its financial innovations through its subsidiaries, Municipal & General Securities and Transatlantic & General Securities, of which he was chairman from 1931 until December 1943.

Booth and Burton-Baldry had been horrified by the crash of pyramided investment trusts in New York in 1929, and wanted to experiment with the concept of a fixed unit trust. On 23 April 1931 they made the initial issue of the First British Fixed Trust at 31s 9d per unit, of which Lloyds Bank were trustees conditional upon Booth acting as manager. Only £80,000 of the units were sold in the first fourteen months, and there was little improvement until the conversion of a war loan in June 1933. Under the trust deed of this fixed trust, the investment portfolio was immutable, which later proved inconvenient, as some investments turned out badly and others too splendidly, thus wrecking the trust's claim to have a good level spread. Booth therefore introduced the flexible unit trust in 1934, in which year also, at the suggestion of Montagu Norman (qv), he made the first issue of a unit trust of foreign government bonds (FGB Trust). This was a less successful departure, as the market in such bonds was narrow, and was utterly dislocated in 1939: Booth wound up the FGB Trust in 1950. In total, Municipal & General Securities issued nine unit trusts in 1931-39, although they did not receive their first stock exchange quotation until 1951. After the war, control of M&GS passed to a charitable trust promoting knowledge about investments, but Booth remained a director until 1965.

Booth was also a director of the Sao Paolo Brazilian Railway, succeeding Oliver Bury as chairman in 1943, and serving until its nationalisation by the Brazilian Government. He was founding chairman of the Brazilian Chamber of Commerce & Economic Affairs in Britain (1942-45), and received the Brazilian Order of the Southern Cross in 1947. As befitted the god-father and guardian of Peter Pan (Peter Llewelyn-Davies) he had a vigorous old age and remained on the boards of the Manaos, White Drummond and M&GS companies until 1965.

Booth shared his father's charitable and sociological interests, becoming in 1910 a member of the Tailoring Trade Board set up to impose a minimum wage in the sweated trades. During 1916-21 he paid a considerable amount of R G Tawney's salary at the Workers' Educational Association. He was a director of the Bank of England in 1915-47, was a leading member of its Building Committee in 1920-39, and high sheriff of the City of London in 1936.

In 1906 G M Booth married his cousin Margaret (1880-1959), second daughter of Daniel Meinertzhagen (1842-1910), senior partner in the merchant bankers Frederick Huth & Co, and his wife Georgina, daughter of Richard Potter, former chairman of the Great Western Railway. George and Margy Booth's vast cousinry included the Trevelyans, the Holts, and progressive politicians such as Leonard Courtney, Beatrice Webb, Lord Parmoor and his son Stafford Cripps. They had three sons and three daughters. G M Booth died at Chichester on 10 March 1971 aged ninety-four, leaving £8,002 gross.

R P T DAVENPORT-HINES

Writings:

Poem on tercentenary of discovery of Hudson River *Westminster Gazette* September 1909.

letter on management of unit trusts *Times* 25 Jan 1937.

letter on future of unit trusts *ibid* 24 Aug 1942.

Sources:

Unpublished

Bank of England archives, Threadneedle Street, London.

Bodleian Library, Oxford, papers of Lord Addison.

BLPES, papers of Lady Passfield.

House of Lords RO, papers of David Lloyd George.

PRO, papers of Lord Kitchener, of the Ministry of Munitions, Foreign Office and War Office.

Trinity College, Cambridge, papers of Edwin Montagu.

Published

R J Q Adams, *Arms and the Wizard* (Cassell, 1978).

Burke's Peerage 1970.

Burke's Landed Gentry 1965.

Duncan Crow, *A Man of Push and Go: the Life of George Macaulay Booth* (Rupert Hart-Davis, 1965).

Arthur John, *A Liverpool Merchant House: Being the History of Alfred Booth and Company 1863-1958* (Allen & Unwin, 1959).

Lord and Lady Simey, *Charles Booth, Social Scientist* (Oxford: Oxford University Press, 1960).

WWW.

BOOTH, Sir Robert Camm

(1916-)

Organiser of the National Exhibition Centre

Sir Robert Booth (courtesy of the National Exhibition Centre Ltd).

Robert Camm Booth was born in Southport on 9 May 1916, the elder of two sons of Robert Wainhouse Booth, master packer and exporter of textiles, and Annie Gladys née Taylor. He was educated at Altrincham Grammar School and Manchester University, where he graduated in law in 1936. After a short spell in the family business he became a student at Gray's Inn in 1939, and resumed his Bar studies again after the War. He was subsequently called to the Bar in 1949, though he never practiced as a barrister. He chose law through an interest in problems of equity and justice.

During the Second World War he served with the Manchester Regiment in Europe and the Middle East, rising to the rank of major by the age of twenty-six. He returned to the Manchester Chamber of Commerce in 1946, as an assistant secretary, with an added interest in personnel and organisation, and in 1948 he became deputy secretary.

Booth's early Lancastrian pre-occupation with the problem of exports, especially textiles, was intensified when in 1950 he went to the USA on a marketing mission with a team from Lancashire. Soon after he became secretary of the Birmingham Chamber of Industry and Commerce in 1958, he was asked to consider the future of the old Industrial Fair Buildings at Castle Bromwich. He did not think them commercially viable and encouraged instead the development of export missions. His promotion to the directorship of the Birmingham Chamber of Commerce in 1965 recognised the success of this policy.

To this initial background and experience can be traced Robert Booth's remarkable part in the creation of the National Exhibition Centre (NEC) at Birmingham. In 1968, during a visit from a Select Committee of the House of Commons on export promotion, the chairman asked for views on such a centre, the presumption being that it would be in London. Booth wrote a memorandum proposing that it be near Birmingham, at the Bickenhill site: his legal and administrative skills were effectively employed in the subsequent process of gaining support for the idea from government ministers and civil servants. The NEC, which Booth later described as analogous to the inception of the Manchester Ship Canal, was set up as a £40 million investment with 100 per cent gearing, of which £1.5 million was government grant, the rest loan stock, with one stockholder, the City of Birmingham. Booth was in effect an 'acting unpaid' director of the company. In 1975 Booth succeeded the chairman (Frank Cole), and the general manager, and became both chairman and chief executive of the NEC: in 1978 he relinquished the position of chief executive to a successor, but remained chairman until his retirement in March 1982. The previous year 1980-81, the NEC made just over £8 million gross profit on turnover of £18 million, and a net profit after tax of

The National Exhibition Centre hall complex of 5 halls (right) with Birmingham Metropole Hotel and Conference Complex in foreground (courtesy of the National Exhibition Centre Ltd).

just over £1 million. In recognition of his services Booth was accorded the honour, unusual for a former officer of the Chamber, of being elected president of the Birmingham Chamber of Commerce in 1978-79.

During the 1970s his business interests widened: he became a local non-executive director of Barclays Bank, and a board member of the Legal & General Assurance Society and of British Rail (Midlands and North Western). The CBE conferred on him in 1967, and the knighthood in 1977, were both for services to exports. The Légion d'Honneur was awarded for his efforts to promote economic co-operation between Britain and France.

Robert Booth's experience in the administration of the Chamber of Commerce and at the head of a large enterprise, together with his wide general interests, drew him into various avenues of public service. From 1974 until 1979 he was a member of the West Midlands Economic Planning Council; from 1975 until 1982, of the British Overseas Trade

Advisory Council. He served on the Council of Birmingham University, 1973-78 and is a life member of Court of the University. His particular interest in continuing education was reflected in his chairmanship, 1975-76, of the University's Committee on Post-Experience Training. He was made an honorary FRSA in 1975: in that year also, Aston University conferred on him an honorary DSc. On his retirement from the NEC he was made the first honorary member of the British Exhibitions Promotion Council.

Robert Booth in 1939 married Veronica Courtenay née Lamb; they had one son and three daughters.

A L MINKES

Writings:

'Marketing Cotton Textiles in the USA' (Manchester Chamber of Commerce, 1950).

'Protection of Textile Designs in Japan' (Manchester Chamber of Commerce, 1957).

'Trading with Japan' joint study with the London Chamber of Commerce (Birmingham Chamber of Commerce, 1961).

Sources:

Unpublished

BCe.

Personal conversation and correspondence with Sir Robert Booth.

Published

Birmingham Post Year Book.

PP, HC 1967-68 (365) X, Report of SC on Estimates on Promotion of Exports.

WW 1982.

BORTHWICK, Sir Thomas

(1835-1912)

Meat importer

Thomas Borthwick was born at Musselburgh near Edinburgh on 11 January 1835, the son of Thomas Borthwick Sr of Edinburgh. Borthwick worked his way up from apprentice butcher in the family business nearby at Ratho.

At an early age it was clear that Borthwick's real talent lay in assessing livestock, and he was soon an acknowledged expert. It was said he could walk into a pen of sheep of 500 or more and tell the weight and value of any of them at a glance; he was later to become a judge at the Royal Agricultural Show. He was only twenty-two when he established himself as a livestock agent, initially in Midlothian, but since he also handled Irish cattle landed at Liverpool he was attracted by the prospects there and in 1863 moved to Liverpool. In 1870 he rented a farm near Llanwryst in North Wales, and it was from there that he established a flourishing trade with Liverpool butchers. An indication of his drive is that, occasionally dissatisfied with prices, he slaughtered animals and sold direct to the consumer.

The 1860s and 1870s were years of experimentation in transporting meat long distances, from overseas suppliers. When refrigeration finally made it possible to bring meat across the equator from Australasia and Argentina (the first consignments of frozen meat were arriving by the late 1870s, the first from New Zealand arrived in 1882), Borthwick was quick to recognise the possibilities of international trade in the product. In 1883 he became the selling agent for the New Zealand Loan & Mercantile Agency Co Ltd. He opened meat depots in Liverpool, Manchester, Glasgow and Birmingham and in 1892 transferred the firm's headquarters to London, and at the same time secured a stall in Smithfield. This was the real beginning of the large wholesale and distribution business that covered the major livestock products of meat, wool and tallow. But the main business was meat, and Borthwick was a leading figure in promoting the trade, especially in experimenting with chilling (as opposed to freezing) techniques, which indirectly made him responsible for improving the quality of exported beef from Australasia.

Borthwick married Letitia Banks of Liverpool in 1872, and had four sons and three daughters. The first son, also Thomas (and later Lord Whitburgh) was born in 1875. All the sons went into the business; Thomas, the eldest son, went to Australia and New Zealand in 1904, purchasing meat works and establishing branch offices at Sydney, Melbourne, Brisbane and Christchurch. That same year the firm became a limited liability company under the name of Thomas Borthwick & Sons Ltd, registered with a capital of £300,000. More meat works were added later and the company continued to prosper until the early 1980s, dominating the Australasian meat trade, together with the Vesteys (qv). At the time of his death in 1912 Thomas Borthwick was still chairman of Thomas Borthwick & Sons Ltd, a director of Lancashire Cold Storage Co Ltd, Thames Cold Storage Co Ltd, and Thomas Borthwick & Sons (Australasia) Ltd.

Thomas Borthwick was a staunch Presbyterian throughout his life, and contributed to church activities both in Midlothian and at Regent Square Presbyterian Church, London. He was in his late sixties before he took an active part in local Midlothian politics. In 1902 he was appointed chairman of the Midlothian Liberal Association, a post he held until his death, and in 1908 he was knighted for his services to the Liberals. He was known as being a plain and blunt man, and while he probably lacked any serious political ambition, he was certainly not without friends in high places, being a close friend of Gladstone and later Lloyd George and Asquith. Weeks before he died he was named as baron in the birthday honours and so the title of Lord Whitburgh passed to his eldest son. Sir Thomas Borthwick died on 31 July 1912.

FORREST CAPIE

Sources:

Unpublished

Notes from Sir John Borthwick, Bt.

PrC.

Published

Austin Chadwick, *The Meat Trade* (3 vols, Gresham Publishing Co, 1934).

James T Critchell and Joseph Raymond, *A History of the Frozen Meat Trade* (Constable & Co, 1912).

Godfrey P Harrison, *Borthwicks, A Century in the Meat Trade 1863-1963* (Thomas Borthwick & Sons, 1963).

New Zealand Journal of Agriculture 1909, 1911.

Times 2 Aug 1912.

WWW.

BOSTOCK, Henry John

(1870-1956)
Shoe manufacturer

Henry John Bostock was born at Stafford on 6 January 1870, the eldest son of Henry Bostock (1833-1923), a shoe manufacturer, and Alice Susannah née Marson. He was educated at King's School, Chester.

In 1887 he joined the family firm of Edwin Bostock & Co of Stafford and Stone: Stafford's premier firm. After a practical grounding in both production and management techniques, he specialised in the marketing and sales aspects of the business. When a limited company was formed in 1898, he joined his father and uncle Thomas (d 1908) on the board as the sales director. Increased competition and rising costs in the period underlined the strategic importance of the marketing and sales function within the industry. Henry's contribution to these techniques, both within his own company, and the industry generally, was significant. He was pre-eminent amongst the pioneers of the modern 'in-stock system', which enabled shoe retailers to draw on stocks held by manufacturers as required, rather than the traditional practice of placing advanced orders. This enabled the manufacturer to improve stock controls and regulate seasonal fluctuations in the levels of manufacturing activity; it also obviated the need amongst retailers to commit working capital to large stocks. At the same time the system forced the manufacturer to concentrate his energies on a smaller range of shoes which in turn strained his capital resources and there is some evidence that E Bostock Ltd felt this constraint.

It was due to Bostock's inspiration that a new subsidiary, Lotus Shoemakers Ltd, was formed in 1903 to market their leading branded products, the Lotus and the Delta Boot: this was the first firm to adopt the in-stock system. Henry became its managing director. The branded products of the two family companies, Edwin Bostock Ltd, based at Stafford, and Frederick Bostock & Co, based at Northampton, were now marketed by Lotus. Ladies' footwear was supplied from Stafford, and menswear from Northampton. Traditionally, firms at each footwear centre in Britain had tended to concern themselves primarily with the manufacture and distribution of either men's or women's wear. The Bostock collaboration reflected a currently general trend towards eradicating this historic, and in retailing terms, outmoded product specialisation.

With Henry's direction and energy the two family firms continued to draw closer together. In 1911 Frederick Bostock & Co established a manufacturing subsidiary, Sutor Ltd, to provide additional capacity for producing Lotus menswear. A separate factory was acquired, the company being under the initial direction of Henry's cousins, Neville (1886-1962) and Eric (1889-1918) Bostock. In 1912, inter-company co-operation was advanced a stage further when Frederick Bostock & Co was floated as a public company. The principal directors at Stafford and Northampton joined the boards of all four companies: in addition, Lotus Shoemakers acquired a minority share-holding in Sutor Ltd. A virtual merger of control in matters of general policy was achieved, prompted chiefly by marketing considerations.

Lotus Shoemakers (the name was changed in 1914 to simply Lotus Ltd) made substantial headway after 1912: nominal capital was increased on three occasions between 1913 and 1918 (from £10,000 to £100,000). Then, in 1919, a further substantial increase to £1 million was sanctioned to provide working and development capital consequent upon Lotus' acquisition of the other Bostock concerns. At the same time Lotus was floated as a public limited company with an issued capital of £998,890; its assets were then £904,114, against its liabilities of £170,000. Net profit in 1919 was £120,430.

Elected joint managing director of the reconstructed company, Henry also became its chairman in 1923 on the death of his father. He relinquished the former post in 1945, but continued as chairman until 1953, when his eldest son, James F Bostock, took over: he retained the title chairman emeritus until his death. In 1953 the company's total assets were £3.668 million, against liabilities of £1.144 million; consolidated profits were then £346,178.

Although several members of the family continued to share the control of the company, Henry Bostock was the dominant personality. He was responsible for directing the successful post-merger rationalisation of the company's productive capacity, and played a key role in its inter-war growth in both home and overseas markets. Lotus under his chairmanship became one of the brand leaders in the twentieth century footwear industry. His energy and pragmatism were revealed in changing company policy regarding sales promotions and advertising, which relied heavily on shop display features and advertisements rather than public relations or close links with retailers, and in technical advances in production, workers' welfare and industrial relations. Throughout this time he maintained a strong tie with trade associations, being a president of the Incorporated Federation of Boot and Shoe Manufacturers, 1922-25; the then infant British Boot, Shoe and Allied Trade Research Association, to which he gave particular encouragement; and the British Boot and Shoe Institute, of which he was a fellow.

Despite sustained business commitments, however, he nurtured '... a broadminded and vital interest in everything that happened in the world ...' {*Times* 8 Jan 1957}. He was noted for his encyclopaedic general knowledge. A Conservative, he was first elected to Stafford Borough Council in 1902, being elected mayor in 1914, and then alderman and JP in 1942. He also sat on the Staffordshire County Council in 1919-22, again in 1925-28, and finally in 1934-36. He was High Sheriff of the county in 1948-49, and was awarded the CBE in 1953, in recognition of his public services.

He maintained to his last years '... a fine physique and energetic habits ... allied with an alert, enquiring and mature mind ...' {*Stafford Newsletter* 5 Jan 1957}. His business and public success he attributed to a contented family life, and strong religious belief. He was an active Anglican lay reader. Personally unostentatious, he sought quiet leisure pursuits, principally horticulture, and bicycled the three miles between home and office until shortly before his retirement.

He married Eleanor, daughter of James Hardley, a JP of Garston, Liverpool, in 1900; they had three sons and one daughter. His sons, James, Gilbert, and Godfrey, all entered the firm. He died at home, Shawms, Redford Rise, Stafford, on 27 December 1956. His estate was valued at £65,267 gross.

KEITH BROOKER

Sources:

Unpublished

PRO, Edwin Bostock & Co Ltd company file (BT 31/10943/97852); Frederick Bostock & Co Ltd company file (BT 31/20790/123106).

C Reg: Lotus Ltd (78,857); Sutor Ltd (119,040).

BCe.

MCe.

PrC.

Published

Shoe Manufacturers Monthly Jan 1957.

Staffordshire Advertiser and Chronicle 3 Jan 1957.

Staffordshire Newsletter 29 Dec 1956, 5 Jan 1957.

Times 28 Dec 1956, 1, 8 Jan 1957.

VCH Staffordshire.

WWW.

BOTTOMLEY, Horatio William

(1860-1933)

Promoter of companies and dubious speculations, and publisher

Horatio W Bottomley addressing a crowd on the Victoria Embankment, London, from the deck of the ex-German submarine Deutschland *(from Henry J Houston OBE,* The Real Horatio Bottomley *(Hurst & Blackett Ltd, 1923).*

Horatio William Bottomley was born at Bethnal Green, London on 23 March 1860. His father, William King Bottomley, a tailor's cutter, died insane in July 1863; his mother Elizabeth, née Holyoake, the sister of George Holyoake, one of the founders of the Co-operative Movement, died in 1865. Horatio's sister Grace was adopted, while George Holyoake used his contacts to obtain a place for Horatio in Sir Josiah Mason's (qv) orphanage in Birmingham. Here he stayed from the age of ten until he was fourteen, showing an aptitude for arithmetic and sprinting, but little else.

On leaving the orphanage, Horatio settled in London. He held a variety of jobs as an office boy, including two in solicitors' offices, where he began to acquire a knowledge of court procedure, and learned shorthand. In 1880 he joined Walpoles, a firm of legal shorthand writers. Bottomley enrolled as a member of the Institute of Shorthand Writers Practising in The High Court, and the firm soon became Walpole & Bottomley. His years in the law courts as a shorthand writer provided him with a knowledge of the law and of the intricacies of legal argument which would stand him in excellent stead in future years. During these years he also acquired a wife, marrying Elizabeth Norton (d 1930), the daughter of Samuel Norton, a collector for Sarson's vinegar brewery, in May 1880. They had one daughter, Florence.

Bottomley's first essays in company promotion, starting in 1885, were in printing and publishing. This stage of his career ended in May 1891 with Bottomley's first petition for bankruptcy, after a debenture corporation that had underwritten £250,000 of debentures of one of his companies, the Hansard Publishing Union, brought in the Receiver when their interest was not paid. The bankruptcy proceedings brought to light the inadequacy of Bottomley's accounting, and the fact that £85,000, given to him by the board of another of his promotions, the Anglo-Austrian Printing & Publishing Union, to purchase printing firms in Vienna, had simply disappeared. However Bottomley turned disaster into triumph by a tour de force of audacity and persuasive power in court, demonstrating an ability to win over not only juries but judges and magistrates as well.

His triumph in court also helped him obtain the rescinding of the receiving order in 1893, and he was free to resume his career as a company promoter with the help of a loan of £2,000 from Osborne O'Hagan (qv) who had been associated with him in the Hansard Union. Now he concentrated on companies to mine gold in Western Australia. From 1894 to 1903 he launched companies with a nominal capital of about £25 million. Often these were 'reconstructions' of earlier companies. Some of the £25 million capital was not taken up, much was duplicated in the various reconstructions, but still some millions must have come into Bottomley's hands, and very little was spent on buying mining rights in Western Australia.

By 1903 the public had grown weary of throwing their money down unproductive goldmines, and Bottomley returned to publishing with the purchase of a London evening newspaper, the *Sun*. This was never financially rewarding, and he soon disposed of it. It was not until he founded the weekly paper *John Bull* in 1906 that his reputation as an editor and journalist was firmly established. The paper was sharp, often aggressive in style, and frequently libellous, although sometimes, perhaps fortuitously, uncomfortable truths were revealed. Bottomley had some difficulty in obtaining financial backing for the project until he approached the printing firm Odhams, managed by J S Elias (qv). Elias, ambitious for the expansion of the business, agreed to undertake the printing, carefully providing in the contract against liability in libel actions. *John Bull* was a success with the public but, under Bottomley's business direction, a financial disaster. The printing bill remained unpaid, and sometimes Bottomley's staff would have been unpaid too had not Elias taken care of their wages. In 1907 Elias persuaded Bottomley to let Odhams take over the publishing of the paper, handing over the receipts from sales and advertisements to Bottomley after subtracting Odhams' charges. Despite all Elias's efforts, Bottomley could still not be prevented from, literally, dipping his hands into the petty cash, but Elias was now paid for a printing contract he could no longer afford to relinquish. Bottomley got an assured platform from which he could invite participation in his various money-raising schemes.

The year before the first appearance of *John Bull*, Bottomley achieved a long-standing ambition by his election as Liberal MP for South Hackney.

He attached great importance to his membership of the Commons. It provided another means of attracting public attention, and increased his defensive cover against creditors and those he had libelled in *John Bull*.

Some of the companies Bottomley had started in the 1890s were still functioning in some form or other, including one which had been known since 1903 as the Joint Stock Trust & Finance Co. For his own purposes Bottomley wanted to liquidate it in 1906, but the circumstances of its dissolution aroused the suspicions of the Official Receiver. Books went missing, papers that had been carefully sorted by the Receiver's officials mysteriously became unsorted, but at length the investigators came to the conclusion that the Trust had issued nearly 10 million shares in excess of the stated capital and that hundreds of innocent investors had been cheated. In November 1908 Bottomley was charged with conspiracy to defraud. At the trial Bottomley conducted his own defence in a masterly way. He was able to take advantage of the very confusion of the affairs of the Joint Stock Trust, for it was difficult for the prosecution to give precise details of specific irregularities. The judge dismissed the case, but suspicions had been aroused. Bottomley lost three subsequent cases brought by individual victims of his financial manipulations.

However, even before these cases were out of the way, Bottomley held the inaugural meeting of the John Bull League, which was, he proclaimed, opposed to cant, and favoured the 'introduction of common-sense business methods into the government of the country' {Symons (1955) 97}. The League provided a useful rallying point for his supporters in his political activities, including his own re-election in 1910.

Some of the business methods Bottomley had studied were those of E T Hooley (qv). Bottomley took pains to keep his association with Hooley, which began in 1905, fairly quiet. But the personal approach to gullible individuals with money to invest, which was something of a Hooley speciality, led to trouble for Bottomley. A prosecution by the executrix of a man called Master, who had lost over £100,000 by his investment in various Bottomley companies, resulted in a verdict against Bottomley and a fine of £50,000.

In the hope of warding off further claims on him by his victims, Bottomley once again filed a petition for bankruptcy. Unfortunately among his creditors was the Prudential Assurance Co, one of many companies which had been vilified in articles in *John Bull*. So great was the nuisance value of such attacks that even blameless companies often dealt with them by paying large sums to *John Bull* either directly, or by placing advertisements. The Prudential countered Bottomley by sending out a circular. Bottomley issued a writ for libel but, having just lost the Master case, decided to withdraw the action. The Prudential demanded payment of their £1,559 costs, and Bottomley found himself in the London Bankruptcy Court in February 1912. Four days of cross-examination by the Prudential's counsel left no hope for Bottomley that his own scheme for dealing with his affairs would be accepted, and no alternative but to resign his seat in the Commons. His public career was in ruins.

Yet there were still plenty of people prepared to believe in Bottomley the opposer of cant, the champion of the 'bottom dog'. He also had the reputation of a sportsman: though no judge of horses he was devoted to horse-racing (and betting) and owned a string of racehorses which earned him considerable popularity in circles unaffected by admiration for his moral posturing. It was not long before he had hit on a very lucrative source of income, in competitions and sweepstakes run through *John Bull*. (Sweepstakes were illegal in Britain and these had to be run from Switzerland.) They seem to have been highly lucrative, even when Bottomley did not fix the prizes.

When the outbreak of war in 1914 curtailed these schemes Bottomley had been only a couple of sweepstakes away from the annulment of his bankruptcy, but he soon found another way of exploiting his popularity with the crowds. A government recruiting rally in London gave him the idea of holding his own recruiting meetings. He was not paid for these meetings (although he drew substantial expenses from *John Bull*, which did receive valuable publicity from them) and he soon abandoned recruiting for patriotic war lectures, for which he was paid (as well as receiving expenses from *John Bull*). He developed different speeches for different audiences, depending on how much the meeting was worth to him. His finest flights were reserved for audiences which brought him more than £100. Soon he was giving several lectures a week.

His success as a lecturer brought an invitation from Northcliffe (qv) to write an article in his new *Sunday Pictorial*, launched in 1915. Bottomley's fee soon became £7,800 a year for producing a weekly article, which was often largely 'ghosted' for him (unbeknown to Northcliffe).

Bottomley had had plenty of practice for his patriotic lectures in speaking tours on behalf of his Business Government League (which developed out of the John Bull League) before the war. As soon as he realised a general election was imminent in 1918, he took steps to annul his bankruptcy. Once again he stood for South Hackney, under the slogan 'Bottomley, Brains and Business', and was returned with a large majority. He was later joined in Parliament by other Business Government MPs. Eventually there were seven of them, all except Bottomley respectable, if somewhat naive men.

In 1918 readers of *John Bull* were invited to send in money to be invested in War Stocks and Savings Schemes, with the added Bottomley touch of draws for prizes from the accumulated interest. Some of the money from such schemes had helped to obtain his discharge from bankruptcy. The most successful (at least initially) was the John Bull Victory Bond Club, where Bottomley invited readers to subscribe to Government Victory Bonds. The public response was impressive, with an estimated £900,000 subscribed, but the scheme was badly organised even by Bottomley's standards. As usual, Bottomley had helped himself to large quantities of cash as it had been sent in and had, furthermore, rashly promised Victory Bonds in exchange for the War Stock certificates of those who felt they had not had a fair deal in his earlier schemes. Although at one stage he bought £500,000 of Victory Bonds, this represented nothing like the number he should have held on behalf of subscribers. Even so, he soon had to dispose of some of them for cash, as complaints and demands for refunds flooded in.

In January 1920, after the Victory Bond Club had been operating for six months, Bottomley announced that it was to be merged into a Thrift Bond Prize Club, run from Paris, and investing in French Crédit National Bonds. But the move to Paris failed to stem the flood of complaints or stop the ugly rumours. Once again, in October 1921, Bottomley called in the Receiver. In December Odhams decided the time had come to sever their business connections with Bottomley, and with a payment of £25,000 he ceased to be editor of *John Bull*. He had already sacrificed his substantial income from the *Sunday Pictorial* to his own conceit in 1919, by trying to publish his own Sunday newspaper, the *Sunday Illustrated*. He was convinced the *Illustrated*'s success would be assured simply by transferring his weekly article from the *Pictorial*. However, the magic of his name was not enough to make the badly-managed and inadequately-staffed paper a success, and he soon lost interest in it.

Bottomley's troubles were compounded by the enmity of a bookmaker and printer, Reuben Bigland. Bigland had been of some help to Bottomley in the past and had wanted to be more closely involved with his schemes, but Bottomley had always kept him at a distance. Bigland knew enough to damage Bottomley severely, but Bottomley had failed to take his threats very seriously because Bigland could not reveal what he knew without incriminating himself. Bottomley played into his hands by issuing a libel writ, trying to discredit Bigland by charging him with blackmail as well. But too much was revealed about Bottomley's doings in the subsequent trials, and in late 1921 Bottomley was back at the Old Bailey, yet again charged with fraud. His customary skill in defence deserted him: he was found guilty and sentenced to seven years in prison.

That was the effective end of Bottomley's career. On release from prison he tried to set up a rival publication to *John Bull*, but *John Blunt*, whose first issue appeared in June 1928, was a failure. So were his attempts to give lectures on his prison experiences. He had lost his audience. Soon he was back in the Bankruptcy Court. Bottomley had always been even more skilled at dissipating money, principally on racing, his many mistresses, and champagne, than at extracting it from the gullible public. Now he was penniless. Until his death, he lived largely on small gifts of money from his few remaining friends who had any to spare, including the upright Elias, and Peggy Primrose, his most constant mistress for many years. He died intestate on 26 May 1933.

CHRISTINE SHAW

Selected Writings:

Bottomley's Book (Odhams, 1909).

Great Thoughts of Horatio Bottomley (Holden & Hardingham, 1917).

Full Report of Mr Horatio Bottomley's Speech at the Royal Albert Hall, London, April 27, 1918 (Odhams, 1918).

Convict '13': A Ballad of Maidstone Gaol (Stanley Paul & Co, 1927).

Songs of the Cell (William Southern, 1928).

Humours of Prison Life (William Southern, 1929).

BOTTOMLEY Horatio William

Sources:

Unpublished

BCe.

Published

DNB.

Henry J Houston, *The Real Horatio Bottomley* (Hurst & Blackett, 1925).

Rubeigh J Minney, *Viscount Southwood* (Hurst & Blackett, 1954).

Henry Osborne O'Hagan, *Leaves From My Life* (2 vols, John Lane, 1929).

Julian Symons, *Horatio Bottomley* (Cresset Press, 1955).

Times 27 May 1933.

Aylmer Vallance, *Very Private Enterprise* (Thames & Hudson, 1955).

WWMP.

BOULT, Swinton

(1808-1876)

Insurance company executive

Swinton Boult (courtesy of Hugh Cockerell).

Swinton Boult was born in Liverpool on 3 December 1808, one of the large family of Francis Boult, a shipowner and Unitarian and his wife Anne, née Swanwick. (Another son, Francis Jr, became a prominent shipowner and financial reformer.) At the age of twenty-two he entered business as an agent for London insurance companies. They had recently introduced higher fire rates for Liverpool warehouses and Boult concluded that there was scope for a local company (though a previous one had failed).

In 1836 he founded the Liverpool Fire & Life Insurance Co with the aid of George Holt, a fellow Unitarian and a rich cotton broker and town councillor, who became its chairman. The board was representative of Nonconformist and Whig Liverpool merchants. The paid-up capital was £66,000. Boult, as secretary and chief executive, for some years proceeded cautiously in building up the fire business on which the company chiefly depended. There were occasional setbacks, as in 1842-43, when disastrous fires occurred in Liverpool. These led to the passing of the Liverpool Fire Prevention Act of 1845 and the founding in that city of the insurance companies' own salvage corps, in both of which Boult took a prominent part. Through the need to spread the company's risks geographically the North of England Insurance Co was acquired in 1844 and the London, Edinburgh and Dublin Insurance Co in 1847; thereafter the name Liverpool & London Fire & Life was adopted. Competition reduced premium income until 1851 but entry into the North American market, where the USA had just removed its ban on British fire insurers, opened the way to rapid expansion overseas. The Liverpool & London, already represented in parts of British North America, opened a New York branch and agencies in Charleston, New Orleans and Philadelphia. Boult visited America in 1853. He appointed an agent for the company in Cleveland and made his way overland to San Francisco where the Liverpool & London became the first in the fire insurance field. From there he sailed to Australia where business was also started. In 1851 the company's fire premiums stood at £54,000. Six years later they were £389,000. In 1859 a director resigned in protest at the rapid expansion but a committee of enquiry found that, over the whole of the company's lifetime, foreign business had proved even more profitable than home business.

By 1862 the company's fire premium income reached £436,000 and the need for more capital was apparent. The company merged with the Globe Insurance Co (founded in 1803) whose large capital had not been fully utilised. Globe shareholders were offered the option of ordinary shares or a perpetual 6 per cent debenture. Most chose the debentures, an indication of persistent doubts about the safety of overseas expansion. Boult, who had negotiated the merger, was appointed managing director of the company, renamed the Liverpool & London & Globe. The dividend of 40 per cent, paid at the time of the merger, had to be cut in 1867 and remained lower for some years.

By 1867 the company was the largest fire insurer in the world with a premium income of £836,000. Its UK business was second only to that of the Sun Fire Office which had shunned North America. In Canada the company was the largest fire insurer and in the USA it ranked third only to two domestic companies.

Expansion continued with growing recognition of Boult. A writer in 1871 described him as 'the very Napoleon of fire insurance' {Walford (1871) 354} and the greatest authority on its finance. But Boult had always been critical of reinsurance. He once described it as 'the most pernicious system ever adopted' {*ibid* 355} and maintained that a company should take no more on a risk than it meant to retain, though he did not in practice adhere to this strictly. His philosophy was put to the test by a great fire in Chicago in 1871 which cost his company £654,000 gross, half the year's premium income. The dividend had to be reduced. In 1872 a large fire in Boston cost the company $1.4 million and the dividend had to be passed. Early in 1873 the board decided unanimously not to recommend Boult's reappointment, thus ending his career after thirty-seven years. Boult circularised the shareholders and continued to attend company meetings but no chance of a comeback presented itself, and an attempt by him to form a new insurance company failed. Growth ceased for a few years but profitability returned immediately, thus demonstrating the soundness of the foundations laid by Boult.

He was highly esteemed by his fellow managers and was a prime mover in the formation of the Fire Offices' Committee in 1868, having previously devised and taken the chair of the northern committee of the earlier Fire Tariff Association in 1858. He maintained amicable relations with his rival in Liverpool, the manager of the Tory-sponsored Royal Insurance Co of 1845. A contemporary Liverpool journalist refers to 'the cheery voice, the frank manner, the dignified courtesy, the unfailing tact, the power of assimilation and clarification, which carried his board of directors with him' {*ibid*} but these qualities did not avail him in the end. Boult was not gregarious. He is said to have behaved more like a banker than a merchant, sitting in his office to receive callers, though he made frequent tours of inspection. His success lay in the shrewd selection of agents.

Boult wrote on a number of topics and publicised his views. He was the only insurance manager to object to the Life Assurance Companies Act of 1870 which introduced a measure of consumer protection. The Act offended his laissez-faire principles. In public utterance he was florid but no orator. He had, a contemporary said, 'a sledge-hammer delivery, occasionally toned down by a characteristic sarcasm' {*ibid*}.

Boult married Maria Ann Grundy, oldest child of Rev John Grundy, in 1833. They had three sons. He suffered from gout and died suddenly at Liverpool, where he had lived all his life, on 8 July 1876 leaving nearly £2,000 gross. His wife survived him.

HUGH COCKERELL

Writings:

The Law and Practice Relating to the Constitution and Management of Assurance, Banking, and Other Joint-Stock Companies (J Ridgway & Sons, 1841).

The Income Tax as It Is, Direct Taxation as It Might Be: a Letter to the Right Honourable William Ewart Gladstone (Liverpool: Thomas Baines, 1853).

Trade and Partnership: the Relative Duties and Proper Liabilities of the Merchant and the State (Effingham Wilson, 1855).

PP, HC 1867 (471) X, Report of the Select Committee on Fire Protection.

Sources:

Unpublished

Sir Adrian Boult, letter to author, 30 Dec 1981.

Published

Tom Capes, 'Swinton Boult' *Royal Insurance Newsletter* No 24 Oct/Nov 1975.

DNB.

Benjamin Guinness Orchard, *Liverpool's Legion of Honour* (Birkenhead: the author, 1893).

Post Magazine 1853-76.

Cornelius Walford, *The Insurance Cyclopaedia* (6 vols, C & E Layton 1871-74) I, 3.

BOWATER, Sir Eric (Frederic) Vansittart

(1895-1962)

Paper manufacturer

Sir Eric Bowater (courtesy of the Bowater Corporation PLC).

Eric (a contraction of his given name Frederic) Vansittart Bowater was born at Beckenham, Kent on 16 January 1895, the second of five children (the rest were girls) of Frederick (later Sir Frederick) Bowater and his wife Alice née Sharp.

The Bowaters were a Midland family of good social standing with wide ramifications and strong military connections, including two generals. William Vansittart Bowater (1838-1907), Eric's grandfather, went into the paper trade and by 1881 was in business on his own in London as a paper merchant. By the time Eric was born, W V Bowater had taken three of his sons into partnership, but he seems to have been hard-drinking, bad-tempered and tyrannical, and in about 1900 the three brothers got their father out, taking control themselves. Enormous growth, in the thirty-five years or so before 1914, in the mass-market for periodicals, part-works and popular newspapers, especially the *Daily Mail*, led to a strongly rising demand for newsprint and other printing papers. On that demand W V Bowater & Sons (a private limited company from 1910) flourished, largely through acting as buying agents for Alfred and Harold Harmsworth (qqv), the most successful mass-market publishers of all.

Perhaps with Harmsworth encouragement, the Bowater brothers began to contemplate transforming themselves from merchants into manufacturers. In 1914 they bought a site for a newsprint mill at Northfleet on the Thames near Gravesend, but any plans they may have had for building were blocked by the outbreak of war.

Eric left Charterhouse, spent a few months with a papermaking firm (Peter Dixon of Grimsby), took a Territorial commission in 1913, and went off to the First World War as a gunner subaltern. In September 1915 the roof of a dugout collapsed around him, he spent eighteen hours alone in the dark with two dead men, and was invalided out of the service. That put an end to his first ambition which, he often said in later life, was to make his career in the army. For about three years Eric Bowater seemed to be permanently crippled, but then a neurologist decided that Eric's injuries were psychological, not physical, and ordered him to walk unaided, which he did. Mental illness (shell-shock) was not respectable in 1918 and Eric was deeply ashamed of it. The army being barred to him, he determined, apparently, to prove himself in other ways, and the shell that burst on his dugout propelled him into the family business.

Eric Bowater, tall and very upright, was soldierly in bearing and of a commanding presence, with handsome regular features under red hair turning white in middle age. He had a piercing glance which he could turn at will into a frightening glare, allied to a deep voice which he could use in much the same way, though in moments of affability he would address apprehensive subordinates as 'Dear boy'. Within a very narrow circle he could be relaxed and charming, but as a rule his manner towards men was austere. With women, with several of whom his relations were intimate, he sought and readily found admiration which he greatly enjoyed. He was scarcely ever known to lose his temper, though the result if he did might be terrifying. 'If you lose your temper,' he would say, 'you lose face' {Reader (1981) 90}, and he valued his dignity, finding it very difficult to laugh at himself or to come to terms with mistakes.

As a businessman Eric Bowater displayed the classic qualities of the entrepreneur: judgement both sound and bold; an unresting urge to expand; decisiveness; self-confidence. He sought and paid for the best advice he could find and among his advisers, on both sides of the Atlantic, were his closest personal friends. Nevertheless his decisions were always his own, and from 1927 until he died his authority within the business, derived not from a massive shareholding but from force of character, was absolute. 'I do not wish', he once said, 'to be remembered as a popular chairman but I hope to be remembered as a just one' {Reader (1981) 89}, and among his colleagues and subordinates he inspired both awe and loyalty.

In the 1920s and 1930s British national newspapers were pushing their circulation figures towards previously unheard-of levels (perhaps, by 1937, 10 million copies a day for dailies, 15 million for Sundays) and they required newsprint supplies to match. For making newsprint both Canada and Scandinavia have natural advantages, particularly ample timber and cheap power, which the United Kingdom can never match, but between the wars other circumstances were briefly in favour of the United Kingdom makers. The Scandinavians were chiefly suppliers of woodpulp, not paper. The Canadians in the 1920s were fully occupied with the United States market and after that collapsed, in 1930, the price of pulp fell faster than the price of newsprint in Britain, so that British makers could still compete with imports. Their prices were always rather higher than prices charged by the Canadians, but they could offer deliveries closely matched to daily fluctuations in demand and they prevented the Canadians establishing a monopoly. The newspaper owners, primarily Rothermere, Beaverbrook (qv), Camrose (qv), and Kemsley (qv), were willing and able to pay a premium for these advantages, and it was with their powerful customers' encouragement and support that Bowaters launched into newsprint manufacture.

Eric Bowater, totally untrained technically and with no more than five or six years' commercial experience, was thrust prematurely to the forefront of Bowaters' affairs by the death of his father, aged fifty-six, in 1924. The building of Northfleet Mill by Armstrong, Whitworth, who were better at battleships than paper mills, was badly mismanaged and precipitated a crisis from which Bowaters had to be rescued by the Bank of England, not for their own sake but for the sake of Armstrong, Whitworth. Guided by experts in engineering and finance like Arthur Baker (qv) and Sir Basil Mayhew (qv), both chosen by himself, Eric Bowater pulled his family firm through its troubles, and by 1927 it was soundly established with two newsprint machines in production and two more on order, giving a total capacity, actual or contemplated, of about 120,000 tons a year.

In 1927 Eric Bowater came to the head of the Bowater business, removing his uncles in the process, and over the next dozen years pursued

Bowater's first newsprint mill at Northfleet in 1932 (courtesy of the Bowater Corporation PLC).

a course of expansion which, for audacity and speed, can have few parallels in the history of British business. Between 1927 and 1932, in partnership with Rothermere and later with Beaverbrook also, he doubled Northfleet's capacity and set up a two-machine mill at Ellesmere Port to which in 1933, on his own again, he added two more machines. In 1936 he astonished the paper industry by taking over, from the Berry brothers, the largest newsprint business in Europe, Edward Lloyd Ltd of Kemsley and Sittingbourne in Kent, with a yearly capacity of 320,000 tons of paper, including 275,000 tons of newsprint, and assets valued at a figure 40 per cent greater than Bowaters' own. In 1937, impelled by an urge for self-sufficiency prompted by the activities of cartels in the woodpulp trade, he acquired a pulp mill at Umea in Sweden and set out to acquire timber-cutting rights in Newfoundland. With the encouragement of the Bank of England, he ended by gaining control of a newsprint mill at Corner Brook in Newfoundland with a capacity of about 200,000 tons a year, as well as cutting rights over some 7,000 square miles of forest. At Bowater's Paper Mills' annual meeting in 1938, a little more than twelve years after the first Bowater paper had come off the machines at Northfleet, Eric Bowater was able to claim: 'we are now the largest newsprint manufacturers in the world, the total productive capacity of the mills of your company and its associated mill companies being approximately 800,000 tons per annum.'

To achieve this headlong rate of expansion, far greater than the internal resources of the Bowater business could sustain, Eric Bowater took enormous risks. So great was his hunger for capital and so urgent his drive to expand that between 1927 and 1932 he allowed control of the Bowater business to pass to Lord Rothermere, without whose backing he evidently judged it impossible to raise the preference capital he needed for the doubling of capacity at Northfleet. Rothermere nearly sold Bowaters, over Eric's head, into Canadian ownership and it was extremely lucky for Eric that in 1932 the financial embarrassments of one of Rothermere's companies opened an opportunity for Eric to buy his independence back again.

Since Bowaters' business was not generating profits fast enough for his purposes, Eric Bowater went time and again to the market in the 1930s, for share capital and debentures. The debenture issues were converted, as opportunity offered, to lower rates of interest, but even so by the end of 1936—after Lloyd but before Corner Brook—the ratio of prior-charge capital to ordinary capital in the Bowater group was 8.5:1, requiring nearly 5 per cent on the issued capital of £9.5 million before the ordinary shareholders were entitled to anything.

This was the financial policy of an optimist, leaving little room for unforeseen setbacks. In 1937-38 the pulp-makers' cartels upset Bowaters' profits and from 1939 onward paper controls, increasingly ferocious, reduced the ouput from newsprint machines in the United Kingdom until for a few months in 1942 it was at 15 per cent of pre-war levels. For eleven years, 1937-47 inclusive, Bowater's Paper Mills paid no ordinary dividend.

After the war, how different: in the early 1950s, times were as good for paper-makers as for everyone else whose business could benefit in the sellers' market created by massive, worldwide rises in the standard of living. Demand for newsprint, especially in the USA, tended continually to run ahead of supply, and in 1955-56 actually did so. At the same time there was a rapidly growing market for paper products of all kinds, especially packaging materials, paper towels and tissues.

Eric Bowater's expansionist temperament was exactly suited to these conditions. For a dozen years after the Second World War, he was at the peak of his career. In the United Kingdom, pursuing plans delayed by war, he diversified Bowaters' business away from total dependence on newsprint into packaging and, in partnership with Scott Paper of Pennsylvania, into paper towels and tissues. In North America, even more ambitiously, he advanced from Bowaters' Newfoundland base into manufacture within the USA, the world's largest market for newsprint, hitherto supplied almost entirely from Canada.

The risks were high. In the first place, the timber chosen for Bowaters' raw material was Southern pine, the suitability of which for newsprint had by no means been fully demonstrated. Secondly, finance had to be arranged, which meant heavy borrowing. Eric persuaded American banks and insurance companies to put up about 75 per cent of the initial capital required, leaving Bowaters to supply only the equity capital. In this way, so long as things went well, control remained with Bowaters and the whole undertaking would pass into Bowaters' hands as the bonded debt was paid off. The lenders' conditions, however, were strict, and if things went ill Bowaters might find themselves in serious trouble. Nevertheless in October 1954 Sir Eric Bowater (he had been knighted in 1944 for war

Facial tissue conversion at Bowater-Scott Corporation Ltd's Northfleet mill (courtesy of the Bowater Corporation PLC).

services, chiefly under Beaverbrook in the Ministry of Aircraft Production, and used the title to great effect in the United States) opened a two-machine mill near the small town of Calhoun, Tennessee. He called the mill, which was the foundation of what became the largest newsprint business in the USA, 'the realization of our dream and the crowning joy of my business life' {Reader (1981) 224}, and there is every reason to suppose that he meant it.

From 1957 onward conditions in the market turned decisively against Bowaters. The supply of newsprint overtook demand and there was never again the chronic scarcity which had brought unbroken prosperity and encouraged expansion between 1949 and 1956. This was particularly serious for the newsprint industry in the United Kingdom, exposed at last in all its weakness to the full force of Canadian and Scandinavian competition. Decline, probably irreversible, set in. The Scandinavians, taking advantage of free trade within EFTA as against an 18 per cent tariff if they wanted to export to the EEC, became exceptionally formidable, not only in newsprint but in packaging, which became an overcrowded industry, plagued by over-capacity. Of Bowaters' post-war developments in the United Kingdom only Bowater-Scott, in the late 1950s and early 1960s, was uninterruptedly successful.

Bowater's master plan for newsprint in the United Kingdom faltered and then came to an end, incomplete, in 1959. Apart from that Eric Bowater continued his drive for expansion. In the United Kingdom, growth in newsprint might be halted but growth in packaging went ahead. In Europe, hopeful but ill-executed forays into the EEC carried Bowaters (temporarily, as it turned out, though not in Eric's time) into packaging in Belgium and Italy, newsprint and pulp in France. In North America, a third and then a fourth machine were put up at Calhoun and in 1956 Eric seized an unexpected opportunity, which dismayed his advisers and threw Bowaters' financial planning into disarray, to buy the Mersey Paper Co of Liverpool, Nova Scotia, which he had long coveted. At much the same time, again against expressed misgivings, he insisted on setting up, very expensively, a sulphate pulp mill at Catawba, South Carolina, which was required exclusively to supply raw materials to the United Kingdom (where they were not, in the event, very gratefully received). A hardboard mill was put up, also at Catawba, but the planning was faulty and the project eventually failed. A machine installed at Catawba to supply coated paper to McCalls the magazine publishers, came into production in 1962, but the quality was at first so poor that McCalls refused to accept it, and Bowaters had to admit they were justified.

Not content with producing his own raw materials, Eric decided to provide his own ocean transport, too, and in 1955 the Bowater Steamship Co (which chiefly operated motor vessels) came into existence. Between 1954 and 1961 nine Bowater ships were launched, named after Sir Eric's female relations. Bowaters' house flag was seen from Scandinavia to Sydney Harbour, and on one occasion Eric took some friends on a pleasure cruise in the Caribbean, causing consternation at Bowater House because the ship was not insured for such agreeable diversions. The costs of the steamship company were grossly uneconomic and it looks very much like folie de grandeur.

If Eric Bowater had retired on his sixtieth birthday, soon after opening the Calhoun mill in Tennessee, he would be remembered for a career of almost unbroken success, marked by long views, great boldness, almost uncannily sound judgement and, on occasion, inspired opportunism, as when he bought control of Lloyds in 1936 and of Corner Brook in 1938. His tragedy, like that of others in great positions in business and elsewhere, was that he stayed too long and failed to adapt his policies to changing circumstances.

Again like other outstanding business men, for instance Lord Leverhulme (qv) and Sir Robert Barlow (qv), he showed little interest in organisation, neglected to train a successor, and neither delegated nor shared authority. The business grew too large and too complicated for him to control personally, which he nevertheless went on trying to do, with the result that in his later years ominous signs began to appear of ill-directed planning, indecisiveness and unco-ordinated financial policy, especially as between activities in the United Kingdom and North America. By 1960 it was apparent to Eric's advisers within the business, and to himself, that Bowaters were coming dangerously close to living beyond their means. In the generally depressed state of the market, especially for newsprint and packaging in the United Kingdom, earnings were rising too slowly to cover the interest charges and provision for depreciation generated by expansion at the speed and on the scale which Eric Bowater demanded. Moreover the price of wood pulp was falling, Bowaters' pulp mills were turning out far more than the business required, and the policy of self-sufficiency was becoming very expensive. A cash crisis was approaching, and Eric was warned of it. It came during the last year or so of his life, and by the time he died, in 1962, there was no alternative to drastic modification of the policies of expansion and self-sufficiency by which he set such store.

Outside Bowaters' business, Eric Bowater had few interests, though he was a director of Lloyds Bank and two or three other companies. By way of relaxation he would fairly frequently visit the casino at Le Touquet and at Ascot he would bet inexpertly, but his recreations, unless one includes among them the society of pretty women, do not seem to have been of great importance to him. In politics he disliked Sir Winston Churchill and the post-war Labour Government about equally; resented, as he put it, being 'automatically ... labelled a Conservative' {Reader (1981) 188}; and took a sombre, perhaps all too accurate, view of the likely development of world affairs, being deeply apprehensive of the advance of Communism and of the rise of black power in Africa, where he would never allow Bowaters to become deeply committed.

Eric Bowater courted his shareholders ardently. From 1954 until the end of his life, Bowaters' annual meetings were transformed into outings for thousands of shareholders. There was never enough accommodation for all who wished to come, but those lucky enough to draw tickets found themselves transported by fleets of coaches, by special trains, by Thames steamer, to one or other of Bowaters' factories or some convenient meeting-place nearby. There, the chairman would address the gathering, lunch would be provided and a factory tour would follow. These meetings were the most conspicuous public expression of Eric's personality. They became legendary, for his was a personality which bred legend. Everything he did, he did with style, even magnificence. The last of the meetings, in 1962 when he was tired and ill, was the last gleam of his glory. Their like has never been seen again.

Eric married first, in 1915, Blanche Currie, née de Ville, and secondly, in 1937 after a divorce, Margaret Perkins. He had a daughter by Blanche; a daughter and a son by Margaret. He died on 30 August 1962, leaving £495,181 gross.

W J READER

Writings:

Speeches to company meetings, available at Bowater House, Knightsbridge, London.

Sources:

Unpublished

BCe.

MCe.

Published

DNB.

William J Reader, *Bowater, A History* (Cambridge: Cambridge University Press, 1981) for general source material.

WWW.

BOWDEN, Sir Harold

(1880-1960)

Cycle manufacturer

Harold Bowden was born at San Francisco, California, on 9 July 1880, the eldest son of Frank Bowden, founder of the Raleigh Cycle Co and of Sturmey-Archer Gears Ltd, and his wife Amelia Frances, daughter of Colonel Alexander Houston, one of the pioneers of the State of California. He was educated at Clifton College, Bristol, studied languages at Lausanne and went up to Clare College, Cambridge, but left before taking a degree in order to join the Raleigh Co in 1899, when its affairs were in financial crisis. Initially he was employed in the workshops and commercial department and then travelled for the company in Eastern England. Against the wishes of the majority of the board he was elected a director of the company in November 1905, at the insistence of his father, who held one-third of the voting share capital, and with the support of other shareholders.

For his position in the firm, and his social status outside, Harold Bowden clearly owed much to his father, who developed the Raleigh Cycle Co during the late nineteenth century from the small concern of Woodhead, Angois & Ellis of Nottingham of the 1880s into an enterprise employing about 2,000 workpeople by 1918.

The Raleigh Cycle Co, one of the relatively large, established cycle manufacturing firms, had been floated publicly in 1896 with an issued capital of £200,000, but Frank Bowden retained a substantial shareholding interest. A crisis in 1908 led to the dissolution of the company and its replacement by a 'private' joint stock enterprise with Frank and Harold Bowden having complete ownership and control. Frank Bowden was made a baronet in June 1915 in recognition of his services to early wartime munitions production. Harold succeeded to the baronetcy in April 1921 and followed his father's penchant for outside political, social and intellectual activity. He was an ardent cyclist and motorist. Poor health as a child encouraged him to take up cycling. As a keen motorist he was instrumental in getting the Raleigh Co to make a number of, largely unsuccessful, attempts to enter the motor car trade. He also actively

Harold Bowden (courtesy of TI Raleigh Industries Ltd).

A 1909 Raleigh advertisement (courtesy of TI Raleigh Industries Ltd).

407

supported athletics, engaging in fund raising for the sport and acting as chairman of the Council of the British Olympic Association in 1931-35. He joined the Council of the Cycle and Motor Cycle Manufacturers' and Traders' Union, serving as its president 1921-23, and became a spokesman for the industry during a period of difficulties created by wartime munitions requirements, and the aftermath of reconstruction and reorganization. In the inter-war period, he also became an active propagandist for a reconciliation between capital and labour within British industry, speaking and writing frequently on industrial relations.

Harold Bowden introduced profit sharing in the Raleigh Co in the early 1920s and maintained a sympathetic and paternalistic relationship with his workpeople. He relied heavily on managerial talent, either imported or internally generated, to conduct the Raleigh Co's affairs. Although very active on the sales side, particularly for sporting bicycles, he was no great technological or commercial innovator. He retired in 1938 from the managing directorship which he had inherited, but retained the chairmanship of Raleigh Cycle Holdings Co, formed in 1934, and relied on a series of general managers, in particular G H B Wilson, who during the 1940s and 1950s successfully promoted the company's affairs. Harold Bowden remained actively associated with various cycle industry trade organisations.

He was awarded the Grand Cross of the Order of the Phoenix (Greece) in 1932 and he served as High Sheriff of Nottinghamshire in 1933. His recreations were shooting, fishing and yachting.

His first marriage in 1908 to Vera, daughter of Joseph Whitaker JP, ended in divorce in 1919. The following year he married Muriel Smythe, divorcée and daughter of the late William Douglas. After her death, he married, in 1952, June Schenker, divorcée and daughter of the late Christopher T H Mackay; she died the next year. In 1957 he married a fourth wife, Valerie, widow of Albert Renfrew Porter. By his first marriage he had a son, Frank, and a daughter, Ruth. He died on 24 August 1960, leaving £932,458 gross.

A E HARRISON

Sources:

Unpublished

MCe.

A E Harrison, 'Growth, Entrepreneurship and Capital Formation in the United Kingdom's Cycle and Related Industries, 1870-1914' (York D Phil, 1977).

Published

Burke's Peerage and Baronetage 1959.

A E Harrison, 'Joint Stock Company Flotation in the Cycle, Motor-Vehicle and Related Industries, 1882-1914' *Business History* 23 (1981).

History of Raleigh Industries (pp by firm, nd).

Times 25 Aug 1960.

WWW.

BOWES, John

(1811-1885)

Colliery owner

John Bowes was born in London on 19 June 1811. He was the only, and illegitimate, son of the Tenth Earl of Strathmore, the owner of extensive estates in County Durham and Teesdale, and also in Scotland. His mother, Mary Millner, later Dowager Countess of Strathmore, was the daughter of a village school master. A House of Lords Committee for Privileges, appointed in 1821, rejected John Bowes's claim to his father's title and Scottish inheritance, though confirmed his possession of the estates in the North East of England (amounting to 43,200 acres in Durham and North Yorkshire in 1879). Following preparatory school, he was educated at Eton and Trinity College, Cambridge.

Bowes inherited an interest in mining, in the form of his estates and of a share in Lord Ravensworth & Partners (itself a successor to the Grand Alliance of 1726). In 1838 he engaged Nicholas Wood to sink a new colliery at Marley Hill in Durham. In 1841 the Marley Hill Coal Co was formed with Bowes holding the greater proportion of the shares. This company rapidly became the major producer of coke in Britain, though in its early years it was poorly managed and Bowes, who spent most of his time in Paris, took it into debt. In December 1844 a new partnership (the Marley Hill Coking Co) was formed with Charles Mark Palmer (qv). Palmer, though then only twenty-two, injected new capital and became the company's chief manager, eventually taking the company out of debt. The firm acquired new collieries in the North East, and a greatly expanded coke capacity with ovens in County Durham, at Blackwall in London, at Lowestoft, Dublin and Belfast. By 1855 the company had acquired fourteen collieries, including two in Northumberland. Output of coal by 1884 reached 1.75 million tons.

Bowes's interest in the management of the firm was minimal and it seems likely that his contribution was destructive rather than positive. Prior to 1885 its financial affairs were in considerable disarray, with each partner contracting debts, to which the company was liable, without the others' knowledge or consent. Debts in 1884 amounted to £400,000, and despite the firm's extreme good health (measured in terms of output, expansion and profit) it relied heavily on credit. Limited liability was adopted in July 1886, after Bowes's death; the nominal capital was £600,000.

Bowes's business career had been a minor aspect of his life, though a necessary foundation for his enduring but expensive interests in politics, women, horse-racing and art. He became MP for South Durham in 1832 until he retired from the House of Commons in 1847. He stood as a radical candidate, a 'Reformer', but never spoke in debate in the House. In 1831 he was appointed DL, and later became sheriff, of Durham. Yet he devoted himself mainly to the turf (where he had a number of Derby, Two Thousand Guineas, and St Leger winnings) and to the amassing of an art collection for which he built the Bowes Museum in Barnard Castle.

His first wife, whom he married in 1852, was a French actress, Josephine Benôite Coffin-Chevalier. She died in 1874, and Bowes was re-married in 1877 to Alphonsine de Courten, a Swiss countess. This marriage ended in a legal separation shortly before his death on 9 October 1885. His gross personal estate amounted to £147,875, most of which went to the upkeep of the Bowes Museum. He had no heirs.

A A HALL

Sources:

Unpublished

Newcastle upon Tyne City Library, 'Local Biography', Vol 2.

MCe.

C E Mountford, 'The History of John Bowes and Partners up to 1914' (Durham MA, 1967).

Published

Bateman.

Charles E Hardy, *John Bowes and the Bowes Museum* (Newcastle upon Tyne: Frank Graham, 1970).

George W Havelock, *Local Records of Northern England* (Newcastle upon Tyne: George W Havelock, Examiner Office, 1885).

WWMP.

BOWIE, James Alexander

(1888-1949)

Pioneer of professional management

James Alexander Bowie was born in Aberdeen on 30 November 1888, the third son of William Bowie, a mason, and his wife Jane née Lumsden. He attended Ashley Public School, the Central Secondary School, and Aberdeen University, from which he graduated in philosophy and economic science. After further study at Aberdeen, as a Carnegie Research Scholar, he gained an MA with honours in Commerce (and in 1924 received a DLitt for his publication *Sharing Profits with Employees*). Bowie combined his university studies with business experience: whilst a student at Aberdeen, he was also partner and business manager in the small family firm, Bowie & Son, contractors. His ability to combine successfully two demanding occupations demonstrates a characteristic repeatedly observed by contemporaries: his great capacity and willingness to work.

After the First World War, during which he saw active service with the Royal Artillery in the Near East, Bowie joined the new Department of Industrial Administration of Manchester College of Technology as an assistant lecturer, and became very active in developing both the teaching side and contacts between the department and local industry. The department was the first of its kind in this country, providing an early example of co-operation between industry and education in the training of potential managers. Bowie later enunciated the aims of the department:

> It is the specific purpose of the Department to prepare men to assume responsible positions in industry by instructing them in the practices and problems of the internal organisation of manufacturing concerns. {*The Schoolmaster* Oct 1928}

The University of Manchester recognised industrial administration as a subject appropriate for university study in 1927, and accepted the DIA into the university. In the same year, James Bowie, its new director, founded a full-time, postgraduate course in industrial administration, in which he experimented with new teaching methods. These included practical training for students (in co-operation with the Management Research Group based in Manchester) and the 'Case Method', which he saw in use in American business schools during his visit to the USA in 1931. He left the department 'with many regrets' in 1931 to join the School of Economics in Dundee. At Dundee, he fought to continue and extend the work begun at Manchester. During the Second World War, Bowie served as Honorary Food Executive Officer and as Local Registration Officer for Dundee, 1940-43. In 1943 he joined the staff of Personnel Administration Ltd, a firm of management consultants, returning to the School of Economics in Dundee in 1946.

Lyndall Urwick (qv), who had often found himself cast in the role of adversary, saw Bowie as 'the first British writer of importance on education for management' {Urwick (1963) 259}. Bowie's interest in management education was, however, only part of his wider interest in the movement which, in the inter-war period, was concerned to establish management as a profession. In his major work, *Education for Business Management*, Bowie argued that an effective means of creating responsible and legitimate managerial power was through the professionalisation of management, preferably through the establishment of specialist management institutions. Later he argued for the operation of a 'closed shop' as a means of ensuring professional standards. Professional managers, he believed, in the new role he saw for them as trustees of the community, would help to transform business enterprise into an essentially social institution, with clearly defined social responsibilities.

James Bowie spread his ideas through his writings and through his active membership of the British Association for the Advancement of Science, the British Association for Commercial and Industrial Education, the Institute of Industrial Administration, and, later, the British Institute of Management.

When Bowie died at the relatively young age of sixty-one, the obituarists paid tribute to his contribution to the development of management thought and practice, and to his sincerity and friendliness. In 1954 the Institute of Industrial Administration established the Bowie medal in recognition of his services to management, to be awarded annually to individuals who had made important contributions to management.

Bowie married Rosa née Tatham, daughter of William Henry Tatham, during his stay in Manchester; they had a son and a daughter. James Bowie died on 1 September 1949.

CATHERINE E MEAKIN *and* SHIRLEY KEEBLE

Writings:

Sharing Profits with Employees (Sir I Pitman & Sons, 1922).

'Industrial Management as a Career' *The Schoolmaster* Oct 1928.

'Co-partnership' in J Lee (ed), *Dictionary of Industrial Administration* (Sir I Pitman & Sons, 1928).

Education for Business Management (Oxford: Oxford University Press, 1930).

Rationalisation (Sir I Pitman & Sons, 1931).

'Preparation for Management' in R J MacKay (ed), *Business and Science: Being the Collected Papers Read to the Department of Industrial Co-operation at the Centenary of the British Association for the Advancement of Science* (1931).

American Schools of Business (Sir I Pitman & Sons, 1932).

The Management Factor in Industry: A Manifesto (signatory with others) (1933).

'The Universities and Business' *Labour Management* 17, no 188, (Oct 1935).

'The Ideal Business Manager' *Industry Illustrated* July 1938.

The Future of Scotland (London & Edinburgh: W & R Chambers, 1939).

The Basis of Reconstruction (Oliver & Boyd, 1941).

'The Future of Management' *Journal of the Institute of Industrial Administration* Sept 1942.

'New Opportunities for Training' *Industry Illustrated* Nov 1945.

'Industrial Organisation' *ibid* July 1946.

'Education for Management' *ibid* July 1946.

'Historical Review of Earlier Contributions' *British Management Review* 7, no 3 (1948).

'Management and the Closed Shop' *Industry* Jan 1949.

Reply to B N Seear, 'Do Managers Want a Closed Shop?' *ibid* April 1949.

'Towards a Philosophy of Industry' *ibid* May 1949.

Sources:

Unpublished

University of Manchester Institute of Science and Technology, records of the Department of Industrial Administration.

Scottish BCe.

Published

John Child, *British Management Thought* (George Allen & Unwin, 1969).

H N Munro, 'Training for Management' *British Management Review* 1 (1936).

Lyndall F Urwick (ed), *The Golden Book of Management. A Historical Record of the Life and Work of Seventy Pioneers* (Newman Neame, 1956).

Lyndall F Urwick and Edward F L Brech, *The Making of Scientific Management* (3 vols, Management Publications Trust, 1948-49).

British Institute of Management Bulletin 5 (Oct 1949).

Journal of the Institute of Personnel Management 31 (Sept-Oct 1949).

WWW.

BOWMAN, Sir James

(1898-1978)

Nationalised coal industry chairman

Sir James Bowman. Working drawing by Sir David Low (courtesy of the National Portrait Gallery, London).

James Bowman was born at Great Corby near Carlisle on 8 March 1898, third of five sons of Robert James Bowman (1861-1948), blacksmith, and Mary née Murray (1865-1941). He served in the First World War with the Royal Marines, and after 1918 began work as a coalminer at Ashington in Northumberland. In the early 1920s he joined the branch committee and welfare committee of the Miners' Federation at Ashington. He afterwards became a pit inspector, and then the first full-time trade union official at Ashington with responsibility for five pits and 3,000 miners. At this time union membership stood at under 100 but within three months every miner employed at Ashington became a union member. Bowman was elected secretary of the Northumberland Miners' Mutual Confident Association in 1935, and became a Northumberland magistrate in the same year. In July 1939 he was elected vice-president of the Miners' Federation of Great Britain, the youngest man ever to occupy the post, and was re-elected unchallenged until 1949. He was also a member of the General Council of the Trades Union Congress, 1945-49.

Bowman, together with the miners' president Will Lawther (1889-1976) and secretary Ebby Edwards (1884-1961), was 'startled, as upon the brink of an abyss, to find what backward notions were entertained within the Department of Mines' following the outbreak of war in 1939 {Arnot (1979) 10}, and forced a more accommodating attitude on the Government. Bowman himself was appointed in April 1940 to the Coal Production Council headed by Lord Portal (qv). He was a strong advocate of the nationalisation of the coalmines, and frankly criticised the Government's wartime policy in the industry; despite his fighting rhetoric, he worked hard to keep peace in the mines and to raise wartime productivity and output.

Coal nationalisation in 1946 led to a crisis in the industry. A grave shortage of coal was aggravated by a severe winter and by the upheavals resulting from nationalisation. Some blame lay with Emanuel Shinwell, the Minister of Fuel and Power. 'His officials are in despair at his failure to settle down to a close and objective study of the facts, or to follow a steady line in regard to ... the very tricky issues arising in his Department', wrote one Cabinet colleague, 'He is by far the least attractive member of the Government, always looking round for someone to whom to pass the blame ... a bad administrator [who] will not face the facts squarely' {BLPES, Dalton diary 6, 10 Feb 1947}. In addition to poor political leadership, the industry lost most of its top level management on nationalisation, as the managing directors and other senior administrators of many coal companies refused to enter service with the National Coal Board. This was a heavy blow to the NCB, whose great size and complex business desperately needed talented and experienced leaders. The industry's new hierarchy of group, area, division and board made decision-making much more dilatory and bureaucratic. Moreover, the miners had expected that with the disappearance of mineowners, and the substitution of national for district wage settlements, they would obtain a much better standard of living. They were soon disillusioned, and came to resent the remoteness of NCB headquarters in London: one miner compared the new conditions to working for a ghost. As a result, labour unrest continued.

These difficulties led to the reorganisation of the NCB under the Coal Industry Act of 1949, and as a result of this reform, Bowman was appointed, at the prompting of Shinwell's successor, Hugh Gaitskell, to chair the NCB's Northern Division. The Conservative Government elected in 1951 remained dissatisfied with the industry's efficiency, and in 1953 appointed a committee on NCB organisation headed by Sir Alexander Fleck (qv) of ICI. Six of the NCB board members resigned or were removed around the time of the publication of the Fleck report, and in February 1955 a new board was appointed in accordance with Fleck's recommendations. This comprised six ordinary members with departmental responsibilities, four part-time members, and a chairman and his deputy with general responsibilities. Bowman was appointed deputy chairman, but on the death of Sir Hubert Houldsworth in February 1956, he succeeded as chairman, at a salary of £10,000 per annum. Bowman remained in that post until 1961, and headed a board that was stronger and more experienced than that of Houldsworth's predecessor, Lord Hyndley (qv).

The five years of Bowman's chairmanship of the NCB were complex and difficult. When he took office in 1956 the main task facing his board was to raise production and manpower, but by '1960 the Board's objectives were, broadly, to bring coal production below the level of demand, without involving any substantial measure of hardship to the mining community, and, at the same time, to secure a satisfactory increase in efficiency' {NCB Annual Report (1961) 1}. Thus Bowman and his board had to face a complete reversal in their aims in running the industry while at the same time continuing with the work of mechanisation and improving productivity and industrial relations. The change hit the industry suddenly. In 1957 the NCB reported the recruitment of 4,186 Hungarian workers and in the same year they suffered their first drop in demand. By 1959 they had 36 million tons of stock, and inland consumption of coal had fallen since 1956 by 28 million tons while consumption of black oils increased by the equivalent of about 23.5 million tons of coal.

This reversal in coal policy presented Bowman with four distinct challenges. First he had to try to stimulate demand for coal: marketing for the first time received its due emphasis. This involved attempting to improve the poor public image of coal and evolving a sales service comparable to that of the NCB's competitors in the fuel industry. Large contributions were made to the National Industrial Fuel Efficiency Service and the Coal Utilization Council. Results were slow, but by 1960 consumption had begun to rise again, and stocks of coal held by the board fell during the year by 6.5 million tons.

The second challenge was related: coal was imported from the USA at very high prices and sold in competition with home produced coal, although the NCB itself was unable to export British coal at very much higher prices than it sold for in the British market. This inequity, as Bowman complained to the Commons Select Committee on Nationalised Industries in 1956, highlighted the difficulties met by the NCB because of its anomalous position as neither wholly commercial nor wholly private, but an uneasy mixture. A solution to the problem of the status of nationalised industries eluded Bowman, as it has remained a problem for other leaders of public corporations.

Bowman's third task was to improve, or at least to prevent deterioration in, industrial relations at a time when cuts in labour were inevitable and stoppages could be seen by miners as a way of easing their problems of overproduction. When Bowman became chairman in 1956, labour relations were poor: absenteeism was still as high as it had been at nationalisation, the number of unofficial disputes causing stoppages and go-slows had steadily increased since 1947 from 1,635 to over 3,000 a year in 1956 and tons lost from 1,652,000 in 1947 to 2,146,000 in 1956. In recruiting an ex-trade union official to management the Government hoped to sweeten relations within the industry, but this could not be done so easily: as G A Sparrow, Secretary to the Leicester Colliery Overmen, Deputies & Shotfirers Association wrote of the miners, 'their fathers have eaten sour grapes and it has set the children's teeth on edge' {*Times* 24 Sept 1957}. Unofficial disputes and absenteeism continued. Although the tonnage loss decreased over the period of Bowman's chairmanship by about 27 per cent, the absenteeism increased by about 8 per cent. It is greatly to Bowman's credit, however, that he succeeded in closing 130 pits and cutting manpower from 710,000 to 583,000 without major industrial disturbance. Bowman's great personal achievement lay in wage and other negotiations. He attached enormous importance to industrial relations, believing strongly in participation and attempting to break down the 'them and us' attitude: his greatest achievements were perhaps in this field. His relations with the NUM leaders, especially Arthur Horner, the secretary, and Sam Watson, the Durham leader, were excellent, and enabled negotiations in 1956-61 to be conducted on a more sympathetic and realistic basis than at any time since nationalisation. Bowman, with Joe Gormley, was the first to introduce the redundancy scheme for miners in 1959. This scheme was a forerunner for others introduced throughout industry a decade later.

His final challenge was to improve mining techniques and develop new fuels at a time when the NCB's income was declining but when it was still expected to show an operating profit. This was another area where rationalisation had been expected to solve old problems. Bowman's chairmanship saw the development of the Coal Research Establishment and the Mining Research & Development Establishment. The decline in demand from 1957 meant that there was increased pressure to raise productivity so that coal could be competitive in price, and to improve the end-product so that coal could be competitive in usage. Productivity increased steadily from 25 cwt per man shift for all workers in 1956 to 28 cwt per man shift in 1960. Mechanisation advanced apace. In 1956 15.5 per cent of the total pithead output was power-loaded output; by 1960 the proportion was 38 per cent.

It is hard to evaluate the individual contribution that Bowman brought to these changes, not least since he avoided personal publicity. But it is certain that his understanding of the mining community was clear and sympathetic, that he was an efficient administrator and that he had a keen belief in the importance of technical progress in mining methods. He adapted readily from a union leader to chairman of the NCB Northern Division, possessing a tidy mind and eschewing detailed involvement in day-to-day affairs in favour of the larger administrative issues. As chairman of the NCB he concentrated on public policy, industrial relations, marketing, technical and production developments and relations with senior management in the coalfields. 'He was wonderfully considerate to every single person on his immediate staff', wrote David Kinnersley, 'that is how he got a great deal done without raising his voice in private or public' { *Times* 12 Oct 1978}.

Bowman was a member of the Royal Commission on the Press in 1947-49 and of the governmental enquiry on the organisation of the British Broadcasting Corporation. He was a governor of the Administrative Staff College from 1957, and was a member in the 1950s of the Department of Scientific and Industrial Research. He was made CBE in 1952, KBE in 1957 and was created a baronet on retiring from the NCB in 1961.

He married, in 1923, at Morpeth, Jean, daughter of Henry Brooks of Ashington, Northumberland, by whom he had a son and a daughter. Following his retirement, he returned to Newcastle upon Tyne, where he had kept a home, and died there on 25 September 1978 leaving £21,100 gross.

JENNY DAVENPORT

Writings:

PP, HC 1957-58 (187-1) VI, SC on Nationalised Industries.

Sources:

Unpublished

BLPES, papers of Lord Dalton.

Information from National Coal Board and Sir George Bowman.

Published

Robert Page Arnot, *The Miners in Crisis and War* (Allen & Unwin, 1961).

—, *The Miners* (Allen & Unwin, 1979).

Burke's Peerage 1970.

Reuben Kelf-Cohen, *British Nationalisation 1945-73* (Macmillan, 1973).

National Coal Board *Annual Reports* 1949-61.

Times 24 Sept 1957, 6, 10, 12 Oct 1978.

WWW.

BOWRING, Charles Tricks

(1808-1885)

Shipowner and marine underwriter

Charles T Bowring (courtesy of C T Bowring & Co Ltd).

Charles Tricks Bowring was born at Exeter in 1808, the second of five sons of Benjamin Bowring (1778-1846), a watchmaker and silversmith, and his wife Charlotte née Price, daughter of a Wiveliscombe (Somerset) watchmaker. In spring 1816 Benjamin Bowring took his family to St John's, Newfoundland, where he had decided to set up a watch and clock-maker's business. Once established there, he quickly moved into importing general merchandise. By 1823 he owned a wharf and three ships and had forged trading links with Exeter, London and Liverpool, where he was assisted by kin and Unitarian networks.

Charles and his brothers were brought up in the Unitarian faith at St John's and all entered their father's business as they grew to manhood. In summer 1832 Charles, at his father's suggestion, went to England to meet and marry Harriet Harvey, the daughter of a Devonshire soap maker and tallow chandler with whom Benjamin Bowring did business. Harriet had been the intended bride of Charles's elder brother, William (1804-29), until he was lost at sea. Charles, by now a partner in the family firm, returned to St John's with his wife in spring 1833 to take charge of the Newfoundland business. His father, with the rest of the family, then left the island colony and set up a merchant house in Liverpool. From St John's, Charles sent shipments of cod and oils to Liverpool in the firm's two schooners, *Dove* and *Charlotte*; on the return leg Benjamin sent back various manufactured goods, foodstuffs and salt for the Newfoundland fisheries.

Upon assuming control at St John's, Charles revealed his characteristic independence of mind and boldness of vision. In 1835, for example, contrary to the advice of his father, he decided to go into the seal oil business and built a storage vat at St John's. Despite his father's misgivings regarding the capital risks involved, this venture proved highly successful and the Bowrings soon became a leading firm in the island's seal fishery. They were to retain this position for many years after C T Bowring's death.

On the retirement of Benjamin Bowring in summer 1841, Charles returned to England and became head of the Liverpool merchant house, thenceforth known as C T Bowring & Co, leaving his younger brothers, Henry Price (1815-93) and Edward (1819-75) in charge of Bowring Brothers at St John's. At Liverpool, which was rapidly becoming one of the world's major ports, Charles Tricks Bowring proceeded to direct the remarkable maritime expansion of the Bowring business over the next forty years. From the late 1840s he and his brothers built up a tramp fleet under the red cross house flag that soon became familiar in many of the oceans of the world. The firm moved steadily from chartering to the building of its own ships, the number under Bowring ownership increasing from five to 16 between 1850 and 1860. During these years, the Bowrings also expanded their trading interests to the Mediterranean, South America and Australia. This expansion of its interests gave the firm some immunity from the recurrent economic crises which affected many of its competitors in St John's and Liverpool.

C T Bowring was also largely responsible for developing marine insurance as an important branch of the firm's business. In 1849 Bowring Brothers at St John's had become one of the first overseas agents for the Liverpool & London Fire & Life Insurance Co, founded by Swinton Boult (qv). Doubtless prompted by this, C T Bowring a few years later opened a private marine underwriting account in Liverpool, a not uncommon practice at that time among merchants with marine interests. He probably combined broking with underwriting risks for his own account and placed business for clients in the London market. Although Bowrings' shipowning and trading interests remained predominant in Liverpool, the firm became busily engaged in broking and private underwriting, building a solid foundation for its later prominence in the international insurance market.

As his father had done, C T Bowring introduced his sons into the family firm as soon as they came of age. His first son, Charles, was established at the St John's office; his second son, William Benjamin, was sent to New York to set up a new branch of the company; his third son, Henry, took charge of the Bowring office at Newcastle upon Tyne; his fourth son, George, eventually became head of the London office of the company. While keeping a close watch on his sons to ensure that they carried out their business in the best traditions of the family, Charles Tricks Bowring was often ready to provide them with advice, encouragement and financial support for their various new ventures.

The 1860s saw a rapid growth in the family's shipping interests. In this decade alone C T Bowring and his kinsmen bought or built 19 new ships ranging from small schooners to 1,200 ton iron clippers. In the 1870s another 21 ships, five of which were steamships, joined the family fleet. In the 1880s, with the transition from sail to steam in full swing, no fewer than 22 ships were built, and of these 14 were steamers. In 1860 Bowring inaugurated a line of packets from Liverpool to Rio de Janeiro which soon became famous for the speed of its ships. In 1863 he introduced an Indian run to Bombay with three 'tall ships'. In 1864 he began a service to Auckland, New Zealand, in association with the Liverpool firm of Stoddart Brothers, a senior partner of which Bowring's daughter Charlotte had married two years earlier; and also in association with this firm he started a line of clipper packets between Liverpool and Montreal. In 1866 another line of Bowring packets took up the London to Adelaide trade, while others of the company's ships sailed from Liverpool around the Horn to the west coast of America. In 1876 Bowring Brothers were awarded a contract to operate the whole of Newfoundland's mail steamer service with two Liverpool-built steamships, the *Curlew* and the *Plover*, a service which they continued until 1888. Finally, in 1880 the *Titania*, the first steamship ordered by the firm for regular transoceanic service, was put into service between New York and Newcastle upon Tyne.

While enlarging their various fleets the Bowrings increasingly engaged in the newest and potentially most lucrative traffic of all, namely petroleum, which was used at this time mainly for lubrication and as lamp oil. The exact date when the firm entered the petroleum trade is obscure, as indeed is Charles Tricks Bowring's own role in this development, but it is clear that C T Bowring & Co was one of the pioneer companies for the importation of the mineral oil into Britain. By 1867 the trade was being actively pursued between the Liverpool and New York offices of the company; later, with C T Bowring's encouragement and financial backing, it was also taken on by the London office. The New York-Liverpool-London petroleum trade grew apace, and in 1883 the parent company in Liverpool bought the 850 ton barque *Slieve Bloom* for the express purpose of conveying paraffin in barrels from the United States to Britain.

His public spirit drew C T Bowring into Liverpool's civic affairs at a time when men of vision and energy were urgently needed to carry out far-reaching social improvements. From 1857 until his death he was Liberal representative for St Peter's ward in Liverpool Town Council. As chairman of Liverpool Health Committee he led the drive to eliminate some of the most disgraceful courts, alleys and slum tenements in Britain and replace them with fine new streets and dwellings. Inheriting his father's Unitarian beliefs, he worshipped for many years at the Hope Street Unitarian Church in Liverpool.

C T Bowring and his wife lived long enough to celebrate their golden wedding; they had six daughters and four sons. After several years of declining health he died in Liverpool on 23 September 1885, aged seventy-seven, leaving £106,341 gross.

ALAN J SCARTH

Sources:

Unpublished

Liverpool City RO, William Brown Street, Liverpool, records of C T Bowring & Co Ltd 1830-80, Ref 380 BOW.

Published

David Keir, *The Bowring Story* (The Bodley Head, 1962).

Liverpool Review 26 Sept 1885.

Arthur C Wardle, *Benjamin Bowring and His Descendants: A Record of Mercantile Achievement* (Hodder & Stoughton, 1938).

William Boyd (from Transactions of the North East Coast Institution *35).*

BOYD, William

(1839-1919)

Marine engineer

Wiliam Boyd was born at Arncliffe, Yorkshire, on 17 October 1839, the son of Rev William Boyd, vicar of Arncliffe and Archdeacon of Cleveland, and Isabella née Twining. He was educated at Rugby and King's College, London and then was apprenticed as an engineer to Sharp, Stewart & Co, locomotive engineers of Manchester. After serving his time he became a partner in the marine engineering firm of Thompson, Boyd & Co in Newcastle upon Tyne, 1863-74. In the latter year the partnership was dissolved and Boyd left to become managing director of the Wallsend Slipway Co Ltd. This company had been established in 1871 by representatives of three large Tyneside shipping companies to provide repair facilities for their vessels. The first managing director, C S Swan, had resigned in 1874 to develop his interest in shipbuilding (which was to lead eventually to the creation of Swan, Hunter & Wigham Richardson Ltd, with which firm Wallsend Slipway was subsequently to amalgamate) and Boyd was invited to replace him. Boyd found a firm with 300 employees which was almost entirely involved in ship repair and he immediately developed marine engineering and boiler making, so that in 1878 '& Engineering' was added to the company's title after 'Slipway'. In marine engineering the firm became world famous, providing engine sets for mercantile and naval vessels for many countries. By the time that he resigned as managing director in 1903 (although he remained on the board for several more years) Boyd had seen the labour force grow to 2,000. In 1906 the company constructed the 68,000 horse power turbines for the *Mauretania*.

Boyd played the major role in this development and not only managed and directed the company but also provided technological leadership. He was involved with the development of oil as a fuel for steamships and patented improvements including a method of oil injection. Under his leadership the company pioneered the use of steel for the construction of marine boilers. He was a member of the Technical Committee of Lloyd's Register and was a founding member and first president (1884-86) of the North East Coast Institution of Engineers and Shipbuilders.

In spite of a busy career, Boyd played a major part in local community service and politics. During his apprenticeship he served in the Lancashire Artillery Volunteers and in 1871-79 was colonel of the 1st Newcastle upon Tyne Artillery Volunteers. He served on the Newcastle School Board and in 1894 was made a JP for Northumberland. It was to his adopted town of Wallsend that he gave most significant service, however. He became a member of Wallsend Local Board of Health in 1878 and was its chairman from 1879 until it was replaced in 1894 by Wallsend UDC of which he was also elected chairman. He held this position until Wallsend received a borough charter when he was made an alderman and elected the first mayor, 1901-2.

BOYD William

In 1865 Boyd married Diana, daughter of Edward Hawks of Douglas, Isle of Man; they had two daughters. In 1912 Boyd left Tyneside and moved to Cheltenham where he died on 19 May 1919, leaving an estate valued at £66,757 gross.

D J ROWE

Writings:

'On Experiments Relative to Steel Boilers' *Proceedings of the Institution of Mechanical Engineers* 1878.

'On Slipways' *ibid* 1881.

'Inaugural Address' *Transactions of the North East Coast Institution of Engineers and Shipbuilders* 1 (1884-85).

'Inaugural Address' *ibid* 2 (1885-86).

'The Weight of Machinery in the Mercantile Marine' *ibid* 6 (1889-90).

The Story of the Wallsend Slipway & Engineering Co Ltd, 1871-1897 (Newcastle, 1911).

Sources:

Unpublished

BCe.

Published

Newcastle and Gateshead Incorporated Chamber of Commerce, *Year Book* (1914).

William Richardson, *History of the Parish of Wallsend* (Newcastle: Northumberland Press, 1923).

Transactions of the North East Coast Institution of Engineers and Shipbuilders 35 (1918-19).

BRACKLEY, Herbert George

(1894-1948)

Air transport pioneer and airline manager

Herbert George Brackley was born in Islington, London on 4 October 1894, the second child and eldest son of George Herbert Brackley, master tailor, and his wife Lilian Sarah née Partridge, who had four sons and three daughters. George Brackley came of yeoman farmer stock from Tring in Hertfordshire and Brackley, Northamptonshire. His wife was of Scottish ancestry: her father a manager of the Spottiswood printing company, her mother the daughter of an Essex doctor.

When young George was two years old the Brackley family moved to Westerham in Kent where his father built up a flourishing business. The boy sang in the choir of Westerham parish church, went to the local Brasted school and learned to play the violin before winning a scholarship to Sevenoaks Grammar School. That meant two, 14 mile, cycle rides daily in all weathers. At school he joined the OTC, won prizes for swimming and diving, played cricket, developed his interest in music and a passion for photography which he retained all his life. He also saw his first aeroplane (Bleriot's cross-Channel monoplane) when on holiday in Dover in July 1909. That fired his ambition to fly.

In his last year at school, Brackley contemplated going into the church but, although he always remained a devout Anglo-Catholic, when his family moved back to Harringay in London in 1912, he joined Reuters Press Bureau. At Harringay he became a cadet officer in the Harringay Church Lads Brigade, a violinist in the South Place Orchestra and played rugby for Reuters.

Brackley joined the Royal Naval Air Service in April 1915 and learned to fly on a Maurice Farman of No 4 Wing, RN Air Station, Eastchurch, Kent. One of his instructors was John Alcock (later Sir John, who, with Sir Arthur Whitton-Brown, in June 1919 made the first non-stop Atlantic flight).

'Brackles', as he was known to his friends from his earliest days in the RNAS, qualified for his wings on 27 July 1915, after 4 hours 45 minutes solo. Over the next four years he saw service in France as a bomber pilot on the Western Front.

On 1 April 1918, Brackley transferred to the newly-formed Royal Air Force with the rank of major and took command of No 214 (Bomber) Squadron RAF equipped with the new Handley Page 0/400 twin-engine bomber. Brackley was demobilised in March 1919, having been awarded the DSC and DSO, the French Croix de Guerre and the Belgian Ordre de la Couronne.

Then began for Brackley an interim period of five years in which he was in the forefront of pioneering flight endeavours and overseas adventures. These episodes started when he joined Handley Page Ltd in April 1919, and set out by sea for St John's, Newfoundland, taking with him a

Handley Page V 1500 converted four-engine bomber in packing cases, in an attempt to win the £10,000 *Daily Mail* prize for the first Atlantic flight. Mechanical problems delayed his attempt and meantime Alcock and Brown won the prize. Brackley took his Handley Page to New York where it aroused much enthusiasm as the then largest aeroplane in the world and one of the first British aeroplanes to be seen over New York. After returning to England, Brackley, using another Handley Page, made an abortive attempt in January-February 1920 to win a new *Daily Mail* prize of £10,000 for a flight from London to Cape Town.

Afterwards Major Brackley took over from Col Sholto Douglas as chief pilot of Handley Page Transport Ltd under the managing director, George Woods-Humphery (qv). For the rest of 1920 he flew air services with HP 0/400 aircraft between Cricklewood and Croydon to Paris, Brussels and Cologne and, in August, won the Air Ministry competition for a commercial aeroplane, flying the new HP W-8 G-EAPJ.

Between April 1921 and September 1923, Brackley was a member of a 30-man British Aviation Mission, under Col the Master of Sempill, to the Imperial Japanese Navy. The purpose of the Mission was to train Japanese pilots and ground engineers, to lay aerodromes and to found an aircraft industry building British aircraft under licence including Avro 504s, DH 9s, Sopwith Cuckoos and Short F 5 flying-boats. During this time Brackley made the first deck landings on a Japanese-built aircraft carrier, the *Hosho*, flying Vickers Viking amphibian and Supermarine Seals.

Brackley briefly returned to England and, in September 1922, married Frida Helene Mond, daughter of Sir Robert Mond (qv) of the Mond Nickel Co, having met her in Tokyo in April, 1921. They spent the early months of their marriage in Japan. Brackley followed his wife home (she preceded him for the birth of her first child) after the Tokyo earthquake in which he lost all his personal possessions and his savings in the Bank of Yokohama.

For seven months after his return to England, Major Brackley was out of work in a time of recession for aviation generally. The Brackleys were, however, made welcome at the Mond home at Combe Bank, Sevenoaks, Kent. On 7 May, 1924, Brackley was appointed air superintendent in the newly-formed Imperial Airways Ltd where he was, once again, under George Woods-Humphery, now IAL's general manager.

For the next fifteen years Imperial Airways remained the centre of Brackley's life. As air superintendent (the parallel of marine super-intendent in shipping) Brackley was responsible for all flying staff, for operating standards and for selection and testing of all new aircraft used, or contemplated for use, by the airline. From the start he enjoyed the confidence and respect of all Imperial Airway's pilots — which Woods-Humphery did not. Indeed, Brackley's first task was to heal a rift between the 16 pilots and the general manager, a rift which had its origins in the days of Handley Page Transport. It led to a pilots' strike from the first day of the new company. Brackley thus had to start his new job in difficult and delicate circumstances as an intermediary between the flying staff and the management. His integrity, good sense and blunt straightforwardness smoothed ruffled feathers and Imperial Airways flew its first service (to Paris) on 26 April, 1924.

Inevitably, there continued to be clashes with Woods-Humphery who,

Herbert G Brackley with Sir Alan and Lady Cobham in 1927 (courtesy of Sir Peter Masefield).

in November, 1926, gave Brackley six months' written notice, which he withdrew shortly afterwards. The major problem remained the lack of understanding on the part of the IAL board of the flying side of the business which Brackley represented with unbiased vigour and candour.

From the start Brackley made a major contribution to Imperial Airways' progress in his influence on the requirements and layout for the HP 42 Hannibal and DH 66 Hercules landplanes and the Short Calcutta and Kent flying boats. In July, 1929, however, Wood-Humphery sent him to Cairo to relieve Wooley Dod, the IAL manager there: a three-month assignment which was prolonged to nine months, partly because of problems on Imperial Airways' new routes between Cairo and Karachi and partly because the general manager was, undoubtedly, more comfortable with his forthright air superintendent out of England. When Brackley returned in April, 1930, he wrested from a reluctant board more clearly defined lines of authority and responsibility for the post of air superintendent. He sought, also, some increase in salary after six years' work. It was refused. Throughout its existence Imperial Airways' staff and public relations were poor; made tolerable only by a company-wide dedication to the task of pioneering British air transport.

BRACKLEY Herbert George

A Handley Page HP42 G AAX Heracles at Croydon, 1930s (courtesy of Sir Peter Masefield).

Early in 1931, Brackley test-flew the two new four-engine types of aircraft for Imperial Airways, the HP 42 landplane and the Short Kent flying boat, and supervised their introduction into service. In March he was invited to go to India as deputy director of civil aviation under his old friend, Sir Frederick Tymms, but with children at school in England and other family ties he reluctantly turned the offer down.

For the next eight years, Brackley pressed forward with determination the opening up of Imperial Airways' Empire air routes to South Africa and Australia, at first with landplanes and then with flying boats, in which he developed increasing faith and confidence. In 1931 he flew a DH 66 Hercules to Cape Town, in 1933 an Armstrong Whitworth Atalanta to Karachi and a Short Calcutta flying boat to Durban; in 1935 a Short Kent to Singapore and in 1936, he conducted acceptance tests of the new Short C-Class Empire flying-boats and made survey flights to Australia.

These strenuous expeditions over territory so far covered only by pioneer aviators, were performed by Brackley with no fuss and meticulous care and were recorded in detail in his diary. In all of this he received, however, inadequate support either from the general manager or the board, none of whom at that time appeared to have an understanding of the problems inherent in establishing new routes with few navigational aids or prepared landing grounds, on land or water. Wherever he was, Brackley insisted in an early morning or an evening swim on every possible occasion and on attendance at a church service every Sunday.

In October, 1936, Brackley flew the first of the new Short C-Class Empire boats, *Canopus*, through a series of acceptance tests and then checked out IAL pilots in it. He received the coveted Cumberbatch Trophy of the Guild of Pilots and Air Navigators for the promotion of reliable service in air transport.

In June 1937, the 'all-up' Empire Air Mail Service was inaugurated to Australia with the Empire boat *Centaurus* while Brackley was, concurrently, preparing for the first experimental commercial flight across the North Atlantic. After making all the preparations, Brackley had hoped to make the first flight himself but Woods-Humphery insisted that the honour should go to Captain A S Wilcockson, the senior captain on the projected Atlantic route. Brackley loyally complied and witnessed the take off from Foynes in Ireland on 6 July 1937.

Early in 1938, publication of the Report of the Cadman (qv) Committee on British Civil Aviation stated that 'serious defects in the management of Imperial Airways call for immediate reform; and some changes in the directing personnel may well be involved' {*PP* (1937-38) Cmd 5685, 33}; the statement led to the resignation of George Woods-Humphery and the appointment of Sir John Reith (qv) as chairman, with Brackley now seen as one of the key figures in the Imperial Airways hierarchy.

As a result of the Cadman Committee's recommendations, in March, 1939, the amalgamation was announced of Imperial Airways with the small, privately-owned, British Airways Ltd to form, from 1 April 1940, the new British Overseas Airways Corporation (BOAC). To Major Brackley's dejection and disappointment, Alan Campbell Orde, formerly chief test pilot of Armstrong, Whitworth and then operations manager of British Airways Ltd, was nominated as operations manager of Imperial Airways over the head of Brackley, and the office and title of air superintendent ceased to exist. The secretary and assistant general manager of Imperial Airway, S A Dismore, wrote to Brackley 'It has been my unhappy duty to draft and issue the attached Organisation Bulletin and it is needless to assure you that all your old colleagues of 1924 feel as I do in this matter' {RAF Museum, Brackley papers}. Brackley again loyally accepted the situation and the disappointment and went off on yet another Route Survey to Algiers, Goa, Khartoum, Entebbe, Kora, Lagos, Dakar, and Casablanca. He was hardly back when war was declared and, having seen Imperial Airways landplane services transferred from Croydon to Whitchurch, Bristol, he was released from Imperial Airways. During the fifteen years in which Major H G Brackley was air superintendent of Imperial Airways, from 1924 to 1939, the company carried a total of 575,900 passengers in the course of 512,000 flying hours and operated, in all, 60.62 million revenue load ton-miles while earning a commercial revenue of £9.66 million, plus a government subsidy of £6.97 million. Operating costs thus averaged some £33 a flying hour. Over these years Imperial Airways' traffic increased from 10,300 passengers in 1924-25 to 49,800 passengers in 1938-39 and from 438,000 revenue load ton miles in 1924-25 to 15.12 million revenue load ton miles in 1938-39: an increase in business of almost 35 times.

In October 1939 he joined HQ, RAF Coastal Command, at Northwood, Middlesex, as a squadron leader (RAFVR) under the C-in-C Sir Frederick Bowhill. In October 1941 he was made a CBE. In Coastal Command Brackley was able to use all his flying-boat experience in the development of anti-submarine tactics with Short Sunderland flying-boats, the military development of the Empire boats. Promoted to air commodore in March 1943, he was in at the birth of RAF Transport Command as senior air staff officer. Once again, he was working closely with BOAC and Campbell

Orde and in charge of arrangements for the numerous flights in wartime conditions of HM King George VI, the Prime Minister, Lord Louis Mountbatten and Lord Beaverbrook (qv). In October, 1944, he was a member of the British Delegation to the International Aviation Conference at Chicago and, immediately after the end of the war, he led an Air Ministry Mission to Brazil in an Air Council Avro York as a precursor to the post-war start of British Latin American Airways routes.

He was released from the Royal Air Force on 13 October, 1945, and left the following day on a BOAC Mission to Baghdad and Mosul followed by a visit to New Zealand by way of Cairo, Karachi, Rangoon, Singapore and Sydney, and then to South Africa, now as assistant to Lord Knollys (qv) chairman of BOAC. In April, 1947, he flew round the world on BOAC duties and in September was placed in charge of the air evacuation of 7,000 Pakistan Government servants and their families from Delhi to Karachi; largely by Dakotas, an assignment triumphantly achieved.

Early in 1948 Brackley led a BOAC Mission to Ceylon, to celebrate with the Duke and Duchess of Gloucester the island's independence. On his return he was invited by the Minister of Civil Aviation, Lord Nathan, to take over as chief executive of British South American Airways Corporation in succession to Don Bennett, under the chairmanship of John Booth. So, at the age of fifty-two, after twenty-four years in air transport, Air Commodore H G Brackley reached the summit of his career with great opportunities ahead to develop British air services to West Africa and South America. His promise was not to be realised.

After a few months, in which he vigorously attacked the problems of organising a new airline corporation and ordered new aircraft (including the world's largest and most advanced flying boats, the Saunders Roe 45

Princess Class), and visited West Africa, he went to South America on a tour for the BSAAC and was drowned while swimming from the Copacabana Beach, Rio de Janiero, on 15 November 1948.

Of medium height and stocky build, Brackley was always immaculate in his dress. Though quiet and conscientious and exceedingly modest, he could be a vivid conversationalist on subjects in which he had special interest; aviation and aircraft, photography, the Church and ecclesiastical buildings and aquatic sports.

Through his wife, Frida — by whom he had three children (Mary b, 1923, David, b 1925 and John, b 1926) — he enjoyed a social life when his duties permitted and he was helped in this by his association with the distinguished, artistic British and French circles surrounding his father-in-law, Sir Robert Mond.

In Herbert George Brackley British air transport lost one of its outstanding characters of great honesty of purpose and high integrity, who was trusted and respected by all who knew him. His death came at a time when he was about to make a much needed contribution to post-war air transport, to which he still had much to give. He was buried in the churchyard of St Nicholas Church, Blakeney, Norfolk. His estate was valued at £15,097 gross.

SIR PETER MASEFIELD

Writings:

Lecture to The Royal Aeronautical Society on 'Piloting Commercial Aircraft' *Journal of the Royal Aeronautical Society* Feb 1936.

Sources:

Unpublished

RAF Museum, Hendon, Imperial Airways Archives, Brackley papers.

BCe.

MCe.

PrC.

Personal knowledge.

Published

Frida H Brackley, *'Brackles': Memoirs of a Pioneer of Civil Aviation* (Chatham: W & J Mackay & Co, 1952).

DNB.

Robin Higham, *Britain's Imperial Air Routes: 1918 to 1939* (G T Foulis & Co, 1960).

PP, Report of Committee on the Development of Civil Aviation in the United Kingdom (1937-38) Cmd 5685.

WWW.

Sir John B Braithwaite (courtesy of Foster & Braithwaite).

BRAITHWAITE, Sir John Bevan

(1884-1973)

Stockbroker

John Bevan Braithwaite was born in Islington, London, on 22 November 1884, the younger son of Joseph Bevan Braithwaite (qv), a stockbroker, by his wife Anna Sophia Gillett. He was educated at Leighton Park School. In John Braithwaite's family background and in his connections by marriage the influences of the Society of Friends and of radical politics were strong, contributing to an austerity of outlook not commonly associated with the occupation of stockbroker.

In 1908 he became a partner in the family firm, Foster & Braithwaite, established in 1825. His early experience, profoundly disturbing, helped to determine his approach to business matters for the rest of his life. 'I entered the Firm', he wrote to his father in 1911, 'thinking it was a strong ancient & honoured & impregnable City House. I have learnt that though we remain ancient & in large measure honoured we are now become weak & easily vulnerable.' {Reader (1979) 125-27}

He blamed the policy followed by his father and the other two senior partners. 'We have been overtrading', he wrote. 'We have allowed ourselves to be drawn into schemes & commitments to a greater extent than is legitimate for a Firm with our resources — Overtrading is nothing less than dangerous gambling.' {*ibid*, 126-27} A vision of failure haunted him: 'it has been before my mind like a nightmare day & night more or less continually for the last month & more' {*ibid*, 127}, and a horror of 'gambling' remained lively throughout his career.

Between the wars John Braithwaite was not the senior partner, but Foster & Braithwaites' business was conducted very much according to his way of thinking. The practice, long established, of dealing in securities for the firm's own account as principal, which was very much more risky than the stockbroker's normal business of dealing for clients' accounts on commission, was suppressed. So too was company promotion, though underwriting continued. Underwriting caused the firm embarrassment when C C Hatry (qv) crashed to fraudulent ruin in 1929, though Foster & Braithwaite had no part in the fraud. Throughout the 1920s and 1930s their activities, far less flamboyant than in the old days, were also far more profitable. The firm had been saved, and a good deal of the credit for its salvation should go to John Braithwaite.

As time went on, nevertheless, his relations with the more conservative of his partners grew strained over the question of the admission of new partners, who under the firm's articles had to be chosen from a narrow family circle defined by Isaac Braithwaite, John Braithwaite's great-uncle. Largely, no doubt, for this reason John Braithwaite began to distance himself from the firm's affairs. In 1937 he was elected to the Stock Exchange's governing body, the Committee for General Purposes, and in 1940 he gave notice that he would leave the firm at the end of the war.

This he never did, but in 1949 at the age of sixty-five he was elected chairman of the newly-formed Council of the Stock Exchange, which more or less amounted to the same thing, since he made a full-time job of the chairmanship, attending as best he could to the business of the firm and to his personal affairs, often into the small hours. He held the post for ten years, until 1959. In 1954 he was knighted.

John Braithwaite, using his position as chairman to the full, laid about him with great energy at the enemies of the Stock Exchange, including Ministers in the post-war Labour Governments, for which his wife was an active campaigner. The Stock Exchange, in his view, was an institution of first-class national importance, devoted to 'the efficient exchange of securities' {*ibid*, 171}, and any impious suggestion that it was merely a betting-shop for top people could be guaranteed to draw a thunderous response, the more so if the suggestion had an edge of flippancy, as when Hugh Dalton, in 1951, said that a speech by Hugh Gaitskell had 'thrown the Stock Exchange into complete disorder and that is always good fun.' {*ibid*, 170} 'Good fun' and the Stock Exchange, in Sir John Braithwaite's opinion, did not go together: a pity, because the Stock Exchange never looks so ridiculous as when it is taken too seriously, especially by denying the necessity of an element of gambling in its activities. But then gambling, as we have seen, was abhorrent to John Braithwaite for deep personal reasons.

The Stock Exchange when John Braithwaite was born was a private club for professionals, bound by its own strict rules but recognising no duty to protect investors. From the 1920s onward, especially after the Hatry scandal, a very different view was gaining ground, finding expression in increasingly stringent requirements for the quotation of securities, in increasingly strict rules binding members' dealings with their clients, and later in the part played by the Stock Exchange in formulating the rules governing take-overs. All Sir John's work was based on his deep conviction that the Stock Exchange had a duty to the public running beyond its technical purpose of organising a market. He pressed for the fullest possible disclosure of information by the Stock Exchange itself and in company reports. Against strong opposition he caused a Visitors' Gallery (recommended by a Royal Commission in 1877) to be opened in 1953. He dismayed some of the more conservative members of the House by arranging for the Stock Exchange to employ an advertising agency, J Walter Thompson. Perhaps most important of all, he brought about the establishment, in 1950, of a Compensation Fund to insure members' clients, from Stock Exchange resources, against loss arising from the death or malpractice of a member. His vision of society, not an ignoble one, was evidently of a property-owning democracy, with the share capital of British business widely spread among the British people: a society which would be helped into existence by a Stock Exchange of high efficiency and unblemished reputation.

Sir John's interests outside business lay in music, photography and literature. His home, spiritually as well as physically, was in Hampstead Garden Suburb, an architectural monument to the late Victorian liberal middle class in which social conscience and solid comfort harmoniously intermingled. He did not become head of the family firm until 1963, four years after he ceased to be chairman of the Stock Exchange Council, and his work in that capacity gave him a claim to be remembered as a public servant rather than as a stockbroker, which is no doubt what he would have wished.

Sir John Bevan Braithwaite married in 1908 Maria Janette, daughter of Joseph Allen Baker (1852-1918), an engineer, a member of the LCC from 1895 to 1906 and Liberal MP for Eastern Finsbury from 1905 until his death. They had two sons and one daughter. Sir John retired from the firm in 1971 and died on 5 April 1973, leaving £133,737 gross.

W J READER

Writings:

As chairman of the Stock Exchange Council, Sir John Braithwaite did a great deal of public speaking, especially at the Mansion House every November, and his speeches were usually reported in *The Times* and the *Financial Times*.

Sources:

Unpublished

BCe.

Guildhall Library, London: Foster & Braithwaite's records.

MCe.

Published

Alan Jenkins, *The Stock Exchange Story* (Heinemann, 1973).

Edward Victor Morgan and William A Thomas, *The Stock Exchange, Its History and Functions* (Elek Books, 1962).

William J Reader, *A House in the City: A Study of the City and the Stock Exchange Based on the Records of Foster & Braithwaite 1825-1975* (Batsford, 1979).

WWW.

Joseph Bevan Braithwaite (courtesy of Foster & Braithwaite).

BRAITHWAITE, Joseph Bevan

(1855-1934)

Stockbroker and financier

Joseph Bevan Braithwaite belonged to a great cousinhood of Quakers with connections ranging widely and influentially through banking, railway finance and the City of London. Joseph's father, also Joseph Bevan Braithwaite (1818-1905), was a barrister and a prominent Quaker. His mother Martha (1823-95) was the daughter of Joseph Ashby Gillett (1795-1853), a Quaker banker in Banbury, Oxfordshire. There were three sons and six daughters of the marriage. Joseph was born at 65 Mornington Road, Regent's Park, London on 5 October 1855. After school at Kendal and at the Quaker school at Grove House Tottenham, he read for the Bar, but in 1876 he gave that up and joined Foster & Braithwaite, a firm of stockbrokers in which his uncle Isaac Braithwaite (1810-90) was senior partner. He became a partner in 1880, and in 1888 somewhat unexpectedly (Isaac had two sons in the firm, but they died young) succeeded his uncle as senior partner: a position which he held until he retired in 1922.

Under Joseph Braithwaite and his two cousins, R H Savory (1856-1931) and Cecil Braithwaite (1862-1948), Foster & Braithwaite went enthusiastically into company promotion. That, in the 1890s, was a suspect activity, often with good reason: these eminently respectable Quakers themselves kept colourful company, such as George Herring 'the Bloater', an ex-bookie who left £1.3 million to philanthropic causes. Within the business conventions of the day, Foster & Braithwaite's activities were no doubt entirely honourable but some propositions, to put the matter charitably, were sounder than others and the firm ran into serious difficulties over the financing of the Piccadilly Hotel in 1908-9 and of the Kansas City, Mexico & Orient Railroad a few years later. These misfortunes, combined with the results of the firm's long-established policy of dealing in Stock Exchange securities on its own account, brought Foster & Braithwaite very close to being hammered. In September 1911 Joseph Braithwaite's son John (qv), then a partner and much later (1949-59) chairman of the Stock Exchange Council, asked, in a letter to his father, how the firm's affairs would stand investigation, if it failed, by a Committee of the Society of Friends. 'We should stand condemned', he said, 'as men who had failed culpably through indefensible speculation.' {Reader (1979) 127} Joseph made no comment.

In common with other members of his family, of his own and later generations, Joseph Braithwaite might have succeeded as a scientist or an engineer. He put an astronomical observatory on his house in Muswell Hill, he became a member of the Institution of Electrical Engineers in 1893, and he was closely associated with Emil Garcke (qv), eminent both as an electrical engineer and as 'a vigorous champion of private enterprise' {Hannah (1979) 16}. It is scarcely surprising, therefore, that in the field of company promotion his enthusiasm ran towards the development of

BRAITHWAITE Joseph Bevan

In the offices of Foster & Braithwaite before rebuilding of 1931 (courtesy of Foster & Braithwaite).

certain branches of the electrical industry, where his work prospered and endured.

When electricity first enlivened the Stock Exchange in 1880, Foster & Braithwaite, on Joseph Braithwaite's recommendation, 'brought out' an issue of £400,000 capital for the Anglo-American Brush Electric Light Corporation, later Brush Electrical Engineering Co, of which Joseph Braithwaite was for a time chairman. The firm took up 1,000 fully-paid £10 shares in Brush and were thereby caught when the market in electricity shares collapsed in 1882. In that year, as well as putting electric lighting into his own house, Joseph Braithwaite became chairman of a Brush subsidiary, the Great Western Electric Light & Power Co, and in his own words: 'during the two or three years that I held that position I devoted much time to the development of the early electric lighting stations at Bristol and Cardiff.' {IEE Archives, membership application to IEE}

Fortified, and no doubt educated, by that experience, Joseph Braithwaite, as senior partner, led the firm back into electricity in 1890 when the Electrical & General Investment Corporation was formed to carry out, as its prospectus said, 'the financial and commercial operations of assisting in the promotion and development of electrical undertakings.' The Eighth Duke of Marlborough was chairman and Emil Garcke was on the board, though not, at first, Joseph Braithwaite.

Electrical & General performed some of the functions of a holding company for a cluster of undertakings in electricity supply and electric traction, formed between 1891 and 1905, which all had a special relationship, held carefully short of monopoly, with the Brush Electrical Engineering Co for the manufacture and supply of equipment. The City of London Electric Lighting Co was set up in 1891, the County of London & Brush Provincial Electric Lighting Co in 1894, British Electric Traction in 1896, the Electric Lighting & Traction Co of Australia in 1899, and the Adelaide Electric Supply Co in 1905. Several individuals were directors of several of these companies, but there was only one, Joseph Braithwaite, who was a director and, for varying periods, chairman, of each of them. In 1906 he became chairman of the City of London Co and of Electrical & General, and those offices he held until he died.

As a stockbroker, Joseph Bevan Braithwaite's record was far from exemplary. Under his leadership his firm came very close to disaster, and in the *Financial Times* an obituarist observed that he 'seldom entered the Stock Exchange'. In certain branches of the electrical industry, on the other hand, he has a place among the pioneers, not as a technologist but as a financier. Financial and commercial services are no less essential to industrial success than technology. It was these which Joseph Braithwaite was expert in providing.

Braithwaite married Anna Sophia, daughter of Jonathan Gillett, a banker, in 1881. They had two sons. He died on 30 November 1934 leaving £35,469 gross.

W J READER

Writings:

Who Are We? Notes on the Ancestry of Joseph Bevan and Martha Braithwaite (C E Roberts & Co, 1927).

Sources:

Unpublished

Guildhall Library, London: Foster & Braithwaite's ledgers, journals and papers.

Institution of Electrical Engineers, London, archives.

BCe.

MCe.

PrC.

Published

Leslie Hannah, *Electricity before Nationalisation. A Study of the Development of the Electricity Supply Industry in Britain to 1948* (Macmillan, 1979).

Edward Victor Morgan and William A Thomas, *The Stock Exchange, Its History and Functions* (Elek Books, 1969).

William J Reader, *A House in the City; a Study of the City and the Stock Exchange Based on the Records of Foster & Braithwaite, 1825-1975* (Batsford, 1979).

BRAND, Henry Bouverie William

1st Viscount Hampden

(1814-1892)

Estate developer

Henry Bouverie William Brand was born on 24 December 1814, the second son of Henry Otway Brand, Twenty-first Lord Dacre and Pyne, the daughter of the Hon and Very Rev Maurice Crosbie, Dean of Limerick. He was educated at Eton. His family's inherited estates in Sussex provided an opportunity for his entry into politics, and also a base for diversifying his financial participation into agricultural processing, transport and industry. He took over the management of the Glynde estate (3,300 acres) from his father in 1846 (inheriting it in 1853) and by 1890 he had expanded it to 4,500 acres. A major product of the downland estate was lime and cement, and Brand's membership of the Management Committee for Newhaven Harbour (a successful cross-channel port) and the Ouse Navigation Trust, as well as his good relations with the railway companies, enabled him to widen his markets. During the agricultural depression after 1873 he was therefore able to compensate for the decline of agricultural income by expanding his limeworks and chalk quarry at Glynde, creating a new industrial suburb beside the railway. In 1884 he promoted the Sussex Portland Cement Works, leasing land for a rent plus a share of the turnover. He also built a steam flour mill and a dairy, the latter with a depot in Chelsea, serving the local farmers on his own and other Sussex estates.

Brand married Eliza, daughter of General Robert Ellice in 1838; they had ten children. He entered politics in 1846 as private secretary to the Home Secretary, Sir George Grey. He was Liberal MP for Lewes 1852-68 and for Cambridge 1868-84, acting as party whip 1859-68 and as Parliamentary Secretary to the Treasury 1859-66. He was speaker of the House of Commons from 1872, retiring to become Viscount Hampden in 1884. He passed his estates on to his son when succeeding to his childless elder brother's title of Lord Dacre in 1890. He died on 14 March 1892, leaving £54,752 gross.

SUSAN P FARRANT

Sources:

Unpublished

Susan P Farrant, 'The Role of Landowners and Tenants in Changing Agricultural Practice in the Valley of the River Ouse South of Lewes (Sussex), 1780 to 1930 and the Consequences for the Landscape' (London PhD, 1977).

Published

Burke's Peerage and Baronetage.

DNB.

Susan P Farrant, 'The Management of Four Estates in the Lower Ouse Valley (Sussex) and Agricultural Change, 1840-1920' *Southern History* I (1979).

— 'H B W Brand of Glynde Place and the Development of Industry and Communications in the Ouse Valley, 1846-1890' *Sussex Industrial Archaeology Newsletter* (1978).

A Hampden, *Henry and Eliza* (Glynde, 1981).

Times 16 Mar 1892.

WWMP.

WWW.

Robert H Brand (courtesy of Sir Edward Ford).

BRAND, Robert Henry

1st Lord Brand of Eydon

(1878-1963)

Merchant banker

Robert Henry Brand was born on 30 October 1878, the third son of the Second Viscount Hampden and of his second wife, Susan Henrietta, younger daughter of Lord George Henry Cavendish. He was educated at Marlborough School and at New College, Oxford, where he took a first in modern history in 1901. He was elected a fellow of All Souls, and he remained a fellow (with breaks) until 1963.

Brand spent the years 1902-9 as a member of the Milner 'Kindergarten', working for the Colonial Office in South Africa. He served first as secretary of the Inter-Colonial Council of the Transvaal and Orange River Colony and as secretary of the Railway Committee of the Central South African Railways, and then (1908-9) as secretary of the Transvaal Delegates at the South African National Convention. In the last post he was General Smuts's personal assistant, and together they prepared a draft constitution for the new Union. Brand's period in South Africa strengthened his faith in the British Empire as a force for peace and prosperity in the world. He retained an interest in South African affairs after his return to Britain in 1909, acting as South Africa's Financial Representative at the Genoa Conference in 1922.

In 1909 he joined the merchant bankers Lazard Bros & Co, with a salary of £2,000 plus 5 per cent of the firm's annual profits. Soon after he became a managing director, a position he held until 1944; he remained a director of Lazards until his retirement in 1960. Brand developed a strong belief in international finance as an instrument for international co-operation and peace, and he was one of those who used the skills acquired in, and financial security provided by, merchant banking in carrying out a number of political responsibilities over the period of his working life.

During the First World War Brand was a member of the Imperial Munitions Board of Canada, 1915-18, and deputy chairman of the British War Mission in Washington, 1917-18; during the Paris Peace Conference in 1919 he acted as financial adviser to Lord Robert Cecil, the chairman of the Supreme Economic Council. At this point both Brand and Lazards thought he should concentrate on banking, so he turned down further requests from the British Government to take on other official responsibilities. Nevertheless, he continued to act as adviser or delegate to various European financial conferences during the inter-war years. He initiated the International Financial Conference of the League of Nations in Brussels in 1920, and was himself vice-president. He had long been interested in Germany, having in 1915 written approvingly about the German banking system, and it was therefore appropriate that he was appointed a member both of the Expert Committee which advised the German Government on the stablisation of the mark in 1922 and of the Stillhalte (Standstill) Committee appointed in July 1931 to advise on the means to be taken to deal with the short-term credits caught in the German banking crisis. This approval of Germany, it should be noted, did not extend to Hitler, and Brand was perhaps ahead of many other bankers, and politicians, in deciding by 1933 that Hitler and the Nazis might well pose a threat to the existing international order.

Brand was interested in economics and economic policy beyond the strictly banking sphere, and he served as a member of the Macmillan Committee on Finance and Industry, 1929-31. He argued for cheap money and against wholesale protection, and was generally in sympathy with the liberal ideals of fellow member J M Keynes (qv), supporting him in his close questioning of witnesses. Drawing on his knowledge of German banking, he proposed a closer integration of finance and industry, arguing that what was needed were new first class institutions set up specifically to issue industrial securities, and which, unlike most City institutions, would maintain a close and continuing relationshp with their client companies.

During the Second World War Brand returned to government service, spending the years 1941-46 mainly in Washington. His long experience of North America, and the social and personal contacts provided by his marriage, meant that he moved relatively easily amongst the whirlpools and shoals of wartime Washington. He was head of the British Food Mission, 1941-44, chairman of the British Supply Council in North America in 1942 and again in 1945-46, and British Treasury Representative, 1944-46. As Treasury Representative he joined Keynes in the acrimonious and difficult negotiations for the ending of Lend-Lease and for the US and Canadian Loans to Britain, and as a UK delegate at the Bretton Woods and Savannah Conferences in 1946, which established the International Monetary Fund and the International Bank for Reconstruction and Development. He then returned to Britain.

In 1916 Brand joined the boards of Lloyds Bank and of the North British & Mercantile Insurance Co, resigning from both when he went to Washington during the Second World War. After the war he was re-elected by both, serving as chairman of the North British until 1957 and as director of Lloyds until 1959. He was a director of the Times Publishing Co Ltd, 1925-59, and during the 1930s his anti-Hitler views contrasted startlingly with the pro-appeasement views of the editor of the *Times*, Geoffrey Dawson. He served as a member of the General Advisory Council of the BBC, 1951-56, and as president of the Royal Economic Society, 1952-53.

Brand was one of those quietly powerful men, familiar in British society, who, while not holding elected public office, nevertheless are repeatedly consulted and used by policy-makers both domestic and foreign. He was at home in the worlds of finance and economics and familiar with the politics and politicians of the USA, Europe and the Empire. He was a strong proponent of Anglo-American co-operation, especially in the economic sphere.

Brand received a DCL from Oxford University in 1937 and was created Lord Brand of Eydon in 1946. He married Phyllis Langhorne (Nancy Astor's sister) in 1917; she died in 1937. His only son was killed in action in 1945 but he was survived by two daughters. Lord Brand died on 23 August 1963 leaving an estate of £79,158.

KATHLEEN BURK

Writings:

The Union of South Africa (Oxford University Press, 1909).

War and National Finance (E Arnold & Co, 1921).

Why I am Not a Socialist (The Daily News Ltd, 1923).

The Letters of John Dove (Macmillan, 1938).

Numerous articles, especially in *The Round Table*.

Sources:

Unpublished

Bodleian Library, Oxford, R H Brand papers.

BCe.

MCe.

PrC.

Published

Kathleen Burk, *Britain, America and the Sinews of War 1914-1918* (George Allen & Unwin, 1983).

Burke's Peerage and Baronetage 1981.

DNB.

John Kendle, *The Round Table Movement* (Toronto: University of Toronto Press, 1975).

Times 24 Aug 1963.

WWW.

BRIDGEMAN, Sir Maurice Richard

(1904-1980)

Petroleum company chairman

Sir Maurice Bridgeman, watched by Princess Alexandra, speaking at the opening of the BP Gothenburg refinery (courtesy of BP Co Ltd).

Maurice Richard Bridgeman was born in Marylebone, London on 26 January 1904, third son of William Clive Bridgeman (1864-1935), a Conservative politician who held a number of government posts including that of First Lord of the Admiralty and who was created First Viscount Bridgeman in 1929, and his wife Caroline Beatrix, elder daughter of the Hon Cecil Thomas Parker, second son of the Sixth Earl of Macclesfield. He was educated at Eton and Trinity College, Cambridge, coming down without taking a degree.

Bridgeman had no particular preference for the oil industry, though his father was First Lord of the Admiralty and knew Sir John Cadman (qv), then chairman designate, when he applied for a post with the Anglo-Persian Oil Co (hereafter the Company: APOC until 1935, then the Anglo-Iranian Oil Co until 1955 and British Petroleum thereafter). He accepted a position with the Company as it was more remunerative than other offers. His first post was private secretary to Cadman on the chairman's visit to Tehran in April 1926 for the coronation of Riza Shah. He subsequently served in the operations area in South Persia until he returned home after contracting hepatitis and was employed in the General Department. In 1934, unexpectedly and fortunately he was singled out for promotion and posted to the United States as the second Company representative to serve in New York, where he acquired a good knowledge of the American oil industry and made the acquaintance of many of the leading executives of the principal American oil companies. This experience proved of inestimable value during his government service and later as a director of the Company in international oil negotiations. Bridgeman returned to head office in 1937.

On the outbreak of the Second World War in 1939 he became Petroleum Adviser, Ministry of Economic Warfare. He was then successively in 1940, Assistant Secretary, Petroleum Department, and Joint Secretary Oil Control Board; in 1942, Petroleum Adviser, Government of India; and in

1944-46, Principal Assistant Secretary, Petroleum Division, Ministry of Fuel and Power. Bridgeman thus acquired a comprehensive knowledge of the workings of Whitehall and the place of petroleum in government policy-making, which was invaluable when he resumed his career with the Company. He was appointed managing director of the D'Arcy Exploration Co, which effectively directed and controlled all the Company's exploration activities, particularly in Persia, and its interests in Iraq and Kuwait. This suited his outward-looking view of the international oil industry and enabled him to draw on his experience in the United States and government service. At a time when it appeared to many that the Company was over-rich in crude oil preserves, Bridgeman was a persistent advocate of the need to keep abreast of potentially increasing consumption and he placed great emphasis on the Company strengthening its Middle East activities. This attitude was entirely justified by the Abadan 'crisis' of 1951-54, when the Company was entirely deprived of its Persian sources of crude oil and lost its concessionary position in Persia. It emerged in 1954 with a 40 per cent shareholding in an international consortium which replaced it in Persia. From 1951 he encouraged increasing exploration worldwide and his foresight was ultimately rewarded by the great oil discoveries for the Company in Alaska and the North Sea which are now providing most of the Company's production.

In October 1946 Bridgeman visited Persia for the first time since the war in connection with Persian complaints over sterling convertibility. In 1954, after the Abadan crisis, he was much involved in the arrangements for setting up the international consortium of oil companies which revived the Persian oil industry. During this period as director and deputy chairman of the Company, Bridgeman directed almost exclusively the Middle East policy of the Company, making frequent visits to the area particularly in the emerging oil producing states of the Arab littoral of the Persian Gulf, especially Abu Dhabi and Kuwait, and maintaining his Company's interest in the Iraq Petroleum Co.

Bridgeman became chairman in 1960, the same year that the Organisation of Petroleum Exporting Companies was formed in Baghdad on 14 September. The decade proved to be an exceptional one with tremendous developments in world production, doubling from 22.06 million barrels a day in 1960 to 43.68 million barrels a day in 1969. The provision of increasing supplies of crude oil certainly ensured ample consumption at cheap prices, thereby fuelling a remarkable period of economic growth and a high standard of living in the industrialised world, and growing prosperity in the oil producing countries. However, the excess of production over demand led to lower prices, which, while benefiting consumers, led to lower returns per barrel for producers. This was the period par excellence when the major oil companies performed their function as price and production shock absorbers between the oil producers and consumers. The problem of stable price levels, at a time when the industry needed additional finance for major new investment, led to pressure on the company's returns on capital. Bridgeman was much concerned with this problem, and a celebrated encounter with the British Government over prices for North Sea gas, which he regarded as insufficient, illustrated his preoccupation with the issue.

BRIDGEMAN Sir Maurice Richard

Though long identified with the oil industry, Bridgeman, in his last years as chairman, began to move the Company away from its reliance on an exclusive oil base. In 1967 BP acquired most of the Distillers Co's petrochemical interests, built up by Graham Hayman and Charles Ball (qqv), many of which had been administered in a joint subsidiary company, British Hydrocarbons Ltd. This lowered the British Government's share in BP below 50 per cent, a result favoured by Bridgeman. He also accepted the challenge of a further diversification when he approved of research and development into bio-chemical interests and encouraged the conversion of hydro-carbons into protein.

Bridgeman was much in favour of the interchange of staff within large international organisations, declaring in a report to the board in 1961 that 'The movement of men leads to the exchange of ideas without which no group such as ours can prosper.' {'I Remember' (1969) 30} He was insistent that the non-executive directors should be chosen for professional distinction rather than as sinecurists and he once remarked that the greatest contribution a chairman can make to his company is to ensure his succession. Self-confident, widely experienced, phlegmatic in temperament, Bridgeman was not afraid of taking decisions or living with them. He had an instructive, almost uncanny capacity to go rapidly to the heart of problems and produce his solution without equivocation. Rather imperious in command, often quizzical in manner, he was prepared to delegate much responsibility to those whom he trusted, and to back their judgement with his own personal authority. He was indefatigable in travelling around the operations of BP, recognising that being chairman was 'an absolutely full time job'. He was, however, a member of the Advisory Council on Middle East Trade, 1948-63, and a president of the Middle East Association, 1965-76. He retired from the chair of BP in 1969.

Bridgeman was made KBE in 1964; an honorary fellow of Fitzwilliam College, Cambridge, 1967; Knight of St John, 1961; and an honorary LLD of Leeds University, 1969. The recipient of foreign honours, he was a Knight Grand Cross of the Italian Republic, 1966; Grand Officer, Order of Orange Nassau, 1968; and received the Persian Order of Homayun, 1968.

In his private life Bridgeman was a great follower of the ballet and the arts, a modest ornithologist, a good shot and a dextrous fisherman. Inclined to be distant in company, he was relaxed and gregarious among his friends.

The Hon Maurice Bridgeman married Diana Mary Erica, younger daughter of the late Humphrey Minto Wilson, in 1933. They had four daughters. Sir Maurice Bridgeman died on 18 June 1980 leaving an estate of £343,212 gross.

R W FERRIER

Sources:

Unpublished

BP Co, Britannic House, London, archives.

BCe.

PrC.

Sir David Steel, 'Memorial Address, Given at St Margaret's, Westminster, 22 July 1980' (copy in BP archives).

Published

Burke's Peerage and Baronetage 1980.

'I Remember. Sir Maurice Bridgeman Reflects on His Lifetime with BP. An Interview by John Gearing' *BP Magazine* Nov 1969.

Times 19 June 1980.

WWMP.

WWW.

BRIGGS, Francis Henry

(1865-1952)

Leather manufacturer

Francis Henry Briggs was born in Leeds on 12 May 1865, the sixth child of Joshua Briggs (b 1834), a tanner and leather dresser, and his wife Martha née Phillips (b 1836). His forebears came to Leeds in the 1790s and were all associated with the leather industry, his parents being respectively children of a skin dresser and a currier. Both families played prominent parts in parish activities in the Church of England, a connection F H Briggs maintained throughout his life.

In 1886 F H Briggs, being discontented with his father's refusal to expand the business, after consulting his vicar on his moral justification, took over the managership of Dalrymple & Co in Leicester. In 1891 he became a partner, trading under the style of Dalrymple & Briggs. By 1899 he acquired the remainder of the capital. With his brother, Thomas Norman Briggs, who was associated with Samuel Barrow & Co of Kettering, he founded T N & F H Briggs Ltd. At this point he had a working capital of £12,500 and his brother a slightly smaller sum. The company was mainly concerned with the dressing of East India stock and had an extensive factoring business. The severe depression after the end of the Boer War made business very difficult and even payments of dividend on the preference shares were discontinued. This was rectified in 1910 when the arrears were paid off as well as a 10 per cent dividend on the ordinary shares. Prior to the outbreak of war in 1914, some 80 per cent of the production was exported. This comprised curried leather for heavy footwear, light leather for shoe uppers, lining skins and rolled splits. Much leather in his early days was sold by weight as a 'run'; later, in 1911-12, F H Briggs quickly took advantage of the recently introduced measuring machine and established standard grades to suit the needs of individual customers.

At the outbreak of the First World War he was called upon to organise supplies for the War Office Contracts Directorate, which in 1915 was reorganised under the Ministry of Munitions. Subsequently in 1917 a departmental Leather Control Board was established which assumed virtual control over leather manufacture. For his services F H Briggs was offered a knighthood which he refused on the grounds that nobody should expect any reward for doing his obvious duty.

During this period he was very active in the Federation of Curriers, Light Leather Tanners and Dressers, playing a considerable role in the acquisition of the premises currently occupied. He became president in 1919-20, by which time the title had been changed to the Light Leather Federation. In 1917 he became a freeman of the City of London. In 1918 he became a liveryman of the Leathersellers Company serving as third warden in 1946-47. He was president of the Leather and Hide Trades Benevolent Institution in 1933. Being deeply interested in applied science, he was a founder member of the British Leather Manufacturers Research Association in 1920, serving as a council member for many years and frequently deploring the excessive secrecy of many tanners which hampered the progress of research.

He expected a protective tariff on glazed kid after the war and so reorganised the company as T N & F H Briggs (Tanners) Ltd, with an issued capital of £100,000 (£80,000 in ordinary shares and £20,000 in preference shares). He then doubled the size of the Leicester tannery. The tariff did not, however, materialise and since the scheme was no longer viable, he travelled extensively in the Near and Middle East and India seeking new sources of raw stock, which subsequently formed the basis of a factoring department.

Some export markets were now closed, but accounts were opened in other parts of the world, especially in neglected smaller countries, which proved very remunerative.

In the 1930s production was diversified by introducing full chrome side and calf leathers. As the threat of war approached, the Ministry of Supply required improved properties for service footwear. The semi-chrome process devised became the basis of their specification. Subsequently other leathers with special properties were developed. In the post-war period the output of full chrome leather was increased, together with high class semi-chrome leathers and East India skin products, a large proportion being exported.

F H Briggs attended his Leicester tannery daily until his final illness. He was a man of outstanding ability, extremely industrious and very hospitable, and showed a paternalistic attitude to his 240 employees. He was a keen gardener and widely read in many subjects.

He married firstly in 1893 Charlotte Knibb, daughter of Joseph Knibb, gentleman, and, after her death, Olga Bramley in 1950; by his first wife he had a son and a daughter. F H Briggs died on 29 December 1952 leaving £66,488 gross.

P STANLEY BRIGGS

Sources:

Unpublished

Private collection of Mrs M C Paget, James Phillips Briggs, MS Diary 1885-88.

BCe.

MCe.

PrC.

Information from the British Leather Federation and the Leathersellers Company.

M C Paget, Briggs family tree.

Published

History of the Ministry of Munitions (8 vols, HMSO, 1918-22) 7, part 1.

BRIGGS, Henry Currer

(1829-1881)

Colliery owner and manager

Henry Currer Briggs was born on 2 March 1829, probably at Overton House, near Wakefield, the elder surviving son of Henry Briggs (1797-1868) and of Marianne née Milnes, a colliery co-heiress. His father had, after his failure as a cloth merchant in Leeds and Hamburg, become co-manager in a partnership which worked large collieries, in the adjoining townships of Flockton and Shitlington near Wakefield. H C Briggs (known as Harry) was educated at Worksop and by private tutors at home. As a boy he was an observer of the model social system operated by his father and his partner, involving the provision of facilities well beyond the range of those then usually provided even by enlightened coalmasters: a library, concerts, sports and gymnastic grounds, a theatre, schools and a masters' and employees' discussion class. The famous 1842 employment report had claimed of their provision that

> The Flockton system has given the flattest practical contradiction to the asserted inaccessibility of the poor to kindly and civilizing influences; and equally so to the doctrine that refinements and labour are incompatible {*PP HC* 1842 (381) XVI, 203}.

In 1841 his father, in partnership with Charles Morton (1811-81), a trained mining engineer and later the first regional inspector of mines, took a first lease of coal at Whitwood, near Normanton, sited so as to take advantage of both the newly-opened network of railways connecting Leeds with London and Manchester with Hull, and the adjoining facilities of the Aire & Calder Navigation. His father ultimately withdrew from active interest in the Flockton area collieries ca 1845.

H C Briggs entered into partnership with his father at the Whitwood collieries in 1849, Morton having withdrawn from the partnership about 1846. Father and son took leases of wider areas of coal in 1857 and in January 1860 purchased the Methley Junction colliery for £26,000, admitting new partners in each case. The capital of their whole concern was £75,000, of which almost 70 per cent came from Harry Briggs and his father.

During the early 1860s, a period of widespread industrial unrest, labour relations between the partners and part of their work force deteriorated. Following the Companies Act of 1862, which legalised industrial partnerships, and inspired by Professor H Fawcett's lecture on profit sharing, the Briggs resorted simultaneously to incorporation and profit sharing, as their draft prospectus in 1864 showed. Harry was apparently the partner principally behind the move. A joint stock limited liability company, Henry Briggs & Son Ltd, was registered in 1865 with a nominal capital of £90,000 in £10 shares. The Briggs family retained two-thirds of the shares but offered the rest to officers, agents and workmen of the company. Co-partnership between owners and workpeople and a worker-director were inaugurated, apparently for the first time in a large colliery concern in Britain. By 1881 it was claimed that £40,000 had been distributed as bonus among the employees of the colliery company. Harry Briggs was managing director of the new concern 1865-68.

On the death of his father Harry Briggs became chairman and his younger brother, Archibald, became managing director of the expanding colliery company. Harry Briggs resumed the duties of managing director in 1876. His firm became one of the largest coal producers in the Yorkshire coalfield. Briggs was chairman of the West Yorkshire Coalowners' Association and a director of various companies in Britain, Brazil and Norway, including a partnership in a Dundee jute spinning mill and a major participation, with his younger brother, in the North of England Industrial Iron & Coal Co in Cleveland, which also operated an industrial partnership scheme.

Like his father, Harry Briggs was a liberal in both politics and religion and in 1854 married Catherine Shepherd, a daughter of the liberal and long-serving master of the House of Correction at Wakefield, Edward Shepherd. Both father and son sat under the Unitarian ministry at Wakefield of Rev Goodwyn Barmby, an erstwhile Christian Socialist who married Harry Briggs's wife's sister, and these associations may have also been factors in the establishment of the co-operative colliery system. Old Henry Briggs certainly 'warmly approved' of the new system. Harry Briggs's interest in his employees was also evident in his chairmanship of the local Whitwood School Board after 1870.

In October 1881 Briggs left Leeds, his home town, for Norway, his health having been failing for some time; he died of heart trouble a few days later in Christiana, on 21 October 1881. He was buried in the graveyard of Whitwood Church. He left property worth £47,537 gross.

JOHN GOODCHILD

Writings:

Industrial Partnership, as Carried Out into Practice by Henry Briggs, Son & Co (1868 and a Wakefield edition 1869).

(with Archibald Briggs) *Memorandum on the Industrial Partnership at the Whitwood Collieries 1865-74* (Kegan Paul & Co, 1884).

Sources:

Unpublished

MCe.

Published

Donald H C Briggs, *A Merchant, a Banker and the Coal Trade 1693-1971* (1971).

K M Briggs, *Henry Briggs Son & Company Limited, Adapted From Some Historical Notes* (ca 1935).

Roy A Church, 'Profit Sharing and Labour Relations in England in the Nineteenth Century' *International Review of Social History* 16 (1971).

PP, HC 1842 (381) XVI, RC on Children's Employment (Mines).

David F Schloss, *Report on Profit-Sharing* (Board of Trade, Labour Department, 1894).

Wakefield Express 29 Oct 1881.

BRINDLEY, Harry Samuel Bickerton

(1867-1920)

Consulting engineer and armaments manufacturer

Harry Samuel Bickerton Brindley was born at Handsworth, Birmingham, 21 September 1867, the son of George Samuel Brindley, an engineer, and his wife Ann née Bickerton. He claimed to be related to James Brindley (1716-72), builder of the Bridgewater and Grand Trunk canals. His father later became an instructor at the Japanese Imperial College of Engineering in Tokyo (the Kobudai-gakku), which was then staffed by Europeans and later became part of Tokyo University. Much of Brindley's childhood was spent in Japan, and he received his early technical education at the Japanese Imperial College of Engineering. He was apprenticed to the Birmingham engineering firm of Sir Richard Tangye (qv) for whom in 1888 he designed and executed engineering work connected with projectile and gas vessel plants and solid drawn tube mills.

He next moved to Sheffield where he was employed by Thomas Firth & Co and acquired experience of shell manufacture and the design of hydraulic presses. In the early 1890s he worked for the Leeds hydraulic engineering firm of Henry Berry Ltd, but returned to Japan in 1895 as a consulting engineer and technical adviser. During the following twelve years he designed hydraulic equipment for the Japanese Government, introduced many British engineering firms to business relations with the Japanese authorities, and advised on the building of the Keihan electric tramway. He was also a director of the *London and China Express*'s supplement, *Eastern Engineering*. Returning to Britain in 1907, he established himself as a Westminster consulting engineer in partnership with E T Elbourne. As one of the few Europeans entitled to act as a Japanese patent attorney, he facilitated the patenting of numerous British engineering inventions in Japan during 1907-14. His patent work reflected not only the enterprise of British engineering, but Japanese eagerness to learn.

Brindley was also the London manager of Rees Roturbo Manufacturing Co Ltd of Wolverhampton. This company was formed in 1908 to manufacture centrifugal pumping machinery under patents previously held by its managing director E S G Rees. The chairman of Rees Roturbo was Sir Charles Mander (1852-1929), the Wolverhampton lacquer and varnish manufacturer, and the company's issued capital in 1915 comprised £102,000 ordinary and £13,800 preference shares. It was as a war-time official of Rees Roturbo that Brindley emerged as a leader in munitions engineering.

By an agreement signed on 16 December 1914 Rees Roturbo became the third civilian company (after Dick Kerr the electrical manufacturers, and Messrs J & P Hill), which was not a specialist armaments manufacturer, to receive direct War Office contracts for high-explosive shells. Brindley was responsible for negotiating this pioneering agreement, and arrogated to himself complete control of its execution. Premises at Ponders End (midway between the Royal Ordnance factories at Enfield and Waltham), containing powerful hydraulic presses were bought for £10,000, and Brindley undertook to produce 8 inch shells at a weekly rate of 600 by mid-March 1915, and 6 inch shells at the same weekly rate by mid-April, with the output of both rising to 3,000 shells weekly by mid-June. The War Office advanced 80 per cent of expenditure incurred by Brindley on works and plant up to £80,000 and a capital sum of £137,000 for materials and wages, to be recovered by deducting 50 per cent from payments for shells. Under Brindley's agreement with the War Office, the prices for Ponders End shells were roughly two-thirds of those paid to specialist armourers (viz £9 15s for 8 inch and £4 8s 6d for 6 inch, reduced from July 1915 to £9 3s 4d and £4 2s 6d respectively). Rees Roturbo's example was followed by Herbert Austin (qv) and Dorman Long in February 1915, and by Ebbw Vale Steel in March; and within a few months, both Brindley's financial arrangements and his productive organisation were being widely imitated by other civilian firms entering munitions work.

Rees Roturbo and Messrs Head, Wrightson 'were the first firms outside the circle of the armament firms proper to undertake shell production on a comprehensive scale' {*History of Ministry of Munitions* I, pt I, 115}, and from December 1914 until the end of March 1919, £812,200 was spent on the Ponders End factory. Brindley reached a weekly output capacity of over 8,000 8 inch shells, 250 12 inch shells and 4,000 6 inch shells, plus a quantity of forgings; Ponders End's actual output from 31 March to 31 December 1918 comprised 299,708 8 inch, 700 12 inch and 294,600 6 inch shells. Brindley was despotic, and drove both himself and his workforce with unrelenting fierceness. Although his methods were a national example, he quarrelled with the Rees Roturbo board, and negotiated direct with the Ministry of Munitions for shell contracts, which he always met although they were repudiated by the company. To end these rows, Ponders End was brought under the control of the Government's Gun Ammunition Department in November 1918, with retrospective effect to March 1917.

Brindley's expertise was recognised by his appointment in July 1918 to the Ministry of Munition's committee on the control, administration, organisation and layout of the Woolwich Royal Ordnance Factories, chaired by Thomas McKinnon-Wood MP. This committee had greater collective experience of munitions work than any other body of men previously assembled. It predicted that armaments manufacture 'will not improbably disappear as a speciality' and 'that the country will insist on the production of all armaments being confined to Government factories'; the era of total industrial mobilisation was foreshadowed by the committee's conclusion, 'The real reserve for war is the whole of the manufacturing reserve of the country'. {*PP*, Report on Woolwich Royal Ordnance Factories (1919) 8}

Brindley died of pneumonia on 28 March 1920 at his house, in Westminster, aged fifty-two. Three days later his name appeared in the *London Gazette* as a KBE. His first wife, whom he married in 1897, was Adeline Mary, daughter of John James Bagshawe, a steel merchant; she predeceased him, leaving two daughters, Dariel and Adeline Mary. He was survived by his second wife, Violet Mary. His estate was valued at £28,208 gross.

R P T DAVENPORT-HINES

Sources:

Unpublished

PRO Ministry of Munitions papers.

United Nations Library, Geneva, Lord Noel-Baker, 'The Private Manufacture of Armaments', volume 2.

BCe.

MCe.

PrC.

Published

Eastern Engineering 26 Apr 1920.

Engineering 9 Apr 1920.

History of the Ministry of Munitions (8 vols, HMSO, 1918-22) I, part 1.

London and China Telegraph 6 Apr 1920.

PP, Report on Woolwich Royal Ordnance Factories (1919) Cmd 229.

PP, Report to Minister of Munitions by Committee on Royal Ordnance Factories, Woolwich (1919) Cmd 229.

Times 3 Apr 1920.

BRINSMEAD, John

(1814-1908)
Piano manufacturer

John Brinsmead was born at Weir Gifford, Devon on 13 October 1814, the son of a small farmer and lime burner. Leaving school at the age of twelve, he worked in agriculture for a year and was then apprenticed to a cabinet maker in Torrington for seven years. In 1835 he walked to London and became a journeyman (piano) case maker. After a brief unsuccessful partnership with his older brother he started his own piano manufacturing business in 1837, with the assistance of one man and a boy. A combination of wood-working skills and temperate habits ensured modest success until, for reasons which remain obscure, the firm began to expand vigorously during the 1870s. By 1900, when it became a limited company, Brinsmead employed more than 200 men, and had overtaken Broadwood (qv), the British industry's traditional leader, in the quantity and possibly the value of its output. An essential ingredient of this success was the sedulous cultivation of a 'quality' image, deliberately created by entering, and occasionally winning prizes at, international exhibitions, and by considerable expenditure on adroit advertising and press manipulation.

The instruments, despite exaggerated claims for technological innovation and high quality, were never in the first league, but they were soundly made, at least in John Brinsmead's lifetime. More important, perhaps, they were always efficiently marketed at home and, to some extent, abroad, notably in Australia. Since all this was not common among his British contemporaries, it can be argued that Brinsmead made a substantial contribution to the revival of an industry hitherto demoralised by competition from the superior products of Germany and the USA. Certainly the firm offered leadership and thrust to a new generation of 'medium class' manufacturers at a time when the old established houses were entrenched in obsolete technology and conservative management.

About John Brinsmead's personal achievement there can be no doubt. From the humblest beginnings he had, by 1873, earned a place in the *Royal Blue Book*, and, soon after, a reverential biography in *Fortunes Made in Business: Life Struggles of Successful People*. He died in London on 17 February 1908, leaving a personal estate of £46,127 gross.

CYRIL EHRLICH

Sources:

Published

Edgar Brinsmead, *The History of the Pianoforte* (Simpkin, Marshall & Co, 1889).

Cyril Ehrlich, *The Piano, A History* (Dent, 1976).

Fortunes Made in Business: Life Struggles of Successful People (Sampson Low & Co, 1884).

The New Grove Dictionary of Music and Musicians (20 vols, Macmillan, 1980).

BROADHURST, Sir Edward Tootal

(1858-1922)

Cotton manufacturer

Sir Edward T Broadhurst (courtesy of the Whitworth Art Gallery, University of Manchester).

Edward Tootal Broadhurst was born in Broughton, Lancashire, on 19 August 1858, the second son of Henry Tootal Broadhurst (1822-96) of Prestwich, near Manchester and the first of his three wives, Mary Margaret née Brooke. His father belonged to the second generation associated with the firm which in 1859 became Tootal Broadhurst Lee Co Ltd (hereafter Tootals). Edward was educated at Dr Hungerford's Eagle House, Wimbledon and then at Winchester. In 1876 he joined the family firm.

Between the 1860s and 1880s Tootals grew rapidly as it successfully applied powerlooms to the manufacture of a wide variety of fine and fancy fabrics. By 1887 Tootals was the third largest of the great combined firms of Lancashire: its workforce of ca 5,000 operatives worked 172,000 spindles and 3,500 looms; its merchanting side included offices and warehouses at Bradford, Belfast, Paris and a series of agencies directing the company's goods world-wide. A year later, when the partnership was converted into a limited liability company, Tootals held a unique position as a vertically integrated firm at the upper end of the market.

The four partners of 1859, Henry Tootal Broadhurst, Henry and Joseph Lee (qqv) and Robert Scott, were the major shareholders in the new limited company. However, the younger generation of Lees and Broadhursts, particularly Henry Lee's son Harold (1852-1936), chairman from 1895, and Edward Tootal Broadhurst managed the consolidation of the company's business and finances through the lean years of the 1890s. While Lee directed the mills' management committee, Broadhurst's main area of activity was the finance committee of which he became chairman in 1900. He played key roles in developing the company's new Manchester warehouse and headquarters and in selling the unprofitable sewing cotton business. Also, he represented the company's interests on the board of the British Northrop Loom Co and on the council of the British Cotton Growing Association from its foundation.

After Tootals was successfully turned around with record profits and dividends of 5 per cent and 6 per cent between 1900 and 1906, it required additional capital. In 1907 Broadhurst undertook responsibility for the financial reconstruction which increased nominal share capital from £1 million to £1.2 million and involved the offer of preference shares to the public for the first time.

Later in 1907 Broadhurst became chairman, replacing Harold Lee who had borne the brunt of the 1905-6 weavers' strike at the firm's Sunnyside Mills in Bolton but who carried on as manager of the mills and as deputy chairman. An American slump, a fall in the home demand for fancy fabrics and losses from an earthquake and fire in Kingston, Jamaica forced Tootals to cut dividends on ordinary shares to 4 per cent in 1908 and 2.25

per cent in 1909. Yet, they recovered to 7.5 per cent during the next four years as turnover and profits (averaging £87,320 per annum) again reached record levels.

After the sale of the Black Lane Mills in July 1907, Tootals' production was concentrated throughout the years of Broadhurst's chairmanship in Sunnyside Mills, Bolton and Ten Acres Mills and Hemming Works at Newton Heath, Manchester. However, improvements continued. Sunnyside Mills were changed from steam to electric power in 1912 and two additional weaving sheds were built in 1912 and 1913. Moreover, in 1910 the Manchester warehouse was extended down Great Bridgewater Street.

The company's initial reaction to the outbreak of war in 1914 was wary. However, profits soared during the war and immediate post-war years to reach over £400,000 in 1920. This enabled the company to pay a 10 per cent dividend on ordinary shares in 1916-20 and a weekly war bonus to all employees in 1915-17. Recognising that trade was 'entirely abnormal', Broadhurst built up substantial reserve funds. He commented to shareholders in 1918 that 'some of you may think that we have been over-prudent and conservative in the past ... it is not a bad fault and long may it continue' {*Address to Shareholders* (1918) 2}. The ease with which Tootals covered the loss of £145,000 in 1921 from reserves is a testament to his foresight. Aided in particular by the able Kenneth Lee (qv), Broadhurst also directed substantial funds into the establishment of an advertising department which replaced ad hoc campaigns with 'a new general advertising scheme' {Board Minutes, 9 Feb 1915}; and the setting up of a research department which developed, for example, the successful crease resistant process. In addition, as part of an especially comprehensive array of welfare schemes for employees, Broadhurst promoted employee shareholding and encouraged an educational programme which included one of the first part-time day continuation schools under the 1918 Education Act.

Broadhurst's business leadership extended beyond Tootals and textiles. He was chairman of the Manchester & Liverpool District Bank, and a director of the London & North Western Railway and the Atlas Insurance Co. He was also a member of the executive committee of the Federation of British Industries.

Broadhurst played a particularly influential political role during the general election of 1906 in Manchester North-West where Churchill gained a victory for the Liberals. A Unionist who headed the Free Trade League in the Constituency, Broadhurst argued that 'Free Trade is not a party question' and urged his fellow Conservatives to 'sink personal feeling and party differences' {Clarke (1971) 282}. Two years later Broadhurst and other Unionist Free Traders again supported Churchill in the by-election caused by his appointment as President of the Board of Trade, but the Liberal Government's social legislation proved too great a handicap and Churchill lost. Realizing that the Unionist Free Traders could not offer an independent challenge at the next general election and unable to support the 'ruinous proposals' {*ibid* 289} in the Government's budget, Broadhurst reluctantly retreated to inactive Conservatism in 1909.

Broadhurst, however, remained active in a large number of non-political organisations in the area. Among others, he was president of the

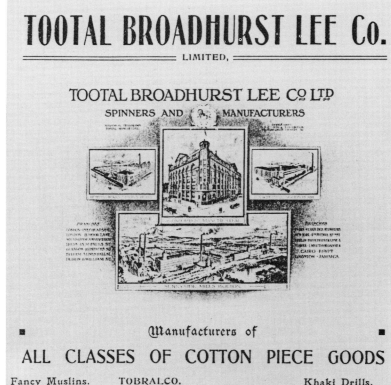

A 1912 Tootal Broadhurst Lee Co Ltd advertisement (from the Lancashire Yearbook of Industries & Commerce, *published by the Manchester Courier, 1912).*

Warehousemen and Clerks Orphan School in Cheadle Hulme and as chairman of its Jubilee Fund Committee he did much to raise the £50,000 subscribed. He was also a member of the council of Manchester University. For eight years he was chairman of the Manchester and Salford Lifeboat Fund. He was High Sheriff of Lancashire 1906-7. He gave unstinting support to the Manchester Athenaeum which he served as president for eighteen years. In addition, he was a member of the board of governors of the Whitworth Institute and Art Gallery established by his aunt, the widow of Sir Joseph Whitworth (qv). He built up a fine collection of early English watercolour paintings which he bequeathed to the Gallery.

Broadhurst took an exceptionally active part in the war effort, receiving a baronetcy in 1918 largely for his local activities. Together with Herbert Dixon (qv) and others he organized the recruitment of the Manchester 'Pals' battalions and he was instrumental in raising funds from Manchester firms to supply the needs of these troops. He also served on the Cotton Control Board and on committees which found work for thousands of discharged officers and men in the North West. In 1919 'as a thank offering for the victory of the Allies, in the winning of which Manchester men — and women also — have played such a glorious part; and in gratitude for all that Manchester has done for me' {letter from Broadhurst, *Manchester Guardian* 7 June 1919}, Broadhurst gave the Manchester Parks Committee 85 acres at Moston for playing fields. Services such as these earned him obituary tributes as a 'great philanthropist', as well as a 'merchant prince' {*Manchester Evening News* 3 Feb 1922}.

Broadhurst married in 1887 Charlotte Jane, the youngest daughter of Thomas Ashton, chairman of the manufacturing firm Ashton Brothers & Co of Hyde; one of her sisters was Lady Bryce, wife of the distinguished scholar and ambassador to the United States. They had no children. His estate of £149,903 gross had many beneficiaries including each of the directors of Tootals and a number of the institutions with which he had been associated.

Broadhurst pursued the lifestyle of a 'country gentleman'. An Anglican, he lived in the Manor House at North Rode near Congleton, Cheshire. He spent August and September of each year at his Scottish grouse moor. Yet, as a dedicated businessman, he regularly chaired the weekly meetings of the board and its committees during the remaining ten months of the year — apart from two extended periods of nervous illness in 1910 and 1912 and another long absence in 1916. These weekly meetings were short and uncontentious. 'Sir Edward said what was going to happen — no disagreement in those years' {interview with Fred Jennings}. However, 'he was not a business tycoon' and was 'satisfied with a small office' on the ground floor of the Manchester headquarters {ibid}. He encouraged younger directors, particulary Kenneth Lee who was able to step in easily as chairman when Broadhurst died unexpectedly on 2 February 1922.

MARGUERITE W DUPREE

Writings:

(with A Herbert Dixon) 'A Record of the Manchester City Battalions' in *Manchester City Battalions of the 90th and 91st Infantry Brigades: Book of Honour* ed S Kempster and H C E Westropp (1916).

BROADHURST Sir Edward Tootal

'Welfare Work in the Cotton Industry' in *Proceedings of the Tenth International Cotton Congress, Zurich* (June 1920).

Address to the Shareholders of Tootal Broadhurst Lee Company Ltd at the Annual Meeting, 3 Sept 1918 (Manchester: pp, 1918).

letter to *Manchester Guardian* 7 June 1919.

Sources:

Unpublished

BL: Add MSS 51158-9, letters Broadhurst to Robert Cecil.

Bodleian Library Oxford: MS Bryce Adds 41-47, correspondence and papers of Lady Bryce.

Bolton Public Library, Tootal Broadhurst Lee Ltd, Sunnyside Mill Business Records.

Manchester Central Library, Local History Room, 'Lancashire's New Sheriff' 3 Nov 1906, newspaper cuttings, f942.7389.M119.

Tootal Group PLC, Manchester, Board Minutes, Mill Management Committee Minutes, Finance Committee Minutes of Tootal Broadhurst Lee Co Ltd 1888-1922; Illuminated Address to Henry Lee 1867, 1886 and Harold Lee 1917.

C Reg: Tootal Broadhurst Lee Co Ltd (25,784).

BCe.

PrC; Wills of Edward Tootal, 22 Sept 1873; Henry Tootal Broadhurst, 16 June 1896; Lady Mary Louisa Whitworth, 26 May 1896; Edward Tootal Broadhurst, 2 Feb 1922; Lady Charlotte Broadhurst, 1 Sept 1924.

Interview with Fred Jennings, the Secretary's Office, Tootal Broadhurst Lee Co Ltd, 1914-65 (on 15 March 1983).

Jill Liddington, Zoe Mumby and Janet Seddon, ' "There's No Room on Daubhill for Me": An Account of the Daubhill Weavers' Strike, Bolton 1906' (unpublished paper, courtesy of Dermot Healy, Manchester Studies Unit, Manchester Polytechnic).

Published

Benjamin S Attwood and J Child (eds), *The Lancashire Yearbook of Industries and Commerce* (Manchester: Manchester Courier Ltd, 1912).

G Baker and J Moss, *Manchester Warehousemen and Clerks Orphan School: A History of Cheadle Hulme School 1855-1955* (Manchester, 1955).

Bolton Journal 10 Feb 1922.

Burke's Peerage and Baronetage 1921.

Peter F Clarke, *Lancashire and the New Liberalism* (Cambridge: Cambridge University Press, 1971).

—, 'The End of Laissez-Faire and the Politics of Cotton' *Historical Journal* 15 (1972).

Douglas A Farnie, 'John Rylands of Manchester' *Bulletin of the John Rylands Library* 56 (1973).

to the car makers. Among these was BRD Ltd (Blade Research & Development at Aldridge, Staffordshire) which he had established in 1951 for the mass-production of aero-engine gas turbine blades. With the end of the Korean War and steadily falling orders, BRD was faced with closure. Brookes, as the company's chairman from 1958 and managing director from its foundation, argued that a new market should be identified. Universal joints, drive shafts and constant velocity joints for front-wheel and four-wheel drives were chosen products with a promising future and one that would consume large quantities of forgings.

Brookes's other directorships of GKN's automotive subsidiaries included: chairman of Scottish Stamping & Engineering (crankshaft forgings) from 1955; chairman of GKN Cwmbran (cylinder blocks and camshafts) from 1959; and chairman of Joseph Sankey & Sons (chassis frames, wheels, body panels, commercial vehicle cabs and later armoured fighting vehicles) from 1961.

GKN developed less as a steel company (in part through the effects of nationalisation) and more as an engineering group committed to the automotive industry. In this functional change the insight and abilities of Brookes became increasingly significant. In 1964 he was appointed managing director (having been deputy managing director from 1962) and in the following year became chairman of GKN, a post that he held until his retirement in 1974, when a new position, life president, was created for him in acknowledgement of his thirty-three years' service.

Under his chairmanship, GKN's published profits and turnover climbed steadily until the Middle East oil crisis of 1973-74 brought difficulties upon their main customers. In 1965 pre-tax profits stood at £30.4 million on a turnover of £353.2 million; by 1974 they increased to £90.4 million on a turnover of £1,137.8 million, a rise that in real terms was only slightly less impressive. A relatively low debt-equity gearing consistently reflected Brookes's dislike of borrowing and the importance he attached to flexibility and independence. This achievement followed his policy of continuing to supply the needs of the motor industry. The decision to take over the Birfield group in 1966 accorded with this strategy because a principal motivation was the acquisition of Hardy, Spicer & Co, the Birmingham manufacturer of drive shafts and constant velocity joints (and, until BRD entered the market, a monopoly producer in the UK), and Laycock Engineering Ltd, the Sheffield firm of clutch, over-drive units, brake cylinders and garage equipment makers. The Birfield merger also resulted in the eventual purchase of a controlling interest in Uni-Cardan AG, then a world leader in constant velocity joint expertise and patents. Brookes supervised the take-over of Vandervell Products (thin wall bearings, bushes and piston assemblies) in 1967 and concluded the amalgamation with the Firth Cleveland group in 1972 for around £27.6 million. Its chairman, Sir Charles Hayward, a friend of Brookes, had wished to see his business placed in responsible hands, while GKN was interested in their fastenings and automotive operations and wished to broaden the market for their steel rod. In December 1973 GKN's stake in the automotive component industry was considerably widened when the group acquired Kirkstall Forge Engineering Ltd, the largest independent manufacturer of heavy-duty axles in the UK, a strength that was to be augmented in February 1974 when Centrax Gears (now renamed Newton

Transmissions), makers of off-highway axles, joined GKN. The total value of acquisitions at their then current prices during Brookes's term of leadership was approximately £162 million, an expenditure that was in part made possible by the compensation payments that followed the re-nationalisation of steel in 1967.

Although closely involved with the motor trade, Brookes did not ignore the company's steel investments. He was responsible for the re-acquisition of Brymbo Steel Works (originally bought by GKN in 1948 but nationalised for a second time in 1967-68) from the British Steel Corporation in February 1974 for £20 million, and the transfer of the Dowlais foundry at Methyr to the BSC. Its special steels were needed for the group's forgings and transmissions factories. In addition, his chairmanship witnessed the initiation of a major investment programme in the GKN's Castle Rod Mill and Tremorfa Steel Works, a scheme that came to fruition, after his retirement, in 1977. Brookes also pursued a policy of moving downstream into stockholding and steel service centres largely through the following acquisitions: Brinton, Adams & Richards Ltd and Roberts, Sparrow & Co Ltd both in 1968, together with Miles, Druce & Co Ltd in 1974.

Concerned that John Lysaght (Australia) Pty Ltd, a GKN overseas subsidiary, had grown up solely as re-rollers of sheet steel with no independent means of raw material supply (they were in fact reliant upon one producer of feedstock, the Broken Hill Proprietary Co), Brookes, appreciating the vulnerability of the group's position in Australia, suggested a 50-50 partnership between GKN and BHP to own Lysaghts and to develop a major new steel works at Westernport, Victoria, so that BHP would have a direct interest in the downstream operations. It took considerable determination and negotiating skill to conclude the arrangement, announced in 1969. The first phase was completed in 1973 and involved the installation of continuous cold reduction mills with related continuous galvanizing and pre-painting plants, while the second phase, completed in 1978, consisted of hot strip mills. The works had high standards of pollution control, were architecturally landscaped and offered efficient and safe operating conditions together with access by road, rail and sea.

As well as these strategic changes of direction, major organisational innovations were undertaken during his period of control. Although limited divisionalisation had occurred late during the chairmanship of Sir Kenneth Peacock (1902-68), GKN had for too long retained a holding-subsidiary company structure, the full implementation of sub-grouping falling to R P Brookes. Following a report by the management consultants, Production Engineering Ltd, the group's subsidiaries were arranged into product-oriented divisions with geographic sub-groups for overseas activities. Two new senior boards were established, GKN (UK) Ltd and GKN (Overseas) Ltd, whose purpose was to provide a 'club' atmosphere and a natural liaison through sub-group leaders. By this means overseas operations were placed on an equal standing with their British counterparts, Brookes believing that there had existed a detrimental distinction in the past. Such activities as could be centralised to gain economies of scale (finance, accounting, strategic planning, economic forecasting, industrial relations, training, personnel and, through the group technological centre, advanced research and development) were concentrated into expanded corporate services. The result was not, however, multi-divisional in the American sense or as manifested by UK firms such as ICI because subsidiaries retained their own boards, names, legal identities and responsibilities, and the sub-groups did not constitute operating companies in their own right.

Brookes's outside appointments included part-time membership of the British Steel Corporation (1967-68), the vice-presidency of the Engineering Employers' Federation (1967-75) and council membership of the CBI between 1968 and 1974. In 1968-70 he was the first president of the British Mechanical Engineering Confederation. A council member of the Society of Motor Manufacturers and Traders (1969-75), he additionally served on its executive committee from 1970 and in 1974-75 was its president. Brookes also became president of the Motor Industry Research Association in 1973-75. From 1972 until 1975 he sat on the Industrial Development Advisory Board and in January 1971 was a member of the Wilberforce Committee of Inquiry into the electricity supply industry dispute. He served on Birmingham University's court of governors (1966-75) and their council (1968-1975). In 1973 Brookes became an honorary fellow of the Institution of Sales Engineers. Other board appointments included ATV Network, chairmanship of Rae Brothers (Isle of Man) Ltd, a non-executive directorship of Plessey Co Ltd, and abroad, AMF Incorporated (1976-79), and membership of the Dubai Aluminium Authority. In 1971 he was knighted for services to export and in December 1975 awarded a life peerage.

He married Florence Edna Sharman, the daughter of Isaac Sharman, a hotel proprietor, in 1937; they had one son.

Possibly because he had gained an extensive experience of the engineering industry from humble beginnings, Lord Brookes took a balanced view of business believing that steady growth was preferable to spectacular profits (which would probably prove short-lived) and that an emphasis on strategic planning should not lose sight of factors other than financial return, such as conditions of employment and social responsibilities. His founding of the GKN Evergreen Association, which services and maintains contact with all retired staff, was one expression of his philosophy that people, whether employees or customers, occupied a prime place in business. His appointment as GKN chairman in 1965 represented an important change in direction for a group which had hitherto seen itself primarily as a steel company in which manufacturing enterprises were considered only as useful adjuncts. Under his guidance steel became subsidiary and engineering, particularly for the automotive industry, came to the fore through investment in existing plant and a series of considered acquistions.

EDGAR JONES

Sources:

Unpublished

GKN, London, various departmental sources.

BROOKES Raymond Percival

BCe.

MCe.

Interview and correspondence with Lord Brookes, 1983.

Published

Derek F Channon, *The Strategy and Structure of British Enterprise* (Macmillan, 1973).

WW 1983.

Edward Brough (courtesy of the Central Library, Newcastle upon Tyne).

BROUGH, Edward

(1846-1933)

Wholesaler of provisions

Edward Brough was born in America on 11 May 1846, and brought to Britain two years later. Nothing is known of his parentage and little of his early life. He lived on Tyneside for the remainder of his life. At the age of twenty he entered the service of Edward R Hume & Co, Newcastle provision importers, but ten years later in 1876 together with a friend he set up the wholesaling business of Frazer & Brough, in High Friar Street, Newcastle, importing chiefly butter and eggs. In 1888 Edward set up independently with his seventeen-year-old eldest son, Joseph William (qv), in their own wholesale provision business with a shop in Farrington Court, Bigg Market. In 1894 Joseph left the partnership to begin provision retailing on his own and was replaced by a younger brother, E Dent Brough. In 1900, however, Edward Brough sold his wholesaling business and brought his experience in that field to the organisation of the supply of goods for his elder son's rapidly expanding retail business. He retired from the day-to-day running of the firm in 1905, although he became chairman when the partnership was converted into a private limited company in 1917. He was also chairman of the General Bill Posting Co Ltd, Dunford Steamship Co Ltd and of James Scott & Son (1926) Ltd.

Edward Brough was a noted philanthropist who was especially involved with the Poor Children's Holiday Association of which he was a governor and vice-president. He financed the building of the Edward Brough Children's Home at South Shields where he was chairman of the local branch of the PCHA. He lived at Ashfield Towers, Gosforth, and was a JP for both Newcastle and Northumberland but apart from being a trustee and member of the Board of Management of Newcastle Savings Bank he

Broughs Stores in 1912 (courtesy of the Central Library, Newcastle upon Tyne).

played little other part in public life. He died on 3 May 1933 and was survived by his second wife, two sons and two daughters. He left a gross estate valued at £123,382.

D J ROWE

Sources:

Unpublished

PrC.

Published

H G Ellis, *Broughs Limited: The Story of a Business* (1952).

BROUGH, Joseph William

(1871-1958)

Food retailer

Joseph William Brough was born at Gateshead on 12 September 1871, the eldest son of Edward Brough (qv), a wholesaler of provisions in Newcastle

BROUGH Joseph William

Joseph W Brough (courtesy of the Central Library, Newcastle upon Tyne).

upon Tyne, and his first wife Mary Brough née Dent. At the age of seventeen, in 1888, Joseph joined his father in the first family wholesale business, based on a shop in Farrington Court, Bigg Market. When, six years later, he left his father's wholesaling business to go into retailing, Joseph had a clear idea of the market at which he was aiming. He opened his shop at 71 Blackett Street, in the centre of Newcastle, with the legend 'Wholesale Cash Store' in huge letters across the window. His prime objective in retailing was to eliminate the middle man and bring basic foodstuffs to working people in large quantities at close to wholesale prices. This was a revolutionary challenge to the co-operatives and the practice of almost daily shopping for small amounts of regularly consumed goods. It was, however, very successful. Warehouse premises were taken in 1896 in Gallowgate, chiefly for the making-up of orders, and then in 1898 the Blackett Street premises were extended and a new shop taken in New Bridge Street as trade expanded.

Brough's pricing policy aimed at a gross profit of 12 per cent and a net profit of 5 per cent, and, therefore, required a large turnover. Price lists were printed weekly and widely circulated and in connection with this Brough became a director of the General Bill Posting Co Ltd, like his father. Delivery by carriers and rail to outlying mining communities in Northumberland and Durham was developed. In 1897 the first traveller was employed on a regular round to gather orders and the firm began to develop its own delivery service to replace independent carriers. As orders from areas away from Tyneside expanded, Joseph opened larger warehouse premises at Oxford Street, Newcastle and decided to open

Broughs Stores at Chester le Street ca 1913 (courtesy of the Central Library, Newcastle upon Tyne).

branch stores, again with no window display and carrying the words 'Wholesale Cash Store'. The first was opened in 1901 at Ashington, while Bedlington, Crook, Gateshead and West Stanley were added by 1906, with eight more branches by 1914. In its turn each store developed its own delivery trade to neighbouring communities. Cash on delivery ensured no bad debts and by 1910 average cash turnover per branch was £850 per week. In 1917 the firm was converted into a private limited company with a capital of £144,000. At this time it had a payroll of over 500 and an annual turnover greater than £1 million. In 1919 the family sold out to Meadow Dairy Co Ltd for the sum of £216,000.

Like his father, Joseph made notable contributions to local charities and especially to the Poor Children's Holiday (from 1952, Homes) Association of which he was a vice-president. He presented the Association with the house at Whickham which became the Edith Brough Children's Home. In 1940 he set aside £25,000 to form the Joseph Brough Trust to provide for deserving employees in cases of illness or hardship. The Trust still exists, with a wider remit to support North-Eastern charities. In later life Joseph lived at Woodside, Wylam, Northumberland and then Thornley Gate, Allendale, where he died on 15 July 1958, leaving an estate valued at £184,750 gross.

D J ROWE

Sources:

Unpublished

BCe.

PrC.

Published

H G Ellis, *Broughs Limited: the Story of a Business* (1952).

Peter Mathias, *Retailing Revolution. A History of Multiple Retailing in the Food Trades Based upon the Allied Suppliers Group of Companies* (Longman, 1967).

Newcastle Journal 4 May 1933.

Sir Stanley Brown (courtesy of the Central Electricity Generating Board).

BROWN, Sir Frederick Herbert Stanley

(1910-)
Electrical engineer and nationalised electricity supply industry chairman

Frederick Herbert Stanley Brown, usually known as Stanley, was born in Handsworth, West Bromwich, on 9 December 1910, the son of Clement Brown and Annie Sophia née Marrian. His father, a mechanical engineer, was a self-made man, proprietor of Brown & Barlow, motor engineers. Stanley was educated at King Edward VI's School, Birmingham, and at Birmingham University, then the leading place for his chosen subject, electrical engineering. He gained a first class honours degree in 1932.

At that time graduate entry to the engineering profession was still rare but Birmingham's municipal electrical engineer was sympathetic and offered Brown a job at £2.50 per week. After initial training, his first years with Birmingham Corporation Electric Supply Department were spent as junior shift engineer at Nechells and Hams Hall power stations. The Department, which was the largest electric utility in the UK, soon offered a chance to widen his scope with work on the design and construction of a Hams Hall extension. In the Second World War, he introduced in Birmingham power stations what has since become known as the STEP factor method of efficiency control. After the war, feeling stale in his current job, he moved back into design and construction, with a spell at the West Midlands Joint Electricity Authority before he went on to Liverpool Corporation to supervise their post-war power station building programme. It was in that capacity that he became acquainted with Josiah Eccles (qv) who was then Liverpool Corporation's electrical engineer and who was to have a considerable influence on his later career.

When the electricity supply industry was nationalised in 1948, Brown remained at his post with responsibility for designing and constructing three power stations on Merseyside, but in 1951 he was asked to transfer to the British Electricity Authority headquarters in London to strengthen the design function in the chief engineer's department. This proved to be his greatest break for, after several years of frustration for Brown, his boss, a rather conservative engineer with no university training, was 'kicked upstairs' and Brown replaced him. His former boss in Liverpool, Eccles, had by then become deputy chairman of the Authority, and they both now pressed for a more adventurous policy in the design of power stations. The size of turbo-alternators was substantially increased (thus substantially reducing their capital costs) and the steam pressures and temperatures were raised (thus considerably improving their thermal efficiency). Central to this policy were the 200 MW sets at High Marnham (Nottinghamshire) power station, proposed by Brown in 1953, first ordered in 1954 and operating by 1959. Their steam conditions of 2350 psi and 1,050°F were in advance of contemporary American practice, and helped get the British national grid back on a path of cheaper, more efficient generation which the conservative policies of his

The turbine hall at High Marnham Power Station, Nottinghamshire, showing the five 200 MW turbo-generator sets, built largely due to Sir Stanley Brown's insistence on advanced engineering standards (courtesy of the Central Electricity Generating Board).

predecessors had compromised. When the chief engineer's post became vacant in 1957, Brown was the youngest candidate for the succession, but his new ideas were appreciated and he got the job. These were the most successful years of his career, in both personal and national terms.

By 1957, however, the Conservative Government had decided to reorganise the industry and shift the emphasis of the construction programme from conventional to nuclear power stations. Brown shared the view of most of the Authority's engineers that the nuclear commitment being made was unwisely large, but the Government established a new Central Electricity Generating Board in 1958, under the nuclear engineer Sir Christopher Hinton (qv). Brown became the new Board's member for engineering, and, pleased to find that Hinton shared his sceptical view about the size of the nuclear programme, was gradually able to reduce the nuclear commitment over the following years. Hinton did, however, dominate policy making and these were frustrating years for Brown, even when in 1959 he became deputy chairman and took responsibility for relations with the Electricity Council, the bulk supply tariff and nuclear safety questions. The major decisions of the Board in the early 1960s (to increase power station construction to meet accelerating growth in demand and to standardise on 500 MW sets) were shared by Brown, though he did not take the initiatives.

When Hinton retired at the end of 1964 Brown succeeded him as chairman of the Central Electricity Generating Board. He was knighted in 1967, became president of the Institution of Electrical Engineers in 1967-68 and joined the Court of his old university, Birmingham in 1969. In the Central Electricity Generating Board, however, these were not easy years. Brown was able to strengthen the management structure and improve labour productivity through a staff status scheme for manual workers and the outlawing of overtime working. But faults in the Board's own organisation and in that of the manufacturers and constructors of power stations became more apparent. In 1965 the Board made disastrous misjudgements in ordering an Advanced Gas-Cooled Reactor, being fooled by the over-optimistic forecasts of the Atomic Energy Authority. They were, however, sensibly able to limit the nuclear commitment to only half the level suggested by the Authority. On the conventional power station side the new advanced 500 MW sets also caused greater troubles than expected, and by the late 1960s the CEGB were occasionally unable to meet the winter peak demand on the grid system. The chairman of the Electricity Council, Sir Ronald Edwards (qv), also persuaded ministers (against Brown's advice) to accept that the Council's control over the CEGB should be increased, though political changes in fact enabled the CEGB to retain their independence. In 1972, frustrated by increasing political interference in the industry on many fronts, Brown resigned prematurely.

He married Marjorie Nancy Brown in 1937; they have two daughters. The Browns live a happy and active retired life in the Cotswolds.

LESLIE HANNAH

Writings:

Electricity Council, Millbank, Intelligence section, a file of the papers published in technical journals and periodicals and Sir Stanley's speeches.

Sources:

Unpublished

BCe.

Central Electricity Generating Board archives.

Interviews with Sir Stanley Brown and his colleagues.

Published

Leslie Hannah, *Engineers Managers and Politicians: The First Fifteen Years of Nationalised Electricity Supply in Britain* (Macmillans, 1982).

WW 1982.

John Brown (courtesy of Sheffield Public Library).

BROWN, Sir John

(1816-1896)

Iron and steel manufacturer

John Brown was born at Fargate in Sheffield on 6 December 1816, the second son of Samuel Brown. There is evidence to suggest that his father was a local slate merchant or builder and, though John's education in a local school was a modest one, Samuel was able to provide the security needed for his first venture into business.

At the age of fourteen John Brown expressed a desire to become a merchant and was accordingly placed with a local firm, Earle Horton & Co, which traded in staple wares. In 1836 the firm built the Hallamshire Works in Orchard Place, Sheffield, and began manufacturing steel. When he came of age John Brown was offered a share in the business and with his father's backing and a £500 loan he launched into spring and file production. A new factory was built in Furnival Street, which he named the Atlas Steel Works.

The rapid expansion of the railways induced John Brown to concentrate on the manufacture of rails, buffers, and other accessories for locomotives and rolling stock. In 1848 he invented and patented the steel helical or volute spring buffer which soon proved a great success. Marketing it with much skill, Brown regarded his buffer as the foundation of his fortune and even incorporated it in a coat of arms. To cope with the demand, manufacturing was extended into several areas of Sheffield. In 1856 new works were acquired in Savile Street; originally costing £23,000, they were purchased for half that sum.

In 1857 John Brown began puddling his own iron for conversion into steel. This method of manufacturing steel, though it was later to be overtaken by the basic bulk steelmaking processes, made an important contribution to the engineering industry by satisfying demand for increased tonnages of steel. The works were once more expanded, as the original number of six puddling furnaces was doubled, surplus production being employed in the manufacture of bridge and boiler plates.

Meanwhile, two partners were taken on: John D Ellis (qv), son of a family of brass founders, and William Bragge, a widely travelled engineer, and the son of a jeweller. It was this partnership that adopted Bessemer's (qv) new steel-making process. Apparently less sceptical than other manufacturers, John Brown was one of the first makers to try the new converter. Despite the initially disappointing results, in 1859 he took out another license from Henry Bessemer and in May 1861 John Brown's Atlas Works rolled the first Bessemer rail made in the ordinary course of business. There were soon large export orders for this product, though the conservatism of the British railways is said to have inhibited demand.

Brown was also a pioneer in the manufacture of rolled armour plate. Though other firms had attempted to roll armour plate, John Brown pioneered the first successful mass-production technique. On one of his

*The John Brown factory in the
1860s (courtesy of Sheffield Public
Library).*

continental tours he noticed a French warship with hammered armour
plate and then decided that thicker, larger and finer quality plates could be
made by rolling. A new rolling mill was laid down under his direction. So
successful was the method that in 1867 it was reported that three-quarters
of the ironclads of the British navy were protected by armour plates made
at the Atlas Works.

In the development of the armour plate plant Brown expended £200,000
and by 1867 the works covered an area of 21 acres. The number of men
employed in 1857 was 200, and in 1867, 4,000. In the first year of the
business the turnover was about £3,000, and by 1867 it reached nearly £1
million. Such was the strain on the firm's resources that on 1 April 1864
John Brown & Co was launched as a limited company with a nominal
capital of £1 million. Capital from outside Sheffield contributed to this
total and two notable recruits to the board were the chemical
manufacturer, Henry Davis Pochin (qv), and a cotton entrepreneur,
Benjamin Whitworth MP, both of Manchester.

Armour plate production accounted for nearly half the output of the
firm and consequently it was adversely affected when naval orders fell
away. The firm turned to steel forgings which necessitated heavy
investment in new equipment. So heavy were capital equipment costs that
cash flow for profits seems to have been affected. In 1867 profits fell to
only £23,000 and new investments were limited to the sums covered by
depreciation allowances. The next year profits recovered, but differences
arose between Brown and the other directors who complained about profit
performance. Through ill-health, the founder's attendance at board
meetings lapsed. In 1871 J D Ellis announced that Brown had parted with

all shares except his preference shares. Brown received £200,000 for goodwill. Later, Brown cut all his links with the company and established a new firm, Brown, Bayley & Dixon, directly competing against his old firm.

In addition to his business interests Brown was heavily involved in civic affairs. In 1856 he became a member of the Sheffield Town Council, he was alderman three years later, and mayor in 1861 and 1862. His commitment to education was attested when he became first chairman of the Sheffield School Board. He was Master Cutler in 1865 and 1866 and contributed £12,000 to All Saints' Church and Schools. He was knighted in 1867.

In his business dealings Sir John Brown gave the impression of being a strong-minded, practical individualist. In his later years these qualities did not bring the kind of success that had enabled him earlier to become one of the world leaders in heavy steel technology. His later ventures in business were much less profitable and his failures were exacerbated by disastrous investments in Spanish iron ore mines.

John Brown married Mary Schofield, the eldest daughter of a local auctioneer, Benjamin Schofield, in 1839. He died without issue on 27 December 1896, at Shortlands, Bromley, Kent, in relative poverty and obscurity, leaving £27,221 gross.

GEOFFREY TWEEDALE

Sources:

Unpublished

British Patent: 1844 (10,343).

MCe.

PrC.

Kenneth C Barraclough, 'The Development of the Early Steelmaking Processes: an Essay in the History of Technology' (Sheffield PhD, 1981).

Information from Paul Nunn.

Published

Sir Henry Bessemer, *Sir Henry Bessemer FRS: An Autobiography. With a Concluding Chapter (by his Son, Henry Bessemer)* (Offices of *Engineering*, 1905).

DNB.

Charlotte J Erickson, *British Industrialists. Steel and Hosiery 1850-1950* (Cambridge: Cambridge University Press, 1959).

Firth Brown Ltd, *100 Years in Steel. Firth Brown Centenary 1837-1937* (Sheffield: T Firth & J Brown, 1937).

Sir Allan Grant, *Steel and Ships. The History of John Brown's* (Michael Joseph, 1950).

William T Jeans, *The Creators of the Age of Steel* (Chapman & Hall, 1884).

Ferdinand Kohn, *Iron and Steel Manufacture* (MacKenzie, 1869).

Peter L Payne, *Rubber and Railways in the Nineteenth Century* (Liverpool: Liverpool University Press, 1961).

J H Stainton, *The Making of Sheffield, 1865-1914* (Sheffield: Weston, 1924).

Mary Walton, *Sheffield, Its Story and Its Achievement* (2nd ed, Sheffield: Sheffield Telegraph & Star, 1949).

Kenneth Warren, 'The Sheffield Rail Trade, 1861-1930: an Episode in the Locational History of the British Steel Industry' *Transactions of the Institute of British Geographers* 34 (1964).

BROWN, Sidney George

(1873-1948)

Electrical and instrument engineer, and inventor

Sidney George Brown was born in Chicago on 6 July 1873. Both his parents, Sidney Brown and Clara née Napier, were English: they had gone to Chicago after the great fire of 1870 to introduce his father's invention of a system of concrete blocks to insulate stove pipes set in wooden walls, a system adopted with enthusiasm in chastened Chicago. The family returned to England in 1879; his father bought land around Bournemouth, and played an important role in the early development of the town. Brown was educated at a private school in Parkstone, near Bournemouth, and later at Harrogate College, Yorkshire. Because of the great interest he showed in mechanical devices, in 1892 his father sent him as a paying pupil to the Chelmsford works of the electrical engineer, R E B Crompton (qv). His pupillage lasted five years in all, broken by two years (1894-96) at University College, London, studying electricity, engineering, mathematics and physics. On the completion of his pupillage he was employed at Cromptons for six months in their calculating department on a salary of £1 a week, before his father's illness forced him to leave the company and return to look after the family's interests in Bournemouth.

Even as a pupil, he had invented a number of improvements in dynamo electrical machinery, and in 1899 he produced the first three of a series of inventions which increased the efficiency, and reduced the costs, of the transmission of messages by submarine cable. Among these, were improvements to condensers which allowed simultaneous signals to be sent from both ends of long submarine cables. In 1906 he formed the Telegraph Condenser Co, with a capital of £2,000, to manufacture them.

In 1908 he married Alice, only daughter of Rev C J Stower of Sudbury, Suffolk. She assisted him in his experiments that produced the first telephone relay for magnifying speech, and a loudspeaker: the Browns were the first to give this name to the instrument. In 1911, he formed S G Brown, to manufacture his inventions in a small factory in Devonshire Street, London. By 1914, the business of this company and of his Telegraph Condenser Co had grown so much that a new factory, covering five acres and employing over a thousand people, was built to accommodate them.

During and after the war, Brown was principally concerned with the invention and development of gyro compasses for use on land and sea and in the air. He invented an entirely new method, called liquid ballistic control, of damping the oscillations set up in a gyro compass by the turning of a ship; this was patented in 1916. He also devised an automatic steering device to work in connection with his compass in 1928.

Altogether Brown took out over 1,000 patents. Since his own inventions were the major asset of his companies, it was important to protect his patents against infringement. Brown bore no rancour towards those who poached his ideas, but then he left the protection of his interests to his wife, Alice, who took the chief part in the actions brought to defend them.

Indeed, though Brown paid close attention to the details of production, visiting his factory workshops daily, he left most of the administration of his businesses to his wife, who was director of both companies. She it was who made most of the financial decisions, for Brown did not wish to be troubled by such matters. It was her business acumen that enabled Brown, who was indifferent to the making or spending of money, to reap the fruits of his inventions. Brown refused all finanical aid towards the invention, development or production of all his devices, preferring to work free of any control.

He and his wife maintained control over the finance and management of their companies. When they wished to raise capital for the Telegraph Condenser Co in 1933, they turned the firm into a public company, but arranged for all the shares sold to be bought by the Charterhouse Investment Trust Ltd. Although the firm produced nearly seven million condensers in 1932 for all purposes from wireless to the distribution of electricity, and made a net profit of £52,744 (the average net profit 1928-32 was £38,554), the private company still had a nominal capital of only £2,000. Brown held 1,200 £1 shares, Alice 600, and the remaining 200 were held by the third director of the company, William Cole. This private company was sold to the new public one for £250,000, which was very largely met by the allotment of shares. Of the new issued capital of £280,000, £100,000 cumulative preference shares and £30,000 ordinary shares were to be bought by Charterhouse Investment Trust, which also agreed to take up another £30,000 preference shares to supply the new company with working capital. Brown was to have a contract as technical adviser for five years at £1,000 a year, as well as his remuneration as a director of £300 a year.

At that time Brown was also chairman and managing director of S G Brown Ltd. Brown was governing director for life, or until he resigned, with powers to act as the sole director of the company; he was paid £2,000 a year, in addition to any royalty or profits from any invention he might authorise the company to use. In 1941 the Admiralty took over direction of S G Brown, under the Defence Regulations of 1939, and Sidney and Alice Brown were replaced as directors by Admiralty nominees.

Brown's health was never very good, and in 1943 he was forced to retire. He sold his interests in the Telegraph Condenser Co to a syndicate, and sold the works of S G Brown Ltd, together with his gyro compass and wireless equipment and all existing patent rights, to the Admiralty.

Brown's brilliance as an inventor was widely recognised; he was elected a Fellow of the Royal Society in 1916. He was a member of the Institution of Electrical Engineers, a fellow of the Institute of Physics, and a fellow of University College, London. Brown was a modest man, who preferred to spend his time producing yet more inventions to writing papers or giving lectures. His chief recreation was the cultivation of orchids. He and Alice had three children, but they all died young. Brown died in Sidmouth, where he and his wife had lived since his retirement, on 7 August 1948. His estate was proved at £140,762 gross.

CHRISTINE SHAW

Writings:

Numerous scientific papers, given before and published by the Royal Society, British Association, Physical Society and Institution of Electrical Engineers.

Sources:

Unpublished

C Reg: S G Brown Ltd (272,806).

PrC.

Information from Gordon Bussey.

Published

Electrical Trades Directory 1916.

Journal of Institution of Electrical Engineers 1948.

Obituary Notices of Fellows of the Royal Society 7 (1951).

Times *Prospectuses* 85 (1933).

Times 9 Aug 1948.

WWW.

BROWNE, Sir Benjamin Chapman

(1839-1917)

Marine engineer and shipbuilder

Sir Benjamin C Browne (courtesy of Tyne & Wear Archives).

Benjamin Chapman Browne was born at Stouts Hill, Uley, Gloucestershire on 26 August 1839, the youngest of three sons of Col B C Browne of the 9th Lancers and later of the Gloucestershire Yeomanry, and of Mary Anne née Baker. On leaving Westminster School he spent a year in the Applied Science Department at King's College, London and in 1856 became an apprentice at the Elswick Works, Newcastle upon Tyne, set up to manufacture hydraulic equipment by Wiliam Armstrong (qv). He worked on the shop floor for four years before spending six months in the drawing office to complete his training as a mechanical engineer.

Browne began his professional career as a civil engineer, firstly at Falmouth Docks, under James Abernethy, then with the Tyne Pier Works and later (1865-69), on the staff of Sir John Coode; finally he worked at Douglas in the Isle of Man. Uncertainties in regard to his future led to discussions with his close friend the banker Thomas Hodgkin (1831-1913), who helped him in the purchase for £60,000 of R & W Hawthorn's Forth Banks Engine Works. Browne raised his quarter-share by changing an annual allowance from his mother into a capital sum and by borrowing from his family. The remainder came equally from a local coal-owner John Straker (1815-85), William Hawthorn (for his son) and the general manager John Scott, and from a mortgage. To provide the technical expertise in marine engines Browne arranged for F C Marshall (qv) to join the partnership at a salary of £1,000 a year, plus a quarter of the profits to build up to a quarter capital holding. The new partnership continued to trade under the title R & W Hawthorn.

The twenty-week long Nine-Hours Strike of 1871 almost ruined the partnership, whose liquid assets were a mere £7,000 and whose workforce was about 1,200; but Browne learned much from this dispute as he showed in later years. Since the intention was to concentrate on marine engine production, a suitable riverside site was acquired for a new works in 1871. This, the St Peter's Works, equipped with the most up-to-date plant, was to dominate the financial success of the partnership until 1885. During those years the effective capital was increased from £45,000 (the £15,000 balance of the purchase price was a mortgage) to £182,400.

In 1885 Andrew Leslie (qv), the senior partner in the Hebburn shipyard wished to retire and the junior partner, Arthur Coote (1841-1906) wanted to form a joint company with a marine engine works. As a result in 1886 R & W Hawthorn, Leslie, & Co Ltd was formed with a capital of £600,000 in £100 shares; 3,810 of the 5,400 shares issued were held by the directors. There was a joint holding of 255 by the Hawthorn partners; Browne personally held shares nos 1-429 and became company chairman. From the outset Browne made it very clear to his fellow directors that they could not behave as though the old partnership conditions operated. Browne's personal salary was £800, which was modest compared with Coote's £2,000, while Marshall's £3,200 indicated just how highly he was rated. Only in 1888 did the company overall make a loss, but dividends were modest and it was not until 1905 that the hoped-for 10 per cent was first declared.

Benjamin Browne led the new company continuously until he retired as chairman in 1915. During this time the annual turnover increased about tenfold, to more than £1.5 million in 1914, when the workforce exceeded 5,250. Browne selected managers and co-ordinated what were almost separate works, building locomotives, marine engines and finally ships. The management of the separate sites, often by partners, was not always easy as their respective profitability varied, and by no means all of Browne's decisions were endorsed, or the locomotive business would have been sold off early. When it became clear that Coote could not manage the shipyard to the satisfaction of his co-directors Browne found Herbert Rowell (qv), the man who was to do for the shipyard what Marshall did for the marine engine works. Later Sir Herbert Rowell succeeded Browne as company chairman.

Generally Browne did not make technical decisions; his introduction of a design of steam tramcar ('tramcar locomotive') was not a commercial success, and although he very early suggested that steps be taken to examine the possibilities of the application of electricity to locomotive propulsion this was not pursued for many years. However, Browne did take the company into a leading position as supplier of marine engines, steam turbines and destroyers to the Admiralty and he was actively concerned with establishing a valuable naval vessel trade with Russia. He was involved with Charles Parsons (qv) in the formation of the Newcastle & District Electric Light Co, and the Cambridge Electric Light Co, both pioneers of the generation of electricity by steam turbine.

Browne played a key role in the work of the national Employers' Federation of Engineering Associations (formed in 1896), and had been previously an active member of the Iron Trades Employers' Association. In the engineering workers' dispute of 1897-98 he regarded himself, quite properly, as representing the 'peace party'. He maintained personal contact with trade union leaders and would remind even his ablest managers that labour dispute issues were his business; he gave constant attention to industrial relations in his speeches and writings. In 1886 as president of the Northern Union of Mechanics' Institutions he welcomed trade unions as beneficial both to workers and employers; in 1904 he expressed similar views to the Royal Commission on Trade Disputes and Trade Combinations.

Benjamin Browne was a member of the Institution of Civil Engineers, the Institution of Mechanical Engineers and the Institution of Naval Architects. He played an important part in the work of the North East Coast Institution of Engineers and Shipbuilders, of which he was a council member for many years and president, 1898-1900. Keenly interested in education and apprentice training, he helped establish the first chair of Mechanical Engineering and Naval Architecture at the Durham College of Science at Newcastle and he later received an honorary DCL from Durham University in recognition of his work in education.

Internal company papers written by him in the early years of the First

World War indicate an appreciation of post-war difficulties for marine production, especially for firms heavily dependent on naval work, problems few others seem to have grasped; he even contemplated the desirability of a take-over of the works by the Admiralty.

A Conservative in politics, Browne was elected to the Newcastle Council in 1879 and served as mayor, 1885-87; he was knighted in 1887. He was also a JP in Newcastle (from 1877), Northumberland and Gloucestershire, and a DL of Northumberland. Always willing to deal with individuals and with personal problems, he was held in high esteem by his fellow employers. With Wigham Richardson (qv), J T Merz and others he found relaxation in Virgil evenings. Influenced by his mother he became a devoted member of the Church of England and a disciple of the Oxford Movement.

Benjamin Browne married Annie, the daughter of R T Atkinson (1807-45) in 1861; they had nine children, of whom seven survived their father. In 1876 Browne became a trustee of the considerable Atkinson properties and five years later the pressure of this administration caused him to consider withdrawing from the active management of R & W Hawthorn-Leslie, a step he did not take. Sir Benjamin Browne died on 1 March 1917 and left an estate valued at £77,415 gross.

J F CLARKE

Writings:

Selected Papers on Social and Economic Questions ed Evelyn M Browne & Helen M Browne (Cambridge: Cambridge University Press, 1918) contains 32 papers from 1886 to 1917.

History of R & W Hawthorn's from 1870 to 1885 (1914).

'The Relations between Capital and Labour; the Standpoint of Capital' in *After-War Problems* ed W H Dawson (Allen & Unwin, 1917).

PP, RC on Trade Disputes and Trade Combinations (1906) Cd 2826.

Sources:

Unpublished

Tyne & Wear Archives, records of Hawthorn-Leslie Ltd; records of the North East Coast Institution of Engineers & Shipbuilders.

BCe.

MCe.

PrC.

Published

Edward Allen, Joseph F Clarke, Norman McCord, David J Rowe, *The North-East Coast Engineers Strike of 1871* (Newcastle upon Tyne: Frank Graham, 1971).

Joseph F Clarke, *Power on Land & Sea: 160 Years of Industrial Enterprise on Tyneside. A history of R & W Hawthorn Leslie & Co Ltd* (Tyne & Wear: Clark Hawthorn Ltd, 1979).

Engineering 103 (1917).

Engineer 123 (1917).

Proceedings of the North East Coast Institution of Engineers and Shipbuilders 33 (1917).

Memoirs of John Wigham Richardson 1837-1908 (Glasgow: Hugh Hopkin, 1911).

Eric L Wigham, *The Power to Manage — a History of the Engineering Employers' Federation* (Macmillan, 1973).

WWW.

BRUCE-GARDNER, Charles
see GARDNER, Charles Bruce

BRUNNER, Sir John Tomlinson

(1842-1919)

Chemical manufacturer

John Tomlinson Brunner was born at Everton, Liverpool, on 8 February 1842. His father, John Brunner, was a Unitarian schoolmaster who had come from Switzerland in 1832 to teach in a friend's school; his mother was Margaret Catherine Curphey, from Ballydroma, Isle of Man.

Brunner attended his father's school, St George's House, and then at the age of fifteen, joined the shipping firm of Edward Estell, a family friend, as a junior clerk. He stayed here four years until the autumn of 1861; in October of that year he joined Hutchinson & Sons, chemical manufacturers at Widnes, still as a clerk, starting with an annual salary of

Sir John T Brunner (courtesy of ICI PLC).

£104. In his twelve years at Hutchinsons he rose to become general office manager, having some responsibility for accounts and supervising the workforce.

At Hutchinsons in 1862 Brunner first met Ludwig Mond (qv). Mond had joined the firm as a research chemist, and the two soon became friends. By the late 1860s both Brunner and Mond were thinking about their future careers, neither being satisfied with his present position. Brunner was ambitious and aware that his job had no real prospects. He and Mond started to consider setting up in business together. They learnt of Ernest and Alfred Solvay's work in Belgium on the ammonia-soda process, and in 1872 Mond went to Belgium and negotiated a licence with Solvay et Cie to manufacture soda by their method in England. Solvays were to give Brunner and Mond all the technical assistance they needed. Brunner and Mond, on the other hand, had to build their works within one year, and start production within two, otherwise the agreement would lapse; and they were to pay Solvays a royalty of 8s for every ton of pure soda produced.

This process promised to be cleaner, cheaper and more efficient than the Leblanc method used in Britain previously, as it produced a purer soda ash with considerably less waste material. Working out the capital required to produce 60 tons of soda ash a week, Brunner calculated that the Solvay method was £3,500 cheaper than the Leblanc method. Soda being one of the major raw materials required in the manufacture of glass, paper, soap and textiles, Brunner anticipated a widespread and enduring demand for the Solvays' cheaper and purer form of soda ash, calcined off to form sodium carbonate.

Brunner's partnership with Mond came legally into existence in February 1873. Next they had to find capital and locate a site suitable for their proposed works. Brunner provided £4,000, borrowed from his father and mother-in-law, and Mond £1,000 out of his own pocket. Together they managed, through loans from friends, mortgages, and a loan from their bank (Parrs' Bank in Warrington), to mobilise an amount sufficient to buy an estate from the Third Lord Stanley for £16,108 freehold. The site at Winnington near Northwich was carefully chosen on the Cheshire brinefields and with access both to the Weaver Navigation to Liverpool and to the Cheshire railway network.

Under their deed of partnership both Brunner and Mond were allowed £10 a week as salary in anticipation of profits. The first year, however, they produced 838 tons of soda ash with a loss of £4,300. This was due mainly to initial teething problems with the manufacturing process and machinery. The next year they broke even, and by 1877 the firm was definitely a going concern and expanding fast.

Whilst Mond generally saw to the scientific and technical side of the business, Brunner, with sixteen years of business experience behind him, acted as the company's salesman, accountant and cashier. His financial foresight and skill quickly built up an excellent commercial organisation. In 1881 Brunner and Mond sold out their partnership for £200,000 to a new public company, Brunner, Mond & Co, with an issued capital of £360,000, half in ordinary and half in preference shares. Brunner and Mond, as managing directors of the new company, retained control by allotting themselves two-thirds of the ordinary shares.

The firm's main product was soda ash, which Brunner at first sold in the UK and in North America, later moving into Australia, the Dutch East Indies, China and Japan, though keeping out of Europe under an agreement reached with Solvays in 1887. By the end of 1890 their average monthly deliveries of soda ash had reached ca 10,000 tons. After a few years they started producing a number of derivatives from the ammonia-soda process, such as soda crystals, bicarbonate and caustic soda, which, though manufactured in smaller quantities, were still profitable.

With John Crosfield (qv) as chairman from 1881, followed by Brunner from 1900, the company's profits rose rapidly; in 1881 they amounted to £30,000; by 1890 they had reached £284,000 and were still rising, reaching £778,472 in 1907. Though the Leblanc manufacturers of alkali had been improving their techniques and though they threateningly merged in 1891 to form the United Alkali Co Ltd, they were still tied to technology inferior to that of Brunner, Mond. Brunner, Mond's most serious competition came from the American Solvay Process Co which got under way in the late 1880s. Any domestic competition which posed a sufficient irritant to Brunner, Mond & Co, or equally, offered chances of expansion, was treated aggressively, as in 1895 when Brunner, Mond & Co took over the ammonia-soda business of Bell Brothers.

By the time Brunner retired as chairman in 1918, the company was one of the leading alkali manufacturers in the world. It was producing 563,548 tons of soda ash a year, had an employed capital of £10,438,719 and a published profit for the year of £1,111,848, having outstripped the UAC's profit levels as early as 1893.

The success of Brunner, Mond & Co must in great part have been due to their efficiency, both technical and commercial. In addition, they were far ahead of their time in general outlook. From the start, they differed from most Victorian firms by recruiting young men of university level or the equivalent to train for senior management posts; it was more common at the time for businessmen to have gradually worked their way up to the top from being junior clerks or office boys. The firm's industrial relations apparently were not unduly troubled and certainly the staff were generously paid and well looked after. Sick benefit was instituted in 1873, and in 1886 a day and evening school was opened for the workers. These developments can all be seen as a direct result of the founders' influence: both Brunner and Mond held liberal political views. Though maintaining complete authority over his men, Brunner was genuinely concerned for their welfare and education. He was also interested in their opinions, and liked to consult both his men and the unions on matters of business.

Brunner was active in politics, entering Parliament as Liberal MP for Northwich in 1885 and, with only one interruption of 13 months, maintaining his seat until he retired from Parliament in 1910. Once Brunner, Mond & Co had been incorporated as a public company, with a staff trained to Brunner's own methods, he allowed himself more time for politics and he always insisted that his role in politics was the most important aspect of his life. In his twenty-five years in the Commons, not only his wealth but the force of his personality won him great standing and influence in the Liberal Party. He campaigned vigorously for Home Rule, advocated temperance legislation, local government reform and religious equality. Devoted to education in Britain, he proposed the establishment and endowment of new universitites at national cost. He was a major figure among the Liberals, supporting many prospective candidates financially, including his own private secretary for many years, Thomas Edward Ellis, who later became MP for Merionethshire (1886-99), Parliamentary Secretary to the Treasury (1894-95), and Chief Opposition 'Whip' (1895-99).

Brunner became a freemason in 1885, and in 1901 became a Past Grand Deacon of England.

He was generous with his money, presenting Northwich with a public library and Runcorn and Winsford with Guildhalls for the use of trade unions, Friendly and other societies. He endowed three chairs at Liverpool University, receiving an honorary degree from that university and becoming pro-chancellor in 1909.

In 1895 he became a baronet, and he was made Privy Councillor in 1906.

Outside his work, Brunner was very much a family man, marrying twice, first in 1864 Salome Davies of Liverpool, and after her death, Jane Wyman of Kettering in 1875. He had seven children, and his youngest son, Roscoe Brunner, succeeded his father as chairman of the company in 1918. Sir John Brunner died on 1 July 1919, the year after he retired as chairman of his company, leaving £906,454 gross.

ALEXANDRA KIDNER

Writings:

A Scheme for the Redistribution of Cheshire, with Remarks on the Proposals of the Boundary Commissioners (Liverpool: 1885).

(with Thomas E Ellis) *Public Education in Cheshire* (Manchester: J Heywood, 1890).

(with John Lawrence Hammond) *Public Education in Cheshire in 1896* (Manchester: J Heywood, 1896).

Copy Conveyance of Land and Buildings to be Used as a Village Hall and School ... at Barnton ... 8th January 1898 (Liverpool: G C Walmsley, 1898).

Unveiling of the Statue of the late Dr. Ludwig Mond, F.R.S., at Winnington ... 13th September 1913 (Liverpool: 1913).

Sources:

Unpublished

BCe.

MCe.

PrC.

Published

William J Reader, *Imperial Chemical Industries, A History* (2 vols, Oxford University Press, 1970).

Stephen Koss, *Sir John Brunner: Radical Plutocrat* (Cambridge: Cambridge University Press, 1970).

Representative British Freemasons (Dod's Peerage Ltd, 1915).

John I Watts, *The First 50 Years of Brunner, Mond & Co* (Derby: Brunner, Mond & Co, 1923).

Singer, *History of Technology* 4 and 5.

WWMP.

WWW.

Wilberforce Bryant (courtesy of the Institute of Agricultural History, Reading).

BRYANT, Wilberforce

(1837-1906)

Match manufacturer

Wilberforce Bryant was born at Plymouth on 25 January 1837, the eldest son of William Bryant (1804-74) and his wife Ann Jago née Carkeet. William Bryant, a Wesleyan Methodist who became a Quaker on marriage, had a soap-making and sugar-refining business at Plymouth, and in about 1844 vertically merged his interests, without at first removing from there, with those of Francis May (1803-85), a fellow Quaker and provision merchant in London. The Bryant & May partnership's turning point occurred in 1850, when it became the import agent of the Swedish match manufacturers Carl & Johan Lundstrom. It went on to buy the rights of the Lundstroms' patent safety match-making process; then, after being unable to obtain sufficient quantities of these matches by importing them, it prepared to manufacture on its own account at Bow in London. The well laid-out and ventilated factory and the arrangements for the health and comfort of the workpeople received favourable comment in the report of the 1862 Royal Commission on the Employment of Children in Industry, while a deputation from the London United Workmen's Committee in 1898 learnt that during the previous twenty years only 47 cases of the industrial disease 'phossy-jaw' (phosphorous necrosis) had occurred there, of which over 80 per cent had been fully cured and the others well looked after by the company. In 1900 Bryant & May bought the patent rights of a non-toxic phosphorous, which it then began to use. It offered the process free to its British rivals in 1908, the year in which use of the harmful phosphorous was prohibited by Act of Parliament.

In 1861 Wilberforce, who had been educated at a Quaker school and joined his father's business in the mid 1850s, moved with his family to

A selection of Bryant & May labels from an 1883 catalogue (courtesy of Vesta Publications).

London, and was appointed factory manager of the newly built match works, at a salary of £300 a year. He was subsequently joined by his younger brothers Arthur Charles (1841-84), Frederick Carkeet (1843-88) and Theodore Henry (1843-1913), and all four became partners with their father in 1868, after which they strove to ease Francis May out of the business. In the years following William Bryant's death in 1874, May reluctantly consented to be bought out.

During the 1870s Wilberforce, now the senior partner, master-minded two important developments in Bryant & May. The first was a programme of mechanisation, both to meet the soaring demand for the patent safety matches and to reduce costs in the face of intensive import competition from lower-wage countries, including Sweden. This was followed by the introduction of new products such as wax vestas, mergers with some rival firms and a campaign of intensive advertising.

The second development was diversification into metal containers, both for its own products and for sale to outsiders. In 1877 the firm acquired the patent of the first effective method of printing on tin (the offset litho process) from the printers Barclay & Fry, and employed as manufacturing agents Huntley Boorne & Stevens of Reading, which already supplied it with metal match holders and cases. Huntley Boorne & Stevens thereafter manufactured, under licence, decorated tins for Huntley & Palmers, as well as colour-printed tea caddies and cocoa and other tins for a wide range of firms. However, the period until the patent expired in 1889 was marked by constant friction between the very astute and go-ahead Bryant brothers and the rather complacent Huntley Boorne & Stevens partners who failed to exploit the patent's opportunities to the Bryant brothers' satisfaction.

Its position consolidated by the innovations of the previous decade, Bryant & May during the early 1880s moved into export markets, notably Australia, New Zealand, India and the Far East. An agreement of 1883 with the Diamond Match Co of America, to sell safety matches there, was shortlived owing to the high tariffs in the United States. After the resignation and the death of Arthur Charles Bryant, in 1884 the firm became a limited company with a capital of £300,000 in preference shares and £100,000 debentures. A year later the debentures were paid off and a further £100,000 of preference shares issued at £10 premium. However, it came under criticism in the financial press because of the sparse information it gave in the annual reports and because of insider dealings which were alleged to be used to manipulate the share price.

Wilberforce Bryant was elected the first chairman, and under him the company became the major supplier of matches in Britain. He and the managing director Gilbert Bartholomew were those mainly involved when the match girls' strike broke out in 1888. Thanks to the mediation of the London Trades Council, within a fortnight they agreed to the abolition of the fines and deductions that had been the main grievance, welcomed the establishment of a trade union for the girls and provided them with a dining room. They also set up a girls' club to provide subsidised meals and facilities for recreation and reading, one of the first of its kind in industrial welfare. The Matchmakers' Union, then set up with 700 members, was the largest single all-womens' union in Britain; however, it soon languished, and after staging a wild-cat strike at Bow during 1902, over the introduction of further mechanisation, it was wound up in 1903.

By the 1890s Bryant & May was losing its predominant position in the British market. In 1893 it turned down a proposal by Diamond Match of America for a combination, and later refused to buy the rights in Britain of that company's continuous match-making machinery. Diamond Match therefore set up a British subsidiary and opened a factory at Liverpool, which heavily eroded Bryant & May's market share, notably in northern England. In 1901 the two British companies amalgamated, to combine Wilberforce Bryant's and Gilbert Bartholemew's expertise with the new American technology, whch was at last introduced into the factory at Bow. That merger permitted expansion through the acquisition of interests in match manufacturing in the dominions and South America. In 1903 a subsidiary of Bryant & May, the Match Agency Ltd, became British agents of the Swedish Combine Jonkoping & Vulcan Match Co, a move that helped to contain but did not halt the steady growth in match imports. Then in 1905 the main British manufacturers set up the British Match Makers' Association to fix prices and discounts and introduce a quota system for home output.

By then Wilberforce Bryant, although still chairman, was living in semi-retirement at Stoke Poges. He was a JP and High Sheriff for Bucks in 1892 and president of the local agricultural shows, held in the grounds of his residence Stoke Park, and the local horticultural society. While remaining on the register of the Society of Friends, he was by then a staunch churchman and patron of the Church of England Temperance Society. In politics he was a Conservative; his obituary records that he was fond of driving and an excellent whip, a keen gardener and amateur photographer.

In 1876 he married Margaret, daughter of William Lowson, DL of Perth, by whom he had a son who died in infancy, and three daughters. Through his wife he had another estate at Quarwood, Stow-on-the-Wold. Wilberforce Bryant died on 3 February 1906 and left £98,577 gross; he was the last member of the founding family in Bryant & May.

T A B CORLEY

Sources:

Unpublished

Friends House, London, Quaker records.

Wilkinson Sword Group Ltd, records of Bryant & May Ltd.

C Reg: Bryant & May Ltd (873,671).

Published

Annual Monitor 1907.

Burke's Landed Gentry 1906.

T A B Corley, 'Towards A History of Tin Printing - Some Further Signposts' *Journal of Printing Historical Society* 9 (1975).

Alec Davis, *Package & Print* (Faber, 1967).

—, 'Towards A History of Tin-Printing', *Journal of Printing Historical Society* 8 (1972).

Hakan Lindgren, *Corporate Growth. The Swedish Match Industry in Its Global Setting* (Stockholm: Liber Foreag, 1979).

PP, HC 1952–53 (161) XV, Monopolies Commission Report on the Supply and Export of Matches and the Supply of Match-Making Machinery.

Royal Album of Arts and Industries of Great Britain (1887).

Norbert C Solden, *Women in British Trade Unions 1874-1976* (Macmillan, 1978).

Slough Observer 10 Feb 1906.

The Link 1888.

Beryl Williams, *Quakers in Reigate 1655-1955* (Reigate: pp, 1980).

BUCKLAND, Lord Buckland of Bwlch
see BERRY, Henry Seymour

BUDD, Sir Cecil Lindsay

(1865-1945)

International metals dealer

Cecil Lindsay Budd was born at Vale Lodge, Leatherhead, Surrey, on 29 September 1865, the sixth child of Edward Budd (1815-86) and Antoinette née Sanderman (d 1922). His father inherited a partnership in Vivian & Sons, a Swansea-based copper smelting firm, and was a director of the London Assurance. Cecil was educated at Winchester College, and then completed his education by travelling on the Continent for a number of years.

In 1893 he became junior partner in the London copper trading firm of Vivian, Younger & Bond (VYB), a firm unconnected, by family at least, with Vivian & Sons of Swansea. Within a few years Budd proved himself a valued member of VYB and of the London Metal Exchange (LME) on which his firm traded. In 1896 he was elected to the board of the latter institution and in 1898, at the age of only thirty-three, was appointed chairman of VYB. Just four years later, in 1902, his growing professional stature was confirmed in his election as chairman of the LME, a post he held for twenty-six years. In the years before the First World War, Budd emerged as the 'chief architect of the fortunes of Vivian, Younger & Bond, and a leading figure in the development of the London Metal Exchange' {Harrison (1959) 31}.

As chairman of VYB, he immediately set out to expand the scope of the firm's activities and in 1898 initiated a joint promotion, with the leading German metals firm Metallgesellschaft, of the Australian Metal Co, VYB taking one-sixth of the issued shares. This new company established plant at the Broken Hill mines, in New South Wales, in order to process the extensive lead-zinc values still held in the waste-tips from former mining operations. However, by 1911, the Australian Metal Co ceased operations, due largely to technological problems, the risk to worker health from the dust-laden process and the eventual introduction of a superior method of extraction by a rival firm. This would appear to have been Budd's only significant business failure in this period and well before 1911 he took VYB into other areas of metals production and trading, with greater success.

In 1907 VYB obtained a stake in Malayan tin smelting, through the promotion of the Eastern Smelting Co Ltd which then purchased, from a Chinese concern, a smelter on the island of Penang. This marked a significant shift away from VYB's traditional concentration in the copper market and its move towards a position of growing importance in the British and Empire tin markets. Budd also attempted an entry into the European market for ferro-manganese and other iron alloys. This took the form of another venture in conjunction with Metallgesellschaft; together with the Rotterdam metal brokers W H Muller & Co, they established the Iron Ore Co Ltd. By 1914 the direct involvement of VYB in this firm had diminished somewhat, as Budd decided to concentrate in the Empire copper and tin trades, but nevertheless the London brokers retained the British and Empire agency for the sale of the ferro alloys marketed by the Iron Ore Co. Budd's increasing interest in the Empire tin trade was confirmed in 1913 with the purchase, by VYB, of the Cornish Tin Smelting Co of Redruth. By this date VYB was one of the leading tin brokers on the LME, as well as remaining one of its leading copper traders.

With the outbreak of war in 1914, Budd headed a delegation of London metal merchants who requested the Government to establish procedures for wartime metals trading and price-setting. Between the autumn of 1914 and early 1916 there appear to have been somewhat strained relations between Government and the members of the LME, with the operations of the latter being suspended on a number of occasions. During this difficult period, Budd emerged both as a trusted spokesman for the interests of the metal broking community and became regarded by government officials, and by Lloyd George, as a competent judge of the metal markets and a potential agent of official policy in that area. To this end, in December 1916, he was appointed to a number of committees of the Ministry of Munitions, having responsibility for strategic metal supplies. In October 1917 Budd was also appointed to the Non-ferrous Metals Committee of the newly-founded Ministry of Reconstruction. In 1918, in recognition of his contribution to the war effort, he was awarded the CBE, followed in 1919 by the KBE. The same year he was decorated further by the French Government, with the award of the Légion d'Honneur. This period was clouded, however, by the death in France of his eldest son Edward.

Following the end of the war, Budd realised there was an urgent need to re-organise the structure of the British and Empire metals trade. This largely arose because prior to 1914, the German Metallgesellschaft had come to control the larger part of Australian lead and zinc ore exports, shipping them to its Belgian and German refineries before sale in Europe and North America. With the outbreak of war, all Metallgesellschaft assets in the Empire had been seized and emergency arrangements made to produce lead and zinc at new refineries at Avonmouth, in Britain. After the autumn of 1918, Budd and other metal traders worked towards the setting up of some permanent arrangement to fill the vacuum left by the demise (if only temporary) of Metallgesellschaft. This led to the establishment, in November 1918, of the British Metal Corporation (BMC), with Sir Cecil Budd as its first chairman. Although there were expressions of government support for the venture, in the prevailing atmosphere of rapid de-control of the economy, there was negligible direct official support, despite some pressing questions raised both inside and outside the House of Commons.

Established with an initial capital of £5 million, raised in Britain and Australia, the BMC had offices in the same building as VYB, at Princes House, Gresham Street, London. Under Budd's able leadership the new corporation set out to promote the development of mining, smelting and metals trading throughout the Empire. Fears amongst members of the LME about the possible monopoly position of the BMC appear to have been allayed by Budd's position as chairman of both institutions and the high regard in which he was held by the London commodity traders.

In 1922 Cecil Budd's second son, John Cecil (b 1899) joined him as a director of VYB. The same year, VYB adopted limited liability status, with the entire capital of £150,000 being taken up by the BMC. Shortly after this, Sir Cecil Budd followed his father's example, entering into insurance broking, in partnership with W A Tennant, in the firm of Tennant & Budd.

Throughout the 1920s, Sir Cecil led the BMC through a phase of steady expansion, particularly in the area of tin smelting, following the lead set by VYB before 1914. This culminated, in December 1929, with the formation of Consolidated Tin Smelters Ltd, with an issued capital of £3.25 million, aimed at rationalising Cornish and Malayan output in a situation of falling world demand and prices. As a result of the policy, initiated by Budd, UK smelter output of tin, dominated by the new concern, fell from 58,000 tonnes in 1929 to 28,000 in 1932.

On 31 December 1928, Sir Cecil Budd retired as chairman of the LME. Within a year, on 31 December 1929, Budd also retired as chairman of both BMC and VYB, at the age of sixty-five. Thereafter, until his death, he served as an ordinary member of the boards of VYB and the Amalgamated Metal Corporation, which took over the activities of the BMC on 1 January 1930. For a number of years he continued to take an active interest in the problems of the metals market; in July 1929 he was appointed to the Iron and Steel Committee of the Economic Advisory Council, which reported in May 1930.

Cecil Budd's success derived from the dynamism of the London mining and commodity trading markets, and from his undoubted personal qualities of integrity, energy and shrewd business sense. He provides an example of a 'gifted amateur' who clearly came to master the complexities of an international market through the successive disruptions of war and depression.

Budd married twice: to Bloom née Tritton in 1892; after her death in 1904, to Muriel née Bevan in 1905 who outlived him, as did three sons and three daughters. Two of his sons, John Cecil and Richard Arthur, continued as directors of VYB after their father's death. Sir Cecil Lindsay Budd died on 27 December 1945, leaving £216,473 gross.

CHRISTOPHER J SCHMITZ

Sources:

Unpublished

BCe.

MCe.

PrC.

Published

Geoffrey Blainey, *The Rush that Never Ended: a History of Australian Mining* (2nd ed, Melbourne: Melbourne University Press, 1969).

Burke's Landed Gentry 1937.

Harry G Cordero and Leslie H Tarring, *Babylon to Birmingham: an Historical Survey of the Development of the World's Non-ferrous Metal and Iron and Steel Industries and of the Commerce in Metals since the Earliest Times* (Quin Press, 1960).

Economist 109 (1929), 110 (1930).

Economist Intelligence Unit, *The London Metal Exchange* (1958).

Robert Gibson-Jarvie, *The London Metal Exchange: a Commodity Market* (Cambridge: Woodhead-Faulkner for Metallgesellschaft AG, 1976).

Godfrey Harrison, *VYB. A Century of Metal Broking 1859-1959* (1959).

Susan Howson and Donald Winch, *The Economic Advisory Council, 1930-1939* (Cambridge: Cambridge University Press, 1977).

PD, 5th ser 110 (15 Oct-21 Nov 1918).

Walter E Skinner (ed), *Mining Year Book* (Skinner; Financial Times, 1949).

Times 28 Dec 1945.

WWW.

BULLOCK, William Edward

(1877-1968)

Motor car manufacturer

William Edward Bullock was born at Handsworth, Birmingham on 14 March 1877, the son of William Bullock, a smith, and his wife Beatrice Caroline née Barnett. Educated at Smethwick Technical School he became a toolmaker's assistant with the firm of Dennison & Wigley of Handsworth. His subsequent training included working for an electrical engineer and other toolmakers in the Birmingham area. About 1899 he became works manager of the recently formed Wigley-Mulliner Engineering Co. This firm expanded rapidly during the Boer War with munitions contracts (for which Bullock prepared gun carriage designs) and subsequently became the nucleus of the Coventry Ordnance Works. During Bullock's time with this firm, new machinery was rapidly introduced and labour relations deteriorated. Bullock moved to Coventry with his employer and remained there until 1909 when, at the age of thirty-two, he became works manager at Singer & Co. Two years earlier he was elected a member of the Institution of Mechanical Engineers.

The Singer company, established in Coventry in 1876 by George Singer, was one of the foundation firms of the Midlands cycle trade. It was a traditional engineering business with a strong sense of community. A works band was established in the early 1880s and the football team formed in 1883 was a predecessor of the city team. The firm grew rapidly in the 1890s when cycle demand was at a peak. After the collapse of the boom the firm experimented with motor cycles and added cars in 1904-5. These new developments were unprofitable and the company was reconstructed in 1903 and 1909.

When Bullock joined Singer in 1909 the firm had an authorised capital of £50,500 and employed 600 workers in a medium-sized plant in the centre of the city. Four car models were being made at this time: one 2 cylinder vehicle and three 4 cylinder cars ranging from 8 to 25 horsepower. The company became a pioneer in the production of an early light car, the Singer Ten, which made its appearance at the 1912 Motor Show. Bullock's role in the development of this vehicle is not known, but he must have been significant in providing the production facilities for its manufacture. By 1913 Singer was making 1,350 cars annually, a figure which placed the firm in the ten largest British motor manufacturers. The Singer Ten performed with great success in reliability trials and speed tests: one vehicle maintained an average speed of 62 mph for 24 hours on the Brooklands test track. The Singer light car design was followed by other manufacturers in 1912-14.

Singer produced some cars for the army during the First World War but the main emphasis of the works was on munitions production. After 1913 the company began to pay dividends to its shareholders, rising from 10 per cent in 1914 to 25 per cent in 1917. The authorized capital was increased to £101,000 in 1917 and to £500,000 in 1920. By 1919 Bullock

W E Bullock in front of a Singer 1919 10hp coupé — known more widely as a doctor's coupé (courtesy of Mrs M Jones).

was managing director of the company. Under the direction of 'WEB', as he was known in the factory, Singer expanded considerably in the 1920s. The firm made the transition from a small engineering-based manufacturing business to a medium-sized mass-producer during this decade.

Production facilities were expanded by acquisitions: Coventry Premier Co Ltd in 1920; Coventry Repetition Co in 1922; Sparkbrook Manufacturing Co in 1925; and the Calcott factory in 1926. By this time Singer was producing about 9,000 cars a year, a sizeable volume for the cramped and somewhat inefficient facilities being operated. Bullock introduced gravity conveyors for materials and an advanced enamelling plant for body parts. Many components were interchangeable between the two models then being built. In common with other traditional engineering motor firms a very high proportion of components was made in the Singer factories. During the 1920s Singer paid respectable dividends to shareholders and included bonuses in the years from 1924 to 1928.

Limited capacity, compared to British mass-producers like Austin and Morris, held back the company's expansion in the mid 1920s but Bullock prepared some ambitious plans for growth in 1927. The authorised capital was increased to £1 million in May 1927 and raised again to £1.5 million in September 1928. Much of the new investment capital went into the acquisition of a larger wartime factory of Daimler at Coventry Road, Small Heath, Birmingham. This was refurbished with new machinery and equipped with a travelling track assembly system. Assembly work was transferred from Coventry to the new plant. A final acquisition in 1928 was the Aster Engineering Works in Wembley which became the London service depot. This fresh investment raised Singer's production capacity to new levels. In 1929 the company produced an estimated 28,000 cars, about 15 per cent of national output. With 8,000 employees and seven factories covering 50 acres of floor space, Singer was the third largest British motor manufacturer.

W E Bullock presenting a Singer 1929 Senior Six model to Princess Alice of Athlone and Prince Arthur (courtesy of Mrs M Jones).

However this successful and rapid growth of the 1920s was not sustained in the next decade. Singer was unable to maintain its rank with the largest producers such as Austin and Morris which were joined by the Rootes Brothers, Standard, and the revitalised American concerns of Ford and Vauxhall. Singers' market share fell rapidly, dividends were paid only in 1931-32 and Bullock's leadership of the company was increasingly questioned. When a loss of £129,292 was reported at the annual general meeting in May 1936 there was heavy criticism from shareholders. One critic claimed that £13,000 invested in the company in 1927 would have been worth only £2,000 in 1936; a similar amount invested in Austin would have been worth as much as £400,000. Bullock was not re-elected to the board and shortly afterwards left the company. The company was re-organised in 1937 as Singer Motors Ltd with a reduced capital base. Ouput in 1938 amounted to no more than 9,000, and although the company retained its independence until 1955 (when it joined the Rootes Group), it never recovered the position achieved in the late 1920s.

William Bullock was 'of less than average height' and possessed 'a chin which was a caricaturist's delight' {Davison (1931) 41}. A vice-president of the Society of Motor Manufacturers and Traders, he was a personality of the motor trade in the 1920s. An energetic man, he was always at his office by 8 am, where he personally scanned the entire business mail of the company. Like many of the leaders of the motor industry of this period he was a man of many parts. While a production engineer by training, he was innovative in car design, especially in colour and appeal to the role of women in car buying. In this connection he advocated advertising. He fostered the introduction of the sliding head roof, backed early British experiments in fabric bodies and was one of the first car makers to offer safety glass, four-brakes, low pressure tyres and rear-mounted petrol tanks as standard equipment. Bullock was an early proponent of moving assembly lines, years ahead of Morris for example (but not Austin). He was the first British car manufacturer to employ an artist to design body work in his own exclusive studio. Bullock was interested in the export trade and an active supporter of the McKenna duties, first introduced on vehicle imports in 1915. The continued imposition of the duties, which protected British manufacturers from a flood of US and Canadian imports, was never absolutely secure in the 1920s. Bullock's support of the duties may have been motivated by a perception that the tariff benefited the economy as a whole, not merely the motor industry.

Singer's fall from high rank was perhaps due to Bullock's weakness in financial matters. Church has suggested that the firm was over-committed at the end of a major phase of the industry's growth and that the Small Heath plant was uneconomic for the production volumes reached. This was illustrated by the Singer 'Junior' model in 1926 and the short-lived 'Singer Industrial Motors' range of cars of 1929-32. As in so many business decisions the question of timing was critical. If the former Daimler factory had been bought by Singers three years earlier, the subsequent history of the British motor industry might have had a different shape, with the firm occupying a more dominant and secure position in 1929.

Bullock's interests outside the industry were largely limited to his garden although he was a member of the Coventry City Council in 1919. He was married three times: in 1902 to Nellie Elizabeth Parsons, daughter of Cornelius Parsons, a moulder (she died in 1934), by whom he had a son William Edmund, and a daughter Marjorie Beatrice Mary; in 1936 (the day after his resignation from Singers) to Mrs Margaret F Van Driest née Whynant, a divorcée and daughter of a veterinary surgeon; then (after he and his second wife divorced) to Mrs Parsons, widow of his first wife's brother. William Edmund (b 1902) was educated at Malvern College and joined his father at Singers, first as an apprentice, then as a production engineer (1925), assistant to the managing director (1928) and then as director and general manager (1932-36). William Edmund Bullock left Singers with his father in 1936 and joined Guy Motors, Wolverhampton as director and general manager, remaining until 1957; he then moved to W G Allen & Sons as deputy chairman.

After leaving Singers in 1936, Bullock worked with a Mr Aaron on the development of firepumps, but when the blitz began he left Coventry and spent the war years working on the Warwickshire farm belonging to his daughter and her husband, Aubrey Jones. After his third marriage he retired completely. William Edward Bullock died on 17 March 1968.

G T BLOOMFIELD

Sources

Unpublished

Autobiographical notes by W E Bullock in the possession of Mrs Aubrey Jones (subject's daughter); xerox in *DBB* files.

BULLOCK William Edward

BCe.

MCe.

DCe.

Information from William Edmund Bullock.

Published

Roy Church, *Herbert Austin: The British Motor Car Industry to 1941* (Europa, 1979).

Pauline L Cook (ed), *The Effects of Mergers. Six Studies* (Allen & Unwin, 1959).

Geoffrey S Davison, *At the Wheel. Impressions of the Leaders of Britain's Greatest Industry* (Industrial Transport Publications, 1931).

James Foreman-Peck, 'Tariff Protection and Economics of Scale: the British Motor Industry before 1939' *Oxford Economic Papers* 31 (1979).

George N Georgano (ed), *The Complete Encyclopaedia of Motorcars, 1885 to the Present* (3rd ed, Ebury Press, 1982).

—, *Complete Encyclopaedia of Commercial Vehicles* (Iola, Wisconsin: Kraus Publications, 1979).

Midland Daily Telegraph 27 May, 14 Sept 1936.

Kenneth Richardson, *Twentieth-Century Coventry* (Macmillan, 1972).

—, *The British Motor Industry, 1896-1939* (Macmillan, 1977).

Stock Exchange Year Book 1929.

'The Works of Singer and Company Ltd' *The Automobile Engineer* Mar 1926.

BULLOUGH, Sir George

(1870-1939)

Textile machinery manufacturer

George Bullough was born at Accrington on 28 February 1870, the eldest child of John Bullough (qv) who controlled Howard & Bullough, the textile machinery makers of Accrington, and Alice née Schmidlin. He went to Harrow, after which he undertook no further formal study. On the death of his father, in 1891, he became the head of the family firm.

By the terms of his father's will the firm was registered as a private limited company, with a capital of £500,000, divided into £100 shares; George inherited 50 per cent of the equity. He remained chairman of the firm until his death. During his lifetime Howard & Bullough remained the largest English producer of ring spinning frames, and until the late 1920s almost invariably declared dividends equal to or in excess of 10 per cent. The trading difficulties of the inter-war years witnessed the formation of a new merged company, Textile Machinery Makers, in which Howard & Bullough controlled 25 per cent of the capital, being second in importance to Platt Bros, which held 46 per cent. It appears that George Bullough was generally not involved in the daily management of the firm before or after the merger. Instead it was ably run by a small number of managers, primarily Alfred Hitchon, William Smith, E Horne and John Redman. However, Bullough was regularly informed of the firm's performance and took an interest in questions concerning general policy particularly in the inter-war years when his support was instrumental in effecting the merger.

During the First World War Bullough served on the Engineering Trades New Industries Committee and was chairman of the Textile Machinery sub-committee.

Bullough received a knighthood in 1901 for offering the Government his services during the Boer War, when he allowed his luxury yacht to be converted into a floating hospital. He pursued a brief military career in 1908-11, serving in the Scottish Horse Imperial Yeomanry, reaching the rank of captain; in the First World War he held the rank of major and was superintendent of the Remount Department before retiring in 1915. He received a baronetcy in 1916 for his services to the nation, after having publicly loaned £50,000 to the Government at no interest.

Bullough was a lifelong member of the Conservative Party and the Accrington branch (in which his father had been prominent) selected him as their Parliamentary candidate; although he initially accepted, he later rejected the invitation, since he preferred a more passive role. His political interests, like his business commitments, were secondary to his pursuit of social status. He was a leading member of both the Jockey Club and the National Hunt Committee, and one of his horses won the 'War' Grand National at Gatwick in 1917.

Bullough died suddenly on 26 July 1939, while on holiday in France. He was survived by his wife, Monica Lilly, the eldest daughter of the Fourth Marquis de la Pasture, whom he married in 1903, and a daughter, Hermione. He left an estate valued at £714,639 gross.

R M KIRK

Sources:

Unpublished

Lancashire RO, Platt-Saco-Lowell Archive.

PRO, Howard & Bullough company file, BT 31/5101/34346.

BCe.

Published

Accrington Observer 2 Mar 1891.

Accrington Observer and Times 12 Nov 1901, 30 Sept 1902, 29 July 1939.

Richard S Crossley, *Accrington Captains of Industry* (Accrington: Wardleworth, 1930).

Manchester Guardian 27 July 1939.

Times 27 July, 4 Aug 1939.

WWW.

BULLOUGH, John

(1837-1891)

Textile machinery manufacturer

John Bullough was born in Blackburn and baptised on 10 December 1837, the third son of James Bullough and his wife Martha née Mellor. James was employed at Hornbys & Kenworthy, cotton manufacturers, where in conjunction with W Kenworthy, he worked on the technical improvement of weaving machinery. When John was six his father entered into a short-lived partnership in a cotton mill, after which he owned and managed a cotton manufacturing firm. In 1856 James Bullough began a partnership with John Howard to organize the Globe Works, Accrington, which built textile machinery and employed approximately 150 persons.

John was educated at Queenwood College, Hampshire, and Glasgow University, where he registered for an Arts degree but never graduated. In 1859 he commenced work at his father's firm and began to familiarize himself with the technical details of production and design. The deaths of John Howard (1866) and James Bullough (1867) left him as the proprietor of the engineering enterprise which now employed over 300 and produced a full complement of cotton spinning machinery. The rapid expansion of the works, from 1880, was largely a result of the successful marketing of the ring frame. Bullough took a close interest in the management of the firm by supervising many technical improvements, the most important being improvements to flat carding engines and an electric stop motion, and by travelling widely to promote sales. Although Bullough was the sole owner of the firm, he devolved responsibility to a small number of efficient managers and salesmen, especially Edmund and Samuel Tweedale, Joseph Smalley (qv), Joseph Newton and Alfred Hitchon. The willingness of Bullough to allocate the duties of management both improved the internal efficiency of the firm and allowed him gradually to spend more time away from the works on his 32,000 acre estate, Castle

Meggernie, near Bridge of Balgie, Perth, which he purchased in 1883. By the time of his death (1891) Howard & Bullough employed nearly 2,000 workers and were the world's largest producers of ring spinning frames.

John played an active role in local politics as a Conservative. Because of his importance as an employer of labour, even his more intemperate comments received wide circulation. Three themes, all of which he emphatically upheld, recurred in his speeches: laissez-faire capitalism; self-help; and the Union with Ireland. In 1881 Bullough improved the provision of technical education in Accrington by opening a school at the works, teaching scientific and technical subjects; he also encouraged the Mechanics' Institute by donating money for the purchase of books.

John married Alice Schmidlin, daughter of a Swiss cotton manufacturer, in 1868; they had two children, George (qv) and Bertha (b 1872). After divorcing his first wife, he married in 1884, Miss Alexandra Marion McKenzie, daughter of a prominent Stornaway banker, by whom he also had two children, John and Gladys. John Bullough died on 25 February 1891, leaving an estate of £1,228,183 gross in the UK.

ROBERT KIRK

Writings:

Speeches and Letters ed Alec Bullough (3 vols, Manchester: pp, 1892).

Sources:

Unpublished

Lancashire R O, Platt-Saco-Lowell Archive; Parish Register, St John's Blackburn DRB/2/16; Will of John Bullough wLa/1/55.

PRO, Howard & Bullough company file, BT31 5101/34346.

A Hand, 'The Development of Technical Education in Accrington' (Certificate of Education Dissertation, Bolton Training College, 1963).

Published

Accrington Gazette 26 Feb 1921.

Accrington Observer 3 Oct 1888, 27 Feb, 2 Mar, 14 Mar 1891.

Accrington Times 15 Aug 1868, 8 May, 26 June 1880, 15 Mar 1884, 27 June 1885.

Richard S Crossley, *Accrington Captains of Industry* (Accrington: Wardleworth, 1930).

Textile Manufacturer 15 Mar 1891.

Textile Mercury 14, 21, 28 Mar 1891.

Textile Recorder 14 Mar 1891.

BULMER, Edward Frederick

(1865-1941)

Cider manufacturer

Edward F Bulmer ca 1935-40 (courtesy of the Hereford Cider Museum Trust).

Edward Frederick 'Fred' Bulmer was born at Credenhill, near Hereford, on 26 May 1865, the elder son of Rev Charles Henry Bulmer, Rector of Credenhill, whose family were wine merchants skilled in cidermaking, and of Mary Grace Parnel Cockrem, daughter of a Torquay newspaper proprietor.

Educated at Hereford Cathedral and Shrewsbury Schools, he won a classical exhibition to King's College, Cambridge, where he found widespread questioning of accepted Victorian ideas. He gained an honours degree in classics, a half blue for running and friends who would later invest money in his business.

In 1887 he helped his younger brother, Percy, to make cider commercially at Credenhill, and then in Hereford. In June 1889 he joined Percy on a permanent basis. Percy borrowed £1,760 on the security of his father's life insurance policy, bought land and in 1888 built a small factory in Ryelands Street, Hereford. The firm was now called H P Bulmer & Co.

Both young men did the hard manual work of cidermaking with one employee, but from the start Percy specialised in production, Fred on buying apples and on marketing. Each January he set off to tackle wine merchants in the Midlands and North where cider was then virtually unknown. After many rebuffs he built up a substantial trade in draught and bottled ciders. He also attacked the market by circularising landowners and professional men; friends and relatives helped by asking for Bulmers' cider at hotels, clubs and on the railways.

For thirty years Fred and Percy worked as close partners, pioneering modern methods of manufacture and improving control of fermentation. When in 1918 Percy was dying of cancer, the partnership was turned into a private company. After Percy's death in 1919 Fred became chairman and managing director. His style was highly personal; he opened all the firm's mail himself before breakfast and twice a day walked round every department. He had a sharp eye, a ready grasp of the essentials of a problem, and a great sense of humour and compassion. In 1938 with some of his own shares he formed a trust to provide family allowances before state allowances existed.

Under his guidance between 1919 and 1937 the annual sales increased from £79,000 to over £360,000. This period included the introduction of Bulmers' well-known Woodpecker brand which rapidly gained national distribution. In 1937, the firm's golden jubilee, he withdrew from day-to-day management, but remained chairman.

From 1898 Fred Bulmer found time for public work on Hereford City and County Councils, and was twice mayor of Hereford; in 1934 he became High Sheriff of the county. He was a local JP and chairman of the governors of the Girls' High School. In a speech as mayor in 1925 he said that business should be regarded primarily as a social service, rather than a means of personal gain.

He married in 1899 Sophie Fredericka Rittner, daughter of a Liverpool merchant, George Sebastian Rittner, who gave him great support and happiness, and bore him three sons and three daughters. He retired from the chairmanship of Bulmers in March 1941 and died on 2 September the same year, leaving £48,369 gross.

R H BULMER

Writings:

'The Evolution of Herefordshire Cyder' *Memorials of Old Herefordshire* ed Rev Compton Reade (George Allen & Sons, 1904).

'Rural England from Within' *Independent Review* 6 (Aug 1905).

Early Days of Cider Making (Hereford: pp, 1937).

Early Days of Cider Making with notes by R H Bulmer (Hereford: Hereford Cider Museum Trust, 1980).

Sources:

Unpublished

King's College Library, Cambridge, E F Bulmer and N Wedd, letters (1889-1939).

BCe.

MCe.

PrC.

Published

Annual Report of Council of King's College, Cambridge 1941.

R H Bulmer, 'E F Bulmer: a Man of Unique Capabilities' *Hereford Times* 9 June 1978.

Hereford Times 6, 13 Sept 1941.

Times 4 Sept 1941.

WWW.

BUNTING, John

(1839-1923)

Sharebroker and company director

John Bunting ca 1881 (from Souvenir of the Primitive Methodist Chapel and Schools, Henshaw Street, Oldham, *1909).*

Shares

WANTED, Central, Royton, Sun, Green-acres Borough, Westwood, and other shares. TO SELL Parkside, &c. All kinds of shares negotiated on reasonable terms.—J. BUNTING, 56, Newton-street.

An advertisement for shares from the Oldham Chronicle *14 August 1875.*

John Bunting was born at Carrington Field, Stockport, on 28 December 1839, the son of John Bunting and of Kerenhappuch née Hill. His father, a brickmaker, supplied bricks to the Stockport Railway Viaduct (completed across the Mersey in 1842) and then migrated to Crewe, where he became a leading builder of cottages and shops in the new railway town. The son attended a private school at Bunbury and then worked in his father's brickyard 1848-53. The sudden death of the older Bunting apparently required that his business be wound up and forced his widow to become a shopkeeper in order to earn her living. In 1853 the son left Crewe at the age of fourteen to make his fortune elsewhere: he went to Oldham, his mother's birthplace, and was apprenticed as a blacksmith. Through employment at two ironworks and at an engineering works he acquired a large practical knowledge of machinery.

In 1854 John Bunting joined the Primitive Methodists and soon became a Sunday School teacher and secretary. In 1868 he was made joint circuit steward, treasurer of the Benevolent Fund and one of the twenty trustees of Oldham Primitive Methodist Chapel. He became a leading promoter of the construction of Oldham's fourth and largest Primitive Methodist Chapel in Henshaw Street (1868-71). During the boom of 1873-75 he changed his trade from one of the oldest in the world to one of the newest: he began investing his savings in mill shares and then he became a sharebroker, first as a part-time dabbler and then as a full-time operator, publishing his first advertisement for shares in the *Oldham Chronicle* of 14 August 1875. He became a founder-member of the Lancashire Sharebrokers' Association formed in 1880 and, like David Chadwick (qv), established close links with a clientele of rich investors, especially in the business world of Oldham and Rochdale. His success as a sharebroker was the more remarkable because he did not drink and was therefore excluded from the taverns in which much share-dealing was undertaken. He maintained and extended his business and became the leading authority on mill shares, compiling a regular weekly survey of the share market, first for private circulation and then from 1879 for the local press.

In 1882 Bunting issued two-thirds of the shares of the Dowry Spinning Co and established links with the vendors of its land, the Oldham Estate Co, founded in 1874. By 1884 he had become wealthy and ambitious enough to project the flotation of a new ring spinning company, which proved abortive. In 1885 he marketed the shares of the Peel Spinning Co, which gave Bury its first modern cotton mill in 1887. In the boom of 1889-90 Bunting began a new career as a company-promoter and a company director, turning to advantage the knowledge gained as a sharebroker. He promoted three companies in Oldham (the Empire, Summervale and Neville) and two in Rochdale (the Eagle and Moss). Those five companies were all existing firms purchased from private owners so that their fixed costs remained low: all had large mills, averaging 96,000 spindles, and their productive capacity was increased by re-equipment with new machinery. In their flotation Bunting was supported by the advice of a mill manager, James Smith, and by the capital of a small coterie of tradesmen including William P Hartley (qv), the Aintree jam manufacturer and a fellow Primitive Methodist, and Hartley's son-in-law the Congregationalist, J S Higham (1857-1932), cotton spinner and manufacturer of Accrington. Two of the five companies did not issue balance-sheets and all passed their dividends during the depression of 1891-93, paying dividends only from 1894-95.

In 1898 Bunting floated the Times Mill Co Ltd of Middleton and made it into a great financial success by raising the ratio of loans (raised mostly from local shareholders) to shares, paying a first dividend of 39 per cent: in 1907 he built a second mill, raising the firm's spindleage to 264,000 and making it into the fifth largest spinning firm in Lancashire. From 1904 Bunting first ventured upon mill-building in Oldham, floating the Bell Mill in 1904 and then the nearby Iris Mill, which was built in the record time of forty days in 1907. From 1911 he developed a more exclusive approach to financial management, no longer publishing balance-sheets and using a very high ratio of loan to equity capital in order to raise the level of dividends: from 1912 his mills regularly paid dividends which were higher than average while one mill, the Iris, paid an average annual dividend of 86 per cent in the period 1912-20.

Bunting also became a 'company doctor' from 1911, rescuing enterprises in difficulty. Thus he enabled the Fox Mill, built in Oldham in 1907, to complete its equipment through the issue in 1911 of 12.5 per cent preference shares. The success of that issue led him to buy at public auction four Oldham mills floated earlier by contractors, the Glen (1902), Magnet (1902), Majestic (1903) and Laurel Mills (1905), and to rescue them from their parlous financial state by the issue in 1912-13 of preference shares. He also helped the Palm Mill (1884) of Oldham and the Irwell Bank Spinning Co (1892) of Farnworth out of difficulty through the issue of preference shares, so extending the range of financial techniques used by the cotton industry. In 1914 he established the Neva Mills Ltd (at Middleton) from the remaining mills of the Middleton & Tonge Spinning Co and so completed the construction of one of the earliest groups of mills in the cotton industry. The Bunting Group was not the first of its kind but it was one of the largest and the most successful. By 1916 John Bunting had become the biggest individual millowner in Lancashire and controlled, through separate companies united by the person of the chairman, twenty of the finest and most profitable mills. His companies mustered in the aggregate 2,347,068 spindles or four per cent of the capacity of the industry and nine per cent of the spindles of the Oldham, Rochdale and Middleton districts. 'No man was better known in the Lancashire cotton trade and no man played a bigger part in it during the last forty years' {*Oldham Standard* 24 Feb 1923}.

The postwar boom carried the group to the heights of its success. The first preference dividends were paid in 1918-19 on the four companies salvaged in 1912-13. The Textile Mill, Chadderton, was bought in 1919 from a private company formed in 1882 and paid a first dividend of 100 per cent on its ordinary shares. The average annual ordinary dividend paid by fourteen mills averaged 51 per cent in 1918-20 while unpublished dividends soared in 1920 to 600 per cent for the Times and to 800 per cent for the Bell. Such dividends evoked some unfavourable comment but also earned Bunting inclusion in the *Directory of Directors* for 1921. He sold his interest in the Irwell Bank Spinning Co in 1920 and made his last purchases in 1921, those of two small private firms in Oldham which combined weaving and spinning. His mills had paid an average dividend of 5.2 per cent in the period 1894-1911 against a general average of 5.9 per cent, but one of 22 per cent in the years 1912-20, or almost double the general average of 12 per cent. In the climactic year of 1920 an average dividend of 85 per cent was declared by fourteen of his mills.

The secret of his success was to maintain the confidence of investors. An active director and chairman, he had both technical and financial capacity, reinforced by energy, pertinacity and shrewdness. He secured more backing than any other millowner in the trade, since 4 per cent on loans in his mills was regarded as a gilt-edged investment, and he could often afford to pay only 3 per cent on loans. He appointed good managers and insisted that profits be made only at the mill, avoiding speculation in raw cotton and participation in the postwar recapitalization boom. He depreciated his machinery at a healthy rate of 6 per cent but paid out all profits in dividends and avoided accumulating reserves for the future. He paid his operatives well and was rarely afflicted by strikes. A true individualist, he remained a stubborn opponent of the Oldham Master Cotton Spinners' Association and of the Federation of Master Cotton Spinners' Associations: he would never join in any short-time movement and he worked his mills full-time until the depression of 1921.

A staunch Conservative and a devoted Primitive Methodist, he recognised the commercial shrewdness of his fellow 'Ranters' but believed that his church 'existed to make character, not merely to gather money' {*Oldham Evening Chronicle*, 26 Nov 1909}. He remained a lifelong adherent of the cause of temperance and supported the work of the Salvation Army in Oldham. He was reputed to work harder than any other man in the town and he certainly lived frugally, accumulating one of the largest fortunes of any Oldham cotton magnate or Primitive Methodist. He died at the age of eighty-three on 22 February 1923 after a tramcar accident, leaving his widow Sarah née Jackson, (daughter of James Jackson, a cotton spinner), whom he had married in 1871, one of the richest women in Lancashire. She however, left only £56,000 when she died at the age of eighty-three in 1928. It is not known what proportion of his wealth came from sharebroking and what proportion from dividends and fees but the gross value of his estate was £742,940.

Bunting's death was providential, occurring before depression in the cotton trade of Oldham became permanent. He had no true successors, though he was survived by one son and two daughters. James Henry Bunting (1874-1929) followed in his father's steps as a sharebroker but promoted four mills (1904-15) independently and entered into public life, unlike his father, becoming a town councillor (1904-10) and a magistrate in 1924. He recapitalized two of his mills in 1919-20 and became the heir to the nineteen directorships of his father, as well as the victim of the depression, leaving on his death an estate of only £14,958. His brother-in-law, William Cheetham (1869-1942) was the son of a sharebroker turned mill-manager: he worked his own way up from piecer to manager, married Eliza, Bunting's eldest daughter, and became in 1900 a trustee of the Henshaw Street Primitive Methodist Church. He became a director of eighteen mills of the group and left an estate of £109,880 gross.

D A FARNIE

Writings:

'Oldham Share Market: Weekly Report' *Oldham Chronicle* (Saturday's issues), 13 Dec 1879 — 31 July 1920.

Sources:

Unpublished

Manchester Central Library, Archives Department, Henshaw Street Primitive Methodist Church, Register of Baptisms, 1860-74; 1875-1919.

C Reg(w): Company files of the Empire Cotton Spinning Co Ltd (1889-1933), Summervale Mill Co Ltd (1890-1934), Neville Mill Co Ltd (1890-1932), Moss Spinning Co Ltd (1890-1935), and Eagle Spinning Co Ltd (1890).

BCe.

MCe.

Private information from H Horton and W H Chaloner.

F Jones, 'The Cotton Spinning Industry in the Oldham District from 1896 to 1914' (Manchester MA Econ, 1959).

Published

William H Chaloner, *The Social and Economic Development of Crewe 1780-1923* (Manchester: Manchester University Press, 1950).

Douglas A Farnie, 'The Emergence of Victorian Oldham as the Centre of the Cotton Spinning Industry' *Saddleworth Historical Society Bulletin* 12 (1982).

Manchester Guardian 23 Feb 1923.

Oldham Chronicle 26 Nov 1909, 14 Feb 1921, 2, 22, 26 Feb 1923, 31 Dec 1929, 7, 12, 26 Sept 1942.

Oldham Standard 20 July, 14 Sept 1907, 22, 26 Feb 1923.

Arthur S Peake, *The Life of Sir William Hartley* (Hodder, 1926).

Primitive Methodist Leader 1 Mar 1923.

Rochdale Observer 24 Feb 1923.

Souvenir of the Primitive Methodist Chapel and Schools, Henshaw Street, Oldham (Oldham: Fish, 1909).

W Tattersall, *Cotton Trade Circular* 1895-1923.

Textile Manufacturer 15 May, 15 June 1884.

Textile Mercury 24 Feb 1923.

William A Thomas, *The Provincial Stock Exchanges* (Cass, 1973).

Times 27 Feb, 28 Mar 1923.

White's *Directory of Cheshire* 1860.

Carl W von Wieser, *Der Finanzielle Aufbau der Englischen Industrie* (Jena: Fischer, 1919).

Worrall's *Directory of Oldham* 1875, 1880, 1884.

BURBIDGE, Sir Richard

(1847-1917)

Managing director of department store

Sir Richard Burbidge (courtesy of House of Fraser PLC).

Richard Burbidge was born at South Wraxall in Wiltshire on 2 March 1847, the fourth of nine sons and one daughter of George Burbidge, a farmer, and his wife Elizabeth née Clarke. He attended schools in Devizes for four years and spent a further two years at Spa Villa Academy in Melksham.

In 1861, when his father died, Burbidge was sent to London to learn the trade of grocer and provision merchant with Wiltshireman Jonathan Puckeridge at his shop in Oxford Street. After four years as apprentice and one as assistant, he left Puckeridge and opened his own wine and grocery business at 35-36 Upper George Street. In 1879, eager for a more exacting managerial position, Burbidge sold his shop, which had not been wholly successful, and joined the South Kensington Co-operative Stores. He remained sole owner of a small wine merchanting business until admitting his brother as a partner in 1881. In 1880 Burbidge joined the Army & Navy Provision Market Ltd in Regent Street and the following year moved to a position at the Army & Navy Auxiliary Supply in Westminster. In 1882 he was appointed manager of the provisions department at William Whiteley's (qv) Bayswater emporium where he learned about the operation of a large departmental store. In 1890 he moved to the West Kensington Stores but soon left when the firm fell into disrepute.

In 1889 Harrods stores of Knightsbridge was sold by Charles Digby Harrod to a limited liability company capitalised at £140,000. The shop was large and stocked a diverse range of goods but the business was not a high-class one. The new company was in financial difficulties when Burbidge was appointed general manager in March 1891. By this time Burbidge had worked in many of the most advanced retail businesses in

Harrods in 1901 (courtesy of House of Fraser PLC).

London. He was accustomed to trading on the new principle of ready money and quick returns, which had been the basis of Harrod's own success, and he was devoted to the idea of the large department store. Within three years he had been given a seat on the board and was appointed managing director in 1894. Burbidge worked hard and efficiently and his period of administration was one of continuous growth. Until the acquisition of the island site was completed in 1911 Burbidge negotiated for the purchase and redevelopment of adjoining premises at every opportunity. Between 1891 and 1917 the frontage was extended from 35 to 350 feet. The investment was funded by the establishment of Harrods Founders Shares Ltd in 1895. Burbidge's ambitions were not restricted to the Knightsbridge store. He also built a depository at Barnes in 1894, established Harrods Buenos Aires in 1913 and acquired Dickins & Jones of Regent Street in 1914.

Burbidge realised that Harrods had to attract a larger and better clientele in order to support the store's growth. He introduced new departments and services. By 1894 a theatre ticket agency, a restaurant and a hairdressing salon had been opened and the store was operating one of London's first twenty-four hour telephone services. Burbidge was also convinced of the value of good advertising. He introduced the circulation of the comprehensive illustrated catalogue and, in 1894, took his first full page advertisement in the *Telegraph*. The quality of Harrods' promotional events improved as Burbidge began to use more aggressive American techniques after a visit to Macys of New York in 1904 and the opening of Gordon Selfridge's (qv) new London store in 1909. The hire of special shopping trains to bring in country customers and the staging of exhibitions in the store were amongst the many new devices employed. By 1913 Harrods had abandoned its co-operative image and had assumed a new exclusiveness which was reflected in the award of its first Royal Warrant. The results of Burbidge's efforts were remarkable. Between 1891 and 1913 annual profits rose from £16,071 to £309,227 and the number of staff increased from 200 to 6,000.

Burbidge recognised that good conditions of work were a pre-requisite of an efficient workforce. In his first year as general manager he abolished lateness fines and introduced early closing, cost price meals and a provident fund for the lower grades. He continued to reduce hours of work in later years and as a trustee of the Early Closing Movement he spoke before several Parliamentary Committees on shop work. He was also committed to staff training and re-organised the managerial structure within the store in order to improve both performance and promotional opportunities. In 1905 he opened an athletics club at Barnes and a few years later introduced a pension scheme for managers. In his will Burbidge made generous provision for a staff benefit fund. These were progressive measures pre-dating statutory requirements.

In 1901 Burbidge bought Littleton Park, an 11,000 acre estate near Shepperton, which already supplied the store's food halls with fresh produce. He continued to work in London where he maintained a residence. Besides the managing directorship of Harrods London and Harrods Buenos Aires, Burbidge was also chairman of the Hudson Bay Co of Canada.

Outside business he performed many public services. He was a JP for the County of London, a member of the Committee on Post Office Wages, honorary treasurer of the Tariff Commission (which he strongly supported), trustee of the Crystal Palace and president of the Society of Wiltshiremen in London. He also acted for many military organisations. During the Boer War Burbidge equipped the City Imperial Volunteers and afterwards supported the development of the Territorial Movement. He was chairman of the Royal Aircraft Factory and Invalid Kitchens Committees and a member of the Munitions Advisory Committee, the Board of Control for Regimental Institutes, Queen Alexandra's Field Force Fund Committee and many others. During the First World War Harrods supplied a hospital at the Western Front and goods to the troops and encouraged staff to join up. In 1916 2,000 were on war service. For this work Burbidge was awarded a baronetcy in 1916.

Burbidge, a committed Anglican, was a benefactor of Littleton parish church (where he built a family vault). In 1868 Burbidge married Emily Woodman of Melksham, Wiltshire, by whom he had two sons and four daughters. His first wife died in 1905, and in 1910 he married Lilian Preece of Herefordshire; they had no children. Sir Richard Burbidge died on 31 May 1917 at his London residence, Hans Mansions, leaving £186,262 gross; besides the Manor of Littleton, he owned 1,500 acres in Middlesex, property in Canada and 52,000 acres in Western Australia. He was succeeded as managing director of Harrods Stores by his son, Woodman Burbidge.

ALISON TURTON

Writings:

PP, Report of Committee on Royal Aircraft Factory (1916) Cd 8191.

BLPES, Tariff Commission papers, TC3 1/301 (evidence to the Commission).

Sources:

Unpublished

Glasgow University, House of Fraser Archive HF 6/14/1, correspondence relating to the appointment of Richard Burbidge to the Army and Navy Auxiliary Supply Ltd, 1880-1882.

—, House of Fraser Archive HF 9/1/1 — 9/1/5, Harrods Stores Ltd, minutes, 1890-1921.

—, House of Fraser Archive HF 9/7/2, Harrods Stores Ltd, annual reports, 1890-1917.

BCe.

Gilbert Frankau, 'Great Store' (nd), unpublished history of Harrods, Harrods Archive 1/44, Harrods, Knightsbridge, London.

Published

In Memoriam: Sir Richard Burbidge Bart (1917) (Harrods, 1917).

Mrs Stuart Menzies, *Modern Men of Mark* (Herbert Jenkins, 1921).

PP, Departmental Committee on the Truck Acts (1908) Cd 4442, 4443, 4444 and (1909) Cd 4568.

PP, First Report of the Committee on the War Organisation of the Wholesale and Retail Distributing Trades in Scotland with reference to Enlistment and other National Services 1914-16 (1915) Cd 7987.

Times 2 June 1917.

WWW.

BURMAN, Sir Stephen France

(1904-)

Manufacturer of motor vehicle and specialist engineering components

Stephen France Burman was born at Edgbaston, Birmingham, on 27 December 1904, the son of Henry Burman and his wife Marion Isobel née France. In 1888 Henry Burman with his brother Thomas had joined their

Sir Stephen F Burman (courtesy of Sir S F Burman).

father, William Burman, on the dissolution of the latter's partnership with T L Phipps, in William's implement manufacturing business. To the range of rakes, hooks, scrapers and other implements was added a power-operated horse-clipper, which remained an important product for a long period, finally being phased out in the 1950s. The firm, employing about 50 people, entered the field of automotive engineering in 1913, when the bankrupt Illston concern was acquired and motorcycle gear-box manufacture began.

After education at Oundle, to which he won a scholarship, Stephen Burman joined the family firm in 1923, serving a five year mechanical engineering apprenticeship. During the 1920s the firm supplied gearboxes to most major motor cycle manufacturers. In 1928 Burman joined the firm's management and in the slump of 1931-32 played a major part in the 'ruthless pruning' {Burman (1966) 261}, which reduced the business by 75 per cent, and reinvestment which provided the basis for new product lines. In 1931 he negotiated the purchase and application of the Douglas patent for the production of phosphor bronze nut and worm steering gears for cars. Initially these were supplied to Singer & Co and later to Fords. The decision to move from motorcycle gearbox to car steering gear manufacture was taken in the belief that the latter was an 'open' market, whereas any move into car gearbox production would have encountered strong resistance. Similar market appraisal lay behind Burman's move into oil pump production in the 1940s: in this case the first customer was the Austin Motor Co, to which pumps were supplied at a cost 40 per cent below Longbridge production costs.

Despite heavy commitments elsewhere, Burman continued to manage his own firm until he retired in 1969. Steering gear designs were improved with the introduction of recirculating ball units, half nut for cars and full nut units for commercial vehicles. In 1957 the production of power steering units for Jaguar commenced. Heavy vehicle companies supplied with steering gear by Burmans included Massey-Ferguson. Between 1932 and 1960 the firm's turnover rose from £100,000 to over £5 million and its workforce from 100 to 1,500. Until 1955 Burman & Sons Ltd was a private company. In that year it was sold to the industrial holding company, Vono Industrial Products Ltd, which changed its name in 1956 to Duport Ltd. In 1978 Duport, to finance its investment programme, sold Burmans to the Adwest Group.

Burman embarked on a demanding period of public service in 1944 when he became a governor of the Birmingham Children's Hospital. This led in 1948 to the chairmanship of the United Birmingham Hospitals Board set up under the newly formed National Health Service. As the chairman of a group of teaching hospitals he became a member of the Council of Birmingham University in 1949 and was Pro-Chancellor of Birmingham University, 1955-66. He was also involved in planning for the new universities of Aston and Warwick.

Burman served as General Commissioner for Income Tax, 1950-68, and on the Royal Commission on the Civil Service, 1953-56. He was chairman of the Birmingham and District Advisory Committee for Industry 1947-49, and a member of the Midland Regional Board for Industry 1949-65, and later its vice-chairman, 1951-65. In 1950-51 Burman was president of the Birmingham Chamber of Commerce, which he tried unsuccessfully to merge with the FBI's local organisation. Contacts here and on the Midlands Electricity Board (of which he was a member, 1948-65) with leading Midlands industrialists resulted in his election as a director of several major companies. In 1951 he joined Averys' board, in 1952 Lucas's, and in 1953 ICI's. He was also a director of Imperial Metal Industries Ltd, 1962-75, and the valedictory address by Sir Michael Clapham when Burman retired from that directorship made clear the value of his contribution to the boards and public bodies on which he sat. Burman's own views on management are clearly set out in his contribution to *The Accounting Field* (1954).

Burman was awarded the MBE in 1943, the CBE in 1954 and was knighted in 1973. He married Joan Margaret Rogers, daughter of John Henry Rogers, a chartered accountant, in 1931; there were two sons of the marriage.

RICHARD A STOREY *and* ALISTAIR G TOUGH

Writings:

'Management - the Director's Viewpoint' in D Cousins (ed), *The Accounting Field* (English Universities Press, 1954).

'Design, Manufacture, and Marketing of Specialist Engineering Components' in Ronald S Edwards and Harry Townsend (eds), *Business Growth* (Macmillan, 1966).

Sources:

Unpublished

BCe.

MCe.

Interview with Sir Stephen Burman.

Published

Thomas Burman, *Short History of Burman & Sons Ltd* (pp, 1944).

Kelly's Directory for Birmingham.

WW 1982.

BURNEY, Sir Charles Dennistoun

(1888-1968)

Promoter of the airship

Charles Dennis Burney (he assumed the name of Dennistoun around 1918) was born in Bermuda on 28 December 1888, the only son of Admiral Jellicoe's second-in-command at the battle of Jutland, Admiral Sir Cecil Burney. His father was created a baronet in 1921 and Dennistoun inherited the title in 1929. His mother was Lucinda Marion, second daughter of George R Burnett.

Burney appears to have entered the Navy in the normal way and by 1909-10 was serving aboard the destroyers *Afridi* and *Crusader*. In the meantime his father had become chairman of the Anti-Submarine Committee under the very active first sea lord, Admiral 'Jacky' Fisher. The *Crusader* was assigned to the Committee. Young Burney very much enjoyed this experimental work and especially towing explosives to deter submarines. On one occasion he went up in a new-fangled aeroplane to locate a sunken submarine. So intrigued was he by this experience that he went on half pay in 1911 to pursue research at Sir George White's (qv) Bristol Aviation Works. On each of his next two appointments, to the battleship *Venerable* and to the cruiser *Black Prince*, he only reported in order to apply once more to be placed upon half pay and then to return to Bristol. In August 1912, however, upon being selected for the gunnery course at HMS *Excellent*, he reported for duty, and when a year later he completed the work, he went on to HMS *President* to do experimental work in anti-submarine defence and seaplane construction. One of the earliest known of his writings was an article in the then secret and recently founded *Naval Review* of May 1913 on the future role of aircraft in naval warfare. In conjunction with Bristols and at his own expense, he built a seaplane at Pembroke Dock and tested it for carrying wireless.

The outbreak of war ended this work. Burney was given command of the destroyer *Velox* on Channel patrol but his connections and abilities persuaded the C-in-C Portsmouth to let him, while still in command of the *Velox*, engage in experiments which led to the development of the first successful paravane, a torpedo-shaped float towed submerged from a ship's bow and able to cut mine moorings. Following successful trials, the Admiralty ordered paravanes and transferred Burney to HMS *Vernon* in 1915, to establish the paravane department and supervise the fitting of this protective cutter to all naval vessels. A similar device was developed for merchant ships. Both devices probably saved some 50 warships and 40 merchantmen during the First World War. For his work, the Royal Commission on Awards to Inventors in 1920 gave Burney credit, but as he had been allowed to patent the devices and with Sir Stanley White (1882-1964) had reaped the huge sum of £350,000 in royalties, no monetary grant was made. In the meantime, in 1917 while still a lieutenant, he had been made a CMG. He retired in 1920 as a lieutenant-commander and was promoted to commander on the retired list on reaching the age of forty in 1928.

In 1922 Burney was elected Conservative MP for Uxbridge, a constituency he served until 1929 and one which gave him a suitable platform for his next venture: a rigid airship service to the ends of the Empire and across the North Atlantic. The idea was not new, for Vickers had tried to emulate the success of Germany's Zeppelins as early as 1911 and two years later, under the influence of Trevor Dawson (qv), had set up an Airship Department which set out to build transatlantic airships after the war. Burney's scheme was a renewed initiative in this campaign to sell the airship as an inter-continental form of transport. Technically feasible, the scheme was delayed by political and economic difficulties and the complexity of Burney's legal arrangements, which separated government subsidies from a construction company, so that overseas sales would be unhampered. In addition the Admiralty used the airship debate as a means of preserving control of naval aviation against the wishes of the Air Ministry. The creation of the private Imperial Airways in 1924 caused the new Labour Government to split Burney's proposal into rival capitalist and socialist experimental ships, the former, *R-100*, built by Vickers and the latter, *R-101*, by the Royal Airship Works at Cardington. Burney himself worked closely with Vickers, Zeppelin and Goodyear, and was Vickers' representative on the acceptance flight of *R-100*, designed by Barnes Wallis (1887-1979), to Montreal and back in 1930. In fact Burney in the airship campaign was as much as anything the financial frontman and political liaison representative for Vickers. The project failed partly because of the disastrous crash of *R-101* in 1930 and partly because the technological revolution in aviation gave the aeroplane the edge over the airship. For *R-100* Vickers received the fixed price of £350,000, leaving the firm with a loss of £220,000.

Burney also patented a method for erecting concrete homes in the 1920s. In 1930 he designed the Burney Streamlined Motor Car, which was produced in limited numbers, the Prince of Wales buying one of these expensive automobiles.

Burney then lived quietly at Carlton House Terrace, SW1, surrounded by paintings, photographs, and parts, memorabilia of his previous achievements. He was still sure that aviation was going to be important at sea and he spent considerable time trying to perfect a means of launching torpedoes from a higher altitude than was then possible. Trials with live winged weapons carried on into the war years. He also worked on improving fishing trawlers.

In the 1950s he became interested in the possibilities of transporting methane gas to the UK for heating and other uses and to this end he helped design and develop ships which could carry liquid menthane in tanks both below and above decks, an idea which came to fruition in the 1960s.

In the 1930s and later he maintained a home at Baynards Park, Cranleigh, Surrey; in 1950 he had residences in Southern Rhodesia and at Camberley, Surrey; later he moved to Bracknell, Berkshire. In London he belonged to the Marlborough-Windham Club. He lived well, as a naval officer and gentleman should, if quietly, and he enjoyed tennis on his own court.

Burney married Gladys, the younger daughter of George Henry High of Lake Shore Drive, Chicago, USA; they had one son, Cecil Denniston (b 1923). Sir Dennistoun Burney died at Hamilton, Bermuda on 11 November 1968.

ROBIN HIGHAM

Writings:

letter on Imperial airship scheme *Times* 21 July 1922.

letter on Royal Navy's relations with RAF *ibid* 18 Aug 1922.

letters on Burney airship scheme *ibid* 11 and 15 Mar 1924.

letter on allowance for suspension of season tickets *ibid* 2 Dec 1924.

letter on airship policy *ibid* 25 Feb 1925.

article 'The Pre-facto System' on concrete houses *Times Housing Supplement* 7 Apr 1925.

The World, the Air, and the Future (Alfred A Knopf, 1929).

letter on airship and sea-liner *Times* 4 Sept 1930.

letter on war debts and reparations *ibid* 3 June 1932.

Sources:

Unpublished

PrC.

Richard P T Davenport-Hines 'The British Armaments Industry during disarmament 1918-36' (Cambridge PhD, 1979).

Personal knowledge.

Published

DNB.

Robin Higham, *The British Rigid Airship, 1908-1931: a Study in Weapons Policy* (G T Foulis, 1961).

Arthur Marder, *From the Dreadnought to Scapa Flow, II* (Oxford University Press, 1965).

The Times 14 Nov 1968.

WWMP.

WWW.

BURNHAM, 1st Lord
see LAWSON, Edward

BURR, Arthur

(1849-1919)

Developer of the Kent coalfield

Arthur Burr was born at Canonbury, Islington, London, on 4 June 1849, the son of William Burr, a merchant, and his wife Ellen née Crook. Nothing is known of his early life before 1870, when with his brother William Alfred Burr, he started trading as Burrs & Co, metal brokers and merchants, from premises in Gracechurch Street, London. The undertaking terminated four years later in what was to be the first of Burr's five bankruptcies, when the company became insolvent with the collapse of E B and A T Pitchford of the Island Lead Works, Limehouse. His four subsequent bankruptcies resulted from a series of highly speculative ventures: as a colliery proprietor in North Wales (1880), as a land agent operating particularly in the Lingfield-East Grinstead area (1891), and twice in connection with the Kent coalfield (1898 and 1917). As an undischarged bankrupt, Burr in the 1880s and 1890s deliberately avoided keeping regular sets of business records and accounts, and often operated through third parties such as his stockbroker brother-in-law, Henry Thomas Potter, or various female relatives.

With Potter's assistance Burr made his first entry into the Kent coalfield, when in 1896 he attempted to sink a colliery at Dover, on the site of the suspended Channel Tunnel workings, where coal had been discovered in a deep boring six years earlier. Although Burr had no financial resources of his own to devote to this, or subsequent, Kent undertakings, he possessed a remarkable ability to raise funds from thousands of small-scale investors, who were attracted by the prospects of a coalfield close to the growing South-Eastern and Continental markets. Because at this stage no coal had been proved to exist beyond the Dover boring, it was not altogether surprising that large industrial and financial investors regarded Kent as being too risky for their capital. Their judgement seemed to be confirmed by Burr's failure to sink his colliery through what proved to be heavily waterlogged strata. This venture resulted in both Burr's fourth bankruptcy (1898) and his removal from office by the shareholders because of his implication in bogus share sales.

Burr was not deterred by this setback, and in 1904 he embarked upon his grand design to prove and develop the Kent coalfield. The plan entailed the formation of a number of interrelated limited liability companies known as the Kent Coal Concessions group. Its purposes were to try to acquire, by purchase or lease, a monopoly of mineral rights in areas to the north of Dover; to initiate borings to prove the coal under these areas; and to promote subsidiary companies to sink collieries, or to sell sections of the proved areas to other investors wishing to establish collieries. In this way the profits from organising the colliery companies and from the general development of the coalfield would accrue not to local landowners, but to Burr and those who had risked their capital. Burr later added to his scheme the formation of the East Kent Light Railway, an electric power company and the building of three garden villages to house the miners. His method of financing this risky long-term venture, in what was as yet an unproved and completely concealed coalfield, was somewhat ingenious: four separate companies were formed to acquire the mineral rights; some of the expensive exploratory boring was then entrusted to a subsidiary company, which was to receive payment only when it proved the existence of coal; and a third set of companies was formed to sink and equip the collieries. In this way Burr hoped to attract risk capital in stages without diluting the profit prospects of those who had invested earlier. The scheme received approval from such a well-informed contemporary observer of the coal industry as H Stanley Jevons.

By the end of 1913 the Concessions companies had raised some £1.5 million from investors, of which nearly half was for sinking and equipping the group's three main collieries. Although, according to Burr, this capital enabled the mineral companies to gain control of some three-fifths of the 150 square miles of proved coalfield (excluding under-sea areas), it was not sufficient to give the three main colliery developments more than a hand-to-mouth existence. Serious underground water problems caused delays and difficulties in sinking operations, and raised development costs well above the original estimates. Even when two of these collieries commenced production in 1913 the hoped-for success was short-lived. Further water problems in the 1,500 foot-deep workings raised operation costs above expectation, while the coal proved to be unsuitable for what would have been the lucrative household market of South-East England. Nevertheless, in 1913 Burr received the freedom of Dover in recognition of his services to the borough in developing the coalfield.

The Concessions companies were not a success from the investor's point of view and, starting in 1914, Burr was progressively removed from office by dissatisfied shareholders. He was subsequently declared bankrupt on account of funds owed to one of his companies. At his death, six legal actions against him remained undecided.

Through the Concessions group Burr had put down boreholes, found coal and spent money far in excess of any other entrepreneur. The result had been two collieries that fell into receivership, four uncompleted collieries that fell into decay, a virtually useless 16 miles of railways, and thirteen financially impotent companies. As a catalogue of failure it could hardly be more complete. Without Burr, the coalfield might have been developed to a much greater extent; it is equally possible that there might never have been a working coalfield at all.

Little is known of Burr's family life other than that he had a son Malcolm (1878-1954), who trained as a mining engineer and ably supported his father. Arthur Burr died in Hampstead on 29 August 1919 after a long illness which prevented him from attending his final bankruptcy hearing. In the next decade the Kent coalfield was acquired and developed by large industrial investors.

WALFORD JOHNSON

Sources:

Unpublished

BCe.

DCe.

Information from Dr Clive G Down.

W Johnson, 'The Development of the Kent Coalfield, 1896-1946' (Kent PhD, 1972).

Published

Colliery Guardian 1 Mar 1901.

Herbert Stanley Jevons, *The British Coal Trade* (1915 ed, repr Newton Abbot: David & Charles, 1969).

Mining Magazine Nov 1913.

Arthur E Ritchie, *The Kent Coalfield: Its Evolution and Development (The Iron and Coal Trades Review,* 1919).

Times 31 May 1873, 19, 20 Jan, 26 Mar, 20 Apr, 7 Nov 1874, 13 Nov 1891, 29 Jan 1892, 1 May 1897, 24 Feb, 30 June 1899, 8 Feb 1901, 21 Oct 1904, 23 Feb 1907, 30 Nov, 21 Dec 1911, 6 June 1913, 27 Mar, 2 Sept 1919, 15 July 1954.

BURRELL, Charles

(1817-1906)

Traction engine and agricultural machinery manufacturer

Charles Burrell was born at Thetford, Norfolk in 1817, the son of James Burrell, owner of a small agricultural engineering business at Thetford

Charles Burrell (courtesy of the Institute of Agricultural History, Reading).

founded in turn by his father, Joseph Burrell, in 1770. When James Burrell died in 1836, Charles found himself head of the concern at the tender age of nineteen, a position he was to occupy until his retirement in 1900.

In 1836 the firm was producing mostly simple agricultural implements, abetted by the usual local trade in constructional ironwork. However during the 1840s Burrell turned his mechanical bent to the two pieces of equipment that came to epitomise British agricultural engineering achievement. In 1848 Burrell exhibited the first-ever combined steam driven thrashing machine, capable of both thrashing and finishing the grain; three years earlier the firm were among the pioneer producers of the portable steam engine. In neither instance did Burrell go ahead to exploit fully in commmercial terms his pioneering technical work, as other engine and thrasher producers, such as Claytons and Ransomes, most certainly did. Instead Burrell turned his technical interests towards self-moving steam engines, and in 1856 the firm produced the first-ever heavy duty steam road haulage engine.

From the 1860s onwards, self-moving steam engines became the firm's speciality, particularly traction engines, road locomotives, ploughing engines and showman's engines. Overseas customers included the Governments of Russia, France, Turkey, Egypt, Peru, Venezuela and Hungary. Yet even in this specialised area Burrells could not rival the output of R H Fowler (qv) or T L Aveling (qv). During the period 1867-1904, Burrells built about 2,300 engines, mostly self-moving, compared to about 10,000 Fowler engines during the same period. It seems that Charles Burrell's main commitment was to technology rather than commerce. His firm relied on the custom building of specially tailored machines with their own idiosyncracies and variations in design.

Burrells seem to have suffered worse than some of their competitors from the slump in the agricultural engineering trade in the mid 1880s. They did survive however, helped by the capital raised in the formation of two private limited companies. In 1884 Charles Burrell & Sons Ltd was formed, with a nominal capital of £100,000, to handle the firm's principal business, while in 1887 Burrells Hiring Co Ltd was created to handle hire-purchase sales of their engines. Charles Burrell finally retired in 1900, leaving his son, Charles, in charge of the firm, with the assistance of two other sons, Robert and Frederick. His fourth son, William, became a solicitor.

Burrell died a few years later on 28 June, 1906, leaving a very modest estate of £13,500. Most of Burrell's activities were devoted to the family business, so that he took little part in public life. Burrell's successors were never able to counteract his baneful influence and the firm fell into a precipitous decline in the 1920s, blinded as ever by the prestige of their own technology.

DAVID C PHILLIPS

Sources:

Unpublished

PrC.

Published

Ronald H Clark, *Chronicles of a Country Works* (Percival Marshall, 1952).

The Engineer 102 (1906).

The Implement and Machinery Review 32 (1906-7).

Sir George M Burt (courtesy of John Mowlem & Co Ltd).

BURT, Sir George Mowlem

(1884-1964)

Civil engineer and building contractor

George Mowlem Burt was born in Grosvenor Road, Westminster on 10 January 1884, the son of George Burt (1851-1919), a contractor, and Emily Stewart née Arbon. His paternal grandfather was George Burt (1816-94), a nephew and partner of John Mowlem (1788-1868), the founder of John Mowlem & Co Ltd, builders and contractors. The business was incorporated in 1903 and converted into a private company in 1908, though the firm started trading as builders in Marylebone in 1822.

George M Burt attended Clifton College and then in 1902 joined the family firm, entering the joiner's shop in the firm's Millbank depot as an apprentice. He received his practical training under Sir George Humphries MICE and Harold Jones. His first supervisory position came in 1906 when he was assistant foreman and timekeeper on the construction of the Admiralty Block and Admiralty Arch, part of the National Memorial to Queen Victoria, contracts worth over £160,000 to the firm. In 1913 he joined the board of John Mowlem & Co Ltd and over the next seven years handled projects which included the diversion of the low-level sewer at Millbank for the London County Council. After the demise of his uncle, Sir John Mowlem Burt (1845-1918), George Burt became supervising director in full charge of all engineering and building contracts. In 1925 the firm became a public company with an authorised capital of £500,000 and an issued capital of £350,000 (£30,000 in £100 preference shares and the rest in £1 ordinary shares). Profits in 1920-25 allowed the payment of a dividend of 7.5 per cent, free of income tax, in addition to the 4.5 per cent fixed dividend on the preference shares and in 1925 the firm's reserve fund stood at £75,000.

Under George Burt the firm's turnover showed a marked upward movement, averaging £1.53 million per annum in the 1920s and £3.47 million in the 1930s. Maintenance contracts, for the Office of Works and the Port of London Authority, and the contract for ICI's headquarters at Millbank (£1.6 million) figured among the largest jobs in the 1920s; in the 1930s large projects like the Southampton Graving Dock for the Southern Railway and the larger maintenance contracts were augmented by rearmament work, the biggest rearmament contract being that for the Royal Ordnance Factory at Swynnerton in 1939-42, worth £4 million. This upward turnover trend continued during the Second World War when Mowlems won nearly £29 million worth of contracts, 1940-45 inclusive, the most valuable jobs being runways for the Air Ministry, Phoenix units for the Mulberry Harbours and various government tunnelling contracts.

During the Second World War George Burt served on a number of crucial government committees and missions concerned with building and contracting including the Ministry of Health Central Housing Advisory Committee; the Central Council for Works and Buildings (Ministry of Works), appointed to report on the Placing and Management of Building Contracts, chaired by Sir Ernest Simon, in 1944; the mission under Viscount Portal (qv) which went to America in 1942 to study building methods; and the Inter Departmental Committee on Alternative Forms of House Construction, of which Burt himself was chairman. After the war he served on other committees concerned with industry: the Working Party on Building Operations (Ministry of Works) in 1948, and the National Consultative Council and the Plant Advisory Committee, both reporting to the Minister of Works. For these services Burt was knighted in 1942 and created KBE in 1955.

In the post-war reconstruction period, Sir George Burt moved his firm into more complex projects including the power station at Braehead near Glasgow (a £2.39 million contract in 1946) and the foundations for the Shellhaven refinery (a £3.66 million project in 1948). Over the period 1946-51 the firm's contracts averaged £9 million per annum. This fell to £6.97 million, 1952-64. In the late 1950s Mowlem gained a large subcontract, worth £9.34 million, for Hunterston nuclear power station. By 1961 when Sir George Burt retired as chairman but became company president, his firm ranked eleventh in the construction industry, with net assets of £3.612 million. In 1964, the year of Sir George's death, the company won contracts worth £7.507 million (excluding long term contracts already under way); its pre-tax profits were £690,000.

George Burt was actively involved in promoting the professional and commercial interests of his industry. He was one of the 23 contractors who met under the chairmanship of Weetman Pearson, Viscount Cowdray (qv), in 1919 to form the Federation of Civil Engineering Contractors. From the outset Burt was a council member of the FCEC, its chairman in 1932-33 and its president, 1946-48 and 1951-56. On the building side of the industry he was president of the London Master Builders Association in 1921 and of the International Federation of Building and Public Works in 1930, when Britain hosted the IFBPW's fifth conference. He sat on the board of the Building Research Station (ten years as chairman), ca 1936-56; on the board of the Road Research Laboratory, in the early 1950s; and on the Fire Research Board, 1947-56. He became a member of the Institution of Civil Engineers in 1943 and he was a Fellow of the Institute of Builders.

Burt was a keen sportsman. In 1922 he was British épée champion and represented Great Britain at the épée in the Olympic Games in 1920 and 1924. He was master of the Old Surrey and Burstow Hunt, 1931-37 and was an enthusiastic salmon fisherman.

George Burt married Olive Charlotte Sortain, daughter of Frederich E Hulbert, in 1911; they had one son. Sir George Mowlem Burt died on 1 September 1964 leaving £294,247 gross.

D G CARPENTER *and* DAVID J JEREMY

Writings:

'Machinery and Plant in Connexion with Civil Engineering' *Journal of the Institution of Civil Engineers* 22 (May 1944).

'Modern Road Building' *Financial Times* supplement 25 Feb 1957.

Sources:

Unpublished

John Mowlem & Co PLC Brentford, Middlesex, company papers, including 'The Principal Engineering, Building and Road Works Executed by John Mowlem & Co Ltd 1874-1968' (typescript, np, nd).

Kenneth R Burt (second cousin of Sir George Burt), Sussex, family papers and oral information.

BCe.

MCe.

PrC.

Information on company profits from R F Erith of Savory Milln & Co Ltd.

Published

J R Colclough, *The Construction Industry of Great Britain* (Butterworths, 1965).

Proceedings of the Institution of Civil Engineers 34 (June 1965).

Times 3 Sept 1964.

Times *Prospectuses* 69 (1925).

WWW.

BURTON, Sir Montague Maurice

(1885-1952)

Clothing manufacturer and retailer

Sir Montague Burton (courtesy of Hudson Road Mills).

Montague Maurice Burton was born in the small town of Kurkel in Lithuania on 15 August 1885, the only son of Hyman Judah Ossinsky, a bookseller, and his wife Rachel Edith née Ashe. His parents were Jewish. His father was sixty years old when he was born and the boy was brought up by an uncle, who was a timber merchant and from whom probably he borrowed the £100 with which he began business in 1904 (though there have been others who claimed this distinction).

He was educated in a Yeshiva (an Orthodox Jewish parochial school in which heavy emphasis was placed upon Talmudic scholarship). At the age of fifteen, in 1900, he migrated alone from Lithuania to England as so many Jews had done earlier in the face of Russian pogroms; he arrived, unaccompanied, in Chesterfield, Derbyshire, where he began learning the English language and the business of shopkeeping.

In 1904 (when he adopted the name of Montague Maurice Burton) he was sufficiently advanced to begin business in retail clothing in Chesterfield. Shortly after his marriage in 1909 he moved to Sheffield where he lived at Violet Bank Road, trading at 101-103 South Street, Moor, Sheffield, in ready-made men's clothing purchased from wholesale clothiers.

By 1910 the firm had shops in Chesterfield, Sheffield, Manchester, Leeds and Mansfield. Since Leeds was the principal national centre for the wholesale manufacture of men's clothing, it made sense to move there. Further, there were advantages for a retailing organisation to integrate backwards into the manufacture of men's clothing. This had been done by 1913. Having been joined by his younger brother Bernard, the firm now traded as Burton & Burton, clothiers.

Burton Brothers, wholesale clothiers at 41 Camp Road, Leeds, were joined by Ellis Hurwitz, a tailor, who took charge of manufacturing for the next forty years. From this point the firm expanded rapidly in both retailing and manufacture. A factory was taken in Concord Street, Leeds, in 1914 which produced ready made uniforms. Further factories were added between 1914 and 1919 in Byron Street, Millroyd Street, Woodhouse Lane and Melbourne Street, Leeds. The factory of Albrecht & Albrecht in Hudson Road, acquired in 1921, provided the site for a vast operation in which production was concentrated in the largest clothing factory in Europe employing 5,000 workers by 1925.

On the retail side, the firm grew to 51 shops by 1918, including eight in Ireland. The combination of retailing and manufacturing was designed to produce good quality men's clothing at low prices suitable for popular consumption, by eliminating the middle-man's costs and profits. The business developed strongly on the wholesale bespoke type of production: a combination of bespoke tailoring with the economies of large scale production of made-to-measure suits catering for the individual customer.

By 1925 this type of product accounted for 75 per cent of the firm's sales with the balance consisting of ready made clothing. The firm was then producing about a fifth of the national supply of bespoke tailored men's suits.

Burton converted his business into a public company under the title 'Montague Burton, the Tailor of Taste, Ltd,' in March 1929, with an authorised capital of £4 million (equally divided between 10 shilling ordinary shares and 7 per cent £1 cumulative preference shares). The public company acquired assets with a combined total value of £3,225,000 from the vendors, Montague Burton Ltd, Key Estates Ltd and Montague Burton himself. Profits (before interest and tax) had risen from £283,348 in 1926 (ending 31 March) to £419,091 in 1928. Integration had been carried a stage further and Burtons were one of the few clothing manufacturers or retailers who produced a proportion of their own cloth. The expansion of the Hudson Road factory, because of its magnitude, was completed only by 1934, when the canteen was opened by the Princess Royal. It provided meals priced between 4d and 10d for 8,000 workers at a sitting, and replaced earlier facilities which the expansion of the labour force had outgrown.

Burton's business organisation embodied in practice the welfare provisions for workers which were an expression of his business principles and beliefs about the organisation of industrial relations, which strongly emphasised co-operation between capital and labour. Welfare services freely available to workers included attendance by a resident doctor, a dental surgery, optical department, chiropodist, sun ray clinic and rest rooms, several of which dated back to the early 1920s. There was also a voluntary sick club for employees and a savings bank deposit scheme begun in 1926.

A committed temperance advocate, Montague Burton excluded alcohol from his firm's premises and this was reflected in his retail shops (which were well sited in prominent central town locations). Wherever possible, he originally provided a billiards saloon above the shop, directing the attention of its male patrons to the clothes displayed in his windows and offering leisure outlets as an alternative to the public house.

The 51 shops of 1918 grew to 364 by 1928 and increased further to 600 by 1939. The acquisition of valuable retail premises was one of Montague Burton's principal expressions of business acumen and the assets which they represented were to be of great assistance to the firm's financial position in the difficult trading conditions affecting their branch of the clothing industry in the years following the Second World War.

Burton's high street shops were a distinctive contribution to the urban scene in the inter-war period. 'Every Montague Burton shop has the same outward appearance, both in its window dressing and in the name of the firm uniformly presented in bronze lettering on fine marble. The exterior stonework is always of emerald pearl granite, with shafts of Scotch grey granite. The interior fittings of oak and gunmetal, quiet and dignified, are the same at every branch' {Fraser (1925) 62}.

Although the economy was still suffering from the heavy unemployment characterising the years after 1920, the rising real wages of the large majority who remained in employment during the 1930s provided especially favourable demand conditions for the Leeds wholesale

Grand Buildings, Trafalgar Square, London (from Ideals in Industry, *1951).*

clothing industry in general and in particular for that section of the market catered for by Burtons. By the mid-1930s the firm was experiencing problems in recruiting sufficient labour to the Hudson Road factory. Their nationwide retailing enterprise helped to balance different degrees of prosperity and consequently the demand for their products in different regions.

The firm's market was essentially British (but with shops in Eire and one in Copenhagen). In addition to the publicity value of the firm's own distinctive shops, press advertising was keenly exploited, with full page insertions in national daily newspapers. In addition, advertisements were sent out by the firm's branches to all male voters on the electoral lists.

Consequent upon the firm's retailing success, new factories were opened in Lancashire at Walkenden, Worsley and Bolton so that by 1939 over

One of the vast workrooms at Hudson Road Mills (from Ideals in Industry, *1951).*

6,000 workers were employed, in addition to the 10,500 at Hudson Road and the 4,000 employed in distribution and retailing. The firm which began with £100 by 1939 had a working capital of some £12 million. None of the directors serving in 1929 had attended school beyond the age of sixteen.

During the Second World War Burtons produced 13,524,634 garments for the armed forces, about one quarter of what was needed, and at its end about a third of men's demobilisation clothing which absorbed 90 per cent of the firm's productive capacity.

The pre-war expansion of output which enabled the firm to play so vital a role in equipping British and Allied forces during the Second World War also saw the expansion of the firm's control over the production of the cloth which it used, including Calverley Worsted Mills; Hobsons of Huddersfield; Sykes Marsden, Honley; James Croysdale Ltd, Bramley; and the Pontefract Burling & Mending Co. After the Second World War trade was good and Burtons entered into long term contracts, one of their biggest suppliers being Salts of Saltaire.

Trimmings such as linings were obtained directly as early as the 1920s from A W Roberts Ltd, a Manchester firm of merchant convertors. In 1940 the firm purchased a button factory in Ightham in Kent, capable by 1950 of producing over half a million buttons weekly. The expansion which had been so dramatic before 1939 was obviously more constrained by the stringent trading conditions, including clothes rationing, after 1945.

By 1950, shortly before Burton's death, the firm's working capital was £15 million. It controlled eleven factories and had launched into the women's clothing trade with the purchase in 1946 of Peter Robinson Ltd, and Stagg & Russell Ltd, famous West End stores. In all by 1950 the firm employed directly 20,000 workers and it was estimated that 'a fifth of the British male population was clothed by Burtons'. {Redmayne (1951) 241}

The management style of Sir Montague Burton (he was knighted in 1939) as head of his firm may be described as authoritative though benevolently patriarchal with a willingness to delegate that authority, provided that its source was clearly recognised. He usually worked for fourteen hours a day and was rarely without a secretary in attendance. Outside the firm he had four directorships, including the Sun Insurance Co.

Sir Montague Burton was not in a fundamental sense technologically or organisationally innovative. Wholesale bespoke tailoring had existed before he took it up. His success lay in his ability to integrate, with great managerial and entrepreneurial flair, the functions associated with the manufacture and sale of clothing on an unprecedented and unequalled scale; in his keen sense of retail site opportunities; and in the humanity of his relationships with the work force, especially when seen in the context of an industry which historically has been too frequently characterised by gross exploitation. Not alone but in a large measure, he transformed the nation's clothing, especially of working class customers, by placing good quality, reasonably priced garments within reach of those who had hitherto relied on shoddy and frequently second-hand clothes.

Widely travelled and well read, his love of letters and scholarship was reflected in honours received: a fellowship of the Royal Society of Arts; Doctor of Letters, University of Leeds; membership of the Pen Club. His benefactions, echoing his interests, included endowed chairs of industrial relations at Leeds, Cardiff and Cambridge; a visiting chair of international relations at Edinburgh; full chairs of international relations at the Hebrew University in Jerusalem, the London School of Economics and Oxford; and endowed lectureships in the same subjects at Nottingham and Leeds.

Montague Burton was an enthusiastic Zionist who took a keen interest in the development of the Jewish nation state, including charitable donations and the Hebrew University chair. In faith an Orthodox Jew, he was president of the Harrogate Hebrew Congregation in 1941 and became its honorary life president in 1948. Montague Burton was a pioneer supporter of the League of Nations and United Nations activities (his firm's branch, established in 1922, became the biggest UN Association branch in 1950 with 1,600 members). In addition he was a freemason, and a Merchant Adventurer of the City of York, a supporter of the abstinence movement, an enthusiastic supporter of the New Commonwealth Society and a keen golfer. While he was not a member of any political party much in his view of life was attuned to a Liberal outlook.

In 1909 Montague Burton married Sophia Amelia Marks whose father Maurice Marks, a furniture dealer, was a leader of the Chesterfield Jewish community and Worshipful Master of the Pelham Masonic Lodge and father of fourteen children.

On 21 September 1952 Sir Montague Burton collapsed and died in

Leeds, leaving his widow, a daughter and three sons. His estate was valued at £687,495 gross.

ERIC M SIGSWORTH

Writings:

Globe Girdling (2 vols, Leeds: Petty & Sons, 1935, 1937).
The Middle Path (Leeds: Petty & Sons, 1943).

Sources:

Unpublished
MCe.
PrC.

Published
DNB.
Sir John Foster Fraser, *Goodwill in Industry* (pp, 1925).
An Historic Occasion (Leeds, 1934).
'Men Who Made Leeds: Sir Montague Burton — Tailor, 1885-1952' *Leeds Journal* 31 (1960).
Ronald Redmayne (ed), *Ideals in Industry* (Leeds: Montague Burton, 1951).
Times *Prospectuses* 77 (1929).
WWW.

BUTLER, Sir Robert Reginald Frederick

(1866-1933)

Milk and dairy products wholesaler and retailer

Robert Reginald Frederick Butler was born at Shepton Mallet, Somerset on 19 June 1866, the son of Frederick James Butler, a farmer, and Susan née Swanson. He was educated at Bedford School and entered the milk trade as manager of the North Wiltshire Dairy Co's depot at Eastcourt Street, Devizes. Business grew rapidly with the accelerated demand of

London's milk trade, and in 1896 Butler helped to organize Wilts United Dairies, of which he became a principal shareholder. His partner, Charles Maggs, died in 1899, but Reginald Butler helped make the new company one of the most successful in the trade. In 1901 he bought a wholesale milk business at the Paddington terminus of the GWR and made Joseph Maggs (qv) son of Charles, its manager. By 1911 they were able to buy the established firm of Freeth & Pocock Ltd, and in 1915 Reginald Butler engineered a major re-structuring of the trade in the form of a new company, United Dairies.

United Dairies was an amalgamation of the most powerful wholesale firms in London, including the Dairy Supply Co Ltd, Great Western & Metropolitan Dairies Ltd, Wilts United Dairies Ltd, and F W Gilbert Ltd. It was thought best under the then prevailing war conditions to reduce the inefficiency of overlapping rounds and undesirable competition. In 1917 some of the leading retail companies also joined, such as Welford & Sons, the Aylesbury Dairy Co, the London, Gloucester & North Hants Dairies, Curtis Bros & Dumbrill, R Higgs & Son, Welford's Surrey Dairies, West London Dairy Co, Ben Davies & Son, Eastern Counties Dairy Farmers, Emerton & Sons, and many more. In the same year Butler became chairman of this unprecedentedly large dairy combine, a post he held until succeeded by Joseph Maggs in 1922. By the end of the war United Dairies controlled about two-thirds of London's wholesale milk supply, and had been able to cut by 30 per cent the number of its rounds, creating in the process what amounted to a virtual monopoly in some areas. Within a year the group was subject to an excess profit duty.

Sir Reginald (he was granted a baronetcy in 1922) was also active outside the boardroom. As a result of his efforts the National Milk Publicity Council was founded in 1920, and he was at various times president of the National Federation of Dairymen's Associations, and the Metropolitan Dairymen's Benevolent Institution. He was also a leading promoter of the Young Farmers' Club movement.

After his retirement from the chairmanship of United Dairies in 1922, Butler kept interests in a wide sphere of business concerns in the catering and confectionery trades. He became, for instance, a director of the Aerated Bread Co (ABC), and with some friends acquired the rights in several countries of the Hayes gear.

The successful career of Reginald Butler was a result not only of the fortunate circumstances of being in a trade that was expanding rapidly. He was an energetic, astute and forceful businessman to whom 'mediocrity, inefficiency, and any suggestion of failure were abhorrent' {*Milk Industry* 14 (1933) 33}. His talent for organisation was a key asset, although his direct manner was known to cause occasional embarrassment to colleagues.

Butler married in 1895 Rose née Rich, daughter of Thomas Godwin Rich, a farmer; they had one son who, as Lieutenant Reginald Thomas Butler RN, succeeded to the baronetcy, and one daughter, Mrs Wayland-Smith. Sir Reginald Butler died on 19 November 1933 leaving £115,555 gross.

PETER J ATKINS

Sources:

Unpublished

BCe.

MCe.

PrC.

Peter J Atkins, 'The Milk Industry of London, ca 1790-1914' (Cambridge PhD, 1977).

Published

Arthur G Enock, *This Milk Business: A Study from 1895 to 1943* (H K Lewis & Co, 1943).

Alan Jenkins, *Drinka Pinta: the Story of Milk and the Industry That Serves It* (Heinemann, 1970).

Milk Industry 14 (1933).

Bryan S Morgan, *Express Journey, 1864-1964* (Newman Neame, 1964).

Times 20 Nov 1933.

WWW.

BUTLER, Sir William Waters

(1866-1939)

Brewer

William Waters Butler was born at the *London Works* tavern, Smethwick, near Birmingham on 14 December 1866, the eldest son of William Butler, licensed victualler, of Birmingham, and his wife Mary Jane née Ewing. He was educated at King Edward VI School, Birmingham, and at the Birmingham and Midland Institute. He qualified as a chemist and then joined his father's business, known then as Butler's Crown Brewery Ltd. By the time of the merger with Henry Mitchell & Co Ltd of Smethwick in 1897, Butler was a director of his family firm; he became deputy chairman of the new firm in 1907 and chairman in 1914, on the death of Henry Mitchell. He combined the posts of chairman and managing director, a fairly common practice in the brewing industry in this era.

Under his control, Mitchells & Butlers Ltd continued the steady progress which his predecessor, Henry Mitchell, initiated. Between 1900 and 1914 the company doubled its annual output to 600,000 barrels of beer which placed it in sixth position in the brewing industry, by output. Between 1918 and 1939 the company consolidated its reputation as one of the safest investments in the industry. Its financial strategy was consistently and severely conservative.

Butler's most important role, however, was that of 'trade statesman'. He was elected chairman of the Brewers' Society in 1907 and held office during the great and successful struggle against the Asquith Government's Licensing Bill in 1908. From then on he played a prominent part in the politics of the liquor trade. He was the first representative of the brewing industry to be appointed to the Liquor Control Board (1916) and was closely involved in the scheme to nationalise the trade in the Carlisle and Gretna districts. It was partly as a result of his experience as a member of the State Management Authority that he became a leading advocate of 'rationalisation'. He correctly diagnosed that most of the pre-war problems of the brewing industry were attributable to excessive competition, which arose in turn from the existence of too many licensed houses and too many brewers. At his company's annual general meeting in 1917 he said:

> Healthy competition is good for all industries but under existing conditions in the retail licensed trade, competition is excessive and the results arising therefrom damage the whole trade in the estimation of the public.
> {Company report (1917) 9-10}

The crux of his argument was that an excessive number of licensed houses encouraged drunkenness and discouraged the improvement of amenities. This in turn prevented the liquor trade from regaining the social respectability which it had once had, but from the 1850s onwards had largely forfeited in the face of attacks by the temperance movement.

Butler's belief that only the state could take the necessary steps to rationalise the trade, however, was neither shared by his fellow brewers nor was it acted upon by subsequent Governments. Indeed, Butler himself showed that in those areas where licensed outlets were concentrated in relatively few hands and, equally important, where the local licensing magistrates were prepared to support the brewers' attempts to improve their public houses, much could be done to restore the respectability as well as the profitability of the trade. The Birmingham brewers' maxim of 'fewer and better' proved to be the forerunner of a progressive approach to licensing reform which was ultimately adopted by practically every licensing bench in England and Wales. Although his enthusiasm for the Carlisle experiment later cooled, he remained, along with other prominent brewers such as Francis Whitbread (qv) and Sir Richard Garton (qv), a leading advocate of rationalisation and social responsibility.

Unlike many other brewers, however, he took an active interest in brewing science. President of the Institute of Brewing in 1906, he made a substantial financial contribution both to the foundation of the Birmingham University School of Brewing and Malting in 1899 and to the establishment of a chair of brewing. He was also active in philanthropic causes and it was partly in recognition of this involvement that he was made a baronet in 1926. Although he never held any political office, he was a lifelong friend of the Chamberlain family and, like most other brewers, actively supported the Conservative Party.

He married Emily Mary Brown in 1893. They had two daughters and a son, William Owen, who died in 1935. The family interest in Mitchells & Butlers Ltd was preserved up to the early 1960s through Butler's brothers, nephews and other relatives. Sir William Butler died on 5 April 1939 leaving an estate of £552,615 gross.

KEVIN HAWKINS

Sources:

Unpublished

Mitchells & Butlers Ltd, Company Report Aug 1917.

BCe.

PrC.

Published

John Vaizey, *The Brewing Industry, 1886-1951* (Pitman, 1960).

WWW.

BUTLIN, Sir William Heygate Edmund Colbourne

(1899-1980)

Pioneer in the mass leisure industry

Sir Billy Butlin ca 1975 (courtesy of Peter Dacre).

William Heygate Edmund Colbourne Butlin, 'Billy Butlin', was born in Cape Town, on 27 September 1899, the offspring of an ill-matched marriage between William Butlin, engineer and son of Anglican clergyman William Heygate Butlin (d 1906), and Bertha née Hill, daughter of a travelling baker and showman who played the fairs of Gloucestershire and Somerset. Billy's parents had married against their families' wishes and then emigrated to South Africa where William Butlin's efforts to run a cycle business collapsed during the Boer War. When Billy was five his mother brought him back to her family in England; eventually she obtained a divorce and in 1910 remarried. His stepfather, Charlie Rowbotham, a gas fitter with the Bristol Gas Co, took Billy's mother to Canada, leaving the boy with a widow at Redcliffe, near Bristol. For over a year Billy attended St Mary Redcliffe school, and then in 1912 his parents sent for him.

Billy completed his schooling in Toronto and started work in Eatons, a large department store, pushing wickerwork trucks along basement tunnels: a task he accelerated by wearing roller skates. In 1915 he joined the Canadian army as a boy bugler and saw service in France with the 3rd Canadian Mounted Rifles. By the time he returned to Toronto in 1919 his stepfather had died and his mother was working for Eatons. Billy secured a job in the store's advertising department but found it hard to settle down. With a few pounds from his mother, he worked his passage on a cattle boat back to England, arriving in February 1921 with £5 in his pocket.

He headed for Dorney's Yard (now Locke's Yard), Bedminster, near Bristol, the winter quarters of the area's fairground families, and found a warm welcome among his mother's relatives. His uncle, Marshall Hill, equipped him with a few poles and some canvas and the 'swag merchants' of Hounsditch, London, provided him with £10 worth of prizes, mostly cheap watches, on credit. His first hoop-la stall took £20 the first day because Billy accidentally made it easy to win and discovered the secret of small margins on high turnover. In the summer of 1921 he earned £25 net a week. The following year he had an assistant and a second stall, painted blue and yellow, in which goldfish bowls were won by throwing ping pong balls and Billy himself started wearing a white coat emblazoned with a large B. After visiting Olympia, where Bertram Mills (qv) was adding sideshows to his spectacular circus, Butlin carefully selected and then, for £40, in 1922 hired a prime site at the circus entrance for a hoop-la stall with 'love birds' (budgerigars) for prizes. That winter he made a net profit of more than £200. When, in the mid-1920s, he fell foul of the big owners and organisers of fairground rides (riding masters), for forming a Stallholders Association to resist increased rents, Billy confined his summer activities to smaller fairs in the West of England.

Travelling around, he observed a spreading recreation: charabanc day excursions to the seaside. One showman mentioned that Skegness attracted a lot of free-spending holidaymakers, so in 1927 he went there and set up four stalls, a tower slide, a haunted house and an electric car track. Soon he had two amusement parks at Skegness and Mablethorpe, and a workforce of 30 men. He stopped following the fairs and lived with his first wife and his mother (brought back from Canada in 1924) in caravans on his sites. Then he heard of an exciting new attraction in America, the Dodgem car. For £2,000 (£1,800 his own savings) he purchased a batch of Dodgems along with the monopolistic concession to operate them in Britain. Dodgem rinks became leading attractions in the amusement parks Butlin had at Skegness, Mablethorpe (opened in 1928), Bognor Regis (in 1930), Felixstowe, Hayling Island and Southsea (in 1931), and Littlehampton (in 1932). Other sensational rides followed, like the Big Dipper, the Figure Eight, which he bought from France and then copied, and the Wall of Death, which came from Australia in 1935. Next to each of the parks he set up small zoos.

By 1930, with the support of a Barclays bank manager who lent him

£2,000, he went back to Bertram Mills and secured the concession for all the amusements at Olympia (for an outlay of £10,000), soon acquiring another for the amusements at Kelvin Hall, Glasgow. By 1933 he had 900 men in his permanent employ and 2,000 during the six months' summer season; his profits were reported in the *Sunday Express* (15 January 1933) at £20,000 to £25,000 a year.

The idea of a holiday camp first came to Billy Butlin in the early 1920s while on a boarding-house holiday on Barry Island; he found himself turned out each day in rain that lasted a week, which triggered unfavourable comparisons with lakeside holiday huts in Canada. With capital from his amusement parks, he bought 48 acres of turnip fields near Skegness in 1935 and built, over the winter of 1935-36, a camp comprising dining and recreation halls, club rooms and a gymnasium (all concrete buildings) and 800 timber and concrete chalets equipped with electric light and water. Tennis courts, bowling and putting greens, a swimming pool and a boating lake, formed by excavations needed to reinforce the sea wall, were added. The first visitors arrived on Easter Saturday 1936 though the camp was not completed until the following year when over 2,000 visitors were accommodated each week; by 1939 it held 5,000 campers.

Billy Butlin with his Auben car and a bevy of beauties at Skegness, 1937 (courtesy of Peter Dacre).

The Skegness holiday camp quickly became profitable. It cost £100,000 to build (half this sum coming from Barclays Bank and half from Butlin's own savings), and between 9 April and 30 September 1936 it realised a gross profit of £18,021. Butlin, already owner of three small private companies in the amusement industry (Butlin's Auto-Cars Ltd, the Dodgem concern; Butlin's Coastal Rides Ltd; and Entertainments Development Corporation Ltd), decided on a massive expansion, raising capital by a public flotation. Butlin's Ltd, formed early in 1937 with an authorised share capital of £220,000, offered 400,000 5s ordinary shares to the public at 6s each and £100,000 of 5.5 per cent first mortgage debenture stock at par. The issue was over-subscribed in five minutes. The new company paid Butlin £242,400 (nearly £124,000 in cash and the rest in ordinary shares by which he retained voting control) for his existing businesses and he became managing director of the new company with a salary of £3,000 a year. The business then mushroomed. To his first holiday camp Butlin in 1938 added another at Clacton (also on a 48 acre site), funded by the issue of 100,000 £1 preference shares and 180,000 5s ordinary shares (offered at 7s 6d each). He was planning a third camp at Filey, near Scarborough, when war broke out. By October 1938 the total net assets of Butlins Ltd stood at nearly £876,500 and that year's gross profits at nearly £121,000.

Holiday camps, and Butlin's in particular, proved an immense success in the late 1930s for several reasons. A growing number of wage earners, 3 million by 1938 and 11 million by 1939 (under the Holidays with Pay Act of 1938), were entitled to an annual week's holiday with pay. Since a good proportion of the 9 million working class families in Britain had a weekly income of £3 to £4, a camp holiday at 35 shillings to £3 a head (depending on the time in the season) was within the means of a large number of them. In addition, charabancs, and to a small extent the motor car, opened remote campsites to holiday makers. By 1939 there were nearly 100 holiday camps in Britain and Billy Butlin's two camps at Skegness and Clacton were the largest.

Butlin secured the market lead in various ways. His camps were next door to his amusement parks where campers could enjoy free rides. From the start he persuaded the London & North Eastern Railway, which served both Skegness and Clacton, to pay for half his advertising costs. His camps were comfortable and respectable, despite press stories to the contrary. Nurseries and play gardens were a powerful attraction for working class mothers. Wholesome family entertainment, punctuated by Sunday services (on which Billy consulted the Archbishop of York in 1945), distinguished Butlin camps. So too did a heavily-organised camp programme, heartily enforced by squads of 'Redcoats'. Wearing red blazers and white flannels these members of the camp staff had the task of ensuring that everyone enjoyed themselves in group entertainment, which ranged from chants to games to serious sports coaching, ballroom dancing, films and big name entertainment. Billy Butlin's sense of showmanship infused everything that publicised his camp, from camp décor and beauty competitions to the publicity visits of celebrities including Amy Johnson, Gracie Fields and Len Hutton.

After the outbreak of war in 1939 the armed forces moved into the Skegness and Clacton camps. When the War Office discovered that Billy

Butlin's building costs were 30 per cent lower than their own estimates, they contracted with him to complete his camp at Filey for the Army on the understanding that he could purchase it back at the war's end for three-fifths of its cost. On this risky basis Billy Butlin constructed two more camps, at Pwllheli and Ayr, for the Admiralty. Butlin's talents and resources were appropriately utilised during the remaining war years. For eighteen months he served under Lord Beaverbrook (qv) at the Ministry of Supply, as Director-General of Hostels, brightening the living accommodation and routines of 50,000 women and girls engaged on war production. For this he received the MBE. Then, at the request of various towns and cities, he took his fairground rides out of mothballs and organised Holidays at Home weeks for the immobile civilian population. Butlin ended the war as Honorary Advisor to Montgomery's 21st Army Group, organising Leave Centres across Belgium, Holland and Germany for battle-weary troops.

Although the Filey camp opened in summer 1945, admitting some 50,000 campers during a short season, the other four holiday camps were not ready until the next season. The costs of renovation and the climate of post-war austerity hurt the Butlin company's profit performance, although 1.6 million people each year spent their holidays in Butlin's five holiday camps by the late 1940s. At this point Billy Butlin boldly decided to expand overseas, and in so doing nearly lost his holiday empire.

He began in 1946 when, on a rare holiday, he acquired two luxury hotels in Bermuda, purchased and refurbished for £1.1 million, money mostly borrowed from Barclays. Then, uncharacteristically, he formed a partnership with Brigadier-General Alfred C Critchley (qv) and registered Butlin's (Bahamas) Ltd, to build and operate a luxury holiday village on Grand Bahama, 80 miles from Miami, for middle-income Americans. It foundered on three obstacles. Estimated to cost £1.5 million, its cost rose by 25 per cent as a result of devaluation of sterling in 1949. Local hotel and business interests prevented Butlin from receiving a Bahamian Government subsidy for half the cost of building an airport essential for his holiday traffic. And the group of City financiers, who held half the preference shares, increasingly unimpressed by Butlin's performance, refused to provide their promised £500,000 worth of equity capital which would have kept the scheme going. While Billy was trying to sell his holiday village (it was taken over and successfully operated by a Texas hotel chain after the company was liquidated in 1953), his City backers, managers of large investment funds, carpeted and proposed sacking him. True to form, Billy Butlin fought back, appealing to a multitude of small shareholders in arguing that 'there must be room for instinct, flair and vision that is not always copper-bottomed' {Butlin (1982) 198}. In a dramatic AGM the City financiers were repulsed. Billy Butlin gave up all his outside directorships and his £5,000 a year salary as managing director of Butlin's Ltd (until a 100 per cent dividend was paid) and devoted himself entirely to Butlin's Ltd. Throughout the 1950s he held his AGMs at one of the holiday camps and, until he retired in 1968, maintained a very close grip on the business.

During the 1950s, before cheap air travel opened up foreign holidays, Butlin's camps regularly received over a million bookings a year. As tastes became more educated, Butlin adjusted his camp programme to keep in line with his changing market, modifying his early working class image. Alongside the established regime of organised physical games, fairground fun, ballroom dancing and media humour, he introduced occasional performances by the San Carlo Opera Co, the Bristol Old Vic, the International Ballet and the London Symphony Orchestra. On the other hand, a number of popular media stars began their careers as Redcoats and resident camp entertainers. Des O'Connor, Dave Allen, Roy Hudd, Charlie Drake and Cliff Richard had spells as Redcoats; though on first hearing the last-named, Billy opined 'Good-looking boy, but I don't like the way he sings' {North (1962) 61}.

Billy Butlin recovered from his Caribbean disaster. He built two more holiday camps, at Bognor in 1959 and at Minehead in 1962. Together with his amusement park at Littlehampton and two hotels, the seven holiday camps had an asset value of £22.75 million in 1965 and the previous year pre-tax profits reached a healthy £4.732 million. Billy's showmanship played an important part in his success. He figured prominently in a range of publicity stunts, from the annual Cross Channel swims he sponsored from 1953 onwards to the transportation of his elephant, Big Charlie, between Ayr and Filey in 1957, to the marathon walk from John O'Groats to Land's End he promoted in 1960. He took the Queen and the Duke of Edinburgh on a tour of the Pwllheli camp in 1963.

Cheap air travel and foreign package holidays started to hurt the Butlin holiday camp business in 1965. In 1965-66 bookings were 900,000 and a year later slipped again to 740,000. Butlin made his son Bobby a joint managing director but old habits died hard and the shift to smaller sites and self-catering did not come until Billy retired in 1968. To the end he remained an autocratic boss, deciding even the colour of chalet doors. Friction developed as Billy found it hard to relinquish power.

The prospect of a massive tax bill forced Billy Butlin to resign suddenly. His income in 1965-66 was £232,000 and his tax bill £200,000; by 1968 past tax flows were exceeding current income. Faced with a negative cash flow, he handed over to his son Bobby in April 1968 and went to live in Jersey, a tax haven. The Butlins holiday business was eventually sold in 1972 to the Rank Organisation for £43 million.

Billy Butlin undertook an enormous amount of work for charity, particularly for underprivileged children. Whether or not this was motivated by guilt over the neglect he had shown towards the children of his first and second wives, the fact remains that he gave away an estimated £5 million. Of this, £2 million went to the children's charities of the Variety Club, which he joined in 1952, becoming Chief Barker (fund raiser) three times and indirectly inspiring bigger givers like Charles Clore (qv). He gave £100,000 to establish the Police Dependents' Trust and another £100,000 to the Duke of Edinburgh's Award Scheme. In recognition of his work for youth and charitable organisations he was knighted in 1964. In the 1970s he twice served as president of the Printers' Pension Corporation.

Until his third liaison and marriage, Billy Butlin's private life was distinctly unhappy, largely because his work obsessed him. He married first, in 1927, Dorothy 'Dolly' Mabel Cheriton, daughter of a Tiverton carpenter, whom he met at a West Country fair. They had a daughter, Shirley. After separating from Dolly in the early 1930s he lived with

Norah, Dolly's sister, by whom he had three children, Bobby (b 1934), Cherry and Sandra. Though marrying Norah in 1959 he turned to Sheila Devine, later Lady Butlin, by whom he had two children, Bill Jr and Jacquie, before they were able to marry in 1976. Sir Billy Butlin died in Jersey on 12 June 1980.

DAVID J JEREMY

Writings:

(with Peter Dacre) *The Billy Butlin Story. 'A Showman to the End'* (Robson Books, 1982).

Sources:

Unpublished

MCe.

C Reg: Butlins Ltd (323,698).

Published

Elizabeth Brunner, *Holiday Making and the Holiday Trades* (Oxford: Oxford University Press, 1945).

Ruth Manning-Sanders, *Seaside England* (Batsford, 1951).

Charles L Mowat, *Britain between the Wars* (Methuen, 1966).

Rex North, *The Butlin Story* (Jarrolds, 1962).

J A R Pimlott, *The Englishman's Holiday. A Social History* (Faber & Faber, 1947).

Sunday Express 15 Jan 1933.

Times 13 June 1964, 19, 30 June 1980.

Times *Prospectuses* 93 (1937), 95 (1938).

WWW.

BUTTERWORTH, Sir Alexander Kaye

(1854-1946)

Railway manager

Alexander Kaye Butterworth was born at Clifton, Bristol, on 4 December 1854, the son of George Butterworth, curate of Henbury, Clifton, and his wife, Frances Maria née Kaye, younger daughter of a bishop of Lincoln. Educated at Marlborough College and the University of London, he obtained an LLB degree prior to being called to the Bar in 1878. He joined the legal staff of the Great Western Railway in 1883 and quickly became an acknowledged expert on railway rates, playing an important part in the railway companies' collective deliberations over the Railway and Canal Traffic Act of 1888.

In 1891, after a brief period as clerk to Bedfordshire County Council, Butterworth was appointed solicitor to the North Eastern Railway at a salary of £1,500 per annum, and in 1906 succeeded Sir George Gibb (qv) as general manager at an annual salary of £5,000.

On the North Eastern Railway his ability in the analysis and negotiation of legal and financial matters was manifested between 1906 and 1914 in the successful development of procedural arrangements for the regulation of conditions of service for hourly paid grades and a firm but realistic handling of the rash of strikes that occurred on the system between 1910 and 1913. His expertise in this field made him an important witness in 1911 to the Royal Commission on the Conciliation and Arbitration scheme of 1907, whilst in his specialist field of rates and competition he contributed to the Board of Trade Railway Conference of 1909 and the Departmental Committee of the Board of Trade on Railway Agreements and Amalgamations of 1911. While the North Eastern under Gibb came to dominate Tyneside, under Butterworth it re-established its position on Humberside and gained a firm footing in south Yorkshire.

Knighted in 1914, Butterworth rendered important service throughout the war as a member of the Railway Executive Committee through which state control of the railways was exercised. At the same time he remained responsible to his board for the management of the North Eastern within the framework of government control: a demanding task since the effect of the war on the region was to double traffic volumes over peak pre-war levels at a time when five of the company's top management team were taken into government service.

In many ways, however, the peak of Butterworth's career was the key role he played in the restructuring of a substantial part of the railway industry under the Railways Act of 1921. The dominant position of the North Eastern in the 'Eastern' group created by this act made it the fulcrum of negotiations leading to the eventual creation of the London & North Eastern Railway and much of the onerous task of representing the company's interest in finance, organisation and top management placement was delegated to Butterworth. At the same time he was required to settle satisfactorily the North Eastern's claim against the post-war Railway Compensation Account. He completed these tasks without intruding any personal ambitions. To protect the North Eastern's interest and facilitate R L Wedgwood's (qv) claim to the top executive post in the new company, Butterworth resigned voluntarily his post of general manager late in 1921 remaining with the North Eastern to guide the board on all issues relating to the negotiation of amalgamation. On the completion of the negotiation in December 1922, he was rewarded with a payment of £20,000 and an annuity equivalent to half pay. It was, the *Times* judged, largely through his work in negotiation and consultation that the merger which created the LNER in 1923 was brought to a successful conclusion.

Butterworth became a director of Armstrong-Whitworth in 1926, as part of the emergency reconstruction during its financial crisis. Outside business he rendered long service to the London Chest Hospital (as its chairman 1916-35), as a director of Welwyn Garden City and as chairman of the Pedestrians' Association, 1930-39.

Butterworth was twice married: firstly in 1884 to Julia, daughter of George Wigan MD; after her death in 1911, to Dorothea Mavor in 1916, daughter of Luke Ionides, a stockbroker, and widow of Ebenezer Mavor. Butterworth died on 23 January 1946 leaving £32,584 gross.

ROBERT J IRVING

Writings:

The Practice of the Railway and Canal Commission (Butterworths, 1889).

A Treatise on the Laws Relating to Rates and Traffic on Railways and Canals (Butterworths, 1889).

The Law Relating to Maximum Rates and Charges on Railways (Butterworth & Co, 1897).

Road Accidents. A Pedestrian's Grievance (Pedestrians' Association, 1923).

Sources:

Unpublished

PRO, RAIL 527, Records of the North Eastern Railway Co, 1891-1923.

BCe.

MCe.

PrC.

Published

Cecil J Allen, *The London & North Eastern Railway Company* (Allan, 1966).

Robert Bell, *Twenty Five Years of the North Eastern Railway Company, 1898-1922* (Railway Gazette, 1951).

Robert J Irving, *The North Eastern Railway Company, 1870-1914* (Leicester: Leicester University Press, 1976).

Edwin A Pratt, *British Railways and the Great War* (Selwyn & Blount, 1921).

WWW.

BYTHELL, John Kenworthy

(1840-1916)

Chairman of the Manchester Ship Canal Co

John K Bythell ca 1887-94 (courtesy of the Manchester Ship Canal Co).

John Kenworthy Bythell was born in Hulme, Manchester on 20 April 1840, to James Bythell, a calenderer and maker-up, and Sarah Southell. He joined the Manchester merchant firm of Gaddum & Co and served as resident partner in Bombay from 1864 during the cotton boom induced by the American Civil War. There he acquired a thorough knowledge of the links between commerce, shipping, railways and ports. He became a prime mover in the construction of the great harbour works of the port, was elected chairman of the Bombay Chamber of Commerce in 1872 and became a member of the Bombay Port Trust in 1873, as well as a member of the Bombay Legislative Council. He secured the reduction of railway rates and, after his return to Manchester in 1875, advocated the extension of railways in India.

In 1886 Bythell became a founder-member of the Manchester Ship Canal Consultative Committee and was converted by the evidence from disbelief in the project to faith in its practicality. He agreed to join the board of the Canal Co if Daniel Adamson (qv), the original promoter, ceased to be chairman. On 10 February 1887 Adamson resigned and Bythell became a director, chairman of the finance committee and a member of the executive committee. During the financial crisis of 1891 he acted as deputy-chairman in place of Sir Joseph C Lee (qv). From 1893 he became chairman of the traffic committee, which was the only one of six sub-committees of the Canal board left by the Manchester Corporation under the control of the shareholders' directors. On 20 July 1894 he was elected chairman in succession to Lord Egerton of Tatton (1832-1909). As such he became the first paid, resident and full-time chief executive in the history of the company, earning a salary of £3,000 as the manager of the city's largest firm at a time when the Town Clerk received only £2,500.

Bythell assumed office six months after the opening of the Canal and at a critical juncture in its affairs, created by the bitter opposition of

Liverpool and by the unanticipated competitive reduction of rates. His first task was to avert bankruptcy and to enable the company to survive. To that end he paid the interest due to the Manchester Corporation on its debentures in 1894-96 out of the revenues of the Bridgewater Canal. Then he persuaded the Corporation to levy a special Ship Canal rate from 1896. Finally, he established in 1904 a permanent partnership with the Corporation at the price of conceding to it a perpetual majority upon the board of directors. At the same time Bythell sought to attract trade by wooing railways, shipowners and merchants and by extending the facilities of the port. He supplied the driving energy which was essential to attract and retain paying traffic, even at the price of extending the functions of the company far outside the normal range of a port authority. In order to draw the import of raw cotton away from Liverpool, he encouraged the establishment in 1894 of the Manchester Cotton Association and became its vice-president as well as chairman of the executive committee. In 1895 he persuaded his directors to begin chartering steamers to carry cotton from the Gulf ports to Manchester. From 1896 he also chartered vessels to load in Irish ports for Manchester. Through negotiation with his friends amongst the Hindu merchants of Bombay he secured the conclusion of the crucial contract of 29 December 1894 for the shipment of piece-goods direct from Manchester to Bombay. He also inspired the foundation of the Manchester Ship Canal Warehousing Co Ltd in 1895 in order to provide the port with warehouses and, in 1898, with the largest grain elevator in Europe, through a system of lease and sub-lease. He also founded the Manchester Dock & Warehouse Extension Co Ltd in order to finance the construction of Dock No 9 (1902-5). He had already organised a shipping line for the new port in Manchester Liners Ltd, registered in 1898, with the support of Christopher Furness (qv) and the Canadian Government. That year Bythell, against the opposition of his board, concluded an agreement with Trafford Park Estates Ltd for the construction of a rail link between the dock area and the new industrial estate.

Bythell's talents were primarily those of a merchant, a financier and a diplomat. His grasp of detail was sure, his decisions were made after careful deliberation and his policy was executed with firmness and tenacity. His unresting activity helped to raise Manchester from the status of the sixteenth port of the kingdom in 1894 to that of the fourth in 1906. Manchester ranked second in the export of cotton yarn from 1894, second in that of piece-goods from 1895 and third in that of salt from 1896; it became the second largest importer of raw cotton from 1896, the second importer of petroleum from 1903, the seventh importer of timber from 1898 and the seventh importer of grain from 1900. Bythell declined to give evidence before the Royal Commission on Shipping Rings but a year later in 1908 he inspired the foundation of the Manchester Association of Importers and Exporters and became its vice-chairman. From 1910 the company was able to pay in full the interest on the Corporation debentures and Bythell launched a publicity campaign with the slogan of 'Manchester Goods for Manchester Docks'.

J K Bythell was pre-eminently responsible for the development of the port of Manchester, translating a legal concept and an engineering achievement into a commercial reality. Between 1894 and 1915 the volume of imports rose sevenfold, the volume of exports eightfold and the receipts of the company eightfold. He shattered Liverpool's historic monopoly and crowned his career by paying a first dividend, for the year 1915, to his loyal ordinary shareholders.

A Liberal in politics and a Presbyterian in religion, he devoted all his energies to business and lived entirely for the Ship Canal. He became a JP from 1895 but did not become a director of other companies save as a representative of the Canal Co, serving from 1898 on the boards of the Manchester Chamber of Commerce and the Manchester Dry Docks Co Ltd. In February 1916 he retired partially from administration, having guided the destinies of the company for twenty-two years, without personal publicity: he declined all national honours. John Kenworthy Bythell died on 18 August 1916, leaving an estate of £18,563 gross.

D A FARNIE

Writings:

PP, HC 1884 (284) XI, SC on East India Railway Communication.

'Railways in India: their Advantages and the Necessity for their Extension' *Journal of the Manchester Geographical Society*, 2 March 1887, (repr, Manchester Guardian Printing Works, 1887).

'Manchester Ship Canal Traffic. Important Report to the Directors' *Manchester Guardian*, 9 June 1894.

'Ship Canal Affairs' *Manchester Guardian* 24 April 1895.

PP, RC on Canals and Waterways, Minutes of Evidence (1909) Cd 4840.

Sources:

Unpublished

City of Manchester Central Library, archives, Manchester Association of Importers and Exporters, Minutes, 1908-16. Manchester Cotton Association, Minutes of the Board, 1894-1917.

Lancashire RO, Preston, Papers of J W G Beaumont (1869-1960), confidential secretary to J K Bythell.

Greater Manchester Council Archives, Manchester Ship Canal Co, Minute Books of the Board of Directors, 1887-1916.

BCe.

PrC.

Published

Douglas A Farnie, 'The Manchester Ship Canal, 1894-1913', in W H Chaloner (ed), *Trade and Transport* (Manchester: Manchester University Press, 1977).

Douglas A Farnie, *The Manchester Ship Canal and the Rise of the Port of Manchester, 1894-1975* (Manchester: Manchester University Press, 1980).

Manchester City News 19 Aug 1916.

Manchester Faces and Places 10 (Jan 1894).

Manchester Guardian 19, 23 Aug 1916.

Manchester Ship Canal Co, *Reports of Shareholders' Meetings* 1894-1917.

Northern Finance and Trade 2 Feb 1898.

Salford Chronicle 18 Aug 1894.

W B Tracey and W T Pike, *Manchester and Salford at the Close of the Nineteenth Century* (Brighton: Pike, 1899).

C

CADBURY, George

(1839-1922)

Chocolate manufacturer

George Cadbury (courtesy of Cadbury Schweppes PLC).

George Cadbury was born in Edgbaston, Birmingham on 19 September 1839. He was the third son of John Cadbury, who started as a tea and coffee dealer in Birmingham in 1824 and founded the family cocoa and chocolate business in 1831, and his second wife Candia, daughter of George Barrow, a merchant and shipowner from Lancaster. Unlike his brothers who went to boarding school, George attended a Quaker day school in Birmingham and at the age of fifteen joined his elder brother Richard in his father's business.

His character and ambitions owed much to his Quaker faith and his father's example. For more than twenty years John Cadbury combined successful promotion of his business with notable public service in Birmingham. As a cocoa and chocolate manufacturer he received a Royal Warrant in 1853. The cleanliness of his Bridge Street factory and his care for his workers were praised by Chambers' *Edinburgh Journal* (30 Oct 1852). In civic affairs he was a Street Commissioner (forerunners of elected

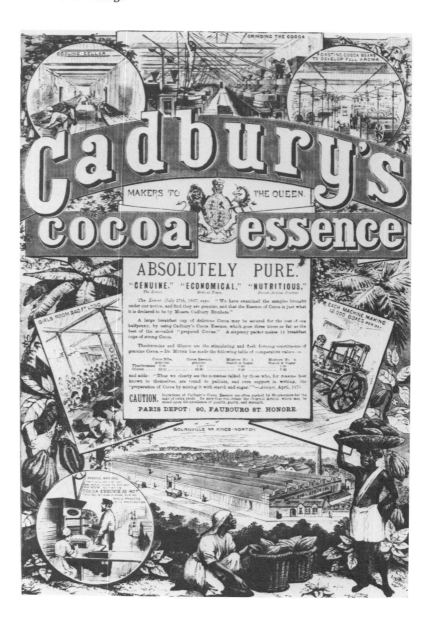

An early Cadbury's advertisement (courtesy of Cadbury Schweppes PLC).

Councillors) and an Overseer and Guardian of the Poor. His health and vigour declined after his wife died in 1855, and his business was near collapse when in 1861 he handed it over to Richard, then aged twenty-five and George, aged twenty-one.

To rescue the business the young partners worked from 8.00 am to 7.30 pm, Saturdays included, and every Sunday morning George taught at the Severn Street Adult School. The breakthrough came in 1866 when

Cadbury's Cocoa Essence was launched as the first pure, that is, unadulterated, cocoa to be sold in Britain. Previously all cocoas required additives such as various forms of flour, sago and even treacle to offset the unpleasant taste of the cocoa butter which could not be removed from the raw cacao bean. George Cadbury learnt that a Dutch firm, Van Houten, had developed a machine press which extracted most of the butter and eliminated the need for additives. Realising the potential of this machine, he went to Holland and bought one.

His timing was propitious because adulteration of food was an important issue in the mid-nineteenth century and the Adulteration Act of 1872, which required manufacturers to specify ingredients, worked to the advantage of Cocoa Essence. Its quality was recognised by the medical profession and quotations from the *Lancet* became a feature of Cocoa Essence advertisements supporting the slogan 'Absolutely pure: therefore best'. Cocoa Essence became the springboard for the firm's growth not only because it allowed persuasive advertising but also because surplus butter from its manufacture raised the output and quality of eating chocolate, which requires a higher proportion of cocoa butter than is contained in the bean. An early ledger records total receipts in 1860 as £27,800; by 1879 they reached £103,000, a modest growth by later standards but sufficient to demonstrate that Cadbury Brothers had outgrown the Bridge Street factory. In the latter year the turnover of Fry's of Bristol, a large chocolate manufacturer and an older Quaker firm, was £266,000.

Between 1861 and 1879 employees increased from 20 to over 200. Like their father, Richard and George were benevolent masters. They were the first employers in Birmingham to make Saturday a half-day, and they closed the factory on bank holidays. George introduced a piece-rate system which he correctly anticipated would increase both output and wages. Small additional sums were paid for punctuality and abstention from eating chocolates, while fines were imposed for misdemeanours and slovenly work. In the Creme Room in 1874 'using any but square tin (kept for purpose) under chocolate ladle' incurred a 2d fine. Under another rule when a girl (all females in the Cadbury employ were known as 'girls') married, her employment ceased; George Cadbury was, and remained, adamant that a wife's proper place was at home. He had also observed that a wage-earning wife encouraged idleness in a husband.

The need for new premises enabled George to put into practice his belief that a healthy working environment would benefit both employees and the firm. After an extensive search he and his brother in June 1878 purchased 14.5 acres of open country near the Bourn stream four miles south-west of the city. Determined that the factory should be purpose-built George Cadbury drew up initial plans as a brief for the architect. Direct labour was employed and with the aid of a professional foreman the two brothers supervised the building. George was particularly active, having moved temporarily to a nearby cottage in order to keep an eye on progress, after finishing the day's work at Bridge Street.

The old premises were vacated in July 1879, and when the 230 employees arrived at Bournville they found a playing field for men, a garden for girls and welfare facilities, such as a kitchen for heating food and provision for drying wet clothes.

Packing chocolates 1912. Works forewoman (Fanny Price) standing in the gangway (courtesy of Cadbury Schweppes PLC).

Sales increased, and by 1890 factory space had virtually doubled. By 1900 it had trebled and sales exceeded £1 million. Because chocolate manufacture was so labour-intensive the number of employees increased to approximately 1,500 in 1890 and to a precise 3,023 in 1900 (2,177 girls and 846 men). Bournville wages were normally higher than those which trade unions could negotiate with other employers, and George Cadbury was in favour of unions and of the right to strike. As far as possible the partners maintained their personal contacts with the workforce. They were accessible to everyone, and George supervised manufacturing processes in some detail. An office manager described the proprietors' regime as a 'kindly duocracy'. By the late 1890s Barrow and William, sons of Richard, and Edward and George Jr, sons of George, joined the firm. Their presence helped to maintain the family relationship; they acquired extensive departmental experience but initially were not partners in the business.

Richard and George Cadbury had agreed that on the death of either the firm should become a private limited company. Following Richard's unexpected death in 1899 (from diptheria while visiting Palestine) Cadbury Brothers Ltd was incorporated in June 1899 with a capital of £950,000. George was appointed chairman, a position he held until his death; the other directors were Barrow, William, Edward and George Jr, each being responsible for specific sections of the business as managing directors. Barrow was responsible for 'travellers' (sales), William for cocoa buying and factory functions, Edward for employment and export. George Jr, the youngest director, had mainly administrative roles in 1900 but quickly acquired responsibility for certain manufacturing processes, specifically the development of Cadbury's Dairy Milk Chocolate launched in 1905.

Until the early years of the present century Fry's annual turnover exceeded that of Cadbury. But from 1908 when Cadbury sales were £1.6 million compared with Fry's £1.5 million, the Bournville firm progressively outpaced the Bristol one. By 1912, when sales reached £2 million, Cadbury employees numbered 6,200 and substantial additions had been made to buildings and plant. Authorised capital stood at £2.15 million with £1.2 million subscribed, but further working capital was required to meet continued growth. In February 1912 the firm became a public company, and in the following month 200,000 £1 preference shares were offered to the public with priority given to customers and staff. The shares, which were over-subscribed, were allocated 75 per cent to customers, 15 per cent to senior staff and 10 per cent to directors. That no ordinary shares were offered was a reflection of George Cadbury's belief that family control was in the best interest of the expanding business, which by 1920 achieved a turnover of £8.1 million.

The approach to industrial relations originally conceived by George Cadbury and his brother was further developed during the early years of the present century, and was described in Edward Cadbury's *Experiments in Industrial Organisation* published in 1912. Among major developments were an employee suggestion scheme started in 1902 and the introduction of men's and women's pension schemes in 1906 and 1911 respectively. The works committees introduced in 1905, a year after Crosfields and contemporary with Rowntrees, later became works councils with elected worker representatives.

George's most far-reaching achievement was the Bournville Village. He was not the originator of the garden village concept. Robert Owen had explored the idea and William Lever (qv) had built Port Sunlight with tied houses for his workers. Apart from the scale of its subsequent development, the distinctive feature of Bournville was that the estate houses were not, and never have been, restricted to Cadbury employees. In 1895 George Cadbury bought 140 acres of undeveloped land roughly a mile from the factory and within a year 200 houses were built, at first for sale and then, after speculative purchasers emerged, for rent. All the properties, their layout, size and gardens, and intervening spaces, were specified by George himself. The result was a spacious housing estate broken by lawns, trees, flower gardens and ponds. In 1905 he built the village schools at a cost of £30,000. When he surrendered his private interest to the Bournville Village Trust in 1901 the estate and the buildings were valued at £172,000. The Trust now (1982) owns a much enlarged estate in south-west Birmingham comprising more than 7,000 houses.

Bournville General Office 1912. Note the time-recording clock in the foreground (courtesy of Cadbury Schweppes PLC).

The partnership of Richard and George Cadbury lasted for nearly fifty years until the former's death. They shared many common ideals and religious faith, and each had his own distinctive talents. Richard had the wider interests, was fond of travel and music and had some artistic ability. George Cadbury's interests were less diverse but possibly deeper. At the age of twenty-two he began a fifty-year association with the Adult School movement. He taught hundreds of men to read and write, visited their homes and saw at first hand the slum conditions endured by Birmingham's working classes. This experience kindled his lifelong concern for temperance and social reform, and led in later years to his practice of applying much of the wealth he acquired from the business to furthering the social and religious causes in which he believed.

Throughout their careers Richard and George Cadbury took their philanthropic duties seriously. The firm's growing prosperity during the 1890s enabled George to increase his support for religious and social causes. Examples are the gift of his former home, Woodbrooke, to the

Society of Friends as a centre for religious studies; the purchase and conversion of a large house as an open air hospital for Birmingham Cripples Union; and the building of a convalescent home for children. But George Cadbury did not parade his benevolence and 'it is impossible to estimate the sum of his benefactions' {Owen (1965) 434}.

Until 1901 George Cadbury's activities had centred around Birmingham. He declined suggestions from Gladstone in 1892 and from Lord Rosebery in 1895 to stand for Parliament. For a very brief period in 1878-79 he was a member of Birmingham City Council but preferred to pursue his radical ideas outside the arena of party politics. However, his strong opposition to the Boer War led to his involvement in national politics. The national Conservative press vigorously supported the war and there was no effective news medium expressing the opposing Liberal and radical view. In 1901 Lloyd George persuaded George Cadbury and other sponsors to purchase and develop the *Daily News* as a strong Liberal voice. This policy led to a rapid loss of the newspaper's advertising revenue, and when some sponsors withdrew their support George Cadbury reluctantly agreed to become sole owner, at an investment of £40,000. For several years he had to bear substantial annual losses, on one occasion up to £60,000. His strong views on social issues brought personal hostility from political and industrial opponents, but he continued his support and in 1910 purchased an evening paper, *The Star*, from the Rowntree family to reinforce the Liberal cause. A year later at the age of seventy-two he handed over his press ownership to the Daily News Trust of which his son, Edward, was the first chairman.

One key to his achievement was his shrewdness as a businessman. He could identify a crucial opportunity for advancing his business, seize it and then develop the potential, as with Cocoa Essence in 1866. Equally shrewd was his recognition of the shared interests of employer and employed; a better life for the latter contributed significantly to the fortunes of the former. He accepted responsibility for the *Daily News* as a social and political duty, but temperamentally he could never have been a 'press baron' because in his view the justice of the causes he supported outweighed all other considerations.

In private life he was fond of gardens and enjoyed outdoor activities. He had a strong affection for children and at his Northfield home large parties were entertained almost daily during the summer. Perhaps inevitably he had little time for art, literature or music. His personal life was relatively spartan and in a Quaker tradition he declined any public honours. In appearance he was an arresting figure: spare, upright and active of frame, with a beard grown from his youth.

George Cadbury married Mary Tylor in 1873 and they had three sons and two daughters before Mary died in 1887. The following year he married Elizabeth Mary Taylor (later Dame Elizabeth Cadbury), and there were three sons and three daughters of this marriage. George Cadbury died at his home, the Manor House at Northfield near Birmingham, on 24 October 1922 aged eighty-three. His estate was valued at £1,071,100 gross.

BASIL G MURRAY

Sources:

Unpublished

Cadbury Archives, Bournville, 'Bridge Street Factory Ledger 1855-79'.

PrC.

Published

Bournville Works Magazine Dec 1922.

Edward Cadbury, *Experiments in Industrial Organization* (Longmans & Co, 1912).

A Century of Progress 1831-1931 (Bournville, Cadbury Bros, 1931).

DNB.

Edinburgh Journal 30 Oct 1852.

Alfred G Gardiner, *Life of George Cadbury* (Cassell & Co, 1923).

T Insull, *John Cadbury* (pp, 1979).

David Owen, *English Philanthropy, 1660-1960* (Cambridge, Massachusetts: Belknap Press of Harvard University Press, 1965).

Iolo A Williams, *The Firm of Cadbury 1831-1931* (Constable & Co, 1931).

WWW.

Laurence J Cadbury, portrait by E I Halliday 1959 (courtesy of Cadbury Schweppes PLC).

CADBURY, Laurence John

(1889-1982)

Chocolate manufacturer

Laurence John Cadbury was born in Birmingham on 30 March 1889, the fourth son of George Cadbury (qv), chairman of Cadbury Brothers Ltd, and the first child of George's second wife, Elizabeth Mary née Taylor. Laurence Cadbury was educated at a Quaker school, Leighton Park, and at Trinity College, Cambridge, where he read economics, graduating in 1911. In the same year he joined the family business at Bournville and in 1913 spent a year in America studying business methods. During the First World War he served in France with Friends Ambulance Units and was awarded the Croix de Guerre and the OBE.

At the end of the First World War senior members of the Cadbury board were suffering from strain and George Cadbury was nearly eighty years old. On his return to Bournville in 1919 Laurence Cadbury was appointed a managing director with a wide range of responsibilities including engineering and production. Existing factory buildings were inadequate for the anticipated post-war expansion of the business, and under Laurence Cadbury's direction long-term plans were prepared to replace existing premises with multi-storey blocks designed for lengthy layouts of mass-production machinery. New six-storey buildings provided 2.5 times the floor space of the factory units they replaced. In 1927 a far-reaching development was the installation of automatic moulding machines for milk chocolate production under an arrangement with the makers Boggild & Jacobsen of Denmark, whereby Cadbury obtained exclusive use of these machines for a four-year period. The resulting improvements in productivity and also vigorous promotion led in the early 1930s to the rising sales and reductions in price which secured Cadbury's dominance of the moulded chocolate market.

For many years Laurence Cadbury was responsible for wage and employment policies. He was a member of the first Confectionery Industrial Reconstruction Committee which was the forerunner of the Joint Industrial Council, and with Ernest Bevin was one of the signatories of the first agreement to stabilize the wages structure and working conditions of the chocolate and confectionery industry. He took particular interest in the investment of Cadbury pension funds. He became a trustee of the men's fund in 1920 and chairman of the trustees in 1932, a position he retained until his retirement.

He played a leading role in the co-ordination of the Cadbury and Fry businesses following the merger of their financial interests in the British Cocoa & Chocolate Co Ltd in 1919. He was appointed a director of the BC & CC in 1921 and was a member of the joint board which co-ordinated the two businesses until 1936 when the Fry company became a wholly-owned subsidiary of Cadbury Brothers.

Development of overseas business was also a major concern of Laurence Cadbury. Prior to 1914 a substantial export trade had been built up with former Empire countries; after the war these countries imposed severe import tariffs. Laurence Cadbury joined the firm's committee formed in 1920 to plan the setting up of overseas subsidiaries behind the tariff walls. An Australian factory, opened in 1922, was followed by others in New Zealand (1930), Eire (1934) and South Africa (1939). The Canadian factory dating from 1920 was originally a Fry enterprise.

During the Second World War chocolate production was severely curtailed and rationing introduced. Manufacturers pooled their resources and considerable factory space became available for other purposes. A substantial proportion of the Bournville factory was converted to production of war materials for the Ministry of Supply. A company was set up called Bournville Utilities Ltd under Laurence Cadbury's chairmanship, and employees were re-trained to make gas masks, aeroplane wings, petrol jerricans and a variety of machine tools. Apart from assisting the war effort Bournville Utilities helped to maintain employment for personnel not required by the armed forces. In 1944 Laurence Cadbury succeeded his elder brother, Edward, as chairman of Cadbury Brothers and in the same year became chairman of the British Cocoa & Chocolate Co. In 1959 he retired from the Cadbury board and

Cadbury Dairy Milk blocks emerging from the cooler and awaiting wrapping, 1930 (courtesy of Cadbury Schweppes PLC).

from the chairmanship of the BC & CC. By that date the number of employees worldwide in the BC & CC group had grown from 16,000 in 1939 to 27,000 and over the same period sales rose from £14 million to £85 million. Group profits after tax rose from £1.017 million in 1944 on sales of £8.912 million (during wartime rationing and when figures related only to UK and export) to £4.119 million in 1958 on sales of £84.246 million. Laurence Cadbury remained a director of the BC & CC until 1964 and chaired its finance committee until 1962, the year the firm's ordinary shares were first quoted on the London Stock Exchange.

His business activities were by no means confined to the family chocolate firm. In 1922 on the death of his father he joined the board of the Daily News Ltd, the holding company for the *News Chronicle* and the *Star*, and subsequently was its chairman until the business was sold to Associated Newspapers in 1960. He was a director of the Bank of England in 1936-38 and 1941-61. In 1941 he was head of the Economic section of the Gvernment Mission to Moscow led by Sir Stafford Cripps. He was High Sheriff of the County of London in 1947-48 and in 1959-60.

This breadth of experience reinforced by his training as an economist was used to good effect by Laurence Cadbury during his chairmanship of Cadbury Brothers and of the British Cocoa & Chocolate Co. Here his main contribution was to guide Cadbury's transition from a home-based family chocolate business to a professionally-managed, international public company. In the post-war period the growth of full employment, of greater spending power and of wider consumer choice demanded major business re-appraisal. The home market for chocolate confectionery had become relatively static, and new markets had to be found overseas or by moving, as Cadbury did in the 1960s, to new product areas in the UK. Television advertising, the decline of independent shops, the growth of multiple grocers and the erosion of resale price maintenance altered the whole pattern of marketing and distribution. Labour-intensive processes gave way to capital-intensive ones and the company's financial and pricing policies had to adapt to continuous inflation. Finally the company needed to come to terms with the separation of ownership and management through the introduction of outside shareholders.

Laurence Cadbury played a similar role in the Bournville Village Trust of which he was chairman from 1954 to 1978; his predecessors as chairman had been his father, George Cadbury, and his mother, Dame Elizabeth. The Trust had to adapt from pioneering the development of the Bournville Estate to working in partnership with the City of Birmingham and with Government to use public funds for joint housing projects. In effect the Trust's experience in housing management became its most important resource and the organisation had to reflect this change in emphasis.

As chairman of the Daily News Trust, Laurence Cadbury supported Liberal causes, though his personal interests lay more in economic affairs than politics. His other interests included membership for many years of the Council of Birmingham University, from which he received an honorary LLD in 1970. He was treasurer of the Populations Investigation Committee from 1936 to 1976 and a trustee of the Historic Churches Preservation Committee. He collected old furniture and guns and built up his own library. As a young man he excelled at a variety of sporting activities including sculling, skiing and motor racing.

In 1925 he married Joyce Mathews; there are two surviving sons and a daughter. His eldest son, Sir Adrian Cadbury, is now (1983) chairman of Cadbury Schweppes PLC. Laurence Cadbury died on 5 November 1982.

BASIL G MURRAY

CADBURY Laurence John

Writings:

This Question of Population. Europe in 1970 ('News Chronicle' Publications Department, 1945).

Post War Problems in the Cocoa and Chocolate Industry Address at a Conference of Sales Representatives of Cadbury Brothers Ltd by Mr L Cadbury and Mr W M Hood, Bournville, 31 May 1946 (Bournville, 1946).

The Newsprint Shortage Statement made at the Annual General Meeting of the Daily News Ltd by the chairman, Mr L J Cadbury (Caxton Press, 1948).

Sources:

Published

Bournville Works Magazine Dec 1959.

Industrial Challenge 1964.

Industrial Record 1947.

Times 9, 17 Nov 1982.

Iolo A Williams, *The Firm of Cadbury 1831-1931* (Constable & Co, 1931).

WW 1982.

CADMAN, John

1st Lord Cadman of Silverdale

(1877-1941)

Petroleum company chairman

John Cadman, 1st Lord Cadman of Silverdale (courtesy of BP Co Ltd).

John Cadman was born in the Staffordshire mining town of Silverdale on 7 September 1877, the second child and eldest son of a family of thirteen. His father, James Cope Cadman, was a mining surveyor, manager of the Silverdale Collieries, who became president of the Institution of Mining Engineers; his mother was Betty née Kelling. His paternal grandfather, John Furnival Cadman, was manager of the Northwood Colliery, Hanwood.

His upbringing was comfortable, with mining the chief topic of conversation and music the main relaxation. Cadman was a competent violinist. He attended the High School, Newcastle under Lyme, and mining classes held by Staffordshire County Council and then won a scholarship to Durham College of Science, obtaining a BSc (Hons) and an MSc. His first post was assistant manager to his father at the Silverdale Collieries but three years later in 1892 he was appointed Assistant Inspector of Mines and sent to work in Fife and the Lothians, where he first became acquainted with oil from the shale deposits: an interesting but not a congenial experience as it lacked sufficient stimulus for his inquisitive mind. He returned to Staffordshire with the same status. In September 1904 he was seconded as Chief Inspector of Mines to the Colony of Trinidad and Tobago and became acquainted with oil for the second time in the bitumen of the great asphalt lakes. Within a short while he was involved as an expert witness in a major gas disaster. His interest turned to the potential oil-bearing areas of the island, but once again his lively intellect felt constricted. Returning to England he was introduced by Dr J S, later Sir James, Haldane, who had a high opinion of Cadman's professional ability, to the Royal Commission on Mines, for which he carried out special investigations into gases and mine ventilation on which he had become very knowledgeable. On more than one occasion he was commended for his bravery in disasters as he sought to determine their causes.

In June 1908 he addressed the Institution of Mining Engineers and in the same year he was appointed Professor of Mining at Birmingham University. Although his primary concern was with mining engineering, he soon organised a degree course in petroleum technology against much opposition. 'It is grossly unfair', wrote Sir Thomas Holland, Professor of Geology at Manchester University, speaking against the projected new course, 'to entice young men into a blind alley and saddle them with a freak title that will handicap every attempt that they make in after-life to specialise in a recognised branch of technology.' {Rowland and Cadman (1960) 55} It is only fair to add that later Sir Thomas became an admirer and close colleague of Cadman in scientific circles. Educationally, no less than scientifically, Cadman was ahead of the time, for, no less than Sir Boverton Redwood (qv), he laid the foundations of the technical appreciation of the petroleum industry in the United Kingdom.

In 1913 Cadman was appointed to the Admiralty Commission, chaired by Admiral Sir Edmund Slade (qv), which was set up by Winston Churchill, First Lord of the Admiralty, to investigate and report on the oil prospects of Persia and the operations there of the Anglo-Persian Oil Co (hereafter the Company: APOC until 1935, the Anglo-Iranian Oil Co until 1955 and the British Petroleum Co thereafter), in connection with a supply contract for naval fuel oil supplies and the possible acquisition of a shareholding in the company by the British Government. The Report was favourable and in July 1914 Parliament approved the government shareholding in the Company of which Cadman later became a dominant figure.

During the First World War Cadman at first acted as an adviser on a number of petroleum matters and became a member of the Advisory Council for Scientific and Industrial Research in 1916. In 1917 he was appointed petroleum assistant to Walter Long, then Secretary of State for the Colonies, who had been charged by the Prime Minister, Lloyd George, with co-ordinating petroleum activities. Shortly afterwards a government department, the Petroleum Executive, was created, charged with the overall supervision of petroleum affairs and Cadman was appointed the first executive head, an appointment in which he showed conspicuous success and received remarkable acclaim. It was the first time that any statistical information on the British consumption and supply situation had been collected, as well as oil production figures from other countries.

Cadman was appointed chairman of the Inter-Allied Petroleum Conference which was set up in May 1918 and he became a close and esteemed colleague of the French representative, Sénateur Henri Bérenger.

Also in 1918, partly at Cadman's instigation, an inter-departmental committee with representatives from other industries under the chairmanship of Lewis Harcourt, was appointed by Walter Long. The purpose of the Harcourt Committee was

> to formulate a policy by which His Majesty's Government shall be guided in all matters relating to the advancement and direction of petroleum industries ... elaborating a general policy which shall be applicable in all cases and shall form a basis which will enable His Majesty's Government to deal uniformly with all questions relating to the industry whether departmental or commercial which may arise for decisions and settlement in the future. {PRO, FO 368/2255}

The brief was extensive and important, but the results fell below expectations. Too much time was expended in trying to reconcile the respective interests of the APOC, Burmah Oil Co and the Royal Dutch-Shell group and the Committee never succeeded in tackling the structural and strategic issues of a British oil industry. Cadman was deeply disappointed but became absorbed in a series of diplomatic negotiations on behalf of the British Government with French representatives, notably Henri Bérenger, which eventually resulted in the San Remo Agreement of 24 April 1920. This settled Anglo-French oil relations and ultimately enabled the Turkish Petroleum Co to be reconstituted with French and later American participation. Cadman's war-time services were honoured in 1918 with the bestowal of a KCMG.

After the war in the midst of his diplomatic activities he was appointed Technical Adviser on Oil to the British Government and as his absences from Birmingham University became longer and more frequent, he felt obliged to resign his chair, which he did from 30 September 1920. In the autumn of the same year he visited the United States where he widened his understanding of the latest technical developments in the American oil industry. He was now approaching a major turning point in his life, comparable only to his earlier academic appointment. With the ending of the war, the conclusion of the San Remo Agreement, the retirement of Walter Long and the slackening of government interest in the Petroleum Executive which had become a department within the Board of Trade, Cadman felt uneasy and frustrated. The role of a government official after the excitement of the previous half-dozen years, when he had been advising some of the most influential politicians, associating with some of the most eminent scientists and negotiating on some of the most important aspects of international petroleum affairs, left him dissatisfied. Unlike

France, no constituted oil industry was likely to emerge in Britain and therefore Cadman had diminishing hopes of playing a decisive part in relations between Government and the oil industry. In 1921, therefore, he accepted the post of Technical Adviser to the APOC offered to him by Sir Charles Greenway (qv). Greenway since late 1919 had been re-organising the Company and recognised that it needed the infusion of new scientific skills and a comprehensive policy of technical development. This was Cadman's new challenge.

He moved to London to a house in Highgate in 1921. Towards the end of that year, whilst keeping a discreet 'official' watch upon the Washington negotiations, Cadman undertook his first business assignment to the United States. He was empowered by Greenway to discuss collaborative action with Standard Oil over a concession in North Persia with which both countries had become associated. At the same time Cadman made the first overtures for American participation in the Turkish Petroleum Co. It was a successful mission, cementing earlier relations which Cadman had made with American officials and oil executives during his period of government service. It was also a period of intense diplomatic activity over the 'Open Door' controversy and anxiety about the American oil reserves' position on which many pessimistic assessments were being made. Cadman's personal and impartial intervention moderated the acrimony and improved the mutual understanding.

In 1923 Cadman became a managing director of the Company and began to make his influence strongly felt within it. He had already re-organised the technical departments and made them more cohesive and interrelated. He imparted new directions and a better application of scientific principles to exploration activities. He reviewed the refinery processes being operated and the functioning of the research centre. He was respected not only because of his authoritative presence, but also because he understood the technical basis of the problems and the scientfic relevance of the solutions proposed. He did not instruct, he informed, preferring a better approach to emerge in a co-operative effort from those involved rather than being imposed by those in charge. He was a practical scientist who deprecated any rigid classifications of 'pure' and 'theoretical' science. He was, however, determined in his differentiation of responsibilities to maintain a clearly defined line of managerial control and a proper appreciation of the cost effectiveness of all technical operations. He was later, as chairman of the Company, to apply these practical principles to all phases of the Company's activities within an overall harmonisation of effort and objectives. The more each person understood his personal involvement and corporate policy, the greater would be the total output, and the less individual friction. He applied budgeting criteria and cost analysis on a comprehensive scale, but he generously encouraged personal initiative. His concept of managerial expertise may seem mundane in present terms, but in his time his managerial practices were innovative in his country and constituted one of the elements which contributed to the growth of the Company.

Some of his ideas and the strength of his personality did not commend him to some of his colleagues on the board, who had tried unsuccessfully to block his appointment as a managing director and were equally determined to prevent his appointment as chairman. Nevertheless, to Greenway's satisfaction and the relief of many, Cadman became deputy chairman and finally on 27 March 1927, chairman on Greenway's retirement. It was a notable appointment, for Cadman's background and expertise were academic and scientific, not financial or administrative. By this time he had already visited the company's installations in Persia in 1924 and attended the coronation of the Riza Shah in Tehran in April 1926. He investigated the Company's properties in Argentina in 1923. His time as chairman of APOC was marked by extensive negotiations, 1928-32, with the Persian Government to improve the concessionary relationship, and included his offer of participation to the Persian Government in the shareholding of the Company, and the final establishment of the Iraq Petroleum Co under its working agreement of 1928 and its modified concessionary arrangements in 1932.

Cadman was a key figure in the attempts to introduce a measure of self-regulation into the oil industry at a time of over-production, excessive competition and falling prices. At Achnacarry Castle in August 1928 Cadman met with Deterding (qv) and Teagle to discuss measures of rationalisation. The 'As Is' agreement proposed stabilising production levels and market shares on the basis of those actually achieved in 1928, with agreed increases thereafter. These moves were partly vitiated by the failure to restrain production in the USA, by the restrictions placed on American companies by anti-trust legislation, and by the difficulties in restraining local management from increasing their market shares.

Cadman also took part in the negotiation of a new concession with the Persian Government in April 1933, following the cancellation of the D'Arcy Concession on 26 November 1932; discussions in Italy with Mussolini and petroleum officials in 1928 and 1932; organising the First World Petroleum Congress which took place in London in July 1933; encouraging exploration for oil in the UK which resulted in the Petroleum Act of 1934, the first drilling by the Company at Portsdown in Hampshire in March 1936 and the first discovery at Eakring in Nottinghamshire, 1939; and visits to Australia in 1934, Tehran in 1934 and 1939 and frequently to Paris. It was a busy schedule and the pace certainly affected his health, which needed serious attention in 1938, and doubtless curtailed his life.

Cadman not only devoted all his talents to the Company but found time to be a director of the Great Western Railway and the Compagnie Universelle du Canal Maritime de Suez in 1935. He sat on (and later chaired) the Commission on Televison which was the first body to appreciate the potential significance of the new form of communication. He also served as vice-chairman of an Advisory Committee set up to monitor its subsequent development. In 1937 he was asked to chair a government committee into the workings of the Imperial Airways, which reported critically on its management and policies amid general approval. He also served on the Air Advisory Panel, the Economic Advisory Council, the Industrial Transference Board, the Coal Advisory Committee, the Fuel Research Board, the safety in Mines Board, the Committee on Inquiry into the Post Office, the Industrial Research Association, the Ministry of Information Committee, the Government Petroleum Board and the Institute of Petroleum, of which he was president 1916-17 and 1935-37. He was also a prolific lecturer addressing many professional societies and took a great interest in the proceedings of the Royal Institute.

Honours continued to be conferred on John Cadman. In 1934 he received the honorary degree of LLD from Birmingham University. In 1937 he was elevated to the peerage as Lord Cadman of Silverdale and in 1940 he was elected a Fellow of the Royal Society. These were fitting testimonials to his educational, public and scientific interests and services. He was appreciated for his humanity, his sense of humour, his friendliness and his practical faith. Throughout his life he was a devout Anglican. He was respected for his scientific acumen and technological understanding which he applied to his Company and shared with men of vision in industry and in Government, young and old. In business circles he is remembered not only for his leadership of the APOC and his prominent role in the international oil industry, but for his integrity, his spirit of reconciliation and his personal sympathy and enthusiastic natural talents in an industry which had been prone to animosity, rivalry and sharp practices and into which he instilled a sense of international responsibility. The warmth of his personality and the breadth of his talents brought him an extraordinarily wide range of friends.

In February 1907 Cadman married Lilian Harrigan, daughter of the Magistrate of Port of Spain; they had two sons and two daughters. Lord Cadman died at the age of sixty-three on 31 May 1941 leaving £234,748 gross.

R W FERRIER

Writings:

Many lectures published.

Sources:

Unpublished

PRO, FO 368/2255, Report and Proceedings of the Petroleum Imperial Policy Committee.

BCe.

MCe.

PrC.

Published

Addresses of the recipients of the Cadman Memorial Medal in the *Journal of the Institute of Petroleum* 1946-82.

DNB.

Ronald W Ferrier, *The History of The British Petroleum Company*, vol 1 *The Developing Years* (Cambridge: Cambridge University Press, 1982).

The Journal of the Institute of Petroleum 1941.

CADMAN John

'The Late Lord Cadman' *The Naft*.

Obituary Notices of Fellows of the Royal Society 3 (1941).

John Rowland and Basil, Second Baron Cadman, *Ambassador for Oil: The Life of John, First Baron Cadman* (Jenkins, 1960).

WWW.

CAILLARD, Sir Vincent Henry Penalver

(1856-1930)

Industrialist

Sir Vincent Caillard (courtesy of the National Portrait Gallery, London).

Vincent Henry Penalver Caillard was born in Kensington, London on 23 October 1856. His father, Camille Felix Desiré Caillard, of Trowbridge, Wiltshire, was a County Court judge who left £1,629; his mother Emma Louisa née Reynolds was second cousin to Benjamin Disraeli. Caillard was educated at Eton and Woolwich, where he won the Pollock Medal, and was commissioned in the Royal Engineers in 1875.

From April 1879 to March 1880 he served on the Montenegrin Frontier Commission and the Arab Tabia Bridge Commission; and from July 1880 to October 1883 he was an intelligence officer in the Eastern Mediterranean. In October 1883, because of his linguistic facility and knowledge of the Ottoman Empire, he was appointed Financial Representative of Great Britain, Holland and Belgium on the Ottoman Public Debt Council in Constantinople. Here Caillard gained the experience of international politics and high finance which were the principal assets he brought to his business career. Until his retirement in 1898 he alternated with the French representative as President of the Council, which managed part of the Ottoman revenues in order to protect the interests of foreign creditors. Caillard was responsible for reorganising the administration of the revenues, and the reform of indirect taxation over which he presided encouraged the revival of the silk, salt, and winegrowing industries. He also acted as an intermediary between the Sultan (Abdul Hamid) and the British Government, most notably in making financial arrangements for British participation in the Baghdad Railway scheme (a proposal eventually abandoned in 1903).

In 1898 Caillard resigned from the Debt Council to enter private business. He became a director of the newly-formed National Bank of Egypt, taking an active part in its early development and remaining on the board until 1908. He also became chairman of two companies interested in agricultural development in the Ottoman Empire, the Daira Sanieh Co and the Irrigation Investment Co, and was briefly a director of La Banque Internationale de Commerce et de l'Industrie (Brussels). He also joined the board of Vickers Ltd, lending his financial and political expertise to an expanding armaments manufacturer which now needed an infusion of talent to supplement the skills of an ageing and family-dominated board. In 1903 Sigismund Loewe, who had presided as finance director over the major issues of share capital marking Vickers' rapid expansion in the 1890s, died; his responsibilities for financial control were gradually assumed by Caillard, who became finance director in 1906 and thereafter made Vickers his principal, though never his only, business interest. His main contribution was to encourage the full use of the company's assets, and to use his contacts in international banking circles and in the Near East to arrange finance for Vickers' customers, thereby maximising the company's share of a volatile and difficult market. Though Francis Barker and Basil Zaharoff were the company's principal salesmen, Caillard used his connections in Constantinople to secure the order for the reconstruction of the Turkish fleet, won by Vickers in 1914.

The First World War overturned the political and financial world which had seen Vickers' greatest success, and set Caillard's particular talents at a discount. Against the claims of his obituarist that it was 'chiefly due to his initiative and organising ability' {*Times* 18 Mar 1930} that Vickers contributed so largely to the output of munitions, must be set the collapse of the company's internal accounting system, of which Caillard was in charge. Under war conditions Vickers' profits of over £4 million for 1916 to 1919 were respectable, but the company could not say how or when they had been made. This uncertainty about the company's financial position contributed to the most damaging mistake of buying British Westinghouse, the electrical interests of the Metropolitan Carriage, Wagon & Finance Co from Dudley Docker (qv), a close political associate of Caillard. The purchase price of £19 million in 1919 was more than Vickers could afford and was believed in City circles to be almost double what the interests were worth. The subsequent mismanagement and loose financial control of those subsidiaries, contributed heavily to Vickers' losses; together with unprofitable expansion into Roumania (Aciéries et Domaines de Reçsiçta) and Poland (the Starachowice company), they so weakened Vickers financially that a major writing-down of capital was forced on the board in 1926. In 1927 Caillard left the board, to be succeeded by Sir Mark Webster Jenkinson (qv).

Besides Vickers and banking, Caillard had extensive railway interests as director of Mexican Central Railways Securities (1900-8), of Bath Electric Tramways (chairman, 1904-10) and of the London, Chatham & Dover Railway (1905-22). After the amalgamation of the railways (1921–23) he served as director of the Southern Railway Co until his death. His most significant railway interest was as director (1903-23) and chairman (1904-20) of Beyer Peacock & Co, a well-established locomotive manufacturing and general engineering firm which was reconstructed and floated on the Stock Exchange in 1903. Beyer Peacock's poor profit record was heavily criticised in the financial press between flotation and the outbreak of war. Caillard's miscellaneous interests included the Canada Steamship Co, the Trust & Loan Co of Canada, and the World Auxiliary Insurance Co.

A strong, if fitful, dynastic sense marked much of Caillard's business life. In 1910 he handed over the chairmanship of Bath Electric Tramways to his brother Esmond (1861-1930), who also became a director of James Booth & Co, a metal manufacturer bought by Vickers in 1918. Caillard's son Bernard (1882-1966) joined the board of Wolseley Motors in 1914 and the main board of Vickers in 1919, leaving both in 1925. He was also managing director of British Lighting & Ignition Co, which Vickers formed in 1917 and a director of the Variable Speed Gear Co, another Vickers subsidiary. At various times Caillard himself joined his relatives on the boards of these companies, finally taking over the chairmanship of British Lighting & Ignition Co in 1925, shortly before it ceased trading.

After 1914 Caillard's time was increasingly occupied with political activity. He was a convinced tariff reformer, and had sat on the Tariff Commission, of which he was chairman in 1904 and president in 1920; in 1906 he contested Central Bradford as a Unionist. During the war he was disturbed by labour militancy and excited by the prospects of a protectionist reconstruction of post-war commercial policy. He joined Dudley Docker in the foundation of the Federation of British Industries in 1916, and with two Vickers directors (Sir Trevor Dawson (qv) and Francis Barker) and others established the London Imperialists, later the British Commonwealth Union, in December of the same year. He led an outspoken and disgruntled protectionist faction in the FBI, and served as the Federation's third president in 1919. During the war he maintained a steady correspondence with David Lloyd George, both as Minister of Munitions and Prime Minister, on the subject of labour subversion; and he acted as an intermediary between Lloyd George and Basil Zaharoff in 1917 when the latter was entrusted with negotiations to end the war with Turkey by the payment of £10 million in gold to certain Turkish politicians.

Caillard married Eliza Hanham, his stepsister, in 1881; they had a son and a daughter. Eliza Caillard commanded a Red Cross hospital during the war and received the OBE. She died in 1926. In 1927 Caillard married Zoé, widow of John Oakley Maund, who outlived her second husband and published in 1933 *Sir Vincent Caillard Speaks from the Spirit World*, which reported little about his business life. Caillard was a man of eclectic cultural interests. He composed a number of unremembered songs and a setting of Blake's 'Songs of Innocence', and he published several short stories. He was a fierce controversialist for tariff reform whose style is perhaps best illustrated by the observation, in a letter to the *Times* on 28 October 1925, that 'I am convinced that free-traders and protectionists have their brains so differently constructed that they never can meet in argument on the same plane.' He was a major backer of the *Empire Mail*, a periodical journal which appeared in various forms from 1911 to 1934, stridently advocating economic nationalism based on the Empire. His principal published work, *Imperial Fiscal Reform*, was an expansion of articles appearing in the *National Review* from February to April 1903 in anticipation of the launching of the tariff reform campaign by Joseph Chamberlain (qv). Caillard was knighted in 1896. He was a DL and JP for Wiltshire. He died on 18 March 1930, leaving £92,261 gross.

JOHN TURNER

Writings:

Report on the Revenues Ceded by Turkey to the Bond Holders of the Ottoman Public Debt ... and Some Remarks on Cognate Subjects (Effingham Wilson, 1888).

letter on the Transvaal crisis *Times* 3 Oct 1899.

'Some Considerations on Imperial Finance' *National Review* 38 (Feb 1902).

'Foreign Trade and Home Markets' *ibid* 39 (Mar 1902).

'Some Suggestions towards an Imperial Tariff' *ibid* 39 (Apr 1902).

'Free Trade and its Defenders' *ibid* 41 (May 1903).

Imperial Fiscal Reform (Edward Arnold, 1903).

letter on German indemnities *Times* 16 Dec 1918.

'A New Force in Industrial Legislation' *Empire Review* 32 (Nov 1918).

'Premier's Indefinite Policy: Risk of Disorganising Production' *Times* Trade Supplement 23 Aug 1919.

'Industry and Production' *National Review* 75 (1920).

letter on industrial relations *Times* 30 Aug 1923.

letter on inter-Imperial preferential trading *ibid* 22 Nov 1923.

letter on fiscal policy and industry's handicaps *ibid* 22 Apr 1924.

letter on Baron d'Estournelles de Constant *ibid* 20 May 1924.

letter on coal dispute *ibid* 28 July 1925.

letter on tariff protection of industries *ibid* 28 Oct 1925.

letter on English view of American War of Independence *ibid* 5 Aug 1926.

letter on Anglo-Saxon church at Bradford-on-Avon *ibid* 24 Feb 1927.

letter on time reckonings *ibid* 15, 19 Dec 1928.

letter on taxation of thrift *ibid* 10 Oct 1928.

A New Conception of Love by Sir V Caillard, written on his Communigraph and transcribed with an appendix by Lady Caillard (Rider & Co, 1934).

This is a selection of his writings.

Sources:

Unpublished

BLPES, Tariff Commission papers.

House of Lords RO, P J Hannon papers; Lloyd George papers.

Modern Records Centre, University of Warwick Library, FBI papers.

Vickers Ltd, Millbank Tower, London SW1, Vickers papers.

BCe.

PrC.

H S W Corrigan, 'British, French and German Interests in Asiatic Turkey, 1888-1914' (London PhD, 1954).

R P T Davenport-Hines, 'The Armaments Industry under Disarmament, 1919-36' (Cambridge PhD, 1979).

Published

Lady Zoé Caillard, *Sir Vincent Caillard Speaks from the Spirit World* (Rider & Co, 1932).

DNB.

FBI *Bulletin* 1917-20.

Herbert Feis, *Europe, The World's Banker* (New Haven, Connecticut: Yale University Press, 1930).

Investor's Journal 1904-27.

John D Scott, *Vickers, a History* (Weidenfeld & Nicolson, 1962).

Times 18 Mar, 1 Aug 1930 and 1903-30 passim.

Clive Trebilcock, *The Vickers Brothers: Armaments and Enterprise* (Europa Publications, 1977).

WWW.

CALLENDER, Sir Thomas Octavius

(1855-1938)

Electrical cable manufacturer

Sir Thomas O Callender ca 1928 (courtesy of BICC PLC).

Thomas Octavius Callender was born in Glasgow on 9 April 1855, the eldest son of the family of five boys and five girls of William Ormiston Callender and his wife Jean née Marshall, both of whom had close connections with the leather trade in Scotland. In 1859 the family moved south to Hammersmith where William acted as agent for several Scottish textile mills. Later, he established a connection with the Val de Travers Asphalte Co of Neuchâtel and obtained an interest in the import of bitumen from Trinidad.

Thomas or 'Tom' as he was known, was educated at Greenock, London and at a school in Boulogne-sur-Mer. His schooling in France, only terminated by the outbreak of the Franco-Prussian War in 1870, was the beginning of his life-long interest in modern languages which was encouraged still further by his wide business travels to India (seven times), much of Africa, America and the West Indies, in addition to Russia and Rumania and the Continent generally.

Laying Callender mains at Aalborg, 1895. Tom Callender holding plans (courtesy of BICC PLC).

Returning to London, he entered his father's office, and when Callender & Sons was formed in 1877 for asphalt paving and the refining of bitumen, Tom and his brother William joined their father as partners. The refinery was situated on the River Thames at Millwall where it remained until 1880 when a four-and-a-half acre site was purchased at Erith, Kent.

At the instigation of Tom, who had been much impressed by the electric lighting at the St Petersburg Opera House when he visited it in 1880, the company turned their attention to cables. When, in 1882, Callender's Bitumen, Telegraph & Waterproof Co was formed with a share capital of £40,000 in £1 ordinary shares, together with £13,000 debenture stock, Tom was appointed manager and devoted all his energies to the development of cables insulated with vulcanized bitumen (patented by his father) and to a method of laying these solid in asphalt. Shortly after the company's formation, W O Callender sold out his interest in the Trinidad lake to Ami Lorenzo Barber (1843-1909) in the USA, one of the leaders in the paving industry in that country. In 1896, Callender's Cable & Construction Co was formed with Tom Callender as managing director, a position he held for forty-two years. That year the firm's sales totalled £95,764, of which 94 per cent came from cables. By 1932, the company's capital comprised £1,116,000 of ordinary shares, £800,000 of preference stock, and £300,000 of debentures; its sales were then £1,368,387.

Callender held directorates in a number of related companies which included Callender's Share & Investment Trust, the Lancashire Electric Power Co, the Yorkshire Electric Power Co, the Scottish Electric Power Co, St Helen's Cable & Rubber Co, Herne Bay & District Electric Supply Co, Anchor Cable Co, Enfield Cable Works, W T Glover & Co and Thomas Bolton & Sons.

In 1893 Tom was elected a member of the Institution of Electrical Engineers, on the council of which he served from 1903 to 1906. In 1915 he was made a JP for the county of Kent and in 1918 was knighted in recognition of his public work and services to the nation. In 1921 he became president of the Electrical Trades Benevolent Institution, in which he had taken a close personal interest. He also served as vice-president of the Federation of British Industries and in 1900 was a founder member of the Cable Makers' Association.

His recreations were travelling, modern languages, motoring and philately. His outstanding characteristics were his tremendous driving force and energy.

In 1884 Tom married Bessie Emmeline Pinnock of Erith, by whom he had one son, Thomas Ormiston (d 1941). Sir Thomas Callender died on 2 December 1938, at his home, Bidborough Court, Kent, leaving £383,276 gross.

R M BLACK

Writings:

Evidence before the Tariff Commission, BLPES, Tariff Commission papers TC 1/27.

'Recollections at IEE Commemoration Meetings, 1922' *Journal of the Institution of Electrical Engineers* 60 (1922).

Sources:

Unpublished

BICC, Prescot, Merseyside, archives, board minute books 1882-1945.

MCe.

PrC.

Waldo J Clements, 'B I-Callender History' (4 vols, typescript, ca 1970, in BICC archives).

Published

Robert M Black, *Electric Cables in Victorian Times* (Science Museum, 1972).

DAB.

Electrical Review 123 (Dec 1938).

Philip V Hunter and James Temple Hazell, *Development of Power Cables* (George Newnes, 1956).

Journal of the Institution of Electrical Engineers 85 (1938).

Robert M Morgan, *Callender's, 1882-1945* (Prescot, Merseyside: BICC PLC, 1982).

The Story of Callenders 1882-1932, Callenders Cable and Construction Company Ltd (pp, 1932).

WWW.

CAMM, Sir Sydney

(1893-1966)

Aircraft designer and manufacturer

Sydney Camm was born in New Windsor, Berkshire, on 5 August 1893, the eldest of 12 children of Frederick William Camm, carpenter and joiner, and his wife Mary née Smith.

Sydney went to the Royal Free School in Windsor where he acquired an early interest in aeronautics through the construction of flying models. Early in 1912, as an apprentice carpenter, he was a founder member and secretary of the Windsor Model Aeroplane and Gliding Club. In December 1912 the Club, led by Sydney Camm, designed and built two successful full-size biplane gliders. The second of these was being adapted to take a 25 hp Anzani engine when war broke out in August 1914. Later that year Camm joined Martin & Handasyde Ltd of Maybury Hill, Woking, and Brooklands, Weybridge, to work under A A Fletcher on the Martinsyde S I single-seat scout biplane of which 11 were delivered to the Royal Flying Corps by the end of the year. This type was followed in 1915 by the Martinsyde G 100 Scout, which formed the equipment of No 27 Squadron RFC, as a fighter-bomber and, in 1916, the G 102 with a 160 hp Beardmore engine which saw service in the Middle East as the Martinsyde Elephant.

Camm gained early design and construction experience of single-seat fighters under H P Martin, George H Handasyde and A A Fletcher, culminating in 1917, in the Martinsyde F 3 and F 4 Buzzard single-seat fighters, judged in their day to be superior to any contemporary type. With a 300 hp Hispano Suza engine the Buzzard had a top speed of 144 miles an hour, the fastest British aircraft in production when the war ended. By that time Camm was assistant chief designer with much practical experience, supplementing his modest salary by writing articles for model aircraft magazines. Indeed, he described himself as a 'technical journalist' when he was elected to the Royal Aeronautical Society in 1918.

The Martinsyde company went into liquidation in May 1921, but Camm stayed on with George Handasyde and Hamilton Fulton of the newly-formed Handasyde Aircraft Co and, in September 1922, with Fred Raynham (Martinsyde's chief pilot) he reconditioned a Martinsyde F 6 which won second place in the first Kings Cup Air Race at Croydon, with Raynham as pilot and Camm as navigator mechanic. In October 1922, Handasyde and Camm collaborated in the design of an exceptionally clean, unbraced cantilever monoplane glider which did well at the International Itford Gliding Meeting. When Raynham moved in early 1923 to the new H G Hawker Engineering Co Ltd at Brooklands (a successor to the Sopwith Aviation Co Ltd) Sydney Camm went too as a senior draughtsman under the chief designer, W G Carter.

At once Camm showed his enthusiasm, practical experience and a design artistry in work on a single-seat fighter development of the Sopwith

Hawker Hurricane II, 1940 (courtesy of Sir Peter Masefield).

Snipe, the Hawker Woodcock. As a sideline, Carter gave Camm the job of designing an ultra-light aeroplane for the Air Ministry's Light Aeroplane Competition of 1924 for a prize of £3,000. This was Camm's first 'solo' design and, like all his subsequent projects, a 'good looker'. Named the Cygnet, it was a neat two-seat biplane first powered with a 34 hp Anzani two-cylinder engine and, as a result of meticulous attention to detail, weighed only 373 lb empty, the lightest in the competition. The two aircraft built gained third and fourth places in the competition as a whole and would have won but for engine unreliability. Camm thus showed his competence and originality and, when Carter moved to the Gloster Aircraft Co in 1925, Sydney Camm was appointed Hawkers' chief designer, a position which he occupied with distinction for thirty-four years until 1959 when he became chief engineer.

Camm's first military design, the Hawker Danecock (of which 15 were delivered to Denmark), revealed both Martinsyde and Sopwith influence and was a logical follow-up to the Woodcock.

Camm then moved on from wood to metal construction and, in the Hawker Heron, first flown in 1925, founded a long line of Hawker single-seat fighters with simple steel and duralumin tubes swaged to rectangular sections at their ends to form joints through flat steel plates, riveted and bolted. Camm straightaway established a reputation for structural strength in the new metal construction and never cut corners in this, or other, respects.

Hawker's production lines were now filled and Camm turned to a range of projects, including bombers, which culminated in December 1926, in a design study for a clean and graceful two-seat day-bomber biplane to replace the vintage DH 9s still in service with the Royal Air Force. The first flight of this significant new aircraft, designed around the 450 hp Rolls Royce F Engine, was in June 1928. This was the Hawker Hart which showed in convincing fashion Camm's eye for line and symmetry of form which was to characterise all his subsequent aircraft. In its various developed forms — Hart, Demon, Osprey, Audax, Hardy, Hartbee, Hind and Hector — a total of more than 2,800 aircraft were built in ten years to the same basic design and delivered to 20 air forces throughout the world, in addition to squadrons of the Royal Air Force and the Fleet Air Arm.

Concurrently, in 1929, Camm produced an advanced new single-seat fighter biplane prototype, to the Air Ministry's F 20/27 specification, named by Hawkers the Hornet. Designed, like the Hart, around the Rolls Royce F engine with 'the eversharp nose' the Hornet was the first fighter to exceed 200 miles an hour in level flight. After extensive trials, the new Hawker single-seat fighter was ordered as the standard single-seat interceptor fighter for the Royal Air Force and named the Fury. In developed forms, Furies remained in RAF service until 1939. In all, 284 Furies, and the Naval version, the Nimrod, were built and delivered to nine air forces, as the peak of biplane fighter performance. The fastest, the High Speed Fury of 1936, attained 242 mph at 15,000 feet.

By 1934, however, there was a move to supersede the traditional braced biplanes with cantilever monoplane fighters. The result was Camm's prototype F 36/34 'Interceptor Monoplane' (K 5083) powered with the new 1,000 hp Rolls Royce Merlin engine, fitted with a retractable undercarriage and designed as an eight gun fighter, first flown by P W S Bulman on 6 November 1935. This most significant aeroplane which became the Hawker Hurricane, represented a leap forward in performance and received a production order for 600 aircraft in June 1936.

Thanks to the Hawker system of construction, the Hurricane was easy to build and, by July 1944, when Hurricane production ceased, a total of 14,533 Hurricanes of a dozen different Marks had been completed. When the Battle of Britain began in August 1940, RAF Fighter Command had 32 Hurricane squadrons and by March 1942, a peak production rate was reached of 77 Hurricanes a week. To the Hurricanes must go the major credit for the winning of the Battle of Britain and to Camm the credit for designing an aeroplane which (by contrast with the Spitfire) could be built simply in sufficient numbers while retaining a performance to make that desirable.

In 1937, when the first production Hurricanes were coming into service, Camm and his design team set to work on a 'Hurricane replacement', around the Rolls Royce Vulture or the Napier Sabre engine of twice the power of the original Merlin. This aircraft, to Specification F 18/37, was the Hawker Tornado, first flown with the Vulture engine by Philip Lucas on 6 October 1939, and 500 were ordered from A V Roe & Co. Production was, however, switched to the 12-gun Sabre-powered Hawker Typhoon, a variant of the Tornado, first flown on 24 February 1940, and of which 3,300 were built before a developed variant the Tempest, took over with both the Sabre and the Bristol Centaurus engine (1,395 built). Tempests shot down more than 600 V1 flying bombs and saved London from much devastation. It was followed by the F2/43 Fury and Sea Fury monoplanes, the peak of piston fighter design, of which 1,460 were completed. With these designs, speeds reached 485 mph at 1,800 feet.

Camm was now established as the leading exponent of single-seat fighter design and development — indeed as the world's greatest designer of

Hawker Harrier prototype with Hawker Hart on the ground, 1966 (courtesy of Sir Peter Masefield).

fighter aircraft. Naturally he moved to the revolutionary new power-plant, the jet engine, with enthusiasm and, on 2 September 1947, the P 1040 prototype jet fighter was flown at Boscombe Down, powered with a 4,500 lb thrust Rolls Royce Nene engine. In production form for the Royal Navy the P 1040 became the Sea Hawk, of which 536 were built with a top speed now raised to 550 mph at 36,000 feet.

Last of Camm's great line of conventional fighters came the Hawker Hunter, again displaying his eye for elegance of line, and first flown on 20 July, 1951 as the P 1067. In all, 1,985 Hunters were built for the Royal Air Force and six other air forces. It remained in service, as the Hunter Mark 9, into the 1970s.

With the development, by a Bristol-Siddeley team led by Dr Stanley Hooker, of the BS 53 jet engine, later the Pegasus, in which jet afflux was discharged through two pairs of rotatable nozzles as well as from the normal jet pipe, in 1957 Sydney Camm embarked upon his most advanced and revolutionary design which started as a Hawker Private Venture. It was the P 1127 Vertical Take-Off and Landing (VTOL) shoulder-wing, fighter. A tethered, hovering, first flight of the P 1127 was performed by Bill Bedford on 21 October 1960, at Dunsfold and its first conventional take-off on 13 March 1961, at the Royal Aircraft Establishment, Bedford. Named the Kestrel, the prototype was developed by 1966 into the Harrier GR MK 1 V/STOL fighter which brought a new dimension into air warfare with the capability of operating from small cleared areas or ships at sea.

Camm continued to press forward his concepts for advanced fighters with a new project always on the drawing-board before the previous prototype had flown and, in 1963, he laid out a new design for a supersonic VTOL fighter, the P 1154, to fly at Mach 2. Regrettably, initial orders for this potentially outstanding strike-fighter were, unwisely, cancelled with other advanced projects by the new Labour Government in 1965, to a serious loss in export orders and employment and to Camm's vigorously expressed dismay.

Sydney Camm had been elected to the board of Hawker Siddeley Aviation Ltd as director of design in 1935 and to the Hawker Siddeley Group board in 1963 on which he remained until his death. Tall, lean, determined, hard-working and autocratic, though shy and inherently modest, Camm, as he gained confidence in himself and his design team in the early 1930s, pursued an unwavering path towards single-engine military aircraft development, with special emphasis on both fighters and the, so-called, day bombers.

Hawker Siddeley's fortunes in both home and export markets were founded upon Camm's designs and he had the satisfaction of being, to a large extent, responsible for the winning of one of the decisive battles of world history. He was in close accord with Royal Air Force policy and procurement in the fifteen years between 1938 and 1953. Thereafter he became increasingly critical of what he regarded, with some justice, as the inadequately informed aviation bureaucracy. This hostility to officialdom reached its zenith with the timid approach of both the Services and the Air Ministry towards his supersonic fighter proposals and, in particular, with the political rejection of his supersonic V/STOL P 1154. He was always ready to listen to people who knew their job and always ready to offer a forthright opinion.

Camm was elected a fellow of the Royal Aeronautical Society in 1932 and an honorary fellow in 1961. He served on the council of the Society from 1943 and became president in 1954-55. He was a regular attender at its meetings and cherished greatly his contacts with fellow members of the aeronautical profession there. He received the British gold medal for Aeronautics in 1949 and the Royal Aeronautical Society's gold medal in 1958. Camm was appointed CBE in 1941 and knighted in 1953.

He married Hilda Rose Starnes (d 1977) on Christmas Day 1915, at the parish church of Wooburn, Buckinghamshire, describing himself then as 'aeroplane mechanic of Bourne End'. They had one daughter.

Sir Sydney Camm died on 12 March 1966, while playing golf at Richmond, Surrey. He left £67,614.

SIR PETER MASEFIELD

Sources:

Unpublished

BCe.

MCe.

PrC.

Personal knowledge.

Published

The Centenary Journal of the Royal Aeronautical Society 1866-1966 Jan 1966.

DNB.

Flight International 17 Mar, 7 Apr 1966.

Peter Lewis, *The British Fighter since 1912* (Putnam & Co Ltd, 1965).

Francis K Mason, *Hawker Aircraft since 1920* (Putnam & Co Ltd, 1961).

WWW.

CAMMELL, Charles

(1810-1879)

Steel manufacturer

Charles Cammell was born in Sculcoates, Hull on 8 January 1810, the fourth son of George Cammell, a shipmaster with Scots connections, and his wife Hannah (d 1825). He was apprenticed to an ironmonger before joining the Sheffield firm of Ibbotson Brothers in 1830. Employed as a commercial traveller for the products of their Globe Works, he remained in their employment until 1837. As a traveller he was successful, and developed great confidence in his own abilities. In the crisis of the American market, which badly affected the firm, he left with Thomas Johnson, the former head bookkeeper at the Globe Works, and set up a partnership with him and his brother Henry, as Johnson, Cammell & Co, steel and file manufacturers and merchants in Furnival Street. Reasons for the departure are unclear, but given his character, the rumours that he quarrelled with his employer over seeking to marry his daughter should not be dismissed.

Besides the traditional products of steel and files, the firm benefited from the great growth in demand for railway materials, especially after the severe trade depression of 1843. By May 1845 they obtained a lease on a site on Savile Street, east of the new station of the Sheffield to Rotherham railway. There they erected the Cyclops Works, one of the earliest of the large steel plants to be built east of the old and crowded central area of Sheffield. The terms obtained from the Duke of Norfolk at that time were advantageous, as his agent Michael Ellison sought to induce industrial and residential development in the eastern area to boost estate rental. This changed pattern of location was repeated by John Brown (qv), Vickers and other Sheffield steelmakers.

Cammell was an accomplished salesman with marked entrepreneurial abilities, who depended upon others for technical expertise. In 1852 Thomas Johnson died and Edward Bury, a former locomotive engineer of the London & Birmingham Railway, became a partner until 1855. From 1846 Cammell was helped by George Wilson (1829-85). Another Scot, he had been sent by his family from Hough Mill, Fife, to the Collegiate School in Sheffield; it seems probable that this occurred at Cammell's instigation, as Wilson was only nine years old at the time and Cammell was a distant relative of the family. He studied chemistry and mathematics at St Andrews and Edinburgh Universities before joining Johnson-Cammell and then spent two years travelling for them in New York. Wilson and Cammell then formed a powerful business alliance which lasted through Cammell's life. Wilson married Cammell's wife's niece, and managed the firm 1864-85.

After 1845 the firm benefited greatly from its spacious site, located close to the railway which supplied iron ore and coal, and which increasingly became vital to the transport of heavy finished products. The initial two acre site quickly became four, and in the late 1850s the works expanded further in size, employment and output.

The firm was a rapid follower, rather than leader, in adopting some of the main innovatory processes. Its Bessemer rail production, begun in 1861, followed John Brown and Bessemer himself locally. Similarly the production of iron armour plate in 1863 followed the example of a neighbouring firm, which had plated its first ships in 1859. The first ships with Cammell armour plates, the *Lord Clyde* and *Lord Alfred*, were launched in 1864. Probably the importance of the Cammell developments lay rather in their responsiveness to the changing market and the rapid increases which were made in the scale of operations to satisfy it. By 1864 the firm produced a very wide range of products of high quality, and the works were greatly enlarged and modernized.

Like John Brown, Cammell adopted limited liability. Registered in 1864 as Charles Cammell & Co Ltd, the company had a nominal capital of £1 million of which £800,000 was paid up. Charles Cammell, chairman of the new company (with George Wilson as managing director), received £200,000 for goodwill as part of the arrangement. A proportion of the other capital raised by conversion into a limited company was used for expansion. Some 15 acres of additional industrial land were developed soon afterwards, and a further 15 acres acquired for future use. After 1865 large-sized steel ingots were produced in the new Grimesthorpe plant. The Cyclops Works was expanded, so that it absorbed the Howard and Agenovia works close by, and new Bessemer plant was installed at the Penistone 'Yorkshire Iron and Steel Works' purchased in 1865. Further rapid expansion in the boom of 1871-73 reduced the costs of production dramatically while demand and prices reached a peak.

Innovations now emerged from the process of development and from the specialisations of the different departments. By 1872 the company produced ten feet thick armour plates, when six feet had been the usual limit in the early 1860s. New handling plant included power cranes, and there was widespread use of gas in the furnaces, for which great efficiency was claimed. The company produced 1,200 to 1,500 tons of finished Bessemer steel per week, and at Grimesthorpe new railway spring and buffer works were in operation, while tyres and axles amounting to 250 tons per week were made. The company employed 4,000 men, 800 more than in the previous year, 1871. At Penistone, where much of the Bessemer material was produced, 700 men were employed, producing metal and rails, tyres and forgings. In the boom the company's directors were also involved in the purchase of the Old and New Oaks Colleries near Barnsley, giving them access to 1,200 acres of the nine foot Barnsley seam of coal, and also as shareholders or directors in the new Wilson-Cammell Patent Wheel Co Ltd, which set up a modern plant employing about 500-600 people in Dronfield.

In all these business expansions the relative entrepreneurial roles of Charles Cammell and George Wilson are hard to distinguish. Charles Cammell attended directors' meetings regularly, but Wilson held the reins, and exercised ever greater power, becoming one of Sheffield's most prominent citizens by the 1870s. He was in turn increasingly helped by his brother Alexander Wilson, who played a key role in the development of the firm. By 1875 three of the eight directors were Manchester men, Thomas Vickers, Alfred Peck and James Harvey, while Charles Vickers became a shareholder in Wilson-Cammell.

By 1873 the boom broke and in 1875, after two years of bad trade, extreme competition and heavy losses (especially on two contracts with an American railway company), reduced profits and a dividend of only £6 per share was paid. Cammell and John Brown reacted in similar ways to the crisis. Alexander Wilson and John Devonshire Ellis (qv) both patented different methods of producing compound armour plates in 1876-77 and thereby laid the groundwork for subsequent recovery based upon a monopoly of that market until the late 1880s. Both firms had by now sprung ahead of their British rivals technologically, and had the know-how and technological momentum to keep a substantial lead at home — though technically Krupp was already developing a similar momentum which would eventually outstrip them both in this field in the 1890s.

Charles Cammell, who had laid the firm's foundations and recruited his technically capable successors, the Wilsons, was no longer much involved. He had moved from an early residence in Watery Lane opposite Portmahon Chapel to a house in the more salubrious Clarkehouse Road not far from the new Botanical Gardens. He then bought Wadeley House, but eventually purchased the Norton Hall estate of the failed banker Samuel Shore from Shore's assignees. Before this, in 1846, Cammell married a widow, Mrs Wright of Birmingham, by whom he eventually had six sons and one daughter. By 1857 he was living at Norton Hall, and was Lord of the Manor of Norton. Subsequently he bought 2,000 acres at Ditchingham in Hampshire and the Brookefield Hall estate near Hathersage in Derbyshire, to which his third son George succeeded after his death in 1879. That year Charles owned 6,563 acres with a gross annual value of £5,925.

Although he served as a JP and a Conservative member of the Sheffield Council (representing Brightside) for three years (1857-60), Cammell avoided all other offices and involvements, except for his membership of the Institution of Mechanical Engineers from 1847. He sponsored a school in Woodseats, but does not appear to have been over-generous to charity.

In later life Charles Cammell suffered from an unidentified but painful internal disease and died in London, whence he had removed for medical treatment, on 13 January 1879. He left an estate valued at under £250,000 gross.

One of his sons, Bernard, was then a managing director of Wilson-Cammell (with George Wilson's son) and after his father's death took a seat on the board of Charles Cammell & Co Ltd.

PAUL NUNN

Sources:

Unpublished

Humberside CRO, Beverley, Sculcoates, baptismal register.

Sheffield Central Library, Charles Cammell & Co Ltd, Report and Balance Sheet, 31 Mar 1875; Henry Tatton, 'Old Sheffield' (3 vols of handwritten notes, comp 1920-36).

Sheffield, Newton Chambers & Co Ltd, archives, M Chambers to Messrs Newton 13, 20 May 1843.

Kenneth C Barraclough, 'The Development of the Early Steelmaking Processes — An Essay in the History of Technology' (Sheffield PhD, 1981).

Published

John Austin and Malcolm Ford, *Steel Town. Dronfield and Wilson Cammell 1873-1883* (Sheffield: Scarsdale Publications, 1983).

Boase.

Duncan Burn, *The Economic History of Steelmaking 1867-1939: A Study in Competition* (Cambridge: Cambridge University Press, 1940).

Charles Cammell & Co Ltd (Charles Cammell & Co Ltd, 1900).

Philip Cottrell, *Industrial Finance, 1830-1914. The Finance and Organisation of English Manufacturing Industry* (Methuen, 1980).

Engineering 24 Jan 1879.

William Odom, *Hallamshire Worthies: Characteristics and Work of Notable Sheffield Men and Women* (Sheffield: J W Northend, 1926).

Sidney Pollard and Paul Robertson, *The British Shipbuilding Industry 1870-1914* (Cambridge, Massachusetts: Harvard University Press, 1979).

Ryland's Iron Trade Circular 12 Feb 1876.

Sheffield and Rotherham Illustrated Update 1897.

Sheffield and Rotherham Independent 6 Jan 1872, 14 Jan 1879.

Sheffield Telegraph 13 Jan 1879.

James H Stainton, *The Making of Sheffield* (Sheffield: E Weston & Son, 1924).

CAMPBELL, Lord Campbell of Eskan
see **CAMPBELL, John Middleton**

CAMPBELL, Colin Frederick

1st Lord Colgrain

(1866-1954)

Clearing banker

Colin Frederick Campbell was born in Scotland on 13 June 1866, the son of George W Campbell, a younger son of Colin Campbell of Colgrain, near Helensburgh. His mother was the second daughter of Sir James Weir Hogg, Bt. Campbell was educated at Eton and began his career in the City of London in the old family business of Finlay, Campbell & Co, East India merchants. He spent several years in India studying the business there and was admitted to a partnership in the firm on his return to England. In 1903 Finlay, Campbell & Co amalgamated with Forbes, Forbes & Co, one of the oldest merchant houses in Bombay, under the style of Forbes, Forbes, Campbell & Co, of which Campbell was chairman for many years. In 1903 he joined the board of the National Provincial Bank, beginning an association of over fifty years.

When his father died in 1897 Campbell succeeded him as a director of the London Assurance and was Governor of that company, 1914-33. Other chairmanships included Alexander's Discount Co (chairman, 1916-50) and the Telegraph Construction & Maintenance Co (chairman from 1932), on whose board his father had also served. Campbell's experience of Far Eastern affairs was of great value to the board of the Chartered Bank of India, Australia & China of which he was a member for many years.

Campbell's father-in-law was senior partner in Messrs Coutts & Co and the link was instrumental in bringing this old banking partnership into affiliation with the National Provincial Bank in 1920.

Campbell's distinguished career was chiefly associated with the National Provincial Bank. During his half-century on the board he saw it grow from the National Provincial Bank of England with fewer than 300 branches and deposits of £50 million to one of the 'Big Five' banks controlling some 1,500 branches and deposits exceeding £800 million. He became deputy chairman in 1929 and succeeded Sir Harry Goschen as chairman in 1933, holding this post until 1946. Under his chairmanship the National Provincial further consolidated its strong position in the country and surmounted the problems of the Second World War. During the war he was chairman of the British Bankers' Association and the Clearing House, while remaining chairman of the National Provincial Bank. His wartime services were recognised in 1946 by his elevation to the peerage as First Baron Colgrain.

At the annual meeting of the bank's shareholders in 1946 Captain Eric Smith (qv), deputy chairman, pointed to the significance of Lord Colgrain's wartime role:

> 'It is a fact, not always realised, that wars if they are to be brought to a successful conclusion, must have behind the combatant forces employed in battle a civilian structure capable of withstanding the strain of interruption and dislocation. An essential component of such civilian structure is an adequate banking system.'

Lord Colgrain remained active as a director until his death, maintaining his contacts with the representatives of the Bank's staff amongst whom his dignified and fair-minded presence appears to have engendered affection as well as respect.

Outside his work he was JP for Kent from 1905, and a member of the Bishop of London's Commission on City Churches.

He married in 1890 Lady Angela Mary Alice Ryder (died 1939), second daughter of the Fourth Earl of Harrowby. They had two sons and two daughters. Lord Colgrain died on 3 November 1954, leaving an estate of £95,648 gross.

RICHARD REED

Sources:

Unpublished

National Westminister Bank, London, archives.

PrC.

Published

Burke's Peerage.

Sir Theodore E G Gregory, *The Westminster Bank through a Century* (2 vols, Oxford University Press, 1936).

'Natproban' (staff magazine) Spring 1946, Winter 1954.

Times 4 Nov 1954.

WWW.

CAMPBELL, Colin Minton

(1827-1885)

Pottery manufacturer

Colin Minton Campbell was born in Liverpool on 27 August 1827, the son of John Campbell and his wife Mary, eldest daughter of Thomas Minton (1765-1836), founder of the Minton Pottery Co. He began to work for Minton at Stoke-on-Trent, under his uncle, Herbert Minton, in 1842, becoming a partner six years later.

After the death of Herbert in 1858, Colin Minton Campbell took control of the firm. He set out to consolidate Minton's international reputation, established when it was awarded the only Council Medal at the Great Exhibition of 1851.

Minton Campbell recognised the popularity of Continental ceramic design and obtained for Minton the skills of a number of Continental artists. Antonin Boullemier, a skilled artist particularly renowned for his paintings of cherubs, came to Stoke-on-Trent in 1872, followed by Désiré Leroy in 1874. Perhaps the most important recruit was Frenchman Louis Marc Solon from Sèvres in 1870, master of the pâte-sur-pâte decorative technique. This technique involved building up an image in relief on a tinted Parian body by painting on successive layers of slip, or liquid clay. The delicate and laborious process defied imitation by Minton's competitors and achieved great popularity. Furthermore, the Art Pottery studio established in South Kensington, 1871-75, kept the factory in touch with contemporary developments in art and design.

Minton Campbell was also quick to utilise the latest technological advances. In 1863 James Leigh Hughes was granted Letters Patent by Royal Warrant for an invention, later known as the acid gold process, which was to revolutionise the ceramic industry. It enabled a rich gold decoration in bas relief to be produced for the first time. Recognising the potential of this invention, Minton Campbell soon obtained the patent rights for Minton. Another great success was the Minton Patent Ceramic Oven, developed by Léon Arnoux, and sold worldwide to most of the major ceramic manufacturers.

These developments secured Minton's international reputation, and the firm was awarded the coveted Diploma of Honour at the Vienna Exhibition of 1875, adding to its gold medals from the Paris Exhibitions of 1867 and 1878. Minton Campbell's contribution to these achievements met with personal recognition and honours. He was made a Commander of the Order of Franz Josef by the Emperor of Austria in 1874, and a member of the Légion d'Honneur at Paris in 1878.

Keenly aware of the importance of having close connections with the major retailers, Minton Campbell established good relations with the London retail trade. So much so, that in 1878 Thomas Goodes bought Minton's entire Paris display and exhibited it in London.

By the time of his death, Minton Campbell had established an expanding and successful company. Its workforce was over 2,000, its turnover £111,000 and its annual profits £2,000, levels not surpassed within the firm until John Campbell assumed control of the company in 1902. Shortly before his death Minton Campbell converted the firm into a limited liability company, admitting several old and valued servants as shareholders.

In addition to managing the affairs of the factory, Minton Campbell enjoyed an extremely active public life. He was a JP for Staffordshire and Derbyshire and a DL of Staffordshire; mayor of Stoke, 1880-83, Conservative MP for North Staffordshire, 1874-80, captain of a battalion of Rifle Volunteers, and chairman of North Staffordshire Railways, 1873-83.

His marriage to Louisa Wilmot, daughter of Rev William A Cave-Browne-Cave of Stretton-in-le-field, in 1853 produced 11 children, only four of whom were alive when their father died at home in Woodseat, near Uttoxeter, on 7 February 1885. He left £189,921 gross.

KEVIN WILSON

Sources:

Unpublished

Minton Museum, Stoke-on-Trent, Minton archives.

MCe.

PrC.

Published

Paul Atterbury, *The Story of Minton from 1793 to the Present Day* (Royal Doulton Tableware Ltd, 1978).
WWMP.

CAMPBELL, John Middleton

Lord Campbell of Eskan

(1912-)

Commodity merchant

John Middleton Campbell, known as 'Jock', was born in London on 8 August 1912, the eldest of the five children of Colin Algernon Campbell, a partner in Curtis Campbell & Co, West India merchants of London, and

CAMPBELL John Middleton

John M Campbell, Lord Campbell of Eskan, aged sixty-five (courtesy of Booker McConnell Ltd).

his wife Gladys née Barrington. The family firm had traded with and owned sugar plantations in British Guiana for over a century.

On his father's side, there were strong banking traditions: his father was a director of the Westminster Bank for over forty years; his grandfather Governor of the Bank of England from 1907 to 1909; and his grandmother was the eldest daughter of the first chairman of Barclays Bank. His mother was descended on both sides from Irish landowners, her mother being a Bayly. In Campbell there was a combination of the hard Scottish head and the romantic Irish heart. As a small boy in Ireland during 'the bad times', he heard views from 'downstairs' as well as 'upstairs' and learnt early how the same events were capable of totally different interpretation from different stand-points.

He was educated at Eton and Exeter College, Oxford, where he did not complete his degree. From childhood he had a stammer which in later years somehow increased the appeal and impact of his speech. In adolescence he was seriously incapacitated for a spell with polio which allowed him to develop his voracious appetite for reading. Although he did not achieve academic distinction, he had great intellectual ability. He was chosen to be the editor of Torquemada's 112 Best Crossword Puzzles, after he had composed a 'revenge' puzzle which Powys Mather considered the most brilliant and the most 'Torquemada-ish' of the many he received. Throughout his business life, Campbell's intellectual ability has been complemented by great skills in getting things done, by a relentless desire to win, a constant search for high standards, a fastidiousness about detail and an enormous capacity to inspire loyalty and devotion from all walks of life.

Jock Campbell joined the family firm, Curtis Campbell, in 1933 and a year later first visited British Guiana where he was profoundly shaken by the social conditions he found. In 1939 the firm, with Campbell as a partner, merged with Booker Brothers, McConnell & Co, a small public company which from a number of family concerns had become the major sugar producer and trader in British Guiana.

The legacy of his polio prevented Campbell joining the armed services during the Second World War and for some time he worked in the Economic Section of the Colonial Office where he contributed his knowledge of sugar and enhanced his understanding of the West Indies. This experience gave him an insight into the working of the political and administrative machine in Whitehall. Although it was mooted that he stay on as a permanent civil servant he declined the opportunity in order to return to business.

He became a managing director of Booker Brothers, McConnell in 1945, vice-chairman in 1947 and chairman in 1952. Whilst he had long family connections with Curtis Campbell, his family had only a small shareholding in the company. His appointments were above all due to the recognition by the board of his leadership, his outstanding ability and energy. He retired in June 1967 and was president (an honorary office), 1967-79.

Campbell had a clear vision of what he wanted for Bookers in British Guiana. Through force of personality, sometimes autocratic, always thoughtful, he transformed the business, the organisation and the attitudes in the decade of the 1950s. At the end of the Second World War, Bookers in Campbell's eyes was 'a shapeless, incoherent conglomeration of variegated activities ... it was almost impossible to make out who and what made a profit or loss, who or what was efficient or inefficient' {Campbell (1959)}.

The businesses were reorganised on a functional basis with companies established for each economic activity. Campbell also began spreading Bookers' investment outside Guiana as hedges against the agricultural and, above all, political hazards of the colony. The most important of these investments were: United Rum Merchants (London), 1949; Motor Car Supply Co of Canada (Alberta), 1954; Coe Group, coastal shipping (Liverpool), 1955; George Fletcher & Co, sugar machinery manufacturers (Derby), 1956; Alfred Button & Sons, wholesale and retail food distributors (London), 1957; Estate Industries, manufacturers of the coffee liqueur Tia Maria (Jamaica), 1957; Sigmund Pumps, pump manufacturers (Gateshead), 1958. These businesses set the pattern for Bookers in the 1960s and 1970s with divisional activities in tropical agriculture, wholesale and retail food distribution, alcohol production and marketing, shipping and engineering. To an extent they were a geographical diversification of activities which had been carried on in the comparatively small economy of British Guiana. At the same time, Bookers' sugar production increased from 125,000 tons per annum in the period 1940-1950 to 175,000 tons in 1952 and to 283,000 in 1967. With additional investments in Jamaica, Trinidad and Barbados, the proportion of Booker assets employed in the West Indies fell only from 60 per cent to 55 per cent between 1950 and 1967.

In 1947 when Campbell was effectively first appointed chief executive of Bookers, shareholders' capital employed was £2.8 million, after-tax profits were £208,000 and 800 shareholders received dividends totalling £80,000. In 1967, the year of Campbell's retirement, shareholders' capital employed was £24 million, after-tax profits £1,692,000 and the dividend totalled just over £1 million paid to 9,000 shareholders. Campbell's policy was continued by his successors, so that when all the Booker businesses in Guyana (renamed after independence in 1966) were acquired by the Government of Guyana in 1976, Booker McConnell continued as an active medium-sized multinational business.

Following the dramatic change in business organisation and clarification of objectives, Campbell strove with all his exceptional energy to make Bookers more acceptable to the people of Guyana and to increase the return on capital employed. His objectives were many: to achieve acceptable profits for Booker shareholders; to improve the material and social circumstances of the employees; to fit the business to the requirements of the Guyanese economy since for much of the period Bookers produced around one-third of the country's GDP; and to assuage and repair the hurts and wrongs of the past, much of which he attributed to racial discrimination and the short-term concern for profits. He knew that Bookers could never be loved or even liked, but he did believe that it could be understood and respected as an efficient productive enterprise. He was amongst the first to stress the four-fold responsibilities of a company to the shareholders, to employees, to customers and to the community. The company improved its public regard in Guyana especially by actively ensuring that Guyanese replaced expatriates in the management of the business. The recruitment and training policies which he designed were models for developing countries. With great fluency he rammed home his theme: 'People are more important than ships or shops or sugar estates' {*ibid*}. Campbell modernised Booker McConnell, created a group of managers well aware that the tide of independence would overcome old-style colonial businesses, and began the process by which Booker McConnell survived cut-off from its roots in British Guiana.

His concern for the developing world was seen in his leadership of the Commonwealth Sugar Producers, which resulted in the Commonwealth Sugar Agreement of 1951. This assured reasonably remunerative prices for the greater part of their sugar production. His continued leadership of the Commonwealth Sugar Producers from 1951 until the present (1982) is an outstanding and unique record. Every British Government and many Commonwealth Governments have turned to him for advice and guidance on sugar matters for thirty years. His special concern with the Caribbean is reflected in his presidency of the West India Committee from 1957 to 1977. His wider interest in developing countries was shown by his work for the Africa Bureau; his numerous private meetings and relationships with leaders of the newly independent West Indian and African countries; and his membership of the Councils of the Overseas Development Institute, and of the University of the West Indies.

His widening political and social interests led him to join the Labour Party but although his advice was sought especially by members of the Wilson Governments, Conservative administrations also welcomed his expert views on sugar affairs. He became director and then chairman of the *New Statesman*, a trustee of Chequers, a director (and deputy chairman) of London Weekend TV, and a director (and nearly chairman) of the Commonwealth Development Corporation. He retired early from Booker McConnell to take up an appointment as chairman of the Milton Keynes Development Corporation, perhaps a little disheartened that the new look he had brought to Booker McConnell was not fully reflected in either its commercial success or in commonsensical behaviour in Guyana as a whole. He brought to the building of Milton Keynes great energy and care of detail, and the ability to inspire and weld a group of managers to a common theme.

Campbell was knighted in 1957 and created a life peer in 1966. Throughout his life, he derived great pleasure from winning ball games — tennis, table-tennis, croquet and golf.

He married first in 1938 Barbara Noel, daughter of Leslie Arden Roffey; they had two sons and two daughters. Secondly, in 1949 he married Phyllis Jacqueline Gilmour Taylor, daughter of Henry Boyd, CBE.

M H CAINE

Writings:

'Why Does Man Work?' Address to Duke of Edinburgh's Study Conference, Oxford 1956 (Oxford University Press, 1957).

'Development and Organisation of Booker Brothers, McConnell & Co Ltd' Edwards Seminar paper 248, Nov 1959.

'The New Africa' Africa Bureau Anniversary address, Nov 1962.

'Attitudes on Africa' *Tropic* Oct 1960.

'£250 million Invested in Ten years in Commonwealth Sugar' *Achievement* Nov 1960.

'Facing up to Facts in the Caribbean' *Times* 9 May 1962.

'The Role of Big Business in the New Nations' *Optima* Dec 1963, reprinted in *Investment and Development: the Role of Private Investment in Developing Countries* (ODI, 1965).

'Private Enterprise and Public Morality' *New Statesman* 27 May 1966.

'Britain, Sugar and the EEC' *Venture* Feb 1967.

Sources:

Unpublished

Booker McConnell's Annual Report and Accounts.

Personal information.

Published

WW 1982.

CAMROSE, 1st Viscount
see **BERRY, William Ewert**

CANDLISH, John

(1816-1874)

Glass manufacturer

John Candlish was born at Bellingham in Northumberland in 1816, the son of John Candlish, a small farmer, who came originally from the south of Scotland. When Candlish was about five his father, attracted to a manufacturing town by the prospect of more lucrative employment, moved to Ayres Quay near Sunderland where his brother was already employed as the manager of the Ayres Quay bottle works belonging to Richard Pemberton. Through the influence of his brother, Candlish's father was employed as a labourer in the bottle works, never earning more than 14s a week according to his son. Despite the poverty of the family Candlish was given a good schooling; at Bellingham he received tuition from Mr Dodds, later Dr Dodds, of North Shields, and his education continued at a small school at Ayres Quay where he distinguished himself as an outstanding scholar.

In 1829, aged eleven, he was put to work in the bottle works as a bottle carrier but thanks to the influence of his uncle was instead apprenticed to a draper. In 1836 Candlish and a partner established their own drapery business in Sunderland but lack of capital led to failure and in 1837 Candlish embarked on a series of not altogether successful ventures including a spell as a commercial traveller for a Bradford firm; the purchase, in 1838, of a small Sunderland newspaper; a partnership in a coal exporting business; and, in 1848, a partnership in a ship-building yard. Candlish eventually became secretary to the Sunderland Gas Co but resigned in 1853 having purchased a small bottle works at Seaham Harbour in partnership with Thomas Greenwell. This was the turning point of Candlish's career. He soon became the principal partner and practically sole owner of the Seaham Harbour works, also known as the Londonderry Bottle Works, and realised a large fortune from the concern. By the 1850s the manufacture of black bottles for the wine and beer trades was already well established in the Sunderland area and during the following two decades the local industry profited greatly from the growing export of bottled beer to the colonies. Candlish secured favourable contracts with several large brewing firms and also supplied bottles by appointment to the Government. In 1860 he purchased an additional bottle works at Diamond Hall near Sunderland which established him as one of the largest manufacturers of black bottles in the country. By 1870 the manufacture of black bottles was largely confined to the North East while other bottle-manufacturing areas such as Yorkshire and Lancashire concentrated on the manufacture of pale bottles for the soft drinks trade. Candlish's works then consisted of ten four-pot furnaces (six at Seaham Harbour and four at Diamond Hall): two furnaces more than his largest local rival, the Ayres Quay Bottle Co.

Profits from bottles enabled Candlish to continue speculating in a variety of other enterprises. He became an extensive ship owner in partnership with Ralph Milbanke Hudson with whom he also established a spelter works. Less successful were his involvements in the Middlesbrough iron ship builders, Candlish Fox & Co, through which he lost money, and the Thornley Colliery Co.

During his lifetime Candlish's religious and political views altered. He had been brought up a Presbyterian, but whilst still a young man became a Baptist lay preacher. His early conservative views were exchanged for more radical ones during the anti-Corn Law agitation of the 1840s and throughout the last half of his life he was a tireless promoter of radical causes at both local and national levels. In 1848 he was elected to

Sunderland Town Council and thereafter took an active part as the leader of the advanced section of the council, as opposed to the conservative section led by James Hartley (qv). He energetically advocated reforms in sanitary and financial administration and took a prominent part in securing the Sunderland Improvement Act of 1851.

Hartley and Candlish had many political clashes, notably in 1861 when Candlish narrowly beat Hartley in the mayoral election, and in 1865 when Hartley beat Candlish in the parliamentary elections. Candlish won the Sunderland parliamentary seat in 1866 and held it until ill-health forced his resignation in 1873. As an MP he was apparently self-conscious about his lack of education. Nevertheless, his attendance rate at Westminster was high. Most notably he chaired the Select Committee investigating the costs of the Abyssinian expedition of 1868. Candlish was also a generous donor to philanthropic institutions, notably the Ragged Schools and the Free Library which he helped to found; a free library and reading room were also provided for his workforce at the Londonderry Bottle Works. In 1862 Candlish became a borough, and subsequently a county, JP. Although Candlish was, according to James Hartley, a 'glutton for work' {*Newcastle Daily Chronicle* 19 Mar 1874}, during his later life the task of managing the Londonderry Bottle Works was given to his brother Robert who inherited the works on Candlish's death.

In 1845 Candlish married his cousin, Elizabeth, daughter of Robert Candlish of Ayres Quay; they had one daughter who married William Shepherd Allen, the MP for Newcastle under Lyme, in 1869. John Candlish died in Cannes on 17 March 1874 from heart disease and hereditary scrofula, leaving effects valued at under £40,000. He was buried in Sunderland with great public mourning.

CATHERINE ROSS

Writings:

PP, HC 1868-69 (180) VI, SC on the Abyssinian War (chairman).

PP, HC 1870 (401) V, SC on Cost of War with Abyssinia (chairman).

Political Life and Speeches of John Candlish, Member for Sunderland from 1866 to 1874 (Sunderland: William Duncan, 1886).

Sources:

Unpublished

MCe.

PrC.

Published

W Brockie, *Sunderland Notables* (Sunderland, 1894).

Newcastle Daily Chronicle 19 Mar 1874.

Newcastle Weekly Chronicle 21 May 1864.

Sunderland Daily Echo 19 Mar 1874.

PP, RC on Labour (1893-94) C 6894.

WWMP.

Sir John T Cargill (courtesy of the Burmah Oil Co Ltd).

CARGILL, Sir John Traill

(1867-1954)

Petroleum industry entrepreneur

John Traill Cargill was born in Glasgow on 10 January 1867, the second son of David Sime Cargill (1826-1904), an East India merchant and founder of the Burmah Oil Co (1886), by his first wife Margaret née Traill. John Cargill was educated at Glasgow Academy and, like his father, had an office training in the city. From 1890 to 1893 he served an apprenticeship in Rangoon with Finlay Fleming & Co, managing agents of Burmah Oil. He then returned to the company's Glasgow office; there he specialised in the accounts side and in 1902, the year he became a director, acted as liquidator when the company was dissolved and re-formed to give it a more realistic assets structure. The following year his father's mortal illness and the premature death of Kirkman Finlay, managing director in London (who was not replaced until 1920), unexpectedly projected him into the daunting position of supremo of a £2 million company.

Motherless at the age of five, he later admitted to having had a deprived childhood; he was left feeling very unsure of himself and yet inflexible on matters where he believed he was in the right. His father's death in 1904 gave him the succession to the chairmanship. He was exceptionally fortunate to have three able and experienced advisers, Sir Boverton Redwood, the oil consultant, C W Wallace and R I Watson (qqv), whose guidance over the years he appreciated and readily acknowledged. Deeply pessimistic, he almost invariably turned down any proposition of substance, such as participation in oil interests outside Burma, that was put to him. Often, very reluctantly, he had to be talked round by his more robust associates.

Even so, in the far-reaching developments in the company after 1903, he was a good deal more than simply a figurehead. His businesslike but open manner, with a hint of having just vacated the grouse moor, went down extremely well in the corridors of Whitehall, where he soon found himself being summoned for negotiations over a long-term fuel oil contract for the Royal Navy: Burmah Oil was then the only major oil producer with deposits in the British Empire. That contract, finally signed in 1905, incidentally led to Burmah Oil being asked to take responsibility for oil prospecting in Persia, for which W K D'Arcy (qv) held the concession. After some years of disappointment and financial drain, in May 1908 Cargill was greatly relieved when substantial oil deposits were located there. As a separate company was required to work those deposits, the Anglo-Persian Oil Co Ltd was registered in April 1909, as an almost wholly-owned subsidiary of Burmah Oil. Cargill became a non-executive director of the new company. In 1912, when Anglo-Persian was still experiencing grave financial and production difficulties, Cargill's refusal to commit a further £2 million of Burmah Oil funds led Charles Greenway (qv) to seek from the British Government either a loan or a stake in Anglo-Persian. Two years later the Treasury subscribed just over £2 million to that company, which in turn signed a contract to supply fuel oil.

After 1912, when R I Watson joined the London office, Cargill, who continued to reside in Glasgow, was decreasingly involved in Burmah Oil's day-to-day affairs, and in 1920 Watson became managing director. Cargill thankfully accepted his new role well above the fray. He had many outside directorships, including those of the Anglo-Sumatra Rubber Co, the Changkat Salak Rubber & Tin Co, the Caledonian Trust Co, the Clydesdale Investment Co and the Scottish Western Investment Co. He was also a director of the Glasgow Chamber of Commerce. Like his father he was a committed Conservative.

In 1928 he loyally agreed to Watson's proposal to terminate the managing agency of Finlay Fleming & Co and establish a branch office in Rangoon, at the same time as the Burmah-Shell marketing agreement was being implemented for oil products in India; for him personally it was a poignant break with the past.

Cargill was never quite the same man after his wife's death in 1929. By then Burmah Oil's Glasgow office had become a little run down, with all departments (apart from the accounts and share registration) being centralised in London. It was Watson who, when all the company's installations in Burma had to be demolished in 1942 to deny them to the advancing Japanese armies, declared that the firm's overriding policy was to return and rebuild the industry as soon as possible after the war. Immediately before the demolition, refinery throughput, which had been 2 million barrels in 1904, had risen to over 5 million barrels. Between 1904 and 1943 net profit rose from £264,000 to £2,230,000; by 1943 half the gross profits were from dividends and interest, notably from the Anglo-Iranian (formerly Anglo-Persian) shares.

Among Cargill's many benefactions was one of £20,000 to establish in 1920 the Cargill Chair of Applied Physics at Glasgow University, and in 1927 £7,500 towards Rangoon University endowment fund, followed by a gift of £100,000 by Burmah Oil to found a College of Mining and Engineering there. He was given a baronetcy in 1920.

John Cargill in 1895 married Mary Hope Walker Grierson, daughter of George Moncrieff Grierson, a Glasgow merchant and sister of General Sir James Grierson (1859-1914): they had one daughter. After retiring from the chairmanship in 1943, Sir John Cargill left Glasgow to live quietly in Edinburgh, where he died on 24 January 1954. He left £296,766 gross.

T A B CORLEY

Sources:

Unpublished

Burmah Oil Co Ltd, Swindon, Wiltshire, archives.

BCe (Scots).

MCe (Scots).

PrC (Scots).

Interview with Mrs Alison Greenlees (Sir John Cargill's daughter).

Published

The Bailie (Glasgow) 91 (20 Feb 1918) 'Men You Know', No 2366.

Burke's Peerage, Baronetage and Knightage 1949.

T A B Corley, *A History of the Burmah Oil Company 1886-1924* (Heinemann, 1983).

Ronald W Ferrier, *The History of the British Petroleum Company* vol 1 *The Developing Years, 1901-1932* (Cambridge: Cambridge University Press, 1982).

Glasgow Weekly Herald 9 July 1932, 'Men You Know', No 15.

Journal of Institute of Petroleum 40 (1954).

WWW.

CARMICHAEL, Sir James

(1858-1934)

Builder and contractor

James Carmichael was born at Meikleour, a small village in Perthshire on 19 February 1858, one of four sons of Robert Carmichael, the local shoemaker, and his wife Jane née Kynoch. James was apprenticed as a joiner and served his time at Meigle, a small town ten miles away; during his apprenticeship there he walked home every weekend.

At the end ·of his apprenticeship he began to look further afield. Edinburgh attracted him and after gaining further experience there he came to London with Charles McIntosh, another joiner, in 1885. They rented a large shed in the garden of a house at 314 Trinity Road, Wandsworth, and started to produce handmade joinery to orders from

Sir James Carmichael (courtesy of James Carmichael (Contractors) Ltd).

building firms. The premises opposite, 331 Trinity Road, were occupied by George Neal, a large cartage contractor with a fleet of horse-drawn vehicles used by local authorities and building contractors for the transport of materials. Part of these premises was leased to James's uncle, a man named Kynoch, who operated a small and relatively unsuccessful building business. In 1889 this business closed down and the two joiners took over the premises under the name of 'James Carmichael, Builder'.

At the turn of the century the business was well established and in 1901 a tender for the construction of an extension to the Hotel Cecil was won. The contract sum, £85,000, was a very large one, comparable to these being won by the larger London builders like John Mowlem & Co Ltd. Between 1908 and 1910 Carmichael had 11 Scottish derrick cranes erected and working on various jobs in the London area. This type of crane, introduced into London by James Carmichael, was the forerunner of the present tower crane. A contract for the erection of new offices for the Liverpool Victoria Friendly Society, in the region of one million pounds, was the largest carried out during his lifetime. In May 1921, partly due to the death of both his sons Carmichael formed a private limited liability company, James Carmichael (Contractors) Ltd. He remained active as head of the company until his death.

James Carmichael was president of the London Master Builders Association in 1904 and of the Institute of Builders in 1908. During the First World War, he was a member of the Government Surplus Property Disposal Board in 1918, and chairman of the Munitions Works Board of the Ministry of Munitions, 1917-19. He was also a member of the Standing Council of the Ministry of Reconstruction in 1918, chairman of the Building Materials Supply Committee of the Ministry of Reconstruction in 1919 and Director-General of Housing in England and Wales, 1918-20. He was knighted in 1919 for his services during the war.

Throughout his life he maintained a warm interest in his native village of Meikleour and three years before his death he presented the village with a handsomely-furnished Hall and Institute, partly as a memorial to his parents whom he held in high esteem.

Sir James did a great deal of philanthropic work and was a governor of no fewer than seven hospitals, especially Bolingbroke Hospital, Wandsworth. He joined the board in 1900 and became vice-chairman in 1920 and chairman in 1924. His gifts to that hospital during the last seven years of his life amounted to nearly £40,000. He was also a member of the Board of Management and a generous supporter of the Royal Hospital and Home for Incurables, Putney.

James Carmichael was a staunch member of the Congregational Church. Both he and his wife were assiduous in aiding Surrey and Metropolitan churches, especially East Hill Congregational Church, Wandsworth. He served on the General Purposes and Finance Committees of the Congregational Union of England and Wales and was chairman and treasurer of the Church Building and Extension Committee.

James Carmichael married Annie Reid of Ruthven in 1884. She was a teacher, and the daughter of a farmer, James Reid. They had two daughters and two sons. Their first daughter only lived three months; their elder son Douglas, a captain in the Rifle Brigade, was killed in action near Ypres in 1915; their younger son, Stewart Reid, was killed in a road accident a year later.

Sir James died on 9 April 1934 leaving an estate valued at £286,452 gross.

H B KERR

Writings:

PP, Report of the Building Materials Supply Committee (1918) Cd 9197 (chairman).

Sources:

Unpublished

The Company's archives were partly destroyed by enemy bombing during the Second World War and all the early documents in the Companies House file have been weeded.

BCe (Scots).

MCe (Scots).

PrC.

W N Rumsby, 'This Is Your Firm' (a survey of the firm's history from the author's own recollections of fifty years of service, during the latter part of which he was a director; completed ca 1971-72). Copy in firm's possession.

Published

Times 11 Apr 1934.

Wandsworth Borough News 13 Apr 1934.

WWW.

CARR, Arthur

(1855-1947)
Biscuit manufacturer

Arthur Carr was born at Barton, Westmorland (near Penrith), on 16 August 1855, the younger son of John Carr, 'gentleman', and his wife

Arthur Carr (courtesy of T A B Corley).

Harriet née Ellis. John Carr (1824-1912) was a brother of Jonathan Dodgson Carr (qv), founder of Carr & Co, millers and biscuit manufacturers of Carlisle. Having trained in the firm, John Carr was told by his two elder brothers that there was no place for him there; he therefore withdrew from the business. In 1860 he was invited by James Peek, who three years earlier had established the biscuit-making firm Peek Frean & Co, to join that firm at Bermondsey in London.

As a Quaker, Arthur Carr would have been educated at a Friends' school near the family home in Clapham, but its identity is not known. After he and his elder brother Ellis (1852-1930) had spent nearly a year in Germany, to learn the language, he joined Peek Frean as an apprentice in 1872. He became a partner in 1877, two years after his brother.

From about 1880 until the late 1890s Peek Frean was a troubled firm, under the control of James Peek's son-in-law Thomas Stone and Thomas's two sons. This unloved trio displayed a depressing combination of mental rigidity and poor commercial judgement, and their era was long remembered without regret. Turnover, having risen from £500,000 in 1880 to £775,000 in 1891, then fell to £550,000 on average in 1896-98, with average annual profits between 1880 and 1898 of no more than £34,000. However, Arthur Carr was responsible in 1885 for introducing female clerks into the office: believed to be one of the earliest examples in British industry of women in clerical posts.

In 1901, when Peek Frean & Co Ltd was established with an issued capital of £500,000, John Carr and his sons took charge of the company, Arthur and Ellis becoming joint managing directors. The more retiring Ellis Carr concentrated on the production side; Arthur, who became chairman and sole managing director in 1904, following his father's retirement, thereafter dominated the company's overall policy.

Two main lines of strategy characterised Arthur Carr's lengthy reign at Peek Frean from 1904 to 1927. The first was to set the company on a sure course of growth after the era of relative ossification, by launching some attractive new varieties of biscuit and by advertising intensively for the first time. In 1902 he introduced one of the company's most successful varieties, the Pat-a-Cake, with the slogan 'For goodness sake, eat Pat-a-Cake': this was claimed to be the first-ever shortcake type put out in Britain. He went on to produce the first cream-sandwich biscuit, the Bourbon, in 1910 and the Custard Cream in 1913, and also pioneered the packing up of assortments.

On the marketing side, he supplemented the conventional outlets of newspaper and display advertising with some rather startling publicity devices, such as taking over the Crystal Palace to conduct a sales promotion for 20,000 London grocers one afternoon in 1904, and two years later despatching nearly 200,000 picture postcards to housewives throughout the country, making free (some considered over-free) offers of the company's biscuits. Combined with some much-needed overhauling of production and office methods, these steps raised turnover from £620,000 in 1900 to £1,193,000 in 1913, with profits of £112,000, and to £1,992,000 turnover and £229,000 profit in 1927. Whereas biscuit tonnage produced in 1900 was only 45 per cent of that of the company's main quality rival, Huntley & Palmers Ltd, by 1927 it was 108 per cent.

The second line of policy consistently pursued by Arthur Carr was to promote far closer co-operation between the chief biscuit manufacturers. In response to declining demand, over-capacity after the irruption into England of several Scottish manufacturers early in the century, and the countervailing power of multiple grocers and grocers' federations, in 1903 the Association of Biscuit Manufacturers was set up. Peek Frean did not join this trade association as Arthur Carr disagreed with its discount policy, but he maintained friendly contacts with it. Instead, over the next twenty years he made periodical efforts to weld the leading firms into a combine, similar to the Imperial Tobacco Co Ltd, which he hoped would be led by the prestigious Huntley & Palmers. In 1912 he met representatives of three Scottish companies and W R Jacob & Co Ltd and persuaded most of them to participate in a very tentative feasibility study. His objects were three-fold: to ensure continuity of top management, to build up reasonable profits by the abandonment of cut-throat competition, and to bring about an improvement in the low wages paid to employees. Huntley & Palmers had already declined to co-operate and the proposal foundered.

Not until 1919 was the merger scheme revived, this time by the Huntley & Palmers' directors, concerned about the potential impact on their company of high income taxes and death duties. Arthur Carr once again sought to interest the Scottish manufacturers, but in 1921 it was only Huntley & Palmers and Peek Frean which became subsidiaries of a newly-formed public holding company, The Associated Biscuit Manufacturers Ltd. Both companies maintained separate production and marketing arrangements. Arthur Carr was the first vice-chairman of Associated Biscuits, becoming chairman in 1923. In 1924-25 he strove hard to bring Jacobs into the combine, but difficulties over the divided structure of the firm (being in both Dublin and Liverpool) made the talks abortive.

In 1927 Arthur Carr retired, to the end remaining a Victorian. At work he sported the pince-nez and high collars of his youth and he never reconciled himself to the more informal manners of the telephone and of visitors dropping in without appointment. In the firm he kept up the Quaker spirit of benevolent paternalism, although he became a member of the Church of England in the 1880s. Medical facilities had been provided since 1889, but he introduced a full-time doctor and free dental and ophthalmic services in 1905, the year in which he helped to found a sports club. In 1922 he and Ellis Carr jointly gave £10,000 to set up an employees' benevolent fund, and seven years later they gave £130,000 for a properly funded pensions scheme. He shunned publicity; although he is known to have made many outside benefactions, these are nowhere recorded. When he died at Wimbledon on 23 May 1947, no local or national newspaper is known to have given him an obituary.

He married Marie Georgette Baumann in 1881. They had two sons: John Carr Jr (1882-1923) who was managing director from 1910 until his premature death, and Philip Carr (1884-1968) who succeeded his father as chairman of Peek·Frean. He left £630,206 gross.

T A B CORLEY

Sources:

Unpublished

BCe.

MCe.

PrC.

F C Davis, 'Historical Survey of Peek Frean & Co Ltd 1857-1957' (typescript, 1957).

Reading University Library, Peek Frean & Co Ltd archives.

Published

'Souvenir of Mr Arthur Carr's Fifty Years' Association with Peek Frean & Co' *The Biscuit Box* (Journal of the Employees of Peek Frean) 5 (Dec 1922) supplement.

Ellis Carr, 'Reminiscences', *ibid* 16-17 (Jan 1933-June 1934).

T A B Corley, *Quaker Enterprise in Biscuits: Huntley & Palmers of Reading 1822-1972* (Hutchinson, 1972).

CARR, Jonathan Dodgson

(1806-1884)

Biscuit manufacturer

Jonathan Dodgson Carr (courtesy of Carrs, Milling Industries Ltd).

Jonathan Dodgson Carr was born in Kendal on 9 December 1806, the second son of Jonathan Carr (1776-1849) and his wife Jane née Dodgson. Both his mother and father belonged to the Society of Friends and J D Carr was himself a strict Quaker until he resigned from the Society in 1869.

The forebears of J D Carr had been weavers, probably originating from Yorkshire, but his father was a wholesale grocer and tea-dealer and his maternal grandfather was also a grocer. J D Carr and his brothers were therefore brought up in the grocery trade but while the eldest brother Henry followed in his father's footsteps and opened his own grocer's shop, Jonathan was apprenticed to a baker. For a short time J D Carr was actually in business in Kendal as a baker and biscuit maker. By 1831, however, he had decided that Carlisle offered more opportunities for trade — at this date the city, with a population of 19,000, was expanding rapidly. One story records that Carr set off to walk the fifty miles from Kendal to Carlisle but on the way was offered a lift by Thomas Brockbank, a tea-

CARR Jonathan Dodgson

Carrs Biscuit Factory, Bread Bakery, Shop and Flour Mill in Caldewgate, Carlisle, by Hudson Scott, Printer, ca 1850 (from Carrs House Magazine Topper Off*).*

merchant in the city. Thus Carr arrived in Carlisle having already made a business contact and eventual friend.

In June 1831 Carr commenced business as a baker and dealer in meal and flour in Castle Street, Carlisle. Within three years, however, he was building new premises in Caldewgate, a working-class township on the western side of the city; these incorporated a bakery and retail shop, a biscuit factory and a flour mill to supply all the flour needed for the works. The whole establishment was powered by steam and included several innovative pieces of machinery designed by Carr himself. It was in full operation by 1837. The exact reasons for the sudden expansion of the business and, more importantly, for the decision to embark on large scale biscuit manufacture are not known. Carr, however, had considerable business acumen and courage and probably saw, even at that early date, the potential market for sweet biscuits for general consumption. Until the early nineteenth century biscuit making was a slow process (all the biscuits had to be cut by hand) and in Britain it was largely confined to making 'ships biscuits'. In his new factory Carr had a machine for cutting biscuits which he had adapted from a hand-operated printing machine with the aid of a fellow Quaker businessman in Carlisle, the printer and metal-box manufacturer, Hudson Scott (1808-91).

Although flour milling and bread-baking long remained part of Carr & Co's activities, it was the manufacture of biscuits which took the firm into world markets. By 1841 J D Carr was sufficiently well-established to have obtained the royal warrant, through the good offices, of Philip Henry Howard (1801-83), MP for Carlisle, 1830-47 and 1848-52. In the 1840s output increased yearly, although only two varieties of sweet biscuit were made (one of these was the famous 'Alphabet Range') as well as 'ships biscuits'. In 1846 total biscuit production was 400 tons and there were about 90 employees. By 1860, however, Carrs were producing 72 kinds of

Interior of Carrs Biscuit Factory, Carlisle, showing number 2 icing and decorating room ca 1908 (courtesy of the County Record Office, Carlisle).

sweet biscuit and had built up a considerable export trade. Particular emphasis was placed on packing by the firm and from an early date tins were designed and supplied by Hudson Scott. In addition to printing labels and handbills for Carr, Hudson Scott in the 1870s began to make transfer-painted tins, and in the late 1880s offset-painted tins for the firm.

J D Carr's brothers went into partnership with him as a result of the expansion of the firm. Henry Carr gave up his grocery business in Kendal to come to Carlisle. George Carr also left the grocery trade to take charge of the offices and the youngest brother John was trained in biscuit manufacture from an early age. Eventually, John left the firm in the 1850s and took over the running of the London based biscuit company Peek, Frean & Co, which was later run by his son Arthur (qv). In 1833 J D Carr had married Jane Nicholson of Whitehaven, also a Quaker. Three of their four sons, Henry, James Nicholson and Thomas William also entered the firm in the 1850s and 1860s.

When the biscuit works and flour mill commenced working J D Carr was able to put into practice his ideas about the health and welfare of his employees. Several contemporary writers attest to the relatively good working conditions in the Carlisle factory, such as clean, airy surroundings and shorter working hours. He built houses for his workpeople, provided hot baths and instituted an evening school, a library and a reading room in the neighbourhood of the factory. On Sundays the men and boys were invited to his own house for religious instruction and discussion. From an early date, probably about 1840, there was an annual works outing: the surviving account of one of these excursions (in the 1850s) shows that a whole day was spent by the workpeople and their families in the Lake District, together with the Carr family.

J D Carr was involved in several public controversies which concerned the Society of Friends in the nineteenth century: the anti-slavery and anti-militia campaigns and the temperance movement. His political sympathies were 'liberal' and after the passing of the Reform Act in 1832 he gave each prisoner in Carlisle Gaol a fruit loaf. He also supported the campaign to repeal the Corn Laws, convinced that a cheap loaf would benefit the poor. When the last of the laws was repealed in 1849 he gave all his employees a day's holiday and a tea-drinking was held in the factory to celebrate the occasion.

Although he would never accept any municipal office in Carlisle, Carr was very active and influential in local affairs, particularly anything to do with social improvement. He was a founder of the Cumberland Building Society, helped to establish gas and water supplies in the town and was a patron of the Cumberland Infirmary. He was also a partner in the Silloth Dock Co and a promoter of the Carlisle to Silloth railway. So actively did the Carr family help to develop the town of Silloth, that by the 1880s they decided to concentrate their flour-milling activities there, building a new mill on the dock-side to replace the Caldewgate mill and others which they had acquired in Carlisle. The Silloth mill was opened in 1887, three years after J D Carr's death, and is still (1983) run by one of his descendants.

The firm of Carr & Co owed much of its style to Jonathan Dodgson Carr's strong character and beliefs. There is little doubt that the source from which he drew this strength was his religion. Like other Quaker businessmen, his success was in large part due to his reputation for honesty, plain-dealing and concern for others which earned him the trust and respect of many people. However, on 20 May 1869 Carr and his wife Jane resigned from the Society of Friends and by 1874 joined the Brethren Assembly in Carlisle. The leading members of the Carr family had for some time been diverging from Quaker practice and belief (for example, Jonathan Dodgson wished to read his Bible at the Meeting which was not acceptable to Friends). In 1868 his two eldest sons were disowned by the Carlisle Meeting and this led to a spate of Carr family resignations culminating in those of Jonathan Dodgson and his wife. All became leading members of the Brethren Assembly in Carlisle, to which the family of John W Laing (qv) also belonged.

Carr died in Carlisle on 6 April 1884 and the Bishop of Carlisle, preaching in the Holy Trinity Church, said after his death 'he caused a light to shine and it is a light which will be very much missed' {*Carlisle Journal* 8 Apr 1884}. J D Carr left £38,552 gross.

SUSAN I DENCH

Sources

Unpublished

Cumbria CRO, 'A list of the members of Carlisle Monthly Meeting in the County of Cumberland, 1837-1963' D/FCF/3/102.

MCe.

PrC.

Clare Burgess et al, 'Carrs: the Family and the Enterprise' (1971, a copy in the possession of Carr's Milling Industries Ltd).

Published

Carlisle Journal 16 June 1832, 2 Feb 1849, 8 Apr 1884.

Chambers Edinburgh Journal 1846, 1848.

Roy Coad, *'Laing'. The Biography of Sir John W Laing CBE (1879-1978)* (Hodder and Stoughton, 1979).

M J Franklin, *British Biscuit Tins 1868-1939: An Aspect of Decorative Packaging* (New Cavendish Books, 1979).

David Griffith, *Decorated Printed Tins: The Golden Age of Printed Tin Packaging* (Studio Vista, 1979).

'Jonathan 'Printed' His Biscuits' *The Evening News* 26 Mar 1958.

Journal of the History of Friends Society 20 (1923).

CASH, John   and   CASH, Joseph

(1822-1880)   (1826-1880)

Silk ribbon manufacturers

John and Joseph Cash were both born at Sherbourne House, Coventry, John on 16 February 1822, Joseph on 28 October 1826, the elder sons of Joseph Cash, a Quaker stuff-merchant. Their father was a leading businessman in the city, a founder member of Coventry Mechanics Institute (1828) and Coventry Industrial School (1846), and an active opponent of church rates; he was also a director of the Coventry Steam Power Society, formed in 1835 to promote the use of steam engines.

The brothers served seven year apprenticeships with stuff-merchants which entitled them to become freemen of the city. During the early 1840s they operated a ribbon business on the outwork system, from a warehouse in Hertford Street. However, they became one of the first dozen factory masters in Coventry when in 1846 they built a factory at West Orchard, largely equipped with Jacquard looms powered by steam. At the same time they recruited French designers to design their ribbons. By 1856 they employed 200 weavers in the factory. Quaker ideals were expressed in the paternalistic management of the employees, which included a sickness benefit club and organised outings for employees' holidays. Cashs paid some of the highest wages in the Coventry ribbon trade until 1857, when they were forced to adopt the list of lower wage rates imposed by Coventry masters.

However, the factory system was not readily accepted at Coventry as out-weavers fought to maintain their wages at rates equal to those of factory-weavers. In this situation, and influenced and encouraged in part by their philosopher-journalist friend Charles Bray, and in part by their Quaker principles, the Cash brothers drew up plans to build a factory in which they hoped to combine the old outwork method of weaving with the advantages of factory organization.

They bought a seven acre field in the country a mile from the city centre and planned to build one hundred 'top shops', or cottage factories, arranged around a square with their attic-level looms powered by a central beam engine. Water for power and for the dyehouse was to be taken from the canal which bordered the land and which also provided transport for coal from the nearby collieries. Capital came from relatives (particularly the brothers' in-laws) and fellow Quaker businessmen. However, the trade boom did not last long and only 48 terraced houses, started in 1857, were actually built at Kingfield. Here the Cashs encouraged the formation of a dramatic society, sports clubs and evening classes.

The labour struggle over the degradation of work ended in 1860 when the Anglo-French Trade Treaty of 1860 brought an overwhelming influx of high-quality, low-priced French ribbons. Many Coventry firms, unable to compete, collapsed. Losses for the J & J Cash partnership necessitated drastic changes. The top shops were reorganised to operate along factory lines and a departmental structure set up to accommodate the manufacture of a new product. John and Joseph were quick to recognise the need for some diversification and in September 1860 they took out a patent for the manufacture of narrow frillings. The firm pulled through the ensuing depression and emerged in a strong position. This was due largely to the Cash brothers' prudent business practices. Their accounting was careful, employing advanced depreciation techniques. Their capital came from relatively safe sources. They controlled labour by means of paternalistic and authoritarian techniques. In addition to a knowledge of French techniques and designs, machinery and expertise were imported but probably the most important reason for their survival was their product diversification, into other fabric types. For some time the Cashs preserved their image as benevolent employers, refusing, for example, to lock out their employees during the 1860 strike. However, by 1862 the collapse of trade made them more arbitrary, exacting and harsher, according to their manager, William Andrews.

The philanthropy of the Cash brothers extended throughout Coventry. Joseph was the founder of St Thomas's Infant School. Both brothers made handsome contributions to, and were trustees of, numerous local charities such as Moores Charity, Hospital Saturday Fund (1874) and Gulson Hospital Fund. In addition John served as a Liberal on Coventry City Council, representing Earl Street Ward, 1868-76.

John Cash's work with and for Independent Nonconformists (he established the Vicar Lane Independent Chapel) caused him to be disowned by the Quakers in 1844. He married Mary Sibree, the daughter of an Independent minister in 1852. Joseph in 1851 married Sarah Iliffe, and like his brother had a large family. They both died in 1880, John on 9 September, leaving a personal estate of less than £60,000, and Joseph on 14 October, leaving an estate of under £45,000. John's son Sidney (1856-1931) and his cousin Joseph (1853-1927) took over the partnership.

S A VERTIGAN

Sources:

Unpublished

Coventry RO, MS Accession 562/1-22 business papers of J & J Cash; diary of William Andrews (manager and designer for J & J Cash at times between 1857 and 1863).

British Patents: 1860 (2,292), 1862 (2,799), 1867 (513), 1868 (417), 1869 (3,083), 1872 (2,424).

P Searby, 'Weavers and Freemen in Coventry 1820-61: Social and Political Traditionalism in an Early Victorian Town' (Warwick PhD, 1972).

N Tiratsoo, 'Coventry's Ribbon Trade in the Mid-Victorian Period; Some Social and Economic Responses to Industrial Development and Decay' (London PhD, 1980).

Sean A Vertigan, 'J & J Cash Limited: a Business History 1846-1928' (Nottingham BA thesis, 1982).

Published

Coventry Standard 3 Sept 1858, 17 Sept 1880, 15 Oct 1880.

PP, HC 1864 (567) LII, Ribbon Manufactories.

PP, HC 1865 (38) XX, Reports of Inspectors of Factories.

John Prest, *The Industrial Revolution in Coventry* (Oxford: Clarendon Press, 1960).

CASSEL, Sir Ernest Joseph

(1852-1921)

Merchant banker and international financier

Sir Ernest J Cassell. Etching by Anders Leonard Zorn, dated 1909 (courtesy of the National Portrait Gallery, London).

Ernest Cassel was born at Cologne on 3 March 1852, the youngest of the three children of Jacob Cassel and Amalia née Rosenheim. Jacob Cassel had a small banking business in Cologne, which provided the family with a comfortable though modest income. This business had been founded by Jacob's father, Moses, in 1822. Since at least the late seventeenth century Cassels had been active in financial affairs in the Rhineland, several of them as advisors or agents for the Prince Electors. In later life Cassel gave entirely conflicting accounts of the atmosphere of his early home life. His elder brother, Max, died in 1875; he had one sister, Wilhelmina (later Schoenbrunn).

Ernest was educated at Cologne until the age of fourteen, when he started work with the banking firm of Eltzbacher; but in 1869 he migrated to Liverpool, arriving with a bag of clothes and his violin, and no apparent arrangements to take up a post. He soon found a job with the German grain merchants, Blessing, Braun & Co, in Liverpool, but after a little over a year he moved again, to a clerkship with the Anglo-Egyptian Bank in Paris. The outbreak, shortly afterwards, of the Franco-Prussian War forced him, as a German subject, to return to England, this time to a clerkship in the London merchant bank, Bischoffsheim & Goldschmidt, which also had interests in Egyptian affairs. This move was probably facilitated by an introduction from the powerful European financier Baron Moritz de Hirsch, who was associated with the Paris bank and related by marriage to the Bischoffsheims. Cassel was closely associated with Hirsch in his later life and business dealings (he was an executor of Hirsch's estate after the latter's death in 1896) and may even have modelled his career of independent and enterprising international financial dealing upon that of Hirsch.

Within a year, Cassel, still aged only nineteen, had demonstrated his flair by rapidly saving the affairs of a Jewish firm in Constantinople in which Bischoffsheims had an interest. In 1874 he was appointed manager at a salary said to have been £5,000 a year, following a series of highly successful negotiations on behalf of the house, especially in connection with some complicated and risky Latin American loans. In addition to his salary Cassel obtained substantial commission from the rescue or liquidation of troublesome ventures, which he rescued on Bischoffsheims' behalf. Such activities also gained him an international network of contacts, notably his lifelong friendship with Jacob H Schiff, of Kuhn, Loeb & Co (New York), an American railroad financier, who became an invaluable source of advice to Cassel on American affairs; Cassel reciprocating with European information. Through use of such contacts Cassel became profitably involved on his own account in American and other overseas enterprises. When his father died in 1875 leaving Ernest a half-share, with his sister, of RM 91,286 (20 RM = £1 in the 1870s), Cassel could afford to settle more than his own half (RM 60,000) upon his sister, now divorced, and her two children. When he married, in 1878, he was able to put aside capital of £150,000.

He married Annette, daughter of Robert Thompson Maxwell, of Croft House, Croft, Darlington, and on the day of his marriage became a naturalized British subject. Mrs Cassel died of tuberculosis three years later; they had one daughter, Maud. Mrs Cassel had been a convert to Roman Catholicism and by her wish Cassel, never a devout Jew, was himself received into the Roman Church shortly after her death. His devotion to his new religion was never very apparent, nor was his conversion widely known until, at his appointment to the Privy Council in 1902, he chose, to general surprise, to be sworn in on the Catholic Bible. He never re-married. At his wife's death his sister, with her children Anna (later Jenkins) and Felix (later Sir Felix, a prominent lawyer and Conservative Assistant Attorney-General), came to live with him and adopted the name of Cassel.

Thereafter Cassel devoted his life to international finance, to his daughter and to his own entry into high society. His opportunity to increase his fortune vastly came rapidly. Bischoffsheim & Goldschmidt had interests in three unprofitable Swedish railway lines which linked the phosphorous iron ore deposits of Grangesborg with the Baltic port of Oxelsund. There was little potential demand for this ore until the invention, in 1878-79, of the Gilchrist-Thomas process. Cassel was not alone in recognising the gains to be made from introducing this process into Sweden, but only he was prepared to take the considerable risks of investing in the mining and transportation of Swedish ore and of facing Swedish opposition to foreign intervention in their economy. Around 1882 he acquired the Swedish rights in the Gilchrist-Thomas process and bought a substantial personal interest in the Grangesborg mines, in the railway companies and in Swedish steel mills. When the new process was introduced, Swedish iron ore sales expanded rapidly.

This activity in Sweden laid the foundation of Cassel's independent fortune. Equally important was his extensive and growing involvement in American railways. The rapid expansion of railways in a society with limited sources of domestic capital made the American railway companies heavily dependent upon European finance during the 1880s and 1890s. As Jacob Schiff became an important figure in United States railroad finance his relationship with Cassel was to their growing mutual benefit. They both had moderate investments in the construction stock of the Canadian Pacific from 1883; jointly they reorganized the finances of the Texas & Pacific after the US railroad crisis of 1884. In 1885 they bought securities in the New York, Ontario & Western and were active also in trying to resolve its financial difficulties. In the early 1880s his association with Bischoffsheims was on a profit-sharing rather than a salaried basis (he never became a partner) and in 1884 he left the firm, although he continued to occupy part of their offices in Throgmorton Street, whilst working on his own account. He did not join another finance house until 1910, preferring to work independently or in association with consortia of financiers formed for specific projects.

He remained active in Swedish affairs for two decades as a board member of prominent mining and transportation companies. In 1896, in association with Frederic Warburg of Hamburg, he was the architect of the Grangesborg Oxelsund Traffic Co which owned railway lines, the harbour installations at Oxelsund, Baltic shipping interests and the Grangesborg ore mines, with a capital of £995,000, the bulk of the shares initially owned by Cassel. He faced considerable opposition to his activities from such influential Swedish sources as the Wallenberg banking family. He overcame it by refraining from joining the board of the new company, allowing it to be dominated by Swedes, and also by selling many of his fast-rising shares in the company to Swedish friends, bankers, politicians and journalists, at below market prices, though still at considerable profit. 'Cassel's greasing system' as his enemies called it, bought support for his speculative ventures, as well as further antagonism, but there is no doubt that his activities benefited the Swedish economy. Share issues in his companies helped to create a Swedish capital market and he played a crucial role in the early development of the iron industry on which so much of Sweden's later economic expansion was based.

Also from the mid-1880s Cassel expanded his wider international activities. In 1888, 1890 and 1893 he negotiated loans for the Mexican Government and from 1885 co-operated with Jacob Schiff in financing Mexican enterprises, especially railways, notably the Mexican Central Railway, the major Mexican railway whose finances he arranged for some years. In 1899 he formed the Mexican Central Railway Securities Co through which he acquired a dominant interest in the American company. In 1888-89, in association with Carl Meyer, long a close friend and associate of Cassel (and later First Lord Shortgrove), chief clerk of N M Rothschild, he arranged loans for the Governments of Egypt, Brazil, Argentina and Uruguay. In 1895 he issued a 6 per cent loan for the Chinese Government and in 1896 another 5 per cent loan for Uruguay. His interests in, and profits from US railways continued at least to 1914. By 1891, again in association with Schiff, and with Wertheim & Gompertz of Amsterdam, he successfully reorganised the Louisville & Nashville Railroad Co and handled the sale of their shares in London. He was a frequent visitor to the United States in these years. In 1893 he and Schiff successfully negotiated the extension of maturing bonds in the New York, Pennsylvania & Ohio Railroad, which was in trouble. From 1890 Cassel's mining interests also extended into America when he bought shares in Anaconda.

Up to this time Cassel appears to have taken no significant interest in home investment. However, his penchant for risk-laden speculation attracted him into taking a leading part in financing the Electric Traction Co Ltd, formed in 1894, which in 1895 became the main contractor and underwrote the construction of the Central London underground line connecting the Bank and Shepherds Bush. More cautious financiers, such as Rothschilds, had refused to participate in this risky venture. From the financial point of view they were right, since it was never a source of much profit to Cassel or others, despite the considerable gain to transport users.

More profitably in 1897 Cassel began a long association with Vickers Sons & Co derived from his friendly relationship with Albert Vickers (qv). In 1897 he arranged the purchase of the Barrow Naval & Shipbuilding Co for amalgamation with Vickers; and after the merger of the Maxim Gun

financial and commercial interests. Where it was not, as in Turkey, financial and commercial interests were subordinated to political and diplomatic priorities. Consequently Cassel, who had the vision and the capacity to bring great benefits to the Turkish economy, was prevented from doing so, to his intense frustration.

The year 1910-11 was as difficult a time in Cassel's personal as in his business life. In 1910 King Edward VII died, to Cassel's great personal grief; at Edward's request he was one of the last people to see the King alive. With Edward, Cassel lost much of his social and political influence, to the undisguised glee of certain members of high society who disliked Edward's cosmopolitan entourage.

More heartbreaking still, in 1911 Cassel's only daughter, Maud, died after a long battle with tuberculosis. Cassel had devoted much care and attention to her in her last years. In 1901 she had married Lt Col Wilfred Ashley, grandson of the great Earl of Shaftesbury and great-grandson of Lady Palmerston, through whom he had inherited Broadlands House in Hampshire. Long attached to the Conservative party and to the anti-socialist union, Ashley became Conservative MP for Blackpool in 1906, Minister of Transport in 1924-29 and Lord Mount Temple in 1932. Ashley's relationship with Cassel was friendly, Cassel providing financial advice, as always to his friends and relatives. After his daughter's death Cassel's affections centred upon his two grand-daughters, especially the elder, Edwina Ashley.

Amidst these personal tragedies, Cassel decided late in 1910 to give up his City office, to reduce the volume of his activity and once more to join a merchant bank. He became a partner in the firm of S Japhet & Co, bringing in capital of £200,000. Saemy Japhet had gradually transferred his business from his native Frankfurt and sought a British replacement for his previous backers, the Darmstadter Bank, in which Cassel also had an interest. Technically Cassel was a 'sleeping partner' and did not work from Japhets but frequently visited the firm and was an invaluable source of advice on most of the firm's activities whilst maintaining his wide range of independent interests. His own office was now at Green Street near Grosvenor Square, close to his new and sumptuous home, Brook House in Park Lane. This had taken three years to renovate. It had six marble-lined kitchens, an oak-panelled dining room, designed to seat 100 in comfort; the entrance hall was panelled in lapis lazuli alternating with green veined cream coloured marble: 'the giant's lavatory' Edwina's irreverent young friends christened it. Until his death Cassel lived there much of the time, though also frequented his flat in Paris, his Swiss villa, his villa in the South of France, his stud farm at Newmarket and three country houses which he purchased between 1912 and 1917.

After 1911 Cassel certainly curtailed his activities, though he remained very active in the affairs of Japhet. The extent to which he was motivated by anticipation of war to withdraw from European business can only be matter for speculation. Certainly his personal investments were concentrated in America by 1914, apart from the investment in small British landed estates noted above. He was strongly aware of the danger of war with Germany as early as 1908 and strove harder than most to avoid it. Both as a businessman and as a German by birth he disliked the prospect of war. Between 1908 and 1912 he co-operated with Albert Ballin, head of the Hamburg-Amerika shipping line, a leading figure in the development of the German merchant fleet and a friend of the Kaiser, in attempts to bring together British and German political leaders to decelerate the naval race and diminish the prospects of war. The efforts culminated in a secret visit by Haldane (Secretary for War), and Cassel to Berlin in 1912, which only revealed the poor prospects for Anglo-German agreement.

Cassel made one of the largest subscriptions to the war loan and was a member of the Anglo-French financial mission to the USA in 1915, headed by Rufus Isaacs, Lord Reading, which resulted in the large American loan. Such patriotic activities did not protect Cassel from suffering constant attack within Britain for his German birth, nor from an attempt in 1915 to remove him and Sir Edgar Speyer from the Privy Council. The verdict of a court, also headed by Lord Reading (a personal friend of Cassel), went in his and Speyer's favour.

Thereafter, until his death on 21 September 1921, Cassel confined his attention to a limited range of American business and to racing and shooting parties with old friends, cared for by his grand-daughter Edwina. He died sitting at his desk at Brook House, in the loneliness that characterised much of his life. Shortly afterwards, Edwina married Lord Louis Mountatten (Earl Mountbatten of Burma) bringing Broadlands House, which she inherited on her father's death, into the Mountbatten family.

Cassel left an estate worth £7,333,411 gross, most of it to his immediate family. He left small items to a list of 'old and valued friends', whose very names describe the social, political and business circles in which he moved. They included the Asquiths, Lord Birkenhead, Mrs Bischoffsheim, Mr and Mrs Winston Churchill, Mrs Keppel, Lord Revelstoke, the Schiffs, Babington-Smith, Lord and Lady Reading, the Warburgs and the Marchioness of Winchester.

Cassel had penetrated the social élite with the same determination, and using some of the same methods, by which he achieved business success. From the time of his marriage he cultivated, at a succession of rented and, later, owned country houses, the gentry and aristocracy in the milieux in which they were most at ease: the hunting-field, the shooting-party, the racecourse and the card-table. He learned to hunt despite a certain dislike of horses and a tendency to fall off them. He owned and bred racehorses with no outstanding success on the course. It took him thirteen years to achieve election to the Jockey Club, in 1908. The patronage of King Edward VII gave Cassel the entrée to circles otherwise closed to a largely self-made man of German and Jewish origins, but it could not win for him entire acceptance.

Politicians were less exclusive. Both Winston Churchill and his father were good friends, as were the Asquiths, although Cassel's own politics were Conservative. He was never, however, active in politics. Like other prominent City financiers his advice was sought on financial issues by politicians of both parties and by Treasury civil servants, but a certain aloofness in public towards party politics was one of the keys to his business success. In 1909, at the height of the Budget crisis, when the City was organising against Lloyd George's new taxes, Cassel wrote to his Conservative son-in-law emphasising his 'absolute loyalty to whatever government I happen to be serving, and if whoever happened to be in power could not be certain of this he would not give me, and I certainly should not wish, his confidence' {Broadlands Archive, Cassel papers, Folder X6, Cassel to Sir Wilfred Ashley 18 Nov 1909}: an entirely accurate description of his approach. He did not sign the City's anti-Budget petition in 1909.

Especially in his earlier years Cassel also mixed widely in theatrical and artistic circles. Beerbohm Tree (qv) was a close friend; Alma-Tadema and Burne-Jones were both grateful to Cassel for his friendship and patronage in hard times. He also amassed an impressive collection of old masters, French and English furniture, Renaissance bronzes, Dresden china, Chinese jade and old English silver.

Sir Ernest Cassel gave away at least £2 million in charitable donations. Apart from his philanthropic activity in Egypt, he gave £200,000 in 1902 for the founding of the King Edward VII Sanatorium for Consumption, Midhurst, and a further £20,000 in 1913; £10,000 in 1907 for the Imperial College of Science and Technology; in 1909 a £46,000 half-share (with Edward Cecil Guinness, Lord Iveagh (qv)) for founding the Radium Institute; £210,000 in 1911 for creating the King Edward VII British-German Foundation for the aid of distressed English people in Germany and vice versa; £30,000 for distressed workmen in Swedish mines; £50,000 to Hampshire hospitals in his daughter's memory; in 1913, £10,000 to Egyptian hospitals and £50,000 for the sick and needy of Cologne; during the First World War, he gave at least £400,000 for medical services and the relief of the families of servicemen. In 1919 he donated £500,000 for educational purposes. The funds were administered by a trust (whose members included Haldane, Asquith, Balfour, Sidney Webb and Philippa Fawcett), and were used to establish a faculty of commerce at the London School of Economics; to support the Workers' Educational Association; to finance scholarships for the technical and commercial education of working men; to promote the study of foreign languages by the establishment of professorships, lectureships and scholarships; and to support the higher education of women.

Cassel's was a remarkable career. He was among the minority of City of London financiers who relied on independent methods of operation in the very risky business of financing and promoting projects overseas. Much of his success derived from his judgement of risks, which proved to be more shrewd than that of established merchant bankers. Withal Cassel allied immense skill and a large capacity for hard work. He was therefore able to benefit from a world economy expanding as never before, and to play an important role in that expansion.

P THANE

Sources:

Unpublished

American Jewish Archive, Cincinnati, Ohio, USA, papers of Jacob H Schiff.

Broadlands Archive, Broadlands House, Hants, papers of Sir Ernest Cassel.

Trinity College, Cambridge, papers of Sir Henry Babington-Smith.

MCe.

PrC; Will.

Published

Theodore C Barker and Michael Robbins, *A History of London Transport* (2 vols, George Allen & Unwin, 1963 and 1974) I.

DNB.

K Grunwald, '"Windsor Cassel" — The Last Court Jew' *Yearbook of the Leo Baeck Institute* 14 (1969).

Saemy Japhet, *Recollections of My Business Life* (pp, 1931).

Marian Kent, 'Agent of Empire? The National Bank of Turkey and British Foreign Policy' *Historical Journal* 18 (1975).

WWW.

CASTNER, Hamilton Young

(1858-1899)

Chemical manufacturer

Hamilton Young Castner was born in Brooklyn, New York on 11 September 1858. Educated at the Brooklyn Polytechnic Institute and Columbia University, he trained as a chemist, and after graduating in 1879, set up a practice as a consultant chemist in Pine Street, New York. His interests, however, turned more and more to the design and improvement of chemical manufacturing methods and machinery. In 1885 he sold his successful business to three of his colleagues, Elliot, Mattison and Hopke, in order to devote more time and energy to research in this field.

He began by successfully patenting a number of his inventions, the most important being his new process for the manufacture of sodium by the reduction of caustic soda with iron and carbon. Unable to obtain the necessary financial backing to develop it in America, however, in 1886 he came to England. Here he found support among a group of wealthy and well-connected Englishmen, including Gerald Balfour MP, Professor Sir Henry Roscoe MP and William Mather MP (qv). With their help and money a small factory was built. It was successful, and soon attracted the attentions of the Aluminium Crown Metal Co (formed 1877) of

Birmingham who were using large quantities of sodium in their manufacture of aluminium. Castner, by his new process, was able to lower the price of sodium from 14s a pound to under 1s a pound.

As a result a new company, the Aluminium Co, was formed in 1887 by Balfour and his colleagues; it had an initial authorised capital of £400,000. Castner was managing director, whilst G Balfour and Sir Henry Roscoe were among the directors. The new company bought Castner's patents for £140,000, of which £100,000 was paid in shares, and a factory was built at Oldbury in 1888. Their declared aim was firstly to produce sodium under Castner's patents, and secondly, to manufacture aluminium using James Fernley Webster's method. The potential annual output was to be 100,000 pounds of aluminium a year.

The company prospered for two years, until 1889, when a new method of manufacturing aluminium, invented simultaneously by Hall in America and by Heroult in France, appeared. The new method, the electrolysis of a solution of alumina in molten cryolite, proved considerably cheaper than that of the Aluminium Co, who found themselves no longer competitive.

With a new factory built specifically for the manufacture of sodium and aluminium this appeared to be a considerable setback. Castner persevered, however, and turned to the manufacture of various sodium compounds. He began to manufacture sodium peroxide, cyanide, electrolytic sodium, caustic soda and chlorine; eventually production of aluminium ceased entirely. The growing world-wide market for these sodium compounds soon led to recovery and renewed prosperity for the firm.

In 1890 Castner devised a new process for obtaining sodium by the electrolysis of molten caustic soda. In order to produce caustic soda of the required purity for this process, he devised his famous mercury rocking cell which became his most successful invention. A pilot plant at Oldbury was built to demonstrate this process, and Castner, in the Aluminium Co's name, patented it throughout the world, with the one exception of Germany. Here a similar invention had already been filed by Carl Kellner, the patent being owned by Solvay & Cie of Brussels. Solvays were interested in both Castner's and Kellner's patents, and in October 1895 an agreement was reached whereby the two companies agreed to an exchange of rights and processes. Solvays paid the Aluminium Co £5,000 for the right to use Castner's patents on the continent whilst the Aluminium Co retained the English market. Both parties reserved the rights for the USA and Canada.

To work this agreement, the Castner-Kellner Alkali Co was formed in 1895, with an initial capital of £300,000 in shares of £1 each, financed jointly by Solvay & Cie and the Aluminium Co. The latter retained a third of the shares themselves; the other 200,000 shares were left open for public subscription. A site was bought at Weston Point for £5,650. William Platt, chairman of Mather & Platt, engineers, was the first chairman of the new company, while Castner was one of the directors. Production capacity was to be 18.5 tons of pure caustic soda and 40 tons of bleaching powder daily.

The company did well and by 1900 profits were rising rapidly. In this year the Aluminium Co went into voluntary liquidation and its assets were bought by the Castner-Kellner Alkali Co for £130,000. The latter's capital was in the same year increased to £450,000.

Castner's process, the first to produce soda of such a high purity, was of great importance; caustic soda, a heavy chemical, was used in many other industries besides that of sodium manufacture, including soap making and textile manufacture. Castner, unfortunately, did not live to see the success of the Castner-Kellner Alkali Co which was taken over by Brunner Mond & Co in 1920 and so was taken into ICI in 1926.

Said to be quiet and unassuming in manner and always immaculately dressed, Castner was a keen sportsman until he contracted tuberculosis. He died on 11 October 1899, aged forty-one, while wintering at Saranac Lake, New York, and was survived by his wife, Cora Marian Castner. He left £13,431 gross.

ALEXANDRA KIDNER

Sources:

Unpublished

PrC.

Published

William J Reader, *Imperial Chemical Industries. A History* (2 vols, Oxford University Press, 1970) 1.

Fifty Years of Progress 1895-1945 (Birmingham: Castner-Kellner Alkali Company, 1945).

Singer, *History of Technology* 5.

CATTO Thomas Sivewright

1st Lord Catto of Cairncatto

(1879-1959)

Governor of the Bank of England

Thomas Sivewright Catto was born at Newcastle upon Tyne on 15 March 1879, fifth son and seventh child of William Catto (1834-79), shipwright, and his wife Isabella née Yule (1842-1930), a sea captain's daughter. His father died when he was a few months old and he was brought up by his mother, who continued to support and encourage him in his early career.

Sir Thomas S Catto, 1st baron Catto of Cairncatto (courtesy of the Bank of England).

He was educated at Peterhead Academy, and then had a council scholarship at Heaton School, later Rutherford College, in Newcastle. At the age of fifteen or sixteen he became a clerk with the Gordon Steam Shipping Co of Newcastle at a salary of £24 per annum and had a grounding in commerce and shipping. Having taught himself shorthand in the evenings, after Gordons acquired a typewriter he learned to pick its lock and practised typewriting when the other staff had gone home.

In February 1898, at a salary of £8 per month, he became personal assistant at Batoum to William Horwood Stuart, the managing director of F A Mattievich & Co, agents for cargo and tank steamers at Batoum and shipping merchants in southern Russia and the Near and Middle East. Stuart (who was murdered at Batoum in 1906) made Catto his manager on his twenty-first birthday in 1900, and the young man lived at Batoum and Baku, during which period he learned Russian. In 1904 Catto became European sales manager of the Scottish-American firm of MacAndrews & Forbes, Russian and Near Eastern merchants and manufacturers at Camden, New Jersey, of large paper and cardboard mills. His remuneration was then £400 per annum plus 2.5 per cent on sales, and Catto, who became a member of the Baltic Exchange at this time, was responsible for opening the London office of MacAndrews & Forbes. In 1906 he was transferred to Smyrna as general manager in charge of sales in Europe and Asia Minor, and in 1908 he was moved to New York as a director of MacAndrews & Forbes, serving as a vice-president in 1909-19. The largest individual shareholder in the company was James Buchanan Duke of British American Tobacco, and Catto participated in some of Duke's more peripheral interests, serving for example as president of a Mexican oil company launched by Duke.

Catto's knowledge of Russian and American business conditions proved invaluable after the outbreak of war in 1914. He was British Admiralty representative to the Russian supply commission in the United States, 1915-17, and moved to the British Food Mission in the USA following the Russian revolution in 1917. He served as chairman of the British & Allied Provisions Commission and head of the British Ministry of Food in the USA and Canada in 1918-19, for which he was made CBE in 1918 and a baronet in 1921. He was also appointed a Commander of the Order of Leopold of Belgium in 1919. One of his close associates in wartime supply work was George Macaulay Booth (qv) who became a lifelong friend.

In 1919-31 Catto was Calcutta head of the great Anglo-Indian mercantile house of Andrew Yule & Co. This had been formed in the 1860s by two Scots brothers, Andrew and George Yule, but its driving force had been their nephew David Yule (qv), who joined them at the age of seventeen, and eventually bought out his uncles. In 1917, while remaining head of the business in London, David Yule sold control of Messrs Andrew Yule to Morgan Grenfell, the London merchant bankers. One of the latter's leading directors was an old friend of Catto from Russian days, Vivian Smith (qv), and he suggested that Catto should be appointed head of the firm in Calcutta. J P Morgans had a high regard for Catto (especially in his wartime procurement work in which they had been involved), and Catto himself was attracted by the coincidence that his mother's maiden name was Yule, although he was not related to David Yule.

Catto went out to Calcutta in 1919, and soon became a dominant figure in India and the Orient, although he spent increasing time in London after his appointment as a managing director of Morgan Grenfell in 1928. The firm of Andrew Yule was renamed Yule, Catto in the 1920s, and after Sir David Yule's death in 1928, Vivian Smith became its chairman. Catto favoured Dominion Status for India, believing like 'the majority of British business men in India' that 'sooner or later it had to come in that form or events would force an even more advanced form' {Catto (1962) 79}. His views on the Indian political question, his sense that the Anglo-Indian die-hards' obstruction was counter-productive, probably influenced his strategy in 1945-46 when as Governor of the Bank of England he had to meet the Labour Government's nationalisation proposals in a helpful, realistic and conciliatory spirit.

Although Catto and Yule had not met until the former arrived in Calcutta in 1919, they became close colleagues and a formidable business partnership. It was through Yule that Catto obtained several other important board appointments, including a directorship of the Royal Exchange Assurance (where Yule also had a seat), serving as chairman 1935-40. Catto was also associated with Yule in buying control of the *Daily Chronicle* from Lloyd George in 1926, and running it as a Liberal newspaper. The *Daily Chronicle* was later fused with the *Daily News*, but the Daily Chronicle Investment Corporation was the financial medium for the purchases in the 1930s and 1940s of Liberal provincial newspapers by the United Newspapers group headed by Harley Drayton (qv).

Catto was a member of the Indian Government retrenchment committee of 1922-23, chaired by Lord Inchcape (qv), and of the committee on co-operative sales of coal (1926), chaired by Sir Frederick Lewis (qv). This committee, whose other members included Hugo Hirst (qv) and Sir Alfred Mond (qv), considered the possibility of creating a British coal-selling cartel on the lines of the Rhenish Westphalian Coal Syndicate, but its recommendations were resisted by the backward-looking and mutually jealous coal-owners. After the arrest of Lord Kylsant (qv), Catto at the request of Montagu Norman (qv) of the Bank of England became deeply involved in the reconstruction of the Royal Mail and Elder Dempster shipping companies, and in 1936 was co-opted onto the board of the Union Castle Mail Steamship Co. He received a barony in 1936, and until 1944 'sat on the Liberal benches in the House of Lords, partly from family convention and partly because there was more room there' {Catto (1962) 91}. After 1944 he was a crossbencher: his parliamentary speeches were usually on Indian or financial topics, and were always heard with interest and respect.

In March 1940 he became a director of the Bank of England, and a fortnight later replaced Lord Woolton as director-general of equipment and stores at the Ministry of Supply, joining the Supply Council. Three months later, however, the Chancellor of the Exchequer appointed him to the specially created and unpaid war position of financial adviser to the Treasury, which job required him to resign all his business interests and leave the Ministry of Supply before he had made any real impact. Catto was intended to add solid commercial and banking experience to the wartime team of economists and publicists who were being given temporary appointments in the Treasury, and although his position was ill-defined in its powers, he had a major part in both domestic and overseas financial policy. His proximity to Keynes in these dealings produced for them the nicknames of 'Catto and Doggo'. In April 1944 he returned to the Bank of England, succeeding Norman as Governor, and was confronted by many pressing problems. He was involved in launching both the Finance Corporation for Industry and the Industrial & Commercial Finance Corporation which were intended to provide some of the finance for post-war business reconstruction, and to meet the common criticism of gaps in the capital market. In 1945-46 he represented the Bank in its negotiations with the Labour Government over nationalisation. Catto approached these discussions in an accommodating spirit which angered the more reactionary members of the City, but his policy was vindicated by the final arrangements which left the Bank with uncompromised operational independence. The Bank entered public ownership in March 1946, and Catto continued to serve as Governor until February 1949 when he was succeeded by C F Cobbold (qv).

The only business connections which he resumed after 1949 were with Yule, Catto and with REA. In 1950-52 he chaired a government committee on Scotland's financial and economic relations with the rest of the United Kingdom, in which he drew on his pre-war experience as an Extraordinary Director of the Royal Bank of Scotland. Catto was, indeed, a proud Scot, who extensively restored his Aberdeenshire home, The House of Schivas at Ythanbank, in 1931-37, and was delighted to be made first Freeman of Peterhead in 1957. He was also a member of the Order of St John of Jerusalem, was elected as a distinguished member to the Athenaeum in 1945, received an honorary LL D from Manchester University in 1945, and was sworn to the Privy Council in 1947.

As a young man Catto owed much to his mother's support and encouragement. He was of diminuitive stature and quiet manner, but his quick wit and determined will impressed almost everyone with whom he worked, including Maynard Keynes. He was sensitive to criticism, and suffered anxiety at the sniping of City diehards in 1946, but his tact and sense preserved the individuality, independence and organisation of the Bank despite the change of ownership. Dalton, as Chancellor of the Exchequer, has left an account of Catto 'trotting along like a small kitten' to a press conference in Washington DC: asked how they should describe him he replied 'You can describe me as a small man with grey hair and an Aberdeen accent' {Dalton diary 26 Sept 1946}.

In 1910, while in Smyrna, Catto married Gladys Forbes Gordon, daughter of Stephen Gordon, a Scotsman who was MacAndrews & Forbes's partner at Smyrna. Their only son, Stephen (1923), was a managing director of Morgan Grenfell, and a director of both the Mercantile Bank and Yule, Catto. Catto died on 23 August 1959 at his house at Holmbury St Mary leaving £501,805 gross.

R P T DAVENPORT-HINES

Writings:

letter pleading for settled policy in Russia *Times* 4 Sept 1920.

letter criticising Lloyd George's Eastern policy *ibid* 29 Sept 1922.

letter on war experience of State trading in food *ibid* 15 Oct 1924.

letter on Indian policy *ibid* 8 Nov 1924.

letter on businessman's view of India *ibid* 11 Nov 1930.

article 'Milestones in India: Reform by Stages' *ibid* 17 Dec 1934.

letter suggesting final settlement of war debts to USA *ibid* 30 July 1938.

letter on Indian famine *ibid* 22 Nov 1943.

PP, Committee on Scottish Financial and Trade Statistics (1952) Cmd 8609 (chairman).

'Personal Memoir' in Sir Humphrey Baskerville Mynors, *Thomas Sivewright Catto, Baron Catto of Cairncatto, 1879-1959* (Edinburgh: T & A Constable, 1962).

Sources:

Unpublished

Bank of England archives, Threadneedle Street, London.

BLPES, papers of Lord Dalton.

Published

Bankers' Magazine Sept 1959.

Complete Peerage.

DNB.

Elizabeth Johnson and Donald Moggridge (eds), *The Collected Writings of John Maynard Keynes* (in progress, Macmillan, 1971-) 26.

Sir Humphrey Baskerville Mynors, *Thomas Sivewright Catto, Baron Catto of Cairncatto, 1879-1959* (Edinburgh: T & A Constable, 1962).

Richard S Sayers, *Financial Policy, 1939-45* (HMSO, 1956).

—, *The Bank of England 1890-1944* (3 vols, Cambridge: Cambridge University Press, 1977).

Times 24 Aug 1959.

WWW.

William Cavendish, 7th Duke of Devonshire (courtesy of Barrow in Furness Central Library).

CAVENDISH, William

7th Duke of Devonshire

(1808-1891)

Industrial and urban estate developer

William Cavendish, Seventh Duke of Devonshire and Second Earl of Burlington, was born in London on 27 April 1808, the eldest son of William Cavendish (1783-1812) and Louisa, daughter of the First Lord Lismore, and the grandson of Lord George Augustus Henry Cavendish, First Earl of Burlington (1754-1834). He was educated at Eton and Trinity College, Oxford, graduating in mathematics in 1829 as Second Wrangler, and eighth in the first class of the Classical Tripos, becoming a Smith's Prizeman and an MA in the same year, 1829. His intellectual standing has some relevance to his industrial and business exploits, and, as an estate developer, he has few equals in Victorian history. He was steered into estate management and business administration when, on 9 May 1834, he succeeded his grandfather as Second Earl of Burlington, thereby becoming responsible for considerable estates in North Lancashire, and, in particular, for the Burlington Slate Quarry at Kirkby-in-Furness, which still (1982) operates under that title. Much of his early manhood, however, was devoted to the improvement of those Cavendish estates attached to Holker Hall, Cartmel, and he became one of the founders of the Royal Agricultural Society (1838). The death of his young wife, the former Lady Blanche Howard (whom he married in 1829), on 29 April 1840, drove the Earl, as his personal diary shows, into tragic and lonely preoccupation with the Holker estates, and this accident was to have a profound effect upon the history of the nearby Furness area. Holker remained his favourite family retreat.

During the next few years, the future of the Burlington Quarries seemed uncertain, and the economic recovery of the years 1843-45 prompted the Earl, together with his legal advisers, Benjamin and Arthur Currey, to consider a railway to take ore and slate to the then tiny port of Barrow. The Currey family were afterwards to play a large if sometimes partially hidden part in many of his business decisions. The Duke of Buccleuch and friends or agents of his and the Earl's families joined in the scheme, and the Furness Railway — which the Earl at first saw principally as benefiting his slate quarries — was opened in 1846, to become one of the most successful iron ore lines in Britain. His belief in the success of the railway was far from total, and in 1849 he was, as his diary shows, on the point of agreeing to its leasing-out. Thereafter, its success was steadily more marked, and his chairmanship of the company was more rewarding. The Earl was sufficiently conscientious to learn to read its detailed accounts. His interest in business matters was sharply quickened when, following his accession to the Dukedom of Devonshire (at the death of the Sixth Duke, his cousin, on 15 January 1858), he found that the massive

Cavendish estates were encumbered to the value of roughly £750,000 with family debts in excess of £1 million.

But fortunately, Furness Railway receipts were improving and, moreover, the new Duke's annual income from land — the Cavendish estates amounted to 198,572 acres in 1873 — was soon in excess of £94,000 (1863). Determined estate improvement, as in the case of the Holker territories, soon sent this income to a higher level, and the 'improvement' comprehended some spectacular ventures, notably that of the industrial development of Barrow-in-Furness, part of which lay on the Duke's land. More covertly, he pursued the promotion of Eastbourne, also on Cavendish land, and Buxton, which lay near his great family seat of Chatsworth. The Duke did not at first invest heavily in these towns as communities, and his business strategy was to let the resorts finance their own development as far as possible. Even at Barrow, where his industrial investments were heavy only after 1870, he had, on 1 January 1866, an initial shareholding of only £26,000 out of a total capital of £500,000 recorded by the newly formed Barrow Haematite Steel Co, of which the Duke was chairman. But the rapid success of this company, which moved early into the steel rail market, and which was helped by its association with Midland and North-Eastern Railway magnates, encouraged much more serious support from the Duke and his family, who, between them (1871), held £190,750 in stock in the Steel Co, or some 27 per cent of all holdings. The Duke, influenced by a tight entourage of businessmen concerned in Barrow affairs, notably Sir James Ramsden (qv) and H W Schneider (qv), was very soon legitimising Barrow decisions if not always making them, and he became (January 1871) chairman of the new Barrow Shipbuilding Co, in which he held some 26 per cent of the £17,400 stock issued, and was more involved in the Barrow Flax & Jute Mill Co, promoted by Sir James Ramsden to employ women's labour in the town; the Duke and his family held shares in this to the value of £15,000 or 26 per cent.

The Barrow Shipbuilding Co was associated indirectly with the Barrow Ocean Shipping Co (1872), and the Eastern Steamship Co (1871), and these ventures were, in turn, related to the Furness Railway's immensely heavy investment in Barrow Docks from 1863; the new port was driven to attract shipping and shipbuilding alike, just as its promoters sought to strengthen its industrial base. The Duke could only follow the dangerous logic posed by a complex of interlocking enterprises. His income from dividends increased twelve-fold between 1863 and 1874, the income for the latter year being £169,361, greater than his total land rental income. The family fortunes seemed to be well on the way to rehabilitation, and 90 per cent of total investment revenue came from Barrow industries.

Meanwhile, the Duke found time to become a conscientious Chancellor of the University of Cambridge (from 1861 to his death), contributing signally to the foundation of the Cavendish Laboratory, and was equipped to fill the role of a keenly interested first president of the Iron and Steel Institute (1868), and president of the Royal Agricultural Society (1869-70). In addition, he travelled much about his numerous family seats throughout Britain, and remained interested in his Irish estates at Lismore and Waterford, in which he had invested heavily, especially via railway promotion.

A Liberal Whig in politics, the Duke remained detached from active participation in campaigning or debate, but was on friendly terms with Gladstone until he parted company with the latter over Home Rule in 1885. His improving attitude to landownership was in part transferred to matters of town welfare and amelioration, but, as a serious-minded Anglican, he was more interested in church-building than in hospitals. Tidy administration appealed to him, as did civic self-reliance.

His moral resources were severely tested in the years following 1874. Barrow demands for capital expenditure had been so vast that the Duke's indebtedness still exceeded £1.2 million in that year. In the following year, the dividends of the Furness Railway and the Steel Co began to slide downwards, commencing a collapse that was temporarily broken only in the early 1880s. Devonshire found himself required in 1877 to 'find a great deal of money to prevent a smash' {Chatsworth House, MS Diary of the Duke}, and responded in face of a refusal by the London & Westminster Bank to extend further credit to Barrow industries. Both the Barrow Shipbuilding Co and the Flax & Jute Co were saved from immediate disaster by him, and even the steelworks was in severe difficulties. By 1888, the Duke's Barrow-derived income was £8,487, as compared with £151,820 in 1874, while the interest on the Duke's debts stood at over £80,000. It was fortunate that his net estate rental exceeded the £106,000 mark, and that the administration and development of Eastbourne and Buxton did not provide extra burdens; it is clear, indeed, that a less able and a less cautious man would have been in desperate straits. Nor was his life immune from other tragedies; his favourite son Lord Frederick Cavendish ('Freddie') was assassinated in Phoenix Park, Dublin, in May 1882, and his third son, Lord Edward Cavendish (1838-91) pre-deceased him.

During these personal trials, the Duke was ably advised by William Currey, the family's solicitor, between the death of the latter's father, Benjamin Currey, in 1848, and 1886. Currey was an efficient secretary to the Barrow and other Cavendish enterprises. The Duke's interests were too wide-ranging and complex for unilateral or unassisted decision-making: a matter of great interest in this case, for the Seventh Duke, as a Fellow of the Royal Society and a Senior Wrangler, was a man of striking intellectual merit in any company. Yet he was obliged to remain dependent on others, and was often fortunate in his agents and advisers. Sir James Ramsden, Barrow's most notable grandee, was regarded somewhat distantly by the Duke even before the profitability of Barrow investments had reached its maximum ca 1870, but Ramsden was responsible for the direction or misdirection of great sums of Cavendish money; the influence of G A Wallis in Eastbourne was similar in kind if less expensive and controversial, as was that of E W Wilmott in Buxton. Without their influence, and that of excellent estate stewards, the Cavendish fortunes might have suffered more drastically than in fact happened.

The Duke died at Holker Hall on 21 December 1891. His gross personal estate was valued at £1,863,800. His son Spencer Compton Cavendish (1833-1908), the Marquess of Hartington of Gladstone's cabinet, 1868-74, succeeded him as Eighth Duke.

JOHN D MARSHALL

CAVENDISH William

Writings:

Opening Address at Owens College, Manchester, 1874.

Catalogue of the Library at Chatsworth (Chiswick Press, 1879).

Sources:

Unpublished

Chatsworth House, Devonshire Papers including MS Diary of the 7th Duke of Devonshire.

Lancashire RO, Holker Estate Papers, DDCa.

PRO, Furness Railway papers, Directors' Minutes; BT/31 Companies Registration Office, files of Dissolved Companies.

PrC.

Published

David Cannadine, 'The Landowner as Millionaire: the Finances of the Dukes of Devonshire c 1800-c 1926' *Agricultural History Review* 25 (1977).

David Cannadine, *Lords and Landlords: the Aristocracy and the Towns, 1774-1967* (Leicester: Leicester University Press, 1980).

Complete Peerage.

DNB.

Robert G Heape, *Buxton under the Dukes of Devonshire* (Robert Hale, 1948).

John D Marshall, *Furness and the Industrial Revolution* (2nd ed, Cumbria: M J Moon, 1981).

Sidney Pollard, 'Town Planning in the Nineteenth Century: the Beginning of Modern Barrow-in-Furness' *Transactions of the Lancashire and Cheshire Antiquarian Society* 63 (1952-53).

—, 'Barrow-in-Furness and the Seventh Duke of Devonshire' *Economic History Review* 2nd ser 8 (1955).

Proceedings of the Royal Society 51 (1892).

David Chadwick (courtesy of Cheshire County Library).

CHADWICK, David

(1821-1895)

Company promoter

David Chadwick was born at Macclesfield on 23 December 1821, the ninth and youngest child of John Chadwick, an accountant, and his wife Rebecca. David followed the same career as his father, remedying the problems caused by only a short period of schooling and employment at an early age in a warehouse, by attending evening classes. After serving as a clerk, he began business as a professional accountant in 1843 and the following year was elected treasurer to the Corporation of Salford; he was treasurer also to the City's magistrates and its gasworks and waterworks.

During the 1850s Chadwick published widely on urban affairs and conditions. He was especially interested in the sanitary question, in statistics and in the provision of a wide range of educational institutions. A number of patents covering water meters, six of which were taken out between 1853 and 1860, were registered in the name of David Chadwick. He took a prominent role in the establishment of both the Salford Royal Free Library and Museum and the Salford Working Men's College and acted as the first treasurer of both institutions. His advice was taken by the sponsors of the Act which enabled municipal bodies to establish public libraries and museums. Later, in 1876, Chadwick presented a library containing 10,000 volumes to his home town, Macclesfield. Following his move to London in the mid-1860s, he was consulted about the building of the Royal Holloway College, acted as a trustee of its estate, and on the nomination of its founder was made a governor of the college.

Chadwick's best-known statistical work was *On the Rate of Wages in 200 Trades*, the result of an enquiry suggested by William Newmarch, which was read as a paper to the Statistical Society of London in 1859 and then published at the request of the Manchester Chamber of Commerce. Chadwick was a member of the council of the London Statistical Society and between 1865 and 1867 was the president of the Manchester Statistical Society, after previously serving as its secretary. In the 1860s he wrote and published three more papers on local social statistics and statistical methods. His final achievement in this area was the appointment of a Medical Officer of Health to Manchester in 1868 which was largely due to his advocacy.

What can be termed as his 'Salford period' started to come to an end in 1860 when Chadwick decided to practise accounting privately once more and became the local agent and superintendent of the Globe Insurance Co. Initially he worked from an office in Manchester: in 1863 in partnership with Alexander Hathorn, in 1864 with John Adamson under the style Chadwick, Adamson & Co. In 1864 or 1865 a London office was opened and during the mid-1860s the partnership was titled Chadwick, Adamson, McKenna & Co; W C McKenna, a London financial agent who was related to J N McKenna, a director of the National Bank and company promoter, was probably a partner. In 1868 John Adamson withdrew to start business on his own account and Chadwick was joined by John Oldfield Chadwick and Edwin Collier of Hulme, Manchester in a practice titled Chadwick, Adamson, Collier & Co; in 1880 it consisted of four partners: David Chadwick, John Oldfield Chadwick, Edwin Collier and Francis Emmanuel Moore Beardsall. In 1883 the practice was split in three: Chadwick, Boardman & Co consisting of David Chadwick and James Boardman with offices in London and Manchester; Edwin Collier, Beardsall & Co of Manchester; and John Oldfield Chadwick & Co of London. In all David Chadwick had ten partners between 1860 and 1892 and from seven he was separated by lawsuits. In one obituary it was commented that he 'found excitement in litigiousness' rather than from operating on the Stock Exchange, racing, betting or gambling {*Proceedings of the Institution of Civil Engineers* 123 (1895) 450}. On his death in 1895 David Chadwick's practice was acquired by Mellors, Basden, chartered accountants of London and Nottingham, who purchased the assets and book debts for £75 and agreed to pay Chadwick's widow 12 per cent of the net receipts arising from any transferred business.

Chadwick played an important role in the professionalisation of accountancy. He was a founder member and fellow of the Institute of Accountants (London) and was the first president of the Manchester Institute of Chartered Accountants, giving its inaugural address on 3 April 1871. When the Institute of Chartered Accountants in England and Wales was established in 1880, Chadwick was one of the first council members, a position which he retained until his death.

Chadwick was no ordinary accountant. Between 1862 and 1874 he was involved in the formation of at least 47 limited companies, most of which were the conversion of family-owned industrial concerns. At the centre of his promotions were the most important mid-Victorian iron, steel and coal concerns, such as Staveley Coal & Iron, Charles Cammell, Ebbw Vale, John Brown and Bolckow, Vaughan. Most of these conversions were undertaken privately with Chadwick acting for the vendors, charging a 1 per cent commission for his services, and offering the companies' shares to his firm's 'friends'.

It has often been stated that the spur to Chadwick's activities in this area was the passage of the 1862 Company Act. Actually he began his career as a financier two years earlier when he established the Manchester Water Meter Co which acquired patent rights held by Chadwick and Herbert Frost. This company represented a bridge between Chadwick's involvement in the 1850s with the sanitary question and his post-1862 career as a company promoter. His interest in sanitary engineering can be dated to 1854 when, with the Borough Surveyor of Salford, Chadwick took out a patent for a stench-trap grid. During the same year he read a technical paper on water meters to the Institution of Civil Engineers for which he was awarded a premium by the ICE Council.

Chadwick's circle of acquaintances and friends in Salford and Manchester provided the capital for the water meter company and this group also provided the core of the equity funds which went into Chadwick's industrial conversions in the mid-1860s and the early 1870s. In the case of ten companies established as limited concerns between 1863 and 1868, on average 63.45 per cent of their shares were taken up by shareholders residing in the North West, with the averages for Manchester and the cotton towns being 43.53 per cent and 14.97 per cent respectively. Although Chadwick had to rely more heavily on public prospectuses for flotations in the early 1870s, south-east Lancashire continued to be the most important regional source of subscriptions for the companies that he converted. Chadwick's Mancunian circle of investors were not only substantial equity holders in his converted companies but also went on to the boards of these companies, and so constituted a block of interlocking shareholdings and directorships which continued until at least 1914, as shares and positions were retained within families. The most prominent members of this group were J Ashbury, the carriage and waggon builder; J Holden, a merchant; H J Leppoc, a merchant; H E Leo, a merchant; H D Pochin (qv), a manufacturing chemist; Benjamin Whitworth, a merchant and cotton manufacturer; T Vickers, a manufacturing chemist; and G Wood, a merchant and cotton dealer. Accordingly Chadwick provided a largely informal mechanism which channelled the profits earned in the cotton industry and trade into the iron, steel, coal and engineering industries during the 1860s and 1870s.

In the mid-1860s Chadwick's iron, steel and coal conversions were geographically concentrated in Sheffield, its immediate locality, and the north Midlands: John Brown, Charles Cammell, Parkgate Iron, Sheepbridge Coal & Iron, Staveley Coal & Iron, Vickers, Sons & Co and Yorkshire Engine. It has been asserted that this was a planned affair undertaken by 'a circle of businessmen in Manchester' who cherished 'ambitious projects of railway development at home and abroad, who, to assure control of the necessary material equipment, interested themselves in the acquisition or establishment of iron and steel works in Cleveland (Bolckow, Vaughan and Palmers) and in the neighbourhood of Sheffield.' {Newbold et al (1927) 19} H D Pochin, the father-in-law of Lord Aberconway (qv), the chairman of John Brown in the 1920s, has been portrayed as the head of this group with interests in Bolckow, Vaughan, John Brown, Palmers, Staveley, Sheepbridge, and the Tredegar Iron & Coal Co. Further, a link has been drawn between Pochin, who was the deputy chairman of the Metropolitan Railway Co and a director of the Manchester, Sheffield & Lincolnshire Railway, and the ambitions of E W Watkin (qv) in the creation of the Great Central and the opening-up of the South Yorkshire coalfield. It has not been possible to establish any definite connection between Watkin and Chadwick, except that Chadwick investigated the accounts of the Hudson's Bay Co in 1863 on behalf of the International Financial Society, which was to buy out the proprietors of the chartered company so that Watkin then could extend the Canadian Grand Trunk railway westward.

Although there does appear to be considerable circumstantial evidence for a Manchester railway supplies syndicate, there is, as yet, no substantiating documentary evidence. The only pointer is that Chadwick's first industrial conversion, undertaken in 1862, was the Ashbury Railway Carriage Co, a Manchester firm. An alternative hypothesis would be that this firm's inter-industry links brought the accountant into contact with such Sheffield firms as John Brown and Charles Cammell. Both produced rolling stock parts and both required capital in the early 1860s to finance investment projects for the production of armour plate and the development of the Bessemer process. Such outlets for savings would have been attractive to Mancunian business circles in the mid-1860s with the domestic boom in railway construction and steamship building coupled with the uncertainty hanging over the cotton industry as a result of the American Civil War.

If Chadwick did have partners outside his Manchester group then it was with the circle of merchants, bankers and financiers which had at its centre the International Financial Society and the London private bank Glyn, Mills, which was important in the finances of many domestic railway companies and the Canadian Provinces. The initial link may have been William Newmarch, the manager of Glyn, Mills with whom Chadwick had become acquainted through both the Globe Insurance Co and the statistical societies of London and Manchester. Palmer's proprietorship, after the company's conversion by Chadwick, contained a significant group which were allied to Glyn, Mills and one of the private bank's associates, L M Rate, went on to the board of the shipbuilding undertaking. Further, Glyns acted as bankers to many of the concerns converted by Chadwick, such as John Brown, Staveley Coal & Iron and Vickers.

Chadwick's links with this London group became clear during the aftermath of the 1866 crisis when along with Newmarch and W R Drake (a partner in Birchams and solicitor to the International Financial Society), he attempted to obtain legislation to remedy the problem of 'unlimited limited liability'. This arose from the practice in the mid-1860s flotation boom of forming companies with large share denominations on which only a small proportion was called up. With the crisis these shares became unmarketable as potentially they were subject to having large calls made upon them. Newmarch estimated that between £20 million and £30 million had been invested in such shares and legislation was required because the 1862 Act, unlike the 1856 Act, contained no provision whereby companies could either reduce their nominal capitals or subdivide their shares. Chadwick petitioned the President of the Board of Trade for the necessary amending bill in November 1866. It passed the Commons but failed in the Lords. Drake prepared a fresh bill which was considered by the Select Committee on the Limited Liability Acts which sat during the spring of 1867. This committee contained a large 'City' contingent, some of whom like Goschen and G G Glyn either knew personally or had strong business connections with Drake, Newmarch and Chadwick. It recommended that companies should be given powers to reduce both their nominal capitals and the values of their shares and these were adopted in the 1867 Act. Only three of the companies converted by Chadwick (Palmers, Yorkshire Engine and Samuel Dewhurst, a cotton enterprise) took advantage of the 1867 Act and only one immediately following its passage. Although Chadwick made great play about the position of Bolckow, Vaughan before the 1867 committee, this company continued with a nominal capital of £2.5 million divided into £100 shares. However, the Ebbw Vale Co, with £50 shares on which £10 had been called, had been unable to await the modification of the 1862 Act and consequently was forced to go through the expensive business of liquidation and reconstitution.

While pressing for the modification of company law, Chadwick's firm was involved in the resuscitation of four banks which had failed during the 1866 crisis: the Agra & Masterman's, the Bank of London, the Consolidated Bank and the Preston Bank.

Chadwick's experience with the 1867 Companies Act may have spurred his political ambition. He had unsuccessfully contested Macclesfield as a Liberal in 1865 but gained the seat as the junior member in December 1868 and was re-elected in 1874 and 1880. He voted for the disestablishment of the Irish Church in 1869 and was 'in favour of the reduction of the national expenditure' {*Macclesfield Courier* 31 Jan 1874}. He headed his 1880 letter to electors with the slogan 'Peace, Retrenchment and Reform', although at this election he was accused of 'recent indifference to the interests of the borough'. In fact in 1880 he was unseated, along with the other Liberal candidate, as the result of a petition lodged by the Conservative agent which contained charges of bribery, treating, undue influence and personation.

The main feature of Chadwick's parliamentary career was his campaign for the reform of company law. Before the 1867 Select Committee he asked that the Registrar of Joint Stock Companies be given the same powers as the Registrar of Friendly Societies and suggested that the model structure of articles of association, contained in the 1862 Act, should be mandatory, any deviations from it requiring special permission from the Registrar. On entering the House, Chadwick's first successful piece of legislation was an amendment to the Joint Stock Companies Arrangement Act of 1870 which dealt with winding-up procedure, an area in which Chadwick's firm had been heavily involved during the late 1860s. It was not until 1876 that his campaign took definite legislative shape with the introduction of a bill to repeal the unsatisfactory disclosure clause of the 1867 Act and replace it by a far more wide-ranging yet highly specific measure. Chadwick's concerns were to make the details of company flotation public knowledge, to ensure that companies had sufficient capital with which to commence business and to see that every company published uniform profit and loss accounts, balance sheets and annual reports. His campaign was blunted by the decision of the Master of the Rolls, in a case affecting the Ebbw Vale Co, that under the 1867 Act a company could only reduce the unpaid portion of its nominal capital. This ruling raised immediate difficulties for overcapitalised iron and steel companies during the severe slump of the late 1870s and diverted attention from the need to reform company law to protect shareholders from unscrupulous promoters. As a result of this Chancery decision, Chadwick introduced two bills in 1877. This and representations to the Board of Trade from both MPs and large Northern coal, iron and steel companies, many of which had been promoted by Chadwick, prompted the Government to introduce its own bill empowering companies to reduce their paid-up capital.

Chadwick was both a member of the 1877 Select Committee on the Companies Acts and gave evidence before it. His own bill received support from a large number of the other witnesses but it was heavily criticised by the Master of the Rolls. The committee, in its report, recommended the abandonment of the bill, but did urge some checks to prevent frauds against shareholders. Chadwick's bill was revived, but by others, in 1884 and again in 1887.

Chadwick's own promotional methods were discussed before the Select

Committees of 1867 and 1877 and came under legal scrutiny as a result of litigation in the late 1870s and early 1880s arising from the flotation of the Blochairn Iron Co in May 1873. Chadwick finally won the legal case, the action against him being dismissed with costs and costs of appeal. Actually Chadwick represented the best of mid-Victorian domestic company promotion: his commission of 1 per cent was low compared to the usual 5 or 6 per cent, which occasionally rose to 50 per cent. Unlike most other promoters, Chadwick employed professional valuers when he converted companies and did not inflate the price of the assets to be transferred by having them sold initially to 'dummy' vendors.

Whereas in the mid-1860s Chadwick had been concerned solely with domestic industrial affairs, during the financial boom of the early 1870s his firm's activities covered a very wide range of securities including domestic and American railway shares and bonds, American land sales, and shares of overseas mining, telegraph and tramway companies as well as domestic commercial and public utility companies. This activity became increasingly public as a result of Chadwick's publication of prospectuses and, between 3 September 1870 and 16 August 1875, a monthly *Investment Circular*, which replaced the earlier private communications made to the firm's established clients.

With the decline in domestic flotations in the mid-1870s, Chadwick's energies were absorbed in his parliamentary campaign for company law reform and the Blochairn litigation. His unseating in 1880 ended his political career and the break-up of his firm into three in 1883 possibly indicates some waning of his entrepreneurial energies. He continued to write articles in *The Accountant* and publish pamphlets occasionally: in 1878 on the causes of the industrial depression; in 1887 on changes in real wages over the previous half-century; and finally in 1890 on profit-sharing.

Another break occurred in 1877 with the death of his first wife, Louisa née Bow, youngest daughter of William Bow of Broughton, Manchester, whom he had married in 1844. They had a son and two daughters who survived Chadwick. Chadwick married again in 1878, to Ursula, the eldest daughter of Thomas Sopwith FRS. In his later life Chadwick may have been hard to live with. Apart from billiards, he had no hobbies or private interests. Increasingly self-assurance became the dominant trait of his character, revealed in an 'aversion to criticism, advice or opposition, or even to listen to caution' {*Proceedings of the Institution of Civil Engineers* 123 (1895) 450}. During the 1880s he continued to act as an accountant for the companies that he had converted ten or twenty years earlier and, as in the case of the Staveley undertaking, this could lead to public clashes with the board. From 1890 he was a shadow of his former self and suffered from impaired vision and increasing deafness. David Chadwick died on 19 September 1895, leaving an estate valued at £2,726 gross.

PHILIP L COTTRELL

The principal conversions undertaken by Chadwick, 1862-75:
Ancoats Vale Rubber Co

However, Chamberlain considered that the patent process used by Endurance was a failure.

Arthur Chamberlain's main contribution to business was at Kynoch. By 1888 the cartridge business of George Kynoch (qv), floated as a limited company in 1884, was sinking into confusion and loss. The shareholders and main board in London, following the recommendations of a committee of investigation, in September 1888 appointed Arthur Chamberlain, Simon Leitner and J P Lacy to overlook affairs in Birmingham and George Kynoch resigned as managing director. Chamberlain became chairman in 1889, remaining so for the rest of his life (and was succeeded by his son for another ten years). He immediately instituted economies to bring the business on to a sound base before launching a great expansion. He took over a desperately sick ammunition factory and saw to its recovery and growth. He made a clean sweep, paying attention to the operation of the works, costs, stock and purchasing, making many workers redundant. Quality control was introduced to eliminate cartridge rejection and to regain the reputation of the company. A metallurgist was appointed. Advertising was used. Annie Oakley, for instance, was seen using Kynoch's Eley cartridges. Many of the old board of directors were replaced. Chamberlain sold the lamp and gun factories, bought up the rolling mill and another, too, to insure the supply and quality of his metal. Already he was beginning to expand. He bought 85 acres of land at Witton and at Streetley, ten miles away. In 1893, he went into the explosives business by buying Shortridge & Wright at Worsboro Dale, near Barnsley; in 1895, he decided to make cordite at Arklow in Ireland and also at what became Kynochtown on the Thames in Essex. At Witton, glycerine, soap and candles were added as products associated with nitroglycerine production. On the metal side, a Siemens-Martin steel melting plant and a rolling-mill were added. After eight years, he had doubled capacity in existing products and added many new lines, pushing further into the munitions business.

The company was reconstructed as Kynoch Ltd in 1897 and expansion continued thereafter. Cycle components, brass casting and rolling, machine guns, and the Kynoch press (to print cartridge wrappings) were added plus, at Kynochtown, 52 houses, a hotel, school and playground and, nearby at Canvey Island, a hotel resort. In 1905 the electrification of Kynoch works was completed. After 1901 Kynochs took over Hadley & Shorthouse, Forward Engineering, Accles and their factories as well as one at Stirchley to make shells and a paper mill in Dublin. Employment rose from 2,000 in 1892 to 4,000 in 1897 and 6,000 in 1904, in nine works scattered round the UK. A branch factory was opened in Natal in 1908 while Chamberlain was on sick leave there.

Perhaps this pace of expansion was too much even for Arthur Chamberlain to digest, despite the assistance of his son and of A T Cocking; during 1906-12, profits fell, contracts were lost (culminating in 1909 in the law case against the War Office over 'impure' cordite contracts) and workers made redundant. Money was lost on copper stocks when the market fell. Chamberlain's attempt to introduce metric measurements to the Kynoch empire failed too during these difficult years. Soon after the tide turned, Chamberlain died and then the war changed prospects for munitions manufacturers. But, by then, he had built the foundation of the metals and explosives division of what became, via Nobel Industries, ICI, and survives, hived off, as IMI Ltd, Birmingham.

Chamberlain became director of the Corringham Light Railway Co and Ammonia Soda Co, the former owning the line that linked Kynochtown and the Thames estuary. He also became chairman of Hadley & Shorthouse but his interest in this preceded the acquisition by Kynoch. The Birmingham Trust Ltd, an investment trust with which the Chamberlains were closely concerned, had bought £14,000 shares in Felix Hadley & Co, nailmakers, and Chamberlain, after criticising the management with his customary candour, became chairman in 1896 to sort the company out. He was, thus, in a good position to sell out to Kynoch in 1901 after arranging Hadley's merger with B & G Shorthouse in 1898.

One of Chamberlain's problems and contributions at Kynoch lay in the matter of middle management. The virtual absence of this was a common problem in business at this time. Chamberlain strengthened management, provided an open plan office building and female clerks and, also, for example, 20 costing clerks.

Chamberlain's responsibilities and achievements at Kynoch seem enough for one man. However, over the same period, he was also busy rescuing Weldless Tubes Ltd, another Birmingham firm. Like Kynoch, this had been mismanaged. Four tube concerns, Climax, New Credenda, Star and St Helen's Metal, were merged into Weldless Tubes in 1897 to exploit Stiefel & Robertson's patents for weldless or seamless drawn steel cycle tubes. When the cycle boom crashed, ruining their market, they switched to engineering tubes but the existing suppliers fought back and prices collapsed, to 92.5 per cent off list price. The Birmingham Trust and Chamberlain had acquired a large interest in the firm and, after its reconstruction as Tubes Ltd in 1898, Chamberlain became director and chairman, with McFarlane from Armstrong, Whitworth as engineer and manager. The old board withdrew, leaving Chamberlain to cope with a loss of £52,000 and a completely unreal goodwill of £758,000 on the balance sheet. He found no plan of the Tube Co's works, an absence of office staff, machinery in disrepair and severe competition.

By 1904, cycle tubes had ceased to be an important part of the business largely because three works had been closed down. In 1905, losses were still being made but Chamberlain, characteristically, refused to consider joining a 'ring' to hold up the price of tubes, down 55 per cent in three years. He held off the debenture holders and reconstructed the company again in 1906. He himself at this time owned 43,000 ordinary shares, 43,000 preference shares, £23,000 of debentures and a debt of £4,750 in the old company and, therefore, he obtained a large share of the new £100,000 capital. He remained chairman, with J H Aston as his main assistant. The company survived, just, to form the nucleus of Tube Investments in 1919. His son and grandson, both called Arthur Chamberlain, were concerned with its management into the 1950s.

One of the companies referred to in the House of Commons debate in 1900 mentioned below was Hoskins & Son, makers of ships' berths, in Birmingham. Arthur Chamberlain had bought this company earlier and 'handed it to my brother, J C' {*Book of Business*, 23}. However, neither Arthur nor Joseph Chamberlain seem to have been concerned with

Hoskins except as shareholders. It was Neville Chamberlain who owned and managed it. Elliotts Metal, makers of ships' sheathing, in Birmingham, was another investment in which other Chamberlains were directors.

In December 1900 Lloyd George attacked the Chamberlains concerning the propriety of their shareholdings in companies with government contracts. The Birmingham Trust, Tubes, Elliotts Metal, Kynoch and Hoskins were referred to specifically. Joseph Chamberlain countered by mentioning the very real problem he had faced when investing the money taken out of Nettlefolds in ways compatible with a political career. Some capital had almost inevitably ended up in such companies. This criticism ignored the rights of his relatives not involved in political careers to carry on their normal business affairs.

Arthur Chamberlain's business views emerged in various ways. He gave evidence on behalf of the Birmingham Chamber of Commerce to the Departmental Committee on Income Tax in 1905, and discussed the issues of tax evasion, unfairness and the need for allowances against tax for obsolescence of machinery and for patent exhaustion. (Chamberlain served on the council of the Chamber, 1903-6, and represented it at the Association of UK Chambers of Commerce and the Empire. The Chamber apparently was an acceptable form of association to Chamberlain, but not one to which he gave much time in practice.) Thanks to Chamberlain's *Book of Business* printed privately in 1899 for the confidential use of his children and their children, his personal views on business management survive. The *Book* filled a gap for them on the general principles of the 'master's part' in a business and, in 1982, would still serve an entrepreneur or investor well (especially if he wished to stay clear of the government 'assistance' so common nowadays and so rare in 1899). Chamberlain told his children that for him

> The real interest of business ... consists, not in money making, but its variety, and the constant calls it makes on your courage, your judgement, your energy, or your patience, at uncertain, and unexpected, but very frequent intervals. Constantly at such times, *the human element*, in your workmen, your customers, your opponents, your colleagues, or yourself, is the main factor: and of the human element which enters then so largely into business, it is impossible for me to predict anything with certainty, except, that you can control it, *if you know how* {*ibid*, 1}.

He also believed that 'idleness is the father of all curses'. He defined a 'well-managed and well-established business' as one that 'can support the unexpected absence of the principal ... without injury'. The 'certain taint' attached to commerce had, in his view, no foundation in reason {*ibid*, 1}.

He advised his children not to 'sit on addled eggs' or, in modern parlance, invest in lame ducks. They should expect 10 per cent or 20 per cent on capital employed in a new venture, before subtracting their own fees but after all other charges including the manager's salary, depreciation and bad debts, and should insist on seeing the income tax returns for verification of the true position. He added that the average Birmingham business of that time was earning 12.5 per cent {*ibid*, 22, 23, 28}. An investor should be a pessimist, ready to lose one good venture to escape nine bad. New ventures were best considered as a 'lottery'. He ranked both Chamberlain & Hookham and Endurance as new, the first because it made an absolutely new product, electric meters, and the second because it introduced a new tubemaking process, which proved a failure.

However, this advice given confidentially to his children was rather different from that given publicly at the same date. The latter advice was never to buy shares in new companies, nor in mines, nor in patents worked for less than ten years nor in anything offering 10 per cent or more on the investment {*Ironmonger*, 27 May 1899}. Someone seems to have seen the confidential advice but misquoted it a little.

Arthur Chamberlain was interested in the education and training of businessmen. In the *Book of Business* he was sharply critical of the 'modern' side of many school courses. While he thought Greek and Latin or mathematics or chemistry were as good as anything else as preparation for a business career, schools often failed to provide the needed mastery in these subjects {*Book of Business* 9}. For a commercial career as a manager, the young man needed to be a trained accountant up to the level of passing the professional examinations, to have command of two foreign languages, preferably French and Spanish (as the Germans controlled no colonies, that language was less useful), involving three months' residence in each country, and to be a good shorthand writer. After two years' experience in business, the potential commercial manager should spend a year in foreign travel. His main criticism of technical (as distinct from commercial) courses was that they taught 'nothing about the British workman, his habits and customs, his strengths and his weaknesses, his vices and his virtues'. This was a 'great and almost fatal omission' for 'the British workman is the most important of all the machines' in the factory in the manager's charge. Each technical manager should spend six months in a machine shop to overcome this omission. {*ibid*, 16}.

In the plans for a Faculty of Commerce in the new university being engineered by his brother at Birmingham at this time, Arthur Chamberlain's part was limited to an executive, temporary and investigatory role rather than an innovating one. It is not known when his relations with his brother Joseph started to deteriorate over the protection issue, but that may have been a factor. The practical business syllabus Arthur proposed may well have influenced the Faculty's first dean, William Ashley, and in turn may have been influenced by that of the Birmingham Chamber of Commerce and of Mason College in 1899. He recommended a three-year course, taken on top of an arts degree with fees at £50 per annum; the main problem he foresaw was to find a suitable professor to run the course. He then seems to have dropped out of the proceedings, apart from becoming a life governor and apparently advising Ashley that 'if Tommy goes home and talks about balance sheets, father will think there is something in it' {*ibid*, 20n}.

Chamberlain came out clearly against both employers' associations and trade unions, seeing them as mutually generated. He wanted free bargaining on both sides with no conflicts of loyalty with peer groups. However, he recommended treating unions with goodwill and courtesy, though with a watchful eye on their effect on profitability {*ibid*, 116}. No worker who quit should be re-employed and no loyal worker be discharged.

The *Book of Business* expressed his private principles and these can be measured against his actions in relation to his own workforces. He was a strict paternalist. He opposed trade unionism but, on the other hand, introduced improvements to working conditions and pay earlier than many other manufacturers and before the unions were strong enough to obtain them. As early as 1872 he led his industry on the wages front. At the arbitration meeting in the Birmingham chandelier and gas fittings trade, he sat on the platform because Smith & Chamberlain were leaders in the trade and were reported to have been the first to grant the 15 per cent bonus on wage rates awarded then. However, in 1881, Smith & Chamberlain were paying 25 per cent below the wage list prices and were in dispute with the Brassworkers Union over this. Chamberlain reacted by establishing a trade benefit society for non-unionists only; all workers were pressed to join and all union members discharged.

After the Rowntree inquiry had shown that a man, wife and three children could not live on less than 21s 8d a week, Chamberlain in 1903 introduced a living wage at Kynoch. He put wages up to 22s a week for male workers aged 22-54 and about 200 had a rise. When, in July 1891, Kynoch faced a works stoppage which started in the fitting shop over the manager's displacement of skilled toolmakers by apprentices, Chamberlain stood by his manager. He refused in future to employ any members of a 'trade society' or to vary the printed pay scales. In consequence, the whole 3,000 strong labour force joined the strike, but returned to work two weeks later though they had to re-apply for their jobs. Another dispute, equally unpopular with Chamberlain, occurred at Kynoch in 1896. Then 160 operatives belonging to the National Society of Amalgamated Metal, Wire & Tubemakers went on strike to force Kynoch to join the Metal Trades Alliance.

On a rather different issue, Chamberlain acted in a way that, on several occasions, promoted the use of female labour, though probably because it was cheaper than male. He gave evidence, for Smith & Chamberlain, to the factory inquiry in 1876 on his employment of women on men's work such as lathe turning in his brassfoundry. He wanted freedom to employ either sex on all jobs and at all hours. He argued later that women had lost an estimated 25 per cent on their pay scales simply because the 'blind limitations' of the law saw fit to 'protect' them and restrict their working.

While Chamberlain was tough with trade unionists and strikers, he was paternal to the sick and needy. A notice appeared in the Kynoch works in 1891 drawing attention to the availability of 'sick clubs'. Witton workers in the early 1900s were vaccinated against smallpox and a convalescent home was opened for them at Llandudno. As the vaccination operation took place in the dining hall, it is evident that canteen facilities were also provided (long before they became a requirement during the First World War). However, the convalescent home was closed during the economy phase a few years later.

Chamberlain also recognised the manufacturer's self-interest in shorter hours of work. He was one of the first to introduce a forty-eight hour week. He started with a half day on Saturday in 1891, and extended this cut to an eight-and-a-quarter hour day and forty-eight hour week, with no cut in pay, in 1894. The cut in hours was said to be an economic proposition: 'it does not seriously, if at all, increase the percentage of wages to the cost of production, whilst it diminishes loss through waste and improves the general average of quality' {*Under Five Flags*, 30}.

However, at Smith & Chamberlain, he went further with the reduction of working hours. While seventy-two hours were common in other firms, there they worked sixty hours a week, often including fourteen hours a day at the end of the week. Chamberlain cut the week to forty-eight hours in 1890. Later he introduced the four-hour gang system (probably at Smith & Chamberlain), by which gangs worked either 6am-10am plus 2pm-6pm, or 10am-2pm plus 6pm-10pm, going home (or into the pub, Chamberlain noted regretfully) in between, indicating how near by they all lived in the 1890s. The machinery worked round the clock, a system in which female labour was illegal, and the men did a forty-four hour week.

He also provided his clerks and foremen at Kynoch with paid holidays, fourteen days a year plus customary holidays after one year's service, sick pay and a pension after ten years' service. However, this seems to have been limited to those on the staff.

Chamberlain significantly improved the safety record at Kynoch, the firm being complimented by the factory inspectors. In the days of George Kynoch, explosions had been endemic in the shops where child workers cooked their breakfasts over candles amongst the gunpowder waiting to be fed into the cartridges.

In the political field, Arthur Chamberlain supported his brother Joseph's views on Ireland but after 1900 came to oppose publicly his views on protection. This rift emerged between 1903 and 1906 and perhaps came earlier. In 1903 Arthur argued that competition was an incentive to invention. He preached this to his employees and shareholders and to a wider audience through the *Manchester Guardian* and *Birmingham Post*. Kynoch workers, Chamberlain & Hookham workers and Tubes shareholders were urged to support free trade and to oppose protectionist candidates in the 1906 election. Arthur argued that protection would reduce earnings: the taxes on food and manufactures would cut consumer spending power and divert it to food away from manufactures and, thus, cut jobs. It would also hit British exports as they would be kept out of markets in retaliation. Workers would suffer both from a higher cost of living and fewer jobs. Since Tubes bought its steel from Sweden, it could not benefit from colonial preference while, in a heavy industry like that, its workers needed to be well fed to work properly. Thus, Arthur Chamberlain differed profoundly from his brother Joseph and, in 1906, unsuccessfully supported the Liberal and Free Trade candidate in the Aston constituency in which Tubes and Kynoch were situated. His words had to be written to his workpeople because he was in Siam and Burma at election time.

Arthur Chamberlain was a free trader in other spheres as well. When Kynoch became involved in soap production, he was finally forced by the retailers to accept the idea of soap coupons and advertising. Kynoch published a circular opposing the soap trust. He also stood out against combines in other trades, including the Birmingham alliances as mentioned above. On the other hand, he supported resale price maintenance on Kynoch's Eley cartridges both in the press and in a law case against an underselling firm.

Chamberlain wanted to be free of control by statute or by his peers. He said, for example, that

> we are tied round with red tape, we are battened on by inspectors, we are cramped at every turn. And then these people who are responsible for this state of affairs, in another of their moods, ask, 'Why is it the English business men have no longer that initiative, that energy, that self-reliance which used so to distinguish our race? {*ibid*, 47}

He was prepared to take the 'lash of bad trade' considering 'this lash is to my mind the natural punishment for past faults, and their only effective cure' {*Book of Business*, 110-11}. Hence his attachment to free trade and market forces.

Arthur Chamberlain, who became a Birmingham JP in 1884, was chairman of the Licensing Committee in Birmingham from 1893 to 1903. In an effort to curb drunkeness (which he had seen firsthand when, in disguise, he made a survey of public houses), Arthur Chamberlain negotiated with the Birmingham and Midland Counties Wholesale Brewers Association in 1896 about his scheme for the voluntary surrender of licenses. The retiring licensee in over-licensed parts of the city would be compensated by the survivors for the value of his business. Half the licenses in some areas were surrendered under the scheme and 298 had been eliminated by 1903. However, opposition developed from those who wanted a quicker, compulsory scheme backed by state compensation and act of Parliament and from the brewers' lobby (and also, perhaps, the air-gun clubs whom Chamberlain proposed to exclude from licensed premises). Consequently in 1903 Chamberlain was not re-elected by his fellow magistrates and the Birmingham surrender scheme lapsed.

Arthur Chamberlain had an

> ascetic appearance and grave demeanour [and] his most striking characteristics were an almost pathological probity, a faculty of detachment which at times came perilously near ruthlessness, and a fervent conviction that of all sins Intemperance was by far the most deadly. The reaction he evoked in those around him varied from violent resentment to reluctant respect {*Under Five Flags*, 29}.

He was said to have a 'larger-than-life personality and an unusual repertoire of eccentricities, not all of them amiable' {*ibid*, 51}. Perhaps it was his 'unwearied patience in the care of details' and the fact that he 'worked by and to time' that established the success of most of his ventures. However, for relaxation, he read yellow-backed whodunits as he travelled in the brougham that he preferred to more modern forms of transport.

Arthur Chamberlain was a Unitarian like his brother, attending the Church of the Messiah in Broad Street, Birmingham. Like so many in his family, he married a Kenrick, marrying Louisa, daughter of Timothy Kenrick, in 1870; they had two sons and seven daughters before Louisa died in 1892. Their sons were Arthur (ca 1880-1941), who succeeded his father as chairman of Kynoch, and John (1881-1917), who was killed in Flanders. One of the daughters married J S Nettlefold. Arthur Sr lived at Moor Green Hall in Moseley in Birmingham, his garden adjoining that of brother Joseph.

Arthur Chamberlain died on 19 October 1913, at Cadhay House, Ottery

CHAMBERLAIN Arthur

St Mary in Devon, where he lived during the winter, after three or four years of ill-health following influenza. He left £142,718 gross.

BARBARA M D SMITH

Writings:

PP, RC on Factory and Workshop Acts (1876) C 1443.

The Book of Business (pp, 1899).

Commercial Education (pp, 1900).

PP, HC 1900 (313) IX, War Office Contracts.

Licensing in the City of Birmingham. Birmingham Surrender Scheme (Birmingham: Cornish Bros, 2nd ed, 1902; 3rd ed, 1903).

In the Matter of the Drink Trade ... a Speech, May 6, 1903 (Birmingham, 1903).

Speech by Arthur Chamberlain, Justice of the Peace for the City of Birmingham, 14th April 1904 (1904).

Notes on the Government Licensing Bill of 1904 (Birmingham, 1904).

On Free Trade and Protection. A Few Words to the Witton Workpeople of Kynoch Ltd. December 21, 1905 (Birmingham: Kynoch Press, 1905).

PP, Departmental Committee on Income Tax (1905) Cd 2575.

Sources:

Unpublished

BCe.

MCe.

PrC.

Barbara M D Smith (comp), 'Bibliography of Birmingham Industrial History' (copies in Birmingham Reference and University Libraries).

'Newspaper Cuttings in Birmingham Biography', vol 8, and other volumes (Birmingham Reference Library).

Published

Birmingham Mail 29 Apr 1899.

Birmingham Post 25 May 1881, 7 Sept 1886, 18 Nov 1888.

Birmingham Red Book.

Directory of Directors.

Engineer 24 Sept 1886.

Ironmonger July 1863, 17 Apr 1866, Oct 1869, 1 Aug 1881, 28 Aug 1883, 17 Apr, 8 June, 23 Aug 1886, 30 June 1888, 7 Nov 1891, 3 Feb 1894, 2 May 1896, 10 Dec 1898, 21 Jan, 27 May, 16 Dec 1899, 8 Aug 1903, 6 Feb, 3 Nov, 22 Dec 1906.

Kynoch Journal, 1899-1900 and 1902-3.

PP, Children's Employment Commission, 3rd Report, Appendix: Metal Manufacturers of the Birmingham District (1864) 3414.

Barbara M D Smith, *Education for Management: its Conception and Implementation in the Faculty of Commerce at Birmingham Mainly in the 1900s* (Centre for Urban and Regional Studies, Research Memorandum 37, 1974).

The Stock Exchange Year-Book.

Under Five Flags. The Story of Kynoch Works, Witton, Birmingham 1862-1962 (Birmingham: Kynoch Press, 1962).

Eric W Vincent and Percival Hinton, *The University of Birmingham. Its History and Significance* (Birmingham: Cornish Bros, 1947).

WWW.

CHAMBERLAIN, Joseph

(1836-1914)

Screw manufacturer

Joseph Chamberlain as a young businessman (courtesy of J B Kenrick).

Joseph Chamberlain was born in Camberwell, Surrey on 8 July 1836, the son of Joseph Chamberlain, a shoe manufacturer, and his wife Catherine née Harben, daughter of a provision merchant. Joseph Jr was educated at University College School and then spent two years in his father's London office. At the age of eighteen, in 1854, he went to Birmingham to join an uncle by marriage, in a move designed to exploit a technological break-through in screw manufacturing.

At the Great Exhibition of 1851 in the Crystal Palace, his uncle, John Sutton Nettlefold, had seen a pair of machines patented by Thomas J Sloan, an American, which fully mechanized the technique of making wood screws. The process of making small, fairly standard goods from wire was ripe for full automation, but the opportunity entailed a dauntingly high investment of capital. The initial price for exclusive rights to the patent in Britain plus enough machines to begin to exploit its potential was set at £30,000, and upkeep of the machines would be expensive. For three years Nettlefold hesitated. Then, in 1854, he took the plunge by raising a third of the initial purchase price from his wife's brother, Joseph Chamberlain Sr.

Joseph Chamberlain Sr raised the £10,000 without encroaching upon the capital of his own shoe manufacturing or cordwaining business and eventually he assumed an equal share with Nettlefold in the screw manufacturing enterprise, now called Nettlefold & Chamberlain. He, rather than his son was the leading Chamberlain in the new enterprise during its first years. But he was not the man on the spot. As soon as he agreed to the initial investment, he despatched Joseph Jr to Birmingham to look after his interests.

Young Joseph started on the shop floor, where he learned to tend one of the new machines. He then spent a longer apprenticeship in the book-keeping office, where he acquired the tiny, regular, oblique handwriting which marked him apart after he left business for politics. With this experience behind him, young Joseph assumed day-to-day responsibility for the firm's wholesaling and eventually for its commercial policy. His father did not move to Birmingham until after he sold the cordwaining business in 1863. Before the death of John Sutton Nettlefold in 1866, effective control of the enterprise passed to the sons of the original partners: Joseph Nettlefold was in charge of production, Joseph Chamberlain of marketing.

In the mid-1860s, before the transition from the fathers to the sons was complete, the four men together took a group of decisions which enabled them to dominate the British and, to a lesser extent, the world-wide screw market. Their purchase of the Sloan patent had not been enough to give them the dominance they desired. A rival firm in Birmingham, James & Avery, had made independent technological advances, not to the level of the Sloan patent, but enough to give them a goodly share of the industry's expanded production. The exclusive rights of Nettlefold & Chamberlain to the Sloan patent did not extend to the American market where it originated, nor to France, Germany and Russia, where the patent had been sold to other buyers. Frustrated by the limits to their achievement, the Nettlefold and Chamberlain fathers and sons integrated and extended their production vertically to include the manufacture of wire from which screws were made and eventually also production of their own iron rods. In 1864, they purchased a wire-making works situated in Birmingham, the Imperial Mills. Now able to reduce the price of their final product, they persuaded their main rivals in Birmingham to sell out to them.

Meanwhile young Joseph Chamberlain threw himself into a related banking venture in association with the uncle of his first wife (and father of his second), Timothy Kenrick, the leading hollow-ware manufacturer of the West Midlands. Kenrick assumed the chairmanship of the provisional committee which transformed Lloyds of Birmingham, hitherto a private bank, into a public joint stock concern. Chamberlain also took a lead on that committee.

Together with the purchase of the Sloan patent, the extension of Nettlefold & Chamberlain's enterprise in the mid-1860s laid the foundations of their eventual near-monopoly. They now produced nearly 70 per cent of Birmingham's output of screws. The reduced wholesale prices which their own wire as well as mass production enabled them to offer (a tenth of what prices had been at the beginning of the century) opened up the prospect of almost limitless expansion of their market, already doubled since mid-century.

Chamberlain moved quickly to expand the sales of the firm beyond Britain. His first marketing voyage took to him Ireland. Whenever he went on the Continental holidays he loved, he carried his order book with him. It always came back full. Foreign travel alerted him to the preferences of potential foreign buyers. The French were used to screws nicked and wormed but not turned like English ones; so Chamberlain had Nettlefold make some accordingly. The French were also used to blue wrapping paper, which Chamberlain gave them, and they liked the measurements of the gauges of the screws to be hand-written on the packages, which was therefore done. But handwritten specifications aroused the suspicions of the Scots, so Chamberlain made sure that they got machine printed numbering, and also the green wrapping paper which they preferred.

The addition of new kinds of products went hand in hand with expansion of the market. Apart from a vast array of designs, qualities and sizes of screw, Nettlefold & Chamberlain sold whatever wire the Imperial Mills produced beyond their own needs. They were even prepared to sell the automatic machines for which they held the patent, confident that they could make a profit on the sale and still produce screws more cheaply than the buyer. The increasing complexity of the firm's array of wares prompted Chamberlain to initiate an effectively illustrated as well as detailed price list.

Chamberlain's enterprise extended into other fields. He negotiated with the neighbouring railway and canal companies for special rates for his goods in return for his employment of their facilities. Eventually he arranged with the Great Western Railway for a rebate on its charges, and he joined the board of directors of the Midland Railway. Yet he never attempted to raise his enterprise to a higher level of merger by taking over the transport and banking concerns with which he was involved.

He was less concerned with extension of the firm at home than with promotion of its sales abroad. The stiffest competition for the lucrative Continental market came from two French firms. With the lesser of the two, Le Comptoir de Ferches, Chamberlain negotiated in 1869 for a territorial division of the Continental market; Nettlefold & Chamberlain took maritime countries, leaving landlocked nations to the Comptoir. But he could not make headway against the great Parisian firm of Japy Frères until it was cut off from its buyers by the siege of Paris during the Franco-Prussian War.

The expansion of sales overseas was Chamberlain's most spectacular and profitable achievement in business. However the part of the business that caught his imagination lay outside his allocated responsibilities. Joseph Nettlefold was in charge of the firm's factories and their workforce, not Chamberlain. But as cost accountant for the firm, Chamberlain began in 1864 to keep a periodic abstract of how the wages paid at the main mill in Smethwick contributed to the cost per unit of its products. At the same time, with remarkable quickness, he perceived, as he put it, that 'a revolution is taking place in the principal hardware trades, and ... is assimilating (Birmingham) to the great seats of manufacture in the North, and depriving it of its special characteristic, viz., the number of its small manufacturers, which has hitherto materially influenced its social and commercial prosperity as well as its politics.' {Timmins (1866) 604-5} The revolution Chamberlain was talking about had to do with the factory system, the creation of great mills such as his own which gathered together all the processes of manufacture of a particular range of goods for mass production. That revolution put the civic genius of Birmingham at risk.

Chamberlain recognised the risk. Yet, in addition to the economic advantage to himself, he saw social benefit in the change. The new system would undoubtedly lead 'to the extinction of the small manufacturers'. But in all other regards, he argued, the change was 'really an almost unmixed good. At all events, the following advantages will spring from its consummation: healthier work-places, regularity of hours, economy of labour, increased demand, lower prices, and at the same time higher wages.' {ibid} He sought to substantiate his prophecy, partly through exercises in class collaboration such as the Smethwick Working Men's Club, Institute, and Benefit Society which he instigated in informal association with the mill, and more substantially by sharing the prosperity of the firm with its workforce through concessions such as the nine-hour day in 1872 before they were demanded.

The most serious challenge to the dominance of Nettlefold & Chamberlain over their industry arose in 1870, with the formation of the Birmingham Screw Co. The new company brought together a number of the ingredients of Nettlefold & Chamberlain's success. Alfred Field, a wholesaler in the trade market, bought rights to an American patent for what was claimed to be a better automatic machine than the one which Nettlefold & Chamberlain used. Field secured capital to exploit the invention from John Cornforth, a local manufacturer of wire which could be used in the business, and from Josiah Mason (qv), the immensely rich manufacturer of steel pens. In order to begin business even before they could fit out a plant for their own production, Field ordered a supply of screws from Chamberlain's French rival, Japy, not yet menaced by war. One of Nettlefold's foremen undertook to supervise the building and equipping of the new firm's mill.

Chamberlain rose to the challenge with the same mixture of angry impulse followed by sharp response and tenacious pursuit which would characterise his career in politics. The plan which he hammered out called for high prices and profit-taking by Nettlefold & Chamberlain for however long the new company took to get into production. This profit would then be used to tide Nettlefold and Chamberlain over while they slashed their prices in order to deny the new company a profit and hence exhaust the patience of its shareholders. Chamberlain worked out his line of thought in tables of statistics. He sought advice widely among his friends and associates in Birmingham. He gathered information by every device he could think up, until he knew as much about the new company as its own promoters. He contacted Nettlefold's skilled workmen, and also made clever use of the press to discourage would-be investors in the new enterprise. Each day he conveyed his findings to his partner in a way intended to stiffen Nettlefold's spine. 'We have got to smash the new Company' was the repeated refrain.

The Birmingham Screw Co managed to get off the ground, but it never really flew. Within weeks of its formation, the Franco-Prussian War broke out, vastly expanding Chamberlain's foreign sales and cutting the Birmingham Screw Co off from its interim supplier. In 1871 and 1872, Nettlefold & Chamberlain pushed their prices up by as much as 50 per cent. They rolled in much greater profits than Chamberlain had predicted, for, even apart from the Franco-Prussian War, the early 1870s saw a worldwide economic boom.

Yet while Chamberlain thus achieved his greatest wealth in industry, his mind was turning to other things. He was already a leader among the aggressive Radicals on Birmingham's Town Council and of the National Education League in its fight against the Act of 1870. In 1873, now Mayor of Birmingham and prospective candidate for election to Parliament at Sheffield, he handed the records of his commercial transactions and a précis of his accounting methods over to Nettlefold. Marginally damaged by his connection with the business in his unsuccessful bid for election at Sheffield, Chamberlain and his brothers sold their half of the partnership to the Nettlefolds in 1874 for a reputed £600,000.

The concerns which Chamberlain had imbibed and the methods he had learned during his career in business permeated his second, much more famous career in politics. None of Nettlefold & Chamberlain's successes in taking over their competition were as spectacular as the take-overs of the local gas companies and then of the water companies by Birmingham's Town Council in the mid-1870s at Chamberlain's behest. The financial arrangements he made, which enabled the municipalised gas company to return a profit almost immediately to the tax payers and reduced the cost of good water to the consumer, dazzled the Town Council and gained for Birmingham a reputation as the best governed city in the world. His transformation of some of the worst slums in central Birmingham into a handsome thoroughfare for the commercial and professional life of the town proved more controversial. The plans for the development made inadequate provision for the displaced slum dwellers; and in the depressed 1880s, after Chamberlain had left the Town Council for the House of Commons, the mounting costs of Corporation Street threatened to outweigh its diffused dividends. His efforts as Colonial Secretary, in 1895-1903, to cultivate economically undeveloped or depressed stretches of the Empire overseas produced similarly equivocal results.

The most effective bond between Chamberlain's business and political careers lay in his enduring sensitivity to the economic needs and industrial society of Birmingham. He was arguably the greatest constituency representative in British Parliamentary history. Not only did he use his political influence steadily to advance the city's major business interests, particularly its munitions industry, in which some of his family were involved. The small, inner circle of his lifelong friends was composed of men, most of them linked to him by marriage, who had made and in some cases were continuing to build their fortunes in Birmingham businesses, usually involving some form of metal manufacturing. At the same time the particular constituency which he represented, West Birmingham, a single seat constituency (which he held, 1886-1914, after sitting as one of Birmingham's three MPs, 1876-85) embraced a largely working-class electorate in the old jewellery quarter of the city. Chamberlain returned again and again to the annual dinner of the jewellers, to keep in touch with the electors whom he represented, and to reflect upon and apply their interests to the questions of state with which he was concerned in a succession of speeches to which the nation at large paid close heed. The campaign for imperial tariff protection on which he embarked in 1903 closely reflected the sentiments and economic well-being of his city.

CHAMBERLAIN Joseph

Throughout his political career, the industrial society of Birmingham shaped Chamberlain's conception of the needs of Britain and its Empire.

His personal business acumen was, nonetheless, dulled by disuse. The income from his investments soared through the 1880s. Then he invested and lost heavily in an abortive sisal-growing venture on the island of Andros in the Bahamas. That loss, compounded by sagging returns from his other investments, reduced his wealth by the mid-1890s far enough for him to contemplate withdrawal from public life. But the thought was fleeting. His wealth remained sufficient to allow him to resign as Colonial Secretary over tariff reform in 1903 without serious dismay at the loss of official income. Though he had to reduce his public donations at that time, financial worries did not impinge upon him until he suffered a stroke in 1906. Limp with paralysis, which silenced him in the Commons, he endured until 1914.

Joseph Chamberlain married firstly, in 1861, Harriet Kenrick, by whom he had one son and a daughter; after Harriet's death in 1863 he married, in 1868, her cousin Florence, by whom he had one son and three daughters. After Florence's death in 1875, he married Mary Endicott, daughter of William C Endicott (1876-1900) the American Secretary of War, 1885-89. Joseph Chamberlain died on 2 July 1914 leaving £125,495 gross.

PETER T MARSH

Writings:

'Manufacture of Iron Wood Screws' in Samuel Timmins (ed), *The Resources, Products, and Industrial History of Birmingham and the Midland Hardware District* (1866).

Sources:

Unpublished

Birmingham University Library, Joseph and Neville Chamberlain papers.

GKN, London headquarters and Smethwick, archives.

Lloyds Bank archives, London headquarters and Colmore Row, Birmingham.

Published

DNB.

James L Garvin and H Julian Amery, *The Life of Joseph Chamberlain* (5 vols, Macmillan, 1932-1951).

Ernest P Hennock, *Fit and Proper Persons* (Edward Arnold, 1973).

WWMP.

WWW.

Sir Paul Chambers (courtesy of ICI PLC).

CHAMBERS, Sir Stanley Paul

(1904-1981)

Chemical manufacturing company chairman

Stanley Paul Chambers, usually known as Paul, was born in Southgate, Middlesex on 2 April 1904. His father, Philip Chambers, was a commercial clerk, and later a City wine merchant; his mother was Catherine née Abbott. He was educated at the City of London School, and then as an evening student at the London School of Economics in 1923-26, and again in 1930-35, taking a B Com in 1928 and an MSc in 1934.

His career started in 1927, in the Inland Revenue Department. He has been described as 'one of the most brilliant Inspectors of Taxes the Inland Revenue had ever produced' {*Times* 5 Jan 1982}, and his rise in the service was rapid. In 1935, he became a member of the Indian Income Tax Inquiry Committee and later Taxation Adviser to the Government of India with the rank of Joint Secretary. During this time he became a member of the Indian Legislative Assembly and later of the Council of State; for his services in India he was created a Companion of the Order of the Indian Empire. Returning to the UK in 1940, Chambers was appointed Director of Statistics and Intelligence and Assistant Secretary to the Board of Inland Revenue. In 1942 he became Secretary to, and a member of, the Board of Inland Revenue. The PAYE (Pay As You Earn) system of taxation was largely his brain-child: it was heralded as 'ingenious in construction and simple to operate' {*Economist* 25 Sept 1943}, was of immense assistance in raising war revenue, and has remained the basic method of collection for income tax, but it may be doubted whether many businessmen would thank him for thus enlisting their wages departments in the labours of tax collection. He was also responsible for the development of the Inland Revenue statistical service, which after the war furnished much of the information on which plans for the management of the national economy were based. For his Inland Revenue work he was created a CB in 1944. In that year he visited Washington in connection with the negotiations for the comprehensive double taxation agreement which was signed between the United States and Britain in 1945.

Just before the end of the war, Chambers was appointed Chief of the Finance Division of the British Element of the Control Commission for Germany, a post he held until he left the public service in 1947. That year he moved to ICI which had, and still has, a tradition of recruiting Inland Revenue officials among whom Josiah Stamp (qv) was his most distinguished predecessor. Within a year Chambers became finance director, in 1952 one of three deputy chairmen, and chairman in 1960. He was the first, and so far the only, chairman to have come from outside ICI.

With his enquiring mind, his curiosity and his adaptability of thought, Paul Chambers quickly made his mark in ICI. He led the company at a time of great change when the chemical industry was going over from coal to oil as its basic raw material and when the market was changing from a seller's to a buyer's one.

He insisted that ICI should modernise its thinking about profits, profitability and profit margins, arguing that the company was in danger of not recognising post-war inflation, and insisting on a revaluation of its plants and assets.

His approach to ICI's affairs is well-encapsulated in a report he produced after chairing a committee charged with examining the company's objectives in the broadest sense. One of the main conclusions of his lengthy study of ICI's industrial and social objectives, and of its duties and obligations to its shareholders, employees, and to the communities in which it operated, was that ICI's main purposes could best be fulfilled by acting in the best interests of its stockholders. By maintaining a reasonable and continuing profitability, and developing an efficient business, ICI was more likely to serve the public interest than by the pursuit of vaguer objectives. To many in a company where a scientific rather than a financial ethos had been dominant, this approach came as something of a shock.

In accordance with this philosophy Chambers worked purposefully both as finance director and subsequently as chairman, to raise the company's capital gearing. By comparison with many of its major international competitors ICI had low borrowings in relation to its equity, and he believed this unnecessarily constrained its growth at a time when the industry as a whole was increasing production capacity and output at a rate approaching 10 per cent a year. This comparison was particularly striking in relation to the I G Farben successor companies in Germany which had very little equity after the Second World War but nevertheless grew rapidly, predominantly on the basis of loans. The Japanese provided an even sharper contrast to the low capital gearing of ICI (and of many major American companies) in the 1950s and 1960s.

The new emphasis on finance was also shown by the introduction of special courses on finance and taxation, and the institution of an investment committee. The functions of the main board were changed to give more power to the divisional chairmen, and allow the directors of the main board more time to think about the long-term objectives and problems of the company. Chambers called in McKinseys, the management consultants, to advise on the reorganisation; this consultation of outside experts was another shock to the corporate psychology, for many of those bred within ICI found it hard to believe outsiders could have anything to teach them.

Nonetheless, Chambers had a healthy scepticism about 'planning'. Corporate planning was becoming more widely practised during his chairmanship and ICI was one of the first companies to adopt it. Although it was not entirely novel in concept, corporate planning was becoming more clearly recognised and developing a more coherent form and methodology. He was not opposed to the concept, but he needed to be convinced, having a suspicion that formal planning might reduce the company's ability to respond quickly and flexibly to changes in the economic and political environment. Moreover, he tended to associate planning with excessive intervention by Government in industrial affairs, and to associate this with some aspects of socialist philosophy.

Paul Chambers will always be associated with the attempt by ICI to take over Courtaulds which took place in 1961-62. Chambers opened discussions with Courtaulds soon after he became chairman, and headed the negotiations personally. Public disquiet about the prospect of a merger between two of the largest companies in the British economy found echoes even within ICI. Many ICI staff were also disturbed by Chambers's public statements about the proposals, which had far more to say about the anticipated financial benefits to the companies than about the effect of the merger on their employees or on the public. These widespread doubts about the merger, and Chambers's miscalculation of the price he needed to offer to attract sufficient Courtaulds shareholders, so that he was forced publicly to revise his 'final' offer more than once, strengthened the hand of the Courtaulds board led by Sir John Hanbury-Williams (qv). Their defeat of Chambers's bid left his company with a 38 per cent holding in a company controlled by a board whose policies he had attacked publicly, and joint owner with Courtaulds of British Nylon Spinners, which had 85 per cent of the nylon market in Britain. This embarrassing situation was resolved in 1964, when ICI surrendered their shares in Courtaulds in exchange for Courtaulds' shares in British Nylon Spinners; in addition ICI was to pay Courtaulds £2 million a year for five years, to provide capital for their development of nylon. This deal could not repair the damage that had been done, both to ICI's public image and to Chambers's reputation within his own company. Nonetheless, the attempted merger had been a bold and imaginative move; had it succeeded, the shape of British industry would have been changed in a major way.

Chambers was not a man to be daunted by such a setback. He pressed ahead with his efforts to equip the company to face an increasingly competitive international market, and to remind the staff that even ICI could not afford complacently to assume that past triumphs guaranteed an untroubled future. But even he absorbed a notion prevalent in ICI, that so long as a project was technically sound, the money to realise it could always be provided. In 1966, through faulty planning procedures for which Chambers cannot be absolved from some responsibility, the board suddenly faced the scarcely credible possibility that ICI might run out of cash. Expensive borrowing put matters right, as a first-aid measure, but the episode was yet another shock to the system and another blow to Chambers's reputation.

His style during his ICI chairmanship was simple, approachable and refreshingly open, in contrast with the aura of remote majesty cultivated by some of his predecessors. He was probably at his best on the major public occasions, like the annual general meeting, and set a high standard for his successors to follow.

Chambers was an ideal ambassador-at-large, and made contact with people at all levels in the countries in which ICI operated. His ability to get on with people, his photographic memory and quickness of mind, and his astonishing stamina during long, crowded visits made him a 'natural' on such occasions. He was a strong advocate of Britain's entry into the Common Market and the development of its international trade. Under his chairmanship, ICI's exports doubled in value, from £96.6 million out of total sales of £558 million in 1960, to £200 million out of £816 million in 1968.

Following his retirement from ICI in 1968, he became chairman of three insurance companies: the Royal Insurance, the Liverpool, London & Globe, and the London & Lancashire, from 1968 to 1974.

He was president of the National Institute of Economic and Social Research from 1955 to 1962, president of the British Shippers' Council from 1963 to 1968 and president of the Institute of Directors from January 1964 to November 1968. He was appointed president of the Advertising Association in April 1968 and treasurer of the Open University in April 1969. He was also a member of several government committees, notably those formed to investigate the supply organisation of the Board of Customs and Excise and the disposal of government archives. In 1953 he was chairman of a Committee of Inquiry into London Transport. He was a part-time member of the National Coal Board from 1 January 1956 until 11 May 1969, and was president of the Royal Statistical Society in 1964-65. Chambers was created a KBE in June 1965.

Although his salary as chairman of ICI, about £50,000 a year, was one of the highest in British industry at the time, he lived unpretentiously; he liked to spend his evenings playing bridge or scrabble, and enjoyed gardening. He was married twice, firstly in 1926 to Dorothy Copp, and in 1955 after the termination of this marriage, to Mrs Edith Pollack. There were two daughters of this second marriage. He died on 23 December 1981, leaving an estate proved at £339,873 gross.

SIR MAURICE HODGSON *and* CHRISTINE SHAW

Writings:

'The Financial Control of Imperial Chemical Industries Limited' (Edwards seminar paper 133, 24 Feb 1953).

Report of the Committee of Enquiry into London Transport (HMSO, 1955).

Sources:

Unpublished

BCe.

PrC.

Information from Dr W J Reader.

Published

Donald C Coleman, *Courtaulds. An Economic and Social History* (3 vols, Oxford: Clarendon Press, 1969-80) 3.

Economist 25 Sept 1943, 1 Apr 1961, 12 Apr 1969.

William J Reader, *Imperial Chemical Industries. A History* (2 vols, Oxford: Oxford University Press, 1970 and 1975) 2.

Anthony T S Sampson, *Anatomy of Britain Today* (Hodder & Stoughton, 1965).

Times 29 Dec 1981, 5 Jan 1982.

WW 1981.

CHANCE, Sir James Timmins

(1814-1902)

Glass manufacturer

James Timmins Chance was born in Birmingham on 22 March 1814, the eldest son of William Chance, the prominent merchant and glass manufacturer, and his wife Phoebe née Timmins, daughter of a toy manufacturer. His father's prosperity and commitment to the cause of education combined with his own outstanding scholarly abilities to provide James with a depth and breadth of academic training highly unusual in an entrepreneur of his generation. After Totteridge School and University College, London, he went to Trinity College, Cambridge in 1833 to read mathematics. In these early years he also studied classics, divinity, modern languages, law, and science, and James's reluctance to take up a commercial career is clearly shown in his withdrawal from his father's merchant house after a brief taste of business in 1831.

By 1838 however, the lack of reliable managerial support at the glass works was putting great strain on Robert Lucas Chance, the driving force of the firm in entrepreneurial and commercial terms, and his nephew James was summoned from Cambridge to take charge of daily production problems which R L Chance could not effectively supervise. But as late as 1850 R L Chance was still demanding 'that every case of (breakage) should be instantly laid before me or J T Chance, and don't rely on that, but tell me also' {Chance (1919) 93}, which suggests a continuing junior status for James a decade at least after he was admitted a partner. His uncle seems to have been an exacting chief; in July 1845, James was admonished for lack of close attention to the manufacture and a consequent '£10,000 — lost through this negligence' {*ibid*}, and ordered back from his honeymoon. Such details suggest a bright young man not fully reconciled to the drudgery, as it seemed, of production management, and James's innovative enthusiasm during these early years lends support to such a view.

Before 1852 he took out seven patents of which three marked important innovations. The earliest, in 1838, specified the bedding of plate glass in a foundation of damp leather which held it perfectly flat for easier and better smoothing and polishing. The process produced high quality polished glass marketed by Chances as 'patent plate'. The sales of this climbed impressively from the 1840s to the 1850s, until in 1854-55 it supplied 17.6 per cent of the firm's net returns. Chances made 900,000 square feet of this glass for the Crystal Palace which housed the Great Exhibition of 1851. James also improved Chances' polishing machinery, introduced to the firm the continental advances in kiln development, and devised a process for continuous flattening and annealing of sheet, or cylinder, glass. Like his father William, James disparaged R L Chance's faith in Bessemer's (qv) attempts to produce continuous rolled plate in the 1850s (in fact the attempt failed completely). However, in 1861, with his father now dead and his uncle aged and infirm, it was clearly James who took the adventurous decision to test and then employ at the Spon Lane glass works, the Siemens regenerative gas furnace, the patents for which had only been taken out three years earlier. The motivation for this innovation almost certainly came from the growing pressure of domestic and Belgian competition in the glass trade from the mid-1840s, which halted Chances' growth and rendered unit cost-cutting essential to keep afloat.

It is tempting to see James Chance's increasing preoccupation with lighthouse work, which filled the years 1859-72, both as a compensation for the businessman who was by nature less commercial than scientific in temperament, and as part of the explanation of the glass firm's relative failure in these years. In the first place, as his biographer writes, 'heavily burdened at the time with private business, ... he yet gave up to the construction and improvement of light-house apparatus nights as well as days at the Works ...', noting elsewhere that James was 'fired by the attraction of scientific work undertaken in the service of the country ... to his own honour indeed, and that of his firm, but to the detriment of its more profitable undertakings, from which his attention was necessarily diverted' {*ibid*}. The *Dictionary of National Biography* details James's worthy endeavours on behalf of the nation's sailors in the cause of advanced dioptrics, and his wresting of home and overseas contracts for lighthouse equipment from the French. He read learned papers on dioptrics to the Institution of Civil Engineers in 1867 and 1879, worked closely with the Trinity House Commissioners, and demonstrated the superiority of British dioptric apparatus at the Paris Exhibition of 1867. Certainly he would have felt himself somewhat cushioned by the growth in the partnership's capital, which rose from £360,000 in 1853 to £420,000 in 1861; of these sums he held nearly £52,000 and £124,000 respectively.

In spite of the active involvement of R L Chance's sons, W E and Alexander Chance, in the firm's management after 1861, production methods at Spon Lane were not the most efficient, and the firm made an unfortunate investment in the purchase in May 1870 of the Nailsea Glass Works, for the sum of £14,000. By 1876 production had entirely ceased there and the works were valued at only £3,250. Moreover, in these years, the chance to develop the new Siemens' tank furnaces was rejected by Chances on grounds of quality and profits, a decision which has been regarded as a 'major error of judgement' {Barker (1977) 139}. Undoubtedly in his preoccupation with dioptrics J T Chance as head of the firm robbed it of guidance at what was arguably the crucial era in the firm's growth. The lighthouse works, to which he gave most attention, seems to have made a consistent loss between 1858 and 1882.

James Chance retired from active management in 1879, and moved with his family to Prince's Gate, London. He remained a director until 1889 when the firm became a limited company. Before and after retirement he was active in local and county affairs, and played a prominent part in the movement for the advancement of education in Smethwick, Birmingham and at national level. He gave evidence to the 1868 Select Committee on Scientific Instruction, and was a founder member of the National Education League. His endowments included the gift of West Smethwick

Park to the town of Smethwick in 1895, and of the Chance School of Engineering to Birmingham University in 1900. In addition to numerous governerships and directorships, James Chance was High Sheriff of Staffordshire in 1868, DL for Staffordshire and Worcestershire, and a borough and county magistrate. He was created a baronet in June 1900.

Chance married, in 1845, Elizabeth née Ferguson, daughter of George Ferguson of Houghton Hall, Carlisle. They had three sons and five daughters.

Sir James Chance died, aged eighty-seven, on 6 January 1902, leaving an estate of £246,654 gross.

LINDA JONES

Writings:

'On Optical Apparatus used in Lighthouses' *Minutes of Proceedings of the Institution of Civil Engineers* 26 (1867).

PP, HC 1867-68 (432) XV, SC on Scientific Instruction.

'Dioptric Apparatus in Lighthouses for the Electric Light' *Minutes of Proceedings of the Institution of Civil Engineers* 50 (1879).

British Patents: 1838 (7618), 1842 (9407), 1846 (11,185), 1847 (11,749), 1848 (12,067), 1851 (13,699), 1852 (14,048); all these deal with the manufacture of glass.

Sources:

Unpublished

Birmingham University Library, Sir James T Chance, private ledger, 1838-75.

Published

Theodore C Barker, *The Glassmakers. Pilkington: The Rise of an International Company 1826-1976* (Weidenfeld & Nicholson, 1977).

Birmingham Daily Post Jan 1902.

James F Chance, *The Lighthouse Work of Sir James Chance Bart* (Smith, Elder & Co, 1902).

—, *A History of the Firm of Chance Bros & Co* (pp, 1919).

W H S Chance, 'A Family Business — the Early Years' *Proceedings of the Worcester Archaeological Society* 7 (1973).

DNB.

Raymond McGrath and Albert C Frost, *Glass in Architecture and Decoration* (Architectural Press, 1961).

Times Jan 1902.

WWW.

CHANCELLOR Sir Christopher John Howard

(1904-)

News agency manager, publisher, and paper manufacturer

Sir Christopher Chancellor (from Graham Storey, Reuters Century 1851–1951, *Max Parrish, 1951).*

Christopher John Howard Chancellor was born at Cobham, Surrey, on 29 March 1904, the eldest of the three children of John Robert Chancellor and Elizabeth Mary née Thompson. At the time of Christopher's birth, John Chancellor was a captain in the Royal Engineers; his distinguished later career included secondment to the Colonial Office, 1911-31, as Governor and Commander-in-Chief of four important colonies, including Southern Rhodesia and Palestine.

Christopher Chancellor was educated at Eton and Trinity College, Cambridge, where he took a first in history. Although his family background and education at the heart of the establishment seemed to point to a career in government service, he began work in a business firm. However, he did not really enjoy it, and in 1930 he joined Reuters news agency in the Editorial Department.

At his interview he had impressed the chairman, Sir Roderick Jones (1877-1962), with his energy and intelligence, and his 'executive outlook' {Jones (1951) 385}, and Jones kept an eye on him as a likely candidate for rapid promotion. After Chancellor had been eighteen months on the London staff, he was sent to Shanghai as general manager for the Far East. It was a challenging assignment, for Chancellor had to maintain and extend the firm's excellent network of contacts, through the hazards and difficulties of the war between Japan and China which began with the Japanese invasion of Manchuria in the autumn of 1931. The Sino-Japanese war meant a considerable increase in demand for news from the Far East, but Chancellor and his staff, in the face of competition from government-subsidised Russian, German and French agencies won credit for their efficient and impartial news service. Chancellor succeeded in keeping on friendly terms with leading figures in both China and Japan, including the head of the Japanese news agency, although the Japanese Government was convinced he was a British spy, and watched his movements closely.

In 1939 Jones recalled Chancellor to London, where at Jones's invitation he attended three meetings of the Reuters board. At the third, Jones announced that he had appointed Chancellor as the third general manager of the company, to be resident in London. The directors accepted the fait accompli, although they protested to Jones about his failure to consult them. Jones's partiality for Chancellor might have been more of a hindrance than a help to Chancellor's career. Not only were Jones's autocratic ways arousing ill-feeling, but there was also increasing unease within Reuters, and in the Press Association (who held practically all Reuters' shares except for a few held by Jones himself), about the degree to which Jones was able or willing to resist pressure from the Ministry of Information for control over the Agency's output. But Chancellor's own abilities were so evident that even after Jones's resignation from Reuters in

February 1941, followed by a new agreement in October 1941 by which the Newspaper Proprietors' Association became equal partners with the Press Association in the ownership of Reuters, his career progressed much as Jones had hoped. One of the three general managers retired just after the new ownership structure had been established, and a second retired in 1944. They were not replaced, and Chancellor was left as the sole general manager of Reuters, in effective charge of all the agency's operations.

At the beginning of 1942, Chancellor had been given responsibility for all Reuters' editorial services. He appointed Walton Cole, night editor of the Press Association as joint editor of Reuters, and together they reorganised the whole of Reuters' editorial system. They revitalised Reuters by bringing in new men recruited from provincial newspapers in Britain, and replacing local dignitaries by trained reporters as their correspondents abroad. Administrative costs in London were cut to the bone to release all available funds for strengthening the reporting staff, especially the war correspondents. By 1943 the British press was commenting on the transformation of Reuters, on the new spirit of enterprise and confidence.

Continuing pressure from the Government to suppress news unfavourable to the national cause was resisted. Following a meeting between the Foreign Secretary, Anthony Eden, and Chancellor in June 1943, a memorandum was sent to all British embassies, emphasising Reuters' independence and insisting on a sympathetic understanding of the position of the agency's correspondents abroad. Under Jones, the independence and impartiality of Reuters had been compromised in the eyes of the press in many countries; it had come to be seen by some as the mouthpiece of the British Government. Chancellor attached great importance to reburnishing Reuters' tarnished reputation, emphasising the agency's independence in speeches, in personal meetings with representatives of the press of other countries, and in the wording of agreements with national agencies in Europe and the English-speaking world. In 1946 the Australian Associated Press and the New Zealand Press Agency (like the Press Association, co-operative news agencies owned by the press) took shares in Reuters. Chancellor considered that bringing the news agencies of Australia and New Zealand into Reuters was the most important achievement of his career. They were joined in 1948 by the newly-formed Press Trust of India although this agreement ended four years later.

According to the articles drawn up in 1941, Reuters was to be regarded by the PA and NPA as a trust, rather than an investment. But if Chancellor did not have to produce profits to content shareholders, the agency had to pay its way. Inflation and increased transmission costs, as well as the expansion of services, increased Reuters' expenditure from £478,000 in 1937 to about £1.4 million in 1948. Reuters had always offered commercial and financial news, but these services had been rather eclipsed by the main news services. Chancellor began to build up the economic news service, beginning with the purchase in 1944 of Comtelburo, a private company founded in 1869, which had had for many years a virtual monopoly in reporting commercial prices between England and South America. Reuters' commercial services were renamed Comtelburo, and they came to be of increasing importance in financing the general news service. Chancellor also diversified the main news services by establishing two joint subsidiaries with the Press Association, PA-Reuter Photos and PA-Reuter Features.

After fifteen strenuous years as chief executive, a post which entailed continuous travelling around the world, Chancellor was ready to leave Reuters, though he served as a trustee, 1960-65. He received an invitation in June 1959 to join the board of Odhams Press as deputy chairman, and succeeded as chairman of Odhams in 1960. Odhams Press, together with two recently acquired subsidiaries, the Hulton Press and George Newnes, was the largest magazine-publishing house in the world. It also published the *Daily Herald*, a persistent commercial problem which had made a profit in only six of the thirty years it had been published by Odhams, and the highly successful Sunday newspaper, *The People*. As chairman, Chancellor's main effort was to try to revive the *Daily Herald*. While he believed it should be an important organ of opinion, he wanted to loosen its bonds to the TUC which held 49 per cent of the shares, and determined the policy of the paper. Chancellor believed the paper could be made successful, and was prepared to invest about £7 million over six years, but he wanted to end the TUC's control over policy, and warned them that, if the paper continued to make losses, Odhams must reserve the right to give one year's notice to discontinue publication. After prolonged negotiations he succeeded in convincing the TUC of the need for change.

Chancellor's efforts to revive the *Herald* soon began to bear fruit, but barely six months after he became chairman, he found himself plunged into one of the most controversial take-over battles of the 1960s. Cecil King (qv), chairman of the Daily Mirror Group and a friend of Chancellor (he had been a director of Reuters for many years), suggested to Chancellor that their two companies should come to some arrangement to rationalise the highly-lucrative but over-crowded field of women's magazines, in which Odhams' subsidiary Newnes and the Mirror Group's Fleetway magazines were far and away the market leaders. In January 1961 King developed this idea, proposing a merger of Odhams and Fleetway. Chancellor had listened to what he had interpreted as a proposal that Odhams should buy Fleetway, but neither he nor his board liked the idea of a merger with the Daily Mirror Group. Thinking Odhams was in danger of a take-over bid, they turned to Roy Thomson (qv). (Just before taking over the chair of Odhams, Chancellor had suggested to Thomson that he should buy Odhams newspapers, but when Thomson elaborated a scheme for a merger between Odhams and Thomson Newspapers, it had been rejected out of hand.) The Mirror Group responded to the announcement of the planned merger between Odhams and Thomsons by making a bid for Odhams. The enormous concentration of magazine ownership in the Mirror Group that could result from a successful bid, and the fears of Labour politicians for the future of the *Daily Herald*, brought demands for government intervention and for a public enquiry into the proposals, but the Prime Minister, Macmillan, refused to intervene. Although the Odhams board had advised against acceptance of the first Mirror offer to their shareholders, a higher offer published on 17 February was too attractive financially for the shareholders to continue to oppose the Mirror bid. Thomson withdrew, and by 22 March over 90 per cent of Odhams' shareholders had accepted King's final offer. In June

Chancellor resigned from his brief chairmanship of Odhams and its subsidiaries. He did not like the merger, because he thought it was bad for advertisers, journalists and the public that so many magazines should be in one company, and told the Royal Commission on the Press held soon after this episode, that he favoured the introduction of anti-trust legislation.

After his resignation from Odhams, Chancellor became chairman of Madame Tussaud's Waxworks and a director of several other companies, including the *Observer*. Even before his resignation, in May 1961, he had been approached by Sir Eric Bowater (qv). Odhams was one of the most important British customers for Bowaters' newsprint, and earlier that year Sir Eric, fearful lest Odhams' contracts should be transferred by King to the paper firm of Albert E Reed, in which Daily Mirror Newspapers had a large holding, had contemplated joining Thomson in the takeover of Odhams. In November 1961, after some hesitation because of his age, Chancellor accepted an invitation to join the board of Bowater Paper Corporation, as a full-time executive director. His extensive contacts with newspaper proprietors and publishers in Britain and overseas, acquired during his years at Reuters, were considered to be a great asset at a time when Bowaters were having difficulties selling their newsprint in the UK against strong competition from Canada and Scandinavia. From the first he was thought of as a possible successor to Sir Eric, who had long dominated the company. Coming from the outside onto a board largely composed of men who had worked their way up through the business, Chancellor could bring a fresh approach to the problems created by Sir Eric's over-enthusiastic expansion of Bowaters' capacity, particularly in the UK, and was less under the spell of Sir Eric's powerful personality. When Sir Eric died in August 1962, Chancellor was elected chairman and chief executive.

Chancellor set about the unpleasant but essential task of streamlining and reorganising the administration and structure of Bowaters, and cutting the inflated overheads, particularly those for advertising and public relations. The UK organisation was decentralised, the headquarters staff halved, and the principles governing trading between the different companies of the organisation revised. It was essential to reduce Bowaters' dependence on newsprint by developing the manufacture of other paper products, but the British and world markets for the obvious alternative product, packaging, were becoming as over-crowded as those for newsprint. Attempts to establish packaging plants in Italy and France foundered. However, demand for paper tissues was rising by 10 per cent a year, and Bowater-Scott, the most successful of Bowaters' joint enterprises, founded in 1956, paid its first dividend in 1963. In 1966 plans for a new mill were announced; it was opened in 1968 at Barrow-in-Furness. Chancellor's efforts to pull Bowaters through a difficult period of adjustment in unfavourable trading conditions were greatly assisted by the consistent profits of Bowaters' North American business. Its success probably encouraged the major programme of expansion in British Columbia launched in 1965, to safeguard future supplies of raw materials. This joint venture with a leading Canadian packaging firm, Bathurst Paper of Montreal, was named Bulkley Valley Forest Industry. Plans to build a large pulp and paper mill were abandoned when it became clear there was no immediate need for it, but a sawmill was begun in 1969. Chancellor had retired before it became clear that production costs at the mill were far greater than had been anticipated. In 1971, the ambitious programme ended with the sale of Bulkley Valley Forest Industry to Northwood Pulp Ltd; Bowaters' share of the losses was at least £7.5 million.

However, in 1969, the year of Chancellor's retirement, Bowater's profits before tax of £19.2 million were greater than ever before, and though the company's prosperity was not yet assured, Chancellor had done much to help it survive the difficult transition from Sir Eric's personal autocracy.

Chancellor served as chairman of the Appeal and Publicity Committee for the King George VI National Memorial Fund, 1952-54, and as deputy chairman of its executive committee in 1955-56. He was also deputy chairman of St Paul's Cathedral Trust, 1954-62, vice-president of the National Council of Social Service, 1959-71, chairman of the Pilgrims Society, 1962-69, and deputy chairman of the Council of Bath University. He was awarded the CMG in 1948, knighted in 1951, and received honours from several foreign governments, including the Légion d'Honneur.

In 1926 he married Sylvia, daughter of Sir Richard Paget, Bt, and Lady Muriel Finch-Hatton, daughter of the Twelfth Earl of Winchelsea and Nottingham. They had two sons and two daughters.

CHRISTINE SHAW

Writings:

PP, HC, RC on Press (1947-48) Cmnd 7379.

PP, HC, RC on Press (1961-62) Cmnd 1812.

Sources:

Unpublished

BCe.

Information from Sir Christopher Chancellor.

Joseph Oliver Boyd-Barrett, 'The World-Wide News Agencies: Development, Organisation, Competition, Markets, and Products' (Open University PhD, 1976).

Published

Oliver Boyd-Barrett, 'Market Control and Wholesale News: The Case of Reuters', in George Boyce, James Curran and Pauline Wingate (eds), *Newspaper History from the Seventeenth Century to the Present Day* (Constable, 1978).

Hugh Cudlipp, *At Your Peril* (Weidenfeld & Nicolson, 1962).

Sir Roderick Jones, *A Life in Reuters* (Hodder & Stoughton, 1951).

Cecil H King, *Strictly Personal* (Weidenfeld & Nicolson, 1969).

William J Reader, *Bowater. A History* (Cambridge: Cambridge University Press, 1981).

Anthony T S Sampson, *Anatomy of Britain Today* (Hodder & Stoughton, 1965).

George Scott, *Reporter Anonymous, the Story of the Press Association* (Hutchinson, 1968)

Graham Storey, *Reuters' Century, 1851-1951* (Max Parrish, 1951).

Lord Thomson of Fleet, *After I was Sixty: A Chapter of Autobiography* (Hamish Hamilton, 1975).

WW 1982.

CHANDOS, 1st Viscount
see LYTTELTON, Oliver

CHARLESWORTH, John Charlesworth Dodgson

(1815-1880)

Colliery owner

John Charlesworth Dodgson Charlesworth was born at Chapelthorpe Hall near Wakefield, Yorkshire in 1815, the son of John Dodgson Charlesworth (1777-1850). His grandfather Joseph Charlesworth (ca 1749-1822) founded a colliery business which was expanded by his sons, John Dodgson and Joseph (1784-1845).

   J C D Charlesworth was a forceful character who became intimately involved in local social and political life in a way in which no other family member ever seems to have done. He was the first of the family to be educated at a major public school, Sedbergh, and from thence he went up, again as the first of the family to receive a university education, to St John's College, Cambridge, where in 1837 he took a BA. In 1850, on his father's death, he succeeded to the estate and to a half-share in the colliery business, although he had for some time been managing the business on his father's behalf.

In J C D Charlesworth's early youth his father and uncle were rapidly developing their colliery empire in various parts of both West and South Yorkshire — at Netherton, Flockton, Robin Hood, East Moor (near Wakefield) and East Ardsley in the former area; and at Billingley, Silkstone, Dodworth, Warren Vale and Darton in the latter, as well as running the large and old-established Rothwell Haigh colliery near Leeds from 1820 and the Wakefield Outwood colliery from 1845.

Comparatively little is known of the relationship between the partners in the firm of J & J Charlesworth and their officials and workmen prior to incorporation in 1888, although what little information there is suggests that the active partners regularly frequented the collieries and had contact with the labour force. Not everything ran smoothly: there were colliers' convictions for combination in 1844, some trouble in 1853 and again in 1857 when Charlesworth suggested employing 'a delegate' to speak at the union meetings to counteract the effect of the miners' own leaders. Yet in 1880 its 'singular freedom from strikes' was noted by a local newspaper — and in 1874 the safety record at Charlesworth's Rothwell collieries was reported as excellent. In 1879 the firm was operating collieries near Rotherham, and between Leeds and Wakefield, and in 1892 the firm was described as 'one of the largest vendors of coal in England' {*Colliery Guardian* 63 (1892) 15}. No production figures appear to be available, unfortunately.

In 1850 Charlesworth became a West Riding magistrate and ultimately was very active as a visiting justice of the West Riding House of Correction, of the Pauper Lunatic Asylum and of private asylums; he was a member of the Police Committee and chairman of the Assessment Committee, as well as being frequently chairman of the Wakefield Bench. Additionally, Charlesworth was a governor of the Wakefield Charities and Grammar School, and as their Spokesman (annual chairman) he was active in promoting the establishment of a weekly, as against the earlier fortnightly, cattle market on their estate in Wakefield Ings, in 1849. In 1853 he was appointed a DL; he was also honorary colonel of the Wakefield Volunteers and from 1873 honorary colonel of the 3rd Administrative Battalion of the West Riding Volunteers. His interests extended to sport, and he held offices varying from the presidency of the Wakefield Cricket Club to the chairmanship of the Hunt Committee of the local Badsworth Hunt; he purchased the Grinton Lodge estate in Swaledale, in the North Riding, and was the first of the family to have a 'country place'.

Charlesworth was an Anglican and a Tory. He was also a freemason, a Past Master of the Wakefield Lodge no 495 (in 1860) and a member of the Lodge of Unanimity no 154, for which he had been proposed in 1844 and 1857, but which he only joined in about 1863 as a joining member from Friendly Lodge, Barnsley. When in 1876, as president of the Clayton Hospital, Wakefield, he laid the foundation stone of a new (still existing) hospital in that town, it was laid with masonic honours. It was, however, more with local politics that he was associated in the public mind. He was elected Conservative MP for the Borough of Wakefield at the general election in March 1857, unopposed, on the retirement of the Liberal candidate. Two years later he was defeated by the Liberal, W H Leatham, a banker at Wakefield and Pontefract, but corruption had been so extensive on both sides, that a Tory petition, which was followed by a Parliamentary Corrupt Practices Inquiry, resulted in the disfranchisement of the borough for some years as a penalty.

The investments he held in 1880 reflected Charlesworth's prosperity and included shares in the Midland, Great Northern, Lancashire & Yorkshire, North Eastern, Great Western, Great Indian Peninsular and Dutch Rhenish railway companies, the Yorkshire Conservative Newspaper Co, John Brown & Co (Sheffield steel and South Yorkshire coal), Aire & Calder Navigation, York United Gas Co, Wakefield Gas Light Co, Wakefield Public Baths Association, York Club Chambers Co Ltd, Wakefield Exchange Buildings Co, Hurlingham Club, Ebbw Vale Steel Co, London & St Catherine's Docks Co, Bolckow, Vaughan & Co Ltd (North East steel) and the National Reversionary Investment Co; it also included Italian Government bonds. In addition Charlesworth owned 3,469 acres (with a gross annual value of £9,126 in 1879) in Yorkshire, Worcestershire and Shropshire and held a shareholding in the experimental West Riding Steam Ploughing, Cultivating & Thrashing Co.

Charlesworth in 1847 married Sarah, the second daughter of Walter Featherstonhaugh of Chester-le-Street, County Durham; they had at least one son and three daughters. His wife's sister became the second wife of the Fourth Lord Hawke. J C D Charlesworth died on 21 March 1880, leaving under £200,000 gross.

JOHN GOODCHILD

Sources:

Unpublished

City of Wakefield Metropolitan District Archives, indexes and Goodchild Loan MSS.

PrC.

Published

Bateman.

Burke's Landed Gentry 1906.

Colliery Guardian 63 (1892).

John Goodchild, *Coal Kings of Yorkshire* (Wakefield: Wakefield Historical Publications, 1978).

PP, Reports of Inspectors of Mines (1880) C 2604.

WWMP.

CHILDE, Rowland

(1826-1886)

Consultant mining engineer

Rowland Childe was born at Flockton, near Wakefield, in 1826, the eldest son of Joseph Childe, engineer to the Flockton Collieries. He was articled to Henry Holt of Wakefield, at that time one of the foremost engineers in the West Riding, and during the railway mania of the 1840s worked with him on projecting (or opposing) numbers of lines throughout the country and subsequently in laying out and sinking several collieries in Yorkshire.

After Holt's death, Childe bought out the junior partner in the firm for £750 in 1871 and expanded the business. He worked from his office in Wakefield for many of the great landowners of the West Yorkshire coalfield (for some on a retainer basis), and undertook surveying work for lawyers in Wakefield, Leeds, Barnsley and Dewsbury and for a wide range of colliery owners, large and small, as well as for the North Eastern Railway Co. His professional profits, recorded in a personal ledger, rose from £223 in 1870-71 to £1,419 in 1875, £2,002 in 1880 and £2,168 in 1885. By 1878 he employed four or five clerks and assistants and in 1882 Childe's nephew and adopted son, Henry Slade Childe (d 1925), himself to become a major figure in the British world of mining engineering, became an employee and subsequently a partner.

By 1886 Childe had a wide portfolio of modest investments, the largest of which were £2,510 in Henry Briggs, Son & Co, Ltd (colliery owners), £1,265 in the Lancashire & Yorkshire Railway and £1,760 in (Briggs') North of England Industrial Iron & Coal Co. He invested less in local shares, in various steamship companies, in land (only £361) and in small loans at interest.

Childe became a member of the North of England Institute of Mining Engineers and later of the Midland Institute too. In December 1883 he was elected a member of the Institution of Civil Engineers. He was an Anglican and a Tory, a prominent freemason, and lived latterly at Calder Grove, just outside Wakefield.

In 1852 he married Rosa Wigney, daughter of William Wigney, gentleman, of Huddersfield; they had no children and Childe was succeeded by his adopted son, H S Childe. Rowland Childe died on 30 July 1886 leaving £15,896 gross.

JOHN GOODCHILD

Sources:

Unpublished

City of Wakefield Metropolitan District Archives, Goodchild Loan MSS, index cards and notes.

MCe.

PrC.

Published

Proceedings of the Institution of Civil Engineers 87 (1886).

CHIVERS, John

(1857-1929)

Jam manufacturer

John Chivers was born in Histon, Cambridgeshire on 27 June 1857, into a family of farmers who specialised in fruit growing. He was the third son of Stephen Chivers (1824-1907), who had founded the family business of Chivers & Sons, and Rebecca née Frohock from Waterbeach, Cambridgeshire.

After the arrival of the railway at Histon in 1847, the Chivers sought wider markets for their fruit. One was reached through a distribution centre and depot in Bradford, Yorkshire, set up in 1871 and managed by John's elder brother William. John first became involved in the business on this side, helping during his school holidays; later he joined his brother at Bradford on a permanent basis. In Bradford, the Chivers brothers sold fruit over a market stall and also distributed it in quantity to local jam manufacturers. Inspired by the example of these Yorkshire jam makers, the Chivers family started their own jam manufacturing business in Histon and neighbouring Impington. The first boil of Chivers' jam took place in a disused barn on an Impington farm in 1873, and William returned to assist with the new venture, leaving John in Bradford. The business proved so successful that within two years John joined the rest of the family in Histon permanently. The business was run by William (as managing director) and John jointly, until William's premature death in 1902 when John took over full responsibility for the factory.

In his time as managing director, the number of employees rose from 1,000 in 1902 to 3,000 in 1929, while the output of jams and jellies alone rose from just under 2,800 tons in 1906 to 4,600 tons in 1929. This expansion owed much to John Chivers's style of management. His support for research and development was a key contributory factor because R & D improved the quality of the firm's existing products, and introduced new ones. Thus around 1900 the firm was diversifying into the manufacture of jellies, custard powders and, most notably, canned fruit. By 1925, the firm's expansion led to the opening of a new Chivers factory in Montrose in Scotland to deal almost exclusively with the canning of raspberries.

Another key aspect of John Chivers's successful management was his approach to industrial relations. Adopting a stance of domineering benevolence, a managerial style reminiscent of nineteenth century paternalists, he succeeded in achieving harmonious industrial relations. From his workers he expected loyalty and commitment to the firm's goals, and he successfully avoided significant trade union activity in his works. In return, he provided such welfare provisions as a factory nurse, a surgery, a subsidised workers' canteen and model villas for some of his employees. A profit-sharing scheme for male employees, established in 1891, was carried on as a 'co-partnership' scheme, so that by 1923 over 600 workers had acquired share capital to a total value of £40,000. Moreover, his paternalistic tendencies did not lead him to resist new forms of consultative management once his workforce reached a size where continual personal contact was no longer possible. Thus, in 1918 he authorised his welfare officer to set up a workers' committee which would serve as a formalised mediating body between management and the workforce.

John Chivers also took a keen interest in the affairs and conditions of the local community as a whole. In 1903 he financed the first Histon Social Institute and donated a field for the local football and cricket clubs. In 1909 he purchased premises for evening classes for his employees and local people, and in 1920 he was instrumental in setting up the Histon & District Co-operative Homes Society.

His private interests mainly involved religion and politics. Throughout his life he was a supporter and benefactor of the Histon Baptist Church, founded by his father in 1858. He was honoured with the office of life deacon, like his father before him, in 1928. As a young man, John was organist and choirmaster and Sunday School superintendent. He served as treasurer of the Cambridgeshire Baptist Association and he was a member of the Cambridgeshire Band of Hope Union. He also served on the Council of the Baptist Union in London for a number of years.

As a lifelong Liberal, John Chivers was president of the Histon and Impington Liberal Association for twenty years, and president of the County Liberal Association for a term. John Chivers's essentially quiet and modest nature probably prevented him from ever embarking on a parliamentary career himself. He was also a JP.

John Chivers married Emily Ann, daughter of Ephraim Barker Batterson, a farmer, in 1891; they had four children. After a prolonged illness, he died in Histon on 15 March 1929 leaving £54,540 gross.

ZUZANA BURIANOVA

Sources:

Unpublished

BCe.

MCe.

PrC.

Cadbury-Schweppes archives, Dollis Hill, London: Chivers company papers. Information from Stanley Chivers.

Published

William H Beable, *Romance of Great Businesses* (2 vols, Heath Cranton, 1926) 2.

H Rider Haggard, *Rural England* (2 vols, Longmans & Greene & Co, 1902) 2.

Walter McLennan Citrine, Lord Citrine (courtesy of The Electricity Council).

CITRINE, Walter McLennan

Lord Citrine

(1887-1983)

Nationalised electricity industry chairman

Walter McLennan Citrine was born in Liverpool on 22 August 1887, one of a family of six children. His father, Alfred Citrine, a seafarer, worked variously as a master rigger, pilot and salvage worker, and was at times a heavy drinker and careless with money; his mother Isabella née McLennan, was a gentle and caring woman in the more respectable working class mould. Although her churchgoing was not regular, her Presbyterian teetotal background influenced the young man, and he forswore alcohol (taking up 'social' drinking only when he was thirty-eight). Initially a weakly infant, he had a conventional elementary schooling, enjoying history and literature, and also attended the Oakdale Presbyterian Mission. At twelve and a half and now rather more robust, he left school, briefly worked in a local flour mill and then gained an apprenticeship with a firm of electrical contractors, on the relatively generous terms (usually a premium had to be paid) of no wages for the first six months, followed by 2s 6d a week. It was not a likely start in life for someone who was to rise to control the largest capital spender in the British economy.

The key to his rise to business power was his intellectual energy and painstaking application to any problem: his vehicle for success was the trade union movement. In 1911 he joined the Liverpool branch of the Electrical Trades Union, read widely, studied avidly and taught himself Gregg shorthand with his fiancée's help, and thus began his rise to power in the Labour movement, first in the ETU (of which he became the first full-time district secretary in 1914 and assistant general secretary in Manchester in 1920) and then in the Trades Union Congress headquarters. Moving to the TUC in London in 1924 as assistant secretary, he became general secretary in 1926 and consolidated his position as the administrator par excellence of the trade union movement in the years of reconstruction following the disastrous General Strike of that year. In the international field he became president of the International Federation of Trade Unions in 1928, a post he held for ten years; president of the World Anti-Nazi Council; and later president of the World Federation of Trade Unions. His services were recognised by a knighthood in 1935, and by an increasing influence in the inner councils of the Labour movement. He served on several government inquiries and in wartime his role as a Labour representative on government committees increased, with the need of Government to incorporate Labour into the decision-making process. He became a member of the Privy Council in 1940. His powerful contribution as a chairman and committeeman and his overwhelming skill in debate became well known in political circles.

In this part of his career, however, his experience of business, apart from his service between 1922 and 1946 as a director of Labour's newspaper the *Daily Herald*, had all been indirect. He had, however, come to admire some of the more liberal-minded industrial statesmen with whom he had to deal, like Mond (qv) of ICI and Hirst (qv) of GEC. With Labour's first overall majority in Parliament, achieved in 1945, moreover, he felt the time had come for the movement to show that socialist enterprises could be created which could build on and improve the solid achievements which (he was sufficient of a realist to recognise) had been possible under capitalism. He therefore welcomed the extensive nationalisation programme of Attlee's Government (and had indeed been involved in much earlier committee work preparing for it). When in November 1945 he was invited to become a member of the newly created National Coal Board, with responsibilty for recruitment, education, training and safety and the general welfare of miners, he was strongly tempted to take up this new career which capitalised on his previous commitment to labour interests. He was careful to get the permission of the TUC to take up this full-time job, and also obtained a guarantee that they would take him back to a job of equivalent status if the NCB position was terminated (an unusual option which he claimed greatly strengthened his power with future Governments). A peerage followed in 1946.

Shortly afterwards, however, word reached ministers that Citrine was restive in a subordinate position to Hyndley (qv) at the NCB, and Attlee asked him to move to wider responsibilities in the nationalised electricity industry, this time as chairman-designate of the newly created British Electricity Authority at a salary of £7,000 pa. The responsibilities of this new job in the (subsequently unequalled) period of ten years in which he held it were daunting: it involved the development of the most rapidly growing industry in England and Wales and (until 1955 when a separate Scottish organisation was set up) in the South of Scotland. Given the failure to invest adequately in wartime and the industry's ageing capital stock, there was a substantial backlog of capital works in power stations and distribution systems to make up. Moreover, this rapid capital expansion programme had to be accomplished in the context of amalgamating nearly 600 formerly independent municipal and company undertakings into twelve new area boards for distribution and a central authority for generation, transmission and general policy development. Inevitably there were strains in this reorganisation (no such merger has ever occurred without them and many mergers of less than that size, indeed, have simply collapsed), but Citrine successfully built on the existing esprit de corps of the industry. Helped by Self (qv), Hacking (qv) and Eccles (qv) as his deputy chairmen, he overcame many of the problems and created a powerful centralised organisation.

Labour relations were his particular interest, and he insisted from the start on a positive commitment to collective bargaining with the recognised unions, strongly discouraging the unofficial movements, but backing up the official unions with managerial authority. The system of joint consultation which he imposed has been singled out as one of the most successful initiatives in bridging the gap between management and workers in this period in Britain. Unfortunately, the unions used their increasingly entrenched power to intensify restrictive practices, and the productivity record of the industry in this period was very poor. Criticisms were also made about other policies being followed by the industry: notably that it was failing to adopt the most advanced technology of generation and that its pricing policy failed to reflect the underlying costs of supply, particularly for domestic consumers. Citrine was able to support those, like Eccles and Stanley Brown (qv), who changed the former, but his own prejudices in favour of cheap electricity and low profits delayed the emergence of rational electricity pricing policies until he was succeeded by Ronald Edwards (qv).

Although Citrine's contract was renewed by the Conservative Governments of the 1950s, they were increasingly uneasy at the policies being pursued by Citrine and his colleagues, and by 1954-57 his power was increasingly weakened by political sniping from the sidelines. He strongly resisted government intervention where he could, and he was successful in this, particularly in labour relations, but from 1955 he had to give way on several issues, notably by pressing his colleagues to accept a (sensible) shift from coal to oil and a (somewhat less defensible) overcommitment to an unwisely large nuclear power programme in 1957, against the advice of engineers like Eccles. He retired at the age of seventy, when the Conservatives reorganised the industry at the end of 1957. Between nationalisation in 1948 and the reorganisation of 1957 the electricity supply industry which he controlled accounted for around 7 per cent of UK domestic capital formation, making him the biggest businessman in Britain's history in terms of corporate spending power; over the same period employment rose from 151,000 to 199,000.

He married Doris Slade, after a five year courtship, in 1913; they had two sons: the elder becoming a solicitor and the younger a doctor. His retirement in 1958 was initially only partial, as he served as a part-time member of both the Electricity Council and the Atomic Energy Authority and participated in the proceedings of the House of Lords. Following his wife's death in 1973, he was less active, living at Brixham in Devon until his death on 22 January 1983.

LESLIE HANNAH

CITRINE Walter McLennan

Writings:

The Labour Chairman and Speaker's Companion Guide to the Conduct of Trade Union and Labour Meetings, etc (Labour Publishing Co, 1921).

Die Gewerkschaftsbewegung Grossbritanniens (Amsterdam: Internationale Gewerkschafts-bibliotek, 1926).

Labour and the Community (Ernest Benn, 1928).

'The Martyrs of Tolpuddle' in *The Book of the Martyrs of Tolpuddle 1834-1934* (TUC General Council, 1934).

Ein Jahr Schuschnigg. Dokumente einer Diktatur (Brussels: Maison d'Edition L'Eglantine, 1935).

I Search for Truth in Russia (G Routledge & Sons, 1936).

Under the Heel of Hitler. The Dictatorship over Sport in Nazi Germany (TUC General Council, 1936).

A la Recherche de la Verité en Russie (Paris, 1937).

A B C of Chairmanship. All about Meetings and Conferences (Many editions, and translations to date; 1st: Co-operative Printing Society, 1939).

The T.U.C. in War-Time. An Informal Record of Three Months Progress (Dec 1939-April 1945).

Citrine and Others v Pountney. Full summary with extracts from verbatim evidence etc (The Daily Worker libel case) (Modern Books, 1940).

My Finnish Diary (Harmondsworth, Penguin Books, 1940).

My American Diary (G Routledge & Sons, 1941).

British Trade Unions (William Collins, 1942).

'Presidential Address' *Proceedings of the British Electrical Power Convention* 1949.

Men and Work, An Autobiography (Hutchinson, 1964).

Two Careers, An Autobiography (Hutchinson, 1967).

Ceremony of Unveiling Memorial to James Ramsay Macdonald, 1886-1937, at Westminster Abbey, March 12 1968 (1968).

A full collection of Citrine's writings on the electricity industry and related business matters is available in the Electricity Council Intelligence Section files.

Sources:

Unpublished

BCe.

Interviews with Lord Citrine and his business colleagues.

Published

Leslie Hannah, *Engineers, Managers and Politicians. The First Fifteen Years of Nationalised Electricity Supply in Britain* (Macmillan, 1982).

Times 26 Jan 1983.

WW 1982.

(which favourably compared to the Gramophone Co's turnover in 1929-30 of £2.989 million). In April 1941 Clark stepped down as managing director and was replaced by Sir Robert McLean (qv). Clark continued as chairman. After McLean retired in March 1944, Clark and Sir Alexander Aikman became joint managing directors. Clark retired as chairman and managing director on 19 March 1945, but remained on the board. He was apppointed the first president of EMI in April 1946, but five months later, as a result of a fierce quarrel with the board, in which he defended American interests, he resigned as president and as director. Clark remained bitter against the company for the rest of his life.

Within the firm Clark was responsible for setting up a structure of committees which proved unwieldy. As a boss Clark was not generally popular. In his latter years he was not particularly innovative. Within the industry Clark served as the first president of the Radio Industry Council.

He was twice married: his first wife was Florence Beecher née Crouse (later divorced); his second wife was the journalist and author Gertrude Ivy Sanders, daughter of Haydon Sanders 'of independent means' {MCe}, whom he married in 1921. Clark became a British subject in 1928.

Alfred Clark died on 16 June 1950 at the age of seventy-six, leaving £73,758 gross.

RAYMOND R WILE and DAVID J JEREMY

Sources:

Unpublished

Edison National Historic Site, West Orange, New Jersey, various files of correspondence and legal papers.

EMI Music Archives, Hayes, Middlesex, company archives, company reports and accounts.

University of Wyoming, Laramie, Wyoming, manuscript collections, Eldridge R Johnson papers.

US Gramophone, Annual Report, 1898.

MCe.

PrC.

Information from Leonard Petts.

Alfred Clark, 'His Master's Voice: A Memoir' (carbon ribbon typescript of the first six chapters of this unpublished memoir, University of Wyoming).

Dale Kramer, 'Eldridge Reeves Johnson: A Biography' (typescript of unpublished biography, University of Wyoming).

Published

B L Aldridge, *The Victor Talking Machine Company* (RCA Sales Corp, 1964).

V K Chew, *Talking Machines* (HMSO, 1981).

Frederick W Gaisberg, 'Emile Berliner Picks a Winner' *Gramophone* (Dec 1943).

—, *The Music Goes Round* (New York: Macmillan, 1942), republished in London as *Music on Record* (Robert Hale, 1946).

Gramophone News (August 1903) (in the collection of Gordon Bussey).

Jerrold Northorp Moore, *A Voice in Time: The Gramophone of Fred Gaisberg 1873-1951* (Hamish Hamilton, 1976).

New York Times 11 Sept 1930, 18 June 1950.

Statist 30 Apr 1931, 10 Mar, 19 May 1934.

WWW.

CLARK, Sir Allen George

(1898-1962)

Electrical and electronic components manufacturer

Sir Allen G Clark (courtesy of Charles Barker Lyons Ltd).

Allen George Clark was born at Brookline, Massachusetts on 24 August 1898, the elder child of Byron George Clark and Helen née Peirce. Byron Clark was an executive of the United Shoe Machinery Corporation, in charge of liaison with the company's factories in Europe. In 1905 he brought his wife, son and daughter to England, where the family settled. Allen Clark was educated at Felsted from 1913 to 1915, and then served with the London Scottish Regiment before being commissioned in the Royal Flying Corps in 1918.

Allen Clark's business career began in 1920 when his father bought him a share in a small tool-making business in Ilford, Essex, the Plessey Co Ltd, which had been formed two years before. When Clark joined the company, only half a dozen people were employed. The first contract of importance Clark obtained for the firm was one from Marconi, to design and produce one of the first radio-receivers on the UK market. A new factory was built in Ilford on the proceeds of this contract. In 1925 a new private company, Plessey Co (1925) Ltd, was formed with a capital of £20,000. Clark was joint managing director with a talented mechanical engineer of German origin, W O Heyne. Although he sometimes described himself as an engineer, the ebullient Clark was well aware of his own limitations in that field, and concentrated on an activity for which he was well suited, the selling of Plessey's services to other companies. Among the products Plessey made in the 1920s were the first portable radio sets in Britain, for Marconi, and the first commercially-produced television set in the world, for Baird. By 1931 Plessey employed about 500 people on a wide range of electrical and mechanical engineering projects.

It was Clark who brought this business in. His confidence in his own ability as a salesman matched his confidence in the ability of Heyne and his team to manufacture more cheaply and efficiently any part that Clark brought to them. At the same time, Clark believed strongly that the right way for the company to keep abreast of the latest technical developments in their field was to take out licences for products developed by other firms. Many of the licences Plessey held were from American firms. Clark attributed the solid growth and steady prosperity of Plessey, even in the difficult years of the 1930s, to his policy of never manufacturing anything that had to be sold directly to the public. By adhering to this policy he avoided incurring the costs of marketing, and the commercial risks and uncertainties of selling to the public. The wide range of goods manufactured by Plessey protected the firm from fluctuations in the fortunes of individual trades. He was also careful to restrict his sales to financially-sound companies, thus avoiding the considerable risks of bad debts. In March 1937 Plessey became a public company and the issued capital was increased to £500,000.

The technical licences Clark acquired for Plessey, including some from Germany, helped the firm to make an important contribution to Britain's war effort. Fuel pumps for Spitfires, and electrical connectors that enabled electrical wiring to be built into aircraft at an early stage of the construction of the frame, thus accelerating production rates, were both the outcome of American licences. During the war Clark also developed the company's own expertise in electronic systems, particularly in radio and direction-finding equipment.

Like other engineering firms whose production during the war had been wholly geared to munitions and military equipment, Plessey needed a year or two to get back to the track of its peacetime development. From a wartime peak of nearly 11,500 workers, the number of employees dropped to under 5,250. Heyne retired, because of ill-health, in 1946. But Clark quickly re-established Plessey on the course it had been following so successfully in the 1930s. As before the war, his policy was to avoid selling direct to the public, but rather to seek out industries which required products Plessey was equipped to make, or into the manufacture of which Plessey could sensibly extend. Contracts would be negotiated, usually comparatively long-term contracts, with manufacturers in the industries concerned, and Plessey would then work to produce the appliances or components required in the most economic way. The success of this policy depended on speed, efficiency and a continuous regard for the reduction of expenses.

By the early 1950s, Plessey was growing rapidly; the workforce reached, and then surpassed wartime levels. Turnover in 1951 was over £10 million. The company was producing a greater variety and volume of products than ever before. About one-quarter of output was radio components, and the rest was largely composed of a variety of domestic and Service radio equipment, and components for aircraft. Profit before tax for 1951 was about £600,000. Greater attention was being paid to research and development within the company: Clark wanted his team to anticipate the significant developments of ten or fifteen years ahead (Plessey was involved in research into silicon technology as early as 1952). Greater attention was also being paid to sales abroad: Plessey International Ltd was formed in 1948 specifically to develop exports.

Clark, with his eye on further expansion, could not finance this growth, as he had done in the past, largely by ploughing back profits. Increased taxation (which, he lamented, tended to stifle initiative and drive) left little money for investment. Instead he began to raise capital. The nominal capital of the company was raised from £500,000 to £1.5 million in 1947, and to £2.05 million in 1954, £2.45 million in 1956, and £3.45 million in 1957. Steadily increasing production costs were offset partly by restricting profits by keeping prices down, because Clark was anxious not to price Plessey's products out of world markets. Sometimes he kept the company's finances stretched so tight, he was forced to borrow money from his own employees. By 1959, however, the increased investment in research and development, the employment of the additional capital, and the long-standing policy of widening the range of products made to avoid being unduly affected by fluctuations in any one industry, were all bearing fruit in record profits of £2.236 million in 1959, and £4.3 million in 1960. (In 1959-60 the nominal capital was £7.75 million, increased to £14.25 million in the course of 1960).

By 1960, the growth of the company and its increased geographical spread (there were now 16 manufacturing plants and three research establishments, mainly in Ilford, Havant, Northampton and Swindon) had made necessary its decentralisation into groups and divisions. There was an Aircraft and Automotive Group (Clark claimed that no British-made aircraft flying did not include some Plessey equipment); an Electronics Group, with substantial telecommunications contracts for the Services, which was beginning to expand into industrial electronics; a Components Group; Plessey Nucleonics Ltd, formed in 1956, and entirely engaged in designing and manufacturing control equipment for atomic power stations; and the Plessey Development Co, which saw to the early stages of development of products manufactured under licence from abroad.

Plessey then held about 65 licencing agreements with foreign firms, despite the increasing importance of its own research and development activities, which now accounted for over 15 per cent of the total wagebill. Since the latter part of the war Plessey had made something of a speciality of taking American designs and 'anglicising' them, that is, studying them and revising their specifications so that they could be made by Plessey in the UK from British products. Clark also began to make other types of agreements with overseas companies. In 1957 a new company, Semiconductors Ltd, was formed jointly with the Philco Corporation of Philadelphia for the manufacture of transistors and semiconductors, and in 1959 Hagan Controls Ltd was formed in association with Hagan Chemicals & Controls Inc to manufacture control devices for British industry. In July 1959 a German subsidiary was formed, Plessey Maschinen Elemente GmbH.

In 1960, Clark began to consider takeovers as a means to the further expansion of his company. Garrard Engineering & Manufacturing Co Ltd, which made components for record-players near the Plessey plant at Swindon, and had an issued capital of £1,083,460, was acquired by an exchange of shares. Much more ambitious was Clark's purchase the following year of two manufacturers of telephone equipment, Automatic Telephone & Electric (issued capital £6 million), and Ericsson Telephones (issued capital £2.6 million). Plessey already had contracts to make telephone handsets, and Clark hoped the merger would allow substantial economies in research and manufacture. The purchase of these companies doubled the size of Plessey (its nominal capital became £27.5 million), but also multiplied the problems of the board when Clark died in June 1962, before the companies had been properly assimilated.

Clark's success as a salesman had, in part, been due to his ability to win the liking of his customers; even as the company grew, he still negotiated many of the larger deals in person. He made a powerful impression: six feet tall, heavily built, supremely self-confident, highly extrovert, with a taste for Stetson hats, big cigars and monogrammed shirts that belied the fact he had been a naturalised British citizen since 1927. His relations with those who worked for him were not always so warm and friendly. He worked hard and with dedication, habitually arriving at his office before 8am (both office and works started at 8am) and keeping an eye on latecomers. He expected equal dedication from all his staff, and since he believed strongly in management keeping in close personal touch with the work-force, he was often seen on the shopfloor of his factories. One of the consequences of growth that he deplored was that he perforce began to lose touch with his company: even Clark could not keep a personal eye on a work-force which numbered 50,000 at his death. These visits must have caused some apprehension, because he was not slow to criticise those whose performance he found lacking — and even his senior executives found him intimidating. The other side of this coin was that he believed in rewarding talent. Rewards were geared to results, at every level of the company.

Clark clearly intended his elder son John to succeed him as chairman. John and his brother Michael had joined the board in 1953 and John was appointed joint managing director during his father's last illness. But the brothers were both still in their thirties, and held less than 5 per cent of Plessey's shares between them. There were three resignations from the board before they emerged in effective control of the business. Sir Harold Wernher, the chairman of Ericsson Telephones, was appointed chairman of Plessey Co, which became a holding company, John became chairman of Plessey Group Management Ltd, and Michael chairman of Plessey (UK) Ltd, which took over the operating functions of the Plessey Co.

Clark did not have a very active public life outside his company, apart from serving as a council member of the Telecommunication Engineering and Manufacturing Association from 1943, and of the Society of British Aircraft Constructors from 1960. His main recreations were sporting, particularly fishing, golf and shooting. An excellent shot, he was a member of the English clay-pigeon shooting team in 1935-39 and in 1948-50. He was knighted in 1961.

In 1925 he married Jocelyn, the daughter of Percy Culverhouse, the chief architect of the Great Western Railway. They had a daughter, as well as their two sons. They subsequently divorced, but he did not remarry. He died on 30 June 1962, leaving an estate proved at £583,086 gross.

CHRISTINE SHAW

Sources:

Unpublished

MCe.

PrC.

Published

DNB.

Economist 6 Jan 1951, 5 Jan, 13 Dec 1952, 2 Jan 1954, 8 Jan 1955, 7 Jan 1956, 5 Jan 1957, 4 Jan 1958, 3 Jan 1959, 2 Jan 1960, 7 Jan, 7 Oct 1961, 4 Aug 1962.

M J Lipman, *Memoirs of a Socialist Businessman* (Lipman Trust, 1980).

Plessey Co Ltd, *The Electronics and Equipment Group of the Plessey Company Limited* (Ilford: Plessey, 1960).

Times 2, 10, 28 July, 4 Aug 1962.

Graham Turner, *Business in Britain* (Eyre & Spottiswoode, 1969).

WWW.

CLARK, George

(1843-1901)

Marine engine manufacturer

George Clark was born in Sunderland on 14 June 1843, the son of George Clark (1815-83) and Jane née Lockie (1820-82). His father, in the second generation of an iron manufacturing family, joined with an elder brother and others to form John Clark & Co in 1840. This partnership did not last many years and was followed by a brief period when George Sr managed a small Wearside works, after which he worked for the Consett Iron Co as an engineer. In 1848 George Sr established his Sunderland general engineering business, and in February 1852 the first iron ship on the River Wear was constructed there with the help of shipbuilder John Barkes. Two years later the works produced the first marine engine built at Sunderland, and became the second marine engineering firm on the Wear, following John Dickinson & Sons who commenced this activity in 1852.

George Jr at about the age of fourteen began his engineering apprenticeship in his father's works in North Bridge Street and completed his training at the famous London engineering company of Penn of

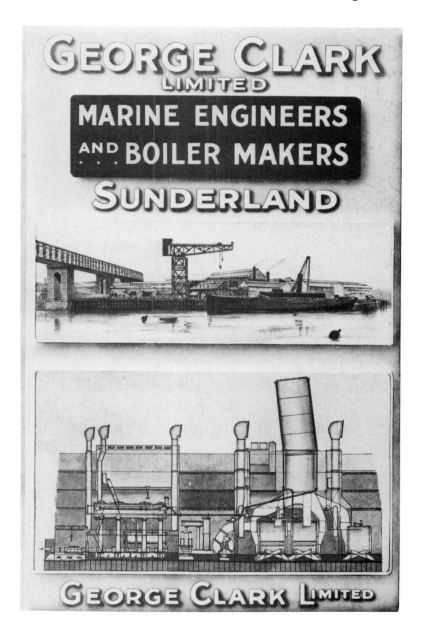

An early 20th century advertisement of George Clark Ltd (courtesy of Tyne & Wear Museum Service).

Greenwich. On his return to Sunderland in 1864 George Jr began to play a major role in the management of the works and not long afterwards took sole charge, due to the crippling effects of severe asthma on his father. Clark gained 'an enviable reputation' {*Newcastle Daily Journal* 5 Mar 1901} as a marine engineer at a time when shipbuilders on the River Wear were beginning to change from wood to iron shipbuilding. The expansion of engine building led to the acquisition of a nine acre site at Southwick,

681

with a 700 foot quay frontage, in 1872. Over the next decade Clarks became the largest engine works on the Wear, employing at least 300 workers. In 1883 the works was the starting point for a most prolonged strike over the issue of the ratio of craftsmen to apprentices. The formation of the Wearside Engine Builders Association followed and Clark was very active in this and other engineering employers' organisations, frequently representing Wearside in regional discussions. He also played an important part in local conciliation boards, where his judgements were such as to inspire 'esteem in representatives of the men' {*ibid*}. Outside the marine engineering industry Clark's business interests included a directorship of the Sunderland & South Shields Water Co. George Clark joined the Institution of Mechanical Engineers in 1867 and was also a member of the Institution of Naval Architects. He was founder member of the North East Coast Institution of Engineers and Shipbuilders and for many years one of its vice-presidents.

A Liberal, although disagreeing with Gladstone on Home Rule, Clark was involved for many years in local politics, serving on the Sunderland Town Council and representing Southwick on the Durham County Council for six years, where his principal interest was education. He was also a freemason. His health was, however, indifferent following a major surgical operation in the late 1880s.

In 1864 he married Jessie Maud, daughter of a schoolmaster, James McFarlane Chalmers; they had five sons and three daughters. The eldest son George (1868-1937) and George Clark's brother, Fred, were both active in the firm's management. George Clark died on 4 March 1901, leaving an estate valued at £105,948 gross.

J F CLARKE

Sources:

Unpublished

Joseph F Clarke, 'Labour Relations in Engineering and Shipbuilding on the North-East Coast ca 1850-1906' (Newcastle upon Tyne MA, 1967).

BCe.

PrC.

Published

Newcastle Daily Journal 5 Mar 1901.

Transactions of the North East Coast Institution of Engineers and Shipbuilders 17 (1900-1).

Proceedings of the Institution of Mechanical Engineers 1883, 1901.

J W Smith and T S Holden, *Where Ships Are Born* (Sunderland: Thomas Reed & Co, 1946).

Sunderland Echo 4 Mar 1901.

CLARK, Sir George Smith

(1861-1935)

Shipbuilder

George Smith Clark was born in Paisley, Renfrewshire, Scotland on 8 November 1861, the son of James Clark (d 1910), a partner in the firm of J & J Clark, thread manufacturers, and his first wife Jane Smith (1837-68), daughter of George Smith (1803-76), the Glasgow shipowner and founder of the City Line. Raised as a Presbyterian, George Clark was educated at Merchiston Castle School, Edinburgh and then trained in the Belfast shipyard of Harland & Wolff. Here he met Frank Workman (qv) and in 1880 he entered into a partnership with Workman who had established a small shipyard on the Lagan in 1877.

For Workman the attraction was almost certainly the injection of fresh capital, as well as the forging of a useful relationship with a prominent shipowning family (the parallels with Harland & Wolff are striking). The original site of the yard occupied only four acres on the north side of the river. In its first year 150 men were employed and two small ships launched, the *Ethel* of 400 tons and the *William Hinde* of 450 tons. It is clear that family connections were very important in the initial stages of the business's growth as the first substantial vessel the yard built, the 2,576 ton *City of Cambridge*, was constructed for Clark's uncle, George Smith, who continued to provide useful orders, particularly for larger ships.

The firm expanded steadily until 1891 when the partnership became Workman, Clark & Co Ltd. At this time Charles E Allan (d 1933) of Glasgow joined the firm. Allan was a relative of Clark and belonged to a Scottish family of shipowners, whose Allan Line had 31 vessels by 1909. This was an important step in the firm's development as it meant that, besides extending its links with shipowners, it established an engineering department with Allan as its first director; previously it had imported its engines. From this point Workman, Clark's progress was extremely rapid. By 1895 annual output had risen to 34,000 tons and the firm employed 3,500 men. By 1902 the yards covered 50 acres and the company launched more tonnage than any other shipbuilder in the world (75,800 tons), a performance it repeated in 1909 with 88,200 tons. The firm were pioneers in two areas: firstly the development of Charles Parson's (qv) turbine engine, in which Clark took a personal interest (the *Victorian*, built for the Allan Line was the first turbine-propelled ocean steamer); and secondly the construction of insulated and refrigerated fruit carriers. It established useful connections with the United Fruit Co of Boston for which it built over 40 ships. Its other major customers were Alfred Holt & Co (51 vessels), J P Corry & Co Ltd, and the Tyser Line (33), Ellerman Lines Ltd (26), and Lloyd Brasiliero (21). Thus the firm specialized not, as has recently been suggested, in passenger liners {Pollard and Robertson (1979) 84-85}, but rather in medium-sized cargo boats, or cargo and

683

passenger combined, and rarely launched a vessel over 10,000 tons. Of the 534 ships launched between 1880 and 1933, 19 were described as passenger liners {Workman, Clark (1933) 58-65}.

During the First World War, particularly after 1916, the firm concentrated on Admiralty work producing mainly smaller types of ship such as boom defence vessels, patrol boats and sloops. In 1917 Clark received a baronetcy for his services to the industry during the war. By 1920 the acreage of the yard had increased to 100 and the payroll to 10,000. Clark's part in this progress was obviously substantial. The firm remained a limited company and control lay largely with the Workman and Clark families. It is true that the business was operating against a background of growing world trade and a rising demand for new tonnage, but Workman, Clark had prospered more than most shipbuilders. The proportion of UK tonnage launched from its yards rose from 5 per cent in 1895 to 14 per cent in 1909. Given the shorter timespan in which the company had been operational, the achievements of Workman and Clark were quite comparable with those of Harland, Wolff and Pirrie (qqv).

In early 1920, then, the firm seemed set to achieve even greater expansion. Its books were full with 37 ships on order and its labour force was not only greater than ever before, but one of the most efficient in the world. (In 1918 one of its workers, Mr J Moir, hammered home in nine hours 11,209 rivets, a world record.) Within seven years, however, the firm was on the verge of bankruptcy and Sir George Clark was accused with his fellow directors of misrepresentation, fraud, conspiracy, breach of trust and breach of contract. Part of the company's difficulties stemmed from the changed economic environment: world trade was stagnating and shipbuilding capacity became far too large for the reduced demand. But the firm's problems were also a result of a financial operation in February 1920. In that month it became involved in a complex manoeuvre in which the business was taken over by the Northumberland Shipping Co, which acquired complete control of the shareholding. A new debenture loan for £3 million at 7 per cent was floated, ostensibly to develop and extend the activities of Workman, Clark. In fact the proceeds of the issue were used to repay a loan of the shipping company to Kleinwort's Bank. Clark, apparently, opposed this move and together with his son, George Ernest, resigned, though the latter was to rejoin the board between 1924 and 1927. Although Clark (albeit unwillingly) was made a very rich man by this manoeuvre, the firm was saddled with a huge burden of fixed interest debt which made it financially vulnerable. In 1927 the company was sued in the courts on the grounds that the prospectus it had issued in 1920 was misleading and fraudulent. The case was a complex and lengthy one and went, eventually, to the Northern Ireland Court of Appeal. Although the original trial judge ruled that there was no evidence against Clark and the former directors of the pre-takeover company, this was reversed on appeal. Effectively the company lost (settling out of court in what was a test case) and went into temporary liquidation. It was briefly revived in the shape of Workman, Clark (1928) Ltd under the chairmanship of William Strachan, a former director and secretary of the old company, but it could not survive the world depression which began in 1929. In 1935 it was taken over and closed by the National Shipbuilders Security Ltd; part of its facilities were acquired by Harland & Wolff.

Clark's interests were not confined to shipbuilding. Like many Ulster businessmen Clark had been drawn into politics by the issue of Home Rule for Ireland. In 1907 he became MP for North Belfast, a position which he vacated in 1910 to devote more attention to his business affairs. His commitment to Unionism, however, remained deep. In 1913 Clark became chairman of the committee set up in Ulster to smuggle guns, 'the shipyard providing excellent cover for the importation of arms' {Stewart (1967) 96}. Clark, along with Workman and Allan, donated considerable sums to the Ulster Volunteer Force. The war, of course, temporarily shelved the 'national question'. In 1919, however, it once more came to the fore, and this time involved considerable violence. Assassinations of policemen and soldiers were followed by reprisals, and in 1920 the workers of Workman, Clark led the movement to expel Roman Catholics from the shipyards and other major factories in the city. In 1925 Clark became a Unionist Senator in the Northern Ireland Parliament, a position he retained until his death.

Clark held many other business appointments. He was a director of Henry Matier & Co Ltd, linen manufacturers, a position he held by virtue of his marriage in 1881 to Frances Elizabeth Matier. His other directorates comprised the Bank of Ireland, the Irish Shipowners Co Ltd, the Ardan Shipping Co Ltd and the Scottish Maritime Investment Co Ltd. He was a Belfast Harbour Commissioner, a member of the Committee of the British Corporation for the Survey and Registry of Shipping, a DL for the city and county of Belfast, and a prominent Orangeman.

Clark's career falls into two distinct phases. The first forty years were brilliantly successful; thereafter the position of the firm he helped to create steadily deteriorated. He died on 23 March 1935, six years after the death of his wife. The elder of his two sons, George Ernest, inherited the baronetcy. In his will Sir George Clark left £1,544,439 gross; two months after his death the firm of Workman, Clark ceased to exist.

DAVID JOHNSON

Writings:

PD 1907-10.

Official Report of the Debates of the Parliament of Northern Ireland (Senate) vols 7-11 (1926-29).

Sources:

Unpublished

Glasgow University Archives, 'Calendar of Confirmations' 1876, 1910, 1915.

Paisley Central Library, 'The Clark Genealogy'.

Published

Belfast News Letter 25 Mar 1935.

Belfast Telegraph 14 June 1935.

Glasgow Herald 4 Mar 1876, 4 Apr 1892, 7 Mar 1910, 25 Mar 1935.

Memoirs and Portraits of One Hundred Glasgow Men (2 vols, Glasgow: MacLehose, 1886) 2.

Henry Patterson, *Class Conflict and Sectarianism: The Protestant Working Class and the Belfast Labour Movement 1868-1920* (Belfast: Blackstaff Press, 1980).

Sidney Pollard and Paul Robertson, *The British Shipbuilding Industry 1870-1914* (Cambridge, Massachusetts: Harvard University Press, 1979).

Shipbuilding and Shipping Records April 1914, 31 Aug 1933, 28 Mar 1935.

Anthony T Q Stewart, *The Ulster Crisis* (Faber, 1967).

Times 1927-28 passim.

Urquart v Stacey and Others reported in *Northern Ireland Law Reports 1928*.

Workman, Clark (1928) Ltd, *Shipbuilding at Belfast 1880-1933* (Belfast: Workman, Clark, 1935).

WWMP.
WWW.

CLARK, George Thomas

(1809-1898)

Iron and steel firm manager

George Thomas Clark, born in London on 26 May 1809, was the son of George Clark (1777-1848), chaplain at Chelsea Hospital, and Clara née Dicey, a relative of the constitutional lawyer, A V Dicey. Educated at Charterhouse, he started first towards medicine and then switched to become an engineer. He worked on the building of the Great Western Railway under I K Brunel and then spent a few years (ca 1843-47) in India, reporting on sewerage at Bombay and advocating the construction of the first railway in India (Bombay to Tannah). He was offered the post of chief engineer to the Great Indian Peninsular Railway, but instead accepted an appointment at home with the Board of Health in 1848, first as a superintending inspector and then as one of the Board's three Commissioners. His career was diverted to the Dowlais Iron Co in South Wales in 1852 when he became a trustee of the estate of his friend Sir Josiah John Guest (1785-1852).

Over a period of forty years Guest had made Dowlais (by 1845) reputedly the largest ironworks in the world, with himself (by 1851) its sole owner. Under his will the works passed during her widowhood to Lady Charlotte Guest (1812-95), in trust for the ten children. After some time the second trustee, Edward Divett, withdrew and Clark then enlisted Henry Austin Bruce, later Lord Aberdare (1815-95). The active management was at first in the hands of Lady Charlotte, as it had been in the last years of her husband's life. She gradually withdrew, even before her re-marriage in 1855, and in 1856 the autocratic general manager, Thomas Evans, retired. Clark, who had become increasingly involved, then took charge of the works.

The task of controlling a works employing well over 10,000 men was necessarily formidable. It was intensified by the run-down of capital investment during a long dispute between Guest and his landlord, the Second Marquess of Bute, over the renewal of the Dowlais lease, a dispute not settled until 1848. In addition, Clark had no experience of the iron and steel trade or, indeed, of business at all. Many, especially the other Merthyr ironmasters at Cyfarthfa, Penydarren and Plymouth, expected him to sell. Yet forty years later, when his active involvement with the company ended (when Clark was in his eighties), Dowlais was a flourishing concern whereas Penydarren and Plymouth had disappeared as iron and steel makers, and Cyfarthfa had long been limping.

In the Dowlais success Clark determined the basic strategy and ensured that it was carried out, but against considerable difficulties at first. The example of Lady Charlotte, whose investments in the business had been unsuccessful, and the opposition of the Guest family and his co-trustee, did not encourage the pursuit of expansion and efficiency, but Clark persisted in a policy of major capital investment commencing in the late 1850s.

He accepted his lack of practical experience and sought to overcome this by avoiding the day-to-day running of the works. Instead he gave time and care to the selection of a general manager and, with him, to the appointment of managers to each of the various departments, and also to choosing foremen and other supervisory workmen. He was shrewd, or fortunate, in his choices. His general manager from 1856 to 1882 was William Menelaus (qv), an engineer at Dowlais since 1851. The Martin brothers, Edward Williams and William Jenkins (qv) were other first-class managers recruited under Clark. Clark's hand-picked managers reported back to him through Menelaus on a regular basis. The stress of these reports was on the costs involved in each process, which served both as a means of exercising a tight financial control and as a way of identifying particular problems or bottlenecks.

In the process of innovation Clark was a promoter rather than initiator, beyond the purely administrative area of office organisation. At the technical level the initiative both for experiment and adoption normally came from the divisional managers and especially from William Menelaus, to whom Clark invariably lent his support for innovations at Dowlais. These were continuous and unobtrusive. For example, the records show that in the 1850s and 1860s the amount of coal used to produce a ton of pig iron was substantially reduced not by any one dramatic discovery but by a series of small improvements in practice developed at Dowlais or learnt from elsewhere.

In the case of discrete and major innovations, Clark's correspondence reveals his close and constant involvement through discussions with the general manager of the works. The most famous example was the encouragement given by Dowlais to Bessemer (qv), who was afforded facilities to pursue his process for making malleable iron direct from the ore, commencing in 1856. Dowlais, also prompt in adopting David Mushet's improvements to the Bessemer process, produced the first rail ever rolled without the use of the puddling process, in 1858; it was also first in the field in the production of steel rails (1865). Clark's scientific background must have helped during the long delays in developing the Bessemer process because the experiments were subjected to close chemical analysis by a company chemist, Edward Riley. Eventually, when the rush towards steel gathered pace in the 1870s, Dowlais, almost alone of the Welsh works, was well placed to take part.

After the 1870s coal sales were a major source of company profits, largely because Clark successfully overcame the problems of coal supply. In 1856 he singled out as a central problem the high cost and deficient quantity of coal readily available to support an expansion at Dowlais. He then attacked the problem on all fronts: economies in fuel; contracts with outside firms for coal supplies at reasonable prices; a programme of heavy capital investment in new pits; and in 1859 the purchase of the Penydarren works as an immediate source of cheap coal. Then he developed coal sales. Despite the Welsh ironmasters' disdain for the coal trade, even in the 1860s, Clark established special agencies to sell Dowlais coal; pressed his co-trustee Bruce to use political influence to secure the inclusion of Dowlais coal on the prestigious Admiralty list; and accelerated efforts to use more small coal (unacceptable in the coal trade) at the ironworks in order to free a greater proportion of the large coal for sale.

A similar search for new sources took place over iron ore. Faced with inadequate local supplies, Clark embarked on the bold solution of investing to develop Spanish mines, and joined with the Consett Iron Co and with Krupps of Essen to form the Orconara Iron Ore Co Ltd in 1873 to own and work iron ore tracts at Bilbao.

Clark's last, and perhaps boldest, coup was to build a new Dowlais iron works, not at Merthyr, but at the dock-side in Cardiff. This enterprise was started after the retirement and death of Menelaus, and perhaps serves to confirm that Clark's innovatory tendency did not simply reflect the formidable genius of his first general manager. Clark and Edward Pritchard Martin planned the move in 1889 and the first iron was made in Cardiff in early 1891. (The works later became the East Moors Works of Guest, Keen & Nettlefolds which continued in operation until 1978.)

Clark retired from control in 1892, in his eighty-third year, suggesting a source of managerial weakness: the inability to let go. Associated with this was Clark's antagonism, on principle, towards joint stock companies. He successfully repulsed several proposals by the family to liquidate their assets by selling the company. The issue was not that ownership should not be separated from control (the trust had already done that), but that he thought limited companies did not permit the single, unified control ('despotic management' was his frequently-used phrase) that he thought essential. For a long time success was his justification, but towards the end of his reign, with no obvious successor in sight, this was not enough. A year after his death Dowlais became a limited company and three years later the two mergers necessary to create Guest, Keen & Nettlefolds had been effected.

Clark's importance in the industry was professionally recognised by his election as first president of the British Iron Trades Association in 1876, but outside his firm his field of action was local rather than national. During his long ascendancy Clark engaged in numerous local activities. Besides serving, mostly as chairman, on the Poor Law Guardians from 1859 to 1881, on the Board of Health from 1857 to 1868, and on the School Board from 1871 to 1881, he also spent a great deal of time extending and over-seeing the already famous Dowlais Works Schools, organising a Volunteer corps based on the works, and building a hospital at Dowlais. He also contributed enormously to sanitary improvement and the provision of a pure water supply for Dowlais, although his authoritarian attempts to control the cholera outbreak in 1866 by burning bedding and clothing met with fierce opposition from the people and had to be abandoned. In 1867-68 he was High Sheriff of Glamorgan.

His concern with sanitation was professional; in poor law administration he aimed to minimise the rates paid by the Dowlais Part of his educational involvement reflected a belief that it would secure a more efficient workforce, one that was disciplined and malleable; but there was also a strong human concern and, as a devout and ardent churchman, religious motivation.

Above all, Clark nurtured a life-long interest in archaeology and mediaeval history. He helped to found the Archaeological Association (later Royal Archaeological Institute) and became a trustee of the Cambrian Archaeological Association. He wrote numerous books and articles, the first in 1834 on Caerphilly Castle. Some of these remain standard works.

Clark married Ann Price, second daughter of Henry Lewis of Greenmeadow, near Cardiff, and co-heiress of Wyndham Lewis; she died in 1885 leaving a son and a daughter. Clark died on 31 January 1898, with an estate valued at £333,305 gross.

L J WILLIAMS

Writings:

A Guide Book to the Great Western Railway (1839).

The History and Description of the Great Western Railway (1846).

A Description and History of the Castles of Kidwelly and Caerphilly, and of Castell Coch (W Pickering, 1852).

Some Account of Morlais Castle (Tenby: R Mason, 1858).

Thirteen Views of the Castle of St Donat's, Glamorganshire, with a Notice of the Stradling Family (Shrewsbury: Adnitt & Naunton, 1871).

The Earls, Earldom, and Castle of Pembroke (Tenby: R Mason, 1880).

CLARK George Thomas

Some Account of Sir Robert Mansel ... and of Admiral Sir Thomas Button ... (Dowlais: pp, 1883).

The Land of Morgan (Whiting & Co, 1883).

Medieval Military Archaeology in England (2 vols, Wyman & Sons, 1884).

Limbus Patrum Morganiae et Glamorganiae (Wyman & Sons, 1886).

Cartae et Alia Munimenta Quae ad Dominium de Glamorgan Pertinent (4 vols, Dowlais: William Lewis, 1885-93).

'Heraldry' *Encyclopedia Britannica* (1880) vol 11.

Numerous Reports to the General Board of Health.

Sources:

Unpublished

Glamorgan RO, Dowlais MSS.

National Library of Wales, Clark MSS.

PrC.

M Lewis, 'G T Clark and the Dowlais Iron Co' (University of Wales, M Sc Econ 1983).

Published

DNB.

DWB.

John R Edwards and Colin Baber, 'Dowlais Iron Company: Accounting Policies, and Procedures for Profit Measurement and Reporting Purposes' *Accounting and Business Research* 34 (1978-79).

Madeleine Elsas, *Iron in the Making: Dowlais Iron Company Letters, 1782-1860* (Glamorgan Co Council and Guest Keen Iron & Steel Co, 1960).

John A Owen, *History of the Dowlais Iron Works, 1759-1930* (Risca, Gwent: Starling Press, 1977).

South Wales Daily News 2 Feb 1898.

Times 2 Feb 1898.

Western Mail 2 Feb 1898.

CLARK, William Stephens

(1839-1925)

Shoe manufacturer

William S Clark (courtesy of C & J Clark Ltd).

William Stephens Clark was born in Street, near Glastonbury, Somerset, on 22 February 1839, third of the fourteen children of James C Clark, described on the birth certificate as a rug manufacturer, and his wife Eleanor née Stephens. He attended two Quaker schools: Sidcot School, Somerset, 1848-50 and Bootham School, York, 1850-54. At Christmas 1854 William joined the family firm of C & J Clark in 1855 at the age of sixteen. His father, James, and his uncle, Cyrus, were then riding high on a business which had been making good profits for a decade by making and selling a whole range of sheepskin products and footwear. Their starting point in the 1820s had been sheepskins, made into slippers, rugs, mops, ottoman covers, gloves and so forth, but during the 1840s the production and sale of footwear became their major business and the company was trading throughout Britain.

In the late 1850s it was, however, on the point of collapse. The brothers were excellent salesmen and technically very able, but were indifferent financial controllers and tried to buy their way out of continual capital shortages by ill-considered expansion including a disastrous investment in exports to Australia. By 1863 the business was virtually insolvent and the family and its Quaker friends and creditors, principally Thomas Simpson (a Preston cotton spinner who had retired to Street) unceremoniously 'dumped' Cyrus, kicked James upstairs and gave William, who had clearly impressed, full and sole charge of the business under their general supervision. The business never looked back and at the time of William's death in 1925 'Clarks of Street' was a household name both at home and abroad.

The Clarks were originally a Quaker farming family in the Polden Hills near Street in Somerset, and William was brought up firmly in the Quaker tradition. His community was close-knit, of yeoman stock, with a high standard of personal and business morality. There is no question that his religion and upbringing were extremely important in forging the man who had to rescue his family's fortunes.

He was also, however, a man with rare business talents. From the first he imposed strict control over all key elements of spending and set up productivity measurements of his own invention and of a type unique in his part of the world. These included the allocation of departmental costs to specific components and work-groups; the analysis of direct and indirect costs; and the widespread use of percentage ratios to analyse costs and profit margins. He understood the importance of branding and firmly established the name of 'Clark' as a premium name in a crowded market. He led the way in offering a large range of fittings and styles. He was much impressed by American progress in machinery design and supported attempts to develop a British sewing-machine. Clarks were

CLARK William Stephens

ahead of their Northampton and Stafford competitors in introducing American technology and team methods; one unwelcome consequence was a short strike in 1880. He started Britain's first synthetic sole factory, based on the new 'magic' material called gutta-percha. This material revolutionised golf, but not shoemaking. In persevering with such 'new-fangled' ideas William was demonstrating that willingness to think strategically which is the hallmark of a successful businessman. Clarks quadrupled in size, from sales of £38,000 to £154,000, whilst he ran the company and it has continued to grow in the eighty years which have followed.

William retired from the leadership in 1903, leaving the reins in the hands of his son, John Bright Clark. William was a cultured and immensely enthusiastic man, and extremely active, especially after his retirement from business, in the fields of education and local government. He founded Strode School in Street and was for many years chairman of the Central Education Committee of the Society of Friends. He was a county alderman, a magistrate, and presided over the local urban council for thirty years. His contribution to the social and educational life of his town was immense but his chief interest in life, and legacy, was the firm which still bears his family name. He was not widely known outside his industry, or even outside Somerset, except within the closely-knit Quaker community.

In 1866 William Clark married Helen Priestman Bright, daughter of the cotton manufacturer and free trader, John Bright. He died on 20 November 1925 leaving £96,280 gross.

G BARRY SUTTON

Sources:

Unpublished

BCe.

MCe.

PrC.

Published

George B Sutton, *A History of Shoe Making in Street, Somerset. C & J Clark 1833-1903* (York: William Sessions Ltd, 1979).

CLAYTON, Nathaniel

(1811-1890)

Manufacturer of portable steam engines and thrashing machines

Nathaniel Clayton, from a painting at Shuttleworth Agricultural College, Bedfordshire (courtesy of the Institute of Agricultural History, Reading).

Nathaniel Clayton was born in Lincoln on 25 August 1811, the second son of Nathaniel Clayton Sr, a packet captain who plied a horse-drawn boat on the River Witham between Lincoln and Boston. Nathaniel Jr trained at the Butterley Ironworks near Ripley, Derbyshire, and he kept an interest in the iron trade which included a connection with the Boston engineer William Howden.

Returning to Lincoln, Clayton set up a foundry at Stamp End and became a boat owner and proprietor of two steam packets, one the *Celerity*, which he maintained in his own yard. Then in 1842 he formed a partnership with his brother-in-law Joseph Shuttleworth (qv), who already owned a boat-yard next to Clayton's foundry. They established their first engineering works at Waterside, Lincoln, on a one-and-a-half acre site of which two-thirds was frequently under water, and in 1845 built their first portable steam engine, a double cylinder 8 nominal hp design with 6 inch diameter horizontal cylinders. Four years later the partners built their first steam-powered thrashing machine. In these two agricultural equipment markets, steam engines and steam thrashing machines, Clayton & Shuttleworth became the leading mid-Victorian business.

By 1890 they had built 26,000 steam engines and 24,000 steam thrashing machines. Their works occupied 20 acres by 1885 and in 1870 they had a workforce of 1,200. With the decline of the home market in the late 1870s and early 1880s the export trade became important. Clayton & Shuttleworth formed a branch in Vienna as early as 1857 and by 1890 had other branches at Pesth, Prague, Cracow, Lemberg and Crajova, as well as numerous agencies.

A number of their competitors, like the firms of Ruston (qv), Foster, Cooke, Rainforth, Penney and Coultas set up in Lincoln, making it the centre of the English agricultural engineering industry.

Clayton, in Lincoln as the dominant partner, initially contributed his skill as an ironmaster but over the years took charge of the commercial side of the business, leaving technical development to Shuttleworth. After the founders' deaths the firm's innovational impetus faltered, and by the 1920s foreign markets were lost and the business was poorly equipped to deal with the challenge of the internal combustion engine.

Clayton was much involved in the general commercial life of Lincoln and took an active part in politics. He served his turn as mayor in 1857 even though Lincoln City Council was under the control of the Tories and Clayton was a professed and vigorous Liberal. By the mid-1850s he had been 'received' into local society and became a county JP in Lindsey. In 1875 he bought a substantial agricultural estate at Withcall in the Lincolnshire Wolds, but as an investment, for he lived in some state 'Above hill' at Lincoln, in Eastcliffe House. He served as High Sheriff in 1881.

Clayton's wealth was used in several philanthropic ventures in Lincoln. He was much interested in many improvements — better sanitation, education and hospitals — most of which he effected as the dominant member of various Corporation committees.

Nathaniel Clayton married Hannah Shortcliffe in 1837; they had three daughters, one of whom married Shuttleworth's son Alfred. Clayton died on 21 December 1890 leaving an estate of £1,365,496 gross.

J HOLDERNESS *and* D C PHILLIPS

Sources:

Unpublished

Reading University, Institute of Agricultural History and Museum of English Rural Life, Clayton & Shuttleworth production records.

PrC.

Published

The Engineer 71 (1891).

J W Francis Hill, *Victorian Lincoln* (Cambridge: Cambridge University Press, 1974).

The Implement and Machinery Review 16 (1890-91), 23 (1897-98).

Journal of the Royal Agricultural Society of England 2nd series 19 (1883).

Kelly's Directory of Lincolnshire various dates.

Lincolnshire Chronicle Supplement, 1854.

Stamford Mercury 20 June 1856.

William Tritton, 'The Origin of the Thrashing Machine' *Lincolnshire Magazine* II (1934-36).

White's Directory of Lincolnshire various dates.

Harry Clifford-Turner (courtesy of Clifford-Turner).

CLIFFORD-TURNER, Harry

(1876-1941)

Solicitor

Harry Clifford Turner was born in Dalston, Hackney, East London on 10 October 1876, the fifth of six children of Everett Turner (1837-1932), a ladies' set and collar manufacturer, and of Everett's second wife, Frances née Greaves (1842-96). The Turner family came from Lavenham in Suffolk, but Everett Turner had migrated to London at an early age.

Clifford Turner attended a school called Merton College and, after leaving at about the age of fourteen, got a job as a solicitor's clerk for which he was paid 5s a week. He was not articled as his family could not afford the £80 for the stamp duty then payable on articles. He entered articles in 1895 and on qualifying as a solicitor in 1900 set up his own firm at 68 Finsbury Pavement with Sidney Slater, the brother of his former principal. The firm was called H Clifford Turner & Co and most of its work was small litigation.

In 1905 Slater retired and was replaced by Ulric Hopton and the name of the firm was changed to Clifford Turner & Hopton. Hopton had some experience of company law, a field the importance of which Clifford Turner was quick to recognise, and in 1906 the firm's name appeared for the first time on a company prospectus. By 1910 Clifford Turner was earning over £3,000 a year and by the outbreak of the First World War the firm had acted on several prospectuses.

After the war activity in the new issue market revived and Clifford Turner quickly established a reputation in this field. By 1921 the firm had a staff of about 25. Because he was generally known as Clifford Turner, and in order to preserve the goodwill attaching to the firm's name, in January 1925 Clifford Turner changed his surname from Turner to Clifford-Turner. In 1926 Sir Alexander Lawrence Bt, the chief assistant solicitor to the Treasury, joined the firm and its name was changed to Clifford-Turner, Hopton & Lawrence.

The company promotion and prospectus work flourished in the 1920s and the firm acted on the flotation of Imperial Airways and also on the incorporation of ICI. In 1928, a particularly active year, the firm's profits, of which Clifford-Turner was entitled to the lion's share, amounted to £90,032 but three years later, in spite of the addition of two more partners, the profits were down to £27,554. After the slump of 1931, business again expanded and in 1934, when the name of the firm was changed to Clifford-Turner & Co, there were seven partners.

From his early thirties, when he was becoming well established, Clifford-Turner had to husband his strength because of the septicaemia and other illness by which he was increasingly afflicted. His ambition was not to be a great lawyer but to build a successful 'business': the word he used rather than 'practice'. He was a competent lawyer, but his great strength lay in his perception of the financial and business aspects of corporate transactions, and his ability to combine financial and legal advice.

In the early 1930s Clifford-Turner became financially interested in several property developments, including the development of an office building at 11 Old Jewry in the City. The firm moved there in 1934, but Clifford-Turner sold his interest in the property early in the Second World War. In 1935 Clifford-Turner bought Heathfield Park, a large house in Sussex.

By the outbreak of the war in 1939, the firm had nine partners and a staff of over 60 but by this time Clifford-Turner was increasingly suffering from ill-health. On medical advice he left London and did not attend the office, but he continued to take a close interest in the firm and to exercise a considerable degree of control over it until he died two years later.

Many of the leading figures of his day in the professions and in industry were his friends but, in spite of his gift for anticipating future trends, he was less successful in equipping the firm for the future as many clients looked to him personally for advice rather than to the firm as a whole. Apart from his family, the firm was his life; and since his death it has continued to grow and maintain its position as a leading firm of City solicitors.

Clifford-Turner in 1899 married Emmy Marion Louise Davis (1873-1940), the daughter of Joseph Davis, a masonic jeweller; they had five children, four boys and a girl who died in infancy. Only the third son, Raymond (b 1906), went into the law, succeeding his father as senior partner in 1941. Harry Clifford-Turner died at Inkpen near Newbury on 11 June 1941 and left an estate valued at £232,686 gross.

J W SCOTT

Sources:

Unpublished

Clifford-Turner family papers.

Clifford-Turner, London, company archives.

BCe.

MCe.

Published

John Scott, *Legibus* (pp, King, Thorne & Stace Ltd, 1980).

Sir Charles Clore (courtesy of Sears Holdings PLC).

CLORE, Sir Charles

(1904-1979)

Property developer and industrialist

Charles Clore was born in Mile End, East London on 24 December 1904, the son of Israel Clore and his wife Yetta née Abrahams. They were Russian Jewish immigrants who had arrived in Liverpool some years earlier, and then moved to London. By the time Charles Clore was born his father had established himself as a modestly successful textile manufacturer in the East End of London, supplying department stores and shops. His father also dabbled in a small way in property. After education at a local elementary school (which produced a number of Jewish children from similar backgrounds who made their way in the commercial field), Charles spent some time in his father's business and acquired experience which proved of value to him in later years, in textiles, shops, stores and property.

At the age of twenty he went to South Africa and lived with a cousin who was engaged in fruit farming on a large scale and there developed an interest in agriculture. He also became interested in the possibilities offered by the cinematograph industry which in South Africa at that time was controlled by the Schlesinger interests. Back in England, the young Clore succeeded in buying the South African rights to the film of the World Championship fight between Jack Dempsey and Gene Tunney and on his return to South Africa resold them at a profit.

He returned to England in 1927 and became interested in property transactions. With financial help from his family, in 1930 he bought a derelict skating rink in Cricklewood where he had learnt to skate as a youth, and in a few years turned it into a successful concern. In the 1930s he found a number of business opportunities, some of which he bought and was able to turn over at a profit, while others he had to relinquish through lack of available finance. He had an extremely acute eye for opportunity and his motto at the time was 'Find your opportunity and work hard and success is almost inevitable'.

In 1930 the lease of the Prince of Wales Theatre which had about seven years to run was put up for auction and Charles Clore bought it for £700. As it was impossible to obtain a profitable rent for it he found some associates to run the theatre and thus entered the field of theatre management. The theatre was rebuilt; it stayed open throughout the Second World War and remained in the ownership of one of Clore's companies, City and Central Investments Ltd, which was eventually merged into Land Securities Investment Trust Ltd.

In 1939 Charles Clore had a certain amount of capital available as the result of some profitable property transactions (he had been involved in a number of developments, chiefly of industrial premises) and he made a substantial investment in Lydenburg Estates, a South African gold mining company, which he had bought on the advice of his contacts in that country. He kept these shares through the vicissitudes of the war and subsequently made a substantial profit on this investment.

During the war he began building premises for the Government. He continued to do this after the war, putting together sites for office buildings to be let to the Government, using his own construction company, Token Constructions Ltd, to develop the sites. These properties eventually were brought into City & Central Investments Ltd, a property company. One of the most notable developments by City & Central was the London Hilton Hotel, built at a cost of about £5 million. Clore made no apology for the fact that in developing property he built above all for profit: he said that he did 'not believe in any great architectural triumphs which end up in bankruptcy' {Marriott (1967) 271}.

After the war Clore acquired a 50,000 acre estate, Balmacaan, in Scotland (which included some Loch Ness fishing rights), for £500,000; he subsequently broke it up and sold it at a substantial profit. A coachworks at Park Royal was bought and floated as a public company. In 1946 he bought woollen textile mills employing nearly 4,000 people in Yorkshire. Clore also became involved in stores in 1946 by buying the bankrupt Richards Shops chain of dress outlets (which he expanded vigorously from 30 to 46 shops) and a department store, Heelas of Reading. He sold the latter two investments at a substantial profit and in 1951 bought Furness Shipbuilding for about £3-4 million. He reorganized the company, which was extremely profitable until the shipbuilding slump; in 1969 he sold the Furness yard to Swan Hunter. In 1952 he bought a controlling interest in the knitting machinery business of Bentley Engineering, which had previously acquired Wildt & Co, hosiery machine makers, from Clore in 1949. In 1954 he brought Mellor, Bromley & Co, hosiery and textile manufacturers into the Bentley Engineering Group.

Clore in 1953 bought about 70 per cent of the equity of J Sears (True-Form Boot) Co as it was then known, which owned the True-Form and Freeman, Hardy & Willis footwear business with some 900 shops and a number of footwear factories. Later, other shoe retailers were added, including the well-known firms of Dolcis, with 250 shops (acquired in 1956 for £5.8 million), Manfield, with 200 shops (acquired in 1956 as well, for just under £3.5 million), and Lilley & Skinner. These businesses were combined into the British Shoe Corporation, to form the largest footwear concern in the UK, with nearly one-quarter of the industry's total retail trade. By the late 1960s, it had 2,000 shops.

Soon after Clore became chairman of Sears in February 1953, the company sold off a substantial proportion of its freeholds and took back long leases in their stead. Sears was turned into a holding company, with some funds invested in the footwear business and other funds now available for other investments. In 1954, he sold his holdings in Furness and Bentley Engineering to Sears. By the middle of 1955, Clore headed a group employing 20,000 workers, with trading profits of £3 million a year.

In 1956 he entered the road transport industry. After a considerable battle with Hugh Fraser he bought Scottish Motor Traction and a year later added to it the firm of Shaw & Kilburn Ltd by an exchange of shares worth £375,000, subsequently acquiring Gilbert Rice & Co, and later adding to this group Silcock & Colling, transporters of motor vehicles.

Charles Clore attracted a great deal of criticism at the time of his bid for

Sears in 1953 as it was then not considered appropriate for someone to bid for a company over the heads of its directors. He regarded the position as being one where the entrenched directors were not making adequate use of their assets and on completing these acquisitions he set himself the task of making the assets work. 'In some business [sic] the profits earned show that existing assets are not being employed in the fullest capacity. I maintain that neither this country nor any business can afford to have its resources remaining stagnant.' {*Fortune* (Sept 1957) 102} Typically he reduced the assets by selling the premises and leasing them back. The business would thus be subjected to proper market rent and the funds released would be reinvested in more profitable investment than property. This did not conflict with his substantial interest in property where he regarded himself as a developer rather than as an investor. He felt that property investment was appropriate for financial institutions and pension funds, but that businesses should normally show profit after paying or being charged with a proper rent. One of the criticisms was that he was 'milking' a company, but it was a fact that he never bought a company merely to sell its assets, only to put them to more profitable use.

Perhaps the greatest legacy of his promotion of contested takeover bids is the incentive it has provided to boards more generally to exploit fully the assets under their control if they are to maintain that control: a discipline all the more necessary with the weakening of shareholder power consequent on the divorce of ownership and control in modern corporations. For all the criticisms, City institutions thus proved willing to invest in the companies for which he was showing results and his actions were soon recognised as being in the interests of efficiency.

The footwear company, which changed its name to Sears Holdings Ltd in 1955, became the main company in the group and absorbed the other companies which Sir Charles then controlled, except the property development companies which were entirely separate. Subsequent acquisitions included a jewellery group, Mappin & Webb, in 1957, to which Garrards, the Crown Jewellers, were added. A further contested bid resulted in the acquisition in 1965 of the Lewis's Investment Trust (the Selfridges/Lewis store group) which adopted a policy of modernisation and expansion. In 1971 he bought the William Hills organisation, one of the world's biggest bookmakers, for £20 million. However, his most ambitious bid, for the brewery group of Watney Mann in 1959, was unsuccessful. When Clore acquired control of Sears Holdings Ltd in 1953 its profits were about £1.4 million before tax. In the year of his death, the pre-tax profits for 1979-80 were in excess of £90 million.

In 1959 Clore offered some shares in his property company, City & Central Investments, to the public for the first time. It is a measure of the City's confidence in him, despite the controversy over his takeover tactics, that in 1960 the Prudential Assurance Co took 10 per cent of the capital of City & Central and agreed to advance £13 million of long-term mortgage finance. A few days later, it was announced that City & Central was to merge with City Centre Properties which was run by Jack Cotton (qv). Clore's share of the new City Centre Properties was estimated at £10 million (of £65 million). But the partnership between Cotton and Clore was not a happy one as the personalities and styles of the two men were diametrically opposite. Jack Cotton was an effervescent extrovert and

Charles Clore was a cautious and thoughtful introvert. After a number of unhappy years the company was merged in late 1968 with Land Securities Investment Trust Ltd, making it the largest property company in the UK. At this point Clore retired from participation in any public property company, concentrating on a comparatively small number of property investments by some of his private companies.

Clore made very considerable donations to charities; from the early 1960s, he gave away £500,000 a year. Most of these donations were made quietly, and often anonymously. Important donations were made to London University, the London Zoo and University College Hospital. He was a committed Zionist, making large donations to Israeli institutions and serving as a member of the British Council for Israel. His knighthood in 1971 was given in recognition of his charitable gifts.

In later years, Clore relaxed by farming at Stype Grange, Hungerford, where he had a stud farm. (He thought of land as an investment too: in 1961 he bought a 16,627 acre estate in Herefordshire from Guy's Hospital for a reputed £3.25 million; after reorganisation and considerable expense in improvements he sold it to the Prudential Assurance Co in May 1979 for £20.5 million.) He became an expert on antique furniture and accumulated an impressive collection of paintings.

He was a withdrawn man, shunning publicity, refusing all interviews with journalists. He was rarely a happy man, especially after his divorce in 1957 from his wife Francine Rachel Halphen, whom he had married in 1943. She had been awarded the Croix de Guerre for her work in the French Resistance during the war. They had one son and one daughter. Clore died on 26 July 1979 in a London clinic. He left to charity an estate valued in excess of £50 million, his family having been provided for during his lifetime.

LEONARD SAINER

Sources:

Unpublished

BCe.

MCe.

PrC.

Personal knowledge.

Published

George Bull and Antony Vice, *Bid for Power* (Elek, 1958).

Daily Telegraph 27 July 1979.

Edward Erdman, *People and Property* (Batsford, 1982).

Fortune Sept 1957.

Oliver Marriott, *The Property Boom* (Hamish Hamilton, 1967).

the hands of three of his four sons (the other being a solicitor), the second son, Ralph (1843-1912) being the most hard-working and successful as a surveyor. No partners from outside the family were taken into Messrs Clutton until 1909, and the partnership has continued to include direct descendants of John Clutton.

The attainment of professional status by surveyors owed a great deal to the example, and to the efforts, of John Clutton. He appreciated the value, both social and professional, of associations, becoming a member of the Royal Agricultural Society in 1838 on its foundation, being elected to the exclusive Land Surveyors' Club in 1839, and being recruited as an associate of the Council of the Institution of Civil Engineers in 1848. In 1868 he took the lead in gathering together 49 leading surveyors, who formed themselves into the Institution of Surveyors (now the Royal Institution of Chartered Surveyors) and elected John Clutton their first president.

He retired from his last professional appointment, that of Crown Receiver, in 1889, and made a final appearance before a Select Committee in 1890, that on the woods, forests, and land revenues of the Crown, retiring to live at Woodhatch House, Reigate, where he died on 1 March 1896, survived by four sons and one daughter. He left an estate valued at £148,000 gross.

F M L THOMPSON

Writings:

PP, HL 1845 (420) X, SC Compensation for Lands taken by Railways.

PP, HC 1847-48 (645) VII, Ecclesiastical Commission.

PP, HC 1849 (513, 514) XX, SC Woods, Forests, and Land Revenues of the Crown.

PP, HL 1851 (589) XIX, Episcopal and Capitular Estates.

PP, HC 1854 (377) X, SC Crown Forests in England.

PP, HC 1890 (333) XVIII, SC Woods, Forests, and Land Revenues of the Crown.

Sources:

Unpublished

Messrs Clutton's archives, 5 Great College Street, London.

'Cluttons 1765-1965' (typescript, 1965, the firm).

Published

Cluttons: Some Historical Notes Put together in 1948 (pp, 1950).

Julian C Rogers, 'Memoir of John Clutton' *Transactions of the Surveyors' Institution* 29 (1896-97).

F M L Thompson, *Chartered Surveyors. The Growth of a Profession* (Routledge & Kegan Paul, 1968).

Times 5 Mar 1896.

COATES, John Bernard Maurice

(1908-)

Printing ink and chemical coatings manufacturer

John B M Coates, CBE, Group Chairman 1956–1977 (courtesy of Coates Brothers & Co Ltd).

John Bernard Maurice Coates was born in Coulsdon, Surrey on 16 August 1908. He was the eldest grandson of George Coates, the founder of the business of Coates Brothers (established 1877), manufacturers of printing inks and lithographic stones. After education at Oundle School and Trinity Hall, Cambridge, he joined the family company, then under the chairmanship of his grandfather and still very small (with a turnover of £75,019), in August 1929.

In his last year at Cambridge, John Coates had been afflicted by ankylosing spondylitis, a painful and disabling disease of the spine, and his early years in the company were marred by serious ill-health. However, despite, and perhaps partly because of this handicap, he set out to expand and modernise the company, with his father, Maurice's, active encouragement. Their boldness bore fruit and, in the teeth of the serious business depression, Coates Brothers embarked upon a period of continuous growth which led to its becoming by 1939 one of the largest manufacturers of printing ink in Europe, with branch factories around the UK, in South Africa and India. After the war the momentum continued; factories were established in all the former British Empire territories except Canada, and the manufacturing base was diversified to include synthetic resins, industrial finishes, lithographic plates and, later, reprographic materials.

John Coates became chief executive of the company in 1938 at the early age of thirty. The growth of Coates Brothers over the ensuing forty-odd years was achieved with no important acquisitions and financed almost entirely out of retained profits. By the time John Coates retired in the company's centenary year, 1977, his grandfather's small business (which in 1938 had shareholders' funds (issued share capital plus reserves) of £129,000) had become a large multinational public company and a leading world influence in its chosen fields, shareholders' funds amounting to £32,471,000. Under John Coates the firm established 24 factories in 14 territories of the Empire; their subsidiary companies became major importers of intermediate products manufactured by the UK company. For services to export he was awarded the CBE in 1973.

John Coates believed that the task of management was to provide opportunities for the right level of self-expression for each individual. This required a sensitive appreciation of other people's circumstances and aspirations, but in the long run, he felt, attention to that factor would bring financial success.

Apart from his business activities John Coates has played an active part in three medical charities. For nine years he was chairman of the British Rheumatism and Arthritis Association, now renamed Arthritis Care, and more recently has been chairman of the Research Committee and a member of the council of the Back Pain Association. He is also president of the Ankylosing Spondylitis Society. When the active phase of his own spondylitis ended, he took up sailing again and he is still active in keel boat racing in the Solent and at Falmouth.

J B M COATES

Writings:

Coates Brothers. A History 1877-1977 (Westerham Press Ltd, 1977).

Sources:

Unpublished

BCe.

Published

J B M Coates, *Coates Brothers. A History 1877-1977* (Westerham Press, 1977).

COATES, Sir William Henry

(1882-1963)

Chemical industry manager

William ('Billy') Henry Coates was born at Runcorn on 31 May 1882, son of T Mallalieu Coates, a veterinary surgeon, and of Esther Sarah née Tough. He was educated at Loughborough Grammar School and entered

Sir William H Coates (courtesy of ICI PLC).

the civil service in 1900. He took an external degree at London University on a part-time basis.

After a spell in the War Office, he went to the Inland Revenue, where he was Director of Statistics and Intelligence, 1919-25. In that period he worked with Josiah Stamp (qv) on tax matters and it was Stamp who invited him in November 1925 to take an industrial post as secretary of Nobel Industries. When Nobels joined the Imperial Chemical Industries merger of the following year he became ICI treasurer. Coates became a director of ICI in 1929 and served as deputy chairman in 1945-50.

His most important contribution to the development of ICI was in the field of finance. He knew more than the other board members about economic theory and taxation, and was considered by some of them to have rather too pernickety a mind and to be donnish. (He kept up his studies with Stamp and examined economics at the LSE, serving on the Senate of London University, 1929-33.) He was, however, a skilled administrative foil to the flamboyant Harry McGowan (qv), in a period when ICI was developing its world position in a network of cartels in the traditional chemical sectors and hesitantly expanding into new sectors.

As W J Reader in his study of ICI stressed, the firm (though in the private sector) had a highly developed symbiotic relationship with Government, and Coates played a significant part in this. He served on various government committees on taxation, agricultural support, and other matters. He was more frequently consulted informally: it was Coates, for example, who drew up the wartime plans for transport nationalisation which were subsequently to result in the Labour Government's creation of the British Transport Commission. He was knighted in 1947. He also represented ICI at the Federation of British Industries and was chairman of an FBI committee which defended cartels on classic Schumpeterian grounds.

When he retired from ICI in 1950 he continued to serve on various government committees and joined the boards of the Carpet Manufacturing Co (1950-55) and the National Westminster Bank (deputy chairman 1950-57). Keen on golf, he retired to the Burlington Hotel, Eastbourne.

Coates married Claire Ferris, daughter of a deceased clerk, in 1909. They had two daughters. He died in the Esperance Nursing Home at Eastbourne on 7 February 1963 leaving £119,427 gross.

LESLIE HANNAH

Writings:

'Administration and Capital' *British Management Review* 3 (1938).

His Inland Revenue work was often published but only rarely surfaced under his own name, eg in his evidence to the Colwyn committee (*Minutes of Evidence Taken Before the Committee on National Debt and Taxation* (2 vols, HMSO, 1927) 2).

Sources:

Unpublished

Business History Unit, Management Research Group Papers.

ICI, Millbank, London, archives.

PRO, MT 64 10.

BCe.

MCe.

PrC.

Published

William J Reader, *ICI: A History* (2 vols, Oxford University Press, 1970 and 1975) 2.

Times 9,10 Feb 1963.

WWW.

COBBOLD, Cameron Fromanteel

1st Lord Cobbold

(1904-)

Banker

Cameron F Cobbold, 1st Lord Cobbold (courtesy of the Bank of England).

Cameron Fromanteel Cobbold was born in Mayfair, London, on 14 September 1904, elder son of Lieutenant Colonel Clement John Fromanteel Cobbold (1882-1961) and only child of his first wife, Stella Willoughby Saville Cameron (1882-1918). His father was a barrister at the Inner Temple, before acting as secretary of the Royal Cancer Hospital, 1933-44; he left £422 in 1961. Cobbold's great-grandfather John Chevalier Cobbold (1797-1882), MP for Ipswich 1847-68, was a brewer who left £138,505. Cobbold was educated in Leonard Todd's house at Eton in 1917-23, and at King's College, Cambridge, where he was a scholar and prizeman, but left without taking a degree in his second year. He was afterwards fellow of Eton in 1951-67 and Steward of the Courts at Eton from 1973. After leaving Cambridge, Cobbold served as a lieutenant in the London Rifle Brigade in 1925-29, and worked with a firm of accountants in London and Paris before joining one of their clients, C E Heath & Excess Insurance. He then became general manager of the Italian Excess Insurance Co in Milan, and was involved in the rescue operation mounted in 1929-30 by the Bank of England of the Banco Italo Britannica.

During the First World War an Italian-born Hungarian national, I George A P C E Manzi-Fé, then with the Credito Italiano Bank, agitated British financial and industrial circles with schemes for an Anglo-Italian trading bank to loosen the grip of German exporters on Italian markets. Following his testimony in May 1917 to Lord Balfour of Burleigh's committee on post-war commercial and industrial policy, the British-Italian Banking Corporation was formed with 80 British shareholders including the Westminster, National Provincial and Lloyd's clearing banks. This Corporation ranked as fourth or fifth among Italian commercial banks. Manzi-Fé was managing director of both Italo Britannica and the British-Italian Banking Corporation, but (like the similar British Trade Corporation of Lord Faringdon (qv) in Yugoslavia) heavy losses were sustained through managerial incompetence, fraud and ill-judged speculation. Manzi-Fé was arrested at Le Touquet in July 1929, and the Bank of England supported British shareholders in preventing a crash which would have reacted on British credit overseas.

Cobbold's adeptness in this affair impressed Threadneedle Street and he entered the Bank in 1933, becoming Executive Director in 1938 and Deputy Governor in 1945. In the former position he held great responsibility during the wartime Governorship of Montagu Norman (qv), and he also had critical influence during the difficult post-war transition period when Lord Catto (qv) was Governor. Cobbold was much involved in the most important historical event in the Bank during this period, its nationalisation, but Hugh Dalton, the Chancellor of the Exchequer, 'totally lost all confidence in Cobbold' after he 'made a bloomer' over the terms of a 2.5 per cent tap issue in 1946 {Dalton diary, 20 May 1946}, and perhaps unfairly favoured the appointment of Lord Piercy (qv) or Sir Clarence Sadd as Governor in succession to Catto. His successor as Chancellor of the Exchequer, Sir Stafford Cripps, first approached Sir John Hanbury-Williams (qv), but Cobbold's appointment as Governor was confirmed with effect from 1949. His selection was welcomed in the City since he was a lively and forceful personality and was one of the few leading figures of the Bank of England who distrusted Keynesian economics.

Cobbold's suspicion of Keynesian economics was manifest. In 1951-64 successive Conservative Governments reacted against the controls of Dalton and Cripps and practised a limited form of monetary policy. At a time when the National Debt was increasing absolutely and was abnormally liquid, Conservative Chancellors met their commitment to maintain a high and stable level of employment by the policy of stop-go which Cobbold did not unreservedly approve. Thus, though a close friend of Harold Macmillan as both Chancellor and Prime Minister, Cobbold thought him 'dangerously unorthodox' in 1956 in his plans to expand the economy and government spending {Macmillan (1971) 9}, and he regretted that as Governor he did not have more influence on hire-purchase restrictions to restrain demand.

Cobbold sympathised with the traditional City view that 'one of the essentials of the ideal Governor is that successful management and control of his institution and of the financial situation, rather than frequent public speeches, should be his leading attribute' {*Bankers' Magazine* 108 (1919) 391}. The Bank was regarded by many politicians, economists and journalists as obsessively secretive, and although some of this criticism was self-serving, it is undeniable that the Bank's Annual Reports, and Cobbold's public pronouncements, were uninformative. Cobbold's tendency to treat the workings of monetary policy, and especially the Bank Rate, as mysterious arcana was criticised by Lord Kahn, among others, and was by no means wholly endorsed by the report of Lord Radcliffe's committee on the Working of the Monetary System in 1959. On the other hand, Cobbold made an increasing number of speeches in London and other cities, was the first Governor to appear on television, and initiated the making of a film about the workings of the Bank. As to the relations between the Bank and the Treasury, Cobbold told Radcliffe that he 'found it very difficult to say just where any particular idea starts and finishes, or exactly where the initiative comes from' {*PP* (1958–59) Cmnd 827, Q 260}; in July 1956 he objected to Macmillan calling the Clearing Bankers and other financiers to the Treasury for a meeting 'since he regards himself as the right person to deal with these institutions' {Macmillan (1971) 52}. His successor as Governor, Lord Cromer, was certainly more open and less of a votary of the Bank's mystique. Foreign exchange management, and other aspects of Bank of England business with international ramifications, took up about half of Cobbold's time as Governor. He attended monthly meetings of the Bank of International Settlements at Basle, had intimate relations with Commonwealth, European and American central bank Governors, and in later years helped to form central banks in Commonwealth countries as they became independent. In many of these tasks he was assisted by Sir George Bolton (qv).

Cobbold retired as Governor in 1961, and in February 1962 was appointed by Macmillan as chairman of a commission of enquiry to investigate the attitude of the people of Sarawak and North Borneo to the plan for a Greater Malaysia. Their report was concluded by July 1962. After his retirement as Governor, Cobbold became a director of Royal Exchange Assurance (1961), Hudson's Bay Co, and British Petroleum (1962). He was a member of the Advisory Board of the Chemical Bank New York Trust from 1966.

He was High Sheriff of London, 1946-47, DL for Hertfordshire from 1972, Lord Chamberlain, 1963-71, and Chancellor of the Royal Victorian Order, 1963-71. A supporter of medical charities, he was chairman of Middlesex Hospital, 1963-74, and president of the British Heart Foundation until 1976. An honorary fellow of the Institute of Bankers, he received an LL D from McGill University in 1961, and after giving the Lord Stamp Memorial Lecture in 1962, was made DSc of London University in 1963. He was sworn of the Privy Council in 1959, created a baron in 1960, GVCO in 1963 and Knight of the Garter in 1970.

He married at Knebworth, Hertfordshire, in 1930, Lady Hermione Bulwer-Lytton (b 1905), elder daughter of the Second Earl of Lytton, KG, PC, temporary Viceroy of India in 1925, and after his father-in-law's death in 1947, settled on the Lytton estate at Knebworth. He has two sons and a daughter.

R P T DAVENPORT-HINES

COBBOLD Cameron Fromanteel

Writings:

PP, Radcliffe Committee on the Working of the Monetary System (1958-59) Cmnd 827.

Report of the Commission of Inquiry, North Borneo and Sarawak (1962) Cmnd 1794 (chairman).

Some Thoughts on Central Banking (Athlone Press, 1962).

Sources:

Unpublished

Bank of England Archives, Threadneedle Street.

BLPES, papers of Lord Dalton.

PRO, Foreign Office and Treasury papers.

Information from Lord Cobbold.

Published

Bankers' Magazine.

Harold Macmillan, *Riding the Storm* (Macmillan, 1971).

The Old Public School-boys' Who's Who: Eton (St James's Press, 1933).

Henry Roseveare, *The Treasury* (Allen Lane, 1969).

Richard S Sayers, *Financial Policy 1939-45* (HMSO, 1956).

—, *Bank of England 1890-1944* (3 vols, Cambridge University Press, 1976).

Times 30 June 1961.

George D N Worswick and P H Ady, *The British Economy in the 1950s* (Oxford University Press, 1962).

WW 1982.

COBHAM, Sir Alan John

(1894-1973)
Pioneer of in-flight refuelling

Alan John Cobham was born in Camberwell, London on 6 May 1894, the elder of two children of Frederick Cobham, a 'town traveller', and Elizabeth née Burrows. He attended Wilson's Grammar School, leaving at

Sir Alan J Cobham in 1926.
Portrait by Frank O Salisbury
(courtesy of the National Portrait
Gallery, London).

fifteen to become a junior clerk in Hitchcock & Williams, textile wholesalers in the City. He then started an agricultural apprenticeship but after a year returned to the City. At the outbreak of war in 1914 Cobham volunteered for the Veterinary Corps and saw action in France; eventually in 1917, with the help of a family friend in the War Office, he transferred to the Royal Flying Corps as a cadet sergeant. He gained his 'wings' and was commissioned in the Royal Air Force in 1918, as a flying instructor, his first and only appointment in the RAF.

On demobilisation he worked briefly for British Aerial Transport before going into partnership with Jack Holmes, an ex-RFC pilot, to form the Cobham & Holmes Aviation Co, offering air displays and joyriding. Initially the venture was very successful but later failed through lack of capital. Cobham next joined the Aircraft Manufacturing Co run by George Holt Thomas (qv). After it became Geoffrey de Havilland's (qv) De Havilland Aircraft Co in 1920, Cobham stayed on as an aerial survey, test and air charter pilot, undertaking all De Havilland's long-range charter flights to Europe and beyond. He also won the King's Cup Air Race in 1924 and flew Sir Sefton Brancker, Director General of Civil Aviation, to India in 1925 for the Imperial Airship Conference. He then undertook two more long-range flights to prove the viability of the aeroplane, rather than the airship, as a means of improving imperial communications: to the Cape and back (1925-26), and to Australia and back (1926) sponsored by Sir Charles Wakefield (qv). For these flights he was awarded, both in 1926, the AFC and KBE respectively.

After leaving De Havilland, Sir Alan Cobham established in 1927 his own holding company, Alan Cobham Aviation Ltd, for consultancy and survey work in civil and general aviation. Financed and supported in kind variously by Wakefield, Imperial Airways, and the Air Ministry, Short Brothers and other interested parties, he flew survey flights round Africa in a Short Brothers Singapore flying boat (1927-28); to Salisbury, Rhodesia in a DH 61 (1929); and to Lake Kivu in a Short Brothers Valetta seaplane (1931). He jointly founded in 1927, with Robert Blackburn (qv) and with the promise of co-operation from Imperial Airways, Cobham-Blackburn Airlines Ltd to operate scheduled air services in Africa. However, government policy forced the company to sell their hard-won operating concessions to Imperial Airways for a substantial sum in 1930 after which the company went into voluntary liquidation. During this period Cobham was also deeply involved in the promotion of municipal aerodromes, becoming chairman of Bournemouth Airport Ltd, although he was to be disappointed by the comparative failure of the campaign to provide every major town and city in Britain with an aerodrome.

His most notable pre-war contributions to aviation in Britain were possibly his 'Youth of Britain' Tour of 1929 followed by his National Aviation Day tours of 1932-35 which gave thousands of people their first taste of flying. He claimed that an RAF officer responsible for air crew recruitment interviews during the Second World War told him that a substantial number of interviewees stated that their desire to fly had been aroused by visiting 'Cobham's Flying Circus'.

Partly as a means of keeping his NAD staff active during the winter months he started serious experiments with in-flight refuelling in 1932 in order to make a non-stop flight to Australia in 1934. The aircraft to be

An Airspeed Courier G ABXN refuelling from a Handley Page W10 airliner, 1934 (courtesy of Flight Refuelling Ltd).

employed was the purpose-designed Airspeed Courier. Cobham had become a founder director with Hessell Tiltman and N S Norway (later the popular novelist, Nevil Shute) of Airspeed Ltd in 1931. This company was in the forefront of aircraft design for nearly ten years but, owing to the Government's restrictive policies on military aircraft procurement, it was never able to secure valuable fighter contracts. As a result it was in constant financial difficulties.

Following his abortive non-stop flight to India in 1934 and the demise of Cobham Air Routes, established to provide services between the South Coast and Guernsey, Cobham decided to devote most of his considerable energies to the further development of in-flight refuelling for civil applications. With the prospect of backing from Imperial Airways (provided in 1935) and Air Ministry contracts, he founded Flight Refuelling Ltd in 1934. In-flight refuelling was a method of overcoming the poor range, payload and take-off performance and safety of contemporary aircraft to give them economically viable transatlantic performance. In 1937 Imperial Airways sold their interest to Shell as it was thought inappropriate for a company which would sell refuelling services to airlines to be owned by one of those airlines. Cobham was retained as managing director. Despite successful transatlantic flight-refuelled trials before and after the war, by variants of the looped-hose system, opposition from airline pilots and improvements in aircraft performance stopped its civil adoption.

During the Second World War Flight Refuelling was employed by the Ministry of Aircraft Production on research and development including materials' testing, wing de-icing, the towing of fighters, the prototype installation for the Telecommunications Research Establishment of RAF radars and electronic warfare equipment and, towards the end of the war, the manufacture of in-flight refuelling equipment for the 1,250 aircraft of the Far East Tiger Force (a project subsequently cancelled). It was one of Cobham's greatest regrets that use was never made of in-flight refuelling for long-range patrols during the Battle of the Atlantic, a measure which would have closed the mid-ocean gap that aircraft could not reach. Airspeed, the other company Cobham was associated with, undertook the mass production of the Oxford trainer during the war.

After the war Flight Refuelling existed on Ministry of Civil Aviation and minor Air Ministry contracts and in 1948 Shell sold their controlling interest to Cobham for the original purchase price. At this stage Flight Refuelling Ltd nearly collapsed. It was saved only by a contract from the United States Air Force for looped-hose equipment for their strategic nuclear bombers and the Berlin Airlift. The USAF's order for bomber refuelling resulted in the development of the highly successful probe and drogue method. During the Airlift of 1948-49 the company carried 26,091 short tons of liquid fuel into Berlin. However Cobham needed a new backer to support his plans for an American company, Flight Refuelling Inc, to manufacture equipment for the USAF and US Navy. The merchant bankers Robert Benson Lonsdale (later Kleinwort Benson) took control of the company in 1949 and held a 51 per cent interest until 1953. Then, chafing under what had been the necessary restrictions of control by bankers, Cobham bought the company back, shortly afterwards converting it, with the help of Robert Benson Lonsdale, into a publicly quoted company by using the defunct Manitoba & North West Lands Corporation as a shell. Thereafter, as Flight Refuelling (Holdings) Ltd, the company continued developing very healthily, winning Air Ministry and Royal Navy contracts for in-flight refuelling equipment for V-Bombers, fighter aircraft and helicopters. Unfortunately, the security regulations in force in America in the 1950s concerning foreign ownership of strategic defence contractors forced Flight Refuelling to sell a majority holding in their American subsidiary, the Rockefeller Group acquiring the relevant stock. From the mid-1950s the company diversified, undertaking the design and manufacture of aerospace components, drone aircraft, nuclear engineering and, in the 1960s, fuel filtration and electronic switching. Sir Alan Cobham resigned as managing director in 1964 but continued as chairman until 1969 when he was elected life president.

Outside business Cobham had numerous cultural and charitable interests. He invested in property in the British Virgin Islands, was chairman of the Air Transport section of the London Chamber of Commerce and was Master of the Guild of Air Pilots and Navigators, 1964-65. He was chairman of the Western Orchestral Society (Bournemouth Symphony Orchestra) and did much to save it from financial ruin in the late 1950s. He was also an avid film maker, broadcaster and journalist, particularly before the Second World War. Although his reputation was made as a pilot, his greatest gifts were as an energetic leader of men and as a propagandist.

He married in 1922 Gladys Marie née Lloyd (d 1961), daughter of William Lloyd, a bayonet manufacturer; she played a very active part in all his business activities, and provided a strong element of domestic stability and a sense of fun which helped to moderate his enthusiasms.

Sir Alan Cobham died on 21 October 1973 and was survived by his two sons Geoffrey and Michael; the latter succeeded his father. He left an estate valued at £81,899 gross in England and $US 1,200,680 in the British Virgin Islands.

CHRIS FARQUHARSON-ROBERTS

Writings:

Skyways (Nisbet & Co, 1925).

My Flight to the Cape and Back (A & C Black, 1926).

Australia and Back (A & C Black, 1926).

Twenty Thousand Miles in a Flying Boat: My Flight Round Africa (G G Harrap & Co, 1930).

'Refuelling in the Air' *The Aeroplane* 10 Oct 1934.

'Something Attempted, Something Done' *Flight* 11 Oct 1934.

(ed Sir Alan Cobham, written by R S Lyons) *Sir Alan Cobham's Book of the Air* (Blackie & Sons, 1938).

'The Atlantic Service Refuelled' *Flight* 2 Nov 1939.

(with M Langley) 'The History and Progress of Refuelling in Flight' *Journal of the Royal Aeronautical Society* July 1940.

(et al) *Tight Corners, Tales of Adventure of Land, Sea and in the Air* (George Allen & Unwin, 1940).

'Refuelling in Flight' *Interavia* 2 May 1947.

'North Atlantic Refuelling Trials' *Flight* 15 Apr 1948.

Aviation 1916-1966 (Royal Aeronautical Society, Centenary symposium of the Graduates' and Students' Section, 15-16 July 1966).

(ed Christopher Derrick) *A Time to Fly, Sir Alan Cobham's Autobiography* (Shepheard-Walwyn, 1978).

Films and Television:

With Cobham to the Cape (1926).

Flight Commander (1927).

With Cobham to Kivu (1932).

The Flying Years (BBC Television 1960).

Sources:

Unpublished

Flight Refuelling Ltd, Wimborne, Dorset, Cobham Archives.

National Film Archives.

British Patents: 21 Feb 1938 (480,276), 30 July 1952 (676,430).

BCe.

MCe.

PrC.

Published

Aubrey J Jackson, *De Havilland Aircraft since 1915* (Putnam, 1962).

Cecil Hugh Latimer Needham, 'Flight Refuelling in the Future' *Shell Aviation News* Nov 1947.

—, 'Flight Refuelling and the Problem of Range' *Journal of the Royal Aeronautical Society* 54 (1950).

—, *Refuelling in Flight* (Sir Isaac Pitman, 1950).

—, 'Refuelling in Flight by the Probe and Drogue Method' *Engineering* 27 Apr 1951.

Norman Macmillan, 'Flight Refuelling, Its Development and Current Uses' *Journal of the Royal United Services Institute* 100 (1955).

Nevil S Norway (Nevil Shute), *Round the Bend* (W Heinemann, 1951). This work of fiction paints a very fine picture of the life and routine of the National Aviation Day tours of the early 1930s.

—, *Slide Rule: The Autobiography of an Engineer* (Heinemann, 1954).

Harold A Taylor, *Airspeed Aircraft since 1931* (Putnam, 1970).

Times 22 Oct 1973, 2 June 1975.

'Twenty-One Years of Flight Refuelling' *Flight* 23 Dec 1955, and passim.

WWW.

COCHRAN, Sir Charles Blake

(1872-1951)

Theatrical entrepreneur and showman

Charles Blake Cochran was born in Brighton on 25 September 1872. He was the son of a tea-merchant, James Elphinstone Cochran and of Matilda Walton, the daughter of a merchant-navy officer, who had been married before. The Cochrans had nine children; Charles was the fourth child and eldest son. He was educated at Upperton College, Eastbourne, from which he was expelled for sneaking out to see a fireworks display (his love of spectacle, it seems, was already developing) and then at Brighton Grammar School. When Charles was sixteen, his father had to sell his

Sir Charles B Cochran. Pencil sketch by Powys Evans (courtesy of the National Portrait Gallery, London).

business to pay his gambling debts, and Charles and his elder sisters had to earn their own living.

The surveyor's office in which he began his working life was not to his taste, but an attempt to find an alternative career as a music-hall comedian resulted in his being booed off the stage at Dover on his first appearance at the age of eighteen. In December 1890, after some escapade whose details he never revealed in later life, Cochran ran away to America. He scraped a living acting small parts with touring companies until he caught the eye of the actor-manager, Richard Mansfield, who detected Cochran's abilities as an organiser and made him his private secretary. This association gave him invaluable experience and contacts, but a quarrel resulted in Cochran leaving Mansfield, first to try his hand as a partner in a school of acting in New York, and then bringing out his first production, of *John Gabriel Borkman* by Ibsen. This was not a success and that year, 1897, he returned home to London, now earning his living as a journalist and theatre critic. After a brief period in America working for Mansfield again, he came to London once more and refused to return when Mansfield summoned him back.

Cochran set up in Chancery Lane as a theatrical agent, and gradually began to achieve success as a promoter of boxing and wrestling matches and of concerts. It was as the promoter of Houdini, the great 'escapist', and of the wrestler Hackenschmidt that he first made his name. His first two attempts at theatrical production in London flopped and bankrupted him in 1903. Hackenschmidt rescued him by guaranteeing his creditors £15 a week until the debts were paid off and Cochran was soon discharged from bankruptcy.

In the years before the First World War, Cochran promoted a wide range of entertainments, from roller-skating to circuses, while continuing to promote boxing and wrestling. In 1911 he brought to the Olympia Max Reinhardt's extraordinary production *The Miracle*, a theatrical and musical extravaganza with a religious theme which represented Cochran's real beginning as a 'showman' (an epithet of which he was very proud), no longer merely giving the public what they wanted, but what he felt they ought to have.

The First World War brought a great demand for bright and lively entertainment and Cochran produced a series of successful reviews; the first, *Odds and Ends*, ran for nearly 500 nights, and brought Cochran £500 a week profit. Among the other attractions he promoted during the war was Horatio Bottomley (qv), in his guise as patriotic orator.

After the war, he began promoting boxing matches at the Holborn Stadium (his first promotion there in 1919 brought Cochran a personal profit of £2,500) and at Olympia. Usually, each fight made several thousand pounds for him. In 1924 he presented a rodeo at the British Empire Exhibition at Wembley which, he claimed, saved the exhibition from threatened financial failure, by raising the average daily attendance from 60,000 to 200,000. However, the rodeo itself just about broke even.

His theatrical productions in the years after the war (mostly in London though some shows were also put on in New York) were many and various. The best-known were probably a series of reviews, particularly those put on at the London Pavilion from 1918 to 1931. On balance his gains outweighed his losses. He also began to bring over to England famous artists and companies from abroad. Though they gave him great personal satisfaction, most of these productions resulted in a financial loss to him: a ten-week season of the Russian ballet of Stravinsky and Diaghilev, for example, lost £5,000. Much more serious losses were incurred by Cochran's remodelling of a London theatre, the New Oxford Music Hall. An earlier venture, the redecoration of the London Pavilion in 1918, had been a great financial success, enabling London Pavilion Ltd, of which he became chairman and managing director, to show a profit of over £12,000 on the year, after the cost of decoration and improvements. His productions at the New Oxford had enabled the owners to declare a 31 per cent dividend for three years, to pay off £33,000 of debt and to spend £10,000 on renovations. This success proved his undoing. Cochran agreed to lease the theatre for a long period at a fixed sum which would guarantee the shareholders a regular 10 per cent, and on condition that he spent a large sum on improvements. But while he had planned to spend £25,000, in the event the reconstruction cost over £80,000 as well as involving repeated postponements which cost £400 a night in lost receipts; his total losses on this venture rose to £98,000. These expenses, combined with some heavy losses on shows, brought his financial affairs to a crisis which the Wembley rodeo failed to resolve as he had hoped. In January 1925 he became bankrupt for the second time, with liabilities of £109,284 and assets of £2,316.

But Cochran had a great reputation and many friends. He was invited by Montague Gluckstein (qv) of Lyons & Co to manage the cabaret at the Trocadero club for £50 a week. He wrote a volume of memoirs which earned him some useful royalties (he only ever turned to writing when his finances were at a low ebb). Backers were still willing to give him money, and artists to join his productions, and he was soon back in his stride. In 1925, the very year of his bankruptcy, he began a long and fruitful collaboration with Noel Coward with the review *On With The Dance* and, continuing to champion the work of serious playwrights, he also presented a season of Pirandello.

Cochran's activity as a major sports promoter virtually ended in 1927, after he lost over £15,000 on a World Championship boxing match. He had already become rather disenchanted with the shadier aspects of boxing promotion and the unreliability of many fighters and their managers, and henceforth he largely confined his activities to the theatre. Another milestone for Cochran in 1927 was his appointment as manager of the Royal Albert Hall in July. He was proud of the appointment, but because of the traditions restricting the use of the Hall, it was an all but impossible business proposition. Legislation was necessary to ease some of these restrictions, particularly the problem of 1,300 proprietary seats (reserved for their owners), and after the introduction of a Royal Albert Hall Bill, and the appointment of a Select Committee of the House of Lords, to which Cochran gave evidence, a supplemental charter was granted. This did not free Cochran's hand as much as he would have liked in choosing the sort of entertainment he wished to put on there, but it did do something to help the finances of the Hall. The shows he put on ranged from classical concerts to Charleston Balls, and, breaking his own resolution to have done with boxing promotion for good, a little boxing. He served two five-year terms as manager of the Hall before resigning; his memoirs do not reveal how successful he had been in restoring its ailing finances.

In the mid-1930s, Cochran's fortunes began to wane. His ten-year partnership with Coward, which had brought such shows as *Private Lives* and *Cavalcade* to the stage, ended. He seemed to have lost his touch in the choice of theatrical material. Audiences were in any case less plentiful in the 1930s, and there was increasing competition from the cinema. From 1932 entertainment taxes became a serious burden; Cochran had to pay £13,000 tax on one production alone, a revival of *The Miracle* that actually lost £17,000. The effect of these taxes on the British theatre in general can be gauged from the fall in the number of touring companies in the United Kingdom from 184 in 1932 to 37 in 1933.

Moreover, Cochran was ill, with an arthritic hip, and often in considerable pain. The efforts of Equity, the actors' union, to impose standard contracts for their members on theatre managements angered and upset him. He had always paid all those who worked for him well, but he liked freedom to negotiate. Without that freedom much of his pleasure in organising shows and dealing with his artists would be lost. In 1935, when Equity organised a campaign against him, he even declared he would abandon all his theatrical ventures.

During the Second World War the withdrawal of the Trocadero Cabaret, which he had managed since 1925, ended his last regular source of income. He and his wife were now living in a small flat, and the fine collection of Impressionist paintings he had built up had been sold to finance a show in the late 1930s. There was little he could do during the war to recover his position. He produced a series of broadcasts, *Cock-a-Doodle-Doo* (the title was based on his nickname 'Cockie', though he preferred to be known as 'CB'), for the BBC in the summer of 1940. He also ran a successful provincial tour with a review called *Lights Up*, and organised various entertainments for charities or the troops.

In 1946, with money raised for a film of his life, which was in fact never made, he put on a musical show, *Big Ben*. Cochran himself was too ill to attend the opening night: he had an operation for the removal of a kidney the following day. While recovering from this, and encouraged by the success of *Big Ben*, which ran for five months, he planned perhaps the biggest success of his career. The musical *Bless the Bride* played for two and a half years in London, and four years later was still playing to capacity audiences in the provinces. Cochran became bored with the London show, and took it off while it was still going well. But then followed a couple of failures, including his last show, *Ivory Towers*, which ran for only eight nights. To help finance it, Cochran formed a company, Cochran Productions Ltd, with a nominal capital of £5,250.

He was acknowledged to have a good visual sense, and a good ear for music, but some felt his sense of humour was less well-developed. Cochran openly admired beautiful young women, but there was no scandal in his relations with them. Indeed he much enjoyed the company of all the many varieties of performers who worked for him, and they liked and trusted him. He was invariably courteous, never swore, and was said to have only lost his temper twice in his life. Cochran never set out to make a personal fortune, nor did he draw any lessons from his father's financial failure. He was generous to all who worked for him and spared no expense in bringing his entertainments before the public. His ambition was to be known as the most artistic producer of all time, and it was his skills as an entertainer, not as a businessman, that made his reputation as *the* 'showman'. He was knighted in 1948 for his services to the theatre.

His wife, with whom he eloped in 1903, was Evelyn née Dade, daughter of a merchant navy captain; she brought him a long and happy marriage, not least perhaps because she was a noted wit.

Sir Charles Cochran was planning several new productions when he had a fatal accident, being terribly scalded in his bath because he was too crippled by arthritis to be able to turn off the hot tap. He died in hospital on 31 January 1951, leaving an estate proved at £22,921 gross.

CHRISTINE SHAW

Writings:

Secrets of a Showman (William Heinemann, 1925).

(ed) *Review of Revues, and Other Matters* (Jonathan Cape, 1930).

I Had Almost Forgotten (Hutchinson & Co, 1932).

Cock-a-Doodle-Do (J M Dent, 1941).

Showman Looks On (J M Dent, 1945).

Sources:

Unpublished

PrC.

Published

DNB.

Vivian Ellis, *I'm on a See-Saw* (Michael Joseph, 1953).

Charles Graves, *The Cochran Story: A Biography of Sir Charles Blake Cochran, Kt* (W H Allen, 1951).

Sheridan Morley, *A Talent to Amuse: a Biography of Noel Coward* (Heinemann, 1969).

The Oxford Companion to the Theatre, ed Phyllis Hartnoll (3rd ed, Oxford University Press, 1967).

Times 1 Feb 1951.

WWW.

WWW Theatre.

COCHRANE, Sir Henry

(1836-1904)

Mineral water manufacturer

Henry Cochrane was born in Virginia, County Cavan, Ireland in 1836. His father William Cochrane, was a farmer and a member of the Church of Ireland. After a rudimentary education Henry worked first in a Belfast linen mill and then as a shop assistant. In the 1850s he moved to Dublin where he was fortunate enough to be employed by James Weir, a Scotsman who, starting with very little, entered the wine and spirit trade and made a considerable fortune, leaving £100,000 to charity. Cochrane gained promotion under Weir and subsequently joined the whiskey-blending firm of Kinahans.

The decisive moment in his career came in 1867 when he responded to a newspaper advertisement placed by Thomas Cantrell (fl 1820-84), an apothecary who had manufactured aerated water in Belfast since 1852. It was to prove something of an irony that someone trained in the liquor trade should make his fortune out of one of the drinks favoured by the temperance movement. Cantrell and Cochrane formed a partnership, and with the injection of the latter's capital, a new artesian well, costing £2,000, was sunk in Belfast to take advantage of the fine natural spring water the city possessed. In 1869 the firm established a branch in Dublin where Cochrane took up residence, and in 1885 after Cantrell's death he became sole proprietor in the business. The late nineteenth century was a favourable period for the growth in the mineral water trade. Incomes were rising and, partly under the influence of the temperance movement, alcohol consumption was falling. By the late 1880s the firm had 500 employees; using Riley bottling machines it produced over 160,000 bottles of table waters a day. 'C&C', as they subsequently became known, achieved a world-wide reputation for soda waters, ginger ales (which the firm claimed to have invented) and 'Sparkling Montserrat', 'the drink par excellence for the gouty and rheumatic' {*Industries of Ireland* (1891) 81}. In 1889 the firm won a medal at the prestigious 'Paris Exposition Universelle'. On Cochrane's death in 1904, the business became a limited liability company capitalised at £200,000. By this time C&C were the largest of the 25 mineral water manufacturers in Belfast.

From the 1880s Cochrane used his wealth to advance his political and social ambitions. He became an alderman of the City of Dublin and in 1887 was knighted by Queen Victoria on her visit to the city. He became the High Sheriff for Wicklow (1897) and then Cavan (1900), a JP for three Irish counties, and DL for the City of Dublin.

In 1892, in an attempt to take advantage of a split between Parnellite and anti-Parnellite nationalists, Cochrane stood for Parliament in the College Green division of Dublin, but was beaten into third place. He was also an active freemason, and a member of the Grand Lodge of Ireland. In 1903 following a lavish gift of £5,000 to Sir Horace Plunkett's Irish Agricultural

Organisation Society, Cochrane became a baronet. It was rumoured that the two events were not unconnected.

Cochrane in 1865 married Margaret Gilchrist, by whom he had two sons and two daughters. He was succeeded as chairman of the company by his elder son, Ernest, who later achieved more fame as a playwright than as an entrepreneur. In 1923, the firm was acquired by E J Burke Ltd, whiskey exporters and bottlers of Guinness stout. The Dublin part of the business was sold in 1927 to a consortium, Mineral Distributors Ltd. Today, although 'C&C' products are still marketed under the old brand name throughout Britain and Ireland, the ownership of the company is dispersed.

Sir Henry Cochrane died on 11 September 1904 leaving £47,358 gross.

DAVID JOHNSON

Sources:

Unpublished

PrC.

Cantrell & Cochrane, 'The Story of Cantrell and Cochrane' (nd, Belfast).

Published

Belfast Newsletter 12 Sept 1904.

Freeman's Journal 12 Sept 1904.

The Industries of Ireland: Part I, Belfast and the Towns of the North (Historical Publishing Co, 1891).

Irish Times 12 Sept 1904.

Northern Whig 12 Sept 1904.

PP, *HC* 1905 (244) LXXIII, Return of Joint Stock Companies and Limited Liability Companies in ... the City of Dublin.

COCKSHUT, John

(1837-1912)

Wallpaper manufacturer

John Cockshut was born at Tong with Haulgh, near Bolton, on 4 November 1837, the son of John Cockshut, a plumber and glazier, and his wife Alice née Bromiley. It is not known where he was educated, if indeed he had any formal schooling at all. He began work when he was about eight years old at Potters wallpaper mill in Darwen. After a few years he went to a cotton mill but then returned to Potters, where he was joined by his brother, James.

When Cockshut was about twenty, he and his brother moved to the wallpaper mill belonging to their uncle, Henry Lightbown, at Pendleton, Lancashire. Lightbown's firm, Lightbown, Aspinall & Co (Aspinall had sold out in the early days of the firm) had grown rapidly from a small block-printing shop opened in 1851, as he turned from the production of block-printed wallpaper to the manufacture of machine-made paper. The adaptation of machinery for printing wallpaper, pioneered by the Potters of Darwen, made it possible to produce wallpaper much more cheaply, and enabled the manufacturers to supply a much wider market than before.

While James was a dedicated and talented designer, John was an equally dedicated and talented salesman. Lightbown himself perfected several devices to improve the manufacture of wallpaper, including one for registering the lengths of wallpaper pieces prior to final packaging, which he patented in 1871, and which was still in general use fifty years later. Business grew rapidly under the stimulus of this useful combination of family talents, and warehouses were opened in Manchester, Leeds, Glasgow, Leipzig and London. John Cockshut was the first manager of the London warehouse in Cannon Street, from which he built up a large export trade. From his base in London he continued to supply his brother with suggestions and collaborate with him on new designs.

In 1880-81 the brothers were responsible for a very successful innovation in their uncle's business. Wallpaper production was largely divided between cheap goods produced by machine, and hand-printed paper, much of it imported from the Continent. The brothers saw an opening for a new, machine-made range of intermediate quality and cost. Their new, medium-grade, 'Early English' style, was printed on superfine paper and had a distinctive embossed finish, new to wallpaper. A French firm, Corbière, challenged their right to some of the production methods, and began legal proceedings, but the lawsuit was settled by a compromise entailing the withdrawal of certain designs, and gave the new venture considerable publicity throughout the trade. A new factory, with additional, larger printing machines was required to cope with demand, and the continuing success of the 'Early English' range encouraged Lightbown to introduce finer grades and designs in machine and hand printed papers. Lightbown, Aspinall also laid claim to the introduction of multi-colour printing in 'sanitary' (that is, washable) wallpapers in 1884, but other firms were working on the development of similar processes and brought out coloured 'sanitaries' at much the same time.

The Cockshut brothers left Lightbown in 1888, when they bought John Allan & Sons, an old wallpaper firm with a factory at Old Ford in London. The name of the firm was changed to Allan, Cockshut & Co. Determined on expansion, the Cockshuts began building a greatly enlarged mill, nearly 400 feet long, including warehouses and a fireproof basement for the storage of print rollers. A 'sanitary' machine-room was added later which took over the printing of designs on those goods which under Allan had been put out to other mills. The quality of the papers produced was considerably improved, and Allan, Cockshut became known for the high quality of their products. Soon it became the most serious competitor of the largest wallpaper manufacturers, Potters of Darwen. The staff of the mill grew from 140 in 1888 to 600 a few years later. Relations with their employees were always good, and John Cockshut had a gift for picking capable staff. He directed the commercial side of the business, attaching great importance to the personal connections his salesmen established with their customers. One of the best salesmen was his son Harry, who ranged as far as Australia and New Zealand in his quest for new business.

In 1896 the Cockshuts bought up the rights to manufacture a raised material, Lignomur, an American product which had been manufactured in England at Shepherds Bush, with mixed success at best, since about 1892. Production was moved to Old Ford in 1897, and the Cockshuts, with the experience gained from the production of Lignomur, began to diversify into manufacturing their own raised paper for wall and ceiling decoration.

Allan, Cockshut was one of the 31 wallpaper firms that amalgamated to form Wallpaper Manufacturers in 1900. Including three other houses with which the new company had working agreements, it was said to conduct 98 per cent of the wallpaper trade in Britain. All the ordinary and deferred shares went to the vendors, for a total purchase price of £4.2 million; they were also to hold one-third of the preference and debenture stock. WPM was one of the largest firms in the British economy, ranking within the top thirty by capital (£14.14 million) and the top hundred by employment (3,400 in 1903). John Cockshut took a very active part in the formation of WPM, together with the first chairman of the company, W B Huntington. John, James and Henry Cockshut all joined the board, and John Cockshut served as chairman in 1901-3. He emphasised the need to use the resources of the company to strengthen its position, rather than to pay large dividends to the holders of ordinary and deferred shares, and argued that the savings from combination should permit WPM to sell at prices which would be profitable for their company, but with which other manufacturers could not compete. He also stressed that these advantages should benefit the merchants and customers as well as the shareholders.

The death of his brother James in 1905 was followed by another severe personal blow for Cockshut, the death of his only son Harry in 1909. He continued to direct the Ford business, aided by James's sons Cheetham and Percy, but after Harry's death he lost much of his former striking vigour.

Both John and James Cockshut had been dedicated to the manufacture of wallpaper, finding in it their hobby as well as their work. They also shared a passion for old prints, engravings and china. John's reputation as a collector stood particularly high; his collection was shown at the Franco-British exhibition at the White City in 1908, a considerable honour for a private collector and specimens from his collection were also exhibited abroad. He was an active Presbyterian, generous in his charitable donations to his local church at Willesden and to individuals. He was appointed a JP in 1895.

His first wife was Alice Cheetham, whom he married before 1865; his second wife Leah survived him. There were five daughters, as well as the son Harry, of these marriages. Cockshut died on 11 November 1912, leaving an estate proved at £149,705 gross.

CHRISTINE SHAW

Sources:

Unpublished

BLPES, Tariff Commission papers, TC4 35/1, TC4 34/8.

SSRC Elites data.

BCe.

PrC.

Published

Henry W Macrosty, *The Trust Movement in British Industry* (Longmans, 1907).

Alan Sugden and John Edmondson, *A History of English Wallpaper 1509-1914* (Batsford, 1926).

Statist 24 Feb 1900, 30 Nov 1901, 20 Nov 1902.
Times 13 Nov 1912.

Willesden Citizen 15 Nov 1912.

World's Paper Trade Review 22 Nov 1912.

COHEN, Sir John Edward

(1898-1979)

Retail entrepreneur and pioneer of self-service stores

John Edward Cohen (he changed his name by deed poll from Jacob Kohen in 1937) was born at St George-in-the-East, London, on 6 October 1898, the second son (among six children) of an East End journeyman tailor and immigrant Polish Jew, Avroam Kohen (who could not write English at the time his second son was born), by his first wife Sime née Garinda. Until he was fourteen Jack, as he was known, attended the local London County Council Elementary School in Rutland Street in the St George-in-the-East

Sir John E Cohen (courtesy of the Tesco Group of Companies).

district, and then dutifully joined his father. Though he became especially adept on a Singer buttonholing machine, he found the work irksome. After his mother's death in 1915 and the ensuing conflicts between stepmother and children, Jack seized the earliest opportunity to escape from home. He joined the Royal Flying Corps, which employed his tailoring skills on balloon and aircraft canvas, and then served in the Middle East, being almost drowned when his troop carrier was sunk off Alexandria. In this period also he had a nose operation which left him with the distinctive features of a pugilist.

Jack Cohen returned to London in March 1919, demobilised early because of malarial infection, with a weekly medical pension of 6s 8d and a £30 demobilisation gratuity. Unable to find an office job in the City and determined to avoid tailoring, he turned to street trading, influenced by the example of a brother-in-law. He went to wholesalers and importers in Eastcheap and invested his £30 in surplus NAAFI foodstuffs, chiefly paste, syrup and condensed milk. On his first day, in spring 1919, he sold £4 worth of goods and made £1 profit. At his coster's stall Cohen soon discovered his natural abilities for selling: self-confidence and cheek, good humour, persuasiveness and a loud voice. Within a few months he added an old ambulance to his barrow and later rented a warehouse under railway arches in Upper Clapton Road.

On 29 January 1924 (when his occupation was recorded as grocery salesman) he married in South Hackney synagogue Sarah ('Cissie') Fox, daughter of Benjamin Fox, a master tailor and immigrant Russian Jew. His wife brought him not only a dowry of £500 (added to £130 of cash as wedding presents), but a partner of independent spirit who supported his business ambitions. Together they agreed that Jack should set up as a wholesaler. His first attempt, an investment in several tons of soap, collapsed when selling agents absconded with his soap. Despite the loss of his £130, Jack searched for new lines and found a winner in tea. With his supplier, Mr T E Stockwell of Torring & Stockwell of Mincing Lane, he coined the brand name formed from Stockwell's initials and his own surname: Tesco.

While he edged into wholesaling, Cohen remained essentially a street trader throughout the 1920s. He and his wife's two teenage brothers went round the morning markets of Hammersmith, Hackney and Bermondsey and the Caledonian Cattle Market (where he paid the local authority 2s for his stand and took as much as £100 a day). On a Saturday he went south to the Croydon market. Afternoons were spent on the wholesaling side, searching and negotiating for goods. The main obstacles to expansion, until he stopped giving credit in 1925, were unreliable market traders. When the application of the London County Council Powers Act of 1927 prevented Jack from retaining his Monday pitch at Hammersmith he moved further into wholesaling. In 1929 his turnover was about £23,000: he relied heavily on cash transactions, keeping no account books.

From his accounting chaos Cohen was rescued in 1930 when he recruited Arthur Albert Carpenter, a City clerk. Carpenter's work in the business office released Cohen to buy more expansively. One purchase, of 100,000 cases of Snowflake milk (from Amalgamated Dairies), lifted his turnover to over £50,000 in 1930. He acquired a van and two trucks and to his market stalls and warehouse added a stand in a new arcade in Tooting, close to the spreading estates at Merton. He operated this permanent stand in partnership with another market trader who took Cohen's stock on a credit arrangement, auctioned it from the stand and divided the profits with Jack. Soon he secured two more shops as outlets for his wholesale goods, both run by members of his wife's family. Noticeably Jack Cohen was trying to transfer street market vending techniques to the new shopping arcades around London. The first store under the Tesco name opened at Watling Avenue, Burnt Oak in 1931, immediately followed by one at Green Lanes, Becontree. At this time Daisy Hyams joined him as secretary and general assistant. With four shops, and on the advice of his solicitor, he formed two private companies, Tesco Stores Ltd (registered 28 January 1932), to run the stores, and J E Cohen & Co Ltd (registered 24 January 1933), to operate the wholesaling and property aspects of the business. At the same time Cohen recruited Thomas Edward Freake, a traditional grocer, as his first retail lieutenant; Freake balanced Jack's vision and impetuosity with attention to detail and restraint. Under Freake's guidance Cohen abandoned the auctioneering technique of selling cut-price goods and instead piled them in two pyramids on a counter open to the street, being protected by roller shutters rather than plate glass. Cohen moved his base from the Upper Clapton Road to a new central warehouse off the North Circular Road at Edmonton, in 1935. By 1939 Tesco had a hundred stores in the London area when net profits for the two companies were £12,600 (J E Cohen & Co. Ltd) and £19,000 (Tesco Stores Ltd).

During the Second World War Jack Cohen responded to food shortages by moving into farming, buying a market-garden at Cheshunt and then

Exterior of an early Tesco store (courtesy of the Tesco Group of Companies).

Interior of an early Tesco store (courtesy of the Tesco Group of Companies).

two farms at Goldhanger on the Essex coast, where he set up a modest jam factory.

New directions for Tesco's expansion followed Jack Cohen's visit to the United States in 1947. The practice of self-service trading, which he had first observed on a visit there in 1935, was now sweeping the American retail trade: gleaming, low-cost and large scale premises; slashed prices; customer-selection from shelved goods removed with the aid of trolleys; payment at turnstile exits; and loud publicity for bargains on offer: in a word, the supermarket. When he returned to England, however, he discovered that American methods were obstructed by food shortages, rationing, building restrictions and lack of co-ordination between manufacturer and wholesaler. Despite this Cohen prepared for expansion, resting his hopes on a strategy of low prices and low profit margins on high volume sales, which self-service promised. His first experiment in self-service, at St. Albans in 1947, was premature, for rationing choked demand. Undeterred, he formed a public holding company, Tesco Stores (Holdings) Ltd, in 1947 to take over his two operating subsidiaries (with a combined nominal capital of £11,425 and assets of £295,537); his holding company's capital of £300,000 was divided into 5s ordinary shares which were offered to the market at 15s a share. When the company went public in 1946, net profits were estimated at £64,840, compared to £50,885 in 1939 and £28,183 in 1937. Cohen brought his son-in-law Hyman Kreitman on to the board as executive director. Freake served as assistant managing director but, unhappy with the ascendancy of Kreitman, left Tesco in 1950 and set up on his own.

In 1949 the St. Albans shop resumed its self-service character and by the end of 1950 Tesco had 20 self-service units. After the Conservative

Government dismantled controls and rationing in 1953 a fast cash-trade quickly developed. The company spread from Greater London to Bristol, Reading, and Maldon. In 1959 the headquarters offices and warehouse facilities were moved to Cheshunt to serve the group's 185 stores (over 140 of which were self-service), and drapery and household goods were soon added to food sales. A new technique, the loss-leader (a cut price item to attract customers), was adopted. Net profits, which moved up from £78,000 in 1952 to £947,000 in 1959, evidenced Cohen's successful expansion of Tesco.

A personal setback Jack Cohen kept secret was a colostomy operation which he had in 1958. Two months later 'Jack the Slasher' was back in business, nagging his subordinates, dropping in on store managers and negotiating the bulk purchase of Golden Circle canned pineapples. And he came back to mount the major campaign of his career: the battle against resale price maintenance.

RPM effectively held back supermarket sales by inhibiting price-cutting. While manufacturers served injunctions on retailers, Jack Cohen advertised manufacturers' profit margins on list prices and continued to cut where he could. RPM finally crumbled in the trading stamp war of the early 1960s. After the Fine Fare supermarket chain owned by Garfield Weston (qv) adopted the pink trading stamps of the American company, Sperry & Hutchinson, and other supermarkets followed, the Tesco board took action. In October 1963 Cohen clinched a deal with Green Shield Trading Stamp Co, set up by Granville Richard Tompkins. Tesco's rivals united in the Distributive Trades Alliance, mobilised by Lord Sainsbury (qv), against trading stamps; then suppliers, like Imperial Tobacco and the Distillers' Co, stepped in. A tangle of litigation built up. Eventually, early in 1964, the Heath Government intervened, bringing in a bill to abolish RPM. Cohen hastened the demise of the system which lingered in food retailing by defiantly price-cutting at every opportunity, until 1967 when the Restrictive Practices Court pronounced against the big five sweet manufacturers.

The abolition of RPM permitted new expansion for Tesco. Cheshunt became the centre of a network of warehouses and packing stations from which a fleet of lorries supplied a growing number of supermarkets. Efficient stock control allowed the sale of goods before they were paid for, so that Jack Cohen's capital soon turned over twenty times a year, earning 3 per cent each time.

Financed by increases in the company's capitalisation, which rose from £2 million in 1960 to £14 million in 1968, the 1960s saw growth by takeover. It began with the takeover of John Irwin, Sons & Co, a chain of 212 traditional grocery stores in Lancashire, Cheshire and North Wales, purchased in 1960 for £1,127,000 and 1.5 million Tesco shares. This took Tesco into the North of England. Meantime Cohen faced internal problems at board level. Hyman Kreitman, his cool and dependable lieutenant, resigned from the post of joint managing director. Then in 1963 Jack stepped down as managing director of the Tesco holding company, brought Kreitman back to the top position and simultaneously elevated his other son-in-law Leslie Porter (recruited in 1960 to develop non-food products) as assistant managing director. At last the succession was secured.

Between them Cohen, Kreitman and Porter steered the company through the 'Great Trading Stamp War' and then a series of takeovers culminating in 1968 with the absorption of Tesco's major rival, Victor Value (by an exchange of shares which valued the addition at £8.5 million). The merger gave Tesco a total of 834 self-service stores placing it fourth in size behind the Co-op, Fine Fare and Allied Suppliers. Tesco's turnover in the takeover decade 1961-70 dramatically increased from £21.4 million to £238.4 million and its net profits mounted in proportion from £607,000 to £6,657,000.

Jack Cohen was knighted for services to retailing in 1969. When he retired from the chairmanship of Tesco the following year, assuming the title of Life President (being succeeded as chairman by Kreitman), his company had a stock market value of £120 million; he and his family held personal and trust interests in 40 million shares whose market value was put at £22 million.

As an individual Jack Cohen was outgoing but mercurial, relying on more stable partners, his wife in the home and his lieutenants in business, to absorb his moods and modulate his decision-making. Much of his emotional, as well as his economic, strength derived from the circle of his family and also from his life-long Jewish faith. He supported many charities including homes for poor and elderly Jews. He regularly visited Israel, having first been impressed by the Zionist cause when befriended by the Jews of Alexandria during the First World War. In addition, he was a freemason (attaining London Grand Rank in 1963) and a member of the Company of Carmen. He died on 24 March 1979 leaving £1,957,640 gross.

DAVID J JEREMY

Sources:

Unpublished

C Reg: Tesco Stores Ltd (262,254). Tesco (Wholesale) Ltd (272,240). Tesco Stores (Holdings) Ltd (445,790).

BCe.

MCe.

PrC.

Published

Maurice Corina, *Pile It High, Sell It Cheap. The Authorised Biography of Sir Jack Cohen, Founder of Tesco* (2nd ed, Weidenfeld & Nicolson, 1978).

Daily Telegraph 26 Mar 1979.
Times 19 Nov 1979.

Times *Prospectuses* 101 (1947).

WWW.

Lewis C Cohen, ca 1950 (courtesy of the Alliance Building Society).

COHEN, Lewis Coleman

Lord Cohen of Brighton

(1897-1966)

Building society manager

Lewis Coleman Cohen was born at Hastings on 28 March 1897, the son of Hyam Cohen, a local jeweller, and his wife Esther née Szapira. He started his education in Hastings, later moving to Brighton Grammar School. He left school at thirteen and a half to become an articled clerk with a Brighton estate agency, Reason & Tickle, and later moved to another estate agent before starting his own agency in 1920.

Cohen tried a number of commercial sidelines in the late 1920s. With a barrister friend, a Mr Gordon, he invested in a photomatic device, which yielded £11,000 profit. This was in turn invested in a device to close doors quietly, a scheme that did not prosper. He tried three more commercial opportunities in 1929. Firstly he purchased the firm of Reason & Tickle for £1,500. Secondly, with Gordon, he invested in a London theatre property, the Duchess Theatre. Thirdly he became secretary of the Brighton & Sussex Building Society, at this time a very small society with assets of only £60,000. Using £400 salvaged from the 'door closing' scheme as compensation, Cohen reorganised the building society's board, with Sir Hubert Carden as chairman. In 1931 the financial crisis led to the calling in of the mortgage on the Duchess Theatre and the forced sale left a loss of £30,000. Thereafter Cohen concentrated on property investment through the building society, the estate agency and an interest in Brabons Ltd, a firm of builders.

The Brighton & Sussex Building Society soon embarked on rapid expansion both in its own activities and by amalgamating with, or taking over the engagements of, other societies. There were six such moves in the last two years before the war and a further 11 between 1944 and 1949. In 1944 the Society changed its name, appropriately, to the Alliance; its headquarters remained in Brighton. Cohen was inspired by the example of commercial banking amalgamations in the nineteenth century but scarcely needed the warning given in 1939 by the Chief Registrar of Building Societies against amalgamations which compensated directors of the small societies taken over but which neglected the interests of their other members. From £66,000 in 1929, assets of the Alliance and its predecessor rose to £3.7 million in 1937 and £6.9 million in 1945. Assets of £100 million were reached by 1962 and they doubled again before Cohen's death in 1966. Over the period since 1945 the Alliance achieved the highest rate of growth of any British building society and became the sixth largest society. After 1950 amalgamations played no significant part in the Alliance's progress; instead there was a rapid expansion of its branch network. Cohen moved from secretary to managing director in 1933 and board chairman in 1939.

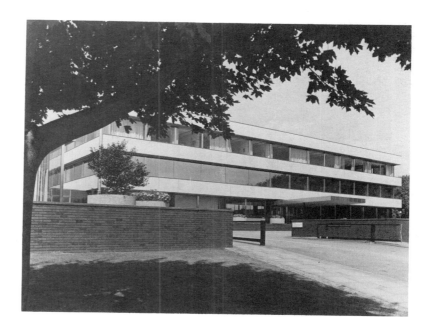

The Alliance Building Society's Head Office, Hove Park, completed in 1967, one year after the death of Lewis C Cohen (courtesy of the Alliance Building Society).

Though there were no striking innovations in any particular direction the Society pushed hard in most aspects of business. It was quick to extend the term of years for which it would lend; indeed Cohen was an advocate of linking the terms of the loan to the life of the house rather than to the life of the borrower. He quickly appreciated after 1945 that rising property values allowed the society to increase the proportion of a house's value that could safely be lent. Being prepared to make some larger loans at higher than normal interest rates, the Society was able to be fully competitive in attracting investment in a variety of shares.

Long interested in politics, Cohen joined the Labour Party in 1914, despite a strong Conservative tradition in the family that included a Brighton town commissioner (a grandfather) and two aldermen (cousins). In Brighton he was elected to the Council, at the fourth attempt, in 1930. He gave it long service, eventually as mayor (1956) and alderman (1964). Nationally he was less successful. He contested six of the seven general elections from 1931 to 1959; 1945 was the exception. He was five times unsuccessful in Brighton and once in Hastings. He was made a life peer by Harold Wilson in 1965 and made the most of what was to be a brief parliamentary career. He frequently contributed to debates, especially on housing matters. In 1965 he was appointed chairman of the Agrément Board, newly established by the Ministry of Works to certify new materials and techniques for use in the construction industry. Cohen was a respected figure in the Labour Party and persuaded it to view owner-occupation less unfavourably.

Despite the striking growth in the size of his society and the useful link he would have provided with the Labour Party, Cohen was never a member of the Building Societies Association Council. His society did not always implement the recommendations of the Association and some of the ideas he propagated did not find wide acceptance. For instance, he favoured providing societies with liquidity by creating a government agency to advance money temporarily against the deposit of mortgage deeds, thus enabling societies to reduce the resources tied up in quickly realisable securities. He also advocated lower reserves to release funds for lending, and he wanted the law altered to allow building societies to help housing associations more actively.

Among his voluntary activities he was chairman of the Brighton Housing Society, which provided rented accommodation for the aged, and of the Brighton Theatre Royal. He was council member of Sussex University where he chaired the building committee. He was a keen traveller, flying on the first of his visits to Russia in 1922; he also visited the United States, Finland, Turkey, Hungary, Israel and South Africa where he had business interests. He was a fellow of the Society of Auctioneers and Landed Property Agents, of the Corporation of Insurance Agents and of the Building Societies Institute.

The *Times* in its obituary wrote of a tall, sociable extrovert, a good speaker and talker, with a liking for public occasions, and a ready wit, devoid of rancour. He had a flair for publicity for his building society and was not embarrassed if some of the limelight fell on himself.

He married in 1939 Sonya née Lawson, by whom he had a son and two daughters. After that marriage was dissolved he married in 1961 Renee née Frieze, the widow of Leonard Bodlander.

After his early failures his business interests, as well as the building society, prospered and the *Building Societies Gazette* described his career as a progress from articled clerk at 5s a week to millionaire. His estate was valued at £130,565 gross. Something at least of the substantial gap may be explained by a trust that was created in 1941. He died in a London hospital as the result of a heart attack on 21 October 1966.

ESMOND J CLEARY

Sources:

Unpublished

BCe.

Published

Brighton and Hove Gazette 28 Oct 1966.

Brighton and Hove Herald 28 Oct 1966.

Building Societies Gazette May 1942, July, Aug 1963; June, Nov 1966.

Economist 15 Apr 1939.

Times 8, 22 Oct, 4 Nov 1966, 9 Feb 1967.

WWW.

Eric K Cole (courtesy of Gordon Bussey).

COLE, Eric Kirkham

(1901-1966)

Radio and electronic equipment manufacturer

Eric Kirkham Cole was born at Prittlewell, Southend-on-Sea, Essex on 4 July 1901, the only child of Henry Cole, a dairyman, and Alice Laura née Kirkham. After attending Southend Day Technical School he served a three-year apprenticeship to a local electrical firm and subsequently went into partnership as an electrical engineer with his father. Henry Cole retired in 1922 and Eric began trading as E Kirkham Cole from a single room in nearby Westcliff. Public broadcasting was imminent and Eric, assisted by his future wife, Muriel Bradshaw, manufactured a weekly average of six two-valve receivers. Under the name 'EKCO', these sold at £6 10s, including headphones and batteries. Batteries were expensive and the requirements of an invalid schoolteacher, William S Verrells, led Eric to devise a method of powering the radio from the mains and then to patent a mains-driven H T eliminator. Still on sale thirty years later, this proved so successful in 1924 that his business expanded whilst other small firms collapsed. Eric married Muriel in 1925 and in the same year went into partnership with Verrells who became salesman. On 22 October 1926, a private company, E K Cole Ltd was formed with an authorised capital of £2,500, with Verrells as chairman. John A Maxwell, an amusement park caterer, Henry J Manners, a local builder and estate developer, and E R Pring, a local milkman, joined the board. In 1927 a factory employing about 50 was built at Leigh-on-Sea, followed in 1930 by a yet larger one at Southend. By 1929 profits of around £30,000 were reached. A 1932 gazetteer entry lists Southend as 'Seaside Resort: Wireless factory'. E K Cole Ltd was converted to a public limited company on 25 April 1930 when it employed 1,500 people in a 100,000 square foot factory. At this point Cole and Verrells, realising the limitations of their staff (mostly local amateurs and electricians) recruited further technical staff from firms like Marconi and AEG. Their new chief engineer, John Wyborn, came from HMV.

Stamping machinery at the ECKO plastics division (courtesy of Gordon Bussey).

Three hydraulic Bakelite moulding presses were installed in 1932 and well-known designers (Wells Coates and Serge Chermayeff) developed a distinctive style of cabinet for EKCO: sets in moulded plastic with bold, rounded lines and wide, clear station-name dials became a pattern for competitors. In 1934 the firm had a turnover of £1 million. Advances followed in home disc-recording, car-radio and later, television. The company began to diversify into heating, lighting and valves.

In 1939, war intervened and a rapid expansion took place, with employment rising to 7,000. New factories in Malmesbury, Aylesbury, Preston, Woking and Rutherglen produced items ranging from radar to plastic practice bombs. The firm's output of radar and radio equipment alone, 1939-45, amounted to £17.5 million. After 1945 the firm resumed manufacture of radios and TVs and in the 1950s diversified into nuclear instruments and industrial ventilation. EKCO emerged from the war 'woefully weak in its top management' {Lipman (1980) 173} and never really recovered its early entrepreneurial dynamism. For example in the television tube market it was beaten by Jules Thorn (qv). Overseas, between 1947 and 1956, manufacturing was started in India and Australia but the former operation made losses and the latter never properly started. Assembly plants were opened in Ireland, South Africa and New Zealand.

EKCO took over Dynatron in 1955 and Ferranti Radio & Television in 1957 and in 1958 employed 8,000. However the failings of top management led at the end of 1960 to a merger with Pye to form British Electronic Industries Ltd, which effectively swallowed up EKCO. Eric K Cole was appointed deputy chairman but retired in 1961 following a boardroom disagreement. For a short time Cole was chairman of Robinson Rentals, a TV rental firm.

Eric K Cole was awarded the CBE in 1958. His wife died in 1965, leaving Eric with his son Derek and daughter Anne. He did not have much time for leisure pursuits, although he occasionally enjoyed shooting and was a keen cameraman. He died in a bathing accident in Barbados on 18 November 1966. His will was proved at £100,885 gross in England, and the estate was divided between his two children.

GORDON BUSSEY

Sources:

Unpublished

British Patent, 1926 (262,567).

Eric K Cole destroyed most of his business documents when the company merged with Pye. However, some documents were discovered and are now in the author's possession.

BCe.

PrC.

Published

Gordon Bussey, *The Story of Pye Wireless* (Pye Ltd, 1979).

Essex Weekly News 16 Aug 1935.

Donald Glennie, *Our Town. An Encyclopaedia of Southend-on-Sea and District* (Southend-on-Sea: Civic Publications, 1947).

COLE Eric Kirkham

Kelly's Directory of Southend-on-Sea 1922-31.

Michael I Lipman, *Memoirs of a Socialist Business Man* (Lipman Trust, 1980).

Southend Standard 25 Aug 1932, 24 Nov 1966.

WWW.

COLES, Henry James

(1847-1905)

Crane manufacturer

Henry James Coles was born in London on 24 June 1847, the second son of Lewis Coles, a tailor, and his wife Helen Marion née Penny. At thirteen he was apprenticed to S Worssam & Co, of Chelsea, manufacturers of saw-mill equipment. He was five years in the workshop there and five years in the drawing office. In 1870 he went to Maudslay, Sons & Field, where he spent two years as a marine engineer. Then he joined Appleby Bros, general engineers, specialising in steam cranes, where he became assistant manager in 1875. Late in 1878 Appleby Bros decided to move from Southwark to East Greenwich. Henry Coles, with three of his brothers also on the staff of Appleby, took over one of their former workshops in 1879 to begin trading independently. Within two years he took out the first of a dozen patents relating to cranes, baling presses, steam engines, grab buckets and rock drills. He became an associate of the Institution of Civil Engineers in 1877 and a member in 1890. His proposal for the Institution refers to the design and manufacture of all classes of lifting machinery, rock-drilling and dredging machinery, and to considerable contracts for Woolwich Arsenal, Chatham Dockyard and Lisbon Central Station. The firm exported widely from the outset, presumably helped by the fact that London was at that time the centre for international contracting; Coles himself appears to have gone abroad only once. In 1898 Henry Coles moved the firm to Derby with the whole of his workforce and two of his brothers. Despite the obvious heavy demands of such an undertaking for capital, he remained a sole trader.

In the late 1880s and early 1890s Henry Coles was involved in local political and charitable work in London, especially through his association with Southwark Cathedral, and he engaged in similar work in Derby after his move there.

Coles married Amy Elizabeth née Burks by whom he had at least five children. He collapsed at the age of fifty-seven and died within a week, on

29 April 1905, leaving £6,314 gross. The business passed to his relations; in 1907 a limited company was formed, under the chairmanship of Henry James Coles Jr, but was sold out of the family in the 1920s.

RICHARD STOREY

Sources:

Unpublished

PrC.

British Patents: 1884 (2,302), improvements in the method of revolving or slewing cranes; other patents included his last of 1900 (15,696) for an improved brake on rail cranes.

Published

M Wilson and K Spink, *Coles 100 Years. The Growth of Europe's Leading Crane Manufacturer, 1879-1979* (Uxbridge: Coles Cranes Ltd, 1978).

COLGRAIN, 1st Lord Colgrain
see CAMPBELL, Colin Frederick

COLLINS, Douglas Raymond

(1912-1972)

Perfume manufacturer

Douglas Raymond Collins was born at Waltham St Lawrence in Berkshire on 31 August 1912. His father, Richard Collins, was a member of a Glasgow paper-making firm, but had left the family business after only a year and lived on a gradually dwindling private income. His mother was Adelaide née Cressy-Hall. Douglas was the youngest of three children; his parents separated when he was two, and he did not meet his father again until he was seventeen. The family lived in a number of towns on the South Coast, apart from a few years spent in Canada and four years, from 1923, in Vevey in Switzerland. Douglas attended the Collège de Vevey, and in 1925-26 was sent to Zurich to learn German. When the family returned to England in 1927 Collins took a commercial course (really a glorified shorthand and typing course) at Brighton Technical College for a year. The examinations at the end of it were the only ones he ever passed, or indeed took. After three months at Perugia University learning Italian, he returned to England but left home in September 1928, as he felt that living with his kind-hearted but domineering mother made independence of thought or action impossible.

For the next few years Collins's wandering life continued as he took a variety of jobs acquired through family or personal contacts. Several months working as a clerk in hotels in the South of France first aroused his interest in perfume (one of his duties was checking consignments of perfume for a hotel shop), and he visited several perfume oil factories in Grasse. This was followed by two years in a paint factory in Birmingham as a clerk and then as a traveller, discovering a taste for the challenge of selling. On holiday in early 1931 he met the daughter of Henry Loebl, a co-founder of the stockbroking firm of Shaw, Loebl & Co, who gave Collins a job as a trainee. He found the work interesting, and the training and insight into company finance it provided was very useful to him later. Nevertheless after a year he decided he wanted to 'make things' rather than work in an office.

At that time in the early 1930s, when jobs were hard to find and poorly-paid, many young men were founding their own business, borrowing a little capital from their families. With a friend, Collins formed Douglas Collins & Co with a capital of £100 in 1933. They took a small workshop in Camden Town and, inspired by the memory of an acquaintance at Brighton Polytechnic who had made his own haircream, Collins began to make toilet preparations for hairdressers, selling largely to men's hairdressers in the East End. He produced his first perfume in 1934 when, through Henry Loebl's sister, he got a small order to produce a perfume for Jaeger shops. The ingredients of perfume were not in themselves very costly, and Collins wanted to sell perfume without expensive packaging; he hit on the idea of offering a small plain bottle, for the low price of one shilling. The success of this fragrance, 'Bracken', could not arrest the decline of the company. In 1935 Collins sold his interest in Douglas Collins & Co for £300, keeping the right to take over the manufacture of Jaeger 'Bracken' if he started his own business again.

After an unsuccessful attempt to run a greengrocer's shop, Collins started to make perfume again, using £50 from a friend who became his partner and a £50 bank loan. He ran the business from his mother's house in Brighton, producing fifteen different perfumes during 1936 under the name Lafontaine.

His new company was a little more successful, making enough in the first year to pay Collins £100 as a salary, and repay the bank loan. He dissolved his partnership, and in March 1937 started D R Collins Ltd with another partner, Bill Barratt, whom he had met in Brighton. Each held 50 shares in the company, which had a nominal capital of £100; Barratt agreed to put up £600 in all. Four rooms in White Horse Street off Piccadilly provided the workshop, the office, Collins's bedsitting-room, and the excuse to put 'Lafontaine, Piccadilly' on the packages.

Previous experience had taught him the need to concentrate on selling branded goods to build up customer loyalty, and not to try to sell a luxury product too cheaply. He changed his trade-name to Goya, not after the painter, whom he had never even heard of, but because he wanted a short name that could be easily pronounced anywhere in the world. Sales in the first year totalled £1,592, on which a loss of £192 was made. In 1938, when the company employed only one part-time packer and Collins himself was still filling all the bottles with a fountain-pen filler, his assiduously-cultivated press contacts resulted in an offer from the Associated Press's *Woman's Journal* to distribute 225,000 phials of his 'Gardenia' perfume as a free gift. With extra staff and a lot of personal effort the order was completed with four days to spare. Two more orders for Associated Press, each for 250,000 phials, followed and with the boost for Goya they provided sales began to average £2,000 a month. On the strength of this Barratt provided another £4,000 preference capital during 1938 and 1939, and Collins increased his own salary from £4 to £8 a week.

During the war Collins served in the Navy, rising to the rank of lieutenant-commander. Goya kept ticking over, with annual sales averaging about £23,000. On his return in 1945 the factory was moved to Amersham from Buckingham (where it had been evacuated in 1940), a London office was opened in Bond Street, and the company began to make new lines such as talcum powder. Barratt put in a further £14,000, the last capital, apart from bank loans, to be put into Goya. The time had come to put to use the experience, contacts and reputation that had been built up.

In the circumstances of 1946, far more effort was needed for acquiring materials than for selling, but much money was spent on advertising to build up the name of Goya. This, combined with the scrapping of old stocks as better materials became available, cut profits to only £4,300 on sales of £222,000 in 1946. For the next few years, Collins concentrated on the problems of production, but as supplies of materials became easier, devoted more and more time to designing and developing Goya's increasing range of products. Collins's fertile mind produced a continuous stream of new products, perfumes and cosmetics. Goya marketed far more products than its competitors. Mistakes were made, but every success could pay for several failures. The aim was still to supply a little of something good for a low price, and this policy gave Goya a far larger market than the firms selling expensively-priced perfumes, and consequently the opportunity to grow much bigger than these rivals could hope to do.

By 1951, annual sales had risen to £661,000 and profits to £105,000 before tax. After a disagreement with Collins, Barratt had sold out for £60,000. Barratt's interest was bought by Sir John Keeling (co-founder of London & Yorkshire Trust and vice-chairman of Bowaters), who had been introduced to Collins by his auditor. Collins ran the business, just as he had always done. In 1952 an old soap-making firm, J C & J Field, was acquired in a reverse takeover: Collins received 200,000 shares in Fields (44.4 per cent) and £50,000 cash. Fields' business was moved to Amersham. With the dividend from his shares in Fields, Collins's income was now about £20,000 a year.

By 1957, however, the business was becoming too large for him to manage in the personal way he favoured. The combined turnover of Goya and Fields was £1.5 million a year in the late 1950s; Goya perfumes were outselling any other English brand, though Goya cosmetics had made less progress in a highly competitive market. Sales were growing faster than the factories could be enlarged to cope with the increase. By then nearly 1,000 people were employed at the Amersham factories and the supply of local labour was running out. To avoid problems of currency exchange and duties, Goya perfumes were also being manufactured in fifteen countries around the world (it was comparatively simple to ship the raw materials to be mixed together on the spot). Though Goya could easily have grown into a group several times larger, Collins did not want to be responsible to shareholders, and preferred close control of a smaller company to running a much larger business of which he would own only a small part.

In contrast to Goya's sales, Fields' turnover of £500,000 lost money. In February 1958 another complicated deal resulted in Collins in effect selling Fields to Griffiths, Hughes of Manchester, and just running his own companies again.

By the end of 1959 the reduction in turnover due to the disposal of Fields had been more than made up, and annual sales exceeded £2 million for the first time. Collins by now had able directors and executives who took care of the routine management, while his own work was confined largely to advertising and the development and design of new products. His own fertility of ideas continually frustrated his intention of simplifying the business, of slowing down the pace of development. He launched a new perfume every other year. Each time one was introduced, production of another ceased but Goya was still the only perfume manufacturer to sell approximately equal quantities of four or five perfumes at any one time, most firms relying on one fragrance for 80-90 per cent of their sales.

In early 1960 Collins was approached by Reckitts who were interested in buying Goya. He had no real intention of selling, but could not resist finding out how much would be offered. When a price was settled, he found it too good to refuse: Goya was sold for £1.5 million, of which about £850,000 represented goodwill. Collins was to stay on the Goya board for at least five years.

Gradually, however, he became less involved in the management of Goya, and was ready to seize the opportunity of moving into another business when it was offered to him. The ageing members of the old-established family firm of Suttons Seeds of Reading, while maintaining Suttons' excellent reputation among horticulturalists, were finding it difficult to cope with changing business conditions. In 1964 Collins bought 45 per cent of Suttons' shares, and began to help run the business. In 1965 he became managing director and his impact on the firm began to show. Again, an original approach to packaging was the key to success. Using machinery first developed for packing dried soups, seeds were packed and sealed in moisture-free conditions, enabling them to be stored for many years without deterioration. New sales methods were also introduced. Sales had been almost exclusively by mail order; by 1966 almost 3,000 retail outlets and agents had been found. By 1967 Suttons' losses had been turned into a profit of £77,000. The Collins family then owned nearly 100 per cent of the shares.

Meanwhile although exports of Goya products were doing well for Reckitts, the home trade was doing badly: in 1967 it made a loss of about £100,000. In 1968 Collins half-seriously suggested to the board of Reckitts that they should sell Goya back to him. When Reckitts replied that they would, Collins quickly agreed. His decision was influenced by the desire of his eldest son Christopher, who had qualified as an accountant in 1965 but had devoted most of his energy so far to a very successful career as an amateur steeplechase jockey, to go into business. The Collins paid £800,000 for Goya; Reckitts retained the rights to market Goya lines outside the British Isles, the European Economic Community and North America. The firm became a subsidiary of Suttons, so that its losses could be set against Suttons' profits for tax purposes.

Goya was reorganised and streamlined, the number of products being reduced from 246 to 41, and Christopher Collins became managing director. The speedy recovery of Goya was aided by the launching of a highly successful product range, 'Aqua Manda', in 1969. By 1972 the company was making a profit of £250,000 a year. Suttons too continued to flourish, though profits remained about £100,000 a year because, despite increasing turnover, prices were deliberately kept stable. In 1970 it was agreed that Christopher should sell his share of Suttons (now 16 per cent) to his father and to a family trust, and with the proceeds increase his share of Goya to 70 per cent. Douglas Collins remained chairman of Goya and it was run much as before, while Christopher continued to become involved in projects at Suttons.

Christopher was not the only member of his family to have worked with Douglas Collins. His first wife, Patricia ('Patsy') née Backhouse, the daughter of a director of Thomas Cook, whom he married in 1938, was an able business woman. She was a director of Goya almost from the start until 1960, and took charge of Goya's cosmetic lines. They had five children before their divorce in 1961. His second wife, Elisabeth née Worswick, was a 'creative' director of Goya, and took part with Douglas and Christopher Collins in the development of the Aqua Manda products. There were three children of this second marriage.

Douglas Collins much enjoyed spending time with his children. During the war he wrote some children's books, and he also wrote a book about sailing, a favourite relaxation of his. In later years he enjoyed making and restoring furniture. In 1953 he bought a farm near Amersham; though he ran it to make a profit, he found the lack of competition in farming a welcome relief from his business life.

A desire to do some public work led him to stand for election as a Labour councillor in Chelsea in 1946. When he moved to Amersham in 1949 he resigned his seat and had no further political ambitions. In 1954 Sir Jack Keeling, chairman of the National Film Finance Corporation, invited him on to the board. In December 1957 he became chairman of the NFFC's subsidiary film distribution company, British Lion. Executives were changed, economies made, and by 1961 British Lion, which had made a loss of £337,000 in 1957-58 made a profit of £318,000. Collins found the work fascinating, but expensive (he would not accept any expenses, salary or fee because he was doing the work as a form of public service). In February 1961 he resigned from British Lion and the NFFC after a disagreement with the President of the Board of Trade. For some years he served as chairman of the National Seed Development Organisation.

By 1972 Collins was thinking of retiring to the South of France leaving his son to manage Suttons as well as Goya, but before arrangements were completed for this, he died of a heart attack on 4 March 1972. He left an estate proved at £610,408 gross.

CHRISTINE SHAW

Writings:

Sailing in Helen (E Arnold & Co, 1946).

'Mr Mole' series of children's books (Collins, 1947-50).

A Nose for Money: How to Make a Million (Michael Joseph, 1963).

Sources:

Unpublished

BCe.

PrC.

Information from Mr Christopher Collins.

Published

Times 4 Oct 1965, 4 Jan, 18 Feb 1966, 3 Nov 1967, 9 Apr, 20 Aug 1968, 12 Aug 1969, 10 Oct 1970, 14 May, 22 Nov 1971, 6 May 1972.

WWW.

COLLS, John Howard

(1846-1910)

Builder

John Howard Colls was born in Camberwell, London on 30 August 1846, the second son of Benjamin Colls (1813-78) and Elizabeth née Jackson. Little is known about his education or early life except that he spent some time in his father's joinery workshop. His father, a painter in the 1840s, left in 1878 an estate of less than £18,000 gross and a relatively small building business relying mainly on artisan house construction in Camberwell and office building in the City of London, supplemented by occasional church and school building contracts. Benjamin had served on the Camberwell Vestry and the Camberwell Board of Guardians and, from 1867 until his death, on the Common Council of the Corporation of London; at his death, he was chairman of the City Lands Committee and hence 'first commoner' of the Corporation of London.

The family business passed to Howard (as he was known) Colls and his elder brother William Abraham Colls (1842-93) jointly and equally in 1878. Hereafter Colls & Sons specialised in building City offices, banks and similar premises. They retained workshops at 240 Camberwell Road but withdrew from local work. They also established premises at Dorking in Surrey from which prepared work, particularly joinery, was brought to be fixed on jobs in the City. As the wages payable to craftsmen in Dorking were substantially below London rates, this represented an astute move which competitors were surprisingly slow to imitate. The Dorking 'branch', as it was later called, was for very many years managed by Henry T Challacombe who became one of the first technical directors of the successor firm Trollope & Colls in 1930 and a full director in 1938, retiring ultimately in 1946.

Although the emphasis of Colls & Sons' building activities was, from the 1880s onwards, on City office building, other work was carried out. Notable in this respect were extensions and alterations executed at Stratfield Saye for the Duke of Wellington. Amongst their finest City buildings was that for the Institute of Chartered Accountants, constructed 1889-92.

In trade affairs Howard Colls was more active than his brother. Howard was vice-president of the National Association of Master Builders of Great Britain, 1885-89, and president of that body, 1889-90; during his presidential term he also served on the Association's committee on the complex and contentious question of the form of contract between builder and architect, though it is not clear whether he formulated the standard form of building contract agreed in 1903, as has been claimed. He was also president of the Institute of Builders (the title adopted by the long established Builders' Society on its incorporation in 1884), 1887-88. He was president of the Central Association of Master Builders of London in 1890-91. As its leader, Howard Colls was directly involved in the eight-hour-day dispute with the London United Trade Committee of Carpenters and Joiners.

His term of office ended before the commencement of the strike and lock-out which virtually paralysed building in London between May and November 1891 but he took a forceful part in the deliberations and negotiations which preceded it and represented the Association at the arbitration which brought the dispute to a close in November. After seven months on the streets the woodworkers agreed to arbitration by the president of the RIBA. The verbatim minutes of the arbitration show Howard Colls not only as shrewd, forceful and highly knowledgeable but also courteous towards his opponents as well as his peers. In the main, the master builders were successful at the arbitration: the hours of work were reduced but the rate of payment remained unchanged. For Colls & Sons, however, the arbitrator's decision to increase overtime rates was a setback. Much of their business consisted of alterations and extensions to City offices and this work could only be executed outside the working hours of City clerks.

If there were any inequalities in ability or achievement between Howard Colls and his elder brother William, there would appear to have been no resentment on the part of the older man. Quite the contrary, in fact, for when he died at the unusually young age of fifty-one, William Abraham Colls was at pains to ensure that his testamentary settlement would facilitate the continuance of the firm of Colls & Sons under the control of Howard Colls. Of William Abraham Colls's effects of £100,000 a mere £4,000 was earmarked for Howard Benjamin Colls, his older son. Neither of William Abraham Colls's two sons was given any direct part in Colls & Sons. Instead the whole estate was put into trust under the effective control of Howard Colls; the other trustees were Colls & Sons' solicitor and Frederick Hazell, a surveyor to whom one of William Abraham Colls's daughters was married.

Following his brother's death in 1893 Howard Colls appears to have withdrawn from active involvement in the affairs of the various builders' associations named above. He did, however, give his support to some charitable bodies including the Camberwell & Dulwich Pension Society of which he was president in 1908.

Howard Colls's last significant service to the building trades came with the celebrated case of *Colls v Home & Colonial Stores Ltd* which went to the House of Lords in 1904. The issue at stake was that of 'ancient lights', the rights of the proprietor of an existing building over light and air and against interference with light and air from new building. The new building in question was erected in Worship Street, Finsbury, by Colls & Sons. At the outset the Home & Colonial Stores had sought an injunction to prohibit its erection but this had been refused. After Colls completed the building the Appeal Court overturned the original ruling and ordered its demolition. Colls in his turn appealed to the House of Lords which ruled that the Home & Colonial Stores were entitled to sufficient air and light for ordinary purposes but had no proprietorial right to the same amount as they had previously enjoyed, and, in the circumstances, had no claim against Colls & Sons. Thus the law was substantially modified. Previously many of those who claimed grievances and sought injunctions did so in order to extort compensation and were in reality little concerned with air or light. Referring to the case of *Colls v Home & Colonial Stores Ltd*, the editor of the *Builder* offered ' ... a word of recognition of the public service which Messrs Colls & Sons have done in persisting, at the risk of heavy loss to themselves ...' {*Builder* 86 (1904) 485}. Interestingly, the National Association of Master Builders of Great Britain did not discuss the case and offered Colls no financial support. When, however, the matter was settled his fellow master builders presented Colls with his portrait in oils by W Q Orchardson, RA as a token of their appreciation.

Howard Colls became a member of Joseph Chamberlain's Tariff Commission and served alongside his son-in-law, Francis Elgar, managing director of the Fairfield Engineering & Shipbuilding Co. Appearing before the Tariff Commission as a witness, Colls urged the imposition of tariffs on timber, iron girders and joists, cement, glass and slates and argued that this would reduce unemployment.

At the end of 1903 the firm of Colls & Sons ceased to exist, being incorporated in the new firm of George Trollope & Sons and Colls & Sons, a name commonly shortened to Trollope & Colls. John Howard Colls became joint chairman with George Haward Trollope (qv). The other four members of the board were Trollope's two sons; Howard Colls's only son, Archibald Benjamin Howard Colls; and another Colls' nominee, Wallace Elliot. The agreement for the sale of the assets of Colls & Sons to Trollope & Colls, excluding freehold and leasehold property, stipulated a purchase price of £165,375 10s, consisting of 10,417 £10 ordinary shares and £61,205 10s cash. By comparison the purchase price of the assets of George Trollope & Sons was set at £234,624 10s consisting of 14,283 £10 ordinary shares and £91,794 10s cash. Clearly the Trollopes were the dominant partners in the new firm. The joint profits of the two component firms had exceeded £44,000 in each of the preceding three years.

In the last years of his life, Howard Colls was an ardent opponent of the reforming Liberal administration. He protested against Lloyd George's proposals for land taxation, contained in the 1909 budget, and believed they had dampened investment in building. He put this view in a letter to the secretary of Peckham, Nunhead and Brixton Lodge of the General Union of Carpenters and Joiners.

John Howard Colls married Annie M McMillan, daughter of shipbuilder Archibald McMillan, in 1867; they had at least seven daughters and one son. He died of a heart attack at or near Buenos Aires, Argentina, on 29 December 1910 while on a sea cruise for his health's sake. His estate was valued at £419,797 gross.

ALISTAIR G TOUGH

Writings:

letters in *Times* 15 Oct 1879, 8 Jan 1904, 8 July 1909.

COLLS John Howard

Sources:

Unpublished

BLPES, Tariff Commission papers, summary of the evidence of J H Colls, 9 Nov 1904.

National Federation of Building Trades Employers, minute books of the Council of the National Association of Master Builders of Great Britain (1894-1910).

University of Warwick, Modern Records Centre, MSS 78/ASW/6/LMC/1 and /16, records of London United Trades Committee of Carpenters and Joiners.

C Reg: Trollope & Colls Ltd (79,287).

BCe.

MCe.

PrC.

Information from Andrew Marrison, Manchester University.

Published

Builder, passim.

Harold James Dyos, *Victorian Suburb: a Study of the Growth of Camberwell* (Leicester: Leicester University Press, 1961).

National Federation of Building Trades Employers, *An Outline History of the National Federation of Building Trades Employers 1878-1978* (NFBTE, 1978).

Christopher G Powell, *An Economic History of the British Building Industry, 1815-1979* (Methuen, 1982).

Richard Price, *Masters, Unions and Men. Work Control in Building and the Rise of Labour, 1830-1914* (Cambridge: Cambridge University Press, 1980).

Sir John Newenham Summerson, *The London Building World of the Eighteen-Sixties* (Thames & Hudson, 1973).

Times 9 Nov 1909, 31 Dec 1910.

Trollope & Colls Ltd, *City Builders for 200 years, 1778-1978. The History of Trollope & Colls* (Precision Press, 1978).

WWW.

Cecil Colman (courtesy of Sutton Library).

COLMAN, Cecil

(1878-1954)

Shoe manufacturer and retailer

Cecil Colman, born at Bournemouth on 30 May 1878, was one of the nine children of Rev Robert Colman JP, a Baptist minister, and his wife Sophia née Allen. His father, a son of Edward Colman (partner in the Norwich mustard firm of J & J Colman), won the Gold Medal for Analytical Chemistry at London University in 1861, but forsook science to train at Regent's Park Baptist College. At Bournemouth Rev Robert Colman became a leading promoter of municipal enterprise: he sat on the Board of Improvement Commissioners; supported the inauguration of omnibus services, became involved in speculative building for the growing resort; and, an ardent temperance worker, he initiated the formation of Bournemouth's Coffee Taverns & Temperance Hotels.

Cecil Colman was educated privately and at Christchurch School, Hampshire. A moderate scholar, he was apprenticed at seventeen to Moore Bros, a large Salisbury retail footwear concern of which his father was a director, at a starting salary of 2s 6d per week. Although practically trained, he quickly developed a flair for the marketing and sales of shoes. In 1897 Moore Bros went into liquidation, and Colman, with his brother Robert, set up briefly as shoe factors in Bournemouth. National trade connections were quickly established, and commission agencies for the marketing of American and Austrian products established. A London office was opened. Merely moderate financial success, however, resulted in the termination of their business association, but not before Cecil's business ability had been recognised. In 1901 he joined the prominent Norwich-based firm of boot and shoe manufacturers and wholesalers, Howlett & White, as their London sales manager and export agent: exports accounted for most of their sales at this time. His starting salary was £300 a year, plus commission. This association was to last for over fifty years, during which time Colman was to be continually linked with the company's success, and the London office, rather than the production base at Norwich. W G Nase and Cecil Colman became the first senior employees to be appointed to the main board of Howlett & White, in 1909 and 1912 respectively. After the death of Sir George White (qv) in 1912, Colman, in close collaboration with Sir Ernest White (Sir George's son), emerged as the dominant force for change.

Beyond his continued financial control of purchasing and sales from the London office, Colman increased the size of the firm by takeover, and integrated manufacture with wholesale and retail distribution, between 1912 and 1935. This was accomplished in three ways. Firstly, he negotiated the successful absorption of four subsidiaries into the firm's operations: the Mansfield Shoe Co in 1919; Oakeshott & Finnemore of Northampton in 1922; S L Witton of Norwich in 1934; and John Marlow

& Son of Northampton in 1948. For varying periods of time he served on the reconstituted boards of all four concerns. He also served on the board of a retail subsidiary company, C H Baber Ltd. Secondly, he helped to reshape advertising and retailing techniques. In 1913, the board accepted his proposal to adopt the Norvic trade mark and national advertising campaigns. Over time, he gave greater prominence to advertising and the development of lines of branded, specialty goods, which were central to inter-war growth. In the early 1930s, Colman initiated a refinement in established retail trading practice, which originated from the USA, known as the Norvic Concentration Plan. Essentially a financial partnership between manufacturer and independent retailer, it sought to provide the distinctively styled premises, stocking arrangements and 'back-up' services commonly found in the retail chain.

Lastly, and above all, Colman inspired and carried into effect the complex re-organisation of the Howlett interests to form the Norvic group of companies, 'and supplied a great deal of the ideas and driving force which built it to its present size' {*Shoe & Leather Record* 18 Mar 1954}. The Norvic Shoe Co Ltd was floated as a public company on 26 October 1935, with an issued share capital of £2.6 million, to acquire the parent company and its subsidiaries. Colman, who then held £20,000 of deferred ordinary and £28,700 of preferred ordinary shares, was the first joint managing director, and deputy chairman to Sir Ernest White. The organisational pattern Colman introduced combined the central control of general administration, policy and finance by the Norvic board, with the decentralised control of production and daily management of each subsidiary under the local resident directorate. This enabled each factory to enjoy relative autonomy, yet at the same time effective liaison was maintained by the chairman and managing directors of Norvic becoming, ipso facto, members of all the associate boards.

Colman progressively reorganised the central administration after 1947 when he became chairman. Gradually sales, marketing, advertising and retailing functions were concentrated at the London offices. Following war damage the Rathbone Place premises were remodelled, and Norvic House was constructed in Grosvenor Street to become the company's headquarters.

Trade matters claimed some of Colman's attention: he was a president of the Federated Association of Boot and Shoe Manufacturers of Great Britain, and during the Second World War chaired the government-sponsored Branded Retailers' Advisory Bureau. Colman was very much a London man. He was a member of Lloyd's, the National Liberal Club, and active in the London Rotarians. He lived for many years at Sutton, Surrey, where he took an active part in local affairs. He was successively councillor, alderman and mayor (1935) of the borough and elected a JP in 1933. He was chairman of the local juvenile court; president of the Sutton and Cheam General Hospital, of its Elderly People's Homes, and of its Chamber of Trade. For many years he was the president of the Epsom Division Liberal Association.

Cecil Colman married Florence Beatrice, daughter of Henry Alfred Laws, 'gentleman' of Bournemouth, at Westcliff Baptist Tabernacle, Bournemouth in 1903. They had four sons and one daughter; the elder son, Cecil Ralph, became an assistant managing director of Norvic. Cecil

Colman died at Cheam on 11 March 1954, leaving an estate of £397,724 gross.

KEITH B BROOKER

Sources:

Unpublished

PRO, Howlett & White company file, BT 31/31678/60575.

C Reg: Norvic Shoe Co Ltd (1,875,348).

BCe.

MCe.

PrC.

Published

Cox's County Who's Who 1912: Norfolk, Suffolk and Cambridgeshire.

Directory of Directors 1954.

Eastern Daily Press 12 Mar 1954.

Ernest Gaskell, *Norfolk Leaders: Social and Political* (pp, ca 1907).

C B Hawkins, *Norwich: A Social Study* (P L Warner, 1910).

'Historical Survey of Shoe making in Norwich' *Footwear Organiser* Feb 1932.

Kelly's Directory of Norwich ca 1850 – ca 1950.

Shoe and Leather News 18 Mar 1954.

W L Sparks, *Story of Shoemaking in Norwich* (Norwich, 1948).

The Stock Exchange Official Year-Book 1979.

Times 12 Mar, 11 June 1954.

Frederick W Wheldon, *A Norvic Century and the Men Who Made It* (Norwich: Jarrold & Sons, 1947).

WWW.

COLMAN, Jeremiah James

(1830-1898)

Mustard and starch manufacturer

Jeremiah J Colman (courtesy of Colmans of Norwich).

Jeremiah James Colman was born at Stoke Holy Cross near Norwich on 14 June 1830, the only son of James Colman and his wife Mary née Burlingham. His father was a partner, since 1823, in a flour and mustard milling business started by his great uncle, Jeremiah Colman. Jeremiah James was educated privately until the age of seventeen after which he pursued his own education through mutual improvement societies and evening classes, being brought up in a family of Baptists with strong Whig tendencies.

By 1850, Jeremiah James was closely involved in the family business which then employed about 250 men. He showed no conspicuous signs of business aptitude, preferring vigorous sports and natural history. But, following the deaths of his great uncle and father in 1851 and 1854 respectively, he developed an enormous capacity for work which enabled him to fulfil existing plans for moving the business from Stoke to a large site at Carrow on the outskirts of Norwich.

When production at Stoke finally ceased in 1862, mustard and flour, starch and laundry blue mills were operational at the Carrow Works. Over the next twenty years ancillary plants, including a tin shop, paper mill, cooperage, sawmill and printing department were established and the product range was extended to cover cornflour. Jeremiah James was a firm believer in advertising and the late 1870s saw the setting up of an advertising department to deal with annual promotions, in-store and outdoor advertising. During the 1880s and 1890s, medicinal mustard products, the famous penny oval mustard tin and Self-Rising (sic) flour were developed.

In expanding the business, Jeremiah James displayed considerable organisational skill, an ability to pick able staff (like his successive general managers, Samuel Harvard and Robert Haslewood) and a managerial style which commanded his employees' loyalty. He had a reputation for strict integrity in business relationships and was renowned for his thoroughness. He was heavily involved in the day-to-day running of the firm but was substantially helped by his wife Caroline née Cozens-Hardy, daughter of William Hardy Cozens-Hardy, gentleman, whom he married in 1856. She catered for the welfare needs of the workforce, organising meals, medical services, schools and welfare benefits of every description.

In 1896, the firm was converted into a private limited liability company with a capital of £1,350,000 of which £350,000 was in ordinary shares and £1 million in 5 per cent cumulative preference shares. In 1898, an amalgamation of J & J Colman Ltd, Reckitt & Sons Ltd, and Keen, Robinson & Co was discussed, but no agreement reached. By this time the firm employed nearly 3,000 men and was the biggest employer in Norwich.

River Frontage, Colman's Carrow Works ca 1857, with Mustard Mill on left (courtesy of Colmans of Norwich).

There were constant claims on Colman's time of a religious, educational, charitable and political kind. He was Mayor of Norwich, JP, DL of Norfolk and an Honorary Freeman of the City of Norwich. He was instrumental in starting the *Eastern Daily Press* and had long-standing interests in local schools and hospitals. A deacon in St Mary's Baptist Chapel, Norwich, 1861-70, he deplored the divisions between Nonconformist denominations and emphasised Freechurchmanship. In 1871, partly through his wife's influence, he joined Princes Street Congregational Church in Norwich. Jeremiah James Colman was a staunch supporter of Gladstone, a generous contributor to Liberal party funds and MP for Norwich, 1871-95. He was offered a baronetcy which he declined.

A Collection of mustard packaging ca 1890 (courtesy of Colmans of Norwich).

COLMAN Jeremiah James

Jeremiah James Colman died at his seaside home at Corton in Suffolk on 18 September 1898, leaving £883,380 gross. He was survived by his son Russell and four daughters. He bequeathed £2,000 annually for twenty years for helping employees, ex-employees or their wives in cases of sickness, old age or infirmity. In 1900, the Carrow Works Old Age Pension Scheme and Savings Fund was founded as a memorial to him.

HONOR GODFREY

Sources:

Unpublished

Research notes compiled by Ethel and Helen Colman.

MCe.

PrC.

Published

David W Bebbington, 'Baptist MPs in the Nineteenth Century' *The Baptist Quarterly* 29 (1981).

E and W L Burgess, *Men Who Have Made Norwich* (1904).

Helen Caroline Colman, *Jeremiah James Colman: A Memoir* (pp, 1905).

J & J Colman, *Souvenir of Carrow Works, Norwich* (Norwich: 1888, ca 1890, 1901).

Lesser Columbus, 'An East Anglian Colony' *Commerce* 15 Nov 1893.

Commerce 21 Sept 1898.

Eastern Evening News 19 Sept 1898.

Grocer 24 Sept 1898.

Norfolk Daily Standard 22 Sept 1898.

Pentagon, 'A Leading British Industry: The Works on the Wensum. A Visit to Messrs J & J Colman Limited at Norwich' *Grocery* Apr 1899.

Laura E Stuart, *In Memoriam Caroline Colman* (Norwich: pp, 1896).

Times 19 Sept 1898.

WWMP.

COLSON, Alfred

(1849-1910)

Gas manager and engineering consultant

Alfred Colson was born at Newport, Monmouthshire on 31 January 1849, the son of Henry Colson, an engineer with the London & SouthWestern Railway Co, and Sarah Harriet née Richards. He received private education and was later articled to his father, subsequently joining the staff of the engineering contractor John Aird (qv). In 1871 Colson was engaged as clerk of works to assist Robert Morton, engineer to the London Gas Co, in the construction of the first gas-holder at Battersea. Moving to the Midlands in 1873 as assistant engineer to the Birmingham Gas Co, he assisted Charles Hunt for the next ten years in managing the Windsor Street Works. The experience gained in the construction of new plant was no doubt largely responsible for his appointment in 1882 as engineer to the Leicester Corporation's gas undertaking, the latter having been municipalised in 1878.

His appointment not only marked the end of a long period of dominance over the Leicester gas undertaking by the Robinson family, but also coincided with the newly-emerging threat to gas from electricity, particularly for lighting. Colson demonstrated a progressive approach, displaying not only skill in dealing with technical, financial, and sales matters but also adaptability in meeting the challenge presented by the growth of the socialist and trade union movements. These qualities made him eminently suitable for the dual role of engineer and manager, a successful blend which was the envy of many other gas undertakings.

Colson was an extremely capable engineer, designing and supervising two major extension programmes at Leicester before 1900 in his efforts to keep pace with the rising demand for gas both in Leicester and in its surrounding areas. In this context he masterminded the Corporation's case before a select committee of the House of Commons in 1897 with great success. His skill and ability generated demand for his services as a consultant, and in this capacity he designed and supervised the erection of new stations at several gas undertakings. He displayed good judgement and business acumen in the introduction of innovations at Leicester, examining closely and extensively, both at home and abroad, all the latest designs, seemingly with a great knack for introducing new ideas at the right time. He avoided, for instance, the temptation to employ inclined retorts in his expansion programme of the late 1890s even though they were fashionable on the continent and had been introduced at some places in this country. In 1909 he examined the new systems of vertical retorts, of Arthur Duckham (qv) and others, which were under experimental use in England, and particularly in Germany; he recommended the serious consideration of this method of coal-carbonisation after visiting Germany and Switzerland in 1909. His previous caution proved rewarding for the Leicester undertaking which began the installation of vertical retorts two years after his death, at a time when many of the initial problems of this system had been overcome. As a designer he was noted for his prepayment meter cash box and for his method of removing the extremely troublesome deposits of naphthalene by treating the gas with light creosote oil.

As an administrator, Colson appreciated the great importance of good relations with staff and workers. The provision of mess rooms, toilets and baths, and leisure facilities were given high priority. He organised concerts, talks, dramatics and the like, during the winter, and was instrumental in the formation of a cricket club, band, and first aid department, and a sickness and funeral allowance society funded by the gas department. This close contact with the workers enabled him to minimise the impact of militancy by the gas workers during 1889 and 1890. Strikes were avoided at Leicester by Colson's adept handling of negotiations between the gas committee and the workers.

Within his profession Colson was highly regarded, being a member of the Midland Association of Gas Managers, a member of the Institution of Civil Engineers, and of the Institution of Electrical Engineers. In 1876 he joined the British Association of Gas Managers, and later helped form the Incorporated Institution of Gas Engineers, being elected president in 1894. He joined the re-organised Institution of Gas Engineers at its formation in 1902. In 1898 he was elected president of the Leicester Literary and Philosophical Society and chaired the reception committee for the meeting of the British Association at Leicester in 1907.

Alfred Colson was married and had two daughters and two sons. He died on 27 May 1910 leaving £24,228 gross.

DAVID E ROBERTS

Writings:

'The Leicester Gas-Works Extensions' *Incorporated Institution of Gas Engineers* 1891.

'Ten Years' Experience with the Prepayment Meter at Leicester' *ibid* 1904.

Sources:

Unpublished

John Doran Museum, EMGAS, Leicester: Correspondence re sulphate plant, coal supplies, and long boat at Leicester, 1886-1893; drawings and designs of various sewer and building projects; ledgers: Earl Shilton, Syston and Thurmaston Gas undertakings; quotations and specifications prepared by A Colson; reports, accounts and notices of Sickness and Funeral Allowance Society, Leicester, 1889-1910.

—, and Leicester CRO (EMGAS Collection): Memoranda for Engineers and Managers from Committees and Sub-Committees (Leicester), 1887-1910.

Leicester CRO: Minutes of Evidence of House of Commons Committees on Leicester Gas, 1897, 1902, 1908.

BCe.

PrC.

Published

Journal of the Institution of Gas Engineers 1910.

Leicester Corporation Acts 1884, 1897, 1902, 1908.

Leicester Corporation Bills (Gas Section) 1897, 1902.

David E Roberts, *The Leicester Gas Undertaking, 1821-1921* (Leicester: EM GAS, 1978).

John Storey, *Historical Sketch of Some of the Principal Works and Undertakings of the Council* (Leicester: W H Lead, 1895).

COLSTON, Sir Charles Blampied

(1891-1969)

Electrical appliance manufacturer

Charles Blampied Colston was born at Gerrards Cross, Chalfont St Peter on 31 October 1891, the son of Charles Edward Colston, a schoolmaster and his wife Rosala Jane Colston née Blampied. He was educated at Colston's School, Bristol and the City and Guilds Technical College, Finsbury, London.

After distinguished wartime service in the Royal Engineers (he won the DCM and MC), Charles Colston joined the newly-formed Hoover company in June 1919, subsequently rising to become managing director in 1928 and chairman in 1937. The company, under his control, grew from a minor subsidiary of an American giant to a major international holding company with a turnover that rivalled that of its American parent. The UK subsidiary was formed in 1919 as a private British company, with £20,000 capital, one office and a staff of six. By 1954, the year Charles Colston resigned, Hoover was a £12 million empire with eight factories in the UK, over 12,000 employees and subsidiaries throughout the world. Net trading profits were £297,807 in 1938, when it was first quoted as a public company (on 11 March 1937 Hoover Ltd was registered as a public company, acquiring the business of the private company for £1,324,401). By 1954 profits had risen to £2,005,496.

Hoover Ltd was formed as a private British company by the Hoover Co in 1919 to market the holding company's vacuum cleaners in this country. Manufacturing in Britain was introduced to overcome the effects upon US imports of British abandonment of free trade and of the gold standard. Initially, Hoover reacted to the changed circumstances by importing vacuum cleaners from the parent company's Canadian factories (these were allowed in duty free by Empire preference). Production in this country followed almost immediately, at first using imported parts, and from 1933 with entirely British-made products at the Perivale factory in Middlesex (a factory subsequently celebrated as a model of inter-war industrial architecture). During the inter-war period Hoover manufactured and marketed only one product: the electric vacuum cleaner. The company quickly established a dominant position in the British vacuum cleaner market, its main rivals being Electrolux, Goblin and BVC. By heavy advertising and hard-pressure selling (Charles Colston was an enthusiastic supporter of hire-purchase sales), the company educated British housewives to regard the American electric cleaner as an indispensable household accessory. Sales rose from 2,252 in 1919 to 203,243 in 1938 and the company's name became synonymous with the electric vacuum cleaner.

During the Second World War, Colston directed the change to manufacturing rotary transformers, electrical plugs and sockets, complete wiring installations for aircraft, fractional horsepower motors, engine starters and speed indicators. There was also a switch in the location of production. Colston quickly realised that most of the wartime labour force would be female and that women with domestic ties would need to work close to their homes. Small workplaces were erected in the villages around Perivale enabling women to contribute to Hoover's output without expensive travelling.

Charles Colston had sometimes been criticised in the pre-war decades for the narrow product base of the company. However, he brought about a transformation of the company's activities after the war. The late 1940s and early 1950s witnessed considerable diversification. The company still claimed to sell more electric cleaners than all the other British makers combined in 1954, but vacuum cleaners no longer dominated production. In 1946 the manufacture of fractional horsepower motors began in Scotland and in 1948 the Hoover electric washing-machine was launched. By 1954 the washing-machine accounted for substantially more income than did vacuum cleaners and Hoover sold one and a half times as many electric washing-machines in Britain as all the other manufacturers combined. An electric polisher was brought on to the market in 1951 and the Hoover electric steam and dry iron and the Mark II washing-machine followed in 1953. During the post-war period Colston directed the expansion of the company's overseas activities. Hoover became a major exporting enterprise, and an international holding company with subsidiaries in Belgium, West Germany, Italy, France, Holland, Switzerland, Australia, New Zealand and South Africa. By 1954 the British company was trading in 90 countries and was exporting nearly 60 per cent of production.

Three features of Hoover's manufacturing and marketing activities can be largely attributed to Charles Colston: the quality of the product, high-pressure selling and the service department. He took a particular interest in the Hoover Research Department and the quality of the Hoover product was constantly being improved in terms of mechanical and electrical efficiency and styling. A believer in incentives at all levels, he offered particular incentives to sales and service staff. By 1939 the company claimed to have the largest salaried outside sales force in Great Britain. By 1954 bonuses (apart from piece-work incentives and sales commissions) amounted to £754,000. The success of the company can also be attributed to its policy of specialisation and its financial resources. Hoover at the outset did obtain financial backing from its American parent company, but its growth was the result of Colston's policy of ploughing back profits.

The period was not, however, one of uninterrupted growth. In the early 1950s, a time of high purchase tax and deflationary measures at home coupled with severe import restrictions in many of the company's overseas markets, net trading profits fell from £928,503 in 1951 to £510,697 in 1952. This temporary setback may have contributed to Charles Colston's forced resignation from Hoover in 1954. There were two other possible explanations (neither of them substantiated). The first was that Colston had built up a turnover several times greater than that of the parent company in America. This may not have endeared him to Herbert Hoover Jr, grandson of the company's founder. A barely-concealed row in 1954 precipitated the resignation. A second reason can perhaps be found in the volatile nature of Herbert Hoover Jr, who at this time appears to have been set upon introducing sweeping changes from the ways of the past.

After thirty-five years with Hoover, Colston terminated this part of his career with a golden handshake of £83,575 (an amount which earned him a place in the *Guinness Book of Records* and was not exceeded for ten years). He now moved independently into the dishwashing-machine business, setting up Charles Colston Ltd, of which he was chairman, with his son Michael in 1955. In 1959 the company marketed its first dishwasher and by the early 1960s (before the big electrical companies like Bosch, Hotpoint and Hoover moved in) held about 70 per cent of the market.

In November 1961 Colston made an agreement with John Bloom to form Rolls Colston Appliances, each partner putting up £125,000. By 1961 Bloom, the thirty-year-old son of a London jobbing tailor, had merged his own company, Electromatic Washing Co, with Rolls Razor (his appointment in 1961 as managing director of Rolls Razor being a precondition of that merger) and was looking for additional supplies of washing-machines, new products and respectable names to add to the Rolls Razor board. Colston meanwhile needed to reduce distribution costs to take his dishwasher out of the the luxury appliance class and into the mass market: Bloom's renowned direct-selling methods offered the way to do this. By December 1961 the new company, of which Colston was chairman and joint managing director, was selling dishwashers direct to the housewife at 49 guineas, a 54.4 per cent reduction on the previous Colston price. Six months later the connection was extended when Tallent Engineering, a subsidiary of the Colston group, started making washing-machines for Rolls Razor.

Colston's business involvement with John Bloom was however a strained and short-lived affair. He was never entirely happy with Bloom's direct-selling methods (he reverted to using retailers after 1964). In 1963 he resigned from the board of Rolls Razor. Bloom had just concluded a deal with Pressed Steel for the supply of washing-machines which Colston viewed as a threat to his own Tallent Engineering. By the middle of the same year the joint Bloom-Colston dishwashing venture was over. Sales were not reaching Bloom's targets and the maintenance of low prices was not giving Rolls Razor sufficient return on its investment. Colston purchased Rolls Razor's 50 per cent interest for £40,000, renaming the company Colston Appliances. The connection with Bloom was not, however, entirely severed. Tallent Engineering continued making washing machines for Rolls Razor, turning out 80,000 during 1963, and there was another six month period in early 1964 when Charles Colston served on the board of Rolls Razor (a precondition of Tallent Engineering taking over the whole of the production of washing machines after the failure of Pressed Steel). By this time, however, the days of Bloom's empire were numbered. On 27 July Colston resigned from the Rolls Razor board. A resolution placing Rolls Razor in voluntary liquidation was passed on 27 August 1964, Tallent Engineering claiming (but not receiving) the sum of £866,194 damages for washing-machines which they said Rolls Razor had contracted to buy over the next five years. Colston's group survived the Rolls Razor crash, continuing to make dishwashers, washing machines and other domestic appliances until 1979 when the domestic appliances division was sold by his son Michael to the Italian company, Merloni, to raise capital in order to fund the expansion of the components division.

Charles Colston had a reputation for looking after his employees. In 1935 a Hoover staff pension and a group assurance scheme were launched and in 1947 a free superannuation scheme covered all employees who did not come within the staff scheme. The Charles Colston Trust was founded and endowed in 1948 for the purpose of assisting Hoover employees and ex-employees. By 1954 the capital value of this trust amounted to £400,000. In 1956, however, this trust was wound up due to income tax complications and its assets were transferred to an educational trust from which New Hall, Cambridge, Bristol University, Colston's School, Bristol and Stowe School, Buckinghamshire, were the beneficiaries.

Charles Colston's other activities included his appointment as Regional Controller, Ministry of Production and chairman of the London and South East Regional Board, 1942-45 and the deputy chairmanship of the Independent Television Authority, August to December 1954.

He married Eliza Foster Shaw, daughter of William Alexander Shaw, a retired fishmonger, in 1924. They had one son and three daughters. His first wife died in 1964. On 20 September 1968 he married Margaret Sim. Charles Colston died on 14 February 1969, leaving £28,356 gross.

SUSAN BOWDEN

Sources:

Unpublished

BCe.

MCe.

PrC.

Hoover, Perivale, Middlesex, archives.

Published

John Bloom, *It's No Sin to Make a Profit* (W H Allen, 1971).

T A B Corley, *Domestic Electrical Appliances* (Jonathan Cape, 1966).

John H Dunning, *American Investment in British Manufacturing Industry* (George Allen & Unwin, 1958).

Economist 11, 18 Mar 1950, 13 Mar 1954, 2 June 1963, 21 Mar 1964, 25 July 1964.

Electrical Times 1919-69.

Electrical Trading 1919-69.

Financial Times 1937-79.

Garcke's Manual of Electrial Undertakings 1937-38.

Investors Chronicle 22 Mar 1947, 18 Mar 1950, 24 Jan, 17 Nov 1964.

The Stock Exchange Official Year-Book 1955, 1961-69.

Sunday Telegraph 21 Jan 1979.

Times 1937-69 passim.

WWW.

COMBE, Simon Harvey

(1903-1965)
Brewery company chairman

Simon Harvey Combe was born at Frensham in Surrey on 4 May 1903, the second son of Major Boyce Combe and his wife Katherine Mabel, the daughter of Major-General Sir Henry Tombs. He was educated at Eton. After leaving school in 1921 he spent a year in France before joining Watney, Combe, Reid & Co.

Apart from his service in the Second World War as a captain in the Irish Guards (during which he was awarded the MC at Anzio), Combe spent his entire business life in the family firm. He was appointed an 'annual' director in 1926, and a full director in 1931.

In 1950, he was appointed chairman, and faced the task of guiding Watneys through a period when technological and social changes were

Simon Harvey Combe (courtesy of The Brewers' Society).

having a considerable effect on the structure of the brewing industry. Technological changes were emphasising the advantages of economies of scale in production, and permitting greater standardisation of brews between one brewery and another. These developments encouraged brewers to look for mergers which would permit the rationalisation of production. Changing social patterns, including increased leisure, increasing consumption of wines and spirits, the fact that far more women were going regularly to public houses, made it necessary for breweries and their publicans to provide new facilities, a wider range of services and a more congenial atmosphere.

A number of small breweries were acquired in the early 1950s, expanding Watneys' coverage of Sussex and East Hampshire, but much the most important merger was that with Mann, Crossman & Paulin in 1958. Combe approached Manns because it had been decided to close Watneys' large Stag Brewery in Westminster, in order to develop the valuable site. However, Watneys' other London brewery at Mortlake would not be able to cope alone with the full demand for Watneys' beers, so either a new brewery had to be built or an arrangement had to be made with another company which already had a brewery in East London. Mann, Crossman & Paulin, with their Albion Brewery in Whitechapel, fitted the bill well. The two companies combined by an exchange of shares. Manns had an issued capital of £3,801,538 (£2,250,000 issued ordinary and preference shares, and £1,551,538 outstanding debentures), while Watneys had an issued capital of £15,455,553 (£8,516,659 issued ordinary and preference shares, and £6,938,894 outstanding debentures). The directors of both companies joined the board of the new Watney Mann; Combe was chairman of the board.

In 1959 the Stag Brewery, the last brewery in the City of Westminster, was closed. Combe and his fellow directors were not only concerned with the development of the valuable Stag Brewery site, but also considered a number of public houses which, because of their sites, were likely to have greater value if put to other uses. Combe announced the board's intention to form a separate property company to deal with these matters on 14 May 1959. Eleven days later, Charles Clore (qv) announced his intention of making an offer for 75 per cent of the ordinary capital of Watney Mann. However, the board had already demonstrated to their shareholders that they were just as aware as Clore of the value, actual and potential, of their real property, and they also enjoyed the support of their staff, and of the rest of the industry. Before the bid, Watney Manns' shares had stood at about 40 shillings; by mid-June they had risen to over 70 shillings, much higher than Clore expected, or was willing to pay. After a meeting between Combe and Clore arranged by Lionel Fraser (qv), Clore withdrew his bid. Watney Mann Property Co, formally registered as a private company in August 1959, became a public company in January 1960. It bought properties to the value of £4,656,750 from Watney Manns, which held about 51 per cent of the £4,650,000 share capital. While a new head office, opened in April 1962, was built on part of the Stag Brewery site, the rest was leased to the City of London Real Property Co Ltd.

The amalgamation with Manns had extended Watneys' interests north of the Thames considerably; Manns had houses up to the Coventry area. Increasing sales, especially to the free trade, were beginning to strain

Watneys' brewing capacity. As it was now possible to match brews between one brewery and another, Watneys' popular keg beer 'Red Barrel' could be made at different locations. Combe negotiated a number of amalgamations with breweries in Manchester, Trowbridge, East Anglia, Northampton and Edinburgh, which not only helped to minimise distribution costs by brewing at a number of different locations, but added 3,000 public houses to Watneys' estate. By 1965 it was the largest owner of public house property in the country, with about 8,000 of the 60,000 hotels and public houses owned by breweries. This expansion brought a substantial increase in Watney Mann's capital, to £63,485,674 (£35,439,001 issued ordinary and preference shares, and £28,046,673 outstanding debentures). Combe denied that Watneys were expanding simply in order to own the largest number of licenced premises in the country. Their aim, he said, was to build up the most efficient group; this entailed the acquisition of bases in picked locations, from which their customers could be supplied. The board was sure that the best way of doing this was to amalgamate with efficiently-run concerns which had strong local connections in the right areas.

Combe succeeded in limiting the capital expenditure Watneys needed to undertake to meet the growing popularity of lager, by exchanging supplies of Red Barrel keg bitter for lager brewed by other companies. E P Taylor, the Canadian businessman, entered the brewing industry in the UK about the time of the Clore bid for Watneys, and announced his intention of establishing a large brewing group with Carlings lager as one of its principal products. Watney Manns concluded an arrangement with Taylor to introduce Carlings as a preferred lager product throughout the tied and free trade of Watney Mann, in exchange for Taylor's group accepting Red Barrel as the principal keg bitter. A similar arrangement was reached by Combe with Allied Breweries. Thus, all three companies, Watney Manns, Taylor's group (which started as Northern Breweries and eventually became Bass Charringtons), and Allied Breweries could each limit their capital expenditure on new plant and distribution facilities by concentrating on one product rather than two.

Watneys had also to reckon with the increasing popularity of wines and spirits, especially for consumption at home. Watneys' first venture into the off-licence trade had been with the establishment in 1929 of the Westminster Wine Co, which had three shops in the London area. More off-licence shops had been acquired with some of the breweries that had been taken over. Mann, Chapman & Paulin had also been expanding their interests in this field before the amalgamation with Watneys. After the merger it was decided to conduct all Watneys' wine and spirit business under the name Brown & Pank Ltd, which had been used by Manns since they acquired this London firm in 1952. The sales force was enlarged, and new brands were introduced. By 1965 Watney Mann had one of the largest wine and spirit businesses in the country.

Combe also ensured that Watneys had a share in the booming trade in the soft drink Coca Cola. In 1953 Watneys and the Beecham Group acquired the franchise for Coca Cola for the greater part of Southern and North-Western England. In 1956 it was decided, for reasons of administrative convenience, to divide the franchise, and a wholly-owned Watneys' subsidiary, Coca-Cola Southern Bottlers Ltd took over the trade for the South, while the Beechams Group retained the North West. The purchase in 1961 of the brewery of Morgans of East Anglia, brought with it Coca Cola Eastern Bottlers Ltd, which was owned by Morgans.

Under Combe, Watneys diversified their business in other ways, too. In 1955 they opened their first motel, as a joint venture with Graham Lyon, the pioneer of motels in the UK. Four other motels were built before the formation of Watney-Lyon Motels Ltd in 1961. That same year, the formation of another company, Swifts Garages, was announced. In order to provide better facilities for motorists and tourists, it was decided to take advantage of the large sites on which many Watneys houses stood, to build garages.

Extensive rebuilding and refurbishing of Watneys' premises was undertaken, once restrictions on building after the war were lifted in 1954. In 1958, a design policy was devised so that each house, while retaining its individual character, was clearly a Watneys house. The expansion of trade in the 1950s meant that poster advertising was no longer really enough. In 1953 Watneys began several provincial press campaigns; in 1955, national newspapers began to be used. A commercial for Watneys was among the first ever broadcast in the UK in September 1955, and from then on television became the main Watneys advertising medium.

Thus, Combe directed Watneys through a period of great change for the company. During his chairmanship, Watneys was firmly established as the largest brewery company in the UK, operating on a national scale.

Apart from his activity with Watneys, Combe was also an important figure in the industry. He was elected to the Council of the Brewers' Society in 1945 and was one of the first brewers' representatives on the Central Panels instituted in 1948 by Sir Hugh Beaver (qv). In 1953 he was elected vice-chairman of the Brewers' Society and served as chairman in 1955-56. He was a vice-president of the Brewers' Society from 1956 until his death.

He was an enthusiastic and knowledgeable gardener, and created a fine garden around his home at King's Lynn; he also took a personal interest in the management of his farm. He was a good shot, and a keen golfer. He married Lady Sylvia Beatrice Coke, the elder daughter of the Fourth Earl of Leicester, in 1932. They had one son, and one daughter. The son, Robin Harvey Combe, joined the board of Watney Manns in 1960.

Simon Combe died on 1 April 1965, leaving an estate proved at £18,243 gross.

TOM CORRAN *and* CHRISTINE SHAW

Sources

Unpublished

Information from M G T Webster.

BCe.

PrC.

Published

Brewery Trade Review 1 Apr 1965.

Tom H Corran, *The Brewing Industry* (forthcoming).

Henry H Janes, *The Red Barrel: A History of Watney Mann* (John Murray, 1963).

H A Monckton, *A History of English Ale and Beer* (Bodley Head, 1966).

Times 2 Apr 1965.

WWW.

COOK, John Mason

(1834-1899)

Travel agent

John Mason Cook ca 1880-1890 (courtesy of Thomas Cook & Son Ltd).

John Mason Cook was born at Market Harborough, Leicestershire, in 1834, the son of Thomas Cook (qv) and his wife Marianne née Mason. Almost nothing is known of his early life. By 1851 he had joined his father in his excursion business at Leicester, taking a strenuous part in the arrangements for bringing up travellers by the Midland Railway to London for the Great Exhibition. In 1856 he went into the service of the Midland Co as excursion traffic superintendent at £75 a year. Then in 1859 he became a printer on his own account in Leicester and helped his father part-time. He went back to his father's business in 1864 and remained with it for the rest of his life. Its headquarters were removed to London in 1865.

Thomas at first continued to direct affairs, with his son as his assistant. Thus in 1865 the father made an exploratory journey to the United States, and the son conducted the first excursion party there in 1866. But this role cannot have satisfied the younger man, already over thirty and fully conscious of his powers, and there was much friction between the two. Thomas's energies were flagging by 1871, when he took his son formally into partnership. For the next seven years the struggle between them went on quietly within the firm and drew into it, on both sides, the differing sympathies of the family. In 1878 Thomas retired, deriving henceforth a fixed annuity from the business.

John Mason Cook was by this time making his own reputation. He organised the dispatch of supplies sent from England for the relief of Parisians after the siege of 1870-71. He devoted much attention to developing the firm's business in Egypt, opening an office in Cairo in 1873

A song sheet cover of the 1880s showing John Mason Cook guiding a tour up Vesuvius, Italy (courtesy of Thomas Cook & Son Ltd).

and an hotel at Luxor two years later. This led to his undertaking two important public commissions: one for the transport of the sick and wounded after the battle of Tel-el-Kebir in 1882, the other the enormous operation of conveying 10,000 troops and 200,000 tons of stores and coal from England to Wadi Halfa for the Gordon Relief Expedition in 1884.

Under his direction the business of the firm now extended even further. Its first office in Australia was opened in 1879, at Melbourne. He went twice to India, in 1880 and 1885, and established its business there. A by-product of those journeys was a contract for conveying pilgrims to Mecca. The firm grew into a great international enterprise. It set up a Banking and Exchange Department in 1879. By 1891, when it celebrated its jubilee, John Mason could point out that its salaried staff amounted to 1,714, with 169 offices and agencies across the world. When the business had opened in London twenty-six years earlier its employees, besides his father and himself, numbered two.

John Mason Cook and his father had some qualities in common. Both were exceptionally energetic, and capable of long spells of uninterrupted hard work. But their minds and temperaments were quite different. Thomas was in his own field an original genius, a man who always dealt in ideas; John Mason a first-rate administrator, daunted by no challenge to his powers of organisation. If the son's mind eventually concentrated itself into a coarse-grained hardness, that was in part because he found his father's interest and concerns exasperatingly diffuse. But they had between them the range of thinking and executive power that established and kept Thomas Cook & Son well ahead of all its rivals in Britain and Europe.

John Mason Cook in 1861 married Emma, daughter of Thomas Hodges, a wealthy elastic-web manufacturer of Leicester; they had three sons, who all went into the family business. He died at Walton-on-Thames on 4 March 1899 leaving £622,534 gross.

JACK SIMMONS

Sources:

Unpublished

The archives of the firm, in terms of personal papers, are disappointing. They include a few documents concerning the internal differences of the 1870s, perhaps the most important of them a long memorandum by John Mason Cook, dated 19 January 1878: Guard Book Folio no 13, pp 290-306. The firm also has a good, though not complete, run of *The Excursionist*, which announces its programmes, from 1851 onwards, and a most valuable collection of handbills.

PrC.

Published

DNB.

John S Pudney, *The Thomas Cook Story* (Michael Joseph, 1953).

W Fraser Rae, *The Business of Travel* (Thomas Cook & Son, 1891).

Edmund Swinglehurst, *The Romantic Journey* (Pica Editions, 1974).

—, *Cook's Tours* (Blandford Press, 1982).

Thomas Cook ca 1850 (courtesy of Thomas Cook & Son Ltd).

COOK, Thomas

(1808-1892)

Travel agent

Thomas Cook was born at Melbourne, Derbyshire, on 22 November 1808, the only son of John Cook and Elizabeth née Perkins, the daughter of a Baptist minister. His parents were poor, and after his father died when he was four years old, his mother brought him up. He had some schooling but went to work at the age of ten, and at fourteen became a wood-turner. He served as a Baptist 'village missionary' in the counties of Rutland, Northampton, and Lincoln in 1828-31, covering over 2,000 miles on foot in 1829, and then set up as a cabinet-maker at Market Harborough, Leicestershire. Here in 1833 he married Marianne née Mason, daughter of a farmer and worker in the Baptist Chapel, and grew increasingly absorbed in the cause of temperance, distributing, writing and printing temperance tracts, and opening a book depository in 1839.

In 1841 he worked out a plan for conveying a large body of people by railway from Leicester to a temperance fête at Loughborough. With the ready collaboration of the Midland Counties Railway Co the idea was carried into effect with entire success on 5 July 1841, when 570 passengers paid a shilling each for their return fare. It was not the first railway excursion. But Cook now began to use the facilities offered by railways in a new way. He assumed the role of an agent who organised the excursion, under an agreement with the railway. He himself bore personal responsibility for those who took tickets by travelling with the trains; he even provided them with small guide-books, of his own writing.

Cook moved to Leicester in late 1841 as a printer and publicist for the South Midland Temperance Association, and organized further excursions of the same sort in 1842-44. In 1845 he took them further afield, to Liverpool and North Wales. Next year he offered a trip to Scotland, the first of a series running almost without a break to 1862. Cook secured the agency for the Midland Railway's excursion traffic to the Great Exhibition in 1851, to which he brought a total of 165,000 people or 2.75 per cent of the Exhibition's six million visitors. He began to give his full time to the excursion business in 1854. He had by then extended his operations to Ireland, and he moved across the Channel in 1855-56. After some difficulties he came to terms with the Eastern Counties and London Brighton & South Coast Railways, taking his travellers to the Continent by Harwich and Newhaven.

He went through much trouble in 1862-63 (when the Scottish companies withdrew the facilities he had enjoyed and the Midland refused to give him any exclusive agency for the traffic to the second Exhibition, of 1862), but he recovered his initiative boldly. Hitherto his whole business had been managed from Leicester. In 1865 he acquired premises in Fleet Street, London, and opened an office there with his son John Mason Cook (qv) as manager.

OPENING
OF THE
MELBOURNE RAILWAY
MR. THOMAS COOK
(Formerly of Melbourne)
Respectfully intimates to his old Friends and Fellow Townspeople that, in connection with the visit of his
FIRST EXCURSION PARTY,
FROM LEICESTER,
ON THURSDAY, SEPTEMBER 10th, 1868,
(To arrive at about 4-0 p.m.)
HE WILL GIVE AN
ADDRESS
IN THE ATHENÆUM,
TO INHABITANTS & VISITORS,
Briefly recapitulating some of the events of his EXCURSION and TOURIST LIFE, since leaving Melbourne nearly 40 years ago; and anticipatory of his approaching Trips to
ITALY, EGYPT & PALESTINE.
FREE ADMISSION
AFTER TEA, AT HALF-PAST SEVEN O'CLOCK.
T. COOK, Printer, Granby Street, Leicester.

An early Thomas Cook advertisement (courtesy of Thomas Cook & Son Ltd).

Cook was a pioneer not only in the promotion of a new kind of travel but also in providing for his customers' accommodation. His wife had run a temperance boarding-house in Leicester and for a time he also owned one in Great Russell Street, opposite the British Museum. He supplied, by various expedients, accommodation for many of the working-class visitors he brought to London for the two Exhibitions. About 1864 he began entering into arrangements with hotel keepers to accept his coupons in payment for board and lodging, which allowed him to offer excursions at fully inclusive prices, and became the originator of the 'package tour'.

His horizons now extended beyond Europe. In 1865 he went to the United States, armed with letters of introduction from John Bright and W

Thomas Cook (seated fourth from right) at Pompeii on one of his earliest Italian tours, ca 1864/5 (courtesy of Thomas Cook & Son Ltd).

E Forster, and a tour there followed in the next year. In 1868 another series started, to Egypt and Palestine.

The firm changed its title to Thomas Cook & Son in 1871, and that was a proper acknowledgment of the part John Mason Cook was now playing in it. Unhappily divergences of opinion now developed between father and son. Thomas withdrew from the active direction of the firm in 1878.

Though the firm he founded had its rivals, it quite outdistanced them all. Thomas Cook was not an impeccable man of business; there his son was much his superior. But no one ever justly called his integrity into question, and on that his whole life's work rested. He did more than any other one man to open up for the English middle classes, and to some extent for working men too, the notion of organised travel, in their own country and abroad. He was trusted because he performed what he had undertaken; and he was enabled to perform because he took the infinite pains necessary to prepare each operation in advance.

Thomas Cook lost his only daughter tragically in 1880, and his wife in 1884; he himself was then going blind. He retained all his enthusiasm for the temperance cause. He died at Leicester on 18 July 1892, leaving the curiously small fortune of £2,731 gross.

JACK SIMMONS

Writings:

Cook's Scottish Tourist Official Directory (W Tweedie; W H Smith & Son, 1861).

A Collection of Temperance Melodies and Hymns, Original and Select, Compiled under the Direction of the Committee of the Leicester Temperance Society (Leicester: E T Lawrence, 1863).

Guide to Cook's Excursions to Paris; and Directory of Excursions and Tours in Switzerland and Italy (Thomas Cook, London and Leicester, 1865).

Handbook to International Tours (Cook's Tourist Office, 1865).

Letters to His Royal Highness the Prince of Wales, and to the Rt Hon the Earl of Clarendon, Foreign Secretary of State: In Reply to Various Misstatements and Calumnies Contained in 'A Diary in the East' by W H Russell, LLD; and to Certain Papers by 'Cornelius O'Dowd' — Charles Lever ... in 'Blackwood's Magazine' (Cook's Tourist & Publication Office, 1870).

Anti-smoker Selections. First Series. Science v Tobacco: A Selection of Original Medical Testimonies, Chiefly by John Higginbottom, Contributed to the Anti-smoker (Elliot Stock, 1874?).

Anti-smoker Selections. Second Series. Religion and Commonsense v Tobacco: Selected Articles from the Anti-smoker (Elliot Stock, 1874?).

Temperance Jubilee Celebrations at Leicester and Market Harborough, from Nov 13 to 18 1886 (Depot of the National Temperance League, 1886).

Temperance Testimonies (National Temperance League Publication Depot, 1893).

Sources:

Unpublished

For the records of the firm see under 'John Mason Cook'.

PrC.

Published

DNB.

John Pudney, *The Thomas Cook Story* (Michael Joseph, 1953).

W Fraser Rae, *The Business of Travel* (Thomas Cook & Son, 1891).

Jack Simmons, 'Thomas Cook of Leicester' *Transactions of the Leicestershire Archaeological and Historical Society* 49 (1973-74).

Edmund Swinglehurst, *The Romantic Journey* (Pica Editions, 1974).

—, *Cook's Tours* (Blandford Press, 1982).

Clive Cookson (courtesy of the Central Library, Newcastle upon Tyne).

COOKSON, Clive

(1879-1971)

Lead manufacturer

Clive Cookson was born at Hexham, Northumberland, on 16 September 1879, the third son of Norman Charles Cookson (qv) and his wife Phoebe née Newall. He was educated at Harrow, and subsequently went gold-prospecting before joining the family firm. He followed his father as chairman of Cookson & Co Ltd in 1909, and although other members of the family were directors of the company, Clive Cookson was the dominant figure after his father's death until his own retirement. He took on a successful company and made it the single most powerful firm in the lead manufacturing industry. Although it remained a private company until 1924, he modernised it by bringing in non-family managers and directors, paying particular attention to the recruitment of science graduates even before 1914. Despite this policy, he remained very actively the chief executive of the firm, a dominating paternalist universely known to the labour force as 'Mr Clive'.

In the early 1920s he was responsible for pursuing an amalgamation which produced Associated Lead Manufacturers Ltd in 1924, a company which by 1930 dominated the lead manufacturing industry, having taken over most of the major firms. Clive Cookson was its first chairman and in 1930 he took it into a merger with the Liverpool paint manufacturers, Goodlass Wall & Co Ltd, to form Goodlass Wall & Lead Industries Ltd (from 1967 Lead Industries Group Ltd; from 1982 Cookson Group PLC). Cookson remained chairman of the new group until he retired in 1947. By that time he had been responsible for the rationalisation of the lead companies, with the closure of a great deal of surplus capacity and, in recognition of the declining demand for some lead products, had laid down a policy of diversification. This was to be into fields analogous to the existing interests of the company and took the form of development in other non-ferrous metals and in ceramics, commencing with the purchase in 1944 of Fry's Metal Foundries Ltd. Net profits of Associated Lead Manufacturers rose from £83,000 in 1925 to £522,000 in 1949.

Apart from his involvement in the lead industry, which brought him a number of chairmanships and directorships of companies which became part of Goodlass Wall & Lead Industries Ltd and also led to his appointment as chairman of the Lead Employers' Council, Cookson had many other industrial activities, especially on Tyneside. He was elected to the board of Consett Iron Co Ltd in 1922 and appointed chairman in 1937, a post which he retained until 1957, having guided the company through a very difficult period. He also continued the family involvement with the coal industry until nationalisation in 1947. He was chairman of the Mickley Group, which included the Mickley Coal Co Ltd, Acomb Coal Co Ltd, Cowpen Coal Co Ltd, Hazelrigg and Burradon Coal Co Ltd, and Wm Benson & Sons Ltd. As a result of these interests, he was appointed Northern Region Fuel and Power Controller and coal production adviser for Northumberland and Durham during the Second World War. He was chairman of the local board of the North British & Mercantile Assurance Co Ltd and of the Northumberland Sea Fisheries Committee. He was a vice-president of the Federation of British Industries, 1925-57, and was chairman of its Northern Regional Council.

In 1913 Cookson moved from his father's old home of 'Oakwood' to the nearby estate of 'Nether Warden', near Hexham, where he lived until his death. He also owned land in Northumberland, where he pursued his interest in forestry. Apart from shooting and fishing, his recreational activities were centred on his home: he was (like his father) a keen gardener; he bred goldfish; and he was a serious collector of pictures, pottery and silver. Made an honorary Doctor of Civil Law by the University of Durham in 1945, he was a member of Brook's and the Northern Counties and Union (Newcastle) Clubs.

Cookson in 1913 married Marion Amy James, daughter of Archibald Hubert James, a landowner; they had two sons and one daughter.

He died on 14 February 1971, leaving an estate valued at £398,904 gross.

D J ROWE

Writings:

'Antimony' in George B Richardson and William W Tomlinson (eds), *Official Handbook to Newcastle and District* (Newcastle upon Tyne: British Association for the Advancement of Science, 1916).

Sources:

Unpublished

Tyne and Wear RO, Associated Lead Manufacturers Ltd, uncatalogued papers.

BCe.

MCe.

Published

Burke's Landed Gentry 1965.

Evening Chronicle (Newcastle) 15 Feb 1971.

Newcastle Journal 15 Feb 1971.

David J Rowe, *Lead Manufacturing in Britain. A History* (Croom Helm, 1983).

Water Life and Aquaria World Oct 1947.

WWW.

COOKSON, Norman Charles

(1841-1909)

Lead manufacturer

Norman Charles Cookson was born in Newcastle upon Tyne on 26 November 1841, the second son of William Isaac Cookson (1812-88) and his wife Jane Anne née Cuthbert, daughter of his own father's partner. The Cookson family's glass manufacturing interests were sold in 1846 (as a result of growing competition following the abolition of the excise duty on glass in 1845) and William Cookson, with his partners John and William Cuthbert, moved into the chemical industry; here William Cookson's patents for the manufacture of sulphuric acid (1844) and the use of iron oxide in the reduction of lead ores (1854) gave him a foothold in the lead industry. In the 1850s the partners developed two works at Hayhole and Howdon on the Tyne for the manufacture of a variety of lead products.

Norman Cookson was educated at Harrow before joining the family firm. From the mid-1860s he and his brother, George John, were responsible for running the firm, although Norman was the dominant partner and George retired to Devon in 1889. From 1868 the brothers each received a salary of £300 per annum, plus 5 per cent of profits which averaged £7,500 per annum over the next six years, and in 1869 they were made partners. Considerable changes were now made. William Cookson's original Gateshead works was closed in 1869 and antimony and Venetian red production transferred to a vacant part of the Howdon site, thus reducing overheads. New processes were introduced, such as the replacement in 1874 of Pattinson desilverising plant by the Rozan process, while in 1876 a lead rolling mill was installed and in 1882 the manufacture of lead pipe introduced. Perhaps more than any other partner in lead manufacture in the country at this time, Norman was technically competent. He took out patents in 1876 for improvements in the manufacture of white lead and gave evidence to the 1878 Royal Commission on Noxious Vapours. In 1885 he took out a patent for improvements in the smelting of antimony sulphide, and in 1889 one for improvements in coating iron with antimony, while his work in electricity led to patents for improvements in secondary batteries in 1882.

Perhaps the most significant result of Cookson's interest in research and development was his firm's installation in 1898 of plant to manufacture white lead by the chamber process (after two decades of experimentation) to add to its capacity in the traditional 'stack' process. The firm was the only UK manufacturer to adopt a satisfactory new process in this field before 1914 and by that date its output accounted for about 25 per cent of that of the UK industry. In 1914 the firm's total employment was over 500 and a measure of Norman Cookson's impact is the growth of the number of monthly salaried staff from eight in 1875, to 16 in 1890, to 50 in 1908. Norman's salary rose from £300 plus a share in profits of about £400 per annum in the early 1870s, to £1,000 salary by 1889, together with a profit from the firm (which in a good year such as 1889 was £18,000).

Cookson had a number of other business interests. Between 1863 and 1872 he was a partner in the Newcastle engineering firm of John Jameson & Co; from 1865 he was a director and later chairman of the Tyne General Ferry Co Ltd and he was subsequently a major shareholder in and director of Parsons Marine Steam Turbine Co Ltd. He was also chairman of the Mickley Coal Co Ltd and of the Wallsend & Hebburn Coal Co Ltd from its formation in 1892, and a director of the Cowpen Coal Co Ltd. He was a director and chairman of W C Gibson & Co (later Adamsez of Scotswood), 1895-1905. He was a member of the Newcastle Chemical Society, 1875-82 and a founder member of the Institute of Metals in 1908 and was made a vice-president in the following year.

In his spare time Cookson was best known as an internationally recognised grower of, and authority on, orchids, and he was a vice-president of the Royal Horticultural Society. He was also well-known for his contributions to local charities. He was president of the Northern Scientific Club and a member of the Linnaean Society and the Northern Counties Club.

Cookson married in 1873 Phoebe, daughter of Robert Stirling Newall, FRS of Gateshead; they had four sons and two daughters. From 1879 Cookson lived at 'Oakwood', Wylam, Northumberland, where he died on 15 May 1909, leaving an estate of £201,403 gross.

D J ROWE

Writings:

'On Rozan's Process for Desilverising Lead' *Transactions of the Newcastle Chemical Society* 4 (1877-80).

PP, RC Noxious Vapours (1878) C 2159-I.

'Lead' and 'Antimony' in Wigham Richardson (ed), *Visit of the British Association to Newcastle upon Tyne 1889, Official Local Guide. Industrial Section* (Newcastle upon Tyne, 1889).

British Patents:
1876 (708 and 709).
1882 (3,941 and 4,428).
1885 (3,386).
1889 (4,428).

Sources:

Unpublished

Tyne and Wear RO, Associated Lead Manufacturers Ltd, uncatalogued papers.
PrC.

Published

Burke's Landed Gentry 1965.

Newcastle Evening Chronicle 17 May 1909.

David J Rowe, *Lead Manufacturing in Britain. A History* (Croom Helm, 1983).

Roland A Cookson (courtesy of the Central Library, Newcastle upon Tyne).

COOKSON, Roland Antony

(1908-)

Lead manufacturer

Roland Antony Cookson was born at Chesterton, Cambridgeshire, on 12 December 1908, the son of Bryan Cookson, an assistant in astrophysics at Cambridge University, and his wife Millicent née Elliot. He was the grandson of Norman Cookson (qv). Like his father, he was educated at Harrow and Magdalen College, Oxford, where he read chemistry and Modern Greats. Unlike his father, however, who had become lecturer in astronomy at the University of Cambridge, he elected to enter the family firm in 1930.

Initially working in the Cookson works and offices and also as manager (1936-37) of the Perivale Research Laboratories of Goodlass Wall & Lead Industries Ltd, he became a director of that company in 1948 and a managing director in 1952. This was a period in which the company was beginning a major diversification and he was responsible for developing and greatly extending the policy begun by his uncle, Clive Cookson (qv). He played a considerable part in the introduction of the manufacture of zircon and zircon products at Cookson's Howdon works on Tyneside in 1950 and its subsequent development as the only British producer and, with several overseas plants, possibly the world's major producer. In 1962 he became chairman of the group (by then only just outside the top 100 British companies by turnover), a position which he retained until his retirement in 1973, although he remained on the board of Lead Industries Group Ltd, as a non-executive director until 1980. In his time as chairman the policy of diversification by takeover was continued with major expansion into the field of ceramics. Between 1962 and 1973 Lead Industries Group sales rose from just over £33 million to £95 million.

Roland Cookson was the natural Tyneside industrialist to assume the activities of Clive Cookson, when the latter retired. In 1955 he was appointed a director of Consett Iron Co Ltd and he became chairman from 1964 until nationalisation in 1967. Until the coal industry's nationalisation in 1946 he was a director of the family coal interests: Acomb Coal Co Ltd, Wm Benson & Son Ltd, Cowpen Coal Co Ltd, Hazelrigg & Burradon Coal Co Ltd, and Mickley Coal Co Ltd. He was appointed a director of Lloyds Bank Ltd in 1964 and became chairman of its Northern Regional board in 1966, a post he held until 1979. He had previously been a member of the North-Eastern Regional board of Martins Bank Ltd. Among his other directorships were the North East Electricity Supply Co (until nationalisation in 1947) and Basinghall Mining Syndicate Ltd. He was a member of the Port of Tyne Authority from 1968 to 1974; a member of the Newcastle and Gateshead Chamber of Commerce and its president, 1955-57; vice-chairman of the Northern Regional Board for Industry, 1949-65, and member of the Northern Economic Planning Council, 1965-68. He was a member of the Northern

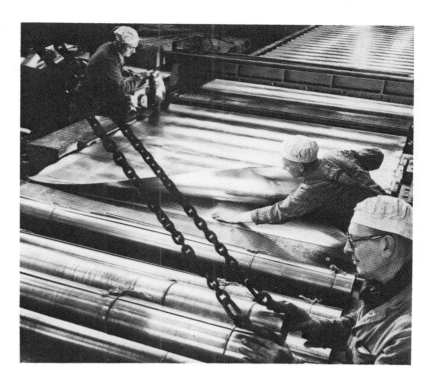

A pair of finished sheets of lead on mill, preparatory to coiling, Millwall, 1949 (courtesy of Associated Lead Manufacturers Ltd).

Regional Council of the Confederation of British Industries, its vice-chairman, 1968-70, and chairman, 1970-72. He was chairman of the Northern Industrial Development Board, 1976-80.

He has taken a great interest in higher education in the region and especially in establishing links between the universities and industry. Between 1962 and 1973 he was chairman of the Appointments Board of the Universities of Durham and Newcastle upon Tyne and he is a member of both Court and Council of the latter. In 1946 he was made OBE and in 1974 CBE and in the latter year he was made an honorary Doctor of Civil Law of the University of Newcastle upon Tyne. He lived at Howden Dene, Corbridge until 1980, when he moved to Wylam.

He married in 1931 Rosamond Gwladys, elder daughter of Sir John Storey Barwick, Bt; they had one daughter. His wife died in 1973 and he married secondly in 1974 Dr Anne Aitchison, widow of Sir Stephen Aitchison, Bt.

D J ROWE

Sources:

Unpublished

BCe.

COOKSON Roland Antony

Published

Burke's Landed Gentry 1965.

Newcastle & Gateshead Incorporated Chamber of Commerce, *Industrial Tyneside* 33 (May 1955).

David J Rowe, *Lead Manufacturing in Britain. A History* (Croom Helm, 1983).

WW 1982.

Arthur Cooper (courtesy of Coopers & Lybrand).

COOPER, Arthur

(1833-1892)

Accountant

Arthur Cooper was born in 1833, the second son of Emanuel Cooper (d 1851), a staunch Quaker and one of the founders, and later deputy chairman, of the London & County Bank (1841-48). His parents instilled their strong religious teaching into their sons, who translated their Nonconformist ethics into business practice. Both Arthur and his elder brother William started as clerks with the City accountants Quilter, Ball & Co. William left in 1854, taking two rooms at 13 George Street, Mansion House, to set up on his own. Shortly afterwards Arthur joined him and became a partner in 1857, when the style W & A Cooper was adopted, being changed to Cooper Brothers & Co in 1861. On William Cooper's death in 1871, Arthur became the senior partner, his two younger brothers Francis (d 1893) and Ernest (qv) having become partners in 1871 and 1872 respectively; Arthur remained in charge of the firm until his death.

Arthur Cooper was involved in a number of important insolvencies, the major source of employment for accountants in the mid-nineteenth century until the 1856 and 1862 Companies Acts expanded the volume of audit work. For example, he liquidated the Oriental Commercial Bank, and was receiver of the Swedish & Norwegian Railway. An obituary suggested that as a Trustee in Bankruptcy Cooper had 'probably more and larger estates than any other London accountant' {*Accountant* (1892)}. With the spread of public limited liability companies after the 1850s he also secured a share of the growing market in auditing, and concentrated largely on a number of relatively small-scale banks like the Anglo-Egyptian Bank (established 1867), Direktion der Diskonto-Gesellschaft, Mercantile Bank of India (1892), Bank of Mauritius (1894), and the Mines & Banking Corporation (1895), the last two being obtained after his death. Other partners also audited bank accounts. Ernest Cooper was joint auditor of the London & Provincial Bank. E H Fletcher (a partner in Cooper Brothers from 1873) audited the London & South Western Bank, while the audit of the National Bank of India (now Grindlays Bank) was acquired in 1871, the audit report being signed jointly by C N Cooke and

Francis Cooper, the fee a mere 50 guineas. In addition, William Cooper had become joint auditor of the Bombay, Baroda & Central India Railway. A number of important audit clients were obtained during the late 1880s as Cooper Brothers acted for Brin's Oxygen Co Ltd (now BOC International) from its formation in 1886, while the Guardian Assurance Ltd (now Guardian Royal Exchange Assurance), Stewarts & Lloyds, the steel makers, and the British South Africa Co were all added in 1889, together with Babcock & Wilcox in 1890.

Arthur Cooper became a Council member of the Institute of Accountants in London in 1876; when the English Institute of Chartered Accountants received its royal charter in 1880 he occupied a Council seat, serving as its vice-president in 1882-83 and its third president in 1883-84. He was especially concerned with devising the Institute's by-laws (designed to regulate members' conduct) and until 1892 was chairman of its building committee whose planning produced the present structure in Moorgate Place. He served as vice-president of the Chartered Accountants' Benevolent Association, to which he donated his fees earned as an Institute examiner. In addition, Arthur Cooper was a member of the committee of five appointed by the profession to make recommendations to the Board of Trade about the Bankruptcy Bill that finally resulted in the 1883 Act. Not only were his suggestions important in this respect, but in addition a court case in which he was involved (*Titterton v Cooper*) also contributed to the legislation. Arthur Cooper was the trustee of a bankrupt who had pledged a lease to a creditor. As the law then stood the trustee could not disclaim the lease without injuring the creditor to whom it was pledged. The landlord sued the trustee for rent and delapidations, and the trustee was held personally liable. Arthur Cooper brought the position to the notice of Joseph Chamberlain (qv), President of the Board of Trade, and although the Bankruptcy Bill had then already passed the Commons, the latter arranged for an amendment to be added in the House of Lords, whereby a trustee, with the leave of the court, could disclaim his interest.

In the family, Arthur Cooper was regarded as the ablest of the four brothers and had a fine legal mind, honed on and critical in insolvency work. An obituary reiterated the point: 'combining as he did the knowledge of the lawyer with that of a clever expert in accounts; great industry with sound common sense; splendid organizing powers with sentry-like watchfulness; his services for the welfare of the profession can scarcely be exaggerated, or sufficiently acknowledged.' {*ibid*}

He married in 1869 Maria Cole, daughter of Edward Joseph Cole, a merchant. They had three sons and three daughters; his son Harold Arthur Cooper entered the firm to become a partner in 1910. Arthur Cooper died on 22 August 1892 leaving £32,223 gross.

EDGAR JONES

Sources:

Unpublished

MCe.

COOPER Arthur

PrC.

Published

The Accountant No 925, 27 Aug 1892.

C & L Journal June 1979.

A History of Cooper Brothers & Co 1854-1954 (Batsford, for Coopers, 1954).

Titterton versus Cooper, 9 Queen's Bench Division 473 (1881-82).

COOPER, Ernest

(1848-1926)

Accountant

Portrait of Ernest Cooper (courtesy of Coopers & Lybrand).

Ernest Cooper was born in 1848, the fourth son of Emanuel Cooper (d 1851), deputy chairman of the London & County Bank, 1841-48. Ernest, as the youngest of 13 children, in August 1864 joined his brothers William, Arthur (qv) and Francis, in the family's City accountancy practice, founded by William in 1854. Ernest became a partner in 1872, remaining so until retirement in 1923. Like his brothers he followed his father's Quaker religion, incorporating his beliefs into the business's principles. Surprisingly, however, Ernest recalled in later life that he had been in part educated abroad at a Roman Catholic school.

Ernest Cooper was probably responsible for his firm's long association with Lever Brothers Ltd, as William Hesketh Lever (qv), was introduced to him by the District Bank. When Lever's family soap-making business in Birkenhead became a public company in 1894, it was most likely that Ernest Cooper prepared the accountant's report for the first prospectus of Lever Brothers Ltd. The audit fee in this initial year was £200. Later Francis D'Arcy Cooper (qv), his nephew, left the partnership in 1923 to join the board of Lever Brothers, becoming chairman in 1925.

Recalling his own career in later life, Ernest Cooper observed that 'business journeys have taken my firm to all the five continents. Personally, I have visited on business all but two or three of the European countries, and only North and South Africa and North America. My brother William in the early 'sixties paid a long visit on business to Russia' {Cooper (1921) 52}. These trips were often for English clients with overseas interests and involved the collection of debts. His first overseas assignment had been in 1874 to Hamburg where he investigated the accounts of a firm associated with an insolvent business in London. Visits to Frankfurt, Bremen and Venice were supplemented by two to

Egypt and one to the diamond mines of South Africa, whilst several journeys to Greece had probably been occasioned by his reconstruction of the Ionian Bank in 1879.

In recalling the low social standing of accountants in the 1860s Ernest Cooper suggested that this related to their heavy involvement with insolvency work: 'we may disregard the then current gibes that if an accountant were required he would be found at the bar of the nearest tavern to the Bankruptcy Court in Basinghall Street' {*ibid*, 43}. He himself undertook many insolvencies covering a wide variety of enterprises including the liquidation of a salt works (possibly the Victoria Salt Co which from 1872 shared premises with Coopers at 13 George Street, as did their audit client the British South Africa Co). Other insolvency commissions embraced a major London marine engine business, a Texas cattle ranch, a Canadian lumber property, a hotel in South Wales, asbestos mines in Sicily, a colliery and a Yorkshire brewery.

When Arthur Cooper died, Ernest took over as senior partner in 1892-93 and unlike his predecessor, who rejected the notion of territorial expansion on the grounds that the partners must be able personally to supervise all the firm's work, gradually opened a number of branch offices beginning with Liverpool in 1920. This particular branch was designed to assist the Lever audit. Others followed at Brussels in 1921 (presumably to deal with Levers' factories in Belgium and the Netherlands) and at New York in 1926 after a request from their client Cunards. Overseas growth continued throughout the inter-war years particularly in the African continent. It is difficult to estimate the size of Cooper Brothers' London office staff though the fact that 59 joined the armed forces in the First World War suggests that it was not particularly large. However, in establishing a separate tax section in the mid-1920s as part of a policy of departmentalisation, Coopers were in advance of common practice.

Ernest Cooper was himself concerned in a libel case following the failure of Barker's Bank, after having been criticised in the press for his role as that bank's special manager and trustee. He took the matter to court in 1892 winning damages of £2,000 which resulted in the bankruptcy of the newspaper in question. Another event of much comment concerned their client, the Marconi's Wireless Telegraph Co. For the last three years of Ernest Cooper's period as senior partner the firm had, on the issue of inter-company investments, been qualifying the audit report. Subsequently in 1927 when events reached a crisis, and following a protracted investigation, a meeting of shareholders opposed Cooper Brothers' re-election and the firm withdrew as auditors, an occurrence of considerable rarity and public comment. During the First World War, along with other leading City accountants, Ernest Cooper helped to administer a number of enemy banks established in Britain, including the Deutsche Bank.

Like his elder brother Arthur, Ernest Cooper earned a considerable reputation as a legal expert, and published a series of articles on the notion of profit and the nature of the auditor's role. Amongst his writings was a virtually unique autobiographical study of an early chartered accountant's career. Entitled 'Fifty-seven Years in an Accountant's Office', this lucid and evocative text offered a revealing insight into the workings of his profession and the character of his many rivals in the City.

COOPER Ernest

Much involved in the profession's organization, Ernest Cooper joined the Institute of Accountants in London in 1876. He was a founder member of the Institute of Chartered Accountants in England and Wales and was elected to its Council in 1891, his publications, it was said, having been influential in this respect. He became the Institute's vice-president in 1898-99 and president in 1899-1901, remaining on the Council for a total of thirty-three years.

By his wife Edith Isabella he had at least one son, Stuart Ranson Cooper, and one daughter, May Isabel. Ernest Cooper died on 4 January 1926, leaving £194,403 gross.

EDGAR JONES

Writings:

'Chartered Accountants as Auditors of Companies' *The Accountant* 12, no 623 (1886).

'What is Profit of a Company?' *ibid* 14, no 727 (1888).

'Notes on Mr Welton's paper "On the Profit of Companies Available for Distribution" *ibid* 17, no 839 (1891).

'Chartered Accountants and the Profit Question' *ibid* 20, no 1042 (1894).

'Fifty-seven Years in an Accountant's Office' *Institute of Chartered Accountants in England and Wales, Proceedings of the Autumnal Meeting Held in London on 11th ... October 1921* (1921) (reprinted in *The Accountant* 65, no 2446 (1921)).

Sources:

Unpublished

PrC; Will.

Published

The Accountant no 2666 (9 Jan 1926).

Thomas A Lee and R H Parker, *The Evolution of Corporate Financial Accounting* (Sunbury on Thames: Nelson, 1979).

A History of Cooper Brothers & Co 1854-1954 (Batsford, for Coopers, 1954).

*Sir Francis D'Arcy Cooper
(courtesy of Unilever PLC).*

COOPER, Sir Francis D'Arcy

(1882-1941)

Accountant and industrial manager

Francis D'Arcy Cooper was born at Cumberland Terrace, London on 17 November 1882, the son of Francis Cooper, partner in the accounting firm Cooper Brothers & Co, and Ada Frances née Power. He was educated at a private school, and Wellington College; he then spent a year in Paris before joining the family firm in early 1899.

Cooper Brothers & Co had been founded in 1854 by Francis Cooper's brother William. Francis Cooper himself became a partner in the firm in 1872. D'Arcy Cooper (as he was known) was not particularly attracted towards accountancy, and became an accountant probably only because it was his father's chosen profession. He took his articles with the family firm, was admitted to the Institute of Chartered Accountants in England and Wales in 1904, and became a partner in 1910. During the First World War he served in the Royal Field Artillery, and was seriously wounded on the Somme. After a year in hospital, he worked at the War Office until January 1919 when he rejoined Cooper Brothers, soon becoming its senior partner. During the next four years he did much to improve the position and prestige of the firm, which had suffered from the absence of its partners in the services.

One of the firm's largest clients was Lever Brothers, soap manufacturers, whose chairman was William Lever, the First Lord Leverhulme (qv). Cooper initially obtained the confidence of this famous entrepreneur (in Cooper's words he became Leverhulme's 'blue-eyed boy') by producing an impressive report on a German company that Leverhulme was considering acquiring in 1910. The two men possessed very different personalities; Leverhulme was extrovert, ebullient and autocratic, whereas Cooper was a naturally shy man, reserved, unaffected and less dominating in manner. Nevertheless, they developed a strong mutual regard, and Leverhulme once remarked that Cooper was 'one of the type of men that I consider most resemble a warm fire and people naturally seem to come up to him for warmth' {Wilson (1954) I 269}. Other assessments of Cooper show that he was forceful, imaginative and that he had a lively sense of humour.

Lever Brothers, formed in 1885 and incorporated as a private company in 1890, had become probably Britain's largest holding company by 1920. Throughout much of this period the company functioned as a one-man business under Leverhulme's dictatorship, and the principal theme of his corporate strategy was expansion. In the immediate post-war period, Leverhulme seemed to lose his commercial sense, and excessive optimism concerning future prospects caused insufficient consideration to be given either to profitability or to the financial implications of growth. The vulnerability of the company was further aggravated by Leverhulme's desire to retain control of the ordinary share capital, since this resulted in large issues of preference shares carrying a fixed dividend entitlement. Matters came to a head in 1920 as the result of the disastrous purchase of the Niger Co, for over £8 million, without even taking the precaution of examining that company's accounts. The Niger Co was bought in an effort to guarantee Lever Brothers' supply of oils and fats, but shortly after the purchase, the prices of these raw materials collapsed; and it was discovered the Niger Co had an overdraft of £2 million. The banks refused to provide urgently-needed finance, and made it clear that they were alarmed by what seemed to them to be Leverhulme's reckless improvidence. The chairman turned to Cooper for help, and it says much for the accountant's personality and reputation in the City of London that he was able to persuade the banks to provide Lever Brothers with the finance they needed to avoid probable liquidation. The bankers regarded Cooper's continuing influence on the policy of Lever Brothers as their guarantee of the safety of their money. Initially Leverhulme resented having this check imposed upon his control of the company, but gradually he was won over by Cooper's tact, integrity and quiet charm.

In 1921 Cooper was asked to join the policy-making 'inner cabinet' recently established by Leverhulme. From that date Cooper possessed the authority of a director, though it was not until 1923 that he formally resigned from the family firm to take up the appointment of vice-chairman of Lever Brothers. This must have been a difficult decision. There is little doubt that the family firm suffered a serious loss as a result of his leaving, but the new post represented an exciting challenge.

Leverhulme had groomed his son to succeed him as chairman, and it is generally agreed that Hulme Lever was a capable businessman who did valuable work within the company. But by the time the First Lord Leverhulme died in 1925, it was clear that Cooper was the man for the job. Apparently Hulme Lever fully concurred with this popular assessment, and Cooper continued to enjoy excellent relations with the Second Lord Leverhulme, who accepted the post of Governor of the company.

Following his appointment as chairman, it became Cooper's responsibility to convert this ill-organised collection of companies into an efficient, modern industrial organisation. Before he became chairman, Cooper had already persuaded Leverhulme to set up a number of specialised committees to review various aspects of the operation of the company, including one to supervise the operation of the manufacturing companies, one to coordinate financial matters, and one to discuss the affairs of the overseas companies. Thus, some steps had been taken even before Leverhulme's death in the 'complete metamorphosis of Lever Brothers from a private empire owned and controlled by one man into a public company administered by a professional management' {Wilson (1977) 132}, a process Cooper's appointment confirmed and extended.

Cooper set about completing the rationalisation of the management structure of Lever Brothers. He encouraged managers to set their sights clearly on efficiency in production and sales. Companies within the group were no longer encouraged to compete with one another, a favourite policy of Leverhulme's which, before his death, Cooper had brought him to see must be modified. To help re-establish the financial health of the company, Cooper decided there would be no ordinary dividend for 1925 or 1926; all surplus property belonging to the company around the world was sold off. More graduates were recruited for management. Cooper joined the Cambridge University Appointments Board, indicating the importance he attached to this influx of new blood into the company. He had a gift for developing a sense of personal responsibility in his subordinates, a gift the autocratic Leverhulme had lacked.

By 1929 Lever Brothers' record profits of £5.5 million showed that Cooper's methods were having some success. The only company within the group that made a loss that year was Planters' margarine, which was under severe pressure from the Dutch combine, Margarine Unie, formed in 1927 by the merger of Jurgens and Van den Burgh. As in Lever Brothers, professional managers had taken over the direction of these Dutch margarine manufacturers from the founding families; with old family rivalries no longer a stumbling-block, the way was clear for the merger with Margarine Unie signed on 2 September 1929. Margarine Unie had first approached Lever Brothers in 1928, proposing to buy Planters'. Lever Brothers had replied with a counter-proposal to buy Margarine Unie's soap interests in Europe. Proposals and counter-proposals followed for many months, until eventually a scheme for the full amalgamation of the two companies emerged. There were to be two parent companies, Unilever Ltd and Unilever nv; the boards of the two holding companies were always to be identical. The nominal issued capital of the whole Unilever complex was nearly £100 million, making it one of the largest companies in Europe.

As chairman of Unilever Ltd, Cooper played a crucial role in guiding the new group through the problems of amalgamation, at a most difficult period for the world economy. His integrity, his clarity of mind, his insistence on the appointment of the best man for the job, regardless of nationality or business origins, won the respect and trust of his new Dutch colleagues. His commitment to the unity of the firm, and to the long-term interests of the united firm, was demonstrated when the necessity for the reorganisation of the structure of Unilever became clear in the late 1930s. The proportion of profits contributed by the Dutch and British parts of the company had changed significantly: in 1929, one-third of the profits had come from the British business; by 1937, owing to the increasing difficulties the Dutch group was having in trading in Europe, particularly in Germany, British interests contributed two-thirds of the profits. The redistribution of the assets of the two groups, so that they were more nearly equal, involved the sale of virtually all the Lever companies' assets outside the British Empire, including the highly profitable Lever Brothers' interests in the USA, to the Dutch company. Cooper's patient advocacy of the long-term advantages of this proposal, at first sight so unfavourable to the British company, gradually won over his colleagues and shareholders.

In the 1920s, Cooper's reforms had been directed at the reorganisation of the central control of Lever Brothers. Little had been done to reorganise production, although before Leverhulme's death the workforce at Port Sunlight had been reduced from 8,000 to 5,000; by 1927 the number of man-hours needed to produce a ton of soap had fallen from 115 to 61. Cooper proceeded cautiously, despite his growing conviction that the soap trade, still the bastion of the business, needed to be reformed. The UK market had ceased to grow, but within a static level of consumption, the demand for the older, hard soaps was declining, and that for the new flakes and powders increasing. But it was not until 1931, when Geoffrey Heyworth (qv), Cooper's most trusted subordinate, produced a plan for rationalising Unilever Ltd's 49 manufacturing companies and 48 separate sales organisations that these essential reforms were undertaken. Cooper accepted this plan at once, though it would take twenty years to be implemented fully.

Despite leaving the profession for industry in 1923, Cooper remained an active participant in discussions concerning the development of corporate financial reporting procedures. Sir Gilbert Garnsey's (qv) 1922 lecture criticised holding companies for failing to publish financial information concerning their subsidiaries, while the Greene Committee on Company Law Amendment (1925) was asked to consider whether the financial information published by holding companies should extend beyond the legal boundaries of the reporting unit. As the chairman of Lever Brothers, Cooper was well-qualified to contribute to this debate, and it is thought that the committee was closely guided by his opinions.

Cooper's letters written to the *Times* (3 June 1925) and the Greene Committee (24 June 1925), and verbal evidence given before the Greene Committee, strongly opposed the view, favoured by many accountants, that companies should be legally required to publish consolidated accounts. Cooper believed that corporate reporting procedures should be allowed to develop on a voluntary basis rather than be the subject of legislative compulsion, and his letter to the *Times* claimed that 'if directors considered that the publication of an amalgamated balance sheet was in the interests of their shareholders, they would no doubt publish it.' It is doubtful whether corporate management always behaves in such an altruistic manner, but it is likely that Cooper's arguments helped delay, until 1948, the introduction of a legal requirement for companies to publish group accounts.

Cooper's career with Lever Brothers is an early example of a chartered accountant transferring his skills to industry at top managerial level. It was the increased complexity and fragmentation of industrial companies, during the inter-war period, which demanded more sophisticated procedures for controlling and reporting the financial effects of business transactions. As companies expanded, partly through merger and partly through internal growth, there was a growing appreciation of the accountant's contribution to the efficient conduct of business operations. The achievements of people like Cooper were no doubt an important factor causing accountants to leave the profession for industry in increasing numbers.

Despite his heavy business commitments, Cooper devoted a great deal of energy to public work. He was a member of the Royal Commission on the Distribution of the Industrial Population, 1939-40, and vice-chairman of the Permanent Hops Committee. Before the Second World War he was a member of the Prime Minister's Industries Advisory Panel on Rearmament. From the early months of the war, although still nominally the chairman of Unilever Ltd, his time was largely taken up with his work as chairman of the executive committee of the Export Council of the Board of Trade, set up in early 1940. In this capacity he was responsible for the reorganisation of Britain's export trade, taking a leading part in the export drive. Although he never really recovered from a serious illness he suffered in 1939, and was often in considerable pain, he worked hard at this task. He was made a baronet in June 1941.

He married Evelyn, elder daughter of Arthur Radford, in 1913; they had no children. His recreations were shooting and golf. He died on 18 December 1941, leaving an estate proved at £648,012 gross.

J R EDWARDS

Writings:

(Oral and written evidence) *Companies Acts, 1908 to 1917: Minutes of Evidence Taken before the Departmental Committee Appointed by the Board of Trade to Consider and Report What Amendments are Desirable* (HMSO, 1925).

letter on publication of company accounts *Times* 3 June 1925.

Sources:

Unpublished

BCe.

PrC.

Published

The Accountant 27 Dec 1941.

DNB.

A History of Cooper Brothers & Co 1854-1954 (Batsford, for Coopers, 1954).

J Kitchen, 'The Accounts of British Holding Company Groups: Developments and Attitudes to Disclosure in the Early Years' *Accounting and Business Research* (Spring 1972).

Andrew Knox, *Coming Clean* (Heinemann, 1976).

Times 19 Dec 1941.

Charles Wilson, *The History of Unilever: A Study in Economic Growth and Social Change* (2 vols, Cassell, 1954).

—, 'Management and Policy in Large-Scale Enterprise: Lever Brothers and Unilever, 1918-1938' in Barry Supple (ed), *Essays in British Business History* (Oxford: Clarendon Press, 1977).

WWW.

COPELAND, Richard Ronald John

(1884-1958)

Bone china and earthenware manufacturer

Richard Ronald John Copeland was born at Kibblestone Hall near Stone, Staffordshire on 9 February 1884, the second son of Richard Pirie Copeland, the proprietor of W T Copeland & Sons, and Emily Henrietta née Wood. Since 1833 the Copeland family had owned the Spode firm, manufacturers of fine English bone china and earthenware in Stoke-on-Trent; William Copeland, Ronald's grandfather, started working for Josiah Spode at his London warehouse in 1784. Ronald, as he was known, was educated at Harrow School, after which he entered the family business.

Following the death of his father in 1913 Ronald Copeland with his younger brother, Gresham, directed the fortunes of the firm through the difficult war years and the recession which followed, though in 1915 he served in the Red Cross with the French Third Army, behind Verdun. While Gresham was responsible for the factory management, Ronald travelled to obtain orders and was especially successful in the United States where in 1923 he selected Sydney Thompson to act as sole distributing agent for Spode wares. His judgement in this case proved of inestimable value to the firm because Thompson established the Spode product in all the country's leading stores and extended its world-wide reputation.

Covered temple jars in Spode Fine Bone China (courtesy of Spode Ltd).

Copeland regarded his position as head of this business as carrying responsibilities also in the field of public duty. He was DL for Staffordshire from 1939 and also a JP. He assisted Robert Heath in the founding of the Biddulph Children's Orthopaedic Hospital at Biddulph, Staffordshire, and he was a member of the executive committee of the Stoke-on-Trent Children's Convalescent Home at Rhyl. He was dedicated to the Boy Scout movement, being its principal benefactor in North Staffordshire where he gave a large area of land for the establishment of a permanent camp at Kibblestone, near Stone. He was County Commissioner of the North Staffordshire Boy Scouts Association from 1921.

A knowledgeable authority on the decorative arts, Ronald Copeland formed one of the finest collections of Spode bone china as well as building up the collection of the Spode Factory Museum. He was a member in 1934-36 of the Council of Art and Industry, and a member of the Pottery Section Committee of the Royal Society of Arts. He followed the family tradition in becoming a liveryman of the Goldsmiths Company in 1919, and prime warden in 1946. His recreations were scouting, fishing and gardening, as well as collecting antique china and silver.

In 1915 he married Ida (d 1964), daughter of C Fenzi and Mrs Leonard Cunliffe; she was Unionist MP for the Stoke division of Stoke-on-Trent, 1931-35, and was also very interested in the Girl Guide movement. They had two sons, one of whom predeceased them. Copeland died on 22 August 1958, leaving £71,053 gross.

ROBERT COPELAND

Sources:

Unpublished

BCe.

PrC.

Personal knowledge.

Published

Times 26 Aug, 10 Sept 1958.

WWMP.

WWW.

COPEMAN, Henry John

(1851-1938)

Wholesale grocer

Henry John Copeman was born in Norwich on 21 October 1851, the son of John Copeman Jr (1811-1899) and his wife Ann Elizabeth née Buck. After being educated at a private school in Ipswich at the age of sixteen he entered the family firm of Copeman & Sons, wholesale grocers and provision merchants, of Norwich. Seven years later he became a partner, his father then being the senior partner. The firm had decided to specialise in the wholesale grocery and provision trades, servicing the Eastern counties, and sold off, in 1873, their retail grocery shop in the Walk in Norwich to another local family firm of grocers, Charles Underhill & Co. To accommodate an expansion of trade, the firm's wholesale and office facilities on the same site were extended in 1874, and in the following year they bought out another wholesale grocer in Norwich, Henry Butcher & Co. Successively as partner (1874-99), senior partner (1899-1917) and first chairman (1917-38) of the incorporated company, Henry Copeman steered the firm to a dominant position in the Eastern counties' wholesale provisions and grocery trade.

His first aim was to extend the firm's range of business and trade throughout East Anglia. He forged trading links with London, Ireland and Cheshire for home-produced provisions, and with Holland and the United States via the provision markets and import houses in London for colonial and Far Eastern products. Copemans specialised in teas and coffees, as well as in numerous types of dried fruits and spices. They had excellent connections at this time with the London importing trade: Henry's uncle, Jonathan Davey Copeman, had left the family firm in 1847 and built up a large importing and wholesale provision business in London; J D Copeman became the first chairman of the Home and Foreign Produce Exchange, later known as the London Provision Exchange.

Henry Copeman also made changes in the firm's trading techniques and business organisation. In the 1870s distinctive trade marks were registered for the firm, particularly for their specialist items such as coffees. In 1876 they issued their 'Copeman's Parisian Coffee' and 'The Royal Exhibition Coffee', and claimed to be the first firm to pack coffee in tins. At the same time they also registered 'The Star Baking Powder' as their own brand name. Early in 1894 the firm began to issue a monthly list of priced products, their 'Prices Current', which continued until the Second World War.

The firm's premises had to be extended considerably, and were rebuilt with cold-storage facilities in 1903 on the original site. A further major expansion in trade occurred during the First World War. Henry Copeman with his cousin, Charles Copeman, as a partner, worked with the War Office supplying army units stationed around Norwich, running canteens for some 30,000 troops. After these canteens were taken over by the Army

Canteen Committee, Copemans continued to act as suppliers to several army units. In 1917 the firm became a limited company under the name of John Copeman & Sons Ltd, which safeguarded the family interest in and control of the business.

After the First World War, under Henry Copeman's chairmanship, the firm expanded its trading activities further and modernised its marketing. A fleet of lorries was bought for regular deliveries of products to numerous retailers in the Eastern Counties. In 1930 a branch depot was set up at Ely for the Cambridgeshire trade, and another in 1936 at Stowmarket in Suffolk. A further indication of the firm's continuing enterprise was the formation of a subsidiary trading company in 1933, Mancroft Food Products Ltd, which launched a number of products under the 'Mancroft' trade mark or label. They were commodities manufactured by or packaged for the firm, including for instance 'Mancroft Self-Raising Flour'. Henry Copeman was still chairman at his death in 1938.

Of a Liberal Nonconformist background, he remained throughout his life an active member of his political party, combining trade with serving on Norwich City Council for over forty years. He was first elected as a local councillor in 1889, became an alderman, and held the office of sheriff in 1902-3, and of lord mayor in 1911-12. He was leader of the Liberal party on the City Council 1904-32 and unsuccessfully stood for Norwich at the general election of 1923. He was also a local magistrate. Two of his main interests as a local councillor were housing and flood control, and he was particularly associated with the development of municipal housing in the years following the First World War. A Congregationalist, Copeman was for sixty-six years a member of Chapel-in-the-Field, Norwich, its treasurer and senior deacon; he also strongly supported the Congregational Union and the London Missionary Society.

Henry John Copeman married Harriet née Monement in 1886; they had no children and he was succeeded by his nephew William Oliver Copeman, son of Charles Copeman. At his death on 21 July 1938 Henry John Copeman left £109,870 gross.

JANET M BLACKMAN

Sources:

Unpublished

BCe.

PrC.

Published

Copeman's of Norwich, 1789-1946 (Norwich: pp for firm, 1946).

Eastern Daily Press 21 Sept, 14 Oct 1932, 22, 25, 26 July 1938.

Evening Mercury (Norwich) 22 Nov 1919.

Norfolk Chronicle 24 Sept 1932.

Norwich Mercury 28 Aug 1926, 22 Oct 1932, 23, 30 July 1938.

COSSOR, Alfred Charles
(1861-1922)

Electronic valve manufacturer

Alfred Charles Cossor was born in Islington, London on 8 July 1861, the son of Alfred Charles Cossor Sr, a thermometer maker, and his wife Elizabeth née Freeman. In 1875 he joined the family business making barometers and thermometers and glass-blowing, set up by his father in 1859 at 26 Gloucester Street, Clerkenwell, London.

In 1890 he left his father and younger brother Frank, who continued the business, and established himself as a scientific glass-blower at 56 Farringdon Road, Clerkenwell. Here and at 59-61 Clerkenwell Road, where he subsequently moved, he produced fluorescent tubes for Sir William Crookes and Sir Oliver Lodge's high tension valves and advertised as the first maker of X-ray tubes in England.

He developed and produced electro-medical apparatus, infra-red equipment, radium spinthariscopes devised by Sir William Crookes and experimental wireless apparatus for the young Guglielmo Marconi (qv). In 1902 he made the first British examples of the Braun-type cathode ray tube, the forerunner of the tubes later used in television and radar. Other vacuum products he made at the beginning of the twentieth century included miniature electric bulbs for surgical probes, and relatively large quantities of bulbs for miners' lamps and eventually motor cars.

Cossor did not make the first valve, a diode: this was invented in 1904 by Ambrose Fleming when he was employed by the Edison Swan Electric Co at Ponders End, Middlesex and it was undoubtedly made by that company. However A C Cossor quickly followed Fleming and from about

An early Cossor advertisement (from Half a Century of Progress, *published by A C Cossor Ltd, 1947).*

1907 Cossor's experimental valves began to appear. Production for the armed services during the First World War necessitated a move to Highbury in North London in 1918.

About 1907 Alfred Cossor was joined by a young man, W R Bullimore. Together they formed a limited company, A C Cossor Ltd, in 1908. Soon afterwards Cossor moved to Fawley, Hampshire, leaving the running of the company to Bullimore but continuing as chairman of A C Cossor Ltd until his death. Bullimore built up, and eventually acquired control of, the company, which became nationally known after the start of broadcasting by the BBC in 1922. By this time Cossors manufactured valves of a unique construction, as well as radios and cathode ray tubes. The original business started by the father is still (1983) family-owned and trades sucessfully as A C Cossor & Son (Surgical) Ltd in North London, producing sphygmomanometers (blood pressure testers) for which it has a world-wide reputation.

At Fawley Cossor served as churchwarden (1911-22), and as harbour master. He was keenly interested in the locality, especially in its conservation and preservation, and was associated with the restoration of Fawley parish church. Cossor was a member of the London Lodge of freemasons.

Alfred Cossor married twice, firstly in 1892 to Alice Parker, daughter of George Parker, an estate bailiff, and secondly to Elsie M Vincent in 1919. He died at Fawley on 27 May 1922 leaving £17,007 gross.

FRANK BRITTAIN

Sources:

Unpublished

BCe.

MCe.

PrC.

Information from Clifford Gulvin.

Published

Half a Century of Progress (A C Cossor Ltd, 1947).

Hampshire Advertiser 7 June 1922.

Hampshire Independent 9 June 1922.

1859-1959 (A C Cossor & Son (Surgical) Ltd, 1959).

COSTAIN, Sir Richard Rylandes

(1902-1966)

Builder and contractor

*Sir Richard R Costain in 1965
(courtesy of Richard Costain Ltd).*

Richard Rylandes Costain was born at Great Crosby, Liverpool, on 20 November 1902, the elder son of William Percy Costain, a house builder and contractor, and his wife Maud May née Smith. The third Costain in the building business, he was known as R R. After being educated at the Merchant Taylors' School, Crosby, and then Rydal School in Colwyn Bay he trained as a building craftsman, working as a joiner and bricklayer. He took a short architectural course in Rome and then, in 1920, joined the family firm.

The business was founded by his grandfather, Richard Costain (1839-1902), a joiner who moved in 1865 from the family farm in Colby, Isle of Man, to Blundellsands on the edge of Liverpool, where he set up as a small local builder in partnership with his brother-in-law, Richard Kneen. The two parted amicably in 1888 and Richard Costain was joined by three of his sons, Richard A, William P, and John Kneen Costain. Between 1902 and the First World War Richard Costain & Sons spread their activities into North Wales and the Isle of Man as well as Lancashire. They built some of the first blocks of artisan flats in Liverpool. During the First World War the firm built houses for steel workers at Redcar and for munition workers in South Wales while their joinery works at Blundellsands manufactured ammunition boxes.

When R R Costain joined the firm in 1920 his father was becoming aware, like John Laing (qv), of the growing construction market represented by London and the South East, due to population drift and the rise of new industries. Under the direction of William P Costain a London branch was established in 1922 and a year later the private limited company, Richard Costain & Sons Ltd, was formed. The next fifteen years saw the firm expand into a large business, particularly under the leadership of R R Costain who, on his father's death in 1928, succeeded as managing director, despite his relatively youthful age of twenty-seven. His uncle, Richard A Costain, was appointed chairman and his younger brother Albert (b 1910) became director of production.

The London business started with the construction of a housing estate at Kingswood in Surrey and others, of 1,000 houses in Cricklewood and 800 at Croydon. At first Costain built more expensive houses, ranging from £350 to £4,000, purchasing the land and then selling the houses as freehold properties. The southern operation expanded rapidly, with the pre-tax and pre-interest profits of its three companies (Walton Heath Land Co, Costain Ltd, and the London side of Richard Costain & Sons Ltd) starting at £102,620 in 1929, dipping to £60,629 in the lowest depression year of 1931, and recovering to £90,145 in 1932. In 1933 a public company, Richard Costain Ltd, with an authorised capital of £600,000, was floated to take over the net assets of the three private firms, amounting to £377,507. Of the 450,000 £1 ordinary shares, 290,058 were retained by seven members of the family including R R who held 27,119. The Liverpool company remained in the family under the name R Costain & Sons (Liverpool) Ltd and still (1982) trades in the North West independently of the main group.

The public company, Costain, continued to build estates during the 1930s: an estate of 1,400 houses at Sudbury, another of 1,600 at Dagenham and a large one of 5,000 houses at Elm Park, for example. But R R Costain decided that the firm, although it was 'one of the largest speculative house builders and estate developers in this country before the war' {Bowley (1966) 210n}, should avoid dependence on house building, so vulnerable to domestic cyclical fluctuations. He secured other forms of construction work: for blocks of flats in Bloomsbury, Streatham and Highgate; for sewage works at Becton and Hornchurch; a laboratory for Glaxo; and the Trans-Iranian Railway in Persia. The largest Costain contract of the 1930s, however, was for the Dolphin Square project. In 1933 R R Costain speculatively bought from an American (who had paid the deposit but could not find the balance of the price) seven acres of land on the Embankment in Pimlico, London, on the site of the old army clothing depot. He planned to build a block of 1,250 flats for Pimlico bed-sitters. Novel in being a self-contained flat community, with its own shops and social amenities, it was a large project which eventually cost over £1 million. The company's capital was increased to £1 million in 1935 and construction commenced soon after. The flats were completed in October 1937 but the demand for tenancies from middle and upper class customers persuaded R R Costain to depart from the original specifications and equip them with better finishings and fittings. War and rent restrictions reduced the profitability of the Dolphin Square project and the flats were sold in 1958 to Maxwell Joseph (qv) for £2.5 million. Soon after they were sold again at a considerable profit, much to the chagrin of R R Costain.

The record of R R Costain and his company during the 1930s placed his firm on the War Office List and himself in the Ministry of Works first as Deputy Director of Emergency Works and then as Deputy Director of Works. This consequently removed him from an active role in his company's operations. For his wartime services R R Costain was awarded the CBE in 1946. While he served in Whitehall, his firm took on numerous wartime civil engineering contracts which 'set the company on its feet in the contracting business' {Catherwood (1966) 273}. Costain primarily built airfields, of which they constructed 26, but also fabricated 18 of the largest reinforced hangars, besides some coastal defence works; they were the first to complete their quota of 12 Mulberry Units for the D-Day invasion in 1944.

In 1945 R R Costain succeeded his uncle as chairman of the company and determined to move the firm into overseas markets. A consultancy agreement for the Anglo-Iranian Oil Co continued in Iran and by 1947 the firm had offices in Nigeria, Rhodesia and Turkey. Rather more business came at home: 10,000 prefabricated concrete houses, 7,500 steel prefabs and 10,000 aluminium houses were built during the chronic housing shortage after 1945.

One major building job after 1945 was a £2 million government office block in Whitehall, followed by the South Bank river wall and then the contract to build for the Festival of Britain. The firm's net profits rose from £81,000 to £101,000 between 1945 and 1956 (turnover figures are unavailable).

A serious illness in 1951 kept R R Costain away from the firm for almost a year. Soon after, he concluded that it was no longer possible to run the company on the basis of centralised control by members of the family. By 1955 the firm was spread across a wide variety of projects and countries: it was 'engaged in opencast coal, a £4 million hydro-electric scheme in Scotland, a £4 million harbour in Nigeria, two power stations in Nigeria, a £1.5 million earth dam in Wales, roads in Iraq, concrete works in the UK, a new venture in Canada, a return to house-building in the UK, and of course the ordinary contracting business in Rhodesia, Nigeria and the UK' {Catherwood (1966) 275}. (Rhodesia was R R Costain's special interest and he was often there. He was a friend of Sir Roy Welensky, the Prime Minister, and the company, which undertook various contracts there like the Kariba Dam township, owned an interest in an hotel in Malinde, Kenya, which he much enjoyed.)

Costain therefore decentralised the business into twelve operating divisions, covering separate markets and having separate managements but all under a group general manager. These divisions spanned buildings, civil engineering, housing, concrete manufacture and property investment; eventually they became subsidiary companies. The results of this growth were impressive: between 1956 and 1965 net profits rose from £101,000 to £600,000 and by 1961 Richard Costain Ltd ranked the third largest firm, behind Wimpeys and Laings, in the UK building industry with net assets of £9.2 million and a turnover of £61 million. Between 1955 and 1958 Costain's group trading profits trebled (from £403,287 up to £1,330,806), a growth rate unmatched by its rivals, Wimpey, Taylor Woodrow and Laings.

In the 1950s and 1960s Costain had a high percentage of its workload abroad and was one of the leading UK companies in the international construction market. Much of the credit for this must go to R R Costain who was well able to take risks, as he needed to in that business, but was himself well informed, partly by his many friends all over the world. He was basically a 'hunch' man in the best sense: knowing many of the relevant facts and then fearlessly backing his own judgement.

His nervous breakdown in the early 1950s convinced R R Costain of the need to look after the health of his staff for he recognised the vital importance to a contracting company of its managers. He invited Lord Taylor whom he knew from his work with Harlow New Town to carry out intensive annual medical checks, lasting about two hours and including a cardiogram, of all his senior staff regardless of age.

Outside his firm, R R Costain was president of the London Master Builders Association in 1950 and chairman of the Harlow Development Corporation (from 1950 until his death). He brought to the HDC his knowledge of running large organisations and of co-ordinating the services of technical experts in building and contracting. He was especially concerned about the town's social development and was responsible for Harlow's golf course, laid out by his friend Henry Cotton. For his work at Harlow and in the building industry R R Costain was knighted in 1954. In

1955-57 Sir Richard Costain was chairman of the Export Group for Constructional Industries.

During the whole of his life he was an outstanding sportsman, playing for the Waterloo rugby team, and reaching the English trials. When he was too old to play rugby, he took up golf seriously and played three or four rounds each weekend and sometimes on Wednesdays. He always claimed this was the time when he left his colleagues to get on with the job, and when he took the chance to think up ideas for the future.

He married Gertrude Minto, daughter of William John Minto, 'gentleman' {MCe}, of Waterloo near Crosby, in 1927. They had one son and two daughters. Sir Richard Rylandes Costain died suddenly at his home on 26 March 1966, aged sixty-three, leaving an estate valued at £58,521 gross.

DAVID BURRAGE and DAVID J JEREMY

Sources:

Unpublished

C Reg: Richard Costain Ltd (274,453).

BCe.

MCe.

PrC.

Company performance data from R F Erith of Savory Milln & Co.

Information from A P Costain MP and Dr Patricia M Hillebrandt.

Published

Marian Bowley, *The British Building Industry. Four Studies in Response and Resistance to Change* (Cambridge: Cambridge University Press, 1966).

Henry F R Catherwood, 'Development and Organisation of Richard Costain Ltd' in Ronald S Edwards and Harry Townsend (eds), *Business Growth* (Macmillan, 1966).

John R Colclough, *The Construction Industry of Great Britain* (Butterworths, 1965).

DNB.

Frederick Gibberd et al, *Harlow. The Story of a New Town* (Publications for Companies, 1980).

Charles M Kohan, *Works and Buildings: The History of the Second World War, UK Civil Series* (HMSO, 1952).

Oliver Marriott, *The Property Boom* (Hamish Hamilton, 1967).

Times 28 Mar, 1 Apr 1966.

Times *Prospectuses* 85 (1933).

WWW.

COTTON, Jack

(1903-1964)

Property developer

Jack Cotton. Working drawing by Sir David Low (courtesy of the National Portrait Gallery, London).

Jack Cotton was born at Edgbaston, Birmingham, on 1 January 1903, third son of Benjamin Marcus Cotton, an import-export merchant who had enjoyed a flourishing trade in silver plate cutlery with South Africa before the Boer War, and his wife Caroline Josephine née Rudelsheim. He was educated at King Edward VI's Grammar School, Birmingham (which he later pulled down when the school moved to Edgbaston) and in the Jewish house at Cheltenham College. At the age of eighteen he was articled as a clerk with a Birmingham firm of estate agents, and subsequently passed the examinations of the Auctioneer's Institute. Despite his father's opposition, his mother lent him £50 and on his twenty-first birthday he opened an estate agency in Birmingham. For two years he worked single-handed as estate agent, auctioneer, rent collector and typist, only taking on additional staff in 1926.

With the growth of his estate agency in the early 1930s, Cotton founded the architectural firm of Cotton, Ballard & Blow, which later had offices in London, Birmingham and Newcastle upon Tyne. He laid the basis for his fortune with suburban ribbon development around Birmingham. He was an adept middleman between the farmers and speculative builders who put up the small and ugly semi-detached houses around the outskirts of Birmingham, and often acted as the estate agent selling the houses for the builder. In the late 1930s Cotton moved into commercial development, and with the backing of a Birmingham solicitor named Joseph Cohen, built King Edward House on the site of his old school in New Street, Birmingham. This redevelopment scheme cost £1 million, and in 1935 was one of the biggest and most daring schemes ever seen in Britain. The great success of the scheme enriched Cotton, and enhanced his reputation, and in the remaining years of peace, he developed other office blocks in central Birmingham, such as Somerset House, Neville House and Cavendish House. Such was Cotton's hold on the Birmingham property market that in 1938 the Air Ministry approached him when it needed to find a large shadow armaments factory in a hurry. He and Joseph Cohen also headed the syndicate which developed Birmingham's first block of luxury flats, Kenilworth Court, in 1935; but the market for the flats proved sluggish, and Cotton eschewed the development of flats thereafter.

During the war, Cotton was a member of the Home Guard, and in 1945 he was a delegate in the British section of the World Jewish Congress at the Emergency War Conference, and visited the USA to help Zionist emigration to Palestine. He became a major benefactor of Jewish and Zionist charities, endowing chairs of Architecture and Fine Arts at the Hebrew University in Jerusalem, and the chair of Biochemistry at the Weizmann Institute of Science in Israel.

After the war, Cotton moved to London, living in a suite at the Dorchester Hotel in Park Lane, and formed the City of Birmingham Real

Property Co to redevelop the blitzed sites of the Midlands and elsewhere. In 1947 he bought control, through nominees, of Mansion House Chambers Co Ltd, a property company on the verge of liquidation whose one property in the City of London had been destroyed during the war. Cotton did not join the board of Mansion House Chambers, appointing his accountant Freddie Lindgren as chairman, but he used this shell company, with its useful quotation on the London Stock Exchange, as a means of breaking into the London property market. In 1953 Cotton merged City of Birmingham Real Property Co Ltd with another London company, Chesham House (Regent Street) Co Ltd, of which he had taken control around 1949. In 1954 his interests also acquired Central Commercial Properties Co, and the following year, having sold Chesham House in Regent Street at a profit of £424,000, he consolidated his group in a new company, City Centre Properties. Although all the deals and developments of this company were his ideas, and he was their major shareholder, he avoided publicity and did not sit on their boards until 1958, when he became chairman of City Centre at the insistence of its institutional shareholders who required the man who ran the company to sit on its board.

Wartime building restrictions continued until 1954, and Cotton made a great deal of money out of the shortage of government office space. He was one of the first developers to enter the 'Building Lessor Scheme' in which Office Development Permits were issued for the erection of civil service office blocks at a rent based on a pre-determined rate of interest on the actual cost as disclosed by the developer. Office Development Permits were also issued to major exporting businesses, or those working in the national interest, who could provide a certificate from the Board of Trade. Cotton developed various large schemes under these provisions, of which Shell BP House in Birmingham is notable, in its financial provisions, for being one of the earliest sale-and-leaseback agreements to include rent revision clauses.

Cotton was also a pioneer in involving insurance offices in property development. Insurance companies had been providing mortgages as a long-term investment since the eighteenth century, but by 1955 his schemes were so big that they could only be financed by institutional participation. For his proposed £7 million development of the Monico site in Piccadilly, Cotton took Legal & General Assurance as partner in 1955, and although the Monico scheme was prevented by local and national opposition, in 1956-57 he formed another joint development with Pearl Assurance. This departure was soon widely copied. Cotton was also the first developer to realise that large pension funds were ideal partners for property companies because their investment managers could take a longer view than those in life assurance offices, and more significantly, because their investments had been tax-free since the Finance Act of 1921. In July 1960 Cotton reached an agreement for a joint development company with Britain's biggest private pension fund, that of ICI, and he soon settled similar deals with the Unilever, AEI and Imperial Tobacco pension funds. Neither the assurance offices nor the pension funds felt any responsibility for the aesthetics of the tower-blocks which they financed, nor did they accept the criticism that the national economy would have been stronger if their funds had been put into industrial investment.

The Church Commissioners were other (and unlikely) partners in his deals, and in 1958-59 he launched a programme of developments in South Africa and the West Indies in which Barclays Bank (Dominion, Colonial & Overseas) took a 20 per cent interest. In 1959 City Centre took a half-interest in the $100 million scheme for the 59-storey Pan Am building over Grand Central Station in Manhattan: the project was particularly dear to Cotton's heart and he commissioned a song commemorating it, with the refrain

Hoi, but its big/Its gotta be big;/Why does it have to *be* so big? {Whitehouse (1964) 33}

It had to be big because Cotton could think in no other way. 'Property is my life', he once said, 'I would not know what else to do' {*Daily Mirror* 23 Mar 1964}; 'there's not enough money in the world for me' {Marriott (1967) 137}.

Early in 1960 City Centre bought 30 per cent of the shares of Murrayfield Properties, run by Walter Flack, and in October 1960, the group merged with City & Central Investments headed by Charles Clore (qv). Cotton remained chairman of the combined company, City Centre, whose stock market valuation stood at the inflated figure of £65 million (City Centre shares worth 7s 7d in 1958 stood at 72s in 1959). Cotton's business methods proved quite unsuitable to working with Clore and Flack. At the time of the merger in 1960, City Centre's staff comprised a handful of accountants, typists and clerks, none of whom knew details of current deals which were kept in Cotton's head, or had access to the important company files, which were piled on the spare bed of Cotton's bedroom at the Dorchester. He had great mental difficulty in adjusting to the new conditions, and in 1961-63 the City Centre board was wracked with rows and a power struggle between Clore, Cotton and Flack and institutional shareholders. Early in 1963 Flack resigned and committed suicide, and in June Cotton was removed as chairman of City Centre, while remaining a director until February 1964. In November 1963, however, his shares in City Centre, held by family trusts, were sold for about £8.5 million to a consortium headed by Sir Isaac Wolfson (qv) and Sir Kenneth Keith.

Cotton was a showman of extremely gregarious personality, who detested being alone and was always a steady social drinker. But in the late 1950s the visitors to his Dorchester suite, where he held informal court, included regulars who were cunning sycophants, egged him to drink and then made business propositions or sought other favours. There is no doubt that they induced him to believe some of the preposterously extravagant press estimates of his capabilities, and that they aggravated his drinking, and to this extent they were responsible for the folie de grandeur which was increasingly evident in him after 1959. Indeed, the coup against him at City Centre in June 1963 was only possible because the company's main institutional investors had decided that he was too erratic in judgement to remain chairman.

Cotton was an ebullient and noisy man whose chief interest was his business. Although he collected Impressionist paintings, his justification for buying Renoir's 'La Pensée' for £72,000 — 'I bought it because it makes me think' {Marriott (1967) 138} — and the unrelenting ugliness of every building that he erected suggests that he had no artistic feeling, and an imagination that was merely pecuniary. In developing the Park Lane site which became the Playboy Club, Cotton employed Walter Gropius as architect for the prestige: this decision reputedly raised the cost by £150,000 to £800,000 and produced one of the most unpleasant-looking buildings in Mayfair. His other schemes, such as the rebuilding of Notting Hill Gate in a scheme with the Greater London Council, or the Top Site development in Birmingham, had no ruling criterion except for size, and are visual monuments by which no man would wish to be remembered. Cotton gave part of his fortune to Zionism, as well as £250,000 to London Zoo and £100,000 to the Royal College of Surgeons, but did not receive the knighthood for which he longed.

Cotton married Marjorie Rachel Mindleson in 1928, by whom he had three sons and a daughter; he proved a difficult husband, and separated from his wife in the 1940s. Having led an unhealthy life for years, he died of heart disease on 21 March 1964 at Nassau in the Bahamas. His fortune was tied in family trusts, but his personalty was valued at £1,176,074 gross.

R P T DAVENPORT-HINES

Sources:

Unpublished
BCe.
PrC.
Private information.

Published
Stephen Aris, *The Jews in Business* (Cape, 1970).

Christopher J P Booker, *The Neophiliacs* (Collins, 1969).

Derek Channon, *The Service Industries* (Macmillan, 1978).

Daily Mirror 23 Mar 1964.

DNB.

Edward L Erdman, *People and Property* (Batsford, 1982).

Simon Jenkins, *Landlords to London* (Constable, 1975).

Oliver J D Marriott, *The Property Boom* (Hamish Hamilton, 1967).

Observer colour magazine 13 June 1965.

Anthony T S Sampson, *Anatomy of Britain* (Hodder & Stoughton, 1962).

Times 23 Mar 1964.

Brian P Whitehouse, *Partners in Property: A History and Analysis of the Provision of Institutional Finance for Property Development* (Birn Shaw, 1964).

WWW.

Samuel Courtauld III (courtesy of Courtaulds PLC).

COURTAULD III, Samuel

(1793-1881)

Silk manufacturer

Samuel Courtauld III was the third of that name in a family of French Huguenot origin and is not to be confused with his better-known great-nephew, Samuel Courtauld IV (qv). He was born in Albany, New York, on 1 June 1793. His father, George (1761-1823), was the first member of the family to have been concerned with textiles. The Courtaulds had been traders and small landowners on the Isle d'Olèron and came to England as refugees at the end of the seventeenth century. For three generations they worked and prospered as silversmiths in London and a number of fine examples of their work can be seen today. George Courtauld, a younger son, after having been apprenticed to a Spitalfields silk weaver in 1775, set up as a silk throwster in London but in 1785 made the first of a number of trips to America. Here he farmed in New York State where in 1789 he married Ruth Minton, daughter of Stephen Minton of Cork, Ireland. Of the eight children she bore him, three sons and four daughters survived to maturity; Samuel was the eldest son. Shortly after Samuel's birth his parents returned to England and to the silk industry. In 1807, at the age of fourteen, Samuel was working in a silk-throwing mill at Pebmarsh in Essex which his father managed for a London firm. Two years later his father quitted this post and became manager, and later partner, in a silk-throwing and weaving enterprise at nearby Braintree. For a time Samuel worked here but in about 1811 he left home and tried his luck as a clerk in a London hardware firm of which his uncle was a partner. Then, in 1816, he took the crucial step in his own business career: he returned to the Bocking-Braintree area and set up as a silk throwster on his own account.

His decision to take this step was strongly influenced by the behaviour of his father. The latter, who had become a dedicated Unitarian with politically radical sympathies, was an impracticable idealist and an incompetent businessman. He managed to fall out with his partner, his wife, some of his daughters and certainly his eldest son. By 1816, as a consequence of action taken by his infuriated partner, George Courtauld's position and that of his family was financially perilous. His son's new enterprise was part of a scheme to rescue the family and to restore it to what the ambitious Samuel saw as its rightful social position. George Courtauld's partnership was dissolved in 1818; after trying his hand at sundry activities in this country and in America, he finally set off to try to found a community of immigrants in Ohio, and died there in 1823. His eldest son, meanwhile, was moving into a position of ascendancy in the family as his mother, brothers and sisters returned from America and became dependent upon his growing prosperity.

The path to that prosperity was not immediately straightforward. Initial success and the acquisition of a lease of a water-powered mill at Bocking was quickly followed by acute financial difficulties, as the silk industry in

Courtauld's mourning crape — a modern photograph of a piece made in the 1890s (courtesy of Courtaulds PLC).

general and Samuel Courtauld in particular experienced a sharp down-turn in their fortunes. In 1820-21 he was vainly trying to sell the business. However, he survived to enjoy the up-turn in 1823-25 and to start a further venture in 1825, the conversion for silk-throwing of an old corn mill at Halstead, a few miles from Bocking. In 1828 there began a long-enduring partnership comprising Samuel Courtauld, Peter Alfred Taylor (cousin and doubly brother-in-law, Taylor having married Samuel's sister and Samuel having married Taylor's sister), George Courtauld II (Samuel's younger brother) and Andrew Taylor (an unrelated London silk broker who brought in more capital). The firm, formally known as Courtauld, Taylors & Courtauld, soon became known to the public as what it was in reality: Samuel Courtauld & Co. To silk throwing was added handloom weaving and, the first foundation of the family's wealth, the power-loom weaving, dyeing and finishing of black silk crape used for mourning. By the middle of the nineteenth century Samuel Courtauld was the biggest manufacturer of this curious product for which there developed a remarkable boom in Victorian England as the ancient ritual of mourning was formalized, publicized and commercialized. After the mid-century the partners changed as the children of George II and Peter Taylor replaced the older generation. But meanwhile mourning crape, in its heyday and until it began to fall from fashion in the 1880s, was regularly earning those partners some 30-50 per cent on their capital. As the senior partner, Samuel Courtauld in the last decade of his life was drawing an income from the business alone of around £46,000 a year.

In an age of family businesses, Samuel Courtauld & Co was quintessentially a family business. The family was given cohesion at the time by a shared belief in Unitarianism; and family and firm alike were totally dominated by Samuel Courtauld himself. His contribution, as a businessman, lay neither in the provision of credit and capital (though he found ways of borrowing it through the family) nor in technical innovation (his brother George was the engineer of the business and was responsible for the firm's workshops which produced their own powerlooms). What Samuel provided was organising ability and a driving ambition which, allied to a shrewd, practical intelligence and an immense capacity for hard work, propelled him forward towards the satisfaction of his own urgent need for achievement. His letters often reveal paranoid tendencies as he fluctuated between euphoria, self-confidence and highly autocratic behaviour, on the one hand, and gloom, dejection and self-deprecation, on the other. He quarrelled from time to time with his partners, especially some of the younger generation of nephews and cousins for whose business abilities he had little regard. In his younger days he had taken some part in local radical activities; and he later played an important part in the famous Braintree Church Rates Case which ran from 1834 until 1853 and led ultimately in 1868 to the abolition of Church rates and was thus a notable victory for the principle of religious freedom. But his other attempts at political involvement bore little fruit. Stiff and domineering in manner, yet sensitive to insult, he lacked the resilience necessary for politics. As the *Times* observed in its obituary, 'had the death of Mr Courtauld happened some 30 or 40 years ago a popular hero would have passed away' but he lived on 'to be almost forgotten' {*Times* 24 Mar 1881}.

By the 1880s his firm employed over 3,000 persons and was easily the biggest industrial employer in the area. His attitude to his workers was characteristic of the day: a benevolent despotism informed by a profound belief in the merits of free enterprise; a concern to instil 'orderly and industrious habits' amongst the working poor by a system of fines and rewards; and a ruthless determination to stamp out incipient strikes or other symptoms of insubordination. The firm pursued a welfare policy of an earnestly Nonconformist nature; various members of the family, notably Mrs Samuel Courtauld, were active in local charitable activities.

In 1854 Samuel Courtauld had bought the substantial mansion of Gosfield Hall, between Halstead and Bocking, with 2,000 acres, an estate which was augmented by subsequent purchases. He had a London house and a yacht. At his death on 21 March 1881 his estate was proved at under £700,000. Apart from legacies of £30,000-£35,000 apiece to two nephews and sundry lesser bequests, he left the bulk of his estate to two adopted children, his only child having died in infancy.

D C COLEMAN

Sources:

Unpublished

PrC.

Published

Donald C Coleman, *Courtaulds. An Economic and Social History* (3 vols, Oxford: Clarendon Press, 1969-80).

S L (Sir Stephen) Courtauld, *The Huguenot Family of Courtauld* (3 vols, pp, 1957, 1966 and 1967).

COURTAULD IV, Samuel

(1876-1947)

Rayon manufacturer and patron of the arts

Samuel Courtauld IV (courtesy of Courtaulds PLC).

Samuel Courtauld IV was born at Bocking, Essex on 7 May 1876, the second son of Sydney Courtauld and his wife Sarah Lucy née Sharp. His father — son of George Courtauld II who was the younger brother of Samuel III (qv) and one of the original partners of Samuel Courtauld & Co — worked throughout his life in the family silk business. Samuel, great-nephew of the founder, followed precedent and in 1898 joined the company. He had meanwhile been schooled at Rugby and then sent to Crefeld and Lyons to learn the techniques of textile manufacture. In 1901, the year he married Elizabeth Theresa Frances Kelsey, he became manager of the company's weaving mill at Halstead and in 1908 general manager of all the textile mills. This promotion was not mere nepotism. He was the only member of the family in the business to have earned the approbation of H G Tetley (qv), who was by this time the dominant power in the company which he had already set on its rayon course. By the time that Sam (as he was generally called) joined the board of Courtaulds Ltd in 1916 all the steps had been taken which were to shape the company's future in the next two decades: the viscose rayon patents had been bought; the new venture, with its pioneering plant at Coventry, had proved so successful that profits from the sales of rayon yarn already far exceeded those from textile fabrics; and the American subsidiary was already showing promise of its immense future profitability. When Tetley died in August 1921 the chairmanship was offered to his ageing deputy, Sir Thomas Latham. He declined it, thereby opening the way for Sam Courtauld who was in effect the only other suitable internal candidate.

The company which he took over was earning a very high rate of return on capital but was just beginning to face the big international rayon boom, as the patents ran out, the First World War ended, and the competitors moved in. Sam Courtauld's response to the boom, evident alike in acts of policy, in his public speeches, and in surviving correspondence, exhibited certain central facets of his character. Clear, knowledgeable and authoritative in his statements, he strove for conciliation, compromise, agreement, limits on competition, ordered growth. Bold, aggressive and risky business ventures of the sort which his great-uncle or Tetley had pursued were anathema to him. So it was wholly in keeping with his ideas that the investments which Courtaulds made in France, Germany and Italy during the 1920s and the informal agreements which they entered into with overseas producers should have been primarily designed to stabilise prices and variously to restrain competitive enthusiasm; and that in 1928 he should have concluded a gentleman's agreement with Lord Melchett (qv) of ICI that the two companies should keep out of each other's fields of interest. The 1920s boom saw a surge of new rayon companies in Britain and the 1930s slump brought many of these creations crashing down. In 1931 Sam Courtauld voiced his disapproval of what he called 'the senseless increase in production resulting from the orgy of company-promoting and speculation' and observed loftily that it was 'a discreditable chapter in industrial history' {Coleman (1969) II, 219}. So now he refused overtures for price-maintenance in order to keep surviving domestic competitors alive; and in 1934, when recovery was setting in, he announced, with appropriate publicity, a cut in prices. Thereby he was able both to hit at his competitors and at the same time satisfy his principles and sense of social responsibility by passing on to the consumer his own company's success in reducing costs.

Under Sam Courtauld's leadership the company which bore his family name became a highly respected industrial giant, a 'blue-chip' security. It pursued a policy of financial conservatism, building up very large reserves and adopting a cautious dividend policy. But it always paid a dividend and its growth was entirely financed out of profits of which an average of 38 per cent from 1921 to 1940 came from its American subsidiary, the American Viscose Corporation. His own lengthy and forthright speeches at annual general meetings were something of an event in the business calendar. He became a public figure, yet he characteristically turned down the offer of a barony in 1937. A few years later one newspaper described him as a 'shy, arty, philanthropic rayon millionaire' {Coleman (1980) III, 15-16}. His ideas on a variety of subjects were disseminated in numerous letters to the *Times* and, especially during the Second World War, by sundry articles and pronouncements on industry and the state and on capital-labour relations. Some of these, such as his advocacy of a greater degree of government control of the economy and of a more sympathetic regard for the claims of labour to a share in management and the rewards of industry, did not go down well with many of his fellow businessmen, including members of his own board. He publicly expressed disapproval of massive advertising; he was worried about waste and saw big newspapers as an example of it. America, ironically, excited his disapprobation: 'I doubt whether American ideals of living, purely materialistic as they are, will finally lead to a contented working nation anywhere when the excitement of constant expansion has come to an end' {Coleman (1969) II, 218}.

The fact that he was in so many ways the antithesis of the adventurous entrepreneur owed much to his serious-minded upbringing. His parents retained longer than others of their generation a profound regard for the family Unitarianism. He inherited from his father an interest in the technical side of the business, from his mother an appreciation of art and literature. The latter found its outlet in his picture collecting and in his acqaintanceship with many prominent figures of the literary and artistic world such as the Sitwells, T S Eliot, Charles Morgan, as well as Maynard Keynes (qv), a link between Bloomsbury and business. His collecting started well before he became a rich man and showed an adventurousness not evident in his business career, for it resulted in the building up of what had become in the 1920s the finest collection in the country of French impressionist paintings. He followed a gift to the Tate Gallery for the purchase of similar works by the creation and handsome endowment in 1931 of the Courtauld Institute of Art in the University of London (which conferred on him an honorary D Litt). On the death of his wife in the same year he provided the Institute with his splendid Adam house in Portman Square and a substantial part of his own collection. He was a trustee of the Tate Gallery from 1927 to 1937 and of the National Gallery from 1931 to 1947. He continued to give or lend money for these purposes and in his will made further gifts of paintings to the Institute. He and his wife also gave financial support to the Covent Garden opera and to music and concert-going in London. In the 1930s he became much enamoured of Christabel Maclaren, Lady Aberconway, and his self-doubt and private quest for truth and beauty can be seen in many letters to her, letters often charged with a rather heavy sententiousness of a markedly Victorian flavour. Perhaps it is hardly surprising that Edith Sitwell should have recorded that he made her feel 'unpardonably flippant' {Glendinning (1981) 172}.

If there were benefits from Sam Courtauld's idealism and concern for stability in business there were also costs. For his firm there were two of real consequence. One was that under his dignified and respected leadership Courtaulds lacked dynamism. Not until the end of 1938 did he come to appreciate the need to rectify the company's complacency and its neglect of research. The advent of the Second World War frustrated his efforts to bring about change in this area; and it was not until 1945, with the appointment of a distinguished scientist, Alan Wilson (qv), to direct research and development, that they bore fruit. The second consequence was a failure to understand the need for changes in organisation, management and personnel as the firm grew into a big multinational enterprise. Both in the UK and in the American subsidiary much was left in the hands of unimaginative bosses whose rough and ready methods had worked in the past and who remained contemptuous of change. Again, it was only in the later 1930s that the faults became evident to the chairman. His own attempts to engender cost-consciousness and to attract university graduates into the firm were real enough but were too little and too late. Despite his interest in capital-labour relations it took a long time to rid his firm's yarn mills of the malign influence of old-style foremen and mill managers. Not until after the Second World War, at the very end of his life, did some of the changes, which he had earlier seen the need for, begin to happen. A newly-appointed outside director said of Courtaulds in December 1946 that it was like 'a big Empire on the decline' {Coleman (1980) III, 16}. There was truth in the comment and some part of the responsibility for that state of affairs lay at the door of the then recently retired chairman.

In May 1946 Sam Courtauld suffered a severe illness and in October resigned from the chairmanship. He remained on the board but died in December 1947. His will was proved at £1,030,126 gross. After various legacies much of his property went to his only daughter Sydney and to her husband Richard Austen Butler (later Lord Butler of Saffron Walden) whom she had married in 1926.

D C COLEMAN

Writings:

The Businessman's Inspiration and *Coming Industrial Changes* (two talks) (Industrial Christian Fellowship, 1943).

A number of Samuel Courtauld's occasional pieces, including his best-known article, 'An Industrialist's Reflection on the Future Relations of Government and Industry' *Economic Journal* (1942), were collected together and published posthumously as *Ideals and Industry* (Cambridge, 1949) with a preface by Charles Morgan.

Sources:

Unpublished

British Library, MSS 52432-5, letters written by Samuel Courtauld to Lady Aberconway, 1929-47.

BCe.

PrC.

Published

Donald C Coleman, *Courtaulds. An Economic and Social History* (3 vols, Oxford: Clarendon Press, 1969-80).

DNB.

Victoria Glendinning, *Edith Sitwell* (Weidenfeld & Nicolson, 1981).

WWW.

Arthur B Coussmaker (courtesy of Johnson, Matthey & Co Ltd).

COUSSMAKER, Arthur Blakeney

(1885-1974)

Executive and chairman of precious metals firm

Arthur Blakeney Coussmaker was born at Hamstall Ridware, Staffordshire on 27 July 1885, the son of Rev John Octavius Coussmaker, Rector of Hamstall Ridware, and descendant of a family of Dutch bankers prominent in the City of London since the seventeenth century, and of Mary Coussmaker née Blakeney. He was educated at King's School, Ely, and, undecided about a career, he went to Canada to spend some time with an uncle who was engaged in gold mining. He decided that this was the type of work he would take up. He therefore returned to England and enrolled at the Camborne School of Mines in Cornwall where he studied for three years. He then obtained a position as assayer and mining engineer to the Siberian Exploration Syndicate and became knowledgeable in the platinum mines in the Urals.

On his return to England in 1909 he was introduced to Johnson Matthey who were seeking a mining engineer to investigate a platinum proposition in Brazil. He went out there, unmasked a fraud, and was asked to assist the company further, joining the staff in 1911. Among his early assignments were a visit to the Urals to negotiate with the Russian platinum mining concerns and, in 1912, the inspection of another platinum project in British Columbia.

On the outbreak of the First World War he returned from Russia and was commissioned in the South Wales Borderers, serving with them on the Somme and being severely wounded in 1916. Later he served in Mesopotamia and at the end of 1918 was sent on a military mission to Russia. Here he found himself in familiar territory, and he took the opportunity of making himself known to Maxim Litvinov, later the Soviet Foreign Minister, and of representing to him, without success then, Johnson Matthey's position in the platinum industry. This position had been gravely damaged by the war, and Coussmaker resolved to restore the firm's leadership in the platinum world by any means open to him, and above all to find a new and reliable source.

In July 1925 he was invited to join the Johnson Matthey board, at a difficult and trying time of internal reconstruction and external doubt. In 1924 the huge platinum bearing reef that bears his name had been discovered in the Transvaal by Dr Hans Merensky, first in the areas of Potgietersrust and Lydenburg and a little later at Rustenburg. This led to a platinum boom, with a great many mining companies being floated, but a slump was soon in evidence, and by 1929 there were only two companies left in the field, Waterval Platinum controlled by Consolidated Goldfields, and Potgietersrust Platinum controlled by Johannesburg Consolidated Investment, both working adjacent properties in the Rustenburg area. Coussmaker had already made a thorough survey of the new platinum prospects, and considered that this was the most promising part of the Merensky reef.

He therefore took the initiative in persuading these two important mining houses to merge their platinum interests, and in due course this was brought about with the formation of Rustenburg Platinum Mines, with Johnson Matthey as refiners and in charge of marketing arrangements.

In the meantime Coussmaker had organised a research programme to establish a satisfactory process for the extraction of the platinum metals and the copper and nickel from the Rustenburg ore body. This was completely successful, whereas others who had been retained to devise a process were unsuccessful. The first smelting plant was built at Brimsdown. Coussmaker's vision of putting Johnson Matthey firmly in a position of leadership in the platinum industry was on the way to being realised.

But this was by no means his sole contribution to the progress of the company. He was also responsible for the acquisition of their American subsidiary, then known as J Bishop & Co Platinum Works, and for securing for them the refining contract for the alluvial platinum from Goodnews Bay in Alaska.

In 1944 he took charge of Johnson Matthey's Mechanical Production Division, at that time scattered over a number of small units. He put forward ideas for rationalisation and, with some involuntary help from the Government of the day, secured new and larger equipment for rolling, wire drawing and tube production for a large new plant at Harlow in Essex.

In 1948 he became chairman of the executive committee of the board and retired from executive duties two years later. He continued to be a member of the general board and in 1960 was elected chairman, a position he held until 1963.

Throughout his long career with the company, he displayed remarkable gifts of foresight and determination, coupled with great reserve and modesty. His guiding principle was always the need to foster the industrial uses of platinum and the other precious metals, and almost invariably he had the satisfaction of seeing his imaginative planning brought to successful fruition.

On a visit to a silver mine in Yugoslavia, he met Militza Misic, and married her in Belgrade Cathedral in June 1925. Arthur Coussmaker died on 16 March 1974 leaving £260,535 gross.

L B HUNT

Sources:

Unpublished

BCe.

PrC.

Personal knowledge.

Published

Leslie B Hunt, 'Mr A B Coussmaker — Hatton Garden' *Johnson Matthey Bulletin* July 1974.

Donald McDonald and Leslie B Hunt, *A History of Platinum and Its Allied Metals* (Johnson Matthey, 1982).

COWLIN, Sir Francis Nicholas

(1868-1945)

Builder

Francis Nicholas Cowlin was born in Bristol on 23 September 1868. His father, William Henry Cowlin was the son and partner of William Cowlin, who had founded a building firm under his own name in 1834. His mother, Annie née Scull, was the daughter of a local plumbing contractor.

'Frank', the second eldest of ten children, appears to have been educated privately in Bristol and joined William Cowlin & Son at the age of nineteen. In 1889, he enrolled in a weekly night class (probably in joinery) at the University College in Bristol, whilst continuing to work in the firm's recently-acquired joinery shop. On the death of his father in 1890, he and his elder brother, William Henry Cowlin Jr, became sole partners in the family business.

The fact that both brothers had received some advanced technical training enhanced their local image as innovators. By the early 1890s William Cowlin & Son had earned the reputation for modernity in both the decorative and civil engineering branches of building work. Before his untimely death in 1896, William Henry Jr enjoyed considerable local prestige as a town councillor and Guardian of the Poor. On his brother's death, Francis Cowlin became senior member of a partnership which now included a younger brother, Charles.

Under Francis Cowlin's direction, the firm grew steadily, its total working capital of £36,000 in 1900 increasing to over £212,000 by 1946. Before the First World War, William Cowlin & Son restored a number of important medieval churches and erected some prestigious commercial buildings, mainly (though not exclusively) in the Bristol region. The business also integrated related business functions under Francis Cowlin and by 1915, included an established estate agency, a stone mason's yard and auction rooms.

But it was as an innovative 'ferro-concrete contractor' that Cowlin secured some important pre-war contracts outside Britain. For example, the firm was invited to Kingston, Jamaica to rebuild (in reinforced concrete) government buildings destroyed in the 1907 earthquake. The firm built other administrative buildings (also in concrete) in Brazil, where Bristol staff personally supervised a native labour force supplemented by West Indians. A number of other projects were also completed in Canada, but after the First World War, Cowlin seems increasingly to have confined its operations to the South West of England.

In 1920, the firm built some of Bristol's first council houses. Municipal schemes were not as financially attractive as private ones, but after much negotiation Cowlin contracted to build experimental steel frame and concrete houses which earned praise from *The Builder* and a less enthusiastic response from consumer groups.

By 1924, William Cowlin & Son became a limited company, with Francis Cowlin and his two younger brothers, Charles and Conrad, as directors. Throughout the inter-war period Cowlin continued to build many of the most important non-residential buildings in Bristol (several of them in concrete), including the well-known municipal tobacco bond warehouses, the Filton offices of the Bristol Aeroplane Co, 'Electricity House', and a number of university buildings, banks and offices.

Francis Cowlin's outside directorships and social connections may well have served his building business. For over thirty years (1911-1944), he was a director and sometime chairman of what is now the Bristol & West of England Building Society. In 1939, his firm, which held substantial shares in the Bristol & West as early as 1925, won the contract to build the Society's Bristol offices. Again, Francis Cowlin was one of eight directors of the Bristol Gas Co from 1929 until 1944, and his firm built several gas showrooms in the West of England, as well as the architecturally-acclaimed Bristol Gas Showrooms; it also undertook important repair work for the BGCo during the blitz. Cowlin's acquaintance with Sir Edward Mountain (qv), chairman of Eagle Star Insurance, reportedly predated Cowlins' erection of Eagle House, Bristol, in 1936. Francis Cowlin was a local director of Eagle Star, 1940-44. The Cowlin family's long-standing friendship with the Wills family is evidenced by the offices and other buildings Francis and his predecessors erected for the Wills and Imperial Tobacco companies. Besides these business connections, Cowlin held the presidency of the local Commercial Rooms in 1917 and by the early 1920s belonged to the Bristol Chamber of Commerce and was chairman of the Bristol Waterworks Co.

As an active member and sometime chairman of the local and regional branches of the Federation of Building Trades Employers from 1893, Cowlin was often involved in negotiations with building operatives' unions. In his own firm, Cowlin appears to have employed union labour (certainly he did so when building council housing) but it is unlikely that he kept a closed shop. A study of Federation minutes and company accounts suggests that he was a paternalistic employer who as early as 1910 instituted a modest pension fund for two of his employees, probably clerical or supervisory workers.

Francis Cowlin held a variety of civic and philanthropic posts and honours. In 1908, he became a founder member, along with other local Liberals, of the Bristol Garden Suburb Association which by the 1920s had become Bristol Housing Ltd, a low-cost housing scheme intended as an alternative to subsidised housing for the working class. Francis Cowlin plainly preferred philanthropy to collectivism, and was president of such venerable Bristol charities as the Anchor and Grateful Societies and several churches and hospital boards. He was perhaps most fondly remembered as 'the Grand Old Man of Rugby', because of his generous patronage of the local club and Playing Fields Association.

He was also Bristol's Liberal Sheriff in 1921, a fellow of the Royal Society of Arts and a fellow of the Institute of Builders. In 1935, Francis Cowlin became the first Bristol builder to receive a knighthood.

Sir Francis Cowlin died in Bristol on 26 July 1945, a bachelor, leaving £170,730 gross. His successor as chairman of William Cowlin & Son Ltd was his first cousin J R Scull. Today (in 1981) the firm (now a subsidiary of William Cowlin (Holdings) Ltd) is still headed by a member of the Cowlin family.

MADGE DRESSER

Sources:

Unpublished

Bristol Association of Building Trade Employers Office, 22 Richmond Hill, Bristol, Bristol Association of Building Trades Employers (formerly Bristol Master Builders Association) Minutes and Reports.

South West Gas Archive, Regional Office, Riverside, Temple Street, Keynsham, Bristol, Bristol Gas Company Minutes.

University of Bristol Research Library, University College, Bristol, Calendar for the Session 1889-90.

William Cowlin & Son Ltd Office, Stratton Street, Bristol, Accounts and Misc. Papers.

BCe.

PrC.

Information from E J C Parsons, present chairman of Willam Cowlin & Son Ltd, grand-nephew of Sir Francis Cowlin; Brian Norris, head of research, Bristol & West Building Society; and Jim Whitcombe, administrative supervisor, Eagle Star Insurance Group.

Madge J Dresser Summerbell, 'Bristol's Housing Policy, 1919-1930' (Bristol MSc, 1980).

Published

Bristol Evening Post 27 June 1945.

'Bristol Gas Showroom' Architecture Illustrated Apr 1935.

Extel Statistical Survey Ltd 1 Apr 1980.

Journal of the Bristol Chamber of Commerce 1921-1939.

Key British Enterprises, the Top 20,000 Companies, 1981 (Dun & Bradstreet Ltd, 1981).

Edward Liveing, 'William Cowlin & Son' *Bristol Times and Mirror* 23 Mar 1923.

'New Companies' *Investors' Guardian* 11 Oct 1924.

'Ports of the Bristol Channel' *Progress and Commerce* 1893.

A Record of Building (William Cowlin & Son Ltd) (pp, 1928).

Times 28 July 1945.

Western Daily Press 3, 4, 27 June 1945.

'William Cowlin & Sons Ltd' *Illustrated Bristol News* May 1963.

WWW.

CRAWFORD, Sir William

(1840-1922)

Linen manufacturer

William Crawford was born at Randalstown, Ulster on 19 May 1840, the son of Rev Alexander Crawford, a Presbyterian clergyman, and his wife Anna née Gardiner. When just sixteen years old he commenced an apprenticeship with the York Street Flax Spinning Co, Belfast, a firm with which he remained for the rest of his working life. During his apprenticeship he displayed exceptional aptitude, initiative and diligence with the result that in 1862 he was asked by the directors of the company to take in hand the re-organisation of the Paris branch of the firm. The successful completion of this task was a significant step in Crawford's rise to the position of managing director of the firm, for in an industry dominated by overseas demand (like the Irish linen industry) the successful operation of overseas branches was seen as being of paramount importance. He was then appointed the company's representative in Paris, a post he retained until 1887. While in Paris he spent two years as the president of the British Chamber of Commerce there.

In 1887 he was made managing director of the firm and returned to Belfast to take up the position. He remained a director of the firm for thirty years and in 1913 he became chairman, a post he held until June 1918.

During Crawford's period as managing director the York Street Flax Spinning Co flourished, despite the general recession in the Irish linen trade. The foundations for this success were laid as early as 1864 when the firm became one of the earliest limited liability companies in the Irish linen industry with a nominal share value of £500,000 and a properly constituted board of directors. Thus when the industry was hit by recession from the mid-1870s the firm could raise more capital from its uncalled subscriptions and on the stock market (which the majority of linen firms which had remained in family hands could not do). It also had a broader spectrum of managerial expertise than most other businesses in the industry. Furthermore, the firm was one of the few vertically integrated concerns in the industry carrying out all the processes from preparing the flax to selling the finished consumer product. Thus the firm was able to undercut the price of goods being sold by single sector firms. By 1882 the firm was the largest vertically integrated linen spinning and weaving firm in the world. It operated 55,000 spindles and 1,000 powerlooms and employed 4,000 operatives. It also owned and operated the Muckamore Bleaching and Finishing Works in Co Antrim, and had branch houses in New York, Paris, Berlin, Melbourne, London and Manchester.

Crawford was well aware of the serious threat to linen posed by the development of cotton and was constantly on the lookout for new uses to which linen could be put. In his book *Irish Linen and Some Features of Its Production* published in 1910 he advocated its use in mesh underwear. Furthermore his many years spent running the Paris branch of the firm had taught him the importance of successful marketing overseas. Crawford's success at business has been attributed not only to his ability and his unique knowledge of the linen trade but also to his transparent honesty and uprightness of character. {*Belfast Newsletter* 13 May 1922}

William Crawford was also very active in public life. The well-established managerial structure which had existed in the firm since its incorporation facilitated delegation of authority and control of the business by subordinates, thus leaving him free to concern himself in public affairs. He held office in many of the commercial associations connected with the linen industry including the Linen Merchants Association, the Flax Supply Association and the Linen Section of the Textile Institute. In 1910 he was president of the Belfast Chamber of Commerce. He was also a director of the Midland Railway Co. However he was particularly involved in the building of the new Royal Victoria Hospital in Belfast, one of the largest of its kind in the United Kingdom. For his services to the hospital he was knighted in 1906. He was also active in the Irish Presbyterian Church.

Crawford married in 1866 Annie Coulston, daughter of Rev James Glasgow DD, a missionary to India. They had four sons and a daughter. Sir William Crawford died on 12 May 1922, leaving an estate valued at over £42,000. William Crawford's career was mostly untypical of the Irish linen entrepreneurs in the nineteenth century. He entered an industry, totally dominated not only by family firms but also by inter-family connections and relationships, as an ordinary apprentice when just a young man, and rose to be the managing director and chairman of the largest linen firm in the world, without the aid of family links.

EMILY BOYLE

Writings:

Irish Linen and Some Features of Its Production (Belfast: Queen's University, 1910).

Sources:

Unpublished

PrC.

Emily J Boyle, 'The Economic Development of the Irish Linen Industry, 1825-1913' (Queen's University, Belfast PhD, 1979).

Published

Belfast Newsletter and Northern Whig 13 May 1922.

The Home and Foreign Linen Trade Directory (Belfast, 1892).

WWW.

R M Young, *Belfast and the Province of Ulster* (Brighton: W T Pike & Co, 1910).

CRAWFORD, Sir William Smith

(1878-1950)
Advertising agent

Sir William S Crawford (courtesy of the History of Advertising Trust).

William Smith Crawford was born in Glasgow in 1878, son of Robert Crawford, DL, LLD, JP, and brother of Archibald, later to become a noted barrister. After education at Lenzie Academy, Blair Lodge, Neuwied-am-Rhein, and Frankfurt-am-Main, he entered the fancy goods business in which his father was a partner. When his father retired in 1902, William joined a firm of opticians, but later moved to London to look for a job in advertising.

In 1906 he was working as a space canvasser for the De Wynter Co, moving to the Frederick E Potter advertising agency when De Wynters failed. In March 1914 he set up his own agency, W S Crawford Ltd, with the help of friends, and in 1919 acquired the advertising agency of W H Smith & Son.

Crawford built his agency into one of the most important in the world. He saw the advantage to major international companies of being able to deal with an international agency network, and by his death had built up a chain of 37 associate offices around the globe. He was particularly successful in attracting business from American companies seeking a co-ordinated approach to their advertising in Europe.

He made an outstanding contribution to the improvement of advertising techniques, in terms both of planning and execution. He studied the allocation of advertising expenditure within and between media, realising in particular the value of large press spaces at a time when many companies still clung to the classified columns, and evolved a planning formula (concentration, domination, repetition) which is still used today.

He also did a good deal to raise creative standards. The agency commissioned work from leading artists and designers in Britain, Europe, and the United States. It took the lead in supplying advertisements to the press with the type already set, so making it an integral part of the overall design, instead of letting publishers do the job in whatever faces they happened to have. To this end the agency imported new typefaces, particularly from Germany, and also designed its own in collaboration with the Monotype Corporation.

Crawford was further notable for his enlightened approach to the employment of women in positions of importance, his agency having women as vice-chairman, company secretary and creative director. He is quoted as saying 'I never think of men and women in separate categories: as far as I am concerned, whoever does the job best can have it'. {Mills (1954) 50}

The rapid success of Crawford's agency brought him considerable personal recognition. In 1923 he became a member of the Advisory Publicity Committee to the Ministry of Health. He was a member of the Imperial Economic Committee, 1925-26, and of the Empire Marketing Board, 1926-31. In 1931 he also acted as chairman of the 'Buy British' campaign though he privately disagreed with the underlying concept, describing it as like looking at world economics through the wrong end of a telescope. He became publicity advisor to the Ministry of Agriculture in 1929, and chairman of the Post Office Publicity Committee in 1931. His work for the Empire Marketing Board in particular was recognised in 1927 when he was made a KCBE.

Crawford also did much to increase the standing of the advertising business. He took a leading part in organising the World Advertising Convention at Wembley in 1924, and was chairman of the organising committee of the Advertising and Marketing Exhibition at Olympia in 1933. He was a member of the council of the Association of British Advertising Agents, was president of the Institute of Incorporated Practitioners in Advertising, 1937-40, and a member of the executive council of the Advertising Association from its foundation in 1926. He became chairman of the National Advertising Benevolent Society in 1933, and in addition was an active member of several advertising clubs.

He married in 1907 Marion, daughter of William Whitelaw MD, JP, of Kirkintilloch; they had one son and two daughters. Sir William Smith Crawford died on 19 November 1950, leaving £66,910 gross.

T R NEVETT

Writings:

How to Succeed in Advertising (World's Press News, 1931).

(with Sir Herbert Broadley) *The People's Food* (W Heinemann, 1938).

Sources:

Unpublished

PrC.

Conversations with Hubert Oughton, OBE, and R J Cowen, both formerly of W S Crawford Ltd.

Information from T Baker-Jones, W H Smith & Son.

Published

Advertiser's Weekly 23 Nov 1950.

Godfrey H Saxon Mills, *There IS a Tide* (W Heinemann, 1954).

T R Nevett, *Advertising in Britain. A History* (Heinemann, 1982).

Times 21, 24, 30 Nov 1950.

World Press News 24 Nov 1950.

WWW.

CRAWFORD, 27th Earl of Crawford
see LINDSAY, David Alexander Edward

CRAWSHAY, George

(1821-1896)

Iron and heavy engineering equipment manufacturer

George Crawshay was born in London in 1821, the son of George Crawshay Sr, a London iron merchant, and his French wife. He was nephew of William Crawshay II (1788-1867), the Cyfarthfa ironmaster.

George Crawshay, from the Newcastle Daily Chronicle *Mar 1896 (courtesy of the Central Library, Newcastle upon Tyne).*

George Jr was educated at North End House School, Hampstead and Trinity College, Cambridge. He spent a year on the Continent doing the Grand Tour before going to Cambridge and was fluent in several languages, including French (in which he was bilingual) and German.

Intended for the Bar, he passed the relevant examinations but never practised, probably because an accident directed his career to industry. In 1843 the death of his brother-in-law, Frank Stanley, after a fall from a horse, brought the latter's share in Hawks, Stanley & Co, a Gateshead firm of ironfounders and engineers, into Crawshay hands. Together with his brother, Edmond, George was sent to Gateshead by his father, at first to join with, and then take over from, George Hawks in the management of the firm. Established in the area for nearly a century and employing about 1,000 workmen, the firm was well placed to benefit from the secondary phase of industrialisation with expansion in the capital goods industries in which the North East was to play a notable part. Although the firm did not possess the dynamism of the new companies, such as Armstrongs and Palmers, and unlike them did not diversify into shipbuilding and armaments, it undertook considerable expansion in a wide range of iron products. It was perhaps best known as a bridge contractor, building bridges in many parts of the world, as well as the High Level Bridge at Newcastle. Other items of manufacture included lighthouses, boilers and chains as well as a wide range of iron semi-manufactures. In these years the firm appears to have been fairly progressive. For instance, in 1844, the year after the Crawshays' arrival, the firm installed the first Nasmyth steam hammer in the North East, which was subsequently used for driving the piles of the High Level Bridge. Under the impact of rising demand for engineering products the firm's employment reached 1,500 in 1863 and in 1889 2,000 were employed, making it probably the largest employer in Gateshead.

In somewhat mysterious circumstances, however, the firm closed suddenly in 1889. It is usually said that this was a result of a shortage of capital and the impact of competition from steel on iron. The firm had, however, installed Siemens-Martin open hearth equipment not long before its closure. Although the firm's creditors were paid in full it would appear that this had to be done from George Crawshay's private resources, since he died almost penniless (as did his brother). Surprisingly, in 1889, there was no attempt to sell the firm to the public and the works were dismantled.

George Crawshay was active in political affairs and was a friend and correspondent of many leading liberals both at home and abroad. On his arrival on Tyneside he threw himself into the campaign for the repeal of the Corn Laws, became involved with local suffrage reformers, such as Joseph Cowen, and was active in sponsoring local Mechanics' Institutes, to which he lectured frequently on a variety of political subjects, as well as on mathematics which he had studied at Cambridge. He became a member of Gateshead Council in 1854 and an alderman in 1862 and was mayor of the town in 1856, 1859 and 1863. He was, however, best known for his involvement in foreign affairs and for championing liberal causes throughout Europe. In the early 1850s he came under the spell of the Russophobe, David Urquhart, and was his chief assistant in setting up Foreign Affairs Committees agitating for support of Turkey and reform of

British policy during the Crimean War. While his interest lay particularly in the Middle East and he became Turkish Consul in Newcastle (and was said to be the first man in England to have a Turkish bath, which was installed at his house in Tynemouth), he wrote pamphlets and lectured on many aspects of international relations. He also had a considerable interest in literature and contributed both prose and poetry to local newspapers as well as writing, shortly before his death, a pleasant autobiographical recollection of an early romance.

He married a daughter of Sir John Fife (1795-1891), prominent Tyneside physician, reformer and mayor of Newcastle, and they had two sons and a daughter. Initially living at Tynemouth House, Tynemouth, they moved in about 1862 to the splendours of Haughton Castle, with its estate on the North Tyne in Northumberland. Growing financial pressures in the business led to the sale of the estate in the late 1880s and George returned briefly to Tynemouth. After the closure of the firm, however, he went to live with his daughter at Horsted Keynes in Sussex, where he died on 13 March 1896, leaving assets of only £25.

D J ROWE

Writings:

Speech Delivered at a Meeting in Gateshead. Monday 26 May 1845. Containing a Vindication of the Conduct of the Gateshead Free Trade Society (Newcastle: John & James Selkirk, 1845).

The Catastrophe of the East India Company (1858).

The Immediate Cause of the Indian Mutiny (Effingham Wilson, 1858).

Proselytism Destructive of Christianity and Incompatible with Political Dominion (Effingham Wilson, 1858).

The European Complication Explained (Newcastle: Horn & Story, 1859).

The Treaty of London (Newcastle: Daily Journal Office, 1864).

A Run with the Tyndale Hounds: a Romantic Drama by A Fox (Edinburgh: W Blackwood & Sons, 1884).

In What Consists the Change from the Old 'Law of Nations' to Modern 'International Law' (1891).

A Silver Shape. Recollections of a Victorian Romance ed E Esdaile (Athenaeum, 1980).

Sources:

Unpublished

PrC.

Published

Newcastle Daily Chronicle 16 Mar 1896.

Sketches of Public Men of the North (1855).

Times 23 Mar 1896.

CREED, Frederick George

(1871-1957)

Telegraph equipment inventor and manufacturer

Frederick G Creed (courtesy of Creed & Co Ltd).

Frederick George Creed was born at Mill Village, Nova Scotia, on 6 October 1871, one of six children born to humble parents who had emigrated to Canada from Scotland.

Frederick Creed left school at fourteen to become a check boy with the Western Union Telegraph Co at Canso, Nova Scotia; here he qualified as a telegraph operator. Three years later, he took a similar post with the Central & South American Telegraph Co in Peru. Later, he was transferred to the company's telegraph office in Iquique, Chile. While in Peru Frederick Creed met his future wife, Jane (Jeannie) Russell, who was working there as a Free Church of Scotland missionary. The couple were married in Halifax, Nova Scotia, in October 1896, after Creed's company posted him back to Canada.

At that time, Morse code signals were transmitted from punched paper tape which involved the use of a Morse 'stick' perforator, a device with three keys which were hit by hand-held wooden punches. The method was slow and tedious and often damaging to the operator's hands. Creed suffered a permanently distorted right hand as a result of this employment, and his experience forced him to think about alternative methods.

In search of new techniques and opportunities, Creed resigned from his job in 1897, and set sail with his wife for Glasgow, her home. Here he approached Lord Kelvin with an idea for a Morse-based telegraphic keyboard perforator, but the well-known physicist and inventor dismissed the project. Having obtained work as a telegraph operator with the *Glasgow Herald*, Creed also outlined his idea to Alexander Ewing, the newspaper's assistant editor, but received a similar rejection. Undaunted, Creed bought an old Barlock typewriter for 15s and spent much of his leisure time over the following year converting it into a pneumatically powered keyboard perforator. Eventually he returned to Lord Kelvin who was sufficiently impressed with the device to offer him some technical facilities.

By 1904, Creed had left his job with the *Herald* and had rented a top-floor workshop at 156 St Vincent Street, Glasgow, advertising his business with the words 'Creed — Makers of Telegraphic Equipment'. An early success was the sale of 12 keyboard perforators to the General Post Office. In 1906, he was able to sell a number of his machines to his old employer the *Glasgow Herald*. Creed was given the freedom of the *Herald* offices to test his later inventions: a receiving perforator (reperforator), which recorded incoming signals on perforated tape identical to that used at the other end of the line for transmission; and a printer which accepted the received message tape and decoded it into plain language characters on ordinary paper tape. Creed & Co's turnover for the years 1906, 1907, 1908

Frederick Creed's original Morse keyboard tape perforator (courtesy of Creed & Co Ltd).

and 1910 were (rounded off) £1,720, £888, £2,570 and £2,633 respectively. Creed apparently had a small number of employees working with him at this time; total salaries and wages for September 1910, for example, came to £94 1s 9d.

In 1909, Creed, with six mechanics, set out for Croydon, where he opened a small factory. This took him into the vicinity of London where he could more conveniently negotiate with the Post Office management which had appeared strangely reluctant to follow up their initial order for 12 keyboard perforators. In Croydon, Creed, a devout Christian (probably Presbyterian), was horrified to find people at work or drinking in public houses on Sundays. He felt it a duty to shield his workforce from these practices. New employees, without exception, had to sign a pledge to stay teetotal, and Creed would sometimes scour the streets, searching for transgressors, who were usually sacked. Smoking was strongly discouraged. But he would often visit sick employees: six feet four inches tall, black-bearded and with a long, black coat and black, wide-brimmed hat, his sudden appearance on the doorsteps of the sick apparently unnerved some spouses. He was also known to despatch certain convalescing employees on holiday at no expense to themselves.

In the struggle for the survival of his business Creed was helped through contact with Harald Bille, an innovative Danish telegraph engineer. A partnership developed, and in 1912, Creed, Bille & Co Ltd was incorporated with a share capital of £100,000. The new company paid £53,525 for the assets of Creed & Co. Boosted by additional capital, the company, with Frederick Creed and Harald Bille as joint managing directors and around 60 employees, began to benefit from its growing network of overseas agents. In its first year of business, the new company received a fillip when the *Daily Mail* offices in London and Manchester were completely equipped with Creed telegraphy instruments. Over subsequent years, other newspapers followed the lead of the *Mail*. After the outbreak of the First World War the firm received substantial orders for telegraph equipment and also for shell fuses, radio tube amplifiers, bomb release gear and air compasses. The expansion in business led to the acquisition of new factory premises in Croydon.

In August 1916, Harald Bille died in a train accident. It was a great loss, but the company, dropping the name 'Bille' from its title, continued to progress. In 1923, Frederick Creed designed Europe's first 'start-stop' 5-unit code teleprinter, the 1P. An improved version, the 2P, quickly followed. The machine was Creed's response to the Morkrum Teletype machine from the USA. In 1925, Creed acquired the patents of the successful Murray Multiplex Telegraphy System and in the following year, he introduced the 6S automatic tape transmitter. In 1927 came one of the company's most successful products, the Model 3 send/receive teleprinter. Thousands were sold in the following years.

Later that year, Creed & Co was acquired by the International Telephone & Telegraph Corporation (now ITT Corporation) for just over £250,000. Frederick Creed remained on the board until 1930, when, at the age of fifty-nine, he suddenly resigned. A factor in this decision appears to have been the parent company's readiness to permit employees to use their sports field on Sundays, although there was also evidence of a growing rift between Creed and his American employers.

Frederick Creed now turned his inventive capabilities to a number of products, such as various types of catamaran and a twin-hulled seadrome for refuelling aeroplanes on transatlantic flights, but none was accepted in the commercial world.

Following his resignation, Frederick Creed made a number of unfortunate investments, and, over the years, inventive ideas and patenting them proved a constant drain on his resources. His last years were spent preventing his descent into bankruptcy.

Creed's first wife died in May 1945; there were six children from the marriage. He married his second wife, Valerie Leopoldina Gisella Layton, in 1947. Frederick Creed died on 11 December 1957, leaving £1,496 gross.

JOHN RACKHAM

Sources:

Unpublished

ITT Creed Ltd, Hollingbury, Brighton, Creed & Co minute books, 1912 to 1928.

Family letters, collected by the author.

PrC.

Published

The Breath of Invention. The Story of Frederick G Creed (Hollingbury, Brighton: ITT Creed Ltd, 1976).

Hovering Craft and Hydrofoil Magazine Aug 1979.

CRISP, Charles Birch

(1867-1958)

Company promoter and financier

Charles Birch Crisp was born at Dove Street, Bristol on 5 September 1867, the son of Charles Birch Crisp, a common law clerk, and his wife, Clara Isabella née Peterkin. Raised in Bristol, he worked as a journalist in his youth. He had become a newspaper manager in London by December 1893, when he married, at Hampstead, Beatrice Marion (b 1872), daughter of Edwin Chapple. Crisp was a self-styled 'Tory Democrat', and together with Winston Churchill contested the two-member constituency of Oldham for the Unionists in the general election of 1900: both then and in the next election of 1906 he was defeated.

He became a member of the London Stock Exchange in 1897, with Ernest William Broadbent later acting as his junior partner. In the decade that followed he was an active company promoter, and in 1909 he became chairman of the South American Railway Construction Co Ltd, whose interests included the Creara railway in Brazil. His ambition to become an international financier was realised by 1909. In March he visited St Petersburg to discuss finance for the municipality's proposed drainage system to eliminate cholera; and arising from this visit, in June 1909, Crisp and the London, City & Midland Bank placed £3,544,960 worth of Armavir-Touapse railway bonds on the London market, backed by a Russian Government guarantee. In July 1909 Crisp visited Copenhagen as the representative of Lloyds, Parrs and other banks to tender for the London flotation of the Danish State Loan worth £2,240,000; but a French banking syndicate secured the business. Crisp also worked jointly at this time with the Russo-Chinoise Bank and made unsuccessful overtures to both Barings and Rothschilds about Russian finance.

He next bought 30 per cent of the 100,000 shares in the Russian Commercial & Industrial Bank (Russki Torgovi Promishlenni Bank, founded 1890 and capitalised at 35 million roubles). This holding, which he valued at £680,000, was the main asset of the Anglo-Russian Trust, which he formed in 1909 and chaired from 1910. He also became the London director of the Russki Bank in 1910, and in January 1911 launched the Anglo-Russian Bank, the name of which was changed in October 1912 to the British Bank for Foreign Trade (BBFT). Crisp was chairman of BBFT in 1912-27, and his co-directors included Almeric Paget MP (created Lord Queenborough 1918) who remained a close associate for many years; Sir Charles Delmé-Radcliffe, formerly Military Attaché in Rome and then agent in China of Marcus Samuel (qv) of Shell; and Charles Greenway (qv), chairman of the Anglo-Persian Oil Co. BBFT's staff included Samuel Pepys Cockerell (1880-1915), who had served at the Foreign Office until 1910.

Crisp's professed aim was for the Anglo-Russian Trust and BBFT to follow the German and French example of putting capital into Russia in order to draw increased Russian industrial orders to Britain. The Trust paid 10 per cent dividends on £1 million capital in 1910-12, and 6 per cent in 1913 after the issue of £500,000 4.5 per cent debentures in May 1913. The BBFT, with £1.2 million issued capital, paid 5 per cent for 1911-12 and 6 per cent for 1912-14.

In 1910 Crisp was briefly a director of the ailing motor-car manufacturers, A Darracq (1905) Ltd, and was succeeded on the Darracq board by Almeric Paget 'an amiable Grand Seigneur ... of immense vigour' {James (1967) 191, 358}.

The public highlight of his career came with the so-called Birch Crisp Loan of 1912. Banking interests from Britain, France, Germany and the USA, supported by their respective Governments, had formed the 'Four Power Consortium' to regulate financial business with China in 1910. To this consortium Russian and Japanese bankers were admitted in 1912. The intention was that the participating powers would prevent their nationals who were outside the consortium from making unsound loans to China which would increase Chinese indebtedness haphazardly. The only British bank which the Foreign Office would support for Chinese loans was the Hongkong & Shanghai Bank (the sole British bank inside the consortium). Crisp, with his loan of 1912, now assailed this banking monopoly.

In July 1912 the Chinese Government signed a preliminary loan agreement with an American financial syndicate. Birch Crisp was then introduced to the deal by (Sir) Harry Brittain, the imperial publicist, and took on the loan with the encouragement of Dr G E Morrison, formerly the *Times* correspondent in Peking and then special adviser to the Chinese Government. On 23 August Crisp informed the British Foreign Office that he was heading a syndicate to lend £10 million to China, and was informed that the British Government still adhered to their policy of exclusive support for the Hongkong & Shanghai Bank. In September he concluded the loan agreement despite further warnings that the Foreign Office utterly opposed it. Subsequently he stated in the press that the Office had not objected to his loan, though this was forcefully denied by them. In the convulsion that followed Sir Eyre Crowe of the Foreign Office wrote that it was 'notorious' that the loan's promoters knew 'little' about China, and were relying 'on security of most doubtful value, against the wishes of the government, who consider that such loans are doing harm to British interests in circumstances of which the government alone can really judge' {PRO, FO 371/1322, minute of 26 September 1912}. The contrary view was put by Dr Morrison, who called Birch Crisp

> a man of high character, who had rendered important services to Russia and ... materially assisted in the Anglo-Russian rapprochement ... To compare him to his disparagement to Sir Carl Meyer Bart — the most active of the Hongkong & Shanghai Bank, a Hamburg Israelite who bought his baronetcy, and ... to whom no such words as integrity ... could be applied - seems ... unjust {Morrison (1978) 65}.

This anti-semitic and anti-German tincture recurred throughout the affair, as when Pepys Cockerell alleged 'that it was notorious in the City ... that the Hongkong & Shanghai Bank had practically passed into the control of the Deutsche Bank' {PRO, FO 371/1322, Crowe to Sir Edward Grey, 13 July 1912}.

The Foreign Office's opposition hindered the flotation of the first loan instalment of £5 million in September 1912 and made it impossible for Crisp to arrange a further issue. In December he persuaded the Chinese to pay him £150,000 for surrendering his right to issue the second loan instalment and for waiving his option to handle the proposed £25 million Reorganisation Loan of 1913 — neither of which he was in fact able to raise. He thus received £150,000 of the loan's proceeds for the privilege of breaking his own contractual obligations, as well as interest on £520,000 of the first instalment which he held for six months. The Chinese were also forced to pay £150,000 in compensation to the Consortium, while the Hongkong & Shanghai Bank (confronted by the City's sympathies for Crisp's aims) reluctantly admitted four other London banks to share in Chinese business.

Between 1908 and 1914 Crisp and the BBFT placed £20 million of Russian bonds and other securities in London, and at the outbreak of war the BBFT itself held over £1 million in Russian Government guaranteed and municipal bonds. The war wrecked Crisp's Russian business, BBFT paid no dividends in 1914-21, and £840,000 of its issued capital was written off in 1920. His most important war-time deal was to buy the Siemens electrical factory at Stafford (1917). Under the Trading with the Enemy Acts, this had been confiscated from German ownership by the Public Trustee, and the Board of Trade had hoped in 1916 that it would be bought by Dudley Docker (qv). Crisp and Queenborough became directors of Siemens in 1917 and Crisp superintended an elaborate capital reconstruction of the company which in 1919 joined the English Electric merger led by W L Hichens (qv).

In 1918 Crisp organised another controversial Chinese debt known as the Marconi loan. China borrowed £600,000 at 8 per cent interest in order to erect Marconi wireless stations, but there was soon a complete default of interest payments. Attempts to resolve this confusion continued throughout the 1920s. In April 1923, in association with the Sino-Scandinavian Bank, Crisp made another attempt to break the consortium monopoly by offering to lend £20 million to China (including an advance of £1 million at the start of negotiations), but this proposition fortunately lapsed. Birch Crisp nevertheless remained proud of his Chinese transactions, and when the College of Arms granted armorial bearings to his family in 1922, these featured 'a Chinese dragon' and 'two horseshoes' (a superstitious reference to the luck needed by a company promoter).

From 1917 Crisp was entangled in the problem of Russian debts. In order to prevent the value of its holding in Russian securities from falling to zero, BBFT bought large parcels of securities on the open market, and jointly with Crisp's stockbroking firm became 'the largest individual holders of Russian securities' in Britain {PRO,FO 371/10503, Crisp to Sidney Webb, 20 March 1924}. Crisp represented the British bondholders of the Wolmar railway in Latvia, and was member of the Russian committee of the Foreign Bondholders Council until forced to resign on the committee's discovery that, contrary to its rules, he had conducted private negotiations in June 1924 with Scheinman, president of the Russia State Bank, and Rakovsky, leader of the Russian trade delegation to Britain. BBFT passed its dividends throughout 1922-28 and had no hope of prosperity without an Anglo-Russian political and debt settlement. Crisp saw the Conservative party's anti-bolshevism as an obstacle to this end, and therefore resigned from the Carlton club to contest Windsor as a Liberal in the general elections of 1922 and 1923. (He lived nearby at Binfield.)

The accession of a Labour Government in 1924 coincided with a visit by Crisp to Russia, and encouraged him to approach Labour leaders such as Ramsay MacDonald, Arthur Ponsonby and Sidney Webb about methods of Anglo-Soviet settlement and the abandonment of the Chinese consortium policy. Claiming that 'big interests which resented my firm's activities in the past have succeeded in keeping me out of the Conferences' {PRO, FO 371/10503, Crisp to Mrs Rose Rosenberg, 19 March 1924}, he had a series of meetings with the Prime Minister on ways to 'clear up the Russian mess' {PRO, MacDonald papers, 30/69/2, Crisp to Ramsay MacDonald, 1 September 1924}. When a general election was called in 1924, before the Anglo-Russian commercial treaty could be concluded, Crisp arranged for BBFT to lend £5,000 to the Labour party, and personally provided £750 to pay for Labour to fight the three parliamentary divisions in Berkshire: the first Labour candidacies in the county. His son (Christopher Norman Birch Crisp, b 1900) stood for Labour at Windsor, and MacDonald was instructed that 'the fight [must be] made to turn exclusively upon the Treaty' {*ibid*, Crisp to MacDonald, 5 October 1924}.

Crisp retired in 1927 aged sixty and went to Australia for several years. He later claimed, 'When I resigned from the Carlton Club my firm lost many clients, and when I fought the Windsor division as a Liberal Free Trader more clients fell away, and when my son stood ... as a Labour candidate my business suffered an eclipse which led me later to leave the Stock Exchange' {PRO, MacDonald papers 30/69/676, Crisp to Hugh Dalton, 21 July 1930}. He thereafter sank into obscurity, and his entry was removed from *Who's Who* in 1948. He died in a London hospital on 7 November 1958 aged ninety-one. No details of his will or estate are recorded in the probate calendars at Somerset House, for the period 1958-65.

R P T DAVENPORT-HINES

CRISP Charles Birch

Writings:

letter on Explanations of Unionist Defeat *Times* 26 Jan 1906.

full page advertisement The Anglo-Russian Trust: the Investment of British Capital in Russia *ibid* 20 Nov 1911.

letter on Chinese Loan Dispute *ibid* 31 Oct 1912.

letter on The Restoration of Anglo-Russian Commerce: Recognition problems for the Conference *Manchester Guardian* Trade Supplement 20 Mar 1924.

open letter to Liberal party officials on Russian treaty and Mr Lloyd George *Times* 27 Sept 1924.

Sources:

Unpublished

House of Lords RO, papers of A Bonar Law (BL 33/2/30).

Midland Bank Archives, Poultry, London EC2, diaries of S B Murray.

Mitchell Library, Sydney, NSW, Australia, papers of Dr G E Morrison (vols 70, 74, 81 and especially 152).

PRO, papers of Board of Trade and Foreign Office, Ramsay MacDonald.

Sheffield University Library, papers of W A S Hewins (59/102-112).

University of Toronto, Thomas Fisher Library, papers of J O P Bland.

BCe.

MCe.

Published

John O P Bland, *Recent Events and Present Policies in China* (W Heinemann, 1912).

Randolph F E S Churchill, *Winston Churchill: Young Statesman* (Heinemann, 1966-7) companion vol 2, part 1 (1969).

Roberta Allbert Dayer, *Bankers and Diplomats in China 1917-25* (Cass, 1981).

Documents of British Foreign Policy 2nd series, 8 (HMSO, 1960), documents 1 and 95.

Economist 17 July 1909, 21 Jan, 29 Apr 1911, 21, 28 Sept 1912, 12 Oct 1918.

Arthur C Fox-Davies, *Armorial Families* 1 (Hurst & Blackett, 1929).

Gabriel Gorodetsky, *The Precarious Truce: Anglo-Soviet Relations 1924-27* (Cambridge: Cambridge University Press, 1977).

Robert Rhodes James (ed), *Chips: the Diaries of Sir Henry Channon* (Weidenfeld, 1967).

Robert Jones and Oliver J D Marriott, *Anatomy of a Merger* (J Cape, 1970).

George E Morrison, *Correspondence* (2 vols, Cambridge: Cambridge University Press, 1976-78).

Cyril A Pearl, *Morrison of Peking* (Sydney: Angus & Robertson, 1967).

PP, Correspondence Respecting Chinese Loan Negotiations (1912-13) Cd 6446.

John D Scott, *Siemens* (Weidenfeld & Nicolson, 1958).

Times 5 Jan 1906, 24, 25, 27 Sept, 16, 31 Oct, 8, 9 Nov 1912, 20 Feb 1913, 23 July 1919, 29 Apr, 1 Dec 1920, 3, 29 May 1923, 31 Oct 1923, 16 Mar 1928, 10 Nov 1958. *WW* 1942.

*Brigadier General Critchley
(courtesy of G R Monk).*

CRITCHLEY, Alfred Cecil

(1890-1963)

Greyhound racing promoter and industrialist

Alfred Cecil Critchley, born on a ranch near Calgary, Canada, in 1890, was the elder son of Oswald Asheton Critchley (d 1935) an immigrant rancher whose family hailed from Salwick Hall, Preston, and his first wife Marie Cecil née Newbolt, daughter of Col Newbolt of the Royal Horse Artillery. Raised on the prairies, Alfred had no formal education until he, his brother Walter and a half-brother (the son of Alfred's step-mother, Winifred née Holt, of the Liverpool shipping family) were sent to England in 1899. They rioted their way through several preparatory schools until 1906 when further additions to the family prevented him going to Sandhurst. Instead, his father found him a junior clerk's job with the Bank of Montreal. After twelve months Alfred, who found bank work 'mentally stultifying' {Critchley (1961) 25}, escaped by passing into the Royal Military College at Kingston, Ontario. When war broke out in 1914 Critchley was a subaltern with Lord Strathcona's Horse at Winnipeg; by the end of the war he was a brigadier-general. After being wounded and gaining the DSO in 1916 he achieved rapid promotion for his extremely efficient organisation of a Canadian Corps officers' training school in England. He was seconded to the RFC in 1918 to take charge of the ground training of air crews (and himself learned to fly), recording that by the end of the war he had trained nearly 100,000 men. For this he was awarded the CMG in 1919.

Weary of war, Critchley decided to go into business, taking charge of the Mexican interests of 'a well-known British financier' {*ibid*, 89}, presumably those of Weetman Pearson (qv), including oil drilling. Bandits and a bout of dysentery forced him back to London where the Wallenberg group introduced him to Henry Horne, a financier then trying to buy 600,000 shares of the Associated Portland Cement Manufacturers Co which dominated the expanding British cement industry. Critchley in 1924, through his friend William C Potter, vice-president of the Guaranty Trust Co of New York, arranged a short term loan of £300,000. Then he and Sir Philip Nash, as nominees of the financiers controlling a majority of APCM shares, joined the interlocking board of the APCM and the British Portland Cement Manufacturers, which together formed an unwieldy amalgamation of nearly 60 companies. In his characteristically forceful and direct manner, Critchley demanded restructuring and a centralised management. The APCM and BPCM capitulated. The main board was reduced in size with P Malcolm Stewart (qv) as chairman, Nash as deputy chairman, Alfred Stevens in charge of finance, Harold Anderson, sales, and A C Davis, works. Critchley took over publicity, transport and personnel. A few months later Malcolm Stewart and his associates bought Horne's shares from the Guaranty Trust Co and set about the reorganisation Critchley wanted. Critchley remained on the APCM and BPCM boards until the early 1960s; one of his first and most enduring changes was the blue circle advertising logo for the companies' products, symbolising a seal of quality achieved under the new British Standard Specifications of 1920.

Sometime in 1926 Critchley, through golfing acquaintances, met an American, Charlie Munn, who showed him photographs of greyhounds chasing a mechanical hare in Oklahoma City. 'It immediately occurred to me that this might prove to be the poor man's racecourse' {*ibid*, 131}. There had been earlier attempts to use mechanical hares; but only whippet racing, chiefly in the North of England, was popular. Critchley therefore chose a Northern site for a new move to introduce greyhound racing, this time with a circular track, a mechanical hare and handicap arrangements to sharpen the competition. With Munn and his American friends Critchley and his associates raised £14,000. When the management of Bellevue Gardens, Manchester, refused to lease their football field, the group leased 12 acres on the opposite side of the road and built their own stands and track. Critchley borrowed an extra £500 from the Westminster Bank (for which his branch manager was nearly sacked) and on 24 July 1926 the stadium opened. After the first few meetings attendances improved from 2,500 to 4,000 or more; 35 meetings in 1926 attracted a total of 333,375 attendances. Critchley formed a private company, Greyhound Racing Association Ltd. Working full time for APCM, he decided to close down over winter and to look for a London site. For £125,000 he acquired the lease of the dilapidated White City arena, originally built for the Olympic Games of 1908; later he bought the freehold from the Ecclesiastical Commissioners for another £75,000. At the same time Critchley took an option on 23 acres at Harringay, on a site where earth from tube excavations had been dumped. The White City Stadium was a spectacular success, with 40,000 spectators a night for 50 consecutive nights. The promoters decided to go public, forming the Greyhound Racing Association Trust Ltd in December 1927. Critchley became vice-chairman and managing director; Sir W B Gentle became chairman and his son F S Gentle, assistant managing director. Of the £1 million share capital, 530,400 8 per cent cumulative participating £1 preference shares and 1,326,000 one shilling ordinary shares were set aside for the purchase of GRA Ltd while another £283,080 of shares (including 269,600 of the 4 million one shilling ordinary shares) were offered to and oversubscribed by the public, allowing the White City and Harringay

Stadiums to be completed. Stadiums at Stamford Bridge and later New Cross, both in London, at Hall Green, Birmingham and at Powderhall Marine Gardens and Stenhouse, Edinburgh were built or acquired by 1939. The GRA Trust owned the racecourse properties and controlled a number of subsidiary companies which managed the various racecourses, including the Greyhound Racing Association Ltd.

To ensure the highest possible standards in the sport, the National Greyhound Racing Society was formed and Critchley's father, a senior steward of horse-racing in Western Canada, joined Alfred in drafting the rules, doing so 'with such clarity that they are still in force today in their entirety' {*ibid*, 138}. O A Critchley served as the Society's first senior steward. The Critchleys, their associates (like Sir William Gentle and his son Frank) and other operators in the industry succeeded in excluding corruption on any scale from the sport and a favourable police report on the new greyhound tracks stifled the impact of protests from church leaders. Julius Totalizators, which continuously recorded the aggregate of bets on each dog, were early installed, but the Leeds bookmakers, feeling threatened by a more efficient technique for publicising betting odds, went to court and forced a suspension. When Critchley became an MP in 1934, he later recalled, 'One of the main efforts of my parliamentary career was directed to the introduction of the totalizator to the greyhound tracks' {*ibid*, 154}. He secured this in the Betting and Lotteries Act of 1934. Critchley retired from the managing directorship of the GRA Trust to join the war effort in 1939; he returned as ordinary director in 1946. The trading profits of GRA Ltd rose from £36,000 in 1928 to £250,000 in 1939 and £1.7 million in 1946, a boom year; when Critchley left the board in May 1957 the trading profit was £194,000.

During the Second World War Critchley, with the rank of air commodore, had charge of initial training of air crews for the RAF in 1939-43 and for this was awarded the CBE. Then as Director General of BOAC 1943-46 (appointed at Churchill's request), he was responsible for selecting the site of a new London airport at Heathrow, and for its initial construction. Under Critchley discipline in BOAC was tightened and loss turned into profit, partly because of the changing fortunes of war, partly because he insisted on charging realistic prices to the Post Office for the carriage of mails. He resigned in January 1946 when it became clear that the Labour Government intended to divide BOAC into different corporations, which Critchley regarded as administratively extravagant in a period of wartime stringency and structurally weak in the face of long-term international competition.

Critchley then moved into the management of a private charter airline initially for flying personnel and materials between Britain and the Persian Gulf. With £400,000 put up by Harley Drayton (qv) and the support of Sir Alan Cobham (qv), Critchley and one of his BOAC pilots, Captain Ronald Ashley, formed Skyways, operating out of Dunsfold Aerodrome near Guildford. Services to the Far East, East Africa and the Mediterranean were established. The firm took the leading British share in the Berlin Airlift of 1948-49. Eventually however, under the Civil Aviation Act of 1946 and the Air Corporations Act of 1949, Skyways' licences were withdrawn and the business handed over to the subsidised national corporations. About this time too, Critchley became involved with Billy Butlin (qv) in a disastrous project to develop a holiday village in the Bahamas, about which Critchley is singularly silent in his memoirs.

Critchley twice stood for Parliament, as Conservative in the Gorton division of Manchester in 1929 and as United Empire candidate in the Islington by-election of 1931. Eventually he sat as National Conservative MP for Twickenham, 1934-35 but after serving his interests in greyhound racing he withdrew at the 1935 general election in order to sustain his business career.

A keen horseman in his youth, Critchley took up golf seriously in 1925 and in the 1930s won a string of domestic and European amateur titles, playing on various occasions with the Prince of Wales, Henry Longhurst and Dai Rees.

Critchley married three times: first in 1916, Maryon, elder daughter of John Galt, Canadian tea importer and banker, by whom he had one son, John (killed in the Western Desert in 1941); after his first marriage broke up he married in 1927 Joan, younger daughter of Mrs Reginald Foster by whom he had a son and a daughter; thirdly in 1938 he married Diana Fishwick, British Ladies Open Golf Champion, by whom he had a son and a daughter.

At the age of sixty-three Critchley suddenly became blind but courageously preserved an involvement in his cement and greyhound racing companies for several more years. He died on 9 February 1963 leaving £23,331 gross.

DAVID J JEREMY

Writings:

Critch! The Memoirs of Brigadier-General A C Critchley CMG, CBE, DSO (Hutchinson, 1961).

Sources:

Unpublished

Churchill College, Cambridge, papers of Sir Edward Spears, ten letters and one telegram from Critchley and his wife, 1946-62.

MCe.

PrC.

Information from E J Monk of the GRA Group.

Published

P Lesley Cook and Ruth Cohen, *Effects of Mergers. Six Studies* (George Allen & Unwin, 1958).

Benjamin Seebohm Rowntree and G R Lavers, *English Life and Leisure: A Social Study* (Longmans, 1951).

The Stock Exchange Official Year-Book 1939, 1945, 1946, 1947.

The Stock Exchange Year-Book 1928.

Times *Prospectuses* 74 (1927).

WWMP.

WWW.

Francis H Crittall. Sketch by Sir Alfred J Munnings (courtesy of Miss E Crittall).

CRITTALL, Francis Henry

(1860-1935)

Metal window frame manufacturer

Francis Henry Crittall was born at Braintree, Essex, on 27 July 1860, the eighth of the 11 children of Francis Berrington Crittall and his wife Fanny Morris née Godfrey. His father came to Braintree from Kent in 1849 to buy a small ironmonger's shop in Bank Street (then the High Street). There he built up his business in the shop and in a small rear workshop where he carried out metal work and general plumbing.

F H Crittall was educated at private schools in Braintree and Witham. His parents became regular attenders at the Congregational chapel on coming to Braintree and brought up their family as Nonconformists. In later life F H Crittall was indifferent to all organised religion. He left school in 1876 and joined his father and elder brother, Richard, in the shop. For the next five years he learnt the many-sided activities of his father's business.

His father died in 1879, leaving most of his estate to Richard, and a £1,000 interest in the business to Francis Henry. In 1881 F H Crittall, who was not in sympathy with his brother, left Braintree for new experience in Birmingham. There he worked as a clerk in a firm of iron-bedstead manufacturers. He also attended evening classes and generally took advantage of the freer, more tolerant atmosphere of a big city. In Birmingham he met his future wife, Ellen Laura Carter, who, although of the same social class, came from a more cultivated, less narrow family background. They married in 1883 and with her social and artistic gifts she made an outstanding contribution to her husband's career. They had four sons and one daughter.

In 1882 F H Crittall left Birmingham to open a small ironmonger's business in Chester. In 1883, however, his brother left Braintree for London and F H Crittall returned to take over the Bank Street business and live above the shop. For the next fifteen years all his energy went into building up the business. Richard left a small investment in it and a local tradesman, Arthur Dyer, put in a larger one, but F H Crittall was constantly on a financial knife edge. He diversified and increased his stock in trade, but he saw that his best hope of success lay in the rear workshop. There with a handful of skilled craftsmen he took on metal work of all descriptions as well as contracting for drainage and street-lighting schemes. In his search for orders he travelled far beyond the boundaries of Braintree and by 1889 had a sufficient reputation to win large orders for fireproof doors and roofing in Liverpool and Birkenhead.

At this point he realised that to survive he must develop a specialised trade. The product that he hit upon for this was the metal window. These were already being made as and when required by the blacksmiths in the rear workshop, but in the 1880s one of the craftsmen discovered a way of making an improved window which suggested the possibility of large-scale production.

It was now decided to divide the business between two separate private limited companies. A manager and co-director was found for the shop, which became Crittall & Winterton Ltd, and still (1981) trades on the same site. For the manufacturing side a second company was formed on 30 April 1889 as the Crittall Manufacturing Co Ltd with a share capital of £5,000. For some years Richard Crittall kept an interest in this company but in 1898 F H Crittall acquired his brother's shares and became chief shareholder and managing director. Arthur Dyer, who had invested in the early business, became chairman of the new board but played little part in the manufacturing development of the company.

By the early 1890s the Bank Street workshop was totally inadequate for the amount of work coming in and a new factory, later the Manor Works, was built in Braintree. Some 60 employees moved from the old premises to the new. F H Crittall's early success owed much to the skills of these craftsmen and to his own ability to keep their support through thick and thin. In essence he retained the same relationship with his workforce for the rest of his life. To his family and many of his employees he was known as 'the Governor', a title conveying affection and respect. But his dedication to his business and his independent character made him for a time unpopular with some ranks of Braintree society.

After the move to the new factory F H Crittall applied himself to perfecting manufacturing techniques and to finding new markets for his products. Before the end of the century several important orders were won, among them the doors and windows for the Public Record Office in London and the kitchens of the Houses of Parliament. Steady expansion began after 1900. The Manor Works were enlarged, a London office opened, business overseas begun, and manufacturing improvements introduced. Just before the outbreak of the First World War F H Crittall was joined by his two eldest sons. Both were to have a great influence upon the firm, Valentine George (1884-1961) in the spheres of finance and administration, Walter Francis (1887-1956) in the field of design and technical invention. The two younger sons also entered the firm in due course.

At the beginning of the war F H Crittall campaigned vigorously against the monopoly of the 'armaments ring' and with William Stokes (later Sir William) of Ransomes & Rapier Ltd, Ipswich, formed in 1915 the East Anglian Munitions Committee. His firm was redeployed on munitions and throughout the war he was the committee's joint manager. He was utterly opposed to any idea of profiteering and immediately the war was over insisted upon the cancellation of all outstanding contracts. In recognition of his work the committee presented him in 1919 with a portrait of himself by Augustus John and one of his wife by Charles Sims. It was an appropriate tribute, for he had developed an interest in art and later gave practical encouragement to a number of young artists.

The decade following the war was one of enormous growth for the firm. This was partly due to the development of the standard metal window, designed for the smaller private house and for large-scale housing schemes. But there was also a demand for purpose-made windows for the factories, department stores, and public buildings being built, or rebuilt, after the war.

During the 1920s the Braintree factory was enlarged, two new factories built in Essex, and several subsidiary companies formed. The office administration was reorganised and depots opened throughout the country. In 1922 F H Crittall resigned as managing director in favour of his eldest son, but throughout this period of growth he remained as chairman and governing director. In 1924 the company went public with an authorised share capital of £450,000. In 1929 there were about 3,500 employees.

Already before 1914 business agreements had been made with firms in America, Canada, and the Far East. After the war expansion overseas at least matched that at home with agencies or subsidiary companies established in, among other places, India, China, Egypt, Australia, New Zealand and South Africa. In Europe there had long been a link with a Dutch firm, and in 1927 a partnership with a German firm was formed. At the end of the 1920s the company acquired with Messrs Dorman Long & Co of Middlesbrough an equal share in the Darlington Rolling Mills, so freeing itself from dependence upon Belgium and Germany for its raw material.

F H Crittall first encountered trade union activity about 1905. After initial resistance, he came to accept completely the place of the unions in industry. In 1919 his became the first engineering firm to implement the closed shop policy, and in 1921 he left the Engineering Employers Federation which was opposed to that policy. In the same year, because of his dislike of price fixing, he resigned from the Steel Window Association of which he was chairman and co-founder.

F H Crittall's concern for employee welfare developed after the war. Rates of pay were above average. Saturday working was ended in 1926. Welfare and personnel departments were expanded during the 1920s. Among other amenities, training and pension schemes were introduced, medical and dental surgeries were opened, and sports fields and social clubs built. The largest of his schemes was the creation between 1926 and 1928 of the garden village of Silver End to provide houses for his workers. A Development Co, of which he was chairman, was formed and a self-supporting community planned with school, churches, shop and hotel. Characteristically some of the more progressive architects of the day were employed. Included in the plan was a factory to make fittings where disabled workers could be employed. In 1930 the population was about 2,000.

Even though the business remained based on his native town, F H Crittall played little part in local affairs, although he became a JP in 1904. He was for a time chairman of the Divisional Liberal Party but in 1918 he joined the Labour Party. He was not, however, aggressively political. He is said to have been keen on sport in his youth but his stocky, round-shouldered figure in later life makes it hard to credit him with much prowess. He was extremely hospitable and enjoyed good living. In his last years he took an interest in the farms attached to Silver End. His business, however, was his life and when the scale of his achievement is considered it could hardly have been otherwise.

He resigned as chairman in 1930 when the firm was hard hit by the slump and left the board in 1933 when improvement was in sight. His wife died in 1934. He died on 9 March 1935 on board ship, returning from a cruise in the Caribbean, leaving £18,255 gross.

ELIZABETH CRITTALL

Writings:

(with E L Crittall) *Fifty Years of Work and Play* (Constable & Co, 1934).

Sources:

Unpublished

BCe.

PrC.

P E Austin, 'History of the Crittall Company' (in firm's possession).

Published

Crittall Centenary leaflet and various company leaflets and magazines.

Times 12 Mar 1935.

WWW.

CROMPTON, Rookes Evelyn Bell

(1845-1940)

Electrical equipment manufacturer and consulting engineer

Rookes E B Crompton (courtesy of the Science Museum, London).

Rookes Evelyn Bell Crompton (or REB, as he was known) was born at Sion Hill, near Thirsk in Yorkshire on 31 May 1845, the fourth son and youngest child of a widely-travelled diplomat, Joshua Samuel Crompton, who had retired into the country and become a Whig MP after the Reform Act of 1832, and his first wife Mary, daughter of Sir Claud Alexander.

During the Crimean War Crompton's father went to Gibraltar in 1855 as commander of the West Yorkshire Light Infantry Militia, taking his family with him. Young Crompton sailed to Sebastopol, in a ship commanded by a relation, who took him aboard as a guest and enrolled him as a cadet. He visited his elder brother in the trenches and, although only eleven, qualified for the Crimean Medal and Sebastopol clasp. On returning to England he was sent to Harrow (1858-60), where he displayed an aptitude for engineering. In his holidays he made a steam road engine, 'Bluebell', in the workshops of his father's estate. He was commissioned into the Rifle Brigade in 1864 and spent four years in India; vexed by the slowness of bullock teams, he had his tools sent out from England and persuaded the Viceroy, R S Bourke, Earl of Mayo, to sponsor a system of steam road haulage which Crompton engineered.

On leaving the army in 1875 he bought for £5,000 a one-third share in the agricultural and general engineering firm of T H P Dennis & Co of Chelmsford, intending to develop his interests in transport. His attention, however, was drawn to the newly developing technology of electric lighting. Electric lighting on a large scale was first seen in Britain in 1878, when a French company lit part of the Victoria Embankment in London. France then held the lead in electric lighting, and Crompton began by importing French equipment. He soon decided that he could make better equipment himself. In March 1879 he engaged A P Lundberg as his first foreman of electrical apparatus at a salary of £3 a week, and Dennis & Co was transformed into Crompton & Co, electrical engineers.

Crompton quickly established himself as an authority on lighting, at first supplying equipment for street lighting and for lighting large buildings, such as markets and railway stations. He was closely associated with Joseph Swan (qv), in the development of filament lamp manufacture, and with the beginnings of the public electricity supply industry. In 1882 he was involved with the financier Cuthbert Quilter in the formation of the Swan United Electric Light Co, which took over the old Swan's Electric Light Co. With its capital of £1 million the United Co could finance large lighting contracts, such as at the new Law Courts in the Strand, London, where Cromptons' undertook the installation. The burning of the Ring Theatre in Vienna in 1883 gave Crompton the opportunity of carrying out a large electrical installation. After the fire the Emperor Franz Josef decided that a number of theatres and public

Crompton's Blue Bell *in India (courtesy of the Science Museum, London).*

buildings should be lit electrically. Crompton supplied them from a single, central power station although some were more than a mile apart. It was a time when electricity supply in England was inhibited by the Electric Lighting Act of 1882, one effect of which was to discourage investment in electricity supply schemes. The successful conclusion of the Vienna contract at the end of 1886 brought Crompton consultancy work in several continental cities. He was unable, however, to obtain many contracts for actual installations because other contractors, especially the German Allgemeine Elektrizitäts Gesellschaft (AEG), received far more help from their bankers than the English banks would give Cromptons.

In 1892 Cromptons was converted from a partnership into a limited liability company. Crompton himself later lamented the change in his own position: as senior partner he had 'enjoyed practically complete freedom of action', now he had to consult a board of directors 'whose judgement did not always coincide with my own' {Crompton (1928) 207}. Disagreements arose between Crompton and the other directors, and during his absences abroad the rift widened. Eventually Crompton lost control of the business through a revolt of the directors. By the end of the nineteenth century Crompton & Co Ltd supplied about 8 per cent of the generating capacity of British power stations and had sales of electrical machinery worth £290,000 per annum.

Crompton visited India in 1896 and again in 1899 to advise on electricity supply projects, mainly utilizing hydro-electric power. Between those visits he was actively involved with John Hopkinson (qv) in the formation of the Electrical Engineers Volunteer Corps of the Royal Engineers. When Hopkinson was killed in a climbing accident in 1898, Crompton succeeded him as commander. After the outbreak of the Boer War in the

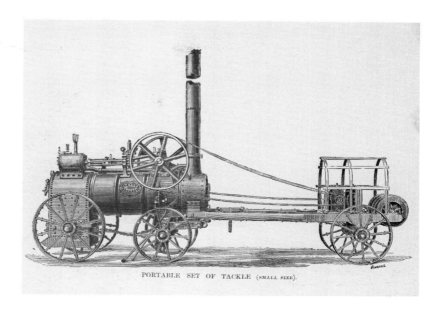

PORTABLE SET OF TACKLE (SMALL SIZE).

A Crompton portable generating set (courtesy of the Science Museum, London).

autumn of 1899, Crompton, now well over fifty, took the Corps to South Africa, where their work included the provision and maintenance of telegraphs and arc lights for the army and for essential reconstruction work on the railways.

On returning to England he launched out on his own again, this time as a consulting engineer. A founder member of the Royal Automobile Club in 1896 and a judge at the first Motor Show in 1903, he designed road vehicles, worked on the engineering aspects of road construction, and was appointed engineer· to the new Road Board in 1910. During the First World War he worked for the Government on engineering problems associated with munitions and the development of tanks. He was a firm believer in the value of engineering standards, and became the first secretary of the International Electrotechnical Commission in 1906.

In 1927 Cromptons merged with another firm to become Crompton, Parkinson & Co Ltd and 'the Colonel', as he was known, although over eighty, stayed on the board. At a dinner in his honour held in 1931 he was made an honorary member of the three principal engineering bodies (the Institutions of Civil, Mechanical and Electrical Engineers), having twice been president of the Electrical Engineers (in 1895 and 1908); he was elected an FRS in 1933.

R E B Crompton married in 1871 Elizabeth Gertrude (d 1939), daughter of George Clarke of Tanfield, near Ripon; they had two sons, one of whom predeceased his father, and three daughters. Crompton died at the age of ninety-five on 15 February 1940, leaving £28,329 gross.

BRIAN BOWERS

Writings:

Reminiscences (Constable, 1928). This includes a list of his earlier publications on pp 228-29.

Sources:

Unpublished

BCe.

MCe.

PrC.

Published

Brian Bowers, *REB Crompton. Pioneer Electrical Engineer* (HMSO, 1969).

Ian C R Byatt, *The British Electrical Industry, 1875-1914* (Oxford: Clarendon Press, 1979).

DNB.

John H Johnson and Wilfred L Randell, *Colonel Crompton and the Evolution of the Electrical Industry* (Longmans & Co, 1945).

WWW.

CRONSHAW, Cecil John Turrell

(1889-1961)

Chemical industry manager

Cecil John Turrell Cronshaw was born at Heywood in Lancashire on 13 June 1889, the son of William Robert Cronshaw, a cashier at a paper mill, and his wife Ann Elizabeth née Turrell. Educated at Bury Grammar School and later at Manchester University, where he graduated with first class honours in chemistry, he joined Levinstein Ltd as a research chemist in 1915. There he was a member of a small research team under James Baddiley with whom he formed a close working relationship that was to last for some thirty years and inspire and guide the re-development of the long neglected British dyestuffs industry. His interest in research continued for the whole of his life.

Levinstein Ltd acquired the former Meister Lucius & Bruning indigo factory at Ellesmere Port in 1916. This factory had been designed to run on chemical intermediate (a product of one process used as the raw material for a subsequent process) phenyl glycine, imported from Germany and not manufactured in Britain. Cronshaw's first major task was to bring this factory with all its significance for the British war effort into production again. This he and his colleagues did within the remarkably short time of three months.

In 1917 he worked briefly in the United States helping in the exchange of technical information with Du Pont. After the war ended, Cronshaw was appointed Chemical Controller of the Rhineland Area Factories in Germany where he was able to examine more closely the technical developments in this field and meet the leading members of the German dyestuffs industry who later came to regard him as the leader of the industry that he was to do so much to re-invigorate. Upon his return to England, Cronshaw became assistant to Dr Herbert Levinstein then managing director of the British Dyestuffs Corporation newly formed from the merger of Levinstein Ltd with British Dyes Ltd. In 1921 he became works manager of the Corporation's Blackley Factory, engaged in the manufacture of some of the earliest rubber chemicals made on a commercial scale in Britain. Three years later he was appointed the Corporation's technical manager and, on the firm's merger into ICI in 1926, Cronshaw became the first technical director of ICI's Dyestuffs Group. In 1931 he became managing director of the Group and served as chairman from 1939 until 1943. During the 1930s Cronshaw did much to enlarge the size and scope of the Group, recruiting intakes of able graduates to build up the level of research and inventiveness on which Dyestuffs' prosperity and survival depended. Trading profits of the group grew from £50,000 on sales of £1.7 million in 1927, to £1.56 million on sales of £8.3 million in 1942; return on capital employed increased from 2 per cent to 17 per cent during the same period.

Cronshaw's appointment to the board of ICI in 1943, the first from the Dyestuffs Group, brought in a new technical mind with distinctly different views from those of the dominant heavy chemical men, who were more experienced in the continuous production of large tonnages of inorganic chemicals. This turned out to be of great value in the post-war period when ICI changed course towards organic chemistry and rose to eminence in man-made fibres, plastics and pharmaceuticals. However he insisted on 'learning by doing', even when information could be bought or gained by licences to manufacture. The attitude probably derived from his early days at BDC when the only way for a company to get into the international dyestuffs business was to invent its way in. Many companies however adopted a different approach, particularly in the pharmaceutical industry where company acquisition and licensing, particularly in penicillin development, was used to expand their businesses. ICI concentrated on its own pharmaceutical research following the Second World War, spending considerable sums of money. Modest profits in some years outweighed losses in others. An integrated team of medical, pharmaceutical, biological, chemical and engineering staff was developed for the first time in the company and this period up to Cronshaw's retirement in 1952 produced important drugs — Sulphamezathine (1942),

Paludrine (1946), Antrycide (1949) and Mysoline (1952) — which were to form the bedrock of a subsequently highly successful international pharmaceuticals business for ICI.

In pursuit of the same self-reliance theme, Cronshaw also inspired the ICI board's decisions in August 1945 to provide heavy organic chemicals from petroleum and to set up its own cracking plant, rather than rely on the oil industry. The result was the Wilton plant on Teesside, opened in 1949. At the same time, Cronshaw was responsible in 1944 for obtaining for ICI the patent rights to 'Terylene' (polyethylene terephthalate), a fibre-forming material in the same class as nylon and developed after 1939 in the industrial research laboratory of the Calico Printers Association by J R Whinfield and J T Dickson. In all of this, and as personnel director on the staff side, Cronshaw was conspicuously successful until bad health caught up with him.

'Of small stature, he was fizzing with energy in his prime. Whilst he loved the broad humour of the North of England and could tell a dialect story effectively, he had a natural relish for satire. He himself had a lightning and sometimes astringent wit but was always happy to take as good as he gave. Unless it was unavoidable he never missed the annual smoking concert in which his staff lampooned with good-humoured satire the foibles of the organisation he had created.' {*Journal of the Society of Dyers* (Apr 1981) 164} He was very good with younger people and never made the error of talking down to them.

A man of considerable energy and wide-ranging interests, Dr Cronshaw found time for a multitude of external activities and public works and as a governor he retained an association with his former school and university. He was a director of the Manchester Ship Canal Co and of the District Bank Ltd, Manchester, as well as a part-time member of the North Western Gas Board. He was a member of the Worshipful Company of Dyers and was the Prime Warden in 1949-50. He played an active role in the Society of Dyers and Colourists and served as its president during the difficult years of the Second World War. There he did much to strengthen the link between the Society and the individual member and to encourage the young. The Society's award to him of its Perkin Medal was an acknowledgement of his exceptional services both to it and to the industry it represented. He remained first and foremost a chemist and this was recognised by the University of Leeds which conferred on him an honorary DSc in 1938.

Cronshaw married Annie née Downham, daughter of John Downham, a consulting engineer, in 1917; they had two sons. He died on 5 January 1961, leaving £70,717 gross.

SIR PETER ALLEN

Writings:

Through Chemistry, Adornment (*Fifth Dalton Lecture*) (Royal Institute of Chemistry, 1949).

Sources:

Unpublished

BCe.

MCe.

PrC.

Published

Journal of the Society of Dyers and Colourists 77 (April 1981).

William J Reader, *Imperial Chemical Industries. A History* (2 vols, Oxford University Press, 1970-75).

WWW.

CROS
see DU CROS

CROSFIELD, John

(1832-1901)

Soap manufacturer

John Crosfield was born at Warrington on 11 February 1832, the eighth of ten children of Joseph Crosfield (1792-1844), founder of the family soap- and candle-making firm, and his wife Elizabeth née Goad. Joseph had set up the family business at Bank Quay, Warrington in 1814. John was only twelve when his father died in 1844, and management of the firm was left in the hands of trustees who included his elder brother George. John's association with the business began in 1847 and continued until his death.

Joseph felt strongly that his sons should have a thorough education, and one reflecting the Quaker tradition of the family. After attending a local Quaker school at Penketh, Cheshire, John was sent to Bootham School in

York and later to Glasgow High School. In 1847 he followed his brothers, George and Morland, into the family business, the name of which was changed in 1847 to Joseph Crosfield & Son. Six years later, soon after his twenty-first birthday, John was taken into partnership. His elder brother George was mainly responsible for the development of Crosfields until 1875 when he left for London following Morland's premature death. Thereafter John took a principal role in the firm and by 1882 had sole responsibility.

Repeal of the soap duty in 1853 gave an impetus to all British soap manufacturers including Crosfields. Although not particularly inventive themselves, the Crosfields were always ready to improve both the range of their products and the method of production. Following patents by the Widnes soap manufacturer, William Gossage (qv), Crosfields took a leading role in the manufacture of silicated soap (prompted by the shortage of Russian tallow during the Crimean War) and marbled (or mottled) soap.

The availability and cost of raw materials were also a constant concern. Soda was an essential raw material for making soap and was produced by the Leblanc process until after 1874 when John Brunner and Ludwig Mond (qqv) established their works at Winnington, Cheshire for the manufacture of soda by the ammonia-soda process. The soda produced by this process was considerably cheaper than hitherto and the method of production avoided the unpleasant and harmful by-products of the Leblanc process. When Brunner, Mond & Co was changed to a limited company in 1881 John Crosfield became the first chairman, thereby forging an important link with his raw materials supplier, which gave him soda on very favourable terms; Crosfields became the largest user of Brunner, Mond soda-ash at about 10,000 tons per annum. John Crosfield invested £10,000 in Brunner, Mond & Co, and although he relinquished the chairmanship in 1891 he remained a director until his death, at which time the value of his investment was put at £89,000.

The relationship between the two firms was fruitful in another direction. Though Crosfields were dependent on Brunner, Mond for soda-ash they were continuing to develop their caustic soda production. In 1890 Dr Karl Markel, a German chemist working at Brunner, Mond, was transferred to Crosfields (no doubt at the instigation of John Crosfield) to held develop the caustic soda side of the business. John Crosfield, clearly impressed with Markel's work, retained his services and later appointed him works manager.

Although Crosfields had tried to keep the works up-to-date with silicate plant (about 1863), a black-ash revolver (about 1877), glycerine recovery plant (about 1884), steam power and electric light, and were steadily increasing the number of soap pans (from 16 in 1870 to 23 by 1886), the geographical location of the works and the lack of readily-available land restricted expansion of the business. What was required was a thorough rationalisation in which the development of the works could be considered as a whole, rather than just by adding or making alterations to the existing buildings. John Crosfield had the foresight to see that this planning required the services of people like Dr Markel with a high level of scientific training.

To raise capital for rationalising and expanding the business a limited liability company, Joseph Crosfield & Sons Ltd, with a share capital of £300,000, was formed in July 1896 with John Crosfield as chairman and his two sons, Arthur H and Joseph John, and Dr Markel as directors. Active management of the firm had been transferred by John in 1894 to his sons and Markel.

During the second half of the nineteenth century Crosfields' production of soap increased steadily (with minor fluctuations from year to year): 1855, 3,200 tons; 1865, 8,918 tons; 1873, 11,450 tons; 1893, 15,000 tons. This growth in production gave Crosfields an increased share of the national production, except during the last quarter of the century when their share began to fall, clearly indicating the need for Markel's rationalisation plan.

The range of soap products grew to include household soaps, scented and coloured toilet soaps, mottled soaps, silicated soaps and 'dry soap' powders (by about 1895). Following the Trade Mark Act of 1875 Crosfields soon imitated William Lever's aggressive marketing activities. One of their household tablet soaps was stamped 'Perfection', and wrapped and boxed with appropriate colourful advertising. When Crosfields became a limited company in 1896 over 300 of their trade marks were registered and these included: Honey, Castile, Rainbow, Good Judge, Uncle Toby and Miracle. Many of these trade marks were registered in countries throughout the world. Besides soap products Crosfields also diversified their chemical products to include silicate of soda, caustic soda and glycerine. Candle production was steadily run down during the 1860s.

Even though production methods were improved and steam-powered machinery introduced, the work force was rapidly increased in the 1890s: from 16 men in 1837, to 120 in 1871, about 250 in 1885 and to over 800 by 1896. This growth in the number of employees reflected not only the expansion of production in soap and chemicals, but also the need to promote and market the products in the wider markets in Britain and abroad.

John Crosfield appeared to have a good working relationship with his employees. An obituary noted that he 'earned for himself the reputation as a kind and considerate employer of labour. To him, his work people were not so many "hands": he knew most of them by name, he freely conversed with them, and those who had grown grey in his service retired on a pension' {Musson (1965) 117}. He also respected the part both employers and employees play in the success of a business: 'that capital and labour were dependent upon each other, and labour was no use without capital, nor capital without labour' {Musson (1965) 118}.

John Crosfield, like his father and brothers, was a staunch Liberal and helped to set up the Liberal Club and Liberal Association in Warrington. He was a director of the publishing company which in 1869 started the *Warrington Examiner* as a Liberal Party newspaper. As a Liberal, John Crosfield admired Gladstone and supported Irish Home Rule Bills, and was an ardent campaigner through membership of the Liverpool Financial Reform Association and the Warrington branch of the National Reform Union. In July 1886 John Crosfield stood as the Liberal candidate for Warrington but was defeated by about 500 votes by the Tory, Sir Gilbert Greenall.

John Crosfield was proud to be a Warringtonian and freely contributed his time (and often money) to many ventures in the town, including the Workingmen's Mission, numerous schools (he believed in non-sectarian education), the library, museum, building societies, savings bank, dispensary, and infirmary, and in 1888 the Warrington branch of the National Association for the Promotion of Technical Instruction. He was a supporter of the Temperance Society, and although not a particularly good public speaker, frequently addressed meetings on the evils of excessive drink. He also gave considerable time as a councillor and a magistrate, serving on the town council for all but nine years between 1866 and 1890, being mayor in 1882, and alderman in 1885; in 1891 he was made a freeman of the borough. He became a JP for the borough in 1874 and for the county in 1884.

Behind his actions and beliefs lay strong religious feelings cultivated by his Quaker background. However, John (like his brother Morland) married a non-Quaker, Eliza Dickson (who came from an Ulster Protestant family in the cotton trade) in Belfast in 1864; although he became a practising Anglican he never forgot his Quaker roots. His first wife had five sons (two dying young) and four daughters. She died in 1882 and six years later John married her sister, Gertrude; they had no children.

In his later years John travelled widely, notably to the South of France, Italy, the West Indies, China, Japan and India, but his health steadily declined. He died from bronchitis on 26 December 1901 at his home, Walton Lea. His will showed shareholdings in Joseph Crosfield & Sons Ltd, Brunner, Mond & Co Ltd, and Salt Union Ltd. The total value of his estate was £157,262 gross and most of this went to his second wife and his children.

PETER N REED

Sources:

Unpublished

Joseph Crosfield & Sons Ltd, Warrington, company archives.

Unilever Ltd, Port Sunlight, papers of Joseph Crosfield & Sons Ltd.

Warrington Library, papers of Joseph Crosfield & Sons Ltd.

PrC.

Published

A E Musson, *Enterprise in Soap and Chemicals* (Manchester: Manchester University Press, 1965).

The Illustrated London News 13 Nov 1886.

Warrington Examiner 28 Dec 1901.

Warrington Guardian 28 Dec 1901.

Charles Wilson, *The History of Unilever* (2 vols, Cassell, 1954).

CROSS, Herbert Shepherd

(1847-1916)

Textile bleacher

Herbert Cross was born on New Year's Day 1847, the third son of Thomas Cross (1805-79), a bleacher, cotton spinner and banker of Bolton, Lancashire, and grandson of James Cross (1771-1850), a solicitor and founding partner of Hardcastle, Cross & Co, the Bolton bank. Herbert was educated at Worksop School in Nottinghamshire, Harrow School and Exeter College, Oxford, graduating BA in 1869, MA 1873. He entered the Inner Temple in 1867. In 1870 he married Lucy, only child of Rev Shepherd Birley, one of the well-connected Birleys of Kirkham, Lancashire. Cross, who took the name of Shepherd on his father-in-law's death in 1884, hoped to follow a family tradition of legal service until illness ended his studies for the Bar. He then returned to Bolton and the family business.

Shepherd-Cross and his two brothers (a fourth died in infancy) formed a partnership and took over their father's bleaching concern. Illness removed the younger brother, Alfred (1849-86), leaving control to Herbert and, principally, the elder brother, James Percival Cross (1843-1906). The Crosses were known for their paternalism; the development of the bleachworks estate as an extensive, alcohol-free model working-class housing community; and the financing of that district's public buildings. Bleaching was a safe trade and enabled the brothers to improve on their inheritance.

Shepherd-Cross's career as a bleacher would have been restricted by his social and political interests. He served on the Bolton School Board, became a JP and a major in the Duke of Lancaster's Own Yeomanry, and actively supported the Anglican Church's education and temperance movements. The Crosses ranked amongst Bolton's leading Tory families and in 1884 Shepherd-Cross was nominated as one of the town's parliamentary candidates. He was elected in 1885 and held the seat until illness (some said differences with his supporters over Chamberlain's programme) led to his retirement in 1906. He spoke in the House on seven occasions, supported his party in the division lobbies, and won a reputation for a good game of chess. National politics changed the style and focus of his life. In 1884 he purchased Hamel's Park, Buntingford, a large Hertfordshire estate, where he raised two families (he remarried in 1895, four years after his first wife's death), enjoyed farming, fishing and shooting, and served his adopted county as a JP and councillor. A London house and membership of the Carlton and Junior Carlton Clubs confirmed his position as a gentleman.

The move to Hertfordshire did not end Shepherd-Cross's business career. His participation as chairman in two small mining ventures, the remunerative Castle Gold Exploration Syndicate Ltd (operating on the Gold Coast, 1896-1902) and the unsuccessful Nelson Copper Fields

Co Ltd (operating in British Columbia, 1898-1901), suggests other commercial interests. However he was best known as a bleacher and through his interests in the family business and his active participation in the Lancashire bleachers' trade asociation, maintained his contacts in the industry. Thomas Cross & Co, Mortfield, the family's Bolton bleachworks, valued at £206,615, was the third largest of the 53 concerns which in 1900 merged to form Bleachers Association Ltd. A family account credits Herbert with the inception of the Bleachers' Association Ltd, on its formation one of Britain's largest industrial companies. To the trade's leaders, some like Shepherd-Cross having partly abandoned business for a life of gentility, the new combine offered reduced competition and less risk, the exchange of assets and responsibilities for shares, and salaries for those proprietors continuing as managers. Shepherd-Cross, perhaps because of his contacts, his firm's standing in the trade, and a reputation for conducting meetings in an exemplary manner, became the Association's first chairman. He received a chairman's fee of £1,000, and a salary of £2,000 for the management of Mortfield, which he delegated, besides share dividends.

Unlike the Bradford Dyers, reputedly the best managed of the great textile combines, with a nominal chairman and an all powerful managerial triumvirate, the Bleachers' Association reserved powers for its chairman and 49 directors, set up a head office headed by two general managers (John Stanning and John Brennand, both successful bleachers and prominent in the textile trade) and, on the whole, left branch management to the original proprietors. There is no evidence of Shepherd-Cross having contributed to the Association's business policy but he did arouse resentment for interfering in matters more properly the concern of the general managers, and, like many of his fellow directors, was over-zealous in representing the interests of his own works. In 1904, following a run of poor results and the death of John Stanning, the Bleachers' articles were amended to delegate the directors' powers to a five-strong board of management which replaced the general managers as the principal decision-making body. In 1906 the new board's powers were checked by the creation of a small finance committee, composed of directors. Shepherd-Cross attended irregularly and the committee's force was its chairman, Henry Whitehead, a Bury bleacher, a director of Armstrong, Whitworth & Co, and sometime chairman of the Lancashire & Yorkshire Bank. The new administrative structure marked a change in the Bleachers' strategy, away from Stanning and Brennand's policy of gradually improving existing works to one aimed at the elimination of competition. Trading profits were improved but were only reflected in higher dividends from 1910. Shepherd-Cross became a nominal chairman, retaining the post until his death at Hamel's Park, 9 January 1916. He left £374,639 gross.

J J MASON

Sources:

Unpublished

Quarry Bank Mill, Styal, Whitecroft Collection (uncatalogued).

MCe.

PrC.

Brigadier E F Audland, 'Shepherd-Cross Pedigree' (typed notes at Bolton Reference Library, ca 1975).

Published

'Pillars-of-Bolton. Mr H Shepherd-Cross, MP' *The Bolton Review* (Bolton, 1897).

Bolton Chronicle obituary notices of: Thomas Cross, 1 Nov 1879; Alfred Cross, 24 Apr 1886; James P Cross, 10 Feb 1906; Herbert Shepherd-Cross, 15 Jan 1916.

DD 1900-16.

Foster, *Alumni Oxonienses*.

Patrick Joyce, *Work, Society and Politics: the Culture of the Factory in Later Victorian England* (Brighton: Harvester Press, 1980).

Henry W Macrosty, *The Trust Movement in British Industry: A Study of Business Organisation* (Longman & Co, 1907).

Stock Exchange Official Intelligence 1896-1910.

The Stock Exchange Year-Book 1896-1910.

Alan J Sykes, *Concerning the Bleaching Industry* (Manchester: Bleachers' Association Ltd, 1925).

WWMP.

WWW.

Sir Francis Crossley (from T and E Baines, Yorkshire: Past and Present *vol 2, 1877).*

CROSSLEY, Sir Francis

(1817-1872)

Carpet manufacturer

Francis (Frank) Crossley was born at Halifax, Yorkshire on 26 October 1817, the eighth and youngest child of John Crossley, carpet manufacturer and former carpet weaver, and his wife Martha née Turner, the daughter of a small farmer near Halifax.

His father founded the family business in Halifax in 1822 after some twenty years in partnership with other carpet manufacturers, and by the time of his death in 1837 the firm, with some 300 employees, probably ranked as the fourth largest in the carpet industry. The three youngest sons, John Jr, Joseph, and Francis, continued the business as John Crossley & Sons. The eldest son had died in infancy and the second and third sons had gone into business in textiles on their own.

Crossley and his two brothers achieved their first major success by the commercial exploitation of a completely new product, Tapestry carpeting. This was a colourful and relatively cheap imitation of Brussels carpeting, which furnished most upper class homes, and though less durable than Brussels it appealed greatly to middle class customers. Richard Whytock of Edinburgh had patented the process in 1832 but technical and commercial success was not achieved until Francis Crossley and his brothers began experiments under licence in 1844. They were mainly responsible for securing a five year extension of the patent and in 1846 purchased the patent rights for £10,000. By 1850, 1,300 Tapestry carpet looms were at work in Great Britain, nearly half of them at Crossleys, which had become the largest firm in the industry.

The dramatic increase in demand for Tapestry carpeting spurred on Crossleys' efforts to mechanise carpet weaving. They recruited George Collier, who had invented a powerloom to weave linen, and a few months later he patented a powerloom for Tapestry and Brussels weaving. The process was improved after negotiations with Erastus B Bigelow of Massachusetts, who exhibited his own Brussels powerloom at the Great Exhibition in London, and in 1852 his patent rights in the UK were purchased for £20,000.

Crossleys defended their patents in a series of lawsuits but readily issued licences and gave technical advice when powerlooms were installed, whilst pursuing a policy of reducing carpet prices to widen the market. As a result, within ten years the output of Brussels and Tapestry carpeting doubled and handlooms were virtually eliminated from this sector of the industry. Crossleys increased their share of carpet production to approximately 30 per cent of the UK total and their profits during 1857-63 exceeded £100,000 a year, including over £24,000 a year from royalties paid by licensees.

The firm was converted into a limited company in September 1864 when, with 4,100 employees and a nominal capital of £1,165,000, it ranked as one of the largest British manufacturing firms. The three brothers retained control as governing directors, with two of their sons and three key employees completing the directorate. Further expansion followed and profits in the years 1866-72 exceeded £150,000 a year. Overseas sales played a vital part in the growth of the firm and by the early 1870s the USA was absorbing nearly half the firm's output.

After Frank Crossley's death the firm lost ground. It was severely shaken by the general decline in carpet exports to the USA during the 1870s, and in the 1880s and 1890s other British carpet manufacturers exploited more vigorously the market for weaving the higher quality Axminster carpeting opened up by the new powerlooms. Nevertheless in 1913 Crossleys accounted for 10 per cent of total output and was the second largest firm in the industry. Since the Second World War the firm has again been one of the industry's leaders.

Frank Crossley sat as a Liberal MP for Halifax, 1852-59, and then for the West Riding of Yorkshire until 1872. He made speeches in Parliament on a variety of commercial and financial subjects and on religious and temperance matters. However, he continued to play an active part in running the firm when in Halifax, arriving at work at 6 am.

His contribution to the firm's success is not easy to separate from that of his two brothers, but it appears that he took the initiative in the development of Tapestry carpeting and in the search for a successful powerloom, persisting with experiments when his brothers were discouraged. The capacity for making bold decisions was allied with careful attention to details and he concerned himself even in later life with quite small matters of policy and administration.

Crossley was a Congregationalist, worshipping regularly at Square Congregational Church which was built in 1855-57 at his expense. He made numerous donations to chapels and schools, gave £10,000 to the London Missionary Society, and established a fund for aged Congregational ministers and their widows. He founded almshouses and, together with his brothers, an orphanage and school, but his most striking gift to Halifax was the People's Park, where his statue was subsequently erected by public subscription. It was mainly in recognition of his charitable gifts that he was made a baronet in 1863.

Sir Frank Crossley died on 5 January 1872. He was survived by his wife, Martha Eliza née Brinton, whom he married in 1845, and a son, Savile Brinton, who became chairman of the company in 1905. He left a personal estate valued at nearly £800,000 gross.

JAMES NEVILLE BARTLETT

Writings:

Canada and the United States. A Lecture Delivered in the Odd Fellows' Hall, Halifax, on Monday 21 January 1856 (Halifax: T & W Birtwhistle, 1856).

Sources:

Unpublished

John Crossley & Sons Ltd, Halifax (a member of Carpets International Ltd), archives. For full details see Bartlett (1978) below.

PRO: C14/641,172; C15/741,213; C16/329,174 (Chancery pleadings); C31/736, 744, 1486, 1555, 1556, 2726, 2727 (Chancery affidavits).

MCe.
PrC.

Published

James Neville Bartlett, 'The Mechanisation of the Kidderminster Carpet Industry' *Business History* 9 (1967).

—, *Carpeting the Millions: The Growth of Britain's Carpet Industry* (Edinburgh: John Donald Publishers Ltd, 1978).

R Bretton, 'Crossleys of Dean Clough', parts 1-3, *Transactions of the Halifax Antiquarian Society* 1950-52.

DNB.

Halifax Courier 6 Jan 1872.

Kidderminster Shuttle 8 June 1872.

Nikolaus Pevsner, *The Buildings of England: Yorkshire, the West Riding* (Harmondsworth: Penguin, 1959).

CROSSLEY, Francis William

(1839-1897)
Internal combustion engine manufacturer

Francis ('Frank') William Crossley was born at Glenburn, Dunmurry, County Antrim on 29 November 1839, the elder son of Major Francis Crossley and his second wife, Elizabeth Helen née Irwin. Major Crossley had been with the East India Company, and served as Governor of the Andaman Islands in 1815. Both sides of his family had been established in Northern Ireland since the seventeenth century.

At the age of eighteen, after a year in the militia, Frank began his apprenticeship at the works of Robert Stephenson & Co in Newcastle upon Tyne. Then he spent a period in the drawing office of William Fawcett in Liverpool. Through the help of an uncle, Hastings Irwin, who was a Liverpool businessman, Frank acquired the business and premises of John M Dunlop, of Great Marlborough Street, Manchester, equipped with machinery for working gutta-percha and india rubber. Several months later Frank was joined by his brother William John (qv) and they formed a partnership in August 1867. The machinery they produced included hydraulic presses, hand- and power-pumps, small steam engines, cotton presses, cotton gins and cotton-seed cleaners. At the end of the first year they just about broke even with Frank making all the drawings and William keeping the books. The office staff consisted of one boy while the works could employ up to 20 men.

Frank, however, was a clever designer and engineer. His patents included one for a rubber thread lathe, which was adopted by virtually every rubber manufacturer in the country, and, prompted by family links with the flax industry, he designed equipment for flax and cotton manufacturing. After two years the business picked up. New markets opened up when the Crossleys became the first manufacturers of the internal combustion engine in Great Britain. A gas engine, created by the Germans Nicolaus August Otto and his partner Eugen Langen, was awarded a gold medal at the Paris Exhibition in 1867. Industry had long wanted a small motive power unit such as this and the engine quickly earned a reputation for itself. Precisely how the Crossley brothers came to hear of Otto and his engine is not known. Possibly William witnessed one of Otto's engines in action whilst in Cologne. Another possibility is that a German consulting engineer, Ludwig August Roosen Runge, with premises in Cross Street, Manchester, introduced the Crossleys to the engine. At that time, Roosen Runge was in correspondence with Langen in Cologne. What is certain, however, is that in 1869 agreements were entered into between Otto & Langen of Cologne and Crossley Brothers of Manchester. The engine made at the time was unusual in its action, but was very successful. Between 1869 and 1876, Crossley Brothers made about 1,400 of these engines, in sizes from one-half to three horse power, which were used for driving workshop machinery in the food industry and in printers' works, among numerous other applications.

In 1876 Otto produced his four-stroke engine and Crossleys, as licensees, became the sole manufacturers in Great Britain. With his subtle improvements in design, Frank Crossley succeeded in making the name of Crossley a household word. By the mid-1880s, almost every firm of note in Britain had at least one Crossley gas engine at work driving its machines. The firm of Crossley Brothers Ltd was registered in 1881 and the following year new premises occupying about ten acres were built at Openshaw, Manchester, where they stand today. Between 200 and 300 people were then employed. The firm became a private limited company in 1881, and went public in 1897 on the death of Frank. At this date the firm employed 1,260 people.

Frank Crossley was an ardent Liberal, following Gladstone on Home Rule. But by the mid-1870s evangelical religion dominated his life far more than politics. Frank began as an Evangelical Anglican, moved to Congregational churches and thence to the Salvation Army and eventually to an independent holiness mission. So generous were his donations to the Salvation Army that he became known as 'The Paymaster'. It has been estimated that his gifts to the Salvation Army exceeded £100,000. In his last decade his life centred on the 'Star Hall' in Ancoats, a former music hall of ill-repute. Frank spent £20,000 on pulling it down and erecting a new hall for meetings with bathrooms and coffee rooms and residences for the social workers. At first he and his wife intended to put the Salvation Army in possession but in the end sold their house at Bowdon, Cheshire, and in 1889 went to live in Star Hall themselves, caring for the sick, poor and underprivileged and running an independent mission church, whilst still sharing in the running of his business. As befitted his religious and social concerns, he was a total abstainer.

Frank Crossley in 1871 married Emily, daughter of Archibald Kerr, whom he met at Union Congregational Chapel, Manchester, then under the ministry of the renowned Dr Alexander McLaren. They had one daughter and four sons who survived. Frank Crossley died on 25 March 1897 in his fifty-eighth year. It was said that his premature death was due to exhaustion. Frank's last wish was that he be buried amongst the poor people of Ancoats in Philips Park Cemetery. A crowd of 15,000 people from Scotland, Ireland and distant parts of England came to pay their tribute. He left £624,456 gross.

K A BARLOW

Writings:

'A Lecture on Prophecy, Delivered in December 1868' (Manchester: J G Kershaw & Co, nd).

'The Ten Virgins' (ca 1868).

'Address before a Vigilance Meeting at Leamington' in J Rendel Harris, *The Life of Francis William Crossley* (James Nisbet & Co, 1900).

Sources:

Unpublished

MCe.

PrC.

Kenneth A Barlow, 'A History of Gas Engines' (Manchester PhD, 1979).

Published

James Rendel Harris, *The Life of Francis William Crossley* (James Nisbet & Co, 1900).

The Stock Exchange Official Intelligence 1899.

CROSSLEY, Sir William John

(1844-1911)

Internal combustion engine and motor vehicle manufacturer

William John Crossley was born at Glenburn, Dunmurry, County Antrim, Ireland on 22 April 1844, the younger son of Major Francis Crossley and his second wife, Elizabeth Helen née Irwin; his elder brother was Francis William Crossley (qv).

William was educated at the Royal School, Dungannon, and in Bonn, Prussia, before serving a four years' engineering apprenticeship with Sir W G Armstrong & Co at Elswick, Newcastle upon Tyne. At the age of twenty-three he joined his brother Frank in Manchester, forming the partnership of Crossley Brothers. William's German connections and his visits to the Continent may have been the means by which the brothers learned about the gas (internal combustion) engine exhibited at Paris in 1867 by Otto and Langen of Cologne. However they heard of Otto's work, William's German experience surely facilitated the licensing agreements of 1869 by which the Crossley brothers secured the rights to manufacture the Otto engine in Britain. For the next two decades the Crossleys dominated the British market for gas engines.

By the late 1880s, when Frank Crossley became preoccupied with Salvation Army and social rescue work, William assumed more responsibility for running the firm. After Frank's death in 1897 William became chairman of Crossley Brothers Ltd and immediately converted it into a public company. The new firm had an authorised capital of £973,700 in £10 shares (£570,310 ordinary and the rest 5 per cent cumulative preference shares). The sum of £973,700 was paid for the private business, £278,200 in cash and the rest in shares (including all the ordinary shares). Fresh expansion was financed by the sale of 27,820 preference shares offered at £10 10s a share.

Frank Crossley, with his flair for design, had anticipated technological developments in internal combustion engines which spread in response to the increasing demands of industry. In addition to the gas engine, oil engines began to appear in the 1890s for use in agriculture. These were followed by diesel engines. Horizontal, vertical, single cylinder and multi-cylinder engines were manufactured and their use extended throughout the whole spectrum of industrial and marine applications. William pursued many of these ideas and in 1906 began to build motor cars, erecting an additional factory for this purpose in Openshaw near Manchester. Private and commercial vehicles were manufactured with Crossley engines. Within four years, such was demand, that it was decided to separate the motor car branch from the expanding business of engine building. In 1910 a public company, Crossley Motors Ltd, was formed with an authorised capital of £140,000 (£108,357 issued) to acquire Crossley's motor manufacturing business and that of Charles Jarratt & Letts Ltd. The directors were William (now Sir William) Crossley (chairman), his son Kenneth Irwin Crossley and W M Letts (qv), managing director. In 1913, two years after Sir William's death, Crossleys, with an annual output of 650 cars, ranked fifteenth in an industry comprising over 65 manufacturers. Outside his own firm, William Crossley was a founder director of the Manchester Ship Canal Co, serving 1886-1906.

William was as active in public service as his brother. In 1901 he was elected a member of Cheshire County Council. The City of Manchester conferred the Freedom of the City upon him in 1903. A Liberal, he became MP for the Altrincham division of Cheshire in 1906 and held the seat until defeated in 1910. He was JP for Manchester and Cheshire and in 1909 received a baronetcy. During his lifetime William Crossley was chairman of the Manchester Hospital for Consumption and of the Crossley Sanatorium which he founded at Delamere. He was also chairman of the Boys and Girls Refuge, Strangeways, and president of the YMCA. The Crossley Lads' Club at Openshaw is still in being today (1982). His recreations were yachting and motoring.

William Crossley in 1876 married Mabel Gordon, daughter of Dr Francis Anderson, previously Inspector General of Hospitals in India. They had one son and two daughters.

Sir William Crossley died on 12 October 1911 leaving £591,636 gross.

K A BARLOW

Sources:

Unpublished

PrC.

Kenneth A Barlow, 'A History of Gas Engines' (Manchester PhD, 1979).

Published

Douglas A Farnie, *The Manchester Ship Canal and the Rise of the Port of Manchester 1894-1975* (Manchester: Manchester University Press, 1980).

Samuel B Saul, 'The Motor Industry in Britain to 1914' *Business History* 5 (1962).

The Stock Exchange Official Intelligence 1899, 1901.

WWMP.

WWW.

Geoffrey Crowther (courtesy of Trusthouse Forte Ltd).

CROWTHER, Geoffrey

Lord Crowther of Headingley

(1907-1972)

Publisher and chairman of hotel-chain

Geoffrey Crowther was born at Headingley, Yorkshire on 13 May 1907, the son of Charles Crowther, a university lecturer in science and Hilda née Reed. He was educated at Leeds Grammar School and Oundle, before going to Clare College, Cambridge where he gained a first in economics and modern languages. A Commonwealth Fund Fellowship which he held from 1929 to 1931 took him to Yale and Columbia universities. He liked the Americans, and the USA; he returned there often and his reputation as a commentator on political and economic affairs came to stand even higher there than it did in Britain. His marriage to Margaret Worth of Claymont, Delaware in 1932, which proved to be a happy union, reinforced his affection for the country. They had two sons and four daughters.

On returning to England in 1931 he spent a year or so with a merchant bank in London. A study of the Irish banking system which he undertook led to an appointment as economic adviser on banking to the Irish Government. But he soon gave up this post to join the editorial staff of the weekly *Economist* in 1932. In 1935 he became assistant editor, and editor in 1938.

chairman. Broackes suggested Crowther; Commercial Union were happy to agree. Crowther himself had his doubts, but accepted.

Trafalgar House (as Eastern International was renamed, after one of its properties) was effectively run by a small executive committee, and Crowther's role was that of helping to reassure Commercial Union that its interests were being looked after, though Commercial Union's chief general manager, Francis Sandilands (qv), also joined the board. Crowther enjoyed his association with Trafalgar House. As his own policies for the *Economist* and Trust Houses showed, he liked building and developing property. (His most notable contribution as a non-executive director of Commercial Union, apart from introducing them to Trafalgar House, was to play a major part in the plans for building a new head office opened in 1965.) About 1964, when finding it difficult to finance the development of Trust Houses at the pace he wanted, he rather tentatively proposed a merger with Trafalgar House. In 1966 he invited Broackes to join the board of Trust Houses with a view to preparing the way for Broackes to succeed him as chairman. However a number of abortive schemes for co-operation between Trust Houses and Trafalgar House in the development of hotels in the West Indies and London (which foundered partly because of opposition to such co-operation among Trust House executives who had doubts about the profitability of West Indian hotels) soured relations between Broackes and Crowther. The executives of Trafalgar House were not prepared to relinquish their plans for hotel development, and it was clear Crowther could not remain as chairman. Crowther resigned from Trafalgar House in June 1969, and Broackes from the board of Trust Houses.

A year after his break with Trafalgar House, Crowther found another way to accomplish the expansion of Trust Houses: a merger with the group built up by Charles Forte. Forte had already proposed such a merger twice before; a renewed approach found Crowther, now more confident his management team could cope with the problems raised by Forte's very different style of management, more receptive. The new group, Trust Houses Forte, had assets of about £100 million: 203 hotels in the United Kingdom and Ireland, and 21 abroad, as well as restaurants, motorway service cafés, amusement arcades and cigarette kiosks. Crowther became chairman, on the understanding he was to hand over the chair to Forte in May 1972. The companies complemented one another well. Trust Houses' strength lay in hotels in the United Kingdom and in industrial catering; Forte's in public catering and foreign hotels. Unfortunately, their managements were not complementary.

Forte's explanation of the group's troubles was that the Trust Houses' men would not 'listen to me and my management formula' {Hennessy (1980) 8}. He found Trust Houses too bureaucratic: there was, he felt, too much paper circulating. He was used to making the decisions he wanted to make; if presented with a carefully-argued report advising against something he wanted to do, he was quite happy to ignore it. This method had served him well in building up his own company, but the Trust Houses men could not get used to it. Nor could Crowther. Once again, however, Crowther was outmanoeuvred. In November 1971 he was forced to resign as chairman. He supported a takeover attempt by Allied Breweries, but Forte successfully resisted it, and two weeks later on 27

January 1972, Crowther and six of his seven supporters on the board resigned. On 5 February, he died of a heart attack.

His death just after he had been driven to resign from the board of the company he had done so much to transform does not mean his career in business was a failure. He left an imprint on every company with which he was involved. Above all he had equipped Trust Houses to deal with the changes in the hotel business, especially the increasing importance of those travelling on business, and by car. Trust Houses might have been the largest hotel-chain, but they could not rely for ever on the attraction of old-world charm to offset inadequate plumbing.

His strength as a businessman lay in his ability to take a long-term view, although sometimes his enthusiasm for new ideas carried his plans beyond the needs of the time. He never worked as an executive and did not really understand the problems of routine management. But he listened to his executives, encouraged discussion, expected argument. Highly intelligent, he was articulate and witty, a master at clarifying an issue or summing up a debate. His warmth and wit aroused great affection and loyalty in many of those who worked with him, and he in turn would stand by them. In the judgement of Sir Francis Sandilands he was 'the ideal non-executive director'.

Contrasted with the clarity of his thought and speech was an emotional approach to people and to problems, which sometimes obscured his judgement. He was stimulated by entrepreneurs, but it is open to doubt whether he understood them. Crowther once said 'Businessmen are on the whole kinder, nicer and more straightforward than intellectuals and professional men; they pay more regard to people's feelings' {Sampson (1965) 548}. One does not need to subscribe to the theory that no decent human being can be successful in business to feel that anyone taking a prominent part in business at a high level with that attitude is destined for disillusion. The setbacks and failures of Crowther's business career were largely due to the fact that he was not playing the game by quite the same rules as those he was dealing with.

Towards the end of his life he appeared to be flagging. In addition to his business responsibilities, he had much work in his capacity as chairman of the Commission on the Constitution from 1969, and of the Committee on Consumer Credit in 1968-71. He was also Chancellor of the Open University, a position he liked because of his long-standing commitment to the expansion of opportunities for higher education. Since he had ceased to be editor of the *Economist*, he had become a non-executive director of a number of American businesses, including Encyclopedia Britannica, and frequently travelled to the USA. He was an enthusiastic traveller (one reason for his liking for the hotel business) but he was overweight and took a perverse pride in his refusal to take any exercise, and this cannot have helped his health and energy. Music was one of his favourite recreations; he also collected pictures. He received a knighthood for his services to journalism in 1957, and became a life-peer in 1968. He left an estate proved at £423,940 gross.

CHRISTINE SHAW

Writings:

(with Sir W T Layton) *An Introduction to the Study of Prices* (Macmillan, 1935).

Ways and Means (Macmillan & Co, 1936).

The Sinews of War (Oxford: Clarendon Press, 1939).

Economics for Democrats (Thomas Nelson & Sons, 1939).

Paying for the War (Oxford: Clarendon Press, 1940).

Ways and Means of War (Oxford: Clarendon Press, 1940).

An Outline of Money (Thomas Nelson & Sons, 1941).

Free Enterprise versus Planned Economy. The Present State of the Argument (Iowa City, 1954).

Balances and Imbalances of Payments The George H Leatherbee Lectures 1957 (Boston: Harvard University Graduate School of Business Administration, 1957).

PP, RC on the Press (1961-62) Cmnd 1812, 1812-9.

PP, Report of the Committee on Consumer Credit (1971) Cmnd 4596 (chairman).

'Trust Houses Limited and the Hotel Industry' (Edwards Seminar paper 386, 7 Mar 1967).

15 to 18. A Report of the Central Advisory Council for Education (England) (2 vols, HMSO, 1959).

Schools and Universities (London School of Economics, 1961).

This is a selection of his more important writings.

Sources:

Unpublished

BCe.

PrC.

Information from Nigel Broackes, J M Pickard, E de Rothschild, Sir Francis Sandilands, Diana Self.

Annual Report Trust Houses, 1966.

Published

Nigel Broackes, *A Growing Concern* (Weidenfeld and Nicolson, 1979).

Economist 2 July 1960, 8 July, 5 Aug, 9 Dec 1961, 30 Mar, 7 Apr, 22 June, 12 Oct, 21 Dec 1963, 22 Feb, 28 Mar 1964, 12 Feb 1972.

Elizabeth Hennessy, *The Entrepreneurs* (Newbury: Scope Books, 1980).

'The Big Build-up at Trust Houses' *Management Today* July 1970.

Oliver Marriott, *The Property Boom* (Hamilton, 1967).

Anthony T S Sampson, *Anatomy of Britain Today* (Hodder & Stoughton, 1965).

Sunday Times 28 Mar 1971.

Times 21 June, 10 July, 6, 19, 28 Dec 1963, 4, 7, 10, 15, 17, 23 Jan 1964, 1 Jan, 3, 6, 31 July, 1, 24 Dec 1965, 7 Feb, 25 Mar 1972.

WWW.

William D Cruddas in 1893 (courtesy of the Central Library, Newcastle upon Tyne).

CRUDDAS, William Donaldson

(1831-1912)

Engineering company director

William Donaldson Cruddas was born on 26 September 1831, the second son of George Cruddas (1788-1879), a Tyneside industrialist and financier. His father in 1846 joined with W G Armstrong (qv) and others to form the company which later became the Tyneside engineering and shipbuilding giant, Sir W G Armstrong, Mitchell & Co Ltd. George Cruddas made a considerable contribution of capital to Armstrongs and ran its financial affairs; he also placed his son in the firm and trained him to take over the company's financial responsibilities on his own retirement. W D Cruddas became a partner in 1861 and controlled Armstrong's financial activities over a period of three decades during which it expanded enormously. It amalgamated with the shipbuilding firm of Charles Mitchell & Co in 1882 and became a limited company (of which Cruddas was financial director) in the same year. When the Association of Employers of Engineering Labour on Tyneside was established in 1883, he was appointed its chairman.

Cruddas had a number of other major activities. He was a director of Newcastle & Gateshead Water Co (formed as the Whitle Dene Water Co in 1845 by Armstrong, George Cruddas and others), 1873-1912, vice-chairman, 1889-94 and chairman, 1894-1912. He was chairman of the *Newcastle Daily Journal*, 1895-1912. In addition to business affairs he had a major involvement in politics as a Conservative. He was a prominent member of the Primrose League and ruling counsellor of the Elswick branch, president of Newcastle Conservative Association and MP for Newcastle, 1895-1900.

Cruddas was also prominent in social affairs on Tyneside. He had an active interest in education in Newcastle and was particularly involved in Christian work. He was a benefactor and chairman of the Newcastle City Mission and was a member of the Bishop's Commission on Church Extension following the establishment of the see of Newcastle in 1882. He was responsible for the building and endowing of St Stephen's, Elswick and St Mark's, Byker. He also gave land at Scotswood to the City of Newcastle in 1890 for use as a recreation ground, which became known as Cruddas Park. He was well known for his charitable contributions to religious, educational, recreational and athletic organisations.

Cruddas was a JP for both Newcastle and Northumberland, was made a DL of the latter county and was High Sheriff in 1903. He was a member of the Carlton, Constitutional and National Clubs. In 1861 Cruddas married Margaret Octavia, daughter of William Nesham of Newcastle, and they had three daughters. They lived at Elswick Dene, Newcastle but also purchased Haughton Castle, Northumberland. He died on 8 February 1912 leaving an estate valued at £1,041,199 gross.

D J ROWE

Sources:

Unpublished

PrC.

Published

Newcastle Daily Journal 9 Feb 1912.

Robert W Rennison, *Water to Tyneside* (Newcastle: Newcastle and Gateshead Water Co, 1979).

WWMP.

WWW.

Walter Cunliffe, 1st Lord Cunliffe (courtesy of the Bank of England).

CUNLIFFE, Walter

1st Lord Cunliffe

(1855-1920)

Governor of the Bank of England

Walter Cunliffe was born at Kensington, London, on 4 December 1855, eldest of the five sons of Roger Cunliffe, later of Tyrrells Wood, Leatherhead and Kensington, and his wife Ann née Edge. He came from a family of bankers. His great-grandfather Roger Cunliffe (d 1824) was a Blackburn manufacturer who, in partnership with William Brooks (1763-1846), established the Lancashire bank of Cunliffe, Brooks in 1792: this bank survived for over a century, latterly with Thomas Brooks, First Lord Crawshaw as senior partner. In 1816 Cunliffe, Brooks opened a London office and bill-broking business, and the firm of Roger Cunliffe, Sons & Co continued until 1942 when it merged with Cater Brightwen (now Cater Ryder). Roger Cunliffe's younger son James (1798-1854) eventually entered the London business; James's son Roger (1824-95), Walter's father, was partner in the Lombard Street bankers of Messrs Alexander Cunliffe and left £1,184,737 in 1895.

Walter Cunliffe was educated at Harrow in 1870-73, where he was in the school shooting eleven, and at Trinity College, Cambridge, where he won the inter-university mile race in 1877, and graduated BA in 1878. After Cambridge he worked for a year as a stockman in Queensland, Australia and subsequently visited all parts of the world except Southern and Central Africa. In later life, he liked to boast of his rough life in mining camps and on big-game shooting expeditions. He entered the City in 1880, and together with his brothers Arthur Cunliffe (1857-1924) and Leonard Daneham Cunliffe (1860-1937) launched in 1890 the merchant bank of Cunliffe Brothers, but remained comparatively unknown and undistinguished for almost another quarter-century.

In 1890 Cunliffe married Mary Agnes (died 1893), younger daughter of Robert Henderson (1807-71), of Sedgwick Park, Horsham and Randall's Park, Leatherhead, a merchant of Mincing Lane who had left almost £400,000. Cunliffe's brothers-in-law Robert Henderson (1851-95) and George W Henderson (1854-1934) were respectively directors of the Bank of England in 1893-95 and 1902-29 (leaving estates of £113,921 and £119,138); and his own election as a Bank director in 1895 filled the vacancy caused by Robert Henderson's death. He re-married, in 1896, Edith Cunningham (1867-1965), fifth daughter of Colonel R T Boothby (1830-97), and sister of Sir Robert Boothby (1871-1941), afterwards manager of the Scottish Provident Institution and director of the Bank of Scotland. They had three sons and three daughters.

By seniority and rotation of the post, Cunliffe became Deputy Governor of the Bank of England in 1911 and Governor in April 1913. He continued the policy of his predecessor, Alfred C Cole (1854-1920), in drawing the joint-stock bankers closer to the Bank, but marred his overtures by rudeness and arrogance. 'An aggressive character, who enjoyed a game of bluff, even when he lost it', Cunliffe 'had the advantage of knowing his own mind, perhaps not a very difficult one to know' {Sayers (1976) 66}. His character was forcibly felt in the Bank in 1911-14, but it was the outbreak of world war that led to the unprecedented prolongation of his Governorship, and his appearance as a power in world finance.

The collapse of the continental bourses in July and August 1914 reacted on both the London Stock Exchange and the joint-stock banks, and Cunliffe was involved in the emergency measures of Lloyd George, as Chancellor of the Exchequer, to prevent collapse and panic in the City. The Bank of England, with government support, announced that it would discount all bills which pre-dated the emergency moratorium declared on 2 August, and was also authorised to make advances to meet maturing bills. It was for his aid in steadying the City that Cunliffe received the first peerage of the war, in December 1914.

During 1915 he attended, and was notoriously taciturn at, conferences with British, French, Italian and Russian finance ministers at Paris, Nice and Boulogne. He was also at the Calais conference (1916), accompanied A J Balfour on his mission to the USA from April to June 1917, and visited Russia and Spain. He received the Order of St Anne (1915), the Crown of Italy (1916), the GBE (1917), the Légion d'Honneur (1918) and the Order of the Rising Sun (1918). He was responsible for the circulation of forged German bank-notes in 1915, and was at the heart of national wartime financial policy. Though he enjoyed a good press as Governor, he had many private critics, and was blamed for the delay in rectifying Anglo-American exchange rates in 1915, and for keeping the Bank Rate unnecessarily high after July 1916, necessitating the issue of further 6 per cent Exchequer Bonds and Treasury bills.

In 1917 Cunliffe had a major personality clash with the Chancellor of the Exchequer, Bonar Law. The origin of their row was the Bank of England's anxiety about its statutory responsibility for the gold standard, and its feeling that the Treasury was inclined to reduce the gold cover in order to meet the Government's outlay on war supplies overseas. Cunliffe had been accustomed to considerable power in both the Bank and the London Exchange Committee (which was responsible for gold reserves), but after three months' absence in the USA, he returned in June 1917 to find, so he alleged, 'that not only have all the means of controlling the Exchanges been taken out of our hands but all information is withheld from us even when we have the Chancellor's permission to obtain it, and requests for telegrams are not only refused but met with absolute incivility'. He claimed that the London Exchange Committee was being supplanted by Sir Robert Chalmers and J M Keynes (qv) of the Treasury, and citing a verbal promise in November 1915 by Reginald McKenna (qv) as Chancellor of the Exchequer 'that Mr Keynes should not meddle again in city matters', demanded the dismissal of both men {HLRO, Bonar Law papers 65/2/26, Cunliffe to Lloyd George, 3 July 1917}. In further self-assertion, on 5 July, without consulting Bonar Law or the Treasury, he ordered that £17.5 million of the Bank of England's gold in Canada should be used to liquidate a long-standing loan of $85 million from J P Morgans and instructed the Canadian Government to disregard any instructions about the gold from the Treasury. Cunliffe was now maintaining 'that in my anxiety to assist the Exchange Committee at a very critical time ... I made an unpardonable mistake ... in allowing anyone to control Gold in the Bank's figures, and I am sure my Court will not only never permit it again, but censure me for having betrayed my trust in ever permitting it' {ibid 65/2/28, Cunliffe to Law, 7 July 1917}. Cunliffe's reprisal against the Treasury over the Canadian gold enraged both Law and Lloyd George, and their tempers were not improved when Cunliffe removed himself to Scotland on 17 July. Cecil Harmsworth reported 'universal satisfaction' in the City at Cunliffe's rumoured resignation {ibid 65/3/20}, but on 12 August, in an attempt to recover his position, Cunliffe tendered Law his humiliatingly unreserved apology. Though the Court of the Bank professed to back the Governor, in November they resolved that Cunliffe would be replaced as Governor by Sir Brien Cokayne, later Lord Cullen of Ashbourne (1864-1932), with effect from April 1918. By intriguing with the clearing bankers, Cunliffe tried to get this decision reversed, and his 'quarrels in the Committee of Treasury [of the bank] became more open and more continuous', with 'violent displays', and 'careful and calculated discourtesy' in public to Montagu Norman (qv) {Sayers (1976) 108}.

After the term of his governorship had ended, Cunliffe remained a director of the Bank until his death. He joined the board of the P&O in November 1919. He was also a director of the North Eastern Railway from 1905, but had little impact on its affairs. A Lieutenant of the City of London, he was made honorary Freeman of the Goldsmith's Company in 1919, and also received an honorary LLD from Columbia University.

Despite his immoderate behaviour in 1917-18, he was entrusted with other official posts. From April 1919 he chaired the influential Fresh Capital Issues Committee; he also chaired the Committee on Currency and Foreign Exchanges after the war, whose interim report of August 1918 is known as the Cunliffe Report. The committee's other members included Sir Charles Addis (qv), Herbert Gibbs (qv), W H N Goschen and Lord Inchcape (qv). They listed the prerequisites for restoring an effective gold standard as the cessation of government borrowing, and the re-introduction of the Bank of England's responsibilities for the discount rate and a fixed note issue. The Cunliffe report proved to be one of the earliest and more erroneous attempts to get 'back to 1914'. After the Armistice, Cunliffe sat on the War Cabinet's committee on German indemnities, and together with Lord Sumner and W M Hughes (the Australian Prime Minister) was British representative on the Reparations Commission at the Paris Peace Conference until June 1919. Cunliffe, 'after talking the matter over in the City', produced the 'wild and fantastic chimera' that Germany could pay £24,000 million in annual instalments of £1,200 million, and this at a time when Treasury investigations indicated Germany's reparations capacity at between £2,000 and £3,000 million *in toto* {Keynes (1971) XVI 336-7}. Keynes's biographer speaks of 'his passionate intellectual contempt for the trash of Hughes and Cunliffe' {Harrod (1951) 237}, while Tom Jones spoke in 1919 of Sumner and Cunliffe as 'both stony hearted men' {Middlemas (1969) 88}.

With effect from 1 January 1920, Cunliffe Brothers was absorbed by the firm of Fruhling & Goschen, and Cunliffe became special partner with Lord Goschen in the new merchant banking house of Goschen & Cunliffe. However, he took no part in the business, dying of septicaemia, after ten days' illness, on 6 January 1920 at Headley Court, Epsom. His estate was sworn at £905,192 gross. He was a rich, arrogant and unimaginative man, of ordinary ability, only remembered because by chance he was Governor of the Bank of England when war erupted.

R P T DAVENPORT-HINES

Writings:

letter on injuring asparagus plants by prematurely cutting foliage *Times* 15 July 1918.

PP, Interim Report of Committee on Currency and Foreign Exchanges after the War (15 Aug 1918) Cd 9182 (chairman).

PP, Final Report of Committee on Currency and Foreign Exchanges after the War (3 Dec 1919) Cmd 464 (chairman).

Sources:

Unpublished

Bank of England Archives, Threadneedle St, London.

House of Lords RO, Bonar Law papers; Lloyd George papers.

PrC.

Published

Banker's Magazine 104 (Aug 1917), 109 (Feb 1920).

Robert Blake, *The Unknown Prime Minister* (Eyre & Spottiswoode, 1955).

Burke's Landed Gentry.

Catalogue of Old English Furniture and Tapestry, the Property of the Late Lord Cunliffe ... Sold by Auction by Messrs Christie ... December 8 1927 (William Clowes, 1927).

Kenneth Clark, *Another Part of the Wood* (Murray, 1974).

Complete Peerage.

Herbert G de Fraine, *Servant of This House: Life in the Old Bank of England* (Constable, 1960).

Sir Henry Roy F Harrod, *Life of John Maynard Keynes* (Macmillan, 1951).

Elizabeth Johnson and Donald Moggridge (eds), *The Collected Writings of John Maynard Keynes* (in progress, Macmillan, 1971-) 16.

Robert K Middlemas (ed), *Thomas Jones, Whitehall Diary* (3 vols, Oxford University Press, 1969) 1.

Richard S Sayers, *The Bank of England 1890-1944* (2 vols, Cambridge: Cambridge University Press, 1977).

WWW.

CUNLIFFE-OWEN, Sir Hugo Von Reitzenstein

(1870-1947)

Tobacco entrepreneur and industrialist

Hugo Von Reitzenstein Cunliffe-Owen was born at Kensington, London, on 16 August 1870, fourth and youngest son of Sir Francis Philip Cunliffe-Owen, KCB, KCMG, CIE (1828-1894), of Lowestoft, and Baroness Jenny Von Reitzenstein, whose father was ADC to King Frederick William IV of Prussia. Hugo's father was sometime Secretary of the Colonial Institute and director of the Victoria and Albert Museum; he left £4,832 gross in 1894. Hugo was educated at Clifton College for a few months in 1885 and at Brighton College, and then was articled as an engineer to Sir John Wolfe-Barry (qv), the public contractor. In 1886 his sister married Henry Herbert Wills (qv), and the latter subsequently recruited him into the export department of the family tobacco business. In 1902 Cunliffe-Owen was on the periphery in negotiating a truce in the tobacco war between Imperial Tobacco and its deadly rival, American Tobacco, which, headed by James Buchanan Duke (1856-1925), monopolised nearly every branch of the huge American tobacco industry.

The outcome of this truce was the formation of the British American

Tobacco Co Ltd and a division of world tobacco markets. Britain was exclusively reserved for Imperial Tobacco, while the rest of the world was allotted to BAT, in which the Americans held two-thirds of the equity. Duke was chairman of BAT from 1902 until 1923 (with an interval around 1910), and appointed Cunliffe-Owen as a director and its first secretary. BAT was 'one of the first organisational units ever created by an American multinational corporation to administer international business' {Cochran (1980) 13}, but in 1911 American Tobacco was forced to sell its interest following the Supreme Court's judgement that, as a combine acting in restraint of trade, it violated anti-trust legislation. By 1915 British interests held a majority of BAT shares, and in 1923 Cunliffe-Owen replaced Duke as chairman, remaining in that office until 1945, when he became titular president of BAT.

BAT's issued capital rose from £5.2 million in 1902 to £21.5 million in 1923, and its worldwide net profits increased from £121,805 in 1902 to £4.6 million in 1922. BAT's world sales in 1923 were 50,000 million cigarettes. Apparently its most lucrative market was China, originally selected by Duke: Chinese cigarette consumption rose from 0.3 billion in 1902 to 25 billion in 1920, 40 billion in 1924 and 87 billion in 1928; BAT's total profits in China (1902-48) were US $380,785,120. BAT owned 97.5 per cent of BAT (China) Ltd, and altogether its Chinese subsidiaries had a capitalisation of Mexican $205,905,000. As one observer wrote in 1910, 'China is decorated with tobacco posters the ever-present evidence of the activities of the BAT ... a Company American in its enterprise and boldness' {NSWL, G E Morrison diary, 23 January 1910}.

Cunliffe-Owen visited China on becoming chairman in 1923, and decentralised BAT (China) Ltd's structure into autonomous regional units which could function when floods or civil war erupted locally. This reorganisation, and the supersession of American domination, led one BAT official, the American James Hutchison, to claim that 'the pioneer days came to an end' under Cunliffe-Owen, who transformed the company 'into a ponderous, unwieldy, old-fashioned English accounting machine' {Cochran (1980) 165}.

Between 1923 and 1937 Cunliffe-Owen lobbied both the British and Chinese Governments in an attempt to minimise the taxation of tobacco, and in 1931 submitted an important memorandum on revenue-raising at the request of T V Soong, the Minister of Finance. In May 1937 he brought to the Midland Bank, of which he was a director from 1925, a Chinese proposal to open a credit account of £4 million, and during the air-raids of 1940-41 he gave refuge at his Sunningdale house to the Chinese Ambassador, with whom he 'had very many talks about business in China' intended to stave off the threat of a Chinese government tobacco sales monopoly {PRO FO 371/31653, Cunliffe-Owen to Sir Horace Seymour, 29 Jan 1942}. BAT's Chinese holdings were nationalised after the Communist takeover in 1949: Chinese Nationalist critics of BAT 'underestimated its financial investments in China or exaggerated its unfortunate economic effects ... because they resented its political privileges and its Western managers' arrogance', but nevertheless 'its use of coercive tactics to destroy or buy out Chinese cigarette companies or block their entrance into the market' did retard native industry {Cochran (1980) 206}.

Cunliffe-Owen was a lifelong friend of Lord Beaverbrook (qv). The latter made him Controller of Eastern Propaganda at the Ministry of Information in 1918, by virtue of BAT's Chinese operations; for his wartime services he received a baronetcy in 1921. Cunliffe-Owen was a director in 1917-19 of Beaverbrook's Colonial Bank, chartered in 1836 and specialising in West African business. At Beaverbrook's instigation he was a director of Provincial Cinematograph Theatres in 1920-21, but resigned, apparently in disappointment at Beaverbrook's discouragement of Adolph Zukor (1873-1976) of Paramount Pictures, and his backer Otto Kahn (1867-1934), the New York banker, who wanted to merge with PCT on a share basis.

In 1928 Cunliffe-Owen created the Tobacco Securities Trust to buy and hold shares in BAT associate and subsidiary companies and to act as an investment interest for himself. Reginald McKenna (qv) of the Midland Bank became chairman, with Cunliffe-Owen as vice-chairman. In May 1933 Tobacco Securities, in association with the Second Lord Trent, bought control of Boots the chemists back to Britain by buying one million shares at £6 15s each from the US combine, Drug Inc, which since 1928 had included L K Liggett & Co, to whom Jesse Boot (qv) had sold out for £2,274,600 in 1920. Cunliffe-Owen also became a director of Eagle Star Insurance in 1941.

With the onset of rearmament in the 1930s, Cunliffe-Owen bought the British manufacturing rights of the much-publicised Burnelli twin-engined flying-wing aircraft which had found no market in the USA where it originated. He formed the Cunliffe-Owen Aircraft Co Ltd, with works at Eastleigh on Southampton Water, spending £120,000 on the factory up to November 1939, at which date he had contracts with the Air Ministry, Lord Rootes (qv), Shorts and Armstrong-Siddeley worth £1.5 million, and other contracts pending worth £1.5 million. In November 1939 he emloyed 850 men with a weekly wage bill of £3,000, but only a month later his staff had risen to 2,000 and the Air Ministry were urging him to take on another 2,000. In 1941 Jim Mollison (1905-59), the aviator, made a famous flight to French Equatorial Africa in a Cunliffe-Owen machine,and their Seafire prototype (a naval version of the Spitfire fighter) was successfully test-flown in September 1943. Until December 1939 Cunliffe-Owen Aircraft had an overdraft with Lloyds Bank Ltd to £30,000, but in January 1940 the Midland Bank extended the overdraft of £75,00, of which Sir Hugo guaranteed £25,000. This limit reached £625,000 by February 1947 when Sir Hugo personally guaranteed £150,000. As to the company's trading results in the latter half of the war, it made a loss of £52,065 in 1943, and profits of £29,948 in 1944, £71,396 in 1945 and £3,441 in 1946. The Midland Bank, in February 1947, declined to extend the overdraft limit to £900,000, as the accounts showed that the company's liquid assets had declined by £220,000 since December 1945, and 'the Bank facility, which should have been used for liquid working-capital, had been used for capital expenditure', such as £155,000 on plant and machinery, and £330,000 on special tooling and the construction of the Concordia prototype {Midland Bank archives, memorandum of Alexander Woods, 21 Feb 1947}.

The Eastleigh factory was ill-organised, and when M J H Bruce was managing director its high-level control was loose. In the summer of 1947

Bruce was replaced by Trevor Westbrook (1901-78), formerly of Supermarine Aviation, and by Cunliffe-Owen's only surviving son, Dudley (born 1923), and an effort was made to win orders in their new lines of pressed steel baths and radiators. All hopes were pinned on their 10-14 seater Concordia aircraft, but its handling by its demonstration pilot at the Radlett flying display in September 1947 led to speculation that it was dangerous at low altitudes. Although British European Airways ordered two Concordia, and the Nawab of Bhopal ordered one, production was suspended in November 1947 when it became clear that there was no possibility of sales in sufficient numbers. Less than one month later Cunliffe-Owen died of a heart attack, on 14 December 1947, at Sunningdale. By the end of the month claims of £450,000 had been registered against the company for breaches of contract through cessation of Concordia production, and the company was dismantled at a loss in 1948.

Cunliffe-Owen described himself as 'a retiring flower [who] dislike[s] seeing my name in prominence' {HLRO Beaverbrook C/106, Cunliffe-Owen to Beaverbrook 8 December 1926}, but he was politically active in the early 1930s. He was treasurer of Lord Beaverbrook's Empire Crusade (himself donating £5,000 in 1930 alone), and supported the attempt of Lord Nuffield (qv) to form a National Council of Industry and Commerce to stop Britain being 'the dumping ground of the world' and to give British workmen who 'were neither Bolshevist nor Socialist ... a real leader' {*Times*, 26 Sept 1930}. In his pamphlet *Industry and the Empire Crusade*, he summarised his views: 'The old system of small firms strenuously competing with each other and interested in limited markets has been replaced by a new order in which the units are vast federations and combines selling their goods on a ... world scale ... The principle of federation, which has proved successful in business, must be extended to [British imperial] politics'. 'Mass production becomes possible only where a large protected market is available', he claimed, blaming free-trade Governments for 'our failure to use the methods of mass production which rule in America and our consequent inability to produce o market our products as cheaply and efficiently as our competitors'. He urged a cartel system throughout the British Empire: 'with a rational division of markets, there would be scope for every factory now standing on British soil to work to capacity' {HLRO Beaverbrook C/106}.

Cunliffe-Owen was a keen racehorse owner, interested in equine breeding, whose horses won the Derby in 1928, and the 1,000 Guineas and Oaks in 1938. He became a member of the Council of Racehorse Owners' and Trainers' Association in 1942. He was also a yachtsman and fond of Great Danes. He married first, in 1918, in Massachusetts, Helen Elizabeth Oliver (1896-1934) of New York, by whom he had two sons and a daughter. He married secondly, in 1935, Mauricia Martha Shaw of San Francisco, from whom he was judicially separated in 1946. He left £1,353,744 gross in 1947, and nineteen days before his death made a new will leaving half his fortune to Marjorie Cunliffe-Owen, a former dancer, who had changed her surname from Daw three weeks before the will was made. In May 1948 his widow brought an action for enticement against Marjorie Cunliffe-Owen, and another suit against his executors.

R P T DAVENPORT-HINES

Writings:

Industry and the Empire Crusade: a Statement to Manufacturers (1930).

letter on world depression and low value of silver *Times* 1 Aug 1931.

letter on gold standard *ibid* 9 Oct 1931.

letter on London-Penang telephone service *ibid* 16 Sept 1933.

letter on the budget *ibid* 14 Oct 1939.

letter on Balkan tobacco *ibid* 20 Jan 1940.

Sources:

Unpublished

House of Lords RO, papers of Lord Beaverbrook.

Midland Bank Archives, Poultry, London EC2.

New South Wales State Library, papers of G E Morrison.

PRO, Foreign Office papers.

Published

Bernard W E Alford, *W D & H O Wills* (Methuen, 1973).

Stanley Chapman, *Jesse Boot* (Hodder & Stoughton, 1973).

Sherman Cochran, *Big Business in China* (Cambridge, Massachusetts: Harvard University Press, 1980).

Maurice Corina, *Trust in Tobacco* (Michael Joseph, 1975).

Alan J P Taylor, *Beaverbrook* (Hamish Hamilton, 1972).

John K Winkler, *Tobacco Tycoon: the Story of J B Duke* (New York: Random House, 1942).

WWW.

CURRIE, Sir Donald

(1825-1909)

Shipping magnate

Donald Currie was born in Greenock on 17 September 1825, the third of ten children of James Currie (1797-1851) and Elizabeth née Martin. His father, a barber, took the family to Belfast in 1826, where between the ages

Sir Donald Currie (from The Journal of Commerce and Shipping Telegraph, *1934).*

of seven and fourteen Donald attended the Belfast Academy and the Royal Belfast Academical Institution. In 1840 he returned to Greenock to work in the shipping office of his uncle, John Martin of Hoyle, Martin & Co. Four years later he moved to Liverpool where he worked for Charles MacIver (qv), family friend and manager of the British & North American Royal Mail Steam Packet Co founded by Samuel Cunard in 1839-40. Currie became head of Cunard's cargo department and opened branches at Paris, Le Havre, Bremen and Antwerp between 1849 and 1854. He left Cunard in 1862 to establish his own company, running sailing vessels between Liverpool, London and Calcutta. From 1863 he was also associated with the Baltic trade through the Leith, Hull & Hamburg Steam Packet Co, in which he became a major shareholder and which was managed by his elder brother James from 1862. With other partners he established the Liverpool & Hamburg Steam Ship Co in 1866.

Difficulties in the Indian trade, and a chance association with the London broker G H Payne, prompted him in 1872 to transfer to the Cape trade in competition with the Union Steam Ship Co which held the mail contract. Four steamers, either chartered or bought from the Leith, Hull & Hamburg Co, were the initial basis for a successful partnership, the Castle Packets Co, established in 1873. A government subsidy from the Cape Colony sustained his challenge to the Union Co from 1874 until 1876. The mail contract was then renewed and divided equally between the two companies. This security and growing traffic prompted expansion. The Castle Co's tonnage increased from 21,000 to 48,000 tons, 1876-81. In 1877 it was reorganised with an authorised capital of £500,000, Donald Currie & Co as managers, and Currie himself as the largest shareholder with 30.3 per cent of the issued shares. Further reorganisation in 1881 brought the public flotation of the Castle Mail Packets Co Ltd. Its subscribed capital was £720,000 of which £504,000 was called up; reserves and insurance funds totalled £240,000 and Currie, appointed as manager in perpetuity, received 5 per cent of gross earnings per annum.

From 1874 Currie began to cultivate political contacts both at Westminster and in South Africa. He played an influential part among shipowners in the reform of mercantile marine legislation in 1876 and became Liberal MP for Perthshire in 1880. For assistance to the Government in South African matters, he was made a CMG in 1877 and KCMG in 1881. His growing personal prosperity was signified by purchase of the adjoining Perthshire estates of Garth and Glen Lyon in 1880 and 1885, and by the diversification of his investments. The first of many lucrative ventures into South African minerals and property was his purchase in 1881 of 75 per cent of the shares of the newly-formed Namaqua Copper Co Ltd for £19,000.

As manager and by far the largest shareholder in Castle Mail, Currie showed a preference for autocratic management and indulged his liking for display and personal prominence. Two structural features of the company he had designed made this possible. Castle Mail's 'Council' was less a board of working directors than a body of acquaintances and others appointed largely at Currie's instigation, useful for their social standing and political connections, particularly in colonial affairs, the Admiralty and telegraphic communications. Financial management hinged on the substantial reserves created in 1881 and their replenishment by generous

Pembroke Castle *(courtesy of the National Maritime Museum, London)*.

annual allowances especially for depreciation. Declared and distributed profits often compared unfavourably with other major companies. Details of earnings and managers' commissions were never disclosed; allowances against depreciation, often not revealed, were regularly estimated in the financial press greatly to exceed what was necessary. This had two results. Financial concealment and meagre dividends bred distrust, and shares were persistently quoted at a substantial discount: after 1881 further capital was raised when necessary not by any increase in ordinary share capital but by issues of debentures, 4.5 per cent cumulative preference shares and loans. By keeping profits within the firm, Currie was able to build high-class vessels often without much regard for timing and economy. Shareholders' losses financed managerial extravagance and self-indulgence, and, despite persistent criticism from journalists and a few investors, no effective opposition emerged.

The second buttress to Currie's position, and his chief contribution to the shipping world, was the South African shipping conference. With great energy and a widely-acknowledged talent for systematic administration, Currie first brought the southern African lines together in 1883 during a severe depression, and sustained the conference against frequent challenges and mounting criticism. Deeds were matched by words, especially in his vigorous defence of its record and the freedom to combine, in his evidence to the Royal Commission on Shipping Rings in 1908.

Other lesser supports also helped. Currie ceaselessly exploited his contacts and position in the conference to secure subsidies and government contracts, not only for mail but for supplies, troops and emigrants. The expanding mining industry was an additional source of such engagements. He developed associated enterprises, such as landing and boating companies at Port Elizabeth, Durban and Beira. His own mainland investments (in exploration and land companies, Transvaal gold mines and diamonds) brought him useful influence and good intelligence in addition to capital gains. Of particular importance was his role in the formation of De Beers Consolidated Mines in 1887-88, following which he was director (1888-1902) and chairman of the London board (1888-91).

The removal in 1899 of the Cape's prohibition on amalgamation of the mail companies finally enabled him to promote a merger with the Union Steam Ship Co, forming the Union-Castle Mail Steam Ship Co Ltd in January 1900. The two companies had been of similar size and their combined tonnage topped 210,000. Demands for transport during the South African War (1899-1902) were high, and further building was undertaken in anticipation of a post-war boom. This proved Currie's largest miscalculation: instead, depression in South Africa, fresh foreign competition and a world-wide slump in freights pressed the new company very hard. As manager and holder of 31 per cent of the 141,841 ordinary £10 shares as well as 26.8 per cent of the preference shares, Currie dictated the company's response, notably an aggressive use of the conference's organisation.

Retiring from Parliament in 1900, he began after 1904 to leave more detailed business to his sons-in-law and other relatives brought into the managing firm since the 1870s. Currie had a passion for steam-yachting and sailed frequently to the Mediterranean. He enjoyed sports, especially shooting, and collected paintings, particularly by J M W Turner. He was also a staunch member of the Free Church of Scotland and between 1902 and 1908 he donated nearly £200,000 to educational and religious causes, including £100,000 to University College Hospital, London.

He married Margaret Miller, daughter of John Miller of Liverpool and Ardencraig, Bute, in 1851; they had three daughters. Sir Donald Currie died on 13 April 1909, leaving virtually his entire estate of £2,432,810 gross to his wife and the families of his daughters.

ANDREW PORTER

Writings:

PP, HC 1873 (334) IX, SC on the Cape of Good Hope and Zanzibar Mail Contracts.

'Maritime Warfare: The Importance to the British Empire of a Complete System of Telegraphs, Coaling Stations, and Graving Docks' *Journal of the Royal United Services Institute* 21 (1877).

'Thoughts upon the Present and Future of South Africa, and Central and East Africa' *Proceedings of the Royal Colonial Institute* 8 (1877).

'Election Letter to Voters' *Greenock Herald* 5 Jan 1878.

The South African Mail Service (1879).

'Maritime Warfare: The Adaptation of Ocean Steamers to War Purposes' *Journal of the Royal United Services Institute* 24 (1880).

Address to constituents at Perth *Times* 30 Nov 1880.

Evidence on 17 May 1881 to *RC on the Defence of British Possessions and Commerce Abroad* (printed but given limited circulation. Copies in PRO Caernarvon papers and National Maritime Museum, Greenwich, Milne papers).

South Africa. Report of Proceedings of the Deputation to the Rt Hon the Earl of Derby, KG (1884).

'South Africa. An Address Delivered by Sir Donald Currie .. 10 Apr 1888 *Proceedings of the Royal Colonial Institute* 19 (Waterlow & Sons, 1888).

PP, Memorandum Submitted for the Consideration of the Commissioners by the Shipowners Engaged in the South and East African Trade, RC on Shipping Rings (1909) Cd 4669.

PP, RC on Shipping Rings (1909) Cd 4685.

PD, 1880-1893/4, 1895, 1897.

PP, HC 1897 (346) XI, SC on Merchandise Marks.

Sources:

Unpublished

Bank of Scotland, Chief Office, Glasgow, Union Bank Records.

British & Commonwealth Shipping Ltd, London, Castle Mail and Union-Castle Co papers.

Cape Archives Depot, Cape Town, South Africa.

H M Customs and Excise Archives, Custom House, Lower Thames Street, London, Customs Bills of Entry.

Natal Archives Dept, Pietermaritzburg, Colonial Secretary archive.

PRO, BT 108 Series II Transcripts, 1860 onwards; BT 109 Series III Transactions, 1860 onwards; CO 48 Cape Colony Original Correspondence, 1872 onwards; CO 417 South Africa Original Correspondence, 1884 onwards; T1 Treasury Board Papers, 1870 onwards; FO 84 Slave Trade, 1875-92; BT 31 Dissolved Companies.

Rhodes House, Oxford, British South Africa Co papers.

South African Library, Cape Town, papers of J X Merriman, P A Molteno and J G Sprigg.

Strathclyde Regional Archives, Barclay Curle & Co papers.

C Reg: Union Castle Mail Steamship Co Ltd (15,671).

PrC.

V E Solomon, 'The South African Shipping Question, 1886-1914' (Rhodes University, Grahamstown PhD, 1978).

Published

DNB.

'Donald Currie, an Illustrated Interview' *Strand Magazine* 8 (1894).

M Murray, *Union-Castle Chronicle 1853-1953* (Longmans, Green & Co, 1953).

'Sir Donald Currie, MP' *South Africa* 10 June 1893.

WWMP.

WWW.

Henry Curry (courtesy of Currys Group PLC).

CURRY, Henry

(1850-1916)

Cycle manufacturer and multiple store retailer

Henry Curry was born in Leicester on 1 May 1850, the son of James Curry (1819-1904), a link maker, and Elizabeth née Linthwaite. After attending a local school he trained as a mechanic in a factory belonging to Corahs, the Leicester hosiery manufacturers. In 1870, when he described himself as an engineer, Henry married Constance Mitchell, daughter of James Mitchell, a framework knitter.

Henry, who was clever with his hands, augmented his income by making fireguards and repairing mangles and penny-farthing bicycles and by 1880, an obituary recorded, he was manager of the Leicester Tricycle Co. When the family moved from Hazel Street to Painter Street, sometime after 1881, Henry had a small shed at the back of the house and in 1884 he turned to building occasional penny-farthings for local customers. In 1885 the 'equal-wheel' or safety cycle designed by James K Starley (qv) appeared. Its growing popularity persuaded Henry Curry to devote himself full-time to the assembly of these new machines, which had about 300 major components. He hand-built one a week in his small workshop. Spurred on by his wife, an energetic and ambitious woman, Henry converted the front room of his tiny house into a shop for selling the bicycles, fireguards and mangles he built. In 1888 a double-fronted shop selling the same merchandise was opened in Belgrave Gate, Leicester. At the same time, a small factory was acquired in Painter Street.

Henry Curry's business grew in response to the cycling boom of the mid-1890s. By this time some of his four sons were assisting their father. In 1897 Henry took his three eldest sons, James (1871-1958), Edwin (1874-1962) and Henry (1879-1953) into partnership as H Curry & Sons, which then had a staff of eight. His fourth son Albert (1886-1950) joined later. At the same time Henry opened a wholesale depot in Halford Street, Leicester.

Henry acquired his first retail branch outside Leicester in 1904 when he opened a shop at Louth in Lincolnshire. Further branches were opened in Boston, King's Lynn, Mansfield and Swadlincote. By 1910 Currys had seven branches with an annual turnover of £16,874. At this point Henry retired.

His four sons took the business into electrical goods, especially crystal sets, loudspeakers and battery operated radios, in the 1920s. The firm became a private limited company in 1922 and had an issued capital of £159,646 when sold in 1927 to a public company, Currys (1927) Ltd, with a capital of £500,000. By 1939 the firm had a turnover of £1.25 million and 221 branches. Largely spread through the market towns and cities of the Midlands and South East England, in pursuit of both cash and credit trade, the firm retailed prams, toys and sports goods but primarily cycles and radios. The Curry family retained total control of ownership and

Curry Cycle Co shop (courtesy of Currys Group PLC).

management, members of the family owning 90 per cent of the public company's ordinary shares and Henry's four sons acting as managing directors, with an unusual degree of unanimity and family solidarity. Their chairman Granville Havelock Bullimore (head of the accounting firm Hogg, Bullimore & Co) had purely nominal power and remained as titular head of the company until 1957. During the 1930s each of the four Curry brothers brought his eldest son into the firm and by 1939 the third generation of Currys joined the board, succeeding their fathers as managing directors. In the late 1950s the business moved into a new phase of growth associated with the retailing of televison sets and then electronic goods.

Henry Curry, the firm founder, was a Congregationalist and attended the Archdeacon Lane Congregational Chapel in Leicester, although he was married in an Anglican church. Unlike Henry, his four sons were total abstainers throughout their lives.

Henry Curry died on 14 May 1916 leaving £3,863 gross.

H J POTTERTON

Sources:

Unpublished

Curry family papers in the possession of author.

Currys, London, company records.

C Reg: Currys (1927) Ltd (222,379).

BCe.

MCe.

Published

C F Caunter, *The History and Development of Cycles* (HMSO, 1955).

The House of Currys, 1884-1964 (np, nd).

The Leicester Daily Post 16 May 1916.

The Leicester Mail 16 May 1916.

Kelsey Van Musschenbroek, 'Why Currys Shops are Hot' *Management Today* Oct 1971.

CZARNIKOW, Julius Caesar

(1838-1909)

Sugar broker

Julius Caesar Czarnikow (he preferred to be called Caesar) was born in Sondershausen, Germany in 1838, the third son of Moritz Czarnikow and Johanne née Bar. His father at that time was court agent to the Prince of Sondershausen, as well as being both Councillor of Commerce and Verderer. Caesar's parents appear to have been comfortably off, though little is known of his early upbringing and education until 1854, when he came to London and took a post as a clerk with a City broker's firm.

Which firm this was is unknown, though there were several German brokers in London at the time with whom he could have gained experience. Ambitious and enterprising, by the 1860s Czarnikow determined to start up a business on his own account, and his first move towards independence was to obtain British nationality. He next completed the necessary formalities for admission as a 'sworn broker', and on 1 March 1861 he opened his office in Philpot Lane under the title of Czarnikow & Co, colonial broker. A year later he moved to larger premises in Mincing Lane.

From the start Czarnikow dealt primarily in cane sugar imported from Java, the Philippines, Cuba and the East and West Indies; later he became the first to import beet sugar from continental Europe. Sugar consumption was steadily increasing. In 1862 the per capita consumption was about 36 lb of sugar a year; ten years later that amount reached 47 lb. In the 1860s and 1870s sugar became less of a luxury largely because prices fell, aided by the high bounties offered by producer Governments and the gradual reduction of high import duties which were finally abolished in 1874.

Czarnikow's business was highly successful. Ten years after setting up his office in London, he established a branch in Glasgow, and in 1881 he set up a similar branch in Liverpool. His business now covered the three main centres of the sugar trade in the UK, but continued to expand still further. In 1888 he established the brokerage and agency business of Czarnikow, MacDougall & Co Ltd in New York, MacDougall managing the business in Czarnikow's absence.

The rapid growth of his business necessitated some delegation of responsibility. A Mr Boog managed his Glasgow agency under the title of Czarnikow & Boog, whilst his partner in Liverpool was George Henry Cox (1848-1935). In London in 1875 he took on Charles Lagemann and Julius Ganzoni, of German and Swiss origins respectively. They were both to be paid on a commission basis of 1 per cent of any profits, and in 1877 both men earned in excess of £200. By then Czarnikow's capital was over £64,000, and he was fast emerging as a leading figure in the sugar industry. His fame was not only due to his commercial achievements, however. From 1863 he had been editing a *Weekly Price Current*, known in the trade as 'Czarnikow's Circular'. Authoritative and informed, it was recognised as being second-to-none for its forecasting of market trends and its listing of news and current prices of sugar, coffee and other commodities.

In 1883 Czarnikow branched out into cotton, opening a new department at his Liverpool branch. Encouraged by this increasing expansion, in 1891 he admitted Messrs Lagemann and Ganzoni as partners in his firm, followed in 1901 by Hubert Nieburg and Theodore Westrik. With five in the partnership altogether (Cox left in 1892), no more additions were made before Czarnikow's death.

In 1888 Czarnikow was actively involved in founding the London Produce Clearing House, an organisation for the registration and clearing of commodities, the forerunner of the International Commodities Clearing House and the first futures market in London. He was its deputy chairman, 1888-1907, and its chairman from 1907 until his death. He was also elected as the first chairman of the Sena Sugar Factory Ltd, incorporated in 1906, which had sugar estates in Mozambique. Most of his energies, however, were directed towards his own business which, by his death, was employing 40 men in its London office alone, and was one of the largest businesses of its kind in the world. Four years later, in 1913, it became a private limited company with a paid-up capital of £500,000.

Despite his delegation of responsibilities among his four partners, it remained very much Czarnikow's own business. He disliked his partners overriding any of his decisions, and expected them to follow his lead in all things. Impulsive and short-tempered at times, he could also be kind and warm-hearted, and with his erratic temperament was quite capable of sacking and re-employing a man in one day. He watched every penny in his account books, and was not known for his generosity, although in 1905 he presented £1,000 to London Zoo for a new aviary. He had a keen interest in animals, at one time buying a young bear to add to his exotic collection of eagles, emus, ponies, monkeys and dogs.

In 1863 Czarnikow married Louisa, daughter of the late Rev Spencer Ashlin; they had two children, a boy and a girl, neither of whom were to join the family business. He died on 17 April 1909, leaving £774,008 gross.

ALEXANDRA KIDNER

Sources:

Unpublished

PrC.

Published

Henry H Janes and H J Sayers, *The Story of Czarnikow* (Harley Publishing Co Ltd, 1963).

John M Hutcheson, *Notes on the Sugar Industry* (Greenock: James Mackelvie & Sons, 1901).

Times 19 Apr 1909.